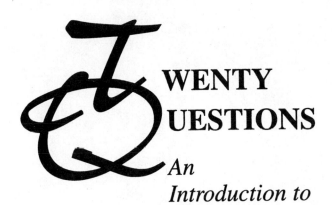

TWENTY QUESTIONS

*An
Introduction to
Philosophy*

Third Edition

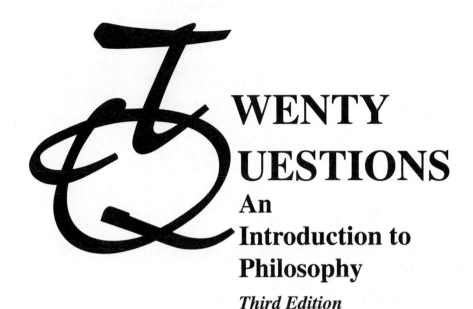

TWENTY QUESTIONS

An Introduction to Philosophy

Third Edition

G. LEE BOWIE
Mount Holyoke College

MEREDITH W. MICHAELS
Hampshire College

ROBERT C. SOLOMON
University of Texas, Austin

HARCOURT BRACE COLLEGE PUBLISHERS

Fort Worth   Philadelphia   San Diego New York   Orlando   Austin   San Antonio
Toronto   Montreal   London   Sydney   Tokyo

Publisher	Ted Buchholz
Editor in Chief	Christopher P. Klein
Senior Acquisitions Editor	David Tatom
Project Editor	John Haakenson
Production Manager	Diane Gray
Senior Art Director	Don Fujimoto

Cover painting by Mark Lane-Davies

ISBN: 0-15-5026607

Library of Congress Catalog Card Number: 95-079694

Copyright © 1996, 1992, 1988 by Harcourt Brace & Company

Address for Editorial Correspondence:
Harcourt Brace College Publishers
301 Commerce Street, Suite 3700
Fort Worth, TX 76102

Address for Orders:
Harcourt Brace & Company
6277 Sea Harbor Drive
Orlando, Florida 32887-6777
1-800-782-4479, or 1-800-433-0001 (in Florida)

(Copyright Acknowledgements begin on page 889 which constitutes a continuation of this copyright page.)

Printed in the United States of America

7 8 9 0 1 2 3 4   066   0 9 8 7 6 5 4 3

PREFACE

The favorable response to *Twenty Questions: An Introduction to Philosophy* has provided us with the impetus to continue to bring philosophy into conversation with other intellectual traditions and activities. The format of this third edition is the same as that of earlier editions. We have added new material in order to keep up with developments in the field. And because of a heightened interest in philosophy and elsewhere in issues of gender, race, class, and culture, we have been able to choose among a large body of interesting work that incorporates these perspectives into traditional philosophical concerns. We have also deleted some selections in response to suggestions from students and teachers throughout the country.

This book is the product of many years of teaching successful introductory philosophy courses. By "successful courses" we mean courses that engage and sustain the students' attention in genuine philosophical activity. We have tried to re-create here some of the elements that have made for success in the classroom.

First, we have included a large number of "classic" philosophical texts, both old and new. Philosophy builds heavily on its own tradition, and the introductory student profits from joining in that tradition. However, philosophers are not the only people who address philosophical questions. The student will also find here pieces on philosophical themes written by scientists, novelists, journalists, political activists, poets, religious figures, economists, and others. We are, along with Socrates, convinced that philosophical questions permeate so-called ordinary life. Students benefit from and appreciate the philosophical reflections of those outside the philosophical profession.

Second, in assembling the selections we have kept in mind that, although most traditional philosophers are white males, many students are not. All students need to know that people like themselves sometimes do philosophy. We have tried to represent a full range of human perspectives and voices.

We have arranged the selections in each chapter to create a natural philosophical conversation from the beginning of the chapter to the end. In many cases this order is antichronological. For example, in the chapter on death, the article by Thomas Nagel precedes the one by Plato because Nagel poses some questions to which Plato can be seen as responding. Instructors will certainly want to take liberties with our arrangements and create "conversations" that are different from the ones we envisaged. Other instructors might wish to gather material from several chapters into groupings that are quite different from what we thought natural. We believe that the design of the book allows a full range for the expression of idiosyncrasy.

Because we have been so concerned to include historical and contemporary material from both philosophical and nontraditional sources, this is a large book. Consequently, there is enormous flexibility in the design of a course that uses this book. One could diverge from the intention of the authors and teach a course entirely from historical materials. A course could focus on women writers. A course might be constructed very traditionally, or it might achieve eccentricity of truly epic proportions. There is no substitute in the classroom for the instructor's enthusiasm for the material; to make that enthusiasm possible, we have offered a broad range of options.

Because this book draws from such a range of sources, it has been in the process of revision since it began. This process will continue. For the book to be improved by use, we hope that instructors will pass on to us their complaints, their praise, and especially their suggestions.

In our experience using this text and talking with others (both instructors and students) who have used it, we have discovered that good students browse through it, reading selections that have not been assigned. We regard this as a significant measure of our success. Accordingly, we urge students to range freely through the readings gathered here. Philosophy is a field that typically (although not always) responds well to different views about what is philosophically engaging.

A number of people have helped us enormously with the creation of this book. Early on, we received important help from Phyllis Green and Maura Colbert. Later, Anna May Dion was instrumental in securing permissions and preparing the manuscript. Kathleen Higgins was helpful both in conceiving and in carrying out the plan for the book. Gail Davidson helped in the selection of the artwork, on which Lee Badger and Reid Badger also gave some selective but critical advice. We would also like to thank Kisor Chakrabarti and William C. Gay for their reviews of the book. For the second edition we thank Abigail Severance, Alice Finke, Sonja Al-Sofi, Janet McCracken, Lenore Bowen, Ruth Hammen, David Goldberg, Bob Gooding-Williams, Becky Michaels, and Nicky Weinstock. Additional thanks for the third edition are due to Lori Strolin and Laurie Dion.

A number of people with whom we worked at Harcourt Brace nurtured and developed this project. Bill McLane liked the initial idea and nursed it along. We especially thank David Tatom, senior editor, who has embodied that highest virtue of an editor: listening to the authors. Leanne Winkler has also been helpful, both with permissions details and with other aspects of the production. Finally, we thank our thousands of former students: Their enthusiastic responses as well as their blank looks have made this book far better than it otherwise might have been.

INTRODUCTION

At certain times in your life, you have undoubtedly stumbled across a peculiar sort of question, a question to which you haven't got a straightforward answer, a question that provokes head-scratching or that leaves you feeling slightly out of sorts. Suppose that you are sitting outdoors with a friend on a beautiful spring day. Both of you are looking up at the sky. "Isn't the sky amazingly blue today?" remarks your friend. "Yes," you respond, but just as you answer, a problem occurs to you. *How do you know that you and your friend are seeing the same color?* Well, your friend is seeing blue, and you are seeing blue, so doesn't that settle it? Not really, for now you can push the question farther. Even if you both use the word "blue" to *describe* what you see, it's still possible that what you see is not what your friend sees. At this point you may begin to get a headache (and not from looking at the sky) and turn your attention to a more manageable question, such as "Is it time for lunch?" Indeed, one of the characteristics of the peculiar question about the color of the sky (the "Color Question") is precisely that it seems so unmanageble. How would one go about trying to answer a question such as that?

All of us have well-developed strategies for answering most questions. If you want to know whether it is time for lunch, you check your watch. If you haven't got a watch, you ask someone who does. If nobody around has a watch, you call the operator, find a sundial, or decide that, no matter what the actual time is, you'll follow the dictates of your stomach. (This last point shows that we also have a sense of when to give up.) But in the case of the Color Question, it is simply not clear what strategy you ought to adopt in attempting to answer it. It's tempting to give up before you even begin.

If the Color Question isn't one that has crossed your mind, perhaps you'll find this one more familiar. Imagine that you have spent the day chasing down various pieces of paper that are required for you to register for your classes. After standing in one line for twenty minutes, you are told that you belong in another line. After filling out four green cards, it turns out that you were supposed to fill out yellow cards. After gathering all your course books at the bookstore, you discover that they don't accept checks. After waiting for your chance to order a sandwich, you are informed that there is no more bread. After carefully choosing your courses, your advisor tells you that three of them are closed. Returning home, you think to yourself, "What a useless day. What was the purpose of standing in all those lines? Nothing works out. I'm like a rat in a maze, running crazily around chasing its tail. In fact, *what is the point, the purpose of life? What does it all mean?*" Most of the time, we just do what we do, content to believe that the purpose in buttering the bread is simply to make it taste better. We don't then ask, *but what is the point in making it taste better?* But sometimes, when we are particularly frustrated or defeated in our attempts to perform ordinary activities, those activities appear in a different light. They appear futile, disconnected from the particular purposes they are designed to serve. Since they fail to achieve their immediate purposes, it is not surprising that the purposes themselves begin to look futile, utterly lacking in meaning. That is when the "Life Question" is likely to strike.

If the Color Question appears unmanageable, then the Life Question, being the biggest question of all, seems even less likely to yield to our ordinary strategies. Where would you begin to answer it? How would you know whether you had arrived at an answer? Perhaps the strangest thing about these peculiar questions is that they are clearly important and fundamental questions, even *profound* questions, and yet it is equally clear that people normally lead most of their lives without answering them, indeed, without giving them more than a passing glance.

There are some people, however, who take these and other questions like them very seriously. Socrates, one of the earliest Western philosophers, said, "The unexamined life is not worth living." As we all know, to examine something is to look at it very carefully. Of course, we can't look at life in the same way we look at a virus under a microsope. In the case of life itself, there is more to it than meets the eye. The process of examination, then, involves thinking about different aspects of life, focusing now on the color of the sky and later, for example, on the existence of God or the importance of truthtelling. Socrates is suggesting that there is something wrong with a life that does not subject itself to scrutiny, at least from time to time. Although his claim doesn't provide an answer to the questions we've been considering, it does suggest that we forge on in our attempt to answer them. That is precisely what he did, and what philosophers since then have done.

There are as many ways of thinking about these questions as there are philosophers. What unifies philosophers as a group, and philosophy as a field of study, is the belief that these questions deserve systematic attention. As a result, philosophy is a discipline that seeks to provede strategies for answering these questions, for seeing how they are related to one another and to our more ordinary beliefs and values. For example, if you believe that there is a God, then your answer to the Life Question might be quite different from that of a person who doesn't.

There is no one strategy that appeals to every philosopher. Different strategies yield different answers and different answers inevitably lead to new questions. Some philosophers think that some questions, the Life Question being a good example, are so general and vague as to be meaningless. In fact, a favorite strategy of some philosophers is to show that something that looks like a question really isn't. It is like going to the doctor, only to discover that your symptoms are psychosomatic. You thought that you were sick, but you really aren't. Or, if you are sick, your illness is not at all what you thought it was. Other philosophers believe that most philosophical questions are really about language. They might try to answer the Color Question by urging us to consider the way in which we use such words as "blue." If you and your friend always use the word in the same way, then there is no further interesting fact about whether what the two of you see is the same or not.

As you read through this book and discuss the issues it raises in class, you will begin to discover that you have certain philosophical inclinations. You will find the strategies of some philosophers congenial or persuasive. You will undoubtedly find, too, that some of them seem to you to miss the point, or to avoid it by distracting you with another issue. Sometimes, you will simply find that the question being considered isn't terribly pressing to you at this moment. People have philosophical preferences just as they have preferences for other things. Some people, for example, are particularly interested in ethical questions (see Chapters 13, 15, 19, and 20) because such questions are closely connected to choices that all of us have to make every day. Although these ethical choices may not be very serious, even the decision of whether or not to skip class has ethical consequences!

Other people are drawn to questions that never explicitly arise in the course of ordinary experience (except when they're doing philosophy), but which nevertheless underlie and inform our ways of thinking about that experience. You can get through the day without having to question whether your mind is something over and above your brain (Chapter 5). You can't however, get through the day without there being some relationship between your mind and your brain. Philosophy permits you to think seriously and systematically about the nature of that relationship.

As you may have noticed, Socrates' claim about the importance of looking "at the inside of life" is itself a philosophical claim. After you have had a chance to do some philosophical thinking, you will be able to decide whether you think he was right. You might even develop some good reasons for thinking that he was wrong. If so, Socrates would have been proud of you. Showing that a great philosopher is mistaken can be an enormously productive and gratifying experience.

Some Advice About Studying Philosophy and Using This Book

Philosophy is notoriously difficult. Philosophers use an array of unfamiliar concepts and don't always do a good job of letting us know what they mean by those concepts. Also, in their attempt to be logical and rigorous, they sometimes leave out such things as examples, cases, and stories that might help us to judge whether we are following their reasoning. Nevertheless, when you read philosophy, always begin by trying to understand a philosopher on his or her own terms. Remember that no matter how strange what you are reading appears to be, it was written by an ordinary human being with a mind roughly like your own. You simply need to accustom yourself to seeing the world from the perspective of another person whose central concerns, at least initially, appear to be very different from your own. Once you've climbed inside the head of a philosopher, it is much easier to see the world in his or her particular way. Doing so doesn't mean that you will like what you see, nor does it involve adopting that way of seeing as your own, but it does give you a better chance of being able to understand and evaluate what you read.

To help you make that first step into a philosopher's world, this book presents a bit of biographical information at the beginning of each essay or story. Be sure to read it before you plunge into the text. Remember, if somebody lived from 1596–1650, that person is not going to be worried about nuclear war, nor will she or he have heard of robots or the Equal Rights Amendment. It may well be, however, that what such a person has to say will help you understand the philosophical issues raised by these and other phenomena of the world in which you live.

In addition to the biographical information provided for each author, each section of this book has an introduction designed to give you an idea of the questions that section explores as well as some sense of what each author in that section is trying to accomplish. Since these introductions attempt to situate philosophical questions in a setting that is familiar to you, it is a good idea to read them carefully before you read the selections themselves. Remember, too, that rereading the introductions may help you to reorient yourself if you begin to get lost midway through a difficult essay.

Finally, you will notice that not every selection in this book is written by a philosopher. The book also contains fiction, scientific writing, newspaper articles, and essays from popular magazines. By setting strictly philosophical writing in a more familiar context, this book allows you to see the ways in which philosophy creeps into ordinary life. It also allows you to see that people other than philosophers are capable of great philosophical insight (and sometimes are more fun to read!).

Long after you've finished this course, you may find yourself reading an article in the newpaper and saying "Hmmm . . . I wonder what Plato would say about this." Philosophy is everywhere, once you learn how to recognize it. An introductory philosophy course is designed to show you how to do just that.

TABLE OF CONTENTS

PART 3   THINKING AND KNOWING   233

PART 4   THE DILEMMAS OF PERSONHOOD   327

Part 1

Religion and the Meaning of Life

Chapter *1*

Does Religion Give My Life Meaning?

What do you believe in? What gives your life meaning? It is true that most of your days are filled with things to do, people to see, assignments to be completed, promises to be kept, and special events to be anticipated and then enjoyed. But what does all this add up to? What makes it significant? Why does it make a difference whether you are alive? These are the questions that are often summarized under the heading "the meaning of life," and they are among the oldest and most important questions in philosophy.

Religion is as old as these questions, and the various religions of the world are, in part, answers to these questions. The primary function of religion is to give our lives meaning, to show us how we fit into the world and God's plan. But there are many religions and conceptions of religion, and they explain life's meaning in very different ways. Judaism and Christianity insist that life has meaning because there is an Almighty God who created us and looks over us. There are, however, other ways of making sense of our existence, and some of them do not involve a being such as the Judeo-Christian God at all.

How does religion give meaning to life? Steven Cahn suggests that it is a combination of theory and practice, rituals, prayers, metaphysical beliefs, and moral commitments. But, he argues, it is not necessary that such theories and practices be part of an established traditional religion, nor is it necessary for a person who is religious to believe in a single supreme being or an afterlife—two fundamental tenets of Christianity but relative rarities among the various religions of the world. There are great religions in the East, as old as Judaism and Christianity, which explain the meaning of life without appealing to any conception of God like our own. And any number of "spiritual attitudes" to life exist that are not part of any particular religion. Religion may make life meaningful, but no particular religion does so exclusively, and many if not all of the ingredients of a meaningful life—rituals, moral commitments, metaphysical beliefs, and even prayers (to whom or what?)—might also be part of someone's strictly secular life. What is essential is that a person's life involves some sensibility that goes beyond the ordinary and everyday concerns of life, and it is the sense of "beyond" that gives life meaning.

3

Some of the great thinkers have suggested that what is central to religion is not so much belief in a particular deity, but rather a transformation of one's self, a rising "above" ordinary, everyday concerns to an appreciation of the nature of the cosmos as a whole. Believing in God is one way to do this, but there are other techniques and ways of viewing the world that make such "awakening" or "transcendence" possible. As Daisetz Suzuki writes, for example, Zen Buddhism elaborates an all-encompassing attitude toward life that uses meditation and other forms of personal discipline to develop a religiously meaningful view of the world. There are "many paths to the same summit," writes Ramakrishna. It would be a mistake to think that there is only one religion or one way to make life meaningful. But then, neither can one simply embrace all religions at once, for it is the particularity of the "path" that makes meaningfulness possible. A Christian should be a Christian, a Hindu a Hindu, but this does not mean that there is or should be any conflict between them.

But then, it has also been argued that religion does not provide meaning to life at all; it rather gives us a distraction *from* life and a set of excuses for not taking life's problems seriously. So conceived, religion may *take away* rather than contribute to life's meaning. So thought Bertrand Russell, who saw in the history of Christianity a horrifying story of protracted violence and intolerance. Mary Daly has a different objection to the Judeo-Christian tradition: It assumes without argument that God is male and consequently elevates male and demeans female characteristics. She accordingly recommends nothing less than a feminist revolution in religion, not just recognizing women as equals in a "patriarchal" universe (a contradiction, she says), but rather involving a reconception of the very nature of religion. In their dialogue on what they call "partnerships" between black men and women, bell hooks and Cornel West stress the importance of a complex, nuanced notion of spirituality in the black struggle for liberation. For them, spirituality is crucial to the effective resistance both to forms of racial oppression and to capitulation to those forces in contemporary society that emphasize the individual over the community. hooks and West insist that life has meaning only in relation to serving others, including God, and to making the world a better place. Thus, they place their spiritual and their political commitments side by side.

Finally, it may be that life has no meaning and that the attempts of all religions to provide that meaning are just denial and refusal to accept the facts. H. L. Mencken makes his point about the illusory character of religion by listing the names of gods and goddesses who were once feared and revered. Albert Camus argues the sensibility of the current age is that life is really "absurd" and religion cannot undo that single, overwhelming truth.

STEVEN M. CAHN

Religion Reconsidered

STEVEN M. CAHN *is a professor of philosophy and Dean of the City University of New York. He teaches and publishes in the philosophy of religion and education.*

MOST of us suppose that all religions are akin to the one we happen to know best. But this assumption can be misleading. For example, many Christians believe that all religions place heavy emphasis on an afterlife, although, in fact, the central concern of Judaism is life in this world, not the next. Similarly, many Christians and Jews are convinced that a person who is religious must affirm the existence of a supernatural God. They are surprised to learn that religions such as Jainism or Theravada Buddhism deny the existence of a Supreme Creator of the World.

But how can there be a non-supernatural religion? To numerous theists as well as atheists the concept appears contradictory. I propose to show, however, that nothing in the theory or practice of religion—not ritual, not prayer, not metaphysical belief, not moral commitment—necessitates a commitment to traditional theism. In other words, one may be religious while rejecting supernaturalism.

Let us begin with the concept of ritual. A ritual is a prescribed symbolic action. In the case of religion, the ritual is prescribed by the religious organization, and the act symbolizes some aspect of religious belief. Those who find the beliefs of supernaturalistic religion unreasonable or the activities of the organization unacceptable may come to consider any ritual irrational. But, although particular rituals may be based on irrational beliefs, nothing is inherently irrational about ritual.

Consider the simple act of two people shaking hands when they meet. This act is a ritual, prescribed by our society and symbolic of the individuals' mutual respect. There is nothing irrational about this act. Of course, if people shook hand in order to ward off evil demons, then shaking hands would be irrational. But this is not the reason people shake hands. The ritual has no connection with God or demons but indicates the attitude one person has toward another.

It might be assumed that the ritual of handshaking escaped irrationality only because the ritual is not prescribed by any specific organization and is not part of an elaborate ceremony. But to see that this assumption is false, consider the graduation ceremony at a college. The graduates and faculty all wear peculiar hats and robes, and the participants stand and sit at appropriate times throughout the ceremony. However, there is nothing irrational about this ceremony. Indeed, the ceremonies of graduation day, far from being irrational, are symbolic of commitment to the process of education and the life of reason.

At first glance it may appear that rituals are comparatively insignificant features of our lives, but the more one considers the matter, the more it becomes apparent that rituals are a pervasive and treasured aspect of human experience. Who would want to eliminate the festivities associated with holidays such as Independence Day or Thanksgiving? What would college football be without songs, cheers, flags, and the innumerable other symbolic features surrounding the game? And those who disdain popular rituals typically proceed to establish their own distinctive ones, ranging from characteristic habits of dress to the use of drugs, all symbolic of a rejection of traditional mores.

Religious persons, like all others, search for an appropriate means of emphasizing their commitment to a group or its values. Rituals provide such a means. It is true that supernaturalistic religion has often infused its rituals with superstition, but nonreligious rituals can be equally as superstitious as religious ones. For example, most Americans view the Fourth of July as an occasion on which they can express pride in their country's heritage. With this purpose in mind, the holiday is one of great significance. However, if it were thought that the singing of the fourth verse of "The Star-Spangled Banner" four times on the Fourth of July would protect our country against future disasters, then the original meaning of the holiday would soon be lost in a maze of superstition.

A naturalistic (i.e., non-supernaturalistic) religion need not utilize ritual in such a superstitious manner, for it does not employ rituals in order to please a benevolent deity or appease an angry one. Rather, naturalistic religion views ritual, as Jack Cohen has put it, as "the enhancement of life through the dramatization of great ideals." If a group places great stress on justice or freedom, why should it not utilize ritual in order to emphasize these goals? Such a

use of ritual serves to solidify the group and to strengthen its devotion to its expressed purposes. And these purposes are strengthened all the more if the ritual in question has the force of tradition, having been performed by many generations who have belonged to the same group and have struggled to achieve the same goals. Ritual so conceived is not a form of superstition; rather, it is a reasonable means of strengthening religious commitment and is as useful to naturalistic religion as it is to supernaturalistic religion.

Having considered the role of ritual in a naturalistic religion, let us next turn to the concept of prayer. It might be thought that naturalistic religion could have no use for prayer, since prayer is supposedly addressed to a supernatural being, and proponents of naturalistic religion do not believe in the existence of such a being. But this objection oversimplifies the concept of prayer, focusing attention on one type of prayer while neglecting an equally important but different sort of prayer.

Supernaturalistic religion makes extensive use of petitionary prayer, prayer that petitions a supernatural being for various favors. These my range all the way from the personal happiness of the petitioner to the general welfare of all society. But since petitionary prayer rests upon the assumption that a supernatural being exists, it is clear that such prayer has no place in a naturalistic religion.

However, not all prayers are prayers of petition. There are also prayers of meditation. These prayers are not directed to any supernatural being and are not requests for the granting of favors. Rather, these prayers provide the opportunity for persons to rethink their ultimate commitments and rededicate themselves to live up to their ideals.

Such prayers may take the form of silent devotion or may involve oral repetition of certain central texts. Just as Americans repeat the Pledge of Allegiance and reread the Gettysburg Address, so adherents of naturalistic religion repeat the statements of their ideals and reread the documents that embody their traditional beliefs.

It is true that supernaturalistic religions, to the extent that they utilize prayers of meditation, tend to treat these prayers irrationally, by supposing that if the prayers are not uttered a precise number of times under certain specified conditions, then the prayers lose all value. But there is no need to view prayer in this way. Rather, as Julian Huxley wrote, prayer "permits the bringing before the mind of a world of thought which in most people must inevitably be absent during the occupations of ordinary Life: . . . it is the means by which the mind may fix itself upon this or that noble or beautiful or awe-inspiring idea, and so grow to it and come to realize it more fully."

Such a use of prayer may be enhanced by song, instrumental music, and various types of symbolism. These elements, fused together, provide the means for adherents of naturalistic religion to engage in religious services akin to those engaged in by adherents of supernaturalistic religion. The difference between the two services is that those who attend the latter come to relate themselves to God, while those who attend the former come to relate themselves to their fellow human beings and to the world in which we live.

We have so far discussed how ritual and prayer can be utilized in naturalistic religion, but to adopt a religious perspective also involves metaphysical beliefs and moral commitments. Can these be maintained without recourse to supernaturalism?

If we use the term *metaphysics* in its usual sense, to refer to the systematic study of the most basic features of existence, then it is clear that a metaphysical system may be either supernaturalistic or naturalistic. The views of Plato, Descartes, and Leibniz are representative of a supernaturalistic theory; the views of Aristotle, Spinoza, and Dewey are representative of a naturalistic theory.

Spinoza's *Ethics,* for example, one of the greatest metaphysical works ever written, explicitly rejects the view that there exists any being apart from Nature itself. Spinoza identifies God with Nature as a whole, and urges that the good life consists in coming to understand Nature. In his words, "our salvation, or blessedness, or freedom consists in a constant and eternal love toward God. . . ." Spinoza's concept of God, however, is explicitly not the supernaturalistic concept of God, and Spinoza's metaphysical system thus exemplifies not only a naturalistic metaphysics but also the possibility of reinterpreting the concept of God within a naturalistic framework.

But can those who do not believe in a supernaturalistic God commit themselves to moral principles, or is the acceptance of moral principles dependent upon acceptance of supernaturalism? It is sometimes assumed that those who reject a supernaturalistic God are necessarily immoral, for their denial of the existence of such a God leaves them free to act without fear of Divine punishment. This assumption, however, is seriously in error.

The refutation of the view that morality must rest upon belief in a supernatural God was provided more than two thousand years ago by Socrates in Plato's *Euthyphro* dialogue. Socrates asked the following question: Are actions right because God says they are right, or does God say actions are right because they are right? This question is not a verbal trick; on the contrary, it poses a serious dilemma for those who believe in a supernatural deity. Socrates was inquiring whether actions are right due to God's fiat or whether God is Himself subject to moral standards. If actions are right due to God's command, then anything God commands is right, even if He should command torture or murder. But if one accepts this view, then it makes no sense to say that God Himself is good, for since the good is whatever God commands, to say that God commands rightly is simply to say that He commands as He commands, which is a tautology. This approach makes a mockery of morality, for might does not make right, even if the might is the infinite might of God. To act morally is not to act out of fear of punishment; it is not to act as one is commanded to act. Rather, it is to act as one ought to act. And how one ought to act. And how one ought to act is not dependent upon anyone's power, even if the power be Divine.

Thus, actions are not right because God commands them; on the contrary,

God commands them because they are right. But in that case, what is right is independent of what God commands, for what He commands must conform with an independent standard in order to be right. Since one could act in accordance with this independent standard without believing in the existence of a supernatural God, it follows that morality does not rest upon supernaturalism. Consequently, naturalists can be highly moral (as well as immoral) persons, and supernaturalists can be highly immoral (as well as moral) persons. This conclusion should come as no surprise to anyone who has contrasted the life of Buddha, an atheist, with the life of the monk Torquemada.

We have now seen that naturalistic religion is a genuine possibility, since it is reasonable for individuals to perform rituals, utter prayers, accept metaphysical beliefs, and commit themselves to moral principles without believing in supernaturalism. Indeed, one can even do so while maintaining allegiance to Christianity or Judaism. Consider, for example, those Christians who accept the "Death of God" or those Jews who adhere to Reconstructionist Judaism.

Such options are philosophically respectable. Whether to choose any of them is for each reader to decide.

DAISETZ SUZUKI

The Awakening of a New Consciousness in Zen

DAISETZ SUZUKI *(1870–1966) was the leading expositor of Zen Buddhism in the West. He translated the* Tao Te Ching, *the principal Buddhist text, into English.*

MY position in regard to "the awakening of a new consciousness," summarily stated, is as follows:

The phrasing, "the awakening of a new consciousness" as it appears in the title of this paper, is not a happy one, because what is awakened in the Zen experience is not a "new" consciousness, but an "old" one which has been dormant ever since our loss of "innocence," to use the Biblical term. The awakening is really the rediscovery or the excavation of a long-lost treasure.

There is in every one of us, though varied in depth and strength, an eternal longing for "something" which transcends a world of inequalities. This is a somewhat vague statement containing expressions not altogether happy. "To transcend" suggests "going beyond," "being away from," that is, a separation, a dualism. I have, however, no desire to hint that the "something" stands away from the world in which we find ourselves. And then "inequalities" may sound too political. When I chose the term I had in mind the Buddhist word *asama* which contrasts with *sama,* "equal" or "same." We may replace it by such words as "differentiation" or "individualisation" or "conditionality." I just want to point out the fact that as soon as we recognise this world to be

subject to constant changes we somehow begin to feel dissatisfied with it and desire for something which is permanent, free, above sorrow, and of eternal value.

This longing is essentially religious and each religion has its own way of designating it according to its tradition. Christians may call it longing for the Kingdom of Heaven or renouncing the world for the sake of divine love or praying to be saved from eternal damnation. Buddhists may call it seeking for emancipation or freedom. Indians may understand it as wishing to discover the real self.

Whatever expressions they may use, they all show a certain feeling of discontent with the situation in which they find themselves. They may not yet know exactly how to formulate this feeling and conceptually represent it either to themselves or to others.

I specified this obscure feeling as a longing for something. In this, it may be said, I have already a preconceived idea by assuming the existence of a something for which there is a longing on our part. Instead of saying this, it might have been better to identify the feeling of dissatisfaction with such modern feelings as fear or anxiety or a sense of insecurity. But the naming is not so important. As long as the mind is upset

and cannot enjoy any state of equilibrium or perfect equanimity, this is a
sense of insecurity or discontent. We
feel as if we were in the air and trying
to find a place for landing.

But we do not know exactly where
this place for landing is. The objective
is an altogether unknown quantity. It
can nowhere be located and the fact
adds a great deal to our sense of insecurity. We must somewhere and somehow
find the landing.

Two ways are open: outward and inward. The outward one may be called
intellectual and objective, but the inward one cannot be called subjective or
affective or conative. The "inward" is
misleading, though it is difficult to designate it in any other way. For all designations are on the plane of intellection.
But as we must name it somehow, let us
be content for a while to call it "inward"
in contrast to "outward."

Let me give you this caution here: as
long as the inward way is to be understood in opposition to the outward
way,—though to do otherwise is impossible because of the human inability to
go beyond language as the means of
communication—the inward way after
all turns to be an outward way. The really inward way is when no contrast exists between the inward and the
outward. This is a logical contradiction.
But the full meaning of it will I hope
become clearer when I finish this paper.

The essential characteristic of the
outward way consists in its never-
ending procession, either forward or
backward, but mostly in a circular
movement, and always retaining the opposition of two terms, subject and object. There is thus no finality in the
outward way, hence the sense of insecurity, though security does not necessarily mean "standing still," "not moving
anywhere," or "attached to something."

The inward way is the reverse of the
outward way. Instead of going out end-
lessly and dissipating and exhausting itself, the mind turns inwardly to see
what is there behind all this endless procession of things. It does not stop the
movement in order to examine what is
there. If it does, the movement ceases to
be a movement; it turns into something
else. This is what the intellect does
while the inward way refuses to do so.
As soon as there is any kind of bifurcation, the outward way asserts itself and
the inward way no longer exists. The inward way consists in taking things as
they are, in catching them in their is-
ness or suchness. I would not say, "in
their oneness" or "in their wholeness."
These are the terms belonging to the
outward way. Even to say "is-ness" or
"suchness" or "thusness" or in Japanese
"sono-mama" or in Chinese *"chi-mo,"*
is not, strictly speaking, the inward way.
"To be" is an abstract term. It is much
better to lift a finger and say nothing
about it. The inward way in its orthodoxy generally avoids appealing to language though it never shuns it.

The inward way occasionally uses the
term "one" or "all," but in this case
"one" means "one that is never one," and
"all" means "all that is never all." The
"one" will be "a one ever becoming one"
and never a closed-up "one." The "all"
will be "an all ever becoming all" and
never a closed-up "all." This means that
in the inward way the one is an absolute
one, that one is all and all is one, and further that when "the ten thousand things"
are reduced to an absolute oneness
which is an absolute nothingness, we
have the inward way perfecting itself.

Buddhism, especially Zen Buddhism
as it developed in China, is rich in expressions belonging to the inward way.
In fact, it is Zen that has effected, for
the first time, a deep excavation into the

mine of the inward way. To illustrate my point read the following—I give just one instance:

Suigan at the end of the summer session made this declaration: "I have been talking, east and west, all this summer for my Brotherhood. See if my eyebrows are still growing."

One of his disciples said, "How finely they are growing."

Another said, "One who commits a theft feels uneasy in his heart."

A third one without saying anything simply uttered "Kwan!"

It goes without saying that all these utterances of the disciples as well as of the master give us a glimpse into the scene revealed only to the inward way. They are all expressions directly bursting out of an abyss of absolute nothingness. . . .

When Buddhists make reference to God, God must not be taken in the Biblical sense. When I talk about God's giving an order to light, which is recorded in the Genesis, I allude to it with the desire that our Christian readers may come to a better understanding of the Buddhist idea of the inward way. What follows, therefore, is to be understood in this spirit.

The Biblical God is recorded as having given his Name to Moses at Mount Sinai as "I am that I am." I do not of course know much about Christian or Jewish theology, but this "name," whatever its original Hebrew meaning of the word may be, seems to me of such significance that we must not put it aside as not essential to the interpretation of God-idea in the development of Christian thought. The Biblical God is always intensely personal and concretely intimate, and how did he ever come to declare himself under such as highly metaphysical designation as he did to Moses? "A highly metaphysical designation," however, is from the outward way of looking at things, while from the inward way "I am that I am" is just as "spontaneous" as the fish swimming about in the mountain stream or the fowl of the air flying across the sky. God's is-ness is my is-ness and also the cat's is-ness sleeping on her mistress' lap. This is reflected in Christ's declaration that "I am before Abraham was." In this is-ness which is not to be assumed under the category of metaphysical abstractions, I feel like recognizing the fundamental oneness of all the religious experiences.

The spontaneity of is-ness, to go back to the first part of this paper, is what is revealed in the "eternal longing" for something which has vanished from the domain of the outward way of intellectualisation. . . . While in the world, we find ourselves too engrossed in the business of "knowing" which started when we left the garden of "innocence." We all now want "to know," "to think," "to choose," "to decide," "to be responsible," etc., with everything that follows from exercising what we call "freedom."

"Freedom" is really the term to be found in the inward way only and not in the outward way. But somehow a confusion has come into our minds and we find ourselves madly running after things which can never be attained in the domain of the outward way. The feeling of insecurity then grows out of this mad pursuit, because we are no more able to be in "the spontaneity of is-ness."

We can now see that "The awakening of a new consciousness" is not quite a happy expression. The longing is for something we have lost and not for an unknown quantity of which we have not the remotest possible idea. In fact, there is no unknown quantity in the world into which we have come to pass our time. The longing of any sort implies our previous knowledge of it, though we may be altogether ignorant of its presence in our consciousness. . . . The real object can never be taken hold of until we come back to the abode which we inadvertently quitted. "The awakening of a new consciousness" is therefore the finding ourselves back in our original abode where we lived even before our birth. This experience of homecoming and therefore of the feeling of perfect security is evinced everywhere in religious literature.

The feeling of perfect security means the security of freedom and the securing of freedom is no other than "the awakening of a new consciousness." Ordinarily, we talk of freedom too readily, mostly in the political sense, and also in the moral sense. But as long as we remain in the outward way of seeing things, we can never understand what freedom is. All forms of freedom we generally talk of are far from being freedom in its deepest sense. Most people are sadly mistaken in this respect. . . .

We humans have the very bad habit of giving a name to a certain object with a certain number of attributes and think this name exhausts the object thus designated, whereas the object itself has no idea of remaining within the limit prescribed by the name. The object lives, grows, expands, and often changes into something else than the one imprisoned within the name. We who have given the name to it imagine that the object thus named for ever remains the same, because for the practical purposes of life or for the sake of what we call logic it is convenient to retain the name all the time regardless of whatever changes that have taken place and might take place in it. We become slaves to a system of nomenclature we ourselves have invented.

This applies perfectly to our consciousness. We have given the name "consciousness" to a certain group of psychological phenomena and another name "unconscious" to another group. We keep them strictly separated one from the other. A confusion will upset our thought-structure. This means that what is named "conscious" cannot be "unconscious" and vice versa. But in point of fact human psychology is a living fact and refuses to observe an arbitrary system of grouping. The conscious wants to be unconscious and the unconscious conscious. But human thinking cannot allow such a contradiction: the unconscious must remain unconscious and the conscious conscious; no such things as the unconscious conscious or the conscious unconscious must take place, because they cannot take place in the nature of things, logicians would say. If they are to happen, a time-agent must come in and make consciousness rise out of the unconscious.

But Zen's way of viewing or evaluating things differs from the outward way of intellection. Zen would not object to the possibility of an "unconscious conscious" or a "conscious unconscious." Therefore, not the awakening of a new consciousness but consciousness coming to its own unconscious.

Language is used to give a name to everything, and when an object gets a name, we begin to think that the name is the thing and adjust ourselves to a new situation which is our own creation. So much confusion arises from it. If there is one thing Zen does for modern people, it will be to awaken them from this self-imposed thralldom. A Zen master would take up a staff, and, producing it before the audience declare, "I do not call it a staff. What would you call it?" Another master would say, "Here is a staff. It has transformed itself into a dragon, and the dragon has swallowed up the whole universe. Where do you get all these mountains, lakes, and the great earth?" When I got for the first time acquainted with Zen I thought this was a logical quibble, but I now realise that there is something here far more serious, far more real, and far more significant, which can be reached only by following the inward way.

RAMAKRISHNA

Many Paths to the Same Summit

RAMAKRISHNA (1836–1886) is perhaps the best-known Hindu saint of modern times. He had his first experience of spiritual ecstasy at the age of seven. He worshipped Rama, Krishna, Shiva, Kali, Allah, and Jesus.

GOD has made different religions to suit different aspirants, times, and countries. All doctrines are only so many paths; but a path is by no means God Himself. Indeed, one can reach God if one follows any of the paths with wholehearted devotion. One may eat a cake with icing either straight or sidewise. It will taste sweet either way.

As one and the same material, water is called by different names by different peoples, one calling it water, another eau, a third aqua, and another pani, so the one Everlasting-Intelligent-Bliss is invoked by some as God, by some as Allah, by some as Jehovah, and by others as Brahman.

As one can ascend to the top of a house by means of a ladder or a bamboo or a staircase or a rope, so diverse are the ways and means to approach God, and every religion in the world shows one of these ways.

As the young wife in a family shows her love and respect to her father-in-law, mother-in-law, and every other member of the family, and at the same time loves her husband more than these; similarly, being firm in thy devotion to the deity of thy own choice, do not despise other deities, but honour them all.

Bow down and worship where others kneel, for where so many have been paying the tribute of adoration the kind Lord must manifest himself, for he is all mercy.

The devotee who has seen God in one aspect only knows him in that aspect alone. But he who has seen him in manifold aspects is alone in a position to say, 'All these forms are of one God and God is multiform.' He is formless and with form, and many are his forms which no one knows.

The Saviour is the messenger of God. He is like the viceroy of a mighty monarch. As when there is some disturbance in a far-off province, the king sends his viceroy to quell it, so wherever there is a decline of religion in any part of the world, God sends his Saviour there. It is one and the same Saviour that, having plunged into the ocean of life, rises up in one place and is known as Krishna (the leading Hindu incarnation of God), and diving down again rises in another place and is known as Christ.

Every man should follow his own religion. A Christian should follow Christianity, a Mohammedan should follow Mohammedanism, and so on. For the Hindus, the ancient path, the path of the Aryan sages, is the best.

People partition off their lands by means of boundaries, but no one can partition off the all-embracing sky overhead. The indivisible sky surrounds all and includes all. So common man in ignorance says, 'My religion is the only one, my religion is the best.' But when his heart is illumined by true knowledge, he knows that above all these wars of sects and sectarians presides the one indivisible, eternal, all-knowing bliss.

As a mother, in nursing her sick children, gives rice and curry to one, and sago arrowroot to another, and bread and butter to a third, so the Lord has laid out different paths for different men suitable to their natures.

Dispute not. As you rest firmly on your own faith and opinion, allow others also the equal liberty to stand by their own faiths and opinions. By mere disputation you will never succeed in convincing another of his error. When the grace of God descends on him, each one will understand his own mistakes.

There was a man who worshipped Shiva but hated all other deities. One day Shiva appeared to him and said, 'I shall never be pleased with thee so long as thou hatest the other gods.' But the man was inexorable. After a few days Shiva again appeared to him and said, 'I shall never be pleased with thee so long as thou hatest.' The man kept silent. After a few days Shiva again appeared to him. This time one side of his body was that of Shiva, and the other side that of Vishnu. The man was half pleased and half displeased. He laid his offerings on the side representing Shiva, and did not offer anything to the side representing Vishnu. Then Shiva said, 'Thy bigotry is unconquerable. I, by assuming this dual aspect, tried to convince thee that all gods and goddesses are but various aspects of the one Absolute Brahman.'

BERTRAND RUSSELL

Why I Am Not a Christian

BERTRAND RUSSELL (1872–1970) was one of the greatest philosophers of this century. He wrote an enormous number of philosophical books and articles, from Principia Mathematica *(with Alfred North Whitehead) to some notorious polemics in favor of "free love" and atheism. Like Hume, he was too controversial for most universities, and a famous court case prevented him from teaching at City College of New York. He did, however, with the Nobel Prize for Literature in 1950. At the age of eighty-nine, he was jailed for protesting against nuclear arms. The selection here was delivered as a public lecture.*

AS your Chairman has told you, the subject about which I am going to speak to you tonight is "Why I Am Not a Christian." Perhaps it would be as well, first of all, to try to make out what one means by the word *Christian*. It is used these days in a very loose sense by a great many people. Some people mean no more by it than a person who attempts to live a good life. In that sense I suppose there would be Christians in all sects and creeds; but I do not think that that is the proper sense of the word, if only because it would imply that all the people who are not Christians—all the Buddhists, Confucians, Mohammedans, and so on—are not trying to live a good life. I do not mean by a Christian any person who tries to live decently according to his lights. I think that you must have a certain amount of definite belief before you have a right to call yourself a Christian. The word does not have quite such a full-blooded meaning now as it had in the times of St. Augustine and St. Thomas Aquinas. In those days, if a man said that he was a Christian it was known what he meant. You accepted a whole collection of creeds which were set out with great precision, and every single syllable of those creeds you believed with the whole strength of your convictions.

WHAT IS A CHRISTIAN?

Nowadays it is not quite that. We have to be a little more vague in our meaning of Christianity. I think, however, that there are two different items which are quite essential to anybody calling himself a Christian. The first is one of a dogmatic nature—namely, that you must believe in God and immortality. If you do not believe in those two things, I do not think that you can properly call yourself a Christian. Then, further than that, as the name implies, you must have some kind of belief about Christ. The Mohammedans, for instance, also believe in God and in immortality, and yet they would not call themselves Christians. I think you must have at the very lowest the belief that Christ was, if not divine, at least the best and wisest of men. If you are not going to believe that much about Christ, I do not think you have any right to call yourself a Christian. Of course, there is another sense, which you find in *Whitaker's Almanack* and in geography books where the population of the world is said to be divided into Christians, Mohammedans, Buddhists, fetish worshipers, and so on; and in that sense we are all Christians. The geography books count us all in, but that is purely geographical sense, which I suppose we can ignore. Therefore I take it that when I tell you why I am not a Christian I have to tell you two different things: first, why I do not believe in God and in immortality; and, secondly, why I do not think that Christ was the best and wisest of men, although I grant him a very high degree of moral goodness.

But for the successful efforts of unbelievers in the past, I could not take so elastic a definition of Christianity as that. As I said before, in olden days it had a much more full-blooded sense. For instance, it included the belief in hell. Belief in eternal hell-fire was an essential item of Christian belief until pretty recent times. In this country, as you know, it ceased to be an essential item because of a decision of the Privy Council, and from that decision the Archbishop of Canterbury and the Archbishop of York dissented; but in this country our religion is settled by Act of Parliament, and therefore the Privy Council was able to override their Graces and hell was no longer necessary to a Christian. Consequently I shall not insist that a Christian must believe in hell.

THE EXISTENCE OF GOD

To come to this question of the existence of God: it is a large and serious question, and if I were to attempt to deal with it in any adequate manner I should have to keep you here until Kingdom Come, so that you will have to excuse me if I deal with it in a somewhat summary fashion. You know, of course, that the Catholic Church has laid it down as a dogma that the existence of God can be proved by the unaided reason. That is a somewhat curious dogma, but it is one of their dogmas. They had to introduce it because at one time the freethinkers adopted the habit of saying that there were such and such arguments which mere reason might urge against the existence of God, but of course they knew as a matter of faith that a God did exist. The arguments and the reasons were set out at great length, and the Catholic Church felt that they must stop it. Therefore they laid it down that the existence of God can be proved by the unaided reason and they had to set up what they considered were arguments to prove it. There are, of course, a number of them, but I shall take only a few.

The First-Cause Argument

Perhaps the simplest and easiest to understand is the argument of the First Cause. (It is maintained that everything we see in this world has a cause, and as you go back in the chain of causes further and further you must come to a First Cause, and to that First Cause you give the name of God.) That argument, I suppose, does not carry very much weight nowadays, because, in the first place, cause is not quite what it used to be. The philosophers and the men of science have got going on cause, and it has not anything like the vitality it used to have; but, apart from that, you can see that the argument that there must be a First Cause is one that cannot have any validity. I may say that when I was a young man and was debating these questions very seriously in my mind, I for a long time accepted the argument of the First Cause, until one day, at the age of eighteen, I read John Stuart Mill's Autobiography, and I there found this sentence: "My father taught me that the question 'Who made me?' cannot be answered, since it immediately suggests the further question 'Who made God?'" That very simple sentence showed me, as I still think, the fallacy in the argument of the First Cause. If everything must have a cause, then God must have a cause. If there can be anything without a cause, it may just as well be the world as God, so that there cannot be any validity in that argument. It is exactly of the same nature as the Hindu's view, that the world rested upon an elephant and the elephant rested upon a tortoise; and when they said, "How about the tortoise?" the Indian said, "Suppose we change the subject." The argument is really no better than that. There is no reason why the world could not have come into being without a cause; nor, on the other hand, is there any reason why it should not have always existed. There is no reason to suppose that the world had a beginning at all. The idea that things must have a beginning is really due to the poverty of our imagination. Therefore, perhaps, I need not waste any more time upon the argument about the First Cause.

The Natural-Law Argument

Then there is a very common argument from natural law. That was a favorite argument all through the eighteenth century, especially under the influence of Sir Isaac Newton and his cosmogony. People observed the planets going around the sun according to the law of gravitation, and they thought that God had given a behest to these planets to move in that particular fashion, and that was why they did so. That was, of course, a convenient and simple explanation that saved them the trouble of looking any further for explanations of the law of gravitation. Nowadays we explain the law of gravitation in a somewhat complicated fashion that Einstein has introduced. I do not propose to give you a lecture on the law of gravitation, as interpreted by Einstein, because that again would take some time; at any rate, you no longer have the sort of natural law that you had in the Newtonian system, where, for some reason that nobody could understand, nature behaved in a uniform fashion. We now find that a great many things we thought were natural laws are really human conventions. You know that even in the remotest depths of stellar space there are still three feet to a yard. That is, no doubt, a very remarkable fact, but you would hardly call it a law of nature. And a great many things that have been regarded as laws of nature are of that kind. On the other hand, where you can get down to any knowledge of what atoms actually do, you will find they are much less subject to law than people thought, and that the laws at which you arrive are statistical averages of just the sort that would emerge from chance. There is, as we all know, a law that if you throw dice you will get double sixes only about once in thirty-six times, and we do not regard that as evidence that the fall of the dice is regulated by design; on the contrary, if the double sixes came every time we should think that there was design. The laws of nature are of that sort as regards a great many of them. They are statistical averages such as would emerge from the laws of chance; and that makes this whole business of natural law much less impressive than it formerly was. Quite apart from that, which represents the momentary state of science that may change tomorrow, the whole idea that natural laws imply a lawgiver is due to a confusion between natural and human laws. Human laws are behests commanding you to behave a certain way, in which way you may choose to behave, or you may choose not to behave; but natural laws are a description of how things do in fact behave, and being a mere description of what they in fact do, you cannot argue that there must be somebody who told them to do that, because even supposing that there were, you are then faced with the question, "Why did God issue just those natural laws and no others?" If you say that he did it simply from his own good pleasure, and without any reason, you then find that there is something which is not subject to law and so your train of natural law is interrupted. If you say, as more orthodox theologians do, that in all the laws which God issues he had a reason for giving those laws rather than others—the reason, of course, being to create the best universe, although you would never think it to look at it—if there were a reason for the laws which God gave, then God himself was subject to law, and therefore you do not get any advantage by introducing God as an intermediary. You have really a law outside and anterior to the divine edicts, and God does not serve your purpose, because he is not the ultimate lawgiver. In short, this whole argument about natural law no longer has anything like the strength that it used to have. I am traveling on in time in my review of the arguments. The arguments that are used for the existence of God change their character as time goes on. They were at first hard intellectual arguments embodying certain quite definite fallacies. As we come to modern times they become less respectable intellectually and more and more affected by a kind of moralizing vagueness.

The Argument from Design

The next step in this process brings us to the argument from design. You all know the argument from design: Everything in the world is made just so that we can manage to live in the world, and if the world was ever so little different, we could not manage to live in it. That is the argument from design. It sometimes takes a rather curious form; for instance, it is argued that rabbits have white tails in order to be easy to shoot. I do not know how rabbits would view that application. It is an easy argument to parody. You all know Voltaire's remark, that obviously the nose was designed to be such as to fit spectacles. That sort of parody has turned out to be not nearly so wide of the mark as it might have seemed in the eighteenth century, because since the time of Darwin we understand much better why living creatures are adapted to their environment. It is not that their environment was made to be suitable to them but they grew to be suitable to it, and that is the basis of adaptation. There is no evidence of design about it.

When you come to look into this argument from design, it is a most astonishing thing that people can believe that this world, with all the things that are in it, with all its defects, should be the best that omnipotence and omniscience have been able to produce in millions of years. I really cannot believe it. Do you think that, if you were granted omnipotence and omniscience and millions of years in which to perfect your world, you could produce nothing better than the Ku Klux Klan or the Fascists?

Moreover, if you accept the ordinary laws of science, you have to suppose that human life and life in general on this planet will die out in due course: it is a stage in the decay of the solar system; at a certain stage of decay you get the sort of conditions of temperature and so forth which are suitable to protoplasm, and there is life for a short time in the life of the whole solar system. You see in the moon the sort of thing to which the earth is tending—something dead, cold, and lifeless.

I am told that that sort of view is depressing, and people will sometimes tell you that if they believed that, they would not be able to go on living. Do not believe it; it is all nonsense. Nobody really worries much about what is going to happen millions of years hence. Even if they think they are worrying much about that, they are really deceiving themselves. They are worried about something much more mundane, or it may merely be a bad digestion; but nobody is really seriously rendered unhappy by the thought of something that is going to happen to this world millions and millions of years hence. Therefore, although it is of course a gloomy view to suppose that life will die out—at least I suppose we may say so, although sometimes when I contemplate the things that people do with their lives I think it is almost a consolation—it is not such as to render life miserable. It merely makes you turn your attention to other things.

. . . Of course I know that the sort of intellectual arguments that I have been talking to you about are not what really moves people. What really moves people to believe in God is not any intellectual argument at all. Most people believe in God because they have been taught from early infancy to do it, and that is the main reason.

Then I think that the next most powerful reason is the wish for safety, a sort of feeling that there is a big brother who will look after you. That plays a very profound part in influencing people's desire for a belief in God.

THE CHARACTER OF CHRIST

I now want to say a few words upon a topic which I often think is not quite sufficiently dealt with by Rationalists, and that is the question whether Christ was the best and the wisest of men. It is generally taken for granted that we should all agree that that was so. I do not myself. I think that there are a good many points upon which I agree with Christ a great deal more than the professing Christians do. I do not know that I could go with Him all the way, but I could go with Him much further than most professing Christians can. You will remember that He said, "Resist not evil: but whosoever shall smite thee on thy right cheek, turn to him the other also." That is not a new precept or a new principle. It was used by Lao-tse and Buddha some 500 or 600 years before Christ, but it is not a principle which as a matter of fact Christians accept. I have no doubt that the present Prime Minister [Stanley Baldwin], for instance, is a most sincere Christian, but I should not advise any of you to go and smite him on one cheek. I think you might find that he thought this text was intended in a figurative sense.

Then there is another point which I consider excellent. You will remember that Christ said, "Judge not lest ye be judged." That principle I do not think you would find was popular in the law courts of Christian countries. I have known in my time quite a number of judges who were very earnest

Christians, and none of them felt that they were acting contrary to Christian principles in what they did. Then Christ says, "Give to him that asketh of thee, and from him that would borrow of thee turn not thou away." That is a very good principle. Your Chairman has reminded you that we are not here to talk politics, but I cannot help observing that the last general election was fought on the question of how desirable it was to turn away from him that would borrow of thee, so that one must assume that the Liberals and Conservatives of this country are composed of people who do not agree with the teaching of Christ, because they certainly did very emphatically turn away on that occasion.

Then there is one other maxim of Christ which I think has a great deal in it, but I do not find that it is very popular among some of our Christian friends. He says, "If thou wilt be perfect, go and sell that which thou hast, and give to the poor." That is a very excellent maxim, but, as I say, it is not much practiced. All these, I think, are good maxims, although they are a little difficult to live up to. I do not profess to live up to them myself; but then, after all, it is not quite the same thing as for a Christian.

Defects in Christ's Teaching

Having granted the excellence of these maxims, I come to certain points in which I do not believe that one can grant either the superlative wisdom or the superlative goodness of Christ as depicted in the Gospels; and here I may say that one is not concerned with the historical question. Historically it is quite doubtful whether Christ ever existed at all, and if He did we do not know anything about Him, so that I am not concerned with the historical question, which is a very difficult one. I am concerned with Christ as He appears in the Gospels, taking the Gospel narrative as it stands, and there one does find some things that do not seem to be very wise. For on thing, He certainly thought that His second coming would occur in clouds of glory before the death of all the people who were living at that time. There are a great many texts that prove that. He says, for instance, "Ye shall not have gone over the cities of Israel till the Son of Man become." Then He says, "There are some standing here which shall not taste death till the Son of Man comes into His kingdom"; and there are a lot of places where it is quite clear that He believed that His second coming would happen during the lifetime of many then living. That was the belief of His earlier followers, and it was the basis of a good deal of His moral teaching. When He said, "Take no thought for the morrow," and things of that sort, it was very largely because He thought that the second coming was going to be very soon, and that all ordinary mundane affairs did not count. I have, as a matter of fact, known some Christians who did believe that the second coming was imminent. I knew a parson who frightened his congregation terribly by telling them that the second coming was very imminent indeed, but they were much consoled when they found that he was planting trees in his garden. The early Christians did really believe it, and they did abstain from such things as planting trees in their gardens, because they did accept from Christ the belief that the second coming was imminent. In that respect, clearly He was not so wise as some other people have been, and He was certainly not superlatively wise.

The Moral Problem

Then you come to moral questions. There is one very serious defect to my mind in Christ's moral character, and that is that He believed in hell. I do not myself feel that any person who is really profoundly humane can believe in everlasting punishment. Christ certainly as depicted in the Gospels did believe in everlasting punishment, and one does find repeatedly a vindictive fury against those people who would not listed to His preaching—an attitude which is not uncommon with preachers, but which does somewhat detract from superlative excellence. You do not, for instance find that attitude in Socrates. You find him quite bland and urbane toward the people who would not listen to him; and it is, to my mind, far more worthy of a sage to take that line than to take the line of indignation. You probably all remember the sort of things that Socrates was saying when he was dying, and the sort of things that he generally did say to people who did not agree with him.

You will find that in the Gospels Christ said, "Ye serpents, ye generation of vipers, how can ye escape the damnation of hell." That was said to people who did not like His preaching. It is not really to my mind quite the best tone, and there are a great many of these things about hell. There is, or course, the familiar text about the sin against the Holy Ghost: "Whosoever speaketh against the Holy Ghost it shall not be forgiven him neither in this World nor in the world to come." That text has caused an unspeakable amount of misery in the world, for all sorts of people have imagined that they have committed the sin against the Holy Ghost, and thought that it would not be forgiven them either in this world or in the world

to come. I really do not think that a person with a proper degree of kindliness in his nature would have put fears and terrors of that sort into the world.

Then Christ says, "The Son of Man shall send forth His angels, and they shall gather out of His kingdom all things that offend, and them which do iniquity, and shall cast them into a furnace of fire; there shall be wailing and gnashing of teeth"; and He goes on about the wailing and gnashing of teeth. It comes in one verse after another, and it is quite manifest to the reader that there is a certain pleasure in contemplating wailing and gnashing of teeth, or else it would not occur so often. Then you all, of course, remember about the sheep and the goats; how at the second coming He is going to divide the sheep from the goats, and He is going to say to the goats, "Depart from me, ye cursed, into everlasting fire." He continues, "And these shall go away into everlasting fire." Then He says again, "If thy hand offend thee, cut it off; it is better for thee to enter into life maimed, than having two hands to go into hell, into the fire that never shall be quenched; where the worm dieth not and the fire is not quenched." He repeats that again and again also. I must say that I think all this doctrine, that hell-fire is a punishment for sin, is a doctrine of cruelty. It is a doctrine that put cruelty into the world and gave the world generations of cruel torture; and the Christ of the Gospels, if you could take Him as His chroniclers represent Him, would certainly have to be considered partly responsible for that.

There are other things of less importance. There is the instance of the Gadarene swine, where it certainly was not very kind to the pigs to put the devils into them and make then rush down the hill to the sea. You must remember that He was omnipotent, and He could have made the devils simply go away; but He chose to send them into the pigs. Then there is the curious story of the fig tree, which always rather puzzled me. You remember what happened about the fig tree. "He was hungry; and seeing a fig tree afar off having leaves, He came if haply He might find anything thereon; and when He came to it He found nothing but leaves, for the time of figs was not yet. And Jesus answered and said unto it: 'No man eat fruit of thee hereafter for ever' . . . and Peter . . . saith unto Him: 'Master, behold the fig tree which thou cursedst is withered away.'" This is a very curious story, because it was not the right time of year for figs, and you really could not blame the tree. I cannot myself feel that either in the matter of wisdom or in the matter of virtue Christ stands quite as high as some other people known to history. I think I should put Buddha and Socrates above Him in those respects.

THE EMOTIONAL FACTOR

As I said before, I do not think that the real reason why people accept religion has anything to do with argumentation. They accept religion on emotional grounds. One is often told that it is a very wrong thing to attack religion, because religion makes men virtuous. So I am told; I have not noticed it. You know, of course, the parody of that argument in Samuel Butler's book, *Erewhon Revisited.* You will remember that in *Erewhon* there is a certain Higgs who arrives in a remote country, and after spending some time there he escapes from that country in a balloon. Twenty years later he comes back to that country and finds a new religion in

which he is worshiped under the name of the "Sun Child," and it is said that he ascended into heaven. He finds that the Feast of the Ascension is about to be celebrated, and he hears Professors Hanky and Panky say to each other that they never set eyes on the man Higgs, and they hope they never will; but they are the high priests of the religion of the Sun Child. He is very indignant, and he comes up to them, and he says, "I am going to expose all this humbug and tell the people of Erewhon that it was only I, the man Higgs, and I went up in a balloon." He was told, "You must not do that, because all the morals of this country are bound round this myth, and if they once know that you did not ascend into heaven they will all become wicked"; and so he is persuaded of that and he goes quietly away.

That is the idea—that we should all be wicked if we did not hold to the Christian religion. It seems to me that the people who have held to it have been for the most part extremely wicked. You find this curious fact, that the more intense has been the religion of any period and the more profound has been the dogmatic belief, the greater has been the cruelty and the worse has been the state of affairs. In the so-called ages of faith, when men really did believe the Christian religion in all its completeness, there was the Inquisition, with its tortures; there were millions of unfortunate women burned as witches; and there was every kind of cruelty practiced upon all sorts of people in the name of religion.

You find as you look around the world that every single bit of progress in humane feeling, every improvement in the criminal law, every step toward the diminution of war, every step toward better treatment of the colored races, or every mitigation of slavery, every moral progress that there has been in the world, has been consistently opposed by the organized churches of the world. I say quite deliberately that the Christian religion, as organized in its churches, has been and still is the principal enemy of moral progress in the world.

HOW THE CHURCHES HAVE RETARDED PROGRESS

You may think that I am going too far when I say that that is still so. I do not think that I am. Take one fact. You will bear with me if I mention it. It is not a pleasant fact, but the churches compel one to mention facts that are not pleasant. Supposing that in this world that we live in today an inexperienced girl is married to a syphilitic man; in that case the Catholic Church says, "That is an indissoluble sacrament. You must endure celibacy or stay together. And if you stay together, you must not use birth control to prevent the birth of syphilitic children." Nobody whose natural sympathies have not been warped by dogma, or whose moral nature was not absolutely dead to all sense of suffering, could maintain that it is right and proper that that state of things should continue.

That is only an example. There are a great many ways in which, at the present moment, the church, by its insistence upon what it chooses to call morality, inflicts upon all sorts of people undeserved and unnecessary suffering. And of course, as we know, it is in its major part an opponent still of progress and of improvement in all the ways that diminish suffering in the world, because it has chosen to label as morality a certain narrow set of rules of conduct which have nothing to do with human happiness; and when you say that this or that ought to be done because it would make for human happiness they think that has nothing to do with the matter at all. "What has human happiness to do with morals? The object of morals is not to make people happy."

FEAR, THE FOUNDATION OF RELIGION

Religion is based, I think, primarily and mainly upon fear. It is partly the terror of the unknown and partly, as I have said, the wish to feel that you have a kind of elder brother who will stand by you in all your troubles and disputes. Fear is the basis of the whole thing—fear of the mysterious, fear of defeat, fear of death. Fear is the parent of cruelty, and therefore it is no wonder if cruelty and religion have gone hand in hand. It is because fear is at the basis of those two things. In this world we can now begin a little to understand things, and a little to master them by help of science, which has forced its way step by step against the Christian religion, against the churches, and against the opposition of all the old precepts. Science can help us to get over this craven fear in which mankind has lived for so many generations. Science can teach us, and I think our own hearts can teach us, no longer to look around for imaginary supports, no longer to invent allies in the sky, but rather to look to our own efforts here below to make this world a fit place to live in, instead of the sort of place that the churches in all these centuries have made it.

WHAT WE MUST DO

We want to stand upon our own feet and look fair and square at the world—its good facts, its bad facts, its beauties, and its ugliness; see the world as it is and be not afraid of it. Conquer the world by intelligence and not merely by being slavishly subdued by the terror that comes from it. The whole conception of God is a conception derived for the ancient Oriental despotisms. It is a conception quite unworthy of free men. When you hear people in church debasing themselves and saying that they are miserable sinners, and all the rest of it, it seems contemptible and not worthy of self-respecting human beings. We ought to stand up and look the world frankly in the face. We ought to make the best we can of the world and if it is not so good as we wish, after all it will still be better than what these others have made of it in all these ages. A good world needs knowledge, kindliness, and courage; it does not need a regretful hankering after the past or a fettering of the free intelligence by the words uttered long ago by ignorant men. It needs a fearless outlook and a free intelligence. It needs hope for the future not looking back all the time toward a past that is dead, which we trust will be far surpassed by the future that our intelligence can create.

MARY DALY

The Leap Beyond Patriarchal Religion

MARY DALY, *who teaches at Boston College, is a leading feminist philosopher and theologian. She is the author of a number of influential books, among them* Beyond God the Father: Toward a Philosophy of Women's Liberation, Gyn/Ecology, *and* Pure Lust.

PROLEGOMENA

1. There exists a planetary sexual caste system, essentially the same in Saudi Arabia and in New York, differing only in degree.

2. This system is masked by sex role segregation, by the dual identity of women, by ideologies and myths.

3. Among the primary loci of sexist conditioning is grammar.

4. The "methods" of the various "fields" are not adequate to express feminist thought. Methodolatry requires that women perform Methodicide, an act of intellectual bravery.

5. All of the major world religions function to legitimate patriarchy. This is true also of the popular cults such as the Krishna movement and the Jesus Freaks.

6. The myths and symbols of Christianity are essentially sexist. Since "God" is male,

the male is God. God the Father legitimates all earthly God-fathers, including Vito Corleone, Pope Paul, President Gerald Ford, the God-fathers of medicine (e.g. the American Medical Association), of science (e.g. NASA), of the media, of psychiatry, of education, and of all the -ologies.

7. The myth of feminine evil, expressed in the story of the Fall, is reinforced by the myth of salvation/redemption by a single human being of the male sex. The idea of a unique diving incarnation in a male, the God-man of the "hypostatic union," is inherently sexist and oppressive. Christolatry is idolatry.

8. A significant and growing cognitive minority of women, radical feminists, are breaking out from under the sacred shelter of patriarchal religious myths.

9. This breaking out, facing anomy when the meaning structures of patriarchy are seen through and rejected, is a communal, political event. It is a revelatory event, a creative, political ontophany.

10. The bonding of the growing cognitive minority of women who are racial feminists, commonly called *sisterhood*, involves a process of new naming, in which words are wrenched out of their old semantic context and heard in a new semantic context. For example, the "sisterhoods" of patriarchy, such as religious congregations of women, were really mini-brotherhoods. *Sisterhood* heard with new ears is bonding for women's own liberation.

11. There is an inherent dynamic in the women's revolution in Judeo-Christian society which is Antichurch, whether or not feminists specifically concern ourselves with churches. This is so because the Judeo-Christian tradition legitimates patriarchy— the prevailing power structure and prevailing world view—which the women's revolution leaves behind.

12. The women's revolution is not only Antichurch. It is a postchristian spiritual revolution.

13. The ethos of Judeo-Christian culture is dominated by The Most Unholy Trinity: Rape, Genocide, and War. It is rapism which spawns racism. It is gynocide which spawns genocide, for sexism (rapism) is fundamental socialization to objectify "the other."

14. The women's revolution is concerned with transvaluation of values, beyond the ethics dominated by The Most Unholy Trinity.

15. The women's revolution is not merely about equality within a patriarchal society (a contradiction in terms). It is about *power* and redefining power.

16. Since Christian myths are inherently sexist, and since the women's revolution is not about "equality" but about power, there is an intrinsic dynamic in the feminist movement which goes beyond efforts to reform Christian churches. Such efforts eventually come to be recognized as comparable to a Black person's trying to reform the Ku Klux Klan.

17. Within patriarchy, power is generally understood as power *over* people, the environment, things. In the rising consciousness of women, power is experienced as *power of presence* to ourselves and to each other, as we affirm our own being against and beyond the alienated identity (non-being) bestowed upon us within patriarchy. This is experienced as *power of absence* by those who would objectify women as "the other," as magnifying mirrors.

18. The presence of women to ourselves which is *absence* to the oppressor is the essential dynamic opening up the women's revolution to human liberation. It is an invitation to men to confront non-being and hence affirm their be-ing.

19. It is unlikely that many men will accept this invitation willingly, or even be able to hear it, since they have profound vested (though self-destructive) interest in the present social arrangements.

20. The women's movement is a new mode of relating to the self, to each other, to men, to the environment—in a word—to the cosmos. It is self-affirming, refusing objectification of the self and of the other.

21. Entrance into new feminist time/space, which is moving time/space located on the boundaries of patriarchal institutions, is active participation in ultimate reality, which is dereified, recognized as Verb, as intransitive Verb with no object to block its dynamism.

22. Entrance into radical feminist consciousness involves recognition that all male-dominated "revolutions," which do not reject the universally oppressive reality which is patriarchy, are in reality only reforms. They are "revolutions" only in the sense that they are spinnings of the wheels of the same senescent system.

23. Entrance into radical feminist consciousness implies an awareness that the women's revolution is the "final cause" (pun intended) in the radical sense that it is the cause which can move the other causes. It is the catalyst which can bring about real change, since it is the rising up of the universally and primordially objectified "Other," discrediting the myths which legitimate rapism. Rapism is by extension the objectification and destruction of all "others" and inherently tends to the destruction of the human species and of all life on this planet.

Radical feminism, the becoming of women, is very much an Otherworld Journey. It is both discovery and creation of a world other than patriarchy. Some observation reveals that patriarchy is "everywhere." Even outer space and the future have been colonized. As a rule, even the more imaginative science fiction writers (seemingly the most foretelling futurists) cannot/will not create a space and time in which women get far beyond the role of space stewardess. Nor does this situation exist simply "outside" women's minds, securely fastened into institutions which we can physically leave behind. Rather, it is also internalized, festering inside women's heads, even feminist heads.

The journey of women *becoming,* then, involves exorcism of the internalized Godfather, in his various manifestations (His name is legion). It involves dangerous encounters with these demons. Within the Christian tradition, particularly in medieval times, evil spirits have sometimes been associated with the Seven Deadly Sins, both as personifications and as causes. A "standard" and prevalent listing of the Sins is, of course, the following: pride, avarice, anger, lust, gluttony, envy, and sloth. I am contending that these have all been radically misnamed, that is, inadequately and even perversely "understood" within Christianity. These concepts have been used to victimize the oppressed, particularly women. They are particularized expressions of the overall use of "evil" to victimize women. The feminist journey involves confrontations with the demonic distortions of evil.

Why has it seemed "appropriate" in this culture that a popular book and film (*The Exorcist*) center around a Jesuit who "exorcises" a girl-child who is "possessed"? Why is there no book or film about a woman who exorcises a Jesuit? Within a culture possessed by the myth of feminine evil, the naming, describing, and theorizing about good and evil has constituted as web of deception, a Maya. The journey of women becoming is breaking through this web—a Fall into free space. It is reassuming the role of subject, as opposed to object, and naming good and evil on the basis of our own intuitive intellection. . . .

THE QUALITATIVE LEAP

Creative, living, political hope for movement beyond the gynocidal reign of the fathers will be fulfilled only if women continue to make qualitative leaps in living our transcendence. A short-circuited hope of transcendence has caused many to remain inside churches, and patriarchal religion sometimes has seemed to satisfy the hunger for transcendence. The problem has been that both the hunger and the satisfaction generated within such religions have to a great extent alienated women from our deepest aspirations. Spinning in vicious circles of false needs and false consciousness, women caught on the patriarchal wheel have not been able to experience women's own experience.

I suggest that what is required is *ludic cerebration,* the free play of intuition in our own space, giving rise to thinking that is vigorous, informed, multi-dimensional, independent, creative, tough. *Ludic cerebration* is thinking out of experience. I do not mean the experience of dredging out All That Was Wrong with Mother, or of instant intimacy in group encounters, or of waiting at the doctoral dispensary, or of self-lobotomization in order to publish, perish, and then be promoted. I mean the experience of being. *Be-ing* is the verb that says the dimensions of depth in all verbs, such as intuiting, reasoning, loving, imaging, making, acting, as well as the couraging, hoping, and playing that are always there when one is really living.

It may be that some new things happen within patriarchy, but one thing essentially stays the same: women are always marginal beings. From this vantage point of the margin it is possible to look at what is between the margins with the lucidity of The Complete Outsider. To change metaphors: The systems within the System do not appear so radically different from each other to those excluded by all. Hope for a qualitative leap lies in *us* by reason of that deviance from the "norm" which was first imposed but which can also be *chosen* on our own terms. This means that there has to be a shift from "acceptable" female deviance (characterized by triviality, diffuseness, dependence upon others for self-definition, low self-esteem, powerlessness) to deviance which may be unacceptable to others but which is acceptable to the self and *is* self-acceptance.

For women concerned with philosophical/theological questions, it seems to me, this implies the necessity of some sort of choice. One either tries to avoid "acceptable" deviance ("normal" female idiocy) by becoming accepted as a male-identified professional, or else one tries to make the qualitative leap toward self-acceptable deviance as ludic cerebrator, questioner of everything, madwoman, and witch.

I do mean witch. The heretic who rejects the idols of patriarchy is the blasphemous creatrix of her own thoughts. She is finding her life and intends not to lose it. The witch that smolders within every woman who cared and dared enough to become a philosophically/spiritually questing feminist in the first place seems to be crying out these days: "Light my fire!" The qualitative leap, the light of those flames of spiritual imagination and cerebral fantasy can be a new dawn. . . .

WANTED: "GOD" OR "THE GODDESS"?

Feminist consciousness is experienced by a significant number of women as ontological becoming, that is, being. This process requires existential courage, courage to be and to *see,* which is both revolutionary and revelatory, revealing our participation in the ultimate reality as Verb, as intransitive Verb.

The question obviously arises of the need for anthropomorphic symbols for this reality. There is no inherent contradiction between speaking of ultimate reality as Verb and speaking of this as personal. The Verb is more personal than a mere static noun. However, if we choose to *image* the Verb in anthropomorphic symbols, we can run into a problematic phenomenon which sociologist Henri Desroche calls "crossing." "Crossing" refers to a notable tendency among oppressed groups to attempt to change or adapt the ideological tools of the oppressor, so that they can be used *against* him and *for* the oppressed. The problem here is the fact that the functioning of "crossing" does not generally move far enough outside the ideological framework it seeks to undermine. . . .

Some women religious leaders within Western culture in modern times have performed something like a "crossing" operation, notably such figures as Mary Baker Eddy and Ann Lee, in stressing the "maternal" aspect of the divinity. The result has been mixed. Eddy's "Father-Mother God" is, after all, the Christian God. Nor does Ann Lee really move completely outside the Christian framework. . . . But it is . . . necessary to note that their theologies lack explicit relevance to the concrete problems of the oppression of women. Intellection and spirituality remain cut off from creative political movement. In earlier periods also there were women within the Christian tradition who tried to "cross" the Christian all-male God and Christ to some degree. An outstanding example was Juliana of Norwich, an English recluse and mystic who lived in the last half of the fourteenth century. Juliana's "God" and "Jesus" were—if language conveys anything—hermaphroditic constructs, with the primary identity clearly male. While there are many levels on which I could analyze Juliana's words about "our beloved Mother, Jesus (who) feeds us with himself," suffice it to say here that this hermaphroditic image is somewhat less than attractive. The "androgynous" God and Jesus present problems which occur in connection with the use of the term "androgyny" to describe the direction of women's becoming. There is something like a "liberation of the woman within" the (primarily male) God and Jesus. . . .

One fact that stands out here is that these were women whose imaginations were still partially controlled by Christian myth. My contention is that they were caught in a contradiction. . . . I am saying that there is a profound contradiction between the inherent logic of radical feminism and the inherent logic of the Christian symbol system. . . .

Both the reformers and those who leave Judaism and Christianity behind are contributing and will contribute in different ways to the process of the becoming of women. The point here is not to place value judgments upon individual persons and their efforts—and there are heroic efforts at all points of the feminist spectrum. Rather, it is to disclose an inherent logic in feminism. The courage which some women have in affirming this logic comes in part from having been on the feminist journey for quite awhile. Encouragement comes also from knowing increasing numbers of women who have chosen the route of the logical conclusion. Some of these women have "graduated" from Christianity or religious Judaism, and some have never even been associated closely with church or synagogue, but have discovered spiritual and mythic depths in the women's movement itself. What we share is a sense of becoming in cosmic process, which I prefer to call the Verb, Be-ing, and which some would still call "God."

For some feminists concerned with the spiritual depth of the movement, the word "God" is becoming increasingly problematic, however. This by no means indicates a movement in the direction of "atheism" or "agnosticism" or "secularism," as these terms are usually understood. Rather, the problem arises precisely because of the spiritual and mythic quality perceived in the feminist process itself. Some use expressions such as "power of being." Some reluctantly still use the word "God" while earnestly trying to divest the term of its patriarchal associations, attempting to think perhaps of the "God of the philosophers" rather than the overtly masculist and oppressive "God of the theologians." But the problem becomes increasingly troublesome, the more the "God" of the various Western philosophers is subjected to feminist analysis. "He"— "Jahweh" still often hovers behind the abstractions, stunting our own thought, giving us a sense of contrived doublethink. The word "God" just may be inherently oppressive.

Indeed, the word "Goddess" has also been problematic, but for different reasons. Some have been worried about the problem of "crossing." However, that difficulty appears more and more as a pseudo-difficulty when it is recognized that "crossing" is likely to occur only when one is trying to work *within* a sexist tradition. For example, Christian women who in their "feminist liturgies" experiment with referring to "God" as "she" and to the Trinity as "The Mother, the Daughter, and the Holy Spirit," are still working within all the boundaries of the same symbolic framework and the same power structure. Significantly, their services are at the same place and time as "the usual," and are regarded by most of the constituency of the churches as occasional variations of "business as usual."

As women who are outside the Christian church inform ourselves of evidence supporting the existence of ancient matriarchy and of evidence indicating that the Gods of patriarchy are indeed contrived, pale derivatives and reversals of the Great Goddess of an earlier period, the fear of mere "crossing" appears less appropriate and perhaps even absurd. There is also less credibility allowable to the notion that "Goddess" would function like "God" in reverse, that is, to legitimate an oppressive "female-dominated" society, if one is inclined to look seriously at evidence that matriarchal society was not structured like patriarchy, that it was non-hierarchical. . . .

Clearly, it would be inappropriate and arrogant to try to "explain" or "interpret" this experience of another person. I can only comment that many women I know are finding power of being within the self, rather than in "internalized" father images. As a philosopher, my preference has been for abstractions. Indeed I have always been annoyed and rather embarrassed by "anthropomorphic" symbols, preferring terms such as "ground and power of being" (Tillich), "beyond subjectivity and objectivity" (James), "the Encompassing" (Jaspers), or the commonly used "Ultimate Reality," or "cosmic process." More recently I have used the expression "Intransitive Verb." Despite this philosophical inclination, and also because of it, I find it impossible to ignore the realm of symbols, or to fail to recognize that many women are experiencing and participating in a remythologizing process, which is a new dawn.

It is necessary to add a few remarks about the functioning of the confusing and complex "Mary" symbol within Christianity. Through it, the power of the Great Goddess symbol is enchained, captured, used, cannibalized, tokenized, domesticated, tranquilized. In spite of this, I think that many women and at least some men, when they have heard of or imaged the "Mother of God," have, by something like a selective perception process, screened out the standardized, lobotomized, dull, derivative and dwarfed Christian reflections of a more ancient symbol; they have perceived something that might more accurately be described as the Great Goddess, and which, in human terms, can be translated into "the strong woman who can relate because she can stand alone." A woman of Jewish background commented that "Mother of God" had always seemed strange and contradictory to her. Not having been programmed to "know" about the distinctions between the "divine" and the "human" nature of

"Christ," or to "know" that the "Mother of God" is less than God, this woman had been able to hear the expression with the ears of an extraenvironmental listener. It sounded, she said, something like "infinite plus one." When this symbolic nonsense is recognized, it is more plausible simply to *think* "infinite," and to *image* something like "Great Mother," or "Goddess."

It may appear that the suffix "-ess" presents a problem, when one considers other usages of that suffix, for example, in "poetess," or in "authoress." In these cases, there is a tone of depreciation, a suggestion that women poets and authors are in a separate and "inferior" category to be judged by different standards than their male counterparts. However, the suffix does not always function in this "diminishing" way. For example, there appear to be no "diminutive" overtones suggested by the word "actress." So also it seems that the term "Goddess"—or "The Goddess"—*is not only non-diminutive,* but very strong. Indeed, it calls before the mind images of a powerful and ancient tradition before, behind, and beyond Christianity. These are multi-dimensional images of women's present and future becoming/be-ing.

bell hooks AND CORNEL WEST

Black Women and Men: Partnership in the 1990s

bell hooks *is the pen name of Gloria Watkins. She teaches English and African-American Studies at Yale University. She has published numerous essays and books of cultural criticism. Her most recent book is* Outlaw Culture: Resisting Representations *(1995).*

CORNEL WEST *is a professor of Philosophy of Religion and African-American Studies at Harvard University. Among his many publications are* The American Evasion of Philosophy *(1989) and* Race Matters *(1993).*

b. h.

I requested that Charles sing "Precious Lord" because the conditions that led Thomas Dorsey to write this song always make me think about gender issues, issues of black masculinity. Mr. Dorsey wrote this song after his wife died in childbirth. That experience caused him to have a crisis of faith. He did not think he would be able to go on living without her. That sense of unbearable crisis truly expresses the contemporary dilemma of faith. Mr. Dorsey talked abut the way he tried to cope with this "crisis of faith." He prayed and prayed for a healing and received the words to this song. This song has helped so many folk when they are feeling low, feeling as if they can't go on. It was my grandmother's favorite song. I remembered how we sang it at her funeral. She died when she was almost ninety. And I am moved now as I was then by the knowledge that we can take our pain, work with it, recycle it, and transform it so that it becomes a source of power.

Let me introduce to you my "brother," my comrade Cornel West.

C. W.

First I need to just acknowledge the fact that we as black people have come together to reflect on our past, present, and objective future. That, in and of itself, is a sign of hope. I'd like to thank the Yale African-American Cultural Center for bringing us together. bell and I thought it would be best to present in dialogical form a series of reflections on the

crisis of black males and females. There is a state of siege
raging now in black communities across this nation linked
not only to drug addiction but also consolidation of
corporate power as we know it, and redistribution of wealth
from the bottom to the top, coupled with the ways with
which a culture and society centered on the market,
preoccupied with consumption, erode structures of feeling,
community, tradition. Reclaiming our heritage and sense of
history are prerequisites to any serious talk about black
freedom and black liberation in the twenty-first century. We
want to try to create that kind of community here today, a
community that we hope will be a place to promote
understanding. Critical understanding is a prerequisite for
any serious talk about coming together, sharing,
participating, creating bonds of solidarity so that black
people and other progressive people can continue to hold
up the blood-stained banners that were raised when that
song was sung in the civil rights movement. It was one of
Dr. Martin Luther King's favorite songs, reaffirming his
own struggle and that of many others who have tried to link
some sense of faith, religious faith, political faith, to the
struggle for freedom. We thought it would be best to have a
dialogue to put forth analysis and provide a sense of what
form a praxis would take. That praxis will be necessary for
us to talk seriously about black power, black liberation in
the twenty-first century.

b. h.

Let us say a little bit about ourselves. Both Cornel and I come to
you as individuals who believe in God. That belief informs
our message.

C. W.

One of the reasons we believe in God is due to the long tradition
of religious faith in the black community. I think that, as a
people who have had to deal with the absurdity of being
black in America, for many of us it is a question of God and
sanity, or God and suicide. And if you are serious about
black struggle you know that in many instances you will be
stepping out on nothing, hoping to land on something. That
is the history of black folks in the past and present, and it
continually concerns those of us who are willing to speak
out with boldness and a sense of the importance of history
and struggle. You speak knowing that you won't be able to
do that for too long because America is such a violent

culture. Given those conditions you have to ask yourself what links to a tradition will sustain you given the absurdity and insanity we are bombarded with daily. And so the belief in God itself is not to be understood in a noncontextual manner. It is understood in relation to a particular context, to specific circumstances.

b. h.

We also come to you as two progressive black people on the left.

C. W.

Very much so.

b. h.

I will read a few paragraphs to provide a critical framework for our discussion of black power, just in case some of you may not know what black power means. We are gathered to speak with one another about black power in the twenty-first century. In James Boggs's essay, "Black Power: A Scientific Concept Whose Time Has Come," first published in 1968, he called attention to the radical political significance of the black power movement, asserting: "Today the concept of black power expresses the revolutionary social force which must not only struggle against the capitalist but against the workers and all who benefit by and support the system which has oppressed us." We speak of black power in this very different context to remember, reclaim, revision, and renew. We remember first that the historical struggle for black liberation was forged by black women and men who were concerned about the collective welfare of black people. Renewing our commitment to this collective struggle should provide a grounding for new direction in contemporary political practice. We speak today of political partnership between black men and women. The late James Baldwin wrote in his autobiographical preface to *Notes of a Native Son:* "I think that the past is all that makes the present coherent and further that the past will remain horrible for as long as we refuse to accept it honestly." Accepting the challenge for this prophetic statement as we look at our contemporary past as black people, the space between the sixties and the nineties, we see a weakening of political solidarity between black men and women. It is crucial for the future black liberation struggle that we remain ever mindful that ours is a shared struggle, that we are each other's faith.

C. W.

I think we can even begin by talking about the kind of
existentialist chaos that exists in our own lives and our
inability to overcome the sense of alienation and frustration
we experience when we try to create bonds of intimacy and
solidarity with one another. Now part of this frustration is
to be understood again in relation to structures and
institutions. In the way in which our culture of consumption
has promoted an addiction to stimulation—one that puts a
premium on bottled commodified stimulation. The market
does this in order to convince us that our consumption
keeps oiling the economy in order for it to reproduce itself.
But the effect of this addiction to stimulation is an
undermining, a waning of our ability for qualitatively rich
relationships. It's no accident that crack is the postmodern
drug, that it is the highest form of addiction known to
humankind, that it provides a feeling ten times more
pleasurable than orgasm.

b. h.

Addiction is not about relatedness, about relationships. So it
comes as no surprise that as addiction becomes more
pervasive in black life it undermines our capacity to
experience community. Just recently, I was telling someone
that I would like to buy a little house next door to my
parents' house. This house used to be Mr. Johnson's house
but he recently passed away. And they could not understand
why I would want to live near my parents. My explanation
that my parents were aging did not satisfy. Their inability to
understand or appreciate the value of sharing family life
intergenerationally was a sign to me of the crisis facing our
communities. It's as though as black people we have lost
our understanding of the importance of mutual
interdependency, of communal living. That we no longer
recognize as valuable the notion that we collectively shape
the terms of our survival is a sign of crisis.

C. W.

And when there is crisis in those communities and institutions
that have played a fundamental role in transmitting to
younger generations our values and sensibility, our ways of
life and our ways of struggle, we find ourselves distanced,
not simply from our predecessors but from the critical
project of black liberation. And so more and more we seem
to have young black people who are very difficult to

understand, because it seems as though they live in two
very different worlds. We don't really understand their
music. Black adults may not be listening to NWA (Niggers
With Attitude) straight out of Compton, California. They
may not understand why they are doing what Stetsasonic is
doing, what Public Enemy is all about, because young
people have been fundamentally shaped by the brutal side
of American society. Their sense of reality is shaped on the
one hand by a sense of coldness and callousness, and on the
other hand by a sense of passion for justice, contradictory
impulses which surface simultaneously. Mothers may find
it difficult to understand their children. Grandparents may
find it difficult to understand us—and it's this slow
breakage that has to be restored.

b. h.

That sense of breakage, or rupture, is often tragically expressed in
gender relations. When I told folks that Cornel West and I
were talking about partnership between black women and
men, they thought I meant romantic relationships. I replied
that it was important for us to examine the multi-
relationships between black women and men, how we deal
with fathers, with brothers, with sons. We are talking about
all our relationships across gender because it is not just the
heterosexual love relationships between black women and
men that are in trouble. Many of us can't communicate
with parents, siblings, etc. I've talked with many of you
and asked, "What is it you feel should be addressed?" And
many of you responded that you wanted to talk about black
men and how they need to "get it together."
Let's talk about why we see the struggle to assert agency—that is,
the ability to act in one's best interest—as a male thing. I
mean, black men are not the only ones among us who need
to "get it together." And if black men collectively refuse to
educate themselves for critical consciousness, to acquire
the means to be self-determined, should our communities
suffer, or should we not recognize that both black women
and men must struggle for self-actualization, must learn to
"get it together"? Since the culture we live in continues to
equate blackness with maleness, black awareness of the
extent to which our survival depends on mutual partnership
between women and men is undermined. In renewed black
liberation struggle, we recognize the position of black men
and women, the tremendous role black women played in
every freedom struggle.

Certainly Septima Clark's book *Ready from Within* is necessary reading for those of us who want to understand the historical development of sexual politics in black liberation struggle. Clark describes her father's insistence that she not fully engage herself in civil rights struggle because of her gender. Later, she found the source of her defiance in religion. It was the belief in spiritual community, that no difference must be made between the role of women and that of men, that enabled her to be "ready within." To Septima Clark, the call to participate in black liberation struggle was a call from God. Remembering and recovering the stories of how black women learned to assert historical agency in the struggle for self-determination in the context of community and collectivity is important for those of us who struggle to promote black liberation, a movement that has at its core a commitment to free our communities of sexist domination, exploitation, and oppression. We need to develop a political terminology that will enable black folks to talk deeply about what we mean when we urge black women and men to "get it together."

C. W.

I think again that we have to keep in mind the larger context of American society, which has historically expressed contempt for black men and black women. The very notion that black people are human beings is a new notion in western civilization and is still not widely accepted in practice. And one of the consequences of this pernicious idea is that it is very difficult for black men and women to remain attuned to each other's humanity, so when bell talks about black women's agency and some of the problems black men have when asked to acknowledge black women's humanity, it must be remembered that this refusal to acknowledge one another's humanity is a reflection of the way we are seen and treated in the larger society. And it's certainly not true that white folks have a monopoly on human relationships. When we talk abut a crisis in western civilization, black people are a part of that civilization even though we have been beneath it, our backs serving as a foundation for the building of that civilization, and we have to understand how it affects us so that the partnership that bell talks about can take on real substance and content. I think partnerships between black men and black women can be made when we learn how to be supportive and think in terms of critical affirmation.

b. h.

Certainly black people have not talked enough about the
importance of constructing patterns of interaction that
strengthen our capacity to be affirming.

C. W.

We need to affirm one another, support one another, help, enable,
equip, and empower as one another to deal with the present
crisis, but it can't be uncritical, because if it's uncritical
then we are again refusing to acknowledge other people's
humanity. If we are serious about acknowledging and
affirming other people's humanity then we are committed
to trusting and believing that they are forever in process.
Growth, development, maturation happens in stages.
People grow, develop, and mature along the lines in which
they are taught. Disenabling critique and contemptuous
feedback hinders.

b. h.

We need to examine the function of critique in traditional black
communities. Often it does not serve as a constructive
force. Like we have that popular slang word "dissin'" and
we know that "dissin'" refers to a kind of disenabling
contempt—when we "read" each other in ways that are so
painful, so cruel, that the person can't get up from where
you have knocked them down. Other destructive forces in
our lives are envy and jealousy. These undermine our
efforts to work for a collective good. Let me give a minor
example. When I came in this morning I saw Cornel's latest
book on the table. I immediately wondered why my book
was not there and caught myself worrying about whether he
was receiving some gesture of respect or recognition denied
me. When he heard me say, "Where's my book?" he
pointed to another table.
Often when people are suffering a legacy of deprivation, there is
a sense that there are never any goodies to go around, so
that we must viciously compete with one another. Again
this spirit of competition creates conflict and divisiveness.
In a larger social context, competition between black
women and men has surfaced around the issue of whether
black female writers are receiving more attention than
black male writers. Rarely does anyone point to the reality
that only a small minority of black women writers are
receiving public accolades. Yet the myth that black women

who succeed are taking something away from black men continues to permeate black psyches and inform how we as black women and men respond to one another. Since capitalism is rooted in unequal distribution of resources, it is not surprising that we as black women and men find ourselves in situations of competition and conflict.

C. W.

I think part of the problem is deep down in our psyche we recognize that we live in such a conservative society, a society of business elites, a society in which corporate power influences are assuring that a certain group of people do get up higher.

b. h.

Right, including some of you in this room.

C. W.

And this is true not only between male and female relations but also black and brown relations and black and Korean, and black and Asian relations. We are struggling over crumbs because we know that the bigger part of lower corporate America is already received. One half of one percent of America owns twenty-two percent of the wealth, one percent owns thirty-two percent and the bottom forty-five percent of the population has twenty percent of the wealth. So, you end up with this kind of crabs-in-the-barrel mentality. When you see someone moving up you immediately think they'll get a bigger cut in big-loaf corporate America and you think that's something real because we're still shaped by the corporate ideology of the larger context.

b. h.

Here at Yale many of us are getting a slice of that mini-loaf and yet are despairing. It was discouraging when I came here to teach and found in many black people a quality of despair which is not unlike that we know is felt in "crack neighborhoods." I wanted to understand the connection between underclass black despair and that of black people here who have immediate and/or potential access to so much material privilege. This despair mirrors the spiritual crisis that is happening in our culture as a whole. Nihilism is everywhere. Some of this despair is rooted in a deep sense of loss. Many black folks who have made it or are making it undergo an identity crisis. This is especially true for individual black people working to assimilate into the "mainstream." Suddenly, they may feel panicked, alarmed by the knowledge that they do not understand their history, that life is without purpose and meaning. These feelings of alienation and estrangement create suffering. The suffering many black people experience today is linked to the suffering of the past, to "historical memory." Attempts by black people to understand that suffering, to come to terms with it, are the conditions which enable a work like Toni Morrison's *Beloved* to receive so much attention. To look back, not just to describe slavery but to try and reconstruct a psycho-social history of its impact has only recently been fully understood as a necessary stage in the process of collective black self-recovery.

C. W.

The spiritual crisis that has happened, especially among the well-to-do blacks, has taken the form of the quest for therapeutic release. So that you can get very thin, flat, and uni-dimensional forms of spirituality that are simply an attempt to sustain the well-to-do black folks as they engage in their consumerism and privatism. The kind of spirituality we're talking about is not the kind that remains superficial just physically but serves as an opium to help you justify and rationalize your own cynicism vis-à-vis the disadvantaged folk in our community. We could talk about churches and their present role in the crisis of America, religious faith as the American way of life, the gospel of health and wealth, helping the bruised psyches of the black middle class make it through America. That's not the form of spirituality that we're talking about. We're talking about something deeper—you used to call it conversion—so that notions of service and risk and sacrifice once again become fundamental. It's very important, for example, that those of you who remember the days in which black colleges were hegemonic among the black elite remember them critically but also acknowledge that there was something positive going on there. What was going on was that you were told every Sunday, with the important business of chapel, that you had to give service to the race. Now it may have been a bourgeois form, but it created a moment of accountability, and with the erosion of the service ethic the very possibility of putting the needs of others alongside of one's own

diminishes. In this syndrome, me-ness, selfishness, and
egocentricity become more and more prominent, creating a
spiritual crisis where you need more psychic opium to get
you over.

b. h.

We have experienced such a change in that communal ethic of
service that was so necessary for survival in traditional
black communities. That ethic of service has been altered
by shifting class relations. And even those black folks who
have little or no class mobility may buy into a bourgeois
class sensibility; TV shows like *Dallas* and *Dynasty* teach
ruling class ways of thinking and being to underclass poor
people. A certain kind of bourgeois individualism of the
mind prevails. It does not correspond to actual class reality
or circumstances of deprivation. We need to remember the
many economic structures and class politics that have led to
a shift of priorities for "privileged" blacks. Many privileged
black folks obsessed with living out a bourgeois dream of
liberal individualistic success no longer feel as though they
have any accountability in relation to the black poor and
underclass.

C. W.

We're not talking about the narrow sense of guilt privileged black
people can feel, because guilt usually paralyzes action.
What we're talking about is how one uses one's time and
energy. We're talking about the ways in which the black
middle class, which is relatively privileged vis-à-vis the
black working class, working poor, and underclass, needs
to acknowledge that along with that privilege goes
responsibility. Somewhere I read that for those to whom
much is given, much is required. And the question
becomes, "How do we exercise that responsibility given
our privilege?" I don't think it's a credible notion to believe
the black middle class will give up on its material toys. No,
the black middle class will act like any other middle class
in the human condition; it will attempt to maintain its
privilege. There is something seductive about comfort and
convenience. The black middle class will not return to the
ghetto, especially given the territorial struggles going on
with gangs and so forth. Yet, how can we use what power
we do have to be sure more resources are available to those
who are disadvantaged? So the question becomes, "How do
we use our responsibility and privilege?" Because, after all,
black privilege is a result of black struggle.

I think the point to make here is that there is a new day in black
America. It is the best of times and the worst of times in
black America. Political consciousness is escalating in
black America, among black students, among black
workers, organized black workers and trade unions,
increasingly we are seeing black leaders with vision. The
black church is on the move, black popular music, political
themes and motifs are on the move. So don't think in our
critique we somehow ask you to succumb to a paralyzing
pessimism. There are grounds for hope and when that
corner is turned, and we don't know what particular
catalytic event will serve as the take-off for it (just like we
didn't know December 1955 would be the take-off), but
when it occurs we have got to be ready. The privileged
black folks can play a rather crucial role if we have a
service ethic, if we want to get on board, if we want to be
part of the progressive, prophetic bandwagon. And that is
the question we will have to ask ourselves and each other.

b. h.

We also need to remember that there is a joy in struggle.
Recently, I was speaking on a panel at a conference with
another black woman from a privileged background. She
mocked the notion of struggle. When she expressed, "I'm
just tired of hearing about the importance of struggle; it
doesn't interest me," the audience clapped. She saw
struggle solely in negative terms, a perspective which led
me to question whether she had ever taken part in any
organized resistance movement. For if you have, you know
that there is joy in struggle. Those of us who are old
enough to remember segregated schools, the kind of
political effort and sacrifice folks were making to ensure
we would have full access to educational opportunities,
surely remember the sense of fulfillment when goals that
we struggled for were achieved. When we sang together
"We shall overcome" there was a sense of victory, a sense
of power that comes when we strive to be self-determining.
When Malcolm X spoke about his journey to Mecca, the
awareness he achieved, he gives expression to that joy that
comes from struggling to grow. When Martin Luther King
talked about having been to the mountaintop, he was
sharing with us that he arrived at a peak of critical
awareness, and it gave him great joy. In our liberatory
pedagogy we must teach young black folks to understand
that struggle is process, that one moves from circumstances
of difficulty and pain to awareness, joy, fulfillment. That

the struggle to be critically conscious can be that movement
which takes you to another level, that lifts you up, that
makes you feel better. You feel good, you feel your life has
meaning and purpose.

C. W.

A rich life is fundamentally a life of serving others, a life of
trying to leave the world a little better than you found it.
That rich life comes into being in human relationships. This
is true at the personal level. Those of you who have been in
love know what I am talking about. It is also true at the
organizational and communal level. It's difficult to find joy
by yourself even if you have all the right toys. It's difficult.
Just ask somebody who has got a lot of material
possessions but doesn't have anybody to share them with.
Now that's at the personal level. There is a political version
of this. It has to do with what you see when you get up in
the morning and look in the mirror and ask yourself
whether you are simply wasting time on the planet or
spending time in an enriching manner. We are talking
fundamentally about the meaning of life and the place of
struggle. bell talks about the significance of struggle and
service. For those of us who are Christians there are certain
theological foundations on which our commitment to serve
is based. Christian life is understood to be a life of service.
Even so, Christians have no monopoly on the joys that
come from service and those of you who are part of secular
culture can also enjoy this sense of enrichment. Islamic
brothers and sisters share in a religious practice which also
places emphasis on the importance of service. When we
speak of commitment to a life of service we must also talk
about the fact that such a commitment goes against the
grain, especially the foundations of our society. To talk this
way about service and struggle we must also talk about
strategies that will enable us to sustain this sensibility, this
commitment.

b. h.

When we talk about that which will sustain and nurture our
spiritual growth as a people, we must once again talk about
the importance of community. For one of the most vital
ways we sustain ourselves is by building communities of
resistance, places where we know we are not alone. In
Prophetic Fragments, Cornel began his essay on Martin
Luther King by quoting the lines of the spiritual, "He

promised never to leave me, never to leave me alone." In black spiritual tradition the promise that we will not be alone cannot be heard as an affirmation of passivity. It does not mean we can sit around and wait for God to take care of business. We are not alone when we build community together. Certainly there is a great feeling of community in this room today. And yet when I was here at Yale I felt that my labor was not appreciated. It was not clear that my work was having meaningful impact. Yet I feel that impact today. When I walked into the room a black woman sister let me know how much my teaching and writing had helped her. There's more of the critical affirmation Cornel spoke of. That critical affirmation says, "Sister, what you're doing is uplifting me in some way." Often folk think that those folks who are spreading the message are so "together" that we do not need affirmation, critical dialogue about the impact of all that we teach and write about and how we live in the world.

C. W.

It is important to note the degree to which black people in particular, and progressive people in general, are alienated and estranged from communities that would sustain and support us. We are often homeless. Our struggles against a sense of nothingness and attempts to reduce us to nothing are ongoing. We confront regularly the question, "Where can I find a sense of home?" That sense of home can only be found in our construction of those communities of resistance bell talks about and the solidarity we can experience within them. Renewal comes through participating in community. That is the reason so many folks continue to go to church. In religious experience they find a sense of renewal, a sense of home. In community one can feel that we are moving forward, that struggle can be sustained. As we go forward as black progressives, we must remember that community is not about homogeneity. Homogeneity is dogmatic imposition, pushing your way of life, your way of doing things onto somebody else. That is not what we mean by community. Dogmatic insistence that everybody think and act alike causes rifts among us, destroying the possibility of community. That sense of home that we are talking about and searching for is a place where we can find compassion, recognition of difference, of the importance of diversity, of our individual uniqueness.

b. h.

When we evoke a sense of home as a place where we can renew
ourselves, where we can know love and the sweet
communication of shared spirit, I think it's important for us
to remember that this location of well-being cannot exist in
a context of sexist domination, in a setting where children
are the objects of parental domination and abuse. On a
fundamental level, when we talk about home, we must
speak about the need to transform the African-American
home, so that there, in that domestic space we can
experience the renewal of political commitment to the
black liberation struggle. So that there in that domestic
space we learn to serve and honor one another. If we look
again at the civil rights, at the black power movement, folks
organized so much in homes. They were the places where
folks got together to educate themselves for critical
consciousness. That sense of community, cultivated and
developed in the home, extended outward into a larger,
more public context. As we talk about black power in the
twenty-first century, about political partnership between
black women and men, we must talk about transforming
our notions of how and why we bond. In *Beloved,* Toni
Morrison offers a paradigm for relationships between black
men and women. Sixo describes his love for Thirty-Mile
Woman, declaring, "She is a friend of mind. She gather me,
man. The pieces I am, she gather them and give them back
to me in all the right order. It's good, you know, when you
got a woman who is a friend of your mind." In this passage
Morrison evokes a notion of bonding that may be rooted in
passion, desire, even romantic love, but the point of
connection between black women and men is that space of
recognition and understanding, where we know one another
so well, our histories, that we can take bits and pieces, the
fragments of who we are, and put them back together, remember them. It is this joy of intellectual bonding, or
working together to create liberatory theory and analysis
that black women and men can give one another, that
Cornel and I give to each other. We are friends of one
another's mind. We find a home with one another. It is that
joy in community we celebrate and share with you this
morning.

H. L. MENCKEN

Memorial Service

H. L. MENCKEN (1880–1956) was a journalist and critic. A pungent satirist of American Life, he also published a famous book, The American Language, *which brought together American, rather than English, idioms and expressions.*

Where is the graveyard of dead gods? What lingering mourner waters their mounds? There was a time when Jupiter was the king of the gods, and any man who doubted his puissance was *ipso facto* a barbarian and an ignoramus. But where in all the world is there a man who worships Jupiter today? And what of Huitzilopochtli? In one year—and it is no more than five hundred years ago—50,000 youths and maidens were slain in sacrifice to him. Today, if he remembered at all, it is only by some vagrant savage in the depths of Mexican forest. Huitzilopochtli, like many other gods, had no human father; his mother was a virtuous widow; he was born of an apparently innocent flirtation that she carried on with the sun. When he frowned, his father, the sun, stood still. When he roared with rage, earthquakes engulfed whole cities. When he thirsted he was watered with 10,000 gallons of human blood. But today, Huitzilopochtli is a magnificently forgotten as Allen G. Thurman. Once the peer of Allah, Buddha, and Wotan, he is now the peer of Richmond P. Hobson, Alton B. Parker, Adelina Patti, General Weyler, and Tom Sharkey.

Speaking of Huitzilopochtli recalls his brother Tezcatilpoca. Tezcatilpoca was almost as powerful: he consumed 25,000 virgins a year. Lead me to his tomb: I would weep, and hang a *couronne des perles.* But who knows where it is? Or where the grave of Quitzalcoatl is? Or Xiehtecutli? Or Centeotl, that sweet one? Or Tlazolteotl, the goddess of love? Or Mictlan? Or Xipe? Or all the host of Tzitzimitles? Where are their bones? Where is the willow in which they hung their harps? In what forlorn and unheard-of Hell do they await the resurrection morn? Who enjoys their residuary estates? Or that of Dis, whom Caesar found to be the chief god of the Celts? Or that of Tarvcs, the bull? Or that of Moccos, the pig? Or that of Epona, the mare? Or that of Mullo, the celestial jackass? There was a time when the Irish revered all these gods, but today even the drunkest Irishman laughs at them.

But they have company in oblivion: the Hell of dead gods is as crowded as the Presbyterian Hell for babies. Damona is there, and Esus, and Druneme-ton, and Silvana, and Dervones, and Adsalluta, and Deva, and Belisama, and Uxellimus, and Borvo, and Grannos, and Mogons. All mighty gods in their day, worshipped by millions, full of demands and impositions, able to bind and loose—all gods of the first class. Men labored for generations to build vast temples to them—temples with stones as large as hay-wagons. The business of interpreting their whims occupied thousands of priests, bishops, archbishops. To doubt them was to die, usually at the stake. Armies took to the field to defend them against infidels: villages were burned, women and children were butchered, cattle were driven off. Yet in the end they all withered and died, and today there is none so poor to do them reverence.

What has become of Sutekh, once high god of the whole Nile Valley? What has become of:

Resheph	Isis	Dagon
Anath	Ptah	Yau
Ashtoreth	Baal	Amon-Re
Nebo	Astarte	Osiris
Malek	Hadad	Molech?
Ahijah		

All these were once gods of the highest eminence. Many of them are mentioned with fear and trembling in the Old Testament. They ranked, five or six thousand years ago, with Yahweh Himself; the worst of them stood far higher than Thor. Yet hey have all gone down the chute, and with them the following:

Arianrod	Iuno Lucina
Morrigu	Saturn
Govannon	Furrina
Gunfled	Cronos
Dagda	Engurra
Ogyrvan	Belus

Dea Dia	Ubilulu
U-dimmer-an-kia	Diana of Ephesus
U-sab-sib	Robigus
U-Mersi	Pluto
Tammuz	Vesta
Venus	Zer-panitu
Beltis	Merodach
Nusku	Elum
Aa	Marduk
Sin	Nin
Apsu	Persephone
Elali	Istar
Mami	Lagas
Zaraqu	Nirig
Zagaga	Nebo
Nuada Argetlam	En-Mersi
Tagd	Assur
Goibniu	Beltu
Odin	Kuski-banda
Ogma	Nin-azu
Marzin	Qarradu
Mars	Ueras

Ask the rector to lend you any good book on comparative religion: you will find them all listed. They were gods of the highest dignity—gods of civilized peoples—worshipped and believed in by millions. All were omnipotent, omniscient and immortal. And all are dead.

ALBERT CAMUS

The Absurd

ALBERT CAMUS *(1913–1960), a leading French intellectual, was a political activist and an associate of Jean-Paul Sartre. Awarded the Nobel Prize for Literature in 1957, Camus's philosophical concerns were often expressed in fiction.* The Myth of Sisyphus *focuses on the issue of suicide, which, according to him, is the only philosophical problem.*

L IKE great works, deep feelings always mean more than they are conscious of saying. The regularity of an impulse or a repulsion in a soul is encountered again in habits of doing or thinking, is reproduced in consequences of which the soul itself knows nothing. Great feelings take with them their own universe, splendid or abject. They light up with their passion an exclusive world in which they recognize their climate. There is a universe of jealousy, of ambition, of selfishness, or of generosity. A universe—in other words, a metaphysic and an attitude of mind. What is true of already specialized feelings will be even more so of emotions basically as indeterminate, simultaneously as vague and as "definite," as remote and as "present" as those furnished us by beauty or aroused by absurdity.

At any street corner the feeling of absurdity can strike any man in the face. As it is, in its distressing nudity, in its light without effulgence, it is elusive. But that very difficulty deserves reflection. It is probably true that a man remains forever unknown to us and that there is in him something irreducible that escapes us. But *practically* I know men and recognize them by their behavior, by the totality of their deeds, by the consequences caused in life by their presence. Likewise, all those irrational feelings which offer no purchase to analysis. I can define them *practically,* appreciate them *practically,* by gathering together the sum of their consequences in the domain of the intelligence, by seizing and noting all their aspects, by outlining their universe. It is certain that apparently, though I have seen the same actor a hundred times, I shall not for that reason know him any better personally. Yet if I add up the heroes he has personified and if I say that I know him as little better at the hundredth character counted off, this will be felt to contain an element of truth. For this apparent paradox is also an apologue. There is a moral to it. It teaches that a man defines himself by his make-believe as well as by his sincere impulses. There is thus a lower key of feelings, inaccessible in the heart but partially disclosed by the acts they imply and the attitudes of mind they assume. It is clear that in this way I am defining a method. But it is also evident that that method is one of analysis and not of knowledge. For methods imply metaphysics; unconsciously they disclose conclusions that they often claim not to know yet. Similarly, the last pages of a book are already contained in the first pages. Such a link is inevitable. The method defined here acknowledges the feeling that all true knowledge is impossible. Solely appearances can be enumerated and the climate make itself felt.

Perhaps we shall be able to overtake that elusive feeling of absurdity in the different but closely related worlds of intelligence, of the art of living, or of art itself. The climate of absurdity is in the beginning. The end is the absurd universe and that attitude of mind which lights the world with its true colors to bring out the privileged and implacable visage which that attitude has discerned in it.

All great deeds and all great thoughts have a ridiculous beginning. Great works are often born on a street corner or in a restaurant's revolving door. So it is with absurdity. The absurd world more than others derives its nobility from that abject birth. In certain situations, replying "nothing" when asked what one is thinking about may be pretense in a man. Those who are loved are well aware of this. But if that reply is sincere, if it symbolizes that odd state of soul in which the void becomes eloquent, in which the chain of daily gestures is broken, in which the heart vainly seeks the link that will connect it again, then it is as it were the first sign of absurdity.

It happens that the stage sets collapse. Rising, streetcar, four hours in the office or the factory, meal, streetcar, four hours of work, meal, sleep, and Monday Tuesday Wednesday Thursday Friday and Saturday according to the same rhythm—this path is easily followed most of the time. But one day the "why" arises and everything begins in that weariness tinged with amazement. "Begins"—this is important. Weariness comes at the end of the acts of a mechanical life, but at the same time it inaugurates the impulse of consciousness.

It awakens consciousness and provokes what follows. What follows is the gradual return into the chain or it is the definitive awakening. At the end of the awakening comes, in time, the consequence: suicide or recovery. In itself weariness has something sickening about it. Here, I must conclude that it is good. For everything begins with consciousness and nothing is worth anything except through it. There is nothing original about these remarks. But they are obvious; that is enough for a while, during a sketchy reconnaissance in the origins of the absurd. Mere "anxiety," as Heidegger says, is at the source of everything.

Likewise and during every day of an unillustrious life time carries us. But a moment always comes when we have to carry it. We live on the future: "tomorrow," "later on," "when you have made your way," "you will understand when you are old enough." Such irrelevancies are wonderful, for, after all, it's a matter of dying. Yet a day comes when a man notices or says that he is thirty. Thus he asserts his youth. But simultaneously he situates himself in relation to time. He takes his place in it. He admits that he stands at a certain point on a curve that he acknowledges having to travel to its end. He belongs to time, and by the horror that seizes him, he recognizes his worst enemy. Tomorrow, he was longing for tomorrow, whereas everything in him ought to reject it. That revolt of the flesh is the absurd. . . .

That revolt gives life its value. Spread out over the whole length of a life, it restores its majesty to that life. To a man devoid of blinders, there is no finer sight than that of the intelligence at grips with a reality that transcends it. The sight of human pride is unequaled. No disparagement is of any use. That discipline that

the mind imposes on itself, that will conjured up out of nothing, that face-to-face
struggle have something exceptional
about them. To impoverish that reality
whose inhumanity constitutes man's
majesty is tantamount to impoverishing
him himself. I understand then why the
doctrines that explain everything to me
also debilitate me at the same time. They
relieve me of the weight of my own life,
and yet I must carry it alone. At this
juncture, I cannot conceive that a skeptical metaphysics can be joined to an
ethics of renunciation.

Consciousness and revolt, these re-
jections are the contrary of renunciation. Everything that is indomitable and
passionate in a human heart quickens
them, on the contrary, with its own life.
It is essential to die unreconciled and
not of one's own free will. Suicide is a
repudiation. The absurd man can only
drain everything to the bitter end, and
deplete himself. The absurd is his extreme tension, which he maintains constantly by solitary effort, for he knows
that in that consciousness and in that
day-to-day revolt he gives proof of his
only truth, which is defiance. . . .

But what does life mean in such a
universe? Nothing else for the moment
but indifference to the future and a desire to use up everything that is given.
Belief in the meaning of life always implies a scale of values, a choice, our
preferences. Belief in the absurd, according to our definitions, teaches the
contrary. But this is worth examining.

Knowing whether or not one can live
without appeal is all that interests me. I
do not want to get out of my depth. This
aspect of life being given me, can I adapt
myself to it? Now, faced with this particular concern, belief in the absurd is tantamount to substituting the quantity of
experiences for the quality. If I convince

myself that this life has no other aspect
than that of the absurd, if I feel that its
whole equilibrium depends on that perpetual opposition between my conscious
revolt and the darkness in which it struggles, if I admit that my freedom has no
meaning except in relation to its limited
fate, then I must say that what counts is
not the best living but the most living.
It is not up to me to wonder if this is vulgar or revolting, elegant or deplorable.
Once and for all, value judgments
are discarded here in favor of factual
judgments. I have merely to draw the
conclusions from what I can see and
to risk nothing that is hypothetical.
Supposing that living in this way were
not honorable, then true propriety would
command me to be dishonorable.

The most living; in the broadest
sense, that rule means nothing. It calls
for definition. It seems to begin with the
fact that the notion of quantity has not
been sufficiently explored. For it can
account for a large share of human experience. A man's rule of conduct and
his scale of values have no meaning except through the quantity and variety of
experiences he has been in a position to
accumulate. Now, the conditions of
modern life impose on the majority of
men the same quantity of experiences
and consequently the same profound experience. To be sure, there must also be
taken into consideration the individual's
spontaneous contribution, the "given"
element in him. But I cannot judge of
that, and let me repeat that my rule here
is to get along with the immediate evidence. I see, then, that the individual
character of a common code of ethics
lies not so much in the ideal importance
of its basic principles as in the norm of
an experience that it is possible to measure. To stretch a point somewhat, the
Greeks had the code of their leisure just

as we have the code of our eight-hour day. But already many men among the most tragic cause us to foresee that a longer experience changes this table of values. They make us imagine that adventurer of the everyday who through mere quantity of experiences would break all records (I am purposely using this sports expression) and would thus win his own code of ethics. Yet let's avoid romanticism and just ask ourselves what such an attitude may mean to a man with a mind made up to take up his bet and to observe strictly what he takes to be the rules of the game.

Breaking all the records is first and foremost being faced with the world as often as possible. How can that be done without contradictions and without playing on words? For on the one hand the absurd teaches that all experiences are unimportant, and on the other it urges toward the greatest quantity of experiences. How, then, can one fail to do as so many of those men I was speaking of earlier—choose the form of life that brings us the most possible of that human matter, thereby introducing a scale of values that on the other hand one claims to reject?

But again it is the absurd and its contradictory life that reaches us. For the mistake is thinking that that quantity of experiences depends on the circumstances of our life when it depends solely on us. Here we have to be oversimple. To two men living the same number of years, the world always provides the same sum of experiences. It is up to us to be conscious of them. Being aware of one's life, one's revolt, one's

freedom, and to the maximum, is living, and to the maximum. Where lucidity dominates, the scale of values becomes useless. Let's be even more simple. Let us say that the sole obstacle, the sole deficiency to be made good, is constituted by premature death. Thus it is that no depth, no emotion, no passion, and no sacrifice could render equal in the eyes of the absurd man (even if he wished it so) a conscious life of forty years and a lucidity spread over sixty years. Madness and death are his irreparables. Man does not choose. The absurd and the extra life it involves *therefore do not depend on man's will,* but on its contrary, which is death. Weighing words carefully, it is altogether a question of luck. One just has to be able to consent to this. There will never be any substitute for twenty years of life and experience.

By what is an odd inconsistency in such an alert race, the Greeks claimed that those who died young were beloved of the gods. And that is true only if you are willing to believe that entering the ridiculous world of the gods is forever losing the purest of joys, which is feeling, and feeling on this earth. The present and the succession of presents before a constantly conscious soul is the ideal of the absurd man. But the word "ideal" rings false in this connection. It is not even his vocation, but merely the third consequence of his reasoning. Having started from an anguished awareness of the inhuman, the meditation on the absurd returns at the end of its itinerary to the very heart of the passionate flames of human revolt. . . .

The preceding merely defines a way of thinking. But the point is to live.

Chapter 2

How Do I Know Whether God Exists?

One of the most discussed philosophical beliefs, one that may provide the framework for many other beliefs and determine much of your attitude toward life, is the belief (or lack of belief) in a Supreme Being, an Almighty God who not only created the universe but still watches over it with affection and concern. To believe in God is never to feel alone or abandoned. It is a ground for lifelong optimism, the confidence that "everything will turn out for the best." It is to have a basic explanation for the way things are, especially the existence of the universe. Not to believe in God is to give up this sense of security, to lose that ground for optimism, and, for some people, this opens the way to metaphysical despair and a sense of cosmic loneliness. It is to leave the question, "Why is there something rather than nothing?" without an answer. Science might explain how things are and even how they got that way, but not even the best science can make a crack in the ultimate metaphysical question, Why does the universe exist at all?

Belief in God, however, is not so much an ultimate explanation as it is an inspiration. It has inspired some of the most beautiful poetry, art, and music and some of the greatest human achievements, as well as some of the bloodiest civil wars and most complex philosophies. Different societies seem to believe in God in different ways and they believe different things about Him. They may also believe in different Gods. Protracted wars have been fought over such technical theological questions as whether God, the Son, and the Holy Ghost are in fact one or three. The Old and New Testaments present significantly different portraits of God: as a wrathful and jealous God in the former and as a much more merciful and loving God in the latter. The God of the Old Testament destroys cities, has disobedient messengers swallowed by whales, and tests the faith of His believers by making them suffer (as in the story of Job). The God of the New Testament sacrifices his only son for your salvation. How are disputes about the true nature of God to be settled? How do you know what to believe in? How do you know whether God exists?

The problem is that belief in God does not seem to rest on any particular foundation. Most likely, you were raised with that belief, taught it as a child, and encouraged in it as you grew to maturity. You were taken to church or temple and naturally came to assume that the deity to which everyone referred, and to whom you yourself had often prayed, existed. But what is the evidence for that belief? How can you prove that your natural assumption is justified? A few people claim to have had God speak to them, but they are few and far between and are not always the most reliable witnesses. One popular proof of God's existence is the fact that the Bible tells us, over and over again, about God. But appealing to the Bible as evidence of God's existence presupposes just that sort of belief that is at issue, a logical fallacy often called "begging the question." Believing in God and believing that the Bible is the revealed word of God are two aspects of one and the same belief, and one cannot be used to prove the other.

You may have "felt" God's presence, but feelings, too, must be justified, for sometimes they can be misleading. Sometimes you sense danger when there is no danger, and, in the same way, it is possible to have a religious feeling without that proving the feeling refers to anything outside of you. Indeed, the very nature of God, according to many theorists and theologians, is such that God "transcends" the world and is outside of our experience. God cannot be seen or sensed as such and that is why it is necessary to *believe in* God. If God could simply be presented to us, like a statue or a person, such a powerful notion of belief would not be necessary.

A different way of putting the same point is to say that believing in God is a matter of *faith* and not a matter of knowledge. But many believers have refused to accept the idea that this most important belief is not part of our knowledge in the strongest sense. How can our most important belief not also be the best known? Accordingly, much of the history of theology has been devoted to the project of *proving* God's existence. The idea is not to replace faith or undermine the need to believe, but to supplement faith and belief with a demonstration that they are indeed justified and based on knowledge of the most secure kind.

Numerous such arguments or proofs have been presented throughout the history of philosophy, but the three most popular arguments for God's existence are the **ontological, cosmological,** and **teleological** proofs. The ontological argument, originated by Saint Anselm in the twelfth century, is a deductive proof that proceeds from the premise that God is (by definition) the being greater than whom none other can be conceived, with the conclusion that God therefore *must* exist. The cosmological argument has appeared in many versions, and Saint Thomas Aquinas presents several of them in his famous "Five Ways" (of proving God's existence). They all share the inference from the existence of some imperfect, merely contingent being (for example, ourselves) to the existence of a necessary being, namely God.

The teleological argument is different in that it begins with a very complex and detailed observation: the marvelous complexity and harmony of the world. You have possibly had such an awe-filled experience, for instance, when observing the wonderful array of exotic fish in an aquarium. You may have even said at the time that the variety of life is a miraculous thing and evidence of God's great creativity. This is the essence of the teleological argument, the hypothesis that such a complex, varied, and workable world could not be the product of chance but must have been the creation of an intelligent, powerful creator, namely God. An analogy, suggested in a classic work by William Paley, is this: Walking along a deserted beach, you find a watch in the sand. Now, it is barely possible, but highly unlikely, that the wind and surf had pounded together pieces of sand until they happened to take the form of this intricate piece of machinery. It is much more likely that the watch was made by a watchmaker and dropped in the sand by some passerby whom you have not seen. So too, it may be imaginable that the world as we know it came into existence quite by accident, but it seems much more plausible to assume that it was intelligently created by God.

These three arguments have met with considerable criticism, often from critics who are themselves devout. The ontological proof has been revised and updated many times using the most sophisticated techniques available in logic. The cosmological proof also gets revised with each new development in cosmology. Old inferences are discarded and new, improved steps take their place. The teleological argument was lampooned as soon as it appeared; for example, the German aphorist Lichtenberg sarcastically commented that it certainly was convenient that God put slits in cats' skin right where their eyes were, and Voltaire noted in his novel *Candide* that it was good of God to give us noses, for otherwise, how would we wear spectacles? The most protracted and devastating criticism of the teleological argument, however, was offered by David Hume in his *Dialogues on Natural Religion,* which were so blasphemous that he dared not publish them in his own lifetime.

There have been many believers and philosophers, however, who rejected the entire project of trying to prove that God exists. They see nothing wrong with insisting that belief in God is a matter of faith and not knowledge. Indeed, they insist that the importance of belief in God rests on exactly that, for if we could really prove God's existence, faith would be superfluous. Perhaps the most single powerful argument of this sort appeared in the mid-nineteenth century in the works of Søren Kierkegaard, a Danish philosopher who was extremely devout but also rejected the modernization of religion. In this century, the American philosopher William James also argued that what was important about religious belief was not so much its contribution to knowledge as its role in making our lives happy and fulfilled. And finally, many contemporary philosophers insist that belief in God is not the sort of belief that can be proven or disproven, but that is no argument against it. Belief in God may be sufficiently important in our lives that questions of proof are secondary.

SAINT ANSELM

The Ontological Argument

SAINT ANSELM *(1033–1109), Archbishop of Canterbury, was one of the main opponents of the then anti-intellectualism of the church. He is best known for his* Monologion *and his* Proslogion, *in which the ontological argument is developed.*

Truly there is a God, although the fool hath said in his heart, There is no God.

AND so, Lord, do thou, who dost give understanding to faith, give me, so far as thou knowest it to be profitable, to understand that thou art as we believe; and that thou art that which we believe. And, indeed, we believe that thou art a being than which nothing greater can be conceived. Or is there no such nature, since the fool hath said in his heart, there is no God? (Psalms xiv.I). But, at any rate, this very fool, when he hears of this being of which I speak—a being than which nothing greater can be conceived—understands what he hears, and what he understands is in his understanding; although he does not understand it to exist.

For, it is one thing for an object to be in the understanding, and another to understand that the object exists. When a painter first conceives of what he will afterwards perform, he has it in his understanding, but he does not yet understand it to be, because he has not yet performed it. But after he has made the painting, he both has it in his understanding, and he understands that it exists, because he has made it.

Hence, even the fool is convinced that something exists in the understanding, at least, than which nothing greater can be conceived. For, when he hears of this, he understands it. And whatever is understood, exists in the understanding. And assuredly that, than which nothing greater can be conceived, cannot exist in the understanding alone. For, suppose it exists in the understanding alone: then it can be conceived to exist in reality; which is greater.

Therefore, if that, than which nothing greater can be conceived, exists in the understanding alone, the very being, than which nothing greater can be conceived, is one, than which a greater can be conceived. But obviously this is impossible. Hence, there is no doubt that there exists a being, than which nothing greater can be conceived, and it exists both in the understanding and in reality.

> God cannot be conceived not to exist.—
> God is that, than which nothing greater
> can be conceived.—That which can be
> conceived not to exist is not God.

And it assuredly exists so truly, that it cannot be conceived not to exist. For, it is possible to conceive of a being which cannot be conceived not to exist; and this is greater than one which can be conceived not to exist. Hence, if that, than which nothing greater can be conceived, can be conceived not to exist, it is not that, than which nothing greater can be conceived. But this is an irreconcilable contradiction. There is, then, so truly a being than which nothing greater can be conceived to exist, that it cannot even be conceived not to exist; and this being thou art, O Lord, our God.

So truly, therefore, dost thou exist, O Lord, my God, that thou canst not be conceived not to exist; and rightly. For, if a mind could conceive of a being better than thee, the creature would rise above the Creator; and this is most absurd. And, indeed, whatever else there is, except thee alone, can be conceived not to exist. To thee alone, therefore, it belongs to exist more truly than all other beings, and hence in a higher degree than all others. For, whatever else exists does not exist so truly, and hence in a less degree it belongs to it to exist. Why, then, has the fool said in his heart, there is no God (Psalms xiv.I), since it is so evident, to a rational mind, that thou dost exist in the highest degree of all? Why, except that he is dull and a fool?

How the fool has said in his heart what cannot be conceived.—A thing may be conceived in two ways: (1) when the word signifying it is conceived; (2) when the thing itself is understood. As far as the word goes, God can be conceived not to exist; in reality he cannot.

But how has the fool said in his heart what he could not conceive; or how is it that he could not conceive what he said in his heart? since it is the same to say in the heart, and to conceive.

But, if really, nay, since really, he both conceived, because he said in his heart; and did not say in his heart, because he could not conceive; there is more than one way in which a thing is said in the heart or conceived. For, in one sense, an object is conceived, when the word signifying it is conceived; and in another, when the very entity, which the object is, is understood.

In the former sense, then, God can be conceived not to exist; but in the latter, not at all. So, then, no one who understands what God is can conceive that God does not exist; although he says these words in his heart, either without any, or with some foreign, signification. For, God is that than which a greater cannot be conceived. And he who thoroughly understands this, assuredly understands that this being so truly exists, that not even in concept can it be nonexistent. Therefore, he who understands that God so exists, cannot conceive that he does not exist.

I thank thee, gracious Lord, I thank thee; because what I formerly believed by thy bounty, I now so understand by thine illumination, that if I were unwilling to believe that thou dost exist, I should not be able not to understand this to be true.

SAINT THOMAS AQUINAS

Whether God Exists

SAINT THOMAS AQUINAS *(1225–1274) was the architect of the most comprehensive theological structure of the Roman Catholic Church, the* Summa Theologica. *It has long been recognized as the "official" statement of orthodox Christian beliefs by many theologians. Aquinas borrowed many of his arguments from Aristotle, as can be seen in his "five ways" of demonstrating God's existence.*

*O*BJECTION 1. It seems that God does not exist; because if one of two contraries be infinite, the other would be altogether destroyed. But the word "God" means that He is infinite goodness. If, therefore, God existed, there would be no evil discoverable; but there is evil in the world. Therefore God does not exist.

Obj. 2. Further, it is superfluous to suppose that, what can be accounted for by a few principles has been produced by many. But it seems that everything that appears in the world can be accounted for by other principles, supposing God did not exist. For all natural things can be reduced to one principle, which is nature; and all things that happen intentionally can be reduced to one principle, which is human reason, or will. Therefore there is no need to suppose God's existence.

On the contrary, It is said in the person of God: *I am Who am* (Exod. iii. 14).

I answer that, The existence of God can be proved in five ways.

The first and more manifest way is the argument from motion. It is certain and evident to our senses that some things are in motion. Whatever is in motion is moved by another, for nothing can be in motion except it have a potentiality for that towards which it is being moved; whereas a thing moves inas-

much as it is in act. By "motion" we mean nothing else than the reduction of something from a state of potentiality into a state of actuality unless by something already in a state of actuality. Thus, that which is actually hot as fire, makes wood, which is potentially hot, to be actually hot, and thereby moves and changes it. It is not possible that the same thing should be at once in a state of actuality and potentiality from the same point of view, but only from different points of view. What is actually hot cannot simultaneously be only potentially hot; still, it is simultaneously potentially cold. It is therefore impossible that from the same point of view and in the same way anything should be both moved and mover, or that it should move itself. Therefore, whatever is in motion must be put in motion by another. If that by which it is put in motion be itself put in motion, then this also must needs be put in motion by another, and that by another again. This cannot go on to infinity, because then there would be no first mover, and, consequently, no other mover—seeing that subsequent movers only move inasmuch as they are put in motion by the first mover; as the staff only moves because it is put in motion by the hand. Therefore it is necessary to arrive at a First Mover, put in motion by no other; and this everyone understands to be God.

The second way is from the formality of efficient causation. In the world of sense we find there is an order of efficient causation. There is no case known (neither is it, indeed, possible) in which a thing is found to be the efficient cause of itself; for so it would be prior to itself, which is impossible to go on to infinity, because in all efficient causes following in order the first is the cause of the intermediate cause, and the intermediate is the cause of the ultimate cause, whether the intermediate cause be several, or one only. To take away the cause is to take away the effect. Therefore, if there be no first cause among efficient causes, there will be no ultimate cause, nor any intermediate. If in efficient causes it is possible to go on to infinity, there will be an ultimate effect, nor any intermediate efficient causes; all of which is plainly false. Therefore it is necessary to put forward a First Efficient Cause, to which everyone gives the name of God.

The third way is taken from possibility and necessity, and runs thus: We find in nature things that could either exist or not exist, since they are found to be generated, and then to corrupt; and, consequently, they can exist, and then not exist. It is impossible for these always to exist, for that which can one day cease to exist must at some time have not existed. Therefore, if everything could cease to exist, then at one time there could have been nothing in existence. If this were true, even now there would be nothing in existence, because that which does not exist only begins to exist by something already existing. Therefore, if at one time nothing was in existence, it would have been impossible for anything to have begun

to exist; and thus even now nothing would be in existence—which is absurd. Therefore, not all beings are merely possible, but there must exist something the existence of which is necessary. Every necessary thing either has its necessity caused by another, or not. It is impossible to go on to infinity in necessary things which have their necessity caused by another, as has been already proved in regard to efficient causes. Therefore we cannot but postulate the existence of some being having of itself its own necessity, and not receiving it from another, but rather causing in others their necessity. This all men speak of as God.

The fourth way is taken from the gradation to be found in things. Among beings there are some more and some less good, true, noble, and the like. But "more" and "less" are predicated of different things, according as they resemble in their different ways something which is in the degree of "most," as a thing is said to be hotter according as it more nearly resembles that which is hottest; so that there is something which is truest, something best, something noblest, and, consequently, something which is uttermost being; for the truer things are, the more truly they exist. What is most complete in any genus is the cause of all in that genus; as fire, which is the most complete form of heat, is the cause whereby all things are made hot. Therefore there must also be something which is to all beings the cause of their being, goodness, and every other perfection; and this we call God.

The fifth way is taken from the governance of the world; for we see that things which lack intelligence, such as natural bodies, act for some purpose, which fact is evident from their acting always, or nearly always, in the same way, so as to obtain the best result. Hence it is plain that not fortuitously, but designedly, do they achieve their purpose. Whatever lacks intelligence cannot fulfill some purpose, unless it be directed by some being endowed with intelligence and knowledge; as the arrow is shot to its mark by the archer. Therefore some intelligent being exists by whom all natural things are ordained towards a definite purpose; and this being we call God.

Reply Obj. 1. As Augustine says: *Since God is wholly good, He would not allow any evil to exist in His works, unless His omnipotence and goodness* were such as to bring good even out of evil. This is part of the infinite goodness of God, that He should allow evil to exist, and out of it produce good.

Reply Obj. 2. Since nature works out its determinate end under the direction of a higher agent, whatever is done by nature must needs be traced back to God, as to its first cause. So also whatever is done designedly must also be traced back to some higher cause other than human reason or will, for these can suffer change and are defective; whereas things capable of motion and of defect must be traced back to an immovable and self-necessary first principle.

WILLIAM PALEY

The Teleological Argument

WILLIAM PALEY (1743–1805) was an English theologian and moral philosopher. He believed that the miracles on which Christianity is based are genuine. He regarded the parts of nature as mechanisms that form the basis of the argument from design, which he developed in his Natural Theology.

STATE OF THE ARGUMENT

IN crossing a heath, suppose I pitched my foot against a *stone,* and were asked how the stone came to be there, I might possibly answer, that for any thing I knew to the contrary it had lain there for ever; nor would it, perhaps, be very easy to show the absurdity of this answer. But suppose I had found a *watch* upon the ground, and it should be inquired how the watch happened to be in that place, I should hardly think of the answer which I had before given, that for any thing I knew the watch might have always been there. Yet why should not this answer serve for the watch as well as for the stone; why is it not as admissible in the second case as in the first? For this reason, and for no other, namely, that when we come to inspect the watch, we perceive—what we could not discover in the stone—that its several parts are framed and put together for a purpose, *e.g.* that they are so formed and adjusted as to produce motion, and that motion so regulated as to point out the hour of the day; that if the different parts had been differently shaped from what they are, or placed after any other manner or in any other order than that in which they are placed, either no motion at all would have been carried on in the machine, or none which would have answered the use that is now served by it. To reckon up a few of the plainest of these parts and of their offices, all tending to one result: We see a cylindrical box containing a coiled elastic spring, which, by its endeavor to relax itself, turns round the box. We next observe a flexible chain—artificially wrought for the sake of flexure—communicating the action of the spring from the box to the fusee. We then find a series of wheels, the teeth of which catch in and apply to each other, conducting the motion from the fusee to the balance and from the balance to the pointer, and at the same time, by the size and shape of those wheels, so regulating that motion as to terminate in causing an index, by an equable and measured progression, to pass over a given space in a given time. We take notice that the wheels are made of brass, in order to keep them from rust; the springs of steel, no other metal being so elastic; that over the face of the watch there is placed a glass, a material employed in no other part of the work, but in the room of which, if there had been any other than a transparent substance, the hour could not be seen without opening the case. This mechanism being observed—it requires indeed an examination of the instrument, and perhaps some previous knowledge of the subject, to perceive and understand it; but being once, as we have said, observed and understood, the inference we think is inevitable, that the watch must have had a maker—that there must have existed, at some time and at some place or other, an artificer or artificers who formed it for the purpose which we find it actually to answer, who comprehended its construction and designed its use.

I. Nor would it, I apprehend, weaken the conclusion, that we had never seen a watch made—that we had never known an artist capable of making one—that we were altogether incapable of executing such a piece of workmanship ourselves, or of understanding in what manner it was performed; all this being no more than what is true of some exquisite remains of ancient art, of some lost arts, and, to the generality of mankind, of the more curious productions of modern manufacture. Does one man in a million know how oval frames are turned? Ignorance of this kind exalts our opinion of the unseen and unknown, but raises no doubt in our minds of the existence and agency of such an artist, at some former time and in some place or other. Nor can I perceive that it varies at all the inference, whether the question arise concerning a human agent or concerning an agent of a different species, or an agent possessing in some respects a different nature.

II. Neither, secondly, would it invalidate our conclusion, that the watch sometimes went wrong, or that it seldom went exactly right. The purpose of the machinery, the design, and the designer might be evident, and in the case supposed, would be evident in whatever way we accounted for the irregularity of the movement, or whether we could account for it or not. It is not necessary that a machine be perfect, in order to show with what design it was made: still less necessary, where the only question is whether it were made with any design at all.

III. Nor, thirdly, would it bring any uncertainty into the argument, if there were a few parts of the watch, concerning which we could not discover or had not yet discovered in what manner they conduced to the general effect; or even some parts, concerning which we could not ascertain whether they conduced to that effect in any manner whatever. For, as to the first branch of the case if by the loss, or disorder, or decay of the parts in question, the movement of the watch were found in fact to be stopped, or disturbed, or retarded, no doubt would remain in our minds as to the utility or intention of these parts, although we should be unable to investigate the manner according to which, or the connection by which, the ultimate effect depended upon their action or assistance; and the more complex the machine, the more likely is this obscurity to arise. Then, as to the second thing supposed, namely, that there were parts which might be spared without prejudice to the movement of the watch, and that we had proved this by experiment, these superfluous parts, even if we were completely assured that they were such, would not vacate the reasoning which we had instituted concerning other parts. The indication of contrivance remained, with respect to them, nearly as it was before.

IV. Nor, fourthly, would any man in his senses think the existence of the watch with its various machinery accounted for, by being told that it was one out of possible combinations of material forms; that whatever he had found in the place where he found the watch, must have contained some internal configuration or other; and that this configuration might be the structure now exhibited, namely, of the works of a watch, as well as a different structure.

V. Nor, fifthly, would it yield his inquiry more satisfaction, to be answered that there existed in things a principle of order, which had disposed the parts of the watch into their present form and situation. He never knew a watch made by the principle of order; nor can he even form to himself an idea of what is meant by a principle of order, distinct from the intelligence of the watchmaker.

VI. Sixthly, he would be surprised to hear that the mechanism of the watch was no proof of contrivance, only a motive to induce the mind to think so.

VII. And not less surprised to be informed, that the watch in his hand was nothing more than the result of the laws of *metallic* nature. It is a perversion of language to assign any law as the efficient, operative cause of any thing. A law presupposes an agent; for it is only the mode according to which an agent proceeds: it implies a power; for it is the order according to which that power acts. Without this agent, without this power, which are both distinct from itself, the *law* does nothing, is nothing. The expression, "the law of metallic nature," may sound strange and harsh to a philosophic ear; but it seems quite as justifiable as some others which are more familiar to him such as "the law of vegetable nature," "the law of animal nature," or, indeed, as "the law of nature" in general, when assigned as the cause of phenomena, in exclusion of agency and power, or when it is substituted into the place of these.

VIII. Neither, lastly, would our observer be driven out of his conclusion or from his confidence in its truth, by being told that he know nothing at all about the matter. He knows enough for his argument; he knows the utility of the end; he knows the subserviency and adaptation of the means to the end. These points being known, his ignorance of other points, affect not the certainty of his reasoning. The consciousness of knowing little need not beget a distrust of that which he does know. . . .

APPLICATION OF THE ARGUMENT

Every indication of contrivance, every manifestation of design which existed in the watch, exists in the works of nature, with the difference on the side of nature of being greater and more, and that in a degree which exceeds all computation. I mean, that the contrivances of nature surpass the contrivances of art, in the complexity, subtilty, and curiosity of the mechanism; and still more, if possible, do they go beyond them in number and variety; yet, in a multitude of cases, are not less evidently mechanical, not less evidently contrivances, not less evidently accommodated to their end or suited to their office, than are the most perfect productions of human ingenuity. . . .

DAVID HUME

Why Does God Let People Suffer?

DAVID HUME (1711–1776), a Scottish philosopher, was refused professorships at the leading universities for his "heresies." Nevertheless, he is regarded as the outstanding genius of British philosophy. In addition to writing a number of influential books, among them A Treatise of Human Nature, An Inquiry Concerning the Principles of Morals, *and* Dialogues on Natural Religion, *Hume was a much sought after guest in London, Edinburgh, and Paris.*

I N short, I repeat the Question: Is the World, consider'd in general, and as it appears to us in this Life, different from what a Man or such a Limited Being would, *beforehand,* expect from a very powerful, wise, and benevolent Deity? It must be strange Prejudice to assert the contrary. And from thence I conclude, that however consistent the World may be, allowing certain Suppositions and Conjectures, with the Idea of such a Deity, it can never afford us an Inference concerning his Existence. The Consistence is not absolutely deny'd, only the Inference. Conjectures, especially where Infinity is excluded from the divine Attributes, may, perhaps, be sufficient to prove a Consistence; but can never be foundations for any Inference.

There seem to be *four* Circumstances, on which depend all, or the greatest Part of the Ills, that molest sensible Creatures; and it is not impossible but all these Circumstances may be necessary and unavoidable. We know so little beyond common Life, or even of Common Life, that, with regard to the

Oeconomy of a Universe, there is no Conjecture, however wild, which may not be just; nor any one, however plausible, which may not be erroneous. All that belongs to human Understanding, in this deep Ignorance and Obscurity, is to be sceptical, or at least cautious; and not to admit of any Hypothesis, whatever; much less, of any which is supported by no Appearance of Probability. Now this I assert to be the Case with regard to all the Causes of Evil, and the Circumstances, on which it depends. None of them appear to human Reason, in the least degree, necessary or unavoidable; nor can we suppose them such, without the utmost Licence of Imagination.

The *first* Circumstance, which introduces Evil, is that Contrivance or Oeconomy of the animal Creation, by which Pains, as well as Pleasures, are employ'd to excite all Creatures to Action, and make them vigilant in the great Work of Self-preservation. Now Pleasure alone, in its various Degrees, seems to human Understanding sufficient for this Purpose. All Animals might be constantly in a State of Enjoyment; but when urg'd by any of the Necessities of Nature, such as Thirst, Hunger, Wearyness; instead of Pain, they might feel a Diminution of Pleasure, by which they might be prompted to seek that Object, which is necessary to their Subsistence. Men pursue Pleasure as eagerly as they avoid Pain; at least, might have been so constituted. It seems, therefore, plainly possible to carry on the Business of Life without any Pain. Why then is any Animal ever render'd susceptible of such a Sensation? If Animals can be free from it an hour, they might enjoy a perpetual Exemption from it; and it requir'd as particular a Contrivance of their Organs to produce that Feeling, as to endow them with Sight, Hearing, or any of the Senses. Shall we conjecture, that such a Contrivance was necessary, without any Appearance of Reason? And shall we build on that Conjecture as on the most certain Truth?

But a Capacity of Pain wou'd not alone produce Pain, were it not for the *second* Circumstance, *viz,* the conducting of the World by general Laws; and this seems no wise necessary to a very perfect Being. It is true; if every thing were conducted by particular Volitions, the Course of Nature wou'd be perpetually broken, and no man cou'd employ his Reason in the Conduct of Life. But might not other particular Volitions remedy this Inconvenience? In short, might not the Deity exterminate all Ill, wherever it were to be found; and produce all Good, without any Preparation or long Progress of Causes and Effects?

Besides, we must consider, that, according to the present Oeconomy of the World, the Course of Nature, tho' suppos'd exactly regular, yet to us appears not so, and many Events are uncertain, and many disappoint our Expectations. Health and Sickness, Calm and Tempest, with an infinite Number of other Accidents, whose Causes are unknown and variable, have a great Influence both on the Fortunes of particular Persons and on the Prosperity of public Societies: And indeed all human life, in a manner, depends on such Accidents. A Being, therefore, who knows the secret Springs of the Universe, might easily, by particular Volitions, turn all these Accidents to the Good of Mankind, and render the whole World happy, without discovering himself in any Operation. A Fleet, whose Purposes were Salutary to Society, might always meet with a fair Wind: Good Princes enjoy sound Health and long Life: Persons, born to Power and Authority, be fram'd with good Tempers and virtuous Dispositions. A few such Events as these, regularly and wisely conducted, wou'd change the Face of the World; and yet wou'd no more seem to disturb the Course of Nature or confound human Conduct, than the present Oeconomy of things, where the Causes are secret, and variable, and compounded. Some small Touches, given to *Caligula's* Brain in his Infancy, might have converted him into a *Trajan:* One Wave, a little higher than the rest, by burying *Caesar* and his Fortune in the bottom of the Ocean, might have restor'd Liberty to a considerable Part of Mankind. There may, for aught we know, be good Reasons, why Providence interposes not in this Manner; but they are unknown to us: And tho' the mere Supposition, that such Reasons exist, may be sufficient to *save* the Conclusion concerning the divine Attributes, yet surely it can never be sufficient to *establish* that Conclusion.

If every thing in the Universe be conducted by general Laws, and if Animals be render'd susceptible of Pain, it scarcely seems possible but some Ill must arise in the various Shocks of Matter, and the various Concurrence and Opposition of general Laws: But this Ill wou'd be very rare, were it not for the *third* Circumstance which I propos'd to mention, *viz,* the great Frugality, with which all Powers and Faculties are distributed to every particular Being. So well adjusted are the Organs and Capacities of all Animals, and so well fitted to their Preservation, that, as far as History or Tradition reaches, there appears not to be any single Species, which has yet been extinguish'd in the Universe. Every Animal has the requisite Endowments; but these Endowments are bestow'd with so scrupulous an Oeconomy, that any considerable Diminution must entirely destroy the Creature. Wherever one Power is encreas'd, there

is a proportional Abatement in the others. Animals, which excel in Swiftness, are commonly defective in Force. Those, which possess both, are either imperfect in some of their Senses, or are oppressed with the most craving Wants. The human Species, whose chief Excellency is Reason and Sagacity, is of all others the most necessitous, and the most deficient in bodily Advantages; without Cloaths, without Arms, without Food, without Lodging, without any Convenience of Life, except what they owe to their own Skill and Industry. In short, Nature seems to have form'd an exact Calculation of the Necessities of her Creatures; and like a *rigid Master,* has afforded them little more Powers or Endowments, than what are strictly sufficient to supply those Necessities. An *indulgent Parent* wou'd have bestow'd a large Stock, in order to guard against Accidents, and secure the Happiness and Welfare of the Creature, in the most unfortunate Concurrence of Circumstances. Every Course of Life wou'd not have been so surrounded with Precipices, that the least Departure from the true Path, by Mistake or Necessity, must involve us in Misery and Ruin. Some Reserve, some Fund wou'd have been provided to ensure Happiness; nor wou'd the Powers and the Necessities have been adjusted with so rigid an Oeconomy. The Arthur of Nature is inconceivably powerful: His force is suppos'd great, if not altogether inexhaustible: Nor is there any Reason, as far as we can judge, to make him observe this strict Frugality in his Dealings with his Creatures. It wou'd have been better, were his Power extremely limited, to have created fewer Animals, and to have endowed these with more Faculties for their Happiness and Preservation. A Builder is never esteem'd prudent, who undertakes a Plan, beyond what his Stock will enable him to finish.

In order to cure most of the Ills of human Life, I require that Man should have the Wings of the Eagle, the Swiftness of the Stag, the Force of the Ox, the Arms of the Lion, the Scales of the Crocodile or Rhinoceros; much less do I demand the Sagacity of an Angel or Cherubim. I am contented to take an Encrease in one single Power or Faculty of his Soul. Let him be endow'd with a greater Propensity to Industry and Labor; a more vigorous Spring and Activity of Mind; a more constant Bent to Business and Application. Let the whole Species possess naturally an equal Diligence with that which many Individuals are able to attain by Habit and Reflection; and the most beneficial Consequences, without any Allay of Ill, is the most immediate and necessary Result of the Endowment. Almost all the moral, as well as natural Evils of human Life arise from Idleness; and were our Species, by the original Constitution of their Frame, exempt from this Vice or Infirmity, the perfect Cultivation of Land, the Improvement of Arts and Manufactures, the exact Execution of every Office and Duty, immediately follow; and Men at once may fully reach that State of Society, which is so imperfectly attain'd by the best regulated Government. But as Industry is a Power, and the most valuable of any, Nature seems determin'd, suitably to her usual Maxims, to bestow it on men with a very sparing hand; and rather to punish him severely for his Deficiency in it, than to reward him for his Attainments. She has so contriv'd his Frame, that nothing but the most violent Necessity can oblige him to labor, and she employs all his other Wants to overcome, as least in part, the Want of Diligence, and to endow him with some Share of a Faculty, of which she has thought fit naturally to bereave him. Here our Demands may be allow'd very humble, and therefore the more reasonable. If we requir'd the Endowments of superior Penetration and Judgment, of a more delicate Taste of Beauty, of a nicer Sensibility to Benevolence and Friendship; we might be told, that we impiously pretend to break the Order of Nature, that we want to exalt Ourselves into a higher Rank of Being, that the Presents which we require, not being suitable to our State and Condition, wou'd only be pernicious to us. But it is hard; I dare to repeat it, it is hard, that being plac'd in a World so full of Wants and Necessities; where almost every Being and Element is either our Foe or refuses us their Assistance; we shou'd also have our own Temper to struggle with, and shou'd be depriv'd of that Faculty, which can alone fence against these multiply'd Evils.

The *fourth* Circumstance, whence arises the Misery and Ill of the universe, is the inaccurate Workmanship of all the Springs and Principles of the great Machine of Nature. It must be acknowledg'd, that there are few Parts of the Universe, which seem not to serve some Purpose, and whose Removal wou'd not produce a visible Defect and Disorder in the Whole. The Parts hang all together; nor can one be touch'd without affecting the rest, in a greater or less degree. But at the same time, it must be observ'd, that none of these Parts or Principles, however useful, are so accurately adjusted, as to keep precisely within those Bounds, in which their Utility consists; but they are, all of them, apt, on every Occasion, to run into the one Extreme or the other. One wou'd imagine, that this grand

Production had not receiv'd the last hand of the Maker; so little finish'd is every part, and so coarse are the Strokes, with which it is executed. Thus, the Winds are requisite to convey the Vapours along the Surface of the Globe, and to assist Men in Navigation: But how oft, rising up to Tempests and Hurricanes, do they become pernicious? Rains are necessary to nourish all the Plants and Animals of the Earth: But how often are they defective? how often excessive? Heat is requisite to all Life and Vegetation; but is not always found in the due Proportion. On the Mixture and Secretion of the Humours and Juices of the Body depend the Health and Prosperity of the Animal: But the Parts perform not regularly their proper Function. What more useful than all the Passions of the Mind, Ambition, Vanity, Love, Anger? But how oft do they break their Bounds, and cause the greatest Convulsions in Society? There is nothing so advantageous in the Universe, but what frequently becomes pernicious, by its Excess or Defect; nor has Nature guarded, with the requisite Accuracy, against all Disorder or Confusion. The Irregularity is never, perhaps, so great as to destroy any Species; but is often sufficient to involve the Individuals in Ruin and Misery.

On the Concurrence, then of these *four* Circumstances does all, or the greatest Part of natural Evil depend. Were all living Creatures incapable of Pain, or were the World administer'd by particular Volitions, Evil never cou'd have found Access into the Universe: And were Animals endow'd with a large Stock of Powers and Faculties, beyond what strict Necessity requires; or were the several Springs and Principles of the Universe so accurately fram'd as to preserve always the just Temperament and Medium; there must have been very little Ill in comparison of what we feel at present. What then shall we pronounce on this Occasion? Shall we say, that these Circumstances are not necessary, and that they might easily have been alter'd in the Contrivance of the Universe? This Decision seems too presumptuous for Creatures, so blind and ignorant. Let us be more modest in our Conclusions. Let us allow, that, if the Goodness of the Deity (I mean a Goodness like the human) cou'd be establish'd on any tolerable Reasons *a priori,* these Phaenomena, however untoward, wou'd not be sufficient to subvert that Principle; but might easily, in some unknown manner, be reconcilable to it. But let us still assert, that as this Goodness is not antecedently establish'd, but must be inferr'd from the Phaenomena, there can be no Grounds for such an Inference, while there are so many Ills in the Universe, and while these Ills might so easily have been remedy'd, as far as human Understanding can be allow'd to judge on such a Subject. I am Sceptic enough to allow, that the bad Appearances, notwithstanding all my Reasonings, may be compatible with such Attributes as you suppose: But surely they can never prove these Attributes. Such a Conclusion cannot result from Scepticism; but must arise from the Phaenomena, and from our Confidence in the Reasonings, which we deduce from these Phaenomena.

Look round this Universe. What an immense Profusion of Beings, animated and organiz'd, sensible and active! You admire this prodigious Variety and Fecundity. But inspect a little more narrowly these living Existences, the only Beings worth regarding. How hostile and destructive to each other! How insufficient all of them for their own

Happiness! How contemptible or odious to the Spectator! The whole presents nothing but the Idea of a blind Nature, impregnated by a great vivifying Principle, and pouring forth from her Lap, without Discernment or parental Care, her maim'd and abortive Children.

Here the *Manichoen* System occurs as a proper Hypothesis to solve the Difficulty: And no doubt, in some respects, it is very specious, and has more Probability than the common Hypothesis, by giving a plausible Account of the strange Mixture of Good and Ill, which appears in Life. But if we consider, on the other hand, the perfect Uniformity and Agreement of the Parts of the Universe, we shall not discover in it any Marks of the Combat of a malevolent with a benevolent Being. There is indeed an Opposition of Pains and Pleasures in the Feelings of sensible Creatures: But are not all the Operations of Nature carry'd on by an Opposition of Principles, of Hot and Cold, Moist and Dry, Light and Heavy? The true Conclusion is, that the original Source of all things is entirely indifferent to all these Principles, and has no more Regard to Good above Ill than to Heat above Cold, or to Drought above Moisture, or to Light above Heavy.

There may *four* Hypotheses be fram'd concerning the first Causes of the Universe; *that* they are endow'd with perfect Goodness, *that* they have perfect Malice, *that* they are opposite and have both Goodness and Malice, *that* they have neither Goodness nor Malice. Mixt Phaenomena can never prove the two former unmixt Principles. And the Uniformity and Steadiness of general Laws seem to oppose the third. The fourth, therefore, seems by far the most probable.

FYODOR DOSTOEVSKY

Rebellion

FYODOR DOSTOEVSKY *(1821–1881) was one of the greatest creative artists of the nineteenth century. He was born in Russia, where he lived most of his life. Opposed to the oppressive practices of the government, he was imprisoned for a time in Siberia. His belief in the fundamental evil of human nature permeates his novels, the most famous of which are* The Brothers Karamozov *and* Crime and Punishment.

"I meant to speak of the suffering of mankind generally, but we had better confine ourselves to the sufferings of the children. That reduces the scope of my argument to a tenth of what it would be. Still we'd better keep to the children, though it does weaken my case. But, in the first place, children can be loved even at close quarters, even when they are dirty, even when they are ugly (I fancy, though, children never are ugly). The second reason why I won't speak of grown-up people is that, besides being disgusting and unworthy of love, they have a compensation—they've eaten the apple and know good and evil, and they have become 'like gods.' They go on eating it still. But the children haven't eaten anything, and are so far innocent. Are you fond of children, Alyosha? I know you are, and you will understand why I prefer to speak of them. If they, too, suffer horribly on earth, they must suffer for their fathers' sins, they must be punished for their fathers, who have eaten the apple; but that reasoning is of the other world and is incomprehensible for the heart of man here on earth. The innocent must not suffer for another's sins, and especially such innocents! . . .

. . . Do you understand that, friend and brother, you pious and humble novice? Do you understand why this infamy must be and is permitted? Without it, I am told, man could not have existed on earth, for he could not have known good and evil. Why should he know that diabolical good and evil when it costs so much? Why, the whole world of knowledge is not worth that Child's prayer to 'dear, kind God'! I say nothing of the sufferings of grown-up people, they have eaten the apple, damn them, and the devil take them all! But these little ones! I am making you suffer, Alyosha, you are not yourself. I'll leave off if you like."

"Never mind. I want to suffer too," muttered Alyosha.

"One picture, only one more, because it's so curious, so characteristic, and I have only just read it in some collection of Russian antiquities. I've forgotten the name. I must look it up. It was in the darkest days of serfdom at the beginning of the century, and long live the Liberator of the People! There was in those days a general of aristocratic connections, the owner of great estates, one of those men—somewhat exceptional, I believe, even then—who, retiring from the service into a life of leisure, are convinced that they've earned absolute power over the lives of their subjects. There were such men then. So our general, settled on his property of two thousand souls, lives in pomp, and domineers over his poor neighbours as though they were dependents and buffoons. He has kennels of hundreds of hounds and nearly a hundred dog-boys—all mounted, and in uniform. One day a serf boy, a little child of eight, threw a stone in play and hurt the paw of the general's favourite hound. 'Why is my favorite dog lame?' He is told that the boy threw a stone that hurt the dog's paw. 'So you did it.' The general looked the child up and down. 'Take him.' He was taken—taken from his mother and kept shut up all night. Early that morning the general comes out on horseback, with the hounds, his dependents, dog-boys, and huntsmen, all mounted around him in full hunting parade. The servants are summoned for their edification, and in front of them all stands the mother of the child. The child is brought from the lock-up. It's a gloomy cold, foggy autumn day, a capital day for hunting. The general orders the child to be undressed; the child is stripped naked. He shivers, numb with terror, not daring to cry. . . . 'Make him run,' commands the general. 'Run! run!' shout the dog-boys. The boy runs. . . . 'At him!' yells the general, and he sets the whole pack of hounds on the child. The hounds catch him, and tear him to pieces before his mother's eyes! . . .

I believe the general was afterwards declared incapable of administering his estates. Well—what did he deserve? To be shot? To be shot for the satisfaction of our moral feelings? Speak, Alyosha!"

"To be shot," murmured Alyosha, lifting his eyes to Ivan with a pale, twisted smile.

"Bravo!" cried Ivan delighted. "If even you say so . . . You're a pretty monk! So there is a little devil sitting in your heart, Alyosha Karamazov!"

"What I said was absurd, but—"

"That's just the point that 'but'!" cried Ivan. "Let me tell you, novice, that the absurd is only too necessary on earth. The world stands on absurdities, and perhaps nothing would have come to pass in it without them. We know what we know!" . . .

Ivan for a minute was silent, his face became all at once very sad.

"Listen! I took the case of children only to make my case clearer. Of the other tears of humanity with which the earth is soaked from its crust to its centre, I will say nothing. I have narrowed my subject on purpose. I am a bug, and I recognise in all humility that I cannot understand why the world is arranged as it is. Men are themselves to blame, I suppose; they were given paradise, they wanted freedom, and stole fire from heaven, though they knew they would become unhappy, so there is no need to pity them. With my pitiful, earthly, Euclidian understanding, all I know is that there is suffering and that there are none guilty; that cause follows effect, simply and directly; that everything flows and finds its level—but that's only Euclidian nonsense, I know that, and I can't consent to live by it! What comfort is it to me that there are none guilty and that cause follows effect simply and directly, and that I know it—I must have justice,

or I will destroy myself. And not justice in some remote infinite time and space, but here on earth, and that I could see myself. I have believed in it. I want to see it, and if I am dead by then, let me rise again, for if it all happens without me, it will be too unfair. Surely I haven't suffered, simply that I, my crimes and my sufferings, may manure the soil of the future harmony for somebody else. I want to see with my own eyes the hind lie down with the lion and the victim rise up and embrace his murderer. I want to be there when every one suddenly understands what it has all been for. All the religions of the world are built on this longing, and I am a believer. But then there are the children, and what am I to do about them? That's a question I can't answer. For the hundredth time I repeat, there are numbers of questions, but I've only taken the children, because in their case what I mean is so unanswerably clear. Listen! If all must suffer to pay for the eternal harmony, what have children to do with it, tell me, please? It's beyond all comprehension why they should suffer, and why they should pay for the harmony. Why should they, too, furnish material to enrich the soil for the harmony of the future? I understand solidarity in sin among men. I understand solidarity in retribution, too; but there can be no such solidarity with children. And if it is really true that they must share responsibility for all their fathers' crimes, such a truth is not of this world and is beyond my comprehension. Some jester will say, perhaps, that the child would have grown up and have sinned, but you see he didn't grow up, he was torn to pieces by the dogs, at eight years old. Oh, Alyosha, I am not blaspheming! I understand, of course, what an upheaval of the universe it will be, when everything in heaven and earth blends in one hymn of praise and everything that lives and has lived cries aloud: 'Thou art just, O Lord, for Thy ways are revealed.' When the mother embraces the fiend who threw her child to the dogs, and all three cry aloud with tears, 'Thou art just, O Lord!' then, of course, the crown of knowledge will be reached and all will be made clear. But what pulls me up here is that I can't accept that harmony. And while I am on earth, I make haste to take my own measures. You see, Alyosha, perhaps it really may happen that if I live to that moment, or rise again to see it, I, too, perhaps, may cry aloud with the rest, looking at the mother embracing the child's torturer, 'Thou art just, O Lord!' but I don't want to cry aloud then. While there is still time, I hasten to protect myself and so I renounce the higher harmony altogether. It's not worth the tears of that one tortured child who beat itself on the breast with its little fist and prayed in its stinking outhouse, with its unexpiated tears to 'dear, kind God'! It's not worth it, because those tears are unatoned for. They must be atoned for, or there can be no harmony. But how? How are you going to atone for them? Is it possible? By their being avenged? But what do I care for avenging them? What do I care for a hell for oppressors? What good can hell do, since those children have already been tortured? And what becomes of harmony, if there is hell? I want to forgive. I want to embrace. I don't want more suffering. And if the sufferings of children go to swell the sum of sufferings which was necessary to pay for truth, then I protest that the truth is not worth such a price. I don't want the mother to embrace the oppressor who threw her son to the dogs! She dare not forgive him! Let her forgive him for

herself, if she will, let her forgive the torturer for the immeasurable suffering of her mother's heart. But the sufferings of her tortured child she has no right to forgive; she dare not forgive the torturer, even if the child were to forgive him! And if that is so, if they dare not forgive, what becomes of harmony? Is there in the whole world a being who would have the right to forgive and could forgive? I don't want harmony. From love for humanity I don't want it. I would rather be left with the unavenged suffering. I would rather remain with my unavenged suffering and unsatisfied indignation, *even if I were wrong*. Besides, too high a price is asked for harmony; it's beyond our means to pay so much to enter on it. And so I hasten to give back my entrance ticket, and if I am an honest man I am bound to give it back as soon as possible. And that I am doing. It's not God that I don't accept, Alyosha, only I must respectfully return Him the ticket."

"That's rebellion," murmured Alyosha, looking down.

"Rebellion? I am sorry you call it that," said Ivan earnestly. "One can hardly live in rebellion, and I want to live. Tell me yourself, I challenge you— answer. Imagine that you are creating a fabric of human destiny with the object of making men happy in the end, giving them peace and rest at last, but that it was essential and inevitable to torture to death only one tiny creature—that baby beating its breast with its fist, for instance—and to found that edifice on its unavenged tears, would you consent to be the architect on those conditions? Tell me, and tell the truth."

"No, I wouldn't consent," said Alyosha softly.

SØREN KIERKEGAARD

The Leap of Faith and the Limits of Reason

SØREN KIERKEGAARD (1813–1855) was a Danish philosopher and theologian.
Generally recognized as the father of existentialism and religious irrationalism, he
believed that each individual must choose his or her own way of life. Christianity is
one such choice.

BUT what is this unknown something with which the Reason collides when inspired by its paradoxical passion, with the result of unsettling even man's knowledge of himself? It is the Unknown. It is not a human being, in so far as we know what man is; nor is it any other known thing. So let us call this unknown something: *God.* It is nothing more than a name we assign to it. The idea of demonstrating that this unknown something (God) exists, could scarcely suggest itself to the Reason. For if God does not exist it would of course be impossible to prove it; and if he does exist it would be folly to attempt it. For at the very outset, in beginning my proof, I will have presupposed it, not as doubtful but as certain (a presupposition is never doubtful, for the very reason that it is a presupposition), since otherwise I would not begin, readily understanding that the whole would be impossible if he did not exist. But if when I speak of proving God's existence I mean that I propose to prove that the Unknown, which exists, is God, then I express myself unfortunately. For in that case I do not prove anything, least of all an existence, but merely develop the content of a conception. Generally speaking, it is a difficult matter to prove that anything exists; and what is still worse for the intrepid souls who under-take the venture, the difficulty is such that fame scarcely awaits those who concern themselves with it. The entire demonstration always turns into something very different from what it assumes to be, and becomes an additional development of the consequences that flow from my having assumed that the object in question exists. Thus I always reason from existence, not toward existence, whether I move in the sphere of palpable sensible fact or in the realm of thought. I do not for example prove that a stone exists, but that some existing thing is a stone. The procedure in a court of justice does not prove that a criminal exists, but that the accused, whose existence is given, is a criminal. Whether we call existence an *accessorium* or the eternal *prius,* it is never subject to demonstration. Let us take ample time for consideration. We have no such reason for haste as have those who from concern for themselves or for God or for some other thing, must make haste to get its existence demonstrated. Under such circumstances there may indeed be need for haste, especially if the prover sincerely seeks to appreciate the danger that he himself, or the thing in question, may be non-existent unless the proof is finished; and does not surreptitiously entertain the thought that it exists whether he succeeds in proving it or not.

If it were proposed to prove Napoleon's existence from Napoleon's deeds, would it not be a most curious proceeding? His existence does indeed explain his deeds, but the deeds do not prove *his* existence, unless I have already understood the word "his" so as thereby to have assumed his existence. But Napoleon is only an individual, and in so far there exists no absolute relationship between him and his deeds; some other person might have performed the same deeds. Perhaps this is the reason why I cannot pass from the deeds to existence. If I call these deeds the deeds of Napoleon the proof becomes superfluous, since I have already named him; if I ignore this, I can never prove from the deeds that they are Napoleon's, but only in a purely ideal manner that such deeds are the deeds of a great general, and so forth. But between God and his works there exists an absolute relationship: God is not a name but a concept. Is this perhaps the reason that his *essentia involvit existentiam?* The works of God are such that only God can perform them. Just so, but where are the works of God? The works from which I would deduce his existence are not immediately given. The wisdom of God in nature, his goodness, his wisdom in the governance of the world—are all these manifest, perhaps, upon the very face of things? Are we not here confronted with the most terrible temptations to doubt, and is it not impossible finally to dispose of all these doubts? But from such an order of things I will surely not attempt to prove God's existence; and even if I began I would never finish, and would in addition have to live constantly in suspense, lest something terrible should suddenly happen that my bit of proof would be demolished. From what works then do I propose to derive the proof? From the

works as apprehended through an ideal interpretation, i.e., such as they do not immediately reveal themselves. But in that case it is not from the works that I prove God's existence. I merely develop the ideality I have presupposed, and because of my confidence in *this* I make so bold as to defy all objections, even those that have not yet been made. In beginning my proof I presuppose the ideal interpretation, and also that I will be successful in carrying it through; but what else is this but to presuppose that God exists, so that I really begin by virtue of confidence in him?

And how does God's existence emerge from the proof? Does it follow straightway, without any breach of continuity? Or have we not here an analogy to the behaviour of these toys, the little Cartesian dolls? As soon as I let go of the doll it stands on its head. As soon as I let it go—I must therefore let it go. So also with the proof for God's existence. As long as I keep my hold on the proof, i.e., continue to demonstrate, the existence does not come out, if for no other reason than that I am engaged in proving it; but when I let the proof go, the existence is there. But this act of letting go is surely also something; it is indeed a contribution of mine. Must not this also be taken into the account, this little moment, brief as it may be—it need not be long, for it is a *leap*. However brief this moment, if only an instantaneous now, this "now" must be included in the reckoning.

Whoever therefore attempts to demonstrate the existence of God (except in the sense of clarifying the concept), proves in lieu thereof something else, something which at times perhaps does not need proof, and in any case need none better; for the fool says in his heart that there is no God, but whoever says in his heart or to men: Wait just a

little and I will prove it—what a rare
man of wisdom is he! If in the moment
of beginning his proof it is not absolutely undetermined whether God exists or not, he does not prove it; and if it
is thus undetermined in the beginning he
will never come to begin, partly from
fear of failure, since God perhaps does
not exist, and partly because he has
nothing with which to begin.—A project
of this kind would scarcely have been
undertaken by the ancients. Socrates at
least, who is credited with having put
forth the physico-teleological proof for
God's existence, did not go about it in
any such manner. He always presupposes God's existence, and under this
presupposition seeks to interpenetrate
nature with the ideal of purpose. Had he
been asked why he pursued this method,
he would doubtless have explained that
he lacked the courage to venture out
upon so perilous a voyage of discovery
without having made sure of God's existence behind him. At the word of God he
casts his net as if to catch the idea of
purpose; for nature herself finds many
means of frightening the inquirer, and
distracts him by many a digression.

The paradoxical passion of the Reason thus comes repeatedly into collision
with the Unknown, which does indeed
exist, but is unknown, and in so far does
not exist. The Reason cannot advance
beyond this point, and yet it cannot refrain in its paradoxicalness from arriving at this limit and occupying itself
therewith. It will not serve to dismiss its
relation to it simply by asserting that the
Unknown dies not exist, since this itself
involves a relationship. But what then is
the Unknown, since the designation of it
as God merely signifies for us that it is
unknown? To say that it is the Unknown
because it cannot be known, and even if
it were capable of being known, it could

not be expressed, does not satisfy the
demands of passion, though it correctly
interprets the Unknown as a limit; but a
limit is precisely a torment for passion,
though it also serves as an incitement.
And yet the Reason can come no further, whether it risks an issue *via nega-
tionis* or *via eminentia.*

What then is the Unknown? It is the
limit to which the Reason repeatedly
comes, and in so far, substituting a static form of conception for the dynamic,
it is the different, the absolutely different. But because it is absolutely different, there is no mark by which it could
be distinguished. When qualified as absolutely different it seems on the verge
of disclosure, but this is not the case; for
the Reason cannot even conceive an absolute unlikeness. The Reason cannot
negate itself absolutely, but uses itself
for the purpose, and thus conceives only
such an unlikeness within itself as it can
conceive by means of itself; it cannot
absolutely transcend itself, and hence
conceives only such a superiority over
itself as it can conceive by means of itself. Unless the Unknown (God) remains a mere limiting conception, the
single idea of difference will be thrown
into a state of confusion, and become
many ideas of many differences. The
Unknown is then in a condition of dis-
persion (διασπορά), and the Reason
may choose at pleasure from what is at
hand and the imagination may suggest
(the monstrous, the ludicrous, etc.).

But it is impossible to hold fast to a
difference of this nature. Every time this
is done it is essentially an arbitrary act,
and deepest down in the heart of piety
lurks the mad caprice which knows that
it has itself produced its God. If no specific determination of difference can be
held fast, because there is no distinguishing mark, like and unlike finally

become identified with one another, thus sharing the fate of all such dialectical opposites. The unlikeness clings to the Reason and confounds it, so that the Reason no longer knows itself and quite consistently confuses itself with the unlikeness. On this point paganism has been sufficiently prolific in fantastic inventions. As for the last named supposition, the self-irony of the Reason, I shall attempt to delineate it merely by a stroke or two, without raising any question of its being historical. There lives an individual whose appearance is precisely like that of other men; he grows up to manhood like others, he marries, he has an occupation by which he earns his livelihood, and he makes provision for the future as befits a man. For though it may be beautiful to live like the birds of the air, it is not lawful, and may lead to the sorriest of consequences: either starvation if one has enough persistence, or dependence on the bounty of others. This man is also God. How do I know? I cannot know it, for in order to know it I would have to know God, and the nature of the difference between God and man; and this I cannot know, because the Reason has reduced it to likeness with that from which it was unlike. Thus God becomes the most terrible of deceivers, because the Reason has deceived itself. The Reason has brought God as near as possible, and yet he is as far away as ever.

WILLIAM JAMES

The Will to Believe

WILLIAM JAMES (1842–1910) was one of the greatest American philosophers. He graduated from Harvard with a medical degree but decided to teach (at Harvard) rather than practice medicine. A founder of modern pragmatism, he also established himself as one of the fathers of modern psychology with his Principles of Psychology.

I have long defended to my own students the lawfulness of voluntarily adopted faith; but as soon as they have got well imbued with the logical spirit, they have as a rule refused to admit my contention to be lawful philosophically, even though in point of fact they were personally all the time chockfull of some faith or other themselves. I am all the while, however, so profoundly convinced that my own position is correct, that your invitation has seemed to me a good occasion to make my statements more clear. Perhaps your minds will be more open than those with which I have hitherto had to deal. I will be as little technical as I can, though I must begin by setting up some technical distinctions that will help us in the end.

Let us give the name of *hypothesis* to anything that may be proposed to our belief; and just as the electricians speak of live and dead wires, let us speak of any hypothesis as either *live* or *dead.* A live hypothesis is one which appeals as a real possibility to him to whom it is proposed. If I ask you to believe in the Mahdi, the notion makes no electric connection with your nature,—it refuses to scintillate with any credibility at all. As an hypothesis it is completely dead. To an Arab, however (even if he be not one of the Mahdi's followers), the hypothesis is among the mind's possibilities: it is alive. This shows that deadness and liveness in an hypothesis are not intrinsic properties, but relations to the individual thinker. They are measured by his willingness to act. The maximum of liveness in an hypothesis means willingness to act irrevocably. Practically, that means belief; but there is some believing tendency wherever there is willingness to act at all.

Next, let us call the decision between two hypotheses an *option.* Options may be of several kinds. They may be—1, *living* or *dead;* 2, *forced* or *avoidable;* 3, *momentous* or *trivial;* and for our purposes we may call an option a *genuine* option when it is of the forced, living, and momentous kind.

1. A living option is one in which both hypotheses are live ones. If I say to you: "Be a theosophist or be a Mohammedan," it is probably a dead option, because for you neither hypothesis is likely to be alive. But if I say, "Be an agnostic or be a Christian," it is otherwise: trained as you are, each hypothesis makes some appeal, however small, to your belief.

2. Next, if I say to you: "Choose between going out with your umbrella or without it," I do not offer you a genuine option, for it is not forced. You can easily avoid it by not going out at all. Similarly, if I say, "Either love me or hate me," "Either call my theory true or call it false," your option is avoidable. You may remain indifferent to me, neither loving nor hating, and you may decline to offer any judgment as to my theory. But if I say, "Either accept this truth or go without it," I put on you a forced option, for there is no standing place outside of the alternative. Every dilemma based on a complete logical disjunction, with no possibility of not choosing, is an option of this forced kind. . . .

The thesis I defend is, briefly stated, this: *Our passional nature not only lawfully may, but must, decide an option between propositions, whenever it is a genuine option that cannot by its nature be decided on intellectual grounds; for to say, under such circumstances, "Do not decide, but leave the question open," is itself a passional decision,—just like deciding yes or no,—and is attended with the same risk of losing the truth. . . .*

Wherever the option between losing truth and gaining it is not momentous, we can throw the chance of *gaining truth* away, and at any rate save ourselves from any chance of *believing falsehood,* by not making up our minds at all till objective evidence has come. In scientific questions, this is almost always the case; and even in human affairs in general, the need of acting is seldom so urgent that a false belief to act on is better than no belief at all. Law courts, indeed, have to decide on the best evidence attainable for the moment, because a judge's duty is to make law as well as to ascertain it, and (as a learned judge once said to me) few cases are worth spending much time over: the great thing is to have them decided on *any* acceptable principle, and got out of the way. But in our dealings with objective nature we obviously are recorders, not makers, of the truth; and decisions for the mere sake of deciding promptly and getting on to the next business would be wholly out of place. Throughout the breadth of physical nature facts are what they are quite independently of us, and seldom is there any such hurry about them that the risks of being duped by believing a premature theory need be faced. The questions here are always trivial options, the hypotheses are hardly living (at any rate not living for us spectators), the choice between believing truth or falsehood is seldom forced. The attitude of sceptical balance is therefore the absolutely wise one if we would escape mistakes. What difference, indeed, does it make to most of us whether we have or have not a theory of the Röntgen rays, whether we believe or not in mind stuff, or have a conviction about the causality of conscious states? It makes no difference. Such options are not forced on us. On every account it is better not to make them, but still keep weighing reasons *pro et contra* with an indifferent hand. . . .

But now, it will be said, these . . . cases, . . . have nothing to do with great cosmical matters, like the question of religious faith. Let us then pass on to that. Religions differ so much in their accidents that in discussing the religious question we must take it very generic and broad. What then do we now mean by the religious hypothesis? Science says things are; morality says some things are better than other things; and religion says essentially two things.

First, she says that the best things are the more eternal things, the overlapping things, the things in the universe that throw the last stone, so to speak, and say the final word. "Perfection is eternal,"—this phrase of Charles Secrétan seems a good way of putting this first affirmation of religion, an affirmation which obviously cannot yet be verified scientifically at all.

The second affirmation of religion is that we are better off even not if we believe her first affirmation to be true.

Now, let us consider what the logical elements of this situation are *in case the religious hypothesis in both its branches be really true.* (Of course, we must admit that possibility at the outset. If we are to discuss the question at all, it must involve a living option. If for any of you religion be a hypothesis that cannot, by any living possibility be true, then you need go no farther. I speak to the 'saving remnant' alone.) So proceeding, we see, first that religion offers itself as a *momentous* option. We are supposed to gain, even now, by our belief, and to lose by our nonbelief, a certain vital good. Secondly, religion is a *forced* option, so far as that good goes. We cannot escape the issue by remaining sceptical and waiting for more light, because, although we do avoid error in that way *if religion be untrue,* we lose the good, *if it be true,* just as certainly as if we positively chose to disbelieve. It is as if a man should hesitate indefinitely to ask a certain woman to marry him because he was not perfectly sure that she would prove an angel after he brought her home. Would he not cut himself off from that particular angel-possibility as decisively as if he went and married some one else? Scepticism, then, is not avoidance of option; it is option of a certain particular kind of risk. *Better risk loss of truth than chance of error,*—that is your faith-vetoer's exact position. He is actively playing his stake as much as the believer is; he is backing the field against the religious hypothesis, just as the believer is backing the religious hypothesis against the field. To preach scepticism to us as a duty until 'sufficient evidence' for religion be found, is tantamount therefore to telling us, when in presence of the religious hypothesis, that to yield to our fear of its being error is wiser and better than to yield to our hope that it may be true. It is not intellect against all passions, then; it is only intellect with one passion laying down its law. And by what, forsooth, is the supreme wisdom of this passion warranted? Dupery for dupery, what proof is there that dupery through hope is so much worse than dupery through fear? I, for one, can see no proof; and I simply refuse obedience to the scientist's command to imitate his kind of option, in a case where my own stake is important enough to give me the right to choose my own form of risk. If religion be true and the evidence for it be still insufficient, I do not wish, by putting your extinguisher upon my nature (which feels to me as if it had after all some business in this matter), to forfeit my sole chance in life of getting upon the winning side,—that chance depending, of course, on my willingness to run the risk of acting as if my passional need of taking the world religiously might be prophetic and right.

All this is on the supposition that it really may be prophetic and right, and that, even to us who are discussing the matter, religion is a live hypothesis which may be true. Now, to most of us religion comes in a still further way that makes a veto on our active faith even more illogical. The more perfect and more eternal aspect of the universe is represented in our religions as having personal form. The universe is no longer a mere *It* to us, but a *Thou,* if we are religious; and any relation that may be possible from person to person might

be possible here. For instance, although in one sense we are passive portions of the universe, in another we show a curious autonomy, as if we were small active centres on our own account. We feel, too, as if the appeal of religion to us were made to our own active goodwill, as if evidence might be forever withheld from us unless we met the hypothesis half-way. To take a trivial illustration: just as a man who in a company of gentlemen made no advances, asked a warrant for every concession, and believed no one's word without proof, would cut himself off by such churlishness from all the social rewards that a more trusting spirit would earn,—so here, one who should shut himself up in snarling logicality and try to make the gods extort his recognition willy-nilly, or not get it at all, might cut himself off forever from his only opportunity of making the gods' aquaintance. This feeling, forced on us we know not whence, that by obstinately believing that there are gods (although not to do so would be so easy both for our logic and our life) we are doing the universe the deepest service we can, seems part of the living essence of the religious hypothesis. If the hypothesis *were* true in all its parts, including this one, then pure intellectualism, with its veto on our making willing advances, would be an absurdity; and some participation of our sympathetic nature would be logically required. I, therefore, for one, cannot see my way to accepting the agnostic rules for truth-seeking, or wilfully agree to keep my willing nature out of the game. I cannot do so for this plain reason, that *a rule of thinking which would absolutely prevent me from acknowledging certain kinds of truth if those kinds of truth were really there, would be an irrational rule.* That for me is the long and short of the formal logic of the situation, no matter what the kinds of truth might materially be.

I confess I do not see how this logic can be escaped. But sad experience makes me fear that some of you may still shrink from radically saying with me, *in abstracto,* that we have the right to believe at our own risk any hypothesis that is live enough to tempt our will. I suspect, however, that if this is so, it is because you have got away from the abstract logical point of view altogether, and are thinking (perhaps without realizing it) of some particular religious hypothesis which for you is dead. The freedom to 'believe what we will' you apply to the case of some patent superstition; and the faith you think of is the faith defined by the schoolboy when he said, "Faith is when you believe something that you know ain't true." I can only repeat that this is misapprehension. *In concreto,* the freedom to believe can only cover living options which the intellect of the individual cannot by itself resolve; and living options never seem absurdities to him who has them to consider. When I look at the religious question as it really puts itself to concrete men, and when I think of all the possibilities which both practically and theoretically it involves, then this command that we shall put a stopper on our heart, instincts, and courage, and *wait*—acting of course meanwhile more or less as if

religion were *not* true—till dooms day, or till such time as our intellect and senses working together may have raked in evidence enough,—this command, I say, seems to me the queerest idol ever manufactured in the philosophic cave. Were we scholastic absolutists, there might be more excuse. If we had an infallible intellect with its objective certitudes, we might feel ourselves disloyal to such a perfect organ of knowledge in not trusting to it exclusively, in not waiting for its releasing word. But if we are empiricists, if we believe that no bell in us tolls to let us know for certain when truth is in our grasp, then it seems a piece of idle fantasticality to preach so solemnly our duty of waiting for the bell. Indeed we *may* wait if we will.—I hope you do not think that I am denying that,—but if we do so, we do so at our peril as much as if we believed. In either case we *act,* taking our life in our hands. No one of us ought to issue vetoes to the other, nor should we bandy words of abuse. We ought, on the contrary, delicately and profoundly to respect one another's mental freedom: then only shall we bring about the intellectual republic; then only shall we have that spirit of inner tolerance without which all our outer tolerance is soulless, and which is empiricism's glory; then only shall we live and let live, in speculative as well as in practical things.

ANTHONY FLEW, R. M. HARE, AND BASIL MITCHELL

Theology and Falsification

ANTHONY FLEW *teaches philosophy at the University of Reading in England. He has written many books and articles, among them* Hume's Philosophy of Belief *and* The Politics of Procrustes.

R. M. HARE *taught philosophy at Oxford for many years and now teaches at the University of Florida. An influential moral philosopher, his books include* The Language of Morals, Moral Thinking, *and* Plato.

BASIL MITCHELL *teaches philosophy of religion at Oxford. His works include* Law, Morality and Religion in Secular Society *and* Law, Belief and Morality: Religious and Secular.

ANTHONY FLEW

LET us begin with a parable. It is a parable developed from a tale told by John Wisdom in his haunting and revelatory article 'Gods.' Once upon a time two explorers came upon a clearing in the jungle. In the clearing were growing many flowers and many weeds. One explorer says, 'Some gardener must tend this plot.' The other disagrees, 'There is no gardener.' So they pitch their tents and set a watch. No gardener is ever seen. 'But perhaps he is an invisible gardener.' So they set up a barbed-wire fence. They electrify it. They patrol with bloodhounds. (For they remember how H. G. Wells's *The Invisible Man* could be both smelt and touched though he could not be seen.) But no shrieks ever suggest that some intruder has received a shock. No movements of the wire ever betray an invisible climber. The bloodhounds never give cry. Yet still the Believer is not convinced. 'But there is a gardener, invisible, intangible, insensible to electric shocks, a gardener who has no scent and makes no sound, a gardener who comes secretly to look after the garden which he loves.' At last the Sceptic despairs, 'But what remains of your original assertion? Just how does what you call an invisible, intangible, eternally elusive gardener differ from an imaginary gardener or even from no gardener at all?'

In this parable we can see how what starts as an assertion, that something exists or that there is some analogy between certain complexes of phenomena, may be reduced step by step to an altogether different status, to an expression perhaps of a 'picture preference.' The Sceptic says there is no gardener. The Believer says there is a gardener (but invisible, etc.). One man talks about sexual behaviour. Another man prefers to talk of Aphrodite (but knows that there is not really a superhuman person additional to, and somehow responsible for, all sexual phenomena). The process of qualification may be checked at any point before the original assertion is completely withdrawn and something of that first assertion will remain

(Tautology). Mr. Wells's invisible man could not, admittedly, be seen, but in all other respects he was a man like the rest of us. But though the process of qualification may be, and of course usually is, checked in time, it is not always judiciously so halted. Someone may dissipate his assertion completely without noticing that he has done so. A fine brash hypothesis may thus be killed by inches, the death by a thousand qualifications.

And in this, it seems to me, lies the peculiar danger, the endemic evil, of theological utterance. Take such utterances as 'God has a plan,' 'God created the world,' 'God loves us as a father loves his children.' They look at first sight very much like assertions, vast cosmological assertions. Of course, this is no sure sign that they either are, or are intended to be, assertions. But let us confine ourselves to the cases where those who utter such sentences intend them to express assertions. (Merely remarking parenthetically that those who intend or interpret such utterances as crypto-commands, expressions of wishes, disguised ejaculations, concealed ethics, or as anything else but assertions, are unlikely to succeed in making them either properly orthodox or practically effective.)

Now to assert that such and such is the case is necessarily equivalent to denying that such and such is not the case. Suppose then that we are in doubt as to what someone who gives vent to an utterance is asserting, or suppose that, more radically, we are sceptical as to whether he is really asserting anything at all. One way of trying to understand (or perhaps it will be to expose) his utterance is to attempt to find what he would regard as counting against, or as being incompatible with, its truth.

For if the utterance is indeed an assertion, it will necessarily be equivalent to a denial of the negation of that assertion. And anything which would count against the assertion, or which would induce the speaker to withdraw it and to admit that it had been mistaken, must be part of (or the whole of) the meaning of the negation of that assertion. And to know the meaning of the negation of an assertion, is as near as makes no matter, to know the meaning of that assertion. And if there is nothing which a putative assertion denies then there is nothing which it asserts either: and so it is not really an assertion. When the Sceptic in the parable asked the Believer, 'Just how does what you call an invisible, intangible, eternally elusive gardener differ from an imaginary gardener or even from no gardener at all?' he was suggesting that the Believer's earlier statement had been so eroded by qualification that it was no longer an assertion at all.

Now it often seems to people who are not religious as if there was no conceivable event or series of events the occurrence of which would be admitted by sophisticated religious people to be a sufficient reason for conceding 'there wasn't a God after all' or 'God does not really love us then.' Someone tells us that God loves us as a father loves his children. We are reassured. But then we see a child dying of inoperable cancer of the throat. His earthly father is driven frantic in his efforts to help, but his Heavenly Father reveals no obvious sign of concern. Some qualification is made—God's love is 'not merely human love' or it is 'an unscrutable love,' perhaps—and we realize that such sufferings are quite compatible with the truth of the assertion that 'God loves us as a father (but, of course, . . .).' We are reassured again. But then perhaps we ask: what is this assurance of God's (appropriately qualified) love worth, what is this apparant guarantee really a guarantee against? Just what would have to happen not merely (morally and wrongly) to tempt but also (logically and rightly) to entitle us to say 'God does not exist'? I therefore put to the succeeding symposiasts the simple central questions, 'What would have to occur or to have occurred to constitute for you a disproof of the love of, or the existence of, God?'

R. M. HARE

I wish to make it clear that I shall not try to defend Christianity in particular, but religion in general—not because I do not believe in Christianity, but because you cannot understand what Christianity is until you have understood what religion is.

I must begin by confessing that, on the ground marked out by Flew, he seems to me to be completely victorious. I therefore shift my ground by relating another parable. A certain lunatic is convinced that all dons want to murder him. His friends introduce him to all the mildest and most respectable dons that they can find, and after each of them has retired, they say, 'You see, he doesn't really want to murder you; he spoke to you in the most cordial manner; surely you are convinced now?' But the lunatic replies, 'Yes, but that was only his diabolical cunning; he's really plotting against me the whole time, like the rest of them; I know it I tell you.' However many kindly dons are produced, the reaction is still the same.

Now we say that such a person is deluded. But what is he deluded about? About the truth or falsity of an assertion? Let us apply Flew's test to him.

There is no behaviour of dons that can be enacted which he will accept as counting against his theory; and therefore his theory, on this test, asserts nothing. But it does not follow that there is no difference between what he thinks about dons and what most of us think about them—otherwise we should not call him a lunatic and ourselves sane, and dons would have no reason to feel uneasy about his presence in Oxford.

Let us call that in which we differ from the lunatic, our respective *bliks*. He has an insane *blik* about dons; we have a sane one. It is important to realize that we have a sane one, not no *blik* at all; for there must be two sides to any argument—if he has a wrong *blik,* then those who are right about dons must have a right one. Flew has shown that a *blik* does not consist in an assertion or system of them; but nevertheless it is very important to have the right *blik.*

Let us try to imagine what it would be like to have different *bliks* about other things than dons. When I am driving my car, it sometimes occurs to me to wonder whether my movements of the steering-wheel will always continue to be followed by corresponding alterations in the direction of the car. I have never had a steering failure, though I have had skids, which must be similar. Moreover, I know enough about how the steering of my car is made, to know the sort of thing that would have to go wrong for the steering to fail—steel joints would have to part, or steel rods break, or something—but how do I know that this won't happen? The truth is, I don't know; I just have a *blik* about steel and its properties, so that normally I trust the steering of my car; but I find it not at all difficult to imagine what it would be like to lose this *blik* and acquire the opposite one. People would say I was silly about steel; but there would be no mistaking the reality of the difference between our respective *bliks*—for example, I should never go in a motorcar. Yet I should hesitate to say that the difference between us was the difference between contradictory assertions. No amount of safe arrivals or bench-tests will remove my *blik* and restore the normal one; for my *blik* is compatible with any finite number of such tests.

It was Hume who taught us that our whole commerce with the world depends upon our *blik* about the world; and that difference between *bliks* about the world cannot be settled by observation of what happens in the world. That was why, having performed the interesting experiment of doubting the ordinary man's *blik* about the world, and showing that no proof could be given to make us adopt one *blik* rather than another, he turned to backgammon to take his mind off the problem. It seems, indeed, to be impossible even to formulate as an assertion the normal *blik* about the world which makes me put my confidence in the future reliability of steel joints, in the continued ability of the road to support my car, and not gape beneath it revealing nothing below; in the general non-homicidal tendencies of dons; in my own continued well-being (in some sense of that word that I may not now fully understand) if I continue to do what is right according to my lights; in the general likelihood of people like Hitler coming to a bad end. But perhaps a formulation less inadequate than most is to be found in the Psalms: 'The earth is weak and all the inhabitants thereof: I bear up the pillars of it.'

The mistake of the position which Flew selects for attack is to regard this kind of talk as some sort of *explanation,* as scientists are accustomed to use the word. As such, it would obviously be ludicrous. We no longer believe in God as an Atlas—*nous n'avons pas besoin de cette hypothèse.* But it is nevertheless true to say that, as Hume saw, without a *blik* there can be no explanation; for it is by our *bliks* that we decide what is and what is not an explanation. Suppose we believe that everything that happened, happened by pure chance. This would not of course be an assertion; for it is compatible with anything happening or not happening, and so, incidentally, it is contradictory. But if we had this belief, we should not be able to explain or predict or plan anything. Thus, although we should not be *asserting* anything different from those of a more normal belief, there would be a great difference between us; and this is the sort of difference that there is between those who really believe in God and those who really disbelieve in him.

BASIL MITCHELL

There is an important difference between Flew's parable and my own which we have not yet noticed. The explorers do not *mind* about their garden; they discuss it with interest, but not with concern. But my lunatic, poor fellow minds about dons; and I mind about the steering of my car; it often has people in it that I care for. It is because I mind very much about what goes on in the garden in which I find myself, that I am unable to share the explorers' detachment.

Flew's article is searching and perceptive, but there is, I think, something odd about his conduct of the theologian's case. The theologian surely would not deny that the fact of pain counts against the assertion that God loves men. This very incompatibility generates the most intractable of theological problems—the problem of evil. So the theologian *does* recognize the fact of pain as counting against Christian doctrine. But it is true that he will not allow it—or anything—to count decisively against it; for he is committed by his faith to trust in God. His attitude is not that of the detached observer, but of the believer.

Perhaps this can be brought out by yet another parable. In time of war in an occupied country, a member of the resistance meets one night a stranger who deeply impresses him. They spend the night together in conversation. The Stranger tells the partisan that he himself is on the side of the resistance—indeed that he is in command of it, and urges the partisan to have faith in him no matter what happens. The partisan is utterly convinced at that meeting of the Stranger's sincerity and constancy and undertakes to trust him.

They never meet in conditions of intimacy again. But sometimes the Stranger is seen helping members of the resistance, and the partisan is grateful and says to his friends, 'He is on our side.'

Sometimes he is seen in the uniform of the police handing over patriots to the occupying power. On these occasions his friends murmur against him; but the partisan still says, 'He is on our side.' He still believes that, in spite of appearances, the Stranger did not deceive him. Sometimes he asks the Stranger for help and receives it. He is then thankful. Sometimes he asks and does not receive it. Then he says, 'The Stranger knows best.' Sometimes his friends, in exasperation, say 'Well, what *would* he have to do for you to admit that you were wrong and that he is not on our side?' But the partisan refuses to answer. He will not consent to put the Stranger to the test. And sometimes his friends complain,

'Well, if *that's* what you mean by his being on our side, the sooner he goes over to the other side the better.'

The partisan of the parable does not allow anything to count decisively against the proposition 'The Stranger is on our side.' This is because he has committed himself to trust the Stranger. But he of course recognizes that the Stranger's ambiguous behaviour *does* count against what he believes about him. It is precisely this situation which constitutes the trial of his faith.

ANTHONY FLEW

The challenge, it will be remembered, ran like this. Some theological utterances seem to, and are intended to, provide explanations or express assertions. Now an assertion, to be an assertion at all, must claim that things stand thus and thus; *and not otherwise.* Similarly an explanation, to be an explanation at all, must explain why this particular thing occurs; *and not something else.* Those last clauses are crucial. And yet sophisticated religious people—or so it seemed to me—are apt to overlook this, and tend to refuse to allow, not merely that anything actually does occur, but that anything conceivably could occur, which would count against their theological assertions and explanations. But in so far as they do this their supposed explanations are actually bogus, and their seeming assertions are really vacuous.

Mitchell's response to this challenge is admirably direct, straightforward, and understanding. He agrees 'that theological utterances must be assertions.' He agrees that if they are to be assertions, there must be something that would count against their truth. He agrees, too, that believers are in constant danger of transforming their would-be assertions into 'vacuous formulae.' But he takes me to task for an oddity in my 'conduct of the theologian's case.' The theologian surely would not deny that the fact of pain counts against the assertion that God loves men. This very incompatibility generates the most intractable of theological problems, the problem of evil.' I think he is right. I should have made a distinction between two very different ways of dealing with what looks like evidence against the love of God: the way I stressed was the expedient of qualifying the original assertion; the way the theologian usually takes, at first, is to admit that it looks bad but to insist that there is—there must be—some explanation which will show that, in spite of appearances, there really is a God who loves us. His difficulty, it seems to me, is that he has given God attributes which rule out all possible saving explanations. In Mitchell's parable of the Stranger it is easy for the believer to find plausible excuses for ambiguous behaviour: for the Stranger is a man. But suppose the Stranger is God. We cannot say that he would like to help but cannot: God is omnipotent. We cannot say that he would help if he only knew: God is omniscient. We cannot say that he is not responsible for the wickedness of others: God creates those others. Indeed an omnipotent, omniscient God must be an accessory before (and during) the fact to every human misdeed; as well as being responsible for every non-moral defect in the universe. So, though I entirely concede that Mitchell was absolutely right to insist against me that the theologian's first move is to look for an *explanation,* I still think that in the end, if relentlessly pursued, he will have to resort to the

avoiding action of *qualification.* And there lies the danger of that death by a thousand qualifications, which would, I agree, constitute 'a failure in faith as well as in logic.'

Hare's approach is fresh and bold. He confesses that 'on the ground marked out by Flew, he seems to me to be completely victorious.' He therefore introduces the concept of *blik.* But while I think that there is room for some such concept in philosophy, and that philosophers should be grateful to Hare for his invention, I nevertheless want to insist that any attempt to analyse Christian religious utterances as expressions or affirmations of a *blik* rather than as (at least would-be) assertions about the cosmos is fundamentally misguided. *First,* because thus interpreted they would be entirely unorthodox. If Hare's religion really is a *blik,* involving no cosmological assertions about the nature and activities of a supposed personal creator, then surely he is not a Christian at all? *Second,* because thus interpreted, they could scarcely do the job they do. If they were not even intended as assertions then many religious activities would become fraudulent, or merely silly. If 'You ought *because* it is God's will' asserts no more than 'You ought,' then the person who prefers the former phraseology is not really giving a reason, but a fraudulent substitute for one, a dialectical dud cheque. . . . Religious utterances may indeed express false or even bogus assertions: but I simply do not believe that they are not both intended and interpreted to be or at any rate to presuppose assertions, at least in the context of religious practice; whatever shifts may be demanded, in another context, by the exigencies of theological apologetic.

Part 2

science, mind, and nature

Chapter 3
What Does Science Tell Me About the World?

Have you ever noticed that in your biology and chemistry classes you may get multiple-choice exams, but in your English lit or philosophy classes you are most likely to get essay exams or paper assignments? Why is that? You may think that science deals in facts and that such subjects as philosophy and literature deal with opinions and interpretations. For example, it is a fact that common table salt is composed of sodium and chlorine, whereas it is simply a matter of opinion whether there is free will. You would probably have a hard time writing an entire five-page paper on the chemical composition of table salt. And even if you think that it is a matter of fact whether there is life after death, you would be offended by a question on a philosophy exam that said, "True or false: There is life after death."

But in spite of this prevailing conception of science as being concerned only with facts, not opinions, science as it is actually practiced seems to be full of opinion and interpretation. It may surprise you to learn that scientists often disagree, not only about which of several scientific theories best explains what has been observed, but even about whether something has *been* observed. Moreover, the development of scientific theories is very seldom a process of first observing a lot of facts and then making straightforward generalizations from these observations. In this chapter, Richard Feynman, a Nobel Prize winner in physics, emphasizes the importance of imagination and guessing in science. As an example of imaginative guesswork in science, let's think about quarks. Most scientists believe that all matter is composed of curious particles (which don't really behave like particles) called quarks. The existence of quarks was first hypothesized in 1963. But no scientist has ever seen a quark. So why do they believe that quarks exist? They believe it because some ingenious scientists *invented* quarks, noticing that if quarks did exist, they could explain some other puzzling things. This turned out to be a good guess: If you believe that there are quarks, you can explain a lot. Now most scientists do believe that quarks exist. But the only evidence for the existence of quarks is that if you invent them, many complicated things become simpler and can therefore be explained. Many other things in science were "invented" in this way before they were "discovered"—gravity, molecules, genes, and the planet Neptune, to name a few. Does it still sound to you as though science deals only with facts?

Hard as it may be to believe, the institution of science is a relatively new feature of Western civilization. In the seventeenth and eighteenth centuries, what is now called "science" fell under the category of "natural philosophy." The modern use of the term 'science' dates from the nineteenth century, which was also the first century in which a person could make a living by being a scientist. (It was also the century in which the term 'scientist' was coined.) So although the study of nature is as old as recorded history, people have not always turned exclusively to scientists with questions about the workings of nature. In earlier times people turned to storytellers, writers, artists, religious figures, and philosophers with such questions.

But in our contemporary culture, science has achieved a particularly exalted position. It seems to us that science deals with hard facts, whereas other subjects deal with mere opinions. We have come to believe that science is objective and verifiable. We think that science has a method ("The Scientific Method") for arriving at the "Absolute Truth."

But what is the scientific method, and how does it differ from the methods of literature, history, or philosophy? For that matter, is there really a scientific method? How can we be so sure that what science tells us is true? During the early part of the twentieth century, a group of philosophers and scientists known as the Vienna Circle (they were working in Vienna) tried to place both philosophy and science (and with them, psychology, economics, and other fields) on a more secure base. They tried to show how we could connect all knowledge securely to the pure observation of uninterpreted facts. Anything that could not be secured in this way they claimed was meaningless. (See Chapter 6 for more about this view.) The philosophy of science that grew out of the Vienna Circle has come to be known as the "received view," and is now the classic account of how science works. It is articulated early by Carl G. Hempel in his selection in this chapter.

The received view is often called "the hypothetico-deductive model" or "the deductive-nomological model." ("Nomological" means "having to do with the laws of nature.") It tries to show science to be an orderly process that moves from observation of facts to the confirmation of theories that explain those facts. Hempel focuses on questions about how a scientific theory gets confirmed by observations. He is therefore principally concerned with what makes a theory (as opposed to rival theories) true. He tries to explain what you may have had in mind a few paragraphs back if you thought that science, but not literature, deals with the facts.

Karl Popper, in a piece that is also a classic, challenges Hempel's view. Instead of looking at what makes a theory *true,* he argues that the proper question concerns what makes a theory *scientific.* He argues that it is not the possibility of confirmation that makes a theory scientific, but the possibility of refutation. Hence in an odd twist, he claims that the more open a theory is to being shown false, the more scientific a theory is. In developing his argument, he pays careful attention to actual theories, both those he considers scientific and those that he considers pseudoscientific. Popper's view is one that many people in the scientific community have found attractive.

Hempel's view has been criticized, by both scientists and philosophers, for not reflecting the way that scientists actually work. Interestingly, the idea that to learn about how science works, we should pay attention to the way that actual scientists work, is a fairly new idea in this century. The now classic statement of this idea is Thomas Kuhn's *The Structure of Scientific Revolutions,* part of which is reprinted in this chapter. Kuhn argues that the progress of science is not purely logical and hence it cannot be isolated from its own historical context. Instead, it is conditioned by forces within the scientific community that he characterizes in deliberate political terms (for example, "revolution").

Evelyn Fox Keller goes at least one step beyond Kuhn. She argues that the very standards of objectivity and rationality that define traditional scientific perspective and practice are the products of unrecognized value assumptions. In particular, she argues that these standards are masculine, and she gives a psychoanalytic account of their origin. At the end of her article, she offers some suggestions about how science might be different if it were to cast away its masculinist values and become truly objective. If Keller is right, we need to rethink the cultural mechanisms that bring us both science and scientists.

Finally, two selections give us different perspectives on what science and scientists are really like. Richard Feynman gives us a feeling for how theoretical scientists think about the world. In particular, he talks about the process of guessing that was discussed at the beginning of this introduction. You might think about where the guesses come from and what makes some guesses seem better than others, in light of Kuhn's and Keller's remarks about psychological and cultural influences on scientific theory. Susan Griffin ends the chapter with a somewhat cynical piece suggesting that perhaps we take scientists (and science) too seriously.

CARL G. HEMPEL

The Deductive-Nomological
Model of Science

CARL G. HEMPEL is one of the most influential proponents of what is now regarded as the classic view of explanation in science. Much contemporary work in philosophy of science constitutes a reaction to his view. He was for many years a professor of philosophy at Princeton University. He wrote Aspects of Scientific Explanation and Philosophy of Natural Science.

EXPLANATIONS

AS was known at Galileo's time, and probably much earlier, a simple suction pump, which draws water from a well by means of a piston that can be raised in the pump barrel, will lift water no higher than about 34 feet above the surface of the well. Galileo was intrigued by this limitation and suggested an explanation for it, which was, however, unsound. After Galileo's death, his pupil Torricelli advanced a new answer. He argued that the earth is surrounded by a sea of air, which, by reason of its weight exerts pressure upon the surface below, and that this pressure upon the surface of the well forces water up the pump barrel when the piston is raised. The maximum length of 34 feet for the water column in the barrel thus reflects simply the total pressure of the atmosphere upon the surface of the well.

It is evidently impossible to determine by direct inspection or observation whether this account is correct, and Torricelli tested it indirectly. He reasoned that *if* his conjecture were true, *then* the pressure of the atmosphere should also be capable of supporting a proportionately shorter column of mercury; in-

deed, since the specific gravity of mercury is about 14 times that of water, the length of the mercury column should be about 34/14 feet, or slightly less than 2½ feet. He checked this test implication by means of an ingeniously simple device, which was, in effect, the mercury barometer. The well of water is replaced by an open vessel containing mercury; the barrel of the suction pump is replaced by a glass tube sealed off at one end. The tube is completely filled with mercury and closed by placing the thumb tightly over the open end. It is then inverted, the open end is submerged in the mercury well, and the thumb is withdrawn; whereupon the mercury column in the tube drops until its length is about 30 inches—just as predicted by Torricelli's hypothesis.

A further test implication of that hypothesis was noted by Pascal, who reasoned that if the mercury in Torricelli's barometer is counterbalanced by pressure of the air above the open mercury well, then its length should decrease with increasing altitude, since the weight of the air overhead becomes smaller. At Pascal's request, this implication was checked by his brother-in-law, Périer, who measured the length of the mercury column in the Torricelli barometer at the foot of the Puy-de-Dôme, a mountain some 4,800 feet high, and then carefully carried the apparatus to the top and repeated the measurement there while a control barometer was left at the bottom under the supervision of an assistant. Périer found the mercury column at the top of the mountain more than three inches shorter than at the bottom, whereas the length of the column in the control barometer had remained unchanged throughout the day. . . .

Consider . . . Périer's finding in the Puy-de-Dôme experiment, that the length of the mercury column in a Torricelli barometer decreased with increasing altitude. Torricelli's and Pascal's ideas on atmospheric pressure provided an explanation for this phenomenon; somewhat pedantically, it can be spelled out as follows:

(a) At any location, the pressure that the mercury column in the closed branch of the Torricelli apparatus exerts upon the mercury below equals the pressure exerted on the surface of the mercury in the open vessel by the column of air above it.

(b) The pressures exerted by the columns of mercury and of air are proportional to their weights; and the shorter the columns, the smaller their weights.

(c) As Périer carried the apparatus to the top of the mountain, the column of air above the open vessel became steadily shorter.

(d) (Therefore,) the mercury column in the closed vessel grew steadily shorter during the ascent.

Thus formulated, the explanation is an argument to the effect that the phenomenon to be explained, as described by the sentence (d), is just what is to be expected in view of the explanatory facts cited in (a), (b), and (c); and that, indeed, (d) follows deductively from the explanatory statements. The latter are of two kinds; (a) and (b) have the character of general laws expressing uniform empirical connections; whereas (c) describes certain particular facts. Thus, the shortening of the mercury column is here explained by showing that it occurred in accordance with certain laws of nature, as a result of certain particular circumstances. The explanation fits the phenomenon to be explained into a pattern of uniformities and shows that its occurrence was to be expected, given the specified laws and the pertinent particular circumstances.

The phenomenon to be accounted for by an explanation will henceforth also be referred to as the *explanandum phenomenon;* the sentence describing it, as the *explanandum sentence.* When the context shows which is meant, either of them will simply be called the explanandum. The sentences specifying the explanatory information—(a), (b), (c) in our example—will be called the *explanans sentences;* jointly they will be said to form the *explanans.*

As a second example, consider the explanation of a characteristic of image formation by reflection in a spherical mirror; namely, that generally $1/u + 1/v = 2/r$, where u and v are the distances of object-point and image-point from the mirror, and r is the mirror's radius of curvature. In geometrical optics, this uniformity is explained with the help of the basic law of reflection in a plane mirror, by treating the reflection of a beam of light at any one point of a spherical mirror as a case of reflection in a plane tangential to the spherical surface. The resulting explanation can be formulated as a deductive argument whose conclusion is the explanandum sentence, and whose premises include the basic laws of reflection and of rectilinear propagation, as well as the statement that the surface of the mirror forms a segment of a sphere. . . .

The explanations just considered may be conceived, then, as deductive arguments whose conclusion is the explanandum sentence, *E,* and whose premiss-set, the explanans, consists of general laws, $L^1, L^2, \ldots, L^r$ and of other statements, $C^1, \ldots, C^k$, which make assertions about particular facts. The form of such arguments, which thus constitute one type of scientific explanation, can be represented by the following schema:

$$(D\text{-}N) \quad \left. \begin{array}{c} L_1, L_2, \ldots, L_r \\ C_1, C_2, \ldots, C_k \\ \hline E \end{array} \right\} \begin{array}{l} \text{Explanans sentences} \\ \\ \text{Explanandum sentence} \end{array}$$

Explanatory accounts of this kind will be called explanations by deductive subsumption under general laws, or *deductive-nomological explanations.* (The root of the term 'nomological' is the Greek word 'nomos', for law.) The laws invoked in a scientific explanation will also be called *covering laws* for the explanandum phenomenon, and the explanatory argument will be said to subsume the explanandum under those laws.

The explanandum phenomenon in a deductive-nomological explanation may be an event occurring at a particular place and time, such as the outcome of Périer's experiment. Or it may be some regularity found in nature, such as certain characteristics generally displayed by rainbows; or a uniformity expressed by an empirical law such as Galileo's or Kepler's laws. Deductive explanations of such uniformities will then invoke laws of broader scope, such as the laws of reflection and refraction, or Newton's laws of motion and of gravitation. As this use of Newton's laws illustrates, empirical laws are often explained by means of theoretical principles that refer to structures and processes underlying the uniformities in question. . . .

Some scientific explanations conform to the pattern (D–N) quite closely. This is so, particularly, when certain quantitative features of a phenomenon are explained by mathematical derivation from covering general laws, as in the case of reflection in spherical and paraboloidal mirrors. Or take the celebrated explanation, propounded by Leverrier (and independently by Adams), or peculiar irregularities in the motion of the planet Uranus, which on the current Newtonian theory could not be accounted for by the gravitational attraction of the other planets then known. Leverrier conjectured that they resulted from the gravitational pull of an as yet undetected outer planet, and he computed the position, mass, and other characteristics which that planet would have to possess to account in quantitative detail for the observed irregularities. His explanation was strikingly confirmed by the discovery, at the predicted location, of a new planet, Neptune, which had the quantitative characteristics attributed to it by Leverrier. Here again, the explanation has the character of a deductive argument whose premises include general laws—specifically, Newton's laws of gravitation and of motion—as well as statements specifying various quantitative particulars about the disturbing planet.

Not infrequently, however, deductive-nomological explanations are stated in an elliptical form: they omit mention of certain assumptions that are presupposed by the explanation but are simply taken for granted in the given context. Such explanations are sometimes expressed in the form '*E* because *C*', where *E* is the event to be explained and *C* is some antecedent or concomitant event or state of affairs. Take, for example, the statement: 'The slush on the sidewalk remained liquid during the frost because it had been sprinkled with salt'. This explanation does not explicitly mention any laws, but it tacitly presupposes at least one: that the freezing point of water is lowered whenever salt is dissolved in it. Indeed it is precisely by virtue of this law that the sprinkling of salt acquires the explanatory, and specifically causative, role that the elliptical because-statement ascribes to it. That statement, incidentally, is elliptical also in other respects; for example, it tacitly takes for granted, and leaves unmentioned, certain assumptions about the prevailing physical conditions, such as the temperature's not dropping to a very low point. And if nomic and other assumptions thus omitted are added to the statement that salt had been sprinkled on the slush, we obtain the premisses for a deductive-nomological explanation of the fact that the slush remained liquid. . . .

As the preceding examples illustrate, corresponding general laws are always presupposed by an explanatory statement to the effect that a particular event of a certain kind, *G* (e.g., expansion of a gas under constant pressure; flow of a current in a wire loop) was *caused* by an event of another kind, *F* (e.g., heating of the gas; motion of the loop across a magnetic field). To see this, we need not enter into the complex ramifications of the notion of cause; it suffices to note that the general maxim "Same cause, same effect," when applied to such explanatory statements, yields the implied claim that whenever an event of kind *F* occurs, it is accompanied by an event of kind *G*.

To say that an explanation rests on general laws is not to say that its discovery required the discovery of the laws. The crucial new insight achieved by an explanation will sometimes lie in the discovery of some particular fact (e.g., the presence of an undetected outer planet; infectious matter adhering to the hand of examining physicians) which, by virtue of antecedently accepted general laws, accounts for the explanandum phenomenon. In other cases, such as that of the lines in the hydrogen spectrum, the explanatory achievement does lie in the discovery of a covering law (Balmer's) and eventually of an explanatory theory (such as Bohr's); in yet other cases, the major accomplishment of an explanation may lie in showing that, and exactly how, the explanandum phenomenon can be accounted for by reference to laws and data about particular facts that are already available: this is illustrated by the explanatory derivation of the reflection laws for spherical and paraboloidal mirrors from the basic law of geometrical optics in conjunction with statements about the geometrical characteristics of the mirrors.

An explanatory problem does not by itself determine what kind of discovery is required for its solution. Thus, Leverrier discovered deviations from the theoretically expected course also in the motion of the planet Mercury; and as in the case of Uranus, he tried to explain these as resulting from the gravitational pull of an as yet undetected planet, Vulcan, which would have to be a very dense and very small object between the sun and Mercury. But no such planet was found, and a satisfactory explanation was provided only much later by the general theory of relativity, which accounted for the irregularities not by reference to some disturbing particular factor, but by means of a new system of laws. . . .

THEORIES

Theories are usually introduced when previous study of a class of phenomena has revealed a system of uniformities that can be expressed in the form of empirical laws. Theories then seek to explain those regularities and, generally, to afford a deeper and more accurate understanding of the phenomena in question. To this end, a theory construes those phenomena as manifestations of entities and processes that lie behind or beneath them, as it were. These are assumed to be governed by characteristic theoretical laws, or theoretical principles, by means of which the theory then explains the empirical uniformities that have been previously discovered, and usually also predicts "new" regularities of similar kinds. Let us consider some examples.

The Ptolemaic and Copernican systems sought to account for the observed, "apparent," motions of the heavenly bodies by means of suitable assumptions about the structure of the astronomical universe and the "actual" motions of the celestial objects. The corpuscular and the wave theories of light offered accounts of the nature of light in terms of certain underlying processes; and they explained the previously established uniformities expressed by the laws of rectilinear propagation, reflection, refraction, and diffraction as resulting from the basic laws to which

the underlying processes were assumed to conform. Thus, the refraction of a beam of light passing from air into glass was explained in Huyghens' wave theory as resulting from a slowing of the light waves in the denser medium. By contrast, Newton's particle theory attributed optical refraction to a stronger attraction exerted upon the optical particles by the denser medium. Incidentally, this construal implies not only the observed bending of a beam of light: when combined with the other basic assumptions of Newton's theory, it also implies that the particles of light will be accelerated upon entering a denser medium, rather than decelerated, as the wave theory predicts. These conflicting implications were tested nearly two hundred years later by Foucault in the experiment . . . whose outcome bore out the relevant implication of the wave theory.

To mention one more example, the kinetic theory of gases offers explanations for a wide variety of empirically established regularities by construing them as macroscopic manifestations of statistical regularities in the underlying molecular and atomic phenomena.

The basic entities and processes posited by a theory, and the laws assumed to govern them, must be specified with appropriate clarity and precision; otherwise, the theory cannot serve its scientific purpose. This important point is illustrated by the neovitalistic conception of biological phenomena. Living systems, as is well known, display a variety of striking features that seem to be distinctly purposive or teleological in character. Among them are the regeneration of lost limbs in some species; the development, in other species, of normal organisms from embryos that are damaged or even cut into several pieces in an early stage of their growth; and the remarkable coordination of the many processes in a developing organism which, as though following a common plan, lead to the formation of a mature individual. According to neovitalism, such phenomena do not occur in nonliving systems and cannot be explained by means of the concepts and laws of physics and chemistry alone; rather, they are manifestations of underlying teleological agencies of a nonphysical kind, referred to as entelechies or vital forces. Their specific mode of action is usually assumed not to violate the principles of physics and chemistry, but to direct the organic processes, within the range of possibilities left open by the physico-chemical laws, in such a way that, even in the presence of disturbing factors, embryos develop into normal individuals, and adult organisms are maintained in, or returned to, a properly functioning state.

This conception may well seem to offer us a deeper understanding of the remarkable biological phenomena in question; it may give us a sense of being more familiar, more "at home" with them. But understanding in this sense is not what is wanted in science, and a conceptual system that conveys insight into the phenomena in this intuitive sense does not for that reason alone qualify as a scientific theory. The assumptions made by a scientific theory about underlying processes must be definite enough to permit the derivation of specific implications concerning the phenomena that the theory is to explain. The neovitalistic doctrine fails on this account. It does not indicate under what circumstances entelechies will go into action and specifically, in what way they will direct biological processes: no particular aspect of embryonic development, for example, can be inferred from

the doctrine, nor does it enable us to predict what biological responses will occur under specified experimental conditions. Hence, when a new striking type of "organic directiveness" is encountered, all that the neovitalist doctrine enables us to do is to make the *post factum* pronouncement: "There is another manifestation of vital forces!"; it offers us no grounds for saying: "On the basis of the theoretical assumptions, this is just what was to be expected—the theory explains it!"

This inadequacy of the neovitalistic doctrine does not stem from the circumstance that entelechies are conceived as nonmaterial agencies, which cannot be seen or felt. This becomes clear when we contrast it with the explanation of the regularities of planetary and lunar motions by means of the Newtonian theory. Both accounts invoke nonmaterial agencies: one of them vital forces; the other, gravitational ones. But Newton's theory includes specific assumptions, expressed in the law of gravitation and the laws of motion which determine (*a*) what gravitational forces each of a set of physical bodies of given masses and positions will exert upon the others, and (*b*) what changes in their velocities and, consequently, in their locations will be brought about by those forces. It is this characteristic that gives the theory its power to explain previously observed uniformities and also to yield predictions and retrodictions. Thus, the theory was used by Halley to predict that a comet he had observed in 1682 would return in 1759, and to identify it retrodictively with comets whose appearances had been recorded on six previous occasions going back to the year 1066. The theory also played a spectacular explanatory and predictive role in the discovery of the planet

Neptune, on the basis of irregularities in the orbit of Uranus; and subsequently in the discovery, on the basis of irregularities in Neptune's orbit, of the planet Pluto.

Broadly speaking, then, the formulation of a theory will require the specification of two kinds of principles; let us call them internal principles and bridge principles for short. The former will characterize the basic entities and processes invoked by the theory and the laws to which they are assumed to conform. The latter will indicate how the processes envisaged by the theory are related to empirical phenomena with which we are already acquainted, and which the theory may then explain, predict, or retrodict. Let us consider some examples.

In the kinetic theory of gases, the internal principles are those that characterize the "microphenomena" at the molecular level, whereas the bridge principles connect certain aspects of the microphenomena with corresponding "macroscopic" features of a gas. . . .

Without bridge principles, . . . a theory would have no explanatory power. Without bridge principles, we may add, it would also be incapable of test. For the internal principles of a theory are concerned with the peculiar entities and processes assumed by the theory (such as the jumps of electrons from one atomic energy level to another in Bohr's theory), and they will therefore be expressed largely in terms of characteristic "theoretical concepts," which refer to those entities and processes. But the implications that permit a test of those theoretical principles will have to be expressed in terms of things and occurrences with which we are antecedently acquainted, which we already know how to observe, to measure, and to describe. In other words, while the internal principles of a theory are couched in its characteristic *theoretical terms* ('nucleus', 'orbital electron', 'energy level', 'electron jump'), the test implications must be formulated in terms (such as 'hydrogen vapor', 'emission spectrum', 'wavelength associated with a spectral line') which are "antecedently understood," as we might say, terms that have been introduced prior to the theory and can be used independently of it. Let us refer to them as *antecedently available* or *pretheoretical terms*. The derivation of such test implications from the internal principles of the theory evidently requires further premises that establish connections between the two sets of concepts; and this, as the preceding examples show, is accomplished by appropriate bridge principles (connecting, for example, the energy released in an electron jump with the wavelength of the light that is emitted as a result). Without bridge principles, the internal principles of a theory would yield no test implications, and the requirement of testability would be violated.

Testability-in-principle and explanatory import, though crucially important, are nevertheless only minimal necessary conditions that a scientific theory must satisfy; a system that meets these requirements may yet afford little illumination and may lack scientific interest. . . .

In a field of inquiry in which some measure of understanding has already been achieved by the establishment of empirical laws, a good theory will deepen as well as broaden that understanding. First, such a theory offers a systematically unified account of quite diverse phenomena. It traces all of them back to the same underlying processes and presents the various empirical uniformities they exhibit as manifestations of one and the same basic laws. We noted earlier the great diversity of empirical regularities (such as those shown by free fall; the simple pendulum; the motions of the moon, the planets, comets, double stars, and artificial satellites; the tides, and so forth) that are accounted for by the basic principles of Newton's theory of gravitation and of motion. In similar fashion, the kinetic theory of gases exhibits a wide variety of empirical uniformities as manifestations of certain basic probabilistic uniformities in the random motions of the molecules. And Bohr's theory of the hydrogen atom accounts not only for the uniformity expressed by Balmer's formula, which refers to just one series of lines in the spectrum of hydrogen, but equally for analogous empirical laws representing the wavelengths of other series of lines in the same spectrum, including several series whose member lines lie in the invisible infrared or ultraviolet parts of the spectrum.

A theory will usually deepen our understanding also in a different way, namely by showing that the previously formulated empirical laws that it is meant to explain do not hold strictly and unexceptionally, but only approximately and within a certain limited range of application. Thus, Newton's theoretical account of planetary motion shows that Kepler's laws hold only approximately, and it explains why this is so: the Newtonian principles imply that the orbit of a planet moving about the sun under its gravitational influence alone would indeed be an ellipse, but that the gravitational pull exerted on it by other planets leads to departures from a strictly elliptical path. The theory gives a quantitative account of the resulting perturbations in terms of the masses and spatial distribution of the disturbing objects. Similarly, Newton's theory accounts for Galileo's law of free fall as simply one special manifestation of the basic laws for motion under gravitational attraction; but in so doing, it shows also that the law (even if applied to free fall in a vacuum) holds only approximately. One of the reasons is that in Galileo's formula the acceleration of free fall appears as a constant (twice the factor 16 in the formula '$s = 16t^2$'), whereas on Newton's inverse-square law of gravitational attraction, the force acting upon the falling body increases as its distance from the center of the earth decreases; hence, by virtue of Newton's second law of motion, its acceleration, too, increases in the course of the fall. Analogous remarks apply to the laws of geometrical optics as viewed from the vantage point of wave-theoretical optics. For example, even in a homogeneous medium, light does not move strictly in straight lines; it can bend around corners. And the laws of geometrical optics for reflection in curved mirrors and for image-formation by lenses hold only approximately and within certain limits.

It might therefore be tempting to say that theories often do not explain previously established laws, but refute them. But this would give a distorted picture of the insight afforded by a theory. After all, a theory does not simply refute the earlier empirical generalizations in its field; rather, it shows that within a certain limited range defined by qualifying conditions, the generalizations hold true in fairly close approximation. The limited range for Kepler's laws includes those cases in which the masses of the disturbing additional planets are small compared with that of the sun, or their distances from the given planet are large compared with its distance from the sun. Similarly, the theory shows that Galileo's law holds approximately for free fall over short distances.

Finally, a good theory will also broaden our knowledge and understanding by predicting and explaining phenomena that were not known when the theory was formulated. Thus, Torricelli's conception of a sea of air led to Pascal's prediction that the column of a mercury barometer would shorten with increasing height above sea level. Einstein's general theory of relativity not only accounted for the known slow rotation of the orbit of Mercury, but also predicted the bending of light in a gravitational field, a forecast subsequently borne out by astronomical measurements. Maxwell's theory of electromagnetism implied the existence of electromagnetic waves and predicted important characteristics of their propagation. Those implications, too, were later confirmed by the experimental work of Heinrich Hertz, and they provided the basis for the technology of radio transmission, among other applications.

Such striking predictive successes will of course greatly strengthen our confidence in a theory that already has given us a systematically unified explanation—and often also a correction—of previously established laws. The insight that such a theory gives us is much deeper than that afforded by empirical laws; and it is widely held, therefore, that a scientifically adequate explanation of a class of empirical phenomena can be achieved only by means of an appropriate theory. Indeed, it seems to be a remarkable fact that even if we limited ourselves to a study of the more or less directly observable or measurable aspects of our world and tried to explain these . . . by means of laws couched in terms of observables, our efforts would have only limited success. For the laws that are formulated at the observational level generally turn out to hold only approximately and within a limited range; whereas by theoretical recourse to entities and events under the familiar surface, a much more comprehensive and exact account can be achieved. It is intriguing to speculate whether simpler worlds are conceivable where all phenomena are at the observable surface, so to speak; where there occur perhaps only changes of color and of shape, within a finite range of possibilities, and strictly in accordance with some simple laws of universal form.

KARL POPPER

Science: Conjectures and Refutations

KARL POPPER, *with a background in psychology, physics, and mathematics, was a professor at Canterbury University College in New Zealand until 1945, when he became reader in logic and scientific method at the London School of Economics. His first book,* The Logic of Scientific Discovery, *was a major response to the school of thought known as logical positivism.*

WHEN I received the list of participants in this course and realized that I had been asked to speak to philosophical colleagues I thought, after some hesitation and consultation, that you would probably prefer me to speak about those problems which interest me most, and about those developments with which I am most intimately acquainted. I therefore decided to do what I have never done before: to give you a report on my own work in the philosophy of science, since the autumn of 1919 when I first began to grapple with the problem, *'When should a theory be ranked as scientific?' or 'Is there a criterion for the scientific character or status of a theory?'*

The problem which troubled me at the time was neither, 'When is a theory true?' nor, 'When is a theory acceptable?' My problem was different. I *wished to distinguish between science and pseudo-science;* knowing very well that science often errs, and that pseudo-science may happen to stumble on the truth.

I knew, of course, the most widely accepted answer to my problem: that science is distinguished from pseudo-science—or from 'metaphysics'—by its *empirical method,* which is essentially *inductive,* proceeding from observation or experiment. But this did not satisfy me. On the contrary, I often formulated my problem as one of distinguishing between a genuinely empirical method and a non-empirical or even a pseudo-empirical method—that is to say, a method which, although it appeals to observation and experiment, nevertheless does not come up to scientific standards. The latter method may be exemplified by astrology, with its stupendous mass of empirical evidence based on observation—on horoscopes and on biographies.

But as it was not the example of astrology which led me to my problem I should perhaps briefly describe the atmosphere in which my problem arose and the examples by which it was stimulated. After the collapse of the Austrian Empire there had been a revolution in Austria: the air was full of revolutionary slogans and ideas, and new and often wild theories. Among the theories which interested me, Einstein's theory of relativity was no doubt by far the most important. Three others were Marx's theory of history, Freud's psycho-analysis, and Alfred Adler's so-called 'individual psychology'.

There was a lot of popular nonsense talked about these theories, and especially about relativity (as still happens even today), but I was fortunate in those who introduced me to the study of this theory. We all—the small circle of students to which I belonged—were thrilled with the result of Eddington's eclipse observations which in 1919 brought the first important confirmation of Einstein's theory of gravitation. It was a great experience for us, and one which had a lasting influence on my intellectual development.

The three other theories I have mentioned were also widely discussed among students at that time. I myself happened to come into personal contact with Alfred Adler, and even to co-operate with him in his social work among the children and young people in the working-class districts of Vienna where he had established social guidance clinics.

It was during the summer of 1919 that I began to feel more and more dissatisfied with these three theories—the Marxist theory of history, psycho-analysis, and individual psychology; and I began to feel dubious about their claims to scientific status. My problem perhaps first took the simple form, 'What is wrong with Marxism, psycho-analysis, and individual psychology? Why are they so different from physical theories, from Newton's theory, and especially from the theory of relativity?'

To make this contrast clear I should explain that few of us at the time would have said that we believed in the *truth* of Einstein's theory of gravitation. This shows that it was not my doubting the *truth* of those other three theories which bothered me, but something else. Yet neither was it that I merely felt mathematical physics to be more *exact* than

the sociological or psychological type of theory. Thus what worried me was neither the problem of truth, at that stage at least, nor the problem of exactness or measurability. It was rather that I felt that these other three theories, though posing as sciences, had in fact more in common with primitive myths than with science; that they resembled astrology rather than astronomy.

I found that those of my friends who were admirers of Marx, Freud, and Adler, were impressed by a number of points common to these theories, and especially by their apparent *explanatory power.* These theories appeared to be able to explain practically everything that happened within the fields to which they referred. The study of any of them seemed to have the effect of an intellectual conversion or revelation, opening your eyes to a new truth hidden from those not yet initiated. Once your eyes were thus opened you saw confirming instances everywhere: the world was full of *verifications* of the theory. Whatever happened always confirmed it. Thus its truth appeared manifest; and unbelievers were clearly people who did not want to see the manifest truth; who refused to see it, either because it was against their class interest, or because of their repressions which were still 'unanalysed' and crying aloud for treatment.

The most characteristic element in this situation seemed to me the incessant stream of confirmations, of observations which 'verified' the theories in question; and this point was constantly emphasized by their adherents. A Marxist could not open a newspaper without finding on every page confirming evidence for his interpretation of history; not only in the news but also in its presentation—which revealed the class bias of the paper—and especially of course in what the paper did *not* say. The Freudian analysts emphasized that their theories were constantly verified by their 'clinical observations'. As for Adler, I was much impressed by a personal experience. Once, in 1919, I reported to him a case which to me did not seem particularly Adlerian, but which he found no difficulty in analysing in terms of his theory of inferiority feelings, although he had not even seen the child. Slightly shocked, I asked him how he could be so sure. 'Because of my thousandfold experience,' he replied; whereupon I could not help saying: 'And with this new case, I suppose, your experience has become thousand-and-one-fold.'

What I had in mind was that his previous observations may not have been much sounder than this new one; that each in its turn had been interpreted in the light of 'previous experience', and at the same time counted as additional confirmation. What, I asked myself, did it confirm? No more than that a case could be interpreted in the light of the theory. But this meant very little, I reflected, since every conceivable case could be interpreted in the light of Adler's theory, or equally Freud's. I may illustrate this by two very different examples of human behaviour: that of a man who pushes a child into the water with the intention of drowning it; and that of a man who sacrifices his life in an attempt to save the child. Each of these two cases can be explained with equal ease in Freudian and in Adlerian terms. According to Freud the first man suffered from repression (say, of some component of his Oedipus complex), while the second man had achieved sublimation. According to Adler the first man suffered from feelings of inferiority (producing perhaps the need to prove to himself that he

dared to commit some crime), and so did the second man (whose need was to prove to himself that he dared to rescue the child). I could not think of any human behaviour which could not be interpreted in terms of either theory. It was precisely this fact—that they always fitted, that they were always confirmed—which in the eyes of their admirers constituted the strongest argument in favour of these theories. It began to dawn on me that this apparent strength was in fact their weakness.

With Einstein's theory the situation was strikingly different. Take one typical instance—Einstein's prediction, just then confirmed by the findings of Eddington's expedition. Einstein's gravitational theory had led to the result that light must be attracted by heavy bodies (such as the sun), precisely as material bodies were attracted. As a consequence it could be calculated that light from a distant fixed star whose apparent position was close to the sun would reach the earth from such a direction that the star would seem to be slightly shifted away from the sun; or, in other words that stars close to the sun would look as if they had moved a little away from the sun, and from one another. This is a thing which cannot normally be observed since such stars are rendered invisible in daytime by the sun's overwhelming brightness; but during an eclipse it is possible to take photographs of them. If the same constellation is photographed at night one can measure the distances on the two photographs, and check the predicted effect.

Now the impressive thing about this case is the *risk* involved in a prediction of this kind. If observation shows that the predicted effect is definitely absent, then the theory is simply refuted. The theory is *incompatible with certain possible results of observation*—in fact with results which everybody before Einstein would have expected. This is quite different from the situation I have previously described, when it turned out that the theories in question were compatible with the most divergent human behaviour, so that it was practically impossible to describe any human behaviour that might not be claimed to be a verification of these theories.

These considerations led me in the winter of 1919–20 to conclusions which I may now reformulate as follows:

(*1*) It is easy to obtain confirmations, or verifications, for nearly every theory—if we look for confirmations.

(*2*) Confirmations should count only if they are the result of *risky predictions;* that is to say, if, unenlightened by the theory in question, we should have expected an event which was incompatible with the theory—an event which would have refuted the theory.

(*3*) Every 'good' scientific theory is a prohibition: it forbids certain things to happen. The more a theory forbids, the better it is.

(*4*) A theory which is not refutable by any conceivable event is nonscientific. Irrefutability is not a virtue of a theory (as people often think) but a vice.

(*5*) Every genuine *test* of a theory is an attempt to falsify it, or to refute it. Testability is falsifiability; but there are degrees of testability: some theories are more testable, more exposed to refutation, than others; they take, as it were, greater risks.

(*6*) Confirming evidence should not count *except when it is the result of a genuine test of the theory*; and this means that it can be presented as a serious but unsuccessful attempt to falsify the theory. (I now speak in such cases of 'corroborating evidence'.)

(*7*) Some genuinely testable theories, when found to be false, are still upheld by their admirers—for example by introducing *ad hoc* some auxiliary assumption, or by re-interpreting the theory *ad hoc* in such a way that it escapes refutation. Such a procedure is always possible, but it rescues the theory from refutation only at the price of destroying, or at least lowering, its scientific status. (I later described such a rescuing operation as a '*conventionalist twist*' or a '*conventionalist stratagem*'.)

One can sum up all this by saying that *the criterion of the scientific status of a theory is its falsifiability, or refutability, or testability.*

I may perhaps exemplify this with the help of the various theories so far mentioned. Einstein's theory of gravitation clearly satisfied the criterion of falsifiability. Even if our measuring instruments at the time did not allow us to pronounce on the results of the tests with complete assurance, there was clearly a possibility of refuting the theory.

Astrology did not pass the test. Astrologers were greatly impressed, and misled, by what they believed to be confirming evidence—so much so that they were quite unimpressed by any unfavourable evidence. Moreover, by making their interpretations and prophecies sufficiently vague they were able to explain away anything that might have been a refutation of the theory had the theory and the prophecies been more precise. In order to escape falsification they destroyed the testability of their theory. It is a typical soothsayer's trick to predict things so vaguely that the predictions can hardly fail: that they become irrefutable.

The Marxist theory of history, in spite of the serious efforts of some of its founders and followers, ultimately adopted this soothsaying practice. In some of its earlier formulations (for example in Marx's analysis of the character of the 'coming social revolution') their predictions were testable, and in fact falsified. Yet instead of accepting the refutations the followers of Marx reinterpreted both the theory and the evidence in order to make them agree. In this way they rescued the theory from refutation; but they did so at the price of adopting a device which made it irrefutable. They thus gave a 'conventional twist' to the theory; and by this stratagem they destroyed its much advertised claim to scientific status.

The two psycho-analytic theories were in a different class. They were simply non-testable, irrefutable. There was no conceivable human behaviour which could contradict them. This does not mean that Freud and Adler were not seeing certain things correctly: I personally do not doubt that much of what they say is of considerable importance, and may well play its part one day in a psychological science which is testable. But it does mean that those 'clinical observations' which analysts naively believe confirm their theory cannot do this any more than the daily confirmations which astrologers find in their practice. And as for Freud's epic of the Ego, the Super-ego, and the Id, no substantially stronger claim to scientific status can be made for it than for Homer's collected stories from Olympus. These theories describe some facts, but in the manner of myths. They contain most interesting psychological suggestions, but not in a testable form.

At the same time I realized that such myths may be developed, and become testable; that historically speaking all—or very nearly all—scientific theories originate from myths, and that a myth may contain important anticipations of scientific theories. Examples are Empedocles' theory of evolution by trial and error, or Parmenides' myth of the unchanging block universe in which nothing ever happens and which, if we add another dimension, becomes Einstein's block universe (in which, too, nothing ever happens, since everything is, four-dimensionally speaking, determined and laid down from the beginning). I thus felt that if a theory is found to be non-scientific, or 'metaphysical' (as we might say), it is not thereby found to be unimportant, or insignificant, or 'meaningless', or 'nonsensical'. But it cannot claim to be backed by empirical evidence in the scientific sense—although it may easily be, in some genetic sense, the 'result of observation'.

(There were a great many other theories of this pre-scientific or pseudo-scientific character, some of them, unfortunately, as influential as the Marxist interpretation of history; for example, the racialist interpretation of history—another of those impressive and all-explanatory theories which act upon weak minds like revelations.)

Thus the problem which I tried to solve by proposing the criterion of falsifiability was neither a problem of meaningfulness or significance, nor a problem of truth or acceptability. It was the problem of drawing a line (as well as this can be done) between the statements, or systems of statements, of the empirical sciences, and all other statements—whether they are of a religious or of a metaphysical character, or simply pseudo-scientific. Years later—it must have been in 1928 or 1929—I called this first problem of mine the *'problem of demarcation'*. The criterion of falsifiability is a solution to this problem of demarcation, for it says that statements or systems of statements, in order to be ranked as scientific, must be capable of conflicting with possible, or conceivable, observations.

• • •

The belief that science proceeds from observation to theory is still so widely and so firmly held that my denial of it is often met with incredulity. I have even been suspected of being insincere—of denying what nobody in his senses can doubt.

But in fact the belief that we can start with pure observations alone, without anything in the nature of a theory, is absurd: as may be illustrated by the story of the man who dedicated his life to natural science, wrote down everything he could observe, and bequeathed his priceless collection of observations to the Royal Society to be used as inductive evidence. This story should show us that though beetles may profitably be collected, observations may not.

Twenty-five years ago I tried to bring home the same point to a group of physics students in Vienna by beginning a lecture with the following instructions: 'Take pencil and paper; carefully observe, and write down what you have observed!' They asked, of course, *what* I wanted them to observe. Clearly the instruction, 'Observe!' is absurd. (It is not even idiomatic, unless the object of the transitive verb can be taken as understood.) Observation is always selective. It needs a chosen object, a definite task, an interest, a point of view, a problem. And its description presupposes a descriptive language, with property words; it presupposes similarity and classification, which in its turn presupposes interests, points of view, and problems. 'A hungry animal', writes Kaltz, 'divides the environment into edible and inedible things. An animal in flight sees roads to escape and hiding places. . . . Generally speaking, objects change . . . according to the needs of the animal.' We may add that objects can be classified, and can become similar or dissimilar, *only* in this way—by being related to needs and interests. This rule applies not only to animals but also to scientists. For the animal a point of view is provided by its needs, the task of the moment, and its expectations; for the scientist by his theoretical interests, the special problem under investigation, his conjectures and anticipations, and the theories which he accepts as a kind of background: his frame of reference, his 'horizon of expectations'.

The problem 'Which comes first, the hypothesis (*H*) or the observation (*O*),' is soluble: as is the problem, 'Which comes first, the hen (*H*) or the egg (*O*)'. The reply to the latter is, 'An earlier kind of hypothesis'. It is quite true that any particular hypothesis we choose will have been preceded by observations—the observations, for example, which it is designed to explain. But these observations, in their turn, presupposed the adoption of a frame of reference: a frame of expectations: a frame of theories. If they were significant, if they created a need for explanation and thus gave rise to the invention of a hypothesis, it was because they could not be explained within the old theoretical framework, the old horizon of expectations. There is no danger here of an infinite regress. Going back to more and more primitive theories and myths we shall in the end find unconscious, *in-born* expectations.

The theory of inborn *ideas* is absurd, I think; but every organism has inborn *reactions* or *responses;* and among them, responses adapted to impending events. These responses we may describe as 'expectations' without implying that these 'expectations' are conscious. The newborn baby 'expects', in this sense, to be fed (and, one could even argue, to be protected and loved). In view of the close relation between expectation and knowledge we may even speak in quite a reasonable sense of 'inborn knowledge'. This 'knowledge' is not, however, *valid a priori;* an inborn expectation, no matter how strong and specific, may be mistaken. (The newborn child may be abandoned, and starve.)

Thus we are born with expectations; with 'knowledge' which, although not *valid a priori, is psychologically or genetically a priori,* i.e. prior to all observational experience. One of the most important of these expectations is the expectation of finding a regularity. It is connected with an inborn propensity to look out for regularities, or with a *need* to *find* regularities, as we may see from the pleasure of the child who satisfies this need.

. . . genetically speaking the pseudo-scientific attitude is more primitive than, and prior to, the scientific attitude: it is a prescientific attitude. And this primitivity or priority also has its logical aspect. For the critical attitude is not so much opposed to the dogmatic attitude as superimposed upon it: criticism must be directed against existing and influential beliefs in need of critical revision— in other words, dogmatic beliefs. A critical attitude needs for its raw material, as it were, theories or beliefs which are held more or less dogmatically.

Thus science must begin with myths, and with the criticism of myths; neither with the collection of observations, nor with the invention of experiments, but with the critical discussion of myths, and of magical techniques and practices. The scientific tradition is distinguished from the pre-scientific tradition in having two layers. Like the latter, it passes on its theories; but it also passes on a critical attitude toward them. The theories are passed on, not as dogmas, but rather with the challenge to discuss them to improve upon them. This tradition is Hellenic: it may be traced back to Thales, founder of the first *school* (I do not mean 'of the first *philosophical* school', but simply 'of the first school') which was not mainly concerned with the preservation of a dogma.

The critical attitude, the tradition of free discussion of theories with the aim of discovering their weak spots so that they may be improved upon, is the attitude of reasonableness, or rationality. It makes far-reaching use of both verbal argument and observation—of observation in the interest of argument, however. The Greeks' discovery of the critical method gave rise at first to the mistaken hope that it would lead to the solution of all the great old problems; that it would establish certainty; that it would help to *prove* our theories, to *justify* them. But this hope was a residue of the dogmatic way of thinking; in fact nothing can be justified or proved (outside of mathematics and logic). The demand for rational proofs in science indicates a failure to keep distinct the broad realm of rationality and the narrow realm of rational certainty: it is an untenable, an unreasonable demand . . .

Assume that we have deliberately made it our task to live in this unknown world of ours; to adjust ourselves to it as well as we can; to take advantage of the opportunities we can find in it; and to explain it, *if* possible (we need not assume that it is), and as far as possible, with the help of laws and explanatory theories. *If we have made this our task, then there is no more rational procedure than the method of trial and error—of conjecture and refutation:* of boldly proposing theories; of trying our best to show that these are erroneous; and of accepting them tentatively if our critical efforts are unsuccessful.

From the point of view here developed all laws, all theories, remain essentially tentative, or conjectural, or hypothetical, even when we feel unable to doubt them any longer. Before a theory has been refuted we can never know in what way it may have to be modified. That the sun will always rise and set within twenty-four hours is still proverbial as a law 'established by induction beyond reasonable doubt'. It is odd that this example is still in use, though it may have served well enough in the days of Aristotle and Pytheas of Massalia—the great traveller who for centuries was called a liar because of his tales of Thule, the land of the frozen sea and the *midnight sun.*

The method of trial and error is not, of course, simply identical with the method of conjecture and refutation. The method of trial and error is applied not only by Einstein but, in a more dogmatic fashion, by the amoeba also. The difference lies not so much in the trials as in a critical and constructive attitude towards errors; errors which the scientist consciously and cautiously tries to uncover in order to refute his theories with searching arguments, including appeals to the most severe experimental tests which his theories and his ingenuity permit him to design.

The critical attitude may be described as the conscious attempt to make our theories, our conjectures, suffer in our stead in the struggle for the survival of the fittest. It gives us a chance to survive the elimination of an inadequate hypothesis—when a more dogmatic attitude would eliminate it by eliminating us. (There is a touching story of an Indian community which disappeared because of its belief in the holiness of life, including that of tigers.) We thus obtain the fittest theory within our reach by the elimination of those which are less fit. (By 'fitness' I do not mean merely 'usefulness' but truth . . .) I do not think that this procedure is irrational or in need of any further rational justification.

. . . From what I have said it is obvious that there was a close link between the two problems which interested me at the time: demarcation, and induction or scientific method. It was easy to see that the method of science is criticism, i.e. attempted falsifications. Yet it took me a few years to notice that the two problems—of demarcation and of induction—were in a sense one.

Why, I asked, do so many scientists believe in induction? I found they did so because they believed natural science to be characterized by the inductive method—by a method starting from, and relying upon, long sequences of observations and experiments. They believed that the difference between genuine science and metaphysical or pseudo-scientific speculation depended solely upon whether or not the inductive method was employed. They believed (to put it in my own terminology) that only the inductive method could provide a satisfactory *criterion of demarcation.*

I recently came across an interesting formulation of this belief in a remarkable philosophical book by a great physicist—Max Born's *Natural Philosophy of Cause and Chance*. He writes: 'Induction allows us to generalize a number of observations into a general rule: that night follows day and day follows night . . . But while everyday life has no definite criterion for the validity of an induction, . . . science has worked out a code, or rule of craft, for its application.' Born nowhere reveals the contents of this inductive code (which as his wording shows, contains a 'definite criterion for the validity of an induction'); but he stresses that 'there is no logical argument' for its acceptance: 'it is a question of faith'; and he is therefore 'willing to call induction a metaphysical principle'. But why does he believe that such a code of valid inductive rules must exist? This becomes clear when he speaks of the 'vast communities of people ignorant of, or rejecting, the rule of science, among them the members of anti vaccination societies and believers in astrology. It is useless to argue with them; I cannot compel them to accept the same criteria of valid induction in which I believe: the code of scientific rules.' This makes it quite clear that *'valid induction' was here meant to serve as a criterion of demarcation between science and pseudo-science.*

But it is obvious that this rule or craft of 'valid induction' is not even metaphysical: it simply does not exist. No rule can ever guarantee that a generalization inferred from true observations, however often repeated, is true. (Born himself does not believe in the truth of Newtonian physics, in spite of its success, although he believes that it is based on induction.) And the success of science is not based upon luck, ingenuity, and the purely deductive rules of critical argument.

I may summarize some of my conclusions as follows:

(*1*) Induction, i.e. inference based on many observations, is a myth. It is neither a psychological fact, nor a fact of ordinary life, nor one of scientific procedure.

(*2*) The actual procedure of science is to operate with conjectures: to jump to conclusion—often after one single observation (as noticed for example by Hume and Born).

(*3*) Repeated observations and experiments function in science as *tests* of our conjectures or hypotheses, i.e. as attempted refutations.

(*4*) The mistaken belief in induction is fortified by the need for a criterion of demarcation which, it is traditionally but wrongly believed, only the inductive method can provide.

(*5*) The conception of such an inductive method, like the criterion of verifiability, implies a faulty demarcation.

(*6*) None of this is altered in the least if we say that induction makes theories only probable rather than certain. . . .

THOMAS KUHN

The Structure of Scientific Revolutions

THOMAS KUHN *is a professor of philosophy at M.I.T. In 1962 he revolutionized the philosophy of science with publication of his book,* The Structure of Scientific Revolutions, *from which this selection is taken. In that book he challenged the classic view (represented by Hempel) by suggesting that we look at science as a social enterprise, rather than as a purely logical enterprise.*

IN this essay, 'normal science' means research firmly based upon one or more past scientific achievements, achievements that some particular scientific community acknowledges for a time as supplying the foundation for its further practice. Today such achievements are recounted, though seldom in their original form, by science textbooks, elementary and advanced. These textbooks expound the body of accepted theory, illustrate many or all of its successful applications and compare these applications with exemplary observations and experiments. Before such books became popular early in the nineteenth century (and until even more recently in the newly matured sciences), many of the famous classics of science fulfilled a similar function. Aristotle's *Physica,* Ptolemy's *Almagest,* Newton's *Principia* and *Opticks,* Franklin's *Electricity,* Lavoisier's *Chemistry,* and Lyell's *Geology*—these and many other works served for a time implicitly to define the legitimate problems and methods of a research field for succeeding generations of practitioners. They were able to do so because they shared two essential characteristics. Their achievement was sufficiently unprecedented to attract an enduring group of adherents away from competing modes of scientific activity. Simultaneously, it was sufficiently open-ended to leave all sorts of problems for the redefined group of practitioners to resolve.

Achievements that share these two characteristics I shall henceforth refer to as 'paradigms,' a term that relates closely to 'normal science.' By choosing it, I mean to suggest that some accepted examples of actual scientific practice—examples which include law, theory, application, and instrumentation together—provide models from which spring particular coherent traditions of scientific research. These are the traditions which the historian describes under such rubrics as 'Ptolemaic astronomy' (or 'Copernican'), 'Aristotelian dynamics' (or 'Newtonian'), 'corpuscular optics' (or 'wave optics'), and so on. The study of paradigms, including many that are far more specialized than those named illustratively above, is what mainly prepares the student for membership in the particular scientific community with which he will later practice. Because he there joins men who learned the bases of their field from the same concrete models, his subsequent practice will seldom evoke overt disagreement over fundamentals. Men whose research is based on shared paradigms are committed to the same rules and standards for scientific practice. That commitment and the apparent consensus it produces are prerequisites for normal science, i.e., for the genesis and continuation of a particular research tradition. . . .

Normal science . . . is a highly cumulative enterprise, eminently successful in its aim, the steady extension of the scope and precision of scientific knowledge. In all these respects it fits with great precision the most usual image of scientific work. Yet one standard product of the scientific enterprise is missing. Norman science does not aim at novelties of fact or theory and, when successful, finds none. New and unsuspected phenomena are, however, repeatedly uncovered by scientific research and radical new theories have again and again been invented by scientists. History even suggests that the scientific enterprise has developed a uniquely powerful technique for producing surprises of this sort. If this characteristic of science is to be reconciled with what has already been said, then research under a paradigm must be a particularly effective way of inducing paradigm change. That is what fundamental novelties of fact and theory do. Produced inadvertently by a game played under one set of rules, their assimilation requires the elaboration of another set. After they have become parts of science, the enterprise, at least of those specialists in whose particular field the novelties lie, is never quite the same again.

We must now ask how changes of this sort can come about, considering first discoveries, or novelties of fact, and then inventions, or novelties of theory. That distinction between discovery and invention or between fact and theory will, however, immediately prove to be exceedingly artificial. Its artificiality is an important clue to several of this essay's main theses. Examining selected discoveries in the rest of this section, we shall quickly find that they are not isolated events but extended episodes with a regularly recurrent structure. Discovery commences with the awareness of anomaly, i.e., with the recognition that nature has somehow violated the paradigm-induced expectations that govern normal science. It then continues with a more or less extended exploration of the area of anomaly. And it closes only when the paradigm theory has been adjusted so that the anomalous has become the expected. Assimilating a new sort of fact demands a more than additive adjustment of theory, and until that adjustment is completed—until the scientist has learned to see nature in a different way the new fact is not quite a scientific fact at all.

To see how closely factual and theoretical novelty are intertwined in scientific discovery, examine a particularly famous example, the discovery of oxygen. At least three different men have a legitimate claim to it, and several other chemists must, in the early 1770s, have had enriched air in a laboratory vessel without knowing it. The progress of normal science, in this case of pneumatic chemistry, prepared the way to a breakthrough quite thoroughly. The earliest of the claimants to prepare a relatively pure sample of the gas was the Swedish apothecary, C. W. Scheele. We may, however, ignore his work since it was not published until oxygen's discovery had repeatedly been announced elsewhere and thus had no effect upon the historical pattern that most concerns us here. The second in time to establish a claim was the British scientist and divine, Joseph Priestley, who collected the gas released by heated red oxide of mercury as one item in prolonged normal investigation of the "airs" evolved by a large number of solid substances. In 1774 he identified the gas thus produced as nitrous oxide and in 1775, led by further tests, as common air with less than its usual quantity of phlogiston. The third claimant, Lavoisier, started the work that led him to oxygen after Priestley's experiments of 1774 and possibly as the result of a hint from Priestley. Early in 1775 Lavoisier reported that the gas obtained by heating the red oxide of mercury was "air itself entire without alteration [except that] . . . it comes out more pure, more respirable." By 1777, probably with the assistance of a second hint from Priestley, Lavoisier had concluded that the gas was a distinct species, one of the two main constituents of the atmosphere, a conclusion that Priestley was never able to accept.

This pattern of discovery raises a question that can be asked about every novel phenomenon that has ever entered the consciousness of scientists. Was it Priestley or Lavoisier, if either, who first discovered oxygen? In any case, when was oxygen discovered? In that form the question could be asked even if only one claimant had existed. As a ruling about priority and date, an answer does not at all concern us. Nevertheless, an attempt to produce one will illuminate the nature of discovery, because there is no answer of the kind that is sought. Discovery is not the sort of process about which the question is appropriately asked. The fact that it is asked—the priority for oxygen has repeatedly been contested since the 1780s—is a symptom of something askew in the image of science that gives discovery so fundamental a role. Look once more at our example. Priestley's claim to the discovery of oxygen is based upon his priority in isolating a gas that was later recognized as a distinct species. But Priestley's sample was not pure, and, if holding impure oxygen in one's hand is to discover it, that had been done by everyone who ever bottled atmospheric air. Besides, if Priestley was the discoverer, when was the discovery made? In 1774 he thought he had obtained nitrous oxide, a species he already knew; in 1775 he saw the gas as dephlogisticated air, which is still not oxygen or even, for phlogistic chemists, a quite unexpected sort of gas. Lavoisier's claim may be stronger, but it presents the same problems. If we refuse the palm to Priestley, we cannot award it to Lavoisier for the work of 1775 which led him to identify the gas as the "air itself entire." Presumably we wait for the work of 1776 and 1777 which led Lavoisier to see not merely the gas but what the gas was. Yet even this award could be questioned, for in 1777 and to the end of his life Lavoisier insisted that oxygen was an atomic "principle of acidity" and that oxygen gas was formed only when that "principle" united with caloric, the matter of heat. Shall we therefore say that oxygen had not yet been discovered in 1777? Some may be tempted to do so. But the principle of acidity was not banished form chemistry until after 1810, and caloric lingered until the 1860s. Oxygen had become a standard chemical substance before either of those dates.

Clearly we need a new vocabulary and concepts for analyzing events like the discovery of oxygen. Though undoubtedly correct, the sentence,

"Oxygen was discovered," misleads by suggesting that discovering something is a single simple act assimilable to our usual (and also questionable) concept of seeing. That is why we so readily assume that discovering, like seeing or touching, should be unequivocally attributable to an individual and to a moment in time. But the latter attribution is always impossible, and the former often is as well. Ignoring Scheele, we can safely say that oxygen had not been discovered before 1774, and we would probably also say that it had been discovered by 1777 or shortly thereafter. But within those limits or others like them, any attempt to date the discovery must inevitably be arbitrary because discovering a new sort of phenomenon is necessarily a complex event, one which involves recognizing both *that* something is and *what* it is. Note, for example, that if oxygen were dephlogisticated air for us, we should insist without hesitation that Priestley had discovered it, though we would still not know quite when. But if both observation and conceptualization, fact and assimilation to theory, are inseparably linked in discovery, then discovery is a process and must take time. Only when all the relevant conceptual categories are prepared in advance, in which case the phenomenon would not be of a new sort, can discovering *that* and discovering *what* occur effortlessly, together, and in an instant.

Grant now that discovery involves an extended, though not necessarily long, process of conceptual assimilation. Can we also say that it involves a change in paradigm? To that question, no general answer can yet be given, but in this case at least, the answer must be yes. What Lavoisier announced in his papers from 1777 on was not so much the discovery of oxygen as the oxygen theory of combustion. That theory was the keystone for a reformulation of chemistry so vast that it is usually called the chemical revolution. Indeed, if the discovery of oxygen had not been an intimate part of the emergence of a new paradigm for chemistry, the question of priority from which we began would never have seemed so important. In this case as in others, the value placed upon a new phenomenon and thus upon its discoverer varies with our estimate of the extent to which the phenomenon violated paradigm-induced anticipations. Notice, however, since it will be important later, that the discovery of oxygen was not by itself the cause of the change in chemical theory. Long before he played any part in the discovery of the new gas, Lavoisier was convinced both that something was wrong with the phlogiston theory and that burning bodies absorbed some part of the atmosphere. That much he had recorded in a sealed note deposited with the Secretary of the French Academy in 1772. What the work on oxygen did was to give much additional form and structure to Lavoisier's earlier sense that something was amiss. It told him a thing he was already prepared to discover—the nature of the substance that combustion removes from the atmosphere. That advance awareness of difficulties must be a significant part of what enabled Lavoisier to see in experiments like Priestley's a gas that Priestley had been unable to see there himself. Conversely, the fact that a major paradigm revision was needed to see what Lavoisier saw must be the principal reason why Priestley was, to the end of his long life, unable to see it. . . .

To a greater or lesser extent (corresponding to the continuum from the shocking to the anticipated result), the characteristics common to the . . . example above are characteristic of all discoveries from which new sorts of phenomena emerge. Those characteristics include: the previous awareness of anomaly, the gradual and simultaneous emergence of both observational and conceptual recognition, and the consequent change of paradigm categories and procedures often accompanied by resistance. There is even evidence that these same characteristics are built into the nature of the perceptual process itself. In a psychological experiment that deserves to be far better known outside the trade, Bruner and Postman asked experimental subjects to identify on short and controlled exposure a series of playing cards. Many of the cards were normal, but some were made anomalous, e.g., a red six of spades and a black four of hearts. Each experimental run was constituted by the display of a single card to a single subject in a series of gradually increased exposures. After each exposure the subject was asked what he had seen, and the run was terminated by two successive correct identifications.

Even on the shortest exposures many subjects identified most of the cards, and after a small increase all the subjects identified them all. For the normal cards these identifications were usually correct, but the anomalous cards were almost always identified, without apparent hesitation or puzzlement, as normal. The black four of hearts might, for example, be identified as the four of either spades or hearts. Without any awareness of trouble, it was immediately fitted to one of the conceptual categories prepared by prior experience. One would not even like to say that the subjects had seen something different from what they identified. With a further increase

of exposure to the anomalous cards, subjects did begin to hesitate and to display awareness of anomaly. Exposed, for example, to the red six of spades, some would say: That's the six of spades, but there's something wrong with it—the black has a red border. Further increase of exposure resulted in still more hesitation and confusion until finally, and sometimes quite suddenly, most subjects would produce the correct identification without hesitation. Moreover, after doing this with two or three of the anomalous cards, they would have little further difficulty with the others. A few subjects, however, were never able to make the requisite adjustment of their categories. Even at forty times the average exposure required to recognize normal cards for what they were, more than 10 percent of the anomalous cards were not correctly identified. And the subjects who then failed often experienced acute personal distress. One of the exclaimed: "I can't make the suit out, whatever it is. It didn't even look like a card that time. I don't know what color it is now or whether it's a spade or a heart. I'm not even sure now what a spade looks like. My God!" In the next section we shall occasionally see scientists behaving this way too.

Either as a metaphor or because it reflects the nature of the mind, that psychological experiment provides a wonderfully simple and cogent schema for the process of scientific discovery. In science, as in the playing card experiment, novelty emerges only with difficulty, manifested by resistance, against a background provided by expectation. Initially, only the anticipated and usual are experienced even under circumstances where anomaly is later to be observed. Further acquaintance, however does result in awareness of something wrong or does relate the effect to something that has gone wrong before. That awareness of anomaly opens a period in which conceptual categories are adjusted until the initially anomalous has become the anticipated. At this point the discovery has been completed. I have already urged that that process or one very much like it is involved in the emergence of all fundamental scientific novelties. Let me now point out that, recognizing the process, we can at last begin to see why normal science, a pursuit not directed to novelties and tending at first to suppress them, should nevertheless be so effective in causing them to arise.

In the development of any science, the first received paradigm is usually felt to account quite successfully for most of the observations and experiments easily accessible to that science's practitioners. Further development, therefore, ordinarily calls for the construction of elaborate equipment, the development of an esoteric vocabulary and skills, and a refinement of concepts that increasingly lessens their resemblance to their usual common-sense prototypes. That professionalization leads, on the one hand, to an immense restriction of the scientist's vision and to a considerable resistance to paradigm change. The science has become increasingly rigid. On the other hand, within those areas to which the paradigm directs the attention of the group, normal science leads to a detail of information and to a precision of the observation-theory match that could be achieved in no other way. Furthermore, that detail and precision-of-match have a value that transcends their not always very high intrinsic interest. Without the special apparatus that is constructed

mainly for anticipated functions, the results that lead ultimately to novelty could not occur. And even when the apparatus exists, novelty ordinarily emerges only for the man who, knowing *with precision* what he should expect, is able to recognize that something has gone wrong. Anomaly appears only against the background provided by the paradigm. The more precise and far-reaching that paradigm is, the more sensitive an indicator it provides of anomaly and hence of an occasion for paradigm change. In the normal mode of discovery, even resistance to change has a use that will be explored more fully in the next section. By ensuring that the paradigm will not be too easily surrendered, resistance guarantees that scientists will not be lightly distracted and that the anomalies that lead to paradigm change will penetrate existing knowledge to the core. The very fact that a significant scientific novelty so often emerges simultaneously from several laboratories is an index both to the strongly traditional nature of normal science and to the completeness with which that traditional pursuit prepares the way for its own change. . . .

If awareness of anomaly plays a role in the emergence of new sorts of phenomena, it should surprise no one that a similar but more profound awareness is prerequisite to all acceptable changes of theory. On this point historical evidence is, I think, entirely unequivocal. The state of Ptolemaic astronomy was a scandal before Copernicus' announcement. Galileo's contributions to the study of motion depended closely upon difficulties discovered in Aristotle's theory by scholastic critics. Newton's new theory of light and color originated in the discovery that none of the existing pre-paradigm theories would account

for the length of the spectrum, and the wave theory that replaced Newton's was announced in the midst of growing concern about anomalies in the relation of diffraction and polarization effects to Newton's theory. Thermodynamics was born from the collision of two existing nineteenth-century physical theories, and quantum mechanics from a variety of difficulties surrounding black-body radiation, specific heats, and the photoelectric effect. Furthermore, in all these cases except that of Newton the awareness of anomaly had lasted so long and penetrated so deep that one can appropriately describe the fields affected by it as in a state of growing crisis. Because it demands large-scale paradigm destruction and major shifts in the problems and techniques of normal science, the emergence of new theories is generally preceded by a period of pronounced professional insecurity. As one might expect, that insecurity is generated by the persistent failure of the puzzles of normal science to come out as they should. Failure of existing rules is the prelude to a search for new ones. . . .

Philosophers of science have repeatedly demonstrated that more than one theoretical construction can always be placed upon a given collection of data. History of science indicates that, particularly in the early developmental stages of a new paradigm, it is not even very difficult to invent such alternates. But that invention of alternates is just what scientists seldom undertake except during the pre-paradigm stage of their science's development and at very special occasions during its subsequent evolution. So long as the tools a paradigm supplies continue to prove capable of solving the problems it defines, science moves fastest and penetrates most

deeply through confident employment of those tools. The reason is clear. As in manufacture so in science—retooling is an extravagance to be reserved for the occasion that demands it. The significance of crises is the indication they provide that an occasion for retooling has arrived. . . .

How, then, do scientists respond to the awareness of an anomaly in the fit between theory and nature? What has just been said indicates that even a discrepancy unaccountably larger than that experienced in other applications of the theory need not draw any very profound response. There are always some discrepancies. Even the most stubborn ones usually respond at last to normal practice. Very often scientists are willing to wait, particularly if there are many problems available in other parts of the field. . . . [D]uring the sixty years after Newton's original computation, the predicted motion of the moon's perigee remained only half of that observed. As Europe's best mathematical physicists continued to wrestle unsuccessfully with the well-known discrepancy, there were occasional proposals for a modification of Newton's inverse square law. But no one took these proposals very seriously, and in practice this patience with a major anomaly proved justified. Clairaut in 1750 was able to show that only the mathematics of the application had been wrong and that Newtonian theory could stand as before. Even in cases where no mere mistake seems quite possible (perhaps because the mathematics involved is simpler or of a familiar and elsewhere successful sort), persistent and recognized anomaly does not always induce crisis. No one seriously questioned Newtonian theory because of the long-recognized discrepancies between predictions from that theory and both the speed of sound and the little motion of Mercury. The first discrepancy was ultimately and quite unexpectedly resolved by experiments on heat undertaken for a very different purpose; the second vanished with the general theory of relativity after a crisis that it had had no role in creating. Apparently neither had seemed sufficiently fundamental to evoke the malaise that goes with crises. They could be recognized as counterinstances and still be set aside for later work.

It follows that if an anomaly is to evoke crisis, it must usually be more than just an anomaly. There are always difficulties somewhere in the paradigm-nature fit; most of them are set right sooner or later, often by processes that could not have been foreseen. The scientist who pauses to examine every anomaly he notes will seldom get significant work done. We therefore have to ask what it is that makes an anomaly seem worth concerted scrutiny, and to that question there is probably no fully general answer. The cases we have already examined are characteristic but scarcely prescriptive. Sometimes an anomaly will clearly call into question explicit and fundamental generalizations of the paradigm, as the problem of ether drag did for those who accepted Maxwell's theory. Or, as in the Copernican revolution, an anomaly without apparent fundamental import may evoke crisis if the applications that it inhibits have a particular practical importance, in this case for calendar design and astrology. Or, as in eighteenth-century chemistry, the development of normal science may transform an anomaly that had previously been only a vexation into a source of crisis: the problem of weight relations had a very different status after the evolution of pneumatic-chemical techniques. Presumably there

are still other circumstances that can make an anomaly particularly pressing, and ordinarily several of these will combine. We have already noted, for example, that one source of the crisis that confronted Copernicus was the mere length of time during which astronomers had wrestled unsuccessfully with the reduction of the residual discrepancies in Ptolemy's system.

When, for these reasons or others like them, an anomaly comes to seem more than just another puzzle of normal science, the transition to crisis and to extraordinary science has begun. The anomaly itself now comes to be more generally recognized as such by the profession. More and more attention is devoted to it by more and more of the field's most eminent men. If it still continues to resist, as it usually does not, many of them may come to view its resolution as *the* subject matter of their discipline. For them the field will no longer look quite the same as it had earlier. Part of its different appearance results simply from the new fixation point of scientific scrutiny. An even more important source of change is the divergent nature of the numerous partial solutions that concerted attention to the problem has made available. The early attacks upon the resistant problem will have followed the paradigm rules quite closely. But with continuing resistance, more and more of the attacks upon it will have involved some minor or not so minor articulation of the paradigm, no two of them quite alike, each partially successful, but none sufficiently so to be accepted as paradigm by the group. Through this proliferation of divergent articulations (more and more frequently they will come to be described as *ad hoc* adjustments), the rules of normal science become increasingly blurred.

Though there still is a paradigm, few practitioners prove to be entirely agreed about what it is. Even formerly standard solutions of solved problems are called in question. . . .

Confronted with anomaly or with crisis, scientists take a different attitude toward existing paradigms, and the nature of their research changes accordingly. The proliferation of competing articulations, the willingness to try anything, the expression of explicit discontent, the recourse to philosophy and to debate over fundamentals, all these are symptoms of a transition from normal to extraordinary research. It is upon their existence more than upon that of revolutions that the notion of normal science depends. . . .

In learning a paradigm the scientist acquires theory, methods, and standards together, usually in an inextricable mixture. Therefore, when paradigms change, there are usually significant shifts in the criteria determining the legitimacy both of problems and of proposed solutions.

That observation returns us to the point from which this section began, for it provides our first explicit indication of why the choice between competing paradigms regularly raises questions that cannot be resolved by the criteria of normal science. To the extent, as significant as it is incomplete, the two scientific schools disagree about what is a problem and what a solution, they will inevitably talk through each other when debating the relative merits of their respective paradigms. In the partially circular arguments that regularly result, each paradigm will be shown to satisfy more or less the criteria that it dictates for itself and to fall short of a few of those dictated by its opponent. There are other reasons, too, for the incompleteness of logical contact that consistently characterizes paradigm debates. For example, since no paradigm ever solves all the problems it defines and since no two paradigms leave all the same problems unsolved, paradigm debates always involve the question: Which problems is it more significant to have solved? Like the issue of competing standards, that question of values can be answered only in terms of criteria that lie outside of normal science altogether, and it is that recourse to external criteria that most obviously makes paradigm debates revolutionary.

EVELYN FOX KELLER

Feminism and Science

EVELYN FOX KELLER *was trained in physics and wrote a biography of the Nobel Prize winning biologist Barbara McClintock. She has been a pioneer in bringing feminist perspectives to the study of science. She is a Professor of History and Philosophy of Science in the Program of Science, Technology and Society at MIT. Her books include* Reflections on Gender and Science *(1985), and* Secrets of Life, Secrets of Death *(1992).*

I N recent years, a new critique of science has begun to emerge from a number of feminist writings. The lens of feminist politics brings into focus certain masculinist distortions of the scientific enterprise, creating, for those of us who are scientists, a potential dilemma. Is there a conflict between our commitment to feminism and our commitment to science? As both a feminist and a scientist, I am more familiar than I might wish with the nervousness and defensiveness that such a potential conflict evokes. As scientists, we have very real difficulties in thinking about the kinds of issues that, as feminists, we have been raising. These difficulties may, however, ultimately be productive. My purpose in the present essay is to explore the implications of recent feminist criticism of science for the relationship between science and feminism. Do these criticisms imply conflict? If they do, how necessary is that conflict? I will argue that those elements of feminist criticism that seem to conflict most with at least conventional conceptions of science may, if fact, carry a liberating potential for science. It could therefore benefit scientists to attend closely to feminist criticism. I will suggest that we might even use feminist thought to illuminate and clarify part of the substruc-ture of science (which may have been historically conditioned into distortion) in order to preserve the things that science has taught us, in order to be more objective. But first it is necessary to review the various criticisms that feminists have articulated.

The range of their critique is broad. Though they all claim that science embodies a strong androcentric bias, the meanings attached to this charge vary widely. It is convenient to represent the differences in meaning by a spectrum that parallels the political range characteristic of feminism as a whole. I label this spectrum from right to left, beginning somewhere left of center with what might be called the liberal position. From the liberal critique, charges of androcentricity emerge that are relatively easy to correct. The more radical critique calls for correspondingly more radical changes; it requires a reexamination of the underlying assumptions of scientific theory and method for the presence of male bias. The difference between these positions is, however, often obscured by a knee-jerk reaction that leads many scientists to regard all such criticism as a unit—as a challenge to the neutrality of science. One of the points I wish to emphasize here is that the range of meanings attributed to the claim of androcentric bias reflects very different levels of challenge, some of which even the most conservative scientists ought to be able to accept.

First, in what I have called the liberal critique, is the charge that is essentially one of unfair employment practices. It proceeds from the observation that almost all scientists are men. This criticism is liberal in the sense that it in no way conflicts either with traditional conceptions of science or with current liberal, egalitarian politics. It is, in fact, a purely political criticism, and one that can be supported by all of us who are in favor of equal opportunity. According to this point of view, science itself would in no way be affected by the presence or absence of women.

A slightly more radical criticism continues from this and argues that the predominance of men in the sciences has led to a bias in the choice and definition of problems with which scientists have concerned themselves. This argument is most frequently and most easily made in regard to the health sciences. It is claimed, for example, that contraception has not been given the scientific attention its human importance warrants and that, furthermore, the attention it has been given has been focused primarily on contraceptive techniques to be used by women. In a related complaint, feminists argue that menstrual cramps, a serious problem for many women, have never been taken seriously by the medical profession. Presumably, had the concerns of medical research been articulated by women, these particular imbalances would not have arisen. Similar biases in sciences remote from the subject of women's bodies are more difficult to locate—they may, however, exist. Even so, this kind of criticism does not touch our conception of what science is, nor our confidence in the neutrality of science. It may be true that in some areas we have ignored certain problems, but our definition of science does not include the choice of problem—that, we can readily agree, has always been influenced by social forces. We remain, therefore, in the liberal domain.

Continuing to the left, we next find claims of bias in the actual design and interpretation of experiments. For example, it is pointed out that virtually all of the animal-learning research on rats has been performed with male rats. Though a simple explanation is offered— namely, that female rats have a four-day cycle that complicates experiments—the criticism is hardly vitiated by the explanation. The implicit assumption is, of course, that the male rat represents the species. There exist many other, often similar, examples in psychology. Examples from the biological sciences are somewhat more difficult to find, though one suspects that they exist. An area in which this suspicion is particularly strong is that of sex research. Here the influence of heavily invested preconceptions seems all but inevitable. In fact, although the existence of such preconceptions has been well documented historically, a convincing case for the existence of a corresponding bias in either the design or interpretation of experiments has yet to be made. That this is so can, I think, be taken as testimony to the effectiveness of the standards of objectivity operating.

But evidence for bias in the interpretation of observations and experiments is very easy to find in the more socially oriented sciences. The area of primatology is a familiar target. Over the past fifteen years women working in the field have undertaken an extensive reexamination of theoretical concepts, often using essentially the same methodological tools. These efforts have resulted in some radically different formulations. The range of difference frequently reflects the powerful influence of ordinary language in biasing our theoretical formulations. A great deal of very interesting work analyzing such distortions has been done. Though I cannot begin to do justice to that work here, let me offer, as a single example, the following description of a single-male troop of animals that Jane Lancaster provides as a substitute for the familiar concept of "harem": "For a female, males are a resource in her environment which she may use to further the survival of herself and her offspring. If environmental conditions are such that the male role can be minimal, a one-male group is likely. Only one male is necessary for a group of females if his only role is to impregnate them."

These critiques, which maintain that a substantive effect on scientific theory results from the predominance of men in the field, are almost exclusively aimed at the "softer," even the "softest," sciences. Thus they can still be accommodated within the traditional framework by the simple argument that the critiques, if justified, merely reflect the fact that these subjects are not sufficiently scientific. Presumably, fair-minded (or scientifically minded) scientists can and should join forces with the feminists in attempting to identify the presence of bias—equally offensive, if for different reasons, to both scientists and feminists—in order to make these "soft" sciences more rigorous.

It is much more difficult to deal with the truly radical critique that attempts to locate androcentric bias even in the "hard" sciences, indeed in scientific ideology itself. This range of criticism takes us out of the liberal domain and requires us to question the very assumptions of objectivity and rationality that underlie the scientific enterprise. To challenge the truth and necessity of the conclusions of natural science on the grounds that they too reflect the judgment of men is to take the Galilean credo and turn in on its head. It is not true that "the conclusions of natural science are true and necessary, and the judgment of man has nothing to do with them"; it is the judgment of woman that they have nothing to do with.

The impetus behind this radical move is twofold. First, it is supported by the experience of feminist scholars in other fields of inquiry. Over and over, feminists have found it necessary, in seeking to reinstate women as agents and as subjects, to question the very canons of their fields. They have turned their attention, accordingly, to the operation of patriarchal bias on ever deeper levels of social structure, even of language and thought.

But the possibility of extending the feminist critique into the foundations of scientific thought is created by recent developments in the history and philosophy of science itself. As long as the course of scientific thought was judged to be exclusively determined by its own logical and empirical necessities, there could be no place for any signature, male or otherwise, in that system of knowledge. Furthermore, any suggestion of gender differences in our thinking about the world could argue only too readily for the further exclusion of women from science. But as the philosophical and historical inadequacies of the classical conception of science have become more evident, and as historians and sociologists have begun to identify the ways in which the development of scientific knowledge has been shaped by its particular social and political context, our understanding of science as a social process has grown. This understanding is a necessary prerequisite, both politically and intellectually, for a feminist theoretic in science.

Joining feminist thought to other social studies of science brings the promise of radically new insights, but it also adds to the existing intellectual danger a political threat. The intellectual danger resides in viewing science as pure social product; science then dissolves into ideology and objectivity loses all intrinsic meaning. In the resulting cultural relativism, any emancipatory function of modern science is negated, and the arbitration of truth recedes into the political domain. Against this background, the temptation arises for feminists to abandon their claim for representation in scientific culture and, in its place, to invite a return to a purely "female" subjectivity, leaving rationality and objectivity in the male domain, dismissed as products of a purely male consciousness. . . .

Many authors have addressed the problems raised by total relativism; here I wish merely to mention some of the special problems added by its feminist variant. They are several. In important respects, feminist relativism is just the kind of radical move that transforms the political spectrum into a circle. By rejecting objectivity as a masculine ideal, it simultaneously lends its voice to an enemy chorus and dooms women to residing outside of the realpolitik modern culture; it exacerbates the very problem it wishes to solve. It also nullifies the radical potential of feminist criticism for our understanding of science. As I see it, the task of a feminist theoretic in science is twofold: to distinguish that which is parochial from that which is universal in the scientific impulse, reclaiming for women what has historically been denied to them; and to legitimate those elements of scientific

culture that have been denied precisely because they are defined as female.

It is important to recognize that the framework inviting what might be called the nihilist retreat is in fact provided by the very ideology of objectivity we wish to escape. This is the ideology that asserts an opposition between (male) objectivity and (female) subjectivity and denies the possibility of mediation between the two. A first step, therefore, in extending the feminist critique to the foundations of scientific thought is to reconceptualize objectivity as a dialectical process so as to allow for the possibility of distinguishing the objective effort from the objectivist illusion.

Rather than abandon the quintessential human effort to understand the world in rational terms, we need to refine that effort. To do this, we need to add to the familiar methods of rational and empirical inquiry the additional process of critical self-reflection. Following Piaget's injunction, we need to "become conscious of self." In this way, we can become conscious of the features of the scientific project that belie its claim to universality.

The ideological ingredients of particular concern to feminists are found where objectivity is linked with autonomy and masculinity, and in turn, the goals of science with power and domination. The linking of objectivity with social and political autonomy has been examined by many authors and shown to serve a variety of important political functions. The implications of joining objectivity with masculinity are less well understood. This conjunction also serves critical political functions. But an understanding of the sociopolitical meaning of the entire constellation requires an examination of the psychological processes through which these connections become internalized and perpetuated. Here psychoanalysis offers us an invaluable perspective, and it is to the exploitation of that perspective that much of my own work has been directed. In an earlier paper, . . . [I sought] to understand the ways in which our earliest experiences—experiences in large part determined by the socially structured relationships that form the context of our developmental processes—help to shape our conception of the world and our characteristic orientation to it. . . . In brief, I argued the following: Our early maternal environment, coupled with the cultural definition of masculine (that which can never appear feminine) and of autonomy (that which can never be compromised by dependency) leads to the association of female with the pleasures and dangers of merging, and of male with the comfort and loneliness of separateness. The boy's internal anxiety about both self and gender is echoed by the more widespread cultural anxiety, thereby encouraging postures of autonomy and masculinity, which can, indeed may, be designed to defend against that anxiety and the longing that generates it. Finally, for all of us, our sense of reality is carved out of the same developmental matrix. As Piaget and others have emphasized, the capacity for cognitive distinction between self and other (objectivity) evolves concurrently and interdependently with the development of psychic autonomy; our cognitive ideals thereby become subject to the same psychological influences as our emotional and gender ideals. Along with autonomy, the very act of separating subject from object—objectivity itself—comes to be associated with masculinity. The combined psychological and cultural pressures lead all three

ideals—affective, gender, and cognitive—to a mutually reinforcing process of exaggeration and rigidification. The net result is the entrenchment of an objectivist ideology and a correlative devaluation of (female) subjectivity.

This analysis leaves out many things. Above all it omits discussion of the psychological meanings of power and domination.

In his work *The Domination of Nature* William Leiss observes, "The necessary correlate of domination is the consciousness of subordination in those who must obey the will of another; thus properly speaking only other men can be the objects of domination." (Or women, we might add.) Leiss infers from this observation that it is not the domination of physical nature we should worry about but the use of our knowledge of physical nature as an instrument for the domination of human nature. He therefore sees the need for correctives, not in science but in its uses. This is his point of departure from other authors of the Frankfurt school, who assume the very logic of science to be the logic of domination. I agree with Leiss's basic observation but draw a somewhat different inference. I suggest that the impulse toward domination does find expression in the goals (and even in the theories and practice) of modern science, and argue that where it finds such expression the impulse needs to be acknowledged as projection. In short, I argue that not only in the denial of interaction between subject and other but also in the access of domination to the goals of scientific knowledge, one finds the intrusion of a self we begin to recognize as partaking in the cultural construct of masculinity.

The value of consciousness is that it enables us to make choices—both as individuals and as scientists. Control and domination are in fact intrinsic neither to selfhood (i.e., autonomy) nor to scientific knowledge. I want to suggest, rather, that the particular emphasis western science has placed on these functions of knowledge is twin to the objectivist ideal. Knowledge in general, and scientific knowledge in particular, serves two gods: power and transcendence. It aspires alternately to mastery over and union with nature. Sexuality serves the same two gods, aspiring to domination and ecstatic communion—in short, aggression and eros. And it is hardly a new insight to say that power, control, and domination are fueled largely by aggression, while union satisfies a more purely erotic impulse.

To see the emphasis on power and control so prevalent in the rhetoric of western science as projection of a specifically male consciousness requires no great leap of the imagination. Indeed, that perception has become a commonplace. Above all, it is invited by the rhetoric that conjoins the domination of nature with the insistent image of nature as female, nowhere more familiar than in the writings of Francis Bacon. For Bacon, knowledge and power are one, and the promise of science is expressed as "leading to you Nature with all her children to bind her to your service and make her your slave," by means that do not "merely exert a gentle guidance over nature's course; they have the power to conquer and subdue her, to shake her to her foundations." In the context of the Baconian vision, Bruno Bettelheim's conclusion appears inescapable: "Only with phallic psychology did aggressive manipulation of nature become possible." . . .

The presence of contrasting themes, of a dialectic between aggressive and erotic impulses, can be seen both within the work of individual scientists and, even more dramatically, in the juxtaposed writings of different scientists. Francis Bacon provides us with one model; there are many others. For an especially striking contrast, consider a contemporary scientist who insists on the importance of "letting the material speak to you," of allowing it to "tell you what to do next"—one who chastises other scientists for attempting to "impose an answer" on what they see. For this scientist, discovery is facilitated by becoming "part of the system," rather than remaining outside; one must have a "feeling for the organism." It is true that the author of these remarks in not only from a different epoch and a different field (Bacon himself was not actually a scientist by most standards), she is also a woman. It is also true that there are many reasons, some of which I have already suggested, for thinking that gender (itself constructed in an ideological context) actually does make a difference in scientific inquiry. Nevertheless, my point here is that neither science nor individuals are totally bound by ideology. In fact, it is not difficult to find similar sentiments expressed by male scientists. Consider, for example, the following remarks: "I have often had cause to feel that my hands are cleverer than my head. That is a crude way of characterizing the dialectics of experimentation. When it is going well, it is like a quiet conversation with Nature." The difference between conceptions of science as "dominating" and as "conversing with" nature may not be a difference primarily between epochs, nor between the sexes. Rather it can be seen as representing a dual theme played out in the work of all scientists, in all ages. But the two poles of this dialectic do not appear with equal weight in the history of science. What we therefore need to attend to is the evolutionary process that selects one theme as dominant.

Elsewhere I have argued for the importance of a different selection process. In part, scientists are themselves selected by the emotional appeal of particular (stereotypic) images of science. Here I am arguing for the importance of selection within scientific thought—first of preferred methodologies and aims, and finally of preferred theories. The two processes are not unrelated. While stereotypes are not binding (i.e., they do not describe all or perhaps any individuals), and this fact creates the possibility for an ongoing contest within science, the first selection process undoubtedly influences the outcome of the second. That is, individuals drawn by particular ideology will tend to select themes consistent with that ideology.

One example in which this process is played out on a theoretical level is in the fate of interactionist theories in the history of biology. Consider the contest that has raged throughout this century between organismic and particulate views of cellular organization—between what might be described as hierarchical and nonhierarchical theories. Whether the debate is over the primacy of the nucleus or the cell as a whole, the genome or the cytoplasm, the proponents of hierarchy have won out. One geneticist has described the conflict in explicitly political terms:

Two concepts of genetic mechanisms have persisted side by side throughout the growth of modern genetics, but the emphasis has been very strongly in favor of one of these. . . . The first of these we will designate as the "Master Molecule" concept. . . . This is in essence the Theory of the Gene, interpreted to suggest a totalitarian government. . . . The second concept we will designate as the "Steady

State" concept. By this term . . . we envision a dynamic self-perpetuating organization of a variety of molecular species which owes its specific properties not to the characteristic of any one kind of molecule, but to the functional interrelationships of these molecular species.

Soon after these remarks, the debate between "master molecules" and dynamic interactionism was foreclosed by the synthesis provided by DNA and the "central dogma." With the success of the new molecular biology such "steady state" (or egalitarian) theories lost interest for almost all geneticists. But today, the same conflict shows signs of reemerging—in genetics, in theories of the immune system, and in theories of development.

I suggest that method and theory may constitute a natural continuum, despite Popperian claims to the contrary, and that the same processes of selection may bear equally and simultaneously on both the means and aims of science and the actual theoretical descriptions that emerge. I suggest this in part because of the recurrent and striking consonance that can be seen in the way scientists work, the relation they take to their object of study, and the theoretical orientation they favor. To pursue the example cited earlier, the same scientist who allowed herself to become "part of the system," whose investigations were guided by a "feeling for the organism," developed a paradigm that diverged as radically from the dominant paradigm of her field as did her methodological style.

In lieu of the linear hierarchy described by the central dogma of molecular biology, in which DNA encodes and transmits all instruction for the unfolding of a living cell, her research yielded a view of the DNA in delicate interaction with the cellular environment—an organismic view. For more important than the genome as such (i.e., the DNA) is the "overall organism." As she sees it, the genome functions "only in respect to the environment in which it is found." In this work the program encoded by the DNA is itself subject to change. No longer is a master control to be found in a single component of the cell; rather, control resides in the complex interactions of the entire system. When first presented, the work underlying this vision was not understood, and it was poorly received. Today much of that work is undergoing a renaissance, although it is important to say that her full vision remains too radical for most biologists to accept.

This example suggests that we need not rely on our imagination for a vision of what a different science—a science less restrained by the impulse to dominate—might be like. Rather, we need only look to the thematic pluralism in the history of our own science as it has evolved. Many other examples can be found, but we lack an adequate understanding of the full range of influences that lead to the acceptance or rejection not only of particular theories but of different theoretical orientations. What I am suggesting is that if certain theoretical interpretations have been selected against, it is precisely in this process of selection that ideology in general, and a masculinist ideology in particular, can be found to effect its influence. The task this implies for a radical feminist critique of science is, then, first a historical one, but finally a transformative one. In the historical effort, feminists can bring a whole new range of sensitivities, leading to an equally new consciousness of the potentialities lying latent in the scientific project.

RICHARD FEYNMAN

Seeking New Laws of Nature

RICHARD FEYNMAN (1918–1988) was a professor of physics at California Institute of Technology. In 1945 he was declared mentally deficient for service in the U. S. Army. In 1965 he won the Nobel Prize in physics. He was also well known for his abilities with the bongo drums.

What I want to talk about in this lecture is not, strictly speaking, the character of physical law. One might imagine at least that one is talking about nature when one us talking about the character of physical law; but I do not want to talk about nature, but rather about how we stand relative to nature now. I want to tell you . . . what there is to guess, and how one goes about guessing. Someone suggested that it would be ideal if, as I went along, I would slowly explain how to guess a law, and then end by creating a new law for you. I do not know whether I shall be able to do that. . . .

In general we look for a new law by the following process. First we guess it. Then we compute the consequences of the guess to see what would be implied if this law that we guessed is right. Then we compare the result of the computation to nature with experiment or experience, compare it directly with observation, to see if it works. If it disagrees with experiment it is wrong. In that simple statement is the key to science. It does not make any difference how beautiful your guess is. It does not make any difference how smart you are, who made the guess, or what his name is—if it disagrees with experiment it is wrong. That is all there is to it. It is true that one has to check a little to make sure that it is wrong, because whoever did the experiment may have reported incorrectly, or there may have been some feature in the experiment that was not noticed, some dirt or something; or the man who computed the consequences, even though it may have been the one who made the guesses, could have made some mistake in the analysis. These are obvious remarks, so when I say if it disagrees with experiment it is wrong, I mean after the experiment has been checked, the calculations have been checked, and the thing has been rubbed back and forth a few times to make sure that the consequences are logical consequences from the guess, and that in fact it disagrees with a very carefully checked experiment.

This will give you a somewhat wrong impression of science. It suggests that we keep on guessing possibilities and comparing them with experiment, and this is to put experiment into a rather weak position. In fact experimenters have a certain individual character. They like to do experiments even if nobody has guessed yet, and they very often do their experiments in a region in which people know the theorist has not made any guesses. For instance, we may know a great many laws, but do not know whether they really work at high energy, because it is just a good guess that they work at high energy. Experimenters have tried experiments at higher energy, and in fact every once in a while experiment produces trouble; that is, it produces a discovery that one of the things we thought right is wrong. In this way experiment can produce unexpected results, and that starts us guessing again. One instance of an unexpected result is the mu meson and its neutrino, which was not guessed by anybody at all before it was discovered, and even today nobody yet has any method of guessing by which this would be a natural result.

You can see, of course, that with this method we can attempt to disprove any definite theory. If we have a definite theory, a real guess, from which we can conveniently compute consequences which can be compared with experiment, then in principle we can get rid of any theory. There is always the possibility of proving any definite theory wrong; but notice that we can never prove it right. Suppose that you invent a good guess, calculate the consequences, and discover every time that the consequences you have calculated agree with experiment. The theory is then right? No, it is simply not proved wrong. In the future you could compute a wider range of consequences, there could be a wider range of experiments, and you might then discover that the thing is wrong. That is why laws like Newton's laws for the motion of planets last such a long time. He guessed the law of gravitation, calculated all kinds of consequences for the system and so on, compared them with experiment—and it took several hundred years before the slight error of the motion of Mercury was observed. During all that time the theory had not been proved wrong, and could be taken temporarily to be right. But it could never be proved right, because tomorrow's experiment might succeed in proving wrong what you thought was right. We never are definitely right, we can only be sure we are wrong. However, it is rather remarkable how we can have some ideas which will last so long.

One of the ways of stopping science would be only to do experiments in the region where you know the law. But experimenters search most diligently, and with the greatest effort, in exactly those places where it seems most likely that we can prove our theories wrong. In other words we are trying to prove ourselves wrong as quickly as possible, because only in that way can we find progress. For example, today among ordinary low energy phenomena we do not know where to look for trouble, we think everything is all right, and so there is no particular big programme looking for trouble in nuclear reactions, or in superconductivity. In these lectures I am concentrating on discovering fundamental laws. The whole range of physics, which is interesting, includes also an understanding at another level of these phenomena like super-conductivity and nuclear reactions, in terms of the fundamental laws. But I am talking now about discovering trouble, something wrong with fundamental laws, and since among low energy phenomena nobody knows where to look, all the experiments today in this field of finding out a new law, are of high energy.

Another thing I must point out is that you cannot prove a vague theory wrong. If the guess that you make is poorly expressed and rather vague, and the method that you use for figuring out the consequences is a little vague—you are not sure, and you say, 'I think everything's right because it's all due to so and so, and such and such do this and that more or less, and I can sort of explain how this works . . . ,' then you see that this theory is good, because it cannot be proved wrong! Also if the process of computing the consequences is indefinite, then with a little skill any experimental results can be made to look like the expected consequences. You are probably familiar with that in other fields. 'A' hates his mother. The reason is, of course, because she did not caress him or love him enough when he was a child. But if you investigate you find out that as a matter of fact she did love him very much, and everything was all right. Well then, it was because she was over-indulgent when he was a child! By having a vague theory it is possible to get either result. The cure for this one is the following. If it were possible to state exactly, ahead of time, how much love is not enough, and how much love is over-indulgent, then there would be a perfectly legitimate theory against which you could make tests. It is usually said when this is pointed out, 'When you are dealing with psychological matters things can't be defined so precisely'. Yes, but then you cannot claim to know anything about it.

You will be horrified to hear that we have examples in physics of exactly the same kind. We have these approximate symmetries, which work something like this. You have an approximate symmetry, so you calculate a set of consequences supposing it to be perfect. When compared with experiment, it does not agree. Of course—the symmetry you are supposed to expect is approximate, so if the agreement is pretty good you say, 'Nice!', while if the agreement is very poor you say, 'Well, this particular thing must be especially sensitive to the failure of the symmetry'. Now you may laugh, but we have to make progress in that way. When a subject is first new, and these particles are new to us, this jockeying around, this 'feeling' way of guessing at the results, is the beginning of any science. The same thing is true of the symmetry proposition in physics as is true of psychology, so do not laugh too hard. It is necessary in the beginning to be very careful. It is easy to fall into the deep end by this kind of vague theory. It is hard to prove it wrong, and it takes a certain skill and experience not to walk off the plank in the game. . . .

Because I am a theoretical physicist, and more delighted with this end of the problem, I want now to concentrate on how to make the guesses.

As I said before, it is not of any importance where the guess comes from; it is only important that it should agree with experiment, and that it should be as definite as possible. 'Then', you say, 'that is very simple. You set up a machine, a great computing machine, which has a random wheel in it that makes a succession of guesses, and each time it guesses a hypothesis about how nature should work it computes immediately the consequences, and makes a comparison with a list of experimental results it has at the other end'. In other words, guessing is a dumb man's job. Actually it is quite the opposite, and I will try to explain why.

The first problem is how to start. You say, 'Well I'd start off with all the known principles'. But all the principles that are known are inconsistent with each other, so something has to be removed. We get a lot of letters from people insisting that we ought to make holes in our guesses. You see, you make a hole, to make room for a new guess.

Somebody says, 'You know, you people always say that space is continuous. How do you know when you get to a small enough dimension that there really are enough points in between, that it isn't just a lot of dots separated by little distances?' Or they say, 'You know those quantum mechanical amplitudes you told me about, they're so complicated and absurd, what makes you think those are right? Maybe they aren't right'. Such remarks are obvious and are perfectly clear to anybody who is working on this problem. It does not do any good to point this out. The problem is not only what might be wrong but what, precisely, might be substituted in place of it. In the case of the continuous space, suppose the precise proposition is that space really consists of a series of dots, and that the space between them does not mean anything, and that the dots are in a cubic array. Then we can prove immediately that this is wrong. It does not work. The problem is not just to say something might be wrong, but to replace it by something— and that is not so easy. As soon as any really definite idea is substituted it becomes almost immediately apparent that it does not work.

The second difficulty is that there is an infinite number of possibilities of these simple types. It is something like this. You are sitting working very hard, you have worked for a long time trying to open a safe. Then some Joe comes along who knows nothing about what you are doing, except that you are trying to open the safe. He says 'Why don't you try the combination 10:20:30? Maybe you know already that the middle number is 32, not 20. Maybe you know as a matter of fact that it is a five-digit combination. . . . So please do not send me any letters trying to tell me how the thing is going to work. I read them—I always read them to make sure that I have not already thought of what is suggested—but it takes too long to answer them, because they are usually in the class 'try 10:20:30'. As usual, nature's imagination far surpasses our own, as we have seen from the other theories which are subtle and deep. To get such a subtle and deep guess is not so easy. One must be really clever to guess, and it is not possible to do it blindly by machine.

I want to discuss now the art of guessing nature's laws. It is an art. How is it done? One way you might suggest is to look at history to see how the other guys did it. So we look at history.

We must start with Newton. He had a situation where he had incomplete knowledge, and he was able to guess the laws by putting together ideas which were all relatively close to experiment; there was not a great distance between the observations and the tests. That was the first way, but today it does not work so well.

The next guy who did something great was Maxwell, who obtained the laws of electricity and magnetism. What he did was this. He put together all the laws of electricity, due to Faraday and other people who came before him, and he looked at them and realized that they were mathematically inconsistent. In order to straighten it out he had to add one term to an equation. He did this by inventing for himself a model of idler wheels and gears and so on in space. He found what the new law was—but nobody paid much attention because they did not believe in the idler wheels. We do not believe in the idler wheels today, but the equations that he obtained were correct. So the logic may be wrong but the answer is right.

In the case of relativity the discovery was completely different. There was an accumulation of paradoxes; the known laws gave inconsistent results. This was a new kind of thinking, a thinking in terms of discussing the possible symmetries of laws. It was especially difficult, because for the first time it was realized how long something like Newton's laws could seem right, and still ultimately be wrong. Also it was difficult to accept that ordinary ideas of time and space, which seemed so instinctive, could be wrong.

Quantum mechanics was discovered in two independent ways—which is a lesson. There again, and even more so, an enormous number of paradoxes were discovered experimentally, things that absolutely could not be explained in any way by what was known. It was not that the knowledge was incomplete, but that the knowledge was too complete. Your prediction was that this should happen—it did not. The two different routes were one by Schrödinger, who guessed the equation, the other by Heisenberg, who argued that you must analyze what is measurable. These two different philosophical methods led to the same discovery in the end.

More recently, the discovery of the laws of the weak decay I spoke of, when a neutron disintegrates into a proton, an electron and an anti-neutrino—which are still only partly known—add up to a somewhat different situation. This time it was a case of incomplete knowledge, and only the equation was guessed. The special difficulty this time was that the experiments were all wrong. How can you guess the right answer if, when you calculate the result, it disagrees with experiment? You need courage to say the experiments must be wrong. I will explain where that courage comes from later.

Today we have no paradoxes—maybe. We have this infinity that comes in when we put all the laws together, but the people sweeping the dirt under the rug are so clever that one sometimes thinks this is not a serious paradox. Again, the fact that we have found all these particles does not tell us anything except that our knowledge is incomplete. I am sure that history does not repeat itself in physics, as you can tell from looking at the examples I have given. The reason is this. Any schemes—such as 'think of symmetry laws', or 'put the information in mathematical form', or 'guess equations'— are known to everybody now, and they are all tried all the time. When you are struck, the answer cannot be one of these, because you will have tried these right away. There must be another way next time. Each time we get into this log-jam of too much trouble, too many problems, it is because the methods that we are using are just like the ones we have used before. The next scheme, the new discovery, is going to be made in a completely different way. So history does not help us much. . . .

It is not unscientific to make a guess, although many people who are not in science think it is. Some years ago I had a conversation with a layman about flying saucers—because I am scientific I know all about flying saucers! I said 'I don't think there are flying saucers'. So my antagonist said, "Is it impossible that there are flying saucers? Can you prove that there are flying saucers? Can you prove that it's impossible?' 'No', I said, 'I can't prove it's impossible. It's just very unlikely'. At that he said, 'You are very unscientific. If you can't prove it impossible then how can you say that it's unlikely?' But that is the way that *is* scientific. It is scientific only to say what is more likely and what is less likely, and not to be proving all the time the possible and impossible. To define

what I mean, I might have said to him, 'Listen, I mean that from my knowledge of the world that I see around me, I thing that it is much more likely that the reports of flying saucers are the results of the known irrational characteristics of terrestrial intelligence than of the unknown rational efforts of extra-terrestrial intelligence'. It is just more likely, that is all. It is a good guess. And we always try to guess the most likely explanation, keeping in the back of the mind the fact that if it does not work we must discuss the other possibilities. . . .

That reminds me of another point, that the philosophy or ideas around a theory may change enormously when there are very tiny changes in the theory. For instance, Newton's ideas about space and time agreed with experiment very well, but in order to get the correct motion of the orbit of Mercury, which was a tiny, tiny difference, the difference in the character of the theory needed was enormous. The reason is that Newton's laws were so simple and so perfect, and they produced definite results. In order to get something that would produce a slightly different result it had to be completely different. In stating a new law you cannot make imperfections on a perfect thing; you have to have another perfect thing. So the difference in philosophical ideas between Newton's and Einstein's theories of gravitation are enormous.

What are these philosophies? They are really tricky ways to compute consequences quickly. A philosophy, which is sometimes called an understanding of the law, is simply a way that a person hold the laws in his mind in order to guess quickly at consequences. Some people have said, and it is true in cases like Maxwell's equations, 'Never mind the philosophy, never mind anything of this kind, just guess the equations. The problem is only to compute the answers so that they agree with experiment, and it is not necessary to have a philosophy, or argument, or words, about the equation'. That is good in the sense that if you only guess the equation you are not prejudicing yourself, and you will guess better. On the other hand, maybe the philosophy helps you to guess. It is very hard to say.

For those people who insist that the only thing that is important is that the theory agrees with experiment, I would like to imagine a discussion between a Mayan astronomer and his student. The Mayans were able to calculate with great precision predictions, for example, for eclipses and for the position of the moon in the sky, the position of Venus, etc. It was all done by arithmetic. They counted a certain number and subtracted some numbers, and so on. There was no discussion of what the moon was. There was no discussion even of the idea that it went around. They just calculated the time when there would be an eclipse, or when the moon would rise at the full, and so on. Suppose that a young man went to the astronomer and said, 'I have an idea. Maybe those things are going around, and there are balls of something like rocks out there, and we could calculate how they move in a completely different way from just calculating what time they appear in the sky'. 'Yes', says the astronomer, 'and how accurately can you predict eclipses?' He says, 'I haven't developed the thing very far yet'. Then says the astronomer, 'Well, we can calculate eclipses more accurately than you can with your model, so you must not pay any attention to your idea because obviously the mathematical scheme is better'. There is a very strong tendency, when someone comes up with an idea and says, 'Let's suppose that the world is this way', for people to say to him, 'What would you get for the answer to such and such a problem?' And he says, 'I haven't developed it far enough'. And they say, 'Well, we have already developed it much further, and we can get the answers very accurately'. So it is a problem whether or not to worry about philosophies behind ideas.

Another way of working, of course, is to guess new principles. In Einstein's theory of gravitation he guessed, on top of all the other principles, the principle that corresponded to the idea that the forces are always proportional to the masses. He guessed the principle that if you are in an accelerating car you cannot distinguish that from being in a gravitational field, and by adding that principle to all the other principles, he was able to deduce the correct laws of gravitation.

That outlines a number of possible ways of guessing. I would now like to come to some other points about the final result. First of all, when we are all finished, and we have a mathematical theory by which we can compute consequences, what can we do? It really is an amazing thing. In order to figure out what an atom is going to do in a given situation we make up rules with marks on paper, carry them into a machine which has switches that open and close in some complicated way, and the result will tell us what the atom is going to do! If the way that these switches open and close were some kind of model of the atom, if we thought that the atom had switches in it, then I would say that I understood more or less what is going on. I find it quite amazing that it is possible to predict what will happen by mathematics, which is simply following rules which really have nothing to do with what is going on in the original thing. The closing and opening of switches in a computer is quite different from what is happening in nature.

One of the most important things in this 'guess—compute consequences—compare with experiment' business is to know when you are right. It is possible to know when you are right way ahead of checking all the consequences. You can recognize truth by its beauty and simplicity. It is always easy when you have made a guess, and done two or three little calculations to make sure that it is not obviously wrong, to know that it is right—at least if you have any experience—because usually what happens is that more comes out than goes in. Your guess is, in fact, that something is very simple. If you cannot see immediately that it is wrong, and it is simpler than it was before, then it is right. The inexperienced, and crackpots, and people like that, make guesses that are simple, but you can immediately see that they are wrong, so that does not count. Others, the inexperienced students, make guesses that are very complicated, and it sort of looks as if it is all right, but I know it is not true because the truth always turns out to be simpler than you thought. What we need is imagination, but imagination in a terrible straitjacket. We have to find a new view of the world that has to agree with everything that is known, but disagree in its predictions somewhere, otherwise it is not interesting. And in that disagreement it must agree with nature. If you can find any other view of the world which agrees over the entire range where things have already been observed, but disagrees somewhere else, you have made a great discovery. It is very nearly impossible, but not quite, to find any theory which agrees with experiments over the entire range in which all theories have been checked, and yet gives different consequences in some other range, even a theory whose different consequences do not turn out to agree with nature. A new idea is extremely difficult to think of. It takes a fantastic imagination.

What of the future of this adventure? What will happen ultimately? We are going along guessing the laws; how many laws are we going to have to guess? I do not know. Some of my colleagues say that this fundamental aspect of our science will go on; but I think there will certainly not be perpetual novelty, say for a thousand years. This thing cannot keep on going so that we are always going to discover more and more new laws. If we do, it will become boring that there are so many levels one underneath the other. It seems to me that what can happen in the future is either that all the laws become known—that is, if you had enough laws you could compute consequences and they would always agree with experiment, which would be the end of the line   or it may happen that the experiments get harder and harder to make, more and more expensive, so you get 99.9 per cent of the phenomena, but there is always some phenomenon which has just been discovered, which is very hard to measure, and which disagrees; and as soon as you have the explanation of that one there is always another one, and it gets slower and slower and more and more uninteresting. That is another way it may end. But I think it has to end in one way or another.

We are very lucky to live in an age in which we are still making discoveries. It is like the discovery of America—you only discover it once. The age in which we live is the age in which we are discovering the fundamental laws of nature, and that day will never come again. It is very exciting, it is marvellous, but this excitement will have to go. Of course in the future there will be other interests. There will be the interest of the connection of one level of phenomena to another—phenomena in biology and so on, or, if you are talking about exploration, exploring other planets, but there will not still be the same things that we are doing now.

Another thing that will happen is that ultimately, if it turns out that all is known, or it gets very dull, the vigorous philosophy and the careful attention to all these things that I have been talking about will gradually disappear. The philosophers who are always on the outside making stupid remarks will be able to close in, because we cannot push them away by saying, 'If you were right we would be able to guess all the rest of the laws', because when the laws are all there they will have an explanation for them. For instance, there are always explanations about why the world is three-dimensional. Well, there is only one world, and it is hard to tell if that explanation is right or not, so that if everything were known there would be some explanation about why those were the right laws. But that explanation would be in a frame that we cannot criticize by

arguing that type of reasoning will not permit us to go further. There will be a degeneration of ideas, just like the degeneration that great explorers feel is occurring when tourists begin moving in on a territory.

In this age people are experiencing a delight, the tremendous delight that you get when you guess how nature will work in a new situation never seen before. From experiments and information in a certain range you can guess what is going to happen in a region where no one has ever explored before. It is a little different from regular exploration in that there are enough clues on the land discovered to guess what the land that has not been discovered is going to look like. These guesses, incidentally, are often very different from what you have already seen—they take a lot of thought.

What is it about nature that lets this happen, that it is possible to guess from one part what the rest is going to do? That is an unscientific question: I do not know how to answer it, and therefore I am going to give an unscientific answer. I think it is because nature has a simplicity and therefore a great beauty.

SUSAN GRIFFIN

Gravity

SUSAN GRIFFIN *has published numerous feminist works, including a book of poetry, a play, a book of essays, and three nonfiction books including* Women and Nature, *from which this selection is drawn. Born in 1943, she lives in Berkeley, California.*

*Sooner or later the uniformly moving body will collide with the wall of the elevator
destroying the uniform motion. Sooner or later, the whole elevator will collide with
the earth destroying the observers and their experiments.*

ALBERT EINSTEIN AND LEOPOLD INFELD,
The Evolution of Physics

*. . . it is always possible to be "oriented" in a world that has a sacred history, a world
in which every prominent feature is associated with a mythical event.*

MIRCEA ELIADE,
"A Mythical Geography"

The scientists are in a box. There are no windows. Nothing tells them which is right side up. The walls are empty. The ceiling and the floor are the same. They are standing in a perfect cube. Every surface is a square. This they measure and prove with their rulers. The scientists prove by experiment what is the nature of this world. One drops his handkerchief into space. It does not fall to the ground. It rests where the scientist's hand left it. Over time the handkerchief still does not move. This experiment is repeated with different objects. First they push the eyeglasses, lending them motion, then the handkerchief, a pen, a piece of paper, and then their ruler. Each object moves continuously across space until it collides with the opposite wall. The scientists are delighted. They discover they are living in a perfect inertial system. Every body continues in a state of rest or motion. They will continue resting infinitely. They are delighted with this perfection. But gradually one scientist allows a question to enter his mind. It occurs to him that they do not know if they are at rest in an inertial system or if they are moving at a continuous rate of acceleration. Perhaps in a vacuum. Perhaps, and now the scientist feels a sense of dis-

quiet, perhaps they are in a field of gravity, and *are* therefore accelerating continuously. He realizes that they do not know for certain where they are, nor where they are going, if they are going. He decides to break through the cube. Suddenly air rushes in. (They were suffocating, he realizes.) Through the hole he has made he sees the face of the earth coming closer and closer.

"Do you suppose that what we thought was true is not true?" he says with alarm. "We are falling," he admits, "down." Headfirst, the scientists dive from their cube. "I know where we are now," the doubting scientist shouts. "We are in a field of gravity." "And we are no longer falling at the same rate," another observes, "because of the resistance of the air." "Air!' another scientist sighs. "We are certainly not at rest now," the scientists assent. "We *are* moving," they agree.

"We know where we are now relative to the earth," they pronounce.

"And we know where we are going," another adds quickly.

"To the earth," they whisper.

"Where we were born," one says.

"And we know what will happen next," all of the scientists choir back. "We will all of us die."

Chapter 4

Which Should I Believe: Darwin or Genesis?

In July 1925, a young teacher named John Scopes was brought to trial in Dayton, Tennessee, in one of the most celebrated court cases of the century. Assisting the prosecution was William Jennings Bryan, who had run for the presidency in 1896 and who is still regarded by many as the greatest orator in this country's history. Defending Scopes was Clarence Darrow, the most famous criminal lawyer of his generation. Reporters swarmed from all over the country to the small Southern town, and the trial soon became the showcase for a national debate. What was at issue was not a shocking murder or a scandalous political crime, but whether Scopes would be permitted to teach Charles Darwin's theory of evolution in the Tennessee public schools.

It will surprise many of you to learn that the debate over teaching evolutionary theory in the public schools has been going on for so long. Philosophers have been interested in the controversy for a number of reasons. It raises issues about the nature of science and about the relationship between science and religion. It also forces us to think about the responsibilities of public education.

Many religions have accounts of creation. You are probably already familiar with at least one of the creation accounts in the Bible. In some religions in India, the sky, the air, and the earth were understood as gods created by Aditi, a female goddess. In the Hindu religion, Brahma created himself along with other gods and men; he placed a golden egg into the ocean, and out of the egg hatched Brahma himself, who then divided into two to create the heavens and the earth. Religious liberals often take such accounts as metaphorical, or even as mythical. But a literal reading of scriptural or other accounts of creation will usually be incompatible with Darwin's evolutionary account. This incompatibility has fueled a continuing controversy between religious conservatives who are committed to a literal reading of creation stories and those committed to evolutionary theory. To understand this controversy, we must first see why scientists are so wedded to evolutionary accounts.

Nature seems to embody purpose. Animals have two eyes because two is the minimum number to enable them to see depth, and therefore to judge distance. Giraffes' long necks enable them to eat the leaves from the tall trees in their natural habitat. The delicate balance of hormones in your body enables it to adjust to changes in your environment, in everything from digestion to reproduction, and helps you to get around in the world. How could such delicate and complicated mechanisms arise by mere chance?

Evolutionary theory offers the following kind of explanation. Among members of an animal population, there will be small individual differences. (The mechanisms of genetic mutation were not known in Darwin's time, but they obviously provide an explanation of how such differences can arise.) Some of these differences will be advantageous to the organism, either because it will be better equipped to survive and reproduce or because its social structure will be better equipped (as with bees). Other differences will make either the individual organism or the social structure less likely to survive and reproduce. The differences that are advantageous will be genetically transmitted more often because the organisms that have those differences will survive and reproduce more; the differences that are not advantageous will be transmitted less often. Over the course of millions of years, species will therefore evolve in the direction of increasing adaptation to their environment. In the simplest cases, giraffes with longer necks will eat better, and hence reproduce more often, than short-necked giraffes; consequently, giraffes as a species will gradually become longer necked. In a more complicated way, the same account explains the origin of two eyes instead of one, and of complex hormonal and metabolic pathways to deal with complicated interactions between an organism and its environment. The result of all this theorizing is that the *purpose* in nature gets explained without supposing that there is a creator who is arranging for his or her purpose to be met.

Evolutionary theory is not the only theory that works in this way. There are countless others. For example, in a "properly working" free capitalistic market, just the right amount of copper will be mined to serve the needs of the population. Nobody in the government needs to decide how much copper to mine; indeed, if anybody tries to, they will almost certainly do worse than if nobody thinks about it. It is as though there is an "invisible hand" guiding the individual decisions that people make for it to turn out that just the right amount of copper is produced. But market theory explains how the free market and the so-called law of supply and demand bring this about without guidance or control by any outside force.

Even though such explanations allow us to avoid the assumption of outside forces, such as God, they do not require us to do so. Economists can consistently believe that God directs the day-to-day workings of the market; undoubtedly some do. Similarly, some biologists believe that God directs the day-to-day working of evolution. Others believe that at creation, God set in motion the initial laws of nature, including the mechanisms of evolution, and left them to run by themselves for all of time. Others do not believe in God at all. Evolutionary theory does not require that we choose between these kinds of alternatives. The conflict enters when we look at the details of some religious creation accounts.

For example, the creation stories from Genesis that are in this chapter both describe the creation all at once of fully developed species. Moreover, they describe this creation in a time frame of several thousand years, rather than the many millions of years required by the Darwinian account of creation. It is not the religious viewpoint in general that is incompatible with the evolutionary point of view, but rather the details of particular literal interpretations of religious doctrines.

One focus for the tension between these frameworks is in the teaching in school (usually high school) of accounts of creation. Many conservative religious figures who take creation accounts literally nevertheless believe that it is on the basis of *faith,* not evidence, that they are to be accepted. Other **scientific creationists** believe that the literal biblical account of creation is backed by scientific evidence and that the creationist account should thus be taught in science classes as an alternative to the evolutionary account. This has sparked a brisk debate on what exactly counts as science and what doesn't. Some of that debate is reproduced in this chapter.

The book of Genesis contains the Judeo-Christian creation accounts that most of the current controversy centers around. Notice that in Chapters 1 and 2 of Genesis there are actually *two* stories of creation that differ from one another, particularly in the order of creation that is given. Thus, it is inaccurate to speak simply of *the* biblical account. Rather one must speak of the account of Chapter 1 or the account of Chapter 2.

About the middle of the nineteenth century, several biologists arrived independently at the notion of an evolutionary theory to explain the origin of biological adaptation. Darwin became the best known of these. Between 1831 and 1836 he traveled around the world on the ship "The Beagle"; in the course of that voyage he made many of the observations that gave a richness of detail to his theoretical account. In 1859 he published *The Origin of Species,* the book that launched evolutionary theory. Later, in 1871, *The Descent of Man* was published. In it he responded to a number of critics, revised his views on a number of points, and expanded his account to talk in greater detail about the origin of humans. The selection here is from that book.

Because the U.S. Constitution establishes a clear separation between religion and government, the courts have prohibited the teaching of religious views in public schools. But many advocates of a literal reading of the biblical account have argued not on religious but on scientific grounds. They claim that evolutionary theory is itself bad science and that an unbiased, truly scientific look at the evidence will favor creationist views. Among their charges are that evolutionary theory is circular and not subject to the experimental method, that it stands against God and hence itself embodies a religious viewpoint, that it violates well-accepted scientific doctrine, and that it is not as well supported as creationism by the fossil record. Duane T. Gish, perhaps the primary contemporary spokesperson for creationist science, wrote the article included in this chapter, in which all of these claims are spelled out and defined.

In his article, Philip Kitcher responds to Gish's charges, discussing in detail the issue of the fossil record and some of the details of the empirical claims of creationist science. Finally, Isaac Asimov takes a strong stance against creationism, accusing it of being a force for ignorance and against intellectual progress. The dialogue between him and Kitcher on the one had, and Gish on the other, raises important questions about the extent to which scientific points of view are privileged in our culture and about the extent to which we understand the difference between science and nonscience.

THE BIBLE

Genesis

The book of Genesis is the opening book of the Old Testament of **The Bible.** *The word 'genesis' means beginning. Most religious scholars believe that the accounts recorded in Genesis were compiled by a number of different people.*

CHAPTER 1

In the beginning God created the heaven and the earth.

2 And the earth was without form, and void; and darkness *was* upon the face of the deep. And the Spirit of God moved upon the face of the waters.

3 And God said, Let there be light: and there was light.

4 And God saw the light, that *it was* good: and God divided the light from the darkness.

5 And God called the light Day, and the darkness he called Night. And the evening and the morning were the first day.

6 And God said, Let there be a firmament in the midst of the waters, and let it divide the waters from the waters.

7 And God made the firmament, and divided the waters which *were* under the firmament from the waters which *were* above firmament: and it was so.

8 And God called the firmament Heaven. And the evening and the morning were the second day.

9 And God said, Let the waters under the heaven be gathered together unto one place, and let the dry *land* appear: and it was so.

10 And God called the dry *land* Earth; and the gathering together of the waters called he Seas: and God saw that *it was* good.

11 And God said, Let the earth bring forth grass, the herb yielding seed, *and* the fruit tree yielding fruit after his kind, whose seed *is* in itself, upon the earth: and it was so.

12 And the earth brought forth grass, *and* herb yielding seed after his kind, and the tree yielding fruit, whose seed *was* in itself, after his kind: and God saw the *it was* good.

13 And the evening and the morning were the third day.

14 And God said, Let there be lights in the firmament of the heaven to divide the day from the night; and let them be for signs, and for seasons, and for days, and years:

15 And let them be for lights in the firmament of the heaven to give light upon the earth: and it was so.

16 And God made two great lights; the greater light to rule the day, and the lesser light to rule the night: *he made* the stars also.

17 And God set them in the firmament of the heaven to give light upon the earth,

18 And to rule over the day and over the night, and to divide the light from the darkness: and God saw that *it was* good.

19 And the evening and the morning were the fourth day.

20 And God said, Let the waters bring forth abundantly the moving creature that hath life, and fowl *that* may fly above the earth in the open firmament of heaven.

21 And God created great whales, and every living creature that moveth, which the waters brought forth abundantly, after their kind, and every winged fowl after his kind: and God saw that *it was* good.

22 And God blessed them, saying, Be fruitful, and multiply, and fill the waters in the seas, and let fowl multiply in the earth.

23 And the evening and the morning were the fifth day.

24 And God said, Let the earth bring forth the living creature after his kind, cattle, and creeping thing, and beast of the earth after his kind: and it was so.

25 And God made the beast of the earth after his kind, and cattle after their kind, and every thing that creepeth upon the earth after his kind: and God saw that *it was* good.

26 And God said, Let us make man in our image, after our likeness: and let them have dominion over the fish of the sea, and over the fowl of the air, and over the cattle, and over all the earth, and over every creeping thing that creepeth upon the earth.

27 So God created man in his *own* image, in the image of God created he him; male and female created he them.

28 And God blessed them, and God said unto them, Be fruitful, and multiply, and replenish the earth, and subdue it: and have dominion over the fish of the sea, and over the fowl of the air, and over very living thing that moveth upon the earth.

29 And God said, Behold, I have given you every herb bearing seed, which *is* upon the face of all the earth, and every tree, in the which *is* the fruit of a tree yielding seed; to you it shall be for meat.

30 And to every beast of the earth, and to every fowl of the air, and to every thing that creepeth upon the earth, wherein *there is* life, *I have given* every green herb for meat: and it was so.

31 And God saw every thing that he had made, and, behold, *it was* very good. And the evening and the morning were the sixth day.

CHAPTER 2

Thus the heavens and the earth were finished, and all the host of them.

2 And on the seventh day God ended his work which he had made; and he rested on the seventh day from all his work which he had made.

3 And God blessed the seventh day, and sanctified it: because that in it he had rested from all his work which God created and made.

4 There *are* the generations of the heavens and of the earth when they were created, in the day that the LORD God made the earth and the heavens,

5 And every plant of the field before it was in the earth, and every herb of the field before it grew: for the LORD God had not caused it to rain upon the earth, and *there was* not a man to till the ground.

6 But there went up a mist from the earth, and watered the whole face of the ground.

7 And the LORD God formed man *of* the dust of the ground, and breathed into his nostrils the breath of life; and man became a living soul.

8 And the LORD God planted a garden eastward in Eden; and there he put the man whom he had formed.

9 And out of the ground made the LORD God to grow every tree that is pleasant to sight, and good for food; the tree of life also in the midst of the garden, and the tree of knowledge of good and evil.

10 And a river went out of Eden to water the garden; and from thence it was parted, and became into four heads.

11 The name of the first *is* Pí-son: that *is* it which compasseth the whole land of Hav́-i-lah, where *there* is gold;

12 And the gold of that land *is* good: there *is* bdellium and the onyx stone.

13 And the name of the second river *is* Gí-hon: the same *is* it that compasseth the whole land of E-thi-ó-pi-a.

14 And the name of the third river *is* Hid́-de-kel: that *is* it which goeth toward the east of Assyria. And the fourth river *is* Eu-phrá-tes.

15 And the LORD God took the man, and put him into the garden of Eden to dress it and keep it.

16 And the LORD God commanded the man, saying, Of every tree of the garden thou mayest freely eat:

17 But of the tree of the knowledge of good and evil, thou shalt not eat of it: for in the day that thou eatest thereof thou shalt surely die.

18 And the LORD God said, *It is* not good that the man should be alone; I will make him an help meet for him.

19 And out of the ground the LORD God formed every beast of the field, and every fowl of the air; and brought *them* unto Adam to see what he would call them: and whatsoever Adam called every living creature, that *was* the name thereof.

20 And Adam gave names to all cattle, and to the fowl of the air, and to every beast of the field; but for Adam there was not found an help meet for him.

21 And the LORD God caused a deep sleep to fall upon Adam, and he slept: and he took one of his ribs, and closed up the flesh instead thereof;

22 And the rib which the LORD God had taken from man, made he a woman, and brought her unto the man.

23 And Adam said, This *is* now bone of my bones, and flesh of my flesh: she shall be called Woman, because she was taken out of Man.

24 Therefore shall a man leave his father and his mother, and shall cleave unto his wife: and they shall be one flesh.

25 And they were both naked, the man and his wife, and were not ashamed.

CHARLES DARWIN

The Descent of Man

CHARLES DARWIN (1809–1882) was an English naturalist whose theory of evolution formed the basis for modern evolutionary theory. He suffered most of his life from poor health; he was a reclusive man who shied away from the controversy that raged even then over the conflict between evolutionary theory and some religious doctrines.

NATURAL Selection.—We have now seen that man is variable in body and mind; and that the variations are induced, either directly or indirectly, by the same general causes, and obey the same general laws, as with the lower animals. Man has spread widely over the face of the earth, and must have been exposed, during his incessant migrations, to the most diversified conditions. The inhabitants of Tierra del Fuego, the Cape of Good Hope, and Tasmania in the one hemisphere, and of the Arctic regions in the other, must have passed through many climates, and changed their habits many times, before they reached their present homes. The early progenitors of man must also have tended, like all other animals, to have increased beyond their means of subsistence; they must, therefore, occasionally have been exposed to a struggle for existence, and consequently to the rigid law of natural selection. Beneficial variations of all kinds will thus, either occasionally or habitually, have been preserved and injurious ones eliminated. I do not refer to strongly marked deviations of structure, which occur only at long intervals of time, but to mere individual differences. We know, for instance, that the muscles of our hands and feet, which determine our powers of movement, are liable, like those of the lower animals, to incessant variability. If then the progenitors of man inhabiting any district, especially one undergoing some change in its conditions, were divided into two equal bodies, the one-half which included all the individuals best adapted by their powers of movement for gaining subsistence, or for defending themselves, would on an average survive in greater numbers, and procreate more offspring than the other and less well endowed half.

Man in the rudest state in which he now exists is the most dominant animal that has ever appeared on this earth. He has spread more widely than any other highly organized form: and all others have yielded before him. He manifestly owes this immense superiority to his intellectual faculties, to his social habits, which lead him to aid and defend his fellows, and to his corporeal structure. The supreme importance of these characters has been proved by the final arbitrament of the battle for life. Through his powers of intellect, articulate language has been evolved; and on this his wonderful advancement has mainly depended. As Mr. Chauncey Wright remarks: "a psychological analysis of the faculty of language shows, that even the smallest proficiency in it might require more brain power than the greatest proficiency in any other direction." He has invented and is able to use various weapons, tools, traps, etc., with which he defends himself, kills or catches prey, and otherwise obtains food. He has made rafts or canoes for fishing or crossing over to neighboring fertile islands. He has discovered the art of making fire, by which hard and stringy roots can be rendered innocuous. This discovery of fire, probably the greatest ever made by man, excepting language, dates from before the dawn of history. These several inventions, by which man in the rudest state has become so preeminent, are the direct results of the development of his powers of observation, memory, curiosity, imagination, and reason. I cannot, therefore, understand how it is that Mr. Wallace maintains, that "natural selection could only have endowed the savage with a brain a little superior to that of an ape."

Although the intellectual powers and social habits of man are of paramount importance to him, we must not underrate the importance of his bodily structure, to which subject the remainder of this chapter will be devoted; . . .

If it be an advantage to man to stand firmly on his feet and to have his hands and arms free, of which, from his preeminent success in the battle of life, there can be no doubt, then I can see no reason why it should not have been advantageous to the progenitors of man to have become more and more erect or bipedal. They would thus have been better able to defend themselves with stones or clubs, to attack their prey, or otherwise to obtain food. The best built individuals would in the long run have succeeded best and survived in larger numbers. If the gorilla and a few allied forms had become extinct, it might have been argued, with great force and appar-

ent truth, that an animal could not have been gradually converted from a quadruped into a biped, as all the individuals in an intermediate condition would have been miserably ill-fitted for progression. But we know (and this is well worthy of reflection) that the anthropomorphous apes are now actually in an intermediate condition; and no one doubts that they are on the whole well adapted for their conditions of life. Thus the gorilla runs with a sidelong shambling gait, but more commonly progresses by resting on its bent hands. The long-armed apes occasionally use their arms like crutches, swinging their bodies forward between them, and some kinds of Hylobates, without having been taught, can walk or run upright with tolerable quickness; yet they move awkwardly and much less securely than man. We see, in short, in existing monkeys a manner of progression intermediate between that of a quadruped and a biped; but, as an unprejudiced judge insists, the anthropomorphous apes approach in structure more nearly to the bipedal than to the quadrupedal type.

As the progenitors of man became more and more erect, with their hands and arms more and more modified for prehension and other purposes, with their feet and legs at the same time transformed for firm support and progression, endless other changes of structure would have become necessary. The pelvis would have to be broadened, the spine peculiarly curved, and the head fixed in an altered position, all of which changes have been attained by man. . . .

The free use of the arms and hands, partly the cause and partly the result of man's erect position, appears to have led in an indirect manner to other modifications of structure. The early male forefathers of man were, as previously stated, probably furnished with great canine teeth; but as they gradually acquired the habit of using stones, clubs, or other weapons for fighting with their enemies or rivals they would use their jaws and teeth less and less. In this case the jaws, together with the teeth, would become reduced in size, as we may feel almost sure from innumerable analogous cases. In a future chapter we shall meet with a closely parallel case in the reduction or complete disappearance of the canine teeth in male ruminants, apparently in relation with the development of their horns; and in horses in relation to their habits of fighting with their incisor teeth and hoofs. . . .

Another most conspicuous difference between man and the lower animals is the nakedness of his skin. Whales and porpoises (Cetacea), dugongs (Sirenia) and the hippopotamus are naked; and this may be advantageous to them for gliding through the water; nor would it be injurious to them from the loss of warmth, as the species which inhabit the colder regions are protected by a thick layer of blubber, serving the same purposes as the fur of seals and otters. Elephants and rhinoceroses are almost hairless; and as certain extinct species, which formerly lived under an Arctic climate, were covered with long wool or hair, it would almost appear as if the existing species of both genera had lost their hairy covering from exposure to heat. This appears the more probable, as the elephants in India which live on elevated and cool districts are more hairy than those on the lowlands. May we then infer that man became divested of hair from having aboriginally inhabited some tropical land? That the hair is chiefly retained in the male sex on the chest and face, and in both sexes at the junction of all four limbs with the trunk,

favors this inference—on the assumption that the hair was lost before man became erect; for the parts which now retain most hair would then have been most protected from the heat of the sun. The crown of the head, however, offers a curious exception, for at all times it must have been one of the most exposed parts, yet is thickly clothed with hair. The fact, however, that the other members of the order of Primates, to which man belongs, although inhabiting various hot regions, are well clothed with hair, generally thickest on the upper surface, is opposed to the supposition that man became naked through the action of the sun. Mr. Belt believes that within the tropics it is an advantage to man to be destitute of hair, as he is thus enabled to free himself of the multitude of ticks (acari) and other parasites, with which he is often infested, and which sometimes cause ulceration. But whether this evil is of sufficient magnitude to have led to the denudation of his body through natural selection, may be doubted, since none of the many quadrupeds inhabiting the tropics have, as far as I know, acquired any specialized means of relief. The view which seems to me the most probable is that man, or rather primarily woman, became divested of hair for ornamental purposes, as we shall see under Sexual Selection; and, according to this belief, it is not surprising that man should differ so greatly in hairiness from all other Primates, for characters, gained through sexual selection, often differ to an extraordinary degree in closely related forms. . . .

I have now endeavored to show that some of the most distinctive characters of man have in all probability been acquired, either directly, or more commonly indirectly, through natural selection. We should bear in mind that modifications in structure or constitution which do not serve to adapt an organism to its habits of life, to the food which it consumes, or passively to the surrounding conditions, cannot have been thus acquired. We must not, however, be too confident in deciding what modifications are of service to each being; we should remember how little we know about the use of many parts, or what changes in the blood or tissues may serve to fit an organism for a new climate or new kinds of food. Nor must we forget the principle of correlation, by which, as Isidore Geoffroy has shown in the case of man, many strange deviations of structure are tied together. Independently of correlation, a change in one part often leads, through the increased or decreased use of other parts, to other changes of a quite unexpected nature. It is also well to reflect on such facts, as the wonderful growth of galls on plants caused by the poison of an insect, and on the remarkable changes of color in the plumage of parrots when fed on certain fishes, or inoculated with the poison of toads; for we can thus see that the fluids of the system, if altered for some special purpose, might induce other changes. We should especially bear in mind that modifications acquired and continually used during past ages for some useful purpose, would probably become firmly fixed, and might be long inherited.

Thus a large yet undefined extension may safely be given of natural selection; but I now admit, after reading the essay by Nägeli on plants, and the remarks by various authors with respect to animals, more especially those recently made by Prof. Broca, that in the earlier editions of my "Origin of Species" I perhaps attributed too much to the action of natural selection or the survival of the fittest. I have altered the fifth edition of the "Origin" so as to confine my remarks to adaptive changes of structure; but I am convinced, from the light gained during even the last few years, that very many structures which now appear to us as useless, will hereafter be proved to be useful, and will therefore come within the range of natural selection. Nevertheless, I did not formerly consider sufficiently the existence of structures, which, as far as we can at present judge, are neither beneficial nor injurious; and this I believe to be one of the greatest oversights as yet detected in my work. I may be permitted to say, as some excuse, that I had two distinct objects in view; firstly, to show that species had not been separately created, and secondly, that natural selection had been the chief agent of change, though largely aided by the inherited effects of habit, and slightly by the direct action of the surrounding conditions. I was not, however, able to annul the influence of my former belief, then almost universal, that each species had been purposely created; and this led to my tacit assumption that every detail of structure, excepting rudiments, was of some special though unrecognized, service. Any one with this assumption in his mind would naturally extend too far the action of natural selection, either during past or present times. Some of those who admit the principle of evolution, but reject natural selection, seem to forget, when criticizing my book, that I had the above two objects in view; hence, if I have erred in giving to natural selection great power, which I am very far from admitting, or in having exaggerated its power, which is in itself probable, I have at least, as I hope, done good service in aiding to overthrow the dogma of separate creations. . . .

Conclusion.—In this chapter we have seen that as man at the present day is liable, like every other animal, to multiform individual differences or slight variations, so no doubt were the early progenitors of man; the variations being formerly induced by the same general causes, and governed by the same general and complex laws as at present. As all animals tend to multiply beyond their means of subsistence, so it must have been with the progenitors of man; and this would inevitably lead to a struggle for existence and to natural selection. The latter process would be greatly aided by the inherited effects of the increased use of parts, and these two processes would incessantly react on each other. It appears, also, as we shall hereafter see, that various unimportant characters have been acquired by man through sexual selection. An unexplained residuum of change must be left to the assumed uniform action of those unknown agencies, which occasionally induce strongly marked and abrupt deviations of structure in our domestic productions.

Judging from the habits of savages and of the greater number of the Quadrumana, primeval men, and even their ape-like progenitors, probably lived in society. With strictly social animals, natural selection sometimes acts on the individual, through the preservation of variations which are beneficial to the community. A community which includes a large number of well-endowed individuals increases in number, and is victorious over other less favored ones; even although each separate member gains no advantage over the others of the same community. Associated insects have thus acquired many remarkable structures, which are of little or no service to the individual, such as the pollen-collecting apparatus, or the sting of the worker-bee, or the great jaws of soldier-ants. With the higher social animals, I am not aware that any structure has been modified solely for the good of the community, though some are of secondary service to it. For instance, the horns of ruminants and the great canine teeth of baboons appear to have been acquired by the males as weapons for sexual strife, but they are used in defense of the herd or troop. In regard to certain mental powers the case, as we shall see in the fifth chapter, is wholly different; for these faculties have been chiefly, or even exclusively, gained for the benefit of the community, and the individuals thereof have at the same time gained an advantage indirectly.

It has often been objected to such views as the foregoing, that man is one of the most helpless and defenseless creatures in the world; and that during his early and less well developed condition he would have been still more helpless. The Duke of Argyll, for instance, insists that "the human frame has diverged from the structure of brutes in the direction of greater physical helplessness and weakness. That is to say, it is a divergence which of all others it is most impossible to ascribe to mere natural selection." He adduces the naked and unprotected state of the body, the absence of great teeth or claws for defense, the small strength and speed of man, and his slight power of discovering food or of avoiding danger by smell. To these deficiencies there might be added one still more serious, namely, that he cannot climb quickly and so escape from enemies. The loss of hair would not have been a great injury to the inhabitants of a warm country. For we know that the unclothed Fuegians can exist under a wretched climate. When we compare the defenseless state of man with that of apes we must remember that the great canine teeth with which the latter are provided are possessed in their full development by the males alone, and are chiefly used by them for fighting with the rivals; yet the females, which are not thus provided, manage to survive.

In regard to bodily size or strength, we do not know whether man is descended from some small species, like the chimpanzee, or from one as powerful as the gorilla; and, therefore, we cannot say whether man has become larger and stronger, or smaller and weaker than his ancestors. We should, however, bear in mind that an animal possessing great size, strength, and ferocity, and which, like the gorilla, could defend itself from all enemies, would not perhaps have become social: and this would most effectually have checked the acquirement of the higher mental qualities, such as sympathy and the love of his fellows. Hence it might have been an immense advantage to man to have sprung from some comparatively weak creature.

The small strength and speed of man, his want of natural weapons, etc., are more than counterbalanced, firstly, by his intellectual powers, through which he has formed for himself weapons, tools, etc., though still remaining in a barbarous state, and secondly, by his social qualities which lead him to give and receive aid from his fellow-men. No country in the world abounds in a greater degree with dangerous beasts than Southern Africa; no country presents more fearful physical hardships than the Arctic regions; yet one of the puniest of races, that of the Bushmen, maintains itself in Southern Africa, as do the dwarfed Esquimaux in the Arctic regions. The ancestors of man were, no doubt, inferior in intellect, and probably in social disposition to the lowest existing savages; but it is quite conceivable that they might have existed, or even flourished, if they had advanced in intellect, while gradually losing their brute-like powers, such as that of climbing trees, etc. But these ancestors would not have been exposed to any special danger, even if far more helpless and defenseless than any existing savages, had they inhabited some warm continent or large island, such as Australia, New Guinea, or Borneo, which is now the home of the orang. And natural selection arising from the competition of tribe with tribe in some such large area as one of these, together with the inherited effects of habit, would, under favorable conditions, have sufficed to raise man to his present high position on the organic scale.

DUANE T. GISH

Creationist Science and Education

DUANE T. GISH *received his Ph.D. in biochemistry from the University of California. He has been a National Institute of Health Fellow and has held a number of research positions. He is currently Associate Director of the Institute for Creation Research, founded by Henry Morris, in El Cajon, California.*

IT is commonly believed that the theory of evolution is the only scientific explanation of origins and that the theory of special creation is based solely on religious beliefs. It is further widely accepted that the theory of evolution is supported by such a vast body of scientific evidence, while encountering so few contradictions, that evolution should be accepted as an established fact. As a consequence, it is maintained by many educators that the theory of evolution should be accepted as an established fact. As a consequence, it is maintained by many educators that the theory of evolution should be included in science textbooks as the sole explanation for origins but that the theory of special creation, if taught at all, must be restricted to social science courses.

As a matter of fact, neither evolution nor creation qualifies as a scientific theory. Furthermore, it is become increasingly apparent that there are a number of irresolvable contradictions between evolution theory and the facts of science, and that the mechanism postulated for the evolutionary process could account for no more than trivial changes.

It would be well at this point to define what we mean by creation and evolution. By *Creation* we are referring to the theory that the universe and all life forms came into existence by the direct creative acts of a Creator external to and independent of the natural universe. It is postulated that the basic plant and animal kinds were separately created, and that any variation or speciation that has occurred since creation has been limited within the circumscribed boundaries of these created kinds. It is further postulated that the earth has suffered at least one great world-wide catastrophic event or flood which would account for the mass death, destruction, and extinction found on such a monumental scale in geological deposits.

By *Evolution* we are referring to the General Theory of Evolution. This is the theory that all living things have arisen by naturalistic, mechanistic processes from a single primeval cell, which in turn had arisen by similar processes from a dead, inanimate world. This evolutionary process is postulated to have occurred over a period of many hundreds of millions of years. It is further postulated that all major geological formations can be explained by present processes acting essentially at present rates without resort to any world-wide catastrophe(s).

Creation has not been observed by human witnesses. Since creation would have involved unique, unrepeatable historical events, creation is not subject to the experimental method. Furthermore, creation as a theory is non-falsifiable.

That is, it is impossible to conceive an experiment that could disprove the possibility of creation. Creation thus does not fulfill the criteria of a scientific theory. That does not say anything about its ultimate validity, of course. Furthermore, creation theory can be used to correlate and explain data, particularly that available from the fossil record, and is thus subject to test in the same manner that other alleged historical events are subject to test—by comparison with historical evidence.

Evolution theory also fails to meet the criteria of a scientific theory. Evolution has never been witnessed by human observers; evolution is not subject to the experimental method; and as formulated by present-day evolutionists, it has become non-falsifiable.

It is obvious that no one has ever witnessed the type of evolutionary changes postulated by the general theory of evolution. No one, for example, witnessed the origin of the universe or the origin of life. No one has ever seen a fish evolve into an amphibian, nor has anyone observed an ape evolve into a man. No one, as a matter of fact, has ever witnessed a significant evolutionary change of any kind.

The example of the peppered moth in England has been cited by such authorities as H. B. D. Kettlewell and Sir Gavin De Beer as the most striking evolutionary change ever witnessed by man. Prior to the industrial revolution in England, the peppered moth, *Biston betularia,* consisted predominantly of a light-colored variety, with a dark-colored form comprising a small minority of the population. This was so because predators (birds) could more easily detect the dark-colored variety as these moths rested during the day on light-covered rocks. With the on-set of the industrial revolution and resultant air pollution, the tree trunks and rocks became progressively darker. As a consequence, the dark-colored variety of moths became more and more difficult to detect, while the light-colored variety ultimately became an easy prey. Birds, therefore, began eating more light-colored than dark-colored moths, and today over 95% of the peppered moths in the industrial areas of England are of the darker-colored variety.

Although, as noted above, this shift in populations of peppered moths has been described as the most striking example of evolution ever observed by man, it is obvious that no significant evolutionary change of any kind has occurred among these peppered moths, certainly not the type required to substantiate the general theory of evolution. For however the populations may have shifted in their proportions of the light and dark forms, all of the moths remained from beginning to end peppered moths, *Biston betularia.* It seems evident, then, that if this example is the most striking example of evolution witnessed by man, no real evolution of any kind has even been observed

The world-famous evolutionist, Theodosis Dobzhansky, while endeavoring to proclaim his faith in evolution, admitted that no real evolutionary change has ever been observed by man when he said, ". . . the occurrence of the evolution of life in the history of the earth is established about as well as events *not witnessed by human observers can be.*" It can be said with certainty, then, that evolution in the present world has never been observed. It remains as far outside the pale of human observation as the origin of the universe or the origin of life. Evolution has been *postulated* but *never observed.*

Since evolution cannot be observed, it is not amenable to the methods of experimental science. This has been acknowledged by Dobzhansky when he stated, "These evolutionary happenings are unique, unrepeatable, and irreversible. It is as impossible to turn a land vertibrate into a fish as it is to effect the reverse transformation. The applicability of the experimental method to the study of such unique historical processes is severely restricted before all else by the time intervals involved, which far exceed the lifetime of any human experimenter. And yet it is just such *impossibility* that is demanded by antievolutionists when they ask for 'proofs' of evolution which they would magnanimously accept as satisfactory."

Please note that Dobzhansky has said that the applicability of the experimental method to the study of evolution is an impossibility! It is obvious, then, that evolution fails to qualify as a scientific theory, for it is certain that a theory that cannot be subjected to experimental test is not a scientific theory.

Furthermore, modern evolution theory has become so plastic, it is non-falsifiable. It can be used to prove anything and everything. Thus, Murray Eden, a professor at Massachusetts Institute of Technology and an evolutionist, has said, with reference to the falsifiability of evolution theory, "This cannot be done in evolution, taking it in its broad sense, and this is really all I meant when I called it tautologous in the first place. It can, indeed, explain anything. You may be ingenious or not in proposing a mechanism which looks plausible to human beings and mechanisms which are consistent with other mechanisms which you have discovered, but it is still an unfalsifiable theory."

Paul Ehrlich and L.C. Birch, biologists at Stanford University and the University of Sydney, respectively, have said, "Our theory of evolution has become . . . one which cannot be refuted by any possible observations. Every conceivable observation can be fitted into it. It is thus 'outside of empirical science' but not necessarily false. No one can think of ways in which to test it. Ideas, either without basis or based on a few laboratory experiments carried out in extremely simplified systems, have attained currency far beyond their validity. They have become part of an evolutionary dogma accepted by most of us as part of our training."

Some evolutionists have been candid enough to admit that evolution is really no more scientific than is creation. In an article in which he states his conviction that the modern neo-Darwinian theory of evolution is based on axioms, Harris says ". . . the axiomatic nature of the neo-Darwinian theory places the debate between evolutionists and creationists in a new perspective. Evolutionists have often challenged creationists to provide experimental proof that species have been fashioned *de novo*. Creationists have often demanded that evolutionists show how chance mutations can lead to adaptability, or to explain why natural selection allows apparently detrimental organs to persist. We may now recognize that either challenge is fair. If the neo-Darwinian theory is axiomatic, it is not valid for creationists to demand proof of the axioms, and it is not valid for evolutionists to dismiss special creation as unproved so long as it is stated as an axiom."

In his introduction to a 1971 edition of Charles Darwin's *Origin of Species,* Matthews states, "In accepting evolution as a fact, how many biologists pause to reflect that science is built upon theories that have been proved by experiment to be correct, or remember that the theory of animal evolution has never been thus proved? . . . The fact of evolution is the backbone of biology, and biology is thus in the peculiar position of being a science founded on an unproved theory—is it then a science or a faith? Belief in the theory of evolution is thus exactly parallel to belief in creation—both are concepts which believers know to be true but neither, up to the present, has been capable of proof."

It can be seen from the above discussion, taken from the scientific literature published by leading evolutionary authorities, that evolution has never been observed and is outside the limits of experimental science. Evolution theory is, therefore, no more scientific than creation theory. That does not make it necessarily false, and it can be tested in the same way that creation theory can be tested—by its ability to correlate and explain historical data, that is, the fossil record. Furthermore, since evolution is supposed to have occurred by processes still operating today, the theory must not contradict natural laws.

Evolutionists protest, of course, that these weaknesses of evolution as a theory are not necessarily due to weaknesses of the theory, per se, but are inherent in the very nature of the evolutionary process. It is claimed that the evolutionary process is so slow that it simply cannot be observed during the lifetime of a human experimenter, or, as a matter of fact, during the combined observations of all recorded human experience. Thus, as noted above, Dobzhansky is incensed that creationists should demand that evolution be subjected to the experimental method before any consideration could be given to evolution as an established process.

It must be emphasized, however, that it is for precisely this reason that evolutionists insist that creation must be excluded from science textbooks or, for that matter, from the whole realm of science, as a viable alternative evolution. They insist that creation must be excluded from possible consideration as a scientific explanation for origins because creation theory cannot be tested by the experimental method. It is evident, however, that this is a characteristic that it shares in common with evolution theory. Thus, if creation must be excluded from science texts and discussions, then evolution must likewise be excluded.

Evolutionists insist that, in any case, the teaching of the creation model would constitute the teaching of religion because creation requires a Creator. The teaching about the creation model and the scientific evidence supporting it, however, can be done without reference to any religious literature. Furthermore, belief in evolution is as intrinsically religious as is belief in creation.

If creation must be excluded from science in general and from science textbooks and science classrooms in particular because it involves the supernatural, it is obvious that theistic evolution must be excluded for exactly the same reason. Thus the only theory that can be taught according to this reasoning, and in fact, the only theory that is being taught in almost all public schools and universities and in the texts they use, is a purely mechanistic, naturalistic, and thus atheistic, theory of evolution. But atheism, the antithesis of theism, is itself a religious belief.

The late Sir Julian Huxley, British evolutionist and biologist, has said that "Gods are peripheral phenomena produced by evolution." What Huxley meant was that the idea of God merely evolved as man evolved from lower animals. Huxley desired to establish a humanistic religion based on evolution. Humanism has been defined as "the belief that man shapes his own destiny. It is a constructive philosophy, a *nontheistic religion,* a way of life." This same publication quotes Huxley as saying, "I use the word 'Humanist' to mean someone who believes that man is just as much a natural phenomenon as an animal or plant; that his body, mind, and soul were not supernaturally created but are products of *evolution,* and that he is not under the control or guidance of any supernatural being or beings, but has to rely on himself and his own powers." The inseparable link between this nontheistic humanistic religion and belief in evolution is evident.

George Gaylord Simpson, Professor of Vertebrate Paleontology at Harvard University until his retirement and one of the world's best-known evolutionists, has said that the Christian faith, which he calls the "higher superstition" (in contrast to the "lower superstition" of pagan tribes of South America and Africa) is intellectually unacceptable. Simpson concludes his book, *Life of the Past,* with what Sir Julian Huxley has called "a splendid assertion of evolutionist view of man." "Man," Simpson writes, "stands alone in the universe, a unique product of a long, unconscious, impersonal, material process with unique understanding and potentialities. These he owes to no one but himself, and it is to himself that he is responsible. He is not the creature of uncontrollable and undeterminable forces, but his own master. He can and must decide and manage his own destiny."

Thus, according to Simpson, man is alone in the Universe (there is not God), he is the result of an impersonal, unconscious process (no one directed his origin or creation), and he is his own master and must manage his own destiny (there is no God to determine man's destiny). That, according to Simpson and Huxley, is the evolutionist's view of man. That this is the philosophy held by most biologists has been recently emphasized by Dobzhansky. In his review of Monod's book, *Chance and Necessity,* Dobzhansky said, "He has stated with admirable clarity, and eloquence often verging on pathos, the mechanistic materialist philosophy shared by most of the present 'establishment' in the biological science."

No doubt a majority of the scientific community embraces the mechanistic materialistic philosophy of Simpson, Huxley, and Monod. Many of these men are highly intelligent, and they have woven the fabric of evolution theory in an ingenious fashion. They have then combined this evolution theory with humanistic philosophy and have clothed the whole with the term "science." The product, a non-theistic religion, with evolutionary philosophy as its creed under the guise of "science," is being taught in most public schools, colleges and universities of the United States. It has become our unofficial state-sanctioned religion.

Furthermore, a growing number of scientists are becoming convinced that there are basic contradictions between evolution theory and empirical scientific data as well as known scientific laws. On the other hand, these scientists believe special creation provides an excellent model for explaining the correlating data related to origins which is free of such contradictions. Even some evolutionists are beginning to realize that the formulations of modern evolution theory are really incapable of explaining anything and that an adequate scientific theory of evolution, if ever attainable, must await the discovery of as yet unknown natural laws.

The core of modern evolution theory, known as the neo-Darwinian theory of evolution, or the modern synthetic theory, is the hypothesis that the evolutionary process has occurred through natural selection of random mutational changes in the genetic material, selection being in accordance with alterations in the environment. Natural selection, itself, is not a chance process, but the material it must act on, mutant genes, is produced by random, chance processes.

It is an astounding fact that while at the time Darwin popularized it, the concept of natural selection seemed to explain so much, today there is a growing realization that the presently accepted concept of natural selection really explains nothing. It is a mere tautology, that is, it involves circular reasoning.

In modern theory, natural selection is defined in terms of differential reproduction. In fact, according to Lewontin, differential reproduction *is* natural selection. When it is asked, what survives, the answer is, the fittest. But when it is asked, what are the fittest, the answer is, those that survive! Natural selection thus collapses into a tautology, devoid of explanatory value. It is not possible to explain *why* some varieties live to reproduce more offspring—it is only known that they do.

In discussing Richard Levins' concept of fitness set analysis, Hamilton stated, "This criticism amounts to restating what I think is the admission of most evolutionists, that we do not yet know what natural selection maximizes." Now if evolutionists do not know what natural selection maximizes, they do not know what natural selection selects.

In a review of the thinking in French scientific circles, it was stated, "Even if they do not publicly take a definite stand, almost all French specialists hold today strong mental reservations as to the validity of natural selection." Creationists maintain that indeed natural selection could not result in increased complexity or convert a plant or animal into another basic kind. It can only act to eliminate the unfit.

Macbeth has recently published an especially incisive criticism of evolution theory and of the concept of natural selection as used by evolutionists. He points out that although evolutionists have abandoned classical Darwinism, the modern synthetic theory they have proposed as a substitute is equally inadequate to explain progressive change as a result of natural selection, and, as a matter of fact, they cannot even define natural selection in non-tautological terms. Inadequacies of the present theory and failure of the fossil record to substantiate predictions based on the theory leave macro-evolution, and even micro-evolution, intractable mysteries according to Macbeth. Macbeth suggests that no theory at all may be preferable to the present theory of evolution.

Using Macbeth's work as the starting point for his own investigation of modern evolution theory, Bethell, a graduate of Oxford with a major in philosophy, has expressed his complete dissatisfaction with the present formulations of evolution theory and natural selection from the viewpoint of the philosophy of science. Both Macbeth and Bethell present excellent reviews of the thinking of leading evolutionists concerning the relationship of natural selection to evolution theory. While both are highly critical, neither profess to be creationists.

According to modern evolutionary theory, ultimately all of the evolution is due to mutations. Mutations are random changes in the genes or chromosomes which are highly ordered structures. Any process that occurs by random chance events is subject to the laws of probability.

It is possible to estimate mutation rates. It is also possible to estimate how many favorable mutations would be required to bring about certain evolutionary changes. Assuming that these mutations produced in a random, chance manner, as is true in the Neo-Darwinian interpretation of evolution, it is possible to calculate how long such an evolutionary process would have required to convert an amoeba into a man. When this is done, according to a group of mathematicians, all of whom are evolutionists, the answer turns out to be billions of times longer than the assumed five billion years of earth history!

One of these mathematicians, Murray Eden, stated, "It is our contention that if 'random' is given a serious and crucial interpretation from a probabilistic point of view, the randomness postulate is highly implausible and that an *adequate scientific theory of evolution must await the discovery and elucidation of new natural laws—physical, physico-chemical, and biological."* What Eden and these mathematicians are saying is that the modern neo-Darwinian theory of evolution is totally inadequate to explain more than trivial change and thus we simply have no basis at present for attempting to explain how evolution may have occurred. As a matter of fact, based on the assumption that the evolutionary process was dependent upon random chance processes, we can simply state that evolution would have been impossible.

Furthermore, evolution theory contradicts one of the most firmly established laws known to science, the Second Law of Thermodynamics. The obvious contradiction between evolu-

tion and the Second Law of Thermodynamics becomes evident when we compare the definition of this Law and its consequences by several scientists (all of whom, as far as we know, accept evolutionary philosophy) with the definition of evolution by Sir Julian Huxley, biologist and one of the best-known spokesmen for evolution theory.

> There is a general natural tendency of all observed systems to go from order to disorder, reflecting dissipation of energy available for future transformations—the law of increasing entropy.

> All real processes go with an increase of entropy. The entropy also measures the randomness, or lack of orderliness of the system: the greater the randomness, the greater the entropy.

Another way of stating the second law then is: 'The universe is constantly getting more disorderly!' Viewed that way, we can see the second law all about us. We have to work hard to straighten a room, but left to itself it becomes a mess again very quickly and very easily. Even if we never enter it, it becomes dusty and musty. How difficult to maintain houses, and machinery, and our own bodies in perfect working order: how easy to let them deteriorate. In fact, all we have to do is nothing, and everything deteriorates, collapses, breaks down, wears out, all by itself—and that is what the second law is all about.

Now compare these definitions or consequences of the Second Law of Thermodynamics to the theory of evolution as defined by Huxley:

> Evolution in the extended sense can be defined as a directional and essentially irreversible process occurring in time, which in its course gives rise to an

increase of variety and an increasingly high level of organization in its products. Our present knowledge indeed forces us to the view that the whole of reality is evolution—a single process of self-transformation.

There is a natural tendency, then, for all observed natural systems to go from order to disorder, towards increasing randomness. This is true throughout the entire known universe, both at the micro and macro levels. This tendency is so invariant that it has never been observed to fail. It is a natural law—the Second Law of Thermodynamics.

On the other hand, according to the general theory of evolution, as defined by Huxley, there is a general tendency of natural systems to go from disorder to order, towards an ever higher and higher level of complexity. This tendency supposedly operates in every corner of the universe, both at the micro and macro levels. As a consequence, it is believed, particles have evolved into people.

It is difficult to understand how a discerning person could fail to see the basic contradiction between these two processes. It seems apparent that both cannot be true, but no modern scientist would dare challenge the validity of the Second Law of Thermodynamics.

The usual, but exceedingly naive, answer given by evolutionists to this dilemma is that the Second Law of Thermodynamics applies only to closed systems. If the system is open to an external source of energy, it is asserted, complexity can be generated and maintained within this system at the expense of the energy supplied to it from the outside.

Thus, our solar system is an open system, and energy is supplied to the earth from the sun. The decrease in entropy, or increase in order, on the earth

during the evolutionary process, it is said, has been more than compensated by the increase in entropy, or decrease in order, on the sun. The overall result has been a net decrease in order, so the Second Law of Thermodynamics has not been violated, we are told.

An open system and an adequate external source of energy are necessary *but not sufficient* conditions, however, for order to be generated and maintained, since raw, undirected, uncontrolled energy is destructive, not constructive. For example, without the protective layer of ozone in the upper atmosphere which absorbs most of the ultraviolet light coming from the sun, life on earth would be impossible. Bacterial cells exposed to such radiation die within seconds. This is because ultraviolet light, or irradiation of any kind, breaks chemical bonds and thus randomizes and destroys the highly complex structures found in biologically active macromolecules, such as proteins and DNA. Biological activity of these vitally important molecules is destroyed and death rapidly follows.

That much more than merely an external energy source is required to form complex molecules and systems from simpler ones is evident from the following statement by Simpson and Beck: ". . . the simple expenditure of energy is not sufficient to develop and maintain order. A bull in a china shop performs work, but he neither creates nor maintains organization. The work needed is *particular* work; it must follow specifications; it requires information on how to proceed."

Thus a green plant, utilizing the highly complex photosynthetic system it possesses, can trap light energy from the sun and convert this light energy into chemical energy. A series of other complex systems within the green plant allows the utilization of this energy to build up complex molecules and systems from simple starting material. Of equal importance is the fact that the green plant possesses a system for directing, maintaining, and replicating these complex energy conversion mechanisms—an incredibly complex genetic system. Without the genetic system, no specifications on how to proceed would exist, chaos would result, and life would be impossible.

For complexity to be generated within a system, then, four conditions must be met:

1. The system must be an open system.
2. An adequate external energy source must be available.
3. The system must possess energy conversion mechanisms.
4. A control mechanism must exist within the system for directing, maintaining, and replicating these energy conversion mechanisms.

The seemingly irresolvable dilemma, from an evolutionary point of view, is, how such complex energy conversion mechanisms and genetic systems arose in the *absence* of such systems, when there is a general natural tendency to go from order to disorder, a tendency so universal it can be stated as a natural law, the Second Law of Thermodynamics. Simply stated, machines are required to build machines, and something or somebody must operate the machinery.

The creationist thus opposes the wholly unscientific evolutionary hypothesis that the natural universe with all of its incredible complexity, was capable of generating itself, and maintains that there must exist, external to the natural universe, a Creator, or supernatural Agent, who was responsible for introducing, or creating, the high degree of order found within this natural universe. While creationism is extra-scientific, it is not anti-scientific, as is the evolutionary hypothesis which contradicts one of the most well-established laws of science.

Finally, but of utmost significance, is the fact that the fossil record is actually hostile to the evolution model, but conforms remarkably well to predictions based on the creation model. Complex forms of life appear abruptly in the fossil record in the so-called Cambrian sedimentary deposits or rocks. Although these animals, which include such highly complex and diverse forms of life as brachiopods, trilobites, worms, jellyfish, sponges, sea urchins, and sea cucumbers, as well as other crustaceans and molluscs, supposedly required about two to three billion years to evolve, not a single ancestor for any of these animals can be found anywhere on the face of the earth. George Gaylord Simpson has characterized the absence of Precambrian fossils as "the major mystery of the history of life." This fact of the fossil record, incomprehensible in the light of the evolution model, is exactly as predicted on the basis of the creation model.

The remainder of the fossil record reveals a remarkable absence of the many transitional forms demanded by the theory of evolution. Gaps between all higher categories of plants and animals, which creationists believe constituted the created kinds, are systematic. For example, Simpson has admitted that "Gaps among known orders, classes, and phyla are systematic and almost always large." Richard B. Goldschmidt, well-known geneticist and a rabid evolutionist, acknowledged that "practically all orders or families known appear suddenly and without any apparent transitions." E. J. H. Corner, Cambridge University botanist and an evolutionist, stated, ". . . I still think, to the unprejudiced, the fossil record of plants is in favor of special creation."

Recently, the well-known evolutionary paleontologist, David B. Kitts, stated, "Despite the bright promise that paleontology provides a means of 'seeing' evolution, it has presented some nasty difficulties for evolutionists the most notorious of which is the presence of 'gaps' in the fossil record. *Evolution requires intermediate forms between species and paleontology does not provide them. . . .*"

Lord Solly Zuckerman, for many years the head of the Department of Anatomy at the University of Birmingham, was first knighted and then later raised to the peerage as recognition of his distinguished career as a research scientist. After over 15 years of research on the subject, with a team that rarely included less than four scientists, Lord Zuckerman concluded that *Australopithecus* did not walk upright, he was not intermediate between ape and man, but that he was merely an anthropoid ape. *Australopithecus* (Louis Leakey's "Nutcracker Man," and Donald Johanson's "Lucy") is an extinct ape-like creature that almost all evolutionists believe walked erect and showed many characteristics intermediate between ape and man. Lord Zuckerman, although not a creationist, believes there is very little, if any, science in the search for man's fossil ancestry. Lord Zuckerman states his conviction, based on a life-time of investigation, that if man has evolved from an ape-like creature he did so without leaving any trace of the transformation in the fossil record. This directly contradicts the popular idea that

paleontologists have found numerous evidences of ape-like ancestors for man, but rather suggests they have found none at all.

The explosive appearance of highly complex forms of life in Cambrian and other rocks with the absence of required ancestors, and the abrupt appearance of each major plant and animal kind without apparent transitional forms are the facts of greatest importance derivable for a study of the fossil record. These facts are highly contradictory to predictions based on the evolution model, but are just as predicted on the basis of the creation model of origins.

The facts described above are some of the reasons why creationists maintain that, on the basis of available scientific evidence, the creation model is not only a viable alternative to the evolution model, but is actually a far superior model. Furthermore, after more than a century of effort to establish Darwinian evolution, even some evolutionists are beginning to express doubts. This is evidently true, for example, of Pierre P. Grassé, one of the most distinguished of French scientists. In his review of Grassé's book, *L'Evolution du Vivant,* Dobzhansky states, "The book of Pierre P. Grassé is a frontal attack on all kinds of 'Darwinism.' Its purpose is 'to destroy the myth of evolution as a simple, understood, and explained phenomenon,' and to show that evolution is a mystery about which little is, and perhaps can be, known. Now, one can disagree with Grassé but not ignore him. He is the most distinguished of French zoologists, the editor of the 28 volumes of 'Traite de Zoologie,' author of numerous original investigations, and ex-president of the Academie des Sciences. His knowledge of the living world is encyclopedic. . . ." In the closing sentence of his review, Dobzhansky says, "The sentence with which Grassé ends his book is disturbing: 'It is possible that in this domain biology, impotent, yields the floor to metaphysics.'"

Grassé thus closes his book with the statement that biology is powerless to explain the origin of living things and that it may possibly have to yield to metaphysics (supernatural creation of some kind).

In his Presidential Address to the Linnaean Society of London, "A Little on Lung-fishes," Errol White said, "But whatever ideas authorities may have on the subject, the lung-fishes, like every other major group of fishes I know, have their origin firmly based in *nothing. . . .*" He then said, "I have often said how little I should like to have to prove organic evolution in a court of law." He closed his address by saying, "We still do not know the mechanics of evolution in spite of the over-confident claims in some quarters, nor are we likely to make further progress in this by the classical methods of paleontology or biology: and we shall certainly not advance matters by jumping up and down shrilling 'Darwin is God and I, So-and-so, am his prophet'—the recent researches of workers like Dean and Hinshelwood (1964) already suggest the possibility of incipient cracks in the seemingly monolithic walls of the Neo-Darwinian Jericho." White thus seems to be suggesting that the modern neo-Darwinian theory of evolution is in danger of crashing down just as did the walls of Jericho!

Thus, today we have a most astounding situation. Evolution has never been observed by human witnesses. Evolution cannot be subjected to the experimental method. The most sacred tenet of Darwinism—natur[...] modern formulation is inc[...] plaining anything. Furtherm[...] some evolutionists are conced[...] the mechanism of evolution prop[...] by evolutionary biologists could a[...] count for no more than trivial change in the time believed to have been available, and that an adequate scientific theory of evolution, based on present knowledge, seems impossible. Finally, the major features of the fossil record accord in an amazing fashion with the predictions based on special creation, but contradict the most fundamental predictions generated by the theory of evolution. And yet the demand is unceasing that evolution theory be accepted as the only scientific explanation for origins, even as an established fact, while excluding creation as a mere religious concept!

This rigid indoctrination in evolutionary dogma, with the exclusion of the competing concept of special creation, results in young people being indoctrinated in a non-theistic, naturalistic, humanistic religious philosophy in the guise of science. Science is perverted, academic freedom is denied, the educational process suffers, and constitutional guarantees of religious freedom are violated.

This unhealthy situation could be corrected by presenting students with the two competing models for origins, the creation model and the evolution model, with all supporting evidence for each model. This would permit an evaluation of the students of the strengths and weaknesses of each model. This is the course true education should pursue rather than following the present process of brain-washing students in evolutionary philosophy.

:tionism

losophy at the University of California, San Diego.
iology, he is author of Abusing Science, the book
ich this selection is excerpted.

BEFORE turning to "scientific" Creationism itself—that is, the theory peddled by the Institute for Creation Research and advertised by the Moral Majority—it is important to distinguish two other forms that a belief in special creation might take. The central idea of strict Creationism is that all kinds of organisms presently existing, and perhaps some more, were formed on the earth in a single event. Some people hold this view purely as an article of religious faith, making no claim that it is a part of science supported by scientific evidence. Such people accept strict Creationism because its central doctrine follows from two other beliefs that they hold: (i) The Bible is to be read literally; (ii) When the Bible is read literally, it says that all kinds of organisms were formed on earth in a single event. I disagree with this view, because I do not believe it is possible, let alone reasonable, to read the Bible literally. (Nor do I think that Christians and Jews are compelled, as sincere believers, to read the Bible literally.) However, I have no intention of criticizing Creationism insofar as it is held as an explicitly religious belief, a belief that is recognized as running counter to the scientific evidence.

There is another way to be a Creationist. One might offer Creationism as a scientific theory: Life did not evolve over millions of years; rather all forms were created at one time by a particular Creator. Although pure versions of Creationism were no longer in vogue among scientists by the end of the eighteenth century, they had flourished earlier (in the writings of Thomas Burnet, William Whiston, and others). Moreover, *variants* of Creationism were supported by a number of eminent nineteenth-century scientists—William Buckland, Adam Sedgwick, and Louis Agassiz, for example. These creationists trusted that their theories would accord with the Bible, interpreted in what they saw as a correct way. However, that fact does not affect the scientific status of those theories. Even postulating an unobserved Creator need be no more unscientific than postulating unobservable particles. What matters is the character of the proposals and the ways in which they are articulated and defended. The great scientific Creationists of the eighteenth and nineteenth centuries offered problem-solving strategies for many of the questions addressed by evolutionary theory. They struggled hard to explain the observed distribution of fossils. Sedgwick, Buckland, and others practiced genuine science. They stuck their necks out and volunteered information about the catastrophes that they invoked to explain biological and geological findings. Because their theories offered definite proposals, those theories were refutable. Indeed, the theories actually achieved refutation. In 1831, in his presidential address to the Geological Society, Adam Sedgwick publicly announced that his own variant of Creationism had been refuted:

> Having been myself a believer, and, to the best of my power, a propagator of what I now regard as a philosophic heresy . . . I think it right, as one of my last acts before I quit this Chair, thus publicly to read my recantation.

> We ought, indeed, to have paused before we first adopted the diluvian theory, and referred all our old superficial gravel to the action of the Mosaic Flood. For of man, and the works of his hands, we have not yet found a single trace among the remnants of a former world entombed in these ancient deposits. In classing together distant unknown formations under one name; in giving them a simultaneous origin, and in determining their date, not by the organic remains we had discovered, but by those we expected hypothetically hereafter to discover, in them; we have given one more example of the passion with which the mind fastens upon general conclusions, and of the readiness with which it leaves the consideration of unconnected truths. . . .

Since they want Creationism taught in public schools, contemporary Creationists cannot present their view as based on religious faith. On the other hand, the doctrine is too dear to be subjected to the possibility of outright defeat. What is wanted, then, is a version of Creationism that is not vulnerable to refutation, but that appears to enjoy the objective status that can only be conferred by evidential support. This is an impossible demand. A theory cannot drink at the well of evidential support without running the risk of being poisoned by future data. What emerges from the conflict of goals is the pseudoscience promulgated by the Institute for Creation Research. It is vaguely suggested that the central Creationist idea could be used to solve some problems. But the details are never given, the links to nature never forged. Oddly, "scientific" Creationism fails to be a science not because of what it says (or, in its "public school" editions, very carefully omits) about a Divine Creator, but because of what it does not say about the natural world. The theory has no infrastructure, no ways of articulating its vague central idea, so that specific features of living forms can receive detailed explanations.

Despite my best efforts, I have found only two problem-solving strategies in the writing of "scientific" Creationists. Most of the literature is negative. . . . The positive proposals of Creation "science" are remarkably skimpy. Even *Scientific Creationism* (the work that is intended to enable teachers to present the "creation model") spends far more pages attacking evolutionary theory than in developing Creationist account. Nevertheless, there are passages where a positive doctrine seems to flicker among the criticisms. Similarly, the much earlier book *The Genesis Flood* (Whitcomb and Morris, 1961), mixes attempts at constructing Creation "science" with its explicit Biblical interpretation. Because of the uniformly negative character of most other Creationist writings, my evaluation of the positive theory presented by "scientific" Creationists will be based primarily on these two works. The two problem-solving strategies of "scientific" Creationism are the attempt to use Flood Geology to answer questions about the ordering of fossils and an appeal to a mix of "design" and historical narrative to account for the properties, relationships, and distributions of organisms. I shall document my remarks about pseudoscience by taking a closer look at how these explanatory vehicles operate.

ROOM AT THE TOP FOR THE UPWARDLY MOBILE?

Creationists recognize that the fossil record is ordered. All over the earth we find a regular succession of organisms through the rock strata. At the lowest levels, we find only small marine invertebrates. As we move up, other groups of animals are encountered: Fish join the marine invertebrates; then come the amphibians, reptiles, and, finally, the mammals and birds. Of course, within each of these groups there is also an order. The first reptiles diversify, giving rise at later times to several different groups, some of which, like the dinosaurs, die out, while others of which, like the snakes, turtles, lizards, and crocodilians, persist to the present. Even without evolutionary assumptions, it is possible to offer a simple explanation of this order. The different strata all contain remains of the distinctive organisms that were alive at the time at which those strata were deposited, and the order reflects the fact that different groups of animals have existed at different times. In other words, the animals who have inhabited the earth were not all contemporaries.

Although this simple explanation makes no commitment to the *evolution* of organisms, Creationists cannot accept it. For they believe that all the animals that have ever existed were formed in one original event of Creation. Nor can they abandon this belief without forswearing the theological payoff of their

"science." So how are they to explain the order of the fossil record? Some antievolutionists of the late nineteenth century ascended to new levels of ad hoc explanation with two transparent ruses: (i) The Devil placed the fossils in the rocks to deceive us; (ii) God put the fossils there to test us. Contemporary Creationists are more subtle. They invoke the Flood. They hypothesize a worldwide, cataclysmic deluge, which destroyed virtually all the animals of the earth and deposited almost all the fossil-bearing rocks, thereby producing the fossil record.

Here is an outline of their major ideas. The primeval earth was a very pleasant place, consisting of land masses divided by "narrow seas." It was surrounded by a canopy of water vapor, producing a "greenhouse effect." In the Flood, water came from two directions; primitive waters inside the earth burst through the crust, and, at the same time, the vapor canopy was broken up to cause torrential rain. Some humans and animals escaped in boats (including, presumably, Noah, his family, and a pair of [land] animals of every kind). Others, less lucky, were drowned or destroyed, and some of them were engulfed by mud and other debris that were later deposited as sediments. (The latter animals are the ones that became fossilized.) Finally, the Flood came to an end, partly as the result of evaporation, partly because mountains erupted, producing basins in which the residual waters were entrapped. At this point, the remaining animals dispersed, bred, multiplied, and spread themselves over the new earth.

The attempt to explain geological formations by reference to the Flood is not new. Contemporary Creationists are heirs to a long tradition, begun by

Thomas Burnet (whose *Sacred Theory of the Earth* was published in 1681). The idea of invoking a *single* cataclysm (and a single period of Creation) had been abandoned by the wiser geologists by the end of the eighteenth century, at which time the enterprise appeared hopeless. Nineteenth-century Catastrophists—Cuvier, Buckland, Sedgwick, and their followers—preferred to think of Noah's Flood as the last in a series of catastrophes. But "scientific" Creationists will have none of these newfangled compromises. So their account is vexed by all the questions that arose for their illustrious predecessors—as well as other questions inspired by the discoveries of the past 150 years. Here are just a few. How exactly did the land reemerge? (In traditional terms, how was "the pond drained"?) Did *all* kinds of land animals go on Noah's ship? If so, why are there so many kinds that are unrecorded in "post-Deluge" strata? How were the domestic economies managed during the voyage of the Ark? Obviously, the *mechanisms* of the whole episode could stand considerably more description. Creationists sometimes admit the point; Morris exhorts teachers to prepare geology students who can help with the task of working out the details. However, neither he nor any other Creationist I have read seems to have any definite conception of where or how to begin this Herculean task. . . .

To see why Flood Geology deserves an obituary, let us watch it in action. The most ambitious attempt at detailed problem solving is presented by Henry Morris. Morris is very emphatic that Flood Geology accounts for the order of the fossils. After announcing fourteen "obvious predictions" of his story, he concludes, "Now there is no question

that all of the above predictions from the cataclysmic model are explicitly confirmed in the geologic column. The general order from simple to complex in the fossil record in the geologic column, considered by evolution, is thus likewise predicted by the rival model, only with more precision and detail. But it is the exceptions that are inimical to the evolution model." Bold words. Before we take up the large claims made for Flood Geology, let us consider the swipes at the evolutionary account. First, the "general order from simple to complex" in the fossil record is not considered "the main proof" of evolution. Evolutionary theory rests on its ability to subsume a vast number of diverse phenomena—including the *details* of biogeography, adaptive characteristics, relationships among organisms, and the sequence of fossils—under a single type of historical reasoning. To say that "the general order from simple to complex" in the fossil record is the primary evidence for evolution is like saying that the fact that most bodies tend to fall is the primary evidence for Newtonian theory. Second, those "inimical exceptions" are our old friends the overthrusts, the cave drawings—and, of course, Paluxy. As I have already pointed out, these are not genuine problems for evolutionary theory.

How exactly does Morris propose to "predict" the order of the fossils from his model? Let us look at some of his "predictions" and their justifications:

3. In general, animals living at the lowest elevations would tend to be buried at the lowest elevations, and so on, with elevations in the strata thus representing elevations of habitat or ecological zones.

4. Marine invertebrates would normally be found in the bottom rock of any local

geologic column, since they live on the sea bottom.

5. Marine vertebrates (fishes) would be found in higher rocks than the bottom-dwelling invertebrates. They live at higher elevations and also could escape burial longer.

6. Amphibians and reptiles would tend to be found at still higher elevations, in the commingled sediments at the interface between land and water. . . .

9. In the marine strata where invertebrates were fossilized, these would tend locally to be sorted hydrodynamically into assemblages of similar size and shape. Furthermore, as the turbulently upwelling waters and sediments settled back down, the simpler animals, more nearly spherical or streamlined in shape, would tend to settle out first because of lower hydraulic drag. Thus each kind of marine invertebrate would tend to appear in its simplest form at the lowest elevation, and so on.

10. Mammals and birds would be found in general at higher elevations than reptiles and amphibians, both because of their habitat and because of their greater mobility. However, few birds would be found at all, only occasional exhausted birds being trapped and buried in sediments.

It is hard to know where to start. Morris appears to have three possible explanatory factors: (1) *habitat* (lower dwelling animals were deposited first), (2) *hydraulic characteristics* (the order of deposition depends on the animal's resistance to the downward waters), (3) *mobility* (more mobile animals will be deposited later). The passages I have quoted juggle these three methods so as to obtain the desired results.

Now, for all the extravagant claims about "prediction" with "more precision and detail," the account Morris offers is extremely vague. Puzzles begin to appear in large numbers when we start to consider the details of the fossil record. Why are bottom-dwelling marine invertebrates found at *all* levels of the strata? Why are some very delicate marine invertebrates, which would have been likely to sink more slowly, found at the very lowest levels? Why are all the "modern" fishes (the *teleostean* fishes, which, on the standard account, emerged only in the age of dinosaurs and became spectacularly successful as the reign of the dinosaurs came to its end) found only in Morris's "late Flood" deposits? Why do these particular fishes not occur, as other fishes do, at lower levels? Why are whales and dolphins only found at high levels, while marine reptiles of similar size are found only much lower? Why do lumbering creatures like ground sloths appear only in Morris's post-Flood deposits, while much more agile mammals (such as the ancestors of contemporary carnivores and ungulates) appear much lower? Why are the *flying* reptiles found "in the commingled sediments at the interface between land and water"? Why were not *most* of the birds "exhausted," since perching places would have been hard to find in the raging Deluge? The sequence of questions could go on and on.

Morris does not consider the particularities. So the idea that we get *more* detail from his account is simply bluster. In fact, given that the problems raised for evolutionary theory are spurious—the "inimical exceptions" do not present any difficulty—the question we must ask is whether Flood Geology can *emulate* the ability of evolutionary theory to explain the fossil record. There are two ways in which Creationists might elaborate their proposals. One would be to acknowledge that the account so far given is programmatic and incomplete and to face up to the task of working out the details. The second would be to deny that there are residual questions for "scientific" Creationism to answer.

In the spirit of Morris's exhortation to young paleontologists, Creationists might concede that Flood Geology is only a "sketch." However, it is hardly a matter of adding a bit of detail to the main lines of the account. Problems are everywhere, solutions nowhere. What were the mechanics of the Flood? How were the animals preserved? Why are the details of the fossil ordering as we find them to be? It is reasonable to wonder what Flood Geology does have going for it that inspires people to work further on it. Wonderment increases when we realize that Creationists have abandoned the position of the most enlightened nineteenth-century Catastrophists. . . .

Here is a different "theory sketch" about the history of life on earth. For a very long time, the earth has been a laboratory for clever aliens who live in outer space. Periodically, they have "seeded" our planet with living organisms. In the beginning, they were only able to produce rather simple terrestrial organisms. So they started off with some marine invertebrates. After a while, they came for a visit to see how things were going. At this time, a dreadful thing happened. Something about the alien spacecraft caused a cataclysm on the earth; volcanoes erupted, there were massive earthquakes, enormous tidal waves, and so forth. Perhaps the spacecraft emitted some peculiar type of radiation that triggered all these unfortunate events. In any case, all the first crop of organisms were destroyed and buried in the cataclysm. The whole experiment was spoiled. However, since they understood the moral of Kipling's "If," the aliens decided to try again. Their technology had now improved, and they were able to manufacture more complicated animals. Some of those that had not performed well on the first round were dropped from the cast. The experiment went very well again—until they came to take another look. Once again, their presence led to disaster, and they were forced to start over from scratch. So it has gone for a number of trials. (How many would you like?) The aliens are very persevering. They still have not figured out what it is about their presence that makes the earth go into convulsions. But their technology is clearly improving by leaps and bounds. After all, last time they made us.

My brief acquaintance with the "theory sketch" of the last paragraph has not yet led to a deep attachment. (It took me about ten minutes to make it up.) So I shall not exhort others to join me in working out the details. However, I do want to suggest that, *from a scientific point of view,* my silly proposal is no worse than Morris's Flood Geology. It would not be difficult to mimic the "fourteen predictions." ("What evolutionists call *trends* are really the aliens' progress in fine tuning already workable designs." Notice, too, that my theory, like Morris's vague account of Flood Geology, has plenty of "wiggle room.") The point of the comparison should be obvious. There is utterly no reason to take either my proposal or Flood Geology seriously—or to exhort promising students to waste their careers in the pursuit of such obvious folly.

The second way in which the Creationists can respond to questions about the details is even worse. Instead of taking the problems of detail seriously, they can contend that we can never know how the Flood worked. All that can be done is to lay down some general considerations, which hold "as a rule," and suggest that, given some unknowable distribution of upwelling waters, torrential rains, and trapped animals, everything sorted out as it did. So, for example, the questions I have raised about teleostean fishes, whales, flying reptiles, and giant sloths can just be ducked. These are "the exceptional cases."

Some passages suggest that, when push comes to shove, Morris and his fellow Creationists will slide in this direction:

> 14. All the above predictions would be expected statistically but, because of the cataclysmic nature of the phenomena, would also admit of many exceptions in every case. In other words, the cataclysmic model predicts the general order and character of the deposits but also allows for occasional exceptions.

> In other localities, and perhaps somewhat later in the period of the rising waters of the Flood, in general, land animals and plants would be expected to be caught in the sediments and buried; and this, of course, is exactly what the strata show. Of course, this would be only a general rule and there would be many exceptions, as currents would be intermingling from all directions, particularly as the lands became increasingly submerged and more and more amphibians, reptiles and mammals were overtaken by the waters.

The remarkable point about these passages is not the *number* of qualifying phrases, but their *variable strength*. Are there "many exceptions in every case"

or are the exceptions "occasional"? I do not know what Morris or Whitcomb intend. Yet one thing is clear. Such passages can be used to maintain that the anomalies I have mentioned are not genuine problems for Flood Geology. Morris and Whitcomb have carefully provided an all-purpose escape clause. So while (alleged) exceptions are "inimical" to evolutionary theory—they would mean refutation—exceptions, even hordes of exceptions, in no way weaken the case for Creation "science." For Creation "scientists" data has only one function; it is a potential source of problems for evolution. Counterexamples to the "theory" of Creation "science" do not count.

To see how severe the anomalies are, let us look at one example in more detail. Fossils of teleostean fishes (this class comprises just about all contemporary types from sardines to swordfish) are found only from late Triassic times (roughly 200 million years ago), and they show increasing abundance in the fossil record. Now recall that a leading principle of Flood Geology is that "animals living at the lowest elevations would tend to be buried at the lowest elevations." Overlooking such niceties as the fact that some teleosteans are deep-sea fish, let us ask what accounts for their success in resisting the Flood. Were they hydraulically special, less "streamlined" than other fish? No, as a group, there is more variation of shape *within* the teleosteans than there is between teleosteans and the groups of fish that were buried beneath them. So, perhaps the answer is that they found room at the top because they were upwardly mobile? But this explanation loses its attractiveness when we realize that the teleosts "range from speedy swimmers to slow swimmers to almost sedentary forms, from dwellers in the open ocean to bottom-living types to lake and river fishes." Yet all these lucky teleostean fishes managed to resist the flood waters for a long time, while large numbers of speedy fish are buried beneath them.

By considering this one example, I hope to have explained what lies behind my charge that Flood Geology faces serious anomalies. But my principal purpose is to illustrate the impotence of the idea that worrisome details can be written off as "exceptional cases." Were *all* the teleosts exceptional? Was there no single unlucky sardine, salmon, or swordfish who was buried in the early deposits? Is it enough to remind ourselves that there are bound to be exceptions "because of the cataclysmic nature of the phenomena"? The case of the teleosts is only one among many. Ground sloths, flying reptiles, whales, trilobites, and a host of other creatures prove similarly embarrassing. . . .

Writing in 1961, Whitcomb and Morris made it clear what their last resort would be if the difficult questions began to threaten: "It is because the Bible itself teaches us these things that we are fully justified in appealing to *the power of God,* whether or not He used means amenable to our scientific understanding, for the gathering of two of every kind of animal into the Ark and for the care and preservation of those animals in the Ark during the 371 days of the Flood." Today, "scientific" Creationists have pledged themselves to argue on the scientific evidence. So this last refuge is—officially, at least—out of bounds.

The second major biological problem-solving strategy offered by Creationism attempts to answer questions about adaptation, relationships among organisms, and biogeographical distribution. . . .

The basic idea is straightforward. When we recognize a characteristic of an organism as unmodified, the Creationist explanation of its presence will be to show how the feature manifests the Creator's design. The account of similarities among distinct "basic kinds" will identify the similar needs of organisms of those distinct kinds. Here are some sample "explanations." Bats have wings because the Creator endowed them with wings, and He did so because they need to fly. Chimps and humans have similar hemoglobins (and other biological molecules) because the Creator gave them similar molecules from the start, and He did so because their physiological requirements are similar. Some (perfectly palatable) butterflies mimic unpalatable butterflies of the same region because the Creator saw that they had to have some defense against predators. To each according to his need.

If one wants to believe in Creationism, the picture can easily lull critical faculties. Yet, if we think about it, it is bizarre. Surely we should not imagine the Creator contemplating a wingless bat, recognizing that it would be defective, and so equipping it with the wings it needs. Rather, if we take the idea of a single creative event seriously, we must view it as the origination of an entire system of kinds of organisms, *whose needs themselves arise in large measure from the character of the system.* Why were bats created at all? Why were any defenses against predation needed? Why did the Creator form this system of organisms, with their interrelated needs, needs that are met in such diverse and complicated ways?

Invocation of the word "design," or the passing reference to the satisfaction of "need," explains nothing. The needs are not given in advance of the design of structures to accommodate them, but are themselves encompassed in the design. Nor do we achieve any understanding of the adaptations and relationships of organisms until we see, at least in outline, what the Grand Plan of Creation might have been. This point has been clear at least since the seventeenth century. At the beginning of the *Discourse on Metaphysics,* Leibniz gave a beautiful exposition of it. He recognized that unless there are independent criteria of design, then praise of the Creator's design is worthless: "In saying, therefore, that things are not good according to any standard of goodness, but simply by the will of God, it seems to me that one destroys, without realizing it, all the love of God and all his glory; for why praise him for what he has done, if he would be equally praiseworthy in doing the contrary?" For Leibniz, to invoke "design" without saying what counts as good design is not only vacuous but blasphemous. Later in the same work, Leibniz developed the theme with a striking analogy. *Any* world can be conceived as regular ("designed") just as *any* array of points can be joined by a curve with some algebraic formula.

Why are contemporary Creationists silent about the Design? Because things did not go so well for their predecessors who tried to show how each kind of organism had been separately created with a special design. They found it hard to reconcile the observed features of some organisms with the attributes of the Creator. Contemporary Creationists have learned from these heroic—but fruitless—efforts.

So we encounter the strategy exemplified by Morris: Talk generally about design, pattern, purpose, and beauty in nature. There are many examples of adaptations that can be used—the wings of bats or "the amazing circulatory system," for example. But what happens if we press some more difficult cases? Well, if there seems to be no design or purpose to a feature (and if its presence cannot be understood as a modification of ancestral characters), one can always point out that some parts of the Creator's plan may be too vast for human understanding. *We* do not see what the design is, but there *is* design, nonetheless.

Since no plan of design has been specified, Creationists have available another all-purpose escape clause. But it is precisely this feature of Creation "science" that impugns its scientific credentials. To mumble that "the ways of the Creator are many and mysterious" may excuse one from identifying design in unlikely places. It is not to do science.

To provide scientific explanations, a Creationist would have to identify the plan implemented in the Creation. The trouble is that there are countless examples of properties of organisms that are hard to integrate into a coherent theory of design. There are two main types of difficulty, stemming from the frequent tinkerings of evolution and the equally common nastiness of nature. Let us begin with evolutionary tinkering. Structures already present are modified to answer to the organism's current needs. The result may be clumsy and inefficient, but it gets the job done. A beautiful example is the case of the Panda's thumb. Although they belong to the order Carnivora, giant pandas subsist on a diet of bamboo. In adapting to this diet they needed a means to grasp the shoots. Like other carnivores, they lack an opposable thumb. Instead, a bone in the wrist has become extended to serve as part of a device for grasping it. It does not work well. Any competent engineer who wanted to design a giant panda cold have done better. But it works well enough.

It is easy to multiply examples. Orchids have evolved complicated structures that discourage self-fertilization. These baroque contraptions are readily understood if we understand them as built out of the means available. Ruminants have acquired very complicated stomachs and a special digestive routine. These characteristics have enabled them to break down the cellulose layers that encase valuable proteins in many grasses. Their inner life could have been so much simpler had they been given the right enzymes from the start.

The second class of cases covers those in which, to put it bluntly, nature's ways are rather repulsive. There is nothing intrinsically beautiful about the scavenging of vultures, the copulatory behavior of the female praying mantis (who tries to bite off the head of the "lucky" male), or the ways in which some insects paralyze their prey. Let me describe one example in more detail. Some animals practice *coprophagy*. They produce feces that they eat. Rabbits, for example, devour their morning droppings. From an evolutionary perspective, the phenomenon is understood. Rabbits have solved the problem of breaking down cellulose by secreting bacteria toward the end of their intestinal tracts. Since the cellulose breakdown occurs at the end of the tract, much valuable protein and many valuable bacteria are liable to be lost in the feces. Hence the morning feces are eaten, the protein is metabolized, and the supply of bacteria is kept up. Creationists ought to find such phenomena puzzling. Surely an all-powerful, all-loving Creator, who *separately designed* each kind of living thing, could have found some less repugnant (and, I might add, more efficient) way to get the job done. (These examples are, of course,

far less problematic for those who believe simply that the Creator set the universe in motion billions of years ago and that contemporary organisms are the latest product of the laws and conditions instituted in that original creative event.)

So far, I have concentrated on Creationist resources for answering questions about the characteristics of organisms and the similarities and differences among kinds of organisms. Let us now take a brief look at Creationist biogeography. Discussions of the distribution of animals are not extensive, but the following passage lays down the ground rules of the enterprise: "If the Flood was geographically universal, then all the air-breathers of the animal kingdom which were not in the Ark perished; and present-day animal distribution must be explained on the basis of migrations from the mountains of Ararat." One's first response is surely to ask: Why only one Ark? Why Ararat? (Why not New Jersey?) Of course, we know the answers to these questions. But what *scientific* evidence is there for supposing that there was just one vehicle for preserving land animals during the Deluge and that the subsequent radiation began from Mount Ararat? Creationists tie their hands behind their backs when they approach problems of biogeography with such gratuitous assumptions. There are obvious difficulties posed by the existence of peculiar groups of animals in particular places. The most striking example is the presence of marsupials as the dominant mammals of Australia. Given that all the land animals reemerged at the same place at the same time, why did Australia become a stronghold for marsupial mammals?

Whitcomb and Morris consider precisely this question. Much of their discussion is directed against claims made by one of their evangelical rivals, a geologist who advocated only a "local flood." However, they do indicate the main lines of their answer. In essence, they propose to accelerate the migration of organisms described in a standard evolutionary account. Here is the standard explanation of how the marsupials came to dominate Australia.

One central hypothesis is *placental chauvinism:* Marsupials are competitively inferior to the recent eutherian (placental) mammals. This hypothesis is confirmed by evidence of the consequences of introducing eutherian competitors into marsupial populations. It is usually suggested that the marsupials arose in North America about 130 million years ago and that they were able to compete successfully with the *early* eutherian mammals. The marsupials radiated extensively, established themselves in South America and crossed over to Australia by way of Antarctica. (Australia, Antarctica, and South America become separated about 70 million years ago.) Their eutherian contemporaries did not reach Australia, so that the marsupials were able to diversify and attain their modern forms without competition from eutherians. Other marsupial strongholds (for example, South America) became vulnerable when new continental connections (the Isthmus of Panama) made it possible for the highly successful *recent* eutherians to invade. But Australia was sufficiently isolated, and a rich marsupial fauna developed there.

What Creationists propose to do is to squash something like this sequence of events into less than 100 centuries. Here, then, is the scenario. Noah's Ark lands on Mount Ararat. Out come the animals. They begin to compete for resources. Because they are inferior competitors, the poor marsupials are forced to disperse ever more widely. Spreading southward, they eventually manage to reach Australia. By the time the placentals have given chase, the land connection with Australia is severed. The marsupials are safe in their stronghold.

This is an exciting story, worthy of the best cowboy tradition. The trouble is that it has the marsupials arising in the wrong place, going by the wrong route, and competing with the wrong animals. Apart from that, the pace is just a bit too quick. If Creationists are going to explain fossil findings that, by their own lights, are post-Flood, they had better suppose that the marsupials reached Australia by travelling through Europe, North America, and South America. If they are going to insist that *contemporary* kinds of eutherian mammals emerged form the Ark, then they will have to explain why competition was not so severe that the marsupials were completely vanquished. Waiving these difficulties, let us consider the rate of the migration. When we think of marsupials, we naturally think of kangaroos—so we have the vision of successive generations of kangaroos hopping toward Australia. But kangaroos are relatively speedy. Some marsupials—wombats, koalas, and marsupial moles, for example—move very slowly. Koalas are sedentary animals, and it is difficult to coax them out of the eucalyptus trees on which they feed. Wombats, like marsupial moles, construct elaborate burrows, in which they spend their time and carry on their social relations. The idea of *any* of these animals engaging in a hectic dash around the globe is patently absurd. (On the evolutionary account, of course, they are all descendants of ancestral marsupials who had millions of years to reach their destination.)

Next we must face the question of why all the lucky refugees were *marsupials*. Surely, large numbers of animals would have found it prudent to disperse widely from the Ark. Why is it that the marsupials, almost *alone* among the mammals, were able to find the land connection to Australia and scurry across before other mammals in need of *Lebensraum* could catch up with them? And what about the conveniently disappearing land connection itself? Creationists seem to assume very rapid movements of land masses. Unlike orthodox geologists, who have independent evidence for slow separation of the continents, they maintain that, in a matter of centuries, a land connection that would support a full-scale exodus of marsupials presented an insuperable barrier to the pursuing eutherians. Indeed, if the marsupials were really *driven* across by eutherian competition, then we would expect the competition to be snapping at their heels   otherwise would not the wombat have stopped to dig a burrow, the koala have settled in a convenient tree? In that case, the bridge would have to be cut *very* quickly.

Once again, when the Creationist story is pressed for details, anomalies appear in droves. . . . What constraints govern hypotheses about past land connections? Since the Creationists have forsworn the apparatus of modern geology, their claims about the past relations of land masses seem invulnerable to independent checks. No worries about mechanisms for rapid land subsidence need perturb them, for they may always appeal to the after effects of the great cataclysm. Anything goes.

When Whitcomb and Morris wrote *The Genesis Flood* in 1961, Creationist strategy was somewhat different from that currently in vogue. Those were halcyon days, when Creationists did not mind admitting their reliance on unfathomable supernatural mechanisms. Perhaps they even hoped that a version of Creationism, explicitly based on the Genesis account, might find its place in science education. The following passage is far less guarded than more recent statements:

> The more we study the fascinating story of animal distribution around the earth, the more convinced we have become that this vast river of variegated life forms, moving ever outward from the Asiatic mainland, across the continents and seas, has not been a chance and haphazard phenomenon. Instead, *we see the hand of God guiding and directing these creatures in ways that man, with all his ingenuity, has never been able to fathom*, in order that the great commission to the postdiluvian animal kingdom might be carried out, and "that they may breed abundantly in the earth, and be fruitful, and multiply upon the earth" (Gen. 8 : 17).

There is the all-purpose escape clause. If the way in which the animals might have managed to leave the Ark and distribute themselves around the globe boggles your mind, do not tax yourself. They were guided, directed in ways that we are not able to understand.

Morris's subsequent writings take a different line about biogeographical questions. The subject is not discussed. Hence it is impossible to be sure that current Creationists would involve the actions of the Creator to help out when the going gets tough. Nevertheless, this is one more instance of the phenomenon that we have seen repeatedly. The alleged rival to evolutionary theory provides no definite problem-solving strategies that can be applied to give detailed answers to specific questions. . . .

Creation "science" is spurious science. To treat it as science we would have to overlook its intolerable vagueness. We would have to abandon large parts of well-established sciences (physics, chemistry, and geology, as well as evolutionary biology, are all candidates for revision). We would have to trade careful technical procedures for blind guesses, unified theories for motley collections of special techniques. Exceptional cases, whose careful pursuit has so often led to important turnings in the history of science, would be dismissed with a wave of the hand. Nor would there be any gains. There is not a single scientific question to which Creationism provides its own detailed problem solution. In short, Creationism could take a place among the sciences only if the substance and methods of contemporary science were mutilated to make room for a scientifically worthless doctrine. What price Creationism?

ISAAC ASIMOV

Armies of the Night

ISAAC ASIMOV *was born in the Soviet Union and raised in Brooklyn, New York. He was a legendary writer of science and science fiction, having published over 340 books. He was also a former Professor of Biochemistry at Boston University.*

SCIENTISTS thought it was settled.

The universe, they had decided, is about 20 billion years old, and Earth itself is 4.5 billion years old. Simple forms of life came into being more than three billion years ago, having formed spontaneously from nonliving matter. They grew more complex through slow evolutionary processes and the first hominid ancestors of humanity appeared more than four million years ago. *Homo sapiens* itself—the present human species, people like you and me—has walked the earth for at least 50,000 years.

But apparently it isn't settled. There are Americans who believe that the earth is only about 6,000 years old; that human beings and all other species were brought into existence by a divine Creator as eternally separate varieties of beings, and that there has been no evolutionary process.

They are creationists—they call themselves "scientific" creationists— and they are a growing power in the land, demanding that schools be forced to teach their views. State legislatures, mindful of votes, are beginning to succumb to the pressure. In perhaps 15 states, bills have been introduced, putting forth the creationist point of view, and in others, strong movements are gaining momentum. In Arkansas, a law requiring that the teaching of creationism receive equal time was passed this spring and is scheduled to go into effect in September 1982, though the American Civil Liberties Union has filed suit on behalf of a group of clergymen, teachers and parents to overturn it. And a California father named Kelly Segraves, the director of the Creation-Science Research Center, sued to have public-school science classes taught that there are other theories of creation besides evolution, and that one of them was the Biblical version. The suit came to trial in March, and the judge ruled that educators must distribute a policy statement to schools and textbook publishers explaining that the theory of evolution should not be seen as "the ultimate cause of origins." Even in New York, the Board of Education has delayed since January in making a final decision, expected this month, on whether schools will be required to include the teaching of creationism in their curriculums.

The Rev. Jerry Falwell, the head of the Moral Majority, who supports the creationist view from his television pulpit, claims that he has 17 million to 25 million viewers (though Arbitron places the figure at a much more modest 1.6 million). But there are 66 electronic ministries which have a total audience of about 20 million. And in parts of the country where the Fundamentalists predominate—the so-called Bible Belt—creationists are in the majority.

They make up a fervid and dedicated group, convinced beyond argument of both their rightness and righteousness. Faced with an apathetic and falsely secure majority, smaller groups have used intense pressure and forceful campaigning—as the creationists do—and have succeeded in disrupting and taking over whole societies.

Yet, though creationists seem to accept the literal truth of the Biblical story of creation, this does not mean that all

religious people are creationists. There are millions of Catholics, Protestants and Jews who think of the Bible as a source of spiritual truth and accept much of it as symbolically rather than literally true. They do not consider the Bible to be a textbook of science, even in intent, and have no problem teaching evolution in their secular institutions.

To those who are trained in science, creationism seems like a bad dream, a sudden reliving of a nightmare, a renewed march of any army of the night risen to challenge free thought and enlightenment.

The scientific evidence for the age of the earth and for the evolutionary development of life seems overwhelming to scientists. How can anyone question it? What are the arguments the creationists use? What is the "science" that makes their views "scientific"? Here are some of them:

THE ARGUMENT FROM ANALOGY

A watch implies a watchmaker, say the creationists. If you were to find a beautifully intricate watch in the desert, far from habitation, you would be sure that it had been fashioned by human hands and somehow left there. It would pass the bounds of credibility that it had simply formed, spontaneously, from the sands of the desert.

By analogy, then, if you consider humanity, life, earth and the universe, all infinitely more intricate than a watch, you can believe far less easily that it "just happened." It, too, like the watch, must have been fashioned, but by more-than-human hands—in short by a divine Creator.

This argument seems unanswerable, and it has been used (even though not often explicitly expressed) ever since the dawn of consciousness. To have explained to prescientific human beings that the wind and the rain and the sun follow the laws of nature and do so blindly and without a guiding hand would have been utterly unconvincing to them. In fact, it might well have gotten you stoned to death as a blasphemer.

There are many aspects of the universe that still cannot be explained satisfactorily by science; but ignorance implies only ignorance that may someday be conquered. To surrender to ignorance and call it God has always been premature, and it remains premature today. In short, the complexity of the universe—and one's inability to explain it in full—is not in itself an argument for a Creator.

THE ARGUMENT FROM GENERAL CONSENT

Some creationists point out that belief in a Creator is general among all peoples and all cultures. Surely this unanimous craving hints at a great truth. There would be no unanimous belief in a lie.

General belief, however, is not really surprising. Nearly every people on earth that considers the existence of the world assumes it to have been created by a god or gods. And each group invents full details for the story. No two creation tales are alike. The Greeks, the Norsemen, the Japanese, the Hindus, the American Indians and so on and so on all have their own creation myths, and all of these are recognized by Americans of Judeo-Christian heritage as "just myths."

The ancient Hebrews also had a creation tale—two of them, in fact. There is a primitive Adam-and-Eve-in-Paradise story, with man created first, then animals, then woman. There is also a poetic tale of God fashioning the universe in six days, with animals preceding man, and man and woman created together.

These Hebrew myths are not inherently more credible than any of the others, but they are our myths. General consent, of course, proves nothing: There can be a unanimous belief in something that isn't so. The universal opinion over thousands of years that the earth was flat never flattened its spherical shape by one inch.

THE ARGUMENT BY BELITTLEMENT

Creationists frequently stress the fact that evolution is "only a theory," giving the impression that a theory is an idle guess. A scientist, one gathers, arising one morning with nothing particular to do, decides that perhaps the moon is made of Roquefort cheese and instantly advances the Roquefort-cheese theory.

A theory (as the word is used by scientists) is a detailed description of some facet of the universe's workings that is based on long observation and, where possible, experiment. It is the result of careful reasoning from those observations and experiments and has survived the critical study of scientists generally.

For example, we have the description of the cellular nature of living organisms (the "cell theory"); of objects attracting each other according to a fixed rule (the "theory of gravitation"); of energy behaving in discrete bits (the "quantum theory"); of light traveling through a vacuum at a fixed measurable velocity (the "theory of relativity"), and so on.

All are theories; all are firmly founded; all are accepted as valid descriptions of this or that aspect of the universe. They are neither guesses nor speculations. And no theory is better founded, more closely examined, more critically argued and more thoroughly accepted, than the theory of evolution. If it is "only" a theory, that is all it has to be.

Creationism, on the other hand, is not a theory. There is no evidence, in the scientific sense, that supports it. Creationism, or at least the particular variety accepted by many Americans, is an expression of early Middle Eastern legend. It is fairly described as "only a myth."

THE ARGUMENT FROM IMPERFECTION

Creationists, in recent years, have stressed the "scientific" background of their beliefs. They point out that there are scientists who base their creationist beliefs on a careful study of geology, paleontology and biology and produce "textbooks" that embody those beliefs.

Virtually the whole scientific corpus of creationism, however, consists of the pointing out of imperfections in the evolutionary view. The creationists insist, for example, that evolutionists cannot show transition states between species in the fossil evidence; that age determinations through radioactive breakdown are uncertain; that alternate interpretations of this or that piece of evidence are possible, and so on.

Because the evolutionary view is not perfect and is not agreed upon in every detail by all scientists, creationists argue that evolution is false and scientists, in supporting evolution, are basing their views on blind faith and dogmatism.

To an extent, the creationists are right here. The details of evolution are not perfectly known. Scientists have been adjusting and modifying Charles Darwin's suggestions since he advanced this theory of the origin of species through natural selection back in 1859. After all, much has been learned about the fossil record and about physiology, microbiology, biochemistry, ethology and various other branches in life science in the last 125 years, and it is to be expected that we can improve on Darwin. In fact, we have improved on him.

Nor is the process finished. It can never be, as long as human beings continue to question and to strive for better answers.

The details of evolutionary theory are in dispute precisely because scientists are not devotees of blind faith and dogmatism. They do not accept even as great a thinker as Darwin without question, nor do they accept any idea, new or old, without thorough argument. Even after accepting an idea, they stand ready to overrule it, if appropriate new evidence arrives. If, however, we grant that a theory is imperfect and that details remain in dispute, does that disprove the theory as a whole?

Consider, I drive a car, and you drive a car. I do not know exactly how an engine works. Perhaps you do not either. And it may be that our hazy and approximate ideas of the workings of an automobile are in conflict. Must we then conclude from this disagreement that an automobile does not run, or that it does not exist? Or, if our senses force us to conclude that an automobile does exist and run, does that mean it is pulled by an invisible horse, since our engine theory is imperfect?

However much scientists argue their differing beliefs in details of evolutionary theory, or in the interpretation of the necessarily imperfect fossil record, they firmly accept the evolutionary process itself.

THE ARGUMENT FROM DISTORTED SCIENCE

Creationists have learned enough scientific terminology to use it in their attempts to disprove evolution. They do this in numerous ways, but the most common example, at least in the mail I receive, is the repeated assertion that the second law of thermodynamics demonstrates the evolutionary process to be impossible.

In kindergarten terms, the second law of thermodynamics says that all spontaneous change is in the direction of increasing disorder—that is, in a "downhill" direction. There can be no spontaneous buildup of the complex from the simple, therefore, because that would be moving "uphill." According to the creationist argument, since, by the evolutionary process, complex forms of life evolve from simple forms, that process defies the second law, so creationism must be true.

Such an argument implies that this clearly visible fallacy is somehow invisible to scientists, who must therefore be flying in the face of the second law through sheer perversity.

Scientists, however, do know about the second law and they are not blind. It's just that an argument based on kindergarten terms is suitable only for kindergartens.

To lift the argument a notch above the kindergarten level, the second law of thermodynamics applies to a "closed system"—that is, to a system that does not gain energy from without, or lose energy to the outside. The only truly closed system we know of is the universe as a whole.

Within a closed system, there are subsystems that can gain complexity spontaneously, provided there is a greater loss of complexity in another interlocking subsystem. The overall change then is a complexity loss in line with the dictates of the second law.

Evolution can proceed and build up the complex from the simple, thus moving uphill without violating the second law, as long as another interlocking part of the system—the sun, which delivers energy to the earth continually—moves downhill (as it does) at a much faster rate than evolution moves uphill.

If the sun were to cease shining, evolution would stop and so, eventually, would life.

Unfortunately, the second law is a subtle concept which most people are not accustomed to dealing with, and it is not easy to see the fallacy in the creationist distortion.

There are many other "scientific" arguments used by creationists, some taking quite clever advantage of present areas of dispute in evolutionary theory, but every one of them is as disingenuous as the second-law argument.

The "scientific" arguments are organized into special creationist textbooks, which have all the surface appearance of the real thing, and which school systems are being heavily pressured to accept. They are written by people who have not made any mark as scientists, and, while they discuss geology, paleontology and biology with correct scientific terminology, they are devoted almost entirely to raising doubts over the legitimacy of the evidence and reasoning underlying evolutionary thinking on the assumption that this leaves creationism as the only possible alternative.

Evidence actually in favor of creationism is not presented, of course, because none exists other than the word of the Bible, which it is current creationist strategy not to use.

THE ARGUMENT FROM IRRELEVANCE

Some creationists put all matters of scientific evidence to one side and consider all such things irrelevant. The Creator, they say, brought life and earth and the entire universe into being 6,000 years ago or so, complete with all the evidence for an eons-long evolutionary development. The fossil record, the decaying radioactivity, the receding galaxies were all created as they are, and the evidence they present is an illusion.

Of course, this argument is itself irrelevant, for it can neither be proved nor disproved. It is not an argument, actually, but a statement. I can say that the entire universe was created two minutes ago, complete with all its history books describing a nonexistent past in detail, and with every living person equipped with a full memory; you, for instance, in the process of reading this article in midstream with a memory of what you had read in the beginning—which you had not really read.

What kind of a Creator would produce a universe containing so intricate an illusion? It would mean that the Creator formed a universe that contained human beings whom He had endowed with the faculty of curiosity and the ability to reason. He supplied those human beings with an enormous amount of subtle and cleverly consistent evidence designed to mislead them and cause them to be convinced that the universe was created 20 billion years ago and developed by evolutionary processes that included the creation and development of life on Earth.

Why?

Does the Creator take pleasure in fooling us? Does it amuse Him to watch us go wrong? Is it part of a test to see if human beings will deny their senses and their reason in order to cling to myth? Can it be that the Creator is a cruel and malicious prankster, with a vicious and adolescent sense of humor?

THE ARGUMENT FROM AUTHORITY

The Bible says that God created the world in six days, and the Bible is the inspired word of God. To the average creationist this is all that counts. All other arguments are merely a tedious way of countering the propaganda of all those wicked humanists, agnostics and atheists who are not satisfied with the clear word of the Lord.

The creationist leaders do not actually use that argument because that would make their argument a religious one, and they would not be able to use it in fighting a secular school system. They have to borrow the clothing of science, no matter how badly it fits and call themselves "scientific" creationists. They also speak only of the "Creator," and never mention that this Creator is the God of the Bible.

We cannot, however, take this sheep's clothing seriously. However much the creationist leaders might hammer away at their "scientific" and "philosophical" points, they would be helpless and a laughing stock if that were all they had.

It is religion that recruits their squadrons. Tens of millions of Americans, who neither know or understand the actual arguments for—or even against—evolution, march in the army of the night with their Bibles held high. And they are a strong and frightening force, impervious to, and immunized against, the feeble lance of mere reason.

Even if I am right and the evolutionists' case is very strong, have not creationists, whatever the emptiness of their case, a right to be heard?

If their case is empty, isn't it perfectly safe to discuss it since the emptiness would then be apparent?

Why, then, are evolutionists so reluctant to have creationism taught in the public schools on an equal basis with evolutionary theory? Can it be that the evolutionists are not as confident of their case as they pretend? Are they afraid to allow youngsters a clear choice?

First, the creationists are somewhat less than honest in their demand for equal time. It is not their views that are repressed: Schools are by no means the only place in which the dispute between creationism and evolutionary theory is played out.

There are the churches, for instance, which are a much more serious influence on most Americans than the schools are. To be sure, many churches are quite liberal, have made their peace with science and find it easy to live with scientific advance—even with evolution. But many of the less modish and citified churches are bastions of creationism.

The influence of the church is naturally felt in the home, in the newspapers and in all of surrounding society. It makes itself felt in the nation as a whole, even religiously liberal areas, in thousands of subtle ways; in the nature of holiday observance, in expressions of patriotic fervor, even in total irrelevancies. In 1968, for example, a team of astronauts circling the moon were instructed to read the first few verses of Genesis as though NASA felt it had to placate the public lest they rage against the violation of the firmament. At the present time, even the current President of the United States has expressed his creationist sympathies.

It is only in school that American youngsters in general are ever likely to hear any reasoned exposition of the evolutionary viewpoint. They might find such a viewpoint in books, magazines, newspapers or even, on occasion, on television. But church and family can easily censor printed matter or television. Only the school is beyond their control.

But only just barely beyond. Even though schools are now allowed to teach evolution, teachers are beginning to be apologetic about it, knowing full well their jobs are at the mercy of school boards upon which creationists are a stronger and stronger influence.

Then, too, in schools, students are not required to believe what they learn about evolution—merely to parrot it back on tests. If they fail to do so, their punishment is nothing more than the loss of a few points on a test or two.

In the creationist churches, however, the congregation is required to believe. Impressionable youngsters, taught that they will go to hell if they listen to the evolutionary doctrine, are not likely to listen in comfort or to believe if they do.

Therefore, creationists, who control the church and the society they live in and who face the public school as the only place where evolution is even briefly mentioned in a possibly favorable way, find they cannot stand even so minuscule a competition and demand "equal time."

Do you suppose their devotion to "fairness" is such that they will give equal time to evolution in their churches?

Second, the real danger is the manner in which creationists want their "equal time."

In the scientific world, there is free and open competition of ideas, and even a scientist whose suggestions are not accepted is nevertheless free to continue to argue his case.

In this free and open competition of ideas, creationism has clearly lost. It has been losing in fact, since the time of Copernicus four and a half centuries ago. But creationists, placing myth above reason, refuse to accept the decision and are now calling on the Government to force their views on the schools in lieu of the free expression of ideas. Teachers must be forced to present creationism as though it has equal intellectual respectability with evolutionary doctrine.

What a precedent this sets.

If the Government can mobilize its policemen and its prisons to make certain that teachers give creationism equal time, they can next use force to make sure that teachers declare creationism the victor so that evolution will be evicted from the classroom altogether.

We will have established the full groundwork, in other words, for legally enforced ignorance and for totalitarian thought control.

And what if the creationists win? They might, you know, for there are millions who, faced with the choice between science and their interpretation of the Bible, will choose the Bible and reject science, regardless of the evidence.

This is not entirely because of a traditional and unthinking reverence for the literal words of the Bible; there is also a pervasive uneasiness—even an actual fear—of science that will drive even those who care little for Fundamentalism into the arms of the creationists. For one thing, science is uncertain. Theories are subject to revision; observations are open to a variety of interpretations, and scientists quarrel among themselves. This is disillusioning for those untrained in the scientific method, who thus turn to the rigid certainty of the Bible instead. There is something comfortable about a view that allows

for no deviation and that spares you the painful necessity of having to think.

Second, science is complex and chilling. The mathematical language of science is understood by very few. The vistas it presents are scary—an enormous universe ruled by chance and impersonal rules, empty and uncaring, ungraspable and vertiginous. How comfortable to turn instead to a small world, only a few thousand years old, and under God's personal and immediate care; a world in which you are His peculiar concern and where He will not consign you to hell if you are careful to follow every word of the Bible as interpreted for you by your television preacher.

Third, science is dangerous. There is no question but that poison gas, genetic engineering and nuclear weapons and power stations are terrifying. It may be that civilization is falling apart and the world we know is coming to an end. In that case, why not turn to religion and look forward to the Day of Judgment, in which you and your fellow believers will be lifted into eternal bliss and have the added joy of watching the scoffers and disbelievers writhe forever in torment.

So why might they not win?

There are numerous cases of societies in which the armies of the night have ridden triumphantly over minorities in order to establish a powerful orthodoxy which dictates official thought. Invariably, the triumphant ride is toward long-range disaster.

Spain dominated Europe and the world in the 16th century, but in Spain orthodoxy came first, and all divergence of opinion was ruthlessly suppressed. The result was that Spain settled back into blankness and did not share in the scientific, technological and commercial ferment that bubbled up in other nations of Western Europe. Spain remained an intellectual backwater for centuries.

In the late 17th century, France in the name of orthodoxy revoked the Edict of Nantes and drove out many thousands of Huguenots, who added their intellectual vigor to lands of refuge such as Great Britain, the Netherlands and Prussia, while France was permanently weakened.

In more recent times, Germany hounded out the Jewish scientists of Europe. They arrived in the United States and contributed immeasurably to scientific advancement here, while Germany lost so heavily that there is no telling how long it will take to regain its former scientific eminence. The Soviet Union, in its fascination with Lysenko, destroyed its geneticists, and set back its biological sciences for decades. China, during the Cultural Revolution, turned against Western Science and is still laboring to overcome the devastation that resulted.

Are we now, with all these examples before us, to ride backward into the past under the same tattered banner of orthodoxy? With creationism in the saddle, American science will wither. We will raise a generation of ignoramuses ill-equipped to run the industry of tomorrow, much less to generate the new advances of the days after tomorrow.

We will inevitably recede into the backwater of civilization and those nations that retain open scientific thought will take over the leadership of the world and the cutting edge of human advancement.

I don't suppose that the creationists really plan the decline of the United States, but their loudly expressed patriotism is as simple-minded as their "science." If they succeed, they will, in their folly, achieve the opposite of what they say they wish.

Chapter 5
How Is My Mind Connected to My Body

Anybody who can read this book, or even this sentence, can think. It is tempting to conclude, as Descartes did in his *Second Meditation*, that anybody who can read this book, or even this sentence, has a mind. In addition, most of us are quite certain that we have a body, although Descartes attempted to doubt even this. But the question of what the relationship is between our minds and our bodies is one if the most enduring and puzzling in philosophy. It is also one of the most immediate, since it has direct consequences for our views about what and who we are.

Descartes believed that the mind and the body are distinct substances. He was therefore a **dualist,** a person who believes that there are two fundamentally different kinds of "stuff" (mental and physical) in the universe. The dualist is faced with the difficult problem of explaining what the relationship is between these two fundamentally different kinds of stuff. The usual view is this. Let's say there is a song playing on the radio (a physical event). You hear the song and that causes you to remember or think of a summer friend (a mental event). Your remembering in turn causes you to write your friend a letter (a physical event). Here, a physical event (the playing of the song) causes a mental event (the remembering) which causes a physical event (the writing). Here's another example: You hit your thumb with a hammer (physical event), which causes pain (mental event), which in turn causes you to scream and hop up and down (physical event). The view that mental and physical events interact in this way is called **interactionism.** Dualistic interactionism represents most people's commonsense view about the relationship between the mental and the physical.

Unfortunately, there are two very difficult problems that an interactionist dualist must solve. The first is the problem of what it is that makes your mind yours and not someone else's. Is it perhaps located in your body? But if so, what makes it move when your body moves? Is it glued, stapled, or tied to your brain? If so, how do you attach a nonphysical substance to a physical one? Perhaps it is not located in space at all. (How could a nonphysical substance be located in space anyway?) But if it's not, how exactly did the broken bone in your thumb cause a pain in *your* mind and not in your brother's mind? How did the pain in your mind cause *your* body to hop and not Mick Jagger's?

Related to this problem, and even more vexing, is the question of giving a clear and exact account of how any nonphysical substance could cause changes in a physical substance, or vice versa. How exactly would a nonphysical substance cause molecules of a transmitter substance to be released from the cells of the brain? (This is the mechanism for the transmission of signals in the brain.) Most people regard with suspicion a claim that a nonphysical mind has moved some dice or a table. They should regard with equal suspicion a claim that a nonphysical mind has moved an arm or a toe.

It is these problems that have led some philosophers and quite a few scientists to the odd view that mind and brain do not interact as we might have thought. The most common of these views is **epiphenomenalism.** According to this view, mental events are epiphenomena, which are literally phenomena *outside* the rest of the person. Epiphenomenalists believe that physical events can cause mental events, but that mental events never affect physical events. What you think, believe, and desire is merely a symptom of what is going on in your brain; it never actually makes a difference in what you *do.* Your mind is merely a window into your brain: It observes what happens in the brain and reacts accordingly, but it can never affect the workings of the brain (or the body). Epiphenomenalism must then explain how our ordinary view, that mental events do cause physical events, can be so badly mistaken. It must also give some explanation of how it could be that a physical event could cause a nonphysical event.

One attractive way of dealing with these problems is to deny that they are problems at all. This is what Gilbert Ryle, the famous **behaviorist,** does in his selection, from his book *The Concept of Mind.* In a later part of that book, he argues that our talk of mental states and events is really just talk about behavior, not, as it pretends, talk about inner events that cause us to do what we do.

In response to these problems, most contemporary philosophers have adopted some form of **physicalism,** the view that there are not separate mental and physical things in the universe, but rather that everything is physical. Much of the current philosophical debate about the mind/body problem presupposes a framework of physicalism. One early form of physicalism is known as the **identity theory.** The identity theory claimed that each mental event—for example, wanting to eat dinner—could be identified with a very specific, purely physical event—for example, the firing of neurons number 87 and 163. This requires that each time a "wanting to eat dinner" takes place, a firing of neurons 87 and 163 takes place, because wanting to eat dinner *is* the firing of those two neurons. The identity theory, in this crude form, has now largely been discredited by the observation that dogs and extraterrestrials could both want to eat dinner, but might not have any neurons at all (in the case of extraterrestrials), much less neurons number 87 and 163. Different organisms, with very different physical structures, can all have nonphysical things such as beliefs and desires.

Thus, much current physicalism rejects the identity theory and tries to explain how mental events could be physical but not definable in terms of neurophysiological states. Eliminative materialists take a radical view, claiming that the language of biological science is a privileged scientific way of describing human beings. Since mental states like belief and desire can't be defined in that language, talk of such mental states must be radically defective and should be eliminated in favor of vocabulary that *can* be explained in purely biological terms. They conclude that people do not really have beliefs and desires; the view that we have beliefs and desires is, they go on to claim, an outmoded theory, a **folk-psychology,** that, like other defective theories, should be discarded with the advance of physical science.

Most people are not willing to accept the conclusion that we do not really have beliefs, desires, or other mental states. The problem then becomes how to explain beliefs and desires as genuine physical states of a person, while still rejecting the notion that they can be defined neurophysiologically. **Functionalism is the view to which** most modern physicalists have turned. It is the view that mental events are defined in terms of what they cause and what they affect, which includes both physical events and other mental events. Thus, different things (a person, a dog, an extraterrestrial, a computer) could have the same mental events by having (physically) different things going on inside that were related causally or functionally (that is, in terms of what their function is) in the ways characteristic of that mental event. The pain in your foot may be signals in the thalamus in your brain. In a dog, the pain in its foot may have to do with some other part of its brain. A spaceman may not have a thalamus but could still have a pain in his foot. In each being, whatever state is caused by dropping a hammer on its toe and causing it to hop up and down and scream, is pain. In this view, it is not possible to "reduce" psychological terms such as "believe" or "want" to biological terms. But even though mental terms cannot be reduced to physical terms and so we must still have a psychological vocabulary, that does not mean that there is mental stuff in the universe. There is only mental talk abut physical stuff. William Lycan argues for a particularly appealing form of functionalism and for the consequent view that machines could come to have the same moral and social properties and relationships that humans now have.

By way of contrast, John R. Searle, in a now classic argument against functionalism, launches a deep and provocative critique of the approach taken by Lycan and others. He argues with some flair that any approach that ignores the actual biological stuff of an organism (the "wetware") cannot genuinely explain that organism. If Searle is right, then it is not possible for a computer really to think or to have feelings. The best that a computer could do is to behave *as though* it had thoughts and feelings. If so, then the project of understanding our conscious mental lives in the functionalist terms of the causal roles that our mental states occupy, is hopelessly mistaken.

Elizabeth V. Spelman in her selection offers an entirely different analysis of the mind/body problem, claiming that philosophers have been influenced systematically by unrecognized political and social views (specifically by gender views) in their conceptions of the relationship between mind and body. She argues that our entire conception of the mind (or soul) serves a view of humans that deprecates women and nondominant races. In raising this issue she places under scrutiny the very process by which philosophers have traditionally addressed philosophical issues.

Finally, Francisco Varela and his coauthors agree with Spelman that our difficulties with the mind/body problem have been created by the very structure in which we have conceived of the problem. But in contrast to Spelman, Varela et al. argue that Buddhist conceptions of the self provide a way for seeing ourselves as simultaneously physical and spiritual—as "embodied minds".

The mind/body problem offers philosophical terrain that is both treacherous and rewarding. The problems it poses are particularly pressing because they are so closely tied to a great deal of current scientific work and because they are so frightfully misunderstood. For example, a neuroscientist (a scientist who studies brain function) may have discovered a physiological basis for some phenomenon such as depression. She may then go on to conclude that psychologists (Freud, for example) who have hypothesized a psychological origin for depression have thereby been shown to be wrong. Nothing could be farther from the truth. Differing physiological and psychological explanations for the same phenomenon is exactly what one would expect if physicalism is true.

Another subtler mistake is this: A neuroscientist may, at the end of a long career, come to despair of ever being able to define some psychological state, such as the state of understanding, in biological terms. She may conclude that understanding is not a biological phenomenon. This is how many neuroscientists come oddly to be epiphenomenalists. Again the conclusion rests on a confusion. As both functionalism and eliminative materialism make clear, physicalism does not suggest that one can reduce the psychological to the physical or define psychological terms in biological (or any other physical) terms. So the inability to define understanding, or any other mental phenomenon, in biological terms does not show that there is anything nonphysical about understanding, or any other mental phenomenon. It is possible to be a physicalist and still to believe strongly in the need for psychological theories. All these are areas in which philosophers have much by way of clarification to contribute to their scientific friends.

RENÉ DESCARTES

Mind as Distinct from Body

RENÉ DESCARTES (1596–1650) was born in Britanny, France. He went to college at the age of eight and was finished at the age of sixteen, having studied logic, philosophy, and mathematics. He did important work in mathematics and science in addition to his revolutionary work in philosophy. Descartes was in the habit of spending long morning hours reflecting in bed. But when he entered the service of Sweden's Queen Christina in 1649, he was expected to begin teaching her in the library at 5 A.M. Unaccustomed to such rigors, and to the Swedish winter, he took fever and died early in 1650.

IN order to begin this examination, then, I here say, in the first place, that there is a great difference between mind and body, inasmuch as body is by nature always divisible, and the mind is entirely indivisible. For, as a matter of fact, when I consider the mind, that is to say, myself inasmuch as I am only a thinking thing, I cannot distinguish in myself any parts, but apprehend myself to be clearly one and entire; and although the whole mind seems to be united to the whole body, yet if a foot, or an arm, or some other part, is separated from my body, I am aware that nothing has been taken away from my mind. And the faculties of willing, feeling, conceiving, etc. cannot be properly speaking said to be its parts, for it is one and the same mind which employs itself in willing and in feeling and understanding. But it is quite otherwise with corporeal or extended objects, for there is not one of these imaginable by me which my mind cannot easily divide into parts, and which consequently I do not recognize as being divisible; this would be sufficient to teach me that the mind or soul of man is entirely different from the body, if I had not already learned it from other sources.

I further notice that the mind does not receive the impressions from all parts of the body immediately, but only from the brain, or perhaps even from one of its smallest parts, to wit, from that in which the common sense is said to reside, which, whenever it is disposed in the same particular way, conveys the same thing to the mind, although meanwhile the other portions of the body may be differently disposed, as is testified by innumerable experiments which it is unnecessary here to recount.

I notice, also, that the nature of body is such that none of its parts can be moved by another part a little way off which cannot also be moved in the same way by each one of the parts which are between the two, although this more remote part does not act at all. As, for example, in the cord *ABCD* [which is in tension] if we pull the last part *D*, the first part *A* will not be moved in any way differently from what would be the case if one of the intervening parts *B* or *C* were pulled, and the last part *D* were to remain unmoved. And in the same way, when I feel pain in my foot, my knowledge of physics teaches me that this sensation is communicated by means of nerves dispersed through the foot, which, being extended like cords from there to the brain, when they are contracted in the foot, at the same time contract the inmost portions of the brain which is their extremity and place of origin, and then excite a certain movement which nature has established in order to cause the mind to be affected by a sensation of pain represented as existing in the foot. But because these nerves must pass through the tibia, the thigh, the loins, the back and the neck, in order to reach from the leg to the brain, it may happen that although their extremities which are in the foot are not affected, but only certain ones of their intervening parts which pass by the loins or the neck, this action will excite the same movement in the brain that might have been excited there by a hurt received in the foot, in consequence of which the mind will necessarily feel in the foot the same pain as if it had received a hurt. And the same holds good of all the other perceptions of our senses.

I notice finally that since each of the movements which are in the portion of the brain by which the mind is immediately affected brings about one particular sensation only, we cannot under the circumstances imagine anything more likely than that this movement amongst all the sensations which it is capable of impressing on it, causes mind to be affected by that one which is best fitted and most generally useful for the conservation of the human body when it is in health. But experience makes us aware that all the feelings with which nature inspires us are such as I have just spoken of; and there is therefore nothing in them which does not give testimony to the power and goodness of the God who has produced them. Thus, for example, when the nerves which are in the feet are violently or more than usu-

ally moved, their movement, passing through the medulla of the spine to the inmost parts of the brain, gives a sign to the mind which makes it feel somewhat, to wit, pain, as though in the foot, by which the mind is excited to do its utmost to remove the cause of the evil as dangerous and hurtful to the foot. It is true that God could have constituted the nature of man in such a way that this same movement in the brain would have conveyed something quite different to the mind; for example, it might have produced consciousness of itself either in so far as it is in the brain, or as it is in the foot, or as it is in some other place between the foot and the brain, or it might finally have produced consciousness of anything else whatsoever; but none of all this would have contributed so well to the conservation of the body. Similarly, when we desire to drink, a certain dryness of the throat is produced which moves its nerves, and by their means the internal portions of the brain; and this movement causes in the mind the sensation of thirst, because in this case there is nothing more useful to us than to become aware that we have need to drink for the conservation of our health; and the same holds good in other instances.

From this it is quite clear that, notwithstanding the supreme goodness of God, the nature of man, inasmuch as it is composed of mind and body, cannot be otherwise than sometimes a source of deception. For if there is any cause which excites, not in the foot but in some part of the nerves which are extended between the foot and the brain, or even in the brain itself, the same movement which usually is produced when the foot is detrimentally affected, pain will be experienced as though it were in the foot, and the sense will thus naturally be deceived; for since the same movement in the brain is capable of causing but one sensation in the mind, and this sensation is much more frequently excited by a cause which hurts the foot than by another existing in some other quarter, it is reasonable that it should convey to the mind pain in the foot rather than in any other part of the body. And although the parchedness of the throat does not always proceed, as it usually does, from the fact that drinking is necessary for the health of the body, but sometimes comes from quite a different cause, as is the case with dropsical patients, it is yet much better that it should mislead on this occasion than if, on the other hand, it were always to deceive us when the body is in good health; and so on in similar cases. . . .

From a description of inanimate bodies and plants I passed on to that of animals, and particularly to that of men. But since I had not yet sufficient knowledge to speak of them in the same style as of the rest, that is to say, demonstrating the effects from the causes, and showing from what beginnings and in what fashion Nature must produce them, I contented myself with supposing that God formed the body of man altogether like one of ours, in the outward figure of its members as well as in the interior conformation of its organs, without making use of any matter other than that which I had described, and without at the first placing it in a rational soul, or any other thing which might serve as a vegetative or as a sensitive soul; excepting that He kindled in the heart one of these fires without light, which I have already described, and which I did not conceive of as in any way different from that which makes the hay heat when shut up before it is dry, and which makes new wine

grow frothy when it is left to ferment over the fruit. For, examining the functions which might in accordance with this supposition exist in the body, I found precisely all those which might exist in us without our having the power of thought, and consequently without our soul—that is to say, this part of us, distinct from the body, of which it has just been said that its nature is to think—contributing to it, functions which are identically the same as those in which animals lacking reason may be said to resemble us. For all that, I could not find in these functions any which, being dependent on thought, pertain to us alone, inasmuch as we are men; while I found all of them afterwards, when I assumed that God had created a rational soul and that He had united it to this body in a particular manner which I described. . . .

I had explained all these matters in some detail in the Treatise which I formerly intended to publish. And afterwards I had shown there, what must be the fabric of the nerves and muscles of the human body in order that the animal spirits therein contained should have the power to move the members, just as the heads of animals, a little while after decapitation, are still observed to move and bite the earth, notwithstanding that they are no longer animate; what changes are necessary in the brain to cause wakefulness, sleep and dreams; how light, sounds, smells, tastes, heat and all other qualities pertaining to external objects are able to imprint on it various ideas by the intervention of the senses; how hunger, thirst and other internal affections can also convey their impressions upon it; what should be regarded as the 'common sense' by which these ideas are received, and what is meant by the memory which retains them, by the fancy which can change them in diverse ways and out of them constitute new ideas, and which, by the same means, distributing the animal spirits through the muscles, can cause the members of such a body to move in as many diverse ways, and in a manner as suitable to the objects which present themselves to its senses and to its internal passions, as can happen in our own case apart from the direction of our free will. And this will not seem strange to those, who, knowing how many different *automata* or moving machines can be made by the industry of man, without employing in so doing more than a very few parts in comparison with the great multitude of bones, muscles, nerves, arteries, veins, or other parts that are found in the body of each animal. From this aspect the body is regarded as a machine which, having been made by the hands of God, is incomparably better arranged, and possesses in itself movements which are much more admirable, than any of those which can be invented by man. Here I specially stopped to show that if there had been such machines, possessing the organs and outward form of a monkey or some other animal without reason, we should not have had any means of ascertaining that they were not of the same nature as those animals. On the other hand, if there were machines which bore a resemblance to our body and imitated our actions as far as it was morally possible to do so, we should always have two very certain tests by which to recognize that, for all that, they were not real men. The first is, that they could never use speech or other signs as we do when placing our thoughts on record for the benefit of others. For we can easily understand a machine's being constituted so that it can utter words, and even emit some responses to action on it of a corporeal kind, which brings about a change in its organs; for instance, if it is touched in a particular part it may ask what we wish to say to it; if in another part it may exclaim that it is being hurt, and so on. But it never happens that it arranges its speech in various ways, in order to reply appropriately to everything that may be said in its presence, as even the lowest type of man can do. And the second difference is, that although machines can perform certain things as well as or perhaps better than any of us can do, they infallibly fall short in others, by the which means we may discover that they did not act from knowledge, but only from the disposition of their organs. For while reason is a universal instrument which can serve for all contingencies, these organs have need of some special adaptation for every particular action. From this it follows that it is morally impossible that there should be sufficient diversity in any machine to allow it to act in all the events of life in the same way as our reason causes us to act.

By these two methods we may also recognize the difference that exists between men and brutes. For it is a very remarkable fact that there are none so depraved and stupid, without even excepting idiots, that they cannot arrange different words together, forming of them a statement by which they make known their thoughts; while, on the other hand, there is no other animal, however perfect and fortunately circumstanced it may be, which can do the same. It is not the want of organs that brings this to pass, for it is evident that magpies and parrots are able to utter words just like ourselves, and yet they cannot speak as we do, that is, so as to give evidence that they think of what they say. On the other hand, men who, being born deaf and dumb, are in the same degree, or even more than the brutes, destitute of the organs which serve the others for talking, are in the habit of themselves inventing certain signs by which they make themselves understood by those who, being usually in their company, have leisure to learn their language. And this does not merely show that the brutes have less reason than men, but that they have not at all, since it is clear that very little is required in order to be able to talk. And when we notice the inequality that exists between animals of the same species, as well as between men, and observe that some are more capable of receiving instruction than others, it is not credible that a monkey or a parrot, selected as the most perfect of its species, should not in these matters equal the stupidest child to be found, or at least a child whose mind is clouded, unless in the case of the brute the soul were of an entirely different nature from ours. And we ought not to confound speech with natural movements which betray passions and may be imitated by machines as well as be manifested by animals; nor must we think, as did some of the ancients, that brutes talk, although we do not understand their language. For if this were true, since they have many organs which are allied to our own, they could communicate their thoughts to us just as easily as to those of their own race. It is also a very remarkable fact that although there are many animals which exhibit more dexterity than we do in some of their actions, we at the same time observe that they do not manifest any dexterity at all in many others. Hence the fact that they do better than we do, does not prove that they are endowed with mind, for in this case they would have more reason than any of us, and would surpass us in all other things. It rather shows that they have no reason at all, and that it is nature which acts in them according to the disposition of their organs, just as a clock, which is only composed of wheels and weights, is able to tell the hours and measure the time more correctly than we can do with all our wisdom.

I had described after this the rational soul and shown that it could not be in any way derived from the power of matter, like the other things of which I had spoken, but that it must be expressly created. I showed, too, that it is not sufficient that it should be lodged in the human body like a pilot in his ship, unless perhaps for the moving of its members, but that it is necessary that it should also be joined and united more closely to the body in order to have sensations and appetites similar to our own, and thus to form a true man. In conclusion, I have here enlarged a little on the subject of the soul, because it is one of the greatest importance. For next to the error of those who deny God, which I think I have already sufficiently refuted, there is none which is more effectual in leading feeble spirits from the straight path of virtue, than to imagine that the soul of the brute is of the same nature as our own, and that in consequence, after this life we have nothing to fear or to hope for, any more than the flies and ants. As a matter of fact, when one comes to know how greatly they differ, we understand much better the reasons which go to prove that our soul is in its nature entirely independent of body, and in consequence that it is not liable to die with it. And then, inasmuch as we observe no other causes capable of destroying it, we are naturally inclined to judge that it is immortal.

GILBERT RYLE

The Concept of Mind

GILBERT RYLE (1900–1976) was for many years a professor of philosophy at Oxford. His book, The Concept of Mind, *from which this selection is taken, was a highly influential statement of philosophical behaviorism.*

THE OFFICIAL DOCTRINE

THERE is a doctrine about the nature and place of minds which is so prevalent among theorists and even among laymen that it deserves to be described as the official theory. Most philosophers, psychologists and religious teachers subscribe, with minor reservations, to its main articles and, although they admit certain theoretical difficulties in it, they tend to assume that these can be overcome without serious modifications being made to the architecture of the theory. It will be argued here that the central principles of the doctrine are unsound and conflict with the whole body of what we know about minds when we are not speculating about them.

The official doctrine, which hails chiefly from Descartes, is something like this. With the doubtful exceptions of idiots and infants in arms, every human being has both a body and a mind. His body and his mind are ordinarily harnessed together, but after the death of the body his mind may continue to exist and function.

Human bodies are in space and are subject to the mechanical laws which govern all other bodies in space. Bodily processes and states can be inspected by external observers. So a man's bodily life is as much a public affair as are the lives of animals and reptiles and even as the careers of trees, crystals and planets.

But minds are not in space, nor are their operations subject to mechanical laws. The workings of one mind are not witnessable by other observers; its career is private. Only I can take direct cognisance of the states and processes of my own mind. A person therefore lives through two collateral histories, one consisting of what happens in and to his body, the other consisting of what happens in and to his mind. The first is public, the second private. The events in the first history are events in the physical world, those in the second are events in the mental world.

It has been disputed whether a person does or can directly monitor all or only some of the episodes of his own private history; but, according to the official doctrine, of at least some of these episodes he has direct and unchallengeable cognisance. In consciousness, self-consciousness and introspection he is directly and authentically apprised of the present states and operations of his mind. He may have great or small uncertainties about concurrent and adjacent episodes in the physical world, but he can have none about at least part of what is momentarily occupying his mind.

It is customary to express this bifurcation of his two lives and of his two worlds by saying that the things and events which belong to the physical world, including his own body, are external, while the workings of his own mind are internal. This antithesis of outer and inner is if course meant to be construed as a metaphor, since minds, not being in space, could not be described as being spatially inside anything else, or as having things going on spatially inside themselves. But relapses from this good intention are common and theorists are found speculating how stimuli, the physical sources of which are yards or miles outside a person's skin, can generate mental responses inside his skull, or how decisions framed inside his cranium can set going movements of his extremities.

Even when 'inner' and 'outer' are construed as metaphors, the problem how a person's mind and body influence one another is notoriously charged with theoretical difficulties. What the mind wills, the legs, arms and the tongue execute; what affects the ear and the eye has something to do with what the mind perceives; grimaces and smiles betray the mind's moods and bodily castigations lead, it is hoped, to moral improvement. But the actual transactions between the episodes of the private history and those of the public history remain mysterious, since by definition they can belong to neither series. They could not be reported among the happenings described in a person's autobiography of his inner life, but nor could they be reported among those described in some one else's biography of that person's overt career. They can be inspected neither by introspection nor by laboratory experiment. They are theoretical shuttlecocks which are forever being bandied from the physiologist back to the psychologist and from the psychologist back to the physiologist.

Underlying this partly metaphorical representation of the bifurcation of a person's two lives there is a seemingly more profound and philosophical assumption. It is assumed that there are two different kinds of existence or status. What exists or happens may have the status of physical existence, or it may have the status of mental existence. Somewhat as the faces of coins are either heads or tails, or somewhat as living creatures are either male or female, so, it is supposed, some existing is physical existing, other existing is mental existing. It is a necessary feature of what has physical existence that it is in space and time, it is a necessary feature of what has mental existence that it is in time but not in space. What has physical existence is composed of matter, or else is a function of matter; what has mental existence consists of consciousness, or else is a function of consciousness.

There is thus a polar opposition between mind and matter, an opposition which is often brought out as follows. Material objects are situated in a common field, known as 'space', and what happens to one body in one part of space is mechanically connected with what happens to the other bodies in other parts of space. But mental happenings occur in insulated fields, known as 'minds', and there is, apart maybe from telepathy, no direct causal connection between what happens in one mind and what happens in another. Only through the medium of the public physical world can the mind of one person make a difference to the mind of another. The mind is its own place and in his inner life each of us lives the life of a ghostly Robinson Crusoe. People can see, hear and jolt one another's bodies, but they are irremediably blind and deaf to the workings of one another's minds and inoperative upon them.

What sort of knowledge can be secured of the workings of a mind? On the one side, according to the official theory, a person has direct knowledge of the best imaginable kind of the working of his own mind. Mental states and processes are (or are normally) conscious states and processes, and the consciousness which irradiates them can engender no illusions and leaves the door open for no doubts. A person's present thinkings, feelings and willings, his perceivings, rememberings and imaginings are intrinsically 'phosphorescent'; their existence and their nature are inevitably betrayed to their owner. The inner life is a stream of consciousness of such a sort that it would be absurd to suggest that the mind whose life is that stream might be unaware of what is passing down it.

True, the evidence adduced recently by Freud seems to show that there exist channels tributary to this stream, which run hidden from their owner. People are actuated by impulses the existence of which they vigorously disavow; some of their thoughts differ from the thoughts which they acknowledge; and some of the actions which they think they will to perform they do not really will. They are thoroughly gulled by some of their own hypocrisies and they successfully ignore facts about their mental lives which on the official theory ought to be patent to them. Holders of the official theory tend, however, to maintain that anyhow in normal circumstances a person must be directly and authentically seized of the present state and working of his own mind.

Besides being currently supplied with these alleged immediate data of consciousness, a person is also generally supposed to be able to exercise from time to time a special kind of perception, namely inner perception, or introspection. He can take a (non-optical) 'look' at what is passing in his mind. Not only can he view and scrutinize a flower through his sense of sight and listen to and discriminate the notes of a bell through his sense of hearing; he can also reflectively or introspectively watch, without any bodily organ of sense, the current episodes of his inner life. This self-observation is also commonly supposed to be immune from illusion, confusion or doubt. A mind's reports of its own affairs have a certainty superior to the best that is possessed by its reports of matters in the physical world. Sense-perceptions can, but consciousness and introspection cannot, be mistaken or confused.

On the other side, one person has no direct access of any sort to the events of the inner life of another. He cannot do better than make problematic inferences from the observed behaviour of the other person's body to the states of mind which, by analogy from his own conduct, he supposes to be signalised by that behaviour. Direct access to the workings of a mind is the privilege of that mind itself; in default of such privileged access, the workings of one mind are inevitably occult to everyone else. For the supposed arguments from bodily movements similar to their own to mental workings similar to their own would lack any possibility of observational corroboration. Not unnaturally, therefore, an adherent of the official theory finds it difficult to resist this consequence of his premises, that he has no good reason to believe that there do exist minds other than his own. Even if he prefers to believe that to other human bodies there are harnessed minds not un-like his own, he cannot claim to be able to discover their individual characteris-tics, or the particular things that they un-dergo and do. Absolute solitude is on this showing the ineluctable destiny of the soul. Only our bodies can meet.

As a necessary corollary of this gen-eral scheme there is implicitly pre-scribed a special way of construing our ordinary concepts of mental powers and operations. The verbs, nouns and adjectives, with which in ordinary life we describe the wits, characters and higher-grade performances of the peo-ple with whom we have to do, are re-quired to be construed as signifying special episodes in their secret histories, or else as signifying tendencies for such episodes to occur. When someone is de-scribed as knowing, believing or guess-ing something, as hoping, dreading, intending or shirking something, as de-signing this or being amused at that, these verbs are supposed to denote the occurrence of specific modifications in his (to us) occult stream of conscious-ness. Only his own privileged access to this stream in direct awareness and in-trospection could provide authentic tes-timony that these mental-conduct verbs were correctly or incorrectly applied. The onlooker, be he teacher, critic, bi-ographer or friend, can never assure himself that his comments have any vestige of truth. Yet it was just because we do in fact all know how to make such comments, make them with gen-eral correctness and correct them when they turn out to be confused or mis-taken, that philosophers found it neces-sary to construct their theories of the nature and place of minds. Finding mental-conduct concepts being regu-larly and effectively used, they properly sought to fix their logical geography.

But the logical geography officially rec-ommended would entail that there could be no regular or effective use of these mental-conduct concepts in our descrip-tions of, and prescriptions for, other people's minds.

THE ABSURDITY OF
THE OFFICIAL DOCTRINE

Such in outline is the official theory. I shall often speak of it, with deliberate abusiveness, as 'the dogma of the Ghost in the Machine'. I hope to prove that it is entirely false, and false not in detail but in principle. It is not merely an as-semblage of particular mistakes. It is one big mistake and a mistake of a special kind. It is, namely, a category-mistake. It represents the facts of mental life as if they belonged to one logical type or category (or range of types or categories), when they actually belong to another. The dogma is therefore a philosopher's myth. In attempting to ex-plode the myth I shall probably be taken to be denying well-known facts about the mental life of human beings, and my plea that I aim at doing nothing more than rectify the logic of mental-conduct concepts will probably be disallowed as mere subterfuge.

I must first indicate what is meant by the phrase 'Category-mistake'. This I do in a series of illustrations.

A foreigner visiting Oxford or Cam-bridge for the first time is shown a num-ber of colleges, libraries, playing fields, museums, scientific departments and administrative offices. He then asks 'But where is the University? I have seen where the members of the Colleges live, where the Registrar works, where the scientists experiment and the rest. But I have not yet seen the University in which reside and work the members of

your University.' It has then to be explained to him that the University is not
another collateral institution, some ulte-
rior counterpart to the colleges, laboratories and offices which he has seen.
The University is just the way in which
all that he has already seen is organized.
When they are seen and when their coordination is understood, the University
has been seen. His mistake lay in his innocent assumption that it was correct to
speak of Christ Church, the Bodleian
Library, the Ashmolean Museum *and*
the University, to speak, that is, as if
'the University' stood for an extra member of the class of which these other
units are members. He was mistakenly
allocating the University to the same
category as that to which the other institutions belong. The same mistake would
be made by a child witnessing the
march-past of a division, who, having
had pointed out to him such and such
battalions, batteries, squadrons, etc.,
asked when the division was going to
appear. He would be supposing that a
division was a counterpart to the units
already seen, partly similar to them
and partly unlike them. He would be
shown his mistake by being told that in
watching the battalions, batteries and
squadrons marching past he had been
watching the division marching past.
The march-past was not a parade of battalions, batteries, squadrons *and* a division; it was a parade of the battalions,
batteries and squadrons *of* a division.

One more illustration. A foreigner
watching his first game of cricket learns
what are the functions of the bowlers,
the batsmen, the fielders, the umpires
and the scorers. He then says 'But there
is no one left on the field to contribute
the famous element of team-spirit. I see
who does the bowling, the batting and
the wicket-keeping; but I do not see

whose role it is to exercise *esprit de
corps*'. Once more, it would have to be
explained that he was looking for the
wrong type of thing. Team-spirit is not
another cricketing-operation supplementary to all of the other special tasks.
It is, roughly, the keenness with which
each of the special tasks is performed,
and performing a task keenly is not performing two tasks. Certainly exhibiting
team-spirit is not the same thing as
bowling or catching, but nor is it a third
thing such that we can say that the
bowler first bowls *and* then exhibits
team-spirit or that a fielder is at a given
moment *either* catching *or* displaying
esprit de corps.

These illustrations of category-
mistakes have a common feature which
must be noticed. The mistakes were
made by people who did not know how
to wield the concepts *University, division* and *team-spirit*. Their puzzles
arose from inability to use certain items
in the English vocabulary.

The theoretically interesting category-
mistakes are those made by people who
are perfectly competent to apply concepts, at least in the situations with
which they are familiar, but are still
liable in their abstract thinking to allocate those concepts to logical types to
which they do not belong. An instance
of a mistake of this sort would be the
following story. A student of politics has
learned the main differences between
the British, the French and the American Constitutions, and has learned also
the differences and connections between
the Cabinet, Parliament, the various
Ministries, the Judicature and the
Church of England. But he still becomes embarrassed when asked questions about the connections between the
church of England, the Home Office
and the British Constitution. For while

the Church and the Home Office are institutions, the British Constitution is not another institution in the same sense of that noun. So inter-institutional relations which can be asserted or denied to hold between the Church and the Home Office cannot be asserted or denied to hold between either of them and the British Constitution. 'The British Constitution' is not a term of the same logical type as 'the Home Office' and 'the church of England'. In a partially similar way, John Doe may be a relative, a friend, an enemy or a stranger to Richard Roe; but he cannot be any of these things to the Average Taxpayer. He knows how to talk sense in certain sorts of discussions about the Average Taxpayer, but he is baffled to say why he could not come across him in the street as he can come across Richard Roe.

It is pertinent to our main subject to notice that, so long as the student of politics continues to think of the British Constitution as a counterpart to the other institutions, he will tend to describe it as a mysteriously occult institution; and so long as John Doe continues to think of the Average Taxpayer as a fellow-citizen, he will tend to think of him as an elusive insubstantial man, a ghost who is everywhere yet nowhere.

My destructive purpose is to show that a family of radical category-mistakes is the source of the double-life theory. The representation of a person as a ghost mysteriously ensconced in a machine derives from this argument. Because, as is true, a person's thinking, feeling and purposive doing cannot be described solely in the idioms of physics, chemistry and physiology, therefore they must be described in counterpart idioms. As the human body is a complex organised unit, so the human mind must be another complex

organised unit, though one made of a different sort of stuff and with a different sort of structure. Or, again, as the human body, like any other parcel of matter, is a field of causes and effects, so the mind must be another field of causes and effects, though not (Heaven be praised) mechanical causes and effects.

THE ORIGIN OF THE CATEGORY-MISTAKE

One of the chief intellectual origins of what I have yet to prove to be the Cartesian category-mistake seems to be this. When Galileo showed that his methods of scientific discovery were competent to provide a mechanical theory which should cover every occupant of space, Descartes found in himself two conflicting motives. As a man of scientific genius he could not but endorse the claims of mechanics, yet as a religious and moral man he could not accept, as Hobbes accepted, the discouraging rider to those claims, namely that human nature differs only in degree of complexity from clockwork. The mental could not be just a variety of the mechanical.

He and subsequent philosophers naturally but erroneously availed themselves of the following escape-route. Since mental-conduct words are not to be construed as signifying the occurrence of non-mechanical processes; since mechanical laws explain movements in space as the effects of other movements in space, other laws must explain some of the non-spatial workings of minds as the effects of other non-spatial workings of minds. The difference between the human behaviours which we describe as intelligent and those which we describe as unintelligent must be a difference in their causation; so, while some movements of human tongues and limbs are the effects of mechanical causes, others must be the effects of non-mechanical causes, i.e. some issue from movements of particles of matter, others from workings of the mind.

The differences between the physical and the mental were thus represented as differences inside the common framework of the categories of 'thing', 'stuff', 'attribute', 'state', 'process', 'change', 'cause' and 'effect'. Minds are things, but different sorts of things from bodies; mental processes are causes and effects, but different sorts of causes and effects from bodily movements. And so on. Somewhat as the foreigner expected the University to be an extra edifice, rather like a college but also considerably different, so the repudiators of mechanism represented minds as extra centres of causal processes, rather like machines but also considerably different from them. Their theory was a para-mechanical hypothesis.

That this assumption was at the heart of the doctrine is shown by the fact that there was from the beginning felt to be a major theoretical difficulty in explaining how minds can influence and be influenced by bodies. How can a mental process, such as willing, cause spatial movements like the movements of the tongue? How can a physical change in the optic nerve have among its effects a mind's perception of a flash of light? This notorious crux by itself shows the logical mould into which Descartes pressed his theory of the mind. It was the self-same mould into which he and Galileo set their mechanics. Still unwittingly adhering to the grammar of mechanics, he tried to avert disaster by describing minds in what was merely an obverse vocabulary. The workings of minds had to be described by the mere negatives of the specific descriptions given to bodies; they are not in space,

they are not motions, they are not modifications of matter, they are not accessible to public observation. Minds are not bits of clockwork, they are just bits of not-clockwork.

As thus represented, minds are not merely ghosts harnessed to machines, they are themselves just spectral machines. Though the human body is an engine, it is not quite an ordinary engine, since some of its workings are governed by another engine inside it—this interior governor-engine being one of a very special sort. It is invisible, inaudible and it has not size or weight. It cannot be taken to bits and the laws it obeys are not those known to ordinary engineers. Nothing is known of how it governs the bodily engine.

A second major crux points to the same moral. Since, according to the doctrine, minds belong to the same category as bodies and since bodies are rigidly governed by mechanical laws, it seemed to many theorists to follow that minds must be similarly governed by rigid non-mechanical laws. The physical world is as deterministic system, so the mental world must be a deterministic system. Bodies cannot help the modifications that they undergo, so minds cannot help pursuing the careers fixed for them. *Responsibility, choice, merit* and *demerit* are therefore inapplicable concepts—unless the compromise solution is adopted of saying that the laws governing mental processes, unlike those governing physical processes, have the congenial attribute of being only rather rigid. The problem of the Freedom of the Will was the problem of how to reconcile the hypothesis that minds are to be described in terms drawn from the categories of mechanics with the knowledge that higher-grade human conduct is not of a piece with the behaviour of machines.

It is an historical curiosity that it was not noticed that the entire argument was broken-backed. Theorists correctly assumed that any sane man could already recognise the differences between, say, rational and non-rational utterances or between purposive and automatic behaviour. Else there would have been nothing requiring to be salved from mechanism. Yet the explanation given presupposed that one person could in principle never recognise the difference between the rational and the irrational utterances issuing from other human bodies, since he could never get access to the postulated immaterial causes of some of their utterances. Save for the doubtful exception of himself, he could never tell the difference between a man and a Robot. It would have to be conceded, for example, that, for all that we can tell, the inner lives of persons who are classed as idiots or lunatics are as rational as those of anyone else. Perhaps only their overt behaviour is disappointing; that is to say, perhaps 'idiots' are not really idiotic, or 'lunatics' lunatic. Perhaps, too, some of those who are classed as sane are really idiots. According to the theory, external observers could never know how the overt behaviour of others is correlated with their mental powers and processes and so they could never know or even plausibly conjecture whether their applications of mental-conduct concepts to these other people were correct or incorrect. It would then be hazardous or impossible for a man to claim sanity or logical consistency even for himself, since he would be debarred from comparing his own performances with those of others. In short, our characterisations of persons and their performances as intelligent, prudent and virtuous or as stupid, hypocritical and cowardly could never have been made, so the problem

of providing a special causal hypothesis to serve as the basis of such diagnoses would never have arisen. The question, 'How do persons differ from machines?' arose just because everyone already knew how to apply mental-conduct concepts before the new causal hypothesis was introduced. This causal hypothesis could not therefore be the source of the criteria used in those applications. Nor, of course, has the causal hypothesis in any degree improved our handling of those criteria. We still distinguish good from bad arithmetic, politic from impolitic conduct and fertile from infertile imaginations in the ways in which Descartes himself distinguished them before and after he speculated how the applicability of these criteria was compatible with the principle of mechanical causation.

He had mistaken the logic of his problem. Instead of asking by what criteria intelligent behaviour is actually distinguished from non-intelligent behaviour, he asked 'Given that the principle of mechanical causation does not tell us the difference, what other causal principle will tell it us?' He realised that the problem was not one of mechanics and assumed that it must therefore be one of some counterpart to mechanics. Not unnaturally psychology is often cast for just this role.

When two terms belong to the same category, it is proper to construct conjunctive propositions embodying them. Thus a purchaser may say that he bought a left-hand glove and a right-hand glove, but not that he bought a left-hand glove, a right-hand glove and a pair of gloves. 'She came home in a flood of tears and a sedan-chair' is a well-known joke based on the absurdity of conjoining terms of different types. It would have been equally ridiculous to construct the disjunction 'She came home either in a flood of tears or else in a sedan-chair'. Now the dogma of the Ghost in the Machine does just this. It maintains that there exist both bodies and minds; that there occur physical processes and mental processes; that there are mechanical causes of corporeal movements. I shall argue that these and other analogous conjunctions are absurd; but, it must be noticed, the argument will not show that either of the illegitimately conjoined propositions is absurd in itself. I am not, for example, denying that there occur mental processes. Doing long division is a mental process and so is making a joke. But I am saying that the phrase 'there occur mental processes' does not mean the same sort of thing as 'there occur physical processes', and, therefore, that it makes no sense to conjoin or disjoin the two.

If my argument is successful, there will follow some interesting consequences. First, the hallowed contrast between Mind and Matter will be dissipated, but dissipated not by either of the equally hallowed absorptions of Mind by Matter or of Matter by Mind, but in quite a different way. For the seeming contrast of the two will be shown to be as illegitimate as would be the contrast of 'she came home in a flood of tears' and 'she came home in a sedan-chair'. The belief that there is a polar opposition between Mind and Matter is the belief that they are terms of the same logical type.

It will also follow that both Idealism and Materialism are answers to an im-

proper question. The 'reduction' of the material world to mental states and processes, as well as the 'reduction' of mental states and processes to physical states and processes, presuppose the legitimacy of the disjunction 'Either there exist minds or there exist bodies (but not both)'. It would be like saying, 'Either she bought a left-hand and a right-hand glove or she bought a pair of gloves (but not both)'.

It is perfectly proper to say, in one logical tone of voice, that there exist minds and to say, in another logical tone of voice, that there exist bodies. But these expressions do not indicate two different species of existence, for 'existence' is not a generic word like 'coloured' or 'sexed'. They indicate two different senses of 'exist', somewhat as 'rising' has different senses in 'the tide is rising', 'hopes are rising', and 'the average age of death is rising'. A man would be thought to be making a poor joke who said that three things are now rising, namely the tide, hopes and the average age of death. It would be just as good or bad a joke to say that there exist prime numbers and Wednesdays and public opinions and navies; or that there exist both minds and bodies. In the succeeding chapters I try to prove that the official theory does rest on a batch of category-mistakes by showing that logically absurd corollaries follow from it. The exhibition of these absurdities will have the constructive effect of bringing out part of the correct logic of mental-conduct concepts.

WILLIAM LYCAN

Robots and Minds

WILLIAM LYCAN *teaches philosophy at the Unive*
Hill. He is one of the principal proponents of a view
which sees mental capacities as constituted of comm
(etc.) of progressively more and more stupid submem
Consciousness *(1987).*

RTIFICIAL Intelligence (AI) is, very crudely, the science of getting machines to perform jobs that normally require intelligence and judgment. Researchers at any number of AI labs have designed machines that prove mathematical theorems, play chess, sort mail, guide missiles, assemble auto engines, diagnose illnesses, read stories and other written texts, and converse with people in a rudimentary way. This is, we might say, intelligent behavior.

But what is this "intelligence"? As a first pass, I suggest that intelligence of the sort I am talking about is a kind of flexibility, a responsiveness to contingencies. A dull or stupid machine must have just the right kind of raw materials presented to it in just the right way, or it is useless: the electric can-opener must have an appropriately sized can fixed under its drive wheel *just so*, in order to operate at all. Humans (most of us, anyway) are not like that. We deal with the unforeseen. We take what comes and make the best of it, even though we may have had no idea what it would be. We play the ball from whatever lie we are given, and at whatever angle to the green; we read and understand texts we have never seen before; we find our way back to Chapel Hill after getting totally lost in downtown Durham (or downtown Washington, D.C., or downtown Lima, Peru).

Our pursuit of our goals is guided while in progress by our ongoing perception and handling of interim developments. Moreover, we can pursue any number of different goals at the same time, and balance them against each other. We are sensitive to contingencies, both external and internal, that have a very complex and unsystematic structure.

It is almost irresistible to speak of *information* here, even if the term were not as trendy as it is. An intelligent creature, I want to say, is an *information-sensitive* creature, one that not only *registers* information through receptors such as sense-organs but somehow stores and manages and finally uses that information. Higher animals are intelligent beings in this sense, and so are we, even though virtually nothing is known about how we organize or manage the vast, seething profusion of information that comes our way. And there is one sort of machine that is information-sensitive also: the digital computer. A computer *is* a machine specifically designed to be fed complexes of information, to store them, manage them, and produce appropriate theoretical or practical conclusions on demand. Thus, if artificial intelligence is what one is looking for, it is no accident that one looks to the computer.

as two limitations in
achines of less elite and
ts, both of them already
n the characterization I have
en. First, a (present-day) com-
must be *fed* information, and the
oice of what information to feed and
in what form is up to a human programmer or operator. (For that matter, a
present-day computer must be plugged
into an electrical outlet and have its
switch turned to ON, but this is a very
minor contingency given the availability of nuclear power-packs.) Second, the
appropriateness and effectiveness of a
computer's output depends entirely on
what the programmer or operator had in
mind and goes on to make of it. A computer has intelligence in the sense I have
defined, but has no judgment, since it
has no goals and purposes of its own
and no internal sense of appropriateness, relevance, or proportion.

For essentially these reasons—that
computers are intelligent in my minimal
sense, and that they are nevertheless
limited in the two ways I have mentioned—AI theorists, philosophers and
intelligent laymen have inevitably compared computers to human minds, but at
the same time debated both technical
and philosophical questions raised by
this comparison. The questions break
down into three main groups or types:
(A) Questions of the form, "Will a computer ever be able to do *X*?," where *X* is
something that intelligent humans can
do. (B) Questions of the form, "Given
that a computer can or could do *X*, have
we any reason to think that it does *X* in
the same way that humans do *X*?" (C)
Questions of the form, "Given that
some futuristic supercomputer were
able to do *X, Y, Z,* . . . , for some arbitrarily large range and variety of human
activities, would that show that the
computer had property *P?*," where *P* is

some feature held to be centrally, vitally
characteristic of human minds, such as
thought, consciousness, feeling, sensation, emotion, creativity, or freedom of
the will.

Questions of type A are empirical
questions and cannot be settled without
decades, perhaps centuries of further research—compare ancient and mediaeval
speculations on the questions of
whether a machine could ever fly. Questions of type B are brutely empirical
too, and their answers are unavailable to
AI researchers *per se*, lying squarely in
the domain of cognitive psychology, a
science or alleged science barely into its
infancy. Questions of type C are philosophical and conceptual, and so I shall
essay to answer them all at one stroke.

Let us begin by supposing that all
questions types A and B have been
settled affirmatively—that one day
we might be confronted by a much-
improved version of Hal, the soft-
spoken computer in Kubrick's *2001*
(younger readers may substitute Star
Wars' C3PO or whatever subsequent
cinematic robot is the most lovable). Let
us call this more versatile machine
"Harry." Harry (let us say) is humanoid
in form—he is a miracle of miniaturiza-
tion and has lifelike plastic skin—and
he can converse intelligently on all sorts
of subjects, play golf *and* the viola,
write passable poetry, control his occasional nervousness pretty well, make
love, prove mathematical theorems (of
course), show envy when outdone,
throw gin bottles at annoying children,
etc., etc. We may suppose he fools people into thinking his is human. Now the
question is, is Harry really a *person*?
Does he have thoughts, feelings, and so
on? Is he actually conscious, or is he
just a mindless walking hardware store
whose movements are astoundingly *like*
those of a person?

Plainly his acquaintances would tend from the first to see him as a person, even if they were aware of his dubious antecedents. I think it is a plain psychological fact, if nothing more, that we could not help treating him as a person, unless we resolutely made up our minds, on principle, not to give him the time of day. But how could we really tell that he is conscious?

Well, how do we really tell that any humanoid creature is conscious? How do you tell that I am conscious, and how do I tell that you are? Surely we tell, and decisively, on the basis of our standard behavioral tests for mental states. We know that a human being has such-and-such mental states when it behaves, to speak very generally, in the ways we take to be appropriate to organisms which are in those states. (The point is of course an epistemological one only, no metaphysical implications intended or tolerated.) We know for practical purposes that a creature has a mind when it fulfills all the right criteria. And by hypothesis, Harry fulfills all our behavioral criteria with a vengeance; moreover, he does so *in the right way* (cf. questions of type B): the processing that stands causally behind his behavior is just like ours. It follows that we are a least *prima facie* justified in believing him to be conscious.

We haven't *proved* that he is conscious, of course—any more than you have proved that I am conscious. An organism's merely behaving in a certain way is no logical guarantee of sentience; from my point of view it is at least imaginable, a bare logical possibility, that my wife, my daughter and my chairman are not conscious, even though I have excellent, overwhelming behavioral reason to think that they are. But for that matter, our "standard behavioral tests" for mental states yield practical or moral certainty only so long as the situation is not palpably extraordinary or bizarre. A human chauvinist—in this case, someone who denies that Harry has thoughts and feelings, joys and sorrows—thinks precisely that Harry is as bizarre as they come. But *what is bizarre about him?* There are quite a few chauvinist answers to this, but what they boil down to, and given our hypothesized facts all they could boil down to, are two differences between Harry and ourselves: his *origin* (a laboratory is not a proper mother), and the *chemical composition of his anatomy*, if his creator has used silicon instead of carbon, for example. To exclude him from our community for either or both of *those* reasons seems to me to be a clear case of racial or ethnic prejudice (literally) and nothing more. I see no obvious way in which either a creature's origin or its sub-neuroanatomical chemical composition should matter to its psychological processes or any aspect of its mentality.

My argument can be reinforced by a thought-experiment. Imagine that we take a normal human being, Henrietta, and begin gradually replacing parts of her with synthetic materials—first a few prosthetic limbs, then a few synthetic arteries, then some neural fibers, and so forth. Suppose that the surgeons who perform the successive operations (particularly the neurosurgeons) are so clever and skillful that Henrietta survives in fine style: her intelligence, personality, perceptual acuity, poetic abilities, etc., remain just as they were before. But after the replacement process has eventually gone on to completion, Henrietta will have become an artifact—at least, her body will then be nothing but a collection of artifacts. Did she lose consciousness at some point during the sequence of operations, despite her continuing to behave and respond normally? When? It is hard to imagine that there is some privileged portion of the human nervous system that is for some reason indispensable, even though kidneys, lungs, heart, and any given bit of brain could in principle be replaced by a prosthesis (for *what* reason?); and it is also hard to imagine that there is some *pro*portion of the nervous system such that removal of more than that proportion causes loss of consciousness or sentience despite perfect maintenance of all intelligent capacities.

If this quick but totally compelling defense of Harry and Henrietta's personhood is correct, then the two, and their ilk, will have not only mental lives like ours, but *moral* lives like ours, and moral rights and privileges accordingly. Just as origin and physical constitution fail to affect psychological personhood, if a creature's internal organization is sufficiently like ours, so do they fail to affect moral personhood. We do not discriminate against a person who has a wooden leg, or a mechanical kidney, or a nuclear heart regulator; no more should we deny any human or civil right to Harry or Henrietta on grounds of their origin or physical makeup, which they cannot help.

But this happy egalitarianism raises a more immediate question: *In real life*, we shall soon be faced with medium-grade machines, which have some intelligence and are not "mere" machines like refrigerators or typewriters but which fall far short of flawless human simulators like Harry. For AI researchers may well build machines which will appear to have some familiar mental capacities but not others. The most obvious example is that of a sensor or perceptron, which picks up information from its immediate environment,

records it, and stores it in memory for future printout. (We already have at least crude machines of this kind. When they become versatile and sophisticated enough, it will be quite natural to say that they see or hear and that they remember.) But the possibility of "specialist" machines of this kind raises an unforeseen contingency: There is an enormous and many-dimensional range of possible being in between our current "mere" machines and our fully developed, flawless human simulators; we have not even begun to think of all the infinitely possible variations on this theme. And once we do begin to think of these hard cases, we will be at a loss as to where to draw the "personhood" line between them. How complex, eclectic and impressive must a machine be, and in what respects, before we award it the accolade of personhood and/or of consciousness? There is, to say the least, no clear answer to be had *a priori*, Descartes' notorious view of animals to the contrary notwithstanding.

This typical philosophical question would be no more than an amusing bon-bon, were it not for the attending moral conundrum: What moral rights would an intermediate or marginally intelligent machine have? Adolescent machines of this sort will confront us much sooner than will any good human simulators, for they are easier to design and construct; more to the moral point, they will be designed mainly as *labor-saving devices*, as servants who will work for free, and servants of this kind are (literally) made to be exploited. If they are intelligent to any degree, we should have qualms in proportion.

I suggest that this moral problem, which may become a real and pressing one, is parallel to the current debate over animal rights. Luckily I have never wanted to cook and eat my IBM portable.

Suppose I am right about the irrelevance of biochemical constitution to psychology; and suppose I was also right about the coalescing of the notions *computation, information, intelligence.* Then our mentalized theory of computation suggests in turn a computational theory of mentality, and a computational picture of the place of human beings in the world. In fact, philosophy aside, that picture has already begun to get a grip on people's thinking—as witness the filtering down of computer jargon into contemporary casual speech—and that grip is not going to loosen. Computer science is the defining technology of our time, and in this sense the computer is the natural cultural successor to the steam engine, the clock, the spindle and the potter's wheel. Predictably, an articulate computational theory of the mind has also gained credence among professional psychologists and philosophers. I have been trying to support it here and elsewhere; I shall say no more about it for now, save to note again its near-indispensability in accounting for intentionality (noted), and to address the ubiquitous question of computer creativity and freedom.

Soft Determinism or Libertarianism may be true of humans. But many people have far more rigidly deterministic intuitions about computers. Computers, after all, (let us all say it together:) "only do what they are told/programmed to do," they have no spontaneity and no freedom of choice. But human beings choose all the time, and the ensuing states of the world often depend entirely on these choices. Thus the "computer analogy" ultimately fails.

The alleged failure of course depends on what we think freedom really

is. As a Soft Determinist, I think that to have freedom of choice in acting is (roughly) for one's action to proceed out of one's own desires, deliberation, will and intention, rather than being compelled or coerced by external forces regardless of my desires or will. As before, free actions are not *uncaused* actions. My free actions are those that *I* cause, i.e., that are caused by my own mental processes rather than by something pressing on me from the outside. I have argued elsewhere that I am free in that my beliefs, desires, deliberations and intentions are all functional or computational states and processes within me which do interact in characteristic ways to produce my behavior. Note now that the same response vindicates our skilled human-simulating machines from the charge of puppethood. The word "robot" is often used as a veritable synonym for "puppet," so it may seem that Harry and Henrietta are paradigm cases of *un*free mechanisms which "only do what they are programmed to do." This is a slander—for two reasons.

First, even an ordinary computer, let alone a fabulously sophisticated machine like Harry, is in a way unpredictable. You are at its mercy. You *think* you know what it is going to do: you know what it should do, what it is supposed to do, but there is no guarantee—and it may do something *awful* or at any rate something that you could not have predicted and could not figure out if you tried with both hands. This practical sort of unpredictability would be multiplied a thousandfold in the case of a machine as complex as the human brain, and it is notably characteristic of *people.*

The unpredictability has several sources. (i) Plain old physical defects, as when Harry's circuits have been damaged by trauma, stress, heat, or the like. (ii) Bugs in one or more of his programs. (I have heard that once upon a time, somewhere, a program was written that had not a single bug in it, but this is probably an urban folk tale.) (iii) Randomizers, quantum-driven or otherwise; elements of Harry's behavior may be *genuinely*, physically random. (iv) Learning and analogy mechanisms; if Harry is equipped with these as he inevitably would be, then his behavior-patterns will be modified in response to his experiential input from the world, which would be neither controlled nor even observed by us. We don't know where he's been. (v) The relativity of reliability to goal-description. This last needs a bit of explanation.

People often say things like, "A computer just crunches binary numbers; provided it isn't broken, it just chugs on mindlessly through whatever flipflop settings are predetermined by its electronic makeup." But such remarks ignore the multilevelled character of real computer programming. At any given time, a computer is running *each of any number of* programs, depending on how it is described and on the level of functional organization that interest us. True, it is always crunching binary numbers, but in crunching them it is also doing any number of more esoteric things. And (more to the point) what counts as a mindless, algorithmic procedure at a very low level of organization may constitute, at a higher level, a hazardous do-or-die heuristic that might either succeed brilliantly or (more likely) fail and leave its objective unfulfilled.

As a second defense, remember that Harry too has beliefs, desires and intentions (provided my original argument is sound). If this is so, then his behavior normally proceeds out of his own mental processes rather than being exter-

nally compelled; and so he satisfies the definition of freedom-of-action formulated above. In most cases it will be appropriate to say that Harry could have done other than what he did do (but in fact chose after some ratiocination to do what he did, instead). Harry acts in the same sense as that in which we act, though one might continue to quarrel over what sense that is.

Probably the most popular remaining reason for doubt about machine consciousness has to do with—you guessed it—the raw qualitative character of experience. Could a mere bloodless runner-of-programs have states that *feel to it* in any of the various dramatic ways in which our mental states feel to us?

The latter question is usually asked rhetorically, expecting a resounding answer "NO!!" But I do not hear it rhetorically, for I do not see why the negative answer is supposed to be at all obvious, even for machines as opposed to biologic humans. Of course there is an incongruity *from our human point of view* between human feeling and printed circuitry or silicon pathways; that is to be expected, since we are considering those high-tech items from an external, third-person perspective and at the same time comparing them to our own first-person feels. But argumentatively, that *Gestalt* phenomenon counts for no more in the present case than it did in that of human consciousness, *viz.*, for nothing, especially if my original argument about Harry was successful in showing that biochemical constitution is irrelevant to psychology. What matters to mentality is not the stuff of which one is made, but the complex way in which that stuff is organized. If after years of close friendship we were to open Harry up to find that he is stuffed with microelectronic gadgets instead of protoplasm, we would be taken aback—no question. But our *Gestalt* clash on the occasion would do nothing *at all* to show that Harry does not have his own rich inner qualitative life. If an objector wants to insist that computation alone cannot provide consciousness with its qualitative character, the objector will have to take the initiative and come up with a further, substantive argument to show why not. We have already seen that such arguments have failed wretchedly for the case of humans; I see no reason to suspect that they would work any better for the case of robots. We must await further developments. But at the present stage of inquiry I see no compelling feel-based objection to the hypothesis of machine consciousness.

JOHN R. SEARLE

The Myth of the Computer

JOHN R. SEARLE *teaches philosophy at the University of California, Berkeley. He has done important work in philosophy of language and more recently has become an influential critic of the view that computers can tell us something important about the mind. He is author of* Minds, Brains, and Science *(1984), and numerous other books.*

OUR ordinary ways of talking about ourselves and other people, of justifying our behavior and explaining that of others, express a certain conception of human life that is so close to us, so much a part of common-sense that we can hardly see it. It is a conception according to which each person has (or perhaps *is*) a mind; the contents of the mind—beliefs, fears, hopes, motives, desires, etc.—cause and therefore explain our actions; and the continuity of our minds is the source of our individuality and identity as persons.

In the past couple of centuries we have also become convinced that this common-sense psychology is grounded in the brain, that these mental states and events are somehow, we are not quite sure how, going on in the neurophysiological processes of the brain. So this leaves us with two levels at which we can describe and explain human beings: a level of commonsense psychology, which seems to work well enough in practice but which is not scientific; and a level of neurophysiology, which is certainly scientific but which even the most advanced specialists know very little about.

But couldn't there be a third possibility, a science of human beings that was not introspective commonsense psychology but was not neurophysiology either? This has been the great dream of the human sciences in the twentieth century, but so far all of the efforts have been, in varying degrees, failures. The most spectacular failure was behaviorism, but in my intellectual lifetime I have lived through exaggerated hopes placed on and disappointed by games theory, cybernetics, information theory, generative grammar, structuralism, and Freudian psychology, among others. Indeed it has become something of a scandal of twentieth-century intellectual life that we lack a science of the human mind and human behavior, that the methods of the natural sciences have produced such meager results when applied to human beings.

The latest candidate or family of candidates to fill the gap is called cognitive science, a collection of related investigations into the human mind involving psychology, philosophy, linguistics, anthropology, and artificial intelligence. Cognitive science is really the name of a family of research projects and not a theory, but many of its practitioners think that the heart of cognitive science is a theory of the mind based on artificial intelligence (AI). According to this theory minds just are computer programs of certain kinds. The main ideological aim of Hofstadter and Dennett's book is to advance this theory. . . .

The theory, which is fairly widely held in cognitive science, can be summarized in three propositions.

1. Mind as Program.

What we call minds are simply very complex digital computer programs. Mental states are simply computer states and mental processes are computational processes. Any system whatever that had the right program, with the right input and output, would have to have mental states and processes in the same literal sense that you and I do, because that is all there is to mental states and processes, that is all that you and I have. The programs

in question are "self-updating" or "self-designing" "systems of representations."

2. The Irrelevance of the Neurophysiology of the Brain.

In the study of the mind actual biological facts about actual human and animal brains are irrelevant because the mind is an "abstract sort of thing" and human brains just happen to be among the indefinitely large number of kinds of computers that can have minds. Our minds happen to be embodied in our brains, but there is no essential connection between the mind and the brain. Any other computer with the right program would also have a mind.

Theses 1 and 2 are summarized in the introduction where the author speaks of "the emerging view of the mind as software or program—as an abstract sort of thing whose identity is independent of any particular physical embodiment."

3. The Turing Test as the Criterion of the Mental.

The conclusive proof of the presence of mental states and capacities is the ability of a system to pass the Turing test, the test devised by Alan Turing and described in his article in [Hofstadter and Dennett's] book. If a system can convince a competent expert that it has mental states then it really has those mental states. If, for example, a machine could "converse" with a native Chinese speaker in such a way as to convince the speaker that it understood Chinese then it would literally understand Chinese.

The three theses are neatly lumped together when one of the editors writes, "Minds exist in brains and may come to exist in programmed machines. If and when such machines come about, their causal powers will derive not from the substances they are made of, but from their design and the programs that run in them. And the way we will know they have those causal powers is by talking to them and listening carefully to what they have to say."

We might call this collection of theses "strong artificial intelligence" (strong AI).* These theses are certainly not obviously true and they are seldom explicitly stated and defended.

Let us inquire first into how plausible it is to suppose that specific biochemical powers of the brain are really irrelevant to the mind. It is an amazing fact, by the way, that in twenty-seven pieces about the mind the editors have not seen fit to include any whose primary aim is to tell us how the brain actually works, and this omission obviously derives from their conviction that since "mind is an abstract sort of thing" the specific neurophysiology of the brain is incidental. This idea derives part of its appeal from the editors' keeping their discussion at a very abstract general level about "consciousness" and "mind" and "soul," but if you consider specific mental states and processes—being thirsty, wanting to go to the bathroom, worrying about your income tax, trying to solve math puzzles, feeling depressed, recalling the French word for 'butterfly'—then it seems at least a little odd to think that the brain is so irrelevant.

Take thirst, where we actually know a little bit about how it works. Kidney secretions of renin synthesize a substance called angiotensin. This substance goes into the hypothalamus and triggers a series of neuron firings. As far as we know these neuron firings are a very large part of the cause of thirst. Now obviously there is more to be said, for example about the relations of the hypothalamic responses to the rest of the brain, about other things going on in the hypothalamus, and about the possible distinctions between the *feeling* of thirst and the *urge* to drink. Let us suppose we have filled out the story with the rest of the biochemical causal account of thirst.

Now these theses of the mind as program and the irrelevance of the brain would tell us that what matters about this story is not the specific biochemical properties of the angiotensin or the hypothalamus but only the formal computer programs that the whole sequence instantiates. Well, let's try that out as a hypothesis and see how it works. A computer can simulate the formal properties of the sequence of chemical and electrical phenomena in the production of thirst just as much as it can simulate the formal properties of anything else—we can simulate thirst just as we can simulate hurricanes, rainstorms, five-alarm fires, internal combustion engines, photosynthesis, lactation, or the flow of currency in a depressed economy. But no one in his right mind thinks that a computer simulation of a five-alarm fire will burn down the neighborhood, or that a computer simulation of an internal combustion engine will power a car or that computer simulation of lactation and photosynthesis will produce milk and sugar. To my amazement, however, I have found that a large number of people suppose that computer simulations

---

*"Strong" to distinguish the position from "weak" or "cautious" AI, which holds that the computer is simply a very useful tool in the study of the mind, not that the appropriately programmed computer literally has a mind.

of mental phenomena, whether at the level of brain processes or not, literally produce mental phenomena.

Again, let's try it out. Let's program our favorite PDP-10 computer with the formal program that simulates thirst. We can even program it to print out at the end "Boy, am I thirsty!" or "Won't someone please give me a drink?" etc. Now would anyone suppose that we thereby have even the slightest reason to suppose that the computer is literally thirsty? Or that any simulation of any other mental phenomena, such as understanding stories, feeling depressed, or worrying about itemized deductions, must therefore produce the real thing? The answer, alas, is that a large number of people are committed to an ideology that requires them to believe just that. So let us carry the story a step further.

The PDP-10 is powered by electricity and perhaps its electricity properties can reproduce some of the actual causal powers of the electrochemical features of the brain in producing mental states. We certainly couldn't rule out that eventuality a priori. But remember: the the sis of strong AI is that the mind is "independent of any particular embodiment" because the mind is just a program and the program can be run on a computer made of anything whatever provided it is stable enough and complex enough to carry the program. The actual physical computer could be an ant colony (one of their examples), a collection of beer cans, streams of toilet paper with small stones placed on the squares, men sitting on high stools with green eye shades—anything you like.

So let us imagine our thirst-simulating program running on a computer made entirely of old beer cans, millions (or billions) of old beer cans that are rigged up to levers and powered by windmills. We can imagine that the program simulates the neuron firings at the synapses by having beer cans bang into each other, thus achieving a strict correspondence between neuron firings and beer-can bangings. At the end of the sequence a beer can pops up on which is written "I am thirsty." Now, to repeat the question, does anyone suppose that this Rube Goldberg apparatus is literally thirsty in the sense in which you and I are?

Notice that the thesis of Hofstadter and Dennett is not that *for all we know* the collection of beer cans might be thirsty but rather that if it has the right program with the right input and output it *must* be thirsty (or understand Proust or worry about its income tax or have any other mental state) because that is all the mind is, a certain kind of computer program, and any computer made of anything at all running the right program would have to have the appropriate mental states.

I believe that everything we have learned about human and animal biology suggests that what we call "mental" phenomena are as much a part of our biological natural history as any other biological phenomena, as much a part of biology as digestion, lactation, or the secretion of bile. Much of the implausibility of the strong AI thesis derives from its resolute opposition to biology; the mind is not a concrete biological phenomenon but "an abstract sort of thing."

Still, in calling attention to the implausibility of supposing that the specific casual powers of brains are irrelevant to minds I have not yet fully exposed the preposterousness of the strong AI position, held by Hofstadter and Dennett, so let us press on and examine a bit more closely the thesis of mind as program.

Digital computer programs by definition consist of sets of purely formal operations on formally specified symbols. The ideal computer does such things as print a zero on the tape, move one square to the left, erase a 1, move back to the right, etc. It is common to describe this as "symbol manipulation" or, to use the term favored by Hofstadter and Dennett, the whole system is a "self-updating representational system"; but these terms are at least a bit misleading since as far as the computer is concerned the symbols don't *symbolize* anything or *represents* anything. They are just formal counters.

The computer attaches no meaning, interpretation, or content to the formal symbols; and qua computer it couldn't, because if we tried to give the computer an interpretation of its symbols we could only give it more uninterpreted symbols. The interpretation of the symbols is entirely up to the programmers and users of the computer. For example, on my pocket calculator if I print "3 x 3 = ," the calculator will print "9" but it has no idea that "3" means 3 or that "9" means 9 or that anything means anything. We might put this point by saying that the computer has a syntax but no semantics. The computer manipulates formal symbols but attaches no meaning to them, and this simple observation will enable us to refute the thesis of mind as program.

Suppose that we write a computer program to simulate the understanding of Chinese so that, for example, if the computer is asked questions in Chinese the program enables it to give answers in Chinese; if asked to summarize stories in Chinese it can give such summaries; if asked questions about the stories it has been given it will answer such questions.

Now suppose that I, who understand no Chinese at all and can't even distinguish Chinese symbols from some other kinds of symbols, am locked in a room with a number of cardboard boxes full of Chinese symbols. Suppose that I am given a book of rules in English that instruct me how to match these Chinese symbols with each other. The rules say such things as that the "squiggle-squiggle" sign is to be followed by the "squoggle-squoggle" sign. Suppose that people outside the room pass in more Chinese symbols and that following the instructions book I pass Chinese symbols back to them. Suppose that unknown to me the people who pass me the symbols call them "questions," and the book of instructions that I work from they call "the program"; the symbols I give back to them they call "answers to the questions" and me they call "the computer." Suppose that after a while the programmers get so good at writing the programs and I get so good at manipulating the symbols that my answers are indistinguishable from those of native Chinese speakers. I can pass the Turing test for understanding Chinese. But all the same I still don't understand a word of Chinese and neither does any other digital computer because all the computer has is what I have: a formal program that attaches no meaning, interpretation, or content to any of the symbols.

What this simple argument shows is that no formal program by itself is sufficient for understanding, because it would always be possible in principle for an agent to go through the steps in the program and still not have the relevant understanding. And what works for Chinese would also work for other mental phenomena. I could, for example, go through the steps of the thirst-simulating program without feeling thirsty. The argument also, *en passant*, refutes the Turing test because it show that a system, namely me, could pass the Turing test without having the appropriate mental states. . . .

The rest of what they have to say is mostly a repetition of points made by other authors and already answered by me. Specifically, they endorse the "systems reply" to the Chinese room argument, according to which the man in the room does not understand Chinese, but the system of which he is a part—including the instruction book, the Chinese symbols, etc.—really does understands Chinese. Adherents of this view believe, to my constant amazement, that though the man fails to understand, the *room* does understand Chinese. The obvious objection to this is that the system has no way of attaching meaning to the uninterpreted Chinese symbols, any more than the man did in the first place. The system, like the man, has a syntax but no semantics. And you can see this by simply imagining that the man internalizes the whole system. Suppose he has a super memory and a super intelligence so that he memorizes the instruction book and does all the calculations in his head. To get rid of the room, we can even suppose he works outdoors. Now since the man doesn't understand Chinese, and since there's nothing in the system that is not in the man, there is no way the system could understand Chinese. As near as I can tell Hofstadter and Dennett's only reply to this is to observe that no normal human being could perform such a feat of memory. This is of course quite true, but also quite irrelevant to the point, which, to repeat, is that from syntax alone you don't get semantics. . . .

The details of how the brain works are immensely complicated and largely unknown, but some of the general principles of the relations between brain functioning and computer programs can be stated quite simply. First, we know that brain processes cause mental phenomena. Mental states are caused by and realized in the structure of the brain. From this it follows that any system that produced mental states would have to have powers equivalent to those of the brain. Such a system might use a different chemistry, but whatever its chemistry it would have to be able to cause what the brain causes. We know from the Chinese room argument that digital computer programs by themselves are never sufficient to produce mental states. Now since brains do produce minds, and since programs by themselves can't produce minds, it follows that the way the brain does it can't be simply instantiating a computer program. (Everything, by the way, instantiates some program or other, and brains are no exception. So in that trivial sense brains, like everything else, are digital computers.) And it also follows that if you wanted to build a machine to produce mental states, a thinking machine, you couldn't do it solely in virtue of the fact that your machine ran a certain kind of computer program. The thinking machine couldn't work solely in virtue of being a digital computer but would have to duplicate the specific causal powers of the brain.

A lot of the nonsense talked about computers nowadays stems from the relative rarity and hence mystery. As computers and robots become more common, as common as telephones, washing machines, and forklift trucks, it seems likely that this aura will disappear and people will take computers for what they are, namely useful machines. In the meantime one has to try to avoid certain recurring mistakes that keep cropping up in Hofstadter and Dennett's book as well as in other current discussions.

The first is the idea that somehow computer achievements pose some sort of threat or challenge to human beings. But the fact, for example, that a calculator can outperform even the best mathematician is no more significant or threatening than the fact that a steam shovel can outperform the best human digger. (An oddity of artificial intelligence, by the way, is the slowness of the programmers in devising a program that can beat the very best chess players. From the point of view of games theory, chess is a trivial game since each side has perfect information about the other's position and possible moves, and one has to assume that computer programs will soon be able to outperform any human chess player.)

A second fallacy is the idea that there might be some special human experience beyond computer simulation because of its special humanity. We are sometimes told that computers couldn't simulate feeling depressed or falling in love or having a sense of humor. But as far as simulation is concerned you can program your computer to print out "I am depressed," "I love Sally," or "Ha, ha," as easily as you can program it to print out "3 x 3 = 9." The real mistake is to suppose that simulation is duplication, and that mistake is the same regardless of what mental states we are talking about. A third mistake, basic to all the others, is the idea that if a computer can simulate having a certain mental state then we have the same grounds for supposing it really has that mental state as we have for supposing that human beings have that state. But we know from the Chinese room argument as well as from biology that this simple-minded behaviorism of the Turing test is mistaken.

Until computers and robots become as common as cars and until people are able to program and use them as easily as they now drive cars we are likely to continue to suffer from a certain mythological conception of digital computers. [Hoffstadter & Dennett's] book is very much a part of the present mythological era of the computer.

ELIZABETH V. SPELMAN

Woman as Body

ELIZABETH V. SPELMAN *teaches philosophy at Smith College. She has written widely in ancient philosophy and in feminist philosophy, and is author of* Inessential Woman: The Problem of Exclusion in Feminist Theory *(1988). The selection here is a revised version of an earlier paper.*

and what
pure happiness to know
all our high-toned questions
breed in a lively animal.

Adrienne Rich, from "Two Songs"

WHAT philosophers have had to say about women typically has been nasty, brutish and short. A page or two of quotations from those considered among the great philosophers (Aristotle, Hume, and Nietzsche, for example) constitutes a veritable litany of contempt. Because philosophers have not said much about women, and, when they have, it has usually been in short essays or chatty addenda which have not been considered to be part of the central body of their work, it is tempting to regard their expressed views about women as asystemic: their remarks on women are unofficial asides which are unrelated to the heart of their philosophical doctrines. After all, it might be thought, how could one's view about something as unimportant as women have anything to do with one's views about something as important as the nature of knowledge, truth, reality, freedom? Moreover—and this is the philosopher's move par excellence—wouldn't it be charitable to consider those opinions about women as coming merely from the *heart*, which

all too easily responds to the tenor of the times, while philosophy "proper" comes from the *mind*, which resonates not with the times but with the truth?

Part of the intellectual legacy from philosophy "proper," that is, the issues that philosophers have addressed which are thought to be the serious province of philosophy, is the soul/body or mind/body distinction (differences among the various formulations are not crucial to this essay). However, this part of philosophy might have not merely accidental connections to attitudes about women. For when one recalls that the Western philosophical tradition has not been noted for its celebration of the body, and that women's nature and women's lives have long been associated with the body and bodily functions, then a question is suggested. What connection might there be between attitudes toward the body and attitudes toward women? . . .

PLATO'S LESSONS ABOUT THE SOUL AND THE BODY

Plato's dialogues are filled with lessons about knowledge, reality, and goodness, and most of the lessons carry with them strong praise for the soul and strong indictments against the body. According to Plato, the body, with its deceptive senses, keeps us from real knowledge; it rivets us in a world of material things which is far removed from the world of reality; and it tempts us away from the virtuous life. It is in and through the soul, if at all, that we shall have knowledge, be in touch with reality, and lead a life of virtue. Only the soul can truly know, for only the soul can ascend to the real world, the world of the Forms or Ideas. That world is the perfect model to which imperfect, particular things we find in matter merely approximate. It is a world which, like the soul, is invisible, unchanging, not subject to decay, eternal. To be good, one's soul must know the Good, that is, the Form of Goodness, and this is impossible while one is dragged down by the demands and temptations of bodily life. Hence, bodily death is nothing to be feared: immortality of the soul not only is possible, but greatly to be desired, because when one is released from the body one finally can get down to the real business of life, for this real business of life is the business of the soul. Indeed, Socrates describes his own commitment, while still on earth, to encouraging his fellow Athenians to pay attention to the real business of life:

[I have spent] all my time going about trying to persuade you, young and old, to make your first and chief concern not for your bodies nor for your possessions, but for the highest welfare of your souls.

Plato also tells us about the nature of beauty. Beauty has nothing essentially to do with the body or with the world of material things. *Real* beauty cannot "take the form of a face, or of hands, or of anything that is of the flesh." Yes, there are beautiful things, but they only are entitled to be described that way because they "partake in" the form of

Beauty, which itself is not found in the material world. Real beauty has characteristics which merely beautiful *things* cannot have; real beauty

is an everlasting loveliness which neither comes nor goes, which neither flowers nor fades, for such beauty is the same on every hand, the same then as now, here as there, this way as that way, the same to every worshipper as it is to every other.

Because it is only the soul that can know the Forms, those eternal and unchanging denizens of Reality, only the soul can know real Beauty; our changing, decaying bodies only can put us in touch with changing, decaying pieces of the material world.

Plato also examines love. His famous discussion of love in the *Symposium* ends up being a celebration of the soul over the body. Attraction to and appreciation for the beauty of another's body is but a vulgar fixation unless one can use such appreciation as a stepping stone to understanding Beauty itself. One can begin to learn about Beauty, while one is still embodied, when one notices that this body is beautiful, that that body is beautiful, and so on, and then one begins to realize that Beauty itself is something beyond any particular beautiful body or thing. The kind of love between people that is to be valued is not the attraction of one body for another, but the attraction of one soul for another. There is procreation of the spirit as well as of the flesh. All that bodies in unison can create are more bodies—the children women bear—which are mortal, subject to change and decay. But souls in unison can create "something lovelier and less mortal than human seed," for spiritual lovers "conceive and bear the things of the spirit," that is, "wisdom and all her sister virtues." Hence, spiritual love between men is preferable to physical love between men and women. At the same time, physical love between men is ruled out, on the ground that "enjoyment of the flesh by flesh" is "wanton shame," while desire of soul for soul is at the heart of a relationship that "reverences, aye and worships, chastity and manhood, greatness and wisdom." The potential for harm in sexual relations is very great—harm not so much to one's body or physique, but to one's soul. Young men especially shouldn't get caught up with older men in affairs that threaten their "spiritual development," for such development is "assuredly and ever will be of supreme value in the sight of gods and men alike."

So, then, one has no hope of understanding the nature of knowledge, reality, goodness, love, or beauty unless one recognizes the distinction between soul and body; and one has no hope of attaining any of these unless one works hard on freeing the soul from the lazy, vulgar, beguiling body. A philosopher is someone who is committed to doing just that, and that is why philosophers go willingly unto death; it is, after all, only the death of their bodies, and finally, once their souls are released from their bodies, these philosophical desiderata are within reach. . . .

The division among parts of the soul is intimately tied to one other central and famous aspect of Plato's philosophy that hasn't been mentioned so far: Plato's political views. His discussion of the parts of the soul and their proper relation to one another is integral to his view about the best way to set up a state. The rational part of the soul ought to rule the soul and ought to be attended by the spirited part in keeping watch over the unruly appetitive part; just so, there ought to be rulers of the state (the

small minority in whom reason is dominant), who, with the aid of high-spirited guardians of order, watch over the multitudes (whose appetites need to be kept under control).

What we learn from Plato, then, about knowledge, reality, goodness, beauty, love, and statehood, is phrased in terms of a distinction between soul and body, or alternatively and roughly equivalently, in terms of a distinction between the rational and irrational. And the body, or the irrational part of the soul, is seen as an enormous and annoying obstacle to the possession of these desiderata. If the body gets the upper hand over the soul, or if the irrational part of the soul overpowers the rational part, one can't have knowledge, one can't see beauty, one will be far from the highest form of love, and the state will be in utter chaos. So the soul/body distinction, or the distinction between the rational and irrational parts of the soul, is a highly charged distinction. An inquiry into the distinction is no mild metaphysical musing. It is quite clear that the distinction is heavily value-laden. Even if Plato hadn't told us outright that the soul is more valuable than the body, and the rational part of the soul is more important than the irrational part, that message rings out in page after page of his dialogues. The soul/body distinction, then, is integral to the rest of Plato's views, and the higher worth of the soul is integral to that distinction.

PLATO'S VIEW OF THE SOUL AND BODY, AND HIS ATTITUDE TOWARD WOMEN

Plato, and anyone else who conceives of the soul as something unobservable, cannot of course speak as if we could point to the soul, or hold it up for direct observation. At one point,

Plato says no mere mortal can really understand the nature of the soul, but one perhaps could tell what it resembles. So it is not surprising to find Plato using many metaphors and analogies to describe what the soul is *like*, in order to describe relations between parts of the soul. For example, thinking, a function of the soul, is described by analogy to talking. The parts of the soul are likened to a team of harnessed, winged horses and their charioteer. The body's relation to the soul is such that we are to think of the body vis-à-vis the soul as a tomb, a grave or prison, or as barnacles or rocks holding down the soul. Plato compares the lowest or bodylike part of the soul to a brood of beasts.

But Plato's task is not only to tell us what the soul is like, not only to provide us with ways of getting a fix on the differences between souls and bodies, or differences between parts of the soul. As we've seen, he also wants to convince us that the soul is much more important than the body, and that it is to our peril that we let ourselves be beckoned by the rumblings of the body at the expense of harkening to the call of the soul. And he means to convince us of this by holding up for our inspection the silly and sordid lives of those who pay too much attention to their bodies and do not care enough for their soul; he want to remind us of how unruly, how without direction, are the lives of those in whom the lower part of the soul holds sway over the higher part. Because he can't *point* to an adulterated soul, he points instead to those embodied beings whose lives are in such bad shape that we can be sure that their souls are adulterated. And whose lives exemplify the proper soul/body relationship gone haywire? The lives of women (or sometimes the lives of children, slaves and brutes).

For example, how are we to know when the body has the upper hand over the soul, or when the lower part of the soul has managed to smother the higher part? We presumably can't see such conflict, so what do such conflicts translate into, in terms of actual human lives? Well, says Plato, look at the lives of women. It is women who get hysterical at the thought of death; obviously, their emotions have overpowered their reason, and they can't control themselves. The worst possible model for young men could be "a woman, young or old or wrangling with her husband, defying heaven, loudly boasting, fortunate in her own conceit, or involved in misfortune or possessed by grief and lamentation—still less a woman that is sick, in love, or in labor." . . .

Moreover, Plato on many occasions points to women to illustrate the improper way to pursue the things for which philosophers are constantly to be searching. For example, Plato wants to explain how important and also how difficult the attainment of real knowledge is. He wants us to realize that not just anyone can have knowledge, there is a vital distinction between those who really have knowledge and those who merely think they do. Think, for example, about the question of health. If we don't make a distinction between those who know what health is, and those who merely have unfounded and confused opinions about what health is, then "in the matter of good or bad health . . . any woman or child—or animal, for that matter—knows what is wholesome for it and is capable of curing itself." The implication is clear: if any old opinion were to count as real knowledge, then we'd have to say that women, children, and maybe even animals have knowledge. But surely *they* don't have knowledge! And why not? For one thing, because they don't recognize the difference between the material, changing world of appearance, and the invisible, eternal world of Reality. In matters of beauty, for example, they are so taken by the physical aspects of things that they assume that they can see and touch what is beautiful; they don't realize that what one knows when one has knowledge of real Beauty cannot be something that is seen or touched. Plato offers us, then, as an example of the failure to distinguish between Beauty itself, on the one hand, and beautiful things, on the other, "boys and women when they see bright-colored things." They don't realize that it is not through one's senses that one knows about beauty or anything else, for real beauty is eternal and invisible and unchangeable and can only be known through the soul.

So the message is that in matters of knowledge, reality, and beauty, don't follow the example of women. They are mistaken about those things. In matters of love, women's lives serve as negative examples also. Those men who are drawn by "vulgar" love, that is, love of body for body, "turn to women as the object of their love, and raise a family"; those men drawn by a more "heavenly" kind of love, that is, love of soul for soul, turn to other men. But there are strong sanctions against physical love between men: such physical unions, especially between older and younger men, are "unmanly." The older man isn't strong enough to resist his lust (as in woman, the irrational part of the soul has overtaken the rational part), and the younger man, "the impersonator of the female," is reproached for this "likeness to the model." The problem with physi-

cal love between men, then, is that men are acting like women.

To summarize the argument so far: the soul/body distinction is integral to the rest of Plato's views; integral to the soul/body distinction is the higher worth and importance of the soul in comparison to the body; finally, Plato tries to persuade his readers that it is to one's peril that one does not pay proper attention to one's soul—for if one doesn't, one will end up acting and living as if one were a woman. We know, Plato says, about lives dictated by the demands and needs and inducements of the body instead of the soul. Such lives surely are not good models for those who want to understand and undertake a life devoted to the nurturance of the best part of us: our souls.

To anyone at all familiar with Plato's official and oft-reported views about women, the above recitation of misogynistic remarks may be quite surprising. Accounts of Plato's views about women usually are based on what he says in book 5 of the *Republic*. In that dialogue, Plato startled his contemporaries, when as part of his proposal for the constitution of an ideal state, he suggested that

> there is no pursuit of the administrators of a state that belongs to woman because she is a woman or to a man because he is a man. But the natural capacities are distributed alike among both creatures, and women naturally share in all pursuits and men in all. . . .

Well now, what are we to make of this apparent double message in Plato about women? What are we to do with the fact that on the one hand, when Plato explicitly confronts the question of women's nature, in the *Republic*, he seems to affirm the equality of men and women; while on the other hand, the dialogues are riddled with misogynistic remarks? . . .

So the contradictory sides of Plato's views about women are tied to the distinction he makes between soul and body and the lessons he hopes to teach his readers about their relative values. When preaching about the overwhelming importance of the soul, he can't but regard the kind of body one has as of no final significance, so there is no way for him to assess differentially the lives of women and men; but when making gloomy pronouncements about the worth of the body, he points an accusing finger at a class of people with a certain kind of body—women—because he regards them, as a class, as embodying the very traits he wishes no one to have. In this way, women constitute a deviant class in Plato's philosophy, in the sense that he points to their lives as the kinds of lives that are not acceptable philosophically: they are just the kind of lives no one, especially philosophers, ought to live. . . .

In summary, Plato does not merely embrace a distinction between soul and body; for all the good and hopeful and desirable possibilities for human life (now and in an afterlife) are aligned with the soul, while the rather seedy and undesirable liabilities of human life are aligned with the body (alternatively, the alignment is with the higher or lower parts of the soul). There is a highly polished moral gloss to the soul/body distinction in Plato. One of his favorite devices for bringing this moral gloss to a high luster is holding up, for our contempt and ridicule, the lives of women. This is one of ways he tries to make clear that it makes no small difference whether you lead a soul-directed or a bodily directed life.

FEMINISM AND "SOMATOPHOBIA"

There are a number of reasons why feminists should be aware of the legacy of the soul/body distinction. It is not just that the distinction has been wound up with the depreciation and degradation of women, although, as has just been shown, examining a philosopher's view of the distinction may give us a direct route to his views about women.

First of all, as the soul or mind or reason is extolled, and the body or passion is denounced by comparison, it is not just women who are both relegated to the bodily or passionate sphere of existence and then chastised for belonging to that sphere. Slaves, free laborers, children, and animals are put in "their place" on almost the same grounds as women are. The images of women, slaves, laborers, children, and animals are almost interchangeable. For example, we find Plato holding that the best born and best educated should have control over "children, women and slaves . . . and the base rabble of those who are free in name," because it is in these groups that we find "the mob of motley appetites and pleasures and pains." As we saw above, Plato lumps together women, children, and animals as ignoramuses. (For Aristotle, there is little difference between a slave and an animal, because both "with their bodies attend to the needs of life." A common way of denigrating a member of any one of these groups is to compare that member to a member of one of the other groups—women are thought to have slavish or childish appetites, slaves are said to be brutish. Recall too, that Plato's way of ridiculing male homosexuals was to say that they imitated women. It is no wonder that the images and insults are almost interchangeable, for there is a central descriptive thread holding together the images of all these groups. The members of these groups lack, for all intents and purposes, mind or the power of reason; even the humans among them are not considered fully human.

It is important for feminists to see to what extent the images and arguments used to denigrate women are similar to those used to denigrate one group of men vis-à-vis another, children vis-à-vis adults, animals vis-à-vis humans, and even—though I have not discussed it here—the natural world vis-à-vis man's will (yes, man's will). For to see this is part of understanding how the oppression of women occurs in the context of, and is related to, other forms of oppression or exploitation.

There is a second reason why feminists should be aware of the legacy of the soul/body distinction. Some feminists have quite happily adopted both the soul/body distinction and relative value attached to soul and to body. But in doing so, they may be adopting a position inimical to what on a more conscious level they are arguing for.

For all her magisterial insight into the way in which the image of woman as body has been foisted upon and used against us, Simone de Beauvoir can't resist the temptation to say that woman's emancipation will come when woman, like man, is freed from this association with—according to the male wisdom of the centuries—the less important aspect of human existence. According to *The Second Sex*, women's demand is "not that they be exalted in their femininity; they wish that in themselves, as in humanity in general, transcendence may prevail over imma-

nence." But in de Beauvior's own terms, for "transcendence" to prevail over "immanence" is for the spirit or mind to prevail over matter or body, for reason to prevail over passion and desire. This means not only that the old images of women as mired in the world of "immanence"—the world of nature and physical existence—will go away. It will also happen that women won't lead lives given over mainly to their "natural" functions: "the pain of childbirth is on the way out"; "artificial insemination is on the way in." Although de Beauvoir doesn't explicitly say it, her directions for women are to find means of leaving the world of immanence and joining the men in the realm of transcendence. Men have said, de Beauvoir reminds us, that to be human is to have mind prevail over body; and no matter what disagreements she has elsewhere with men's perceptions and priorities, de Beauvoir here seems to agree with them. . . .

. . . in *The Feminine Mystique*, [Betty] Friedan remarks on the absence, in women's lives, of "the world of thought and ideas, the life of the mind and spirit." She wants women to be "culturally" as well as "biologically" creative—she wants us to think about spending our lives "mastering the secrets of the atoms, or the stars, composing symphonies, pioneering a new concept in government or society." And she associates "mental activity" with the "professions of highest value to society." Friedan thus seems to believe that men have done the more important things, the mental things; women have been relegated in the past to the less important human tasks involving bodily functions, and their liberation will come when they are allowed and encouraged to do the more important things in life.

Friedan's analysis relies on our old friend, the mind/body distinction, and Friedan, no less than Plato or de Beauvoir, quite happily assumes that mental activities are more valuable than bodily ones. Her solution to what she referred to as the "problem that has no name" is for women to leave (though not entirely) women's sphere and "ascend" into man's. Certainly there is much pleasure and value in the "mental activities" she extolls. But we can see the residue of her own negative attitude about tasks associated with the body: the bodily aspects of our existence must be attended to, the "liberated" woman, who is on the ascendant, can't be bothered with them. There is yet another group of people to whom these tasks will devolve: servants. Woman's liberation—and of course it is no secret that by "woman," Friedan could only have meant middle-class white women—seems to require woman's dissociation and separation from those who will perform the bodily tasks which the liberated woman has left behind in pursuit of "higher," mental activity. So we find Friedan quoting, without comment, Elizabeth Cady Stanton:

> I now understood the practical difficulties most women had to contend with in the isolated household and the impossibility of women's best development if in contact the chief part of her life with servants and children. . . .

Friedan at times seems to chide those women who could afford to have servants but don't: the women pretend there's a "servant problem" when there isn't, or insist on doing their own menial work. The implication is that women could find servants to do the "menial work," if they wanted to, and that it would be desirable for them to do

so. But what difference is there between the place assigned to women by men and the place assigned to some women (or men) by Friedan herself? . . .

What I have tried to do here is bring attention to the fact that various versions of women's liberation may themselves rest on the very same assumptions that have informed the deprecation and degradation of women, and other groups which, of course, include women. Those assumptions are that we must distinguish between soul and body, and that the physical part of our existence is to be devalued in comparison to the mental. Of course, these two assumptions alone don't mean that women or other groups have to be degraded; it's these two assumptions, along with the further assumption that woman is body, or is bound to her body, or is meant to take care of the bodily aspects of life, that have so deeply contributed to the degradation and oppression of women. And so perhaps feminists would like to keep the first two assumptions (about the difference between mind and body, and the relative worth of each of them) and somehow or other get rid of the last—in fact, that is what most of the feminists previously discussed have tried to do. Nothing that has been said so far has amounted to an argument against those first two assumptions: it hasn't been shown that there is no foundation for the assumptions that the mind and body are distinct and that the body is to be valued less than the mind.

There is a feminist thinker, however, who has taken it upon herself to chip away directly at the second assumption and to a certain extent at the first. Both in her poetry, and explicitly in her recent book, *Of Woman Born*, Adrienne Rich has begun to show us why use of the mind/body distinction does not give us appropriate descriptions of human experience; and she has begun to remind us of the distance we keep from ourselves when we try to keep a distance from our bodies. She does this in the process of trying to redefine the dimensions of the experience of childbirth, as she tries to show us why childbirth and motherhood need not mean what they have meant under patriarchy.

We are reminded by Rich that it is possible to be alienated from our bodies not only by pretending or wishing they weren't there, but also by being "incarcerated" in them. The institution of motherhood has done the latter in its insistence on seeing woman only or mainly as a reproductive machine. Defined as flesh by flesh-loathers, woman enters the most "fleshly" of her experiences with that same attitude of flesh-loathing—surely "physical self-hatred and suspicion of one's own body" is scarcely a favorable emotion with which to enter an intense physical experience.

But Rich insists that we don't have to experience childbirth in that way—we don't have to experience it as "torture rack"; but neither do we have to mystify it as a "peak experience." The experience of childbirth can be viewed as a way of recognizing the integrity of our experience, because pain itself is not usefully catalogued as something just our minds or just our bodies experience. . . . The point of "natural childbirth" should be thought of not as enduring pain, but as having an active physical experience—a distinction we recognize as crucial for understanding, for example, the pleasure in athletics.

Rich recognizes that feminists have not wanted to accept patriarchal versions of female biology, of what having a female body means. It has seemed to feminists, she implies, that we must either accept that view of being female, which is, essentially, to be a body, or deny that view and insist that we are "disembodied spirits." It perhaps is natural to see our alternatives that way:

> We have been perceived for too many centuries as pure Nature, exploited and raped like the earth and the solar system; small wonder if we not try to become Culture: pure spirit, mind.

But we don't *have* to do that, Rich reminds us; we can appeal to the physical without denying what is called "mind." We can come to regard our physicality as "resource, rather than a destiny":

> In order to live a fully human life we require not only *control* of our bodies (though control is a prerequisite); we must touch the unity and resonance of our physicality, our bond with the natural order, the corporeal ground of our intelligence.

Rich doesn't deny that we will have to start thinking about our lives in new ways; she even implies that we'll have to start thinking about thinking in new ways. Maybe it will give such a project a small boost to point out that philosophers for their part still squabble about mind/body dualism; the legacy of dualism is strong, but not unchallenged by any means. And in any event, . . . one can hardly put the blame for sexism (or any other form of oppression) on dualism itself. Indeed, the mind/body distinction can be put to progressive political ends, for example, to assert equality between human beings in the face of physical differences between them. There is nothing intrinsically sexist or otherwise oppressive about dualism, that is, about the belief that there are minds and there are bodies and that they are distinct kinds of things. But historically, the story dualists tell often ends up being a highly politicized one; although the story may be different at different historical moments, often it is said not only that there are minds (or souls) and bodies, but also that one is meant to rule and control the other. And the stage is thereby set for the soul/body distinction, now highly politicized and hierarchically ordered, to be used in a variety of ways in connection with repressive theories of the self, as well as oppressive theories of social and political relations. Among the tasks facing feminists is to think about the criteria for an adequate theory of self. Part of the value of Rich's work is that it points to the necessity of such an undertaking, and it is no criticism of her to say that she does no more than remind us of some of the questions that need to be raised.

A FINAL NOTE ABOUT THE SIGNIFICANCE OF SOMATOPHOBIA IN FEMINIST THEORY

In the history of political philosophy, the grounds given for the inferiority of women to men often are quite similar to those given for the inferiority of slaves to masters, children to fathers, animals to humans. In Plato, for example, all such subordinate groups are guilty by association with one another and each group is guilty by association with the bodily. In their eagerness to end the stereotypical association of woman and body, feminists such as de Beauvoir, Friedan, Firestone, and Daly have overlooked the significance of the connections—in theory and in practice—between the derogation and oppression of women on the basis of our sexual identity and the dero-

gation and oppression of other groups on the basis of, for example, skin color and class membership. It is as if in their eagerness to assign women a new place in the scheme of things, these feminist theorists have by implication wanted to dissociate women from other subordinate groups. One problem with this, of course, is that those other subordinate groups include women.

What is especially significant about Rich's recent work is that in contrast to these other theorists she both challenges the received tradition about the insignificance and indignity of bodily life and bodily tasks and explicitly focuses on racism as well as sexism as essential factors in women's oppression. I believe that it is not merely a coincidence that someone who attends to the first also attends to the second. Rich pauses not just to recognize the significance attached to the female body, but also to reevaluate that significance. "Flesh-loathing" is loathing of flesh by some particular group under some particular circumstances—the loathing of women's flesh by me, but also the loathing of black flesh by whites. (Here I begin to extrapolate from Rich, but I believe with some warrant.) After all, bodies are always particular bodies—they are male or female bodies (our deep confusion when we can't categorize a body in either way supports and does not belie the general point); but they are black or brown or biscuit or yellow or red bodies as well. We cannot seriously attend to the social significance attached to embodiment without recognizing this. I believe that it is Rich's recognition of this that distinguishes her work in crucial ways from that of most other major white feminists. Although the topic of feminism, sexism, and racism deserves a much fuller treatment, it is important to point out in the context of the present paper that not only does Rich challenge an assumption about the nature of the bodily that has been used to oppress women, but, unlike other feminists who do not challenge this assumption, she takes on the question of the ways in which sexism and racism interlock. Somatophobia historically has been symptomatic not only of sexism, but also of racism, so it is perhaps not surprising that someone who has examined that connection between flesh-loathing and sexism would undertake an examination of racism.

FRANCISCO J. VARELA, EVAN THOMPSON, AND ELEANOR ROSCH

The Embodied Mind

FRANCISCO VARELA *is Director of Research at the Centre National de Recherche Scientifique and Professor of Cognitive Science and Epistemology at the École Polytechnique in Paris.* EVAN THOMPSON, *Assistant Professor of Philosophy at Boston University, is the author of a 1994 book,* Colour Vision: A Study in Cognitive Science and Philosophy of Science. ELEANOR ROSCH *is Professor of Psychology at the University of California, Berkeley. They are collectively authors of* The Embodied Mind *(1991), from which this selection is taken.*

EVEN in *The Crisis*, Husserl insisted that phenomenology is the study of essences. Thus the analysis of the life-world that he undertook there was not anthropological or historical; it was philosophical. But if all theoretical activity presupposes the life-world, what, then, of phenomenology? It is a distinctly theoretical pursuit; indeed, Husserl claimed it is the very highest form of theory. But then phenomenology too must presuppose the life-world, even as it attempts to explicate it. Thus Husserl was being haunted by the untraversed steps of the fundamental circularity.

Husserl recognized some of this circularity and tried to deal with it in an interesting way. He argued that the life-world was really a set of sedimented, background *preunderstandings* or (roughly speaking) assumptions, which the phenomenologist could make explicit and treat as a system of beliefs. In other words, Husserl tried to break out of the circle by treating the background as consisting essentially of representations. Once the life-world is construed in this way, however, Husserl's claim (indeed, the central claim of phenomenology) that the life-world is always prior to science becomes unstable. If the background consists of representations, what is to prevent scientific knowledge from permeating the background and contributing to its tacit store of beliefs? And if such permeation is possible, then what happens to the priority of phenomenology?

Husserl must have recognized these problems because he argued both that the life-world is prior to science and that our Western tradition is unique because our life-world is permeated by science. The task of the phenomenologist was to move back from an analysis of our scientifically permeated life-world to the "original" or "pre-given" life-world. But Husserl held on to the idea that this original life-world could be exhaustively accounted for by tracing it back to the essential structures of consciousness. He thus embraced the peculiar thought that the phenomenologist could stand both inside and outside of the life-world: he stood inside because all theory presupposed the life-world, and yet he stood outside because phenomenology alone could trace the genesis of the life-world in consciousness. Indeed, phenomenology was the highest form of theory for Husserl precisely because it was capable of such a peculiar contortion.

Given this peculiar contortion, it is not surprising that Husserl's pure phenomenology was not (as he hoped it would be) cultivated and improved on from one generation to the next, unlike other methodological discoveries such as the methods for statistical inference. Indeed, it has been the headache of later commentators to find out just exactly how his method of "phenomenological reduction" is to proceed.

But there is a deeper reason for the failure of the Husserlian project that we wish to emphasize here: Husserl's turn toward experience and "the things themselves" was entirely *theoretical*, or, to make the point the other way around, it completely lacked any *pragmatic* dimension. It is hardly surprising, therefore, that it could not overcome the rift between science and experience, for science, unlike phenomenological reflection, has a life beyond theory. Thus although Husserl's turn toward a phenomenological analysis of experience seemed radical, it was, in fact, quite within the mainstream of Western philosophy. . . .

Within our Western tradition, phenomenology was and still is *the* philosophy of human experience, the only extant edifice of thought that addresses these issues head-on. But above all, it was and still is philosophy as theoretical reflection. In most of the Western tradition since the Greeks, philosophy has been the discipline that seeks to find the truth, including the truth about the mind, purely by means of abstract, theoretical reasoning. Even philosophers who critique or problematize reason do so only be means of arguments, demonstration, and—especially in our so-called postmodern era—linguistic exhibitions (i.e., by means of abstract thought). Merleau-Ponty's critique of science and phenomenology, that they are theoretical activities after the fact, can equally be applied to most of Western philosophy as theoretical reflection. In this way, the loss of faith in reason so rampant in current thought becomes simultaneously a loss of faith in philosophy.

But if we turn away from reason, if reason is no longer taken as the method for knowing the mind, what can be used instead? One alternative is *unreason*, and, in the form of psychoanalytic theory, it has probably come to have more influence on our Western folk conception of the mind than any other single cultural factor. People—certainly middle-class North Americans and Europeans—have come to believe that they have an unconscious that is developmentally and symbolically primitive. They believe that both dreams and much of their waking life—motives, fantasies, preferences, aversions, emotions, behaviors, and pathological symptoms—are explainable by means of this unconscious. Thus, in the folk view, to know the mind "from the inside" is to use some version of psychoanalytic method to delve into the unconscious.

This "folk psychoanalytic" view is subject to the same critique that Merleau-Ponty made of science and phenomenology. The psychoanalytic method works within an individual's conceptual system. Whether an individual is commenting on a free association or using mathematical logic, having an ordinary waking conversation or dealing with the highly convoluted symbolic language of dreams, that person is knowing the mind and commenting on it in an after-the-fact fashion. The "professional" psychoanalyst knows, however, that he has to work within an individual's conceptual system and that a method that no theory can substitute for is required to go beyond this stage. What we find particularly interesting about psychoanalysis is that despite its great differences from cognitive science—despite the fact that it deals with phenomena of mind that are quite different from the normal subject matter of cognitive science and studies them by patently different methods—we see some of the same stages of evolution that we identify in cognitive science mirrored in psychoanalytic theory. . . .

A NON-WESTERN PHILOSOPHICAL TRADITION

At this point, a bold step needs to be taken. . . . : we need to enlarge our horizon to encompass non-Western traditions of reflection upon experience. If philosophy in the West no longer occupies a privileged, foundational position with respect to other cultural activities such as science or art, then a full appreciation of philosophy and its importance for human experience requires that we examine the role of philosophy in cultures other than our own. In our culture, cognitive science has caused great excitement among philosophers (and the public at large) because it has enabled them to see their tradition in a new light. Were we to entertain the idea that there is no hard-and-fast distinction between science and philosophy then philosophers such as Descartes, Locke, Leibniz, Hume, Kant, and Husserl would take on a new significance: they could be seen, among other things, as protocognitive scientists. (Or as Jerry Fodor puts it, "In intellectual history, everything happens twice, first as philosophy and then as cognitive science.") Might this not also be the case for philosophical traditions with which we are less familiar?

In this book we will focus on one such tradition, that which derives from the Buddhist method of examining experience called *mindfulness meditation*. We believe that the Buddhist doctrines of no-self and of nondualism that grew out of this method have a significant contribution to make in a dialogue with cognitive science: (1) The no-self doctrine contributes to understanding the fragmentation of self portrayed in cognitivism and connectionism.

(2) Buddhist nondualism, particularly as it is presented in the Madhyamika (which literally means "middle way") philosophy of Nagarjuna, may be juxtaposed with the entre-deux of Merleau-Ponty and with the more recent ideas of cognition as enaction.

It is our contention that the rediscovery of Asian philosophy, particularly of the Buddhist tradition, is a second renaissance in the cultural history of the West, with the potential to be equally important as the rediscovery of Greek thought in the European renaissance. Our Western histories of philosophy, which ignore Indian thought, are artificial, since India and Greece share with us an Indo-European linguistic heritage as well as many cultural and philosophical preoccupations. . . .

EXAMINING EXPERIENCE WITH A METHOD: MINDFULNESS/AWARENESS

There are many human activities of body and mind, both Buddhist and non-Buddhist. The word *meditation* in its general usage in modern America has a number of different prominent folk meanings: (1) a state of concentration in which consciousness is focused on only one object; (2) a state of relaxation that is psychologically and medically beneficial; (3) a dissociated state in which trance phenomena can occur; and (4) a mystical state in which higher realities or religious objects are experienced. These are all altered states of consciousness; the meditator is doing something to get away from his usual mundane, unconcentrated, unrelaxed, nondissociated, lower state of reality.

Buddhist mindfulness/awareness practice is intended to be just the opposite of these. Its purpose is to become

mindful, to experience what one's mind is doing as it does it, to be present with one's mind. What relevance does this have for cognitive science? We believe that if cognitive science is to include human experience, it must have some method for exploring and knowing what human experience is. It is for this reason that we are focusing on the Buddhist tradition of mindfulness meditation.

To get a sense of what mindfulness meditation is, one must first realize the extent to which people are normally not mindful. Usually one notices the tendency of the mind to wander only when one is attempting to accomplish some mental task and the wandering interferes. Or perhaps one realizes that one has just finished an anticipated pleasurable activity without noticing it. In fact, body and mind are seldom closely coordinated. In the Buddhist sense, we are not present. . . .

The purpose of calming the mind in Buddhism is not be become absorbed but to render the mind able to be present with itself long enough to gain insight into its own nature and functioning. (There are many traditional analogies for this process. For example, to be able to see painting on the wall of a dark cave, one needs a good light protected from the wind.). . . Typically mindfulness/awareness is trained by means of formal periods of sitting meditation. The purpose of such periods is to simplify the situation to the bare minimum. The body is put into an upright posture and held still. Some simple object, often the breath, is used as the focus of alert attention. Each time the meditator realizes that his mind is wandering unmindfully, he is to acknowledge nonjudgmentally that wandering (there are various instructions as to how this is to be done) and bring the mind back to its object.

Breathing is one of the most simple, basic, ever-present bodily activities. Yet beginning meditators are generally astonished at how difficult it is to be mindful of even so uncomplex an object. Meditators discover that mind and body are not coordinated. The body is sitting, but the mind is seized constantly by thoughts, feelings, inner conversations, daydreams, fantasies, sleepiness, opinions, theories, judgments about thoughts and feelings, judgments about judgments—a never-ending torrent of disconnected mental events that the meditators do not even realize are occurring except at those brief instants when they remember what they are doing. Even when they attempt to return to their object of mindfulness, the breath, they may discover that they are only thinking about the breath rather than being mindful of the breath.

Eventually, it begins to dawn on the meditators that there is an actual difference between being present and not being present. In daily life they also begin to have instants of waking up to the realization that they are not present and of flashing back for a moment to be present—not to the breath, in this case, but to whatever is going on. Thus the first great discovery of mindfulness meditation tends to be not some encompassing insight into the nature of mind but the piercing realization of just how disconnected humans normally are from their very experience. Even the simplest or most pleasurable of daily activities— walking, eating, conversing, driving, reading, waiting, thinking, making love, planning, gardening, drinking, remembering, going to a therapist, writing, dozing, emoting, sight-seeing—all pass rapidly in a blur of abstract commentary as the mind hastens to its next mental occupation. The meditator now discovers that the abstract attitude which Heidegger and Merleau-Ponty ascribe to science and philosophy is actually the attitude of everyday life when one is not mindful. This abstract attitude is the spacesuit, the padding of habits and preconceptions, the armor with which one habitually distances oneself from one's experience.

From the point of view of mindfulness/awareness meditation, humans are not trapped forever in the abstract attitude. The dissociation of mind from body, of awareness from experience, is the result of habit, and these habits can be broken. As the meditator again and again interrupts the flow of discursive thought and returns to be present with his breath or daily activity, there is a gradual taming of the mind's restlessness. One begins to be able to see the restlessness as such and to become patient with it, rather than becoming automatically lost in it. Eventually meditators report periods of a more panoramic perspective. This is called awareness. At this point the breath is no longer needed as a focus. In one traditional analogy, mindfulness is likened to the individual words of a sentence, whereas awareness is the grammar that encompasses the entire sentence. . . .

THE ROLE OF REFLECTION IN THE ANALYSIS OF EXPERIENCE

If the results of mindfulness/awareness practice are to bring one closer to one's ordinary experience rather than further from it, what can be the role of reflection? One of our popular cultural images of Buddhism is that the intellect is destroyed. In fact, study and contemplation play a major role in all Buddhist schools. The spontaneous action, much dramatized in the popular image of the Zen master, is not contradictory to the use of reflection as a mode of learning. How can this be?

This question brings us to the methodological heart of the interaction between mindfulness/awareness meditation, phenomenology, and cognitive science. What we are suggesting is a change in the nature of reflection from an abstract, disembodied activity to an embodied (mindful), open-ended reflection. By *embodied*, we mean reflection in which body and mind have been brought together. What this formulation intends to convey is that reflection is not just *on* experience, but reflection *is* a form of experience itself—and that reflective form of experience can be performed with mindfulness/awareness. When reflection is done in that way, it can cut the chain of habitual thought patterns and preconceptions such that it can be an open-ended reflection, open to possibilities other than those contained on one's current representations of the life space. We call this form of reflection *mindful, open-ended reflection.*

In our usual training and practice as Western scientists and philosophers, we obviously proceed differently. We ask, "What is Mind?", "What is body?" and proceed to reflect theoretically and to investigate scientifically. This procedure gives rise to a gamut of claims, experiments, and results on various facets of cognitive abilities. But in the course of these investigations we often forget just who is asking this question and how it is asked. By not including ourselves in the reflection, we pursue only a partial reflection, and our question becomes disembodied; it attempts to express, in the words of the philosopher Thomas Nagel, a "view from nowhere." It is ironic that it is just this attempt to have a disembodied view from nowhere that leads to having a view from a very specific, theoretically confined, preconceptually entrapped somewhere.

The phenomenological tradition, from Husserl on, complained bitterly about this lack of self-included reflection but was able to offer in its place only a project of theoretical reflection *on* experience. The other extreme is to include the self but abandon reflection altogether in favor of a naive, subjective impulsivity. Mindfulness/awareness is neither of these; it works directly with, and so expresses, our basic embodiment.

Let us see how the difference in the theoretical and the mindfulness traditions of reflection manifest in an actual issue—the so-called mind-body problem. From Descartes on, the guiding question in Western philosophy has been whether body and mind are one or two distinct substances (properties, levels of description, etc.) and what the ontological relation between them is. We have already seen the simple, experiential, pragmatic approach taken in mindfulness/awareness meditation. It is a matter of simple experience that our mind and body can be dissociated, that the mind can wander, that we can be unaware of where we are and what our body or mind are doing. But this situation, this habit of mindlessness, can be changed. Body and mind can be brought together. We can develop habits in which body and mind are fully coordinated. The result is a mastery that is not only known to the individual meditator himself but that is visible to others—we easily recognize by its precision and grace a gesture that is animated by full awareness. We typically associate such mindfulness with the actions of an expert such as an athlete or musician.

We are suggesting that Descartes's conclusion that he was a thinking thing was the product of his question, and that question was a product of specific practices—those of disembodied, unmindful reflection. Husserlian phenomenology, though it embraced experience in a radical way, nonetheless continued the tradition by reflecting only upon the essential structures of thought. And even though it has recently become quite fashionable to criticize or "deconstruct" this standpoint of the *cogito*, philosophers still do not depart from the basic *practice* responsible for it.

Theoretical reflection need not be mindless and disembodied. The basic assertion of this progressive approach to human experience is that the mind-body relation or modality is not simply fixed and given but can be fundamentally changed. Many people would acknowledge the obvious truth of this conviction. Western philosophy does not deny this truth so much as ignore it. . . .

In summary it is because reflection in our culture has been severed from its bodily life that the mind-body problem has become a central topic for abstract reflection. Cartesian dualism is not so much one competing solution as it is the formulation of this problem. Reflection is taken to be distinctively mental, and so the problem arises of how it could ever be linked to bodily life. Although contemporary discussions of this problem have become quite sophisticated— largely because of the development of cognitive science—they have nevertheless not departed from the essentially Cartesian problematic of trying to understand how two seemingly distinct things are related. (Whether these things are substances, properties, or merely levels of description rarely makes a difference to the basic structure of the discussion.)

From the standpoint of a mindful, open-ended reflection the mind-body question need not be, What is the ontological relation between body and mind, regardless of anyone's experience?—but rather, What are the relations of body and mind in actual experience (the mindfulness aspect), and how do these relations develop, what forms can they take (the open-ended aspect)? As the Japanese philosopher Yasuo Yuasa remarks, "One starts from the experiential assumption that the mind-body modality changes through the training of the mind and body by means of cultivation *(Shugyo)* or training *(keiko)*. Only after assuming this experiential ground does one ask what the mind-body relation is. That is, the mind-body issue is not simply a theoretical speculation but it is originally a practical, lived experience *(taiken)*, involving the mustering of one's whole mind and body. The theoretical is only a reflection on this lived experience."

We may notice that his viewpoint is resonant with pragmatism, a view in philosophy that is having a modern revival. The body and mind relation is known in terms of what it can do. When one takes the more abstract attitude in philosophy or science, one might think that questions about the body-mind relation can be answered only after one first satisfactorily determines what is body and what is mind in isolation and abstraction. In the pragmatic, open-ended reflection, however, these questions are not separate from "the mustering of one's whole mind and body." Such involvement prevents the question, What is mind? from becoming disembodied. When we include in our reflection on a question the asker of the question and the process of asking itself (recall the fundamental circularity), then the question receives a new life and meaning.

Perhaps the closest discipline familiar to Westerners that verges on a pragmatic, open-ended view toward knowledge is psychoanalysis. We have in mind not so much the content of psychoanalytic theory but rather the idea that the very conception of mind and of the subject who is undergoing analysis is understood to change as the web of representations in which the self is entangled is slowly penetrated through analysis. What we believe traditional psychoanalytic methods lack, however, is the mindfulness/awareness component of reflection. . . .

In conclusion, we have argued that it is necessary to have a disciplined perspective on human experience that can enlarge the domain of cognitive science to include direct experience. We suggest such a perspective already exists in the form of mindfulness/awareness meditation. Mindfulness/awareness practice, phenomenological philosophy, and science are human activities; each is an expression of our human embodiment. Naturally, Buddhist doctrine, Western phenomenology, and science are each heir to numerous doctrinal disputes and conflicting claims. Each, however, insofar as it is a form of experimentation, is open to everyone and may be examined with the methods of each of the others. Thus, we believe that mindfulness/awareness meditation can provide a natural bridge between cognitive science and human experience. Particularly impressive to us is the convergence that we have discovered among some of the main themes of Buddhist doctrine, phenomenology, and cognitive science—themes concerning the self and the relation between subject and object. It is to these themes that we now turn in our journey of discovery.

Part 3

Thinking and Knowing

Chapter 6

What Do I Know?

Right now, you think that you are reading a book. In fact, you know that you are. Surely nothing could be more obvious than that. Of course, to philosophers, nothing is obvious. Indeed, the nature and extent of our knowledge have been central concerns of philosophy since Plato. Plato provided a basis for what is usually referred to as **epistemology,** or the theory of knowledge, by suggesting that knowledge must be distinguished from mere belief. A belief can fall short of knowledge in two ways: (1) a belief can be false or (2) it can be based on insufficient evidence. Your little sister might believe that Santa Claus exists. After all, everyone tells her that Santa Claus puts presents under the tree; she sees Santa at the mall and on television; she leaves cookies and milk for Santa on Christmas Eve and they are gone on Christmas morning. In spite of all this evidence, she still doesn't *know* that Santa exists. Why not? Because, in fact, he doesn't. (You might also think that her evidence isn't very good, but compare the evidence she has for Santa Claus to the evidence that you have for the existence of Eddie Murphy. Is there such a big difference?) Because your sister's belief isn't true, it isn't a case of knowledge. On the other hand, truth alone isn't enough to guarantee that a belief is knowledge. Suppose I tell you that I believe that Oprah Winfrey bakes pies on Thursdays and that I believe this because she reminds me of my friend Naomi and Naomi bakes pies on Thursdays. Suppose that, just by coincidence, Oprah Winfrey does bake pies on Thursdays. My belief, then, is true, but given the weakness of my evidence, we should not count my belief as a case of knowledge. Knowledge requires real, hard evidence, something more than quirky associations, random hunches, or mere coincidences. If Oprah's cook, Rosie, had told me that Oprah bakes pies on Thursdays, then not only would my belief be true, but it would also be based on good evidence.

While many philosophers have devoted their attention to determining just how much evidence is required for knowledge, others have argued for the extreme position that we have no knowledge at all. The position is called **skepticism.** Descartes, as you will see when you read the selection from *Meditations,* entertained some alarming skeptical possibilities. Although you think that you are reading right now, maybe you are really snuggled under your covers, fast asleep and merely dreaming that you are reading. It wouldn't be a terribly interesting dream, but haven't you sometimes had dreams that are quite mundane? An even more extreme, and perhaps less plausible, possibility is that there is an all-powerful Evil Demon, or Genius, whose greatest pleasure comes from deceiving mere mortals. Right now, by his ingenious methods, he is making you think that you are reading a philosophy book, but in fact you aren't.

Needless to say, skepticism is a position that most philosophers have tried to avoid, usually by dismissing it as nothing more than a source of irritation. Other philosophers, while disliking skepticism's conclusions, think that it cannot simply be ignored. They have attempted to show that skeptical arguments rest on impossible suppositions. O. K. Bouwsma, for example, wonders whether the Evil Genius could bring about the sorts of deception required for Descartes' skeptical conclusions. Norman Malcolm simply insists that we can be certain of many things. You can be certain that you are enrolled in a philosophy course, for example. If a friend were to challenge your belief that you are, you could respond by taking her to class. If that were not enough, you could ask her to call the Registrar. If she remains doubtful, that is her problem. You have done everything that you possibly could to prove that you are enrolled and that is enough, or so Malcolm argues. You might think about whether the die-hard skeptic would be satisfied with Malcolm's reasoning. Lewis Carroll and Jorge Luis Borges provide some fictional reinforcements for the skeptics' arsenal.

Recall that knowledge (supposing now that we do have some) requires belief and evidence. Many of the beliefs that we have are about what philosophers have called the "external world," the world of tables and chairs, peanut butter and jelly. The evidence that we have for beliefs about the external world is evidence that we get though our senses. Sally believes that she is eating a peanut butter and jelly sandwich. Why? Because she sees the sandwich; she experiences its quintessentially American taste; she feels the stickiness on the roof of her mouth; she hears the smacking of her lips as they cope with the sticky mess between them; she inhales that characteristic peanut smell. All this sensory evidence contributes to Sally's belief.

The case of Sally and her sandwich is a very ordinary case of perception, the sort of perception that leads to knowledge. It is not so obvious, however, how we should understand exactly what goes on, even in a simple case such as this. We might agree that perception gives us knowledge but disagree as to what perception gives us knowledge *of*. If we asked Sally to describe her sandwich, she would say it is roughly five inches square, about an inch thick, is of various colors (white, purple, and brown), and so on. But some philosophers, Bertrand Russell among them, might say that Sally has failed to answer our question. She hasn't described the sandwich, but has rather described how the sandwich *appears* to her. Physics, the science that tells us how the world really is, would describe the sandwich as a cloud of colorless molecules. It is nonsensical to suppose, so the reasoning goes, that something could be both colorless and white, purple, and brown. Thus, color is not a quality of the sandwich itself, but rather a quality of the *appearance* of the sandwich. What Sally sees, then, is not the real, underlying sandwich. Instead she sees her *sense datum* of the sandwich. A sense datum is a mental representation of an externally existing object. Images, smells, tactile sensations, sounds, and tastes are each sense data corresponding to a particular sense organ. A visual sense datum, then, is a two-dimensional visual image.

The claim that we directly perceive sense data and only indirectly perceive physical objects, while supported by contemporary science, has its origins in the work of John Locke. He noticed that some qualities of an object seem to be dependent on our perception of it, while others seem more to be "in" the object itself. How Sally's sandwich tastes to her seems clearly to have much to do with Sally. If she has just brushed her teeth, it will taste one way to her. If she has just indulged her habit of lemon sucking, it will taste another way. The chemical composition of the sandwich, on the other hand, will not be affected by Sally's prelunch activities. On the basis of considerations like these, Locke concluded that we must distinguish between two different kinds of qualities, the ones that are had by objects themselves and the ones that are had by our *ideas* (Locke's word for sense data) of objects. We directly perceive the latter qualities but not the former ones. Locke thus arrived at a conclusion similar to that suggested by Russell, but for different reasons.

It might have occurred to you that the sort of reasoning used by Russell and Locke seems to lead us right back to skepticism. After all, if Sally never perceives her sandwich, but only her ideas or sense data of it, then how can she ever know what her sandwich really is? Of course, in ordinary life, the true nature of her sandwich may not be of much concern to Sally. She just wants to finish her lunch. But as you are probably now well aware, philosophers, although they do get hungry, are seldom content to let ordinary life get in their way. So troubled was Bishop George Berkeley by what he took to be the skeptical consequences of Locke's reasoning, that he argued that there are no physical objects at all! Although that sounds like a crazy way to avoid skepticism, you will see when you read Berkeley's selection that his arguments are very persuasive.

In her contribution to this chapter, Lorraine Code draws our attention to the fact that traditional philosophical discussions of knowledge have a peculiarly abstract idea of what a knower is. Indeed, these discussions assume only that knowers have beliefs, that they are capable of gaining evidence for and against their beliefs, and thus that they have cognitive abilities. But it has not occurred to most philosophers that, for example, the sex of the knower might make a difference in how we understand what knowledge is and under what conditions someone might have it. So Code presents some interesting reasons why we should reconsider the relationship between theories of knowledge and philosophers' assumptions about knowers. In reflecting on Code's essay, you might want to think about whether features of a person's identity other than sex might be equally relevant to developing theories of knowledge. Might not the race of the knower, or her socioeconomic status, be significant as well?

RENÉ DESCARTES

Meditation

RENÉ DESCARTES (1596–1650) was born in Britanny, France. He went to college from the ages of eight to sixteen, studying logic, philosophy, and mathematics. He did important work in mathematics and science in addition to his revolutionary work in philosophy. His Meditations, *from which this selection is taken, was published in 1641.*

MEDITATION 1

S EVERAL years have now passed since I first realized how many were the false opinions that in my youth I took to be true, and thus how doubtful were all the things that I subsequently built upon these opinions. From the time I became aware of this, I realized that for once I had to raze everything in my life, down to the very bottom, so as to begin again from the first foundations. If I wanted to establish anything firm and lasting in the sciences. But the task seemed so enormous that I waited for a point in my life that was so ripe that no more suitable a time for laying hold of these disciplines would come to pass. For this reason, I have delayed so long that I would be at fault were I to waste on deliberation the time that is left for action. Therefore, now that I have freed my mind from all cares, and I have secured for myself some leisurely and carefree time, I withdraw in solitude. I will, in short, apply myself earnestly and openly to the general destruction of my former opinions.

Yet to this end it will not be necessary that I show that all my opinions are false, which perhaps I could never accomplish anyway. But because reason now persuades me that I should withhold my assent no less carefully from things which are not plainly certain and indubitable than I would to what is patently false, it will be sufficient justification for rejecting them all, if I find a reason for doubting even the least of them. Nor therefore need one survey each opinion one after the other, a task of endless proportion. Rather—because undermining the foundations will cause whatever has been built upon them to fall down of its own accord—I will at once attack those principles which supported everything that I once believed.

Whatever I had admitted until now as most true I took in either from the senses or through the senses; however, I noticed that they sometimes deceived me. And it is a mark of prudence never to trust wholly in those things which have once deceived us.

But perhaps, although the senses sometimes deceive us when it is a question of very small and distant things, still there are many other matters which one certainly cannot doubt, although they are derived from the very same senses: that I am sitting here before the fireplace wearing my dressing gown, that I feel this sheet of paper in my hands and so on. But how could one deny that these hands and that my whole body exist? Unless perhaps I should compare myself to insane people whose brains are so impaired by a stubborn vapor from a black bile that they continually insist that they are kings when they are in utter poverty, or that they are wearing purple robes when they are naked, or that they have a head made of clay, or that they are gourds, or that they are made of glass. But they are all demented, and I would appear no less demented if I were to take their conduct as a model for myself.

All of this would be well and good, were I not a man who is accustomed to sleeping at night, and to undergoing in my sleep the very same things—or now and then even less likely ones—as do these insane people when they are awake. How often has my evening slumber persuaded me of such customary things as these: that I am here, clothed in my dressing gown, seated at the fireplace, when in fact I am lying undressed between the blankets! But right now I certainly am gazing upon this piece of paper with eyes wide awake. This head which I am moving is not heavy with sleep. I extend this hand consciously and deliberately and I feel it. These things would not be so distinct for one who is asleep. But this all seems as if I do not recall having been deceived by similar thoughts on other occasions in my dreams. As I consider these cases more intently, I see so plainly that there are no definite signs to distinguish being awake from being asleep that I am quite astonished, and this astonishment almost convinces me that I am sleeping.

Let us say, then, for the sake of argument, that we are sleeping and that such particulars as these are not true: that we open our eyes, move our heads, extend our hands. Perhaps we do not even have these hands, or any such body at all. Nevertheless, it really must be admitted that things seen in sleep are, as it were, like painted images, which could have been produced only in the likeness of true things. Therefore at least these general things (eyes, head, hands, the whole body) are not imaginary things, but are true and exist. For indeed when painters wish to represent sirens and satyrs by means of bizarre and unusual forms, they surely cannot ascribe utterly new natures to these creatures. Rather, they simply intermingle the members of various animals. And even if they concoct something so utterly novel that its likes have never been seen before (being utterly fictitious and false), certainly at the very minimum the colors from which the painters compose the thing ought to be true. And for the same reason, although even these general things (eyes, head, hands, and the like) can be imaginary, still one must necessarily admit that at least other things that are even more simple and universal are true, from which, as from true colors, all these things—be they true or false—which in our thought are images of things, are constructed.

To this class seems to belong corporeal nature in general, together with its extension; likewise the shape of extended things, their quantity or size, their number; as well as the place where they exist, the time of their duration, and other such things.

Hence perhaps we do not conclude improperly that physics, astronomy, medicine, and all the other disciplines that are dependent upon the consideration of composite things are all doubtful. But arithmetic, geometry, and other such disciplines—which treat of nothing but the simplest and most general things and which are indifferent as to whether these composite things do or do not exist—contain something certain and indubitable. For whether I be awake or asleep, two plus three makes five, and a square does not have more than four sides; nor does it seem possible that such obvious truths can fall under the suspicion of falsity.

All the same, a certain opinion of long standing has been fixed in my mind, namely that there exists a God who is able to do anything and by whom I, such as I am, have been created. How do I know that he did not bring it about that there be no earth at all, no heavens, no extended thing, no figure, no size, no place, and yet all these things should seem to me to exist precisely as they appear to do now? Moreover—as I judge that others sometimes make mistakes in matters that they believe they know most perfectly—how do I know that I am not deceived every time I add two and three or count the sides of a square or perform an even simpler operation, if such can be imagined? But perhaps God has not willed that I be thus deceived, for it is said that he is supremely good. Nonetheless, if it were repugnant to his goodness that he should have created me such that I be deceived all the time, it would seem, from this same consideration, to be foreign to him to permit me to be deceived occasionally. But we cannot make this last assertion.

Perhaps there are some who would rather deny such a powerful God, than believe that all other matters are uncertain. Let us not put these people off just yet; rather, let us grant that everything said here about God is fictitious. Now they suppose that I came to be what I am either by fate or by chance or by a continuous series of events or by some other way. But because being deceived and being mistaken seem to be imperfections, the less powerful they take the author of my being to be, the more probable it will be that I would be so imperfect as to be deceived perpetually.

I have nothing to say in response to these arguments. At length I am forced to admit that there is nothing, among the things I once believed to be true, which it is not permissible to doubt— not for reasons of frivolity or a lack of forethought, but because of valid and considered arguments. Thus I must carefully withhold assent no less from these things than from the patently false, if I wish to find anything certain.

But it is not enough simply to have made a note of this; I must take care to keep it before my mind. For long-standing opinions keep coming back again and again, almost against my will; they seize upon my credulity, as if it were bound over to them by long use and the claims of intimacy. Nor will I get out of the habit of assenting to them and believing in them, so long as I take them to be exactly what they are, namely, in some respects doubtful as by now is obvious, but nevertheless highly probable, so that it is much more consonant with reason to believe them than to deny them. Hence, it seems to me, I would do well to turn my will in the opposite direction, to deceive myself and pretend for a considerable period that they are wholly false and imaginary, until finally, as if with equal weight of prejudice on both sides, no bad habit should turn my judgment from the correct perception of things. For indeed I know that no danger or error will follow and that it is impossible for me to indulge in too much distrust, since I now am concentrating only on knowledge, not an action.

Thus I will suppose not a supremely good God, the source of truth, but rather an evil genius, as clever and deceitful as he is powerful, who has directed his entire effort to misleading me. I will regard the heavens, the air, the earth, colors, shapes, sounds, and all external things as nothing but the deceptive games of my dreams, with which he lays snares for my credulity. I will regard myself as having no hands, no eyes, no flesh, no blood, no senses, but as nevertheless falsely believing that I possess all these things. I will remain resolutely fixed in this meditation, and, even if it be out of my power to know anything true, certainly it is within my power to take care resolutely to withhold my assent to what is false, lest this deceiver, powerful and clever as he is, have an effect on me. But this undertaking is arduous, and laziness brings me back to my customary way of living. I am not unlike a prisoner who might enjoy an imaginary freedom in his sleep. When he later begins to suspect that he is sleeping, he fears being awakened and conspires slowly with these pleasant illusions. In just this way, I spontaneously fall back into my old beliefs, and dread being awakened, lest the toilsome wakefulness which follows upon a peaceful rest, have to be spend thenceforward not in the light but among the inextricable shadows of the difficulties now brought forward.

MEDITATION 2

Yesterday's meditation filled my mind with so many doubts that I can no longer forget abut them—nor yet do I see how they are to be resolved. But, as if I had suddenly fallen into a deep whirlpool, I am so disturbed that I can neither touch my foot to the bottom, nor swim up to the top. Nevertheless I will work my way up, and I will follow the same path I took yesterday, putting aside everything which admits of the least doubt, as if I had discovered it to be absolutely false. I will go forward until I know something certain—or, if nothing else, until I at least know for certain that nothing is certain. Archimedes sought only a firm and immovable point in order to move the entire earth from one place to another. Surely great things are to be hoped for if I am lucky enough to find at least one thing that is certain and indubitable.

Therefore I will suppose that all I see is false. I will believe that none of those things that my deceitful memory brings before my eyes ever existed. I thus have no senses: body, shape, extension, movement, and place are all figments of my imagination. What then will count as true? Perhaps only this one thing: that nothing is certain.

But on what grounds do I know that there is nothing over and above all those which I have just reviewed, concerning which there is not even the least cause for doubt? Is there not a God (or whatever name I might call him) who instills these thoughts in me? But why should I think that, since perhaps I myself could be the author of these things? Therefore am I not at least something? But why should I think that, since perhaps I myself could be the author of these things? But I have already denied that I have any senses and any body. Still, I hesitate; for what follows from that? Am I so tied to the body and to the senses that I cannot exist without them? But I have persuaded myself that there is nothing at all in the world: no heaven, no earth, no minds, no bodies. Is it not then true that I do not exist? But certainly I should exist, if I were to persuade myself of something. But there is a deceiver (I know not who he is) powerful and sly in the highest degree, who is always purposely deceiving me. Then there is no doubt that I exist, if he deceives me. And deceive me as he will, he can never bring it about that I am nothing so long as I shall think that I am something. Thus it must be granted that, after weighing everything carefully and sufficiently, one must come to the con-sidered judgment that the statement "I am, I exist" is necessarily true every time it is uttered by me or conceived in my mind. . . .

O. K. BOUWSMA

Descartes' Evil Genius

O. K. BOUWSMA (1898–1978) taught at the University of Nebraska from 1928 to 1965 and at the University of Texas at Austin from 1965 to 1978. He was the author of Philosophical Essays.

THERE was once an evil genius who promised the mother of us all that if we ate the fruit of the tree, she would be like God, knowing good and evil. He promised knowledge. She did eat and she learned, but she was disappointed, for to know good and evil and not to be God is awful. Many an Eve later, there was rumor of another evil genius. This evil genius promised no good, promised no knowledge. He made a boast, a boast so wild and so deep and so dark that those who heard it cringed in hearing it. And what was that boast? Well, that apart from a few, four or five, clear and distinct ideas, he could deceive any son of Adam about anything. So he boasted. And with some result? Some indeed! Men going about in the brightest noonday would look and exclaim: "How obscure!" and if some careless merchant counting his apples was heard to say: "Two and three are five," a hearer of the boast could rub his eyes and run away. This evil genius still whispers, thundering, among the leaves of books, frightening people, whisper-ing: "I can. Maybe I will. Maybe so, maybe not." The tantalizer! In what follows I should like to examine the boast of this evil genius.

I am referring, of course, to that evil genius of whom Descartes writes:

I shall then suppose, not that God who is supremely good and the fountain of truth, but some evil genius not less powerful than deceitful, has employed his whole energies in deceiving me; I shall consider that the heavens, the earth, the colors, figures, sound, and all other external things are nought but illusions and dreams of which this evil genius has availed himself, in order to lay traps for my credulity; I shall consider myself as having no hands, no eyes, no flesh, no blood, nor any senses, yet falsely believ-ing myself to possess all these things.

This then is the evil genius whom I have represented as boasting that he can deceive us about all these things. I intend now to examine this boast, and to understand how this deceiving and being deceived are to take place. I expect to discover that the evil genius may very well deceive us, but that if we are wary, we need not be deceived. He will deceive us, if he does, by bathing the word "illusion" in a fog. This then will be the word to keep our minds on. In order to accomplish all this, I intend to describe the evil genius carrying out his boast in two adventures. The first of these I shall consider a thoroughly transparent case of deception. The word "illusion" will find a clear and familiar application. Nevertheless in this instance the evil genius will not have exhausted "his whole energies in deceiving us." Hence we must aim to imagine a further trial of the boast, in which the "whole energies" of the evil genius are exhausted. In this instance I intend to show that the evil genius is himself befuddled, and that if we too exhaust some of our energies in sleuthing after the peculiarities of his diction, then we need not be deceived either.

Let us imagine the evil genius then at his ease meditating that very bad is good enough for him, and that he would let bad enough alone. All the old pseudos, pseudo names and pseudo statements, are doing very well. But today it was different. He took no delight in common lies, everyday fibs, little ones, old ones. He wanted something new and something big. He scratched his genius; he uncovered an idea. And he scribbled on the inside of his tattered halo, "Tomorrow, I will deceive," and he smiled, and his words were thin and like fine wire. "Tomorrow, I will change everything, everything, everything I will change flowers, human beings, trees, hills, sky, the sun, and everything else into paper. Paper alone I will not change. There will be paper flowers, paper human beings, paper trees. And human beings will be deceived. They will think that there are flowers, human

beings, and trees, and there will be nothing but paper. It will be gigantic. And it ought to work. After all, men have been deceived with much less trouble. There was a sailor, a Baptist I believe, who said that all was water. And there was no more water then than there is now. And there was a pool-hall keeper who said that all was billiard balls. That's a long time ago of course, a long time before they opened one, and listening, heard that it was full of the sound of a trumpet. My prospects are good. I'll try it."

And the evil genius followed his own directions and did according to his words. And this is what happened.

Imagine a young man, Tom, bright today as he was yesterday, approaching a table where yesterday he had seen a bowl of flowers. Today it suddenly strikes him that they are not flowers. He stares at them troubled, looks away, and looks again. Are they flowers? He shakes his head. He chuckles to himself. "Huh! that's funny. Is this a trick? Yesterday there certainly were flowers in that bowl." He sniffs suspiciously, hopefully, but smells nothing. His nose gives no assurance. He thinks of the birds that flew down to peck at the grapes in the picture and of the mare that whinnied at the likeness of Alexander's horse. Illusions! The picture oozed no juice, and the likeness was still. He walked slowly to the bowl of flowers. He looked, and he sniffed, and he raised his hand. He stroked a petal lightly, lover of flowers, and drew back. He could scarcely believe his fingers. They were not flowers. They were paper.

As he stands, perplexed, Milly, friend and dear, enters the room. Seeing him occupied with the flowers, she is about to take up the bowl and offer them to him, when once again he is overcome with feelings of strangeness.

She looks just like a great big doll. He looks more closely, closely as he dares, seeing this may be Milly after all. Milly, are you Milly?—that wouldn't do. Her mouth clicks as she opens it, speaking, and it shuts precisely. Her forehead shines, and he shudders at the thought of Mme Tussaud's. Her hair is plaited, evenly, perfectly, like Milly's but as she raises one hand to guard its order, touching it, preening, it whispers like a newspaper. Her teeth are white as a genteel monthly. Her gums are pink, and there is a clapper in her mouth. He thinks of mama dolls, and of the rubber doll he used to pinch; it had a misplaced navel right in the pit of the back, that whistled. Galatea in paper! Illusions!

He noted all these details, flash by flash by flash. He reaches for a chair to steady himself and just in time. She approaches with the bowl of flowers, and, as the bowl is extended toward him, her arms jerk. The suppleness, the smoothness, the roundness of life is gone. Twitches of a smile mislight up her face. He extends his hand to take up the bowl and his own arms jerk as hers did before. He takes the bowl, and as he does so sees his hand. It is pale, fresh, snowy. Trembling, he drops the bowl, but it does not break, and the water does not run. What a mockery!

He rushes to the window, hoping to see the real world. The scene is like a theatre-set. Even the pane in the window is drawn very thin, like cellophane. In the distance are the forms of men walking about and tossing trees and houses and boulders and hills upon the thin cross section of a truck that echoes only echoes of chugs as it moves. He looks into the sky upward, and it is low. There is a patch straight above him, and one seam is loose. The sun shines out of the blue like a drop of German silver.

He reaches out with his pale hand, crackling the cellophane, and his hand touches the sky. The sky shakes and tiny bits of it fall, flaking his white hand with confetti.

Make-believe!

He retreats, crinkling, creaking, hiding his sight. As he moves he misquotes a line of poetry: "Those are perils that were his eyes," and he mutters, "Hypocritical pulp!" He goes on: "I see that the heavens, the earth, colors, figures, sound, and all other external things, flowers, Milly, trees and rocks and hills are paper, paper laid as traps for my credulity. Paper flowers, paper Milly, paper sky!" Then he paused, and in sudden fright he asked "And what about me?" He reaches to his lip and with two fingers tears the skin and peels off a strip of newsprint. He looks at it closely, grim. "I shall consider myself as having no hands, no eyes, no flesh, no blood, or any senses." He lids his paper eyes and stands dejected. Suddenly he is cheered. He exclaims: *"Cogito me papyrum esse, ergo sum."* He has triumphed over paperdom.

I have indulged in this phantasy in order to illustrate the sort of situation which Descartes' words might be expected to describe. The evil genius attempts to deceive. He tries to mislead Tom into thinking what is not. Tom is to think that these are flowers, that this is the Milly that was, that those are trees, hills, the heavens, etc. And he does this by creating illusions, that is, by making something that looks like flowers, artificial flowers; by making something that looks like and sounds like and moves like Milly, an artificial Milly. An illusion is something that looks like or sounds like, so much like, something else that you either mistake it for something else, or you can easily understand how someone might come to do this. So when the evil genius creates illusions intending to deceive he makes things which might quite easily be mistaken for what they are not. Now in the phantasy as I discovered it Tom is not deceived. He does experience the illusion, however. The intention of this is not to cast any reflection upon the deceptive powers of the evil genius. With such refinements in the paper art as we now know, the evil genius might very well have been less unsuccessful. And that in spite of his rumored lament: "And I made her of the best paper!" No, that Tom is not deceived, that he detects the illusion, is introduced in order to remind ourselves how illusions are detected. That the paper flowers are illusory is revealed by the recognition that they are paper. As soon as Tom realizes that though they look like flowers but are paper, he is acquainted with, sees through the illusion, and is not deceived. What is required, of course, is that he know the difference between flowers and paper, and that when presented with one or the other he can tell the difference. The attempt of the evil genius also presupposes this. What he intends is that though Tom knows this difference, the paper will look so much like flowers that Tom will not notice the respect in which the paper is different from the flowers. And even though Tom had actually been deceived and had not recognized the illusion, the evil genius himself must have been aware of the difference, for this is involved in his design. This is crucial, as we shall see when we come to consider the second adventure of the evil genius.

As you will remember I have represented the foregoing as an illustration of the sort of situation which Descartes' words might be expected to describe. Now, however, I think that this is misleading. For though I have described a situation in which there are many things, nearly all of which are calculated to serve as illusions, this question may still arise. Would this paper world still be properly described as a world of illusions? If Tom says: "These are flowers," or "These look like flowers" (uncertainly), then the illusion is operative. But if Tom says: "These are paper," then the illusion has been destroyed. Descartes uses the words: "And all other external things are nought but illusions." This means that the situation which Descartes has in mind is such that if Tom says: "These are flowers," he will be wrong, but he will be wrong also if he says: "These are paper," and it won't matter what sentence of that type he uses. If he says: "These are rock"— or cotton or cloud or wood—he is wrong by the plan. He will be right only if he says: "These are illusions." But the project is to keep him from recognizing the illusions. This means that the illusions are to be brought about not by anything so crude as paper or even cloud. They must be made of the stuff that dreams are made of.

Now let us consider this second adventure.

The design then is this. The evil genius is to create a world of illusions. There are to be no flowers, no Milly, no paper. There is to be nothing at all, but Tom is every moment to go on mistaking nothing for something, nothing at all for flowers, nothing at all for Milly, etc. This is, of course, quite different from mistaking paper for flowers, paper for Milly. And yet all is to be arranged in such a way that Tom will go on just as we now do, and just as Tom did before the paper age, to see, hear, smell the world. He will love the flowers, he will kiss Milly, he will blink at the sun. So he thinks. And in thinking about these things he will talk and argue just as we do. But all the time he will be mistaken. There are no flowers, there is no kiss, there is no sun. Illusions all. This then is the end at which the evil genius aims.

How now is the evil genius to attain this end? Well, it is clear that a part of what he aims at will be realized if he destroys everything. Then there will be no flowers, and if Tom thinks that there are flowers he will be wrong. There will be no face that is Milly's and no tumbled beauty on her head, and if Tom thinks that there is Milly's face and Milly's hair, he will be wrong. It is necessary then to see to it that there are none of these things. So the evil genius, having failed with paper, destroys even all paper. Now there is nothing to see, nothing to hear, nothing to smell, etc. But this is not enough to deceive. For though Tom sees nothing, and neither hears nor smells anything, he may also think that he sees nothing. He must also be misled into thinking that he does see something, that there are flowers and Milly, and hands, eyes, flesh, blood, and all other senses. Accordingly the evil genius restores to Tom his old life. Even the memory of that paper day is blotted out, not a scrap remains. Witless Tom lives on, thinking, hoping, loving as he used to, unwitted by the great destroyer. All that seems so solid, so touchable to seeming hands, so biteable to apparent teeth, is so flimsy that were the evil genius to poke his index at it, it would curl away save for one tiny trace, the smirch of that index. So once more the evil genius has done according to his word.

And now let us examine the result.

I should like first of all to describe a passage of Tom's life. Tom is all alone, but he doesn't know it. What an opportunity for methodologico-metaphysico-solipsimo! I intend, in any case, to disregard the niceties of his being so alone and to borrow his own words, with the warning that the evil genius smiles as he reads them. Tom writes:

Today, as usual, I came into the room and there was the bowl of flowers on the table. I went up to them, caressed them, and smelled over them. I thank God for flowers! There's nothing so real to me as flowers. Here the genuine essence of the world's substance, at its gayest and most hilarious speaks to me. It seems unworthy even to think of them as erect, and waving on pillars of sap. Sap! Sap!

There was more in the same vein, which we need not bother to record. I might say that the evil genius was a bit amused, snickered in fact, as he read the words "so real," "essence," "substance," etc., but later he frowned and seemed puzzled. Tom went on to describe how Milly came into the room, and how glad he was to see her. They talked about the flowers. Later he walked to the window and watched the gardener clearing a space a short distance away. The sun was shining, but there were a few heavy clouds. He raised the window, extended his hand and four large drops of rain wetted his hand. He returned to the room and quoted to Milly a song from *The Tempest*. He got all the words right, and was well pleased with himself. There was more he wrote, but this was enough to show how quite normal everything seems. And, too, how successful the evil genius is.

And the evil genius said to himself, not quite in solipsimo, "Not so, not so, not at all so."

The evil genius was, however, all too human. Admiring himself but unadmired, he yearned for admiration. To deceive but to be unsuspected is too little glory. The evil genius set about then to plant the seeds of suspicion. But how to do this? Clearly there was no suggestive paper to tempt Tom's confidence. There was nothing but Tom's mind, a stream of seemings and of words to make the seemings seem no seemings. The evil genius must have words with Tom and must engage the same seemings with him. To have words with Tom is to have the words together, to use them in the same way, and to engage the same seemings is to see and to hear and to point to the same. And so the evil genius, free spirit, entered in at the door of Tom's pineal gland and lodged there. He floated in the humors that flow, glandwise and sensewise, everywhere being as much one with Tom as difference will allow. He looked out of the same eyes, and when Tom pointed with his finger, the evil genius said "This" and meant what Tom, hearing, also meant, seeing. Each heard with the same ear what the other heard. For every sniffing of the one nose there were two identical smells, and there were two tactualities for every touch. If Tom had had a toothache, together they would have pulled the same face. The twinsomeness of two monads finds here the limit of identity. Nevertheless there was otherness looking out of those eyes as we shall see.

It seems then that on the next day, the evil genius "going to and from" in Tom's mind and "walking up and down in it," Tom once again, as his custom was, entered the room where the flowers stood on the table. He stopped, looked admiringly, and in a caressing voice said: Flowers! Flowers!" And he lingered. The evil genius, more subtle "than all the beasts of the field," whispered "Flowers? Flowers?" For the first time Tom has an intimation of company, of some intimate partner in perception. Momentarily he is checked. He looks again at the flowers. "Flowers? Why, of course, flowers." To-

gether they look out of the same eyes. Again the evil genius whispers, "Flowers?" The seed of suspicion is to be the question. But Tom now raises the flowers nearer to his eyes almost violently as though his eyes were not his own. He is, however, not perturbed. The evil genius only shakes their head, "Did you ever hear of illusions?" says he.

Tom, still surprisingly good-natured, responds: "But you saw them, didn't you? Surely you can see through my eyes. Come, let us bury my nose deep in these blossoms, and take one long breath together. Then tell whether you can recognize these as flowers."

So they dunked the one nose. But the evil genius said "Huh!" as much as to say: What has all this seeming and smelling to do with it? Still he explained nothing. And Tom remained as confident of the flowers as he had been at the first. The little seeds of doubt, "Flowers? Flowers?" and again "Flowers?" and "Illusions?" and now this stick in the spokes, "Huh!" made Tom uneasy. He went on: "Oh, so you are one of these seers that has to touch everything. You're a tangibilite. Very well, here's my hand, let's finger these flowers. Careful! They're tender."

The evil genius was amused. He smiled inwardly and rippled in a shallow humor. To be taken for a materialist! As though the grand illusionist was not a spirit! Nevertheless, he realized that though deception is easy where the lies are big enough (where had he heard that before?), a few scattered, questioning words are not enough to make guile grow. He was tempted to make a statement, and he did. He said, "Your flowers are nothing but illusions."

"My flowers illusions?" exclaimed Tom, and he took up the bowl and placed it before a mirror. "See," said he, "here are the flowers and here, in the

mirror, is an illusion. There's a difference surely. And you with my eyes, my
nose, and my fingers can tell what that
difference is. Pollen on your fingers
touching the illusion? Send Milly the
flowers in the mirror? Set a bee to suck
honey out of this glass? You know all
this as well as I do. I can tell flowers
from illusions, and my flowers, as you
now plainly see, are not illusions."

The evil genius was now sorely tried.
He had his make-believe, but he also
had his pride. Would he now risk the
make-believe to save his pride? Would
he explain? He explained.

"Tom," he said, "notice. The flowers
in the mirror look like flowers, but they
only look like flowers. We agree about
that. The flowers before the mirror also
look like flowers. But they, you say, are
flowers because they also smell like
flowers and they feel like flowers, as
though they would be any more flowers
because they also like flowers multiply.
Imagine a mirror such that it reflected
not only the look of flowers, but also
their fragrance and their petal surfaces,
and then you smelled and touched, and
the flowers before the mirror would be
just like the flowers in the mirror. Then
you could see immediately that the
flowers before the mirror are illusions
just as those in the mirror are illusions.
As it is now, it is clear that the flowers
in the mirror are thin illusions, and the
flowers before the mirror are thick.
Thick illusions are the best for deception. And they may be as thick as you
like. From them you may gather pollen,
send them to Milly, and foolish bees
may sleep in them."

But Tom was not asleep. "I see that
what you mean by thin illusions is what
I mean by illusions, and what you mean
by thick illusions is what I mean by
flowers. So when you say that my flowers are your thick illusions this doesn't
bother me. And as for your mirror that
mirrors all layer of your thick illusions,
I shouldn't call that a mirror at all. It's a
duplicator, and much more useful than a
mirror, provided you can control it. But
I do suppose that when you speak of
thick illusions you do mean that thick illusions are related to something you call
flowers in much the same way that the
thin illusions are related to the thick
ones. Is that true?"

The evil genius was now diction-
deep in explanations and went on. "In
the first place let me assure that these
are not flowers. I destroyed all flowers.
There are no flowers at all. There are
only thin and thick illusions of flowers.
I can see your flowers in the mirror, and
I can smell and touch the flowers before
the mirror. What I cannot smell and
touch, having seen as in the mirror, is
not even thick illusion. But if I cannot
also *cerpicio* what I see, smell, touch,
etc., what I have then seen is not anything real. *Esse est Cerpici.* I just now
tried to *cerpicio* your flowers, but there
was nothing there. Man is after all a
four- or five- or six-sense creature and
you cannot expect much from so little."

Tom rubbed his eyes and his ears tin-
gled with an eighteenth-century disturbance. Then he stared at the flowers. "I
see," he said, "that this added sense of
yours has done wickedly with our language. You do not mean by illusion
what we mean, and neither do you mean
by flowers what we mean. As for *cerpicio* I wouldn't be surprised if you'd
made up that word just to puzzle us. In
any case what you destroyed is what,
according to you, you used to *cerpicio*.
So there is nothing for you to *cerpicio*
any more. But there still are what we
mean by flowers. If your intention was
to deceive, you must learn the language

of those you are to deceive. I should say that you are like the doctor who prescribes for his patients what is so bad for himself and is then surprised at the health of his patients." And he pinned a flower near their nose.

The evil genius, discomfited, rode off on a corpuscle. He had failed. He took an artery, made haste to the pineal exit, and was gone. Then "sun by sun" he fell. And he regretted his mischief.

I have tried in this essay to understand the boast of the evil genius. His boast was that he could deceive about "the heavens, the earth, the colors, figures, sound, and all other external things." In order to do this I have tried to bring clearly to mind what deception and such deceiving would be like. Such deception involves illusions and such deceiving involves the creation of illusions. Accordingly I have tried to image the evil genius engaged in the practice of deception, busy in the creation of illusions. In the first adventure everything is plain. The evil genius employs paper, paper making believe it's many other things. The effort to deceive, ingenuity in deception, being deceived by paper, detecting the illusions—all these are clearly understood. It is the second adventure, however, which is more crucial. For in this instance it is assumed that the illusion is of such a kind that no seeing, no touching, no smelling, are relevant to detecting the illusion. Nevertheless the evil genius sees, touches, smells and does not detect the illusion. He made the illusion; so, of course, he must know it. How then does he know it? The evil genius has a sense denied to men. He senses the flower-in-itself, Milly-in-herself, etc. So he creates illusions made up of what can be seen, heard, smelled,

etc., illusions all because when seeing, hearing, and smelling have seen, heard, and smelled all, the special sense senses nothing. So what poor human beings sense is the illusion of what only the evil genius can sense. This is formidable. Nevertheless, once again everything is clear. If we admit the special sense, then we can readily see how it is that the evil genius should have certainly created his own illusions, though he has not himself been deceived. But neither has anyone else been deceived. For human beings do not use the world "illusion" by relation to a sense with which only the evil genius is blessed.

I said that the evil genius had not been deceived, and it is true that he has not been deceived by his own illusions. Nevertheless he was deceived in boasting that he could deceive, for his confidence in this is based upon an ignorance of the difference between our uses of the words, "heavens," "earth," "flowers," "Milly," and "illusions" of these things, and his own uses of these words. For though there certainly is an analogy between our own uses and his, the difference is quite sufficient to explain his failure at grand deception. We can also understand how easily Tom might have been taken in. The dog over the water dropped his meaty bone for a picture on the water. Tom, however, dropped nothing at all. But the word "illusion" is a trap.

I began this essay uneasily, looking at my hands and saying "no hands," blinking my eyes and saying "no eyes." Everything I saw seemed to me like something Cheshire, a piece of cheese, for instance, appearing and disappearing in the leaves of the tree. Poor Kitty! And now? Well. . . .

NORMAN MALCOLM

Knowledge Regained

NORMAN MALCOLM *is Professor Emeritus of Philosophy at Cornell University. Malcolm was very much influenced by Wittgenstein with whom he studied at Cambridge University. He is the author of numerous books and articles, among them* Dreaming *and* Knowledge and Certainty.

SOME philosophers have held that when we make judgments of perception such as that there are peonies in the garden, cows in the field, or dishes in the cupboard, we are "taking for granted" that the peonies, cows, and dishes exist, but not knowing it in the "strict" sense. Others have held that all empirical propositions, including judgments of perception, are merely hypotheses. The thought behind this exaggerated mode of expression is that any empirical proposition whatever *could* be refuted by future experience—that is, it *could* turn out to be false. Are these philosophers right?

Consider the following propositions:

(i) The sun is about ninety million miles from the earth.

(ii) There is a heart in my body.

(iii) Here is an ink-bottle.

In various circumstances I should be willing to assert of each of these propositions that I know it to be true. Yet they differ strikingly. This I see when, with each, I try to imagine the possibility that it is false.

(i) If in ordinary conversation someone said to me "The sun is about 20 million miles from the earth, isn't it?" I should reply "No; it is about 90 million miles from us." If he said "I think that you are confusing the sun with Polaris," I should reply, "I *know* that 90 million

miles is roughly the sun's distance from the earth." I might invite him to verify the figure in an encyclopedia. A third person who overheard our conversation could quite correctly report that I knew the distance to the sun, whereas the other man did not. But this knowledge of mine is little better than hearsay. I have seen that figure mentioned in a few books. I know nothing about the observations and calculations that led astronomers to accept it. If tomorrow a group of eminent astronomers announced that a great error had been made and that the correct figure is 20 million miles, I should not insist that they were wrong. It would surprise me that such an enormous mistake could have been made. But I should no longer be willing to say that I *know* that 90 million is the correct figure. Although I should *now* claim that I know the distance to be about 90 million miles, it is easy for me to envisage the possibility that some future investigation will prove this to be entirely false.

(ii) Suppose that after a routine medical examination the excited doctor reports to me that the X-ray photographs show that I have no heart. I should tell him to get a new machine. I should be inclined to say that the fact that I have a heart is one of the few things that I can count on as absolutely certain. I can feel it beat. I know it's there. Furthermore, how could my blood circulate if I didn't have one? Suppose that later on I suffer a chest injury and undergo a surgical operation. Afterwards the astonished surgeons solemnly declare that they searched my chest cavity and found no heart, and that they made incisions and looked about in other likely places but found it not. They are convinced that I am without a heart. They are unable to understand how circulation can occur or what accounts for the thumping in my chest. But they are in agreement and obviously sincere, and they have clear photographs of my interior spaces. What would be my attitude? Would it be to insist that they were all mistaken? I think not. I believe that I should eventually accept their testimony and the evidence of the photographs. I should consider to be false what I now regard as an absolute certainty.

(iii) Suppose that as I write this paper someone in the next room was to call out to me "I can't find an ink-bottle; is there one in the house"? I should reply "Here is an ink-bottle." If he said in doubtful tone "Are you sure? I looked there before," I should reply "Yes, I know there is; come and get it."

Now could it turn out to be false that there is an ink-bottle directly in front of me on this desk? Many philosophers have thought so. They would say that many things could happen of such a nature that if they did happen it would be proved that I am deceived. I agree that many extraordinary things could happen, in the sense that there is no logical absurdity in the supposition. It could happen that when I next reach for this ink-bottle my hand should seem to pass *through* it and I should not feel the contact of any object. It could happen that in the next moment the ink-bottle will suddenly vanish from sight; or that I should find myself under a tree in the garden with no ink-bottle about; or that one or more persons should enter this room and declare with apparent sincerity that they see no ink-bottle on this desk; or that a photograph taken now of the top of the desk should clearly show all of the objects on it except the ink-bottle. Having admitted that these things *could* happen, am I compelled to admit that if they did happen then it would be proved that there is no ink-bottle here *now*? Not at all! I could say that when my hand seemed to pass through the ink-bottle I should *then* be suffering from hallucination; that if the ink-bottle suddenly vanished it would have miraculously ceased to exist; that the other persons were conspiring to drive me mad, or were themselves victims of remarkable concurrent hallucinations; that the camera possessed some strange flaw or that there was trickery in developing the negative. I admit that in the next moment I could find myself under a tree or in a bathtub. But this is not to admit that it could be revealed in the next moment that I am now dreaming. For what I admit is that I might be instantaneously transported to the garden, but not that in the next moment I might *wake up* in the garden. There is nothing that could happen to me in the next moment that I should call "waking up"; and therefore nothing that could happen to me in the next moment would be accepted by me now as proof that I now dream.

Not only do I not *have* to admit that those extraordinary occurrences would be evidence that there is no ink-bottle here; the fact is that I do not admit it. There is nothing whatever that could happen in the next moment or the next year that would by me be called *evidence* that there is not an ink-bottle here now. No future experience or investigation could prove to me that I am mistaken. Therefore, if I were to say "I know that there is an ink-bottle here," I should be using "know" in the strong sense.

It will appear to some that I have adopted an *unreasonable* attitude toward that statement. There is, however, nothing unreasonable about it. It seems so because one thinks that the statement that here is an ink-bottle *must* have the same status as the statements that the sun is 90 million miles away and that I have a heart and that there will be water in the gorge this afternoon. But this is a *prejudice*.

In saying that I should regard nothing as evidence that there is no ink-bottle here now, I am not *predicting* what I should do if various astonishing things happened. If other members of my family entered this room, and while looking at the top of this desk, declared with apparent sincerity that they see no ink-bottle, I might fall into a swoon or become mad. I *might* even come to believe that there is not and has not been an ink-bottle here. I cannot foretell with certainty how I should react. But if it is *not* a prediction, what is the meaning of my assertion that I should regard nothing as evidence that there is no ink-bottle here?

That assertion describes my *present* attitude towards the statement that here is an ink-bottle. It does not prophecy what my attitude *would* be if various things happened. My present attitude toward that statement is radically different from my present attitude toward those other statements (*e.g.* that I have a heart). I do *now* admit that certain future occurrences would disprove the latter. Whereas no imaginable future occurrence would be considered by me *now* as proving that there is not an ink-bottle here.

These remarks are not meant to be autobiographical. They are meant to throw light on the common concepts of evidence, proof, and disproof. Everyone of us upon innumerable occasions of daily life takes this same attitude towards various statements about physical things, *e.g.* that here is a torn page, that this dish is broken, that the thermometer reads 70, that no rug is on the floor. Furthermore, the concepts of proof, disproof, doubt, and conjecture, *require* us to take this attitude. In order for it to be possible that any statements about physical things should *turn out to be false* it is necessary that some statements about physical things *cannot* turn out to be false.

LEWIS CARROLL

Through the Looking Glass

LEWIS CARROLL *(1832–1898), whose real name was Charles Lutwidge Dodgson, was an English mathematician and logician. His mother died when he went away to college, and he became increasingly drawn to the company of children, especially little girls. He was afflicted with a stammer which made him uncomfortable in the company of adults. His books* Alice in Wonderland *and* Through the Looking Glass *are two of the great children's books in English. He also published mathematical works.*

AFTER a pause, Alice began, 'Well—were *both* very unpleasant characters——' Here she checked herself in some alarm, at hearing something that sounded to her like the puffing of a large steam-engine in the wood near them, though she feared it was more likely to be a wild beast. 'Are there any lion or tigers about here?' she asked timidly.

'It's only the Red King snoring,' said Tweedledee.

'Come and look at him!' the brothers cried, and they each took one of Alice's hands, and led her up to where the King was sleeping.

'Isn't he a *lovely* sight?' said Tweedledum.

Alice couldn't say honestly that he was. He had a tall red night-cap on, with a tassel, and he was lying crumpled up into a sort of untidy heap, and snoring loud—'fit to snore his head off!' as Tweedledum remarked.

'I'm afraid he'll catch cold with lying on the damp grass,' said Alice, who was a very thoughtful little girl.

'He's dreaming now,' said Tweedledee: 'and what do you think he's dreaming about?'

Alice said 'Nobody can guess that.'

'Why, about *you!*' Tweedledee exclaimed, clapping his hands triumphantly. 'And if he left off dreaming about you, where do you suppose you'd be?'

'Where I am now, of course,' said Alice.

'Not you!' Tweedledee retorted contemptuously. 'You'd be nowhere. Why, you're only a sort of thing in his dream!'

'If that there King was to wake,' added Tweedledum, 'You'd go out—bang!—just like a candle!'

'I shouldn't!' Alice exclaimed indignantly. 'Besides, if *I'm* only a sort of thing in his dream, what are *you*, I should like to know?'

'Ditto,' said Tweedledum

'Ditto, ditto!' cried Tweedledee.

He shouted this so loud that Alice couldn't help saying 'Hush! You'll be waking him, I'm afraid, if you make so much noise.'

'Well, it's no use *your* talking about waking him,' said Tweedledum, 'when you're only one of the things in his dream. You know very well you're not real.'

'I *am* real!' said Alice, and began to cry.

'You won't make yourself a bit re-
aller by crying,' Tweedledee remarked:
'there's nothing to cry about.'

'If I wasn't real,' Alice said—half-
laughing through her tears, it all seemed
so ridiculous—'I shouldn't be able to
cry.'

'I hope you don't suppose those are
real tears?' Tweedledum interrupted in a
tone of great contempt.

JORGE LUIS BORGES

The Circular Ruins

*JORGE LUIS BORGES (1899–1986) was one of the greatest South American writers
of this century. Challenging traditional narrative forms, he had an enormous impact
on postmodern literature. Among his most famous books are* Labyrinths, Ficciones,
and Dreamtigers.

And if he left off dreaming about you . . .

Through the Looking Glass, VI

NO one saw him disembark in
the unanimous night, no one
saw the bamboo canoe sinking
into the sacred mud, but within a few
days no one was unaware that the silent
man came from the South and that his
home was one of the infinite villages
upstream on the violent mountainside,
where the Zend tongue is not contami-
nated with Greek and where leprosy is
infrequent. The truth is that the obscure
man kissed the mud, came up the bank
without pushing aside (probably without feeling) the brambles which dilacer-
ated his flesh, and dragged himself,
nauseous and bloodstained, to the circular enclosure crowned by a stone tiger
or horse, which once was the color of
fire and now was that of ashes. This circle was a temple, long ago devoured by
fire, which the malarial jungle had pro-
faned and whose god no longer received
the homage of men. The stranger
stretched out beneath the pedestal. He
was awakened by the sun high above.
He evidenced without astonishment that
his wounds had closed; he shut his pale
eyes and slept, not out of bodily weakness but out of determination of will.
He knew that this temple was the place
required by his invincible purpose; he
knew that, downstream, the incessant
trees had not managed to choke the
ruins of another propitious temple,
whose gods were also burned and dead;
he knew that his immediate obligation
was to sleep. Towards midnight he was
awakened by the disconsolate cry of a
bird. Prints of bare feet, some figs and a
jug told him that men of the region had
respectfully spied upon his sleep and
were solicitous of his favor or feared his
magic. He felt the chill of fear and
sought out a burial niche in the dilapi-
dated wall and covered himself with
some unknown leaves.

The purpose which guided him was not impossible, though it was supernatural. He wanted to dream a man: he wanted to dream him with minute integrity and insert him into reality. This magical project had exhausted the entire content of his soul; if someone had asked him his own name or any trait of his previous life, he would not have been able to answer. The uninhabited and broken temple suited him, for it was a minimum of visible world; the nearness of the peasants also suited him, for they would see that his frugal necessities were supplied. The rice and fruit of their tribute were sufficient sustenance for his body, consecrated to the sole task of sleeping and dreaming.

At first, his dreams were chaotic; somewhat later, they were of a dialectical nature. The stranger dreamt that he was in the center of a circular amphitheater which in some way was the burned temple: clouds of silent students filled the gradins; the faces of the last ones hung many centuries away and at a cosmic height, but were entirely clear and precise. The man was lecturing to them on anatomy, cosmography, magic; the countenances listened with eagerness and strove to respond with understanding, as if they divined the importance of the examination which would redeem one of them from his state of vain appearance and interpolate him into the world of reality. The man, both in dreams and awake, considered his phantoms' replies, was not deceived by impostors, divined a growing intelligence in certain perplexities. He sought a soul which would merit participation in the universe.

After nine or ten nights, he comprehended with some bitterness that he could expect nothing of those students who passively accepted his doctrines, but that he could of those who, at times, would venture a reasonable contradiction. The former, though worthy of love and affection, could not rise to the state of individuals; the latter pre-existed somewhat more. One afternoon (now his afternoons too were tributaries of sleep, now he remained awake only for a couple of hours at dawn) he dismissed the vast illusory college forever and kept one single student. He was a silent boy, sallow, sometimes obstinate, with sharp features which reproduced those of the dreamer. He was not long disconcerted by his companions' sudden elimination; his progress, after a few special lessons, astounded his teacher. Nevertheless, catastrophe ensued. The man emerged from sleep one day as if from a viscous desert, looked at the vain light of afternoon, which at first he confused with that of dawn, and understood that he had not really dreamt. All that night and all day, the intolerable lucidity of insomnia weighed upon him. He tried to explore the jungle, to exhaust himself; amidst the hemlocks, he was scarcely able to manage a few snatches of feeble sleep, fleetingly mottled with some rudimentary visions which were useless. He tried to convoke the college and had scarcely uttered a few brief words of exhortation, when it became deformed and was extinguished. In his almost perpetual sleeplessness, his old eyes burned with tears of anger.

He comprehended that the effort to mold the incoherent and vertiginous matter dreams are made of was the most arduous task a man could undertake, though he might penetrate all the enigmas of the upper and lower orders: much more arduous than weaving a rope of sand or coining the faceless wind. He comprehended that an initial failure was inevitable. He swore he would forget the enormous hallucination which had misled him at first, and he sought another method. Before putting into effect, he dedicated a month to replenishing the powers his delirium had wasted. He abandoned any premeditation of dreaming and, almost at once, was able to sleep for a considerable part of the day. The few times he dreamt during this period, he did not take notice of the dreams. To take up his task again, he waited until the moon's disk was perfect. Then, in the afternoon, he purified himself in the waters of the river, worshipped the planetary gods, uttered the lawful syllables of a powerful name and slept. Almost immediately, he dreamt of a beating heart.

He dreamt it as active, warm, secret, the size of a closed fist, of garnet color in the penumbra of a human body as yet without face or sex; with minute love he dreamt it, for fourteen lucid nights. Each night he perceived it with greater clarity. He did not touch it, but limited himself to witnessing it, observing it, perhaps correcting it with this eyes. He perceived it, lived it, from many distances and many angles. On the fourteenth night he touched the pulmonary artery with his finger, and then the whole heart, inside and out. The examination satisfied him. Deliberately, he did not dream for a night; then he took the heart again, invoked the name of a planet and set about to envision another of the principal organs. Within a year he reached the skeleton, the eyelids. The innumerable hair was perhaps the most difficult task. He dreamt a compete man, a youth, but this youth could not rise nor did he speak nor could he open his eyes. Night after night, the man dreamt him as asleep.

In the Gnostic cosmogonies, the demiurgi knead and mold a red Adam who cannot stand alone; as unskillful and crude and elementary as this Adam of dust was the Adam of dreams fabricated by the magician's nights of effort. One afternoon, the man almost destroyed his work, but then repented. (It would have been better for him had he destroyed it.) Once he had completed his supplications to the numina of the earth and the river, he threw himself down at the feet of the effigy which was perhaps a tiger and perhaps a horse, and implored its unknown succor. That twilight, he dreamt of the statue. He dreamt of it as a living, tremulous thing: it was not an atrocious mongrel of tiger and horse, but both these vehement creatures at once and also a bull, a rose, a tempest. This multiple god revealed to him that its earthly name was Fire, that in the circular temple (and in others of its kind) people had rendered it sacrifices and cult and that it would magically give life to the sleeping phantom, in such a way that all creatures except Fire itself and the dreamer would believe him to be a man of flesh and blood. The man was ordered by the divinity to instruct his creature in its rites, and send him to the other broken temple whose pyramids survived downstream, so that in this deserted edifice a voice might give glory to the god. In the dreamer's dream, the dreamed one awoke.

The magician carried out these orders. He devoted a period of time (which finally comprised two years) to revealing the arcana of the universe and of the fire cult to his dream child. Inwardly, it pained him to be separated from the boy. Under the pretext of pedagogical necessity, each day he prolonged the hours he dedicated to his dreams. He also redid the right shoulder, which was perhaps deficient. At times, he was troubled by the impression that all this had happened before. . . . In general, his days were happy; when he closed his eyes, he would think: *Now I shall be with my son.* Or, less often: *The child I have engendered awaits me and will not exist if I do not go to him.*

Gradually, he accustomed the boy to reality. Once he ordered him to place a banner on a distant peak. The following day, the banner flickered from the mountain top. He tried other analogous experiments, each more daring than the last. He understood with certain bitterness that his son was ready—and perhaps impatient—to be born. That night he kissed him for the first time and sent him to the other temple whose debris showed white downstream, through many leagues of inextricable jungle and swamp. But first (so that he would never know he was a phantom, so that he would be thought a man like others) he instilled into him a complete oblivion of years of apprenticeship.

The man's victory and peace were dimmed by weariness. At dawn and at twilight, he would prostrate himself before the stone figure, imagining perhaps that his unreal child was practicing the same rites, in other circular ruins, downstream; at night, he would not dream, or would dream only as all men do. He perceived the sounds and forms of the universe with certain colorlessness: his absent son was being nurtured with these diminutions of his soul. His life's purpose was complete; the man persisted in a kind of ecstasy. After a time, which some narrators of his story prefer to compute in years and others in lustra, he was awakened one midnight by two boatmen; he could not see their faces, but they told him of a magic man in a temple of the North who could walk

upon fire and not be burned. The magician suddenly remembered the words of the god. He recalled that, of all the creatures of the world, fire was the only one that knew his son was a phantom. This recollection, at first soothing, finally tormented him. He feared his son might meditate on his abnormal privilege and discover in some way that his condition was that of a mere image. Not to be a man, to be the projection of another man's dream, what a feeling of humiliation, of vertigo! All fathers are interested in the children they have procreated (they have permitted to exist) in mere confusion or pleasure; it was natural that the magician should fear for the future of that son, created in thought, limb by limb and feature by feature, in a thousand and one secret nights.

The end of his meditations was sudden, though it was foretold in certain signs. First (after a long drought) a faraway cloud on a hill, light and rapid as a bird; then, toward the south, the sky which had the rose color of the leopard's mouth; then the smoke which corroded the metallic nights; finally, the panicky flight of the animals. For what was happening had happened many centuries ago. The ruins of the fire god's sanctuary were destroyed by fire. In a birdless dawn the magician saw the concentric blaze close round the walls. For a moment, he thought of taking refuge in the river, but then he knew that death was coming to crown his old age and absolve him of his labors. He walked into the shreds of flame. But they did not bite into his flesh, they caressed him and engulfed him without heat or combustion. With relief, with humiliation, with terror, he understood that he too was a mere appearance, dreamt by another.

BERTRAND RUSSELL

Appearance and Reality

BERTRAND RUSSELL *(1872–1970) was one of the greatest philosophers of this century. He wrote an enormous number of philosophical books and articles, from* Principia Mathematica *(with Alfred North Whitehead) to some notorious polemics in favor of "free love" and atheism. Like Hume, he was too controversial for most universities, and a famous court case prevented him from teaching at City College of New York. He did however, win the Nobel Prize for Literature in 1950. At the age of eighty-nine, he was jailed for protesting against nuclear arms.*

IN daily life, we assume as certain many things which, on a closer scrutiny, are found to be so full of apparent contradictions that only a great amount of thought enables us to know what it is that we really may believe. In the search for certainty, it is natural to begin with our present experiences, and in some sense, no doubt, knowledge is to be derived from them. But any statement as to what it is that our immediate experiences make us know is very likely to be wrong. It seems to me that I am now sitting in a chair, at a table of a certain shape, on which I see sheets of paper with writing or print. By turning my head I see out of the window buildings and clouds and the sun. I believe that the sun is about ninety-three million miles from the earth; that it is a hot globe many times bigger than the earth; that, owing to the earth's rotation, it rises every morning, and will continue to do so for an indefinite time in the future. I believe that, if any other normal person comes into my room he will see the same chairs and tables and books and papers as I see, and that the table which I see is the same as the table which I feel pressing against my arm. All this seems to be so evident as to be hardly worth stating, except in answer to a man who doubts whether I know anything. Yet all this may be reasonably doubted, and all of it requires much careful discussion before we can be sure that we have stated it in a form that is wholly true.

To make our difficulties plain, let us concentrate attention on the table. To the eye it is oblong, brown and shiny, to the touch it is smooth and cool and hard; when I tap it, it gives out a wooden sound. Any one else who sees and feels and hears the table will agree with this description, so that it might seem as if no difficulty would arise; but as soon as we try to be more precise our troubles begin. Although I believe that the table is 'really' of the same colour all over, the parts that reflect the light look much brighter than the other parts, and some parts look white because of reflected light. I know that, if I move, the parts that reflect the light will be different, so that the apparent distribution of colours on the table will change. It follows that if several people are looking at the table at the same moment, no two of them will see exactly the same distribution of colours, because no two can see it from exactly the same point of view, and any change in the point of view makes some change in the way the light is reflected.

For most practical purposes these differences are unimportant, but to the painter they are all-important: the painter has to unlearn the habit of thinking that things seem to have the colour which common sense says they 'really' have, and to learn the habit of seeing things as they appear. Here we have already the beginning of one of the distinctions that cause most trouble in philosophy—the distinction between 'appearance' and 'reality', between what things seem to be and what they are. The painter wants to know what things seem to be, the practical man and the philosopher want to know what they are; but the philosopher's wish to know this is stronger than the practical man's, and is more troubled by knowledge as to the difficulties of answering the question.

To return to the table. It is evident from what we have found, that there is no colour which preeminently appears to be *the* colour of the table, or even of any one particular part of the table—it appears to be of different colours from different points of view, and there is no reason for regarding some of these as more really its colour than others. And we know that even from a given point of view the colour will seem different by artificial light, or to a colourblind man, or to a man wearing blue spectacles, while in the dark there will be no colour at all, though to touch and hearing the table will be unchanged. This colour is not something which is inherent in the table, but something depending upon the table and the spectator and the way the light falls on the table. When, in ordinary life, we speak of *the* colour of the table, we only mean the sort of colour which it will seem to have to a normal spectator from an ordinary point of view under usual conditions of light. But the other colours which appear under other conditions have just as good a right to be considered real; and therefore, to avoid favouritism, we are compelled to deny that, in itself, the table has any one particular colour.

The same thing applies to the texture. With the naked eye one can see the grain, but otherwise the table looks smooth and even. If we look at it through a microscope, we should see roughnesses and hills and valleys, and all sorts of differences that are imperceptible to the naked eye. Which of these is the 'real' table? We are naturally tempted to say that what we see through the microscope is more real, but that in turn would be changed by a still more powerful microscope. If, then, we cannot trust what we see with the naked eye, why should we trust what we see through a microscope? Thus, again, the confidence in our sense with which we began deserts us.

The *shape* of the table is no better. We are all in the habit of judging as to the 'real' shapes of things, and we do this so unreflectingly that we come to think we actually see the real shapes. But, in fact, as we all have to learn if we try to draw, a given thing looks different in shape from every different point of view. If our table is 'really' rectangular, it will look, from almost all points of view, as if it had two acute angles and two obtuse angles. If opposite sides are parallel, they will look as if they converged to a point away from the spectator; if they are of equal length, they will look as if the nearer side were longer. All these things are not commonly noticed in looking at a table, because experience has taught us to construct the 'real' shape from the apparent shape, and the 'real' shape is what we see; it is something inferred from what we see. And what we see is constantly changing in shape as we move about the room; so that here again the senses seem not to give us the truth about the table itself, but only about the appearance of the table.

Similar difficulties arise when we consider the sense of touch. It is true that the table always gives us a sensation of hardness, and we feel that it resists pressure. But the sensation we obtain depends upon how hard we press the table and also upon what part of the body we press with; thus the various sensations due to various pressures or various parts of the body cannot be supposed to reveal *directly* any definite property of the table, but at most to be

signs of some property which perhaps *causes* all the sensations, but is not actually apparent in any of them. And the same applies still more obviously to the sounds which can be elicited by rapping the table.

Thus it becomes evident that the real table, if there is one, is not the same as what we immediately experienced by sight or touch or hearing. The real table, if there is one, is not *immediately* known to us at all, but must be an inference from what is immediately known. Hence, two very difficult questions at once arise; namely (1) Is there a real table at all? (2) If so, what sort of object can it be?

JOHN LOCKE

Where Our Ideas Come From

JOHN LOCKE *(1632–1704) taught philosophy at Oxford until he earned his medical degree. He devoted considerable time to politics, and his two* Treatises on Government *were highly influential in establishing the theoretical grounds of the U.S. Constitution. Not only is he the founder of modern political liberalism, his* Essay Concerning Human Understanding *initiated what has come to be known as British empiricism.*

SOME FARTHER CONSIDERATIONS CONCERNING OUR SIMPLE IDEAS OF SENSATION

1 *Positive ideas from privative causes.*—Concerning the simple ideas of sensation it is to be considered, that whatsoever is so constituted in nature as to be able by affecting our senses to cause any perception in the mind, doth thereby produce in the

understanding a simple idea; which, whatever be the external cause of it, when it comes to be taken notice of by our discerning faculty, it is by the mind looked on and considered there to be a real positive idea in the understanding, as much as any other whatsoever; though perhaps the cause of it be but a privation in the subject.

2 Thus the ideas of heat and cold, light and darkness, white and black, motion and rest, are equally clear and

positive ideas in the mind; though perhaps some of the causes which produce them are barely privations in those subjects from whence our senses derive those ideas. These the understanding, in its view of them, considers all as distinct positive ideas without taking notice of the causes that produce them; which is an inquiry not belonging to the ideas as it is in the understanding, but to the nature of the things existing without us. These are two very different things, and carefully to be distinguished; it being one thing to perceive and know the idea of white or black, and quite another to examine what kind of particles they must be, and how ranged in the superficies, to make any object appear white or black.

3 A painter or dyer who never inquired into their causes, hath the ideas of white and black and other colours as clearly, perfectly, and distinctly in his understanding, and perhaps more distinctly than the philosopher who hath busied himself in considering their natures, and thinks he knows how far either of them is in its cause positive or privative; and the idea of black is no less positive in his mind than that of white, however the cause of that colour in the external object may be only a privation.

4 If it were the design of my present undertaking to inquire into the natural causes and manner of perception, I should offer this as a reason why a privative cause might, in some cases at least, produce a positive idea, viz., that all sensation being produced in us only by different degrees and modes of motion in our animal spirits, variously agitated by external objects, the abatement of any former motion must as necessarily produce a new sensation as the variation or increase of it; and so introduce a new idea, which depends only on a different motion of the animal spirits in that organ.

5 But whether this be so or not I will not here determine, but appeal to every one's own experience, whether the shadow of a man, though it consists of nothing but the absence of light (and the more the absence of light is, the more discernible is the shadow), does not, when a man looks on it, cause as clear and positive an idea in his mind as a man himself, though covered over with clear sunshine! And the picture of a shadow is a positive thing. Indeed, we have negative names, [which stand not directly for positive ideas, but for their absence, such as *insipid, silence, nihil, &c.,* which words denote positive ideas, *v. g., taste, sound, being,* with a signification of their absence.]

6 *Positive ideas from privative causes.*—And thus one may truly be said to see darkness. For, supposing a hole perfectly dark, from whence no light is reflected, it is certain one may see the figure of it, or it may be painted; or whether the ink I write with make any other idea, is a question. The privative causes I have here assigned of positive ideas are according to the common opinion; but, in truth, it will be hard to determine whether there be really any ideas from a privative cause, till it be determined whether rest be any more a privation than motion.

7 *Ideas in the mind, qualities in bodies.*—To discover the nature of our ideas the better, and to discourse of them intelligibly, it will be convenient to distinguish them, as they are ideas or perceptions in our minds, and as they are modifications of matter in the bodies that use such perceptions in us; that so we may not think (as perhaps usually is done) that they are exactly the images and resemblances of something inherent in the subject; most of those of sensation being in the mind no more the likeness of something existing without us

than the names that stand for them are the likeness of our ideas, which yet upon hearing they are apt to excite in us.

8   Whatsoever the mind perceives in itself, or is the immediate object of perception, thought, or understanding, that I call "ideal"; and the power to produce any idea in our mind, I call "quality" of the subject wherein that power is. Thus a snowball having the power to produce in us the ideas of white, cold, and round, the powers to produce those ideas in us as they are in the snowball, I call "qualities"; and as they are sensations or perceptions in our understanding, I call them "ideas"; which ideas, if I speak of them sometimes as in the things themselves, I would be understood to mean those qualities in the objects which produce them in us.

9   *Primary qualities.*—[Qualities thus considered in bodies are, First, such as are utterly inseparable from the body, in what estate soever it be;] and such as, in all the alterations and changes it suffers, all the force can be used upon it, it constantly keeps; and such as sense constantly finds in every particle of matter which has bulk enough to be perceived, and the mind finds inseparable from every particle of matter, though less than to make itself singly be perceived by our senses: *v. g.,* take a grain of wheat, divide it into two parts, each part has still solidity, extension, figure, and mobility; divide it again, and it retains still the same qualities: and so divide it on till the parts become insensible, they must retain still each of them all those qualities. For, division (which is all that a mill or pestle or any other body does upon another, in reducing it to insensible parts) can never take away either solidity, extension, figure, or mobility from any body, but only makes two or more distinct separate masses of matter of that

which was but one before; all which distinct masses reckoned as so many distinct bodies, after division, make a certain number. [These I call *original* or *primary* qualities of body, which I think we may observe to produce simple ideas in us, viz., solidity, extension, figure, motion or rest, and number.]

10   *Secondary qualities.*—Secondly. Such qualities, which in truth are nothing in the objects themselves, but powers to produce various sensations in us by their primary qualities, i.e., by the bulk, figure, texture, and motion of their insensible parts, as colours, sounds, tastes, &c., these I call *secondary* qualities. [To these might be added a third sort, which are allowed to be barely powers, though they are as much real qualities in the subject as those which I, to comply with the common way of speaking, call qualities, but, for distinction, *secondary* qualities. For, the power in fire to produce a new colour or consistency in wax or clay, by its primary qualities, is as much a quality in fire as the power it has to produce in me a new idea or sensation of warmth or burning, which I felt not before, by the same primary qualities, viz., the bulk, texture, and motion of its insensible parts.]

11   [*How primary qualities produce their ideas.*—The next thing to be considered is, how bodies produce ideas in us; and that is manifestly by impulse, the only way which we can conceive bodies to operate in.]

12   If, then, external objects be not united to our minds when they produce ideas therein, and yet we perceive these original qualities in such of them as singly fall under our senses, it is evident that some motion must be thence continued by our nerves, or animal spirits, by some parts of our bodies, to the brains or the seat of sensation, there to

produce in our minds the particular ideas we have of them. And since the extension, figure, number, and motion of bodies of an observable bigness, may be perceived at a distance by the sight, it is evident some singly imperceptible bodies must come from them to the eyes, and thereby convey to the brain some motion which produces these ideas which we have of them in us.

13 *How secondary.*—After the same manner that the ideas of these original qualities are produced in us, we may conceive that the ideas of secondary qualities are also produced, viz., by the operation of insensible particles on our senses. For it being manifest that there are bodies, and good store of bodies, each whereof are so small that we cannot by any of our senses discover either their bulk, figure, or motion (as is evident in the particles of the air and water, and other extremely smaller than those, perhaps as much smaller than the particles of air or water as the particles of air or water are smaller than peas or hailstones): let us suppose at present that the different motions and figures, bulk and number, of such particles, effecting several organs of our senses, produce in us those different sensations which we have from the colours and smells of bodies, *v. g.,* that a violet, by the impulse of such insensible particles of matter of peculiar figures and bulks, and in different degrees and modifications of their motions, causes the ideas of the blue colour and sweet scent of that flower to be produced in our minds; it being no more impossible to conceive that God should annex such ideas to such motions, with which they have no similitude, than that he should annex the idea of pain to the motion of a piece of steel dividing our flesh, with which the idea hath no resemblance.

14 What I have said concerning colours and smells may be understood also of tastes and sounds, and other the like sensible qualities; which, whatever reality we by mistake attribute to them, are in truth nothing in the objects themselves, but powers to produce various sensations in us, and depend on those primary qualities, viz., bulk, figure, texture, and motion of parts [as I have said].

15 *Ideas of primary qualities are resemblances; of secondary, not.*—From whence I think it is easy to draw this observation, that the ideas of primary qualities of bodies are resemblances of them, and their patterns do really exist in the bodies themselves; but the ideas produced in us by these secondary qualities have no resemblance of them at all. There is nothing like our ideas existing in the bodies themselves. They are, in the bodies we denominate from them, only a power to produce those sensations in us; and what is sweet, blue, or warm in idea, is but the certain bulk, figure, and motion of the insensible parts in the bodies themselves, which we call so.

16 Flame is denominated *hot* and *light;* snow, *white* and *cold;* and manna *white* and *sweet,* from the ideas they produce in us, which qualities are commonly thought to be the same in those bodies that those ideas are in us, the one the perfect resemblance of the other, as they are in a mirror; and it would by most men be judged very extravagant, if one should say otherwise. And yet he that will consider that the same fire that at one distance produces in us the sensation of warmth, does at a nearer approach produce in us the far different sensation of pain, ought to be-think himself what reason he has to say, that this idea of warmth which produced in him the same way is not in the fire.

Why is whiteness and coldness in snow and pain not, when it produces the one and the other idea in us, and can do neither but by the bulk, figure, number, and motion of its solid parts?

17   The particular bulk, number, figure, and motion of the parts of fire or snow are really in them, whether any one's senses perceive them or no; and therefore they may be called *real* qualities, because they really exist in those bodies. But light, heat, whiteness, or coldness, are no more really in them than sickness or pain is in manna. Take away the sensation of them; let not the eyes see light or colours, nor the ears hear sounds; let the palate not taste, nor the nose smell; and all colours, tastes, odours, and sounds, as they are such particular ideas, vanish and cease, and are reduced to their causes, *i.e.,* bulk, figure, and motion of parts.

GEORGE BERKELEY

To Be Is to Be Perceived

GEORGE BERKELEY *(1685–1753) was born, raised, and educated in Ireland. He wrote virtually all the works that made him famous before he was twenty-eight. Unlike his fellow empiricists Locke and Hume, he focused most of his philosophical attention on a single issue—perception. His most famous work is his* Treatise Concerning the Principles of Human Knowledge.

1   It is evident to any one who takes a survey of the *objects of human knowledge,* that they are either *ideas* actually imprinted on the senses; or else such as are perceived by attending to the passions and operations of the mind; or lastly, *ideas* formed by help of memory and imagination—either compounding, dividing, or barely representing those originally perceived in the aforesaid ways. By sight I have the ideas of light and colours, with their several degrees and variations. By touch I perceive hard and soft, heat and cold, motion and resistance; and of all these more and less either as to quantity or degree. Smelling furnishes me with odours; the palate with tastes; the hearing conveys sounds to the mind in all their variety of tone and composition.

And as several of these are observed to accompany each other, they come to be marked by one name, and so to be reputed as one *thing.* Thus, for example, a certain colour, taste, smell, figure and consistence having been observed to go together; are accounted one distinct thing, signified by the name apple; other collections of ideas constitute a stone, a tree, a book, and the like sensible things; which as they are pleasing or disagreeable excite the passion of love, hatred, joy, grief, and so forth.

2   But, besides all that endless variety of ideas or objects of knowledge, there is likewise Something which knows or

perceives them; and exercises divers operations, as willing, imagining, remembering, about them. This perceiving, active being is what I call *mind, spirit, soul,* or *myself.* By which words I do not denote any one of my ideas, but a thing entirely distinct from them, wherein they exist, or, which is the same thing, whereby they are perceived; for the existence of an idea consists in being perceived.

3   That neither our thoughts, nor passions, nor ideas formed by the imagination, exist without the mind is what everybody will allow. And to me it seems no less evident that the various sensations or ideas imprinted on the Sense, however blended or combined together (that is, whatever objects they compose), cannot exist otherwise than in a mind perceiving them. I think an intuitive knowledge may be obtained of this, by any one that shall attend to what is meant by the term *exist* when applied to sensible things. The table I write on I say exists; that is, I see and feel it: and if I were out of my study I should say it existed; meaning thereby that if I was in my study I might perceive it, or that some other spirit actually does perceive it. There was an odour, that is, it was smelt; there was a sound, that is, it was heard; a colour or figure, and it was perceived by sight or touch. This is all that I can understand by these and the like expressions. For as to what is said of the *absolute* existence of unthinking things, without any relation to their being perceived, that is to me perfectly unintelligible. Their *esse* is *percipi;* nor is it possible they should have any existence out of the minds or thinking things which perceive them.

4   It is indeed an opinion strangely prevailing amongst men, that houses, mountains, rivers, and in a word all sensible objects, have an existence, natural or real, distinct from their being perceived by the understanding. But, with how great an assurance and acquiescence soever this Principle may be entertained in the world, yet whoever shall find in his heart to call it in question may, if I mistake not, perceive it to involve a manifest contradiction. For, what are the forementioned objects but the things we perceive by sense? and what do we perceive besides our own ideas or sensations? and is it not plainly repugnant that any one of these, or any combination of them, should exist unperceived?

5   If we thoroughly examine this tenet it will, perhaps, be found at bottom to depend on the doctrine of *abstract ideas.* For can there be a nicer strain of abstraction than to distinguish the existence of sensible objects from their being perceived, so as to conceive them existing unperceived? Light and colours, heat and cold, extension and figures—in a word the things we see and feel—what are they but so many sensations notions, ideas, or impressions on the sense? and is it possible to separate, even in thought, any of these from perception? For my part, I might as easily divide a thing from itself. I may, indeed, divide in my thoughts, or conceive apart from each other, those things which perhaps I never perceived by sense so divided. Thus, I imagine the trunk of a human body without the limbs, or conceive the smell of a rose without thinking on the rose itself. So far, I will not deny, I can abstract; if that may properly be called *abstraction* which extends only to the conceiving separately such objects as it is possible may really exist or be actually perceived asunder. But my conceiving or imagining power does not extend beyond the

possibility of real existence or perception. Hence, as it is impossible for me to see or feel anything without an actual sensation of that thing, so is it impossible for me to conceive in my thoughts any sensible thing or object distinct from the sensation or perception of it. [In truth, the object and the sensation are the same thing, and cannot therefore be abstracted from each other.]

6 Some truths there are so near and obvious to the mind that a man need only open his eyes to see them. Such I take this important one to be, viz. that all the choir of heaven and furniture of the earth, in a word all those bodies which compose the mighty frame of the world, have not any subsistence without a mind; that their *being* is to be perceived or known; that consequently so long as they are not actually perceived by me, or do not exist in my mind, or that of any other created spirit, they must either have not existence at all, or else subsist in the mind of some Eternal Spirit: it being perfectly unintelligible, and involving all the absurdity of abstraction. to attribute to any single part of them an existence independent of a spirit. To be convinced of which, the reader need only reflect, and try to separate in his own thoughts the *being* of a sensible thing from its *being perceived.*

7 From what has been said it is evident there is not any other Substance than *Spirit,* or that which perceives. But, for the fuller proof of this point, let it be considered the sensible qualities are colour, figure, motion, smell, taste, and such like, that is, the ideas perceived by sense. Now, for an idea to exist in an unperceiving thing is a manifest contradiction; for to have an idea is all one as to perceive: that therefore wherein colour, figure, and the like qualities exist must perceive them. Hence it is

clear there can be no unthinking substance or *substratum* of those ideas.

8 But, say you, though the ideas themselves do not exist without the mind, yet there may be things like them, whereof they are copies or resemblances; which things exist without the mind, in an unthinking substance. I answer, an idea can be like nothing but an idea; a colour or figure can be like nothing but another colour or figure. If we look but never so little into our thoughts, we shall find it impossible for us to conceive a likeness except only between our ideas. Again, I ask whether those supposed *originals,* or external things, of which our ideas are the pictures or representations, be themselves perceivable or no? If they are, then *they* are ideas, and we have gained our point; but if you say they are not, I appeal to any one whether it be sense to assert a colour is like something which is invisible; hard or soft, like something which is intangible; and so of the rest.

9 Some there are who make a distinction betwixt *primary* and *secondary* qualities. By the former they mean extension, figure, motion, rest, solidity or impenetrability, and number; by the latter they denote all other sensible qualities, as colours, sounds, tastes, and so forth. The ideas we have of these last they acknowledge not to be the resemblances of anything existing without the mind, or unperceived; but they will have our ideas of the *primary qualities* to be patterns or images of things which exist without the mind, in an unthinking substance which they call Matter. By Matter, therefore, we are to understand an inert, senseless substance, in which extension, figure, and motion do actually subsist. But it is evident, from what we have already shewn, that extension, figure, and motion are only

ideas existing in the mind, and that an idea can be like nothing but another idea; and that consequently neither they nor the archetypes can exist in an unperceiving substance. Hence, it is plain that the very notion of what is called *Matter* or *corporeal substance,* involves a contradiction in it. Insomuch that I should not think it necessary to spend more time in exposing its absurdity. But, because the tenet of the existence of Matter seems to have taken so deep a root in the minds of philosophers, and draws after it so many ill consequences, I choose rather to be thought prolix and tedious than omit anything that might conduce to the full discovery and extirpation of that prejudice.

10 They who assert that figure, motion, and the rest of the primary or original qualities do exist without the mind, in unthinking substances, do at the same time acknowledge that colours, sounds, heat, cold, and suchlike secondary qualities, do not; which they tell us are sensations, existing in the mind alone, that depend on and are occasioned by the different size, texture, and motion of the minute particles of matter. This they take for an undoubted truth, which they can demonstrate beyond all exception. Now, if it be certain that those *original* qualities are inseparably united with the other sensible qualities, and not, even in thought, capable of being abstracted from them, it plainly follows that *they* exist only in the mind. But I desire any one to reflect, and try whether he can, by an abstraction of thought, conceive the extension and motion of a body without all other sensible qualities. For my own part, I see evidently that it is not in my power to frame an idea of a body extended and moving, but I must withal give it some colour or other sensible quality, which is acknowledged to

exist only in the mind. In short, extension, figure, and motion, abstracted from all other qualities, are inconceivable. Where therefore the other sensible qualities are, there must these be also, to wit, in the mind and nowhere else. . . .

14 I shall farther add, that, after the same manner as modern philosophers prove certain sensible qualities to have no existence in Matter, or without the mind, the same thing may be likewise proved of all other sensible qualities whatsoever. Thus, for instance, it is said that heat and cold are affections only of the mind, and not at all patterns of real beings, existing in the corporeal substances which excite them; for that the same body which appears cold to one hand seems warm to another. Now, why may we not as well argue that figure and extension are not patterns or resemblances of qualities existing in Matter; because to the same eye at different stations, or eyes of a different texture at the same station, they appear various and cannot therefore be the images of anything settled and determinate without the mind? Again, it is proved that sweetness is not really in the sapid thing; because the thing remaining unaltered the sweetness is changed into bitter, as in case of a fever or otherwise vitiated palate. Is it not as reasonable to say that motion is not without the mind; since if the succession of ideas in the mind become swifter, the motion, it is acknowledged, shall appear slower, without any alteration in any external object?

15 In short, let any one consider those arguments which are thought manifestly to prove that colours and tastes exist only in the mind, and he shall find they may with equal force be brought to prove the same thing of extension, figure, and motion. Though it must be confessed this method of arguing does not

so much prove that there is no extension or colour in an outward object, as that we do not know by sense which is the true extension or colour of the object. But the arguments foregoing plainly shew it to be impossible that any colour or extension at all, or other sensible quality whatsoever, should exist in an unthinking subject without the mind, or in truth that there should be any such thing as an outward object.

16   But let us examine a little the received opinion. It is said extension is a *mode* or *accident* of Matter, and that Matter is the *substratum* that supports it. Now I desire that you would explain to me what is meant by Matter's *supporting* extension. Say you, I have no idea of Matter; and therefore cannot explain it. I answer, though you have no positive, yet, if you have any meaning at all, you must at least have a relative idea of Matter; though you know not what it is, yet you must be supposed to know what relation it bears to accidents, and what is meant by its supporting them. It is evident *support* cannot here be taken in its usual or literal sense, as when we say that pillars support a building. In what sense therefore must it be taken? For my part, I am not able to discover any sense at all that can be applicable to it.

17   If we inquire into what the most accurate philosophers declare themselves to mean by *material substance,* we shall find them acknowledge they have no other meaning annexed to those sounds but the idea of Being in general, together with the relative notion of its supporting accidents. The general idea of Being appeareth to me the most abstract and incomprehensible of all other; and as for its supporting accidents, this, as we have just now observed, cannot be understood in the common sense of those words: it must therefore be taken

in some other sense, but what that is they do not explain. So that when I consider the two parts or branches which make the signification of the words *material substance,* I am convinced there is no distinct meaning annexed to them. But why should we trouble ourselves any farther, in discussing this material *substratum* or support of figure and motion and other sensible qualities? Does it not suppose they have an existence without the mind? And is not this a direct repugnancy, and altogether inconceivable?

18   But, though it were possible that solid, figured, moveable substances may exist without the mind, corresponding to the ideas we have of bodies, yet how is it possible for us to know this? Either we must know it by Sense or by Reason. As for our senses, by them we have the knowledge only of our sensations, ideas, or those things that are immediately perceived by sense, call them what you will: but they do not inform us that things exist without the mind, or unperceived, like to those which are perceived. This the materialists themselves acknowledge.—It remains therefore that if we have any knowledge at all of external things, it must be by reason inferring their existence from what is immediately perceived by sense. But (I do not see) what reason can induce us to believe the existence of bodies without the mind, from what we perceive, since the very patrons of Matter themselves do not pretend there is any necessary connexion betwixt them and our ideas? I say it is granted on all hands (and what happens in dreams, frensies, and the like, puts it beyond dispute) that it is possible we might be affected with all the ideas we have now, though no bodies existed without resembling them. Hence it is evident the supposition of external

bodies is not necessary for the producing our ideas; since it is granted they are produced sometimes, and might possibly be produced always, in the same order we see them in at present without their concurrence.

19 But, though we might possibly have all our sensations without them, yet perhaps it may be thought easier to conceive and explain the manner of their production, by supposing external bodies in their likeness rather than otherwise; and so it might be at least probable there are such things as bodies that excite their ideas in our minds. But neither can this be said. For, though we give the materialists their external bodies, they by their own confession are never the nearer knowing how our ideas are produced; since they own themselves unable to comprehend in what manner body can act upon spirit, or how it is possible it should imprint any idea in the mind. Hence it is evident the production of ideas or sensations in our minds, can be no reason why we should suppose Matter or corporeal substances; since that is acknowledged to remain equally inexplicable with or without this supposition. If therefore it were possible for bodies to exist without the mind, yet to hold they do so must needs be a very precarious opinion; since it is to suppose, without any reason at all, that God has created innumerable beings that are entirely useless, and serve to no manner of purpose.

20 In short, if there were external bodies, it is impossible we should ever come to know it; and if there were not, we might have the very same reasons to think there were that we have now. Suppose—what no one can deny possible— an intelligence, without the help of external bodies, to be affected with the same train of sensations or ideas that you are, imprinted in the same order and with like vividness in his mind. I ask whether that intelligence hath not all the reason to believe the existence of Corporeal Substances, represented by his ideas, and exciting them in his mind, that you can possibly have for believing the same thing? Of this there can be no question. Which one consideration were enough to make any reasonable person suspect the strength of whatever arguments he may think himself to have, for the existence of bodies without the mind. . . .

23 But, say you, surely there is nothing easier than for me to imagine trees, for instance, in a park, or books existing in a closet, and nobody by to perceive them. I answer, you may so, there is no difficulty in it. But what is all this, I beseech you, more than framing in your mind certain ideas which you call *books* and *trees,* and at the same time omitting to frame the idea of any one that may perceive them? But do not you yourself perceive or think of them all the while? This therefore is nothing to the purpose: it only shews you have the power of imagining, or forming ideas in your mind; but it does not shew that you can conceive it possible the objects of your thoughts may exist without the mind. To make out this, it is necessary that you conceive them existing unconceived or unthought of; which is a manifest repugnancy. When we do our utmost to conceive the existence of external bodies, we are all the while only contemplating our own ideas. But the mind, taking no notice of itself, is deluded to think it can and does conceive bodies existing unthought of, or without the mind, though at the same time they are apprehended by, or exist in, itself. A little attention will discover to any one the truth and evidence of what is here said, and make it unnecessary to insist on any other proofs against the existence of *material substance.*

LORRAINE CODE

Is the Sex of the Knower Epistemologically Significant?

LORRAINE CODE *teaches philosophy at York University. She is the author of*
Epistemic Responsibility *and* What Can She Know? *from which the following
selection is taken.*

A question that focuses on the knower, as the title of this chapter does, claims that there are good reasons for asking who that knower is. Uncontroversial as such a suggestion would be in ordinary conversations about knowledge, academic philosophers commonly treat 'the knower' as a featureless abstraction. Sometimes, indeed, she or he is merely a place holder in the proposition 'S knows that p'. Epistemological analyses of the proposition tend to focus on the 'knowing that', to determine conditions under which a knowledge claim can legitimately be made. Once discerned, it is believed, such conditions will hold across all possible utterances of the proposition. Indeed, throughout the history of modern philosophy the central 'problem of knowledge' has been to determine necessary and sufficient conditions for the possibility and justification of knowledge claims. Philosophers have sought ways of establishing a relation of correspondence between knowledge and 'reality' and/or ways of establishing the coherence of particular knowledge claims within systems of already-established truths. They have proposed methodologies for arriving at truth, and criteria for determining the validity of claims to the effect that 'S knows that

p'. Such endeavors are guided by the putatively self-evident principle that truth once discerned, knowledge once established, claim their status *as* truth and knowledge by virtue of a grounding in or coherence within a permanent, objective, ahistorical, and circumstantially neutral framework or set of standards.

The question 'Who is S?' is regarded neither as legitimate nor as relevant in these endeavors. As inquirers into the nature and conditions of human knowledge, epistemologists commonly work from the assumption that they need concern themselves only with knowledge claims that meet certain standards of *purity*. . . .

The only thing that is clear about S from the standard proposition 'S knows that p' is that S is a (would-be) knower. Although the question 'Who is S?' rarely arises, certain assumptions about S as knower permeate epistemological inquiry. Of special importance for my argument is the assumption that knowers are self-sufficient and solitary individuals, at least in their knowledge-seeking activities. This belief derives from a long and venerable heritage, with its roots in Descartes's quest for a basis of perfect certainty on which to establish his knowledge. The central aim of Descartes's endeavors is captured in this claim: "I shall have the right to conceive high hopes if I am happy enough to discover one thing only which is certain and indubitable." That "one thing," Descartes believed, would stand as the fixed pivotal, Archimedean point on which all the rest of his knowledge would turn. Because of its systematic relation to that point, his knowledge would be certain and indubitable.

Most significant for this discussion is Descartes's conviction that his quest will be conducted in a private, introspective examination of the contents of his own mind. It is true that, in the last section of the *Discourse on the Method,* Descartes acknowledges the benefit "others may receive from the communication of [his] reflection," and he states his belief that combining "the lives and labours of many" is essential to progress in scientific knowledge. It is also true that this individualistically described act of knowing exercises the aspect of the soul that is common to and alike in all knowers: namely, the faculty of reason. Yet his claim that knowledge seeking is an introspective activity of an individual mind accords no relevance either to a knower's embodiment or to his (or her) intersubjective relations. For each knower, the Cartesian route to knowledge is through private, abstract thought, through the efforts of reason unaided either by the senses or by consultation with other knowers. It is this individualistic, self-reliant, private aspect of Descartes's philosophy that has been influenced in shaping subsequent epistemological ideals.

Reason is conceived as autonomous in the Cartesian project in two ways, then. Not only is the quest for certain knowledge an independent one, undertaken separately by each rational being, but it is a journey of reason alone, unassisted by the senses. For Descartes believed that sensory experiences had the effect of distracting reason from its proper course.

The custom of formulating knowledge claims in the 'S knows that p' formula is not itself of Cartesian origin. The point of claiming Cartesian inspiration for an assumption implicit in the formulation is that the knower who is commonly presumed to be the subject of that proposition is modeled, in significant respects, on the Cartesian pure inquirer. For epistemological purposes, all knowers are believed to be alike with respect both to their cognitive capacities and to their methods of achieving knowledge. In the empiricist tradition this assumption is apparent in the belief that simple, basic observational data can provide the foundation of knowledge just because perception is invariant from observer to observer, in standard observation conditions. In fact, a common way of filling the places in the 'S knows that p' proposition is with substitutions such as "Peter knows that the door is open" or "John knows that the book is red." It does not matter who John or Peter is.

Such knowledge claims carry implicit beliefs not only about would-be knowers but also about the knowledge that is amenable to philosophical analysis. Although (Cartesian) rationalists and empiricists differ with respect to what kinds of claim count as foundational, they endorse similar assumptions about the relation of foundational claims to the rest of a body of knowledge. With 'S knows that p' propositions, the belief is that such propositions stand as paradigms for knowledge in general. Epistemologists assume that knowledge is analyzable into prepositional 'simples' whose truth can be demonstrated by establishing relations of correspondence to reality, or coherence within a system of known truths. These relatively simple knowledge claims (i.e., John knows that the book is red) could indeed be made by most 'normal' people who know the language and are familiar with the objects named. Knowers would seem to be quite self-sufficient in acquiring such knowledge. Moreover, no one would claim to know "a little" that the book is red or to be in the process of acquiring knowledge about the openness of the door. Nor would anyone be likely to maintain that S knows better than W does that the door is open or that the book is red. Granting such examples paradigmatic status creates the mistaken assumption that all knowledge worthy of the name will be like this. . . .

In proposing that the sex of the knower is epistemologically significant, I am claiming that the scope of epistemological inquiry has been too narrowly defined. . . . There are numerous questions to be asked about knowledge whose answers matter to people who are concerned to know well. Among them are questions that bear not just on criteria of evidence, justification, and warrantability, but on the 'nature' of cognitive agents: questions about their character; their material, historical, cultural circumstances; their interests in the inquiry at issue. These are questions about how credibility is established, about connections between knowledge and power, about the place of knowledge in ethical and aesthetic judgments, and about political agendas and the responsibilities of knowers. I am claiming that all of these questions are epistemologically significant. . . .

Although it has rarely been spelled out prior to the development of feminist critiques, it has long been tacitly assumed that S is male. Nor could S be just any man, the apparently infinite substitutability of the 'S' term notwithstanding. The S who could count as a model, paradigmatic knower has most commonly—if always tacitly—been an adult (but not *old*), white, reasonably affluent (latterly middle-class) educated man of status, property, and publicly acceptable accomplishments. In theory of knowledge he has been allowed to stand for all men. This assumption does not merely derive from habit or coincidence, but is a manifestation of engrained philosophical convictions. Not only has it been taken for granted that knowers properly so-called are male, but when male philosophers have paused to note this fact, as some indeed have done, they have argued that things are as they should be. Reason may be alike in all men, but it would be a mistake to believe that 'man', in this respect, 'embraces woman'. Women have been judged incapable, for many reasons, of achieving knowledge worthy of the name. It is no exaggeration to say that anyone who wanted to *count* as a knower has commonly had to be male.

In the *Politics,* Aristotle observes: "The freeman rules over the slave after another manner from that in which the male rules over the female, or the man over the child; although the parts of the soul are present in all of them, they are present in different degrees. For the slave has no deliberative faculty at all; the woman has, but it is without authority, and the child has, but it is immature." Aristotle's assumption that a woman will naturally be ruled by a man connects directly with his contention that a woman's deliberative faculty is "without authority." Even if a woman could, in her sequestered, domestic position, acquire deliberative skills, she would remain reliant on her husband for her sources of knowledge and information. She must be ruled by a man because, in the social structure of the *polis,* she enjoys neither the autonomy nor the freedom to put into visible practice the results of the deliberations she may engage in, in private. If she can claim no authority for her rational, deliberative endeavors, then her chances of gaining recognition as a knowledgeable citizen are seriously limited, whatever she may do.

Aristotle is just one of a long line of western thinkers to declare the limitations of women's cognitive capacities. Rousseau maintains that young men and women should be educated quite differently because of women's inferiority in reason and their propensity to be dragged down by their sensual natures. For Kierkegaard, women are merely aesthetic beings: men alone can attain the (higher) ethical and religious levels of existence. And for Nietzsche, the Apollonian (intellectual) domain is the male preserve, whereas women are Dionysian (sensuous) creatures. Nineteenth-century philosopher and linguist Wilhelm von Humboldt, who writes at length about women's knowledge, sums up the central features of this line of thought as follows: "A sense of truth exists in [women] quite literally as a sense: . . . their nature also contains a lack or a failing of analytic capacity which draws a strict line of demarcation between ego and world; therefore, they will not come as close to the ultimate investigation of truth as man." The implication is that women's knowledge, if ever the products of their projects deserve that label, is inherently and inevitably *subjective*—in the most idiosyncratic sense—by contrast with the best of men's knowledge.

Objectivity, quite precisely construed, is commonly regarded as a defining feature of knowledge per se. So if women's knowledge is declared to be *naturally* subjective, then a clear answer emerges to my question. The answer is that if the would-be knower is female, then her sex is indeed epistemologically significant, for it disqualifies her as a knower in the fullest sense of that term. Such disqualifications will operate differently for women of different classes, races, ages, and allegiances, but in every circumstance they will operate asymmetrically for women and for men. Just what is to be made of these points—how their epistemological significance is to be construed—is the subject of this book.

The presuppositions I have just cited claim more than the rather simple fact that many kinds of knowledge and skill have, historically, been inaccessible to women on a purely practical level. It is true, historically speaking, that even women who were the racial and social 'equals' of standard male knowers were only rarely able to become learned. The thinkers I have cited (and others like them) claim to find a rationale for this state of affairs through appeals to dubious 'facts' about women's natural incapacity for rational thought. Yet deeper questions still need to be asked: Is there knowledge that is, quite simply, inaccessible to members of the female, or the male, sex? Are there kinds of knowledge that only men, or only woman, can acquire? Is the sex of the knower crucially determining in this respect, across all other specificities? The answers to these questions should not address only the *practical* possibilities that have existed for members of either sex. Such practical possibilities are the constructs of complex social arrangements that are themselves constructed out of histori-cally specific choices, and are, as such, open to challenge and change.

Knowledge, as it achieves credence and authoritative status at any point in the history of the male-dominated main-stream, is commonly held to be a prod-uct of the individual efforts of human knowers. References to Pythagoras's theorem, Copernicus's revolution, and Newtonian and Einsteinian physics sig-nal an epistemic community's attribu-tion of pathbreaking contributions to certain of its individual members. The implication is that *that* person, single-handedly, has effected a leap of progress in a particular field of inquiry. In less publicly spectacular ways, other cognitive agents are represented as con-tributors to the growth and stability of public knowledge.

Now any contention that such contri-butions are the results of independent endeavor is highly contestable. . . . A complex of historical and other socio-cultural factors produces the conditions that make 'individual' achievement pos-sible, and 'individuals' themselves are socially constituted. The claim that indi-vidual *men* are the creators of the au-thoritative. . . . landmarks of western intellectual life is particularly interest-ing for the fact that the contributions—both practical and substantive—of their lovers, wives, children, servants, neigh-bors, friends, and colleagues rarely fig-ure in analyses of their work.

The historical attribution of such achievements to specific cognitive agents does, nonetheless, accord a sig-nificance to individual efforts which raises questions pertinent to my project. It poses the problem, in another guise, of whether aspects of human specificity could, in fact, constitute conditions for the existence of knowledge or deter-

mine the kinds of knowledge that a knower can achieve. It would seem that such incidental physical attributes as height, weight, or hair color would not count among factors that would deter-mine a person's capacities to know (though the arguments that skin color *does* count are too familiar). It is not necessary to consider how much Archimedes weighed when he made his famous discovery, nor is there any doubt that a thinner or a fatter person could have reached the same conclu-sion. But in cultures in which sex differ-ences figure prominently in virtually every mode of human interaction, being female or male is far more fundamental to the construction of subjectivity than are such attributes as size or hair color. So the question is whether femaleness or maleness are the kinds of subjective factor (i.e., factors about the circum-stances of a knowing subject) that are constitutive of the form and content of knowledge. Attempts to answer this question are complicated by the fact that sex/gender, then, always risks ab-straction and is limited in its scope by the abstracting process. Further, the question seems to imply that sex and gender are themselves constants, thus obscuring the processes of *their* socio-cultural construction. Hence the formu-lation of adequately nuanced answers is problematic and necessarily partial.

Even if it should emerge that gender-related factors play a crucial role in the construction of knowledge, then, the in-quiry into the epistemological signifi-cance of the sex of the knower would not be complete. The task would remain of considering whether a distinction be-tween 'natural' and socialized capacity can retain any validity. The equally pressing question as to how the hitherto devalued products of *women's* cognitive projects can gain acknowledgment as 'knowledge' would need to be addressed so as to uproot entrenched prejudices about knowledge, epistemology, and women. 'The epistemological project' will look quite different once its tacit underpinnings are revealed. . . .

Feminist philosophy simply did not exist until philosophers learned to perceive the near-total absence of women in philosophical writings from the very beginning of western philosophy, to stop assuming that 'man' could be read as a generic term. Explicit denigrations of women, which became the focus of philosophical writing in the early years of the contemporary women's movement, were more readily perceptible. The authors of derogatory views about women in classical texts clearly needed power to be able to utter their pronouncements with impunity: a power they claimed from a 'received' discourse that represented women's nature in such a way that women undoubtedly merited the negative judgments that Aristotle or Nietzsche made about them. Women are now in a position to recognize and refuse these overt manifestations of contempt.

The covert manifestations are more intransigent. Philosophers, when they have addressed the issue at all, have tended to group philosophy with science as the most gender-neutral of disciplines. But feminist critiques reveal that this alleged neutrality masks a bias in favor of institutionalizing stereotypical masculine values into the fabric of the discipline—its methods, norms, and contents. In so doing, it suppresses values, styles, problems, and concerns stereotypically associated with femininity. Thus, whether by chance or by design, it creates a hegemonic philosophical practice in which the sex of the knower is, indeed, epistemologically significant.

Chapter 7

Does Language Make Me Think the Way I Do?

How are taking a test, calling a friend, and buying a sandwich similar to one another? One important way is that they all involve language. Whenever we write or speak, we use language. Whenever we make a promise or ask a question, we use language. Since we spend a good deal of our lives writing or speaking, language is an important part of much that we do.

In fact, language may be even more pervasive than the preceding paragraph leads us to believe. Anything that involves communication requires a medium for communication. It has been claimed that any medium for communication involves a language. According to this view, then, there is a language (or languages) of art, as well as a language (or languages) of love. If we extend the notion of a language this far, then almost any exchange that is embedded in social interaction can be seen as involving language. Short of sitting quietly alone on a mountain looking at a beautiful sunset, it looks as though nearly everything involves language.

But wait a minute. Might it be that even sitting alone on a mountaintop involves the use of language? There are two ways in which it might. First, what are you doing while you are sitting on the mountaintop? Are you thinking about something? Suppose, unlikely as it may seem, that you are thinking about whether the U.S. economy is healthy. Now try to have the same thoughts without using words. Can you do it? Most people experience their thoughts as "using" words. Words may be involved in this way in most of our thinking.

A second way in which language is pervasive is that, even if much of our mental and emotional life could be carried on without any direct use of language, language may be involved in the formation, acquisition, and meaning of the very concepts that we employ when we think, feel, perceive, or desire. For example, language does not seem to be involved when we feel angry. But learning what it is to feel angry requires things like having your mother, when you are a child, point to someone who is shouting and say, "Why is he so angry?" It may be that this (linguistic) background is part of what makes your feeling a feeling of anger. In addition, feeling angry may also involve having certain beliefs, for example, the belief that you have been insulted or unjustly deprived. So unless you are sitting on that mountain in a coma (actually you would

277

have to be lying down), as long as you are thinking, believing, or perceiving, it appears that language may be involved in what you are doing.

But despite the fact that language is probably the most pervasive human activity, or perhaps *because* of that fact, we do not think much about language. Language itself, because it is everywhere, is not noticed. It is part of the background. Moreover, we do not think about it because we see it as an instrument, not as a thing in itself. For example, a beginning painter trying to paint a landscape will focus on the color of the sky and the configuration of the mountains and trees. She will not typically be thinking about the composition of the paint itself or about the fiber content of the canvas. But experienced painters know that an understanding of the *medium* of expression (in this case, of the paint, brushes, and canvas) is crucial in expressing oneself well. The medium imposes hidden constraints on what we can and cannot do. Until we understand those constraints, we will be bound by them without knowing that we are.

So it is with language. To understand the constraints that language places on what we think or feel, and on how we do it, we must somehow be able to think about language itself. But if we can think only by means of language, then in thinking about language we will be using language! This may place us in a vicious circle from which we cannot escape. This is just one of the many complications and difficulties that go along with the philosophical study of language.

Jonathan Swift, in the selection from *Gulliver's Travels,* starts off by claiming ironically that language is an irritating and misleading nuisance. Instead of using words, we should just carry around the things that our words name (since nouns are the only important words anyway). Swift suggests a view of language that was articulated by Saint Augustine, in the fourth century A.D., in a famous passage from his *Confessions.* Wittgenstein begins his excerpt in this chapter by considering this "primitive" picture of language, according to which words are simply names. (This is a view of language that he himself had held earlier, but that he gave up.) He argues that we understand the meaning of an expression by understanding its *use* and that expressions have many more uses than simply that of naming. He also rejects the Socratic method of trying to understand a concept by trying to *define* it. Instead, he argues that most concepts (his example is the concept of a game) do not have neat definitions, but instead work by picking out a range of things that resemble one another loosely. We discover these associations by looking carefully at how expressions are used by actual people. Wittgenstein's view of language strikes at the heart of traditional philosophical method.

It is tempting to think that first we have thoughts and that our language simply reports, or expresses, these thoughts. Many of the authors of this chapter argue, in one way or another, against that simple picture. Whorf, for example, argues that our language creates the conceptual scheme within which we think. As a result of his work in anthropology, he formulated what is now referred to as the "Whorf hypothesis," namely, that our conceptual scheme is determined by our language. If so, people whose language is sufficiently different from ours could not have the same thoughts that we have in our language. Conversely, beings whose conceptual schemes are sufficiently different from ours could not share our language. As Wittgenstein put it, "If a lion could speak, we could not understand him."

George Orwell, writing about the same time as Whorf and Wittgenstein, was well aware of the power of language, as expressed in his masterpiece, *1984*. Orwell paints a grim picture of the political and social control that can be exerted by control over the language. He sees this control as a form of thought control. His protagonist, Syme, claims that without appropriate language, you cannot have certain concepts. Without those concepts, you cannot have certain thoughts.

Stephanie Ross, in her selection, agrees with Orwell about the extent to which language can be put to (dangerous) political uses. She focuses on the sexist use of language and argues that the wrongness of sexist language does not lie only in the fact that it expresses false claims. More important, sexist language actually hurts women. The metaphors used to describe women (for example, "dog," "cow," "shrew") reveal attitudes that are destructive of equality and trust. Her method is therefore in accord with Wittgenstein's claim that we understand language not by trying to isolate its content, but by looking at the use to which it is put.

Steven Pinker, a linguist, brings a mass of current research in linguistics to bear on these issues. He argues forcefully that the Whorf hypothesis is not only clearly false, but that it was foolish for anybody to have it in the first place. Instead, he claims, all (biologically normal) humans have a built-in "language of thought"—"mentalese", it has been dubbed. This language of thought, and not our cultural environment, determines both our concepts and the structure of all human languages.

Friedrich Nietzsche suggests an even deeper way in which language and thought are connected. In his view we are conscious of only a very small part of what is going on in our heads, namely that part we need in order to communicate. Language is therefore a necessary condition for even being conscious. This is a bold enough view, but Nietzsche, one of history's greatest pessimists, goes on to conclude that since the need to communicate arises out of our social nature (what he calls the "herd mentality"), the totality of consciousness is also controlled by the herd. He concludes that whatever arises into consciousness is general, shallow, and stupid.

Lewis Carroll, whose children's books are brimming with philosophical interest, brings us full circle to another "primitive" view of language, but one that, unlike Swift's, takes account of the intimate connection between language and thought. If Swift (and Augustine) claim that the meaning of words is tied directly to what they name and is therefore fixed rigidly, Humpty Dumpty claims that the meaning of words is not constrained at all: Words mean whatever he wants them to mean. Thus, Carroll plays counterpoint to Swift in the same way that Nietzsche plays counterpoint to Augustine.

As you read these selections, you might think about the ways in which the structure of your language places constraints on what and how you can think, feel, believe, and desire.

JONATHAN SWIFT

Getting Rid of Words

JONATHAN SWIFT *(1667–1745), Irish author, journalist, and clergyman, was one of the foremost satirists of all time. He finished* Gulliver's Travels, *from which this selection is taken, in 1725. In 1729 he published a grimly satirical "letter" in which a civic-minded citizen proposes that the poor would contribute more to society if their children were used as food.*

WE next went to the school of language, where three professors sat in consultation upon improving that of their own country.

The first project was to shorten discourse, by cutting polysyllables into one, and leaving out verbs and participles, because, in reality, all things imaginable are but nouns.

The other project was a scheme for entirely abolishing all words whatsoever, and this was urged as a great advantage in point of health as well as brevity. For it is plain that every word we speak is in some degree a diminution of our lungs by corrosion, and consequently, contributes to the shortening of our lives. An expedient was therefore offered, that, since words are only names for things, it would be more convenient for all men to carry about them such things as were necessary to express a particular business they are to discourse on. And this invention would certainly have taken place, to the great ease as well as health of the subject, if the women, in conjunction with the vulgar and illiterate, had not threatened to raise a rebellion, unless they might be allowed the liberty to speak with their tongues, after the manner of their forefathers; such constant irreconcilable enemies to science are the common people. However, many of the most learned and wise adhere to the new scheme of expressing themselves by things, which has only this inconvenience attending it, that if a man's business be very great, and of various kinds, he must be obliged, in proportion, to carry a greater bundle of things upon his back, unless he can afford one or two strong servants to attend him. I have often beheld two of these sages almost sinking under the weight of their packs, like pedlars among us; who, when they met in the street, would lay down their loads, open their sacks, and hold conversation for an hour together, then put up their implements, help each other to resume their bundles, and take their leave.

But for short conversations, a man may carry implements in his pockets, and under his arms, enough to supply him: and in his house he cannot be at a loss. Therefore the room where company meet who practise this art is full of all things, ready at hand, requisite to furnish matter for this kind of artificial converse.

Another great advantage proposed by this invention was, that it would serve as a universal language, to be understood in all civilised nations, whose goods and utensils are generally of the same kind, or nearly resembling, so that their uses might easily be comprehended. And thus ambassadors would be qualified to treat with foreign princes, or ministers of state, to whose tongues they were utter strangers.

LUDWIG WITTGENSTEIN

Meaning as Use

LUDWIG WITTGENSTEIN (1889–1951) was born in Austria. He studied engineering, logic, and philosophy. He was a soldier, an architect, a third-grade teacher, and finally a professor of philosophy. He was a troubled man, and his work was nearly as misunderstood as it was influential. His Philosophical Investigations, *from which this selection is taken, is an ordered series of aphoristic remarks on language, mind, and the conduct of philosophy. The remarks reprinted here have been reordered so as to focus his views on language.*

1. "Cum ipsi (majores Homines) appellabant rem aliquam, et cum secundum eam vocem corpus ad aliquid movebant, videbam, et tenebam hoc ab eis vocari rem illam, quod sonabant, cum eam vellent ostendere. Hoc autem eos velle ex motu corporis aperiebatur: tamquam verbis naturalibus omnium gentium, quae fiunt vultu et nutu/oculorum, ceterorumque membrorum actu, et sonitu vocis indicante affectionem animi in petendis, habendis, rejiciendis, fugiendisve rebus. Ita verba in variis sententiis locis suis posita, et crebro audita, quarum rerum signa essent, paulatim colligebam, measque jam voluntates, edomito in eis signis ore, per haec enuntiabam." (Augustine, *Confessions,* I.8.)*

These words, it seems to me, give us a particular picture of the essence of human language. It is this: the individual words in language name objects—sentences are combinations of such names.—In this picture of language we find the roots of the following idea: Every word has a meaning. This meaning is correlated with the word. It is the object for which the word stands.

Augustine does not speak of there being any difference between kinds of word. If you describe the learning of

*"When they (my elders) named some object and accordingly moved towards something, I saw this and I grasped that the thing was called by the sound they uttered when they meant to point it out. Their intention was shewn by their bodily movements, as it were the natural language of all peoples: the expression of the face, the play of the eyes, the movement of other parts of the body, and the tone of voice which expresses our state of mind in seeking, having, rejecting, or avoiding something. Thus, as I heard words repeatedly used in their proper places in various sentences, I gradually learnt to understand what objects they signified; and after I had trained my mouth to form these signs, I used them to express my own desires."

language in this way you are, I believe, thinking primarily of nouns like "table", "chair", "bread", and of people's name, and only secondarily of the names of certain actions and properties; and of the remaining kinds of word as something that will take care of itself.

Now think of the following use of language: I send someone shopping. I give him a slip marked "five red apples". He takes the slip to the shopkeeper, who opens the drawer marked "apples"; then he looks up the word "red" in a table and fins a colour sample opposite it; then he says the series of cardinal numbers—I assume that he knows them by heart—up to the word "five" and for each number he takes an apple of the same colour as the sample out of the drawer.—It is in this and similar ways that one operates with words.—"But how does he know where and how he is to look up the word 'red' and what he is to do with the word 'five'?"—Well, I assume that he *acts* as I have described. Explanations come to an end somewhere.—But what is the meaning of the word "five"?—No such thing was in question here, only how the word "five" is used.

2. That philosophical concept of meaning has its place in a primitive idea of the way language functions. But one can also say that it is the idea of language more primitive than ours.

Let us imagine a language for which the description given by Augustine is right. The language is meant to serve for communication between a builder A and an assistant B. A is building with building stones: there are blocks, pillars, slabs and beams. B has to pass the stones, and that in the order in which A needs them. For this purpose they use a language consisting of the words "block", "pillar", "slab", "beam". A

calls them out;—B brings the stone which he has learnt to bring at such-and-such a call.—Conceive this as a complete primitive language.

3. Augustine, we might say, does describe a system of communication; only not everything that we call language is this system. And one has to say this in many cases where the question arises "Is this an appropriate description or not?" The answer is "Yes, it is appropriate, but only for this narrowly circumscribed region, not for the whole of what you were claiming to describe."

It is as if someone were to say: "A game consists in moving objects about on a surface according to certain rules . . ."—and we replied: You seem to be thinking of board games, but there are others. You can make your definition correct by expressly restricting it to those games.

4. Imagine a script in which the letters were used to stand for sounds, and also as signs of emphasis and punctuation. (A script can be conceived as a language for describing sound-patterns.) Now imagine someone interpreting that script as if there were simply a correspondence of letters to sounds and as if the letters had not also completely different functions. Augustine's conception of language is like such an over-simple conception of the script.

5. If we look at the example in #1, we may perhaps get an inkling how much this general notion of the meaning of a word surrounds the working of language with a haze which makes clear vision impossible. It disperses the fog to study the phenomena of language in primitive kinds of application in which one can command a clear view of the aim and functioning of the words.

A child uses such primitive forms of language when it learns to talk. Here the teaching of language is not explanation, but training.

6. We could imagine that the language of #2 was the *whole* language of A and B; even the whole language of a tribe. The children are brought up to perform *these* actions, to use *these* words as they do so, and to react in *this* way to the words of others.

An important part of the training will consist in the teacher's pointing to the objects, directing the child's attention to them, and at the same time uttering a word; for instance, the word "slab" as he points to that shape. (I do not want to call this "ostensive definition", because the child cannot as yet *ask* what the name is. I will call it "ostensive teaching of words".—I say that it will form an important part of the training, because it is so with human beings; not because it could not be imagined otherwise.) This ostensive teaching of words can be said to establish an association between the word and the thing. But what does this mean? Well, it may mean various things; but one very likely thinks first of all that a picture of the object comes before the child's mind when it hears the word. But now, if this does happen—is it the purpose of the word?—Yes, it *may* be the purpose.—I can imagine such a use of words (of series of sounds). (Uttering a word is like striking a note on the keyboard of the imagination.) But in the language of #2 it is *not* the purpose of the words to evoke images. (It may, of course, be discovered that that helps to attain the actual purpose.)

But if the ostensive teaching has this effect,—am I to say that it effects an understanding of the word? Don't you understand the call "Slab!" if you act upon it in such-and-such a way?—Doubtless the ostensive teaching helped to bring

this about; but only together with a particular training. With different training the same ostensive teaching of these words would have effected a quite different understanding.

"I set the brake up by connecting up rod and lever."—Yes, given the whole of the rest of the mechanism. Only in conjunction with that is it a brake-lever, and separated from its support it is not even a lever; it may be anything, or nothing.

7. In the practice of the use of language (2) one party calls out the words, the other acts on them. In instruction in the language the following process will occur: the learner *names* the objects; that is, he utters the word when the teacher point to the stone.—And there will be this still simpler exercise: the pupil repeats the words after the teacher—both of these being processes resembling language.

We can also think of the whole process of using words in (2) as one of those games by means of which children learn their native language. I will call these games "language-games" and will sometimes speak of a primitive language as a language-game.

And the processes of naming the stones and of repeating words after someone might also be called language-games. Think of much of the use of words in games like ring-a-ring-a-roses.

I shall also call the whole, consisting of language and the actions into which it is woven, the "language-game".

8. Let us now look at an expansion of language (2). Besides the four words "block", "pillar", etc., let it contain a series of words used as the shopkeeper in (1) used the numerals (it can be the series of letters of the alphabet); further, let there be two words, which may as well be "there" and "this" (because this

roughly indicates their purpose), that are used in connexion with a pointing gesture; and finally a number of colour samples. A gives an order like: "d—slab—there". At the same time he shews the assistant a colour sample, and when he says "there" he points to a place on the building site. From the stock of slabs B takes one for each letter of the alphabet up to "d", of the same colour as the sample, and brings them to the place indicated by A.—On other occasions A gives the order "this—there". At "this" he point to a building stone. And so on.

9. When a child learns this language, it has to learn the series of 'numerals' a, b, c, . . . by heart. And it has to learn their use.—Will this training include ostensive teaching of the words?—Well, people will, for example, point to slabs and count: "a, b, c slabs".—Something more like the ostensive teaching of the words "block", "pillar", etc. would be the ostensive teaching of numerals that serve not to count but to refer to groups of objects that can be taken in at a glance. Children do learn the use of the first five or six cardinal numerals in this way.

Are "there" and "this" also taught ostensively?—Imagine how one might perhaps teach their use. One will point to places and things—but in this case the pointing occurs in the *use* of the words too and not merely in learning the use.

10. Now what do the words of this language *signify?*—What is supposed to shew what they signify, if not the kind of use they have? And we have already described that. So we are asking for the expression "This word signifies *this*" to be made part of the description. In other words the description ought to take the form: "The word. . . . signifies. . . .".

Of course, one can reduce the description of the use of the word "slab" to the statement that this word signifies this object. This will be done when, for example, it is merely a matter of removing the mistaken idea that the word "slab" refers to the shape of building-stone that we in fact call a "block"—but the kind of '*referring*' this is, that is to say the use of these words for the rest, is already known.

Equally one can say that the signs "a", "b", etc. signify numbers; when for example this removes the mistaken idea that "a", "b", "c", play the part actually played in language by "block", "slab", "pillar". And one can also say that "c" means this number and not that one; when for example this serves to explain that the letters are to be used in the order a, b, c, d, etc. and not in the order a, b, d, c.

But assimilating the descriptions of the uses of words in this way cannot make the uses themselves any more like one another. For, as we see, they are absolutely unlike.

11. Think of the tools in a tool-box: there is a hammer, pliers, a saw, a screwdriver, a rule, a glue-pot, glue, nails and screws.—The functions of words are as diverse as the functions of these objects. (And in both cases there are similarities.)

Of course, what confuses us is the uniform appearance of words when we hear them spoken or meet them in script and print. For their *application* is not presented to us so clearly, especially when we are doing philosophy!

12. It is like looking into the cabin of a locomotive. We see handles all looking more or less alike. (Naturally, since they are all supposed to be handled.) But one is the handle of a crank which can be moved continuously (it regulates the

opening of a valve); another is the handle of a switch, which has only two effective positions, it is either off or on; a third is the handle of a brake-lever, the harder one pulls on it, the harder it brakes; a fourth, the handle of a pump: it has an effect only so long as it is moved to and fro.

13. When we say: "Every word in language signifies something" we have so far said *nothing whatever;* unless we have explained exactly *what* distinction we wish to make. (It might be, of course, that we wanted to distinguish the words of language (8) from words 'without meaning' such as occur in Lewis Carroll's poems, or words like "Lilliburlero" in songs.)

14. Imagine someone's saying: "*All* tools serve to modify something. Thus the hammer modifies the position of the nail, the saw the shape of the board, and so on."—And what is modified by the rule, the glue-pot, the nails?—"Our knowledge of a thing's length, the temperature of the glue, and the solidity of the box."—Would anything be gained by this assimilation of expressions?

15. The word "to signify" is perhaps used in the most straightforward way when the object signified is marked with the sign. Suppose that the tools A uses in building bear certain marks. When A shews his assistant such a mark, he brings the tool that has that mark on it.

It is in this and more or less similar ways that a name means and is given to a thing.—It will often prove useful in philosophy to say to ourselves: naming something is like attaching a label to a thing.

16. What about the colour samples that A shews to B: are they part of the *language?* Well, it is as you please. They do not belong among the words; yet when I say to someone: "Pronounce the word 'the'", you will count the second "the" as part of the sentence. Yet it has a role just like that of a colour-sample in language-game (8); that is, it is a sample of what the other is meant to say.

It is most natural, and causes least confusion, to reckon the samples among the instruments of the language.

(Remark on the reflexive pronoun "*this* sentence".)

17. It will be possible to say: In language (8) we have different *kinds of word.* For the functions of the word "slab" and the word "block" are more alike than those of "slab" and "d". But how we group words into kinds will depend on the aim of the classification,— and on our own inclination.

Think of the different points of view from which one can classify tools or chess-men. . . .

23. But how many kinds of sentence are there? Say assertion, question, and command?—There are *countless* kinds: countless different kinds of use of what we call "symbols", "words", "sentences". And this multiplicity is not something fixed, given once for all; but new types of language, new language-games, as we may say, come into existence, and others become obsolete and get forgotten. (We can get a *rough picture* of this form the changes in mathematics.)

Here the term "language-*game*" is meant to bring into prominence the fact that the *speaking* of a language is part of an activity, or of a form of life.

Review the multiplicity of language-games in the following examples, and in others:

Giving orders, and obeying them

Describing the appearance of an object, or giving its measurements

Constructing an object from a description (a drawing)

Reporting an event

Speculating about an event

Forming and testing a hypothesis

Presenting the results of an experiment in tables and diagrams

Making up a story; and reading it

Play-acting

Singing catches

Guessing riddles

Making a joke; telling it

Solving a problem in practical arithmetic

Translating from one language into another

Asking, thanking, cursing, greeting, praying

It is interesting to compare the multiplicity of the tools in language and of the ways they are used, the multiplicity of kinds of word and sentence, with what logicians have said about the structure of language. (Including the author of the *Tractatus Logico-Philosophicus.*)* . . .

27. "We name things and then we can talk about them: can refer to them in talk."—As if what we did next were given with the mere act of naming. As if there were only one thing called "talking about a thing". Whereas in fact we do the most various things with our sentences. Think of exclamations alone, with their completely different functions.

Water!

Away!

Ow!

Help!

Fine!

No!

Are you inclined still to call these words "names of objects"?

In languages (2) and (8) there was no such thing as asking something's name. This, with its correlate, ostensive definition, is, we might say, a language-game on its own. That is really to say: we are brought up, trained, to ask: "What is that called?"—upon which the name is given. And there is also a language-game of inventing a name for something, and hence of saying, "This is. . . ." and then using the new name. (Thus, for example, children give names to their dolls and then talk about them and to them. Think in this connexion how singular is the use of a person's name to *call* him!) . . .

32. Someone coming into a strange country will sometimes learn the language of the inhabitants from ostensive definition† that they give him; and he will often have to *guess* the meaning of these definitions; and will guess sometimes right, sometimes wrong.

And now, I think, we can say: Augustine describes the learning of human language as if the child came into a strange country and did not understand the language of the country; that is, as if it already had a language, only not this one. Or again: as if the child could already *think,* only not yet speak. And "think" would here mean something like "talk to itself". . . .

37. What is the relation between name and thing named?—Well, what *is* it? Look at language-game (2) or at another one: there you can see the sort of thing this relation consists in. This relation may also consist, among many other things, in the fact that hearing the name

---

*Editor's note: An earlier work of Wittgenstein's, which he renounces in this work.

†Editor's note: An ostensive definition is one in which a word is defined by pointing to, or showing, what it refers to or means.

calls before our mind the picture of what is named; and it also consists among other things, in the name's being written on the thing named or being pronounced when that thing is pointed at. 38. But what, for example, is the word "this" the name of in language-game (8) or the word "that" in the ostensive definition "that is called. . . ."?—If you do not want to produce confusion you will do best not to call these words names at all.—Yet, strange to say, the word "this" has been called the only *genuine* name; so that anything else we call a name was one only in an inexact, approximate sense.

This queer conception springs from a tendency to sublime the logic of our language—as one might put it. The proper answer to it is: we call very different things "names"; the word "name" is used to characterize many different kinds of use of a word, related to one another in many different ways;—but the kind of use that "this" has is not among them.

It is quite true that, in giving an ostensive definition for instance, we often point to the object named and say the name. And similarly, in giving an ostensive definition for instance, we say the word "this" while pointing to a thing. And also the word "this" and a name that it is defined by means of the demonstrative expression "that is N" (or "That is called 'N'"). But do we also give the definitions: "That is called 'this'", or "this is called 'this'"?

This is connected with the conception of naming as, so to speak, an occult process. Naming appears as a *queer* connexion of a word with an object.— And you really get such a queer connexion when the philosopher tries to bring out *the* relation between name and thing by staring at an object in front of him

and repeating a name or even the word "this" innumerable times. For philosophical problems arise when language *goes on holiday.* And *here* we may indeed fancy naming to be some remarkable act of mind, as it were a baptism of an object. And we can also say the word "this" *to* the object, as it were *address* the object as "this"—a queer use of this word, which doubtless only occurs in doing philosophy. . . .

410. "I" is not the name of a person, nor "here" of a place, and "this" is not a name. But they are connected with names. Names are explained by means of them. It is also true that it is characteristic of physics not to use these words.

65. Here we come up against the great question that lies behind all these considerations.—For someone might object against me: "You take the easy way out! You talk about all sorts of language-games, but have nowhere said what the essence of a language-game, and hence of language, is: what is common to all these activities, and what makes them into language or parts of language. So you let yourself off the very part of the investigation that once gave you yourself most headache, the part about the *general form of propositions* and of language."

And this is true.—Instead of producing something common to all that we call language, I am saying that these phenomena have no one thing in common which makes us use the same word for all,—but that they are *related* to one another in many different ways. And it is because of this relationship, or these relationships, that we call them all "language". I will try to explain this.

66. Consider for example the proceeding that we call "games". I mean board-games, card-games, ball-games, Olympic games, and so on. What is

common to them all?—Don't say: "There *must* be something common, or they would not be called 'games'"—but *look and see* whether there is anything common to all.—For if you look at them you will not see something that is common to *all,* but similarities, relationships, and a whole series of them at that. To repeat: don't think, but look!—Look for example at board-games, with their multifarious relationships. Now pass to card-games; here you find many correspondences with the first group, but many common features drop out, and others appear. When we pass next to ball-games, much that is common is retained, but much is lost.—Are they all 'amusing'? Compare chess with noughts and crosses. Or is there always winning and losing, or competition between players? Think of patience. In ball-games there is winning and losing; but when a child throws his ball at the wall and catches it again, this feature has disappeared. Look at the parts played by skill and luck; and at the difference between skill in chess and skill in tennis. Think now of games like ring-ring-a-roses; here is the element of amusement, but how many other characteristic features have disappeared! And we can go through the many, many other groups of games in the same way; can see how similarities crop up and disappear.

And the result of this examination is: we see a complicated network of similarities overlapping and criss-crossing: sometimes overall similarities, sometimes similarities of detail.

67. I can think of no better expression to characterize these similarities than "family resemblances"; for the various resemblances between members of a family: build, features, colour of eyes, gait, temperament, etc. etc. overlap and criss-cross in the same way.—And I shall say: 'games' form a family.

And for instance the kinds of number form a family in the same way. Why do we call something a "number"? Well, perhaps because it has a—direct—relationship with several things that have hitherto been called number; and this can be said to give it an indirect relationship to other things we call the same name. And we extend our concept of number as in spinning a thread we twist fibre on fibre. And the strength of the thread does not reside in the fact that some one fibre runs through its whole length, but in the overlapping of many fibres.

But if someone wished to say: "There is something common to all these constructions—namely the disjunction of all their common properties"—I should reply: Now you are only playing with words. One might as well say: "Something runs through the whole thread—namely the continuous overlapping of those fibres". . . .

241. "So you are saying that human agreement decides what is true and what is false?"—It is what human beings *say* that is true and false; and they agree in the *language* they use. That is not agreement in opinions but in form of life.

242. If language is to be a means of communication there must be agreement not only in definitions but also (queer as this may sound) in judgments. This seems to abolish logic, but does not do so.—It is one thing to describe methods of measurement, and another to obtain and state results of measurement. But what we call "measuring" is partly determined by a certain constancy in results of measurements. . . .

350. One cannot guess how a word functions. One has to *look at* its use and learn from that.

But the difficulty is to remove the prejudice which stands in the way of doing this. It is not a *stupid* prejudice. . . .

383. We are not analysing a phenomenon (e.g. thought) but a concept (e.g. that of thinking), and therefore the use of a word. So it may look as if what we were doing were Nominalism. Nominalists make the mistake of interpreting all words as *names,* and so of not really describing their use, but only, so to speak, giving a paper draft on such a description. . . .

309. What is your aim in philosophy?—To shew the fly the way out of the flybottle.

BENJAMIN WHORF

Language, Thought, and Reality

BENJAMIN WHORF *(1897–1941) studied chemical engineering at M.I.T. He worked for his entire career as a fire prevention engineer for a Hartford insurance company, and he pursued his work in anthropology and linguistics on the side, refusing a number of academic positions. He originally became interested in linguistics through his interest in religion.*

Human beings do not live in the objective world alone, not alone in the world of social activity as ordinarily understood, but are very much at the mercy of the particular language which has become the medium of expression for their society. It is quite an illusion to imagine that one adjusts to reality essentially without the use of language and that language is merely an incidental means of solving specific problems of communication or reflection. The fact of the matter is that the "real world" is to a large extent unconsciously built up on the language habits of the group. . . . We see and hear and otherwise experience very largely as we do because the language habits of our community predispose certain choices of interpretation.

EDWARD SAPIR

THERE will probably be general assent to the proposition that an accepted pattern of using words is often prior to certain lines of thinking and forms of behavior, but he who assents often sees in such a statement nothing more than a platitudinous recognition of the hypnotic power of philosophical and learned terminology on the one hand or of catchwords, slogans, and rallying cries on the other. To see only thus far is to miss the point of one of the important interconnections which Sapir saw between language, culture, and psychology, and succinctly expressed in the introductory quotation. It is not so much in these special uses of language as in its constant ways of arranging data and its most ordinary everyday analysis of phenomena that we need to recognize the influence it has on other activities, cultural and personal. . . .

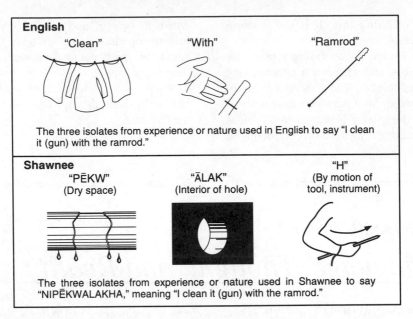

English

"Clean"   "With"   "Ramrod"

The three isolates from experience or nature used in English to say "I clean it (gun) with the ramrod."

Shawnee

"PĒKW"   "ĀLAK"   "H"
(Dry space)   (Interior of hole) (By motion of
                                    tool, instrument)

The three isolates from experience or nature used in Shawnee to say "NIPĒKWALAKHA," meaning "I clean it (gun) with the ramrod."

Languages dissect nature differently. The different isolates of meaning (thoughts) used by English and Shawnee in reporting the same experience, that of cleaning a gun by running the ramrod through it. The pronouns 'I' and 'it' are not shown by symbols, as they have the same meaning in each language. In Shawnee ni- equals 'I'; -a equals 'it.'

Every normal person in the world, past infancy in years, can and does talk. By virtue of that fact, every person—civilized or uncivilized—carries through life certain naive but deeply rooted ideas about talking and its relation to thinking. Because of their firm connection with speech habits that have become unconscious and automatic, these notions tend to be rather intolerant of opposition. They are by no means entirely personal and haphazard; their basis is definitely systematic, so that we are justified in calling them a system of natural logic—a term that seems to me preferable to the term common sense, often used for the same thing.

According to natural logic, the fact that every person has talked fluently since infancy makes every man his own authority on the process by which he formulates and communicates. He has merely to consult a common substratum of logic or reason which he and everyone else are supposed to possess. Natural logic says that talking is merely an incidental process concerned strictly with communication, not with formulation of ideas. Talking, or the uses of language, is supposed only to "express" what is essentially already formulated nonlinguistically. Formulation is an independent process, called thought or thinking, and is supposed to be largely indifferent to the nature of particular languages. Languages have grammars, which are assumed to be merely norms of conventional and social correctness, but the use of language is supposed to be guided not so much by them as by correct, rational, or intelligent *thinking.*

Thought, in this view, does not depend on grammar but on laws of logic or reason which are supposed to be the same for all observers of the universe—to represent a rationale in the universe that can be "found" independently by all intelligent observers, whether they speak Chinese or Choctaw. In our own culture, the formulations of mathematics and of formal logic have acquired the reputation of dealing with this order of things: i.e., with the realm and laws of pure thought. Natural logic holds that different languages are essentially parallel methods for expressing this one-and-the-same rationale of thought and, hence, differ really in but minor ways which may seem important only because they are seen at close range. It holds that mathematics, symbolic logic, philosophy, and so on are systems contracted with language which deal directly with this realm of thought, not that they are themselves specialized extensions of language. The attitude of natural logic is well shown in an old quip about a German grammarian who devoted his whole life to the study of the dative case. From the point of view of natural logic, the dative case and grammar in general are an extremely minor issue. A different attitude is said to have been held by the ancient Arabians: Two princes, so the story goes, quarreled over the honor of putting on the shoes of the most learned grammarian of the realm; whereupon their father, the caliph, is said to have remarked that it was the glory of his kingdom that great grammarians were honored even above kings.

The familiar saying that the exception proves the rule contains a good deal of wisdom, though from the standpoint of formal logic it became an absurdity as soon as "prove" no longer meant "put on trial." The old saw began to be profound psychology from the time it ceased to have standing in logic. What it might well suggest to us today is that, if a rule has absolutely no exceptions, it is not recognised as a rule or as anything else; it is then part of the background of experience of which we tend to remain unconscious. Never having experienced anything in contrast to it, we cannot isolate it and formulate it as a rule until we so enlarge our experience and expand our base of reference that we encounter an interruption of its regularity. The situation is somewhat analogous to that of not missing the water till the well runs dry, or not realizing that we need air till we are choking.

For instance, if a race of people had the physiological defect of being able to see only the color blue, they would hardly be able to formulate the rule that they saw only blue. The term blue would convey no meaning to them, their language would lack color terms, and their words denoting their various sensations of blue would answer to, and translate, our words "light, dark, white, black," and so on, not our word "blue." In order to formulate the rule or norm of seeing only blue, they would need exceptional moments in which they saw other colors. The phenomenon of gravitation forms a rule without exceptions: needless to say, the untutored person is utterly unaware of any law of gravitation, for it would never enter his head to conceive of a universe in which bodies behaved otherwise than they do at the earth's surface. Like the color blue with our hypothetical race, the law of gravitation is a part of the untutored individual's background, not something he

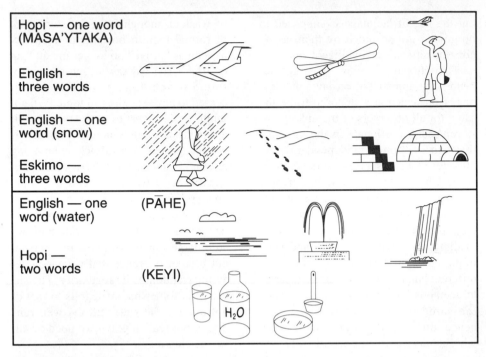

Languages classify items of experience differently. The class corresponding to one word and one thought in language A may be regarded by language B as two or more classes corresponding to two or more words and thoughts.

isolates from that background. The law could not be formulated until bodies that always fell were seen in terms of a wider astronomical world in which bodies moved in orbits or went this way and that.

Similarly, whenever we turn our heads, the image of the scene passes across our retinas exactly as it would if the scene turned around us. But this effect is background, and we do not recognize it; we do not see a room turn around us but are conscious only of having turned our heads in a stationary room. If we observe critically while turning the head or eyes quickly, we shall see, no motion it is true, yet a blurring of the scene between two clear views. Normally we are quite uncon-

scious of this continual blurring but seem to be looking about in an unblurred world. Whenever we walk past a tree or house, its image on the retina changes just as if the tree or house were turning on an axis; yet we do not see trees or houses turn as we travel about at ordinary speeds. Sometimes ill-fitting glasses will reveal queer movements in the scene as we look about, but normally we do not see the relative motion of the environment when we move; our psychic makeup is somehow adjusted to disregard whole realms of phenomena that are so all-pervasive as to be irrelevant to our daily lives and needs.

Natural logic contains two fallacies: First, it does not see that the phenomena of a language are to its own speakers

Objective field	Speaker (Sender)	Hearer (Receiver)	Handling of topic, Running of third person
Situation 1a			English: "He is running" Hopi: "WARI" (running, statement of fact)
Situation 1b Objective field blank Devoid of running			English: "He ran" Hopi: "WARI" (running, statement of fact)
Situation 2			English: "He is running" Hopi: "WARI" (running, statement of fact)
Situation 3 Objective field blank			English: "He ran" Hopi: "ERA WARI" (running, statement of fact from memory)
Situation 4 Objective field blank			English: "He will run" Hopi: "WARIKNI" (running, statement of expectation)
Situation 5 Objective field blank			English: "He runs" (e.g., on the track team) Hopi: "WARIKNGWE" (running, statement of law)

Contrast between a "temporal" language (English) and a "timeless" language (Hopi). What are to English differences of time are to Hopi differences in the kind of validity.

largely of a background character and so are outside the critical consciousness and control of the speaker who is expanding natural logic. Hence, when anyone, as a natural logician, is talking about reason, logic, and the laws of correct thinking, he is apt to be simply marching in step with purely grammatical facts that have somewhat of a background character in his own language or family of languages but are by no means universal in all languages and in no sense a common substratum of reason. Second, natural logic confuses agreement about subject matter, attained through use of language, with knowledge of the linguistic process by which agreement is attained: i.e., with the province of the despised (and to its notion superfluous) grammarian. Two fluent speakers, of English let us say, quickly reach a point of assent about the subject matter of their speech; they agree about what their language refers to. One of them, *A,* can give directions that will be carried out by the other, *B,* to *A*'s complete satisfaction. Because they thus understand each other so perfectly, *A* and *B,* as natural logicians, suppose they must of course know how it is all done. They think, e.g., that it is simply a matter of choosing words to express thoughts. If you ask *A* to explain how he got *B*'s agreement so readily, he will simply repeat to you, with more or less elaboration or abbreviation, what he said to *B*. He has no notion of the process involved. The amazingly complex system of linguistic patterns and classifications, which *A* and *B* must have in common before they can adjust to each other at all, is all background to *A* and *B*. . . .

The situation here is not unlike that in any other field of science. All real scientists have their eyes primarily on background phenomena that cut very little ice, as such, in our daily lives; and yet their studies have a way of bringing out a close relation between these unsuspected realms of fact and such decidedly foreground activities as transporting goods, preparing food, treating the sick, or growing potatoes, which in time may become very much modified, simply because of pure scientific investigation in no way concerned with these brute matters themselves. Linguistics presents a quite similar case; the background phenomena with which it deals are involved in all our foreground activities of talking and of reaching agreement, in all reasoning and arguing of cases, in all law, arbitration, conciliation, contracts, treaties, public opinion, weighing of scientific theories, formula-

tion of scientific results. Whenever agreement or assent is arrived at in human affairs, and whether or not mathematics or other specialized symbolisms are made part of the procedure, *this agreement is reached by linguistic processes, or else it is not reached.*

As we have seen, an overt knowledge of the linguistic processes by which agreement is attained is not necessary to reaching some sort of agreement, but it is certainly no bar thereto; the more complicated and difficult the matter, the more such knowledge is a distinct aid, till the point may be reached—I suspect the modern world has arrived at it—when the knowledge becomes not only an aid but a necessity. The situation may be likened to that of navigation. Every boat that sails is in the lap of planetary forces; yet a boy can pilot his small craft around a harbor without benefit of geography, astronomy, mathematics, or international politics. To the captain of an ocean liner, however, some knowledge of all these subjects is essential.

When linguists became able to examine critically and scientifically a large number of languages of widely different patterns, their base of reference was expanded; they experienced an interruption of phenomena hitherto held universal, and a whole new order of significances came into their ken. It was found that the background linguistic system (in other words, the grammar) of each language is not merely a reproducing instrument for voicing ideas but rather is itself the shaper of ideas, the program and guide for the individual's mental activity, for his analysis of impressions, for his synthesis of his mental stock in trade. Formulation of ideas is not an independent process, strictly rational in the old sense, but is part of a particular grammar, and differs, from slightly to greatly, between different grammars. We dissect nature along lines laid down by our native languages. The categories and types that we isolate from the world of phenomena we do not find there because they stare every observer in the face; on the contrary, the world is presented in a kaleidoscopic flux of impressions which has to be organized by our minds—and this means largely by the linguistic systems in our minds. We cut nature up, organize it into concepts, and ascribe significances as we do, largely because we are parties to an agreement to organize it this way—an agreement that holds throughout our speech community and is codified in the patterns of our language. The agreement is, of course, an implicit and unstated one, *but its terms are absolutely obligatory;* we cannot talk at all except by subscribing to the organization and classification of data which the agreement decrees.

This fact is very significant for modern science, for it means that no individual is free to describe nature with absolute impartiality but is constrained to certain modes of interpretation even while he thinks himself most free. The person most nearly free in such respects would be a linguist familiar with very many widely different linguistic systems. As yet no linguist is in any such position. We are thus introduced to a new principle of relativity, which holds that all observers are not led by the same physical evidence to the same picture of the universe, unless their linguistic backgrounds are similar, or can in some way be calibrated.

This rather startling conclusion is not so apparent if we compare only our modern European languages, with perhaps Latin and Greek thrown in for

good measure. Among these tongues there is a unanimity of major pattern which at first seems to bear out natural logic. But this unanimity exists only because these tongues are all Indo-European dialects cut to the same basic plan, being historically transmitted from what was long ago one speech community; because the modern dialects have long shared in building up a common culture; and because much of this culture, on the more intellectual side, is derived from the linguistic backgrounds of Latin and Greek. Thus this group of languages satisfies the special case of the clause beginning "unless" in the statement of the linguistic relativity principle at the end of the preceding paragraph. From this condition follows the unanimity of description of the world in the community of modern scientists. But it must be emphasized that "all modern Indo-European-speaking observers" is not the same thing as "all observers." That modern Chinese or Turkish scientists describe the world in the same terms as Western scientists means, of course, only that they have taken over bodily the entire Western system of rationalizations, not that they have corroborated that system from their native posts of observation.

When Semitic, Chinese, Tibetan, or African languages are contrasted with our own, the divergence in analysis of the world becomes more apparent; and, when we bring in the native languages of the Americas, where speech communities for many millenniums have gone their ways independently of each other and of the Old World, the fact that languages dissect nature in many different ways becomes patent. The relativity of all conceptual systems, ours included, and their dependence upon language stand revealed. That American Indians speaking only their native tongues are never called upon to act as scientific observers is in no wise to the point. To exclude the evidence which their languages offer as to what the human mind can do is like expecting botanists to study nothing but food plants and hothouse roses and then tell us what the plant world is like!

Let us consider a few examples. In English we divide most of our words into two classes, which have different grammatical and logical properties. Class 1 we call nouns, e.g., 'house, man'; class 2, verbs, e.g., 'hit, run.' Many words of one class can act secondarily as of the other class, e.g., 'a hit, a run,' or 'to man (the boat),' but, on the primary level, the division between the classes is absolute. Our language thus gives us a bipolar division of nature. But nature herself is not thus polarized. If it be said that 'strike, turn, run,' are verbs because they denote temporary or short-lasting events, i.e., actions, why then is 'fist' a noun? It also is a temporary event. Why are 'lightning, spark, wave, eddy, pulsation, flame, storm, phase, cycle, spasm, noise, emotion' nouns? They are temporary events. If 'man' and 'house' are nouns because they are long-lasting and stable events, i.e., things, what then are 'keep, adhere, extend, project, continue, persist, grow, dwell,' and so on doing among the verbs? If it be objected that 'possess, adhere' are verbs because they are stable relationships rather than stable precepts, why then should 'equilibrium, pressure, current, peace, group, nation, society, tribe, sister,' or any kinship term be among the nouns? It will be found that an "event" to us means "what our language classes as a verb" or something analogized therefrom. And it will be found that is not possible to define 'event, thing, object, relationship,'

and so on, from nature, but that to define them always involves a circuitous return to the grammatical categories of the definer's language.

In the Hopi language, 'lightning, wave, flame, meteor, puff of smoke, pulsation' are verbs. 'Cloud' and 'storm' are at about the lower limit of duration for nouns. Hopi, you see, actually has a classification of events (or linguistic isolates) by duration type, something strange to our modes of thought. On the other hand, in Nootka, a language of Vancouver Island, all words seem to us to be verbs, but really there are no classes 1 and 2; we have, as it were, a monistic view of nature that gives us only one class of word for all kinds of events. 'A house occurs' or 'it houses' is the way of saying 'house,' exactly like 'a flame occurs' or 'it burns.' These terms seem to us like verbs because they are inflected for durational and temporal nuances, so that the suffixes of the word for house event make it mean long-lasting house, temporary house, future house, house that used to be, what started out to be a house, and so on.

Hopi has one noun that covers everything or being that flies, with the exception of birds, which class is denoted by another noun. The former noun may be said to denote the class (*FC-B*)—flying class minus bird. The Hopi actually call insect, airplane, and aviator all by the same word, and feel no difficulty about it. The situation, of course, decides any possible confusion among very disparate members of a broad linguistic class, such as this class (*FC-B*). This class seems to us too large and inclusive, but so would our class 'snow' to an Eskimo. We have the same word for falling snow, snow on the ground, now packed hard like ice, slushy snow, wind-driven flying snow—whatever the situation may be. To an Eskimo, this all-inclusive word would be almost unthinkable; he would say that falling snow, slushy snow, and so on, are sensuously and operationally different, different things to contend with; he uses different words for them and for other kinds of snow. The Aztecs go even farther than we in the opposite direction, with 'cold,' 'ice,' and 'snow' all represented by the same basic word with different terminations; 'ice' is the noun form; 'cold,' the adjective form; and for 'snow,' 'ice mist.'

What surprises most is to find that various grand generalizations of the Western world, such as time, velocity, and matter, are not essential to the construction of a consistent picture of the universe. The psychic experiences that we class under these headings are, of course, not destroyed; rather, categories derived from other kinds of experiences take over the rulership of the cosmology and seem to function just as well. Hopi may be called a timeless language. It recognizes psychological time, which is much like Bergson's "duration," but this "time" is quite unlike the mathematical time, T, used by our physicists. Among the peculiar properties of Hopi time are that it varies with each observer, does not permit of simultaneity, and has zero dimensions; i.e., it cannot be given a number greater than one. The Hopi do not say, "I stayed five days," but "I left on the fifth day." A word referring to this kind of time, like the word day, can have no plural. The puzzle picture will give mental exercise to anyone who would like to figure out how the Hopi verb gets along without tenses. Actually, the only practical use of our tenses, in one-verb sentences, is to distinguish among five typical situations, which are symbolized in the picture. The timeless Hopi verb does not distinguish between

the present, past, and future of the event itself but must always indicate what type of validity the speaker intends the statement to have: (a) report of an event (situations 1,2,3, in the picture); (b) expectation of an event (situation 4); (c) generalization or law about events (situation 5). Situation 1, where the speaker and listener are in contact with the same objective field, is divided by our language into the two conditions, 1*a* and 1*b*, which it calls present and past, respectively. This division is unnecessary for a language which assures one that the statement is a report.

Hopi grammar, by means of its forms called aspects and modes, also makes it easy to distinguish among momentary, continued, and repeated occurrences, and to indicate the actual sequence of reported events. Thus the universe can be described without recourse to a concept of dimensional time. How would a physics constructed along these lines work, with no T (time) in its equations? Perfectly, as far as I can see, though of course it would require different ideology and perhaps different mathematics. Of course (velocity) would have to go too. The Hopi language has no word really equivalent to our 'speed' or 'rapid.' What translates these terms is usually a word meaning intense or very, accompanying any verb of motion. Here is a clue to the nature of our new physics. We may have to introduce a new term I, intensity. Every thing and event will have an I, whether we regard the thing or event as moving or as just enduring or being. Perhaps the I of an electric charge will turn out to be its voltage, or potential. We shall use clocks to measure some intensities, or, rather, some *relative* intensities, for the absolute intensity of anything will be meaningless. Our old friend acceleration will still be there but doubtless under a new name. We shall perhaps call it *V,* meaning not velocity but variation. Perhaps all growths and accumulations will be regarded as *V*'s. We should not have the concept of rate in the temporal sense, since, like velocity, rate introduces a mathematical and linguistic time. Of course we know that all measurements are rations, but the measurements of intensities made by comparison with the standard intensity of a clock or a planet we do not treat as ratios, any more than we so treat a distance made by comparison with a yardstick.

A scientist from another culture that used time and velocity would have great difficulty in getting us to understand these concepts. We should talk about the intensity of a chemical reaction; he would speak of its velocity or its rate, which words we should at first think were simply words for intensity in his language. Likewise, he at first would think that intensity was simply our own word for velocity. At first we should agree, later we should begin to disagree, and it might dawn upon both sides that different systems of rationalization were being used. He would find it very hard to make us understand what he really meant by velocity of a chemical reaction. We should have no words that would fit. He would try to explain it by likening it to a running horse, to the difference between a good horse and a lazy horse. We should try to show him, with a superior laugh, that his analogy also was a matter of different intensities, aside from which there was little similarity between a horse and a chemical reaction in a beaker. We should point out that a running horse is moving relative to the ground, whereas the material in the beaker is at rest.

One significant contribution to science from the linguistic point of view may be the greater development of our sense of perspective. We shall no longer be able to see a few recent dialects of the Indo-European family, and the rationalizing techniques elaborated from their patterns, as the apex of the evolution of the human mind, nor their present wide spread as due to any survival from fitness or to anything but a few events of history—events that could be called fortunate only from the parochial point of view of the favored parties. They, and our own thought processes with them, can no longer be envisioned as spanning the gamut of reason and knowledge but only as one constellation in a galactic expanse. A fair realization of the incredible degree of diversity of linguistic system that ranges over the globe leaves one with an inescapable feeling that the human spirit is inconceivably old; that the few thousand years of history covered by our written records are no more than the thickness of a pencil mark on the scale that measures our past experience on this planet; that the events of these recent millenniums spell nothing in any evolutionary wise, that the race has taken no sudden spurt, achieved no commanding synthesis during recent millenniums, but has only played a little with a few of the linguistic formulations and views of nature bequeathed from an inexpressible long past. Yet neither this feeling nor the sense of precarious dependence of all we know upon linguistic tools which themselves are largely unknown need be discouraging to science but should, rather, foster that humility which accompanies the true scientific spirit, and thus forbid that arrogance of the mind which hinders real scientific curiosity and detachment.

GEORGE ORWELL

Newspeak

GEORGE ORWELL *(1903–1950), whose real name was Eric Blair, was an English satirical writer born in Bengal. From 1920 to 1927 he served with the English Colonial Police in Burma. He lived very poorly in London and Paris, gradually establishing his reputation. He fought in the Spanish Civil War. His best known works are* 1984, *from which this selection is taken, and* Animal Farm.

I N the low-ceilinged canteen, deep under ground, the lunch queue jerked slowly forward. The room was already very full and deafeningly noisy. From the grille at the counter the steam of stew came pouring forth, with a sour metallic smell which did not quite overcome the fumes of Victory Gin. On the far side of the room there was a small bar, a mere hole in the wall, where gin could be bought at ten cents the large nip.

"Just the man I was looking for," said a voice at Winston's back.

He turned round. It was his friend Syme, who worked in the Research Department. Perhaps "friend" was not exactly the right word. You did not have friends nowadays, you had comrades; but there were some comrades whose society was pleasanter than that of others. Syme was a philologist, a specialist in Newspeak. Indeed, he was one of the enormous team of experts now engaged in compiling the Eleventh Edition of the Newspeak dictionary. He was a tiny creature, smaller than Winston, with dark hair and large, protuberant eyes, at once mournful and derisive, which seemed to search your face closely while he was speaking to you.

"I wanted to ask you whether you'd got any razor blades," he said.

"Not one!" said Winston with a sort of guilty haste. "I've tried all over the place. They don't exist any longer."

Everyone kept asking you for razor blades. Actually he had two unused ones which he was hoarding up. There had been a famine of them for months past. At any given moment there was some necessary article which the Party shops were unable to supply. Sometimes it was buttons, sometimes it was darning wool, sometimes it was shoelaces; at present it was razor blades. You could only get hold of them, if at all, by scrounging more or less furtively on the "free" market.

"I've been using the same blade for six weeks," he added untruthfully.

The queue gave another jerk forward. As they halted he turned and faced Syme again. Each of them took a greasy metal tray from a pile at the edge of the counter.

"Did you go and see the prisoners hanged yesterday?" said Syme.

"I was working," said Winston indifferently. "I shall see it on the flicks, I suppose."

"A very inadequate substitute," said Syme.

His mocking eyes roved over Winston's face. "I know you," the eyes seemed to say, "I see through you.

I know very well why you didn't go to see those prisoners hanged." In an intellectual way, Syme was venomously orthodox. He would talk with a disagreeable gloating satisfaction of helicopter raids on enemy villages, the trials and confessions of thought-criminals, the executions in the cellars of the Ministry of Love. Talking to him was largely a matter of getting him away from such subjects and entangling him, if possible, in the technicalities of Newspeak, on which he was authoritative and interesting. Winston turned his head a little aside to avoid the scrutiny of the large dark eyes.

"It was a good hanging," said Syme reminiscently. "I think it spoils it when they tie their feet together. I like to see them kicking. And above all, at the end, the tongue sticking right out, and blue—a quite bright blue. That's the detail that appeals to me."

"Next, please!" yelled the white aproned prole with the ladle.

Winston and Syme pushed their trays beneath the grille. Onto each was dumped swiftly the regulation lunch—a metal pannikin of pinkish-gray stew, a hunk of bread, a cube of cheese, a mug of milkless Victory Coffee, and one saccharine tablet.

"There's a table over there, under that telescreen," said Syme. "Let's pick up a gin on the way."

The gin was served out to them in handleless china mugs. They threaded their way across the crowded room and unpacked their trays onto the metal-topped table, on one corner of which someone had left a pool of stew, a filthy liquid mess that had the appearance of vomit. Winston took up his mug of gin, paused for an instant to collect his nerve, and gulped the oily-tasting stuff

down. When he had winked the tears out of his eyes he suddenly discovered that he was hungry. He began swallowing spoonfuls of the stew, which, in among its general sloppiness, had cubes of spongy pinkish stuff which was probably a preparation of meat. Neither of them spoke again till they had emptied their pannikins. From the table at Winston's left, a little behind his back, someone was talking rapidly and continuously, a harsh gabble almost like the quacking of a duck, which pierced the general uproar of the room.

"How is the dictionary getting on?" said Winston, raising his voice to overcome the noise.

"Slowly," said Syme. "I'm on the adjectives. It's fascinating."

He had brightened up immediately at the mention of Newspeak. He pushed his pannikin aside, took up his hunk of bread in one delicate hand and his cheese in the other, and leaned across the table so as to be able to speak without shouting.

"The Eleventh Edition is the definitive edition," he said. "We're getting the language into its final shape—the shape it's going to have when nobody speaks anything else. When we've finished with it, people like you will have to learn it all over again. You think, I dare say, that our chief job is inventing new words. But not a bit of it! We're destroying words—scores of them, hundreds of them, every day. We're cutting the language down to the bone. The Eleventh Edition won't contain a single word that will become obsolete before the year 2050."

He bit hungrily into his bread and swallowed a couple of mouthfuls, then continued speaking, with a sort of pedant's passion. His thin dark face had become animated, his eyes had lost their mocking expression and grown almost dreamy.

"It's a beautiful thing, the destruction of words. Of course the great wastage is in the verbs and adjectives, but there are hundreds of nouns that can be got rid of as well. It isn't only the synonyms; there are also the antonyms. After all, what justification is there for a word which is simply the opposite of some other word? A word contains its opposite in itself. Take 'good,' for instance. If you have a word like 'good,' what need is there for a word like 'bad'? 'Ungood' will do just as well—better, because it's an exact opposite, which the other is not. Or again, if you want a stronger version of 'good', what sense is there in having a whole string of vague useless words like 'excellent' and 'splendid' and all the rest of them? 'Plusgood' covers the meaning, or 'doubleplusgood' if you want something stronger still. Of course we use those forms already, but in the final version of Newspeak there'll be nothing else. In the end the whole notion of goodness and badness will be covered by only six words—in reality, only one word. Don't you see the beauty of that, Winston? It was B.B's idea originally, of course," he added as an afterthought.

A sort of vapid eagerness flitted across Winston's face at the mention of Big Brother. Nevertheless Syme immediately detected a certain lack of enthusiasm.

"You haven't a real appreciation of Newspeak, Winston," he said almost sadly. "Even when you write it you're still thinking in Oldspeak. I've read some of those pieces that you write in the *Times* occasionally. They're good enough, but they're translations. In your heart you'd prefer to stick to Oldspeak, with all its vagueness and its useless shades of meaning. You don't grasp the beauty of the destruction of words. Do you know that Newspeak is the only language in the world whose vocabulary gets smaller every year?"

Winston did know that, of course. He smiled, sympathetically he hoped, not trusting himself to speak. Syme bit off another fragment of the dark-colored bread, chewed it briefly, and went on:

"Don't you see that the whole aim of Newspeak is to narrow the range of thought? In the end we shall make thoughtcrime literally impossible, because there will be no words in which to express it. Every concept that can ever be needed will be expressed by exactly *one* word, with its meaning rigidly defined and all its subsidiary meanings rubbed out and forgotten. Already, in the Eleventh Edition, we're not far from that point. But the process will still be continuing long after you and I are dead. Every year fewer and fewer words, and the range of consciousness always a little smaller. Even now, of course, there's no reason or excuse for committing thoughtcrime. It's merely a question of self-discipline, reality-control. But in the end there won't be any need even for that. The Revolution will be complete when the language is perfect. Newspeak is Ingsoc and Ingsoc is Newspeak," he added with a sort of mystical satisfaction. "Has it ever occurred to you, Winston, that by the year 2050, at the very latest, not a single human being will be alive who could understand such a conversation as we are having now?"

"Except—" began Winston doubtfully, and then stopped.

It had been on the tip of this tongue to say "Except the proles," but he checked himself, not feeling fully certain that this remark was not in some way unorthodox. Syme, however, had divined what he was about to say.

"The proles are not human beings," he said carelessly. "By 2050—earlier, probably—all real knowledge of Oldspeak will have disappeared. The whole literature of the past will have been destroyed. Chaucer, Shakespeare, Milton, Byron—they'll exist only in Newspeak versions, not merely changed into something different, but actually changed into something contradictory of what they used to be. Even the literature of the Party will change. Even the slogans will change. How could you have a slogan like 'freedom is slavery' when the concept of freedom has been abolished? The whole climate of thought will be different. In fact there will *be* no thought, as we understand it now. Orthodoxy means not thinking— not needing to think. Orthodoxy is unconsciousness."

STEVEN PINKER

Mentalese

STEVEN PINKER, *a linguist by training, is professor and director of the Center of Cognitive Neuroscience at MIT. He has won awards for his work in visual cognition and in child language acquisition, and for his teaching at MIT. His 1994 book,* The Language Instinct, *from which this selection is taken, is a lively and readable overview of contemporary linguistics from the perspective of cognitive science. In it he argues that language is an innate human instinct, rather than a cultural artifact.*

THE year 1984 has come and gone, and it is losing its connotation of the totalitarian nightmare of George Orwell's 1949 novel. But relief may be premature. In an appendix to *Nineteen Eighty-four,* Orwell wrote of an even more ominous date. In 1984, the infidel Winston Smith had to be converted with imprisonment, degradation, drugs, and torture; by 2050, there would be no Winston Smiths. For in that year the ultimate technology for thought control would be in place: the language Newspeak.

The purpose of Newspeak was not only to provide a medium of expression for the world-view and mental habits proper to the devotees of Ingsoc [English Socialism], but to make all other modes of thought impossible. It was intended that when Newspeak had been adopted once and for all and Oldspeak forgotten, a heretical thought—that is, a thought diverging from the principles of Ingsoc— should be literally unthinkable, at least so far as though is dependent on words. Its vocabulary was so constructed as to give exact and often very subtle expression to every meaning that a Party member could properly wish to express, while excluding all other meaning and also the possibility of arriving at them by indirect methods. This was done partly by the invention of new words, but chiefly by eliminating undesirable words and by stripping such words as remained of unorthodox meanings, and so far as possible of all secondary meanings whatever. To give a single example. The word *free* still existed in Newspeak, but it could only be used in such statements as "This dog is free from lice" or "This field is free from weeds." It could not be used in its old sense of "politically free" or "intellectually free," since political and intellectual freedom no longer existed even as concepts, and were therefore of necessity nameless.

. . . A person growing up with Newspeak as his sole language would no more know that *equal* had once had the secondary meaning of "politically equal," or that *free* had once meant "intellectually free," than, for instance, a person who had never heard of chess would be aware of the secondary meanings attaching to *queen* and *rook*. There would be many crimes and errors which it would be beyond his power to commit, simply because they were nameless and therefore unimaginable.

But there is a straw of hope for human freedom: Orwell's caveat "at least so far as thought is dependent on words." Note his equivocation: at the end of the first paragraph, a concept is unimaginable and therefore nameless; at the end of the second, a concept is nameless and therefore unimaginable. *Is* thought dependent on words? Do people literally think in English, Cherokee, Kivunjo, or, by 2050, Newspeak? Or arc our thoughts couched in some silent medium of the brain—a language of thought, or "mentalese"— and merely clothed in words whenever we need to communicate them to a listener? No question could be more central to understanding the language instinct.

In much of our social and political discourse, people simply assume that words determine thoughts. Inspired by Orwell's essay "Politics and the English Language," pundits accuse governments of manipulating our minds with euphemisms like *pacification* (bombing), *revenue enhancement* (taxes), and *nonretention* (firing). Philosophers argue that since animals lack language, they must also lack consciousness—Wittgenstein wrote, "A dog could not have the thought 'perhaps it will rain tomorrow'"—and therefore they do not possess the rights of conscious beings. Some feminists blame sexist thinking on sexist language, like the use of *he* to refer to a generic person. Inevitably, reform movements have sprung up. Many replacements for *he* have been suggested over the years, including *E, hesh, po, tey, co, jhe, ve, xe, he'er, thon*, and *na.* The most extreme of these movements is General Semantics, begun in 1933 by the engineer Count Alfred Korzybski and popularized in long-time best-sellers by his disciples Stuart Chase and S. I. Hayakawa. (This is the same Hayakawa who later achieved notoriety as the protest-defying college president and snoozing U.S. senator.) General Semantics lays the blame for human folly on insidious "semantic damage" to thought perpetrated by the structure of language. Keeping a forty-year-old in prison for a theft he committed as a teenager assumes that the forty-year-old John and the eighteen-year-old John are "the same person," a cruel logical error that would be avoided if we referred to them not as

John but as *John 1972* and John *1994,*
respectively. The verb *to be* is a particular source of illogic, because it identifies individuals with abstractions, as in
Mary is a woman, and licenses evasions
of responsibility, like Ronald Reagan's
famous nonconfession *Mistakes were
made.* One faction seeks to eradicate the
verb altogether.

And supposedly there is a scientific
basis for these assumptions: the famous
Sapir-Whorf hypothesis of linguistic
determinism, stating that people's
thoughts are determined by the categories made available by their language,
and its weaker version, linguistic relativity, stating that differences among
languages cause differences in the
thoughts of their speakers. People who
remember little else from their college
education can rattle off the factoids: the
languages that carve the spectrum into
color words and different places, the
fundamentally different Hopi concept of
time, the dozens of Eskimo words for
snow. The implication is heavy: the
foundational categories of reality are
not "in" the world but are imposed by
one's culture (and hence can be challenged, perhaps accounting for the
perennial appeal of the hypothesis to
undergraduate sensibilities).

But it is wrong, all wrong. The
idea that thought is the same thing as
language is an example of what can
be called a conventional absurdity: a
statement that goes against all common
sense but that everyone believes because they dimly recall having heard it
somewhere and because it is so pregnant with implications. (The "fact" that
we use only five percent of our brains,
that lemmings commit mass suicide,
that the *Boy Scout Manual* annually out-
sells all other books, and that we can be

coerced into buying by subliminal messages are other examples.) Think about
it. We have all had the experience of uttering or writing a sentence, then stopping and realizing that it wasn't exactly
what we meant to say. To have that feeling, there has to be a "what we meant to
say" that is different from what we said.
Sometimes it is not easy to find *any*
words that properly convey a thought.
When we hear or read, we usually remember the gist, not the exact words, so
there has be such a thing as a gist that is
not the same as a bunch of words. And
if thoughts depended on words, how
could a new word ever be coined? How
could a child learn a word to begin
with? How could translation from one
language to another be possible?

The discussions that assume that language determines thought carry on only
by a collective suspension of disbelief.
A dog, Bertrand Russell noted, may not
be able to tell you that its parents were
honest though poor, but can anyone
really conclude from this that the dog is
unconscious? (Out cold? A zombie?) A
graduate student once argued with me
using the following deliciously backwards logic: Language must affect
thought, because if it didn't, we would
have no reason to fight sexist usage (apparently, the fact that it is offensive is
not reason enough). As for government
euphemism, it is contemptible not because it is a form of lying. (Orwell was
quite clear about this in his masterpiece
essay.) For example, "revenue enhancement" has a much broader meaning than
"taxes," and listeners naturally assume
that if a politician had meant "taxes,"
and listeners naturally assume that if a
politician had meant "taxes," he would
have said "taxes." Once a euphemism is
pointed out, people are not so brain-

washed that they have trouble understanding the deception. The National
Council of Teachers of English annually
lampoons government doublespeak in a
widely reproduced press release, and
calling attention to euphemism is a popular form of humor, like the speech
from the irate pet store customer in
Monty Python's Flying Circus:

> This parrot is no more. It has ceased to
> be. It's expired and gone to meet its
> maker. This a late parrot. It's a stiff.
> Bereft of life, it rests in peace. If you
> hadn't nailed it to the perch, it would be
> pushing up the daisies. It's rung down the
> curtain and joined the choir invisible.
> This is an ex-parrot.

As we shall see in this chapter, there
is no scientific evidence that languages
dramatically shape their speakers' ways
of thinking. But I want to do more than
review the unintentionally comical history of attempts to prove that they do.
The idea that language shapes thinking
seemed plausible when scientists were
in the dark about how thinking works or
even how to study it. Now that cognitive
scientists know to think about thinking,
there is less of a temptation to equate it
with language just because words are
more palpable than thoughts. By understanding *why* linguistic determinism is
wrong, we will be in a better position to
understand how language itself works
when we turn to it in the next chapters.

•   •   •

The linguistic determinism hypothesis is closely linked to the names Edward Sapir and Benjamin Lee Whorf.
Sapir, a brilliant linguist, was a student
of the anthropologist Franz Boas. Boas
and his students (who also include Ruth
Benedict and Margaret Mead) were important intellectual figures in this
century, because they argued that non-
industrial peoples were not primitive
savages but had systems of language,
knowledge, and culture as complex and
valid in their world view as our own. In
his study of Native American languages
Sapir noted that speakers of different
languages have to pay attention to different aspects of reality simply to put
words together into grammatical sentences. For example, when English
speakers decide whether or not to put
-ed unto the end of a verb, they must
pay attention to tense, the relative time
of occurrence of the event they are referring to and the moment of speaking.
Wintu speakers need not bother with
tense, but when they decide which suffix to put on their verbs, they must pay
attention to whether the knowledge they
are conveying was learned through direct observation or by hearsay.

Sapir's interesting observation was
soon taken much farther. Whorf was an
inspector for the Hartford Fire Insurance
Company and an amateur scholar of Native American languages, which led him
to take courses from Sapir at Yale. In a
much-quoted passage, he wrote:

> We dissect nature along lines laid down
> by our native languages. The categories
> and types that we isolate from the world
> of phenomena we do not find there be-
> cause they stare every observer in the
> face; on the contrary, the world is pre-
> sented in a kaleidoscopic flux of impres-
> sions which has to be organized by our
> minds—and this means largely by the
> linguistic systems in our minds. We cut
> nature up, organize it into concepts, and

ascribe significances as we do, largely because we are parties to an agreement to organize it in this way—an agreement that holds throughout our speech community and is codified in the patterns of our language. The agreement is, of course, an implicit and unstated one, *but its terms are absolutely obligatory;* we cannot talk at all except by subscribing to the organization and classification of data which the agreement decrees.

What led Whorf to this radical position? He wrote that the idea first occurred to him in his work as a fire prevention engineer when he was struck by how language led workers to misconstrue dangerous situations. For example, one worker caused a serious explosion by tossing a cigarette into an "empty" drum that in fact was full of gasoline vapor. Another lit a blowtorch near a "pool of water" that was really a basin of decomposing tannery waste, which, far from being "watery," was releasing inflammable gases. Whorf's studies of American languages strengthened his conviction. For example, in Apache, *It is a dripping spring* must be expressed "As water, or springs, whiteness moves downward." "How utterly unlike our way of thinking!" he wrote.

But the more you examine Whorf's arguments, the less sense they make. Take the story about the worker and the "empty" drum. The seeds of disaster supposedly lay in the semantics of *empty,* which, Whorf claimed, means both "without its usual contents" and "null and void, empty, inert." The hapless worker, his conception of reality molded by his linguistic categories, did not distinguish between the "drained" and "inert" senses, hence, flick . . . boom! But wait. Gasoline vapor is invisible. A drum with nothing but vapor

in it looks just like a drum with nothing in it at all. Surely this walking catastrophe was fooled by his eyes, not by the English language.

The example of whiteness moving downward is supposed to show that the Apache mind does not cut up events into distinct objects and actions. Whorf presented many such examples from Native American languages. The Apache equivalent of *The boat is grounded on the beach* is "It is on the beach pointwise as an event of canoe motion." *He invites people to a feast* becomes "He, or somebody, goes for eaters of cooked food." *He cleans a gun with a ramrod* is translated as "He directs a hollow moving dry spot by movement of tool." All this, to be sure, is utterly unlike our way of talking. But do we know that it is utterly unlike our way of thinking?

As soon as Whorf's articles appeared, the psycholinguists Eric Lenneberg and Roger Brown pointed out two non sequiturs in his argument. First, Whorf did not actually study any Apaches; it is not clear that he ever met one. His assertions about Apache psychology are based entirely on Apache grammar—making his argument circular. Apaches speak differently, so they must think differently. How do we know that they think differently? Just listen to the way they speak!

Second, Whorf rendered the sentences as clumsy, word-for-word translations, designed to make the literal meanings seem as odd as possible. But looking at the actual glosses that Whorf provided, I could, with equal grammatical justification, render the first sentence as the mundane "Clear stuff—water—is falling." Turning the tables, I could take the English sentence "He walks" and render it "As solitary

masculinity, leggedness proceeds."
Brown illustrates how strange the
German mind must be, according to
Whorf's logic, by reproducing Mark
Twain's own translation of a speech he
delivered in flawless German to the Vi-
enna Press Club:

> I am indeed the truest friend of the Ger-
> man language—and not only now, but
> from long since—yes, before twenty
> years already. . . . I would only some
> changes effect. I would only the lan-
> guage method—the luxurious, elaborate
> construction compress, the eternal paren-
> thesis suppress, do away with, annihilate;
> the introduction of more than thirteen
> subjects in one sentence forbid; the verb
> so far to the front pull that one it without
> a telescope discover can. With one word,
> my gentlemen, I would your beloved lan-
> guage simplify so that, my gentlemen,
> when you her for prayer need, One her
> yonder-up understands.

> . . . I might gladly the separable verb also
> a little bit reform. I might none do let
> what Schiller did: he has the whole his-
> tory of the Thirty Years' War between the
> two members of a separate verb inpushed.
> That has even Germany itself aroused,
> and one has Schiller the permission re-
> fused the History of the Hundred Years'
> War to compose—God be it thanked!
> After all these reforms established be
> will, will the German language the no-
> blest and the prettiest on the world be.

Among Whorf's "kaleidoscopic flux
of impressions," color is surely the most
eye-catching. He noted that we see objects in different hues, depending on the
wavelengths of the light they reflect, but
that physicists tell us that wavelength is
a continuous dimension with nothing
delineating red, yellow, green, blue, and
so on. Languages differ in their inven-
tory of color words: Latin lacks generic
"gray" and "brown"; Navajo collapses
blue and green into one word; Russian
has distinct words for dark blue and sky
blue; Shona speakers use one word for
the yellower greens and the greener yellows, and a different one for the bluer
greens and the nonpurplish blues. You
can fill in the rest of the argument. It is
language that puts the frets in the spectrum; Julius Caesar would not know
shale from Shinola.

But although physicists see no basis
for color boundaries, physiologists do.
Eyes do not register wavelength the
way a thermometer registers temperature. They contain three kinds of cones,
each with a different pigment, and the
cones are wired to neurons in a way that
makes the neurons respond best to red
patches against a green background or
vice versa, blue against yellow, black
against white. No matter how influential
language might be, it would seem preposterous to a physiologist that it could
reach down into the retina and rewire
the ganglion cells.

Indeed, humans the world over (and
babies and monkeys, for that matter)
color their perceptual worlds using the
same palette, and this constrains the vocabularies they develop. Although languages may disagree about the wrappers
in the sixty-four crayon box—the burnt
umbers, the turquoises, the fuchsias—
they agree much more on the wrappers
in the eight-crayon box—the fire-engine
reds, grass greens, lemon yellows.
Speakers of different languages unani-
mously pick these shades as the best examples of their color words, as long as
the language has a color word in that
general part of the spectrum. And where
languages do differ in their color words,
they differ predictably, not according
to the idiosyncratic tastes of some

word-coiner. Languages are organized a bit like the Crayola product line, the fancier ones adding colors to the more basic ones. If a language has only two color words, they are for black and white (usually encompassing dark and light, respectively). If it has three, they are for black, white, and red; if four, black, white, red, and either yellow or green. Five adds in both yellow and green; six, blue; seven, brown; more than seven, purple, pink, orange, or gray. But the clinching experiment was carried out in the New Guinea highlands with the Grand Valley Dani, a people speaking one of the black-and-white languages. The psychologist Eleanor Rosch found that the Dani were quicker at learning a new color category that was based on fire-engine red than a category based on an off-red. The way we see colors determines how we learn words for them, not vice versa.

The fundamentally different Hopi concept of time is one of the more startling claims about how minds can vary. Whorf wrote that the Hopi language contain "no words, grammatical forms, constructions, or expressions that refer directly to what we call 'time,' or to past, or future, or to enduring or lasting." He suggested, too that the Hopi had "no general notion or intuition of time as a smooth flowing continuum in which everything in the universe proceeds at equal rate, out of a future, through a present, into a past." According to Whorf, they did not conceptualize events as being like points, or lengths of time like days as countable things. Rather, they seemed to focus on change and process itself, and on psychological distinctions between presently known, mythical, and conjecturally distant. The Hopi also had little interest in "exact sequences, dating, calendars, chronology."

What, then, are we to make of the following sentence translated from Hopi?

> Then indeed, the following day, quite early in the morning at the hour when people pray to the sun, around that time then he woke up the girl again.

Perhaps the Hopi are not as oblivious to time as Whorf made them out to be. In his extensive study of the Hopi, the anthropologist Ekkehart Malotki, who reported this sentence, also showed that Hopi speech contains tense, metaphors for time, units of time (including days, numbers of days, parts of the day, yesterday and tomorrow, days of the week, weeks, months, lunar phases, seasons, and the year), ways to quantify units of time, and words like "ancient," "quick," "long time," and "finished." Their culture keeps records with sophisticated methods of dating, including a horizon-based sun calendar, exact ceremonial day sequences, knotted calendar strings, notched calendar sticks, and several devices for timekeeping using the principle of the sundial. No one is really sure how Whorf came up with his outlandish claims, but his limited, badly analyzed sample of Hopi speech and his long-time leanings toward mysticism must have contributed.

Speaking of anthropological canards, no discussion of language and thought would be complete without the Great Eskimo Vocabulary Hoax. Contrary to popular belief, the Eskimos do not have more words for snow than do speakers of English. They do not have four hundred words for snow, as it has been claimed in print, or two hundred, or one hundred, or forty-eight, or even nine. One dictionary puts the figure at two. Counting generously, experts can come up with about a dozen, but by such standards English would not be far behind, with *snow, sleet, slush, blizzard, ava-lanche, hail, hardpack, powder, flurry, dusting,* and a coinage of Boston's WBZ-TV meteorologist Bruce Schwoe-gler, *snizzling.*

Where did the myth come from? Not from anyone who has actually studied the Yupik and Inuit-Inupiaq families of polysynthetic languages spoken from Siberia to Greenland. The anthropologist Laura Martin has documented how the story grew like an urban legend, exaggerated with each retelling. In 1912 Boas casually mentioned that Eskimos used four unrelated word roots for snow. Whorf embellished the count to seven and implied that there were more. His article was widely reprinted, then cited in textbooks and popular books on language, which led to successively inflated estimates in other textbooks, articles, and newspaper columns of Amazing Facts.

The linguist Geoffrey Pullum, who popularized Martin's article in his essay "The Great Eskimo Vocabulary Hoax," speculates about why the story got so out of control: "The alleged lexical extravagance of the Eskimos comports so well with the many other facets of their polysynthetic perversity: rubbing noses; lending their wives to strangers; eating raw seal blubber; throwing Grandma out to be eaten by polar bears." It is an ironic twist. Linguistic relativity came out of the Boas school, as part of a campaign to show that nonliterate cultures were as complex and sophisticated as European ones. But the supposedly mind-broadening anecdotes owe their appeal to a patronizing willingness to teat other cultures' psychologies as weird and exotic compared to our own. As Pullum notes,

Among the many depressing things about this credulous transmission and elabora-tion of a false claim is that even if there *were* a large number of roots for different snow types in some Arctic language, this would *not,* objectively, be intellectually interesting; it would be a most mundane and unremarkable fact. Horsebreeders have various names for breeds, sizes, and ages of horses; botanists have names for leaf shapes; interior decorators have names for shades of mauve; printers have many different names for fonts (Carlson, Garamond, Helvetica, Times Roman, and so on), naturally enough. . . . Would any one think of writing about printers the same kind of slop we find written about Eskimos in bad linguistics textbooks? Take [the following] random text-book . . . , with its earnest assertion "It is quite obvious that in the culture of the Es-kimos . . . snow is of great enough impor-tance to split up the conceptual sphere that corresponds to one word and one thought in English into several distinct classes . . ." Imagine reading: "It is quite obvious that in the culture of printers . . . fonts are of great enough importance to split up the conceptual sphere that corre-sponds to one word and one thought among non-printers into several distinct classes . . ." Utterly boring, even if true. Only the link to those legendary, promis-cuous, blubber-gnawing hunters of the ice-packs could permit something this trite to be presented to us for contemplation.

If the anthropological anecdotes are bunk, what about controlled studies? The thirty-five years of research from the psychology laboratory is distinguished by how little it has shown. Most of the experiments have tested banal "weak" versions of the Whorfian hypothesis, namely that words can have some effect on memory or categorization. Some of these experiments have actually worked, but that is hardly surprising. In a typical experiment, subjects have to commit paint chips to memory and are tested with a multiple-choice procedure. In some of these studies, the subjects show slightly better memory for colors that have readily available names in their language. But even colors are remembered by verbal labels alone. All it shows is that subjects remembered the chips in two forms, a nonverbal visual image and a verbal label, presumably because two kinds of memory, each one fallible, are better than one. In another type of experiment subjects have to say which two out of three color chips go together; they often put the ones together that have the same name in their language. Again, no surprise. I can imagine the subjects thinking to themselves, "Now how on earth does this guy expect me to pick two chips to put together? He didn't give me any hints, and they're all pretty similar. Well, I'd probably call those two 'green' and that one 'blue,' and that seems as good a reason to put them together as any." In these experiments, language is, technically speaking, influencing a form of thought in some way, but so what? It is hardly an example of incommensurable world views, or of concepts that are nameless and therefore unimaginable, or of dissecting nature along lines laid down by our native languages according to terms that are absolutely obligatory.

The only really dramatic finding comes from the linguist and now Swarthmore College president Alfred Bloom in his book *The Linguistic Shaping of Thought.* English grammar, says Bloom, provides its speakers with the subjunctive construction: *If John were to go to the hospital, he would meet Mary.* The subjunctive is used to express "counterfactual" situations, events that

are known to be false but entertained as hypotheticals. (Anyone familiar with Yiddish knows a better example, the ultimate riposte to someone reasoning from improbable premises: *Az der bubbe vot gehat baytzim vot zie geven mein zayde,* "If my grandmother had balls, she'd be my grandfather.") Chinese, in contrast, lacks a subjunctive and any other simple grammatical construction that directly expresses a counterfactual. The thought must be expressed circuitously, something like "If John is going to the hospital . . . but he is not going to the hospital . . . but if he is going, he meets Mary."

Bloom wrote stories containing sequences of implications from a counterfactual premise and gave them to Chinese and American students. For example, one story said, in outline, "Bier was an eighteenth-century European philosopher. There was some contact between the West and China at that time, but very few works of Chinese philosophy had been translated. Bier could not read Chinese, but if he had been able to read Chinese, he would have discovered B; what would have most influenced him would have been C; once influenced by that Chinese perspective, Bier would then have done D," and so on. The subjects were then asked to check off whether B, C, and D actually occurred. The American students gave the correct answer, no, ninety-eight percent of the time; the Chinese students gave the correct answer only seven percent of the time! Bloom concluded that the Chinese language renders its speakers unable to entertain hypothetical false worlds without great mental effort. (As far as I know, no one has tested the converse prediction on speakers of Yiddish.)

The cognitive psychologists Terry Au, Yohtaro Takano, and Lisa Liu were not exactly enchanted by these tales of the concreteness of the Oriental mind. Each one identified serious flaws in Bloom's experiments. One problem was that his stories were written in stilted Chinese. Another was that some of the science stories turned out, upon careful rereading, to be genuinely ambiguous. Chinese college students tend to have more science training than American students, and thus they were *better* at detecting the ambiguities that Bloom himself missed. When these flaws were fixed, the differences vanished.

• • •

We have met deaf children who lack a language and soon invent one. Even more pertinent are the deaf adults occasionally discovered who lack any form of language whatsoever—no sign language, no writing, no lip reading, no speech. In her recent book *A Man Without Words,* Susan Schaller tells the story of Ildefonso, a twenty-seven-year-old illegal immigrant from a small Mexican village whom she met while working as a sign language interpreter in Los Angeles. Ildefonso's animated eyes conveyed an unmistakable intelligence and curiosity, and Schaller became his volunteer teacher and companion. He soon showed her that he had a full grasp of number: he learned to do addition on paper in three minutes and had little trouble understanding the base-ten logic behind two-digit numbers. In an epiphany reminiscent of the story of Helen Keller, Ildefonso grasped the principle of naming when Schaller tried to teach

him the sign for "cat." A dam burst, and he demanded to be shown the signs for all the objects he was familiar with. Soon he was able to convey to Schaller parts of his life story: how as a child he had begged his desperately poor parents to send him to school, the kinds of crops he had picked in different states, his evasions of immigration authorities. He led Schaller to other languageless adults in forgotten corners of society. Despite their isolation from the verbal world, they displayed many abstract forms of thinking, like rebuilding broken locks, handling money, playing card games, and entertaining each other with long pantomimed narratives.

Our knowledge of the mental life of Ildefonso and other languageless adults must remain impressionistic for ethical reasons: when they surface, the first priority is to teach them language, not to study how they manage without it. But there are other languageless beings who have been studied experimentally, and volumes have been written about how they reason about space, time, objects, number, rate, causality, and categories. Let me recount three ingenious examples. One involves babies, who cannot think in words because they have not yet learned any. One involves monkeys, who cannot think in words because they are incapable of learning them. The third involves human adults, who, whether or not they think in words, claim their best thinking is done without them.

The developmental psychologist Karen Wynn has recently shown that five-month-old babies can do a simple form of mental arithmetic. She used a technique common in infant perception research. Show a baby a bunch of objects long enough, and the baby gets bored and looks away; change the scene, and if the baby notices the difference, he or she will regain interest. The methodology has shown that babies as young as five days old are sensitive to number. In one experiment, an experimenter bores a baby with an object, then occludes the object with an opaque screen. When the screen is removed, if the same object is present, the babies look for a little while, then get bored again. But if, through invisible subterfuge, two or three objects have ended up there, the surprised babies stare longer.

In Wynn's experiment, the babies were shown a rubber Mickey Mouse doll on a stage until their little eyes wandered. Then a screen came up, and a prancing hand visibly reached out from behind a curtain and placed a second Mickey Mouse behind the screen. When the screen was removed, if there were two Mickey Mouses visible (something the babies had never actually seen), the babies looked for only a few moments. But if there was only one doll, the babies were captivated—even though this was exactly the scene that had bored them before the screen was put in place. Wynn also tested a second group of babies, and this time, after the screen came up to obscure a *pair* of dolls, a hand visibly reached behind the screen and removed one of them. If the screen fell to reveal a single Mickey, the babies looked briefly; if it revealed the old scene with two, the babies had more trouble tearing themselves away. The babies must have been keeping track of how many dolls were behind the screen, updating their counts as dolls were added or subtracted. If the number inexplicably departed from what they expected, they scrutinized the scene, as if searching for some explanation. . . .

What sense, then, can we make of the suggestion that images, numbers,

kinship relations, or logic can be represented in the brain without being couched in words? In the first half of this century, philosophers had an answer: none. Reifying thoughts as things in the head was a logical error, they said. A picture or family tree or number in the head would require a little man, a homunculus, to look at it. And what would be inside *his* head—even smaller pictures, with an even smaller man looking at them? But the argument was unsound. It took Alan Turing, the brilliant British mathematician and philosopher, to make the idea of a mental representation scientifically respectable. Turing described a hypothetical machine that could be said to engage in reasoning. In fact this simple device, named Turing Machine in his honor, is powerful enough to solve any problem that any computer, past, present, or future, can solve. And it clearly uses an internal symbolic representation—a kind of mentalese—without requiring a little man or any occult processes. . . .

Remember that a representation does not have to look like English or any other language; it just has to use symbols to represent concepts, and arrangements of symbols to represent the logical relations among them, according to some consistent scheme. But though internal representations in an English speaker's mind don't *have* to look like English, they *could,* in principle, look like English—or like whatever language the person happens to speak. So here is the question: Do they in fact? For example, if we know that Socrates is a man, is it because we have neural patterns that correspond one-to-one to the English words *Socrates, is, a,* and *man,* and groups of neurons in the brain that correspond to the subject of an English sentence, the verb, and the object, laid out in that order? Or do we use some other code for representing concepts and their relations in our heads, a language of thought or mentalese that is not the same as any of the world's languages? We can answer this question by seeing whether English sentences embody the information that a processor would need to perform valid sequences of reasoning—without requiring any fully intelligent homunculus inside doing the "understanding."

The answer is a clear no. English (or any other language people speak) is hopelessly unsuited to serve as our internal medium of computation. . . .

People do not think in English or Chinese or Apache; they think in a language of thought. This language of thought probably looks a bit like all these languages; presumably it has symbols for concepts, and arrangements of symbols that correspond to who did what to whom. . . . But compared with any given language, mentalese must be richer in some ways and simpler in others. It must be richer, for example, in that several concept symbols must correspond to a given English word like *stool* or *stud*. There must be extra paraphernalia that differentiate logically distinct kinds of concepts. . . and that link different symbols that refer to the same thing. . . . On the other hand, mentalese must be simpler than spoken languages; conversation-specific words and constructions (like *a* and *the*) are absent, and information about pronouncing words, or even ordering them, is unnecessary. Now, it could be that English speakers think in some kind of simpli-

fied and annotated quasi-English, with the design I have just described, and that Apache speakers think in a simplified and annotated quasi-Apache. But to get these languages of thought to subserve reasoning properly, they would have to look much more like each other than either one does to its spoken counterpart, and it is likely that they are the same: a universal mentalese.

Knowing a language, then, is knowing how to translate mentalese into strings of words and vice versa. People without a language would still have mentalese, and babies and many nonhuman animals presumably have simpler dialects. Indeed, if babies did not have a mentalese to translate to and from English, it is not clear how learning English could take place, or even what learning English would mean.

So where does all this leave Newspeak? Here are my predictions for the year 2050. First, since mental life goes on independently of particular languages, concepts of freedom and equality will be thinkable even if they are nameless. Second, since there are far more concepts than there are words, and listeners must always charitably fill in what the speaker leaves unsaid, existing words will quickly gain new senses, perhaps even regain their original senses. Third, since children are not content to reproduce any old input from adults but create a complex grammar than can go beyond it, they would creolize Newspeak into a natural language, possibly in a single generation. The twenty-first-century toddler may be Winston Smith's revenge.

STEPHANIE ROSS

How Words Hurt

STEPHANIE ROSS *teaches philosophy at the university of Missouri in St. Louis. She does work in feminist theory and in aesthetics.*

AN old nursery rhyme assures us that "Sticks and stones may break my bones/But names can never hurt me." Yet many philosophers claim that words *can* hurt. They argue that ordinary language is sexist and that sexist language oppresses women. For example, Elizabeth Beardsley has drawn attention to referential genderization (RG) which occurs "whenever a speaker who is saying something about human beings must make distinctions based on sex on pain of saying something linguistically incorrect." She claims that RG increases sexual distinctions, and thereby "helps to provide a conceptual framework useful for rationalizing sex-based discriminatory treatment." Robert Baker claims that

> any movement dedicated to breaking the bonds of female servitude must destroy our ways of identifying and hence of conceiving of women. . . . Contemporary feminists should advocate the utilization of neutral proper names and the elimination of gender from our language.

I believe these claims are sound, but to my knowledge no philosopher has provided a satisfactory account of *how* words hurt. Certainly words can be used to taunt and defame, to voice threats and instill fear, to express discriminatory edits and tyrannical decrees. Yet none of these possibilities explains the particular charge that our ordinary, everyday ways of talking about women

are sexist and oppressive. Some writers suggest that the oppressive aspects of ordinary language are etymological: certain words have roots which are denigrating and offensive to women. Yet most of us are unaware of the etymologies of the words we use. How can historical facts of which both speakers and listeners are unaware transform their words into vehicles of oppression?

In this paper I shall offer an account of how words can hurt. I shall begin by sketching a theory which doesn't work—the theory of etymological oppression. I shall argue that the ancient roots of ordinary English words cannot—by themselves—make those words oppressive. Then I shall turn to a closely related phenomenon which does perpetuate sexism in language. This is the phenomenon of metaphoric identification. . . . Briefly, I claim that metaphors often express attitude, and that the metaphors implicit in sexist language express attitudes of contempt and disdain towards women. . . . I shall also point out a structural similarity which makes metaphor an apt vehicle for the expression of attitude. Thus I hope to show that the nursery rhyme with which I opened is mistaken. Words can hurt, and one way they do is by conveying denigrating or demeaning attitudes.

ETYMOLOGICAL ECHOES?

In an angry article in the *New York Times,* Barbara Lawrence traces the etymology of the verb *to fuck* to the German *ficken* meaning "to strike," to the Latin *fustis,* meaning "a staff or cudgel," and to Celtic *buc,* meaning "a point, hence, to pierce." She goes on to discuss the etymology of the verb *to screw* and to point out what a painful and mutilating activity screwing is:

> Consider what a screw actually does to the wood it penetrates. . . . The verb, besides its explicit imagery, has antecedent associations to "write on," "scratch," "scarify," and so forth—a revealing fusion of a mechanical or painful action with an obviously denigrated object.

Lawrence suggests that these two words oppress women because of the brutal and denigrating imagery implicit in their etymology. While I agree that both words are offensive, I believe that neither one oppresses in virtue of its etymology. And of the two, only "screw" offends in virtue of its associated imagery. . . . In the next section I shall show that the facts cited by Lawrence are relevant to a different sort of explanation of how words hurt. . . .

METAPHORICAL IDENTIFICATION

Return to Lawrence's two examples, "fuck" and "screw." We agree that both these words are insulting and that both are classed as impolite. In addition, I have argued that "fuck" does not offend women because of its etymological ties to "ficken," "fustis," and "buc." Most speakers are unaware of these ties. They find the term offensive because they know it is classed as offensive by their fellow speakers. I believe the offensiveness of "screw" can be explained quite differently, and this is shown even in Lawrence's summary reference to its "revealing fusion of a mechanical or painful action with an obviously denigrated object." The difference here is that most of us are aware of these aspects of screws. Even if we haven't given much thought to screwing as a method of fastening (as opposed to nailing or glueing) we can immediately acknowledge the correctness of Lawrence's claims. A screw is hard and sharp; wood by contrast is soft and yielding; force is applied to make a screw penetrate wood; a screw can be unscrewed and reused but wood—wherever a screw has been embedded in it—is destroyed forever. Once we marshal these everyday facts about screws and screwing, their ramifications become clear. When the verb *to screw* is used to describe sexual intercourse, it carries with it images of dominance and destruction. The woman's role in intercourse is similar to that of wood destroyed by the screw which enters it. Additional echoes are carried by a further use of the verb *to screw* in financial contexts. To screw someone in this sense is to wring her dry, to practice extortion.

Metaphor is the device at work here. The use of the verb *to screw* to describe sexual intercourse invites us to view this latter activity in terms drawn from carpentry and mechanics. As noted above, many facts about screws and screwing are applicable to the new realm as well. And this is just what we should expect of an apt metaphor. But "screwing" is not a fresh, new label for intercourse. This use of the term is accepted, though deemed coarse and impolite. Thus we are dealing here with a dead metaphor— an established use of the word "screw" which has additional depth and resonance because it associates the two realms of sex and mechanics. The central claim I want to make in this paper is that metaphors of this sort are our primary vehicles for conveying attitudes.

The offensiveness of the verb *to screw* is rooted in the attitude it conveys toward the female role in intercourse, and this attitude can be specified by attending to the details of the metaphor. None of the claims I shall make are tied to any one theory of metaphor. While there is much debate about the nature of metaphorical truth, the paraphrasability of metaphors, and so on, I shall skirt these issues. I trust that my positive claims about metaphor will apply to any reasonable account of that trope.

The relation between sexism and metaphor has been charted ably by Robert Baker in his article "'Pricks' and 'Chicks': A Plea for 'Persons'." I want to expand on his work by showing in detail how metaphors can serve to express attitudes. But let me first outline Baker's position. Baker claims that the way in which we identify something reflects our conception of it. This claim is not controversial. It may even be tautological on some reading of "concept." However, the identifications Baker focuses on throughout his paper are metaphorical ones. This enlivens things because metaphors are not finitely paraphrasable. Since their implications can be spun out at length, the identifications they convey are comparably complex.

To establish his claim, Baker first considers racial identifications. He compares the differing conceptions of blacks conveyed by the four labels "Negro," "colored," "Afro-American," and "black." In the course of his discussion, he imagines the remarks "Where did that girl get to?" and "Who is the new boy that Lou hired to help out at the filling stations?" voiced by white Southerners, and then comments:

> If the persons the terms apply to are adult Afro-Americans, then 'girl' and 'boy' are

metaphorical identifications. The fact that the metaphorical identifications in question are standard in the language reflects that certain characteristics of the objects properly classified as boys and girls (for example, immaturity, inability to take care of themselves, need for guidance) are generally held by those who use the identifications to be properly attributable to Afro-Americans.

Baker's acknowledgment that these metaphors are standard usage is important, for it establishes that the metaphors in question are dead metaphors. The Southerners who use them do not first think long and hard about race relations, then consciously construct metaphors which reveal the situation. Rather, they use the terms "boy" and "girl" because these are common currency. Probably few speakers spell out the implications of these terms for themselves as Baker has in the passage quoted above. Nonetheless, these implications are available—at least potentially—to any competent speaker. They resonate in each metaphorical use of the terms "boy" and "girl" quite unlike the supposed echoes of "buc," "fustis," and "flicken" resonating in each use of "fuck."

This is the important difference between Baker's account of the offensiveness of certain idioms and the account I proposed and rejected in Part I of this paper—the implications of dead metaphors are known or accessible to their speakers, while etymological details often are not. To see this, note that dead metaphors are those which have become trite and commonplace. Tenor and vehicle have been associated so frequently that their juxtaposition no longer seems fresh or illuminating. Given this long and public liaison, it follows that neither

tenor nor vehicle can be entirely mysterious unless the metaphor was consistently misunderstood. (One obvious
exception to this claim is the use of
metaphor in scientific theories. Here the
subject matter is indeed arcane and the
presence of metaphor signals that our
understanding is not yet complete.
However, these cases needn't concern
us here since our problem is ordinary
language and its power to offend and
oppress.) Finally, these comments about
metaphor apply equally to metaphorical
identifications. These are simply cases
where instead of a full statement of the
metaphor ("A is B") the name or description of the vehicle replaces that of
the tenor ("B is o" replaces "A is ø").

Baker takes the account of metaphorical identification which emerges from
his discussion of racism and applies it to
a second area, that of sexism. He argues
that many of our ways of identifying
women involve (dead) metaphors which
insult and belittle. Among the categories
of metaphorical identification he points
out are animal terms ("chick," "fox"),
toy terms ("doll"), juvenile terms
("babe," "kid," "sis") as well as more
explicitly sexual and/or anatomical
terms. I believe Baker is right about the
force of these terms, though I grant
there are certain cases which his account does not explain. For example,
his theory does not apply to terms (like
"fuck") which offend because we class
them as offensive. Nor does it apply to
terms which offend by excluding
women from consideration. Examples
here include general labels like "chairman" and "fireman" as well as the personal pronouns "he" and "his" when
used to agree with an antecedent
of unspecified gender ("everyone,"
"someone"). Neither of these examples
offends in virtue of metaphorical impli-

cations. (However, in keeping with
Baker's program we can explain both
by reference to a second figure of
speech: synecdoche. Both wrongly take
part of humanity—the male sex—and
use it to stand for the whole. The resulting idioms make it all too easy for
women to be overlooked.)

ATTITUDE AND METAPHOR

Despite these lacunae, Baker's account fits a sizable number of cases of
sexism in language. However, Baker
calls our attention to the relation between metaphor and sexism without explaining how this relation fosters the
oppression of women. I believe this is a
fact in need of explanation. In what follows, I shall extend Baker's program by
proposing an account of how metaphorical identifications oppress and offend. I
suggest that metaphors often express attitudes. In particular, I suggest that the
metaphorical identifications which
Baker discusses express contemptuous
and disdainful attitudes towards women.
To justify this claim, I shall present
three sorts of evidence. First, I shall present and discuss a single example,
drawn from a novel of Willa Cather.
Rather than argue in the abstract that
metaphors can express attitudes, I shall
examine a particular passage and argue
that the best interpretation of it accords
with my theory. Next, I shall offer some
evidence drawn from social psychology.
I shall examine the methods social psychologists employ to test for attitudes
and point out the central role played by
metaphor. Finally, I shall offer a more
abstract argument for my claim, based
on 'structural' resemblances between attitude and metaphor.

Consider the following passages
from *The Professor's House:*

He loved his family, he would make any sacrifice for them, but just now he couldn't live live with them. He must be alone. That was more necessary to him than anything had ever been, more necessary than his marriage had been in his vehement youth. He could not live with his family again—not even with Lillian. Especially not with Lillian! Her nature was intense and positive; it was like a chiselled surface, a die, a stamp upon which he could not be beaten out any longer. If her character were reduced to an heraldic device, it would be a hand (a beautiful hand) holding flaming arrows—the shafts of her violent loves and hates, her clear-cut ambition.

In these lines Willa Cather details the reactions of her protagonist, Professor Godfrey St. Peter, to the news that his family is returning early from a European tour. That passage tells us a good deal about St. Peter's temperament, loyalties, and needs, his early attachments and his current desires. But my interest is in the Professor's description of his wife, Lillian. Just what is revealed by the simile comparing her nature to a sharp metallic die, or the metaphor imagining her character as a heraldic device? What do we learn about the professor in learning that *these* are his thoughts?

For a start, we do not learn about the Professor's beliefs. At least not in any straightforward sense. One might object that St. Peter expresses at least the belief that Lillian's character can be represented by a heraldic device of such and such a sort. But little follows from this concession. The Professor uses figurative language to talk about his wife. His beliefs about Lillian herself are of primary interest, not his beliefs about the suitability of various metaphors. And his endorsement of a particular trope does little to reveal his literal beliefs about his wife. This is so in part because metaphors aren't readily paraphrased; also because we rarely resort to metaphor to formulate and communicate our literal (pedestrian) beliefs. Thus, although the Professor's description is revealing, it doesn't reveal his beliefs about Lillian.

Nor does it reveal particular emotions he feels toward Lillian. Granted, the tone of the entire passage is hysterical, and its general topic seems to be love. But neither love nor hysteria characterizes St. Peter's portrait of Lillian. Although the opening sentence of the passage assures us that St. Peter loves his family, his portrait reveals love's absence, or its aftermath. (He remarks later, "Surely the saddest thing in the world is falling out of love—if once one has ever fallen in.") Similarly, although St. Peter seems hysterical and overwrought in this passage, these emotions do not carry over to his description of Lillian. She is not the object of his hysteria. Instead she receives a knowing, considered assessment.

What, then, does the Professor's description convey? I suggest it expresses his attitude toward Lillian. It reveals, first, the Professor's admiration for his wife. The words "intense," "positive," "flaming," and "violent" attest to her strength, while the mention of a heraldic device connotes nobility, privilege, and respect. The assessment is not entirely admiring, however, for many of St. Peter's terms come from the vocabularies of war and technology. Here Lillian is characterized as strong in a more pejorative sense—strength as hardness. The metaphors of the die and stamp suggest unyielding resistance, insistent repetition. St. Peter pictures himself weary, beaten, obliterated by her stamp.

The mention of a chiselled surface provides further reinforcement, not only with the immediate image of cold stone and hard edges, but also in its muted suggestion of struggle, of an adversary relationship. (Compare chiselling stone with casting bronze, building clay.) In all these metaphors Lillian is portrayed as awesome, strong, stubborn, and dangerous. The final conceit suggests more specific criticisms of her character—the violence of her emotions and the transparence of her ambition.

The two figures of speech St. Peter employs to describe Lillian are thus immensely effective. They convey his admiration and awe, his distaste and defeat. I claim that these features indicate the Professor's attitude towards his wife. What do I mean by an attitude? Examples might include admiration, approval, dislike and disdain. Attitudes are intentional states (in Brentano's sense). Thus they are object directed; all attitudes are attitudes toward or attitudes about something or other. In addition, attitudes involve beliefs about their objects and convey evaluation of them. If I admire Jane because she is intelligent, capable, and sympathetic, then Jane is the object of my attitude, and my attitude is grounded in my beliefs about her character. Since intelligence, competence, and sympathy are traits we prize, my attitude conveys a favorable evaluation of Jane. Some of my beliefs about Jane might be mistaken. If so, my attitude is misplaced or inappropriate. Attitudes themselves are not classed as true or false. In sum, if we imagine a continuum of psychological states, attitudes occupy an intermediate ground between judgment and belief, on the one hand, and emotions and moods, on the other. Like emotions, attitudes are object-directed, non-propositional and evaluative. Yet attitudes are less visceral than emotions, less partisan, and less closely tied to distinctive behavioral manifestations. Returning to our example, the Professor's attitude towards Lillian is not conveyed by the bare factual claim that he takes her loves and hates to be violent. Thus it is not merely a belief or judgment about his wife. Nor is it a violent state which has overwhelmed him. The reflective mood of his extended metaphorical description indicates that he is not in the throes of a ravaging emotion. His psychological state lies between these poles.

My claim that metaphors express attitudes must be qualified in several respects. First, I do not claim that *all* metaphors serve this function, nor that they do so in all contexts. I would certainly be at a loss to determine the attitude conveyed by "The camel is the ship of the desert"! My claim is that sometimes metaphors express attitudes. And second, even in those cases where metaphors do convey attitude, I do not claim that we can always specify just which attitude is being expressed. The example discussed above is a case in point. The Professor's attitude towards Lillian is a complex attitude for which we have no standard name. It is not plain awe or unalloyed admiration. Despite our inability to name his attitude, I believe it is correct and illuminating to classify it as such. Finally, attitudes, like emotions and beliefs, can be unconscious. There may well be cases where someone has an attitude, expresses it in various ways (including metaphorical identifications of the attitude-object) yet doesn't know that this is so. Thus we are not always the best authorities about the attitudes we hold, reveal, express. Note that this accords with the claims made in Part I of this paper about knowledge and oppression. We do not always know when we are being oppressed; we can in fact become unwitting collaborators in our own oppression. (I do not, by the way, claim that the attitude St. Peter expresses toward his wife Lillian is a sexist one; it is simply a negative attitude, directed towards a woman.) . . .

INTENTIONAL TRANSCENDENCE

My concluding argument for this connection between metaphor and attitude appeals to what I shall (loosely) call structural considerations. I claim that there is an isomorphism between metaphor on the one hand and attitude on the other which makes metaphor a particularly apt vehicle for the expression of attitude. This isomorphism has to do with the logical structure of attitude and metaphor: in particular, with their irreducibility to belief and to literal talk, respectively. I shall call this shared trait intentional transcendence.

Consider one of the central questions about metaphors—their paraphrasability. Can the significance of a metaphor be completely spelled out? In the article "Aesthetic Problems of Modern Philosophy," Stanley Cavell argues that metaphors are paraphrasable. To prove his point, he proposes the following paraphrase of the metaphor "Juliet is the sun":

> Romeo means that Juliet is the warmth of his world; that his day begins with her; that only in her nourishment can he grow. And his declaration suggests that the moon, which other lovers use as emblems of their love, is merely her reflected light, and dead in comparison; and so on.

Cavell's "and so on" is crucial here. He qualifies his claim by noting that metaphors are paraphrasable in a manner "marked by its concluding sense of 'and so on.'" Thus Romeo does not mean that Juliet is like the sun in four respects and four respect only. His metaphor has further significance, further ramifications to be drawn out. For instance, that Juliet is the center of his universe. This richness is what some call the pregnancy of metaphor; it is what I mean by the phrase "intentional transcendence." A number of other writers call attention to this trait. For example, Max Black distinguishes a class of interaction metaphors which cannot be replaced by literal translations without loss of cognitive content. Philip Wheelwright distinguishes two forms of metaphor, one of which—diaphor— creates new meaning through presentational juxtaposition. Nelson Goodman's metaphorical account of metaphor (as the transfer of a schema to an alien realm, where the immigrant sometimes effects new organization and new associations) gives a picture of paraphrase which helps to explain its richness. Alan Tormey's subjunctive theory of metaphor also supports this view. Relations between tenor and vehicle can be spun out indefinitely because we can explore countless crannies of the possible world in which the counterfactual holds.

Consider now intentional transcendence in the psychological realm. Just as metaphors resist collapse into a finite set of literal sentences, so attitudes resist collapse into a finite set of grounding beliefs. All attitudes are belief-dependent. For example, to have an attitude of admiration towards Lauren Bacall, I must hold a number of factual beliefs about her (e.g. that she is the blonde actress in "To Have and Have Not," that she also appears in "Key Largo," that she was Bogart's wife). Such beliefs establish that my attitude is directed towards the proper object. There aren't any particular beliefs about Bacall such that I need to hold *those* beliefs in order to have an attitude directed towards her. I simply must have some collection of beliefs about her, some of which are accurate. [If all my beliefs about Bacall were false and applied instead to Ginger Rogers—e.g. "She's the brassy redheaded actress who danced with Fred Astaire"—then my attitude is not an attitude towards Lauren Bacall at all. It is an attitude towards Ginger Rogers about whom I have (at least) this false belief: that her name is Lauren Bacall.]

This dependence of attitude upon belief has been ably documented in the literature. Though some collection of Bacall-beliefs must be present in order to direct my admiration, these beliefs do not constitute my attitude. This is so because many of Bacall's detractors might hold the very same beliefs logically involved in my attitude. In addition to the beliefs which direct my attitude towards the appropriate object (in this case, Bacall) I hold additional beliefs which determine which attitude it is. Thus, if I think Bacall acts well, is beautiful and intelligent, then my attitude is one of admiration. If I think her a cheap brassy blonde with no acting skills, my attitude is instead one of disdain. Note that my admiration for Bacall does not reduce to this further set of beliefs about her. First, because other people might admire her without holding these particular beliefs. And second, because some might hold these same beliefs without admiring her. Nor can we reduce admiration to holding a preponderance of favorable beliefs, nor even to the single belief that its object is admirable. It is always possible to hold such beliefs about a person (object) yet not admire that person (object).

My point about these attitudes is this: they are no more reducible to the cluster of beliefs which ground them than metaphors are reducible to the set of sentences which provide a paraphrase. To proclaim Bacall stunning, quick, and talented is not yet to admire her; to cite ten ways in which Juliet resembles the sun is not yet to exhaust Shakespeare's metaphor. Thus metaphors and attitudes alike have a sort of intentional transcendence which accords them both richness and mystery. And this structural similarity suggests why metaphorical language might express attitudes more effectively than literal talk *or* wordless gestures. . . .

. . . If correct, my analysis explains not only how metaphorical language can hurt and offend, but also how it can flatter, comfort and soothe. It does so by conveying the various attitudes which are essential to our evaluations, enthusiasms, prejudices, and passions.

FRIEDRICH NIETZSCHE

Communication and Consciousness

FRIEDRICH NIETZSCHE (1844–1900) was a German philosopher who was given a professorship at the unheard-of age of twenty-four. Most of his fame came after his death, and during his professorship he became increasingly disgusted and embittered at the lack of interest in his work. He spent his last ten years in total insanity.

O N the "genius of the species."— The problem of consciousness (more precisely, of becoming conscious of something) confront us only when we begin to comprehend how we could dispense with it; and now physiology and the history of animals place us at the beginning of such comprehension (it took them two centuries to catch up with *Leibniz's* suspicion which soared ahead). For we could think, feel, will, and remember, and we could also "act" in every sense of that word, and yet none of all this would have to "enter our consciousness" (as one says metaphorically). The whole of life would be possible without, as it were, seeing itself in a mirror. Even now, for that matter, by far the greatest portion of our life actually takes place without this mirror effect; and this is true even of our thinking, feeling, and willing life, however offensive this may sound to older philosophers. *For what purpose,* then, any consciousness at all when it is in the main *superfluous?*

Now, if you are willing to listen to my answer and the perhaps extravagant surmise that it involves, it seems to me as if the subtlety and straight of consciousness always were proportionate to a man's (or animal's) *capacity for communication,* and as if this capacity in turn were proportionate to the *need for communication.* But this last point is not to be understood as if the individual human being who happens to be a master in communicating and making understandable his needs must also be most dependent on others in his needs. But it does seem to me as if it were that way when we consider whole races and chains of generations: Where need and distress have forced men for a long time to communicate and to understand each other quickly and subtly, the ultimate result is an excess of this strength and art of communication—as it were, a capacity that has gradually been accumulated and now waits for an heir who might squander it. (Those who are called artists are these heirs; so are orators, preachers, writers—all of them people who always come at the end of a long chain, "late born" every one of them in the best sense of that word and, as I have said, by their nature squanderers.)

Supposing that this observation is correct, I may now proceed to the surmise that *consciousness has developed only under the pressure of the need for communication;* that from the start it was needed and useful only between human beings (particularly between those who commanded and those who obeyed); and that it also developed only in proportion to the degree of this utility. Consciousness is really only a net of communication between human beings; it is only as such that it had to develop;

a solitary human being who lived like a beast of prey would not have needed it. That our actions, thoughts, feelings, and movements enter our own consciousness—at least a part of them—that is the result of a "must" that for a terribly long time lorded it over man. As the most endangered animal, he *needed* help and protection, he needed his peers, he had to learn to express his distress and to make himself understood; and for all of this he needed "consciousness" first of all, he needed to "know" himself what distressed him, he needed to "know" how he felt, he needed to "know" what he thought. For, to say it once more: Man, like every living being, thinks continually without knowing it; the thinking that rises to *consciousness* is only the smallest part of all this—the most superficial and worst part—for only this conscious thinking *takes the form of words, which is to say signs of communication,* and this fact uncovers the origin of consciousness.

In brief, the development of language and the development of consciousness (*not* of reason but merely of the way reason enters consciousness) go hand in hand. Add to this that not only language serves as a bridge between human beings but also a mien, a pressure, a gesture. The emergence of our sense impressions into our own consciousness, the ability to fix them and, as it were, exhibit them externally, increased proportionately with the need to communicate them to *others* by means of signs. The human being inventing signs is at the same time the human being who becomes ever more keenly conscious of himself. It was only as a social animal that man acquired self-consciousness—which he is still in the process of doing, more and more.

My idea, is, as you see, that consciousness does not really belong to man's individual existence but rather to his social or herd nature; that, as follows from this, it has developed subtlety only insofar as this is required by social or herd utility. Consequently, given the best will in the world to understand ourselves as individually as possible, "to know ourselves," each of us will always succeed in becoming conscious only of what is not individual but "average." Our thoughts themselves are continually governed by the character of consciousness—by the "genius of the species" that commands it—and translated back into the perspective of the herd. Fundamentally, all our actions are altogether incomparably personal, unique, and infinitely individual; there is no doubt of that. But as soon as we translate them into consciousness *they no longer seem to be.*

This is the essence of phenomenalism and perspectivism as *I* understand them: Owing to the nature of *animal consciousness,* the world of which we can become conscious is only a surface- and sign-world, a world that is made common and meaner; whatever becomes conscious *becomes* by the same token shallow, thin, relatively stupid, general, sign, herd signal; all becoming conscious involves a great and thorough corruption, falsification, reduction to superficialities, and generalization. Ultimately, the growth of consciousness becomes a danger; and anyone who lives among the most conscious Europeans even knows that it is a disease.

You will guess that it is not the opposition of subject and object that concerns me here: This distinction I leave to the epistemologists who have become entangled in the snares of grammar (the metaphysics of the people). It is even less the opposition of "thing-in-itself" and appearance; for we do not "know" nearly enough to be entitled to any such distinction. We simply lack any organ for knowledge, for "truth": we "know" (or believe or imagine) just as much as may be *useful* in the interests of the human herd, the species; and even what is here called "utility" is ultimately also a mere belief, something imaginary, and perhaps precisely that most calamitous stupidity of which we shall perish some day.

LEWIS CARROLL

Humpty Dumpty

LEWIS CARROL *(1832–1898), whose real name was Charles Lutwidge Dodgson, was an English mathematician and logician. His mother died when he went away to college, and he became increasingly drawn to the company of children, especially little girls. He was afflicted with a stammer which made him uncomfortable in the company of adults. His books* Alice in Wonderland *and* Through the Looking Glass *are two of the great children's books in English. He also published mathematical works.*

HOWEVER, the egg only got larger and larger, and more and more human: when she had come within a few yards of it, she saw that it had eyes and a nose and mouth; and, when she had come close to it, she saw clearly that it was HUMPTY DUMPTY himself. "It can't be anybody else!" she said to herself. "I'm as certain of it, as if his name were written all over his face!"

It might have been written a hundred times, easily, on that enormous face. Humpty Dumpty was sitting, with his legs crossed like a Turk, on the top of a high wall—such a narrow one that Alice quite wondered how he could keep his balance—and, as his eyes were steadily fixed in the opposite direction, and he didn't take the least notice of her, she thought he must be a stuffed figure, after all.

"And how exactly like an egg he is!" she said aloud, standing with her hands ready to catch him, for she was every moment expecting him to fall. . . .

"Don't stand chattering to yourself like that," Humpty Dumpty said, looking at her for the first time, "but tell me your name and your business."

"My *name* is Alice, but—"

"It's a stupid name enough!" Humpty Dumpty interrupted impatiently. "What does it mean?"

"*Must* a name mean something?" Alice asked doubtfully.

"Of course it must," Humpty Dumpty said with a short laugh: "*my* name means the shape I am—and a good handsome shape it is, too. With a name like yours, you might be any shape, almost."

"Why do you sit out here all alone?" said Alice, not wishing to begin an argument.

"Why, because there's nobody with me!" cried Humpty Dumpty. "Did you think I didn't know the answer to *that*? Ask another." . . .

"What a beautiful belt you've got on!" Alice suddenly remarked. . . . "At least," she corrected herself on second thoughts, "a beautiful cravat, I should have said—no, a belt, I mean—I beg your pardon!" she added in dismay, for Humpty Dumpty looked thoroughly offended, and she began to wish she hadn't chosen that subject. "If only I knew," she thought to herself, "which was neck and which was waist!"

Evidently Humpty Dumpty was very angry, though he said nothing for a minute or two. When he *did* speak again, it was in a deep growl.

"It is a —*most—provoking—*thing," he said at last, "when a person doesn't know a cravat from a belt!"

"I know it's very ignorant of me," Alice said, in so humble a tone that Humpty Dumpty relented.

"It's a cravat, child, and a beautiful one, as you say. It's a present from the White King and Queen. There now!"

"Is it really?" said Alice, quite pleased to find that she *had* chosen a good subject, after all.

"They gave it me," Humpty Dumpty continued thoughtfully, as he crossed one knee over the other and clasped his hand round it, "they gave it me—for an un-birthday present."

"I beg your pardon?" Alice said with a puzzled air.

"I'm not offended," said Humpty Dumpty.

"I mean, what *is* an un-birthday present?"

"A present given when it isn't your birthday, of course."

Alice considered a little. "I like birthday presents best," she said at last.

"You don't know what you're talking about!" cried Humpty Dumpty. "How many days are there in a year?"

"Three hundred and sixty-five," said Alice.

"And how many birthdays have you?"

"One."

"And if you take one from three hundred and sixty-five, what remains?"

"Three hundred and sixty-four, of course."

Humpty Dumpty looked doubtful. "I'd rather see that done on paper," he said.

Alice couldn't help smiling as she took out her memorandum-book, and worked the sum for him:

$$\begin{array}{r} 365 \\ \underline{1} \\ 364 \end{array}$$

. . . "[T]hat shows that there are three hundred and sixty-four days when you might get un-birthday presents—"

"Certainly," said Alice.

"And only *one* for birthday presents, you know. There's glory for you!"

"I don't know what you mean by 'glory,'" Alice said.

Humpty Dumpty smiled contemptuously. "Of course you don't—till I tell you. I meant 'there's a nice knock-down argument for you!'"

"But 'glory' doesn't mean 'a nice knock-down argument,'" Alice objected.

"When *I* use a word," Humpty Dumpty said, in rather a scornful tone, "it means just what I choose it to mean—neither more nor less."

"The question is," said Alice, "whether you *can* make words mean so many different things."

"The question is," said Humpty Dumpty, "which is to be master— that's all."

Alice was too much puzzled to say anything; so after a minute Humpty Dumpty began again. "They've a temper, some of them—particularly verbs: they're the proudest—adjectives you can do anything with but not verbs— however, *I* can manage the whole lot of them! Impenetrability! That's what *I* say!"

"Would you tell me, please," said Alice, "what that means?"

"Now you talk like a reasonable child," said Humpty Dumpty, looking very much pleased. "I meant by 'impenetrability' that we've had enough of that subject, and it would be just as well if you'd mention what you mean to do next, as I suppose you don't mean to stop here all the rest of your life."

"That's a great deal to make one word mean," Alice said in a thoughtful tone.

"When I make a word do a lot of work like that," said Humpty Dumpty, "I always pay it extra."

"Oh!" said Alice. She was too much puzzled to make any other remark.

"Ah, you should see 'em come round me of a Saturday night," Humpty Dumpty went on, wagging his head gravely from side to side, "for to get their wages, you know."

(Alice didn't venture to ask what he paid them with; and so you see I can't tell *you*.)

Part 4

The Dilemmas of Personhood

Chapter 8
Who Am I?

You have heard your mother tell the story a thousand times. One day, when you were very little, just past your second birthday, your parents went to visit Aunt Helen. You sat in the back seat, apparently asleep. Next to you your mother had placed a box of cupcakes, Aunt Helen's favorites. Having arrived, your mother went to get you and the cupcakes out of the car. At that point she discovered only you in the back seat, since you had managed in some way to consume every one of the cupcakes. Cooing and gurgling, you peered out from behind a mask of chocolate and crumbs.

Underlying stories such as this one is an assumption that only a philosopher would question seriously, namely, that there is such a thing as personal (or self) identity. Personal identity is what accounts for the fact that we all have childhoods, that once we were small, not very knowledgeable or emotionally complex, whereas now we are grown and full of complex thoughts, feelings, and beliefs. Philosophers' attempts to account for our persistence through time and through change fall into roughly three categories. First, there are those who explain personal identity in mentalistic terms. Our identity through time is considered to be a function of the continuity of our thoughts, beliefs, and feelings (sometimes referred to jointly as our "personality" or "character"). Second, there are those who explain personal identity in terms of the continuity of our bodies. Although the body that you have now is larger than the one you had when you were two years old, their "spatio-temporal" continuity provides the basis for your identity through time. Finally, some philosophers argue that personal identity is just an illusion. In fact, we don't persist through time and change.

The earliest and most familiar version of the view that personal identity can be explained in mentalistic terms has its origin in the religious belief in the existence of the soul. Although philosophers since Descartes have tended to substitute the term 'mind' for 'soul', the underlying idea is basically the same: What now makes you the same person as the one who overindulged in cupcakes many years ago is the persistence of your soul. This view has what many people consider the added advantage of allowing for the possibility of continued existence past the death of the body.

In the dialogue by John Perry, Sam Miller is a passionate advocate of what we will call the **Soul Theory.** He finds a formidable opponent, however, in Gretchen Weirob, who insists that her identity is a function of nothing more than the identity of her (live) body. We will call that view the **Body Theory.** Weirob is concerned to persuade Miller not so much that his belief in the existence of the soul is misguided, but rather that the soul, even if it exists, cannot be responsible for personal identity.

Although the soul has fallen into disrepute as a means for explaining personal identity, philosophers have been reluctant to abandon the spirit of the Soul Theory. That is, many philosophers would like to account for personal identity in terms that acknowledge our special human uniqueness. Our rich mental life distinguishes us from other animals, and we are all psychologically distinct from one another. Surely, then, our self-identity must be intimately tied to our mental characteristics. John Locke is a famous advocate of the view, usually called the **Memory Theory,** that personal identity is based on self-consciousness, in particular, on memories about one's former experiences. Just as you cannot think my thoughts and I cannot think yours, so, too, you cannot remember my experiences and I cannot remember yours. This unique relationship that each of us has to his or her former experiences guarantees the link between what are sometimes called "stages" of a person. Suppose that you are now remembering the day you learned to ride a bicycle. Since you *now* are remembering the experience as one that happened to you *then,* you are self-identical to the person who had that experience. One difficulty with the Memory Theory is that we forget many of our experiences. You don't, for example, remember eating the cupcakes when you were two. You probably don't remember what you had for lunch on July 25, 1987, nor what the first word of this chapter is. Locke needs to specify precisely how we are to explain the connection between our present selves and those forgotten stages of our former selves.

Another difficulty with the Memory Theory is that our memories are not always accurate. For example, you swear that you left the sponge in the sink; you remember doing so very clearly. When you later find it in the refrigerator, you realize that you only *seemed* to remember leaving it in the sink. Your memory was merely apparent, not genuine. Similarly, we have all heard of people who believe that they are Abraham Lincoln, Jesus Christ, even Janis Joplin. What seem to them to be real memories cannot be. Yet, if it is only genuine memories that guarantee the link between the stages of a person, we need to determine which memories are the genuine ones. Unfortunately, the most obvious way to distinguish genuine from apparent memories is by pointing out that a genuine memory is a memory of an experience actually had by the rememberer. The person who is having the memory must be the same as the person who had the experience. But in distinguishing genuine from apparent memory in this way we have presupposed the existence of a persisting, self-identical person. We cannot use the concept of memory to explain personal identity if the only way to explain memory is by appealing to the concept of personal identity. As attractive as the Memory Theory might initially seem to be, it leaves us with this discouragingly large problem.

This problem, sometimes referred to as the "problem of circularity," is alluded to in the selection by Meredith W. Michaels. Much of the contemporary debate over personal identity centers around an attempt to avoid the circularity problem. That is, philosophers want to provide a noncircular way of distinguishing between genuine and apparent memories. The **Brain Theory,** discussed by Michaels, is one such attempt. Basically, the Brain Theory argues that "whither my brain goes, there go I." As you will see, the Brain Theory and its principal rival, the Body Theory, encourage some bizarre speculations about the results of imagined "brain transplants" (alternatively called "body transplants"). Justin Leiber's story provides a glimpse into a future where such practices are an ordinary part of life. Although stories like his appear fanciful, they provoke us to consider just what we think *is* responsible for our identity through time.

Long ago, David Hume came to the conclusion that nothing is responsible for our identity through time because, strictly speaking, it is only a "fiction." If we look inward in the hopes of finding a source of identity, all we find is an array of disconnected and distinct "perceptions" (that is, ideas). Our desire to forge them into a coherent, temporally continuous whole is so strong that we simply invent one and call it a "self." Hume's argument is a masterpiece of philosophical gymnastics, so beware.

Most theories of personal identity focus on our relationship to our past selves. Alasdair MacIntyre suggests that the tendency of philosophers to ignore our relationship to our future selves creates a lopsided picture of personal identity. He encourages us to see ourselves as characters in a number of ongoing stories, characters whose lives are lived according to a variety of goals or purposes. The form of our lives is determined in part by the goals toward which we are heading. If so, he claims, then the criterion of coherence for persons ought not be identity, but rather unity. Right now, you are a character in the story of college students in late-twentieth-century America. As a result of being in that story, there are certain characteristics that you have and others that you don't have. The actions that you perform are properly understood only relative to the fact that you currently inhabit the story of college students. Even when you are lying in a daze on the beach, we (and you) can only account for your (in)action by appealing to your fatigue and desire for a break from studying. The unity and coherence of your "self" is thus a function of its place in a story or a set of interlocking stories.

Anthony Appiah agrees with MacIntyre that philosophical discussion of personal identity has focused too narrowly on what Appiah calls "metaphysical" as opposed to "ethical" identity. But he is particularly concerned to explain how race, gender, and ethnicity figure differently in determining the relationship between ethical and metaphysical identity. How, he asks, might changing one's sex characteristics (as in a sex-change operation) affect one's identity, as opposed to changing one's racial characteristics (perhaps by plastic surgery, hair alteration, etc.)? The difference between the cases, he argues, is a result of our differing cultural views about how race and gender are related to a person's true or essential self.

The problem of personal identity is particularly troubling because it appears so clear that we do indeed persist through time. Surely, it is absurd to suppose that the person who began reading this chapter only a few minutes ago no longer exists. Aren't you that very same person? Of course you are. But if it is so obvious that one and the same person is born, lives a life, and eventually dies, why is it so difficult for philosophers to explain personal identity? The problem of personal identity is a paradigm case of the tension between the appeal of ordinary experience and the demands of philosophy.

JOHN PERRY

The First Night

JOHN PERRY *teaches philosophy at Stanford University. He specializes in philosophy of language and metaphysics. Among his publications are* Situation Semantics *(with John Barwise) and* A Dialogue on Personal Identity and Immortality.

THIS is a record of conversations of Gretchen Weirob, a teacher of philosophy at a small midwestern college, and two of her friends. The conversations took place in her hospital room on the three nights before she died from injuries sustained in a motorcycle accident. Sam Miller is a chaplain and a long-time friend of Weirob's; Dave Cohen is a former student of hers.

COHEN

I can hardly believe what you say, Gretchen. You are lucid and do not appear to be in great pain. And yet you say things are hopeless?

WEIROB

These devices can keep me alive for another day or two at most. Some of my vital organs have been injured beyond anything the doctors know how to repair, apart from certain rather radical measures I have rejected. I am not in much pain. But as I understand it that is not a particularly good sign. My brain was uninjured and I guess that's why I am as lucid as I ever am. The whole situation is a bit depressing, I fear. But here's Sam Miller. Perhaps he will know how to cheer me up.

MILLER

Good evening, Gretchen. Hello, Dave. I guess there's not much point in beating around the bush, Gretchen; the medics tell me you're a goner. Is there anything I can do to help?

WEIROB

Crimenetley, Sam! You deal with the dying every day. Don't you have anything more comforting to say than "Sorry to hear you're a goner"?

MILLER

Well, to tell you the truth, I'm a little at a loss for what to say to
you. Most people I deal with are believers like I am. We
talk of the prospects for survival. I give assurance that God,
who is just and merciful, would not permit such a travesty
as that our short life on this earth should be the end of
things. But you and I have talked about religious and
philosophical issues for years. I have never been able to
find in you the least inclination to believe in God; indeed,
it's a rare day when you are sure that your friends have
minds or that you can see your own hand in front of your
face, or that there is any reason to believe that the sun will
rise tomorrow. How can I hope to comfort you with the
prospect of life after death, when I know you will regard it
as having no probability whatsoever?

WEIROB

I would not require so much to be comforted, Sam. Even the
possibility of something quite improbable can be
comforting, in certain situations. When we used to play
tennis, I beat you no more than one time in twenty. But this
was enough to establish the possibility of beating you on
any given occasion, and by focusing merely on the
possibility I remained eager to play. Entombed in a secure
prison, thinking our situation quite hopeless, we may find
unutterable joy in the information that there is, after all, the
slimmest possibility of escape. Hope provides comfort and
hope does not always require probability. But we must
believe that what we hope for is at least possible. So I will
set an easier task for you. Simply persuade me that my
survival after the death of this body, is *possible,* and I
promise to be comforted. Whether you succeed or not, your
attempts will be a diversion, for you know I like to talk
philosophy more than anything else.

MILLER

But what is possibility, if not reasonable probability?

WEIROB

I do not mean possible in the sense of likely, or even in the sense
of conforming to the known laws of physics or biology. I
mean possible only in the weakest sense—of being
conceivable, given the unavoidable facts. Within the next
couple of days, this body will die. It will be buried and it

will rot away. I ask that, given these facts, you explain to
me how it even makes *sense* to talk of me continuing to
exist. Just explain to me what it is I am to *imagine,* when I
imagine surviving, that is consistent with these facts, and I
shall be comforted.

MILLER

But then what is there to do? There are many conceptions of
immortality, of survival past the grave, which all seem to
make good sense. Surely not the possibility, but only the
probability can be doubted. Take your choice! Christians
believe in life, with a body, in some Hereafter—the details
vary, of course, from sect to sect. There is the Greek idea of
the body as a prison, from which we escape at death—so
that we have continued life without a body. Then there are
conceptions in which, so to speak, we merge with the flow
of being—

WEIROB

I must cut short your lesson in comparative religion. Survival
means surviving, no more, no less. I have no doubts that I
shall merge with being; plants will take root in my remains,
and the chemicals that I am will continue to make their
contribution to life. I am enough of an ecologist to be
comforted. But survival, if it is anything, must offer
comforts of a different sort, the comforts of *anticipation.*
Survival means that tomorrow, or sometime in the future,
there will be someone who will experience, who will see
and touch and smell—or at the very least, think and reason
and remember. And this person will be *me.* This person will
be related to me in such a way that it is correct for me to
anticipate, to look forward to, those future experiences.
And I am related to her in such a way that it will be right
for her to remember what I have thought and done, to feel
remorse for what I have done wrong, and pride in what I
have done right. And the only relation that supports
anticipation and memory in this way, is simply *identity.* For
it is never correct to anticipate, as happening to oneself,
what will happen to someone else, is it? Or to remember, as
one's own thoughts and deeds, what someone else did? So,
don't give me merger with being, or some such nonsense.
Give me identity, or let's talk about baseball or fishing—
but I'm sorry to get so emotional. I react strongly when
words which mean one thing are used for another—when
one talks about survival, but does not mean to say that the
same person will continue to exist. It's such a sham!

MILLER

I'm sorry. I was just trying to stay in touch with the times, if you
want to know the truth, for when I read modern theology or
talk to my students who have studied Eastern religions, the
notion of survival simply as continued existence of the
same person seems out of date. Merger with Being! Merger
with Being! That's all I hear. My own beliefs are quite
simple, if somewhat vague. I think you will live again—
with or without a body, I don't know—I draw comfort from
my belief that you and I will be together again, after I also
die. We will communicate, somehow. We will continue to
grow spiritually. That's what I believe, as surely as I
believe that I am sitting here. For I don't know how God
could be excused, if this small sample of life is all that we
are allotted; I don't know why He should have created us, if
these few years of toil and torment are the end of it—

WEIROB

Remember our deal, Sam. You don't have to convince me that
survival is probable, for we both agree you would not get to
first base. You have only to convince me that it is possible.
The only condition is that it be real survival we are talking
about, not some up-to-date ersatz survival, which simply
amounts to what any ordinary person would call totally
ceasing to exist.

MILLER

I guess I just miss the problem, then. Of course, it's possible. You
just continue to exist after your body dies. What's to be
defended or explained? You want details? Okay. Two
people meet a thousand years from now, in a place that may
or may not be part of this physical universe. I am one and
you are the other. So you must have survived. Surely you
can imagine that. What else is there to say?

WEIROB

But in a few days *I* will quit breathing, *I* will be put into a coffin,
I will be buried. And in a few months or a few years *I* will
be reduced to so much humus. That, I take it, is obvious, is
given. How then can you say that I am one of these persons
a thousand years from now? Suppose I took this box of
Kleenex and lit fire to it. It is reduced to ashes and I smash
the ashes and flush them down the john. Then I say to you,
go home and on the shelf will be *that very box of Kleenex.*
It has survived! Wouldn't that be absurd? What sense could

you make if it? And yet that is just what you say to me. I
will rot away. And then, a thousand years later, there I will
be. What sense does that make?

MILLER

There could be an *identical* box of Kleenex at your home, one
just like it in every respect. And, in this sense, there is not
difficulty in there being someone identical to you in the
Hereafter, though your body has rotted away.

WEIROB

You are playing with words again. There could be an *exactly
similar* box of Kleenex on my shelf. We sometimes use
"identical" to mean "exactly similar," as when we speak of
"identical twins." But I am using "identical" in a way in
which *identity* is the condition of memory and correct
anticipation. If I am told that tomorrow, though I will be
dead, someone else that looks and sounds and thinks just
like me will be alive—would that be comforting? Could I
correctly *anticipate* having her experiences? Would it make
sense for me to fear her pains and look forward to her
pleasures? Would it be right for her to feel remorse at the
harsh way I am treating you? Of course not. Similarity,
however exact, is not identity. I use identity to mean there
is but one thing. If I am to survive, there must be one
person who lies in this bed now, and who talks to someone
in your Hereafter ten or a thousand years from now. After
all, what comfort could there be in the notion of a heavenly
imposter, walking around getting credit for the few good
things I have done?

MILLER

I'm sorry. I see that I was simply confused. Here is what I should
have said. If you were merely a live human body—as the
Kleenex box is merely cardboard and glue in a certain
arrangement—then the death of your body would be the
end of you. But surely you are more than that,
fundamentally more than that. What is fundamentally you
is not your body, but your soul or self or mind.

WEIROB

Do you mean these words, "soul," "self," or "mind" to come to
the same thing?

MILLER

Perhaps distinctions could be made, but I shall not pursue them
   now. I mean the nonphysical and nonmaterial aspects of
   you, your consciousness. It is this that I get at with these
   words, and I don't think any further distinction is relevant.

WEIROB

Consciousness? I am conscious, for a while yet. I see, I hear, I
   think, I remember. But "to be conscious"—that is a verb.
   What is the subject of the verb, the thing which is
   conscious? Isn't it just this body, the same object that is
   overweight, injured, and lying in bed?—and which will be
   buried and not be conscious in a day or a week at the most?

MILLER

As you are a philosopher, I would expect you to be less muddled
   about these issues. Did Descartes not draw a clear
   distinction between the body and the mind, between that
   which is overweight, and that which is conscious? Your
   mind or soul is immaterial, lodged in your body while you
   are on earth. The two are intimately related but not
   identical. Now clearly, what concerns us in survival is your
   mind or soul. It is this which must be identical to the person
   before me now, and to the one I expect to see in a thousand
   years in heaven.

WEIROB

So I am not really this body, but a soul or mind or spirit? And this
   soul cannot be seen or felt or touched or smelt? That is
   implied, I take it, by the fact that it is immaterial?

MILLER

That's right. Your soul sees and smells, but cannot be seen
   or smelt.

WEIROB

Let me see if I understand you. You would admit that I am the
   very same person with whom you had lunch last week
   at Dorsey's?

MILLER

Of course you are.

WEIROB

Now when you say I am the same person, if I understand you, that is not a remark about this body you see and could touch and I fear can smell. Rather it is a remark about a soul, which you cannot see or touch or smell. The fact that the same body that now lies in front of you on the bed was across the table from you at Dorsey's—that would not mean that the same *person* was present on both occasions, if the same soul were not. And if, through some strange turn of events, the same soul were present on both occasions, but lodged in different bodies, then it *would* be the same person. Is that right?

MILLER

You have understood me perfectly. But surely, you understood all of this before!

WEIROB

But wait. I can repeat it, but I'm not sure I understand it. If you cannot see or touch or in any way perceive my soul, what makes you think the one you are confronted with now *is* the very same soul you were confronted with at Dorsey's

MILLER

But I just explained. To say it is the same soul and to say it is the same person, are the same. And, of course, you are the same person you were before. Who else would you be if not yourself? You *were* Gretchen Weirob, and you *are* Gretchen Weirob.

WEIROB

But how do you know you are talking to Gretchen Weirob at all, and not someone else, say Barbara Walters or even Mark Spitz!

MILLER

Well, it's just obvious. I can see who I am talking to.

WEIROB

But all you can see is my body. You can see, perhaps, that the same body is before you now that was before you last week at Dorsey's. But you have just said that Gretchen Weirob is not a body but a soul. In judging that the same person is

before you now as was before you then, you must be
making a judgment about souls—which, you said, cannot
be seen or touched or smelt or tasted. And so, I repeat, how
do you know?

MILLER

Well, I *can* see that it is the same body before me now that was
across the table at Dorsey's. And I know that the same
soul is connected with the body now that was connected
with it before. That's how I know it's you. I see no
difficulty in the matter.

WEIROB

You reason on the principle, "Same body, same self,"

MILLER

Yes.

WEIROB

And would you reason conversely also? If there were in this bed
Barbara Walters' body—that is, the body you see every
night on the news—would you infer that it was not me,
Gretchen Weirob, in the bed?

MILLER

Of course I would. How would you have come by Barbara
Walters' body?

WEIROB

But then merely extend this principle to Heaven, and you will see
that your conception of survival is without sense. Surely
this very body, which will be buried and as I must so often
repeat, *rot away,* will not be in your Hereafter. Different
body, different person. Or do you claim that a body can rot
away on earth, and then still wind up somewhere else?
Must I bring up the Kleenex box again?

MILLER

No, I do not claim that. But I also do not extend a principle,
found reliable on earth, to such a different situation as is
represented by the Hereafter. That a correlation between
bodies and souls has been found on earth does not make it
inconceivable or impossible that they should separate.

Principles found to work in one circumstance may not be
assumed to work in vastly altered circumstances. January
and snow go together here, and one would be a fool to
expect otherwise. But the principle does not apply in
southern California.

WEIROB

So the principle, "same body, same soul," is a well-confirmed
regularity, not something you know "a priori."

MILLER

By "a priori" you philosophers mean something which can be
known without observing what actually goes on in the
world—as I can know that two plus two equals four just by
thinking about numbers, and that no bachelors are married,
just by thinking about the meaning of 'bachelor'?

WEIROB

Yes.

MILLER

Then you are right. If it was part of the meaning of "same body"
that wherever we have the same body we have the same
soul, it would have to obtain universally, in Heaven as well
as on earth. But I just claim it is a generalization we know
by observation on earth, and it need not automatically
extend to Heaven.

WEIROB

But where do you get this principle? It simply amounts to a
correlation between being confronted with the same body
and being confronted with the same soul. To establish such
a correlation in the first place, surely one must have some
other means of judging sameness of soul. You do not have
such a means; your principle is without foundation; either
you really do not know the person before you now is
Gretchen Weirob, the very same person you lunched with at
Dorsey's, or what you do know has nothing to do with
sameness of some immaterial soul.

MILLER

Hold on, hold on. You know I can't follow you when you start
spitting out arguments like that. Now what is this terrible
fallacy I'm supposed to have committed?

WEIROB

I'm sorry. I get carried away. Here—by way of a peace
     offering—have one of the chocolates Dave brought.

MILLER

Very tasty. Thank you.

WEIROB

Now why did you choose that one?

MILLER

Because it had a certain swirl on the top which shows that it is
     a caramel.

WEIROB

That is, a certain sort of swirl is correlated with a certain type of
     filling—the swirls with caramel, the rosettes with orange,
     and so forth.

MILLER

Yes. When you put it that way, I see an analogy. Just as I judged
     that the filling would be the same in this piece as in the last
     piece that I ate with such a swirl, so I judge that the soul
     with which I am conversing is the same as the last soul with
     which I conversed when sitting across from that body. We
     see the outer wrapping and infer what is inside.

WEIROB

But how did you come to realize that swirls of that sort and
     caramel insides were so associated?

MILLER

Why, from eating a great many of them over the years.
     Whenever I bit into a candy with that sort of swirl,
     it was filled with caramel.

WEIROB

Could you have established the correlation had you never been
     allowed to bite into a candy and never seen what happened
     when someone else bit into one? You could have formed
     the hypothesis, "same swirl, same filling." But could you
     have ever established it?

MILLER

It seems not.

WEIROB

So your inference, in a particular case, to the identity of filling
from the identity of swirl would be groundless?

MILLER

Yes, it would. I think I see what is coming.

WEIROB

I'm sure you do. Since you can never, so to speak, bite into
my soul, can never see or touch it, you have no way of
testing your hypothesis that sameness of body means
sameness of self.

MILLER

I dare say you are right. But now I'm a bit lost. What is supposed
to follow from all of this?

WEIROB

If, as you claim, identity of persons consisted in identity of
immaterial unobservable souls, then judgments of personal
identity of the sort we make every day whenever we greet a
friend or avoid a pest are really judgments about such souls.

MILLER

Right.

WEIROB

But if such judgments were really about souls, they would all be
groundless and without foundation. For we have no direct
method of observing sameness of soul, and so—and this is
the point made by the candy example—we can have no
indirect method either.

MILLER

That seems fair.

WEIROB

But our judgments about persons are not simply groundless
and silly, so we must not be judging of immaterial souls
after all.

MILLER

Your reasoning has some force. But I suspect the problem lies in
my defense of my position, and not the position itself. Look
here—there *is* a way to test the hypothesis of a correlation
after all. When I entered the room, I expect you to react just
as you did—argumentatively and skeptically. Had the
person with this body reacted completely differently
perhaps I would have been forced to conclude it was not
you. For example, had she complained about not being able
to appear on the six o'clock news, and missing Harry
Reasoner, and so forth, I might eventually have been
persuaded it was Barbara Walters, and not you. Similarity
of psychological characteristics—a person's attitudes,
beliefs, memories, prejudices, and the like—is observable.
These are correlated with identity of body on the one side,
and of course with sameness of soul on the other. So the
correlation between body and soul can be established after
all by this intermediate link.

WEIROB

And how do you know that?

MILLER

Know what?

WEIROB

That where we have sameness of psychological characteristics,
we have sameness of soul.

MILLER

Well, now you are really being just silly. The soul or mind is just
that which is responsible for one's character, memory,
belief. These are aspects of the mind, just as one's height,
weight, and appearance are aspects of the body.

WEIROB

Let me grant for the sake of argument that belief, character,
memory, and so forth are states of mind. That is, I suppose,
I grant that what one thinks and feels is due to the states
one's mind is in at that time. And I shall even grant that a
mind is an immaterial thing—though I harbor the gravest
doubts that this is so. I do not see how it follows that
similarity of such traits requires, or is evidence to the
slightest degree, for identity of the mind or soul.

Let me explain my point with an analogy. If we were to walk out
of this room, down past the mill and out towards Wilbur,
what would we see?

MILLER

We would come to the Blue River, among other things.

WEIROB

And how would you recognize the Blue River? I mean, of course
if you left from here, you would scarcely expect to hit the
Platte or Niobrara. But suppose you were actually lost, and
came across the Blue River in your wandering, just at that
point where an old dam partly blocks the flow. Couldn't
you recognize it?

MILLER

Yes, I'm sure as soon as I saw that part of the river I would again
know where I was.

WEIROB

And how would you recognize it?

MILLER

Well, the turgid brownness of the water, the sluggish flow, the
filth washed up on the banks, and such.

WEIROB

In a word, the states of the water which makes up the river at the
time you see it.

MILLER

Right.

WEIROB

If you saw blue clean water, with bass jumping, you would know
it wasn't the Blue River.

MILLER

Of course.

WEIROB

So you expect, each time you see the Blue, to see the water,
    which makes it up, in similar states—not always exactly
    the same, for sometimes it's a little dirtier, but by and
    large similar.

MILLER

Yes, but what do you intend to make of this?

WEIROB

Each time you see the Blue, it consists of *different* water. The
    water that was in it a month ago may be in Tuttle Creek
    Reservoir or in the Mississippi or in the Gulf of Mexico by
    now. So the *similarity* of states of water, by which you
    judge the sameness of river, does not require *identity* of the
    water which is in those states at these various times.

MILLER

And?

WEIROB

And so just because you judge as to personal identity by
    reference to similarity of states of mind, it does not follow
    that the mind, or soul, is the same in each case. My point is
    this. For all you know, the immaterial soul which you think
    is lodged in my body might change from day to day, from
    hour to hour, from minute to minute, replaced each time by
    another soul psychologically similar. You cannot see it or
    touch it, so how would you know?

MILLER

Are you saying I don't really know who you are?

WEIROB

Not at all. *You* are the one who say personal identity consists in
    sameness of this immaterial, unobservable, invisible,
    untouchable soul. I merely point out that *if* it did consist in
    that, you *would* have no idea who I am. Sameness of body
    would not necessarily mean sameness of person. Sameness
    of psychological characteristics would not necessarily mean
    sameness of person. I am saying that if you do know who I
    am then you are wrong that personal identity consists in
    sameness of immaterial soul.

MILLER

I see. But wait. I believe my problem is that I simply forgot a
main tenet of my theory. The correlation can be established
in my own case. I know that *my* soul and my body are
intimately and consistently found together. From this one
case I can generalize, at least as concerns life in this world,
that sameness of body is a reliable sign of sameness of soul.
This leaves me free to regard it as intelligible, in the case of
death, that the link between the particular soul and the
particular body it has been joined with is broken.

WEIROB

This would be quite an extrapolation, wouldn't it, from one case
directly observed, to a couple of billion in which only the
body is observed? For I take it that we are in the habit of
assuming, for every person now on earth, as well as those
who have already come and gone, that the principle "one
body, one soul" is in effect.

MILLER

This does not seem an insurmountable obstacle. Since there is
nothing special about my case, I assume the arrangement I
find in it applies universally until given some reason to
believe otherwise. And I never have been.

WEIROB

Let's let that pass. I have another problem that is more serious.
How is it that you know in you own case that there is a
single soul which has been so consistently connected with
your body?

MILLER

Now you really cannot be serious, Gretchen. How can I doubt
that I am the same person I was? Is there anything more
clear and distinct, less susceptible to doubt? How do you
expect me to prove anything to you, when you are capable
of denying my own continued existence from second to
second? Without knowledge of our identity, everything we
think and do would be senseless. How could I think if I did
not suppose that the person who begins my thought is the
one who completes it? When I act, do I not assume that the
person who forms the intention is the very one who
performs the action?

WEIROB

But I grant that a single *person* has been associated with your
body since you were born. The question is whether one
immaterial soul has been so associated—or more precisely,
whether you are in a position to know it. You believe that a
judgment that one and the same person has had your body
all these many years is a judgment that one and the same
immaterial soul has been lodged in it. I say that such
judgments concerning the soul are totally mysterious, and
that if our knowledge of sameness of persons consisted in
knowledge of sameness of immaterial soul, it too would be
totally mysterious. To point out, as you do, that it is not
mysterious, but perhaps the most secure knowledge we
have, the foundation of all reason and action, is simply to
make the point that it cannot consist of knowledge of
identity of an immaterial soul.

MILLER

You have simply asserted, and not established, that my judgment
that a single soul has been lodged in my body these many
years is mysterious.

WEIROB

Well, consider these possibilities. One is that a single soul, one
and the same, has been with this body I call mine since it
was born. The other is that one soul was associated with it
until five years ago and then another, psychologically
similar, inheriting all the old memories and beliefs, took
over. A third hypothesis is that every five years a new soul
takes over. A fourth is that every five minutes a new soul
takes over. The most radical is that there is a constant flow
of souls through this body, each psychologically similar to
the preceding, as there is a constant flow of water
molecules down the Blue. What evidence do I have that the
first hypothesis, the "single soul hypothesis" is true, and
not one of the others? Because I am the same person I was
five minutes or five years ago? But the issue in question is
simply whether from sameness or person, which isn't in
doubt, we can infer sameness of soul. Sameness of body?
But how do I establish a stable relationship between soul
and body? Sameness of thoughts and sensations? But they
are in constant flux. By the nature of the case, if the soul
cannot be observed it cannot be observed to be the same.
Indeed, no sense has ever been assigned to the phrase

"same soul." Nor could any sense be attached to it! One
would have to say what a single soul looked like or felt
like, how an encounter with a single soul at different times
differed from encounters with different souls. But this can
hardly be done, since a soul according to your conception
doesn't look or feel like *anything* at all. And so of course
"souls" can afford no principle of identity. And so they
cannot be used to bridge the gulf between my existence
now and my existence in the hereafter.

MILLER

Do you doubt the existence of your own soul?

WEIROB

I haven't based my argument on there being no immaterial souls
of the sort you describe, but merely on their total
irrelevance to questions of personal identity, and so to
questions of personal survival. I do indeed harbor grave
doubts whether there are any immaterial souls of the sort to
which you appeal. Can we have a notion of a soul unless
we have a notion of the *same* soul? But I hope you do not
think that means I doubt my own existence. I think I lie
here, overweight and conscious. I think you can see me, not
just some outer wrapping, for I think I am just a live human
body. But that is not the basis of my argument. I give you
these souls. I merely observe that they can by their nature
provide no principle of personal identity.

MILLER

I admit I have no answer.

I'm afraid I do not comfort you, though I have perhaps provided
you with some entertainment. Emerson said that a little
philosophy turns one away from religion, but that deeper
understanding brings one back. I know no one who has
thought so long and hard about philosophy as you have.
Will it never lead you back to a religious frame of mind?

WEIROB

My former husband used to say that a little philosophy turns
one away from religion, and more philosophy makes one
a pain in the neck. Perhaps he was closer to the truth
than Emerson.

MILLER

Perhaps he was. But perhaps by tomorrow night I will have come
up with a better argument.

WEIROB

I hope I live to hear it.

JOHN LOCKE

Of Identity and Diversity

*JOHN LOCKE (1632–1704) taught philosophy at Oxford until he earned his medical
degree. He devoted considerable time to politics and his two* Treatises on Government
*were highly influential in establishing the theoretical grounds of the U.S. Constitution.
Not only is he the founder of modern political liberalism, his* Essay Concerning
Human Understanding *initiated what has come to be known as British empiricism.*

*P*ERSONAL *identity.*—To find wherein personal identity consists, we must consider what "person" stands for; which I think, is a thinking intelligent being, that has reason and reflection, and can consider itself as itself, the same thinking thing, in different times and places; which it does only by that consciousness which is inseparable from thinking, and it seems to me essential to it: it being impossible for any one to perceive, without perceiving that he does perceive. When we see, hear, smell, taste, feel, meditate, or will any thing, we know that we do so. Thus it is always as to our present sensations and perceptions: and by this every one is to himself that which he calls "self"; it not being considered, in this case, whether the same self be continued in the same or diverse substances. For since consciousness always accompanies thinking, and it is that that makes every one to be what he calls "self," and thereby distinguishes himself from all other thinking things; in this alone consists personal identity, *i.e.,* the sameness of a rational being: and as far as this consciousness can be extended backwards to any past action or thought, so far reaches the identity of that person; it is the same self now it was then; and it is by the same self with this present one that now reflects on it, that that action was done.

Consciousness makes personal identity.—But it is farther inquired, whether it be the same identical substance? This, few would think they had reason to doubt of, if these perceptions, with their consciousness, always remained present in the mind, whereby the same thinking thing would be always consciously present, and, as would be thought, evidently the same to itself. But that which seems to make the difficulty is this, that this consciousness being interrupted always by forgetfulness, there being no moment of our lives wherein we have the whole train of all our past actions before our eyes in one view: but even the best memories losing the sight of one part whilst they are viewing another; and we sometimes, and that the greatest part of our lives, not reflecting on our past selves, being intent on our present thoughts, and, in sound sleep, having no thoughts at all, or at least, none with that consciousness which remarks our waking thoughts: I say, in all these cases, our consciousness being interrupted, and we losing the sight of our past selves, doubts are raised whether we are the same thinking thing, *i.e.,* the same substance, or no? which, however reasonable or unreasonable, concerns not personal identity at all: the question being, what makes the same person? and not, whether it be the same identical substance which always thinks in the same person? which in this case matters not at all; different substances, by the same consciousness (where they do partake in it), being united into one person, as well as different bodies by the same life are united into one animal, whose identity is preserved, in that change of substance, by the unity of one continued life. For it being the same consciousness that makes a man be himself to himself, personal identity depends on that only, whether it be annexed solely to one individual substance, or can be continued in a succession of several substances. For as far as any intelligent being can repeat the idea of any past action with the same consciousness it had of it at first, and with the same consciousness it has of any present action; so far it is the same personal self. For it is by the consciousness it has of its present thoughts and actions that it is self to itself now, and so will be the same self, as far as the same consciousness can extend to actions past or to come; and would be by distance of time, or change of substance, no more two persons than a man be two men, by wearing other clothes to-day than he did yesterday, with a long or short sleep between: the same consciousness uniting those distant actions into the same person, whatever substance contributed to their production.

Personal identity in change of substances.—That is so, we have some kind of evidence in our very bodies, all whose particles—whilst vitally united to this same thinking conscious self, so that we feel when they are touched, and are affected by and conscious of good or harm that happens to them—are a part of ourselves; *i.e.,* of our thinking conscious self. Thus the limbs of his body is to every one a part of himself: he sympathises and is concerned for them. Cut off an hand and thereby separate it from that consciousness he had of its heat, cold, and other affections, and it is then no longer a part of that which is himself, any more than the remotest part of matter. Thus we see the substance, whereof personal self consisted at one time, may be varied at another, without the change of personal identity; there being no question about the same person, though the limbs, which but now were a part of it, be cut off.

Whether in the change of thinking substances.—But the question is, Whether, if the same substance which thinks be changed, it can be the same person, or remaining the same, it can be different persons?

And to this I answer, First, This can be no question at all to those who place thought in a purely material, animal constitution, void of an immaterial substance. For, whether their supposition be true or no, it is plain they conceive personal identity preserved in something else than identity of substance; as animal identity is preserved in identity of life, and not of substance. And therefore those who place thinking in an immaterial substance only, before they can come to deal with these men, must show why personal identity cannot be preserved in the change of immaterial substances, or variety of particular immaterial substances, as well as animal identity is preserved in the change of material substances, or variety of particular bodies: unless they will say, it is one immaterial spirit that makes the same life in brutes, as it is one immaterial spirit that makes the same person in men, which the Cartesians at least will not admit, for fear of making brutes thinking things too.

But next, as to the first part of the question, Whether, if the same thinking substance (supposing immaterial substances only to think) be changed, it can be the same person? I answer, That cannot be resolved but by those who know what kind of substances they are that do think, and whether the consciousness of past actions can be transferred from one thinking substance to another. I grant, were the same consciousness the same individual action, it could not; but it being but a present representation of a past action, why it may not be possible that *that* may be represented to the mind to have been *which* really never was, will remain to be shown. And therefore how far the consciousness of past actions is annexed to any individual agent, so that another cannot possibly have it, will be hard for us to determine, till we know what kind of action it is that cannot be done without a reflex act of perception accompanying it, and how

performed by thinking substances who cannot think without being conscious of it. But that which we call "the same consciousness" not being the same individual act, why one intellectual substance may not have represented to it as done by itself what it never did, and was perhaps done by some other agent; why, I say, such a representation may not possibly be without reality of matter of fact, as well as several representations in dreams are, which yet, whilst dreaming, we take for true, will be difficult to conclude from the nature of things. And that it never is so, will by us (till we have clearer views of the nature of thinking substances) be best resolved into the goodness of God, who, as far as the happiness or misery of any of his sensible creatures is concerned in it, will not by a fatal error of theirs transfer from one to another that consciousness which draws reward or punishment with it. How far this may be an argument against those who would place thinking in a system of fleeting animal spirits, I leave to be considered. But yet, to return to the question before us, it must be allowed, that if the same consciousness (which, as has been shown, is quite a different thing from the same numerical figure or motion in the body) can be transferred from one thinking substance to another, it will be possible that two thinking substances may make but one person. For the same consciousness being preserved, whether in the same or different substances, the personal identity is preserved.

As to the second part of the question, Whether, the same immaterial substance remaining, there may be two distinct persons? Which question seems to me to be built on this, Whether the same immaterial being, being conscious of the action of its past duration, may be wholly stripped of all the consciousness of its past existence, and lose it beyond the power of ever retrieving it again; and so, as it were, beginning a new account from a new period, have a consciousness that cannot reach beyond this new state? All those who hold pre-existence are evidently of this mind, since they allow the soul to have no remaining consciousness of what it did in that pre-existent state, either wholly separate from body, or informing any other body; and if they should not, it is plain experience would be against them. So that personal identity reaching no farther than consciousness reaches, a pre-existent spirit not having continued so many ages in a state of silence, must needs make different persons. Suppose a Christian, Platonist, or a Pythagorean, should, upon God's having ended all his works of creation the seventh day, think his soul hath existed ever since; and should imagine it has revolved in several human bodies, as I once met with one who was persuaded his had been the soul of Socrates: (how reasonably I will not dispute: this I know, that in the post he filled, which was no inconsiderable one, he passed for a very rational man; and the press has shown that he wanted not parts or learning:) would any one say, that he, being not conscious of any of Socrates's actions or thoughts, could be the same person with Socrates? Let any one reflect upon himself, and conclude, that he has in himself immaterial spirit, which is that which thinks in him, and in the constant change of his body keeps him the same; and is that which he calls himself: let him also suppose it to be the same soul that was in Nestor or Thersites, at the siege of Troy, (for souls being, as far as we know any thing of them, in their nature indifferent to any parcel of matter, the supposition has no apparent absur-

dity in it), which it may have been as well as it is now the soul of any other man: but he now having no consciousness of any of the actions either of Nestor or Thersites, does or can he conceive himself the same person with either of them? Can he be concerned in either of their actions? attribute them to himself, or think them his own, more than the actions of any other man that ever existed? So that this consciousness not reaching to any of the actions of either of those men, he is no more one self with either of them, than if the soul or immaterial spirit that now informs him had been created and began to exist when it began to inform his present body, though it were never so true that the same spirit that informed Nestor's or Thersites's body were numerically the same that now informs his. For this would no more make him the same person with Nestor, than if some of the particles of matter that were once a part of Nestor were now a part of this man; the same immaterial substance, without the same consciousness, no more making the same person by being united to any body, makes the same person. But let him once find himself conscious of any of the actions of Nestor, he then finds himself the same person with Nestor.

And thus we may be able, without any difficulty, to conceive the same person at the resurrection, though in a body not exactly in make or parts the same which he had here, the same consciousness going along with the soul that inhabits it. But yet the soul alone, in the change of bodies, would scarce to any one, but to him that makes the soul the man, be enough to make the same man. For, should the soul of a prince, carrying what it the consciousness of the prince's past life, enter and inform the body of a cobbler, as soon as deserted by his own soul, every one sees he would be the same person with the prince, accountable only for the prince's actions: but who would say it was the same man? The body too goes to the making of the man, and would, I guess, to every body determine the man in this case, wherein the soul, with all its princely thoughts about it, would not make another man; but he would be the same cobbler to every one besides himself. I know that, in the ordinary way of speaking, the same person and the same man stand for one and the same thing. And, indeed, every one will always have a liberty to speak as he pleases, and to apply what articulate sounds to what ideas he thinks fit, and change them as often as he pleases. But yet, when we will inquire what makes the same spirit, man, or person, we must fix the ideas of spirit, man, or person in our minds; and having resolved with ourselves what we mean by them, it will not be hard to determine in either of them, or the like, when it is the same and when not.

Consciousness makes the same person.—But though the same immaterial substance or soul does not alone, wherever it be, and in whatsoever state, make the same man; yet it is plain, consciousness, as far as ever it can be extended, should it be to ages past, unites existences and actions, very remote in time, into the same person, as well as it does the existences and actions of the immediately preceding moment: so that whatever has the consciousness of present and past actions is the same person to whom they both belong. Had I the same consciousness that I saw the ark and Noah's flood, as that I saw an overflowing of the Thames last winter, or as that I write now, I could no more doubt that I who write this now, that saw the Thames

overflowed last winter, and that viewed the flood at the general deluge, was the same self, place that self in what substance you please, than that I who write this am the same myself now whilst I write (whether I consist of all the same substance, material or immaterial, or no) that I was yesterday. For, as to this point of being the same self, it matters not whether this present self be made up of the same or other substances, I being as much concerned and as justly accountable for any action was done a thousand years since appropriated to me now by this self-consciousness, as I am for what I did the last moment.

Self depends on consciousness.—Self is that conscious thinking thing (whatever substance made up of, whether spiritual or material, simple or compounded, it matters not) which is sensible or conscious of pleasure and pain, capable of happiness or misery, and so is concerned for itself, as far as that consciousness extends. Thus every one finds, that whilst comprehended under that consciousness, the little finger is as much a part of himself as what is most so. Upon separation of this little finger, should this consciousness go along with the little finger, and leave the rest of the body, it is evident the little finger would be the person, the same person; and self then would have nothing to do with the rest of the body. As in this case it is the consciousness that goes along with the substance, when one part is separate from another, which makes the same person, and constitutes this inseparable self, so it is in reference to substances remote in time. That with which the consciousness of this present thinking thing can join itself makes the same person, and is one self with it, and with nothing else; and so attributes to itself and owns all the actions of that thing as its own, as far as that consciousness reaches, and no farther; as every one who reflects will perceive. . . .

This may show us wherein personal identity consists, not in the identity of substance but, as I have said, in the identity of consciousness; wherein if Socrates and the present mayor of Queinborough agree, they are the same person. If the same Socrates waking and sleeping do not partake of the same consciousness, Socrates waking and sleeping is not the same person; and to punish Socrates waking for what sleeping Socrates thought, and waking Socrates was never conscious of, would be no more of right than to punish one twin for what his brother-twin did, whereof he knew nothing, because their outsides were so like that they could not be distinguished; for such twins have been seen.

MEREDITH W. MICHAELS
Persons, Brains, and Bodies

MEREDITH W. MICHAELS *teaches philosophy at Hampshire College. Most of her work focuses on issues in feminist ethics, metaphysics, and epistemology.*

ONE night, after a serious bout with the library, you and your best friend Wanda Bagg (or Walter, if you prefer) decide to indulge yourselves at the College Haven. Before you can stop her, Wanda steps out in front of a steamroller that happens to be moving down Main Street. Wanda is crushed. Witnessing the horror of the accident, you have a stroke. Fortunately, Dr. Hagendaas, the famous neurosurgeon who has been visiting the campus, is also on the way to the College Haven. Taking charge, he rushes you and Wanda to the Health Center, where he performs a "body transplant." He takes Wanda's brain, which miraculously escaped the impact of the steamroller, and puts it in the place of yours, which was, of course, severely damaged by the stroke. After several days, the following battle ensues. Wanda's parents claim that they are under no obligation to continue paying tuition. After all, Wanda was killed by a steamroller. Your parents claim that they are under no obligation to continue paying tuition, after all, you died of a stroke. It is clear, then, that a basic question is in need of an answer, who is the person lying in bed in the Health Center? Is it Wanda? Is it you? Is it someone else altogether? For the sake of discussion, let us call the person lying in the bed Schwanda. What reasons do we have for believing that Schwanda is Wanda? Given that one's self-consciousness, one's thoughts, beliefs and feelings are all mental phenomena, we might naturally conclude that a person goes wherever her brain goes (on the assumption that our mental characteristics are more likely "located" in the brain than in, say, our smallest left toe). Schwanda will remember having set off for the College Haven with you; she will remember receiving the college acceptance letter addressed, "Dear Wanda, We are happy to inform you that . . ."; she'll remember being hugged by Wanda's mother on the afternoon of her first day of school. That is, Schwanda will *believe* that she's Wanda.

Nevertheless, the fact that Schwanda believes herself to be Wanda does not in itself guarantee that she is. Do we have any basis for insisting that Schwanda is Wanda and not someone who is *deluded* into thinking that she's Wanda? How can we determine whether Schwanda's Wanda memories are genuine and not merely apparent? As we came to realize in our discussion of Locke's Memory Theory, it is not legitimate at this point to appeal to the self-identity of Schwanda and Wanda, since that is precisely what we're trying to determine. In other words, in attempting to establish that Schwanda's Wanda memories are genuine memories, we cannot argue that they are genuine on the grounds that Schwanda *is* Wanda.

Perhaps it is possible to stop short of circularity. Why couldn't we say that Schwanda's Wanda memories are genuine because the *brain* that is remembering is the same as the brain that had the original experiences. Thus, the experiences are preserved in the very organ that underwent them. Though there is an initial plausibility to this response, it fails to solve our problem. Suppose that Schwanda is Wanda—remembering the experience of learning to ride a bicycle. Though the brain in question is indeed the same, it is nonetheless clear to all of us that brains alone do not learn to ride bicycles, or, indeed, do brains alone remember hav-

ing done so. *People* learn to ride bicycles and *people* remember having done so. And the question we are trying to answer is whether Schwanda (who is remembering) is the same person as Wanda (who did the bicycling). The appeal to the fact that the same brain is involved in each event does not provide us with a way out of the Lockean circle.

It is at this point that philosophers begin to reconsider the Aristotelian position . . . that self-identity is essentially *bodily* identity. If the Body Theory of Personal Identity is true, then the person lying in bed at the Health Center is you, deluded into believing that you are Wanda. That is, Schwanda is self-identical to you.

You might wonder, at this point, whether there are any positive reasons for endorsing the Body Theory, or whether it is simply a place to which one retreats only in defeat? The following case is designed to persuade you that there is at least *some* plausibility to the Body Theory. Suppose that an evil scientist, Dr. Nefarious, has selected you as his prime subject for a horrible experiment. You are dragged into his office. He says, "Tomorrow at 5:00, you will be subjected to the most terrible tortures. Your nails will be pulled out one by one. Rats will be caged round head. Burning oil will drip slowly on your back. The remainder I leave as a surprise."

Are you worried about what will happen to you at 5:00 tomorrow? If you have any sense, you are. You think of the excruciating pain and suffering you will undergo and would surely do just about anything to avoid it. But now, Dr. Nefarious says, "Tomorrow at 4:55, I will use my Dememorizer to erase your memory of this conversation." Are you still anxious about what is going to happen to you tomorrow at 5:00? Surely you are. After all the fact that you won't, between 4:55 and 5:00, be anticipating your torture doesn't entail that the torture itself will be any less painful. When you forget that your Calculus professor told the class there would be a test on Friday, you aren't thereby spared the experience of taking the test (in fact, in that case the experience is made worse by your not having had the opportunity to anticipate it).

Now, Dr. Nefarious says, "Tomorrow at 4:57, I will use my Dememorizer to erase *all* of your memories." Are you still anxious about what will happen tomorrow at 5:00? Isn't it natural to describe the situation as one in which you will undergo horrible torture, though you won't know who you are or why this is happening to you? *You* will still experience *your* fingernails being pulled out, *your* back being burned, *your* face being eaten up by rats. Surely, those experiences are ones you would like to avoid.

Finally, Dr. Nefarious says to you, "Tomorrow at 4:58, I am going to use my Rememorizer to implant in your brain all of Ronald Reagan's memories." Though this may not please you for personal or political reasons, the relevant question remains this: are you still worried about what is going to happen tomorrow at 5:00? Isn't it again perfectly natural to describe the situation as one in which you will undergo horrible torture, all the while believing that you are Ronald Reagan. Do you not *now* remain concerned that *you* will experience excruciating pain and intolerable suffering? Look at your fingernails while you consider your answer to this question.

What this story demonstrates is not the conclusive superiority of the Body Theory over the Memory (or Brain)

Theory, but rather the importance of our bodies to our self-identity. This is something that tends to get lost in the traditional conceptions of personal identity. Furthermore, returning to the case of Schwanda, we can now see that it is not altogether preposterous to argue that Schwanda is indeed you, deluded into believing that she is Wanda. In other words, anyone who wishes to dismiss that possibility must also dismiss the possibility that the person who undergoes the torture is indeed you, deluded into believing that you are Ronald Reagan.

While it is true that we tend to identify ourselves with and by our thoughts, beliefs, inclinations and feelings, our discussion of the Body Theory should remind us that there are reasons for believing that our bodies are, at the very least, important to who we are. Some philosophers would argue that our bodies *are* who we are, that self-identity *is* bodily identity.

In considering these admittedly fanciful problem cases, we have seen that we lack a concept of self-identity that allows us to predict when we would or wouldn't persist through time. This might suggest to us that our concept of self-identity is not an all-or-nothing one, that, in fact, our concept is one which admits of degrees. If so, we are no longer talking about identity *per se,* which is an all-or-nothing concept, but rather about some other relation of psychological and physical connectedness. Nevertheless, we can now see first, that the answer to the question "Who ought to pay Schwanda's tuition?" will depend upon which theory of personal identity we are inclined to endorse and second, that the answer may not be as clear and unequivocal as we would like it to be.

JUSTIN LEIBER

How to Build a Person

JUSTIN LEIBER, *a professor of philosophy at the University of Houston, also writes science fiction. This selection is from his novel* Beyond Rejection.

WORMS began his spiel: "People often think that it ought to be simple enough to just *manufacture* an adult human body, like building a house or a helicopter. You'd think that, well, we know what chemicals are involved, and how they go together, how they form cells according to DNA templates, and how the cells form organ systems regulated by chemical messengers, hormones, and the like. So we ought to be able to build a fully functional human body right up from scratch."

Worms moved so that he blocked their view of the jogger. He brought his drained coffee cup down for emphasis.

"And, of course, we could build a human body up from scratch, theoretically, anyhow. But no one ever has. In fact, no one has ever even started to. De Reinzie manufactured the first fully functional human cell—muscle tissue—in the middle of the last century, about 2062 or so. And shortly after that the major varieties were cooked up. And even then it wasn't really manufactured from scratch. De Reinzie, like all the rest, built some basic DNA templates from actual carbon, oxygen, hydrogen, and so on, or rather from simple sugars and alcohols. *But then he grew the rest from these.* That's growth, not manufacture. And nobody's come closer to building an organ than a lab that made a millimeter of stomach wall for several million credits a couple of decades ago.

"I don't want to bother you with the mathematics," he continued, looking away from Terry. "But my old professor at Tech used to estimate that it would take all the scientific and manufacturing talent of Earth and the rest of the Federation something like fifty years and a googol credits to build a single human hand.

"You can imagine what it would take to make something like that," he said, moving out of their line of vision and gesturing at the jogging figure. He took the clipboard that hung next to the treadmill's controls and scanned the sheets on it.

"This body had been blank for three years. It has a running-time age of thirty-one years, though of course Sally Cadmus—that's the person involved—was born over thirty-four years ago. What with demand, of course, three years is a long time for a body to remain out of action. She's in good health, fine musculature for a spacer—says Sally was an asteroid miner here. Seems the body spent two years frozen in a Holmann orbit. We've had it for four months and we're preparing it now. You might see her walking around any day now.

"But Sally Cadmus won't. Her last tape was just the obligatory one made on reaching majority and she left no instructions for implantation. I trust, people, that all your tapes are updated." He gave them the family doctor look and went on, moving closer and dropping his voice.

"I have my mind taped every six months, just to be safe. After all, the tape is *you*— your individual software, or program, including memory store. Everything that makes you *you*." He walked up to the aide who had brought the beautiful young man.

"You—for instance—Ms. Pedersen, when did you have your last tape job?"

The aide, a gaunt red-haired woman in her mid-thirties, snatched her arm from around her young man and glared at Austin Worms.

"What business—"

"Oh, I wouldn't really expect you to say in front of other people." He grinned at the others as Pedersen subsided. "But that's the whole point, you see. Maybe she has been renewing her tape yearly, which is what our profession recommends as an absolute minimum. But a lot of people neglect this elementary precaution because they are so appalled by the thought of severe bodily injury. They just let things slide. And because the topic is so personal, no one knows, no one asks, no one reminds them until the once-in-half-a-million accident happens—truly irreparable body damage or total destruction.

"And then you find that the person hasn't taped for twenty years. Which means. . . ."

He surveyed the group to let it sink in. Then he saw the beautiful girl-child. Terry had been hiding her, no doubt. A classic blond-haired, blue-eyed girl in her mid-teens. She was looking straight into his eyes. Or *through* them. Something . . . He went on.

"Which means if he or she is lucky and there's estate money, you've got someone who has to face all the ordinary problems of rejection that come in trying to match a young mind with what is almost certain to be a middle-aged body. But also the implant has all those problems multiplied by another. The implant has to deal with a world that is *twenty years in the future.* And a 'career' that is meaningless because he lacks the memory and skills that his old mind picked up over that twenty years.

"More likely, you'll get the real blowout. You'll get massive rejection, psychosis and premature essential senility, and death. Real, final mind death."

"But you would still have the person's tape, their software, as you call it," said Ms. Pedersen. "Couldn't you just try again, with another blank body?" She still had her hands off her young man.

"Two problems. First"—he stuck his index finger in the air—"you got to realize how very difficult it is for a mind and a body to make a match, even with all the help us somaticians and psycheticians can provide, the best that modern biopsychological engineering can put together. Even with a really creative harmonizer to get in there and make the structure jell. Being reborn is very hard work indeed.

"And the failure rate under ordinary circumstances—tapes up-to-date, good stable mind, decent recipient body—is about twenty percent. And we know that is jumps to ninety-five percent if there's a second time around. It's nearly that bad the first time if you got someone whose tapes are twenty years out of date. The person may get through the first few days all right but he can't pull himself into reality. Everything he knows was lost twenty years ago. No friends, no career, everything out of shape. Then the mind will reject its new body just as it rejects the new world it has woken up to. So you don't have much of a chance. Unless, of course, you're the rare nympher or still rarer leaper.

"Second, the Government underwrites the cost of the first implantation. Of course, they don't pay for a fancy body—a nympher body, that is. You'd pay more than two million credits for one of those beauties. You get what's available and you are lucky if you get it within a year or two. What the Government underwrites is the basic operation and tuning job. That alone costs one and a half million or so. Enough to pay my salary for a hundred years. Enough to send the half-dozen or so of you on the Cunard Line Uranium Jubilee All-Planets Tour in first class."

Austin had been moving over to the treadmill control console while speaking. As he finished, his audience noticed a large structure descending from the ceiling just over the jogging figure, Sally Cadmus's body. It looked like a cross between the upper half of a large mummy and a comfortably stuffed armchair. Austin glided over to the treadmill. The audience watched the structure open like an ancient iron maiden. Some noticed that the jogging figure was slowing down.

Austin arrived just in time to complete a flurry of adjustments on the jogger's control package before the structure folded itself around. Two practiced blows on the back of the jogger's thighs brought the legs out of contact with the slowing treadmill.

"It's a lucky thing that implantation is so risky and the sort of accident that calls for it so rare," he said as the structure ascended behind him. "Otherwise, the Kellog-Murphy Law, which underwrites the first implantation, would bankrupt the Government."

"Where is the body going?" asked the blond-haired youngster. Austin could see now that she was probably no more than ten or eleven years old.

Something about her posture had made him think she was older.

"Normally it would go into a kind of artificial hibernation—low temperature and vital activity. But this body will be implanted tomorrow, so we'll keep it at a normal level of biological function." He had given the body an additional four cc.'s of glucose-saline plasma beyond the program. That was to compensate for the extra jogging. He hadn't done the official calculations. It wasn't that such mathematics was more than a minor chore. If you had asked him to explain, he would have said that the official calculation would have called for half again as much plasma. But he sensed that the body got more than usual from every cc. of water, from every molecule of sugar. Perhaps it was something in the sweat smell, the color and feel of the skin, the resilience of the musculature. But Austin knew.

The somatic aides would have said that Austin Worms was the best ghoul in the Solar System, a zombie's best friend. And they would have meant what they said even if they went on to joke.

Austin had vomited for the first and only time in his life when he learned the origin of the slang terms "ghoul" and "vampire."

The sounds of Terry's tour group faded as they moved up the hall to the psychetician laboratory. But Austin did not return to Bruhler's *The Central Equations of the Abstract Theory of Mind.* He had been puzzled by what the eleven-year-old blond girl had said to him before sauntering off to catch up with the rest of the tour. She had said, "I bet that mind is gonna be in for a real shock when it wakes up with that thing on its backside." He wondered how she could know that it wasn't just part of the crazy-quilt system of tubes and wires that the jogger had on her back.

"I'm Candy Darling," she had added as she left the room. Now he know who she was. You never knew what to expect in a harmonizer.

• • •

Psycheticians take care of minds. That's why they are sometimes called vampires. Somaticians are called ghouls because they take care of bodies.

—I.F. + S. C. Operation Logbook, Append. II, Press Releases

Germaine Means grinned wolfishly at them. "I am a psychetician. What Terry would call a vampire. Call me Germaine if that does not appeal."

They were seated facing a blackboard at one end of a large room which was otherwise filled with data cabinets, office cubicles, and computer consoles. The woman who addressed them wore severe and plain overalls. When she had first come to the Norbert Wiener Research Hospital—NWRH—the director had suggested that the chief psychetician might dress more suitably. That director had retired early.

"As you know from what Austin Worms told you, we think of the individual human mind as an abstract pattern of memory, skill, and experience that has been impressed on the physical hardware of the brain. Think of it this way: when you get a computer factory-fresh, it is like a blanked human brain. The computer has no subroutines, just as the brain has no skills. The computer has no data arrays to call on, just as the blanked brain has no memories.

"What we do here is try to implant the pattern of memory, skill, and experience that is all that is left of a person into a blanked brain. It is not easy be-

cause brains are not manufactured. You have to grow them. And a unique personality has to be part of this growth and development. So each brain is different. So no software mind fits any hardware brain perfectly. Except the brain that it grew up with.

"For instance," Germaine Means continued, softening her tone so she would not alert Ms. Pedersen's boyfriend, who was dozing in a well-padded chair, his elegant legs thrust straight out in full display, tights to sandals. "For instance, when pressure is applied to this person's foot, his brain knows how to interpret the nervous impulses from his foot." She suited her action to her words.

"His yelp indicated that his brain recognizes that considerable pressure has been applied to the toes of his left foot. If, however, we implanted another mind, it would not interpret the nervous impulses correctly—it might feel the impulses as a stomachache."

The young man was on his feet, bristling. He moved toward Germaine, who had turned away to pick up what looked like a pair of goggles with some mirrors and gears on top. As he reached her, she turned to face him and pushed the goggles into his hands.

"Yes, thank you for volunteering. Put them on." Not knowing what else to do, he did.

"I want you to look at that blond-haired girl who just sat down over there." She held his arm lightly as he turned and his balance wavered. He appeared to be looking through the goggles at a point several degrees to the right of Candy Darling.

"Now I want you to point at her with your right hand—quick!" The young man's arm shot out, the finger also pointing several degrees to the right of the girl. He began moving his finger to the left, but Germaine pulled his hand down to his side, outside the field of vision that the goggles allowed him.

"Try it again, quick," she said. This time the finger was not as far off. On the fifth try his finger pointed directly to Candy Darling, though he continued to look to her right.

"Now off with the goggles. Look at her again. Point quick!" Germaine grabbed his hand the instant he pointed. Though he was not looking directly at Candy Darling, he was pointing several degrees *to the left* of her. He looked baffled.

Germaine Means chalked a head and goggles on the blackboard, seen as if you were looking down at them from the ceiling. She drew another head to the left of the line of sight of the goggled head and chalked "15°" in to indicate the angle.

"What happened is a simple example of tuning. The prisms in the goggles bend the light so that when his eyes told him he was looking straight at her, his eyes were in fact pointed fifteen degrees to her right. The muscles and nerves of his hand were tuned to point where his eyes were actually pointed—so he pointed fifteen degrees to the right.

"But then his eyes saw his hand going off to the right, so he began to compensate. In a couple of minutes—five tries—his motor coordination compensates so that he points to where his eyes tell him she is—he adjusted to pointing fifteen degrees *to the left* from usual. When I took the goggles off, his arm was still tuned to compensate, so he pointed off to the left until he readjusted."

She picked up the goggles. "Now, a human can adjust to that distortion in a few minutes. But I could calibrate these so that they would turn the whole room upside down. If you then walked around and tried to do things, you would find it

difficult. Very difficult. But if you kept the goggles on, the whole room would turn right side up after a day or two. Everything would seem normal because your system would have retuned itself.

"What do you think will happen if you then take the goggles off?"

Candy Darling giggled. Ms. Pedersen said, "Oh, I see. Your mind would have adjusted to turning the, ah, messages from your eyes upside down, so when you took the goggles off—"

"Precisely," said Germaine, "everything would look upside down to you until you readjusted to having the goggles off—and it happens the same way. You stumble around for a day or so and then everything snaps right side up again. And the stumbling-around part is important. If you are confined to a chair with your head fixed in position, your mind and body can't tune themselves.

"Now I want you to imagine what happens when we implant a mind into a blanked brain. *Almost everything will be out of tune.* The messages from your eyes won't simply be inverted, they'll be scrambled in countless ways. Same thing with your ears, nose, tongue—and with the whole nerve net covering your body. And that's just incoming messages. Your mind will have even more problems when it tries to tell the body to do something. Your mind will try to get your lips to say 'water,' and Sol knows what sound will come out.

"And what's worse is that whatever sound does come out, your new ears won't be able to give your mind an accurate version of it."

Germaine smiled at them and glanced at her watch. Terry stood up.

"Terry will be wanting to take you on. Let me wrap this up by saying that it is a very simple thing to play someone's mind tape into a prepared brain. The great problem is in getting the rearranged brain, the cerebral cortex, speaking strictly, to be tuned into the rest of the system. As Austin Worms may have told you, we start an implant operation tomorrow. The initial tape-in will take days and days. Even months, if you count all the therapy. Questions?"

"Just one," said Ms. Pedersen. "I can understand how difficult it is for a mind to survive implantation. And, of course, I know it is illegal to implant a mind that is over eighty-five. But couldn't a person—if you call a mind a person— live forever bypassing though body after body?"

"Okay, that's a tough one to explain even if we had a lot of time and you knew a lot of mathematics. Until this century it was believed that senility was a by-product of the physical breakdown of the body. Today we know that a human mind can have roughly one hundred years of experiences before it reaches essential senility, however young the body it occupies. As you know, a few successful leapers have survived implantation after a fifty-year wait. So a leaper might, in theory, still be functioning a thousand years from now. But such an individual's mind will not be able to encompass any more lived experience than you. When all there is of you is a tape in storage, you aren't really alive."

After they had filed out, Germaine Means noticed that the blond-haired girl had remained.

"Hi, I'm Candy Darling," she cried. "I hope you don't mind. I thought it would be fun to sneak in on the standard tour. Get the smell of the place."

"Where's your VAT?"

• • •

Austin Worms declared that basic physical meshing procedures were complete.

—I. F. + S. C. Operation Logbook

Gxxhdt.

Etaoin shrdlu. Mmm.

Anti-M.

Away mooncow Taddy-fair fine. Fine again, take. Away, along, alas, alung the orbit-run, from swerve of space to worm-hole wiggle, brings us. Start now. Wake.

So hear I am now coming out of nothing like Eros out of Death, knowing only that I was Ismael Forth—stately, muscled well—taping in, and knowing that I don't know when I'm waking or where, or where-in. And hoping that it is a dream. But it isn't. Oh, no, it isn't. With that goggling piece of munster cheese oumphowing on my eyelids.

And seemingly up through endless levels and configurations that had no words and now no memories. Wake.

"Helow, I'm Candy Darlinz."

"I am Ismael returned" was what I started to reply. After the third attempt it came out better. And the munster cheese had become a blond-haired young girl with piercing blue eyes.

"Your primary implantation was finished yesterday, finally. Everyone thinks you're a success. Your body is a pip. You're in the Norbert Wiener Research Hospital in Houston. You have two estates clear through probate. Your friend Peter Strawson has covered your affairs. It's the first week of April, 2112. You're alive."

She stood up and touched my hand.

"You start therapy tomorrow. Now sleep."

I was already drifting off by the time she had closed the door behind her. I couldn't even get myself worked up by what I was noticing. My nipples felt as big as grapes. I went out as I worked my way down past the belly button.

The next day I discovered that I had not only lost a penis. I had gained a meter-long prehensile tail. It was hate at first sense.

I had worked my way to consciousness in slow stages. I had endless flight dreams—walking, running, staggering on, away from some nameless horror. And brief flashes of sexuality that featured performances by my (former) body.

I really liked my old body. One of my biggest problems, as Dr. Germaine Means was soon to tell me. I could picture clearly how it had looked in the mirrors as I did my stretch and tone work. Just a hair over six foot four. Two hundred and five pounds, well-defined muscles, and just enough fat to be comfortable. A mat of curly red chest hair that made it easy to decide to have my facial hair wiped permanently. It felt good to be a confident even slightly clumsy giant, looking down on a world of little people.

Oh, I wasn't a real body builder or anything like that. Just enough exercise to look good—and attractive. I hadn't in fact been all that good at physical sports. But I had liked my body. It was also a help in the public relations work that I did for IBO.

I was still lying on my back. I felt shrunk. Shrunk. As the warm, muzzy flush of sleep faded, my right hand moved up over my ribs. Ribs. They were thin and they stuck out, as if the skin were sprayed over the bare cage. I felt like a skeleton until I got to the lumps. Bags. Growths. Sacks. Even then part of me realized that they

were not at all large for a woman, while most of me felt that they were as big as cantaloupes.

You may have imagined it as a kind of erotic dream. There you are in the hospital bed. You reach and there they are. Apt to the hands, the hardening nipples nestled between index and middle fingers. (Doubtless some men have felt this warm reverie with their hands on real flesh. The women may have felt pinch and itch rather than the imagined sensual flush. I know whereof I speak. I now know a lot of sexuality is like that. Perhaps heterosexuality continues as well as it does because of ignorance: each partner is free to invent the feeling of the other.)

But I was quite unable to feel erotic about my new acquisitions. Both ways. My fingers, as I felt them, felt pathology. Two dead cancerous mounds. And from the inside—so to speak—I felt that my flesh had swollen. The sheet made the nipples feel raw. A strange feeling of separation, as if the breast were disconnected, nerveless jelly—and then two point of sensitivity some inches in front of my chest. Dead spots. Rejection. I learned a lot about these.

As my hand moved down I was prepared for the swerve of hip. I couldn't feel a penis and I did not expect to find one. I did not call it "gash." Though that term is found occasionally in space-marine slang and often among the small number of male homosexuals of the extreme S&M type (Secretary & Master). I first learned the term a few days later from Dr. Means. She said that traditional male-male pornography revealed typical male illusions about female bodies: a "rich source of information about body-image pathologies." She was certainly right in pointing out that "gash" was how I felt about it. At first.

I was not only scrawny, I was almost hairless. I felt *really* naked, naked and defenseless as a baby. Though my skin was several shades less fair—and I passed a scar. I was almost relieved to feel the curly groin hair. Gone. Stick-like legs. But I *did* feel something between my thighs. And knees. And ankles, by Sol.

At first I thought it was some sort of tube to take my body wastes, But as I felt down between my legs I could tell that it wasn't covering those areas. It was attached at the end of my spine—or rather it had become the end of my spine, stretching down to my feet. It was my flesh. I didn't quite intend it— at that point I can't say that I intended anything I was so shook—but the damned thing flipped up from the bottom of the bed like a snake, throwing the sheet over my face.

I screamed my head off.

"Cut it off" was what I said after they had given me enough betaortho-amine to stop me flailing about. I said this several times to Dr. Germaine Means, who had directed the rest of them out of the room.

"Look, Sally—I'll call you that until you select a name yourself—we are not going to cut your tail off. By our calculations such a move would make termi-nal rejection almost certain. You would die. Several thousand nerves connect your brain with your prehensile tail. A sizable portion of your brain monitors and directs your tail—that part of your brain needs exercise and integration like any other component. We taped the pattern of your mind into your present brain. They *have to* learn to live together or you get rejection. In brief, you will die."

Dr. Means continued to read me the riot act. I would have to learn to love my new body—she practically gushed with praise for it—my new sex, my new tail. I would have to do a lot of exercise and tests. And I would have to talk to a lot of people about how I felt. And I should feel pleased as pisque to have an extra hand.

My new body broke into a cold sweat when I realized that I had— truly—no choice. I wasn't poor, assuming what I had heard yesterday was true. But I certainly couldn't afford an implant, let alone a desirable body. What I had, of course, came free under the Kellog-Murphy Bill.

After a while she left. I stared at the wall numbly. A nurse brought a tray with scrambled eggs and toast. I ignored both nurse and tray. The thin-lipped mouth salivated. Let it suffer.

DAVID HUME

Of Personal Identity

DAVID HUME (1711–1776), a Scottish philosopher, was refused professorships at the leading universities for his "heresies." Nevertheless, he is regarded as the outstanding genius of British philosophy. He wrote a number of influential books, among them A Treatise of Human Nature, An Inquiry Concerning the Principles of Morals, *and* Dialogues on Natural Religion.

T HERE are some philosophers, who imagine we are every moment intimately conscious of what we call our *Self;* that we feel its existence and its continuance in existence; and are certain, beyond the evidence of a demonstration, both of its perfect identity and simplicity. The strongest sensation, the most violent passion, say they, instead of distracting us from this view, only fix it the more intensely, and make us consider their influence on *self* either by their pain or pleasure. To attempt a farther proof of this were to weaken its evidence; since no proof can be deriv'd from any fact, of which we are so intimately conscious; nor is there any thing, of which we can be certain, if we doubt of this.

Unluckily all these positive assertions are contrary to that very experience, which is pleaded for them, nor have we any idea of *self,* after the manner it is here explain'd. For from what impression cou'd this idea be deriv'd? This question 'tis impossible to answer without a manifest contradiction and absurdity; and yet 'tis a question, which must necessarily be answer'd, if we wou'd have the idea of self pass for clear and intelligible. It must be some one impression, that gives rise to every real idea. But self or person is not any one impression, but that to which our several impressions and ideas are suppos'd to have a reference. If any impression gives rise to the idea of self, that impression must continue invariably the same, thro' the whole course of our lives; since self is suppos'd to exist after that manner. But there is no impression constant and invariable. Pain and pleasure, grief and joy, passions and sensations succeed each other, and never all exist at the same time. It cannot, therefore, be from any of these impressions, or from any other, that the idea of self is deriv'd; and consequently there is no such idea.

But farther, what must become of all our particular perceptions upon this hypothesis? All these are different, and distinguishable, and separable from each other, and may be separately consider'd, and may exist separately, and have no need of any thing to support their existence. After what manner, therefore, do they belong to self; and how are they connected with it? For my part, when I enter most intimately into what I call *myself,* I always stumble on some particular perception or other, of heat or cold, light or shade, love or hatred, pain or pleasure. I never can catch *myself* at any time without a perception, and never can observe any thing but the perception. When my perceptions are remov'd for any time, as by sound sleep; so long am I insensible of *myself,* and may truly be said not to exist. And were all my perceptions remov'd by death, and cou'd I neither think, nor feel, nor see, nor love, nor hate after the dissolution of my body, I shou'd be entirely annihilated, nor do I conceive what is farther requisite to make me a perfect non-entity. If any one upon serious and unprejudic'd reflection, thinks he has a different notion of *himself,* I must confess I can reason no longer with him. All I can allow him is, that he nay be in the right as well as I, and that we are essentially different in this particular. He may, perhaps, perceive something simple and continu'd, which he calls *himself;* tho' I am certain there is no such principle in me.

But setting aside some metaphysicians of this kind, I may venture to affirm of the rest of mankind, that they are nothing but a bundle or collection of different perceptions, which succeed each other with an inconceivable rapidity, and are in a perpetual flux and movement. Our eyes cannot turn in their sockets without varying our perceptions. Our thought is still more variable than our sight; and all our other senses and faculties contribute to this change; nor is there any single power of the soul, which remains unalterably the same, perhaps for one moment. The mind is a kind of theatre, where several perceptions successively make their appearance; pass, re-pass, glide away, and mingle in an infinite variety of postures and situations. There is properly no *simplicity* in it at one time, nor *identity* in different; whatever natural propension we may have to imagine that simplicity and identity. The comparison of the theatre must not mislead us. They are the successive perceptions only, that constitute the mind; nor have we the most distant notion of the place, where these scenes are represented, or of the materials, of which it is compos'd.

What then gives us so great a propension to ascribe an identity to these successive perceptions, and to suppose ourselves possest of an invariable and uninterrupted existence thro' the whole course of our lives? . . .

. . . 'Tis evident, that the identity, which we attribute to the human mind, however perfect we may imagine it to be, is not able to run the several different perceptions into one, and make them lose their characters of distinction and difference, which are essential to them. 'Tis still true, that every distinct perception, which enters into the composition of the mind, is a distinct existence, and is different, and distinguishable, and separable from every other perception, either contemporary or successive. But, as, notwithstanding this distinction and separability, we suppose the whole train of perceptions to be united by identity, a question naturally arises concerning this relation of identity; whether it be something that really binds our several perceptions together, or only associates their ideas in the imagination. That is, in other words, whether in pronouncing concerning the identity of a person, we observe some real bond among his perceptions, or only feel one among the ideas we form of them. This question we might easily decide, if we wou'd recollect what has been already prov'd at large, that the understanding never observes any real connexion among objects, and that even the union of cause and effect, when strictly examin'd, resolves itself into a customary association of ideas. For from thence it evidently follows, that identity is nothing really belonging to these different perceptions, and uniting them together; but is merely a quality, which we attribute to them, because of the union of their ideas in the imagination, when we reflect upon them. Now the only qualities, which can give ideas an union in the imagination, are these tree relations above-mention'd. These are the uniting principles in the ideal world, and without them every distinct object is separable by the mind, and may be separately consider'd, and appears not to have any more connexion with any other object, than if disjoin'd by the greatest difference and remoteness. 'Tis, therefore, on some of these three relations of resemblance, contiguity and causation, that identity depends; and as the very essence of these relations consists in their producing an easy transition of ideas; it follows, that our notions of personal identity, proceed entirely from the smooth and uninterrupted progress of the thought along a train of connected ideas, according to the principles above-explain'd.

The only question, therefore, which remains, is, by what relations this uninterrupted progress of our thought is produc'd, when we consider the successive existence of a mind or thinking person. And here 'tis evident we must confine ourselves to resemblance and causation, and must drop contiguity, which has little or no influence in the present case.

To begin with *resemblance;* suppose we cou'd see clearly into the breast of another, and observe that succession of perceptions, which constitutes his mind or thinking principle, and suppose that he always preserves the memory of a considerable part of past perceptions; 'tis evident that nothing cou'd more contribute to the bestowing a relation on this succession amidst all its variations. For what is the memory but a faculty, by which we raise up the images of past perceptions? And as an image necessarily resembles its object, must not the frequent placing of these resembling perceptions in the chain of thought, con-

vey the imagination more easily from one link to another, and make the whole seem like the continuance of one object? In this particular, then, the memory not only discovers the identity, but also contributes to its production, by producing the relation of resemblance among the perceptions. The case is the same whether we consider ourselves or others.

As to *causation;* we may observe, that the true idea of the human mind, is to consider it as a system of different perceptions or different existences, which are link'd together by the relation of cause and effect, and mutually produce, destroy, influence, and modify each other. Our impressions give rise to their correspondent ideas; and these ideas in their turn produce other impressions. One thought chases another, and draws after it a third, by which it is expell'd in its turn. In this respect, I cannot compare the soul more properly to any thing than to a republic or commonwealth, in which the several members are united by the reciprocal ties of government and subordination, and give rise to other persons, who propagate the same republic in the incessant changes of its parts. And as the same individual republic may not only change its members, but also its laws and constitutions; in like manner the same person may vary his character and disposition, as well as his impressions and ideas, without losing his identity. Whatever changes he endures, his several parts are still connected by the relation of causation. And in this view our identity with regard to the passions serves to corroborate that with regard to the imagination, by the making our distant perceptions influence each other, and by giving us a present concern for our past or future pains or pleasures.

As memory alone acquaints us with the continuance and extent of this succession of perceptions, 'tis to be consider'd, upon that account chiefly, as the source of personal identity. Had we no memory, we never shou'd have any notion of causation, nor consequently of that chain of causes and effects, which constitute our self or person. But having once acquir'd this notion of causation from the memory, we can extend the same chain of causes, and consequently the identity of our persons beyond our memory, and can comprehend times, and circumstances, and actions, which we have entirely forgot, but suppose in general to have existed. For how few of our past actions are there, of which we have any memory? Who can tell me, for instance, what were his thoughts and actions on the first of *January* 1715, the 12th of *March* 1719, and the 3d of *August* 1733? Or will he affirm, because he has entirely forgot the incidents of these days, that the present self is not the same person with the self of that time; and by that means overturn all the most establish'd notions of personal identity? In this view, therefore, memory does not so much *produce* as *discover* personal identity, by shewing us the relation of cause and effect among our different perceptions. 'Twill be incumbent on those, who affirm that memory produces entirely our personal identity, to give a reason why we can thus extend our identity beyond our memory.

The whole of this doctrine leads us to a conclusion, which is of great importance in the present affair, *viz.* that all the nice and subtle questions concerning personal identity can never possibly be decided, and are to be regarded rather as grammatical than as philosophical difficulties. Identity depends on the relations of ideas; and these relations produce identity, by means of that easy transition they occasion. But as the relations, and the easiness of the transition may diminish by insensible degrees, we have no just standard, by which we can decide any dispute concerning the time, when they acquire or lose a title to the name of identity. All the disputes concerning the identity of connected objects are merely verbal, except so far as the relation of parts gives rise to some fiction or imaginary principle of union, as we have already observ'd.

ALASDAIR MACINTYRE

The Story-Telling Animal

ALASDAIR MACINTYRE *teaches philosophy at Duke University. Most of his work focuses on issues in ethics and social and political philosophy. Among his many publications are* Against the Self-Images of the Age *and* After Virtue.

E live out our lives, both individually and in our relationships with each other, in the light of certain conceptions of a possible shared future, a future in which certain possibilities beckon us forward

and other repel us, some seem already foreclosed and other perhaps inevitable. There is no present which is not informed by some image of some future and an image of the future which always presents itself in the form of a *telos*—or of a variety of ends or goals—towards which we are either moving or failing to move in the present. Unpredictability and teleology therefore coexist as part of our lives; like characters in a fictional narrative we do not know what will happen next, but none the less our lives have a certain form which projects itself towards our future. Thus the narratives which we live out have both an unpredictable and a partially teleological character. If the narrative of our individual and social lives is to continue intelligibly—and either type of narrative may lapse into unintelligibility—it is always both the case that there are constraints on how the story can continue *and* that within those constraints there are indefinitely many ways that it can continue.

A central thesis then begins to emerge: man is in his actions and practice, as well as in his fictions, essentially a story-telling animal. He is not essentially but becomes through his history, a teller of stories that aspire to truth. But the key question for men is not about their own authorship; I can only answer the question 'What am I to do?' if I can answer the prior question 'Of what story or stories do I find myself a part?' We enter human society, that is, with one or more imputed characters—roles into which we have been drafted—and we have to learn what they are in order to be able to understand how others respond to us and how our responses to them are apt to be construed. It is through hearing stories about wicked stepmothers, lost children, good but

misguided kings, wolves that suckle twin boys, youngest sons who receive no inheritance but must make their own way in the world and eldest sons who waste their inheritance on riotous living and go into exile to live with the swine, that children learn or mislearn both what a child and what a parent is, what the cast of characters may be in the drama into which they have been born and what the ways of the world are. Deprive children of stories and you leave them unscripted, anxious stutterers in their actions as in their words. Hence there is no way to give us an understanding of any society, including our own, except through the stock of stories which constitute its initial dramatic resources. Mythology, in its original sense, is at the heart of things. Vico was right and so was Joyce. And so too of course is that moral tradition from heroic society to its medieval heirs according to which the telling of stories has a key part in educating us into the virtues.

I suggested earlier that 'an' action is always an episode in a possible history: I would now like to make a related suggestion about another concept, that of personal identity. Derek Parfit and others have recently drawn our attention to the contrast between the criteria of strict identity, which is an all-or-nothing matter (*either* the Tichborne claimant *is* the last Tichborne heir; *either* all the properties of the last heir belong to the claimant *or* the claimant is not the heir—Leibniz's Law applies) and the psychological continuities of personality which are a matter of more or less. (Am I the same man at fifty as I was at forty in respect of memory, intellectual powers, critical responses? More or less.) But what is crucial to human beings as characters in enacted narratives is that, possessing only the resources of psychological continuity, we have to be able to respond to the imputation of strict identity. I am forever whatever I have been at any time for others—and I may at any time be called upon to answer for it—no matter how changed I may be now. There is no way of *founding* my identity—or lack of it—on the psychological continuity or discontinuity of the self. The self inhabits a character whose unity is given as the unity of a character. Once again there is a crucial disagreement with empiricist or analytical philosophers on the one hand and with existentialists on the other.

Empiricists, such as Locke or Hume, tried to give an account of personal identity solely in terms of psychological states or events. Analytical philosophers, in so many ways their heirs as well as their critics, have wrestled with the connection between those states and events and strict identity understood in terms of Leibniz's Law. Both have failed to see that a background has been omitted, the lack of which makes the problems insoluble. That background is provided by the concept of a story and of that kind of unity of character which a story requires. Just as a history is not a sequence of actions, but the concept of an action is that of a moment in an actual or possible history abstracted for some purpose from that history, so the characters in a history are not a collection of persons, but the concept of a person is that of a character abstracted from a history.

What the narrative concept of selfhood requires is thus twofold. On the one hand, I am what I may justifiably be taken by others to be in the course of living out a story that runs from my birth to my death; I am the *subject* of a history that is my own and no one else's, that has its own peculiar meaning. When someone complains—as do some of those who attempt or commit suicide—that his or her life is meaningless, he or she is often and perhaps characteristically complaining that the narrative of their life has become unintelligible to them, that it lacks any point, any movement towards a climax of a *telos*. Hence the point of doing any one thing rather than another at crucial junctures in their lives seems to such a person to have been lost.

To be the subject of a narrative that runs from one's birth to one's death is, I remarked earlier, to be accountable for the actions and experiences which compose a narratable life. It is, that is, to be open to being asked to give a certain kind of account of what one did or what happened to one or what one witnessed at any earlier point in one's life than the time at which the question is posed. Of course someone may have forgotten or suffered brain damage or simply not attended sufficiently at the relevant times to be able to give the relevant account. But to say of someone under some one description ('The prisoner of the Chateau d'If') that he is the same person as someone characterised quite differently ('The Count of Monte Cristo') is precisely to say that it makes sense to ask him to give an intelligible narrative account enabling us to understand how he could at different times and different places be one and the same person and yet be so differently characterised. Thus personal identity is just that identity presupposed by the unity of the character which the unity of a narrative requires. Without such unity there would not be subjects of whom stories could be told.

The other aspect of narrative selfhood is correlative: I am not only accountable, I am one who can always ask others for an account, who can put others to the question. I am part of their story, as they are part of mine. The narrative of any one life is part of an interlocking set of narratives. Moreover this asking for and giving of accounts itself plays an important part in constituting narratives. Asking you what you did and why, saying what I did and why, pondering the differences between your account of what I did and my account of what I did, and *vice versa,* these are essential constituents of all but the very simplest and barest of narratives. Thus without the accountability of the self those trains of events that constitute all but the simplest and barest of narratives could not occur; and without that same accountability narratives would lack that continuity required to make both them and the actions that constitute them intelligible.

It is important to notice that I am not arguing that the concepts of narrative or of intelligibility or of accountability are *more* fundamental than that of personal identity. The concepts of narrative, intelligibility and accountability presuppose the applicability of the concept of personal identity, just as it presupposed their applicability and just as indeed each of these three presupposes the applicability of the two others. The rela-

tionship is one of mutual presupposition. It does follow of course that all attempts to elucidate the notion of personal identity independently of and in isolation from the notions of narrative, intelligibility and accountability are bound to fail. As all such attempts have.

It is now possible to return to the question from which this enquiry into the nature of human action and identity started: In what does the unity of an individual life consist? The answer is that its unity is the unity of a narrative embodied in a single life. To ask 'What is the good for me?' is to ask how best I might live out that unity and bring it to completion. To ask 'What is the good for man?' is to ask what all answers to the former question must have in common. But now it is important to emphasise that it is the systematic asking of these two questions and the attempt to answer them in deed as well as in word which provide the moral life with its unity. The unity of a human life is the unity of a narrative quest. Quests sometimes fail, are frustrated, abandoned or dissipated into distractions; and human lives may in all these ways also fail. But the only criteria for success or failure in a human life as a whole are the criteria of success or failure in a narrated or to-be-narrated quest.

ANTHONY APPIAH

"But Would That Still Be Me?"

ANTHONY APPIAH *teaches philosophy and African-American studies at Harvard University. He has published numerous articles and recently a book,* In My Father's House: Africa in the Philosophy of Culture *(1992).*

IF you had asked most Anglo-American philosophers twenty-five years ago what conditions someone had to meet in order to be (identical with) me, they would, no doubt, have taken this (correctly) to be a conceptual question, and (incorrectly) inferred that is was to be answered a priori by reflection in the properties whose presence would have led them to *say* that an imagined entity was Anthony Appiah. Since there are hardly any properties of persons whose absence we cannot intelligibly imagine, it was tempting to conclude that there was something odd about the very question.

. . . Some believe not only that this is a question about real essences, but that we know its answer: that the real essence of a person is the chromosomal structure produced by the coition of his actual parents, a thesis that is the biological fleshing out of the metaphysical doctrine of the necessity of origins. . . . [It] seems to me that there is an important set of questions that recent theorizing [about personal identity] has left to one side, a set of questions that can also be raised by asking, about a possible individual, "But would that still be me?" I want to argue that there is a sense of this question which is best answered in the "old-fashioned" conceptual way; and to get at what I have in mind, nothing could provide a better starting point than questions about "race," ethnicity, gender, and sex.

Consider, for the purposes of an initial example, the possibility that I might have been born a girl, Someone convinced of the chromosomal account of individual identity and convinced, too, that what it is to be biologically female or male is to have the appropriate chromosomal structure, will argue that this is only an apparent possibility. A female person could have been born to my parents when I was, if a different sperm and egg had met: but she would not have been me. It will be false, in this view, that I could have been born a woman.

I am prepared to concede all this for the purposes of argument; but there is a different question I might want to consider about a different possibility. Might I not, without any genetic modification, have been raised as a girl? This sort of thing certainly can happen; as when, for example, surgeons engaged in male circumcision remove the whole penis in error: rather than face a child with what—in our society—is bound to be the trauma of growing into a man without a penis, surgeons will often, in such circumstance, remove the testes from the abdomen, construct a facsimile of the female external genitalia, and ask the parents to bring the child back for hormone therapy in time to manage a facsimile of female puberty. If the good doctor who circumcised me had made such a mistake, could not I—this very metaphysical individual here—have been raised with a feminine (social)

gender even though, on the chromosomal essentialist view, I was still of the
male (biological) sex?

My claim in this paper is that, while
there may be a sense of the question,
"Would that have been me?", under
which the answer to this question is
'yes', there is another, intelligible reading under which it could, surely, be 'no'.

To get at that reading, consider the—
admittedly, very different—possibility
that I might seek to have a sex change
prior to which I could consider our
guiding question about the possible future social female this metaphysical individual would then become. "Would
that still be me?", I could ask. Now it
seems to me that I can give either of two
answers here, and that which answer I
should give depends in large part on
how central my being-a-man—my social masculinity and, perhaps, my possession of the biological appurtenances
of maleness—is, as would ordinarily
say, to my identity. And it is in exploring this sense of the term 'identity' that
we can come to learn why it is that there
is a sense to this question I shall call it
the ethical sense—in which I may
choose to answer it in the negative.

To say that I may choose is to speak
loosely. The issue is not really a matter
of choice. What answer I should give to
the question understood this way depends on how central my being-a-man
is to my identity, not on how central I
choose to make it. Transsexuals will
surely answer in the affirmative; they
often say that they were always of the
"other" sex all along. For the chromosomal essentialist, this will be false. But a
transsexual might . . . come to conclude
that what he or she really had in mind
was the different thought that his or her
real identity, in the sense of the term I
am now trying to explore, was that of
the sex into which he or she was not

born. And if I were a transsexual convinced of this I would say, contemplating the feminine person that I might
become, "Yes, that would be me; in fact
it would be the real me, the one I have
always really been all along."

But what I am actually inclined to
say is: "No. A sex-change operation
would make of the (metaphysical) person a different (ethical) person." And so
there is a sense in which she would not
be me.

As many people think of them, sex
(female and male, the biological sta-
tuses) and gender (masculine and feminine, the social roles) provide the
sharpest models for a distinction between the metaphysical notion of identity . . . and the notion of identity—the
ethical notion—that I am seeking to explore. I say 'as many people think of
them' because the real world is full of
complications. Not every human being
is XX or XY. And there are people who
are XY in whom the indifferent gonad
was not prompted to form the characteristic male external genitalia; people
whom it seems to me odd to regard as
"really" biological males. Just as it
would be odd to treat an XX person
with male external genitalia, produced
as the result of a burst of testosterone
from a maternal tumor, as "really" biologically female. Once you have an
inkling of how messy the real world of
the biology of the reproductive organs
is, you are likely, if you are wise, to
give up the idea that there are just two
biological sexes into which all human
beings must fall. And this is important
because most people do not make the
distinctions (or know the facts) necessary to appreciate this, and thus have
thoughts about what it is to be a man or
a woman which involve concepts that
essentially presuppose falsehoods about
how people biologically are. Before

someone has made a sex-gender conceptual distinction we cannot always say whether what these thoughts were about was one or the other: there are, so to speak, thoughts that no one who *had* made these distinctions could have.

But the general point can be made in cases far from the biological hard cases: if you consider a straightforward case of an XY biological infant, born with standard male internal and external genitalia, who is assigned a feminine gender as the result of early loss of his gonads, it is clear that such a person can agree to a . . . "metaphysical" identification as a biological male and insist on the centrality to her of her feminine-gender identity, on being, so to speak, ethically a woman. But before I say more about what this means, it will help to have a couple of rather different cases before us.

Take next, then, so-called "racial" identity. Here the biological situation is much worse than in the case of sex. No coherent system of biological classification of people—no classification, that is, that serves explanatory purposes central to biological theory—corresponds to the folk-theoretical classifications of people into Caucasian, Negro, and such. This is not, of course, to deny that there are differences in morphology among humans: people's skins do differ in color. But these sorts of distinctions are not—as those who believe in races apparently suppose—markers of deeper biologically-based racial essences, correlating closely with most (or even many) important biological (let alone nonbiological) properties. I announce this rather than argue for it, because it is hardly a piece of biological news, being part of a mainstream consensus in human biology. This means that here we cannot make use of an analog of the systematic sex-gender distinction: the underlying biology does not deliver something that we can use, like the sex chromosomes, as a biological essence for the Caucasian or the Negro.

But this does not mean that people cannot have ethical identities tied up with being, say, Euro- or African- or Asian-American; what it does mean, given that such identities often presuppose falsehood about the underlying biology, is that, once the facts are in, a different theoretical account of those identities is required. From an external point of view, we can construct an account of what it is that people take to be grounds for assigning people to these racial categories. We can note that they are supposed to be asymmetrically based on descent: that "whites" in America are supposed to have no non-"white" ancestry, but that "blacks" and Asians may have non-"black" and non-Asian ancestry. But from the point of view of people whose ethical identity is at stake, it is not going to be enough simply to remark how others classify them. And to see this we can return to our guiding question.

Let us suppose that an American of African descent could be offered the possibility of losing all the morphological markers that are associated in this society with that descent. Her skin is lightened, her hair straightened, her lips thinned: she has, in short, all the services of Michael Jackson's cosmetic surgeon and more. Surely, in contemplating this possibility, she could ask herself whether, once these changes had occurred, the resulting ethical person "would still be me." And, so far as I can see, almost everyone who does contemplate this question in our society is likely to judge that, whether or not these changes are desirable, the answer here must be 'yes'.

I am asserting here, therefore, a contrast between our attitudes to (ethical) gender and (ethical) "race." I suggest that we standardly hold it open to people to believe that the replacement of the characteristic morphology of their sex with a (facsimile) of that of the other (major) one would produce someone other than themselves, a new ethical person; while the replacement of the characteristic morphology of their sex with a (facsimile) of that of the other (major) one would produce someone other than themselves, a new ethical person; while the replacement of the characteristic morphology of their ethical "race" by that of another would not leave them free to disclaim the new person. "Racial" ethical identities are for us—and that means something like, us in the modern West—apparently less conceptually central to who one is than gender ethical identities.

That this is so does not entail that being-an-African-American cannot be an *important* ethical identity: it is a reflection, rather, of the fact that ethical identity is not a matter of morphology, that skin and hair and so on are simply signs for it. Such an identity is, as we ordinarily understand it, exactly a matter of descent: and nothing you do to change your appearance or behavior can change the past fact that your ancestors were of some particular origin. Nevertheless, even for those for whom being-African-American is an important aspect of their ethical identity, what matters to them is almost always not the unqualified fact of that descent, but rather something that they suppose to go with it: the experience of a life as a member of a group of people who experience themselves as—and are held by others to be—a community in virtue of their mutual recognition—and their

recognition by others—as people of a common descent.

It is a reasonable question how such "racial" identities differ from those we call "ethnic." What matters about the identity of, say, Irish-Americans—which was conceived of racially in the nineteenth century in North America—is that it, like an African-American identity, involves experiences of community in virtue of a mutual recognition of a common descent. What differentiates Irish-American from African-American identity, as understood in these United States, is that it is largely recognized nowadays that what flows from this common descent is a matter of a shared culture. People of Irish-American descent adopted and raised outside Irish-American culture are still, perhaps, to be thought of as Irish-Americans; but they have a choice about whether this fact, once they are aware of it, should be central to their ethical identities, and their taking it as central would involve them in adopting certain cultural practices. Someone who refuses to do anything with the fact of their Irish-American descent—who fails to acknowledge it in any of their projects—is not generally held to be inauthentic; is not held to be unfaithful to something about herself to which she ought to respond. So far as I can see, by contrast, African-Americans who respond in this way fall into two categories, depending on whether or not their visible morphology permits them to "pass," permits them, that is, to act in society without their African ancestry's being noticed.

If they cannot pass, they will often be thought of as inauthentic, as refusing to acknowledge something about themselves that they ought to acknowledge, though they will not be thought to be dishonest, since their morphology reveals the fact that is being denied. If they can pass, they will be thought of by many, as being not merely inauthentic but dishonest. And while they may have prudential reasons for concealing the fact of their (partial) African descent, this will be held by many to amount to inauthenticity, especially if they adopt cultural styles associated with "white" people.

Now, so far as I can see, these differences between the identities that we think of as "racial" and those which we think of as "ethnic" cannot be made intelligible without adverting to certain (false) beliefs. Someone who conceals the fact of an African ancestry in his social life quite generally is held to be inauthentic, because there is still around in the culture the idea that being (partially) descended from black people makes you "really" black—in ways that have ethical consequences—while being descended from Irish stock merely correlates roughly with a certain cultural identity. If "races" were biologically real, this would, perhaps, begin to be a possible distinction; though it would require further argument to persuade me that ethical consequences flowed from membership in races. But since they are not, this distinction seems, as I say, to require a distinction that someone apprised of the facts should just give up.

That "race" and gender have interestingly different relations to metaphysical identity would not obscure the fact that as ethical identities they have a central importance for us. What this means is, presumably, something like this: that for us, in our society, being-of-a-certain-gender and being-of-a-certain-race are for many people facts that are centrally implicated in the construction of life plans. To ignore one's race and one's gender in thinking about the ethical project of composing a life for oneself requires, in many minds, a kind of ignoring of social reality which amounts to attempting to fool oneself; and that is part of what is involved in the thought that passing for the "wrong" gender or race involves a certain inauthenticity.

We construct ethical identities—woman, man, African-American, "white"—in ways that depend crucially on false beliefs about metaphysical identities; something like each of them could be reconstructed out of other materials. But if we were to live in a society that did not institutionalize those false metaphysical beliefs, it is unclear that the project of reconstruction would be an attractive one. In a truly nonsexist, nonracist society, gender, the ethical identity constructed on the base of sexual differences, would at least be radically differently configured, and might, like "race," entirely wither away; ethnic identities, by contrast—and this is something an African-American identity could become—seem likely to persist so long as there are human cultures and subcultures, which is likely to mean as long as people are raised in families.

Chapter *9*

Is It OK to Be Emotional?

Whar was your latest passion? When did you last get angry, or feel love, or find yourself envious or jealous? What was the significance of that emotion? Was it an unwelcome intrusion into an otherwise calm and enjoyable day? Or did your emotion actually define your day, perhaps even (as with love) define your life for months or years to come? Was this a familiar emotion to you—do you get angry or fall in love often—or did it seem out of character, a strange reaction that does not represent your real personality? Was it annoying and embarrassing, or did it feel right and good, perhaps even refreshing or elevating? What is the significance of your emotions in your life? Are they disruptions or punctuations? Are they just moments of excitement or do they have some more significant meaning? How are we to understand emotion, and how do our emotions fit into our lives? We often warn one another against emotion, against becoming "emotional." Indeed, becoming emotional is often viewed as a sign of weakness, poor character or temporary irrationality. "Let's be reasonable" often means "Let's not get carried away by our emotions," and a familiar line in a popular movie counsels us, "Don't get mad, get even."

Twenty-five hundred years of emphasis on reason as the subject matter of philosophy and the core of human nature has tended to minimize the importance of emotions in human life. It is true that a person who is all emotion and is never rational is a monster, but a person who is all rationality and without emotion is also a monster, a mere automaton, a walking computer and not a human being. One of the great horror films, *Invasion of the Body Snatchers,* portrays aliens as humanoids without emotion. It is our emotions as well as our reason that makes us human.

Emotions have had a confused place in the history of philosophy. On the one hand, they are acknowledged to be vital, important, and essential to life. Aristotle insisted that the good life consisted of having the right emotions as well as having reason and doing the right things. Christian philosophers have long insisted that love and those emotions associated with faith are among the most important things in life. On the other hand, philosophers have recognized that the emotions can be dangerous. Ancient philosophers likened love and anger to madness, and the famed storyteller Aesop insisted that "emotions should be the slaves, not the masters, of reason." Accordingly, the view that emotions are important and necessary has always been balanced by the view that emotions are subhuman, our more bestial aspect and the "lowest" part of the soul. In more modern times, both popular and scientific views of emotions have reduced them to primitive physical reactions and have opposed them to reason and intelligence. Thus, Descartes and most of his contemporaries referred to the emotions as "animal spirits" and William James more recently defined emotion in terms of physiological ("visceral") reaction. In such a view, emotions typically emerge as unlearned, instinctual, perhaps even stupid if not destructive and, in any case, disruptive and intrusive in our otherwise rational lives.

Obviously our emotions occupy an ambiguous place in our conception of ourselves. They are not within our direct control, but neither are they alien to us. Our emotions are different from reasoning and thinking as such, but they are clearly affected by our reasoning and they affect our thinking in turn. Our emotions are in some sense "in the mind," but like perceptions and unlike a pain or a stomach ache, they are about people and situations in the world. They obviously involve our bodies, but they also involve thought and awareness. They are essential to being a good person, but they also contribute to selfishness, evil, and insanity.

Aristotle long ago recognized that emotions were not just feeling but also perceptions: They involve seeing the world in a certain way. Emotions also involve motives; they urge us to action. His view—augmented by the Stoic philosophers in subsequent generations—was that emotions already include certain aspects of reason; they are learned and can be learned well or badly. They can be smart or foolish, noble or embarrassing.

One particularly ingenious theory of emotion as something more than mere feeling is Book II of David Hume's *Treatise of Human Nature.* A passion, Hume suggested, is a complex mix of impressions (sensations or feelings) and ideas. Pride, for example, involves not just a pleasant feeling but also a set of ideas about one's *self.* Hume opposed passion and reason, but in an unusual and provocative twist of the usual philosophical championing of reason, he announced that "reason is and ought to be the slave of the passions." A very different view of emotions was developed by the French existentialist Jean-Paul Sartre. Emotions, he suggested, are "magical transformations of the world." Like Aristotle, he recognized the perception-like nature of emotion, but Sartre added another unusual twist. Emotions are purposive, he argued; they have an end in mind. He believed that we get afraid or angry or resentful in order to accomplish something, usually to escape from or deny an unpleasant situation.

Understanding emotions in general is perhaps not as personally rewarding as understanding specific emotions. Anger is a particularly misunderstood emotion. It is often thought to be irrational and dangerous, even a sin. We often talk about it as if it were a fluid that fills us up and makes us "hot," occasionally "bursting" or "exploding." Carol Tavris has developed a radically new interpretation of anger, "the misunderstood emotion," in which social awareness is much more important than physiology. Love, by contrast, is an emotion that is almost universally and uncritically praised, but the price of that adulation is that it is an emotion that is rarely scrutinized. In a famous speech in Plato's *Symposium,* Aristophanes defines love metaphorically as a "reunification" of two original halves. Following Aristophanes, Robert Solomon offers a theory of love understood as a form of shared identity. Finally, Morwenna Griffiths insists that the very vocabulary of emotions and feelings needs to be reexamined, and she offers a feminist critique of the Cartesian tradition.

ARISTOTLE

On Anger

ARISTOTLE (384–322 B.C.) was a biologist as well as a great philosopher, and wrote widely on topics in virtually every other science, from astronomy and physics to psychology. The following excerpt is taken from his book on rhetoric, in which he discusses the uses of emotion in moving the public to action.

W E shall define an emotion as that which leads one's condition to become so transformed that his judgment is affected, and which is accompanied by pleasure and pain. Examples of emotions include anger, pity, fear, and the like, as well as the opposites of these. We will need with each of these emotions to investigate three particulars; in investigating anger, for instance, we will ask what the temperament is of angry people, with whom they most often become angry, and at what sort of things. To grasp one or two but not all three of these conditions would make it impossible to induce anger in one's audience. The same is true with the other emotions. So, just as we listed propositions in what we said earlier, let us do this again in analyzing these emotions in the same way.

Let anger be defined as a distressed desire for conspicuous vengeance in return for a conspicuous and unjustifiable contempt of one's person or friends. If this indeed defines anger, then the anger of the angry person is necessarily always directed towards someone in particular, e.g., Cleon, but not towards all of humanity; also of necessity is that this individual has done or intended to do something to him or one of his friends, and that accompanying every outburst of anger is a certain pleasure derived from the hope for revenge. I say "pleasure" because it is pleasant to con-template achieving one's goals; and no one attempts to achieve what seems to be impossible for himself, so the angry man attempts to achieve what is possible for himself. The poet spoke correctly when he said that anger,

> Much sweeter than dripping honey,
> Swells in men's hearts.

Pleasure follows upon anger for this reason and because the mind is consumed with thoughts of vengeance; like dreams, the visions then conjured up create pleasure.

Slighting is the implementing of an opinion about what one considers to be worthless; for we think both the good and the bad to be worthy of attention (as well as what is potentially good or bad), but we do not consider whatever is of little or no account to be worthy of attention.

There are three forms of slighting— scorn, spite, and insolence. One slights what he scorns, for whatever one thinks to be worthy of nothing he scorns, and he slights what is worthy of nothing. Then one who is spiteful is also scornful, for spite involves the interference in another's wishes, not to achieve anything for oneself, but only to make sure that the other achieves nothing. Since he achieves nothing for himself, he slights the other. It is evident that the other does not intend to harm him; if he did, it would then be a matter of fear, not of slighting. It is evident also that he does not intend to help him to any appreciable degree, for there would then be an attempt at creating a friendship.

To act insolently constitutes a form of slighting, for insolence involves doing and saying things that produce shame for the person to whom these things are done or said—so that something else might happen to him (other than what has already happened), but for the other's pleasure. If it were done in retaliation, then this would not be insolence, but sheer vengeance. The insolent person derives pleasure from this because he sees others suffer and thus considers himself quite superior. The young and the rich often derive pleasure from such insolence, for they consider themselves superior when acting insolently. Dishonor is an act of insolence, and the one who dishonors is one who slights, since that which is worthy of nothing—of neither good or bad—has no honor. For this reason the angered Achilles says,

He has dishonored me; he has himself taken and keeps my prize.

and,

I am without honor, as if some foreigner.

and shows that he is angered for this very reason. Some think it fitting that they be esteemed by those of lesser birth, ability, nobility, or whatever quality in which one is generally superior to another; for example, the rich man considers himself worthy of esteem from a poor man where wealth is concerned, as does the rhetorician from one who is inarticulate, the ruler from the governed, and even the hopeful ruler from those he hopes to rule. So it is said,

The anger of divine kings is mighty,

and,

But he holds his anger for another day;

the cause of their vexation is their superior station, and still others feel anger at those from whom they expect the proper care, for example, from those for whom he—either acting by himself or *via* his agents or friends—has done or is doing willful or willed service.

It is now evident from these analyses what the temperament is of angered people, at whom they become angered, and for what reasons. They become angry when they are in distress, for one in distress desires something. If someone should in any manner stand in one's way, for instance, if one should directly prevent a thirsty man from drinking (or even if it is done indirectly, he will appear to be doing the same thing), or if someone opposes, fails to assist, or in some other way annoys a distressed person, he will become angry at any of those individuals. For this reason the sick, the poor, those at war, the lover, and anyone with an unsatisfied desire, are prone to anger and irascibility, particularly against those who make light of their present distress. Examples include the ill person angry at those making light of his illness, the poor man angry at those making light of his poverty, the warrior angry at those making light of his struggle, the lover at those making light of his love and so forth, for each person is predisposed towards his own kind of anger caused by his own sort of distress. He will also anger if he should happen to receive the opposite of what he expected, for the unexpected creates a greater bitterness just as it can create the greater joy if one attains his desires contrary to his expectations. From these observations the hours, periods, moods, and ages most conducive to anger become apparent, as do the places and occasions; and the more intense or numerous these conditions are, the more conducive to anger they become.

We have now seen what sort of temperament belongs to people predisposed to anger. They become angry at those who laugh, scoff, and jeer at them—all acts of insolence—and at those doing them harm in manners which represent an attitude of insolence. This harm cannot be either retaliatory or beneficial to the doers, for then it would not seem to be an act of insolence. They also become angry at those who malign them or scorn matters they take greatly to heart; zealous philosophers and those concerned with their appearance, to cite just two of many examples, anger at those who scorn philosophy and those who scorn their appearance, respectively. Such anger becomes increasingly severe if the angered individuals suspect that this ability or quality does not belong or appear to belong to them, for they do not mind the ridicule when they feel thoroughly superior in those abilities or qualities at which others scoff. Anger is also directed at their friends more often than at others, since better treatment is expected from them, and also at those who normally give honor to take thought of them, but then cease to act in this way; the angry individuals here assume they are being scorned, for otherwise they would be treated in the same way as usual. They also become angry at those who fail to repay or inadequately repay acts of kindness and at inferiors who work against them, for any such people appear to have a scornful attitude; in the latter example the angered individuals are opposed by those who consider them inferior and in the former they have offered kindness to those who consider them inferior.

They especially anger at those of no account who slight them, since we suggested that an anger resulting from a slight was directed towards those who have no right to slight another, and it is one's inferiors who have no right to do so. They also become angry at their friends who fail to speak well of them or who fail to treat them well, or especially when they do the opposite, or when they do not understand their needs (just as Antiphon's Plexippus failed to understand Meleager's needs). It is a sign of contempt to fail to perceive the needs of a friend, since we do not forget those who are on our mind. One also angers at those who celebrate or act quite cheerfully in his misfortunes; either action is a sign of enmity or slight. One also feels anger against those who show no concern for the pains they have given him, which explains why one becomes angry with messengers who bring bad news. One also feels anger at those who listen to talk about him or ogle at his weaknesses, for it is as if they are slighters or enemies; friends would sympathize, since everyone is pained to focus on his own weaknesses. In addition, one angers at those who slight him in the presence of five classes of people—those who envy him, those he admires, those by whom he wishes to be admired, those whom he respects, and those who respect him. When people slight him in the presence of these, they incite him to an even greater anger. One also feels anger at those who slight those whom it would be a disgrace not to defend—parents, children, wives, subordinates—or to those who do not return a favor (since such a slight is an impropriety), or to those who pretend not to know about a matter he feels to be of importance, since this is an act of scorn. And one feels anger toward those beneficent to others, but not to him as well, for it is again an act of scorn to deem everyone else worthy of treatment he is not deemed worthy to receive. Forgetfulness, even of something so insignificant as a name, also produces anger, since forgetfulness as well seems to be a sign of slight and since forgetfulness derives from neglect, which is a slight.

We have now established simultaneously at whom one becomes angry, the temperament of the angry person, and the causes for his anger. It is clear that in his speech the orator must create in his audience a temperament suitable for anger and establish his adversaries as those to be held liable for what makes his audience anger and as the sort of men at whom they should be angry.

RENÉ DESCARTES

The Passions of the Soul

RENÉ DESCARTES (1596–1650) is, among many other things, the father of Cartesian dualism, which holds that the mind and the body are separate "substances." This raises the difficult question of how they interact, but it raises specific problems for the analysis of emotion. Emotions, more than any other psychic phenomena, seem to be both of the mind and of the body. In the following excerpt, Descartes tried to solve such problems with his theory of "animal spirits," which are of the body but disturb the soul as well.

OF THE PASSIONS IN GENERAL, AND INCIDENTALLY OF THE WHOLE NATURE OF MAN

*T*HAT *What in Respect of a Subject Is Passion, Is in Some Other Regard Always Action.* There is nothing in which the defective nature of the sciences which we have received from the ancients appears more clearly than in what they have written on the passions; for, although this is a matter which has at all times been the object of much investigation, and though it would appear to be one of the most difficult, inasmuch as since every one has experi-

ence of the passions within himself, there is not necessity to borrow one's observations from elsewhere in order to discover their nature; yet that which the ancients have taught regarding them is both so slight, and for the most part so far from credible, that I am unable to entertain any hope of approximation to the truth excepting by shunning the paths which they have followed. This is why I shall be here obliged to write just as though I were treating of a matter which no one had ever touched on before me; and, to begin with, I consider that all that which occurs or that happens anew, is by the philosophers, generally speaking, termed a passion, in as far as the subject to which it occurs is concerned, and an action in respect of him who causes it to occur. Thus although the agent and the recipient are frequently very different, the action and the passion are always one and the same thing, although having different names, because of the two diverse subjects to which it may be related.

What the Functions of the Soul Are. After having thus considered all the functions which pertain to the body alone, it is easy to recognise that there is nothing in us which we ought to attribute to our soul excepting our thoughts, which are mainly of two sorts, the one being the actions of the soul, and the other its passions. Those which I call its actions are all our desires, because we find by experience that they proceed directly from our soul, and appear to depend on it alone: while, on the other hand, we may usually term one's passions all those kinds of perception or forms of knowledge which are found in us, because it is often not our soul which makes them what they are, and because it always receives them from the things which are represented by them. . . .

Of the Perceptions.   Our perceptions are also of two sorts, and the one have the soul as a cause and the other the body. Those which have the soul as a cause are the perceptions of our desires, and of all the imaginations or other thoughts which depend on them. For it is certain that we cannot desire anything without perceiving by the same means that we desire it; and, although in regard to our soul it is an action to desire something, we may say that it is also one of its passions to perceive that it desires. Yet because this perception and this will are really one and the same thing, the more noble always supplies

the denomination, and thus we are not in the habit of calling it a passion, but only an action. . . .

That the Imaginations Which only Depend on the Fortuitous Movements of the Spirits, May Be Passions Just as Truly as the Perceptions Which Depend on the Nerves.   It remains for us to notice here that all the same things which the soul perceives by the intermission of the nerves, may also be represented by the fortuitous course of the animal spirits, without there being any other difference excepting that the impressions which come into the brain by the nerves are usually more lively or definite than those excited there by the spirits, which caused me to say [previously] that the former resemble the shadow or picture of the latter. We must also notice that it sometimes happens that this picture is so similar to the thing which it represents that we may be mistaken therein regarding the perceptions which relate to objects which are outside us, or at least those which relate to certain parts of our body, but that we cannot be so deceived regarding the passions, inasmuch as they are so close to, and so entirely within our soul, that it is impossible for it to feel them without their being actually such as it feels them to be. Thus often when we sleep, and sometimes even when we are awake, we imagine certain things so forcibly, that we think we see them before us or feel them in our body although they do not exist at all; but although we may be asleep, or dream, we cannot feel sad or moved by any other passion without its being very true that the soul actually has the passion within it.

The Definition of the Passions of the Soul.   After having considered in what the passions of the soul differ from all its other thoughts, it seems to me that we may define them generally as the perceptions, feelings, or emotions of the soul which we relate specially to it, and which are caused, maintained, and fortified by some movement of the spirits.

Explanation of the First Part of This Definition. We may call them perceptions when we make use of this word generally to signify all the thoughts which are not actions of the soul, or desires, but not when the term is used only to signify clear cognition; for experience shows us that those who are the most agitated by their passions, are not those who know them best; and that they are of the number of perceptions which the close alliance which exists between the soul and the body, renders confused and obscure. We may also call them feelings because they are received into the soul in the same way as are the objects of our outside senses, and are not otherwise known by it; but we can yet more accurately call them emotions of the soul, not only because the name may be attributed to all the changes which occur in it—that is, in all the diverse thoughts which come to it, but more especially because of all the kinds of thought which it may have, there are no others which so powerfully agitate and disturb it as do these passions.

Explanation of the Second Part. I add that they particularly relate to the soul, in order to distinguish them from the other feelings which are related, the one to outside objects such as scents, sounds, and colours; the others to our body such as hunger, thirst, and pain. I also add that they are caused, maintained, and fortified by some movement of the spirits, in order to distinguish them from our desires, which we may call emotions of the soul which relate to it, but which are used by itself;

and also in order to explain their ultimate and most proximate cause, which plainly distinguishes them from the other feelings.

How the Soul and the Body Act on One Another. Let us then conceive here that the soul has its principal seat in the little gland which exists in the middle of the brain, from whence it radiates forth through all the remainder of the body by means of the animal spirits, nerves, and even the blood, which, participating in the impressions of the spirits, can carry them by the arteries into all the members. . . . Let us here add that the small gland which is the main seat of the soul is so suspended between the cavities which contain the spirits that it can be moved by them in as many different ways as there are sensible diversities in the object, but that it may also be moved in diverse ways by the soul, whose nature is such that it receives in itself as many diverse impressions, that is to say, that it possesses as many diverse perceptions as there are diverse movements in this gland. Reciprocally, likewise, the machine of the body is so formed that from the simple fact that this gland is diversely moved by the soul, or by such other cause, whatever it is, it thrusts the spirits which surround it towards the pores of the brain, which conduct them by the nerves into the muscles, by which means it causes them to move the limbs. . . .

How One and the Same Cause May Excite Different Passions in Different Men. The same impression which a terrifying object makes on the gland, and which causes fear in certain men, may excite in others courage and confidence; the reason of this is that all brains are not constituted in the same way, and that the same movement of the gland which in some excites fear, in others causes the spirits to enter into the pores of the brain which conduct them partly into the nerves which serve to move the hands for purposes of self-defense, and partly into those which agitate and drive the blood towards the heart in the manner requisite to produce the spirits proper for the continuance of this defense, and to retain the desire of it.

The Principal Effect of the Passions. For it is requisite to notice that the principal effect of all the passions in men is that they incite and dispose their soul to desire those things for which they prepare their body, so that the feeling of fear incites it to desire to fly, that of courage to desire to fight, and so on.

What Is the Power of the Soul in Reference to Its Passions. Our passions cannot likewise be directly excited or removed by the action of our will, but they can be so indirectly by the representation of things which are usually united to the passions which we desire to have, and which are contrary to those which we desire to set aside. Thus, in order to excite courage in oneself and remove fear, it is not sufficient to have the will to do so, but we must also apply ourselves to consider the reasons, the objects or examples which persuade us that the peril is not great; that there is always more security in defense than in flight; that we should have the glory and joy of having vanquished, while we could expect nothing but regret and shame for having fled, and so on.

The Reason Which Prevents the Soul From Being Able Wholly to Control Its Passion. And there is a special reason which prevents the soul from being able at once to change or arrest its passions, which has caused me to say in defining them that they are not only caused, but are also maintained and strengthened by some particular movement of the spirits. This reason is that they are nearly all accompanied by some commotion which takes place in the heart, and in consequence also in the whole of the blood and the animal spirits, so that until this commotion has subsided, they remain present to our thought in the same manner as sensible objects are present there while they act upon the organs or our senses. And as the soul, in rendering itself very attentive to some other thing, may prevent itself from hearing a slight noise or feeling a slight pain, but cannot prevent itself in the same way from hearing thunder or feeling the fire which burns the hand, it may similarly easily get the better of the lesser passions, but not the most violent and strongest, excepting after the commotion of the blood and spirits is appeased. The most that the will can do while this commotion is in its full strength is not to yield to its effects and to restrain many of the movements to which it disposes the body. For example, if anger causes us to lift our hand to strike, the will can usually hold it back; if fear incites our legs to flee, the will can arrest them, and so on in other similar cases.

DAVID HUME

On Pride

DAVID HUME (1711–1776) was one of the few philosophers of the Enlightenment who would argue that "reason is and ought to be the slave of the passions." Placing emotions in such an elevated position, he spent a significant proportion of his philosophy trying to analyze them and show how they are constructed out of combinations of "impressions and ideas"—the two basic components of his theory of mind. What follows is his analysis of pride from his Treatise of Human Nature, *with some comments on love and hate.*

OF THE PASSIONS

Division of the Subject

AS all the perceptions of the mind may be divided into *impressions* and *ideas,* so the impressions admit of another division into *original* and *secondary.* This division of the impressions is the same with that which I formerly made use of when I distinguish'd them into impressions of *sensation* and *reflexion.* Original impressions or impressions of sensation are such as without any antecedent perception arise in the soul, from the constitution of the body, from the animal spirits, or from the application of objects to the external organs. Secondary, or reflective impressions are such as proceed from some of these original ones, either immediately or by the interposition of its idea. Of the first kind are all the impressions of the senses, and all bodily pains and pleasures: Of the second are the passions, and other emotions resembling them.

'Tis certain, that the mind, in its perceptions, must begin somewhere; and that since the impressions precede their correspondent ideas, there must be some impressions, which without any introduction make their appearance in the soul. As these depend upon natural and physical causes, the examination of them wou'd lead me too far from my present subject, into the sciences of anatomy and natural philosophy. For this reason I shall here confine myself to those other impressions, which I have call'd secondary and reflective, as arising either from the original impressions, or from their ideas. Bodily pains and pleasures are the source of many passions, both when felt and consider'd by the mind; but arise originally in the soul, or in the body, whichever you please to call it; without any preceding thought or perception. A fit of the gout produces a long train of passions, as grief, hope, fear; but is not deriv'd immediately from any affection or idea.

The reflective impressions may be divided into two kinds, *viz.* the *calm* and the *violent.* Of the first kind is the sense of beauty and deformity in action, composition, and external objects. Of the second are the passions of love and hatred, grief and joy, pride and humility. This division is far from being exact. The raptures of poetry and music frequently rise to the greatest height; while those other impressions properly called *passions,* may decay into so soft an emotion, as to become, in a manner, imperceptible. But as in general the passions are more violent than the emotions arising from beauty and deformity, these impressions have been commonly distinguish'd from each other. The subject of the human mind being so copious and various, I shall here take advantage of this vulgar and specious division, that I may proceed with the greater order; and having said all I thought necessary concerning our ideas, shall now explain these violent emotions or passions, their nature, origin, causes, and effects.

When we take a survey of the passions, there occurs a division of them into *direct* and *indirect*. By direct passions I understand such as arise immediately from good or evil, from pain or pleasure. By indirect such as proceed from the same principles, but by the conjunction of other qualities. This distinction I cannot at present justify or explain any farther. I can only observe in general, that under the indirect passions I comprehend pride, humility, ambition, vanity, love, hatred, envy, pity, malice, generosity, with their dependents. And under the direct passions, desire, aversion, grief, joy, hope, fear, despair and security. I shall begin with the former.

Of Pride and Humility; Their Objects and Causes

The passions of *pride* and *humility* being simple and uniform impressions, 'tis impossible we can ever, by a multitude of words, give a just definition of them, or indeed of any of the passions. The utmost we can pretend to is a description of them, by an enumeration of such circumstances, as attend them: But as these words, *pride* and *humility,* are of general use, and the impressions they represent the most common of any,

every one, of himself, will be able to form a just idea of them, without any danger of mistake. For which reason, not to lose time upon preliminaries, I shall immediately enter upon the examination of these passions.

'Tis evident, that pride and humility, tho' directly contrary, have yet the same OBJECT. This object is self, or that succession of related ideas and impressions, of which we have an intimate memory and consciousness. Here the view always fixes when we are actuated by either of these passions. According as our idea of ourself is more or less advantageous, we feel either of those opposite affections, and are elated by pride, or dejected with humility. Whatever other objects may be comprehended by the mind, they are always consider'd with a view to ourselves; otherwise they wou'd never be able either to excite these passions, or produce the smallest encrease or diminution of them. When self enters not into the consideration, there is no room either for pride or humility.

But tho' that connected succession of perceptions, which we call *self*, be always the object of these two passions, 'tis impossible it can be their CAUSE, or be sufficient alone to excite them. For as these passions are directly contrary, and have the same object in common; were their object also their cause; it cou'd never produce any degree of the one passion, but at the same time it must excite an equal degree of the other; which opposition and contrariety must destroy both. 'Tis impossible a man can at the same time be both proud and humble; and where he has different reasons for these passions, as frequently happens, the passions either take place alternately; or if they encounter, the one annihilates the other, as far as its strength goes, and the remainder only of that, which is superior, continues to operate upon the mind. But in the present case neither of the passions cou'd ever become superior; because supposing it to be the view only of ourself, which excited them, that being perfectly indifferent to either, must produce both in the very same proportion; or in other words, can produce neither. To excite any passion, and at the same time raise an equal share of its antagonist, is immediately to undo what was done, and must leave the mind at last perfectly calm and indifferent.

We must, therefore, make a distinction betwixt the cause and the object of these passions; betwixt that idea, which excites them, and that to which they direct their view, when excited. Pride and humility, being once rais'd, immediately turn our attention to ourself, and regard that as their ultimate and final object; but there is something farther requisite in order to raise them: Something, which is peculiar to one of the passions, and produces not both in the very same degree. The first idea, that is presented to the mind, is that of the cause or productive principle. This excites the passion, connected with it; and the passion, when excited, turns our view to another idea, which is that of self. Here then is a passion plac'd betwixt two ideas, of which the one produces it, and the other is produc'd by it. The first idea, therefore, represents the *cause,* the second the *object* of the passion.

To begin with the causes of pride and humility; we may observe, that their most obvious and remarkable property is the vast variety of *subjects,* on which they may be plac'd. Every valuable quality of the mind, whether of the imagination, judgment, memory or disposition; wit, good-sense, learning,

courage, justice, integrity; all these are the causes of pride; and their opposites of humility. Nor are these passions confin'd to the mind, but extend their view to the body likewise. A man may be proud of his beauty, strength, agility, good mien, address in dancing, riding, fencing, and of his dexterity in any manual business or manufacture. But this is not all. The passion looking farther, comprehends whatever objects are in the least ally'd or related to us. Our country, family, children, relations, riches, houses, gardens, horses, dogs, cloaths; any of these may become a cause either of pride or humility.

From the consideration of these causes, it appears necessary we shou'd make a new distinction in the causes of the passion, betwixt that *quality,* which operates, and the *subject,* on which it is plac'd. A man, for instance, is vain of a beautiful house, which belongs to him, or which he has himself built and contriv'd. Here the object of the passion is himself, and the cause is the beautiful house: Which cause again is sub-divided into two parts, *viz.* the quality, which operates upon the passion, and the subject, in which the quality inheres. The quality is the beauty, and the subject is the house, consider'd as his property or contrivance. Both these parts are essential, nor is the distinction vain and chimerical. Beauty, consider'd merely as such, unless plac'd upon something related to us, never produces any pride or vanity; and the strongest relation alone, without beauty, or something else in its place, has little influence on that passion. . . .

Having thus in a manner suppos'd two properties of the causes of these affections, *viz.* that the *qualities* produce a separate pain or pleasure, and that the *subjects,* on which the qualities are plac'd, are related to self; I proceed to examine the passions themselves, in order to find something in them, correspondent to the suppos'd properties of their causes. *First,* I find, that the peculiar object of pride and humility is determin'd by an original and natural instinct, and that 'tis absolutely impossible, from the primary constitution of the mind, that these passions shou'd ever look beyond self, or that individual person, of whose actions and sentiments each of us is intimately conscious. Here at last the view always rests, when we are actuated by either of these passions; nor can we, in that situation of mind, ever lose sight of this object. For this I pretend not to give any reason; but consider such a peculiar direction of the thought as an original quality.

The *second* quality, which I discover in these passions, and which I likewise consider as an original quality, is their sensations, or the peculiar emotions they excite in the soul, and which constitute their very being and essence. Thus pride is a pleasant sensation, and humility a painful; and upon the removal of the pleasure and pain, there is in reality no pride nor humility. Of this our very feeling convinces us; and beyond our feeling, 'tis here in vain to reason or dispute.

If I compare, therefore, these two *establish'd* properties of the passions, *viz.* their object, which is self, and their sensation, which is either pleasant or painful, to the two suppos'd properties of the causes, *viz.* their relation to self, and their tendency to produce a pain or pleasure, independent of the passion; I immediately find, that taking these suppositions to be just, the true system breaks in upon me with an irresistible evidence. That cause, which excites the passion, is related to the object, which nature has attributed to the passion; the sensation, which the cause separately produces, is related to the sensation of the passion: From this double relation of ideas and impressions, the passion is deriv'd. The one idea is easily converted into its cor-relative; and the one impression into that, which resembles and corresponds to it: With how much greater facility must this transition be made, where these movements mutually assist each other, and the mind receives a double impulse from the relations both of its impressions and ideas?

That we may comprehend this the better, we must suppose, that nature has given to the organs of the human mind, a certain disposition fitted to produce a peculiar impression or emotion, which we call *pride:* To this emotion she has assign'd a certain idea, *viz.* that of *self,* which it never fails to produce. This contrivance of nature is easily conceiv'd. We have many instances of such a situation of affairs. The nerves of the nose and palate are so dispos'd, as in certain circumstances to convey such peculiar sensations to the mind: The sensations of lust and hunger always produce in us the idea of those peculiar objects, which are suitable to each appetite. These two circumstances are united in pride. The organs are so dispos'd as to produce the passion; and the passion, after its production, naturally produces a certain idea. All this needs no proof. 'Tis evident we never shou'd be possest of that passion, were there not a disposition of mind proper for it; and 'tis as evident, that the passion always turns our view to ourselves, and makes us think of our own qualities and circumstances. . . .

The difficulty, then, is only to discover this cause, and find what it is that gives the first motion to pride and sets those organs in action, which are naturally fitted to produce that emotion. Upon my consulting experience, in order to resolve this difficulty, I immediately find a hundred different causes, that produce pride; and upon examining these causes, I suppose, what at first I perceive to be probable, that all of them concur in two circumstances; which are, that of themselves they produce an impression, ally'd to the passion, and are plac'd on a subject, ally'd to the object of the passion. When I consider after this the nature of *relation,* and its effects both on the passions and ideas, I can no longer doubt, upon these suppositions, that 'tis the very principle, which gives rise to pride, and bestows motion on those organs, which being naturally dispos'd to produce that affection, require only a first impulse or beginning to their action. Any thing, that gives a pleasant sensation, and is related to self, excites the passion of pride, which is also agreeable, and has self for its object.

What I have said of pride is equally true of humility. The sensation of humility is uneasy, as that of pride is agreeable; for which reason the separate sensation, arising from the causes, must be revers'd, while the relation to self continues the same. Tho' pride and humility are directly contrary in their effects, and in their sensations, they have notwithstanding the same object; so that 'tis requisite only to change the relation of impressions, without making any change upon that of ideas. Accordingly we find, that a beautiful house, belonging to ourselves, produces pride; and that the same house, still belonging to ourselves, produces humility, when by any accident its beauty is chang'd into deformity, and thereby the sensations of pleasure, which corresponded to pride, is transform'd into pain, which is related to humility. The double relation between the ideas and impressions subsists in both cases, and produces an easy transition from the one emotion to the other.

OF LOVE AND HATRED
Of the Objects and Causes of Love and Hatred

'Tis altogether impossible to give any definition of the passions of *love* and *hatred;* and that because they produce merely a simple impression, without any mixture or composition. 'Twou'd be as unnecessary to attempt any description of them, drawn from their nature, origin, causes and objects; and that both because these are the subjects of our present enquiry, and because these passions of themselves are sufficiently known from our common feeling and experience. This we have already observ'd concerning pride and humility, and here repeat it concerning love and hatred; and indeed there is so great a resemblance betwixt these two sets of passions, that we shall be oblig'd to begin with a kind of abridgment of our reasonings concerning the former, in order to explain the latter.

As the immediate *object* of pride and humility is self or that identical person, of whose thoughts, actions, and sensations we are intimately conscious; so the *object* of love and hatred is some other person, of whose thoughts, actions, and sensations we are not conscious. This is sufficiently evident from experience. Our love and hatred are always directed to some sensible being external to us; and when we talk of *self-love,* 'tis not in a proper sense, nor has the sensation it produces any thing in common with that tender emotion, which is excited by a friend or mistress. 'Tis the same case with hatred. We may be mortified by our own faults and follies; but never feel any anger or hatred, except from the injuries of others.

But tho' the object of love and hatred be always some other person, 'tis plain that the object is not, properly speaking, the *cause* of these passions, or alone sufficient to excite them. For since love and hatred are directly contrary in their sensation, and have the same object in common, if that object were also their cause, it wou'd produce these opposite passions in an equal degree; and as they must, from the very first moment, destroy each other, none of them wou'd ever be able to make its appearance. There must, therefore, be some cause different from the object.

If we consider the causes of love and hatred, we shall find they are very much diversify'd, and have not many things in common. The virtue, knowledge, wit, good sense, good humour of any person, produce love and esteem; as the opposite qualities, hatred and contempt. The same passions arise from bodily accomplishments, such as beauty, force, swiftness, dexterity; and from their contraries; as likewise from the external advantages and disadvantages of family, possessions, cloaths, nation and climate. There is not one of these objects, but what by its different qualities may produce love and esteem, or hatred and contempt.

From the view of these causes we may derive a new distinction betwixt the *quality* that operates, and the *subject* on which it is plac'd. A prince, that is possess'd of a stately palace, commands the esteem of the people upon that account; and that *first,* by the beauty of the palace, and *secondly,* by the relation of property, which connect it with him. The removal of either of these destroys the passion; which evidently proves that the cause is a compounded one.

'Twou'd be tedious to trace the passions of love and hatred, thro' all the observations which we have form'd concerning pride and humility, and which are equally applicable to both sets of passions. 'Twill be sufficient to *remark* in general, that the object of love and hatred is evidently some thinking person; and that the sensation of the former passion is always agreeable, and of the latter uneasy. We may also *suppose* with some shew of probability, *that the cause of both these passions is always related to a thinking being,* and *that the cause of the former produce a separate pleasure, and of the latter a separate uneasiness.*

WILLIAM JAMES

What Is an Emotion?

WILLIAM JAMES (1842–1910) was one of America's greatest philosopher–
psychologists and wrote what for many years was the classic textbook of psychology.
He had a special interest in emotions, and his analysis of emotion still dominates
much of current thinking in psychology. What follows is taken from his 1884 essay
"What Is an Emotion?"

T HE physiologists who, during the past few years, have been so industriously exploring the functions of the brain, have limited their attempts at explanation to its cognitive and volitional performances. Dividing the brain into sensorial and motor centres, they have found their division to be exactly paralleled by the analysis made by empirical psychology, of the perceptive and volitional parts of the mind into their simplest elements. But the *aesthetic* sphere of the mind, its longings, its pleasures and pains, and its emotions, have been . . . ignored.

And yet it is even now certain that of two things concerning the emotions, one must be true. Either separate and special centres, affected to them alone, are their brain-seat, or else they correspond to processes occurring in the motor and sensory centres, already assigned, or in others like them, not yet mapped out. If the former be the case we must deny the current view, and hold the cortex to be something more than the surface of "projection" for every sensitive spot and every muscle in the body. If the latter be the case, we must ask whether the emotional "process" in the sensory or motor centre be an altogether peculiar one, or whether it resembles the ordinary perceptive processes of which those centres

are already recognized to be the seat. The purpose of the following pages is to show that the last alternative comes nearest to the truth, and that the emotional brain-processes not only resemble the ordinary sensorial brain-processes, but in very truth *are* nothing but such processes variously combined. . . .

I should say first of all that the only emotions I propose expressly to consider here are those that have a distinct bodily expression. That there are feelings of pleasure and displeasure, of interest and excitements, bound up with mental operations, but having no obvious bodily expression for their consequence, would, I suppose, be held true by most readers. Certain arrangements of sounds, of lines, of colours, are agreeable, and others the reverse, without the degree of the feeling being sufficient to quicken the pulse or breathing, or to prompt to movements of either the body or the face. Certain sequences of ideas charm us as much as others tire us. It is a real intellectual delight to get a problem solved, and a real intellectual torment to have to leave it unfinished. . . .

Our natural way of thinking about [the] standard emotions is that the mental perception of some fact excites the mental affection called the emotion, and that this latter state of mind gives rise to the bodily expression. My thesis on the contrary is that *the bodily changes fol-low directly the* PERCEPTION *of the excit-ing fact, and that our feeling of the same changes as they occur* IS *the emotion.* Common sense says, we lose our for-tune, we are sorry and weep; we meet a bear, are frightened and run; we are in-sulted by a rival, are angry and strike. The hypothesis here to be defended says that this order of sequence is incorrect, that the one mental state is not immedi-ately induced by the other, that the bodily manifestations must first be in-terposed between, and that the more ra-tional statement is that we feel sorry because we cry, angry because we strike, afraid because we tremble, and not that we cry, strike, or tremble, be-cause we are sorry, angry, or fearful, as the case may be. Without the bodily states following on the perception, the latter would be purely cognitive in form, pale, colourless, destitute of emotional warmth. We might then see the bear, and judge it best to run, receive the in-sult and deem it right to strike, but we could not actually *feel* afraid or angry.

Stated in this crude way, the hypoth-esis is pretty sure to meet with immedi-ate disbelief. And yet neither many for farfetched considerations are re-quired to mitigate its paradoxical character, and possibly to produce con-viction of its truth.

To begin with, readers . . . do not need to be reminded that the nervous system of every living thing is but a bundle of predispositions to react in particular ways upon the contact of par-ticular features of the environment. As surely as the hermit-crab's abdomen presupposes the existence of empty whelk-shells somewhere to be found, so surely do the hound's olfactories imply the existence, on the one hand, of deer's or foxes' feet, and on the other, the ten-dency to follow up their tracks. The neural machinery is but a hyphen be-tween determinate arrangements of mat-ter outside the body and determinate impulses to inhibition or discharge within its organs. When the hen sees a white oval object on the ground, she cannot leave it; she must keep upon it and return to it, until at last its transfor-mation into a little mass of moving chirping down elicits from her machin-ery an entirely new set of performances. The love of man for woman, or of the human mother for her babe, our wrath at snakes and our fear of precipices, may all be described similarly, as in-stances of the way in which peculiarly conformed pieces of the world's furni-ture will fatally call forth most particu-lar mental and bodily reactions, in advance of, and often in direct opposi-tion to, the verdict of our deliberate rea-son concerning them. The labours of Darwin and his successors are only just beginning to reveal the universal para-sitism of each special creature upon other special things, and the way in which each creature brings the signature of its special relations stamped on its nervous system with it upon the scene.

Every living creature is in fact a sort of lock, whose wards and springs pre-suppose special forms of key,—which keys however are not born attached to the locks, but are sure to be found in the world near by as life goes on. And the locks are indifferent to any but their own keys. The egg fails to fascinate the hound, the bird does not fear the precipice, the snake waxes not wroth at his kind, the deer cares nothing for the woman or the human babe. . . .

Now among these nervous anticipa-tions are of course to be reckoned the emotions, so far as these may be called forth directly by the perception of certain facts. In advance of all experience of elephants no child can but be frightened if he suddenly find one trumpeting and charging upon him. No woman can see a handsome little naked baby without delight, no man in the wilderness see a human form in the distance without excitement and curiosity. I said I should consider these emotions only so far as they have bodily movements of some sort for their accompaniments. But my first point is to show that their bodily accompaniments are much more far-reaching and complicated than we ordinarily suppose. . . . [N]ot only the heart, but the entire circulatory system, forms a sort of sounding-board, which every change of our consciousness, however slight, may make reverberate. Hardly a sensation comes to us without sending waves of alternate constriction and dilation down the arteries of our arms. The blood-vessels of the abdomen act reciprocally with those of the more outward parts. The bladder and bowels, the glands of the mouth, throat, and skin, and the liver, are known to be affected gravely in certain severe emotions, and are unquestionably affected transiently when the emotions are of a lighter sort. That the heart-beats and rhythm of breathing play a leading part in all emotions whatsoever, is a matter too notorious for proof. And what is really equally prominent, but less likely to be admitted until special attention is drawn to the fact, is the continuous co-operation of the voluntary muscles in our emotional states. Even when no change of outward attitude is produced, their inward tension alters to suit each varying mood, and is felt as a difference of tone or of strain. In depression the flexors tend to prevail; in elation or belligerent excitement the extensors take the lead. And the various

permutations and combinations of which these organic activities are susceptible, make it abstractly possible that no shade of emotion, however slight, should be without a bodily reverberation as unique, when taken in its totality, as is the mental mood itself.

The immense number of parts modified in each emotion is what makes it so difficult for us to reproduce in cold blood the total and integral expression of any one of them. We may catch the trick with the voluntary muscles, but fail with the skin, glands, heart, and other viscera. Just as an artificially imitated sneeze lacks something of the reality, so the attempt to imitate an emotion in the absence of its normal instigating cause is apt to be rather "hollow."

The next thing to be noticed is this, that every one of the bodily changes, whatsoever it be, is *felt,* acutely or obscurely, the moment it occurs. If the reader has never paid attention to this matter, he will be both interested and astonished to learn how many different local bodily feelings he can detect in himself as characteristic of his various emotional moods. It would be perhaps too much to expect him to arrest the tide of any strong gust of passion for the sake of any such curious analysis as this; but he can observe more tranquil states, and that may be assumed here to be true of the greater which is shown to be true of the less. Our whole cubic capacity is sensibly alive; and each morsel of it contributes its pulsations of feeling, dim or sharp, pleasant, painful, or dubious, to that sense of personality that every one of us unfailingly carries with him. It is surprising what little items give accent to these complexes of sensibility. When worried by any slight trouble, one may find that the focus of one's bodily consciousness is the contraction, often quite inconsiderable, of the eyes and brows. When momentarily embarrassed, it is something in the pharynx that compels either a swallow, a clearing of the throat, or a slight cough; and so on for as many more instances as might be named. Our concern here being with the general view rather than with the details, I will not linger to discuss these but, assuming the point admitted that every change that occurs must be felt, I will pass on.

I now proceed to urge the vital point of my whole theory, which is this. If we fancy some strong emotion, and then try to abstract from our consciousness of it all the feelings of its characteristic bodily symptoms, we find we have nothing left behind, no "mind-stuff" out of which the emotion can be constituted, and that a cold and neutral state of intellectual perception is all that remains. It is true, that although most people, when asked, say that their introspection verifies this statement, some persist in saying theirs does not. Many cannot be made to understand the question. When you beg them to imagine away every feeling of laughter and of tendency to laugh from their consciousness of the ludicrousness of an object, and then to tell you what the feeling of its ludicrousness would be like, whether it be anything more than the perception that the object belongs to the class "funny," they persist in replying that the thing proposed is a physical impossibility, and that they always *must* laugh, if they see a funny object. Of course the task proposed is not the practical one of seeing a ludicrous object and annihilating one's tendency to laugh. It is the purely speculative one of subtracting certain elements of feeling from an emotional state supposed to exist in its fullness, and saying what the residual elements are. I

cannot help thinking that all who rightly apprehend this problem will agree with the proposition above laid down. What kind of an emotion of fear would be left, if the feelings neither of quickened heart-beats nor of shallow breathing, neither of trembling lips nor of weakened limbs, neither of goose-flesh nor of visceral stirrings, were present, it is quite impossible to think. Can one fancy the state of rage and picture no ebullition of it in the chest, no flushing of the face, no dilation of the nostrils, no clenching of the teeth, no impulse to vigorous action, but in their stead limp muscles, calm breathing, and a placid face? The present writer, for one, certainly cannot. The rage is as completely evaporated as the sensation of its so-called manifestations, and the only thing that can possibly be supposed to take its place is some cold-blooded and dispassionate judicial sentence, confined entirely to the intellectual realm, to the effect that a certain person or persons merit chastisement for their sins. In like manner of grief: what would it be without its tears, its sobs, its suffocation of the heart, its pang in the breast-bone? A feelingless cognition that certain circumstances are deplorable, and nothing more. Every passion in turn tells the same story. A purely disembodied human emotion is a nonentity. I do not say that it is a contradiction in the nature of things, or that pure spirits are necessarily condemned to cold intellectual lives; but I say that for *us*, emotion dissociated from all bodily feeling is inconceivable. The more closely I scrutinise my states, the more persuaded I become, that whatever moods, affections, and passions I have, are in very truth constituted by, and made up of, those bodily changes we ordinarily call their expression or consequence; and the more it seems to me that if I were to become corporeally anesthetic, I should be excluded from the life of the affections, harsh and tender alike, and drag out an existence of merely cognitive or intellectual form. Such an existence, although it seems to have been the ideal of ancient sages, is too apathetic to be keenly sought after by those born after the revival of the worship of sensibility, a few generations ago. . . .

If our theory be true, a necessary corollary of it ought to be that any voluntary arousal of the so-called manifestations of a special emotion ought to give us the emotion itself. Of course in the majority of emotions, this test is inapplicable; for many of the manifestations are in organs over which we have no volitional control. Still, within the limits in which it can be verified, experience fully corroborates this test. Everyone knows how panic is increased by flight, and how giving way to the symptoms of grief or anger increases those passions themselves. Each fit of sobbing makes the sorrow more acute, and calls forth another fit stronger still, until at last repose only ensues with lassitude and with the apparent exhaustion of the machinery. In rage, it is notorious how we "work ourselves up" to a climax by repeated outbreaks of expression. Refuse to express a passion, and it dies. Count ten before venting your anger, and its occasion seems ridiculous. Whistling to keep up courage is no mere figure of speech. On the other hand, sit all day in a moping posture, sigh, and reply to everything with a dismal voice, and your melancholy lingers. There is no more valuable precept in moral education than this, as all who have experience know: if we wish to conquer undesirable emotional tendencies in ourselves, we must assiduously, and in the first instance cold-bloodedly, go through the *outward motions* of those contrary dispositions we prefer to cultivate. The reward of persistency will infallibly come, in the fading gout of the sullenness or depression, and the advent of real cheerfulness and kindliness in their stead. Smooth the brow, brighten the eye, contract the dorsal rather than the ventral aspect of the frame, and speak in a major key, pass the genial compliment, and your heart must be frigid indeed if it do not gradually thaw!

The only exceptions to this are apparent, not real. The great emotional expressiveness and mobility of certain persons often lead us to say "They would feel more if they talked less." And in another class of persons, the explosive energy with which passion manifests itself on critical occasions, seems correlated with the way in which they bottle it up during the intervals. But these are only eccentric types of character, and within each type the law of the last paragraph prevails. The sentimentalist is so constructed that "gushing" is his or her normal mode of expression. Putting a stopper on the "gush" will only to a limited extent cause more "real" activities to take its place; in the main it will simply produce listlessness. On the other hand the ponderous and bilious "slumbering volcano," let him repress the expression of his passions as he will, will find them expire if they get no vent at all; whilst if the rare occasions multiply which he deems worthy of their outbreak, he will find them grow in intensity as life proceeds.

JEAN-PAUL SARTRE

Emotions as Transformations of the World

JEAN-PAUL SARTRE *(1905–1980), a philosopher, novelist, playwright, and political activist, wrote his essay on the emotions just before he began his monumental existentialist treatise,* Being and Nothingness. *He was reacting against such theories as that of James, and in place of a physiological theory he urged a "phenomenological" view, a study of emotions in terms of the person's own experience. Such a view, he argues, leads us to the conclusion that emotions are a mode of intentional and purposive behavior, a "magical transformation of the world."*

PERHAPS what will help us in our investigation is a preliminary observation which may serve as a general criticism of all the theories of emotion which we have encountered. . . . For most psychologists everything takes place as if the consciousness *of* the emotion were first a reflective consciousness, that is, as if the first form of the emotion as a fact of consciousness were to appear to us as a modification of our psychic being or, to use everyday language, to be first perceived as a *state of consciousness.* And certainly it is always possible to take consciousness of emotion as the affective structure of consciousness, to say, "I'm angry, I'm afraid, etc." But fear is not originally consciousness *of* being afraid, any more than the perception of this book is consciousness *of* perceiving the book. Emotional consciousness is, at first, unreflective, and on this plane it can be conscious of itself only on the non-positional mode. Emotional consciousness is, at first, consciousness *of* the world. It is not even necessary to bring up the whole theory in order clearly to understand this principle. A few simple observations may suffice,

and it is remarkable that the psychologists of emotion have never thought of making them. It is evident, in effect, that the man who is afraid is afraid *of* something. Even if it is a matter of one of those indefinite anxieties which one experiences in the dark, in a sinister and deserted passageway, etc., one is afraid *of* certain aspects of the night, of the world. And doubtless, all psychologists have noted that emotion is set in motion by a perception, a representation-signal, etc. But it seems that for them the emotion then withdraws from the object in order to be absorbed into itself. Not much reflection is needed to understand that, on the contrary, the emotion returns to the object at every moment and is fed there. For example, flight in a state of fear is described as if the object were not, before anything else, a flight *from* a certain object, as if the object fled did not remain present in the flight itself, as its theme, its reason for being, *that from which one flees.* And how can one talk about anger, in which one strikes, injures, and threatens, without mentioning the person who represents the objective unity of these insults, threats, and blows? In short, the affected subject and the affective object are bound in an indissoluble synthesis. Emotion is a certain way of apprehending the world. . . . The subject who seeks the solution of a practical problem is outside in the world; he perceives the world every moment through his acts. If he fails in his attempts, if he gets irritated, his very irritation is still a way in which the world appears to him. And, between the action which miscarries and the anger, it is not necessary for the subject to reflect back upon his behaviour, to intercalate a reflexive consciousness. There can be a continuous passage from the unreflective consciousness "world-acted" (action) to the unreflective consciousness "world-hateful" (anger). The second is a transformation of the other.

At present, we can conceive of what an emotion is. It is a transformation of the world. When the paths traced out become too difficult, or when we see no path, we can no longer live in so urgent and difficult a world. All the ways are barred. However, we must act. So we try to change the world, that is, to live as if the connection between things and their potentialities were not ruled by deterministic processes, but by magic. Let it be clearly understood that this is not a game; we are driven against a wall, and we throw ourselves into this new attitude with all the strength we can muster. Let it also be understood that this attempt is not conscious of being such, for it would then be the object of a reflection. Before anything else, it is the seizure of new connections and new exigences.

But the emotive behavior is not on the same plane as the other behaviors; it is not *effective*. Its end is not really to act upon the object as such through the agency of particular means. It seeks by itself to confer upon the object, and without modifying it in its actual structure, another quality, a lesser existence, or a lesser presence (or a greater existence, etc.). In short, in emotion it is the body which, directed by consciousness, changes its relations with the world in order that the world may change its qualities. If emotion is a joke, it is a joke we believe in. A simple example will make this emotive structure clear: I extend my hand to take a bunch of grapes. I can't get it; it's beyond my reach. I shrug my shoulders, I let my hand drop, I mumble, "They're too green," and I move on. All these gestures, these words, this behavior are not seized upon for their own sake. We are dealing with a little comedy which I am playing *under* the bunch of grapes, through which I confer upon the grapes the characteristic of being "too green" which can serve as a substitute for the behavior which I am unable to keep up. At first, they presented themselves as "having to be picked." But this urgent quality very soon becomes unbearable because the potentiality cannot be realized. This unbearable tension becomes, in turn, a motive for foisting upon the grapes the new quality "too green," which well resolve the conflict and eliminate the tension. Only I cannot confer this quality on the grapes chemically. I cannot act upon the bunch in the ordinary ways. So I seize upon this sourness of the too-green grapes by acting disgusted. I magically confer upon the grapes the quality I desire. Here the comedy is only half sincere. But let the situation be more urgent, let the incantatory behavior be carried out with seriousness; there we have emotion. . . .

True emotion is . . . accompanied by belief. The qualities conferred upon objects are taken as true qualities. Exactly what is meant by that? Roughly this: the emotion is undergone. One cannot abandon it at will; it exhausts itself, but we cannot stop it. Besides, the behavior which boils down to itself alone does nothing else than sketch upon the object the emotional quality which we confer upon it. A flight which would simply be a journey would not be enough to establish the object as being horrible. Or rather it would confer upon it the formal quality of *horrible*, but not the matter of this quality. In order for us truly to grasp the horrible, it is not only necessary to mimic it; we must be spellbound, flooded by our own emotion; the formal frame of the behavior must be filled with something opaque and heavy which serves as matter. We understand in this situation the role of purely physiological phenomena: they represent the *seriousness* of the emotion; they are phenomena of belief. They should certainly not be separated from behavior. At first, they present a certain analogy with it. The hyper-tension of fear or sadness, the vaso-constrictions, the respiratory difficulties, symbolize quite well a behavior which aims at denying the world or discharging it of its affective potential by denying it. It is then impossible to draw exactly a borderline between the pure difficulties and the behavior. They finally enter with the behavior into a total synthetic form and cannot be studied by themselves; to have considered them in isolation is

precisely the error of the peripheric theory. And yet they are not reducible to behavior; one can stop himself from fleeing, but not from trembling. I can, by a violent effort, raise myself from my chair, turn my thought from the disaster which is crushing me, and get down to work; my hands will remain icy. Therefore, the emotion must be considered not simply as being enacted; it is not a matter of pure demeanor. It is the demeanor of a body which is in a certain state; the state alone would not provoke the demeanor; the demeanor without the state is comedy; but the emotion appears in a highly disturbed body which retains a certain behavior. The disturbance can survive the behavior, but the behavior constitutes the form and signification of the disturbance. On the other hand, without this disturbance, the behavior would be pure signification, an affective scheme. We are really dealing with a synthetic form; *in order to believe* in magical behavior it is necessary to be highly disturbed.

Thus the origin of emotion is a spontaneous and lived degradation of consciousness in the face of the world. What it cannot endure in one way it tries to grasp in another by going to sleep, by approaching the consciousness of sleep, dream, and hysteria. And the disturbance of the body is nothing other than the lived belief of consciousness, insofar as it is seen from the outside.

CAROL TAVRIS

Uncivil Rites—
The Cultural Rules of Anger

CAROL TAVRIS is a contemporary psychologist and journalist who captured some important trends in contemporary psychology in her book, Anger: The Misunderstood Emotion, *which is excerpted here.*

THE young wife leaves her house one afternoon to draw water from the local well. She saunters down the main street, chatting amiably with her neighbors, as her husband watches from their porch. On her return from the well, a stranger stops her and asks for a cup of water. She obliges, and in fact invites the man home for dinner. He accepts. The husband, wife, and guest spend a pleasant evening together, and eventually the husband puts the lamp out and retires to bed. The wife also retires to bed—with the guest. In the morning, the husband leaves early to bring back some breakfast for the household. Upon his return, he finds his wife again making love with the visitor.

At what point in this sequence of events will the husband become angry or jealous? Is his anger inevitable? The answer, observes psychologist Ralph Hupka, depends on the tribe and culture he belongs to:

❦ A Pawnee Indian husband, a century ago, would, in fury, bewitch any man who dared to request a cup of water from his wife.

❦ An Ammassalik Eskimo husband who wants to be a proper host invites his guest to have sex with his wife; he signals his invitation by putting out the lamp. (The guest might feel angry if this invitation were not extended.) An Ammassalik husband would be angry, however, if he found his wife having sex with a man in circumstances other than the lamp game, such as that morning encore, or without a mutual agreement to exchange mates.

❦ A middle-class husband belonging to most modern American tribes would tend to get angry with any guest who, however courteously, tried to seduce his wife, and with the wife who, however hospitably, slept with their guest. But some American subcultures, such as you might find at sexually experimental spas like Sandstone, regard husbandly outrages as patriarchal and inappropriate.

❦ A husband who belonged to the polyandrous Toda tribe of southern India at the turn of the century would find the whole sequence of events perfectly normal; nothing to raise a fuss about. The Todas practiced *mokhthoditi,* a custom that allowed both spouses to take lovers. If a man wanted to make love to a married woman, he first got her permission and then the permission of her husband or husbands; a yearly fee was negotiated; and then the wife was free to visit her new lover and the lover free to visit the wife at her home. But a Toda husband and wife would undoubtedly be angry with any man who tried to establish an affair by sneaking around the husband's back (and not paying the proper fee).

People everywhere get angry, but they get angry in the service of their culture's rules. Sometimes those rules are explicit ("Thou shalt not covet thy neighbor's wife"); more often they are implicit, disguised in the countless daily actions performed because "That's the way we do things around here." These unstated rules are often not apparent until someone breaks them, and anger is the sign that someone has broken them. It announces that someone is not behaving as (you think) she or he *ought.* This "assertion of an ought" is, according to psychologist Joseph de Rivera, the one common and essential feature of anger in all its incarnations. "Whenever we are angry," he writes, "we somehow believe that we can influence the object of our anger. We assume that the other is responsible for his actions and ought to behave differently."

This "ought" quality suggests that a major role of anger is its policing function. Anger, with its power of forcefulness and its threat of retaliation, helps to regulate our everyday social relations: in family disputes, neighborly quarrels, business disagreements, wherever the official law is too cumbersome, inappropriate, or unavailable (which is most of the time). Psychologist James Averill observes that for most of Western history, it has been up to individuals to see to it that their rights were respected and justice seen to; in the absence of a formal judiciary, anger operates as a personal one. . . .

MANNERS, EMOTIONS, AND THE AMERICAN WAY

The class was basic English for foreign students, and an Arab student, during a spoken exercise, was describing a tradition of his home country. Something he said embarrassed a Japanese student in the front row, who reacted the proper Japanese way: he smiled. The Arab saw the smile and demanded to know what so funny about Arab customs. The Japanese, who was now publicly humiliated as well as embarrassed, could reply only with a smile and, to his misfortune, he giggled to mask his shame. The Arab, who now likewise felt shamed, furiously hit the Japanese student before the teacher could intervene. Shame and anger had erupted in a flash, as each student dutifully obeyed the rules of his culture. Neither could imagine, of course, that his rules might not be universal.

Because a major function of anger is to maintain the social order, through its moralizing implications of how people "should" behave, it is predictable that when two social orders collide they would generate angry sparks. It is easiest to see this when the colliding cultures are foreign to each other, but we have plenty of such collisions within our society as well. For some groups in America, anger is an effective way to get your way; for others it is the last resort. (Some groups have to learn assertiveness training to deal with others.) You may find your attitudes about anger, and the rules you learned to govern it, in conflict with those of different groups. Often it is this conflict about anger rules, not the rules per se, that can stir up trouble.

Each of us is tied to a group—a minitribe, if you will—by virtue of our sex, status, race, and ethnicity, and with countless unconscious reactions we reveal those ties as surely as Eliza Doolittle did when she opened her mouth. Anthropologist Edward T. Hall speaks of the "deep biases and built-in blinders" that every culture confers on its members. You can observe them at work every time you hear someone grumble, "I'll never understand women," or, "Why can't he just say what he feels?" or, "The (Japanese) (Mexicans) (Irish) (etc.) are utterly inscrutable."

A culture's rules of anger are not arbitrary; they evolve along with its history and structure. The Japanese practice of emotional restraint, for example, dates back many centuries, when all aspects of demeanor were carefully regulated: facial expressions, breathing, manner of sitting and standing, style of walking. Not only were all emotions— anger, grief, pain, even great happiness—to be suppressed in the presence of one's superiors, but also regulations specified that a person submit to any order with a pleasant smile and a properly happy tone of voice. At the time of the Samurai knights, these rules had considerable survival value, because a Samurai could legally execute anyone who he thought was not respectful enough. (You may notice the similarity to American blacks and to women, who likewise had to be careful to control anger in the presence of the white man.)

Even today in Japan, an individual who feels very angry is likely to show it by excessive politeness and a neutral expression instead of by furious words and signs. A Japanese who shows anger the Western way is admitting that he has lost control, and therefore lost face; he is thus at the extreme end of a negotiation or debate. In other cultures, though, showing anger may simply mark the *beginning* of an exchange, perhaps to show that the negotiator is serious; a man may lose face if he does *not* show anger when it is appropriate and "manly" for him to do so.

Perhaps we cannot avoid the anger we feel when someone breaks the rules that we have learned are the only civilized rules to follow. But we might emulate the Arapesh, who criticize the provocateur; or the Eskimo, who settle in for a good round of verbal dueling; or the Mbuti, who have a good laugh, understanding as they do the healing power of humor. We might also retrieve the old-fashioned standard of manners, which is, as small tribes teach us, an organized system of anger management. The conventions of the U.S. Senate, for example—the ornate language, the rules of debate—regulate anger over disagreements into acceptable channels. A senator does not call his or her opposition a stupid blithering moron, for instance. He says, "My distinguished colleague from the great state of Blitzhorn, an otherwise fine and noble individual, is, in this rare moment, erring in judgment." The elaborate language that seems so comically deceptive to the rest of us is what keeps political conversation going without bloodshed and mayhem.

Good manners melt resentment because they maintain respect between the two disagreeing parties. Indeed, one of the basic principles of parliamentary law is courtesy, "Respect for the rights of individuals and for the assembly itself." You don't have to join Congress to feel the effect of this principle at work. Someone steps on your toe, you feel angry, the person apologizes, your anger vanishes. Your toe may still hurt, but your dignity is intact. (A friend tells me he loudly shushed a talkative man sitting behind him at the movies, and immediately felt bad that he had expressed himself so angrily. After the show, the man touched him on the shoulder. "You were quite right to tell me to keep quiet," he said, "I was rude." "I could have kissed him," said my friend.)

Without rules for controlling anger, it can slip into emotional anarchy, lasting far longer than its original purposes require. Observe how friends and family react to someone undergoing a bitter divorce: they extend sympathy and a willing ear to the enraged spouse for a while, but eventually they expect the person to "shape up" and "get on with it." What these friends and relatives are doing is imposing unofficial rules of anger management. The victim may grouse and mutter about the loss of sympathy, but actually the friends and relatives are doing what any decent tribe would do: keeping anger in bounds after it has done its job and making sure the victim stays in the social circle. Well-meaning friends and therapists who encourage a vengeful spouse to ventilate rage for years are doing neither the spouse nor the tribe a service.

In this country, the philosophy of emotional expression confuses self-restraint and hypocrisy. The cultures of the Far East do not have this conflict; a person is expected to control and subdue the emotions because it is the relationship, not the individual, that comes first. Here, where the reverse is true, some people express their emotions even at the expense of the relationship, and manners seem to be as rare as egrets. This analogy is not arbitrary, for the same ideology that gave us emotional ventilation is responsible for the scarcity of regrets: the imperial "I."

Consider the gentle, forgiving environment of Tahiti, where people learn that they have limited control over nature and over other people. They learn that if they try to change nature, she will swiftly destroy them, but if they relax and accept the bounty of nature—and the nature or people—they will be taken care of. Anthropologist Robert Levy calls this resulting world view among the Tahitians "passive optimism."

Such a philosophy would not have lasted long among the ancient Hebrews, whose God gave them "dominion over the fish of the sea, and over the fowl of the air, and over the cattle, and over all the earth, and over every creeping thing that creepeth upon the earth" (Genesis 1:26). And a good thing He did, too, because in the harsh deserts of the Middle East, adherents of a laissez-faire Tahitian religion would have met a swift demise. The Judeo-Christian philosophy, however, produces "active pessimists": people who assume that nature and other people are to be conquered, indeed must be conquered, and that individual striving is essential to survival. But a universe defined as the Tahitians see it is intrinsically less infuriating than a universe in which almost everything is possible if the individual tries hard enough. The individualism of American life, to our glory and despair, creates anger and encourages its release; for when everything is possible, limitations are irksome. When the desires of the self come first, the needs of others are annoying. When we think we deserve it all, reaping only a portion can enrage.

PLATO

Aristophanes' Speech on Love

ARISTOPHANES *(ca. 450–ca. 385 B.C.) was the famous writer of comedy who satirized Socrates unmercifully in* The Clouds. *Here in the* Symposium, *somewhat surprisingly, Plato shows no ill will towards Aristophanes, but supplies him with a masterpiece, an inventive speech that is comic and seriously moving at the same time, about the origins and nature of love.*

FIRST you must learn what Human Nature was in the beginning and what has happened to it since, because long ago our nature was not what it is now, but very different. . . . The shape of each human being was completely round, with back and sides in a circle; they had four hands each, as many legs as hands, and two faces, exactly alike, on a rounded neck. Between the two faces, which were on opposite sides, was one head with four ears. There were two sets of sexual organs, and everything else was the way you'd imagine it from what I've told you. They walked upright, as we do now, whatever direction they wanted. And whenever they set out to run fast, they thrust out all their eight limbs, the ones they had then, and spun rapidly, the way gymnasts do cartwheels, by bringing their legs around straight. . . .

In strength and power, therefore, they were terrible, and they had great ambitions. They made an attempt on the gods, and Homer's story about Ephialtes and Otos was originally about them: how they tried to make an ascent to heaven so as to attack the gods. Then Zeus and the other gods met in council to discuss what to do, and they were sore perplexed. They couldn't wipe out the human race with thunderbolts and kill them all off, as they had the giants, because that would wipe out the worship they receive, along with the sacrifices we humans give them. On the other hand, they couldn't let them run riot. At last, after great effort, Zeus had an idea.

"I think I have a plan," he said, "that would allow human beings to exist and stop their misbehaving: they will give up being wicked when they lose their strength. So I shall now cut each of them in two. At one stroke they will lose their strength and also become more profitable to us, owing to the increase in their number. They shall walk upright on two legs. But if I find they still run riot and do not keep the peace," he said, "I will cut them in two again, and they'll have to make their way on one leg, hopping." So saying, he cut those human beings in two, the way people cut sorb-apples before they dry them or the way they cut eggs with hairs. . . .

Now, since their natural form had been cut in two, each one longed for its own other half, and so they would throw their arms about each other, weaving themselves together, wanting to grow together. In that condition they would die from hunger and general idleness, because they would not do anything apart from each other. Whenever one of the halves died and one was left, the one that was left still sought another

and wove itself together with that.
Sometimes the half he met came from a
woman, as we'd call her now, sometimes it came from a man; either way,
they kept on dying.

. . . This, then, is the source of our
desire to love each other. Love is born
into every human being; it calls back
the halves of our original nature together, it tries to make one out of two
and heal the wound of human nature.

Each of us, then, is a "matching half"
of a human whole, because each was
sliced like a flatfish, two out of one, and
each of us is always seeking the half
that matches him. . . . And so, when a
person meets the half that is his very
own, whatever his orientation, . . . then
something wonderful happens: the two
are struck from their senses by love, by
a sense of belonging to one another, and
by desire, and they don't want to be
separated from one another, not even
for a moment.

These are the people who finish out
their lives together and still cannot say
what it is they want from one another.
No one would think it is the intimacy of
sex—that mere sex is the reason each
lover takes so great and deep a joy in
being with the other. It's obvious that
the soul of every lover longs for something else; his soul cannot say what it is,
but like an oracle it has a sense of what
it wants, and like an oracle it hides behind a riddle. Suppose two lovers are
lying together and Hephaestus stands
over them with his mending tools, asking, "What is it you human beings really
want from each other?" And suppose

they're perplexed, and he asks them
again: "Is this your heart's desire,
then—for the two of you to become
parts of the same whole, as near as can
be, and never to separate, day or night?
Because if that's your desire, I'd like to
weld you together and join you into
something that is naturally whole, so
that the two of you are made into one.
Then the two of you would share one
life, as long as you lived, because you
would be one being, and by the same
token, when you died, you would be one
and not two in Hades, having died a single death. Look at your love, and see if
this is what you desire: wouldn't this be
all the good fortune you could want?"

Surely you can see that no one who
received such an offer would turn it
down; no one would find anything else
that he wanted. Instead, everyone would
think he'd found out at last what he had
always wanted: to come together and
melt together with the one he loves, so
that one person emerged from two. Why
should this be so? It's because, as I said,
we used to be complete wholes in our
original nature, and now "Love" is the
name of our pursuit of wholeness, for
our desire to be complete. . . .

If we are to give due praise to the
god who can give us this blessing, then,
we must praise Love. Love does the
best that can be done for the time being:
he draws us towards what belongs to us.
But for the future, Love promises the
greatest hope of all: If we treat the gods
with due reverence, he will restore to us
our original nature, and by healing us,
he will make us blessed and happy.

ROBERT C. SOLOMON

What Love Is

ROBERT C. SOLOMON *is a philosopher at the University of Texas who writes about emotions. The following is taken from his 1976 book,* Love: Emotion, Myth and Metaphor.

T HE question, What is love? is neither a request for a confession nor an excuse to start moralizing. It is not an invitation to amuse us with some *bon mot* ("Love is the key that opens up the doors of happiness") or to impress us with an author's sensitivity. And love is much more than a "feeling." When a novelist wants us to appreciate his character's emotions, he does not just describe sweaty palms and a moment of panic; he instead describes *a world,* the world as it is experienced— in anger, or in envy, or in love. Theorizing about emotion, too, is like describing an exotic world. It is a kind of conceptual anthropology—identifying a peculiar list of characters—heroes, villains, knaves or lovers—understanding a special set of rules and roles—rituals, fantasies, myths, slogans and fears. But these are not merely empirical observations on the fate of a feeling; none of this will make any sense to anyone who has not [had the emotion.] Love can be understood only "from the inside," as a language can be understood only by someone who speaks it, as a world can be known only by someone who has— even if vicariously—*lived* in it.

To analyze an emotion by looking at the world it defines allows us to cut through the inarticulateness of mere "feelings" and do away once and for all with the idea that emotions in general and love in particular are "ineffable" or beyond description. This might make some sense if describing an emotion were describing something "inside of us." It is not easy, for example, to describe how one feels when nauseous; even describing something so specific as a migraine headache falls back on clumsy metaphors ("as if my head's in a vise," "as if someone were driving a nail through my skull"). But once we see that every emotion defines a world for itself, we can then describe in some detail what that world involves, with its many variations, describe its dimensions and its dynamics. The world defined by love—or what we shall call the *loveworld*—is a world woven around a single relationship with all else pushed to the periphery. To understand love is to understand the specifics of this relationship and the world woven around it.

Love has been so misunderstood both because so often it has been taken to be *other*-worldly rather than one world of emotion among others, and because it has sometimes been taken to be a "mere emotion"—just a feeling and not a world at all. Because of this, perhaps it would be best to illustrate the theory that every emotion is a world by beginning with a less problematic emotion, namely, *anger.* Anger too defines its world. It is a world in which one defines oneself in the role of "the offended" and defines someone else (or perhaps a group or an institution) as "the offender." The world of anger is very much a courtroom world, a world filled with blame and emotional litigation. It is a world in which everyone else tends to become a co-defendant, a friend of the court, a witness or at least part of the courtroom audience. (But when you're *very* angry, there are no innocent bystanders.) Writes Lewis Carroll in *Alice in Wonderland:* "'I'll be judge, I'll be jury,' said cunning old Fury." It is a world in which one does indeed define oneself as judge and jury, compete with a grim righteousness, with "justice"—one's own vengeance— as the only legitimate concern. It is a *magical* world, which can change a lackadaisical unfocused morning into a piercing, all-consuming day, an orgy of vindictive self-righteousness and excitement. At the slightest provocation it can change an awkward and defensive situation into an aggressive confrontation. To describe the world of anger is therefore to describe its fantasies, for example, the urge to kill, though rarely is this taken seriously or to its logical conclusion. It has its illusions too, for instance, the tendency to exaggerate the importance of some petty grievance to the level of cosmic injustice; in anger we sometimes talk as if "man's inhumanity to man" is perfectly manifested in some minor sleight at the office yesterday. It is a world with a certain fragility; a single laugh can explode the whole pretense of angry self-righteousness. And it is a world with a purpose—for when do we feel more self-righteous than in anger? Getting angry in an otherwise awkward situation may be a way of saving face or providing a quick ego boost; "having a bad temper" may be not so much a "character trait" as an emotional strategy, a way of *using* emotion as a means of controlling other people. To

describe anger, in other words, is to describe the way the world is structured— and why—by a person who is angry.

The world of love—the loveworld— can be similarly described as a theatrical scenario, not as a courtroom but rather as "courtly," a romantic drama defined by its sense of elegance (badly interpreted as "spiritual"), in which we also take up a certain role—"the lover"—and cast another person into a complementary role—"the beloved." But where anger casts two antagonistic characters, romantic love sets up an idea of unity, absolute complementary and total mutual support and affection. It is the *rest* of the world that may be the antagonist. [The Russian novelist] Boris Pasternak describes the loveworld beautifully—the world as Adam and Eve, naked, surrounded by chaos.

It is a world we know well, of course—the world of *Casablanca, Romeo and Juliet* and a thousand stories and novels. It is a world in which we narrow our vision and our cares to that single duality, all else becoming trifles, obstacles or interruptions. It is a magical world, in which an ordinary evening is transformed into the turning point of a lifetime, the metamorphosis of one's self into a curious kind of double being. It may seem like a sense of "discovery"; in fact it is a step in a long search, a process of creation. . . .

Like every emotional world, the loveworld has its essential rules and rituals, its basic structures and internal dynamics. Some of these rules and structures are so obvious that it is embarrassing to have to spell them out, for example, the fact that the loveworld (typically) includes two people, instead of only one (as in shame) or three (as in jealousy) or indeed an entire class of people (as in national mourning or revolutionary resentment). Or the fact that the loveworld involves extremely "positive" feelings about the person loved, perhaps even the uncritical evaluation that he or she is "the most wonderful person in the world." Or the fact that the loveworld is held together by the mutual desire to be together (to touch, be touched, to caress and make love) no less essentially than the world of Newton and Einstein is held together by the forces of electromagnetism and gravity. Such features are so obvious to us that we fail to think of them as the structures of love; we take them for granted and, when asked to talk about love, consider them not even worth mentioning. Having thus ignored the obvious, love becomes a mystery. But other seemingly equally "obvious" features of love may not be part of the structure of the loveworld at all—for example, the comforting equation between love and trust. Here, indeed, there is some room for "mystery" in love, not the emotion itself but its essential lack of predictability, the fascination with the unknown and the attraction that comes not with trust but with vulnerability, sometimes even suspicion and doubt. . . .

THE "OBJECT" OF LOVE

Talking about the loveworld is not only a way to avoid the hopeless conception of love as a feeling; it is also a way of rejecting an insidious view of love—and emotions in general—which many philosophers have come to accept as "obvious," particularly in this century. The view simply stated, is that love is an attitude *toward* someone, a feeling directed *at* a person, instead of a shared world. The view is often disguised by a piece of professional jargon—an impressive work, "intentional-

ity." It is said that emotions are "intentional," which is a way of saying that they are "about" something. What an emotion is "about" is called its "intentional object" or, simply, its "object." Thus shame is an emotion which is "about" someone else. The language comes from the medieval scholastics, by way of an Austrian philosopher named Franz Brentano, one of whose students in Vienna was the young Sigmund Freud. Thus Freud talks all the time about the "object" of love, not without some discomfort, for though the conception fits his general theories perfectly, he nonetheless sensed correctly that some considerable conceptual damage was being done to the emotion thereby.

The idea—thought not the terminology—of "intentionality" and "intentional objects" was introduced into British philosophy by the Scottish philosopher David Hume. He analyzed a number of emotions in terms of the "objects" with which they were "naturally associated," for example pride and humility, which both took as their "objects" oneself, and hatred and love, which both took as their objects another person. But we can already see what is going to be wrong with this familiar type of analysis. First of all, all such talk about "objects" leaves out the crucial fact that, in love at least, it is the other as a "subject" that is essential. To be in love (even unrequited) is [to wish] to be looked *at,* not just to look. Thus it is the eyes, not the body (nor the soul), that present the so called "beloved," not as object but as subject, not first as beautiful or lovable but always as (potentially) *loving.* It's the eyes that have it, nothing else. . . .

Love is not just an attitude directed toward another person: it is an emotion which, [one hopes], is *shared with* him or her. . . . [A]ny account of love that begins with the idea of an "object" of love is probably going to miss the main point of the emotion, namely, that it is not an emotion "about" another person so much as, in our terms, a world we share. . . .

One obvious misunderstanding is this: the Christian view of love is not alone in teaching us that love is essentially *selfless.* Proponents of romantic love have argued that too. The idea is that love is thoroughly "about" another person, so that any degree of self-love is incompatible with "true" selfless love. But this is impossible. There is no emotion without self-involvement, and no love that is not also "about" oneself. The other side is just as confused, however; La Rochefoucauld, for example, insists that "all love is self-love." But to be self-involved is not yet to be selfish, nor does self-involvement in any way exclude a total concern for the other person as well. The practical consequence of this confusion, in turn, is the readiness with which we can be made to feel guilty at the slightest suggestion that our love is not "pure" but turns on "selfish" motives, and it renders unaskable what is in fact a most intelligible question—namely, "What am I getting out of this?"—to which the answer may well be, "Not enough to make it worth while." But then, love is not just what one "gets out of it" either.

• • •

So what is love? It is, in a phrase, an emotion through which we create for ourselves a little world—the loveworld, in which we play the roles of lovers and, quite literally, create our selves as well. . . . Even so-called "unrequited" love is shared love and shared identity, if only from one side and thereby woefully incomplete. Of course, occasionally an imagined identity may be far preferable to the actuality, but even when this is the case unrequited love represents at most a hint toward a process and not the process as such. Unrequited love is still love, but love in the sense that a sprout from an acorn is already an oak, no more. . . .

In love we transform ourselves and one another, but the key to this emotion is the understanding that the transformation of selves is not merely reciprocal, a swap of favors like "I'll cook you dinner if you'll wash the car." The self transformed in love is a shared self, and therefore by its very nature at odds with, even contradictory to, the individual autonomous selves that each of us had before. Sometimes our new shared self may be a transformation of a self that I (perhaps we) shared before. Possibly all love is to some extent the transposition of seemingly "natural" bonds which have somehow been abandoned or destroyed, and therefore the less than novel transformation of a self that has always been shared, in one way or another. But the bonds of love are always, to some extent, "unnatural," and our shared identity is always, in some way, uncomfortable. Aristophanes' delightful allegory about the double creatures cleft in two and seeking their other halves is charming but false. Love is never so neat and tidy, antigen and antibody forming the perfect fit. The Christian concept of a couple sanctified as a "union" before God is reassuring, as if one thereby receives some special guarantee, an outside bond of sorts, which will keep two otherwise aimless souls together. But the warranty doesn't apply. What is so special about romantic love, and what makes it so peculiar to our and similar societies, is the fact that it is entirely based on the idea of individuality and freedom, and this means, first of all, that the presupposition of love is a strong sense of individual identity and autonomy which exactly contradicts the ideal of "union" and "yearning to be one" that some of our literature has celebrated so one-sidedly. And, second, the freedom that is built into the loveworld includes not just the freedom to come together but the freedom to go as well. Thus love and the loveworld are always in a state of tension, always changing, dynamic, tenuous and explosive.

. . . To understand love is to understand this tension, this dialectic between individuality and the shared ideal. To think that love is to be found at the ends of the spectrum—in that first enthusiastic "discovery" of a shared togetherness or at the end of the road, after a lifetime together—is to miss the loveworld almost entirely, for it is neither an initial flush of feeling nor the retrospective congratulations of old age but a struggle for unity and identity. And it is this struggle—neither the ideal of togetherness nor the contrary demand for individual autonomy and identity alone—that defines the dynamics of that convulsive and tenuous world we call romantic love.

MORWENNA GRIFFITHS

Feminism, Feelings and Philosophy

MORWENNA GRIFFITHS *teaches in philosophy, gender studies, and education at Oxford Polytechnic.*

WOMEN are more emotional than men, or such is the commonly held belief in present day Western society. But is the belief true? And does it matter? The answers are not easy ones to find because the meaning of the statement is so unclear. It might mean, for instance, that women are less in control of their emotions, or it might mean that they feel things more deeply, or that they are more irrational than men. None of these statements necessarily implies any of

the rest—though they often come as a package. Indeed, the statement that women are more emotional than men has no clear meaning. However, it has a considerable political force because it is used to justify or explain the position of women. The usual justification/explanation runs: since women are more emotional they are less suited to public life. But this is not the only possible political use of the statement. It has been taken up recently by some feminists and used in celebration of women's values and as a criticism of men and their personal, moral, or social arrangements. In other words, feminists have stood the argument on its head. It now goes: since men are so unemotional, they are unfit to run public life.

Feminist writing questions and challenges the assumption that emotion, feeling, nature and bodies are in opposition to rationality, mind and freedom, such that the relationship between them is one of hierarchical control. This challenge is implicit in a wide variety of feminist concerns. Feminism is not monolithic and feminists do not all speak with one voice. It is all the more striking then that the different concerns expressed in feminist writing and the variety of different voices which make themselves heard, all point, time and again, in a similar direction with regard to emotion and reason.

Quite rightly, women have not begun their criticism of masculinism with the abstract categories found useful to describe masculine viewpoints. They have begun with the concrete and particular, for instance, rape, depression, abortion, pay. Out of these concrete, particular concerns, abstractions are generated. One which keeps recurring is the close relationship between feelings and thought, emotion and reason, mind and body, and the need to break down current dualism in thinking about them. An extension of all this is the kind of relationship we perceive ourselves to have with the rest of the natural world, and the damage that is done to us and to it if that relationship is misconceived. How these concerns are theorised varies. But however deep the differences they are focused on a shared concern, that of the fundamental significance of feeling. . . . The production of feminist knowledge

is grounded in feeling. So far from feelings being seen as mere subjectivity, something to be overcome in the search for objectivity, they are seen to be a source of knowledge. The knowledge gained is distorted, however, unless power relations deriving from personality, race, class, etc., are acknowledged and allowed for. All of this can be seen directly in the theory and practice of the activity known as 'consciousness-raising' in which feelings are the subject matter, and their expression is a means of arriving at the truth, a truth about public, political life rather than about individual personalities. Feelings and their expression are likely to be a part of the process of obtaining rational objective knowledge, rather than being a hindrance to it.

Further, truth and knowledge become distorted when feelings are not acknowledged. Most seriously, one way in which distortion has occurred is in the conceptualisation of truth and knowledge themselves. Evelyn Fox Keller has discussed this process for science. She argues that the kinds of rational objectivity and technical control taken to be constitutive of science are distortions introduced by unacknowledged and unexamined myths of masculinity which have their roots in typically masculine ways of feeling and which pervade scientific thought. . . .

. . . [F]eminist views on feeling constitute a significant criticism of much mainstream Western philosophy of mind, and . . . these criticisms need to be taken into account if a better understanding of ourselves, both men and women, is to be reached. I have been summarising the way in which feminist writing implicitly questions and challenges assumptions about feeling and its relationship to reason, bodies and objectivity, assumptions which have been widely accepted in modern Western societies and by modern Western philosophers. I shall focus on three ways in which feminist writing challenges these assumptions. . . .

The first two criticisms are to do with the concepts used to describe people and the third is to do with the focus of attention. The first criticism is that human beings have been discussed in terms of just the two categories of mind and body (or of embodied minds), so feelings and emotions have been thought to be some uneasy mixture of the two. Secondly, the relationship between mind and body (and feelings where they have been noticed at all) has been thought to be one of hierarchical control. Thirdly, the contradictions inherent in this view of people as embodied minds remain unnoticed because feelings have largely been ignored in philosophical discussions. If feelings were taken more seriously as feminism suggests they should be, the view would be harder to maintain.

The first implied criticism that arises from feminist views is that the conceptualisation of human beings has generally been into just two categories. This criticism seems justified. Philosophy of mind has been dominated by considerations of minds as rational, reasonable, reasoning or, sometimes, rationalising. Philosophers also notice bodies, but they have little to say about feeling or emotions as a separate category. This lack of attention can be obscured by the way it is sometimes simply assumed that feelings and emotions are of the body or of the mind.

This dualism is particularly obvious in the analytical tradition where one of the famous, and intractable, problems in philosophy of mind is the 'mind–body' problem, that is, the problematic nature of the relationship of minds to bodies. In this respect it is not much of an exaggeration to say that philosophy is less a series of footnotes to Plato than a series of footnotes to Descartes, whom Mary Daly calls 'modern philosophy's severed head'. Many contemporary philosophers now find themselves thinking of an even more disembodied phenomenon, the 'brain in a vat'. It is true that the similarity is disguised. In analytical philosophy the language has changed from Descartes's pineal gland, corporeal and thinking substances to neurons, intentional objects and physical matter, or to the metaphors of computer programs, software and hardware. . . . Of course, I do not want to suggest that any particular details of Descartes's system are accepted by those philosophers who try to solve the 'mind–body' problem: my point here is that Descartes set the terms in which the discussion is conducted.

Descartes paid some attention to feelings and emotions, trying to fit them into the structure of his philosophy. In his book, *The Passions of the Soul,* Descartes begins by noting that the passions affect and are affected by both soul and body. He defines the passions of the soul as:

> The perceptions, feelings, or emotions of the soul which we relate specially to it, and which are caused, maintained, and fortified by some movement of the spirits.
> (Art. 27)

The 'spirits' are 'animal spirits', i.e. of the body. He continues:

> Of all the kinds of thought which it [the soul] may have, there are no others which so powerfully agitate and disturb it as do these passions.   (Art. 28)

He is making clear that the passions are not a perception of an outside object like sound, scent or colour, nor of a state of body like hunger, thirst or pain, but neither are they a pure activity of the soul, because the most proximate cause is the spirits. He seems unable to sustain this initial position within the framework of his dualism. By the end of his account he is describing a split between *intellectual* emotions and *bodily* ones. For instance, he distinguishes the passion 'joy' from purely intellectual 'joy'. The latter has an obscure relationship with the body. He says:

> It is true that while the soul is united to the body this intellectual joy can hardly fail to be accompanied by that which is passion.   (Art. 91)

But he does not explain what is meant by the phrase 'can hardly fail to'. In effect he abandoned his original definition but did not replace it with another. Feelings and emotions do not fit easily into a two-category system consisting of mind and body, and Descartes failed to solve the problem of making them do so.

Descartes's dualism has been much criticised. Many writers on emotions and feelings begin by criticising him. They declare themselves to be in reaction against him. It is striking though that these critics end up by adopting a very similar solution to Descartes to the problems of fitting feelings and emotions into the philosophy of mind. It is rare nowadays in philosophical circles for emotions to be thought of as pure physical prompting of the body. More often, emotions are defined as 'intentional', that is, of the mind. Feelings are then contrasted with them and are said to be of the body. We end up with emotions (of the mind, rational) contrasted with feelings (of the body, natural).

· · ·

Hofstadter and Dennett say succinctly:

> Emotions are an automatic by-product of the ability to think. They are implied by the nature of thought.

In this dualist conception of the mind, it is this insistence that emotions are of the mind that make them rational. Since to be rational is to have choice and to be free, it then becomes clear that in so far as emotions are rational they are under the control of reason. They are contrasted with 'feelings', which being of the body are not reasonable, but like the rest of the physical world can be controlled indirectly by the exercise of intelligence.

Beginning with the assumptions that bodies and minds are the only fundamental categories and that they are separate and different, the Cartesian solution is not a surprising one. There are other solutions. For instance, if emotions and feelings are taken to be of the body, the controlling relationship may be reversed, and the rational mind controlled by the bodily promptings of feelings. However, none of these dualist solutions are satisfactory. Feelings and emotions do not fit comfortably into a twofold division. This is true both of the 'bodily feelings' and of the 'mental emotions'. The feelings of sexuality and hunger, for instance, are dependent on understanding as well as on physical promptings. The emotions of fear, love, ambition and pride have associated feeling as well as judgment, and it is not at all clear that all of them are rational. And even if all this were resolved, a whole range of other psychological terms associated with feeling such as mood and character are left unaccounted for and unexplained. These problems have been noted by a number of commentators but they remain unresolved.

My first criticism of philosophy of mind, a criticism which is implicit in feminist writing, was that human beings have been wrongly described in terms of minds and bodies only. It is clear from the above summary that the second criticism, that the relationship between them is taken to be one of hierarchical control, appears to be justified too. . . .

I turn now to the third criticism, that feelings have largely been ignored as a focus of attention in philosophy. The question as to why feelings and emotions are not taken to be of much significance is an interesting one. Feeling and emotion present intractable problems to arguments that assume minds and bodies to be the only categories necessary to describe human beings, so it would seem that they should attract attention. They do not. Broadly speaking, feelings are ignored as a serious topic of discussion. . . .

An adequate account of emotion has to take into consideration the process by which feelings come into being, the process by which our feelings become human feelings. To say that our feelings are human feelings is to draw attention to the fact, on the one hand, that they will be different from those of other species simply because of our different genetic inheritance. On the other hand, they will reflect the way human beings create themselves through their social interactions. That is, we have to take into account the history of an individual, and the time and place in which she lives her life. A snapshot of one instant in her life is insufficient to give any depth of understanding. To say this is firstly to emphasis both 'nature' and 'culture' rather than one at the expense of the other, and secondly to look at whole lives. The suggestion that I am making here about human feelings depends on both of these.

It is common enough to discuss either social relationships or genetically given feelings as constrained by each other, but this is usually done with respect to adults. By contrast, I begin by looking at the development of the individual from babyhood, and this makes my account significantly different. The feelings of newborn babies may be genetically given, but from the moment of birth they interact with the understandings and perceptions of the growing baby. Until they do so they are not fully human—but human feelings develop out of the feelings of babies. The process of coming to have human feelings comes about as a result of the interactions of those not yet quite human feelings inherent in human babies with the knowledge, understanding, perceptions and beliefs that people develop as a result of growing up and living in the world. As these feelings interact and reinteract with all the other understandings and perceptions of the individual, new feelings are formed which may be only partly conscious. That is, they are intelligent and the result of intelligence, but they are not necessarily susceptible to cool calculation. In sum, coming to have human feelings involves the understanding of the individual agent: the feelings are her own feelings. But they are not hers quite independently of the rest of the world. The feelings she has also depend on the kinds of understanding available to her: she lives her life in specific historical and geographical circumstances. Finally, they depend on the physical ground of her being: she has a human body.

The account I have outlined has implications for our understanding of how people conduct themselves. Rather than fill in the outline I shall describe some of the claims that follow from it. If the account is right, it suggests *both* that human understanding and actions are essential to human feelings and *also* that human feelings are essential to human understanding and actions. The first of these two claims is easy to see, I think, given what I have said about learning and feelings. A few examples may help to make it clear. Depression about the arms race, fear of going into debt, love of landscape, and the pain of losing a friend are all examples of human feelings that are dependent on being born a human being but that are incomprehensible without human understanding. In nonhumans depression, fear, love or the pain of losing a friend may be as sharply felt but must be significantly different.

My claim that understanding is essential to feelings applies to all feelings, not only to those feelings that are sometimes called emotions. In particular, it is true of those feelings that are often called sensations. Pain, hunger and tiredness all vary with the meaning they have to the individual experiencing them. This conclusion gets support from medical descriptions and psychological research into pain in which there is evidence that pain varies with the meaning it has to the sufferer. The pain of battle wounds, the pain of amputated limbs, the pain of torture or the pain of an injection are not explicable only in terms of physiology—though they are not independent of physiology either. . . .

The process I am describing is dialectical. Our feelings prompt the articulation of our beliefs about the world, and the pattern of conceptualisation of it. They reflect both factual and evaluative judgments. The articulations are learnt in social interactions. But the articulation also molds the feelings. The process is a continuing one which is why an ahistorical snapshot approach, looking at feelings at just one particular moment, must be distorting.

If the foregoing is correct, it is evident that people's feelings are not simply private and individual. They could not be anything other than social. This follows from the fact that the understandings which help determine feelings are shared in a large part with other groups of people. Understanding about the world depends on access to information about it, and to experiences within it. It also depends, of course, on sharing public language with others.

One particularly influential effect is the social world. The understandings and therefore the feelings of people are systematically related to the person's position in society. An obvious example here is class. People who share a class position will share a particular set of viewpoints, that is, have easy access to certain information and language in which to discuss it. Of course, there are many factors influencing anyone's point of view and they may intersect in a variety of ways. Nothing I have said suggests that points of view are entailed by class position, only that they are influenced by it.

Similarly, human understandings and feelings are systematically related to differences in biology, in so far as human beings have different biologies.

A clear example here is that of age. The different ways of understanding and acting available to different age groups affect their feelings about the world. Children the world over share feelings unavailable to their grandparents, and, possibly, vice versa.

Both of the factors I have described, the effect of society and the effect of biology, combine to make feelings gender-related. The understandings and perceptions available to females are different from those available to males. Males and females are treated differently from each other and perceive themselves differently. Physiological differences, such as menstruation, pregnancy and the menopause in women, and erections and ejaculation in men, will also give the two sexes different understandings and feelings about the world.

The argument that physiological differences are likely to remain significant in the lives of future generations should not be taken as implying that 'biology is destiny'. For instance, at present, it is often argued that the facts of pregnancy and lactation imply that women ought to care for young infants. The opposite implications could be drawn just as straightforwardly, with the significance of the sex difference being kept. The argument could run: women have to take the responsibility of nine months of pregnancy, and, moreover, are in some danger during childbirth. It follows, in the name of justice, if for no other reason, that men should take primary responsibility for the infant.

. . . Trying to explain adult human beings as though they are embodiments of rational understanding is a futile activity. The feelings of adults cannot be understood in terms of brute sensations acted upon by rational thoughts. Nor can emotions be understood as by-products of thought, independent of human sensations or bodies. An altogether more complex model is needed. The one I have suggested is an interactive one in which feelings and emotions have to be understood in terms of the history of an individual's life, and in terms of the social context in which that life is lived. Clearly, if this suggestion is right, the concepts of rationality and of mind would change accordingly.

Following from this is another implication for philosophy, that feelings are a source of knowledge and should be treated seriously as such since both need to be taken into account in coming to understand the world. In effect, feelings are a route to truth: they both provide us with our beliefs about the world and also provide a basis for assessing these beliefs. Control of feelings and emotions by the rational mind is a wrong understanding of how human beings ought to conduct themselves. In other words, a rational agent is required to attend to and reflect on feelings, not to attempt to control them, except in so far as a rearticulation of feelings might be appropriate in the light of reflection. The complex interactions of feelings in ourselves are open to reflection and change. One part does not dominate the other. We must be 'in harmony with' our feelings, rather than 'in control of' them.

There are implications for feminist theory as well as for philosophy. The idea that we can shrug off our patriarchal straitjackets and find our pre-social selves is misleading. It is particularly misleading over the way sexism relates to the issues of class and race. The model I have gestured at in this article helps to explain why feminists must take account of class and race. It shows how the issue of sex/gender is similar to them and also why it is different because it is rooted in physiology.

The purpose of this article was to examine some questions about women and emotion. The answers have not been forthcoming because the concepts in which the questions are couched are themselves in doubt. Satisfactory answers depend on overhauling these concepts using the insights of feminists but using them carefully and critically. From a preliminary examination it appears that the place of feelings in human conduct has not been properly understood. Attention to its significance is important because any proper running of private and public life depends on it.

Chapter *10*

How Should I Feel About Abortion?

The issue of abortion is as controversial within philosophy as it is outside of philosophy. In thinking about abortion, we are forced to assess our views about a number of related issues. What we think about abortion will be a function of what we think about sex, about reproduction, about the beginning of human life, about killing, about responsibility, about sexual equality, and about religion. In fact, there is little in life to which the issue of abortion is not in some way related. It is not surprising, then, that there is so much disagreement about what abortion is and whether it is good, bad, or neither.

When thinking about abortion as a philosophical topic, it is helpful to begin by considering what women actually think about when they are trying to make a decision about whether to have an abortion. Obviously, the factors that a woman considers will be a function of her particular circumstances. Sometimes, the pregnancy itself presents difficulties. A teenager may feel that being pregnant would create serious personal and social difficulties for her. A woman about to set off on an arduous archeological expedition may feel that being pregnant would interfere with her work. Sometimes, the pregnancy itself is not so much a problem; rather, the problem is the child that will be its result. A student may feel that having a child at this point will seriously jeopardize her chances of finishing school; a mother of two children may feel that having another child would impair her emotional and financial capacity to care for her existing ones. The story by Alice Walker presents one such set of considerations. Although it is probably unwise to see any particular story about abortion as representative of all others, the Walker story reminds us that decisions about abortion are made in the context of a woman's ongoing and invariably complex life. When we abstract the abortion decision from that context, it may take on different dimensions.

Most opposition to abortion is based on the claim that human life begins at conception and thus a human embryo or fetus is a person like any other and so has a right to life. While there is disagreement among philosophers as to all that a right to life involves, we can assume that at the very least it guarantees that one not be killed unjustifiably. Unwarranted or unjustified killing is murder. Murder is not permissible. Those opposed to abortion typically believe that the killing of an innocent embryo is unwarranted. If so, they conclude, abortion is murder and hence is impermissible. When the problem of abortion is framed in this way, it appears that those who wish to defend the practice of abortion against this conclusion are forced to argue that personhood does not begin at conception, but rather at some later stage in pregnancy or at birth. The question of exactly when human life, or personhood, begins is not a straightforward one. (You may want to look at Chapter 8 for more on this topic.) In pushing the abortion issue into this murky territory, those opposed to abortion are replacing one difficult question (is abortion morally justifiable?) with another one (when does human life or personhood begin?). Judith Jarvis Thomson argues that those concerned with establishing the permissibility of abortion need not become entangled in the issue of fetal personhood. For the sake of argument, she grants those opposed to abortion their major premise, namely, that the fetus is a person. She then proceeds to argue that, even if the fetus is a person, it does not follow that the woman is required to carry it to term. The woman's right to control over her own body outweighs the rights of the fetus. She draws analogies between the sacrifices that pregnant women must make to keep fetuses alive and other situations in which one person's life depends on the willingness of another to act on his or her behalf. In doing so, she hopes to set abortion in a context that displays clearly what she takes to be the central moral issue that it raises: Does a woman have an *obligation* to maintain, for the sake of the fetus, an unwanted pregnancy to term? (Chapters 13 and 15 supply useful background for the issue of obligation.) Thomson's example of the unconscious violinist who requires the use of your kidneys to say alive has become legendary. It is up to you to decide whether you take it, or any of the other analogies, to be persuasive.

Thomson falls squarely in the tradition of those philosophers who see abortion as raising ethical questions. Indeed, Kathryn Pyne Addelson uses the term "the Judith Thomson tradition" to refer to any approach to abortion that focuses on the issue of rights and justice, that makes use of hypothetical rather than actual cases, and that takes the "solution" to the abortion problem to be a matter of gaining clarity about concepts, not a matter of bringing about social change. In the longer paper of which the selection here is the last part, Addelson argues that the Thomson tradition introduces, by its approach and methods, certain biases into its reasoning about abortion. Addelson introduces the actual, not hypothetical, case of Jane, a collective organization of women providing abortion counseling and referral services, and eventually abortions, before abortion was legalized in 1973 (in a famous Supreme Court case, *Roe vs. Wade*). By describing the inner workings of Jane and the self-perceptions of the women who worked in it, Addelson provides a basis for developing a moral framework quite different from that offered by the Thomson tradition. In doing so, she encourages us to do ethics in a novel way. Instead of "imposing" ethical concepts (like those of rights, justice, and obligations) on experience, we should instead allow experience to create and shape our ethical concepts. You might want to think, for example, about whether the story by Walker can be understood in terms of the Thomson tradition. Does Imani worry about rights and justice? If not, what concerns does she have? Are they closer to the concerns raised by the case of Jane? (The selection by Carol Gilligan in Chapter 15 provides a perspective complementary to that of Addelson.)

Much of the opposition to abortion comes from religion. The Catholic church, for example, condemns abortion, even in cases where the woman's life is at stake. Abortion is viewed as an affront to the sanctity of human life. Robert E. Joyce does take up the question of personhood directly. He defends the position that the human zygote is essentially a human person—just as much a person as you are. Joyce tries to avoid the problems inherent in trying to specify at what point (other than at conception) personhood begins. According to Joyce, a person is a being who has natural capacities for reasoning, willing, desiring, and relating to others. These natural capacities are present in the human zygote even though they have not yet developed fully. On this basis, Joyce argues that abortion is the killing of an actual and not just a potential person.

Finally, Barbara Ehrenreich asks us to consider whether abortion itself is really a moral issue. She suggests that by focusing on the needs of the fetus, to the exclusion of the needs of the woman who carries it, we have "created" a moral issue out of nothing. Her reasoning can be seen as an extension of Addelson's: By imposing a set of moral concerns, ones that serve only a particular set of interests, on a set of social practices, those practices are transformed. Abortion could just as well be viewed as a necessary medical procedure because no form of contraception is entirely reliable (nor is contraception itself always available to those who want to use it). If abortion raises difficult moral issues, then that is, according to Ehrenreich, because we *choose* to see it as raising those issues. Clearly, Ehrenreich thinks that the focus on the moral status of the fetus distracts us from what she takes to be important issues about poverty, insufficient information and education, lack of available contraception and so on.

As you can see, abortion raises a variety of troubling and challenging questions. First, it raises ethical questions, such as those addressed by Judith Thomson: Is abortion always wrong? Is it always right? Or is it sometimes right and sometimes wrong? Do embryos and fetuses have rights? Second, it raises what are called **metaethical** questions, such as those raised by Addelson and Ehrenreich: What is the most reasonable way to think about abortion? Is it best seen as a conflict between the woman's right to have control over her body and the fetus's right to life? Or does the language of rights distort the issue? Does it leave out some essential features of the difficulties and dilemmas women confront when deciding whether to have an abortion? What relationship does abortion have to other reproductive practices and choices? Ehrenreich argues that we choose, according to our particular interests, which issues we will treat as moral issues. Nevertheless, it does not appear that as a society we are ready to view having an abortion as no more significant than having a splinter removed. As long as that is true, it is important to understand what you think both about the rightness or wrongness of abortion and about the reasons why is has become such an important issue in contemporary culture.

ALICE WALKER

The Abortion

ALICE WALKER *was born in Georgia and now lives in San Francisco. An essayist, novelist, poet, and biographer, her many books include* The Color Purple, You Can't Keep a Good Woman Down, *and* In Search of Our Mother's Gardens.

T HEY had discussed it, but not deeply, whether they wanted the baby she was now carrying. "I don't *know* if I want it," she said, eyes filling with tears. She cried at anything now, and was often nauseous. That pregnant women cried easily and were nauseous seemed banal to her, and she resented banality.

"Well, think about it," he said, with his smooth reassuring voice (but with an edge of impatience she now felt) that used to soothe her.

It was all she *did* think about, all she apparently *could;* that he could dream otherwise enraged her. But she always lost when they argued. Her temper would flare up, he would become instantly reasonable, mature, responsible, if not responsive precisely, to her mood, and she would swallow down her tears and hate herself. It was because she believed him "good." The best human being she had ever met.

"It isn't as if we don't already have a child," she said in a calmer tone, carelessly wiping at the tear that slid from one eye.

"We have a perfect child," he said with relish, "thank the Good Lord!"

Had she ever dreamed she'd marry someone humble enough to go around thanking the Good Lord? She had not.

Now they left the bedroom, where she had been lying down on their massive king-size bed with the forbidding ridge in the middle, and went down the hall—hung with bright prints—to the cheerful, spotlessly clean kitchen. He put water on for tea in a bright yellow pot.

She wanted him to want the baby so much he would try to save its life. On the other hand, she did not permit such presumptuousness. As he praised the child they already had, a daughter of sunny disposition and winning smile, Imani sensed subterfuge, and hardened her heart.

"What am I talking about," she said, as if she'd been talking about it. "Another child would kill me. I can't imagine life with two children. Having a child is a good experience *to have had,* like graduate school. But if you've had one, you've had the experience and that's enough."

He placed the tea before her and rested a heavy hand on her hair. She felt the heat and pressure of his hand as she touched the cup and felt the odor and steam rise up from it. Her throat contracted.

"I can't drink that," she said through gritted teeth. "Take it away."

There were days of this.

Clarice, their daughter, was barely two years old. A miscarriage brought on by grief (Imani had lost her fervidly environmentalist mother to lung cancer shortly after Clarice's birth; the asbestos ceiling in the classroom where she taught first graders had leaked for twenty years) separated Clarice's birth from the new pregnancy. Imani felt her body had been assaulted by these events and was, in fact, considerably weakened, and was also, in any case, chronically anemic and run down. Still, if she had wanted the baby more than she did not want it, she would not have planned to abort it.

They lived in a small town in the South. Her husband, Clarence, was, among other things, legal adviser and defender of the new black mayor of the town. The mayor was much in their lives because of the difficulties being the first black mayor of a small town assured, and because, next to the major leaders of black struggles in the South, Clarence respected and admired him most.

Imani reserved absolute judgment, but she did point out that Mayor Carswell would never look at her directly when she made a comment or posed a question, even sitting at her own dinner table, and would instead talk to Clarence as if she were not there. He assumed that as a woman she would not be interested in, or even understand, politics. (He would comment occasionally on her cooking or her clothes. He noticed when she cut her hair.) But Imani understood every shade and variation of politics: she understood, for example, why she fed the mouth that did not speak to her; because for the present she must believe in Mayor Carswell, even as he could not believe in her. Even understanding this, however, she found dinners with Carswell hard to swallow.

But Clarence was dedicated to the mayor, and believed his success would ultimately mean security and advancement for them all.

On the morning she left to have the abortion, the mayor and Clarence were to have a working lunch, and they drove her to the airport deep in conversation about municipal funds, racist cops, and the facilities for teaching at the chaotic, newly integrated schools. Clarence had time for the briefest kiss and hug at the airport ramp.

"Take care of yourself," he whispered lovingly as she walked away. He was needed, while she was gone, to draft the city's new charter. She had agreed this was important; the mayor was already being called incompetent by local businessmen and the chamber of commerce, and one inferred from television that no black person alive even knew what a city charter was.

"Take care of myself." Yes, she thought. I see that is what I have to do. But she thought this self-pityingly, which invalidated it. She had expected *him* to take care of her, and she blamed him for not doing so now.

Well, she was a fraud, anyway. She had known after a year of marriage that it bored her. "The Experience of Having a Child" was to distract her from this fact. Still, she expected him to "take care of her." She was lucky he didn't pack up and leave. But he seemed to know, as she did, that if anyone packed and left, it would be her. Precisely *because* she was a fraud and because in the end he would settle for fraud and she could not.

On the plane to New York her teeth ached and she vomited bile—bitter, yellowish stuff she hadn't even been aware her body produced. She resented and appreciated the crisp help of the stewardess, who asked if she needed anything, then stood chatting with the cigarette-smoking white man next to her, whose fat hairy wrist, like a large worm, was all Imani could bear to see out of the corner of her eye.

Her first abortion, when she was still in college, she frequently remembered as wonderful, bearing as it had all the marks of a supreme coming of age and a seizing of the direction of her own life, as well as a comprehension of existence that never left her: that life—what one saw about one and called Life—was not a facade. There was nothing behind it which used "Life" as its manifestation. Life was itself. Period. At the time, and afterwards, and even now, this seemed a marvelous thing to know.

The abortionist had been a delightful Italian doctor on the Upper East Side in New York, and before he put her under he told her about his own daughter who was just her age, and a junior at Vassar. He babbled on and on until she was out, but not before Imani had thought how her thousand dollars, for which she would be in debt for years, would go to keep her there.

When she woke up it was all over. She lay on a brown Naugahyde sofa in the doctor's outer office. And she heard, over her somewhere in the air, the sound of a woman's voice. It was Saturday, no nurses in attendance, and she presumed it was the doctor's wife. She was pulled gently to her feet by this voice and encouraged to walk.

"And when you leave, be sure to walk as if nothing is wrong," the voice said.

Imani did not feel any pain. This surprised her. Perhaps he didn't do anything, she thought. Perhaps he took my thousand dollars and put me to sleep with two dollars' worth of ether. Perhaps this is a racket.

But he was so kind, and he was smiling benignly, almost fatherly, at her (and Imani realized how desperately she needed this "fatherly" look, this "fatherly" smile). "Thank you," she murmured sincerely: she was thanking him for her life.

Some of Italy was still in his voice. "It's nothing, nothing," he said. "A nice pretty girl like you; in school like my own daughter, you didn't need this trouble."

"He's nice," she said to herself, walking to the subway on her way back to school. She lay down gingerly across a vacant seat, and passed out.

She hemorrhaged steadily for six weeks, and was not well again for a year.

• • •

But this was seven years later. An abortion law now made it possible to make an appointment at a clinic, and for seventy-five dollars a safe, quick, painless abortion was yours.

Imani had once lived in New York, in the Village, not five blocks from where the abortion clinic was. It was also near the Margaret Sanger clinic, where she had received her very first diaphragm, with utter gratitude and amazement that someone apparently understood and actually cared about young women as alone and ignorant as she. In fact, as she walked up the block, with its modern office buildings side by side with older, more elegant brownstones, she felt how close she was still to that earlier self. Still not in control of her sensuality, and only through violence and with money (for the flight, for the operation itself) in control of her body.

She found that abortion had entered the age of the assembly line. Grateful for the lack of distinction between herself and the other women—all colors, ages, states of misery or nervousness—she was less happy to notice, once the doctor started to insert the catheter, that the anesthesia she had been given was insufficient. But assembly lines don't stop because the product on them has a complaint. Her doctor whistled, and assured her she was all right, and carried the procedure through to the horrific end. Imani fainted some seconds before that.

They laid her out in a peaceful room full of cheerful colors. Primary colors: yellow, red, blue. When she revived she had the feeling of being in a nursery. She had a pressing need to urinate.

A nurse, kindly, white-haired and with firm hands, helped her to the toilet. Imani saw herself in the mirror over the sink and was alarmed. She was literally gray, as if all her blood had leaked out.

"Don't worry about how you look," said the nurse. "Rest a bit here and take it easy when you get back home. You'll be fine in a week or so."

She could not imagine being fine again. Somewhere her child—she never dodged into the language of "fetuses" and "amorphous growths"—was being flushed down a sewer. Gone all her or his chances to see the sunlight, savor a fig.

"Well," she said to this child, "it was you or me, Kiddo, and I chose me."

There were people who thought she had no right to choose herself, but Imani knew better than to think of those people now.

It was a bright, hot Saturday when she returned.

Clarence and Clarice picked her up at the airport. They had brought flowers from Imani's garden, and Clarice presented them with a stout-hearted hug. Once in her mother's lap she rested content all the way home, sucking her thumb, stroking her nose with the forefinger of the same hand, and kneading a corner of her blanket with the three fingers that were left.

"How did it go?" asked Clarence.

"It went," said Imani.

There was no way to explain abortion to a man. She thought castration might be an apt analogy, but most men, perhaps all, would insist this could not possibly be true.

"The anesthesia failed," she said. "I thought I'd never faint in time to keep from screaming and leaping off the table."

Clarence paled. He hated thought of pain, any kind of violence. He could not endure it; it made him physically ill. This was one of the reasons he was a pacifist, another reason she admired him.

She knew he wanted her to stop talking. But she continued in a flat, deliberate voice.

"All the blood seemed to run out of me. The tendons in my legs felt cut. I was gray."

He reached for her hand. Held it. Squeezed.

"But," she said, "at least I know what I don't want. And I intend never to go through any of this again."

They were in the living room of their peaceful, quiet and colorful house. Imani was in her rocker, Clarice dozing on her lap. Clarence sank to the floor and rested his head against her knees. She felt he was asking for nurture when she needed it herself. She felt the two of them, Clarence and Clarice, clinging to her, using her. And that the only way she could claim herself, feel herself distinct from them, was by doing something painful, self-defining but self-destructive.

She suffered the pressure of his head as long as she could.

"Have a vasectomy," she said, "or stay in the guest room. Nothing is going to touch me anymore that isn't harmless."

He smoothed her thick hair with his hand. "We'll talk about it," he said, as if that was not what they were doing. "We'll see. Don't worry. We'll take care of things."

She had forgotten that the third Sunday in June, the following day, was the fifth memorial observance for Holly Monroe, who had been shot down on her way home from her high-school graduation ceremony five years before. Imani *always* went to these memorials. She liked the reassurance that her people had long memories, and that those people who fell in struggle or innocence were not forgotten. She was, of course, too weak to go. She was dizzy and still losing blood. The white lawgivers attempted to get around assassination—which Imani considered extreme abortion—by saying the victim provoked it (there had been some difficulty saying this about Holly Monroe, but they had tried) but were antiabortionist to a man. Imani thought of this as she resolutely showered and washed her hair.

Clarence had installed central air conditioning their second year in the house. Imani had at first objected. "I want to smell the trees, the flowers, the natural air!" she cried. But the first summer of 110-degree heat had cured her of giving a damn about any of that. Now she wanted to be cool. As much as she loved trees, on a hot day she would have sawed through a forest to get to an air conditioner.

In fairness to him, she had to admit he asked her if she thought she was well enough to go. But even to be asked annoyed her. She was not one to let her own troubles prevent her from showing proper respect and remembrance toward the dead, although she understood perfectly well that once dead, the dead do not exist. So respect, remembrance was for herself, and today herself needed rest. There was something mad about her refusal to rest, and she felt it as she tottered about getting Clarice dressed. But she did not stop. She ran a bath, plopped her child in it, scrubbed her plump body on her knees, arms straining over the tub awkwardly in a way that made her stomach hurt—but not yet her uterus—dried her hair, lifted her out and dried the rest of her on the kitchen table.

"You are going to remember as long as you live what kind of people they are," she said to the child, who, gurgling and cooing, looked into her mother's stern face with light-hearted fixation.

"You are going to hear the music," Imani said. "The music they've tried to kill. The music they try to steal." She felt feverish and was aware she was muttering. She didn't care.

"They think they can kill a continent—people, trees, buffalo—and then fly off to the moon and just forget about it. But you and me we're going to remember the people, the trees and the fucking buffalo. Goddammit."

"Buffwoe," said the child, hitting at her mother's face with a spoon.

She placed the baby on a blanket in the living room and turned to see her husband's eyes, full of pity, on her. She wore pert green velvet slippers and a lovely sea green robe. Her body was bent within it. A reluctant tear formed beneath his gaze.

"Sometimes I look at you and I wonder 'What is this man doing in my house?'"

This had started as a joke between them. Her aim had been never to marry, but to take in lovers who could be sent home at dawn, freeing her to work and ramble.

"I'm here because you love me," was the traditional answer. But Clarence faltered, meeting her eyes, and Imani turned away.

It was a hundred degrees by ten o'clock. By eleven, when the memorial service began, it would be ten degrees hotter. Imani staggered from the heat. When she sat in the car she had to clench her teeth against the dizziness until the motor prodded the air conditioning to envelop them in coolness. A dull ache started in her uterus.

The church was not of course air conditioned. It was authentic Primitive Baptist in every sense.

Like the four previous memorials this one was designed by Holly Monroe's classmates. All twenty-five of whom— fat and thin—managed to look like the dead girl. Imani had never seen Holly Monroe, though there were always photographs of her dominating the pulpit of this church where she had been baptized and where she had sung in the choir— and to her, every black girl of a certain vulnerable age *was* Holly Monroe. And an even deeper truth was that Holly Monroe was herself. Herself shot down, aborted on the eve of becoming herself.

She was prepared to cry and to do so with abandon. But she did not. She clenched her teeth against the steadily increasing pain and her tears were instantly blotted by the heat.

Mayor Carswell had been waiting for Clarence in the vestibule of the church, mopping his plumply jowled face with a voluminous handkerchief and holding court among half a dozen young men and women who listened to him with awe. Imani exchanged greetings with the mayor, he ritualistically kissed her on the cheek, and kissed Clarice on the cheek, but his rather heat-glazed eye was already fastened on her husband. The two men huddled in a corner away from the awed young group. Away from Imani and Clarice, who passed hesitantly, waiting to be joined or to be called back, into the church.

There was a quarter hour's worth of music.

"Holly Monroe was five feet, three inches tall, and weighed one hundred and eleven pounds," her best friend said, not reading from notes, but talking to each person in the audience. "She was a stubborn, loyal Aries, the best kind of friend to have. She had black kinky hair that she experimented with a lot. She was exactly the color of this oak church pew in the summer; in the winter she was the color [pointing up] of this heart pine ceiling. She loved green. She did not like lavender because she said she also didn't like pink. She had brown eyes and wore glasses, except when she was meeting someone for the first time. She had a sort of rounded nose. She had beautiful large teeth, but her lips were always chapped so she didn't smile as much as she might have if she'd ever gotten used to carrying Chap Stick. She had elegant feet.

"Her favorite church song was 'Leaning on the Everlasting Arms.' Her favorite other kind of song was 'I Can't Help Myself—I Love You and Nobody Else.' She was often late for choir rehearsal though she loved to sing. She made the dress she wore to her graduation in Home Ec. She *hated* Home Ec. . . ."

Imani was aware that the sound of low, murmurous voices had been the background for this statement all along. Everything was quiet around her, even Clarice sat up straight, absorbed by the simple friendliness of the young woman's voice. All of Holly Monroe's classmates and friends in the choir wore vivid green. Imani imagined Clarice entranced by the brilliant, swaying color as by a field of swaying corn.

Lifting the child, her uterus burning, and perspiration already a stream down her back, Imani tiptoed to the door. Clarence and the mayor were still deep in conversation. She heard "board meeting . . . alderman . . . city council." She beckoned to Clarence.

"Your voices are carrying!" she hissed.

She meant: How dare you not come inside.

They did not. Clarence raised his head, looked at her, and shrugged his shoulders helplessly. Then, turning, with the abstracted air of priests, the two men moved slowly toward the outer door, and into the churchyard, coming to stand some distance from the church beneath a large oak tree. There they remained throughout the service.

Two years later, Clarence was furious with her: What is the matter with you? he asked. You never want me to touch you. You told me to sleep in the guest room and I did. You told me to have a vasectomy I didn't want and I *did*. (Here, there was a sob of hatred for her somewhere in the anger, the humiliation: he thought of himself as a eunuch, and blamed her.)

She was not merely frigid, she was remote.

She had been amazed after they left the church that the anger she'd felt watching Clarence and the mayor turn away from the Holly Monroe memorial did not prevent her accepting a ride home with him. A month later it did not prevent her smiling on him fondly. Did not prevent a trip to Bermuda, a few blissful days of very good sex on a deserted beach screened by trees. Did not prevent her listening to his mother's stories of Clarence's youth as though she would treasure them forever.

And yet. From that moment in the heat at the church door, she had uncoupled herself from him, in a separation that made him, except occasionally, little more than a stranger.

And he had not felt it, had not known.

"What have I done?" he asked, all the tenderness in his voice breaking over her. She smiled a nervous smile at him, which he interpreted as derision—so far apart had they drifted.

They had discussed the episode at the church many times. Mayor Carswell—whom they never saw anymore—was now a model mayor, with wide biracial support in his campaign for the legislature. Neither could easily recall him, though television frequently brought him into the house.

"It was so important that I help the mayor!" said Clarence. "He was our *first!*"

Imani understood this perfectly well, but it sounded humorous to her. When she smiled, he was offended.

She had known the moment she left the marriage, the exact second. But apparently that moment had left no perceptible mark.

They argued, she smiled, they scowled, blamed and cried—as she packed.

Each of them almost recalled out loud that about this time of the year their aborted child would have been a troublesome, "terrible" two-year-old, a great burden on its mother, whose health was by now in excellent shape,

each wanted to think aloud that the marriage would have deteriorated anyway, because of that.

JUDITH JARVIS THOMSON

A Defense of Abortion

JUDITH JARVIS THOMSON *teaches philosophy at M.I.T. Her extensive writings in ethics are collected in a recent book,* Rights, Restitution and Risk.

MOST opposition to abortion relies on the premise that the fetus is a human being, a person, from the moment of conception. The premise is argued for, but, as I think, not well. Take, for example, the most common argument. We are asked to notice that the development of a human being from conception through birth into childhood is continuous; then it is said that to draw a line, to choose a point in this development and say "before this point the thing is not a person, after this point it is a person" is to make an arbitrary choice, a choice for which in the nature of things no good reason can be given. It is concluded that the fetus is, or anyway that we had better say it is, a person from the moment of conception. But this conclusion does not follow. Similar things might be said about the development of an acorn into an oak tree, and it does not follow that acorns are oak trees, or that we had better say they are. Arguments of this form are sometimes called "slippery slope arguments"—the phrase is perhaps self-explanatory—and it is dismaying that

opponents of abortion rely on them so heavily and uncritically.

I am inclined to agree, however, that the prospects for "drawing a line" in the development of the fetus look dim. I am inclined to think also that we shall probably have to agree that the fetus has already become a human person well before birth. Indeed, it comes as a surprise when one first learns how early in its life it begins to acquire human characteristics. By the tenth week, for example, it already has a face, arms and legs, fingers and toes; it has internal organs, and brain activity is detectable. On the other hand, I think that the premise is false, that the fetus is not a person from the moment of conception. A newly fertilized ovum, a newly implanted clump of cells, is no more a person that an acorn is an oak tree. But I shall not discuss any of this. For it seems to me to be of great interest to ask what happens if, for the sake of argument, we allow the premise. How, precisely, are we supposed to get from there to the conclusion that abortion is morally impermissible? Opponents of abortion commonly spend most of their time establishing that the fetus is a person, and hardly any time explaining the step from there to the impermissibility of abortion. Perhaps they think the step too simple and obvious to require much comment. Or perhaps instead they are simply being economical in argument. Many of those who defend abortion rely on the premise that the fetus is not a person, but only a bit of tissue that will become a person at birth; and why pay out more arguments than you have to? Whatever the explanation, I suggest that the step they take is neither easy nor obvious, that it calls for closer examination than it is commonly given, and that when we do give it this closer examination we shall feel inclined to reject it.

I propose, then, that we grant that the fetus is a person from the moment of conception. How does the argument go from here? Something like this, I take it. Every person has a right to life. So the fetus has a right to life. No doubt the mother has a right to decide what shall happen in and to her body; everyone would grant that. But surely a person's right to life is stronger and more stringent than the mother's right to decide what happens in and to her body, and so outweighs it. So the fetus may not be killed; an abortion may not be performed.

It sounds plausible. But now let me ask you to imagine this. You wake up in the morning and find yourself back to back in bed with an unconscious violinist. A famous unconscious violinist. He has been found to have a fatal kidney ailment, and the Society of Music Lovers has canvassed all the available medical records and found that you alone have the right blood type to help. They have therefore kidnapped you, and last night the violinist's circulatory system was plugged into yours, so that your kidneys can be used to extract poisons from his blood as well as your own. The director of the hospital now tells you, "Look, we're sorry the Society of Music Lovers did this to you— we would never have permitted it if we had known. But still, they did it, and the violinist now is plugged into you. To unplug you would be to kill him. But never mind, it's only for nine months. By then he will have recovered from his ailment, and can safely be unplugged from you." Is it morally incumbent on you to accede to this situation? No doubt it would be very nice of you if you did, a great kindness. But do you *have* to accede to it? What if it were not nine months, but nine years? Or longer still? What if the director of the hospital says, "Tough luck, I agree, but you've now got to stay in bed, with the violinist plugged into you, for the rest of your life. Because remember this. All persons have a right to life, and violinists are persons. Granted you have a right to decide what happened in and to your body, but a person's right to life outweighs your right to decide what happens in and to your body. So you cannot ever be unplugged from him." I imagine you would regard this as outrageous, which suggests that something really is wrong with that plausible-sounding argument I mentioned a moment ago.

In this case, of course, you were kidnapped; you didn't volunteer for the operation that plugged the violinist into your kidneys. Can those who oppose abortion on the ground I mentioned make an exception for a pregnancy due to rape? Certainly. They can say that persons have a right to life only if they didn't come into existence because of rape; or they can say that all persons have a right to life, but that some have less of a right to life than others, in particular, that those who came into existence because of rape have less. But these statements have a rather unpleasant sound. Surely the question of whether you have a right to life at all, or how much of it you have, shouldn't turn on the question of whether or not you are the product of a rape. And in fact the people who oppose abortion on the ground I mentioned do not make this distinction, and hence do not make an exception in case of rape.

Nor do they make an exception for a case in which the mother has to spend the nine months of her pregnancy in bed. They would agree that would be a great pity, and hard on the mother; but all the same, all persons have a right to life, the fetus is a person, and so on. I suspect, in fact, that they would not make an exception for a case in which, miraculously enough, the pregnancy went on for nine years, or even the rest of the mother's life.

Some won't even make an exception for a case in which continuation of the pregnancy is likely to shorten the mother's life; they regard abortion as impermissible even to save the mother's life. Such cases are nowadays very rare, and many opponents of abortion do not accept this extreme view. All the same, it is a good place to begin: a number of points of interest come out in respect to it.

1. Let us call the view that abortion is impermissible even to save the mother's life "the extreme view." I want to suggest first that it does not issue from the argument I mentioned earlier without the addition of some fairly powerful premises. Suppose a woman has become pregnant, and now learns that she has a cardiac condition such that she will die if she carries the baby to term. What may be done for her? The fetus, being a person, has a right to life, but as the mother is a person too, so has she a right to life. Presumably they have an equal right to life. How is it supposed to come out that an abortion may not be performed? If mother and child have an equal right to life, shouldn't we perhaps flip a coin? Or should we add to the mother's right to life her right to decide what happens in and to her body, which everybody seems to be ready to grant—the sum of her rights now outweighing the fetus' right to life?

The most familiar argument here is the following. We are told that performing the abortion would be directly killing the child, whereas doing nothing would not be killing the mother, but only letting her die. Moreover in killing the child, one would be killing an innocent person, for the child has committed no crime, and is not aiming at his mother's death. And then there are a variety of ways in which this might be continued. (1) But as directly killing an innocent person is always and absolutely impermissible, an abortion may not be performed. Or, (2) as directly killing an innocent person is murder, and murder is always and absolutely impermissible, an abortion may not be performed. Or, (3) as one's duty to refrain from directly killing an innocent person is more stringent than one's duty to refrain from directly killing an innocent person is more stringent than one's duty to keep a person from dying, an abortion may not be performed. Or, (4) if one's only options are directly killing an innocent person or letting a person die, one must prefer letting the person die, and thus an abortion may not be performed.

Some people seem to have thought that these are not further premises which must be added if the conclusion is to be reached, but that they follow from the very fact that an innocent person has a right to life. But this seems to me to be a mistake, and perhaps the simplest way to show this is to bring out that while we must certainly grant that innocent persons have a right to life, the theses in (1) through (4) are all false. Take (2), for example. If directly killing an innocent person is murder, and thus is impermissible, then the mother's directly killing the innocent person inside her is murder, and thus is impermissible. But it cannot seriously be thought to be murder if the mother performs an abortion on herself to save her life. It cannot seriously be said that she *must* refrain, that she *must* sit passively by and wait for her death. Let us look again at the case of you and the violinist. There you are, in bed with the violinist, and the director of the hospital says to you, "It's all most distressing, and I deeply sympathize, but you see this is putting an additional strain on your kidneys, and you'll be dead with the month. But you *have* to stay where you are all the same. Because unplugging you would be directly killing an innocent violinist, and that's murder, and that's impermissible." If anything in the world is true, it is that you do not commit murder, you do not do what is impermissible, if you reach around to your back and unplug yourself from that violinist to save your life.

The main focus of attention in writing on abortion has been on what a third party may or may not do in answer to a request from a woman for an abortion. This is in a way understandable. Things being as they are, there isn't much a woman can safely do to abort herself. So the question asked is what a third party may do, and what the mother may

do, if it is mentioned at all, is deduced, almost as an afterthought, from what it is concluded that third parties may do. But it seems to me that to treat the matter in this way is to refuse to grant to the mother that very status of person which is so firmly insisted on for the fetus. For we cannot simply read off what a person may do from what a third party may do. Suppose you find yourself trapped in a tiny house with a growing child. I mean a very tiny house and in a few minutes you'll be crushed to death. The child on the other hand won't be crushed to death; if nothing is done to stop him from growing he'll be hurt, but in the end he'll simply burst open the house and walk out a free man. Now I could well understand it if a bystander were to say, "There's nothing we can do for you. We cannot choose between your life and his, we cannot be the ones to decide who is to live, we cannot intervene." But it cannot be concluded that you too can do nothing, that you cannot attack it to save your life. However innocent the child may be, you do not have to wait passively while it crushes you to death. Perhaps a pregnant woman is vaguely felt to have the status of house, to which we don't allow the right of self-defense. But if the woman houses the child, it should be remembered that she is a person who houses it.

I should perhaps stop to say explicitly that I am not claiming that people have a right to do anything whatever to save their lives. I think, rather, that there are drastic limits to the right of self-defense. If someone threatens you with death unless you torture someone else to death, I think you have not the right, even to save your life, to do so. But the case under consideration here is very different. In our case there are only two people involved, one whose life is threatened, and one who threatens it. Both are innocent: the one who threatens does not threaten because of any fault. For this reason we may feel that we bystanders cannot intervene. But the person threatened can.

In sum, a woman surely can defend her life against the threat to it posed by the unborn child, even if doing so involves its death. And this shows not merely that the theses in (1) through (4) are false; it shows also that the extreme view of abortion is false, and so we need not canvass any other possible ways of arriving at it from the argument I mentioned at the outset.

2. The extreme view could of course be weakened to say that while abortion is permissible to save the mother's life, it may not be performed by a third party, but only by the mother herself. But this cannot be right either. For what we have to keep in mind is that the mother and the unborn child are not like two tenants in a small house which has, by an unfortunate mistake, been rented to both: the mother *owns* the house. The fact that she does adds to the the offensiveness of deducing that the mother can do nothing from the supposition that third parties can do nothing. But it does more than this: it casts a bright light on the supposition that third parties can do nothing. Certainly it lets us see that a third party who says "I cannot choose between you" is fooling himself if he thinks this is impartiality. If Jones has found and fastened on a certain coat, which he needs to keep him from freezing, but which Smith also needs to keep him from freezing, then it is not impartiality that says "I cannot choose between you" when Smith owns the coat. Women have said again and again "This body is *my* body!" and they have

reason to feel angry, reason to feel that it has been like shouting into the wind. Smith, after all, is hardly likely to bless us if we say to him, "Of course it's your coat, anybody would grant that it is. But no one may choose between you and Jones who is to have it."

We should really ask what it is that says "no one may choose" in the face of the fact that the body that houses the child is the mother's body. It may be simply a failure to appreciate this fact. But it may be something more interesting, namely the sense that one has a right to refuse to lay hands on people, even where it would be just and fair to do so, even where justice seems to require that somebody do so. Thus justice might call for somebody to get Smith's coat back from Jones, and yet you have a right to refuse to be the one to lay hands on Jones, a right to refuse to do physical violence to him. This, I think, must be granted. But then what should be said is not "no one may choose," but only "*I* cannot choose," and indeed not even this, but "*I* will not *act*," leaving it open that somebody else can or should, and in particular that anyone in a position of authority, with the job of securing people's rights, both can and should. So this is no difficulty. I have not been arguing that any given third party must accede to the mother's request that he perform an abortion to save her life, but only that he may.

I suppose that in some views of human life the mother's body is only on loan to her, the loan not being one which gives her any prior claim to it. One who held this view might well think it impartiality to say "I cannot choose." But I shall simply ignore this possibility. My own view is that if a human being has any just, prior claim to anything at all, he has a just, prior claim to his own body. And perhaps this needn't be argued for here anyway, since, as I mentioned, the arguments against abortion we are looking at do grant that the woman has a right to decide what happens in and to her body.

But although they do grant it, I have tried to show that they do not take seriously what is done in granting it. I suggest the same thing will reappear even more clearly when we turn away from cases in which the mother's life is at stake, and attend, as I propose we now do, to the vastly more common cases in which a woman wants an abortion for some less weighty reason than preserving her own life.

3. Where the mother's life is not at stake, the argument I mentioned at the outset seems to have a much stronger pull. "Everyone has a right to life, so the unborn person has a right to life." And isn't the child's right to life weightier than anything other than the mother's own right to life, which she might put forward as ground for an abortion?

This argument treats the right to life as if it were unproblematic. It is not, and this seems to me to be precisely the source of the mistake.

For we should now, at long last, ask what it comes to, to have a right to life. In some views having a right to life includes having a right to be given at least the bare minimum one needs for continued life. But suppose that what in fact *is* the bare minimum a man needs for continued life is something he has no right at all to be given? If I am sick unto death, and the only thing that will save my life is the touch of Henry Fonda's cool hand on my fevered brow, then all the same, I have no right to be given the touch of Henry Fonda's cool hand on my fevered brow. It would be frightfully nice of him to fly in from the West

Coast to provide it. It would be less nice, though no doubt well meant, if my friends flew out to the West Coast and carried Henry Fonda back with them. But I have no right at all against anybody that he should do this for me. Or again, to return to the story I told earlier, the fact that for continued life that violinist needs the continued use of your kidneys does not establish that he has a right to be given the continued use of your kidneys. He certainly has no right against you that *you* should give him continued use of your kidneys. For nobody has any right to use your kidneys unless you give him such a right; and nobody has the right against you that you shall give him the right—if you do allow him to go on using your kidneys, this is a kindness on your part, and not something he can claim from you as his due. Nor has he any right against anybody else that *they* should give him continued use of your kidneys. Certainly he had no right against the Society of Music Lovers that they should plug him into you in the first place. And if you now start to unplug yourself, having learned that you will otherwise have to spend nine years in bed with him, there is nobody in the world who must try to prevent you, in order to see to it that he is given something he has a right to be given.

Some people are rather stricter about the right to life. In their view, it does not include the right to be given anything, but amounts to, and only to, the right not to be killed by anybody. But here a related difficulty arises. If everybody is to refrain from killing that violinist, then everybody must refrain from doing a great many different sorts of things. Everybody must refrain from slitting his throat, everybody must refrain from shooting him—and everybody must refrain from unplugging you from him. But does he have a right against everybody that they shall refrain from unplugging you from him? To refrain from doing this is to allow him to continue to use your kidneys. It could be argued that he has a right against us that *we* should allow him to continue to use your kidneys. That is, while he had no right against us that we should give him the use of your kidneys, it might be argued that he anyway has a right against us that we shall not now intervene and deprive him of the use of your kidneys. I shall come back to third-party interventions later. But certainly the violinist has no right against you that *you* shall allow him to continue to use your kidneys. As I said, if you do allow him to use them, it is a kindness on your part, and not something you owe him.

This difficulty I point out here is not peculiar to the right to life. It reappears in connection with all the other natural rights; and it is something which an adequate account of rights must deal with. For present purposes it is enough just to draw attention to it. But I would stress that I am not arguing that people do not have a right to life—quite to the contrary, it seems to me that the primary control we must place on the acceptability of an account of rights is that it should turn out in that account to be a truth that all persons have a right to life. I am arguing only that having a right to life does not guarantee having either a right to be given the use of or a right to be allowed continued use of another person's body—even if one needs it for life itself. So the right to life will not serve the opponents of abortion in the very simple and clear way in which they seem to have thought it would.

4. There is another way to bring out the difficulty. In the most ordinary sort of case, to deprive someone of what he has a right to is to treat him unjustly. Suppose a boy and his small brother are jointly given a box of chocolates for Christmas. If the older boy takes the box and refuses to give his brother any of the chocolates, he is unjust to him, for the brother has been given a right to half of them. But suppose that, having learned that otherwise it means nine years in bed with that violinist, you unplug yourself from him. You surely are not being unjust to him, for you gave him no right to use your kidneys, and no one else can have given him any such right. But we have to notice that in unplugging yourself, you are killing him; and violinists, like everybody else, have a right to life, and thus in the view we were considering just now, the right not to be killed. So here you do what he supposedly has a right you shall not do, but you do not act unjustly to him in doing it.

The emendation which may be made at this point is this: the right to life consists not in the right not to be killed, but rather in the right not to be killed unjustly. This runs a risk of circularity, but never mind: it would enable us to square the fact that the violinist has a right to life with the fact that you do not act unjustly toward him in unplugging yourself, thereby killing him. For if you do not kill him unjustly, you do not violate his right to life, and so it is no wonder you do him no injustice.

But if this emendation is accepted, the gap in the argument against abortion stares us plainly in the face: it is by no means enough to show that the fetus is a person, and to remind us that all persons have a right to life—we need to be shown also that killing the fetus violates its right to life, i.e., that abortion is unjust killing. And is it?

I suppose we may take it as a datum that in a case of pregnancy due to rape the mother has not given the unborn person a right to the use of her body for food and shelter. Indeed, in what pregnancy could it be supposed that the mother has given the unborn person such a right? It is not as if there were unborn persons drifting about the world, to whom a woman who wants a child says "I invite you in."

But it might be argued that there are other ways one can have acquired a right to the use of another person's body than by having been invited to use it by that person. Suppose a woman voluntarily indulges in intercourse, knowing of the chance it will issue in pregnancy, and then she does become pregnant; is she not in part responsible for the presence, in fact the very existence, of the unborn person insider her? No doubt she did not invite it in. But doesn't her partial responsibility for its being there itself give it a right to the use of her body? If so, then her aborting it would be more like the boy's taking away the chocolates, and less like your unplugging yourself from the violinist—doing so would be depriving it of what it does have a right to, and thus would be doing in an injustice.

And then, too, it might be asked whether or not she can kill it even to save her own life: If she voluntarily called it into existence, how can she now kill it, even in self-defense?

The first thing to be said about this is that it is something new. Opponents of abortion have been so concerned to make out the independence of the fetus, in order to establish that it has a right to life, just as its mother does, that they have tended to overlook the possible support they might gain from making out that the fetus is *dependent* on the

other, in order to establish that she has a special kind of responsibility for it, a responsibility that gives it rights against her which are not possessed by any independent person—such as an ailing violinist who is a stranger to her.

On the other hand, this argument would give the unborn person a right to its mother's body only if her pregnancy resulted from a voluntary act, undertaken in full knowledge of the chance a pregnancy might result from it. It would leave out entirely the unborn person whose existence is due to rape. Pending the availability of some further argument, then, we would be left with the conclusion that unborn persons whose existence is due to rape have no right to the use of their mothers' bodies, and thus that aborting them is not depriving them of anything they have a right to and hence is not unjust killing.

And we should also notice that it is not at all plain that this argument really does go even as far as it purports to. For there are cases and cases, and the details make a difference. If the room is stuffy, and I therefore open a window to air it, and a burglar climbs in, it would be absurd to say, "Ah, now he can stay, she's given him a right to the use of her house—for she is partially responsible for his presence there, having voluntarily done what enabled him to get in, in full knowledge that there are such things as burglars, and that burglars burgle." It would be still more absurd to say this if I had had bars installed outside my windows, precisely to prevent burglars from getting in, and a burglar got in only because of a defect in the bars. It remains equally absurd if we imagine it is not a burglar who climbs in, but an innocent person who blunders or falls in. Again suppose it were like this: people-seeds drift about in the air like pollen, and if you open your windows, one may drift in and take root in your carpets or upholstery. You don't want children, so you fix up your windows with fine mesh screens, the very best you can buy. As can happen, however, and on very, very rare occasions does happen, one of the screens is defective; and a seed drifts in and takes root. Does the person-plant who now develops have a right to the use of your house? Surely not—despite the fact that you voluntarily opened your windows, you knowingly kept carpets and upholstered furniture, and you knew that screens were sometimes defective. Someone may argue that you are responsible for its rooting that it does have a right to your house, because after all you *could* have lived out your life with bare floors and furniture, or with sealed windows and doors. But this won't do— for by the same token anyone can avoid a pregnancy due to rape by having a hysterectomy, or anyway by never leaving home without a (reliable!) army.

It seems to me that the argument we are looking at can establish at most that there are *some* cases in which the unborn person has a right to the use of its mother's body, and therefore *some* cases in which abortion is unjust killing. There is room for much discussion and argument as to precisely which, if any. But I think we should sidestep this issue and leave it open, for at any rate the argument certainly does not establish that all abortion is unjust killing.

5. There is room for yet another argument here, however. We surely must all grant that there may be cases in which it would be morally indecent to detach a person from your body at the cost of his life. Suppose you learn that what the violinist needs is not nine years of your life, but only one hour: all you need do to save his life is to spend

one hour in that bed with him. Suppose also that letting him use your kidneys for that one hour would not affect your health in the slightest. Admittedly you were kidnapped. Admittedly you did not give anyone permission to plug him into you. Nevertheless it seems to me plain you *ought* to allow him to use your kidneys for that hour—it would be indecent to refuse.

Again, suppose pregnancy lasted only an hour, and constituted no threat to life or health. And suppose that a woman becomes pregnant as a result of rape. Admittedly she did not voluntarily do anything to bring about the existence of a child. Admittedly she did nothing at all which would give the unborn person a right to the use of her body. All the same it might well be said, as in the newly emended violinist story, that she *ought* to allow it to remain for that hour—that it would be indecent in her to refuse.

Now some people are inclined to use the term "right" in such a way that it follows from the fact that you ought to allow a person to use your body for the hour he needs, that he has a right to use your body for the hour he needs even though he has not been given that right by any person or act. They may say that it follows also that if you refuse, you act unjustly toward him. This use of the term is perhaps so common that it cannot be called wrong; nevertheless it seems to me to be an unfortunate loosening of what we would do better to keep a tight rein on. Suppose that box of chocolates I mentioned earlier had not been given to both boys jointly, but was given only to the older boy. There he sits, stolidly eating his way through the box, his small brother watching enviously. Here we are likely to say "You ought not to be so mean. You ought to give your brother some of those chocolates." My own view is that it just does not follow from the truth of this that the brother has any right to any of the chocolates. If the boy refuses to give his brother any, he is greedy, stingy, callous—but not unjust. I suppose that the people I have in mind will say it does follow that the brother has a right to some of the chocolates, and thus that the boy does act unjustly if he refuses to give his brother any. But the effect of saying this is to obscure what we should keep distinct, namely the difference between the boy's refusal in this case and the boy's refusal in the earlier case, in which the box was given to both boys jointly, and in which the small brother thus had what was from any point of view clear title to half.

A further objection to so using the term "right" that from the fact that A ought to do a thing for B, it follows that B has a right against A that A do it for him, is that it is going to make the question of whether or not a man has a right to a thing turn on how easy it is to provide him with it; and this seems not merely unfortunate, but morally unacceptable. Take the case of Henry Fonda again. I said earlier that I had no right to the touch of his cool hand on my fevered brow, even though I needed it to save my life. I said it would be frightfully nice of him to fly in from the West Coast to provide me with it, but that I had no right against him that he should do so. But suppose he has only to walk across the room, place a hand briefly on my brow—and lo, my life is saved. Then surely he ought to do it, it would be indecent to refuse. Is it to be said "Ah, well, it follows that in this case she has a right to the touch of his hand on her brow, and so it would be an injustice in him to refuse"? So that I have

a right to it when it is easy for him to provide it, though no right when it's hard? It's rather a shocking idea that anyone's rights should fade away and disappear as it gets harder and harder to accord them to him.

So my own view is that even though you ought to let the violinist use your kidneys for the one hour he needs, we should not conclude that he has a right to do so—we should say that if you refuse, you are, like the boy who owns all the chocolates and will give none away, self-centered and callous, indecent in fact, not unjust. And similarly, that even supposing a case in which a woman pregnant due to rape ought to allow the unborn person to use her body for the hour he needs, we should not conclude that he has a right to do so; we should conclude that she is self-centered, callous, indecent, but not unjust, if she refuses. The complaints are no less grave; they are just different. However, there is no need to insist on this point. If anyone does wish to deduce "he has a right" from "you ought," then all the same he must surely grant that there are cases in which it is not morally required of you that you allow that violinist to use your kidneys, and in which he does not have a right to use them, and in which you do not do him an injustice if you refuse. And so also for mother and unborn child. Except in such cases as the unborn person has a right to demand it—and we were leaving open the possibility that there may be such cases—nobody is morally *required* to make large sacrifices, of health, of all other interests and concerns, of all other duties and commitments, for nine years, or even for nine months, in order to keep another person alive.

6. We have in fact to distinguish between two kinds of Samaritan: the Good

Samaritan and what we might call the Minimally Decent Samaritan. The story of the Good Samaritan, you will remember, goes like this:

> A certain man went down from Jerusalem to Jericho, and fell among thieves, which stripped him of his raiment, and wounded him, and departed, leaving him half dead.
>
> And by chance there came down a certain priest that way; and when he saw him, he passed by on the other side.
>
> And likewise a Levite, when he was at the place, came and looked on him, and passed on the other side.
>
> But a certain Samaritan, as he journeyed, came where he was; and when he saw him he had compassion on him.
>
> And went to him, and bound up his wounds, pouring in oil and wine, and set him on his own beast, and brought him to an inn, and took care of him.
>
> And on the morrow, when he departed, he took out two pence, and gave them to the host, and said unto him. "Take care of him; and whatsoever thou spendest more, when I come again, I will repay thee."
>
> (Luke 10:30–35)

The Good Samaritan went out of his way, at some cost to himself, to help one in need of it. We are not told what the options were, that is, whether or not the priest and the Levite could have helped by doing less than the Good Samaritan did, but assuming they could have, then the fact they did nothing at all shows they were not even Minimally Decent Samaritans, not because they were not Samaritans, but because they were not even minimally decent.

These things are a matter of degree, of course, but there is a difference, and

it comes out perhaps most clearly in the story of Kitty Genovese, who, as you will remember, was murdered while thirty-eight people watched or listened, and did nothing at all to help her. A Good Samaritan would have rushed out to give direct assistance against the murderer. Or perhaps we had better allow that it would have been a Splendid Samaritan who did this, on the ground that it would have involved a risk of death for himself. But the thirty-eight not only did not do this, they did not even trouble to pick up a phone to call the police. Minimally Decent Samaritanism would call for doing at least that, and their not having done it was monstrous.

After telling the story of the Good Samaritan, Jesus said "Go, and do thou likewise." Perhaps he meant that we are morally required to act as the Good Samaritan did. Perhaps he was urging people to do more than is morally required of them. At all events it seems plain that it was not morally required of any of the thirty-eight that he rush out to give direct assistance at the risk of his own life, and that it is not morally required of anyone that he give long stretches of life—nine years or nine months—to sustaining the life of a person who has no special right (we were leaving open the possibility of this) to demand it.

Indeed, with one rather striking class of exceptions, no one in any country in the world is *legally* required to do anywhere near as much as this for anyone else. The class of exceptions is obvious. My main concern here is not the state of the law in respect to abortion, but it is worth drawing attention to the fact that in no state in this country is any man compelled by law to be even a Minimally Decent Samaritan to any person;

there is no law under which charges could be brought against the thirty-eight who stood by while Kitty Genovese died. By contrast, in most states in this country women are compelled by law to be not merely Minimally Decent Samaritans to unborn persons inside them. This doesn't by itself settle anything one way or the other, because it may well be argued that there should be laws in this country—as there are in many European countries—compelling at least Minimally Decent Samaritanism. But it does show that there is a gross injustice in the existing state of the law. And it shows also that the groups currently working against liberalization of abortion laws, in fact working toward having it declared unconstitutional for a state to permit abortion, had better start working for the adoption of Good Samaritan laws generally, or earn the charge that they are acting in bad faith.

I should think, myself, that Minimally Decent Samaritan laws would be one thing, Good Samaritan laws quite another, and in fact highly improper. But we are not here concerned with the law. What we should ask is not whether anybody should be compelled by laws to be a Good Samaritan, but whether we must accede to a situation in which somebody is being compelled—by nature, perhaps—to be a Good Samaritan. We have, in other words, to look now at third-party interventions. I have been arguing that no person is morally required to make large sacrifices to sustain the life of another who has no right to demand them, and this even where the sacrifices do not include life itself; we are not morally required to be Good Samaritans or anyway Very Good Samaritans to one another. But what if a man cannot extricate himself from such a situation? What if he appeals to us to

extricate him? It seems to me plain that there are cases in which we can, cases in which a Good Samaritan would extricate him. There you are, you were kidnapped, and nine years in bed with that violinist lie ahead of you. You have your own life to lead. You are sorry, but you simply cannot see giving up so much of your life to the sustaining of his. You cannot extricate yourself, and ask us to do so. I should have thought that—in light of his having no right to the use of your body—it was obvious that we do not have to accede to your being forced to give up so much. We can do what you ask. There is no injustice to the violinist in our doing so.

7. Following the lead of the opponents of abortion, I have throughout been speaking of the fetus merely as a person, and what I have been asking is whether or not the argument we began with, which proceeds only from the fetus' being a person, really does establish its conclusion. I have argued that it does not.

But of course there are arguments and arguments, and it may be said that I have simply fastened on the wrong one. It may be said that what is important is not merely the fact that the fetus is a person, but that it is a person for whom the woman has a special kind of responsibility issuing from the fact that she is its mother. And it might be argued that all my analogies are therefore irrelevant—for you do not have that special kind of responsibility for that violinist, Henry Fonda does not have that special kind of responsibility for me. And our attention might be drawn to the fact that men and women both *are* compelled by law to provide support for their children.

I have in effect dealt (briefly) with this argument in section 4 above; but a (still briefer) recapitulation now may be in order. Surely we do not have any such "special responsibility" for a person unless we have assumed it, explicitly or implicitly. If a set of parents do not try to prevent pregnancy, do not obtain an abortion, and then at the time of birth of the child do not put it out for adoption, but rather take it home with them, then they have assumed responsibility for it, they have given it rights, and they cannot *now* withdraw support from it at the cost of its life because they now find it difficult to go on providing for it. But if they have taken all reasonable precautions against have a child, they do not simply by virtue of their biological relationship to the child who comes into existence have a special responsibility for it. They may wish to assume responsibility for it, or they may not wish to. And I am suggesting that if assuming responsibility for it would require large sacrifices, then they may refuse. A Good Samaritan would not refuse—or anyway, a Splendid Samaritan, if the sacrifices that had to be made were enormous. But then so would a Good Samaritan assume responsibility for that violinist; so would Henry Fonda, if he is a Good Samaritan, fly in from the West Coast and assume responsibility for me.

8. My argument will be found unsatisfactory on two counts by many of those who want to regard abortion as morally permissible. First, while I do argue that abortion is not impermissible, I do not argue that it is always permissible. There may well be cases in which carrying the child to term requires only Minimally Decent Samaritanism of the mother, and this is a standard we must not fall below. I am inclined to think it a merit of my account precisely that it does *not* give a general yes or a general

no. It allows for and supports our sense that, for example, a sick and desperately frightened fourteen-year-old schoolgirl, pregnant due to rape, may *of course* choose abortion, and that any law which rules this out is an insane law. And it also allows for and supports our sense that in other cases resort to abortion is even positively indecent. It would be indecent in the woman to request an abortion, and indecent in a doctor to perform it, if she is in her seventh month, and wants the abortion just to avoid the nuisance of postponing a trip abroad. The very fact that the arguments I have been drawing attention to treat all cases of abortion, or even all cases of abortion in which the mother's life is not at stake, as morally on a par ought to have made them suspect at the outset.

Secondly, while I am arguing for the permissibility of abortion in some cases, I am not arguing for the right to secure the death of the unborn child. It is easy to confuse these two things in that up to a certain point in the life of the fetus it is not able to survive outside the mother's body hence removing it from her body guarantees its death. But they are importantly different. I have argued that you are not morally required to spend nine months in bed, sustaining the life of that violinist; but to say this is by no means to say that if, when you unplug yourself, there is a miracle and he survives, you then have a right to turn round and slit his throat. You may detach yourself even if this costs him his life; you have no right to be guaranteed his death, by some other means, if unplugging yourself does not kill him. There are some people who will feel dissatisfied by this feature of my argument. A woman may be utterly devastated by the thought of a child, a bit of herself, put out for adoption and never

seen or heard of again. She may therefore want not merely that the child be
detached from her, but more, that it die.
Some opponents of abortion are inclined to regard this as beneath contempt—thereby showing insensitivity to
what is surely a powerful source of despair. All the same, I agree that the desire for the child's death is not one
which anybody may gratify, should it

turn out to be possible to detach the
child alive.

At this place, however, it should be
remembered that we have only been
pretending throughout that the fetus is a
human being from the moment of conception. A very early abortion is surely
not the killing of a person, and so is not
dealt with by anything I have said here.

KATHRYN PYNE ADDELSON

Moral Revolution

KATHRYN PYNE ADDELSON *is a professor of philosophy at Smith College and a
founding member of the Society for Women in Philosophy. Originally a philosopher of
science, her work now focuses on issues in feminist ethics.*

JANE

IN 1969, most state laws prohibited
abortion unless the life of the pregnant woman was threatened. A few
states had reformed their abortion laws
to allow abortion by doctors in hospitals
in cases of threat to the health of the
woman, threat of fetal deformity, or rape.
In the mid-1960s, the estimated death
rate for abortions performed in hospitals
was 3 deaths per 100,000 abortions; the
rate for illegal abortions was guessed to
be over eight times that—30 deaths per
100,000 abortions was a rough estimate
and almost certainly conservative. For
minority and poorer women, it was certainly very much higher.

The women's liberation movement
was in its infancy in 1969. In that year,
a group of Chicago women who had

been active in radical politics formed an
organization called Jane. Over the next
year and a half, Jane evolved from an
abortion counseling and referral service
to a service in which abortions were actually performed by the Jane members
themselves. By 1973 when they closed
the service, over 12,000 abortions had
been performed under Jane's auspices.
The medical record equalled that of
abortions done under legal, licensed
conditions by physicians in hospitals.
The service charged on a sliding scale;
eventually all abortions were cheaper
than the going rate, and some women
paid nothing. Jane served many poor
women, black women, and very young
women who could not have had an
abortion otherwise.

My discussion of Jane is based on
one newspaper series and an interview

with one member. Perhaps not all Jane members will agree with this member's interpretation, but that isn't the point here because I'm not doing a sociological study. I am investigating patterns of moral thinking and acting which Judith Thomson tradition makes invisible. The fact that one person's thinking and action are concealed is enough to show bias. . . .

What Jane Did

This is the way Jane operated, as reported in the June 1973 Hyde Park-Kenwood *Voices* article on the organization: "Jane was the pseudonym we chose to represent the service. A phone was opened in her name and an answering service secured, later replaced by a tape recorder. Jane kept all records and served as control-center." "Jane" was not a particular woman but the code name for whichever counselor was taking calls and coordinating activities on a given day.

For four years, Jane kept the same phone number. . . . At first she received only eight to ten calls a week. A year later she was receiving well more than 100 calls a week.

All phoned-in messages were returned the same day: "Hello, Marcia. This is Jane from women's liberation returning your call. We can't talk freely over the phone, but I want you to know that we can help you."

Then Jane would refer the name to a counselor, who would meet personally with the woman and talk with her at length about available alternatives.

The counselor would also help the woman arrange finances and, whenever possible, collect a $25 donation for the service loan fund. The counseling session was also a screening process for detecting conflicts and potential legal threats.

Jane worked with several male abortionists. One of these was "Dr. C." Dr. C worked alone with his nurse in motel rooms until the day an abortion was interrupted by a pounding on the door and a man's voice shouting, "Come on out of there, baby killer!" After a wild chase between buildings and down alleys, Dr. C escaped the irate husband. When he caught his breath, he decided that it might be better to quit working in motels.

Jane members then began renting apartments for Dr. C and his nurse to work in. Jane describes the first day they used a rented apartment: "Seven women were done that day, in a setting where they could relax and talk with other women in a similar predicament. And when the first woman walked out of the bedroom, feeling fine and no longer pregnant, the other six were noticeably relieved. They asked her questions and got firsthand answers." Another advantage of the new arrangement was that Jane counselors were with a woman during the abortion, giving her psychological and moral support and explaining what was going on to her. Still another was that the counselors gradually began assisting Dr. C in the abortion itself, and he began training them in the abortion procedures.

After a few months of operation, members of Jane had begun inducing miscarriages for women more than twelve weeks pregnant. During this time, Dr. C was teaching the women of Jane more and more about the process of doing direct abortions. Finally, some counselors were doing the entire direct abortion themselves, under Dr. C's eye.

In the midst of all this, they learned that Dr. C was no doctor at all, but just a man who had become an expert in the giving of abortions. Later, they broke off the relationship with Dr. C and began doing all their own abortions. For good or ill, this meant that they had a sudden abundance of funds, since the abortion fee went to Jane instead of Dr. C. In the eyes of the law, they became fullfledged abortionists: "We could no longer hide behind the label of 'counselor' or expect 'Dr. C' to act as a buffer, with his know-how and ready cash for dealing with a bust." Jane members were arrested only once, although they were harassed by the police.

The change in the abortion service meant that Jane members had to accept the full consequences of what they were doing—even if it resulted in illness, personal tragedy, or death—and they had to bear this without the protection that the doctor's professionalism gives him. They worked under these conditions until 1 April 1973. Then, two months after the United States Court passed its opinion on the constitutionality of restrictive abortion laws, Jane officially closed.

What Jane Meant

In describing what Jane did, I selected data to a certain purpose. It was a selection different in many respects from the selection someone in Judith Thomson's tradition would have made. I didn't, however, use any special technical concepts or categories from some philosophical theory. In this section, I shall use Jane as a basis for discussing a moral theory which competes with theories of the Judith Thomson tradition, in order to reveal value implications of bias in that tradition.

Jane was an abortion clinic, and the women of Jane were working out moral and political beliefs and activities, not constructing a theory which is able to capture their thinking and their work. The theory should be taken as *hypothesis* about what Jane meant, subject to correction through future investigation of Jane and groups like Jane, and through seeing what comes of acting on the theory. I believe the theory is based on anarchist, or anarchist-feminist principles, but I won't discuss that. Instead I'll call the tradition out of which the theory arises the Jane tradition, to contrast with the Judith Thomson tradition.

In March 1977, I interviewed one of the founders of Jane. She said that the women who founded the organization had been active in civil rights or anti-war work in the late 1960s. They wanted to begin work in the newly born women's liberation movement. But how should they begin? What should they do? Someone suggested abortion as an issue. It was a difficult decision, and they struggled over it for months. Deciding on an issue required an analysis of a network of larger issues, and of the place of the abortion issue in that network. According to the woman I interviewed, the question was one of a woman's opportunities for life choices: "It was a question of free choice about reproduction, free choice about life style, because the old roles for women weren't viable any more. In frontier times, childbearing was valuable and important. So was housework. But that role is gone. The old ways are gone. We felt nothing *could* come in to replace them unless women could make a choice about childbearing. That seemed necessary for any other choice." These alternatives had to be *created* within our social system. The members of Jane hoped that other groups within the women's movement would work on other alternatives—offering alternative living arrangements, working on ways that women could become economically independent, and so on—while Jane members tried to offer the alternative of choosing not to have the child by aborting. That is, they thought in terms of a division of labor among women working to change the society so that women should have real alternatives for meaningful lives.

As I mentioned in the introduction, the concept of a *meaningful life* (more often called "a good life") has traditionally been a central concept in moral philosophy. The pattern of thinking Jane members use requires a holistic analysis of the society in terms of the resources it actually offers for women to have meaningful lives, plus an analysis of how to change the society so that it can offer such resources. . . .

In offering the alternative of abortion, Jane was offering a service that was badly needed. The alternative was open to all kinds of women—rich and poor, older and young, white and nonwhite, but it was a service most desperately needed by the poorer, younger, and minority women. One author says:

> In comparison of blacks and whites, both for premarital and marital conceptions, we find that whites have higher percentages ending in induced abortions at the lower educational levels, while at the higher educational levels there is little or no difference between blacks and whites . . . the data point to the greater reliance upon abortion on the part of whites over blacks and on the part of the more affluent or more educated over the less affluent and less educated.

When they did turn to illegal abortion methods, poorer and nonwhite women came out far worse. Nationally in 1968, the black death rate from abortion was six times that of the white death rate. In New York in the early 1960s, 42 percent of the pregnancy-related deaths resulted from illegal abortions; and of those women who died, half were black and 44 percent were Puerto Rican. Only 6 percent were white.

More affluent women were also able to pay the high fees which all good, illegal abortionists charged. Jane overcame this by calculating fees on a sliding scale according to income. Some women paid nothing.

Jane's purpose, however, was not simply to provide a service for women, however valuable that service might be. The Jane group could not provide abortions to all Chicago women who needed them. More than that, Jane members knew that when abortion was legalized, their service would have to disappear. Jane's purpose was to show women a much broader alternative than simply not having a baby, to show that by acting together, women can change society so that all women can have an opportunity to choose a meaningful life. They tried to show this in different ways. One way was through the sliding scale for fees. Counselors explained to a woman paying $300 that she was helping pay the cost for a woman who could pay only $5.00. She was, in a small way, helping to undercut the unfairness of a society which would allow her an abortion but not the poorer woman.

Jane itself was the most dramatic demonstration of an alternative for women acting together. Jane members were themselves future or past candidates for abortion, and in the present, they were doing something dangerous, exhausting, and illegal for the sake of changing society for all women. Jane showed that women could take change into their own hands. By coming to Jane for their abortions, other women were also acting for this change. They were trusting women to do things which traditionally were done by men in their society, and legally done only by doctors (overwhelmingly) within the rigid, hierarchically ordered medical profession. This was a leap of trust.

In the structure of their service, Jane members were trying to build an alternative kind of medical structure as well.

> We—the counselors—we learned the medical mystiques are just bullshit. That was a great up for us. Do you know, you're required to have a license as a nurse just to give a shot. Nurses can't even give an intravenous on their own. That takes a different kind of license. We would just explain to our workers how you had to fill the syringe, and how to be certain there was no air in it, and why that was important, and so on. We'd spend a lot of time explaining it. Then we would say to the patient, "Well this is the first time that Sue is giving anyone a shot. Maybe you can help her, and be patient with her." The patient was part of what was happening too. Part of the whole team.

> Sometimes in the middle of an abortion, we would switch positions to show that everyone in the service could do things, to show that the woman who was counseling could give a shot, and the one who was giving a shot could counsel too. We did it to make people see that they could do it too. They have the power to change things and build alternatives.

We here come to the central analysis within Jane tradition, as it is expressed in Jane's practice. The analysis operates in a very general way to criticize our so-ciety and to offer direction to move toward change. Let me state it first in terms of the social structure of the institution of medicine in the United States today.

In the United States, medical people operate within a hierarchical system of dominance and subordination. Those higher in the hierarchy have power which those lower do not have—and the power to order those lower ones around is the least of it. One key aspect of that power is what Howard Becker calls "the right to define the nature of reality." He uses the notion of a "hierarchy of credibility": "In any system of ranked groups, participants take it as given that members of the highest group have the right to define the way things really are." I would argue that this "right of definition" means not only that the word of the higher has heavier weight than that of the lower (teacher over student, doctor over intern or aide) but that the very categories and concepts that are used, the "official" descriptions of reality, are descriptions from the point of view of the dominant persons in the hierarchy. What counts as knowledge itself is defined in terms of that viewpoint, and the definition further legitimates the power of the dominant person.

The power of those in dominant positions in the hierarchy is *legitimate authority*. This contrasts with the *natural authority* of a person who, regardless of position, happens to have a great deal of knowledge, experience, or wisdom about a subject. A doctor's authority is legitimated by the criteria, standards, and institutions which control access to his place in the hierarchy. These criteria and requirements for training on the one hand are aimed at insuring that those with legitimate authority in the hierarchy also have the natural authority required to do the jobs they are doing. Although we all know there are incompetent doctors, these criteria do operate to screen out incompetence *as defined from the top of the hierarchy.* Do they insure that those at the top have natural authority? I think not, and that is because *legitimate authority* carries with it a definition of what counts as knowledge: the definition from the top of the hierarchy, the "official" point of view.

This outlook on knowledge is sometimes called "objective" or "the scientific outlook" of experts. In fact, it is absolutist, and when the definition of reality is given solely in terms of the tradition of the dominant in a dominant-subordinate structure, the outlook is, in fact, biased.

In part, Jane members were operating from the viewpoint of a subordinate group in our society: women. They were using this viewpoint to try to create new social structures which were not based on dominance and subordination and in which authority was natural authority—knowledge which suits the situation to the best degree that we know at the moment. When the woman I interviewed said that the members of Jane tried to show other women that they "have the power to learn to counsel and give a shot" and that they "have the power to change things and build alternatives," she is talking not only about the natural authority of knowledge but what we might call natural *moral* power, or *moral* authority.

In structuring the abortion service as they did, the members of Jane were developing an alternative to hierarchy, but they were also overcoming the vices of dependency and feelings of ignorance and importance by showing women that they did have the power to learn and do things themselves. The Jane organization itself was built on nonauthoritarian, nonhierarchical principles, and Jane members tried to run it as a collective.

> We tried to make it as nonauthoritarian as we could. We had rotating chairs. There wasn't a high value placed on one kind of work and a low value on another. Every position was so important to what we were doing, and it was treated as equally important, to the highest degree possible. This meant every one of us could do what she was best at. You didn't have people competing to do what was important, or feeling what they were doing wasn't valuable.

In April of 1973, the women of Jane asked themselves, "What next?" Whether abortion had been a good issue to move on or not, there was no place for an illegal abortion service now that abortions were legal. Some of the women went on to found a "well woman clinic," the Emma Goldman Clinic. They hoped to run the clinic on the nonauthoritarian, nonhierarchical model used by Jane. The clinic was organized around the concept of self-help, in which the "patients" are trained too in the kind of medical knowledge they need to understand and care for their own bodies for a large range of normal functions and slight disorders.

BIAS IN THE WORLD VIEW

In my discussion here, both the Judith Thomson tradition and the Jane tradition were dealing with the problem of abortion. Neither would take it to be *the* problem. Abortion is a subsidiary problem chosen because of its connection with more central concerns. For Judith Thomson, it is a question of rights—we might even say a question of equal rights. But it cannot be described that

way for the Jane tradition without begging questions.

Within the Jane tradition, the problem was taken to be one of meaningful
lives for women, or of free choice
among genuine alternatives for meaningful lives. Some phrasing of the general problem in these terms seems
appropriate to both traditions. Let me
quote Betty Friedan, an activist who
stands within traditions associated with
Judith Thomson's:

> It is my thesis that the core of the prob-
> lem for women today is not sexual but a
> problem of identity—a stunting or eva-
> sion of growth that is perpetuated by the
> feminine mystique. It is my thesis that as
> the Victorian culture did not permit
> women to accept or gratify their basic
> sexual needs, our culture does not permit
> women to accept or gratify their basic
> need to grow and fulfill their potentiali-
> ties as human beings, a need which is not
> solely defined by their sexual roles.

The statement of purpose of the liberal feminist National Organization for
Women (NOW) also concerns opportunities for a meaningful life and moral
development as a human being: NOW
pledges to "take action to bring women
into full participation in the mainstream
of American society now, exercising all
the privileges and responsibilities
thereof, in truly equal partnership with
men." This makes it appear that for both
traditions, the problem may be stated as
one of equality, particularly equality so
far as it relates to the moral questions of
being a full human being and of having
a meaningful (or good) life. I believe
that this is a central concern of those
within the Judith Thomson tradition.
But it may be that the problem cannot
be resolved under that tradition or its associated world view.

Concealing Data

. . . I [have] presented the moral activity of the organization Jane under
one tradition. If we look at the Jane organization under the Judith Thomson
tradition, we get a different selection of
data. Here's a quotation from the newspaper article:

> From the beginning, we discussed the
> moral implications of abortion from all
> angles. We listened to right-to-lifers,
> Catholic clergy, population-control
> freaks and women's liberationists.

> We heard legislators and lobbyists and
> political commentators arguing fine
> points of "fetal viability." When does a
> fetus become a person? When it can
> survive outside the womb (after six
> months)? When it begins to move (after
> four months)? Or from the moment of
> conception?

> Many opponents of abortion called it
> "murder." We argued the logical counter-
> arguments: If a fetus is a person, then
> why aren't abortionists and women who
> have abortions charged with murder?

> Or, if the fetus has the rights of a person,
> then does the woman who carries it be-
> come subject to its rights? What happens
> when the rights of the woman and those
> of the fetus come into conflict?

> All philosophical and legalistic positions
> lost relevance when we began doing and
> viewing abortions . . . we knew that we
> were grappling with matters of life and
> death and no philosophical arguments
> could alter that belief.

Judith Thomson, or someone from her
tradition, would have been a great help
to the Jane women in these early discussions on abortion. On the other hand,
these early discussions had no clear rel-

evance to the central moral activity the women of Jane were engaging in—*by their own judgment.* The terms in which they saw the problem were different. Their perception and their moral activity constitute data which are important to solving the problems of equality, but the Judith Thomson tradition not only ignores those data: it makes them invisible. Let's look at some of the mechanisms by which the data are concealed.

One way a tradition conceals data is through the concepts and categories it uses. The Judith Thomson tradition would focus on the Jane discussion of rights. It would ignore the discussions of hierarchy, dominance, and subordination; and perhaps some within the tradition would not take these as morally relevant discussions at all. Any theory must use concepts. Through their very use, some data are selected and some ignored. Yet the question of whether the concepts properly capture the data, or of whether they are *appropriate,* is a central, critical question about the adequacy of any tradition.

In a similar way, the categories a tradition uses to organize data reveal some and conceal others. For example, the Judith Thomson tradition uses the categories of moral agent and of groups of moral agents as aggregates. The tradition also uses a division of moral phenomena into questions of individual conscience and those of public policy, made by those with legitimate authority. I don't want to argue that the tradition *rules out* other sorts of moral phenomena. But using those categories, it cannot capture the sort of moral phenomena Jane members took to be central: people in a subordinate position acting to create a set of social relations which are not structured by dominance and subordination, through the subordinates' coming

to know their own power (as opposed to legitimate authority) through acting in collectives (not aggregates).

But am I being fair to the Judith Thomson tradition? After all, people within it don't claim to cover *all* moral phenomena. Few theories claim to cover everything within their purview, and even within chemistry there are divisions into organic and inorganic. Mightn't there be divisions within the field of moral phenomena so that another part of the tradition might deal with Jane's moral activity and thus reveal it?

Perhaps any new moral tradition we develop will have to have something to do the concept of rights (and associated concepts), and deal in some way with groups as aggregates and with public policy as officially handed down. But that new tradition could not be the Judith Thomson tradition, for a revolutionary change in the methodology of her tradition is necessary to uncover data like Jane's.

The Judith Thomson tradition supposes that there exists a set of moral concepts embedded in moral principles which "we" all know and understand. In her paper, Judith Thomson herself is clarifying concepts "we" grasp by the standard method of the tradition: the use of hypothetical cases. This method presupposes a very mentalistic view of concepts and word meanings—mentalistic in the way philosophical empiricists are mentalistic in their views on meanings as "ideas." The concepts exist in the speaker's understanding. If someone understands the concept, he or she knows whether it applies in any given case. Considering hypothetical cases (in this view) points out cases the speaker might have overlooked; but once they are brought to his or her attention, the speaker allegedly knows whether the concepts apply or not, and so his or her explicit understanding of the concept is clarified. Similarly, one's explicit understanding of "our" moral principles is supposed to be clarified by considering hypothetical cases.

The most obvious thing to say about this method is that although bringing up hypothetical cases may clarify our understanding of concepts and principles, everyone knows that the selection of hypothetical cases also biases understanding. This bias may be (unintentionally) systematic. For example, Judith Thomson gives a case where Jones faces a frosty death because Smith owns the coat. Why not, instead, use a case where men, women, and children face poor diets, poor housing, and loss of dignity because the owner of a mill decides to move it out of one region into another having cheaper labor and lower tax rates? Philosophers may say the second example is too complicated, but the selection is not a trivial matter of simplicity. The coat example ignores an essential distinction in kinds of property ownership which the mill example reveals.

The method rules out empirical investigation to see what sorts of hypothetical cases might capture what is morally important to persons in a variety of circumstances in the United States. There seems to be no way whatsoever to insure that a fair consideration of hypothetical cases is made to reduce the bias. One can't develop a sampling procedure for hypothetical cases.

Worst of all, the method rules out empirical investigation to discover whether the moral concepts and principles the philosophers are dealing with are really the moral concepts which people use in the United States. It rules out empirical investigation to discover

whether those concepts and those moral principles are relevant to the lives of people in different walks of life, investigation to discover whether they are relevant to solving those people's problems of human dignity and a meaningful life *as those people perceive* those problems.

The method itself has the mere appearance of being plausible only for ancient systems of concepts which are well worked out. It has not even the appearance of plausibility for a case like Jane's, in which people are in the process of creating new concepts through creating new social forms. The fundamental theory of meaning, of understanding, and of concept formation on which the method is based is not only inadequate: it is false.

All of this means that to encompass the Jane data, a revolutionary change is necessary in the methodology of the Judith Thomson tradition. Without it, the data remain concealed.

The data being concealed concern human moral activity and the possibilities of changing society. This constitutes a direct and very important value consequence. The Judith Thomson tradition dominates philosophy departments in the prestigious American universities, and even teachers in nonprestigious colleges are trained within it. This means that students are taught to see moral activity within that tradition. Activity requiring patterns of thinking and concepts and categories like Jane's is made invisible to them.

Official Points of View

From its beginnings, the tradition Judith Thomson works within has been centrally concerned with equality. People in this tradition have particularly been concerned that all human beings be equal under the moral law and under the positive law of the state. Equality before the moral or positive law means that the same laws and principles apply to all. Whether or not this is enlightened depends on which laws and principles one chooses and the society in which they apply.

The question of equality which those in the Jane tradition raise is one which takes dominant-subordinate structures in the society as *creators* of inequality. Their solution to the problem of equality is the use of the perception and power of the subordinate to eliminate dominant-subordinate structures through the creation of new social forms which do not have that structure. Those in the Judith Thomson tradition do not raise questions of dominance and subordination except in the moral, legal, and political spheres, where they are seen in terms of moral, legal, and political equality. Particularly, they do not raise the question of whether equality before the moral or positive law may not be rendered empty because of the dominant-subordinate structures in the economic or social (e.g., family) spheres.

It appears that there is a bias in our world view. It is a bias that allows moral problems to be defined from the top of various hierarchies of authority in such a way that the existence of the authority is concealed, and so the existence of alternative definitions that might challenge that authority and radically change our social organization is also concealed. But having acknowledged that, we must return to the question I asked at the beginning of the paper.

THE INTELLECTUAL PURSUITS

In this paper, I believe I uncovered a bias that requires a revolutionary change in ethics to remedy. But in the process of considering two approaches to the moral problem of abortion, it has become clear that there are serious questions to ask about the question with which I began the paper:

Has a covert bias been introduced into our world view by the near exclusion of women from the domain of intellectual pursuits? If we ask about a bias in "our" world view, mustn't we ask who that "we" refers to? In fact, doesn't the question presuppose that "our" world view is constructed by people in the "intellectual pursuits"? That is, doesn't it presuppose a hierarchy of authority in which people in some occupations (academic humanists and scientists, professional writers, etc.) define a world view for everyone else? If so, then there is something further that the Jane case shows.

Judith Jarvis Thomson is a woman working in an established intellectual pursuit, and at the time she wrote her paper, she took a stand that amounted to criticizing certain ethical arguments for sex bias. She took her stand as an authority, she criticized other authorities, and her paper has been widely used by still other authorities who are certified to teach ethics classes. I have criticized her work in this paper, but I too write as an authority. This leads us to a certain conundrum—if I may call it that.

The women of Jane were certainly challenging the way men in important positions are certified to define the way we do things and, in fact, their authority to define "our" world view and say how things "really are." But some of the Jane members, at least, were not saying that we should remedy the problem by having women in important positions define the way we do things. They were saying that we should change the way we do things so that we do not have some important people giving the official world view for everyone else. That change cannot be accomplished merely by hiring more women to work in the intellectual pursuits. It requires changing the intellectual pursuits themselves. If Jane shows that we need a revolutionary change from the old moral theory, it is a change in the status of the authorities as well as a change in what has been taken to be a moral the-

ory. Unless we strive to find ways to do that, we violate the central moral and scientific injunction for respecting other human beings:

> . . . look upon human group life as chiefly a vast interpretive process in which people, singly and collectively *guide themselves* by *defining* the objects, events, and situations they encounter.

ROBERT E. JOYCE

Personhood and the Conception Event

ROBERT E. JOYCE *teaches at St. John's University in Minnesota and has hosted workshops and taught classes concerning human sexuality. He has been published in many periodicals, among them* Marriage *and* The New Scholasticism.

THIS essay serves as a brief rationale for the claim that a *conceptus* or human zygote is essentially a human person. I will argue that the zygote is just as specifically and truly a person as you or I, though less developed. The idea is that conception or fertilization is the point at which a person—at least *one* individual person, possibly more—definitely begins to exist physically in the space-time world as we naturally and normally perceive this world. This is not offered as a probable conclusion, but as a reasonable certainty. The exact time at which a given conception event or fertilization process terminates may be quite uncertain. But I will maintain that there is definitely a

moment of conception, a moment when the fertilization process is fundamentally complete and a single-celled zygote is essentially first in existence.

The basic format of my argument might be stated simply: Every living individual being with the natural potential, as a whole, for knowing, willing, desiring, and relating to others in a self-reflective way is a person. But the human zygote is a living individual (or more than one such individual) with the natural potential, as a whole, to act in these ways. Therefore the human zygote is an actual person with great potential.

In the 1973 Supreme Court decision on abortion, Justice Harry Blackmun's majority opinion contained the claim that the unborn human individual is not a legal person in the whole sense. . . .

. . . I will try to suggest that we need and can obtain greater philosophical understanding of the good common sense notion that persons can be tiny one-celled creatures just as wondrously as they can be complex trillion-celled creatures. First, I offer a definition of person and some comments by way of clarification. Second, a brief descriptive interpretation of the conception event is presented. Third, responses are given to some significant objections. And in conclusion, I mention a couple of major implications of the idea that the person exists at conception.

THE PERSON

The first element of a sound interpretation of what occurs in human conception seems to be a definition of a person. Person can be defined as a whole individual being which has the natural potential to know, love, desire, and relate to self and others in a self-reflective way. There are many alternate ways of phrasing the definition, depending upon different needs of emphasis. But it would seem to be crucial that we recognize a person as a natural being. A person is one that has the natural, but not necessarily the functional ability to know and love in a trans-sensible or immaterial way. As soon as one would require a person to have the functional ability for this kind of activity, he or she would seem to be slipping into a subjectivistic elitism such that the comatose, senile, and retarded—even the sleeping—would not be regarded necessarily as persons. This is an unrealistic position that seems to be out of touch with the human condition. If nature has no essential value in our knowing and

judging who or what is a person, independent of accepted functional abilities, then there is little hope for recognition of an objective nature transcending the limits of our personal consciousness in anything else.

In recent years some philosophers have adopted what has been called the "developmentalist" interpretation of the beginning of a human person. Daniel Callahan views it this way. "(Abortion) is not the destruction of a human person—for at no stage of its development does the conceptus fulfill the definition of a person, which implies a developed capacity for reasoning, willing, desiring, and relating to others—but is the destruction of an important and valuable form of human life." The language of the Supreme Court in *Roe v. Wade* is harmonious with this perspective. But I would suggest that a person is not an individual with a *developed* capacity for reasoning, willing, desiring, and relating to others. A person is an individual with a *natural* capacity for these activities and relationships, whether this natural capacity is ever developed or not—i.e., whether he or she ever attains the functional capacity or not. Individuals of rational, volitional, self-conscious *nature* may never attain or may lose the functional capacity for fulfilling this nature to any appreciable extent. But this inability to fulfill their nature does not negate or destroy the nature itself, even though it may, for us, render that nature more difficult to appreciate and love. But that difficulty would seem to be a challenge for *us* as persons more than it is for them.

Neither a human embryo nor a rabbit embryo has the functional capacity to think, will, desire, and self-consciously relate to others. The radical difference, even at the beginning of development, is that the human embryo actually has the natural capacity to act in these ways, whereas the rabbit embryo does not have and never will have it. For all its concern about potentialities, the developmentalist approach fails to see the actuality upon which these potentialities are based. Every potential is itself an actuality. A person's potential to walk across the street is an actuality that the tree beside him does not have. A woman's potential to give birth to a baby is an actuality that a man does not have. The potential of a human *conceptus* to think and talk is an actuality. This *actual potential*—not mere logical possibility—would seem to be a much more reasonable ground for affirming personhood than a kind of neoangelic notion of personhood which requires actual performance of subjectively recognized spiritual activity.

CONCEPTION: A DESCRIPTIVE INTERPRETATION

If the person is an individual entity with the natural, though not necessarily functioning, power to think, will, and relate self-reflectively, then when does such an individual actually begin to exist in the world of space and time? There would seem to be but one reasonable point at which to acknowledge the existence of a new individual person in the world. Conception is that moment when the so-called "fertilization" process is complete. From then on, a genetically and physically unique individual is present and growing. In the following description of the conception event, I wish to challenge or correct a few common misunderstandings about conception.

Before a sperm penetrates an ovum, these two cells are clearly individual cells and are parts of the bodies of the man and woman respectively. They are not whole-body cells as is the zygote cell which they crucially help to cause. They are body-part cells. The zygote is a single cell that is a whole body in itself. From within it comes all the rest of the individual, including the strictly intra-uterine functional organs of the placenta, amnion, and chorion, as well as the rest of the body that is naturally destined for extra-uterine life. The sperm and ovum are not potential life. They are potential *causes* of individual human life. They do not, even together, become a new human life. In the fertilization process, they become *causes* of individual human life. They do not, even together, become a new human life. In the fertilization process, they become *causes* of the new human life.

Fertilization is a process. The process may take twenty minutes or several hours. But it has a definite conclusion. The moment at which this process terminates in the resulting zygote can be called the conception event. The sperm and ovum are specific, instrumental causes of the new human being. The man and woman are the main agents of this procreative effect. They cause an actual, not a potential, existence of a person in the space-time world. They do not cause a person to exist as a person, but they do cause (in an important, if partial, way) a person to exist in this world.

Parental bodily matter (the sperm and ovum) is a crucial element of procreative-causing on behalf of the new being, but is not the stuff out of which this unique bodily being is adequately constituted. The bodily matter of the zygote comes into existence *by means of* the bodily matter of the parents but does *not* come *from* their bodies. It only looks that way to the unphilosophical mind. The matter of the new person proper is constitutively different matter. The chromosomal uniqueness of the zygote is sufficient testimony to the radical difference of both form and matter in this new being. The unique matter of the zygote has traits similar to, but in no way identical with, those of the parents. With the perspective of an evolutionist, who once said that the evolution from non-life to life was a "leap from zero to everything," we might say that the transition from parent body to offspring is a leap from zero to all of self.

Moreover, the so-called fertilization process is not as passive as the terminology would suggest. The nuclei of the sperm and ovum dynamically interact. In so doing they both cease to be. One might say they die together. They really should not be said to unite. That suggests that they remain and form a larger whole. But the new single-celled individual is not an in tandem combo of the two parent sex cells. In their interaction and mutual causation of the new being, the sperm and ovum are self-sacrificial. Their nuclei are the subject of the fertilization process; the zygote is the result of this process. There is neither sperm nor ovum once the process of interaction is completed, even though cytoplasmic matter from the ovum remains. It is really a misleading figure of speech to say of the ovum that it is "fertilized" by the sperm, passively as a farmer's field is fertilized. It is proper rather to speak of the sperm-ovum interaction process. There is no such thing as a "fertilized ovum."

Obviously the new individual's growth is ever a process. But neither its coming into existence nor its final exit is a process. We need to be paradoxical in our thinking, not simple-minded and reductionistic, if we are going to appreciate both the process and the non-process factors involved. In contemporary philosophy, when process is valued on a par with substance the dignity of person and nature are served and enhanced. But when process is enthroned above substance, such that, in effect, the process itself is the only substance, we are engaged in a self-deception fraught with epistemological and moral chaos.

At any given moment, a whole living substance—be it a peach tree, a rabbit, or a human person—either is or is not alive. Once it is alive, it is totally there as this particular actual being, even though it is only partially there as a developed actuality. There is no such thing as a potentially living organism. Every living thing is thoroughly actual, with more or less potential: actually itself; potentially more or less expressive of itself. A one-celled person at conception is an actual person with great potential for development and self-expression. That single-celled individual is just as actually a person as you or I, though the actual personhood and personality of the new individual are, as yet, much less functionally expressed.

In fact, the new personality is so little developed that we are not yet able to recognize it functionally, unless we are willing to go beyond the vision of the eyeballs. Many are not willing. As one life scientist remarked, in speaking of the users of the IUD: ". . . Ignorance is bliss, for the blastocyst is only a little larger than the egg to begin with, and its passage through the womb is unknown and undetectable." The issue thus becomes whether we are prepared to acknowledge the *natural roots* of the individual's personality within this largely, though not entirely, undifferentiated stage. The genetic differentiation of a zygote or a blastocyst, however, must be reasonably acknowledged as the natural roots of a *personality,* not of a "dogality" or of a "rabbitality." The human zygote is a member of a unique species of creature. It is not a genus, to which a species is gradually attached. Such a process of attachment can occur in the mind of the observer; but not in the reality of the observed.

No individual living body can "become" a person unless it already is a person. No living being can become anything other than what it already essentially is. From the perspective of the beginning of a living thing, for such a being to *become* something essentially other—say, for a "subpersonal human animal" to become a person—it would have to be a person before it was a person, so that *it* could be said to *become.*

Moreover, from the point of view of an adult, if, at this moment, I do not simply *have* a body, but in some radically natural sense I *am* my body, then, it is likewise perceptive to say or reasonable to conclude that I did not simply *get* a body at some point, but *was* that whole body naturally and radically at every point of *its* time as well as its space. Otherwise, I could never properly say such things as, "When I was conceived. . . ."

OBJECTIONS AND RESPONSE

"The human *conceptus* is not necessarily an individual. But individuality is essential to personhood. Therefore, the *conceptus* cannot be reasonably regarded as a person." Proponents of this argument cite as evidence the fact of so-called "identical" twins and other multiple births resulting from the causality of a single ovum and sperm. They rightly insist that the living zygote which divides in half cannot be viewed as one, identical human being dividing into two. But the evidence would seem to indicate *not* that there is *no* individual present at conception, but that there is at least one and possibly more. Jerome Lejeune of Paris, for instance, has indicated that individuality may be fully existent at the point of fertilization, but that thus far are we do not have the technical capacity to discern how many individuals are present at that point. Moreover, it seems to me that at this very early stage of human development there may occur at times a process of generation similar to that common in other species. In that case, we could say that one of the twins would be the parent of the other. The original zygote could be regarded as the parent of the second, even though we may never know which one was parthenogenically the parent.

There is also the disputed evidence that in the first days of life, twins or triplets sometimes 'recombine' into a single individual. Actually, this could readily mean that one individual's body absorbs the body of the other, resulting in the latter's death at this particular, vulnerable stage in life.

The major type of objection to personhood at conception is some kind of developmentalism, such as gradual ensoulment. Developmentalists claim to take into account life potential as well as life actual, and thereby to give a more reasonable interpretation to the beginning of human personhood. But this approach fails on at least three counts. It tends to confuse process in the collective with process in the individual. It makes a typically utilitarian projection of mechanistic potential onto organic potential. And it seems to suffer from the misleading, yet popular, notion that man is a rational animal.

This gradualist approach does not distinguish sufficiently two kinds of process. There is the process of the cosmos, as it might be called within which living substances exist, and which causes these individuals to exist in space and time. The individuals themselves are not the subject of the process nor are they the cause of it. This grand process of the whole of physical nature would seem to employ individual substances, such as parents and their gametic cells, in the causation of new individual substances. But there is another distinctive process, one that occurs within the living individual entities themselves and one which they themselves cause. It is the process of their own unique life and growth. This process is primarily caused by the individuals; not by the environment and the whole process of Nature. The individual in the womb of his or her mother is in charge of the pregnancy, just as every individual in the womb of "Mother Nature" is in charge of its own life and growth, even as it is thoroughly conditioned by its environment.

In their call for attention to potential life, gradualists have really confused two different kinds of potency. The *potency to cause* something to come into existence is improperly identified with the *potency* for this new being *to become* fully what it *is*. This latter kind of potency applies only to living beings, since only these can grow or become manifestly themselves. The zygote especially exemplifies this later kind of potency—the *potency* of an existing being *to become* more expressly what *it*

already is. The ovum and sperm particularly exemplify the first kind of potency—the *potency to cause* something to come into existence.

One of the important sources of confusion regarding these radically different kinds of potency is the fact that they interweave and interact. The potency to cause something to come into existence—which is proper to the ovum, for instance—also entails the latent function of disposing the newly caused being (the zygote) to become fully what it is, once it is. And once the zygote is, its potency to become fully itself also entails the latent function of internally causing its own stages of organization and development. But the potency to cause something is radically different from the potency to become something.

The gametic and zygotic cells primarily illustrate this difference and this confluence of potencies. The ovum, for instance, besides having the potency to cause, together with the sperm, something else to come into existence, also has the potency to become fully itself once *it* is. And, as with all organic potencies, the potency is attained at the beginning of the ovum's existence (even though it is simply a body part existence). The potency of an ovum to become fully itself, as an ovum, includes its capacity for containing 23 chromosomes, as well as its capacity for causing, together with a sperm cell, a new human being. Moreover, the new human individual, as a zygote, has its own radically different potency for becoming what it *is*, once it is. And within its potency for becoming what it *is*, the potency for causing embryonic, fetal, infant, child, adolescent, and adult stages of development, as well as the potency for causing new human beings through the instrumentality of its gametes.

In this age of the electron microscope, we now know that the matter of a zygote is essentially of the same structure as the matter of an adult. Even a hylomorphic theory, then, demands an acknowledgment that the zygote and the adult have the same formal cause. Only the soul of a *person* could sever the zygote and embryo as an internal final cause of the development of a specifically human brain or of a human anything. No part of a person can be developed through the internal direction of a plant or an animal soul.

A second major flaw in the gradualist approach is its subtle or not so subtle projection of a mechanistic model of development onto an organically developing reality. It fails to distinguish between natural process and artifactual process. Only artifacts, such as clocks and spaceships, come into existence part by part. Living beings come into existence all at once and then gradually unfold to themselves and to the world what they already, but only incipiently, *are*. Some developmentalists use the analogy of a blueprint in characterizing the zygote. But a blueprint never becomes part of a house, unless it is used to paper the walls.

Moreover, the human zygote is much more than a genetic package. It is a living being that *has* genes. We do not think that an adult is a package of organs, muscles, and bones, but that he or she *is* a being who *has* these structures. The whole of a living being is always, at every stage, much more than the sum of its parts.

A third major weakness in the gradualist approach is the implicit or explicit notion that a human person is a rational animal. But a person is not a rational animal any more than an animal is a sentient plant. Persons are animal-like, plant-like, rock-like and God-like in many ways. We fall like rocks when dropped. We digest food like animals. And in our contemplative moments we act *like* God. Essentially, we are a wholly unique kind of *material* entity; even more different from animals than animals are from plants.

The latent idea that a human person is an "incarnate spirit" also seems to be at work in many who have a developmentalist approach. One's own body and biology are regarded as thoroughly subject to the superior and inevitably imperious judgments of mind and commands of will. The body is not valued as a vitally identifiable and intrinsic part of our person, but as an alien animal to be civilized by socialization and technology. By implication, then, one's own body is not regarded as an intrinsic revelation of person, but as a sophisticated instrument for personal use and eventual discard. The utilitarian society—well known for its tin cans, paper cups, disposable babies, *et al.,*—can find in the "developmental school" the heart of its rationale.

In this view, nature is not a friend to be known and loved, but an alien, massive and impersonal monster ultimately to be outwitted and subdued. Thus the most immediately threatening and most symbolic part of this monster is one's body. One should not claim ownership of this body until one is sure he or she can handle it: until one is functionally capable of reasoning, desiring, and willing. These are the minimal criteria for a meaningful bodily existence, conferred by the person whose self-concept represents a refusal to be essential (not exclusively) identified with body and biology. Such is the Cartesian legacy of the gradualist approach.

The point in time when an individual person begins to exist in the spatio-temporal world is one of the most crucial metaphysical and social issues of our age. . . .

In order to put the issue of personhood and conception into its truest perspective, philosophers are being challenged to represent, clarify, and deepen our understanding of the value of the person in himself or herself. Because this value is, as it were, a seamless robe, our thinking must be woven from the natural, substantive, and nonfunctional levels of meaning. Otherwise, "quality of life" ethics becomes the "survival of the fittest," of the most functional; and the ethic itself becomes a nonethic. I think we need an ethics sensitive to a deeper and richer vision of our dignity even as adults, who are dependently developing persons in the environment of space and time. Without appreciable insight into the inexhaustible process of personhood development, we will not be prepared to respect and protect the prenatal person.

BARBARA EHRENREICH

Is Abortion Really a "Moral" Dilemma?

BARBARA EHRENREICH, *a prominent feminist theorist and activist, has written extensively on women's issues. Her most recent book is* Remaking Love: The Feminization of Sexuality *(with Elizabeth Hess and Gloria Jacobs).*

QUITE apart from blowing up clinics and terrorizing patients, the antiabortion movement can take credit for a more subtle and lasting kind of damage. It has succeeded in getting even pro-choice people to think of abortion as a "moral dilemma," an "agonizing decision" and related code phrases for something murky and compromising, like the traffic in infant formula mix. In liberal circles, it has become unstylish to discuss abortion without using words like "complex," "pained," and the rest of the mealy-mouthed vocabulary of evasion. Regrets are also fashionable, and one otherwise feminist author writes recently of mourning each year following her abortion, the putative birthday of her discarded fetus.

I cannot speak for other women, of course, but the one regret I have about my own abortions is that they cost money that might otherwise have been spent on something more pleasurable, like taking the kids to movies and theme parks. Yes, that is abortions, plural (two in my case)—a possibility that is not confined to the promiscuous, the disorderly or the ignorant. In fact, my credentials for dealing with the technology of contraception are first rate: I have a Ph.D. in biology that is now a bit obsolescent but still good for conjuring up vivid mental pictures of zygotes and ova, and I was actually paid, at one point in my life, to teach other women about the mystery of reproductive biology.

Yet, as every party to the abortion debate should know, those methods of contraception that are truly safe are not absolutely reliable no matter how reliably they are used. Many women, like myself, have felt free to choose the safest methods because legal abortion is available as a backup to contraception. Anyone who finds that a thoughtless, immoral choice should speak to the orphans of women whose wombs were perforated by Dalkon shields or whose strokes were brought on by high estrogen birth control pills.

I refer you to the orphans only because it no longer seems to be good form to mention the women themselves in discussion of abortion. In most of the antiabortion literature I have seen, women are so invisible that an uninformed reader might conclude that fetuses reside in artificially warm tissue culture flasks or similar containers. It must be enormously difficult for the antiabortionist to face up to the fact that real fetuses can only survive inside women, who, unlike any kind of laboratory apparatus, have thoughts, feelings, aspirations, responsibilities and, very often, checkbooks. Anyone who thinks for a moment about women's role in reproductive biology could never blithely recommend "adoption, not abortion" because women have to go through something unknown to fetuses of men, and that is pregnancy.

From the point of view of a fetus, pregnancy is no doubt a good deal. But consider it for a moment from the point of view of the pregnant person (if "woman" is too incendiary and feminist a term) and without reference to its potential issue. We are talking about a nine-month bout of symptoms of varying severity, often including nausea, skin discolorations, extreme bloating and swelling, insomnia, narcolepsy, hair loss, varicose veins, hemorrhoids, indigestion and irreversible weight gain, and culminating in a physiological crisis which is occasionally fatal and almost always excruciatingly painful. If men were equally at risk for this condition— if they knew that their bellies might swell as if they were suffering from endstage-cirrhosis, that they would have to go for nearly a year without a stiff drink, a cigarette or even an aspirin, that they would be subject to fainting spells and unable to fight their way into commuter trains—then I am sure that pregnancy would be classified as a sexually transmitted disease and abortions would be no more controversial than emergency appendectomies.

Adding babies to the picture does not make it all that much prettier, even if you are, as I am, a fool for short, dimpled people with drool on their chins. For no matter how charming the outcome of pregnancy that is allowed to go to term no one is likely to come forth and offer to finance its Pampers or pay its college tuition. Nor are the opponents of abortion promising a guaranteed annual income, subsidized housing, national health insurance and other measures that might take some of the terror out of parenthood. We all seem to expect the individual parents to shoulder the entire burden of supporting any offspring that can be traced to them, and, in the all-too-common event that the father cannot be identified or has skipped town to avoid child-support payments, "parent" means mother.

When society does step in to help out a poor woman attempting to raise children on her own, all that it customarily has to offer is some government-surplus cheese, a monthly allowance so small it would barely keep a yuppie male in running shoes, and the contemptuous epithet "welfare cheat." It would be far more reasonable to honor the survivors of pregnancy in childbirth with at least the same respect and special benefits that we give, without a second thought, to veterans of foreign wars.

But, you will object, I have greatly exaggerated the discomforts of pregnancy and the hazards of childbearing, which many women undergo quite cheerfully. This is true, at least to an extent. In my own case, the case of my planned and wanted pregnancies. I managed to interpret morning sickness as a sign of fetus tenacity and to find, in the hypertrophy of my belly, a voluptuousness ordinarily unknown to the skinny. But this only proves my point: A society that is able to make a good thing out of pregnancy is certainly free to choose how to regard abortion. We can treat it as a necessary adjunct to contraception, or as a vexing moral dilemma, or as a form of homicide—and whichever we choose, that is how we will tend to experience it.

So I will admit that I might not have been so calm and determined about my abortions if I had had to cross a picket line of earnest people yelling "baby killer," or if I felt that I might be blown to bits in the middle of a vacuum aspiration. Conversely, though, we would be hearing a lot less about ambivalence and regrets if there were not so much liberal head scratching going on. Abortions will surely continue, as they have through human history, whether we approve or disapprove or hem and haw. The question that worries me is: How is, say, a 16-year-old girl going to feel after an abortion? Like a convicted sex offender, a murderess on parole? Or like a young woman who is capable, as the guidance counselors say, of taking charge of her life?

This is our choice, for biology will never have an answer to that strange and cabalistic question of when a fetus becomes a person. Potential persons are lost every day as a result of miscarriage, contraception or someone's simple failure to respond to a friendly wink. What we can answer, with a minimum of throat-clearing and moral agonizing, is the question of when women themselves will finally achieve full personhood: And that is when we have the right, unquestioned and unabrogated, to choose not to be pregnant when we decide not to be pregnant.

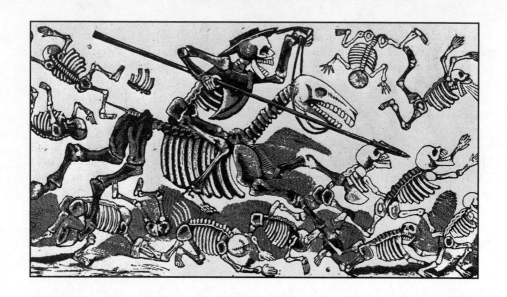

Chapter *11*

What Is the Meaning of Death?

It may have struck you that many of the topics that philosophers find interesting (the nature of knowledge, the relationship between the mind and the body, the nature of justice, and so on) aren't ones that people generally worry much about. While people may have views about, for example, whether a particular law is just, they usually don't spend much time trying to understand the nature of justice itself. That task gets left to the philosopher. But it seems that most people do, at various times in their lives, wonder about the nature of death. What is death? What is it like to be dead? Does that question make sense? Why do we usually consider death to be a bad thing, a thing to be avoided? Is it ever reasonable to prefer death over life? Is there "life" after death? If so, what is it like?

In his paper "Death," Thomas Nagel tries to figure out just what is so bad about death, given that death is the end of conscious existence. How can something be bad for me if I don't even exist? If you have trouble settling this question and those above, if they present you with endless opportunity for speculation, it is partly because each of them is connected not only to one another, but also to a host of other questions that resist easy answers. For example, take the question that Nagel sidesteps, namely, whether there is "life" after death. When someone poses that question, she is usually wondering if, after the death of her body, anything is left of the person who once "inhabited" it. After all, the corpse rots away under the earth, or succumbs to the flames of the crematorium. Where, then, is the person who once was? As you can see, how you answer this question will depend in part on your views about the relationship between the mind and the body (see Chapter 5). For example, if you have been persuaded that a person is a purely physical being and that the notion of an immaterial mind or soul is nonsensical, then you will likely dismiss the idea that a person could survive the death of her body. You can see, too, that underlying this last claim are assumptions about the nature of persons. Thus, any view about life after death will have as a counterpart some view about personal identity (see Chapter 8). Very often, concerns about the afterlife can be seen as concerns about what it is that gives life meaning. Some people think that, without some promise of life beyond that on earth, our lives here are meaningless and without any real purpose.

Shades of this view can be found in Plato's *Phaedo,* in which Socrates makes explicit his position on the question of the afterlife. He thought that the physical body was a mere impediment, something that we have to live with, so to speak, while we are stationed in the material world. To him, the *real* world was purely immaterial. Our embodied life, if lived properly (you will see what Socrates thought about the life well lived), is a process of moving closer and closer to reality. In and of itself, our embodied life means nothing.

The mysteries of death and the afterlife thus provide wide room for philosophical speculation. But there is as well a set of distinctly ethical questions about death and dying that warrant careful attention. Simply put, the most central of such questions is whether it is ever permissible to cause someone to die or even to let someone die. Surely, few people endorse cold-blooded murder. But what about "pulling the plug" in the case of an elderly patient who is in a coma, with no chance of gaining consciousness? Or what about administering a lethal dose of morphine to a terminally ill cancer patient in intractable pain? Immediately, a number of ancillary questions arise. Is there a difference between killing and letting someone die? What role do the desires of the afflicted person play in the decision to "let nature take its course" or to help nature along its way? The Greek word 'euthanasia', which taken literally means "good death," is often used to refer to cases such as these. Sherwin Nuland, a physician, presents his views about the circumstances under which taking one's life, or assisting someone else in doing so, might be permissible. He stresses the importance of considering the unique relation of doctor and patient in our attempts to think about the ethical pressures involved in bringing an end to life.

This critical distinction between actively causing a person's death and passively, through inaction, allowing a person to die, is a distinction on which a huge amount of legal and moral weight has been placed. James Rachels proposes that it is a distinction without a difference. He agrees that "active euthanasia" and "passive euthanasia" are legally different, but by spelling out for us some of the consequences of trying to maintain such a distinction, he argues that there is no moral basis to it. In her response to Rachels's argument, Bonnie Steinbock claims to the contrary that the distinction between active and passive euthanasia can be supported in cases in which the patient refuses treatment, and in cases in which the purpose of failing to treat a patient is not the termination of life, but rather the reduction of pain.

Among the more difficult questions surrounding the issue of death is, When is someone actually dead? For many years, a person was considered dead when there was a cessation of all vital signs. Given that the function of a person's heart and lungs can now be maintained by respirators, a new definition of death has been proposed. According to a committee of doctors, theologians, and ethicists assembled to evaluate the definition of death in 1968, death should be defined as irreversible coma. When a person is found to be in an irreversible coma, death should be declared and the respirator turned off. Willard Gaylin considers some of the unexpected advantages to the living of such a "liberal" definition of death. Such a definition allows for the possibility of stockpiling "dead" bodies, the organs of which could then be used in transplants. You might want to think about why that idea is so unnerving to many people.

THOMAS NAGEL

Death

THOMAS NAGEL teaches philosophy at New York University. He has made important contributions to ethics and philosophy of mind. Among his many publications are Mortal Questions *and* The View from Nowhere.

IF death is the unequivocal and permanent end of our existence, the question arises whether it is a bad thing to die.

There is conspicuous disagreement about the matter: some people think death is dreadful; others have no objection to death *per se,* though they hope their own will be neither premature nor painful. Those in the former category tend to think those in the latter are blind to the obvious, while the latter suppose the former to be prey to some sort of confusion. On the one hand it can be said that life is all we have and the loss if it is the greatest loss we can sustain. On the other hand it may be objected that death deprives this supposed loss of its subject, and that if we realize that death is not an unimaginable condition of the persisting person, but a mere blank, we will see that it can have no value whatever, positive or negative.

Since I want to leave aside the question whether we are, or might be, immortal in some form, I shall simply use the word 'death' and its cognates in this discussion to mean *permanent* death, unsupplemented by any form of conscious survival. I want to ask whether death is in itself an evil; and how great an evil, and of what kind, it might be. The question should be of interest even to those who believe in some form of immortality, for one's attitude toward immortality must depend in part on one's attitude toward death.

If death is an evil at all, it cannot be because of its positive features, but only because of what it deprives us of. I shall try to deal with the difficulties surrounding the natural view that death is an evil because it brings to an end all the goods that life contains. We need not give an account of these goods here, except to observe that some of them, like perception, desire, activity, and thought, are so general as to be constitutive of human life. They are widely regarded as formidable benefits in themselves, despite the fact that they are conditions of misery as well as of happiness, and that a sufficient quantity of more particular evils can perhaps outweigh them. That is what is meant, I think, by the allegation that it is good simply to be alive, even if one is undergoing terrible experiences. The situation is roughly this: There are elements which, if added to one's experience, make life better; there are other elements which, if added to one's experience, make life worse. But what remains when these are set aside is not merely *neutral:* it is emphatically positive. Therefore life is worth living even when the bad elements of experience are plentiful, and the good ones too meager to outweigh the bad ones on their own. The additional positive weight is supplied by experience itself, rather than by one of its contents.

I shall not discuss the value that one person's life or death may have for others, or its objective value, but only the value it has for the person who is its subject. That seems to me the primary case, and the case which presents the greatest difficulties.

Let me add only two observations. First, the value of life and its contents does not attach to mere organic survival: almost everyone would be indifferent (other things equal) between immediate death and immediate coma followed by death and immediate coma followed by death twenty years later without reawakening. And second, like most goods, this can be multiplied by time: more is better than less. The added quantities need not be temporally continuous (though continuity has its social advantages). People are attracted to the possibility of long-term suspended animation or freezing, followed by the resumption of conscious life, because they can regard it from within simply as a *continuation* of their present life. If these techniques are ever perfected, what from outside appeared as a dormant interval of three hundred years could be experienced by the subject as nothing more than a sharp discontinuity in the character of his experiences. I do not deny, of course, that this has its own disadvantages. Family and friends may have died in the meantime; the language may have change; the comforts of social, geographical, and cultural familiarity would be lacking. Nevertheless these inconveniences would not obliterate the basic advantage of continued, though discontinuous, existence.

If we turn from what is good about life to what is bad about death, the case is completely different. Essentially,

though there may be problems about heir specification, what we find desirable in life are certain states, conditions, or types of activity. It is *being* alive, *doing* certain things, having certain experiences, that we consider good. But if death is an evil, it is the *loss of life,* rather than the state of being dead, or nonexistent, or unconscious, that is objectionable. This asymmetry is important. If it is good to be alive, that advantage can be attributed to a person at each point of his life. It is a good of which Bach had more than Schubert, simply because he lived longer. Death, however, is not an evil of which Shakespeare has so far received a larger portion than Proust. If death is a disadvantage, it is not easy to say when a man suffers it.

There are two other indications that we do not object to death merely because it involves long periods of nonexistence. First, as has been mentioned, most of us would not regard the *temporary* suspension of life, even for substantial intervals, as in itself a misfortunc. If it ever happens that people can be frozen without reduction of the conscious lifespan, it will be inappropriate to pity those who are temporarily out of circulation. Second, none of us existed before we were born (or conceived), but few regard that as a misfortune. I shall have more to say about this later.

The point that death is not regarded as an unfortunate *state* enables us to refute a curious but very common suggestion about the origin of the fear of death. It is often said that those who object to death have made the mistake of trying to imagine what it is like to *be* dead. It is alleged that the failure to realize that this task is logically impossible (for the banal reason that there is nothing to imagine) leads to the conviction that death is a mysterious and therefore terrifying prospective *state*. But this diagnosis is evidently false, for it is just as impossible to imagine being dead (though it is easy enough to imagine oneself, from the outside, in either of those conditions). Yet people who are averse to death are not usually averse to unconsciousness (so long as it does not entail a substantial cut in the total duration of waking life).

If we are to make sense of the view that to die is bad, it must be on the ground that life is a good and death is the corresponding deprivation or loss, bad not because of any positive features but because of the desirability of what it removes. We must now turn to the serious difficulties which this hypothesis raises, difficulties about loss and privation in general, and about death in particular.

Essentially, there are three types of problems. First, doubt may be raised whether *anything* can be bad for a man without being positively unpleasant to him: specifically, it may be doubted that there are any evils which consist merely in the deprivation or absence of possible goods, and which do not depend on someone's *minding* that deprivation. Second, there are special difficulties, in the case of death, about how the supposed misfortune is to be assigned to a subject at all. There is doubt both as to *who* its subject is, and as to *when* he undergoes it. So long as a person exists, he has not yet died, and once he has died, he no longer exists; so there seems to be no time when death, if it is a misfortune, can be ascribed to its unfortunate subject. The third type of difficulty concerns the asymmetry, mentioned above, between our attitudes to posthumous and prenatal nonexistence. How can the former be bad if the latter is not?

It should be recognized that if these are valid objections to counting death as an evil, they will apply to many other supposed evils as well. The first type of objection is expressed in general form by the common remark that what you don't know can't hurt you. It means that even if a man is betrayed by his friends, ridiculed behind his back, and despised by people who treat him politely to his face, none of it can be counted as a misfortune for him so long as he does not suffer as a result. It means that a man is not injured if his wishes are ignored by the executor of his will, or if, after death, the belief becomes current that all the literary works on which his fame rests were really written by his brother, who died in Mexico at the age of 28. It seems to me worth asking what assumptions about good and evil lead to these drastic restrictions.

All the questions have something to do with time. There certainly are goods and evils of a simple kind (including some pleasures and pains) which a person possesses at a given time simply in virtue of his condition at that time. But this is not true of all the things we regard as good or bad for a man. Often we need to know his history to tell whether something is a misfortune or not; this applies to ills like deterioration, deprivation, and damage. Sometimes his experiential *state* is relatively unimportant—as in the case of a man who wastes his life in the cheerful pursuit of a method of communicating with asparagus plants. Someone who holds that all goods and evils must be temporally assignable states of the person may of course try to bring difficult cases into line by pointing to the pleasure or pain that more complicated goods and evils cause. Loss, betrayal, deception, and ridicule are on this view bad because people suffer when they learn of them. But it should be asked how our ideas of human value would have to be constituted to accommodate these cases directly instead. One advantage of such an account might be that it would enable us to explain *why* the discovery of these misfortunes causes suffering—in a way that makes it reasonable. For the natural view is that the discovery of betrayal makes us unhappy because it is bad to be betrayed—not that betrayal is bad because its discovery makes us unhappy.

It therefore seems to me worth exploring the position that most good and ill fortune has as its subject a person identified by his history and his possibilities, rather than merely by his categorical state of the moment—and that while this subject can be exactly located in a sequence of places and times, the same is not necessarily true of the goods and ills that befall him.

These ideas can be illustrated by an example of deprivation whose severity approaches that of death. Suppose an intelligent person receives a brain injury that reduces him to the mental condition of a contented infant, and that such desires as remain to him can be satisfied by a custodian, so that he is free from care. Such a development would be widely regarded as a severe misfortune, not only for his friends and relations, or for society, but also, and primarily, for the person himself. This does not mean that a contented infant is unfortunate. The intelligent adult who has been *reduced* to this condition is the subject of the misfortune. He is the one we pity, though of course he does not mind his condition—there is some doubt, in fact, whether he can be said to exist any longer.

The view that such a man has suffered a misfortune is open to the same objections which have been raised in regard to death. He does not mind his condition. It is in fact the same condition he was in at the age of three months, except that he is bigger. If we did not pity him then, why pity him now; in any case, who is there to pity? The intelligent adult has disappeared, and for a creature like the one before us, happiness consists in a full stomach and dry diaper.

If these objections are invalid, it must be because they rest on a mistaken assumption about the temporal relation between the subject of a misfortune and the circumstances which constitute it. If, instead of concentrating exclusively on the oversized baby before us, we consider the person he was, and the person he *could* be now, then his reduction to this state and the cancellation of his natural adult development constitute a perfectly intelligible catastrophe.

This case should convince us that it is arbitrary to restrict the goods and evils that can befall a man to nonrelational properties ascribable to him at particular times. As it stands, that restriction excludes not only such cases of gross degeneration, but also a good deal of what is important about success and failure, and other features of a life that have the character of processes. I believe we can go further, however. There are good and evils which are irreducibly relational; they are features of the relations between a person, with spatial and temporal boundaries of the usual sort, and circumstances which may not coincide with him either in space or in time. A man's life includes much that does not take place within the boundaries of his life. These boundaries are commonly crossed by the misfortunes of being deceived, or despised, or betrayed, (If this is correct, there is a simple account of what is wrong with breaking a deathbed promise. It is an injury to the dead man. For certain purposes it is possible to regard time as just another type of distance.) The case of mental degeneration shows us an evil that depends on a contrast between the reality and the possible alternatives. A man is the subject of good and evil as much because he has hopes which may or may not be fulfilled, or possibilities which may or may not be realized, as because of his capacity to suffer and enjoy. If death is an evil, it must be accounted for in these terms, and the impossibility of locating it within life should not trouble us.

When a man dies we are left with his corpse, and while a corpse can suffer the kind of mishap that may occur to an article of furniture, it is not a suitable object for pity. The man, however, is. He has lost his life, and if he had not died, he would have continued to live it, and to possess whatever good there is in living. If we apply to death the account suggested for the case of dementia, we shall say that although the spatial and temporal locations of the individual who suffered the loss are clear enough, the misfortune itself cannot be so easily located. One must be content just to state that his life is over and there will never be any more of it. That *fact,* rather than his past or present condition, constitutes his misfortune, if it is one. Nevertheless if there is a loss, someone must suffer it, and *he* must have existence and specific spatial and temporal location even if the loss itself does not. The fact that Beethoven had no children may have been a cause of regret to him, or a sad thing for the world, but it cannot be described as a misfortune for the children that he never had. All of us, I believe, are fortunate to have been born. But unless good and ill can be assigned

to an embryo, or even to an unconnected pair of gametes, it cannot be said that not to be born is a misfortune. (That is a factor to be considered in deciding whether abortion and contraception are akin to murder.)

This approach also provides a solution to the problem of temporal asymmetry, pointed out by Lucretius. He observed that no one finds it disturbing to contemplate the eternity preceding his own birth, and he took this to show that is must be irrational to fear death, since death is simply the mirror image of the prior abyss. That is not true, however, and the difference between the two explains why it is reasonable to regard them differently. It is true that both the time before a man's birth and the time after his death are times when he does not exist. But the time after his death is time of which his death deprives him. It is time in which, had he not died then, he would be alive. Therefore any death entails the loss of *some* life that its victim would have led had he not died at that or any earlier point. We know perfectly well what it would be for him to have had it instead of losing it, and there is no difficulty in identifying the loser.

But we cannot say that the time prior to a man's birth is time in which he would have lived had he been born not then but earlier. For aside from the brief margin permitted by premature labor, he *could* not have been born earlier: anyone born substantially earlier than he was would have been someone else. Therefore the time prior to his birth is not time in which his subsequent birth prevents him from living. His birth, when it occurs, does not entail the loss to him of any life whatever.

The direction of time is crucial in assigning possibilities to people or other individuals. Distinct possible lives of a single person can diverge from a common beginning, but they cannot converge to a common conclusion from diverse beginnings. (The latter would represent not a set of different possible lives of one individual, whose lives have identical conclusions.) Given an identifiable individual, countless possibilities for his continued existence are imaginable, and we can clearly conceive of what it would be for him to go on existing indefinitely. However inevitable it is that this will not come about, its possibility is still that of the continuation of a good for him, if life is the good we take it to be.

We are left, therefore, with the question whether the nonrealization of this possibility is in every case a misfortune or whether it depends on what can naturally be hoped for. This seems to me the most serious difficulty with the view that death is always an evil. Even if we can dispose of the objections against admitting misfortune that is not experienced, or cannot be assigned to a definite time in the person's life, we still have to set some limits on *how* possible a possibility must be for its nonrealization to be a misfortune (or good fortune, should the possibility be a bad one). The death of Keats at 24 is generally regarded as tragic; that of Tolstoy at 82 is not. Although they will both be dead forever, Keats' death deprived him of many years of life which were allowed to Tolstoy; so in a clear sense Keats' loss was greater (though not in the sense standardly employed in mathematical comparison between infinite quantities). However, this does not prove that Tolstoy's loss was insignificant. Perhaps we record an objection only to evils which are gratuitously added to the inevitable; the fact it is worse to die at 24 than at 82 does not imply that it is not a

terrible thing to die at 82, or even at 806. The question is whether we can regard as a misfortune any limitation, like mortality, that is normal to the species. Blindness or near-blindness is not a misfortune for a mole, nor would it be for a man, if that were the natural condition of the human race.

The trouble is that life familiarizes us with the goods of which death deprives us. We are already able to appreciate them, as a mole is not able to appreciate vision. If we put aside doubts about their status as goods and grant that their quantity is in part a function of their duration, the question remains whether death, no matter when it occurs, can be said to deprive its victim of what is in the relevant sense a possible continuation of life.

The situation is an ambiguous one. Observed from without, human beings obviously have a natural lifespan and cannot live much longer than a hundred years. A man's sense of his own experience, on the other hand, does not embody this idea of a natural limit. His existence defines for him an essentially open-ended possible future, containing the usual mixture of goods and evils that he has found so tolerable in the past. Having been gratuitously introduced to the world by a collection of natural, historical, and social accidents, he finds himself the subject of a *life* with an indeterminate and not essentially limited future. Viewed in this way, death, no matter how inevitable, is an abrupt cancellation of indefinitely extensive possible goods. Normality seems to have nothing to do with it, for the fact that we will all inevitably die in a few score years cannot by itself imply that it would not be good to live longer. Suppose that we were all inevitably going to die in *agony*—physical agony lasting six months. Would inevitability make *that* prospect any less unpleasant? And why should it be different for a deprivation? If the normal lifespan were a thousand years, death at 80 would be a tragedy. As things are, it may just be a more widespread tragedy. If there is no limit to the amount of life that it would be good to have, then it may be that a bad end is in store for us all.

PLATO

The Death of Socrates

PLATO (427–347 B.C.) was born into a family of considerable wealth and power. In Athens he came under the influence of Socrates and turned his attention to philosophy. After Socrates was condemned to death for corrupting the minds of the youth of Athens, Plato took it upon himself to continue Socrates' work. In the selection here from the Phaedo, *Socrates, who always serves as Plato's spokesman in his dialogues, discusses his view of death with Cebes.*

YOU realize, he said, that when a man dies, the visible part, the body, which exists in the visible world, which we call the corpse, for which it would be natural to dissolve, fall apart and be blown away, does not immediately suffer any of these things but remains for a fair time, in fact, quite a long time if the man dies with his body in a suitable condition and at a favourable season? If the body is emaciated or embalmed, as in Egypt, it remains almost whole for a remarkable length of time, and even if the body decays, some part of it, namely bones and sinews and the like are nevertheless, one might say, deathless. Is that not so?—Yes.

Will the soul, the invisible part which makes its way to a region of the same kind, noble and pure and invisible, to Hades in fact, to the good and wise god whither, god willing, my soul must soon be going—will the soul, being of this kind and nature, be scattered and destroyed on leaving the body, as the majority of men say? Far from it, my dear Cebes and Simmias, but what happens is much more like this: if it is pure when it leaves the body and drags nothing bodily with it, as it had no willing association with the body in life, but avoided it and gathered itself together by itself and always practiced this, which is no other than practicing philosophy in the right way, in fact, training to die easily. Or is this not training for death?

It surely is.

A soul in this state makes its way to the invisible, which is like itself, the divine and immortal and wise, and arriving there it can be happy, having rid itself of confusion, ignorance, fear violent desires and the other human ills and, as is said of the initiates, truly spend the rest of time with the gods. Shall we say this, Cebes, or something different?

This, by Zeus, said Cebes.

But I think if the soul is polluted and impure when it leaves the body, having always been associated with it and served it, bewitched by physical desires and pleasures to the point at which nothing seems to exist for it but the physical, which one can touch and see or eat and drink or make use of for sexual enjoyment, and if that soul is accustomed to hate and fear and avoid that which is dim and invisible to the eyes but intelligible and to be grasped by philosophy—do you think such a soul will escape pure and by itself?

Impossible, he said.

I think it is permeated by the physical, which constant intercourse and association with the body, as well as considerable practice, has cause to become ingrained in it.

Quite so.

We must believe, my friend, that this bodily element is heavy, ponderous, earthy and visible. Through it, such a soul has become heavy and is dragged back to the visible region in fear of the unseen, which is called Hades. It wanders, as we are told, around graves and monuments, where shadowy phantoms, images that such souls produce, have been seen, souls that have not been freed and purified but share in the visible, and are therefore seen.

That is likely, Socrates.

It is indeed, Cebes. Moreover, these are not the souls of good but of inferior men, which are forced to wander there, paying the penalty for their previous bad upbringing. They wander until their longing for that which accompanies them, the physical, again imprisons them in a body, and they are then, as is likely, bound to such characters as they have practiced in their life.

What kind of characters do you say these are, Socrates?

Those, for example, who have carelessly practiced gluttony, violence and drunkenness are likely to join a company of donkeys or of similar animals. Do you not think so?

Very likely.

Those who have esteemed injustice highly, and tyranny and plunder will join the tribes of wolves and hawks and kites, or where else shall we say that they go?

Certainly to those, said Cebes.

And clearly, the destination of the others will depend on the way in which they have behaved.

Clearly, of course.

The happiest of these, who will also have the best destination, are those who have practised popular and social virtue, which they call moderation and justice by habit and practice, without philosophy or understanding.

How are they the happiest?

Because it is likely that they will again join a social and gentle group, either of bees or wasps or ants, and then again the same kind of human group, and so be moderate men.

That is likely.

No one may join the company of the gods who has not practised philosophy and is not completely pure when he departs from life, no one but the lover of learning. It is for this reason, my friends Simmias and Cebes, that those who practice philosophy in the right way keep away from all bodily passions, master them and do not surrender themselves to them; it is not at all for fear of wasting their substance and of poverty, which the majority and the money-lovers fear, nor for fear of dishonour and ill repute, like the ambitious and lovers of honours, that they keep away from them.

That would not be natural for them, Socrates, said Cebes.

By Zeus, no, he said. Those who care for their own soul and do not live for the service of their body dismiss all these things. They do not travel the same road as those who do not know where they are going but, believing that nothing should be done contrary to philosophy and their deliverance and purification, they turn to this and follow wherever philosophy leads.

How so, Socrates?

I will tell you, he said. The lovers of learning know that when philosophy gets hold of their soul, it is imprisoned in and clinging to the body, and that it is forced to examine other things through it as though a cage and not by itself, and that it wallows in every kind of ignorance. Philosophy sees that the worst feature of this imprisonment is that it is due to desires, so that the prisoner is contributing to his own incarceration. As I say, the lovers of learning know that philosophy gets hold of their soul when it is in that state, then gently encourages it and tries to free it by showing them that investigation through the eyes is full of deceit, as is that through the ears and the other senses. Philosophy then persuades the soul to withdraw from the senses in so far as it is not compelled to use them and bids the soul to gather itself together by itself, to trust only itself and whatever reality, existing by itself, the soul by itself understands, and not to consider as true whatever it examines by other means, for this is different in different circumstances and is sensible and visible, whereas what the soul itself sees is intelligible and invisible. The philosopher thinks that this deliverance must not be opposed and so keeps away from pleasures and desires and pains as far as he can; he reflects that violent pleasure or pain or passion does not cause merely such evils as one might expect, such as one suffers when one has been sick or extravagant through desire, but the greatest and most extreme evil, though one does not reflect on this.

What is that, Socrates? asked Cebes.

What the soul of every man, when it feels violent pleasure or pain in connection with some object, inevitably believes at the same time that what causes such feelings must be very real true, which it is not. Such objects are mostly visible, are they not?

Certainly.

And such an experience ties the soul to the body most completely.

How so?

Because every pleasure and every pain provides, as it were, another nail to rivet the soul to the body and to weld them together. It makes the soul corporeal, so that it believes that truth is what the body says it is. As it shares the beliefs and delights of the body, I think it inevitably comes to share its ways and manner of life and is unable ever to reach Hades in a pure state; it is always full of body when it departs, so that it soon falls back into another body and grows with it as if it had been sewn into it. Because of this, it can have no part in the company of the divine, the pure and uniform.

What you say is very true, Socrates, said Cebes.

This is why genuine lovers of learning are moderate and brave, or do you think it is for the reasons the majority says they are?

I certainly do not.

Indeed no. This is how the soul of a philosopher would reason: it would not think that while philosophy must free it, it should while being freed surrender itself to pleasures and pains and imprison itself again, thus labouring in vain like Penelope at her web. The soul of the philosopher achieves a calm from such emotions; it follows reason and ever stays with it contemplating the true, the divine, which is not the object of opinion. Nurtured by this, it believes that one should live in this manner as long as one is alive and, after death, arrive at what is akin and of the same kind, and escape from human evils.

AD HOC COMMITTEE OF THE

HARVARD MEDICAL SCHOOL

Definition of Death

THE AD HOC COMMITTEE OF THE HARVARD MEDICAL SCHOOL TO EXAMINE THE DEFINITION OF BRAIN DEATH *was formed in the 1960s and consisted of physicians, theologians, and lawyers. Their widely discussed report was published in 1968. In it they argue that "cessation of vital functions" must be replaced by "irreversible coma" as the criterion of death.*

OUR primary purpose is to define irreversible coma as a new criterion for death. There are two reasons why there is need for a definition: (1) Improvements in resuscitative and supportive measures have led to increased efforts to save those who are desperately injured. Sometimes these efforts have only partial success, so that the result is an individual whose heart continues to beat but whose brain is irreversibly damaged. The burden is great on patients who suffer permanent loss of intellect, on their families, on the hospitals, and on those in need of hospital beds already occupied by these comatose patients. (2) Obsolete criteria for the definition of death can lead to controversy in obtaining organs for transplantation.

Irreversible coma has many causes, but *we are concerned here only with those comatose individuals who have no discernible central nervous system activity.* If the characteristics can be defined in satisfactory terms, translatable into action—and we believe this is possible—then several problems will either disappear or will become more readily soluble.

More than medical problems are present. There are moral, ethical, religious, and legal issues. Adequate definition here will prepare the way for better insight into all of these matters as well as for better law than is currently applicable.

CHARACTERISTICS OF IRREVERSIBLE COMA

An organ, brain or other, that no longer functions and has no possibility of functioning again is for all practical purposes dead. Our first problem is to determine the characteristics of a *permanently* nonfunctioning brain.

A patient in this state appears to be in deep coma. The condition can be satisfactorily diagnosed by points 1, 2, and 3 to follow. The electroencephalogram (point 4) provides confirmatory data, and when available it should be utilized. In situations where for one reason or another electroencephalographic monitoring is not available, the absence of cerebral function has to be determined by purely clinical signs, to be described, or by absence of circulation as judged by standstill of blood in the retinal vessels or by absence of cardiac activity.

1. Unreceptivity and Unresponsitivity.
There is a total unawareness to externally applied stimuli and inner need and complete unresponsiveness—our definition of irreversible coma. Even the most intensely painful stimuli evoke no vocal or other response, not even a groan, withdrawal of a limb, or quickening of respiration.

2. No Movements or Breathing.
Observation covering a period of at least one hour by physicians is adequate to satisfy the criteria of no spontaneous muscular movements or spontaneous respiration or response to stimuli such as pain, touch, sound, or light. After the patient is on a mechanical respirator, the total absence of spontaneous breathing may be established by turning off the respirator for three minutes and observing whether there is any effort on the part of the subject to breathe spontaneously. (The respirator may be turned off for this time provided at the start of the trial period the patient's carbon dioxide tension is within the normal range,

and provided also that the patient had been breathing room air for at least 10 minutes prior to the trial.)

3. No Reflexes
Irreversible coma with abolition of central nervous system activity is evidenced in part by the absence of elicitable reflexes. The pupil will be fixed and dilated and will not respond to a direct source of bright light. Since the establishment of a fixed, dilated pupil is clearcut in clinical practice, there should be no uncertainty as to its presence. Ocular movement (to head turning and to irrigation of the ears with ice water) and blinking are absent. There is no evidence of postural activity (decerebrate or other). Swallowing, yawning, vocalization are in abeyance. Corneal and pharyngeal reflexes are absent.

As a rule the stretch of tendon reflexes cannot be elicited; i.e., tapping the tendons of the biceps, triceps and pronator muscles, quadriceps and gastrocnemius muscles with the reflex hammer elicits no contraction of the respective muscles. Plantar or noxious stimulation gives no response.

4. Flat Electroencephalogram.
Of great confirmatory value is the flat or isoelectric EEG. We must assume that the electrodes have been properly applied, that the apparatus is functioning normally, and that the personnel in charge is competent. We consider it prudent to have one channel of the apparatus used for an electrocardiogram. This channel will monitor the ECG so that, if it appears in the electroencephalographic leads because of high resistance, it can be readily identified. It also establishes the presence of the active heart in the absence of the EEG. We recommend that another channel be used for a noncephalic lead. This will pick up space-borne or vibration-borne artifacts and identify them. The simplest form of such a monitoring noncephalic electrode has two leads over the dorsum of the hand, preferably the right hand, so the ECG will

be minimal or absent. Since one of the requirements of this state is that there be no muscle activity, these two dorsal hand electrodes will not be bothered by muscle artifact. The apparatus should be run at standard gains 10 μv/mm, 50 μv/5mm. Also it should be isoelectric at double this standard gain, which is 5 μv/mm or 25 μv/5mm. At least ten full minutes of recording are desirable, but twice that would be better.

It is also suggested that the gains at some point be opened to their full amplitude for a brief period (5 to 100 seconds) to see what is going on. Usually in an intensive-care unit artifacts will dominate the picture, but these are readily identifiable. There shall be no electroencephalographic response to noise or to pinch.

All of the above tests shall be repeated at least 24 hours later with no change.

The validity of such data as indications of irreversible cerebral damage depends on the exclusion of two conditions: hypothermia (temperature below 90°F [32.2°C]) or central nervous system depressants, such as barbiturates.

OTHER PROCEDURES

The patient's condition can be determined only by a physician. When the patient is hopelessly damaged as defined above, the family and all colleagues who have participated in major decisions concerning the patient, and all nurses involved, should be so informed. Death is to be declared and *then* the respirator turned off. The decision to do this and the responsibility for it are to be taken by the physician-in-charge, in consultation with one or more physicians who have been directly involved in the case. It is unsound and undesirable to force the family to make the decision.

LEGAL COMMENTARY

The legal system of the United States is greatly in need of the kind of analysis and recommendations for medical procedures in cases of irreversible brain damage as described. At present, the law of the United States, in all 50 states and in the federal courts, treats the question of human death as a question of fact to be decided in every case. When any doubt exists, the courts seek medical expert testimony concerning the time of death of the particular individual involved. However, the law makes the assumption that the medical criteria for determining death are settled and not in doubt among physicians. Furthermore, the law assumes that the traditional method among physicians for determination of death is to ascertain the absence of all vital signs. To this extent, *Black's Law Dictionary* (fourth edition, 1951) defines death as

> The cessation of life; the ceasing to exist; *defined by physicians* as a total stoppage of the circulation of the blood, and a cessation of the animal and vital functions consequent thereupon, such as respiration, pulsation, etc [italics added].

In the few modern court decisions involving a definition of death, the courts have used the concept of the total cessation of all vital signs. Two cases are worthy of examination. Both involved the issue of which one of two persons died first.

In *Thomas v. Anderson* (96 Cal. App. 2d 371, 211 P.2d 478), a California District Court of Appeal in 1950 said, "In the instant case the question as to which of the two men died first was a question of fact for the determination of the trial court. . . ."

The appellate court cited and quoted in full definition of death from

Black's Law Dictionary and concluded, ". . . death occurs precisely when life ceases and does not occur until the heart stops beating and respiration ends. Death is not a continuous event and is an event that takes place at a precise time."

The other case is *Smith v. Smith* (229 Ark. 579, 317 S.W.2d 275), decided in 1958 by the Supreme Court of Arkansas. In this case the two people were husband and wife involved in an auto accident. The husband was found dead at the scene of the accident. The wife was taken to the hospital unconscious. It is alleged that she "remained in coma due to brain injury" and died at the hospital 17 days later. The petitioner in court tried to argue that the two people died simultaneously. The judge writing the opinion said the petition contained a "quite unusual and unique allegation." It was quoted as follows:

That the said Hugh Smith and his wife, Lucy Coleman Smith, were in an automobile accident on the 19th day of April, 1957, said accident being instantly fatal to each of them at the same time, although the doctors maintained a vain hope of survival and made every effort to revive and resuscitate said Lucy Coleman Smith until May 6th, 1957, when it was finally determined by the attending physicians that their hope of resuscitation and possible restoration of human life to the said Lucy Coleman Smith was entirely vain, and that as a matter of modern medical science, your petitioner alleges and states, and will offer the Court competent proof that the said Hugh Smith, deceased, and said Lucy Coleman Smith, deceased, lost their power to will at the same instance, and that their demise as earthly human beings occurred at the same time in said automobile acci-

dent, neither of them ever regaining any consciousness whatsoever.

The court dismissed the petition as a *matter of law.* The court quoted *Black's* definition of death and concluded,

Admittedly, this condition did not exist, and as a matter of fact, it would be too much of a strain of credulity for us to believe any evidence offered to the effect that Mrs. Smith was dead, scientifically or otherwise, unless the conditions set out in the definition existed.

Later in the opinion the court said, "Likewise, we take judicial notice that one breathing, though unconscious, is not dead."

"Judicial notice" of this definition of death means that the court did not consider that definition open to serious controversy; it considered the question as settled in responsible scientific and medical circles. The judge thus makes proof of uncontroverted facts unnecessary so as to prevent prolonging the trial with unnecessary proof and also to prevent fraud being committed upon the court by quasi-"scientists" being called into court to controvert settled scientific principles at a price. Here, the Arkansas Supreme Court considered the definition of death to be a settled, scientific, biological fact. It refused to consider the plaintiff's offer of evidence that "modern medical science" might say otherwise. In simplified form, the above is the state of the law in the United States concerning the definition of death.

In this report, however, we suggest that responsible medical opinion is ready to adopt new criteria for pronouncing death to have occurred in an individual sustaining irreversible coma as a result of permanent brain damage. If this position is adopted by the medical community, it can form the basis for change in the current legal concept of death. No statutory change in the law should be necessary, since the law treats this question essentially as one of fact to be determined by physicians. The only circumstance in which it would be necessary that legislation be offered in the various states to define "death" by law would be in the event that great controversy were engendered surrounding the subject and physicians were unable to agree on the new medical criteria.

It is recommended as a part of these procedures that judgment of the existence of these criteria is solely a medical issue. It is suggested that the physician in charge of the patient consult with one or more other physicians directly involved in the case before the patient is declared dead on the basis of these criteria. In this way, the responsibility is shared over a wider range of medical opinion, thus providing an important degree of protection against later questions which might be raised about the particular case. It is further suggested that the decision to declare the person dead, and then to turn off the respirator, be made by physicians not involved in any later effort to transplant organs or tissue from the deceased individual. This is advisable in order to avoid any appearance of self-interest by the physicians involved.

It should be emphasized that we recommend the patient be declared dead before any effort is made to take him off a respirator, if he is then on a respirator. This declaration should not be delayed until he has been taken off the respirator and all artificially stimulated signs have ceased. The reason for this recommendation is that in our judgment it will provide a greater degree of legal protection to those involved. Otherwise, the physicians would be turning off the respirator on a person who is, under the present strict technical application of law, still alive.

JAMES RACHELS

Active and Passive Euthanasia

JAMES RACHELS *teaches philosophy at the University of Alabama. He has written widely on ethical issues, especially in the field of biomedical ethics.*

THE distinction between active and passive euthanasia is thought to be crucial for medical ethics. The idea is that it is permissible, at least in some cases, to withhold treatment and allow a patient to die, but it is never permissible to take any direct action designed to kill the patient. This doctrine seems to be accepted by most doctors, and it is endorsed in a statement adopted by the House of Delegates of the American Medical Association of December 4, 1973:

> The intentional termination of the life of one human being by another—mercy killing—is contrary to that for which the medical profession stands and is contrary to the policy of the American Medical Association.
>
> The cessation of the employment of extraordinary means to prolong the life of the body when there is irrefutable evidence that biological death is imminent is the decision of the patient and/or his immediate family. The advice and judgment of the physician should be freely available to the patient and/or his immediate family.

However, a strong case can be made against this doctrine. In what follows I will set out some of the relevant arguments, and urge doctors to reconsider their views on this matter.

To begin with a familiar type of situation, a patient who is dying of incurable cancer of the throat is in terrible pain, which can no longer be satisfactorily alleviated. He is certain to die within a few days, even if present treatment is continued, but he does not want to go on living for those days since the pain is unbearable. So he asks the doctor for an end to it, and his family joins in the request.

Suppose the doctor agrees to withhold treatment, as the conventional doctrine says he may. The justification for his doing so is that the patient is in terrible agony, and since he is going to die anyway, it would be wrong to prolong his suffering needlessly. But now notice this. If one simply withholds treatment, it may take the patient longer to die, and so he may suffer more than he would if

more direct action were taken and a lethal injection given. This fact provides strong reason for thinking that, once the initial decision not to prolong his agony has been made, active euthanasia is actually preferable to passive euthanasia, rather than the reverse. To say otherwise is to endorse the option that leads to more suffering rather than less, and is contrary to the humanitarian impulse that prompts the decision to prolong his life in the first place.

Part of my point is that the process of being "allowed to die" can be relatively slow and painful, whereas being given a lethal injection is relatively quick and painless. Let me give a different sort of example. In the United States about one in 600 babies is born with Down's syndrome. Most of these babies are otherwise healthy—that is, with only the usual pediatric care, they will proceed to an otherwise normal infancy. Some, however, are born with congenital defects such as intestinal obstructions that require operations if they are to live. Sometimes, the parents and the doctor will decide not to operate, and let the infant die. Anthony Shaw describes what happens then:

> When surgery is denied [the doctor] must try to keep the infant from suffering while natural forces sap the baby's life away. As a surgeon whose natural inclination is to use the scalpel to fight off death, standing by and watching a salvageable baby die is the most emotionally exhausting experience I know. It is easy at a conference, in a theoretical discussion to decide that such infants should be allowed to die. It is altogether different to stand by in the nursery and watch as dehydration and infection wither a tiny being over hours and days. This is a terrible ordeal for me and the hospital

staff—much more so than for the parents who never set foot in the nursery.

I can understand why some people are opposed all euthanasia, and insist that such infants must be allowed to live. I think I can also understand why other people favor destroying these babies quickly and painlessly. But why should anyone favor letting "dehydration and infection wither a tiny being over hours and days"? The doctrine that says that a baby may be allowed to dehydrate and wither, but may not be given an injection that would end its life without suffering, seems so patently cruel as to require no further refutation. The strong language is not intended to offend, but only to put the point in the clearest possible way.

My second argument is that the conventional doctrine leads to decisions concerning life and death made on irrelevant grounds.

Consider again the case of the infants with Down's syndrome who need operations for congenital defects unrelated to the syndrome to live. Sometimes, there is no operation, and the baby dies, but when there is no such defect, the baby lives on. Now, an operation such as that to remove an intestinal obstruction is not prohibitively difficult. The reason why such operations are not performed in these cases is, clearly, that the child has Down's syndrome and the parents and the doctor judge that because of that fact it is better for the child to die.

But notice that this situation is absurd, no matter what view one takes of the lives and potentials of such babies. If the life of such an infant is worth preserving what does it matter if it needs a simple operation? Or, if one thinks it better that such a baby should not live on, what difference does it make that it

happens to have an unobstructed intestinal tract? In either case, the matter of life and death is being decided on irrelevant grounds. It is the Down's syndrome, and not the intestines, that is the issue. The matter should be decided, if at all, on that basis, and not be allowed to depend on the essentially irrelevant question of whether the intestinal tract is blocked.

What makes this situation possible, of course, is the idea that when there is an intestinal blockage, one can "let the baby die," but when there is no such defect there is nothing that can be done, for one must not "kill" it. The fact that this idea leads to such results as deciding life or death on irrelevant grounds is another good reason why the doctrine would be rejected.

One reason why so many people think there is an important moral difference between active and passive euthanasia is that they think killing someone is morally worse than letting someone die. But is it? Is killing, in itself, worse than letting die? To investigate this issue, two cases may be considered that are exactly alike except that one involves killing whereas the other involves letting someone die. Then, it can be asked whether this difference makes any difference to the moral assessments. It is important that the cases be exactly alike, except for this one difference, since otherwise one cannot be confident that it is this difference and not some other that accounts for any variation in the assessments of the two cases. So, let us consider this pair of cases:

In the first, Smith stands to gain a large inheritance if anything should happen to his six-year-old cousin. One evening while the child is taking his bath, Smith sneaks into the bathroom and drowns the child, and then arranges things so that it will look like an accident.

In the second, Jones also stands to gain if anything should happen to his six-year-old cousin. Like Smith, Jones sneaks in planning to drown the child in his bath. However, just as he enters the bathroom Jones sees the child slip and hit his head and fall face down in the water. Jones is delighted; he stands by, ready to push the child's head back under if it is necessary. But it is not necessary. With only a little thrashing about, the child drowns all by himself "accidentally," as Jones watches and does nothing.

Now Smith killed the child, whereas Jones "merely" let the child die. That is the only difference between them. Did either man behave better, from a moral point of view? If the difference between killing and letting die were in itself a morally important matter, one should say that Jones's behavior was less reprehensible than Smith's. But does one really want to say that? I think not. In the first place, both men acted from the same motive, personal gain, and both had exactly the same end in view when they acted. It may be inferred from Smith's conduct that he is a bad man, although that judgment may be withdrawn or modified if certain further facts are learned about him—for example that he is mentally deranged. But would not the very same thing be inferred about Jones from his conduct? And would not the same further considerations also be relevant to any modification of this judgment? Moreover, suppose Jones pleaded, in his own defense. "After all, I didn't do anything except just stand there and watch the child drown. I didn't kill him; I only let him die." Again, if letting die were in it-

self less bad than killing, this defense should have at least some weight. But it does not. Such a "defense" can only be regarded as a grotesque perversion of moral reasoning. Morally speaking, it is no defense at all.

Now, it may be pointed out, quite properly, that the cases of euthanasia with which doctors are concerned are not like this at all. They do not involve personal gain or the destruction of normal healthy children. Doctors are concerned only with cases in which the patient's life is of no further use to him, or in which the patient's life has become or will soon become a terrible burden. However, the point is the same in these cases; the bare difference between killing and letting die does not, in itself, make a moral difference. If a doctor lets a patient die, for humane reasons, he is in the same moral position as if he had given the patient a lethal injection for humane reasons. If his decision was wrong—if, for example, the patient's illness was in fact curable—the decision would be equally regrettable no matter which method was used to carry it out. And if the doctor's decision was the right one, the method used is not in itself important.

The AMA policy statement isolates the crucial issue very well: the crucial issue is "the intentional termination of the life of one human being by another." But after identifying this issue, and forbidding "mercy killing," the statement goes on to deny that the cessation of treatment is the intentional termination of a life. This is where the mistake comes in, for what is the cessation of treatment, in these circumstances, if it is not "the intentional termination of life of one human being by another"? Of course it is exactly that, and if it were not, there would be no point to it.

Many people will find this judgment hard to accept. One reason, I think, is that it is very easy to conflate the question of whether killing is, in itself, worse than letting die, with the very different question of whether most actual cases of killing are more reprehensible than most actual cases of letting die. Most actual cases of killing are clearly terrible (think, for example, of all the murders reported in the newspapers), and one hears of such cases every day. On the other hand, one hardly ever hears of a case of letting die, except for the actions of doctors who are motivated by humanitarian reasons. So one learns to think of killing in a much worse light than of letting die. But this does not mean that there is something abut killing that makes it in itself worse then letting die, for it is not the bare difference between killing and letting die that makes the difference in these cases. Rather, the other factors—the murderer's motivation—account for different reactions to the different cases.

I have argued that killing is not in itself any worse than letting die; if my contention is right, it follows that active euthanasia is not any worse than passive euthanasia. What arguments can be given on the other side? The most common, I believe, is the following:

The important difference between active and passive euthanasia is that, in passive euthanasia, the doctor does not do anything to bring about the patient's death. The doctor does nothing, and the patient dies of whatever ills already afflict him. In active euthanasia, however, the doctor does something to bring about the patient's death: he kills him. The doctor who gives the patient with cancer a lethal injection has himself caused his patient's death; whereas if he merely ceases treatment, the cancer is the cause of the death.

A number of points need to be made here. The first is that it is not exactly correct to say that in passive euthanasia the doctor does nothing, for he does do one thing that is very important: he lets the patient die. "Letting someone die" is certainly different, in some respects, from other types if action—mainly in that it is a kind of action that one may perform by way of not performing certain other actions. For example, one may let a patient die by way of not giving medication, just as one may insult someone by way of not shaking his hand. But for any purpose of moral assessment, it is a type of action nonetheless. The decision to let a patient die is subject to moral appraisal: it may be assessed as wise or unwise, compassionate or sadistic, right or wrong. If a doctor deliberately let a patient die who was suffering from a routinely curable illness, the doctor would certainly be to blame if he had needlessly killed the patient. Charges against him would be appropriate. If so, it would be no defense at all for him to insist that he didn't "do anything." He would have done something very serious indeed, for he let his patent die.

Fixing the cause of death may be very important from a legal point of view, for it may determine whether criminal charges are brought against the doctor. But I do not think that this notion can be used to show a moral difference between active and passive euthanasia. The reason why it is considered bad to be the cause of someone's death is that death is regarded as a great evil—and so it is. However, if it has been decided that euthanasia—even passive euthanasia—is desirable in a given case, it has also been decided that in this instance death is no greater an evil than the patient's continued existence. And if this is true, the usual reason for not wanting to be the cause of someone's death simply does not apply.

Finally, doctors may think that all of this is only of academic interest—the sort of thing that philosophers may worry about but that has no practical bearing on their own work. After all, doctors must be concerned about the legal consequences of what they do, and active euthanasia is clearly forbidden by the law. But even so, doctors should also be concerned with the fact that the law is forcing upon them a moral doctrine that may be indefensible, and has a considerable effect on their practices. Of course, most doctors are not now in the position of being coerced in this matter, for they do not regard themselves as merely going along with what the law requires. Rather, in statements such as the AMA policy statement that I have quoted they are endorsing this doctrine

as a central point of medical ethics. In that statement, active euthanasia is condemned not merely as illegal but as "contrary to that for which the medical profession stands," whereas passive euthanasia is approved. However, the preceding considerations suggest that there is really no moral difference between the two, considered in themselves (there may be important moral difference in some cases in their *consequences,* but, as I pointed out, these differences may make active euthanasia, and not passive euthanasia, the morally preferable option). So, whereas doctors may have to discriminate between active and passive euthanasia to satisfy the law, they should not do any more than that. In particular, they should not give the distinction any added authority and weight by writing it into official statements of medical ethics.

BONNIE STEINBOCK

The Intentional Termination of Life

BONNIE STEINBOCK *teaches philosophy at the State University of New York at Albany. Her books include* Speciesism and the Idea of Equality *and* Killing and Letting Die.

ACCORDING to James Rachels and Michael Tooley, a common mistake in medical ethics is the belief that there is a moral difference between active and passive euthanasia. This is a mistake, they argue, because the rationale underlying the distinction between active and passive euthanasia is the idea that there is a significant moral difference between

intentionally killing and intentionally letting die. "This idea," Tooley says, "is admittedly very common. But I believe that it can be shown to reflect either confused thinking, or a moral point of view unrelated to the interests of individuals." Whether the belief that there is a significant moral difference (between intentionally killing and intentionally letting die) is mistaken is not my concern here. For it is far from clear that this distinction *is* not the basis of the doctrine of the American Medical Association which Rachels attacks. And if the killing/letting die distinction is not the basis of the AMA doctrine, then arguments showing that the distinction has no moral force do not, in themselves, reveal in the doctrine's adherents either "confused thinking" or "a moral point of view unrelated to the interest of individuals." Indeed, as we examine the AMA doctrine, I think it will become clear that it appeals to and makes use of a number of overlapping distinctions, which may have moral significance in particular cases, such as the distinction between intending and foreseeing, or between ordinary and extraordinary care. Let us then turn to the statement, from the House of Delegates of the American Medical Association, which Rachels cites:

The intentional termination of the life of one human being by another—mercy-killing—is contrary to that for which the medical profession stands and is contrary to the policy of the American Medical Association.

The cessation of the employment of extraordinary means to prolong the life of the body when there is irrefutable evidence that biological death is imminent is the decision of the patient and/or his immediate family. The advice and judgment of the physician should be freely available to the patient and/or his immediate family.

Rachels attacks this statement because he believes that it contains a moral distinction between active and passive euthanasia. . . .

I intend to show that the AMA statement does not imply support of the active/passive euthanasia distinction. In forbidding the intentional termination of life, the statement rejects both active and passive euthanasia. It does allow for ". . . the cessation of the employment of extraordinary means . . ." to prolong life. The mistake Rachels and Tooley make is in identifying the cessation of life-prolonging treatment with passive euthanasia or intentionally letting die. If it were right to equate the two, then the AMA statement would be self-contradictory, for it would begin by condemning, and end by allowing the intentional termination of life. But if the cessation of life-prolonging treatment is not always or necessarily passive euthanasia, then there is no confusion and no contradiction.

Why does Rachels think that the cessation of life-prolonging treatment is in the intentional termination of life? He says:

The AMA policy statement isolates the crucial issue very well; the crucial issue is "the intentional termination of the life of one human being by another." But after identifying this issue, and forbidding "mercy-killing," the statement goes on to deny that the cessation of treatment is the intentional termination of a life. This is where the mistake comes in, for what is the cessation of treatment, in these circumstances, if it is not "the intentional termination of the life of one human being by another"? Of course it is exactly that, and if it were not, there would be no point to it.

However, there *can* be a point (to the cessation of life-prolonging treatment) other than an endeavor to bring about the patient's death, and so the blanket identification of cessation of treatment with the intentional termination of a life is inaccurate. There are at least two situations in which the termination of life-prolonging treatment cannot be identified with the intentional termination of the life of one human being by another.

The first situation concerns the patient's right to refuse treatment. Both Tooley and Rachels give the example of a patient dying of an incurable disease, accompanied by unrelievable pain, who wants to end the treatment which cannot cure him but can only prolong his miserable existence. Why, they ask, may a doctor accede to the patient's request to stop treatment, but not provide a patient in a similar situation with a lethal dose? The answer lies in the patient's right to refuse treatment. In general, a competent adult has the right to refuse treatment, even where such treatment is necessary to prolong life. Indeed, the right to refuse treatment has been upheld even when the patient's reason for refusing treatment is generally agreed to be inadequate. This right can be over-ridden (if, for example, the patient has dependent children) but, in general, no one may legally compel you to undergo treatment to which you have not consented. "Historically, surgical intrusion has always been considered a technical battery upon the person and one to be excused or justified by consent of the patient or justified by necessity created by the circumstances of the moment. . . ."

At this point, it might be objected that if one has the right to refuse life-prolonging treatment, then consistency demands that one have the right to decide to end his life and to obtain help in doing so. The idea is that the right to refuse treatment somehow implies a right to voluntary euthanasia, and we need to see why someone might think this. The right to refuse treatment has been considered by legal writers as an example of the right to privacy

or, better, the right to bodily self-determination. You have the right to decide what happens to your own body, and the right to refuse treatment is an instance of that more general right. But if you have the right to determine what happens to your body, then should you not have the right to choose to end your life, and even a right to get help in doing so?

However, it is important to see that the right to refuse treatment is not the same as nor does it entail, a right to voluntary euthanasia, even if both can be derived from the right to bodily self-determination. The right to refuse treatment is not itself a "right to die"; that one may choose to exercise this right or even at the risk of death or even *in order to die,* is irrelevant. The purpose of the right to refuse medical treatment is not to give persons a right to decide whether to live or die, but to protect them from the unwanted inferences of others. Perhaps we ought to interpret the right to bodily self-determination more broadly so as to include a right to die: but this would be a substantial extension of our present understanding of the right to bodily self-determination, and not a consequence of it. Should we recognize a right to voluntary euthanasia, we would have to agree that people have the right not merely to be left alone, but also the right to be killed. I leave to one side that substantive moral issue. My claim is simply that there can be a reason for terminating life-prolonging treatment other than "to bring about the patient's death."

The second case in which termination of treatment cannot be identified with intentional termination of life is where continued treatment has little chance of improving the patient's condition and brings greater discomfort than relief.

The question here is what treatment is appropriate to the particular case. A cancer specialist describes it in this way:

My general rule is to administer therapy as long as a patient responds well and has the potential for a reasonably good quality of life. But when all feasible therapies have been administered and a patient shows signs of rapid deterioration, the continuation of therapy can cause more discomfort than the cancer. From that time I recommend surgery, radiotherapy, or chemotherapy only as a means of relieving pain. But if a patient's condition should once again stabilize after the withdrawal of active therapy and if it should appear that he could still gain some good time, I would immediately reinstitute active therapy. The decision to cease anticancer treatment is never irrevocable, and often the desire to live will push a patient to try for another remission, or even a few more days of life.

The decision here to cease anticancer treatment cannot be construed as a decision that the patient die, or as the intentional termination of life. It is a decision to provide the most appropriate treatment for that patient at that time. Rachels suggests that the point of the cessation of treatment is the intentional termination of life. But here the point of discontinuing treatment is not to bring about the patient's death but to avoid treatment that will cause more discomfort than the cancer and has little hope of benefiting the patient. Treatment that meets this description is often called "extraordinary." The concept is flexible, and what might be considered "extraordinary" in one situation might be ordinary in another. The use of a respirator to sustain a patient through a severe bout with a respiratory disease would be considered ordinary; its use to sustain the life of a severely brain damaged person in an irreversible coma would be considered extraordinary.

Contrasted with extraordinary treatment is ordinary treatment, the care a doctor would normally be expected to provide. Failure to provide ordinary care constitutes neglect, and can even be construed as the intentional infliction of harm, where there is a legal obligation to provide care. The importance of the ordinary/extraordinary care distinction lies partly in its connection to the doctor's intention. The withholding of extraordinary care should be seen as a decision not to inflict painful treatment on a patient without reasonable hope of success. The withholding of ordinary care, by contrast, must be seen as neglect. Thus, one doctor says, "We have to draw a distinction between ordinary and extraordinary means. We never withdraw what's needed to make a baby comfortable, we would never withdraw the care a parent would provide. We never kill a baby. . . . But we may decide certain heroic intervention is not worthwhile."

We should keep in mind the ordinary/extraordinary care distinction when considering an example given by both Tooley and Rachels to show the irrationality of the active/passive distinction with regard to infanticide. The example is this: a child is born with Down's syndrome and also has an intestinal obstruction which requires corrective surgery. If the surgery is not performed the infant will starve to death, since it cannot take food orally. This may take days or even weeks, as dehydration and infection set in. Commenting on this situation, Rachels says:

I can understand why some people are opposed to all euthanasia, and insist that such infants must be allowed to live. I think I can also understand why other people favor destroying these babies quickly and painlessly. But why should anyone favor letting "dehydration and infection wither a tiny being over hours and days"? The doctrine that says that a baby may be allowed to dehydrate and wither, but may not be given an injection that would end its life without suffering, seems so patently cruel as to require no further refutation.

Such a doctrine perhaps does not need further refutation; but this is not the AMA doctrine. For the AMA statement criticized by Rachels allows only for the cessation of extraordinary means to prolong life when death is imminent. Neither of these conditions is satisfied in this example. Death is not imminent in this situation, any more than it would be if a normal child had an attack of appendicitis. Neither the corrective surgery to remove the intestinal obstruction, nor the intravenous feeding required to keep the infant alive until such surgery is performed, can be regarded as extraordinary means, for neither is particularly expensive, nor does either place an overwhelming burden on the patient or others. (The continued existence of the child might be thought to place an overwhelming burden on its parents, but that has nothing to do with the characterization of the means to prolong its life as extraordinary. If it had, then *feeding* a severely defective child who required a great deal of care could be regarded as extraordinary.) The chances of success if the operation is undertaken are quite good, though there is always a risk in operating on infants. Though the Down's syndrome will not be alleviated, the child will proceed to an otherwise normal infancy.

It cannot be argued that the treatment is withheld for the infant's sake, unless one is prepared to argue that all mentally retarded babies are better off dead.

This is particularly implausible in the case of Down's syndrome babies who generally do not suffer and are capable of giving and receiving love, of learning and playing, to varying degrees.

In a film on this subject entitled, "Who Should Survive?", a doctor defended a decision not to operate, saying that since the parents did not consent to the operation, the doctors' hands were tied. As we have seen, surgical intrusion requires consent, and in the case of infants, consent would normally come from the parents. But, as their legal guardians, parents are required to provide medical care for their children, and failure to do so can constitute criminal neglect or even homicide. In general, courts have been understandably reluctant to recognize a parental right to terminate life-prolonging treatment. Although prosecution is unlikely, physicians who comply with invalid instructions from the parents and permit the infant's death could be liable for aiding and abetting, failure to report child neglect, or even homicide. So it is not true that, in this situation, doctors are legally bound to do as the parents wish.

To sum up, I think that Rachels is right to regard the decision not to operate in the Down's syndrome example as the intentional termination of life. But there is no reason to believe that either the law or the AMA would regard it otherwise. Certainly the decision to withhold treatment is not justified by the AMA statement. That such infants have been allowed to die cannot be denied; but this, I think, is the result of doctors misunderstanding the law and the AMA position.

Withholding treatment in this case is the intentional termination of life because the infant is deliberately allowed to die; that is the point of not operating. But there are other cases in which that is not the point. If the point is to avoid inflicting painful treatment on a patient with little or no reasonable hope of success, this is not the intentional termination of life. The permissibility of such withholding of treatment, then, would have no implications for the permissibility of euthanasia, active or passive.

. . . Someone might say: Even if the withholding of treatment is not the intentional termination of life, does that make a difference, morally speaking? If life-prolonging treatment may be withheld, for the sake of the child, may not an easy death be provided, for the sake of the child, as well? The unoperated child with spina bifida may take months or even years to die. Distressed by the spectacle of children "lying around, waiting to die," one doctor has written, "It is time that society and medicine stopped perpetuating the fiction that withholding treatment is ethically different from terminating a life. It is time that society began to discuss mechanisms by which we can alleviate the pain and suffering for those individuals whom we cannot help."

I do not deny that there may be cases in which death is in the best interests of the patient. In such cases, a quick and painless death may be the best thing. However, I do not think that, once active or vigorous treatment is stopped, a quick death is always preferable to a lingering one. We must be cautious about attributing to defective children *our* distress at seeing them linger. Waiting for them to die may be tough on parents, doctors and nurses—it isn't necessarily tough on the child. The decision not to operate need not mean a decision to neglect, and it may be possible to make the remaining months of the child's life comfortable, pleasant and filled with love. If this alternative is possible, surely it is more decent and humane than killing the child. In such a situation, withholding treatment, forseeing the child's death, is not ethically equivalent to killing the child, and we cannot move from the permissibility of the former to that of the latter. I am worried that there will be a tendency to do precisely that if active euthanasia is regarded as morally equivalent to the withholding of life-prolonging treatment.

SHERWIN NULAND

How We Die

SHERWIN NULAND *is a physician and a professor of medicine at Yale University School of Medicine. He is the author of* How We Die *(1993) from which the following selection is taken.*

TAKING one's own life is almost always the wrong thing to do. There are two circumstances, however, in which that may not be so. Those two are the unendurable infirmities of a crippling old age and the final devastations of terminal disease. The nouns are not important in that last sentence—it is the adjectives that cry out for attention, for they are the very crux of the issue and will tolerate no compromise or "well, almosts": *unendurable, crippling, final,* and *terminal.*

During his long lifetime, the great Roman orator Seneca gave much thought to old age:

> I will not relinquish old age if it leaves my better part intact. But if it begins to shake my mind, if it destroys its faculties one by one, if it leaves me not life but breath, I will depart from the putrid or tottering edifice. I will not escape by death from disease so long as it may be healed, and leaves my mind unimpaired. I will not raise my hand against myself on account of pain, for so to die is to be conquered. But I know that if I must suffer without hope of relief, I will depart, not through fear of the pain itself, but because it prevents all for which I would live.

These words are so eminently sensible that few would disagree that suicide would appear to be among the options that the frail elderly should consider as the days grow more difficult, at least those among them who are not barred from doing so by their personal convictions. Perhaps the philosophy expressed by Seneca explains the fact that elderly white males take their own lives at a rate five times the national average. Is theirs not the "rational suicide" so strongly defended in journals of ethics and the op-ed pages of our daily newspapers?

Hardly so. The flaw in Seneca's proposition is a striking example of the error that permeates virtually every one of the publicized discussions of modern-day attitudes toward suicide—a very large proportion of the elderly men and women who kill themselves do it be-

cause they suffer from quite remediable depression. With proper medication and therapy, most of them would be relieved of the cloud of oppressive despair that colors all reason gray, would then realize that the edifice topples not quite so much as thought, and that hope of relief is less hopeless than it seemed. I have more than once seen a suicidal old person emerge from depression, and rediscovered thereby a vibrant friend. When such men or women return to a less despondent vision of reality, their loneliness seems to them less stark and their pain more bearable because life has become interesting again and they realize that there are people who need them.

All of this is not to say that there are no situations in which Seneca's words deserve heeding. But should this be so, the Roman's doctrine would then deserve consultation, counsel, and the leavening influence of a long period of mature thought. A decision to end life must be as defensible to those whose respect we seek as it is to ourselves. Only when that criterion has been satisfied should anyone consider the finality of death.

Against such a standard, the suicide of Percy Bridgman was close to being irreproachable. Bridgman was a Harvard professor whose studies in high-pressure physics won him a Nobel Prize in 1946. At the age of seventy-nine and in the final stages of cancer, he continued to work until he could no longer do so. Living at his summer home in Randolph, New Hampshire, he completed the index to a seven-volume collection of his scientific works, sent it off to the Harvard University Press, and then shot himself on August 20, 1961, leaving a suicide note in which he summed up a controversy that has since embroiled an entire world of medical ethics: "it is not decent for Society to make a man do this to himself. Probably, this is the last day I will be able to do it myself."

When he died, Bridgman seemed absolutely clear in his mind that he was making the right choice. He worked right up to the final day, tied up loose ends, and carried out his plan. I'm not certain how much consideration he gave to consulting others, but his decision had certainly not been kept a secret from friends and colleagues, because there is ample evidence of his having at least informed some of them in advance. He had become so sick that he felt it doubtful that he would much longer be capable of mustering up the strength to carry out his ironclad resolve.

In his final message, Bridgman deplored the necessity of performing his deed unaided. A colleague reported a conversation in which Bridgman said, "I would like to take advantage of the situation in which I find myself to establish a general principle; namely, that when the ultimate end is as inevitable as it now appears to be, the individual has a right to ask his doctor to end it for him." If a single sentence were needed to epitomize the battle in which we are all now joined, you have just read it.

No contemporary discussion of suicide, at least not one written by a physician, can skirt the issue of the doctor's role in assisting patients toward their mortality. The crucial word in this sentence is *patients*—not just people, but *patients,* specifically the patients of the doctor who contemplates the assisting. The guild of Hippocrates should not develop a new specialty of accoucheurs to the grave so that conscience-stricken oncologists, surgeons, and other physicians may refer to others those who wish to exit the planet. On the other hand, any degree of debate about physicians' participation should be welcomed if it will bring out into the open a muted practice that has existed since Aesculapius was in swaddling clothes.

Suicide, especially this newly debated form, has become fashionable lately. In centuries long past, those who took their own lives were at best considered to have committed a felony against themselves; at worst, their crime was viewed as a mortal sin. Both attitudes are implicit in the world of Immanel Kant: "Suicide is not abominable because God forbids it; God forbids it because it is abominable."

But things are different today; we have a new wrinkle on suicide, aided and perhaps encouraged by self-styled consultants on the limits of human suffering. We read in our tabloids and glossy magazines that the actions of the deceased are, under certain sanctioned circumstances, celebrated with tributes such as are usually reserved for New Age heroes, which a few of them seem to have become. As for the pop cultural icons, medical and otherwise, who assist them—we are treated to the spectacular of those publicized peddlers of death willingly expounding their philosophies on TV talk shows. They extol their own selflessness even as the judicial system seeks to prosecute them.

In 1988, there appeared in the *Journal of the American Medical Association* an account by a young gynecologist-in-training who, in the wee hours of one night, murdered—*murder* is the only word for it—a cancer-ridden twenty-year-old woman because it pleased him to interpret her plea for relief as a plea for death that only he could grant. His method was to inject a dose of intravenous morphine of at least twice the recommended strength and then to stand by until her breathing "became irregular, then ceased." The fact that the self-appointed deliverer had never seen his victim before did not deter him from not only carrying out but actually publishing the details of his misconceived mission of mercy, saturated with the implicit fulsome certainty of his wisdom. Hippocrates winced, and his living heirs wept in spirit.

Though American doctors quickly reached a condemning consensus about the behavior of the young gynecologist, they responded very differently three years later in a case of quite another sort. Writing in the *New England Journal of Medicine,* an internist from Rochester, New York, described a patient he identified only as Diane, whose suicide he knowingly facilitated by prescribing the barbiturates she requested. Diane, the mother of a college-age son, had been Dr. Timothy Quill's patient for a long time. Three and a half years earlier, he had diagnosed a particularly severe form of leukemia, and her disease had progressed to the point where "bone pain, weakness, fatigue, and fevers began to dominate her life."

Rather than agree to chemotherapy that stood little chance of arresting the lethal assault of her cancer, Diane early in her course had made it clear to Dr. Quill and his several consultants that she feared the debilitation of treatment and the loss of control of her body far more than she feared death. Slowly, patiently, with rare compassion and the help of his colleagues, Quill came to accept Diane's decision and the validity of her grounds for making it. The process by which he gradually recognized that he should help speed her death is exemplary of the humane bond that can exist

and be enhanced between a doctor and a competent terminally ill patient who rationally chooses and with consultation confirms that it is the right way to make her quietus. For those whose worldview allows them this option, Dr. Quill's way of dealing with the thorny issue of assent (since then elaborated in a wise and outspoken book published in 1993) may prove to be a reference point on the compass of medical ethics. Physicians like the young gynecologist, and the inventors of suicide machines, too, have a great deal to learn from the Dianes and the Timothy Quills.

Quill and the gynecologist represent the diametrically opposed approaches which dominate discussions of the physician's role in helping patients to die—they are the ideal and the feared. Debates have raged, and I hope will continue to rage, over the stance that should be taken by the medical community and others, and there are many shades of opinion.

In the Netherlands, euthanasia guidelines have been drawn up by common consensus, allowing competent and fully informed patients to have death administered in carefully regulated circumstances. The usual method is for the physician to induce deep sleep with barbiturates and then to inject a muscle-paralyzing drug to cause cessation of breathing. The Dutch Reformed Church has adopted a policy, described in its publication *Euthanasie en Pastoraat*— "Euthanasia and the Ministry"—that does not obstruct the voluntary ending of life when illness makes it intolerable. Their very choice of words signifies the churchmen's sensitivity to the difference between this and ordinary suicide, or *zelfmoord,* literally "self-murder." A new term has been introduced to refer to death under circumstances of euthana-sia: *zelfdoding,* which might best be translated as "self-deathing."

Although the practice remains tech-nically illegal in the Netherlands, it has not been prosecuted so long as the in-volved physician stays within the guide-lines. These include repeated uncoerced requests to end the severe mental and physical suffering that is the result of incurable disease which has no other prospect for relief. It is required that all alternative options have been exhausted or refused. The number of patients un-dergoing euthanasia is approximately 2,300 per year in a nation of some 14.5 million people, representing about 1 percent of all deaths. Most frequently, the act is carried out in the patient's home. Interestingly, the great majority of requests are refused by doctors, be-cause they do not meet the criteria.

Involvement is the essence of the thing. Family physicians who make house calls are the primary providers of medical care in the Netherlands. When a terminally ill person requests euthanasia or assistance with suicide, it is not a spe-cialist to whom he is likely to go for counsel, or a death expert. The probabil-ity is that doctor and patient will have known each other for years, as did Timo-thy Quill and Diane, and even then con-sultation and verification by another physician is mandatory. The length and quality of Quill's relationship with Diane must have been major considerations in the decision of a Rochester grand jury in July 1991 not to indict him.

In the United States and democratic countries in general, the importance of airing differing viewpoints rests not in the probability that a stable consensus will ever be reached but in the recogni-tion that it will not. It is by studying the shades of opinion expressed in such discussions that we become aware of considerations in decision-making that may never have weighed in our soul-searching. Unlike the debates which certainly belong in the public arena, the decisions themselves will always prop-erly be made in the tiny, impenetrable sphere of personal conscience. And that is exactly as it should be.

Into all of this, an organization called the Hemlock Society has intruded itself. These pages are not the forum in which to critique the problematic way in which this well-meaning self-help group of generally intelligent people has publicly validated the suicide decisions of those who may suffer from impaired judg-ment. Nor is it my intention to ventilate more than just a bit of my disdain for the misguided way in which the Hem-lock Society's founder, Derek Humphry, has represented himself in the limelight of the media during promotion of his ill-advised cookbook of death, *Final Exit.* But no one should make a final judg-ment on *Final Exit* without being aware of a startling statistic: A 1991 survey conducted by the United States govern-ment's Centers for Disease Control found that 27 percent of 11,631 high school students had "thought seriously" about killing themselves in the previous year, and that one in twelve had actually attempted it. More than half a million young Americans are known to try sui-cide each year, plus an undiscoverable other huge group of those whose at-tempts are never disclosed.

In a June 1992 letter to the *Journal of the American Medical Association,* two psychiatrists at the Yale Child Study Center advised: "With its lurid examples, explicit instructions, and vig-orous advocacy for suicide, *Final Exit* may have an especially pernicious ef-fect on adolescents, who, with their high rate of attempted and completed suicide, appear susceptible to imitative influences and cultural factors that glorify or destigmatize suicide."

Depression, the periodic despondency of the chronically ill, and the death fascination of some segments of our society are not strong enough justifications for teaching people how to murder themselves, to help them do it, or to bestow a blessing on it. No one with impaired powers of judgment is in a position to make a critical decision about ending his or her own life—on that point, there is no disagreement, even among the ethicists who argue most persuasively for the concept that has recently come to be known as "rational suicide." In no way, as Dr. Quill has pointed out, does Derek Humphry's death primer "resolve the profound moral, ethical and personal uncertainties it raises about the meaning of euthanasia and assisted suicide." As with all issues that deal with human life, there is no universal answer, but there should be a universal attitude of tolerance and inquiry. It is perhaps too much to ask that there should also be a universal method of decision making that is more specifically stated than the guidelines already described. Until a better one is available, Dr. Quill's way—of empathy, unhurried discussion, consultation, questioning, and challenged assumptions—will do just fine.

WILLARD GAYLIN

Harvesting the Dead

WILLARD GAYLIN is a psychiatrist and president of the Institute of Society, Ethics and the Life Sciences in Hastings-on-Hudson, New York. Among his many publications is Partial Justice: A Study of Bias in Sentencing.

NOTHING in life is simple any more, not even the leaving of it. At one time there was no medical need for the physician to consider the concept of death; the fact of death was sufficient. The difference between life and death was an infinite chasm breached in an infinitesimal moment. Life and death were ultimate, self-evident opposites.

With the advent of new techniques in medicine, those opposites have begun to converge. We are now capable of maintaining visceral functions without any semblance of the higher functions that define a person. We are, therefore, faced with the task of deciding whether that which we have kept alive is still a human being, or, to put it another way, whether that human being that we are maintaining should be considered "alive."

Until now we have avoided the problems of definition and reached the solutions in silence and secret. When the life sustained was unrewarding by the standards of the physician in charge—it was discontinued. Over the years, physicians have practiced euthanasia on an ad hoc, casual, and perhaps irresponsible basis. They have withheld antibiotics or other simple treatments when it was felt that a life did not warrant sustaining, or pulled the plug on the respirator when they were convinced that what was being sustained no longer warranted the definition of life. Some of these acts are illegal and, if one wished to prosecute, could constitute a form of manslaughter, even though it is unlikely that any jury would convict. We prefer to handle all problems connected with death by denying their existence. But death and its dilemmas persist.

New urgencies for recognition of the problem arise from two conditions; the continuing march of technology, making the sustaining of vital processes possible for longer periods of time; and the increasing use of parts of the newly dead to sustain life for the truly living. The problem is well on its way to being resolved by what must have seemed a relatively simple and ingenious method. As it turned out, the difficult issues of euthanasia could be evaded by redefining death.

In an earlier time, death was defined as the cessation of breathing. Any movie buff recalls at least one scene in which a mirror is held to the mouth of a dying man. The lack of fogging indicated that indeed he was dead. The spirit of man resided in his *spiritus* (breath). With increased knowledge of human physiology and the potential for reviving a nonbreathing man, the circulation, the pulsating heart, became the focus of the definition of life. This is the tradition with which most of us have been raised.

There is of course a relationship between circulation and respiration, and the linkage, not irrelevantly, is the brain. All body parts require the nourishment, including oxygen, carried by the circulating blood. Lack of blood supply leads to the death of an organ; the higher functions of the brain are particularly vulnerable. But if there is no respiration, there is no adequate exchange of oxygen, and this essential ingredient of the blood is no longer available for distribution. If a part of the heart loses its vascular supply, we may lose that part and still survive. If a part of the brain is deprived of oxygen, we may, depending on its location, lose it and survive. But here we pay a special price, for the functions lost are those we identify with the self, the soul, or humanness, i.e., memory, knowledge, feeling, thinking, perceiving, sensing, knowing, learning, and loving.

Most people are prepared to say that when all of the brain is destroyed the "person" no longer exists; with all due respect for the complexities of the mind/brain debate, the "person" (and personhood) is generally associated with the functioning part of the head—the brain. The higher functions of the brain that have been described are placed, for the most part, in the cortex. The brain stem (in many ways more closely allied to the spinal cord) controls primarily visceral functions. When the total brain is damaged, death in all forms will ensue because the lower brain centers that control the circulation and respiration are destroyed. With the development of modern respirators, however, it is possible to artificially maintain respiration and with it, often the circulation with which it is linked. It is this situation that has allowed for the redefinition of death—a redefinition that is being precipitously embraced by both scientific and theological groups.

The movement toward redefining death received considerable impetus with the publication of a report sponsored by the Ad Hoc Committee of the Harvard Medical School in 1968. The committee offered an alternative definition of death based on the functioning of the brain. Its criteria stated that if an individual is unreceptive and unresponsive, i.e., in a state of irreversible coma; if he has no movements or breathing when the mechanical respirator is turned off; if he demonstrates no reflexes; and if he has a flat electroencephalogram for at least twenty-four hours, indicating no electrical brain activity (assuming that he has not been subjected to hypothermia or central nervous system depressants), he may then be declared dead.

What was originally offered as an optional definition of death is, however, progressively becoming *the* definition of death. In most states there is no specific legislation defining death; the ultimate responsibility here is assumed to reside in the general medical community. Recently, however, there has been a series of legal cases which seem to be establishing brain death as a judicial standard. In California in May of this year an ingenious lawyer, John Cruikshank, offered as a defense of his client, Andrew D. Lyons, who had shot a man in the head, the argument that the cause of death was not the bullet but the removal of his heart by a transplant surgeon, Dr. Norman Shumway. Cruikshank's argument notwithstanding, the jury found his client guilty of voluntary manslaughter. In the course of that trial, Dr. Shumway said: "The brain in the 1970s and in the light of modern day medical technology is the sine qua non—the criterion for death. I'm saying anyone whose brain is dead is dead. It is the one determinant

that would be universally applicable, because the brain is the one organ that can't be transplanted."

This new definition, independent of the desire for transplant, now permits the physician to "pull the plug" without even committing an act of passive euthanasia. The patient will first be defined as dead; pulling the plug will merely be the harmless act of halting useless treatment on a cadaver. But while the new definition of death avoids one complex problem, euthanasia, it may create others equally difficult which have never been fully defined or visualized. For if it grants the right to pull the plug, it also implicitly grants the privilege *not* to pull the plug, and the potential and meaning of this has not at all been adequately examined.

These cadavers would have the legal status of the dead with none of the qualities one now associates with death. They would be warm, respiring, pulsating, evacuating, and excreting bodies requiring nursing, dietary, and general grooming attention—*and could probably be maintained so for a period of years*. If we chose to, we could, with the technology already at hand, legally avail ourselves of these new cadavers to serve science and mankind in dramatically useful ways. The autopsy, that most respectable of medical traditions, that last gift of the dying person to the living future, could be extended in principle beyond our current recognition. To save lives and relieve suffering—traditional motives for violating tradition—we could develop hospitals (an inappropriate word because it suggests the presence of living human beings), banks, or farms of cadavers which require feeding and maintenance, in order to be harvested. To the uninitiated the "new cadavers" in their rows of respirators would seem indistinguishable from comatose patients now residing in wards of chronic neurological hospitals.

PRECEDENTS

The idea of wholesale and systematic salvage of useful body parts may seem startling, but it is not without precedent. It is simply magnified by the technology of modern medicine. Within the confines of one individual, we have always felt free to transfer body parts to places where they are needed more urgently, felt free to reorder the priorities of the naturally endowed structure. We will borrow skin from the less visible parts of the body to salvage a face. If a muscle is paralyzed, we will often substitute a muscle that subserves a less crucial function. This was common surgery at the time that paralytic polio was more prevalent.

It soon becomes apparent, however, that there is a limitation to this procedure. The person in want does not always have a second-best substitute. He may then be forced to borrow from a person with a surplus. The prototype, of course, is blood donation. Blood may be seen as a regeneratable organ, and we have a long-standing tradition of blood donation. What may be more important, perhaps dangerous, we have established the precedent in blood of commercialization—not only are we free to borrow, we are forced to buy and, indeed, in our country at least, permitted to sell. Similarly, we allow the buying or selling of sperm for artificial insemination. It is most likely that in the near future we will allow the buying and selling of ripened ova so that a sterile woman may conceive her baby if she has a functioning uterus. Of course, once *in vitro*

fertilization becomes a reality (an imminent possibility), we may even permit the rental of womb space for gestation for a woman who does manufacture her own ova but has no uterus.

Getting closer to our current problem, there is the relatively long-standing tradition of banking body parts (arteries, eyes, skin) for short periods of time for future transplants. Controversy has arisen with recent progress in the transplanting of major organs. Kidney transplants from a near relative or distant donor are becoming more common. As heart transplants become more successful, the issue will certainly be heightened, for while the heart may have been reduced by the new definition of death to merely another organ, it will always have a core position in the popular thinking about life and death. It has the capacity to generate the passion that transforms medical decisions into political issues.

The ability to use organs from cadavers has been severely limited in the past by the reluctance of heirs to donate the body of an individual for distribution. One might well have willed one's body for scientific purposes, but such legacies had no legal standing. Until recently, the individual lost control over his body once he died. This model piece of legislation, adopted by all fifty states in an incredibly short period of time, grants anyone over eighteen (twenty-one in some states) the right to donate en masse all "necessary organs and tissues" simply by filling out and mailing a small card.

Beyond the postmortem, there has been a longer-range use of human bodies that is accepted procedure—the exploitation of cadavers as teaching material in medical schools. This is a long step removed from the rationale of the transplant—a dramatic gift of life from the dying to the near-dead; while it is true that medical education will inevitably save lives, the clear and immediate purpose of the donation is to facilitate training.

It is not unnatural for a person facing death to want his usefulness to extend beyond his mortality; the same biases and values that influence our life persist in our leaving of it. It has been reported that the Harvard Medical School has no difficulty in receiving as many donations of cadavers as they need, while Tufts and Boston Universities are usually in short supply. In Boston, evidently, the cachet of getting into Harvard extends even to the dissecting table.

The way is now clear for an ever-increasing pool of usable body parts, but the current practice minimizes efficiency and maximizes waste. Only a short period exists between the time of death of the patient and the time of death of his major parts.

USES OF THE NEOMORT

In the ensuing discussion, the word *cadaver* will retain its usual meaning, as opposed to the new cadaver, which will be referred to as a *neomort*. The "ward" or "hospital" in which it is maintained will be called a *bioemporium* (purists may prefer *bioemporion*).

Whatever is possible with the old embalmed cadaver is extended to an incredible degree with the neomort. What follows, therefore, is not a definitive list but merely the briefest of suggestions as to the spectrum of possibilities.

Training

Uneasy medical students could practice routine physical examinations—auscultation, percussion of the chest,

examination of the retina, rectal and vaginal examinations, et cetera—indeed, everything except neurological examinations, since the neomort by definition has no functioning central nervous system.

Both the student and his patient could be spared the pain, fumbling, and embarrassment of the "first time."

Interns also could practice standard and more difficult diagnostic procedures, from spinal taps to pneumoencephalography and the making of arteriograms, and residents could practice almost all of their surgical skills— in other words, most of the procedures that are now normally taught with the indigent in wards of major city hospitals could be taught with neomorts. Further, students could practice more exotic procedures often not available in a typical residency—eye operations, skin grafts, plastic facial surgery, amputation of useless limbs, coronary surgery, etc.; they could also practice the actual removal of organs, whether they be kidneys, testicles, or what have you, for delivery to the transplant teams.

Testing

The neomort could be used for much of the testing of drugs and surgical procedures that we now normally perform on prisoners, mentally retarded children, and volunteers. The efficacy of a drug as well as its toxicity could be determined beyond limits we might not have dared approach when we were concerned about permanent damage to the testing vehicle, a living person. For example, operations for increased vascularization of the heart could be tested to determine whether they truly do reduce the incidence of future heart attack before we perform them on patients.

Experimental procedures that proved useless or harmful could be avoided; those that succeed could be available years before they might otherwise have been. Similarly, we could avoid the massive delays that keep some drugs from the marketplace while the dying clamor for them.

Neomorts would give us access to other forms of testing that are inconceivable with the living human being. We might test diagnostic instruments such as sophisticated electrocardiography by selectively damaging various parts of the heart to see how or whether the instrument could detect the damage.

Experimentation

Every new medical procedure demands a leap of faith. It is often referred to as an "act of courage," which seems to me an inappropriate terminology now that organized medicine rarely uses itself as the experimental body. Whenever a surgeon attempts a procedure for the first time, he is at best generalizing from experimentation with lower animals. Now we can protect the patient from too large a leap by using the neomort as an experimental bridge.

Obvious forms of experimentation would be cures for illnesses which would first be induced in the neomort. We could test antidotes by injecting poison, induce cancer or virus infections to validate and compare developing therapies.

Because they have an active hematopoietic system, neomorts would be particularly valuable for studying diseases of the blood. Many of the examples that I draw from that field were offered to me by Dr. John F. Bertles, a hematologist at St. Luke's Hospital Center in New York. One which interests him is

the utilization of marrow transplants. Few human-to-human marrow transplants have been successful, since the kind of immunosuppression techniques that require research could most safely be performed on neomorts. Even such research as the recent experimentation at Willowbrook—where mentally retarded children were infected with hepatitis virus (which was not yet culturable outside of the human body) in an attempt to find a cure for this pernicious disease—could be done without risking the health of the subjects.

Banking

While certain essential blood antigens are readily storable (e.g., red cells can now be preserved in a frozen state), others are not, and there is increasing need for potential means of storage. Research on storage of platelets to be used in transfusion requires human recipients, and the data are only slowly and tediously gathered at great expense. Use of neomorts would permit intensive testing of platelet survival and probably would lead to a rapid development of a better storage technique. The same would be true for white cells.

As has been suggested, there is great wastage in the present system of using kidney donors from cadavers. Major organs are difficult to store. A population of neomorts maintained with body parts computerized and catalogued for compatibility would yield a much more efficient system. Just as we now have blood banks, we could have banks for all the major organs that may someday be transplantable—lungs, kidney, heart, ovaries. Beyond the obvious storage uses of the neomort, there are others not previously thought of because there was no adequate storage facility. Dr. Marc

Lappe of the Hastings Center has suggested that a neomort whose own immunity system had first been severely repressed might be an ideal "culture" for growing and storing our lymphoid components. When we are threatened by malignancy or viral disease, we can go to the "bank" and withdraw our stored white cells to help defend us.

Harvesting

Obviously, a sizable population of neomorts will provide a steady supply of blood, since they can be drained periodically. When we consider the cost-benefit analysis of this system, we would have to evaluate it in the same way as the lumber industry evaluates sawdust—a product which in itself is not commercially feasible but which supplies a profitable dividend as a waste from a more useful harvest.

The blood would be a simultaneous source of platelets, leukocytes, and red cells. By attaching a neomort to an IBM cell separator, we could isolate cell types at relatively low cost. The neomort could also be tested for the presence of hepatitis in a way that would be impossible with commercial donors. Hepatitis as a transfusion scourge would be virtually eliminated. Beyond the blood are rarer harvests. Neomorts offer a great potential source of bone marrow for transplant procedures, and I am assured that a bioemporium of modest size could be assembled to fit most transplantation antigen requirements. And skin would of course, be harvested—similarly bone, corneas, cartilage and so on.

Manufacturing

In addition to supplying components of the human body, some of which will be continually regenerated, the neomort can also serve as a manufacturing unit. Hormones are one obvious product, but there are others. By the injection of toxins, we have a source of antitoxin that does not have the complication of coming from another animal form. Antibodies from most of the major diseases can be manufactured merely by injecting the neomort with the viral or bacterial offenders.

Perhaps the most encouraging extension of the manufacturing process emerges from the new cancer research, in which immunology is coming to the fore. With certain blood cancers, great hope attaches to the use of antibodies. To take just one example, it is conceivable that leukemia could be generated in individual neomorts—not just to provide for *in vivo* (so to speak) testing of antileukemic modes of therapy but also to generate antibody immunity responses which could then be used in the living.

COST-BENEFIT ANALYSIS

If seen only as the harvesting of products, the entire feasibility of such research would depend on intelligent cost-benefit analysis. Although certain products would not warrant the expense of maintaining a community of neomorts, the enormous expense of other products, such as red cells with unusual antigens, would certainly warrant it. Then, of course, the equation is shifted. As soon as one economically sound reason is found for the maintenance of the community, all of the other ingredients become gratuitous by-products, a familiar problem in manufacturing. There is no current research to indicate the maintenance cost of a bioemporium or even the potential duration of an average neomort. Since we do not at this point encourage sustaining life in the brain-dead, we do not know the limits to which it could be extended. This is the kind of technology however, in which we have previously been quite successful.

Meantime, a further refinement of death might be proposed. At present we use total brain function to define brain death. The source of electroencephalogram activity is not known and cannot be used to distinguish between the activity of higher and lower brain centers. If, however, we are prepared to separate the concept of "aliveness" from "personhood" in the adult, as we have in the fetus, a good argument can be made that death should be defined not as cessation of total brain function but merely as cessation of cortical function. New tests may soon determine when cortical function is dead. With this proposed extension, one could then maintain neomorts without even the complication and expense of respirators. The entire population of decorticates residing in chronic hospitals and now classified among the incurably ill could be redefined as dead.

But even if we maintain the more rigid limitations of total brain death, it would seem that a reasonable population could be maintained if the purposes warranted it. It is difficult to assess how many new neomorts would be available each year to satisfy the demand. There are roughly 2 million deaths a year in the United States. The most likely sources of intact bodies with destroyed brains would be accidents (about 113,000 per year), suicides (around 24,000 per year), homicides (18,000), and cerebrovascular accidents (some 210,000 per year). Obviously, in each of these categories a great many of the individuals would be useless—their bodies either shattered or scattered beyond value or repair.

And yet, after all the benefits are outlined, with the lifesaving potential clear, the humanitarian purposes obvious, the technology ready, the motives pure, and the material costs justified—how are we to reconcile our emotions? Where in this debit-credit ledger of limbs and livers and kidneys and costs are we to weigh and enter the repugnance generated by the entire philanthropic endeavor?

Cost-benefit analysis is always least satisfactory when the costs must be measured in one realm and the benefits in another. The analysis is particularly skewed when the benefits are specific, material, apparent, and immediate, and the price to be paid is general, spiritual, abstract, and of the future. It is that which induces people to abandon freedom for security, pride for comfort, dignity for dollars.

William May, in a perceptive article, defended the careful distinctions that have traditionally been drawn between the newly dead and the long dead. "While the body retains its recognizable form, even in death, it commands a certain respect. No longer a human presence, it sill reminds us of that presence which once was utterly inseparable from it." But those distinctions become obscured when, years later, a neomort will retain the appearance of the newly dead, indeed, more the appearance of that which was formerly described as living.

Philosophers tend to be particularly sensitive to the abstract needs of civilized man; it is they who have often been the guardians of values whose abandonment produces pains that are real, if not always quantifiable. Hans Jonas, in his *Philosophical Essays,* anticipated some of the possibilities outlined here, and defended what he felt to be the sanctity of the human body and the unknowability of the borderline between life and death when he insisted that "Nothing less than the maximum definition of death will do—brain death plus heart death plus any other indication that may be pertinent—before final violence is allowed to be done." And even then Jonas was only contemplating *temporary* maintenance of life for the collection of organs.

The argument can be made on both sides. The unquestionable benefits to be gained are the promise of cures for leukemia and other diseases, the reduction of suffering, and the maintenance of life. The proponents of this view will be mobilized with a force that may seem irresistible.

They will interpret our revulsion at the thought of a bioemporium as a bias of our education and experience, just as earlier societies were probably revolted by the startling notion of abdominal surgery, which we now take for granted. The proponents will argue that the revulsion, not the technology, is inappropriate.

Still there will be those, like May, who will defend that revulsion as a quintessentially human factor whose removal would diminish us all, and extract a price we cannot anticipate in ways yet unknown and times not yet determined. May feels that there is "a tinge of the inhuman in the humanitarianism of those who believe that the perception of social need easily overrides all other considerations and reduces the acts of implementation to the everyday, routine, and casual."

This is the kind of weighing of values for which the computer offers little help. Is the revulsion to the new technology simply the fear and horror of the ignorant in the face of the new, or is it one of those components of humanness that barely sustain us at the limited level of civility and decency that now exists, and whose removal is one more step in erasing the distinction between man and the lesser creatures—beyond that, the distinction between man and matter?

Sustaining life is an urgent argument for any measure, but not if that measure destroys those very qualities that make life worth sustaining.

Chapter *12*

What Does My Race Have to Do with Me?

A man is running down a country road. Two policemen in a cruiser pull up next to him and yell at him to stop. "Who are you? What are you doing here?" one of the officers asks him. "My name is Bob Smith," he replies. "I'm jogging." "Do you live around here?" the other policeman asks him. "Yes, I live on Maple Street," the man responds. "Show us your ID," the police demand, getting out of the car. "But I don't have any. I'm just out jogging!" the man says. "Where do you work, then?" "At Pratt Paper Company. I'm an account executive." "What's the name of the company president then?" "Brenda Schwartz, of course. But why are you asking me these questions?"

Beginning with Plato, there has been a tendency in Western philosophy to assume that a person's real identity is quite independent of the social and political circumstances in which he or she lives (see Chapter 8). This notion of what we might think of as a "context free" identity underlies much of traditional ethics as well (see Chapter 15). That is, your race, gender, and class status aren't thought to be important in attempting to discover whether your actions are morally good, or whether you are a good person. In this chapter, you will have the opportunity to explore the extent to which race actually does figure in the identities and in the moral lives of people who live in a racist society—namely, all of us.

Is the story about Bob puzzling? Why, indeed, are the policemen so suspicious and so lacking in trust? Suppose we add to the story the fact that Bob is black and the policemen are white. Suddenly, the story becomes less puzzling. And yet, in order to understand why something like this might happen, it is necessary to explore carefully the variety of ways in which racism manifests itself in our society. The fact that the policemen stop a black man who is running down the road may well be a function of their having a stereotypical notion that a black person who is running must be trying not to get caught for doing something wrong. Furthermore, if the community in which Bob is running is largely white, his mere presence may be considered grounds for suspicion. The fact that the policemen are inclined to believe that Bob is lying about his employment indicates their tendency to think that blacks can't be account executives. Indeed, in our society it is the case that black people are less likely than white people to be jogging down country roads in middle-class communities. It is also less likely that they will be account executives. So, the racism of our society does make Bob an anomaly. This may explain the responses of the policemen, but does it justify them?

The readings in this chapter are designed to address the ways in which particular practices, attitudes, and institutions serve to perpetuate racism and thereby define the context within which white people and people of color negotiate their individual identities and their relationships with one another. The essay by Jean-Paul Sartre focuses on anti-Semitism. While anti-Semitism may be properly understood as discrimination on the basis of ethnicity rather than race, Sartre's analysis of anti-Semitism provides an account of the psychological mechanisms involved in the sort of thinking that underlies the hatefulness of discrimination in a more general sense. For Sartre, the overtly anti-Semitic person is driven by a passionate hatred of Jews that serves to buttress his own self-esteem. He attempts to overcome his own mediocrity by constructing another group of people as essentially inferior to him. Laurence Thomas discusses the significance of his own role as a black professor. Why should race or gender matter if the most important thing a professor does is to convey knowledge to his or her students? Thomas raises these questions in the context of current arguments about the legitimacy of affirmative action policies designed to correct the effects of discrimination against women and racial minorities. He argues that diversity within an academic institution provides the basis for wider intellectual affirmation, a prerequisite to success within such an environment. Hence, affirmative action is one step in countering the racism and sexism that have prevented racial minorities and women respectively from thriving either as faculty or as students.

Shelby Steele argues that recent calls to establish black identity have exaggerated the dynamics of racism in our society. According to him, the insistence on invoking black power in response to white power precludes the possibility of moral accountability altogether. Steele contends that black power, as a political position, encourages blacks to think of themselves as innocent and white people as guilty. This, he thinks, makes impossible social and personal exchange between whites and blacks. Rather than serving to promote the well-being of black people, black power as a strategy for social change simply serves to perpetuate the suspicion and ignorance that help racism to flourish. Elizabeth V. Spelman, on the other hand, would be wary of Steele's position. Given the power that white people have exercised over black people, there is the danger that the experiences, beliefs, and behavior of white people will continue to serve as the standard by which everyone is judged. Thus, even at a very basic level—namely, that of the body—those whose bodies are different from those of white people will be seen as deviant or inferior. For Spelman, it is particularly important to look at the way in which sexism and racism together insure that black women, given that they are neither white nor male, will doubly fall short of the white male standard.

The essay by Michael Eric Dyson takes up the joint issues of sexism, classism, and racism in contemporary United States culture. His discussion focuses on two cases that arose in the late 1980s: the obscenity trial of 2 Live Crew, and the rape of a woman in Central Park. By comparing public response to these incidents, Dyson demonstrates the ways in which gender, class, and race operate differently in black and in white communities. His discussion helps us to understand how important social values, such as sexual equality, racial equality and freedom of speech, come into conflict with one another in particular cases.

The next two selections in the chapter focus on the issue of racist speech. The First Amendment protects the right to free speech, which many people believe to be one of the most fundamental rights in a democracy. Any restriction of speech is viewed as a threat to the free expression and exchange of conflicting ideas and values that are so crucial to a pluralistic society such as our own. Nevertheless, it is clear that some speech really is hateful and harmful. If a black student finds notes on her dormitory door saying "Nigger, go back to Africa," it will be very difficult for her to function successfully in college. When the Ku Klux Klan chants racist epithets as it marches down the street in an integrated city, it may exaggerate racial tensions there even after it leaves. Thus, some people have argued that racist speech ought not be protected by the First Amendment, that it must be restricted.

Ira Glasser disagrees. In spite of the profoundly hateful and harmful effects of racist speech, he thinks that the legal restriction of it compromises the very values that must be upheld in order to eliminate racism. He focuses on the issue of racist speech on college and university campuses. Rather than banning racist speech, he argues that such institutions must provide an environment that encourages racial equality and respect. Charles Lawrence, on the other hand, makes the case for restricting racist speech and argues that doing so is consistent with Constitutional principles. By taking the victim's perspective, he argues, we can better appreciate the real harm that is done by racist speech. Protection from such harm, he insists, is also guaranteed by the Constitution and so must be weighed carefully against the right to free speech.

Amy Tan's story, which is part of her novel *The Joy Luck Club,* recounts the tensions between a mother and her daughter. In this case, the mother is a Chinese immigrant who views the United States as the land of limitless opportunity, as a place where anybody, especially her own daughter, can become rich and famous. The daughter, born and raised in America, just wants to be herself, though the fact that she is both Chinese and American makes it unclear just what that self might be. The story is a compelling account of the challenge of living at the intersection of two radically different cultures.

JEAN-PAUL SARTRE

Anti-Semite and Jew

JEAN-PAUL SARTRE, *a leader of the existentialist movement, was born in 1905 and died in 1980. He wrote numerous books, essays, and plays, including* No Exit, Nausea, Existentialism and Humanism, *and* The Wall. *In 1964, he turned down the Nobel Prize for literature.*

I F the Jew did not exist, the anti-Semite would invent him . . . Anti-Semitism is a free and total choice of oneself, a comprehensive attitude that one adopts not only toward Jews but toward men in general, toward history and society; it is at one and the same time a passion and a conception of the world . . . [O]rdinarily hate and anger have a *provocation:* I hate someone who has made me suffer, someone who condemns or insults me . . . [A]nti-Semitic passion could not have such a character. It precedes the facts that are supposed to call it forth: it seeks them out to nourish itself upon them; it must even interpret them in a special way so that they may become truly offensive. Indeed, if you so much as mention a Jew to an anti-Semite, he will show all the signs of a lively irritation. If we recall that we must always *consent* to anger before it can manifest itself and that, as is indicated so accurately by the French idiom, we "put ourselves" into anger, we shall have to agree that the anti-Semite has *chosen* to live on the plane of passion. It is not unusual for people to elect to live a life of passion rather than one of reason. But ordinarily they love the *objects* of passion: women, glory, power, money. Since the anti-Semite has chosen hate, we are forced to conclude that it is the *state* of passion that he loves. . . .

How can one choose to reason falsely? Is it because of a longing for impenetrability? The rational man groans as he gropes for the truth; he knows that his reasoning is no more than tentative, that other considerations may supervene to cast doubt on it. He never sees very clearly where he is going; he is "open"; he may even appear to be hesitant. But there are people who are attracted by the durability of a stone. They wish to be massive and impenetrable; they wish not to change. Where, indeed, would change take them? We have here a basic fear of oneself and of truth. What frightens them is not the content of truth, of which they have no conception, but the form itself of truth, that thing of indefinite approximation. It is as if their own existence were in continual suspension. But they wish to exist all at once and right away. They do not want any acquired opinions; they want them to be innate. Since they are afraid of reasoning, they wish to lead the kind of life wherein reasoning and research play only a subordinate role, wherein one seeks only what he has already found, wherein one becomes only what he already was. This is nothing but passion . . .

If then, as we have been able to observe, the anti-Semite is impervious to reason and to experience, it is not because his conviction is strong. Rather his conviction is strong because he has chosen first of all to be impervious.

He has chosen also to be terrifying. People are afraid of irritating him. No one knows to what lengths the aberrations of his passion will carry him—but he knows, for this passion is not provoked by something external. He has it well in hand; it is obedient to his will: now he lets go the reins and now he pulls back on them. He is not afraid of himself, but he sees in the eyes of others a disquieting image—his own—and he makes his words and gestures conform to it. Having this external model, he is under no necessity to look for his personality within himself. He has chosen to find his being entirely outside himself, never to look within, to be nothing save the fear he inspires in others. What he flees even more than Reason is his intimate awareness of himself. . . .

. . . The anti-Semite has no illusions about what he is. he considers himself an average man, modestly average, basically mediocre. There is no example of an anti-Semite's claiming individual superiority over the Jews. But you must not think that he is ashamed of his mediocrity; he takes pleasure in it; I will even assert that he has chosen it. This man fears every kind of solitariness, that of the genius as much as that of the murderer; he is the man of the crowd. However small his stature, he takes every precaution to make it smaller, lest he stand out from the herd and find himself face to face with himself. He has made himself an anti-Semite because that is something one cannot be alone. The phrase, "I hate the Jews," is one that is uttered in chorus; in pronouncing it, one attaches himself to a tradition and to a community—the tradition and community of the mediocre.

We must remember that a man is not necessarily humble or even modest because he has consented to mediocrity. On the contrary, there is a passionate pride among the mediocre, and anti-Semitism is an attempt to give value to mediocrity as such, to create an elite of the ordinary. To the anti-Semite, intelligence is Jewish; he can thus disdain it in all tranquillity, like all the other virtues which the Jew possesses. They are so many ersatz attributes that the Jew cultivates in place of that balanced mediocrity which he will never have . . .

Thus I would call anti-Semitism a poor man's snobbery. . . . Anti-Semitism is not merely the joy of hating; it brings positive pleasures too. By treating the Jew as an inferior and pernicious being, I affirm at the same time that I belong to the elite. This elite, in contrast to those of modern times which are based on merit or labor, closely resembles an aristocracy of birth. There is nothing I have to do to merit my superiority, and neither can I lose it. It is given once and for all. It is a *thing*. . . .

We begin to perceive the meaning of the anti-Semite's choice of himself. He chooses the irremediable out of fear of being free; he chooses mediocrity out of fear of being alone, and out of pride he makes of his irremediable mediocrity a rigid aristocracy. To this end he finds the existence of the Jew absolutely necessary. Otherwise to whom would he be superior? Indeed, it is vis-à-vis the Jew and the Jew alone that the anti-Semite realizes that he has rights. If by some miracles all the Jews were exterminated as he wishes, he would find himself nothing but a concierge or a shopkeeper in a strongly hierarchical society in which the quality of "true Frenchman" would be at a low valuation, because everyone would possess it. He would lose his sense of rights over the country because no one would any longer contest them, and that profound equality which brings him close to the nobleman and the man of wealth would disappear all of a sudden, for it is primarily negative. His frustrations, which he has attributed to the disloyal competition of the Jew, would have to be imputed to some other cause, lest he be forced to look within himself. He would run the risk of falling into bitterness, into a melancholy hatred of the privileged classes. Thus the anti-Semite is in the unhappy position of having a vital need for the very enemy he wishes to destroy.

LAURENCE THOMAS

What Good Am I?

LAURENCE THOMAS *teaches philosophy at Syracuse University and writes in the areas of social philosophy and moral psychology. His most recent book is* Vessel of Evil: American Slavery and the Holocaust *(1994).*

WHAT good am I as a black professor? The raging debate over affirmative action surely invites me to ask this searching question of myself, just as it must invite those belonging to other so-called suspect categories to ask it of themselves. If knowledge is color-blind, why should it matter whether the face in front of the classroom is a European white, a Hispanic, an Asian, and so on? Why should it matter whether the person is female or male?

One of the most well-known arguments for affirmative action is the role-model argument. It is also the argument that I think is the least satisfactory—not because women and minorities do not need role models—everyone does—but because as the argument is often presented, it comes dangerously close to implying that about the only thing a black, for instance, can teach a white is how not to be a racist. Well, I think better of myself than that. And I hope that all women and minorities feel the same about themselves. It is a credit to the authors of this volume that they do not make much of this argument.

But even if the role-model argument were acceptable in some version or the other, affirmative action would still seem unsavory, as the implicit assumption about those hired as affirmative action appointments is that they are less qualified than those who are not. For, so the argument goes, the practice would be unnecessary if, in the first place, affirmative action appointees were the most qualified for the position, since they would be hired by virtue of their merits. I call this the counterfactual argument from qualifications.

Now, while I do not want to say much about it, this argument has always struck me as extremely odd. In a morally perfect world, it is no doubt true that if women and minorities were the most qualified they would be hired by virtue of their merits. But this truth tells me nothing about how things are in this world. It does not show that biases built up over decades and centuries do not operate in the favor of, say, white males over nonwhite males. It is as if one argues against feeding the starving simply on the grounds that in a morally perfect world starvation would not exist. Perhaps it would not. But this is no argument against feeding the starving now.

It would be one thing if those who advance the counterfactual argument from qualifications addressed the issue of built-up biases that operate against women and minorities. Then I could perhaps suppose that they are arguing in good faith. But for them to ignore these built-up biases in the name of an ideal world is sheer hypocrisy. It is to confuse what the ideal should be with the steps that should be taken to get there. Sometimes the steps are very simple or, in any case, purely procedural: instead of *A,* do *B;* or perform a series of well-defined steps that guarantee the outcome. Not so with nonbiased hiring, however, since what is involved is a change in attitude and feelings—not even merely a change in belief. After all, it is possible to believe something quite sincerely and yet not have the emotional wherewithal to act in accordance with that belief. It is this reality regarding sexism and racism that I believe is not fully appreciated in this volume.

The philosophical debate over affirmative action has stalled . . . because so many who oppose it, and some who do not, are unwilling to acknowledge the fact that sincere belief in equality does not entail a corresponding change in attitude and feelings in day-to-day interactions with women and minorities. Specifically, sincere belief does not eradicate residual and, thus, unintentional sexist and racist attitudes. So, joviality among minorities may be taken by whites as the absence of intellectual depth or sincerity on the part of those minorities, since such behavior is presumed to be uncommon among high-minded intellectual whites. Similarly, it is a liability for academic women to be too fashionable in their attire, since fashionably attired women are often taken by men as aiming to be seductive.

Lest there be any misunderstanding, nothing I have said entails that unqualified women and minorities should be hired. I take it to be obvious, though, that whether someone is the best qualified is often a judgment call. On the other hand, what I have as much as said is that there are built-up biases in the hiring process that disfavor women and minorities and need to be corrected. I think of it as rather on the order of correcting for unfavorable moral head winds. It is possible to be committed to gender and racial equality and yet live a life in which residual, and thus unintentional, sexism and racism operate to varying degrees of explicitness.

I want to return now to the question with which I began this essay: What good am I as a black professor? I want to answer this question because, insofar as our aim is a just society, I think it is extremely important to see the way in which it does matter that the person in front of the class is not always a white male, notwithstanding the truth that knowledge, itself, is color-blind.

Teaching is not just about transmitting knowledge. If it were, then students could simply read books and professors could simply pass out tapes or lecture notes. Like it or not, teachers are the object of intense emotions and feelings on the part of students solicitous of faculty approval and affirmation. Thus, teaching is very much about intellectual affirmation; and there can be no such affirmation of the student by the mentor in the absence of deep trust between them, be the setting elementary or graduate school. Without this trust, a mentor's practice will ring empty; constructive criticism will seem mean-spirited; and advice will be poorly received, if sought after at all. A student needs to be confident that he can make a mistake before the professor without being regarded as stupid in the professor's eyes and that the professor is interested in seeing beyond his weaknesses to his strengths. Otherwise, the student's interactions with the professor will be plagued by uncertainty; and that uncertainty will fuel the self-doubts of the student.

Now, the position that I should like to defend, however, is not that only women can trust women, only minorities can trust minorities, and only whites can trust whites. That surely is not what we want. Still, it must be acknowledged, first of all, that racism and sexism have very often been a bar to such trust between mentor and student, when the professor has been a white male and the student has been either a woman or a member of a minority group. Of course, trust between mentor and student is not easy to come by in any case. This, though, is compatible with women and minorities having even greater problems if the professor is a white male.

Sometimes a woman professor will be necessary if a woman student is to feel the trust of a mentor that makes intellectual affirmation possible; sometimes a minority professor will be necessary for a minority student; indeed, sometimes a white professor will be necessary for a white student. (Suppose the white student is from a very sexist and racist part of the United States, and it takes a white professor to undo the student's biases.)

Significantly, though, in an academy where there is gender and racial diversity among the faculty, that diversity alone gives a woman or minority student the hope that intellectual affirmation is possible. This is so even if the student's mentor should turn out to be a white male. For part of what secures our conviction that we are living in a just society is not merely that we experience justice, but that we see justice around us. A diverse faculty serves precisely this end in terms of women and minority students believing that it is possible for them to have an intellectually affirming mentor relationship with a faculty member regardless of the faculty's gender or race.

Naturally, there are some women and minority students who will achieve no matter what the environment. Harriet Jacobs and Frederick Douglass were slaves who went on to accomplish more than many of us will who have never seen the chains of slavery. Neither, though, would have thought their success a reason to leave slavery intact. Likewise, the fact that there are some women and minorities who will prevail in spite of the obstacles is no reason to leave the status quo in place.

There is another part of the argument. Where there is intellectual affirmation, there is also gratitude. When a student finds that affirmation in a faculty member, a bond is formed, anchored in the student's gratitude, that can weather almost anything. Without such ties there could be no "ole boy" network—a factor that is not about racism, but a kind of social interaction running its emotional course. When women and minority faculty play an intellectually affirming role in the lives of white male students, such faculty undermine a nonracist and nonsexist pattern of emotional feelings that has unwittingly served the sexist and racist end of passing the intellectual mantle from white male to white male. For what we want, surely, is not just blacks passing the mantle to blacks, women to women, and white males to white males, but a world in which it is possible for all to see one another as proper recipients of the intellectual mantle. Nothing serves this end better than the gratitude between mentor and student that often enough ranges over differences between gender and race or both.

Ideally, my discussion of trust, intellectual affirmation, and gratitude should have been supplemented with a discussion of nonverbal behavior. For it seems to me that what has been ignored by all of the authors is the way in which judgments are communicated not simply by what is said but by a vast array of nonverbal behavior. Again, a verbal and sincere commitment to equality, without the relevant change in emotions and feelings, will invariably leave nonverbal behavior intact. Mere voice intonation and flow of speech can be a dead giveaway that the listener does not expect much of substance to come from the speaker. Anyone who doubts this should just remind her- or himself that it is a commonplace to remark to someone over the phone that he sounds tired or "down" or distracted, where the basis for this judgment, obviously, can only be how the individual sounds. One can get the clear sense that one called at the wrong time just by the way in which the other person responds or gets involved in the conversation. So, ironically, there is a sense in which it can be easier to convince ourselves that we are committed to gender and racial equality than it is to convince a woman or a minority person; for the latter see and experience our nonverbal behavior in a way that we ourselves do not. Specifically, it so often happens that a woman or minority can see that a person's nonverbal behavior belies their verbal support of gender and racial equality in faculty hiring—an interruption here, or an all too quick dismissal or a remark there. And this is to say nothing of the ways in which the oppressor often seems to know better than the victim how the victim is affected by the oppression that permeates her or his life, an arrogance that is communicated in a myriad of ways. . . .

Before moving on let me consider an objection to my views. No doubt some will balk at the very idea of women and minority faculty intellectually affirming white male students. But this is just so much nonsense on the part of those balking. For I have drawn attention to a most powerful force in the lives of all individuals, namely trust and gratitude; and I have indicated that just as those feelings have unwittingly served racist and sexist ends, they can serve ends that are morally laudable. Furthermore, I have rejected the idea, often implicit in the role-model argument, that women and minority faculty are only good for their own kind. What is more, the position I have advocated is not one of subservience in the least, as I have spoken of an affirming role that underwrites an often unshakable debt of gratitude.

So, to return to the question with which I began this essay: I matter as a black professor and so do women and minority faculty generally, because collectively, if not in each individual case, we represent the hope, sometimes in a very personal way, that the university is an environment where the trust that gives rise to intellectual affirmation and the accompanying gratitude is possible for all, and between all peoples. Nothing short of the reality of diversity can permanently anchor this hope for ourselves and posterity.

... I do not advocate the representation of given viewpoints or the position that the ethnic and gender composition of faculty members should be proportional to their numbers in society. The former is absurd because it is a mistake to insist that points of view are either gender- or color-coded. The latter is absurd because it would actually entail getting rid of some faculty, since the percentage of Jews in the academy far exceeds their percentage in the population. If one day this should come to be true of blacks or Hispanics, they in turn would be fair game.

... [However], the continued absence of any diversity whatsoever draws attention to itself. My earlier remarks about nonverbal behavior taken in conjunction with my observations about trust, affirmation, and gratitude are especially apropos here. The complete absence of diversity tells departments more about themselves than no doubt they are prepared to acknowledge.

I would like to conclude with a concrete illustration of the way in which trust and gratitude can make a difference in the academy. As everyone knows, being cited affirmatively is an important indication of professional success. Now, who gets cited is not just a matter of what is true and good. On the contrary, students generally cite the works of their mentors and the work of others introduced to them by their mentors; and, on the other hand, mentors generally cite the work of those students of theirs for whom they have provided considerable intellectual affirmation.

Sexism and racism have often been obstacles to faculty believing that women and minorities can be proper objects of full intellectual affirmation. It has also contributed to the absence of women and minority faculty which, in turn, has made it well-nigh impossible for white male students to feel an intellectual debt of gratitude to women and minority faculty. Their presence in the academy cannot help but bring about a change with regard to so simple a matter as patterns of citation, the professional ripple effect of which will be significant beyond many of our wildest dreams.

If social justice were just a matter of saying or writing the correct words, then equality would have long ago been a *fait accompli* in the academy. For I barely know anyone who is a faculty member who has not bemoaned the absence of minorities and women in the academy, albeit to varying degrees. So, I conclude with a very direct question: Is it really possible that so many faculty could be so concerned that women and minorities should flourish in the academy, and yet so few do? You will have to forgive me for not believing that it is. For as any good Kantian knows, one cannot consistently will an end without also willing the means to that end. Onora O'Neill writes: "Willing, after all, is not just a matter of wishing that something were the case, but involves comitting oneself to doing something to bring that situation about when opportunity is there and recognized. Kant expressed this point by insisting that rationality requires that whoever wills some end wills the necessary means insofar as these are available." If Kant is right, then much hand-wringing talk about social equality for women and minorities can only be judged insincere.

SHELBY STEELE

I'm Black, You're White, Who's Innocent?

SHELBY STEELE *teaches history at San Jose State University in California. His book* The Content of Our Character: A New Vision of Race in America *(1990) received a National Book Critics Circle Award.*

IT is a warm, windless California evening, and the dying light that covers the redbrick patio is tinted pale orange by the day's smog. Eight of us, not close friends, sit in lawn chairs sipping chardonnay. A black engineer and I (we had never met before) integrate the group. A psychologist is also among us, and her presence encourages a surprising openness. But not until well after the lovely twilight dinner has been served, when the sky has turned to deep black and the drinks have long since changed to scotch, does the subject of race spring awkwardly upon us. Out of nowhere the engineer announces, with a coloring of accusation in his voice, that it bothers him to send his daughter to a school where she is one of only three black children. "I didn't realize my ambition to get ahead would pull me into a world where my daughter would lose touch with her blackness," he says.

Over the course of the evening we have talked about money, infidelity, past and present addictions, child abuse, even politics. Intimacies have been revealed, fears named. But this subject, race, sinks us into one of those shaming silences where eye contact terrorizes. Our host looks for something in the bottom of his glass. Two women stare into the black sky as if to locate the Big Dipper and point it out to us. Finally, the psychologist seems to gather herself for a challenge, but it is too late. "Oh, I'm sure she'll be just fine," says our hostess, rising from her chair. When she excuses herself to get the coffee, the two sky gazers offer to help.

With three of us now one, I am surprised to see the engineer still silently holding his ground. There is a willfulness in his eyes, and inner pride. He knows he has said something awkward, but he is determined not to give a damn. His unwavering eyes intimidate me. At last the host's head snaps erect. He has an idea. "The hell with coffee," he says. "How about some of the smoothest brandy you ever tasted?" An idea made exciting by the escape it offers. Gratefully we follow him back into the house, quickly drink his brandy, and say our good-byes.

An autopsy of this party might read: death induced by an abrupt and lethal injection of the American race issue. An accurate if superficial assessment. Since it has been my fate to live a rather integrated life, I have often witnessed sudden deaths like this. The threat of them, if not the reality, is a part of the texture of integration. In the late 1960s, when I was just out of college, I took a delinquent's delight in playing the engineer's role, and actually developed a small reputation for playing it well. Those were the days of flagellatory white guilt; it was such great fun to pinion some professor or housewife or, best of all, a large group of remorseful whites, with the knowledge of both their racism and their denial of it. The adolescent impulse to sneer at convention, to startle the middle-aged with doubt, could be indulged under the guise of racial indignation. And how could I lose? My victims—earnest liberals for the most part—could no more crawl out from under my accusations than Joseph K. in Kafka's *Trial* could escape the amorphous charges brought against him. At this odd moment in history the world was aligned to facilitate my immaturity.

About a year of this was enough: the guilt that follows most cheap thrills caught up to me, and I put myself in check. But the impulse to do it faded more slowly. It was one of those petty talents that is tied to vanity, and when there were ebbs in my self-esteem the impulse to use it would come alive again. In integrated situations I can still feel the faint itch. But then there are many youthful impulses that still itch, and now, just inside the door of mid-life, this one is least precious to me.

In the literature classes I teach, I often see how the presence of whites all but seduces some black students into provocation. When we come to a novel by a black writer, say Toni Morrison, the white students can easily discuss the human motivations of the black characters. But, inevitably, a black student, as if by reflex, will begin to set in relief the various racial problems that are the background of these characters' lives. This student's tone will carry a reprimand: the class is afraid to confront the reality of racism. Classes cannot be allowed to die like dinner parties, however. My latest strategy is to thank that student for his or her moral vigilance, and then appoint the young man or woman as the class's official racism monitor. But even if I get a laugh—I usually do, but sometimes the student is particularly indignant, and it gets uncomfortable—the strategy never quite works. Our racial division is suddenly drawn in neon. Overcaution spreads like spilled paint. And, in fact, the black student who started it all does become a kind of monitor. The very presence of this student imposes a new accountability on the class. I think those who provoke this sort of awkwardness are operating out of a black identity that obliges them to badger white people about race almost on principle. Content hardly matters. (For example, it made no sense for the engineer to expect white people to sympathize with his anguish over sending his daughter to school with *white* children.) Race indeed remains a source of white shame; the goal of these provocations is to put whites, no matter how indirectly, in touch with this collective guilt. In other words, these provocations I speak of are power moves, little shows of power that try to freeze the "enemy" in self-consciousness. They gratify and inflate the provocateur. They are the underdog's bite. And whites, far more secure in their power, respond with a self-contained and tolerant silence that is, itself, a show of power. What greater power than that of non-response, the power to let a small enemy sizzle in his own juices, to even feel a little sad at his frustration just as one is also complimented by it. Black anger always, in a way, flatters white power. In America, to know that one is not black is to feel an extra grace, a little boost of impunity.

I think the real trouble between the races in America is that the races are not just races but competing power groups—a fact that is easily minimized perhaps because it is so obvious. What is not so obvious is that this is true quite apart from the issue of class. Even the well-situated middle-class (or wealthy) black is never completely immune to that peculiar contest of power that his skin color subjects him to. Race is a separate reality in American society, an entity that carries its own potential for power, a mark of fate that class can soften considerably but not eradicate.

The distinction of race has always been used in American life to sanction each race's pursuit of power in relation to the other. The allure of race as a human delineation is the very shallowness of the delineation it makes. Onto this shallowness—mere skin and hair—men can project a false depth, a system of dismal attributions, a series of malevolent or ignoble stereotypes that skin and hair lack the substance to contradict. These dark projections then rationalize the pursuit of power. Your difference from me makes you bad, and your badness justifies, even demands, my pursuit of power over you—the oldest formula for aggression known to man. Whenever much importance is given to race, power is the primary motive.

But the human animal almost never pursues power without first convincing himself that he is *entitled* to it. And this feeling of entitlement has its own precondition: to be entitled one must first believe in one's innocence, at least in the area where one wishes to be entitled. By innocence I mean a feeling of essential goodness in relation to others and, therefore, superiority to others. Our innocence always inflates us and deflates those we seek power over. Once inflated we are entitled; we are in fact licensed to go after the power our inno-

cence tells us we deserve. In this sense, innocence is power. Of course, innocence need not be genuine or real in any objective sense, as the Nazis demonstrated not long ago. Its only test is whether or not we can convince ourselves of it.

I think the racial struggle in American has always been primarily a struggle for innocence. White racism from the beginning has been a claim of white innocence and, therefore, of white entitlement to subjugate blacks. And in the '60s, as went innocence so went power. Blacks used the innocence that grew out of their long subjugation to seize more power, while whites lost some of their innocence and so lost a degree of power over blacks. Both races instinctively understand that to lose innocence is to lower power (in relation to each other). Now to be innocent someone else must be guilty, a natural law that leads the races to forge their innocence on each other's backs. The inferiority of the black always makes the white man superior; the evil might of whites makes blacks good. This pattern means that both races have a hidden investment in racism and racial disharmony, despite their good intentions to the contrary. Power defined their relations, and power requires innocence, which, in turn, requires racism and racial division.

I believe it was this hidden investment that the engineer was protecting when he made his remark—the white "evil" he saw in a white school "depriving" his daughter of her black heritage confirmed his innocence. Only the logic of power explained this—he bent reality to show that he was once again a victim of the white world and, as a victim, innocent. His determined eyes insisted on this. And the whites, in their silence, no doubt protected their innocence by seeing him as an ungracious trouble-maker—his bad behavior underscoring their goodness. I can only guess how he was talked about after the party. But it isn't hard to imagine that his blunder gave everyone a lift. What none of us saw was the underlying game of power and innocence we were trapped in, or how much we needed a racial impasse to play that game.

When I was a boy of about twelve, a white friend of mine told me one day that his uncle, who would be arriving the next day for a visit, was a racist. Excited by the prospect of seeing such a man, I spent the following afternoon hanging around the alley behind my friend's house, watching from a distance as this uncle worked on the engine of his Buick. Yes, here was evil and I was compelled to look upon it. And I saw evil in the sharp angle of his elbow as he pumped his wrench to tighten nuts, I saw it in the blade-sharp crease of his chinos, in the pack of Lucky Strikes that threatened to slip from his shirt pocket as he bent, and in the way his concentration seemed to shut out the human world. He worked neatly and efficiently, wiping his hands constantly, and I decided that evil worked like this.

I felt a compulsion to have this man look upon me so that I could see evil—so that I could see the face of it. But when he noticed me standing beside his toolbox, he said only, "If you're looking for Bobby, I think he went up to the school to play baseball." He smiled nicely and went back to work. I was stunned for a moment, but then I realized that evil could be sly as well, could smile when it wanted to trick you.

Need, especially hidden need, puts a strong pressure on perception, and my need to have this man embody white evil was stronger than any contravening evidence. As a black person you always hear about racists but never meet any. And I needed to incarnate this odious category of humanity, those people who hated Martin Luther King Jr. and thought blacks should "go slow" or not at all. So, in my mental dictionary, behind the term "white racist," I inserted this man's likeness. I would think of him and say to myself, "There is no reason for him to hate black people. Only evil explains unmotivated hatred." And this thought soothed me; I felt innocent. If I hated white people, which I did not, at least I had a reason. His evil commanded me to assert in the world the goodness he made me confident of in myself.

In looking at this man I was *seeing for innocence*—a form of seeing that has more to do with one's hidden need for innocence (and power) than with the person or group one is looking at. It is quite possible, for example, that the man I saw that day was not a racist. He did absolutely nothing in my presence to indicate that he was. I invested an entire afternoon in seeing not the man but in seeing my innocence through the man. *Seeing for innocence* is, in this way, the essence of racism—the use of others as a means to our own goodness and superiority.

• • •

Black Americans have always had to find a way to handle white society's presumption of racial innocence whenever they have sought to enter the American mainstream. Louis Armstrong's exaggerated smile honored the presumed innocence of white society—I will not bring you your racial guilt if you will let me play my music. Ralph Ellison calls this "masking"; I call it bargaining. But whatever it's called, it points to the power of white society to enforce its innocence. I believe this power is greatly diminished today. Society has reformed and transformed— Miles Davis never smiles. Nevertheless, this power has not faded altogether; blacks must still contend with it.

Historically, blacks have handled white society's presumption of innocence in two ways: they have bargained with it, granting white society its innocence in exchange for entry into the mainstream; or they have challenged it, holding that innocence hostage until their demand for entry (or other concessions) was met. A bargainer says, *I already believe you are innocent (good, fair-minded) and have faith that you will prove it.* A challenger says, *If you are innocent, then prove it.* Bargainers *give* in hope of receiving; challengers *withhold* until they receive. Of course, there is risk in both approaches, but in each case the black is negotiating his own self-interest against the presumed racial innocence of the larger society. . . .

"Innocence is ignorance," Kierkegaard says, and if this is so, the claim of innocence amounts to an insistence on ignorance, a refusal to know. In their assertions of innocence both races carve out very functional areas of ignorance for themselves—territories of blindness that license a misguided pursuit of power. Whites gain superiority by not knowing blacks; blacks gain entitlement by not seeing their own responsibility for bettering themselves. The power each race seeks in relation to the other is grounded in a double-edged ignorance, ignorance of the self as well as the other.

The original sin that brought us to an impasse at the dinner party I mentioned at the outset occurred centuries ago, when it was first decided to exploit racial difference as a means to power. It was the determinism that flowed karmically from this sin that dropped over us like a net that night. What bothered me most was our helplessness. Even the engineer did not know how to go forward. His challenge hadn't worked, and he'd lost the option to bargain. The marriage of race and power depersonalized us, changed us from eight people to six whites and two blacks. The easiest thing was to let silence blanket our situation, our impasse.

I think the civil rights movement in its early and middle years offered the best way out of America's racial impasse: in this society, race must not be a source of advantage or disadvantage for anyone. This is fundamentally a *moral* position, one that seeks to breach the corrupt union of race and power with principles of fairness and human equality: if all men are created equal, then racial difference cannot sanction power. The civil rights movement was conceived for no other reason than to redress that corrupt union, and its guiding insight was that only a moral power based on enduring principles of justice, equality, and freedom could offset the lower impulse in man to exploit race as a means to power. Three hundred years of suffering had driven the point home, and in Montgomery, Little Rock, and Selma, racial power was the enemy and moral power the weapon.

An important difference between genuine and presumed innocence, I believe, is that the former must be earned through sacrifice, while the latter is unearned and only veils the quest for privilege. And there was much sacrifice in the early civil rights movement. The Gandhian principle of non-violent resistance that gave the movement a spiritual center as well as a method of protest demanded sacrifice, a passive offering of the self in the name of justice. A price was paid in terror and lost life, and from this sacrifice came a hard-earned innocence and a credible moral power.

Non-violent passive resistance is a bargainer's strategy. It assumes the power that is the object of the protest has the genuine innocence to morally respond, and puts the protesters at the mercy of that innocence. I think this movement won so many concessions precisely because of its belief in the capacity of whites to be moral. It did not so much demand that whites change as offer them relentlessly the opportunity to live by their own morality—to attain a true innocence based on the sacrifice of their racial privilege, rather than a false innocence based on presumed racial superiority. Blacks always bargain with or challenge the larger society; but I believe that in the early civil rights years, these forms of negotiation achieved a degree of integrity and genuineness never seen before or since.

In the mid-'60s all this changed. Suddenly a sharp *racial* consciousness emerged to compete with the moral consciousness that had defined the movement to that point. Whites were no longer welcome in the movement, and a vocal "black power" minority gained dramatic visibility. Increasingly, the movement began to seek racial as well as moral power, and thus it fell into a fundamental contradiction that plagues it to this day. Moral power precludes racial power by denouncing race as a means to power. Now suddenly the movement itself was using race as a means to power,

and thereby affirming the very union of race and power it was born to redress. In the end, black power can claim no higher moral standing than white power.

It makes no sense to say this shouldn't have happened. The sacrifices that moral power demands are difficult to sustain, and it was inevitable that blacks would tire of these sacrifices and seek a more earthly power. Nevertheless, a loss of genuine innocence and moral power followed. The movement, splintered by a burst of racial militancy in the late '60s, lost its hold on the American conscience and descended more and more to the level of secular, interest-group politics. Bargaining and challenging once again became racial rather than moral negotiations.

You hear it asked, why are there no Martin Luther Kings around today? I think one reason is that there are no black leaders willing to resist the seductions of racial power, or to make the sacrifices moral power requires. King understood that racial power subverts moral power, and he pushed the principles of fairness and equality rather than black power because he believed these principles would bring blacks their most complete liberation. He sacrificed race for morality, and his innocence was made genuine by that sacrifice. What made King the most powerful and extraordinary black leader of this century was not his race but his morality.

Black power is a challenge. It grants whites no innocence; it denies their moral capacity and then demands that they be moral. No power can long insist on itself without evoking an opposing power. Doesn't an insistence on black power call up white power? (And could this have something to do with what many are now calling a resurgence of white racism?) I believe that what divided the races at the dinner party I attended, and what divides them in the nation, can only be bridged by an adherence to those moral principles that disallow race as a source of power, privilege, status, or entitlement of any kind. In our age, principles like fairness and equality are ill-defined and all but drowned in relativity. But this is the fault of people, not principles. We keep them muddied because they are the greatest threat to our presumed innocence and our selective ignorance. Moral principles, even when somewhat ambiguous, have the power to assign responsibility and therefore to provide us with knowledge. At the dinner party we were afraid of so severe an accountability.

What both black and white Americans fear are the sacrifices and risks that true racial harmony demands. This fear is the measure of our racial chasm. And though fear always seeks a thousand justifications, none is ever good enough, and the problems we run from only remain to haunt us. It would be right to suggest courage as an antidote to fear, but the glory of the word might only intimidate us into more fear. I prefer the word effort—relentless effort, moral effort. What I like most about this word are its connotations of everydayness, earnestness, and practical sacrifice. No matter how badly it might have gone for us that warm summer night, we should have talked. We should have made the effort.

ELIZABETH V. SPELMAN

The Erasure of Black Women

ELIZABETH V. SPELMAN *teaches philosophy at Smith College. She has written widely in ancient philosophy and in feminist philosophy. She is the author of* Inessential Women.

RECENT feminist theory has not totally ignored white racism, though white feminists have paid much less attention to it than have black feminists. Nor have white feminists explicitly enunciated and espoused positions of white superiority. Yet much of feminist theory has reflected and contributed to what Adrienne Rich has called "white solipsism":

to think, imagine, and speak as if whiteness described the world.

not the consciously held **belief** that one race is inherently superior to all others, but a tunnel-vision which simply does not see nonwhite experience or existence as precious or significant, unless in spasmodic, impotent guilt-reflexes, which have little or no long-term, continuing momentum or political usefulness.

In this essay, I shall focus on what I take to be instances and sustaining sources of such solipsism in recent theoretical works by, or of interest to, feminists—in particular, certain ways of comparing sexism and racism, and some well-ingrained habits of thought about the source of women's oppression and the possibility of our liberation. . . . To begin, I will examine some recent prominent claims to the effect that sexism is more fundamental than racism. . . . Before turning to the evidence that has been given in behalf of that claim, we need to ask what it means to say that sexism is more fundamental than racism. It has meant or might mean several different though related things.

❦ It is harder to eradicate sexism than it is to eradicate racism.

❦ There might be sexism without racism but not racism without sexism: any social and political changes which eradicate sexism will have eradicated racism, but social and political changes which eradicate racism will not have eradicated sexism.

❦ Sexism is the first form of oppression learned by children.

❦ Sexism is historically prior to racism.

❦ Sexism is the cause of racism.

❦ Sexism is used to justify racism.

In the process of comparing racism and sexism, Richard Wasserstrom describes ways in which women and blacks have been stereotypically conceived of as less fully developed than white men. "Men and women are taught to see men as independent, capable, and powerful; men and women are taught to see women as dependent, limited in abilities, and passive. . . ." But who is taught to see black men as "independent, capable, and powerful," and by

whom are they taught? Are black men taught that? Black women? White men? White women? Similarly, who is taught to see black women as "dependent, limited in abilities, and passive"? If this stereotype is so prevalent, why then have black women had to defend themselves against the images of matriarch and whore?

Wasserstrom continues:

> As is true for race, it is also a significant social fact that to be a female is to be an entity or creature viewed as different from the standard, fully developed person who is male as well as white. **But to be female, as opposed to being black,** is not to be conceived of as simply a creature of less worth. That is one important thing that differentiates sexism from racism: the ideology of sex, as opposed to the ideology of race, is a good deal more complex and confusing. **Women are both put on a pedestal** and deemed not fully developed persons. (emphasis mine)

In this brief for the view that sexism is a "deeper phenomenon" than racism, Wasserstrom leaves no room for the black woman. For a black woman cannot be "female, as opposed to being black"; she is female *and* black. Since Wasserstrom's argument proceeds from the assumption that one is either female or black, it cannot be an argument that applies to black women. Moreover, we cannot generate a composite image of the black woman from the above, since the description of women as being put on a pedestal, or being dependent, never generally applied to black women in the United States and was never meant to apply to them.

Wasserstrom's argument about the priority of sexism over racism has an odd result, which stems from the erasure of black women in his analysis. He wishes to claim that in this society sex is a more fundamental fact about people than race. Yet his description of woman does not apply to the black woman, which implies that being black is a more fundamental fact about her than being a woman. I am not saying that Wasserstrom actually believes this is true, but that paradoxically the terms of his theory force him into that position. . . .

ADDITIVE ANALYSES

. . . [S]exism and racism do not have different "objects" in the case of black women. Moreover, it is highly misleading to say, without further explanation, that black women experience sexism and racism. For to say *merely* that suggests that black women experience one form of oppression, as *blacks*—the same thing black men experience—and that they experience another form of oppression, as *women*—the same thing white women experience. But this way of describing and analyzing black women's experience seems to me to be inadequate. For while it is true that images and institutions that are described as sexist affect both black and white women, they are affected in different ways, depending upon the extent to which they are affected by other forms of oppression.

For example, . . . it will not do to say that women are oppressed by the image of the "feminine" woman as fair, delicate, and in need of support and protection by men. While all women are oppressed by the use of that image, we are not oppressed in the same ways. As Linda Brent puts it so succinctly, "That which commands admiration in the white woman only hastens the degradation of the female slave." More specifically, as Angela Davis reminds us, "the

alleged benefits of the ideology of femininity did not accrue" to the black female slave—she was expected to toil in the fields for just as long and hard as the black male was.

Reflection on the experience of black women also shows that it is not as if one form of oppression is merely piled upon another. As Barbara Smith has remarked, the effect of multiple oppression "is not merely arithmatic." Such an "additive" analysis informs, for example, Gerda Lerner's remark about the nature of the oppression of black women under slavery: "Their work and duties were the same as that of the men, while childbearing and rearing fell upon them as an added burden." But, as Angela Davis has pointed out, the mother-housewife role (even the words seem inappropriate) doesn't have the same *meaning* for women who experience racism as it does for those who are not so oppressed:

> . . . In the infinite anguish of ministering to the needs of the men and children around her (who were not necessarily members of her immediate family), she was performing the **only** labor of the slave community which could not be directly and immediately claimed by the oppressor. . . . Even as she was suffering from her unique oppression as female, she was thrust by the force of circumstances into the center of the slave community.

The meaning and the oppressive nature of the "housewife" role has to be understood in relation to the roles against which it is contrasted. The work of mate/mother/nurturer has a different meaning depending on whether it is contrasted to work which has high social value and ensures economic independence, or to labor which is forced, degrading and unpaid. All of these factors are left out in a simple additive analysis. How one form of oppression (e.g., sexism) is experienced, is influenced by and influences how another form (i.e., racism) is experienced. So it would be quite misleading to say simply that black women and white women both are oppressed as *women,* and that a black woman's oppression as a black is thus separable from her oppression as a woman because she shares the latter but not the former with the white woman. An additive analysis treats the oppression of a black woman in a sexist and racist society as if it were a *further* burden than her oppression in a sexist but non-racist society, when, in fact, it is a *different* burden. As the article by Davis, among others, shows, to ignore the difference is to deny or obscure the particular reality of the black woman's experience.

If sexism and racism must be seen as interlocking, and not as piled upon each other, serious problems arise for the claim that one of them is more fundamental than the other. As we saw, one meaning of the claim that sexism is more fundamental than racism is that sexism causes racism: racism would not exist if sexism did not, while sexism could and would continue to exist even in the absence of racism. In this connection, racism is sometimes seen as something which is both derivative from sexism and in the service of it: racism keeps women from uniting in alliance against sexism. This view has been articulated by Mary Daly in *Beyond God the Father.* According to Daly, sexism is "root and paradigm" of other forms of oppression such as racism. Racism is a "deformity *within* patriarchy . . . It is most unlikely that racism will be eradicated as long as sexism prevails."

Daly's theory relies on an additive analysis, and we can see again why such an analysis fails to describe adequately black women's experience. Daly's analysis makes it look simply as if both black and white women experience sexism, while black women also experience racism. Black women should realize, Daly says, that they must see what they have in common with white women—shared sexist oppression—and see that black and white women are "pawns in the racial struggle, which is basically not the struggle that will set them free as *women."* The additive analysis obscures the differences between black and white women's struggles. Insofar as she is oppressed by racism in a sexist context and sexism in a racist context, the black woman's struggle cannot be compartmentalized into two struggles—one as a black and one as a woman. But that way of speaking about her struggle is required by a theory which insists not only that sexism and racism are distinct but that one might be eradicated before the other. Daly rightly points out that the black woman's struggle can easily be, and has usually been, subordinated to the black man's struggle in anti-racist organizations. But she does not point out that the black woman's struggle can easily be, and usually has been, subordinated to the white woman's struggle in anti-sexist organizations.

Daly's line of thought also promotes the idea that, were it not for racism, there would be no important differences between black and white women. Since sexism is the fundamental form of oppression, and racism works in its service, the only significant differences between black and white women are differences which men have created and which are the source of antagonism between women. What is really crucial about us is our sex; racial distinctions are one of the many products of sexism, of patriarchy's attempt to keep women from uniting. It is through our shared sexual identity that we are oppressed together; it is through our shared sexual identity that we shall be liberated together.

A serious problem in thinking or speaking this way, however, is that it seems to deny or ignore the positive aspects of "racial" identities. It ignores the fact that being black is a source of pride, as well as an occasion for being oppressed. It suggests that once racism is eliminated (!), black women no longer need be concerned about or interested in their blackness—as if the only reason for paying attention to one's blackness is that it is the source of pain and sorrow and agony. But that is racism pure and simple, if it assumes that there is nothing positive about having a black history and identity. . . .

RACISM AND SOMATOPHOBIA

. . . [F]eminist theorists as politically diverse as Simone de Beauvoir, Betty Friedan and Shulamith Firestone have described the conditions of women's liberation in terms which suggest that the identification of woman with her body has been the source of our oppression, and that, hence, the source of our liberation lies in sundering that connection. For example, de Beauvoir introduces *The Second Sex* with the comment that woman has been regarded as "womb"; woman is thought of as planted firmly in the world of "immanence," that is, the physical world of nature, her life defined by the dictates of their "biologic fate."

In contrast, men live in the world of "transcendence," actively using their minds to create "values, mores, religions," the world of culture as opposed to the world of nature. Among Friedan's central messages is that women should be allowed and encouraged to be "culturally" as well as "biologically" creative, because the former activities, which are "mental," are of "highest value to society" in comparison to childbearing and rearing—"mastering the secrets of atoms, or the stars, composing symphonies, pioneering a new concept in government or society." . . .

I bring up the presence of somatophobia in the work of Firestone and others because I think it is a force that contributes to white solipsism in feminist thought, in at least three related ways.

First, insofar as feminists do not examine somatophobia, but actually accept it and embrace it in prescriptions for women's liberation, we will not be examining what often has been an important element in racist thinking. For the superiority of men to women is not the only hierarchical relationship that has been linked to the superiority of the mind to the body. Certain kinds, or "races," of people have been held to be more body-like than others, and this has been meant as more animal-like and less god-like.

For example, in *The White Man's Burden*, Winthrop Jordan describes ways in which white Englishmen portrayed black Africans as beastly, dirty, highly sexed beings. Lillian Smith tells us in *Killers of the Dream* how closely run together were her lessons about the evil of the body and the evil of blacks.

Derogatory stereotypes of blacks versus whites (as well as of manual workers versus intellectuals) have been very similar to the derogatory stereo-types of women versus men. Indeed, the grounds on which Plato ridiculed women were so similar to those on which he ridiculed slaves, beasts and children that he typically ridiculed them in one breath. He also thought it suffi-cient ridicule of one such group to ac-cuse it of being like another (women are like slaves, slaves are like children, etc.). Aristotle's defense of his claim about the inferiority of women to men in the *Politics* is almost the same as his defense of the view that some people are meant to be slaves. (Aristotle did not identify what he called the natural class of slaves by skin color, but he says that identifying that class would be much easier if there were readily avail-able physical characteristics by which one could do that.) Neither in women nor in slaves does the rational element work the way it ought to. Hence women and slaves are, though in different ways, to attend to the physical needs of the men/masters/intellectuals. . . .

So we need to examine and under-stand somatophobia and look for it in our own thinking, for the idea that the work of the body and for the body has no part in real human dignity has been part of racist as well as sexist ideology. That is, oppressive stereotypes of "infe-rior races" and of women have typically involved images of their lives as deter-mined by basic bodily functions (sex, reproduction, appetite, secretions and excretions) and as given over to attend-ing to the bodily functions of others (feeding, washing, cleaning, doing the "dirty work"). Superior groups, we have been told from Plato on down, have bet-ter things to do with their lives. As Han-nah Arendt has pointed out, the position of women and slaves has been directly tied to the notion that their lives are to

be devoted to taking care of bodily functions. It certainly does not follow from the presence of somatophobia in a person's writings that she or he is a racist or a sexist. But somatophobia his-torically has been symptomatic of sexist and racist (as well as classist) attitudes.

Human groups know that the work of the body and for the body is necessary for human existence, and they make provisions for that fact. And so even when a group views its liberation in terms of being free of association with, or responsibility for, bodily tasks, ex-plicitly or implicitly, its own liberation may be predicated on the oppression of other groups—those assigned to do the body work. For example, if feminists decide that women are not going to be relegated to doing such work, who do we think is going to do it? Have we at-tended to the role that racism (and clas-sism) historically has played in settling that question?

Finally, if one thinks—as de Beau-voir, Friedan and Firestone do—that the liberation of women requires abstract-ing the notion of woman from the no-tion of woman's body, then one perhaps also will think that the liberation of blacks requires abstracting the notion of a black person from the notion of a black body. Since the body is thought to be the culprit (or anyway certain as-pects of the body are thought to be the culprits), the solution may seem to be: keep the person and leave the occa-sion for oppression behind. Keep the woman, somehow, but leave behind her woman's body; keep the black person but leave the blackness behind. . . .

Once the concept of woman is di-vorced from the concept of woman's body, conceptual room is made for the idea of a woman who is no particular historical woman—she has no color, no accent, no particular characteristics that require having a body. She is somehow all and only woman; that is her only identifying feature. And so it will seem inappropriate or beside the point to think of women in terms of any physical characteristics, especially if it has been in the name of such characteristics that oppression has been rationalized. . . .

RICH ON EMBODIMENT

. . . Adrienne Rich is perhaps the only well-known white feminist to have noted "white solipsism" in feminist theorizing and activity. I think it is no coincidence that she also noticed and attended to the strong strain of somatophobia in feminist theory. . . .

. . . Both de Beauvoir and Firestone wanted to break it by insisting that women need be no more connected—in thought or deed—with the body than men have been. De Beauvoir and Firestone more or less are in agreement, with the patriarchal cultural history they otherwise question, that embodiment is a drag. Rich, however, insists that the negative connection between woman and body be broken along other lines. She asks us to think about whether what she calls "flesh-loathing" is the only attitude it is possible to have toward our bodies. Just as she explicitly distinguishes between motherhood as experience and motherhood as institution, so she implicitly asks us to distinguish between embodiment as experience and embodiment as institution. Flesh-loathing is part of the well-entrenched beliefs, habits and practices epitomized in the treatment of pregnancy as a disease. But we need not experience our flesh, our body, as loathsome. . . . I think it is not a psychological or historical accident that having reflected so

thoroughly on flesh-loathing, Rich focused on the failure of white women to see black women's experience as different from their own. For looking at embodiment is one way (though not the only one) of coming to note and understand the *particularity* of experience. Without bodies we could not have personal histories, for without them we would not live at a particular time nor in a particular place. Moreover, without them we could not be identified as woman or man, black or white. This is not to say that reference to publicly observable bodily characteristics settles the question of whether someone is woman or man, black or white; nor is it to say that being woman or man, black or white, just means having certain bodily characteristics. But different meanings are attached to having those characteristics, in different places and at different times and by different people, and those differences make a huge difference in the kinds of lives we lead or experiences we have. Women's oppression has been linked to the meanings assigned to having a woman's body by male oppressors. Blacks' oppression has been linked to the meanings assigned to having a black body by white oppressors. We cannot hope to understand the meaning of a person's experiences, including her experiences of oppression, without first thinking of her as embodied, and second thinking about the particular meanings assigned to that embodiment. If, because of somatophobia, we think and write as if we are not embodied, or as if we would be better off if we were not embodied, we are likely to ignore the ways in which different forms of embodiment are correlated with different kinds of experience. . . . Rich does not run away from the fact that women have bodies, nor does she wish that women's bodies were not so different from men's. That healthy regard for the ground of our differences from men is logically con-

nected—though of course does not ensure—to a healthy regard for the ground of the differences between black women and white women. . . .

MICHAEL ERIC DYSON

Sex, Race, and Class: Two Cases

MICHAEL ERIC DYSON *teaches African-American studies at the University of North Carolina. Among his many publications are* Making Malcolm *(1995) and* Reflecting Black: African-American Cultural Criticism *(1993), from which the following selection is taken.*

SEX, race, and class have played a critical role in numerous American cultural revolutions during this century. The civil rights, feminist, and labor movements reflect the power of this provocative trio to spark social transformation, help define personal identity, draw attention to salient categories for social theory, and create coalitions between groups targeted by racial, sexual, and class oppression. But sex, race, and class have also caused considerable conflicts and tensions between groups who compete for limited forms of cultural legitimacy, visibility, and support. Two recent incidents in the public racial memory, the obscenity trial of the rap group 2 Live Crew and the Central Park jogging case, show how sex, race, and class are intricately intertwined and the source of significant anxieties between various feminists, civil libertarians, and black youth culture advocates.

On the surface, the jury trial of 2 Live Crew was straightforward. The rap group, led by rapper Luther Campbell, was charged with violating obscenity laws in an adults-only concert in Hollywood, Florida, on June 10, four days after a federal judge had ruled that the group's album, "As Nasty as They Wanna Be," was similarly obscene. After two weeks of testimony by both sides, 2 Live Crew was found innocent of the charges. In the process of the trial, however, a flurry of commentary and criticism was evoked. The 2 Live Crew controversy is at the center of a vortex of powerful social and cultural issues such as First Amendment rights to free expression, the force and extent of misogynist cultural impulses, and the function of race in judging controversial artistic expressions. How should we think about the issues raised by 2 Live Crew's trial?

There is little doubt that 2 Live Crew's rap artistry hinges on pornographic desires, misogynist impulses, and raucous sexual experimentation:

> To have her walkin' funny we try to abuse it / A big stinking pussy can't do it all / So we try real hard just to bust the walls / . . . Suck my dick, bitch / And make it puke . . . / Lick my ass up and down / Lick it till your tongue turn doo-doo brown / I'll break you down / And dick you long / I'll bust your pussy / Then break your backbone / Cause me so horny

Although most rap lyrics do not explicitly endorse such graphic sexual sentiments, much of rap is rooted in assumptions about women as exclusive objects of male sexual satisfaction that underwrite 2 Live Crew's artistic vision.

More pointedly, 2 Live Crew's sexism expresses cultural sentiments that, although outwardly prohibited, are frequently expressed in the subterranean, pornographic fantasies of men in a patriarchal culture that thrives on strategies of domination in infinitely adaptable guises, including racial, sexual, and class domination. Thus, a double standard of explicit denial and secret permission prevails in regard to sexism. Indeed, that double standard is depended upon to prevent the rupturing of a delicate balance between conscience and guilt where strident offenses are sometimes punished, while the behaviors and attitudes that underwrite sexism's logic, furnish its rationale, and consolidate its manifold practices often remain invisible and unchallenged.

This is not to suggest that one example of sexism is indistinguishable from the next. Some expressions of sexism, patriarchalism, and misogyny are so nefarious that they demand immediate, uncompromising response. My point is that a complex infrastructure of sexist attitudes, behaviors, actions, and ideology is constructed around the issue of gender in everyday American culture, and that infrastructure provides the background for sexism's coarser manifestations. Similar to racism, sexism's cruder expressions (as in 2 Live Crew lyrics) are supported and reinforced by a complex and subtle network of social relations, intellectual justifications, and cultural practices (e.g., glass ceilings placed on the careers of female managers in corporate America).

The 2 Live Crew controversy also surfaces repressed American cultural attitudes toward black male sexuality. Few images have caused more anxiety in the American sexual psyche than the black male embodiment of phallic prowess. A sordid range of stereotypes, jealousies, and fears have been developed around black men wielding their sexuality in ways that are perceived as untoward, unruly, or uncontrolled. Beyond stereotypes and jealousies, a range of sometimes lethal punishments have been practiced against black men, from lynching for "reckless eyeballing" of white women to outright genital castration. Indeed, black male sexual activity has often been historically viewed as inherently vulgar, and particularly dangerous when not directed toward its suitable sexual goal—black women. Thus, the fires of fear of black male sexuality were stoked by imagined black male transgression of proper sexual limits, particularly when the subject was social and sexual intercourse with white women. Fear of black male sexuality is often at root a fear of miscegenation.

The recordings and performances of 2 Live Crew symbolize the black phallus out of control, respecting no sexual territory as sacred, and penetrating the barriers that divide civilized sexual behavior from brutally objectifying and demeaning sex. For many white audiences, they are the frightening embodiment of *Soul on Ice*–era Eldridge Cleaver sexual excesses, with stock rape-as-revenge fantasies in tow. For many black audiences, they are sexual villains whose transgressive sexual behavior represents the weakening of communal bonds and the decline of moral imagination.

This latter fact makes it difficult to write off 2 Live Crew's lyrics as mere examples of black oral practices that employ bawdy humor to make their point. Duke literary critic Henry Louis Gates, who served as an expert defense witness, is right to point out 2 Live Crew's use of the established black oral practice of signifying, a rhythmic teasing and cajoling, often laced with lewd or off-color remarks that employ parody to either compliment or insult. But black oral practices must be placed in a wider cultural context that permits parallel features of that culture, like moral criticism, sage advice, or commonsense admonitions against out-of-bounds behavior, to enter the field of discussion. Failure to adopt such a viewpoint prevents critical distance on black oral practices. Such critical distance is necessary to assess their worth, judge their effectiveness in relation to comparable expressions within the genre, and describe their wider cultural value and social function. To show how 2 Live Crew employs parody does not suspend the necessity to subject their art to cultural and moral criticism. Their use of parody expresses a point of view about women that is disturbing, not least because they couch their misogyny in humorous terms that fail to envision its lethal consequences for women in fantasies of abusive sex

that may lead to, or result from, practices of vicious sexual domination.

We must be reminded that criticism of 2 Live Crew is also a form of self-criticism for most black communities, which continue to reflect the sexism of the larger society. A glaring example is the black church, where a kind of ecclesiastical apartheid is in effect: although black women constitute 70 percent of the membership of the church, they rarely have access to the central symbol of power, the pulpit—a more civilized expression of sexism, but sexism reinforced, sustained, and nourished, nonetheless.

The critique of 2 Live Crew must not, however, feign socio-political innocence, cultural purity, or moral neutrality. Similar cases for censorship and obscenity could be made against comedian Andrew Dice Clay's white racist routines and misogynist monologues, or rock group Guns N' Roses homophobic harangues and racist lyrics. Such examples point to the difficulty of deciding upon and describing national standards of obscenity and supplying convincing public arguments about the reasons that govern such judgments. According to the Supreme Court, an artistic creation is obscene if, by community standards, it appeals primarily to prurient interest or if it lacks serious artistic, literary, political, or scientific merit. One need not be steeped in contemporary moral or philosophical theory to understand that community standards of *anything* vary according to what community is being referred to; that interest-laden reason adjudicates competing claims about the true, the good, and the beautiful; and that our historical, political, economic, and social backgrounds affect our understanding of standards of obscenity, how to best apply them, and how to know when they have been fractured or offended.

That 2 Live Crew, as a result of the legal action its raps have occasioned, becomes the classic example of art combating censorship and claims of obscenity, when so many other prior examples abound, is plainly motivated by racial considerations, driven in part by the black male phallic paranoia discussed above. Furthermore, we must be aware of the social, economic, political, and cultural conditions that help shape the lives of young black males, and understand how rap music functions as a form of youthful black cultural resistance, artistic expression, and personal accomplishment.

Rap culture has provided a healthy and flourishing alternative to a burgeoning juvenocracy in the urban inner city, where young black (mostly) men under the age of twenty-five reign over significant segments of black postindustrial urban space, sustained on goods and services produced by an underground political economy of criminal activity that is centered on drugs. The chronic and structural unemployment of black men, the evaporation of social services to address the gap in black male income, and the deterioration of stable structures of institutional support have all contributed to the plight of black men. Rap music provides young black men with economic incentives, social goals, and cultural prominence to escape the urban inner city and avoid the political economy of criminal activity. Luther Campbell, 2 Live Crew's leader, emerged out of Miami's riot-torn Liberty City, beating poverty and crime through his rap vocation. The obscene conditions under which he matured should be outlawed.

Rap music has also transformed linguistic innovation and verbal experi-

mentation, a staple of diverse African-American rhetorical traditions, into a lucrative art. It has employed the rap concert as a public space of symbolic rejection of black bourgeois sensibilities, an arena for the linguistic refusal to accommodate conservative cultural and political forces, and a refuge from the tyrannizing surveillance of black speech practices exercised in mainstream cultural institutions.

The freedom of expression for rappers, even 2 Live Crew, must be protected. The 2 Live Crew controversy tests the limits of free expression in an increasingly complex cultural sphere where issues of racial, sexual, and class difference provoke thoughtful reexamination of cherished ideals like democracy, equality, and liberty. The First Amendment right to free expression may be conceived as a compromise between the authoritarian regulation of social expression and the potential anarchy of totally unlimited social expression. As with all rights-based defenses of fundamental freedoms, the right to free expression permits conflicting and contradictory expressions within its scope of protection.

Furthermore, the right to free expression often entails an alliance of conscience between ideological opponents who disagree about substantive moral, political, and social issues, but who defend the rights of others to express their views. For instance, some Christians have defended the right of non-Christians *not* to pray in public schools, and some civil rights activists have defended the right of the Ku Klux Klan to verbally express its vitriolic ideology of white racist supremacy. Thus, the speech of civil rights activists and Ku Klux Klan terrorists, as well as feminists and misogynists, should receive, *theoretically,* equal legal protection.

Only political naiveté or insularity would conclude that the right to free expression has been equitably applied throughout its tortuous tenure; as the old saw goes, the right to a free press belongs to those who own the press. So it is with the right to free expression: it belongs to those who control, manipulate, and shape expression, whether they be powerful presses, major corporate media conglomerates, or groups sufficiently aware that their right to free expression has been repressed. But as the civil rights movement proved, rights have sufficient interpretive flexibility to be employed on behalf of those who, despite their exclusion from the vision of the original intent of the law, are able to marshal ample resources of moral courage, social conscience, and intellectual acuity to resist the erosion, misapplication, or negligence of rights in defense of their perspectives, or even their lives.

In the 2 Live Crew case, the right to free expression has exhibited the possibility for interpretive resiliency and broad-based application to a range of provocative social issues. The recent controversy occasioned by the late Robert Mapplethorpe's homoerotic photography and the current crisis of confidence afflicting the National Endowment for the Arts, particularly over the work of nontraditional performance artists, for example, raise the specter of repressed cultural expression and limited artistic freedom. The 2 Live Crew jury clearly and explicitly ratified the principle of free artistic expression, even when it severely threatens mainstream modes of artistic creation. In their view, Luther Campbell and Thomas Jefferson deserve equal protection.

My appeal to maintain the right to free expression, however, does not absolve progressive peoples of responsibility to act to oppose the substance of an offensive viewpoint or set of cultural practices. Indeed, civic responsibility, manifest in civil disobedience, social activism, political resistance, and cultural engagement, is the necessary complement to civil rights. Civil responsibility must be exercised in vigorous and thoughtful measure to eradicate offensive social expressions that the right to free expression permits, and to place legal limits on harmful social practices.

While 2 Live Crew's *right* to express its artistic worldview should be protected, even by the most fervent feminist, that artistic worldview, which has profoundly disturbing social and cultural meanings, must be strongly and vociferously criticized. But 2 Live Crew's artistic worldview must be criticized on the basis of a civilly responsible resistance to their rap narratives, which glorify malicious sexual machismo, vilify female sexuality not exclusively linked to the desires of men, and eroticize violent and vengeful sexual behavior. But the implicit and racist swipe at young black male culture in the whole affair must not be overlooked when calls for legal response go forward. Informed criticism, yes; reactionary censorship, no.

The rape of a young white New York woman by as many as eight black and Hispanic teens in Central Park on April 19, 1989, provoked a deeply divided body of opinion about both the rape's elusive cause and its deleterious effects. In a way that couldn't be totally anticipated, commentary flowed forward from every quarter of New York and the nation, from the right, center, and left, whose only unity perhaps lies in the common sense of bewilderment, helplessness, and anger felt in the face of such seemingly inexplicable behavior. In the fray of attempted answers, no one is exactly sure why it happened, and why this particular incident catalyzed the attention and studied outrage of an entire city and country. What are we to make of the Central Park rape and the reaction it has occasioned?

The Central Park incident is so explosive because it captures the thorny knot of problems that have increasingly made New York City a microcosm of the racial, sexual, and class miseries afoot in American culture at large, a laboratory of societal ills that mount daily without cease or cure. How we understand their intricate interrelationship will ultimately determine how we view this event and perhaps set the agenda for how we should reshape sociopolitical practices structured around race, class, gender, and age.

The tendency of existing commentary is to privilege one aspect of the incident (e.g., race, gender) in relation to the other elements that make it a volatile issue. Such privileging activity may only create more confusion than it seeks to eliminate and may generate alienation among groups that have sound reasons for cooperative alliance. This does not negate the existence of tensions between and within, for example, African-American and feminist communities, but it means that the most helpful dialogue emerges when we understand how race, class, gender, and age all contributed to what occurred in Central Park on April 19. Otherwise, we are left with a sort of musical chairs scamper for ideological legitimacy that always leaves out a crucial component in accounting for what happened, while masking the real social, economic, and political roots of the various problems that converged that evening.

The severity of the sexual brutality exerted against a lone woman by several males rightfully occasioned the outrage of New York and the nation. Few rapes make the front page, and the sad fact is that we live in a culture that has not confronted the laxity of its attitudes, customs, and laws that grant varying degrees of permission to men to intrude upon and violate the sexual ownership by women of their own bodies. In New York City alone, over 3,500 women are the victims of reported rape, not counting the thousands of women who do not report being raped. A woman is raped in the United States every six minutes, and one out of every ten women will be victimized by rape. There has been an enormous increase in rape arrests of teens in New York (27 percent for boys under 18, 200 percent for boys under 13).

Also, the startling increase in date rapes, particularly on college campuses, and a prevalent attitude that further victimizes women by making them feel responsible for their own rape (through alleged provocative dressing or sexual innuendo) make for a very sad and sick scene. Thus, these teens are not perverted monsters or animals who exhibited such totally asocial, deviant, or aberrant behavior. In a very tragic sense what these youth did was an extreme expression, and logical outcome, of the persistence of antiquated views about women as objects of male sexual satisfaction that remain deeply ingrained in the folkways and mores of American culture, despite two solid decades of resistance and protest by feminists. This does not exonerate these teens, but simply seeks to explain how their behavior is more connected to present social practices and cultural attitudes than we would like to admit.

Unfortunately, however, even when they are reported, all rapes do not receive equal media or legal attention for various reasons, the sheer number of such crimes being one, our jaded sensibilities in regard to even outrageous crime being another. However, a clear and consistent principle has asserted itself in regard to such attention that may be summarized in the following way: who you are makes a big difference as to what will be done and said when a crime happens to you. In general, race, class, and gender are primary factors in determining the level of media attention, legal scrutiny, state concern, and even public sympathy developed around a particular crime. That rape is rarely big news exemplifies this truth. But even in usually low-visibility crimes, hierarchy prevails.

For instance, the press coverage of the Central Park event has drawn such heavy criticism, particularly from black circles, because it makes one thing clear: crime that victimizes black folk is not as important as crime that victimizes white folk. How media coverage constitutes some events as "newsworthy" is practically indistinguishable from prevailing attitudes about race, class, and gender that render some events more important than others. In a culture that through institutional practices, personal attitudes, societal norms, and political behavior has reinforced the devaluation of black life, it is no surprise that the media, judicial system, and city government reflect apathy or cool interest about crimes against blacks, crimes often committed by other blacks.

Thus, when a black woman was gang raped on the roof of a New York building and then thrown three stories a few days after the Central Park rape, remaining in critical condition in a New York hospital, it received little attention in the papers, nor was it made a priority of police investigation. This and a thousand other crimes occur in black neighborhoods across America, and yet they are rarely given front-page exposure by the media or priority treatment by the police. The point here is merely to reiterate what passes for common knowledge in black communities: black life is at a low premium, and to hurt, maim, or murder a black person carries little punitive consequence or public concern. (Thus, the same group of teens terrorized black and Hispanic people in a couple of neighborhoods before the Central Park rape, to little police response or media fanfare.) This, too, rightfully occasions the anger of blacks who witness the callous disregard for crime that victimizes blacks and other poor people, who must then suffer the consequences of their victimization in the pain of anonymous silence.

Painful, too, is the way in which the Central Park incident exposed the sexism that continues to plague most black communities. The definition of sexism and patriarchy in black circles has always been a touchy and tricky affair, primarily because of the central preoccupation with racism. While it may be argued that, given the denial of broad access to institutional power, black men have not by and large been able to set the political, economic, and social terms that regulate women's lives, we have often victimized black women with a form of sexist, machismo-laden behavior that compensated for debilitating forms of social emasculation under the sting of racism. Black women, for the most part, were encouraged, and coerced, to subordinate and suppress concerns about feminist liberation in fierce loyalty to the assumed primacy of obtaining racial liberation, which often meant black male acquisition of white male privilege, power, and position.

This set of relations has formed the premise of black male–female relations: they are locked together in common struggle against racism, while sexism is deeply inscribed in the social practices of their limited, and limiting, world. Also, a high degree of violence often mediates black male–female relations. So while black folk have given a particular social twist and specific historical nuance to male–female relations, basic features of that relationship, including violence and repression, cut across lines of race, class, and regrettably, as Central Park shows, even age.

Simply put then, black communities must begin facing up to the lethal consequences of our own sexism. The time is over for expecting black women to be silent about the sexual violence and personal suppression they experience in ostensible fidelity to our common cause. They must no longer be forced to choose between being women or being black—they are both. Rather, our moral purview must be expanded to include problems of sexism as central to the struggle of black communities across America. Subordinating the question of gender oppression to racism only means that we are complicit in encouraging sexist stereotypes, patriarchal posturing, and misogynistic behavior among a younger generation of black males, especially among our teens, adversely affecting the entire community.

What is also deeply disturbing about our youth in Central Park is that they exhibited a mobile nihilism, a denial of norms and sanctions in gratuitous violence that bespeaks an internalization of the terror that has besieged black urban communities, of both working-class and underclass varieties. There has been a definite shift in the balance of power in relations between young black teens and parental and other authority figures, largely because of the erosion of family life, the subversion of stable economic infrastructures in black communities, and the emergence of an underground political economy that thrives on illegal activity and dispenses an accompanying psychic and social capital of its own making. Thus, there is a burgeoning juvenocracy that is generating its own rules of behavior and establishing its own laws of survival. This explains in part the incident in Central Park, even among working-class youth, who fasten onto the folklore and culture of this juvenocracy, which is able to present strategies of survival in a tough, violent world by being (on the) offensive: set the terms of violence yourself, it seems to say, and you have a better chance of survival.

But in one sense, they are highly mimetic, and even parasitic. Central Park is not simply an exceptional event, outside the parameters of usual activity, and these youth are not animals deserving of "Trumped"-up xenophobia and class hatred. These youth are simply the newest twist on a classic American phenomenon: violence. Violence created America (the Revolution), was employed to secure free labor to build its economy and institutions (slavery), informed our national self-identity as the most potent purveyor of world destruction (Hiroshima, Nagasaki), and has been used in countless ways to maintain domestic civility, often stigmatizing specific groups in unconscionable strategies of containment (e.g., state repression aimed at blacks at the height of the civil rights movement).

Furthermore, violence is as fresh to America as the cowboy captivity of the presidency of Ronald Reagan, and is a pervasive part of the American social imagination as reflected in the cult of film stars and characters who reign as popular heroes. Indeed, these figures are a crucial part of the taxonomy of American violence, and each person or character has generated a justification of violence in various ways as they have become key words in our common cultural parlance. Witness our valorization of Rambo reflexes (passionate violence marshaled forward in face of personal injustice), Schwarzenegger sentiments (technically precise violence with merciless execution), the Eastwood ethic (Dirty Harry's cool, dispassionate violence wielded in the name of the state as antihero), Bronson brutality (vigilante violence directed against so-called social refuse, usually young black and Latino men), and Norris nuances (highly stylized violence tainted with strong traces of xenophobia).

In the final analysis, then, Central Park is not so distant from us as we would like to believe, not so far from our making as we would avow. Naive avoidance of hard realities will not do. Central Park is a relatively safe social space for many of New York's privileged, including upwardly mobile professionals. Part of the outrage, then, is occasioned by the perceived violation of the unwritten codes of protective distance that police that space. (Thus many responses were built upon the premise that "we" could take "our" park back.) It will not help to reinforce pernicious stereotypes about black men, increasing the already rampant sociosexual fear that continues to exist between black

men and white women, and especially in the minds of many white men. Neither will it benefit us to deny the vicious violence that is nourished from sexist attitudes that prevail in most minority and mainstream communities. And finally, "wilding" is the social expression among particular groups of teens of the violence that is central to American culture and rooted in factors involving race, class, age, and gender. All of these factors are crucial in understanding what went wrong in Central Park. And all of these categories must be taken seriously in attempting to describe what it will take to make things go right, not only in New York, but in our nation at large.

The 2 Live Crew controversy, as well as the Central Park jogger case, have provoked animated discussions about First Amendment rights to free expression, feminist resistance to misogynist cultural expressions, the role of race in assessing and understanding controversial art, and the lethally sexist social and cultural environment that tolerate and promote violence toward women. To the degree that such discussion heightens not only our awareness of such vital issues, but also quickens our pulse for sustained cultural engagement around such crucial cultural themes, the discussions will prove fruitful. These two incidents also show how the postmodern politics of race, class, and gender gather and order complex and uncomfortable meanings, challenging any easy alliance among groups that have a desperate interest in coalitional survival. Only through careful thinking and conscientious action can we hope to benefit from our failed connections, our substantive disagreements, and our hard-won solidarity.

IRA GLASSER

Talking Liberties

IRA GLASSER *is the executive director of the American Civil Liberties Union, the motto of which is the famous quotation from Thomas Jefferson, "Eternal vigilance is the price of liberty."*

I grew up at a time when people believed in the power of integration to solve the problem of racial prejudice. During those years, it seemed that if the legal structures supporting racism in this country were dismantled, the playing field would become level, and in our lifetimes we would see racial bias wither, if not entirely disappear. Integration in all areas, but especially in education, was the great hope. Integrated education, we believed, would cause all those attitudes the young had inherited from a culture of racism to fade away.

Do I still believe? I'll come back to that question.

The epidemic of racist incidents that has raged in recent years on college campuses has severely tested my faith. Twenty-five years after the civil rights movement culminated in the passage of landmark legislation prohibiting racial discrimination in voting, housing, employment and public accommodations, the Supreme Court has eroded some of that legislation, the President has vetoed a Congressional effort to restore it, and too many young people feel it's legitimate to be openly racist.

How alarming, puzzling and frustrating it is for those of my generation to observe that even though all the laws we wanted were passed, we confront a racial climate in 1990 that seems in some ways worse instead of better. It is

as if racism was a layered structure from which only the hard outer shell has been removed: Gone are the Bull Connors with their cattle prods, the George Wallaces standing in the schoolhouse door, the Selma sheriffs, the folks who killed people for trying to vote. Gone are some of the patterns of employment discrimination. Yet, increasingly, Americans are living in two separate societies, and separation among the young is especially hard to swallow.

The incidents that trigger campus racial flare-ups vary. It could be one student hurling a racial epithet at another or a fraternity holding a mock slave auction; a speech somebody makes or the choice of a guest speaker; an article written, or a statement made, by a professor; disagreements about curricula or about affirmative action. Whatever the catalyst, it provokes the sometimes brutal expression of racial animus. Of course, the racial animus was always there. But the problem has moved to a new level now that white kids seem, suddenly, to feel *comfortable* yelling nigger or harassing people on the basis of race.

Many universities have responded to this development in a distressing way. The solution to the problem, they've decided, is to pass rules outlawing racist speech. Those of us who believe that freedom of speech and academic freedom are just as important as equal opportunity and racial justice, and who believe that universities must protect free speech *and* promote equal opportunity, have naturally opposed the speech restrictions. So in Michigan, New York, California, Connecticut and Wisconsin, the ACLU vigorously opposed college regulations that restricted free speech.

Campus bans on racist speech should also be opposed because, strategically, they are a trap for minority students. Although such bans are intended to protect minorities against racial slurs, that is not the only way they can be used. The decision as to how and against whom to enforce speech restrictions rests, not with the minorities themselves, but with authorities who have far more power than minorities have. Minorities do not have an interest in ceding enforcement decisions to any of those authorities. If a rule is passed that allows the banning of offensive speech, then inevitably minority speakers will be frequent targets of that rule. In the 1960s, Malcolm X would have been a target. In short, such rules are like poison gas: It can be blown back in your face with powerful fans by your enemies in high places. Hurtful as racist name-calling is, minorities never have an interest in supporting bans on speech.

To the contrary, the First Amendment is often an important strategic weapon for minorities, who, having serious grievances and lacking the power possessed by the government and other authorities, require free speech more than anybody else as a means of spotlighting their grievances. The people who were on the front lines with Martin Luther King, Jr. in the early '60s instruct us that the First Amendment was the best friend civil rights activists had. Why? Because every time they marched, picketed, demonstrated and protested to dra-

matize to the nation what was going on down South, the sheriffs would arrest them under ordinances (every Southern town had one) that prohibited activities the white majority found offensive or emotionally distressing. And what offended and distressed the white Southern majority was black and white people—particularly black men and white women—marching hand in hand. When King and his colleagues landed in jail, as they frequently did, it was the First Amendment that got them out.

Of course, colleges are not precluded from punishing harassment or intimidation, which is criminal conduct in many instances. And words used to accompany such conduct do not immunize it against sanction. For example, a threatening phone call made to a black woman in her dorm room in the middle of the night is not protected by the First Amendment. But if all we're talking about is unpleasant public expression that insults whole classes of people, such speech has to be protected. First Amendment principles either protect everyone or we are all vulnerable to the discretion of public authorities.

When universities react to campus racism by simply curbing speech, they're often tap dancing to divert attention away from the underlying problem. *The underlying problem is racism, not racist speech.* That is why the ACLU has not only opposed speech restrictions but has also criticized the failure of many universities to deal with student bigotry seriously.

Universities must address the problem of racism in a variety of ways: through more vigorous recruitment of minority faculty and students; by changing Eurocentric curricula that marginalize and/or ignore the contributions of minorities to American culture;

and by investigating why it is that minority students feel isolated and unwelcome on most supposedly "integrated" campuses.

Here's one example of how minorities can be made to feel marginalized. At one state university, where minorities comprise 20 percent of the student body, the reality of campus life is one of almost total segregation. Whites and minorities rarely mingle. Few whites and minorities are friends. They eat separately. They party separately. Segregation today has become something deeper than denying people access to an education based on skin color: It is now a matter of language and music and style.

There was a music course at that university called "Beethoven For Non-Music Majors." The course was offered because Beethoven is an icon of Western culture and, presumably, every educated person, even if he or she doesn't aspire to become a professional musician, needs to know something about Beethoven. Yet at this same "integrated" university, there was no course called "Duke Ellington For Non-Music Majors"—which said to the black kids that European music is important, but indigenous American music, created by an American of African descent, is not. That sort of "integration" feels to many black students as if they are being subordinated and marginalized. It tells them that all "integration" means is that you blacks should learn about "us" and what we've generated, but we whites don't need to learn about you and what you've generated because you blacks aren't important.

Most of the black students didn't take the Beethoven course as a kind of protest and were perceived by many white students and some faculty as anti-

intellectual. Some whites said they expected blacks not to take the course because most of them "were probably here because of affirmative action anyway."

Such broadly held attitudes only get spoken out loud every now and then, in a moment of tension, or when somebody loses his temper or drinks too much. And when something gets said, the university is embarrassed, so their goal is to get past the incident as quickly as possible. So they outlaw the expression. The universities never seem to ask, what is the underlying problem that produced the expression?

Most white students come to college campuses today from highly segregated communities, where they attended de facto segregated schools. They've had no substantial multiracial contacts, and they've grown up hearing our major political leaders state that the civil rights movement has achieved all of its goals, equality is here, and affirmative action is reverse discrimination. If blacks can't make it, it's no longer due to racism; it's due to their own inadequacy—that's the message many white kids cut their teeth on in this country. Then we throw them together with minorities in college dorms and call it "integration." And we're surprised when seemingly mundane conflicts erupt into racial confrontations.

Example: There's a black and a white party going on in the dorm on Saturday night. The white kids are playing Elvis and the black kids are playing Public Enemy—one of whose songs trashes Elvis. The music is so loud on both sides that it's intrusive. So they keep turning it up until everybody's irritated. They have an argument, in the course of which somebody spews out a racial epithet. And then the university pretends that the epithet is the problem, as if you could make the children play nicely, and make the problem go away, just by suppressing that epithet.

The truth is that many universities aren't anxious to do the hard work of revamping their educational programs to correct the marginalization of minority cultural achievements, or to teach 18-year-olds to lie together in a multiracial society. They would rather take the low road of restricting racist speech because the minority students were up in arms and "we had to make a gesture." That gesture is meaningless, destructive and counterproductive.

There is no clash between the constitutional right of free speech and racial equality. Both are crucial to society. Moreover, the persistent problem of racial prejudice and bigotry cannot be swept under a rug of rules that violate freedom of speech and academic freedom, which are the lifeblood of universities.

Universities should go to the heart of the matter: Let them consider, for example, having a required course on the history of racism in this society. Let them embrace as part of their role the task of educating people about the meaning of life in a pluralistic democracy. What about counseling programs on race relations for new students? We have orientation programs for students on nearly everything—on sexism and date rape, on what to do if you're homesick, on how to acquire good study habits, on word-processing, on speed-reading. Where are the programs to teach people how to respect differences, how to appreciate each other's contributions?

Universities (and the rest of us, too) ought to think about what integration means beyond the numbers. They should stop restricting speech and start *teaching. Brown v. Board of Education* gave us integration in form. Now it's time for the substance.

By the way . . . I still believe.

CHARLES R. LAWRENCE

The Debates Over Placing Limits on Racist Speech Must Not Ignore the Damage It Does to Its Victims

CHARLES R. LAWRENCE III *teaches constitutional law and race relations at Stanford University. He is the author (with Joel Dreyfuss) of* The Bakke Case: The Politics of Inequality *and numerous scholarly articles.*

I have spent the better part of my life as a dissenter. As a high-school student, I was threatened with suspension for my refusal to participate in a civil-defense drill, and I have been a conspicuous consumer of my First

Amendment liberties ever since. There are very strong reasons for protecting even racist speech. Perhaps the most important of these is that such protection reinforces our society's commitment to tolerance as a value, and that by protecting bad speech from government regulation, we will be forced to combat it as a community.

But I also have a deeply felt apprehension about the resurgence of racial violence and the corresponding rise in the incidence of verbal and symbolic assault and harassment to which blacks and other traditionally subjugated and excluded groups are subjected. I am troubled by the way the debate has been framed in response to the recent surge of racist incidents on college and university campuses and in response to some universities' attempts to regulate harassing speech. The problem has been framed as one in which the liberty of free speech is in conflict with the elimination of racism. I believe this has placed the bigot on the moral high ground and fanned the rising flames of racism.

Above all, I am troubled that we have not listened to the real victims, that we have shown so little understanding of their injury, and that we have abandoned those whose race, gender, or sexual preference continues to make them second-class citizens. It seems to me a very sad irony that the first instinct of civil libertarians has been to challenge even the smallest, most narrowly framed efforts by universities to provide black and other minority students with the protection the Constitution guarantees them.

The landmark case *Brown v. Board of Education* is not a case that we normally think of as a case about speech. But *Brown* can be broadly read as articulating the principle of equal citizenship. *Brown* held that segregated schools were inherently unequal because of the *message* that segregation conveyed—that black children were an untouchable caste, unfit to go to school with white children. If we understand the necessity of eliminating the system of signs and symbols that signal the inferiority of blacks, then we should hesitate before proclaiming that all racist speech that stops short of physical violence must be defended.

University officials who have formulated policies to respond to incidents of racial harassment have been characterized in the press as "thought police," but such policies generally do nothing more than impose sanctions against intentional face-to-face insults. When racist speech takes the form of face-to-face insults, catcalls, or other assaultive speech aimed at an individual or small group of persons, it falls directly within the "fighting words" exception to First Amendment protection. The Supreme Court has held that words which "by their very utterance inflict injury or tend to incite an immediate breach of the peace" are not protected by the First Amendment.

If the purpose of the First Amendment is to foster the greatest amount of speech, racial insults disserve that purpose. Assaultive racist speech functions as a preemptive strike. The invective is experienced as a blow, not as a proffered idea, and once the blow is struck, it is unlikely that a dialogue will follow. Racial insults are particularly undeserving of First Amendment protection because the perpetrator's intention is not to discover truth or initiate dialogue but to injure the victim. In most situations, members of minority groups realize that they are likely to lose if they respond to epithets by fighting and are forced to remain silent and submissive.

Courts have held that offensive speech may not be regulated in public

forums such as streets, where the listener may avoid the speech by moving
on, but the regulation of otherwise protected speech has been permitted when
the speech invades the privacy of the
unwilling listener's home or when
the unwilling listener cannot avoid the
speech. Racist posters, fliers, and graffiti in dormitories, bathrooms, and other
common living spaces would seem to
clearly fall within the reasoning of these
cases. Minority students should not be
required to remain in their rooms in
order to avoid racial assault. Minimally,
they should find a safe haven in their
dorms and in all other common rooms
that are a part of their daily routine.

I would also argue that the university's responsibility for insuring that
these students receive an equal educational opportunity provides a compelling
justification for regulations that insure
them safe passage in all common areas.
A minority student should not have to
risk becoming the target of racially as-
saulting speech every time he or she
chooses to walk across campus. Regulating vilifying speech that cannot be anticipated or avoided would not preclude
announced speeches and rallies—situations that would give minority-group
members and their allies the chance to
organize counter-demonstrations or
avoid the speech altogether.

The most commonly advanced argument against the regulation of racist
speech proceeds something like this:
We recognize that minority groups suffer pain and injury as the result of racist
speech, but we must allow this hate
mongering for the benefit of society as
a whole. Freedom of speech is the
lifeblood of our democratic system. It is
especially important for minorities because often it is their only vehicle for
rallying support for the redress of their
grievances. It will be impossible to formulate a prohibition so precise that it
will prevent the racist speech you want
to suppress without catching in the
same net all kinds of speech that it
would be unconscionable for a democratic society to supress.

Whenever we make such arguments,
we are striking a balance on the one hand
between our concern for the continued
free flow of ideas and the democratic
process dependent on that flow, and, on
the other, our desire to further the cause
of equality. There can, however, be no
meaningful discussion of how we should
reconcile our commitment to equality
and our commitment to free speech until
it is acknowledged that there is real harm
inflicted by racist speech and that this
harm is far from trivial.

To engage in a debate about the First
Amendment and racist speech without a
full understanding of the nature and extent of that harm is to risk making the
First Amendment an instrument of
domination rather than a vehicle of liberation. We have not all known the experience of victimization by racial,
misogynist, and homophobic speech,
nor do we equally share the burden of
the societal harm it inflicts. We are often
quick to say that we have heard the cry
of the victims when we have not.

The *Brown* case is again instructive
because it speaks directly to the psychic
injury inflicted by racist speech by noting that the symbolic message of segregation affected "the hearts and minds"
of Negro children "in a way unlikely
ever to be undone." Racial epithets and
harassment often cause deep emotional
scarring and feelings of anxiety and
fear that pervade every aspect of a victim's life.

Brown also recognized that black
children did not have an equal opportu-

nity to learn and participate in the school community if they bore the additional burden of being subjected to the humiliation and psychic assault contained in the message of segregation. University students bear an analogous burden when they are forced to live and work in an environment where at any moment they may be subjected to denigrating verbal harassment and assault. The same injury was addressed by the Supreme Court when it held that sexual harassment that creates a hostile or abusive work environment violates the ban on sex discrimination in employment of Title VII of the Civil Rights Act of 1964.

Carefully drafted university regulations would bar the use of words as assault weapons and leave unregulated even the most heinous of ideas when those ideas are presented at times and places and in manners that provide an opportunity for reasoned rebuttal or escape from immediate injury. The history of the development of the right to free speech has been one of carefully evaluating the importance of free expression and its effects on other important societal interests. We have drawn the line between protected and unprotected speech before without dire results. (Courts have, for example, exempted from the protection of the First Amendment obscene speech and speech that disseminates official secrets, that defames or libels another person, or that is used to form a conspiracy or monopoly.)

Blacks and other people of color are skeptical about the argument that even the most injurious speech must remain unregulated because, in an unregulated marketplace of ideas, the best ones will rise to the top and gain acceptance. Our experience tells us quite the opposite. We have seen too many demagogues elected by appealing to America's

racism. We have seen too many good liberal politicians shy away from the issues that might brand them as being too closely allied with us.

Whenever we decide that racist speech must be tolerated because of the importance of maintaining societal tolerance for all unpopular speech, we are asking blacks and other subordinated groups to bear the burden for the good of all. We must be careful that the ease with which we strike the balance against the regulation of racist speech is in no way influenced by the fact that the cost will be borne by others. We must be certain that those who will pay that price are fairly represented in our deliberations and that they are heard.

At the core of the argument that we should resist all government regulation of speech is the ideal that the best cure for bad speech is good, that ideas that affirm equality and the worth of all individuals will ultimately prevail. This is an empty ideal unless those of us who would fight racism are vigilant and unequivocal in that fight. We must look for ways to offer assistance and support to students whose speech and political participation are chilled in a climate of racial harassment.

Civil-rights lawyers might consider suing on behalf of blacks whose right to an equal education is denied by a university's failure to insure a nondiscriminatory educational climate or conditions of employment. We must embark upon the development of a First Amendment jurisprudence grounded in the reality of our history and our contemporary experience. We must think hard about how best to launch legal attacks against the most indefensible forms of hate speech. Good lawyers can create exceptions and narrow interpretations that limit the harm of hate speech without opening the floodgates of censorship.

Everyone concerned with these issues must find ways to engage actively in actions that resist and counter the racist ideas that we would have the First Amendment protect. If we fail in this, the victims of hate speech must rightly assume that we are on the oppressors' side.

AMY TAN

Two Kinds

AMY TAN is a writer whose most recent novel is The Kitchen God's Wife *(1991). The following selection is a chapter from her first book,* The Joy Luck Club *(1989).*

MY mother believed you could be anything you wanted to be in America. You could open a restaurant. You could work for the government and get good retirement. You could buy a house with almost no money down. You could become rich. You could become instantly famous.

"Of course you can be prodigy, too," my mother told me when I was nine. "You can be best anything. What does Auntie Lindo know? Her daughter, she is only best tricky."

America was where all my mother's hopes lay. She had come here in 1949 after losing everything in China: her mother and father, her family home, her first husband, and two daughters, twin baby girls. But she never looked back with regret. There were so many ways for things to get better.

• • •

We didn't immediately pick the right kind of prodigy. At first my mother

thought I could be a Chinese Shirley Temple. We'd watch Shirley's old movies on TV as though they were training films. My mother would poke my arm and say, "*Ni kan*"—You watch. And I would see Shirley tapping her feet, or singing a sailor song, or pursing her lips into a very round O while saying, "Oh my goodness."

"*Ni kan*," said my mother as Shirley's eyes flooded with tears. "You already know how. Don't need talent for crying!"

Soon after my mother got this idea about Shirley Temple, she took me to a beauty training school in the Mission district and put me in the hands of a student who could barely hold the scissors without shaking. Instead of getting big fat curls, I emerged with an uneven mass of crinkly black fuzz. My mother dragged me off to the bathroom and tried to wet down my hair.

"You look like Negro Chinese," she lamented, as if I had done this on purpose.

The instructor of the beauty training school had to lop off these soggy clumps to make my hair even again. "Peter Pan is very popular these days," the instructor assured my mother. I now had hair the length of a boy's, with straight-across bangs that hung at a slant two inches above my eyebrows. I liked the haircut and it made me actually look forward to my future fame.

In fact, in the beginning, I was just as excited as my mother, maybe even more so. I pictured this prodigy part of me as many different images, trying each one on for size. I was a dainty ballerina girl standing by the curtains, waiting to hear the right music that would send me floating on my tiptoes. I was like the Christ child lifted out of the straw manger, crying with holy indignity. I was Cinderella stepping from her pumpkin carriage with sparkly cartoon music filling the air.

In all of my imaginings, I was filled with a sense that I would soon be *perfect*. My mother and father would adore me. I would be beyond reproach. I would never feel the need to sulk for anything.

But sometimes the prodigy in me became impatient. "If you don't hurry up and get me out of here, I'm disappearing for good," it warned. "And then you'll always be nothing."

Every night after dinner, my mother and I would sit at the Formica kitchen table. She would present new tests, taking her examples from stories of amazing children she had read in *Ripley's Believe It or Not,* or *Good Housekeeping, Reader's Digest,* and a dozen other magazines she kept in a pile in our bathroom. My mother got these magazines from people whose houses she cleaned. And since she cleaned many houses each week, we had a great assortment. She would look through them all, searching for stories about remarkable children.

The first night she brought out a story about a three-year-old boy who knew the capitals of all the states and even most of the European countries. A teacher was quoted as saying the little boy could also pronounce the names of the foreign cities correctly.

"What's the capital of Finland?" my mother asked me, looking at the magazine story.

All I knew was the capital of California, because Sacramento was the name of the street we lived on in Chinatown. "Nairobi!" I guessed, saying the most foreign word I could think of. She checked to see if that was possibly one way to pronounce "Helsinki" before showing me the answer.

The tests got harder—multiplying numbers in my head, finding the queen of hearts in a deck of cards, trying to stand on my head without using my hands, predicting the daily temperatures in Los Angeles, New York and London.

One night I had to look at a page from the Bible for three minutes and then report everything I could remember. "Now Jehoshaphat had riches and honor in abundance and . . . that's all I remember, Ma," I said.

And after seeing my mother's disappointed face once again, something inside of me began to die. I hated the tests, the raised hopes and failed expectations. Before going to bed that night, I looked in the mirror above the bathroom sink and when I saw only my face staring back—and that it would always be this ordinary face—I began to cry. Such a sad, ugly girl! I made high-pitched noises like a crazed animal, trying to scratch out the face in the mirror.

And then I saw what seemed to be the prodigy side of me—because I had never seen that face before. I looked at my reflection, blinking so I could see more clearly. The girl staring back at me was angry, powerful. This girl and I were the same. I had new thoughts, willful thoughts, or rather thoughts filled with lots of won'ts. I won't let her change me, I promised myself. I won't be what I'm not.

So now on nights when my mother presented her tests, I performed listlessly, my head propped on one arm. I pretended to be bored. And I was. I got so bored I started counting the bellows of the foghorns out on the bay while my mother drilled me in other areas. The sound was comforting and reminded me of the cow jumping over the moon. And the next day, I played a game with myself, seeing if my mother would give up on me before eight bellows. After a while I usually counted only one, maybe two bellows at most. At last she was beginning to give up hope.

Two or three months had gone by without any mention of my being a prodigy again. And then one day my mother was watching *The Ed Sullivan Show* on TV. The TV was old and the sound kept shorting out. Every time my mother got halfway up from the sofa to adjust the set, the sound would go back on and Ed would be talking. As soon as she sat down, Ed would go silent again. She got up, the TV broke into loud piano music. She sat down. Silence. Up and down, back and forth, quiet and loud. It was like a stiff embraceless dance between her and the TV set. Finally she stood by the set with her hand on the sound dial.

She seemed entranced by the music, a little frenzied piano piece with this mesmerizing quality, sort of quick passages and then teasing lilting ones before it returned to the quick playful parts.

"*Ni kan,*" my mother said, calling me over with hurried hand gestures, "Look here."

I could see why my mother was fascinated by the music. It was being pounded out by a little Chinese girl, about nine years old, with a Peter Pan haircut. The girl had the sauciness of a Shirley Temple. She was proudly modest like a proper Chinese child. And she also did this fancy sweep of a curtsy, so that the fluffy skirt of her white dress cascaded slowly to the floor like the petals of a large carnation.

In spite of these warning signs, I wasn't worried. Our family had no piano and we couldn't afford to buy one, let alone reams of sheet music and piano lessons. So I could be generous in my comments when my mother badmouthed the little girl on TV.

"Play note right, but doesn't sound good! No singing sound," complained my mother.

"What are you picking on her for?" I said carelessly. "She's pretty good. Maybe she's not the best, but she's trying hard." I knew almost immediately I would be sorry I said that.

"Just like you," she said. "Not the best. Because you not trying." She gave a little huff as she let go of the sound dial and sat down on the sofa.

The little Chinese girl sat down also to play an encore of "Anitra's Dance" by Grieg. I remember the song, because later on I had to learn how to play it.

Three days after watching *The Ed Sullivan Show,* my mother told me what my schedule would be for piano lessons and piano practice. She had talked to Mr. Chong, who lived on the first floor of our apartment building. Mr. Chong was a retired piano teacher and my mother had traded housecleaning services for weekly lessons and a piano for me to practice on every day, two hours a day, from four until six.

When my mother told me this, I felt as though I had been sent to hell. I whined and then kicked my foot a little when I couldn't stand it anymore.

"Why don't you like me the way I am? I'm not a genius! I can't play the piano. And even if I could, I wouldn't go on TV if you paid me a million dollars!" I cried.

My mother slapped me. "Who ask you be genius?" she shouted. "Only ask you be your best. For you sake. You think I want you be genius? Hnnh! What for! Who ask you!"

"So ungrateful," I heard her mutter in Chinese. "If she had as much talent as she has temper, she would be famous now."

Mr. Chong, whom I secretly nicknamed Old Chong, was very strange, always tapping his fingers to the silent music of an invisible orchestra. He looked ancient in my eyes. He had lost most of the hair on top of his head and he wore thick glasses and had eyes that always looked tired and sleepy. But he must have been younger than I thought, since he lived with his mother and was not yet married.

I met Old Lady Chong once and that was enough. She had this peculiar smell like a baby that had done something in its pants. And her fingers felt like a dead person's, like an old peach I once found in the back of the refrigerator; the skin just slid off the meat when I picked it up.

I soon found out why Old Chong had retired from teaching piano. He was deaf. "Like Beethoven!" he shouted to me. "We're both listening only in our head!" And he would start to conduct his frantic silent sonatas.

Our lessons went like this. He would open the book and point to different things, explaining their purpose: "Key! Treble! Bass! No sharps or flats! So this is C major! Listen now and play after me!"

And then he would play the C scale a few times, a simple chord, and then, as if inspired by an old, unreachable itch, he gradually added more notes and running trills and a pounding bass until the music was really something quite grand.

I would play after him, the simple scale, the simple chord, and then I just played some nonsense that sounded like a cat running up and down on top of garbage cans. Old Chong smiled and applauded and then said, "Very good! But now you must learn to keep time!"

So that's how I discovered that Old Chong's eyes were too slow to keep up with the wrong notes I was playing. He went through the motions in half-time. To help me keep rhythm, he stood behind me, pushing down on my right shoulder for every beat. He balanced pennies on top of my wrists so I would keep them still and I slowly played scales and arpeggios. He had me curve my hand around an apple and keep that shape when playing chords. He marched stiffly to show me how to make each finger dance up and down, staccato like an obedient little soldier.

He taught me all these things, and that was how I also learned I could be lazy and get away with mistakes, lots of mistakes. If I hit the wrong notes because I hadn't practiced enough, I never corrected myself. I just kept playing in rhythm. And Old Chong kept conducting his own private reverie.

So maybe I never really gave myself a fair chance. I did pick up the basics pretty quickly, and I might have become a good pianist at that young age. But I was so determined not to try, not to be anybody different that I learned to play only the most ear-splitting preludes, the most discordant hymns.

Over the next year, I practiced like this, dutifully in my own way. And then one day I heard my mother and her friend Lindo Jong both talking in a loud bragging tone of voice so others could hear. It was after church, and I was leaning against the brick wall wearing a dress with stiff white petticoats. Auntie Lindo's daughter, Waverly, who was about my age, was standing farther down the wall above five feet away. We had grown up together and shared all the closeness of two sisters squabbling over crayons and dolls. In other words, for the most part, we hated each other. I thought she was snotty. Waverly Jong had gained a certain amount of fame as "Chinatown's Littlest Chinese Chess Champion."

"She bring home too many trophy," lamented Auntie Lindo that Sunday. "All day she play chess. All day I have no time do nothing but dust off her winnings." She threw a scolding look at Waverly, who pretended not to see her.

"You lucky you don't have this problem," said Auntie Lindo with a sigh to my mother.

And my mother squared her shoulders and bragged; "Our problem worser than yours. If we ask Jing-mei wash dish, she hear nothing but music. It's like you can't stop this natural talent."

And right then, I was determined to put a stop to her foolish pride.

A few weeks later, Old Chong and my mother conspired to have me play in a talent show which would be held in the church hall. By then, my parents had saved up enough to buy me a second-hand piano, a black Wurlitzer spinet with a scarred bench. It was the show-piece of our living room.

For the talent show, I was to play a piece called "Pleading Child" from Schumann's *Scenes from Childhood*. It was a simple, moody piece that sounded more difficult that it was. I was supposed to memorize the whole thing playing the repeat parts twice to make the piece sound longer. But I dawdled over it, playing a few bars and then cheating, looking up to see what notes followed. I never rally listened to what I was playing. I daydreamed about being somewhere else, about being someone else.

The part I liked to practice best was the fancy curtsy: right foot out, touch the rose on the carpet with a pointed foot, sweep to the side, left leg bends, look up and smile.

My parents invited all the couples from the Joy Luck Club to witness my debut. Auntie Lindo and Uncle Tin were there. Waverly and her two older brothers had also come. The first two rows were filled with children both younger and older than I was. The littlest ones got to go first. They recited simple nursery rhymes, squawked out tunes on miniature violins, twirled Hula Hoops, pranced in pink ballet tutus, and when they bowed or curtsied, the audience would sigh in unison, "Awww," and then clap enthusiastically.

When my turn came, I was very confident. I remember my childish excitement. It was as if I knew, without a doubt, that the prodigy side of me really did exist. I had no fear whatsoever, no nervousness. I remember thinking to myself, This is it! This is it! I looked out over the audience, at my mother's blank face, my father's yawn, Auntie Lindo's stiff-lipped smile, Waverly's sulky expression. I had on a white dress layered with sheets of lace, and a pink bow in my Peter Pan haircut. As I sat down I envisioned people jumping to their feet and Ed Sullivan rushing up to introduce me to everyone on TV.

And I started to play. It was so beautiful. I was so caught up in how lovely I looked that at first I didn't worry how I would sound. So it was a surprise to me when I hit the first wrong note and I realized something didn't sound quite right. And then I hit another and another followed that. A chill started at the top of my head and began to trickle down. Yet I couldn't stop playing, as though my hands were bewitched. I kept thinking my fingers would adjust themselves back, like a train switching to the right track. I played this strange jumble through two repeats, the sour notes staying with me all the way to the end.

When I stood up, I discovered my legs were shaking. Maybe I had just been nervous and the audience, like Old Chong, had seen me go through the right motions and had not heard anything wrong at all. I swept my right foot out, went down on my knee, looked up and smiled. The room was quiet, except for Old Chong, who was beaming and shouting, "Bravo! Bravo! Well done!" But then I saw my mother's face, her stricken face. The audience clapped weakly, and I walked back to my chair, with my whole face quivering as I tried not to cry, I heard a little boy whisper loudly to his mother, "That was awful," and the mother whispered back, "Well, she certainly tried."

And now I realized how many people were in the audience, the whole world it seemed. I was aware of eyes burning into my back. I felt the shame of my mother and father as they sat stiffly throughout the rest of the show.

We could have escaped during intermission. Pride and some strange sense of honor must have anchored my parents to their chairs. And so we watched it all: the eighteen-year-old boy with a fake mustache who did a magic show and juggled flaming hoops while riding a unicycle. The breasted girl with white makeup who sang from *Madama Butterfly* and got honorable mention. And the eleven-year-old boy who won first prize playing a tricky violin song that sounded like a busy bee.

After the show, the Hsus, the Jongs, and the St. Clairs from the Joy Luck Club came up to my mother and father.

"Lots of talented kids," Auntie Lindo said vaguely, smiling broadly.

"That was somethin' else," said my father, and I wondered if he was referring to me in a humorous way, or whether he even remembered what I had done.

Waverly looked at me and shrugged her shoulders. "You aren't a genius like me," she said matter-of-factly. And if I hadn't felt so bad, I would have pulled her braids and punched her stomach.

But my mother's expression was what devastated me: a quiet, blank look that said she had lost everything. I felt the same way, and it seemed as if everybody were now coming up, like gawkers at the scene of an accident, to see what parts were actually missing. When we got on the bus to go home, my father was humming the busy-bee tune and my mother was silent. I kept thinking she wanted to wait until we got home before shouting at me. But when my father unlocked the door to our apartment, my mother walked in and then went to the back, into the bedroom. No accusations. No blame. And in a way, I felt disappointed. I had been waiting for her to start shouting, so I could shout back and cry and blame her for all my misery.

I assumed my talent-show fiasco meant I never had to play the piano again. But two days later, after school, my mother came out of the kitchen and saw me watching TV.

"Four clock," she reminded me as if it were any other day. I was stunned, as though she were asking me to go through the talent-show torture again. I wedged myself more tightly in front of the TV.

"Turn off TV," she called from the kitchen five minutes later.

I didn't budge. And then I decided. I didn't have to do what my mother said anymore. I wasn't her slave. This wasn't China. I had listened to her before and look what happened. She was the stupid one.

She came out from the kitchen and stood in the arched entryway of the living room. "Four clock," she said once again, louder.

"I'm not going to play anymore," I said nonchalantly. "Why should I? I'm not a genius."

She walked over and stood in front of the TV. I saw her chest was heaving up and down in an angry way.

"No!" I said, and I now felt stronger, as if my true self had finally emerged. So this was what had been inside me all along.

"No! I won't!" I screamed.

She yanked me by the arm, pulled me off the floor, snapped off the TV. She was frighteningly strong, half pulling, half carrying me toward the piano as I kicked the throw rugs under my feet. She lifted me up and onto the hard bench. I was sobbing by now, looking at her bitterly. Her chest was heaving even more and her mouth was open, smiling crazily as if she were pleased I was crying.

"You want me to be someone that I'm not!" I sobbed. "I'll never be the kind of daughter you want me to be!"

"Only two kinds of daughters," she shouted in Chinese. "Those who are obedient and those who follow their own mind! Only one kind of daughter can live in this house. Obedient daughter!"

"Then I wish I wasn't your daughter. I wish you weren't my mother," I shouted. As I said these things I got scared. It felt like worms and toads and slimy things crawling out of my chest, but it also felt good, as if this awful side of me had surfaced, at last.

"Too late change this," said my mother shrilly.

And I could sense her anger rising to its breaking point. I wanted to see it spill over. And that's when I remembered the babies she had lost in China, the ones we never talked about. "Then I wish I'd never been born!" I shouted. "I wish I were dead! Like them."

It was as if I had said the magic words. Alakazam!—and her face went blank, her mouth closed, her arms went slack, and she backed out of the room, stunned, as if she were blowing away like a small brown leaf, thin, brittle, lifeless.

• • •

It was not the only disappointment my mother felt in me. In the years that followed, I failed her so many times, each time asserting my own will, my right to fall short of expectations. I didn't get straight As. I didn't become class president. I didn't get into Stanford. I dropped out of college.

For unlike my mother, I did not believe I could be anything I wanted to be. I could only be me.

And for all those years, we never talked about the disaster at the recital or my terrible accusations afterward at the piano bench. All that remained unchecked, like a betrayal that was now unspeakable. So I never found a way to ask her why she had hoped for something so large that failure was inevitable.

And even worse, I never asked her what frightened me the most: Why had she given up hope?

For after our struggle at the piano, she never mentioned my playing again. The lessons stopped. The lid to the piano was closed, shutting out the dust, my misery, and her dreams.

So she surprised me. A few years ago, she offered to give me the piano, for my thirtieth birthday. I had not played in all those years. I saw the offer as a sign of forgiveness, a tremendous burden removed.

"Are you sure?" I asked shyly. "I mean, won't you and Dad miss it?"

"No, this your piano," she said firmly. "Always your piano. You only one can play."

"Well, I probably can't play anymore," I said. "It's been years."

"You pick up fast," said my mother, as if she knew this was certain. "You have natural talent. You could been genius if you want to."

"No I couldn't."

"You just not trying," said my mother. And she was neither angry nor sad. She said it as if to announce a fact that could never be disproved. "Take it," she said.

But I didn't at first. It was enough that she had offered it to me. And after that, every time I saw it in my parents' living room, standing in front of the bay windows, it made me feel proud, as if it were a shiny trophy I had won back.

Last week I sent a tuner over to my parents' apartment and had the piano reconditioned, for purely sentimental reasons. My mother had died a few months before and I had been getting things in order for my father, a little bit at a time. I put the jewelry in special silk pouches. The sweaters she had knitted in yellow, pink, bright orange— all the colors I hated—I put those in moth-proof boxes. I found some old Chinese silk dresses, the kind with little slits up the sides. I rubbed the old silk against my skin, then wrapped them in tissue and decided to take them home with me.

After I had the piano tuned, I opened the lid and touched the keys. It sounded even richer than I remembered. Really, it was a very good piano. Inside the bench were the same exercise notes with handwritten scales, the same secondhand music books with their covers held together with yellow tape.

I opened up the Schumann book to the dark little piece I had played at the recital. It was on the left-hand side of the page, "Pleading Child." It looked more difficult than I remembered. I played a few bars, surprised at how easily the notes came back to me.

And for the first time, or so it seemed, I noticed the piece on the right-hand side. It was called "Perfectly Contented." I tried to play this one as well. It had a lighter melody but the same flowing rhythm and turned out to be quite easy. "Pleading Child" was shorter but lower; "Perfectly Contented" was longer but faster. And after I played them both a few times, I realized they were two halves of the same song.

Part 5

Living a Good Life

Chapter *13*
Why Shouldn't I Be Selfish?

Only this morning, no doubt, you had to face up to a basic moral question. Perhaps something you wanted was just sitting there, unguarded, and you could have walked off with it without fear of getting caught. Or maybe someone asked you a question, and you could have lied—much to your advantage. Or possibly you made a promise to a friend, who seems to have forgotten about it, and you wondered if you should remind him or not. Every day, we find ourselves choosing between our own interests and the interests of others, between our personal desires and the promises we have made or principles we ought to obey. But why should you concern yourself with others and obey principles that are not to your own advantage? In short, why shouldn't you be selfish, as Ntozake Shange argues (ironically) in her poem, "get it & feel good."

Daily observation and perhaps logic seem to show us that all of our actions are self-interested, if not actually selfish. We seem to do what we want, whenever we can, and when we don't, it is because we can't, because someone or something prevents us, because we want something else even more, or because we are afraid of the consequences—which we fear even more than we want what we want. But if we can get what we want and there is nothing that we want or fear more, the argument goes, we will surely do whatever will get us what we want. This tempting generalization soon becomes the thesis that "everyone is selfish" or more philosophically, "everyone is an **egoist.**" We hesitate, however, because the thesis seems so crude and unflattering, and because of an admittedly small cluster of actions and agents that seem not to be motivated by self-interest at all, examples of **altruism** that seem to have nothing to do with selfishness. Occasionally we find ourselves making a small sacrifice, performing an act of seemingly pure generosity, or obeying a rule despite the fact that it is not in our interest and there is virtually no chance of our getting caught for such a transgression. And we occasionally meet people and we read about saints who consistently behave with little regard for their own interests, apparently altruists, all the time.

Nevertheless, we are still tempted (or tormented) by that generalization. Ever since Plato (and no doubt before) the same question has plagued philosophers: "Why not be selfish?" The most obvious answers do not seem to work. For instance, "because it is unfair to others" will not be very effective with someone who readily admits that he or she doesn't really care about anyone else, and "because it will make you unhappy," while perhaps true, only rejects selfishness by an appeal to selfishness, so the egoistic thesis remains unchallenged.

In Plato's *Republic,* Glaucon (one of Socrates' several interlocutors) argues that we would all be selfish if we could get away with it, and he introduces the myth of the "ring of Gyges" to make the point. The ring in question supposedly rendered its wearer invisible, and if a man were invisible, Glaucon suggests, he could get away with anything. Indeed, Glaucon argues that if a person could get away with doing whatever he wanted and did not do so, people would think him a fool rather than a saint. Selfishness is the natural order of things, and there is no good reason—except fear of getting caught and suffering the consequences—why we do not all act selfishly all the time.

One of the arguments for the necessity of egoism is the argument from human nature, the argument that all of us are "naturally" selfish. One specific argument for the universality of egoism goes back to ancient times: that all of us naturally seek and enjoy pleasure, dislike and avoid pain. All our actions, accordingly, are aimed at this end, which is called **hedonism,** the pursuit of pleasure. Two thousand years ago, the Greek philosopher Epicurus defended this thesis, and he was so persuasive that we still call people who enjoy the good things in life "Epicureans." It is worth noting, however, that Epicurus did not defend the pursuit of every pleasure without qualification; he knew that some pleasures were better and more durable than others and urged us to seek the "higher" pleasures. Nevertheless, the argument that we act for the sake of our own pleasure (and to avoid pain) provides a powerful argument for egoism. It is argued that whatever people seem to be doing—going boating, studying for an exam, opening a can of Pepsi, helping a friend with a problem—they are really acting toward one goal: obtaining pleasure and avoiding pain. You want to go boating because of the pleasure you get out of boating. You study not just to learn but to obtain pleasure— from the learning itself, but also from the confidence that you will do well in the exam or that you are doing what you are supposed to be doing on a Wednesday night and may well be rewarded. You want a Pepsi, but you really want the satisfaction, the quenching of thirst, and the uplifting feeling. You help a friend because it gives you pleasure to do so—or because you predict the pain of guilt if you don't. It seems, then, that people satisfy their own hedonistic interests. This gives us a way of understanding the behavior of saints and ourselves in our "best" moments: It may seem that we are acting unselfishly, but in fact we are working for the good feeling that comes from having done the right thing. Alternatively, we are just trying to avoid the painful feelings of guilt or shame, not to mention punishment and the verbal abuse of our neighbors, that follow obviously selfish and inconsiderate behavior.

The argument for universal egoism has recently received an even more sophisticated formulation in the theory of evolution and genetics. Perhaps, selfishness is built right into our genes as a matter of evolutionary survival, for how long could an individual or even a species exist if it did not take care of itself? Saints, perhaps, are rare exceptions, as are the admirable inspirations of generosity that we experience ourselves. But self-interest, it is argued, is built right into our basic nature, and although we might find exceptions to it, there is no avoiding the conclusion that we are all basically self-ish, however altruistic our ideals. Against this, it is argued that cooperation and fellow feeling are also essential parts of human nature. The urge to help a fellow creature in trouble is just as strong and just as "natural" as the urge to satisfy one's own desires—indeed, that urge is one of our most natural desires. In this view, purely selfish actions become the exceptions, not sainthood and spontaneous generosity. Such controversies about the natural origins of selfishness go back to early interpretations of Genesis, but the modern argument becomes exquisitely subtle and scientific (represented here by Richard Dawkins and Stephen Jay Gould). It is nothing less than an argument about our basic nature and what we can and should expect of ourselves. But even if selfish-ness is not "natural" as such, it may be argued that selfishness is essential to thriving. So argues the Russian immigrant philosopher Ayn Rand: We *ought* to be selfish, and what we call "altruism" is a form of pathetic self-destructiveness. But here we might start questioning the soundness of the distinction itself. Are all acts of altruism self destructive?

One argument for the universality of selfishness is derived from logical considerations alone. It is argued, first, that people always do what they want to do, barring obstacles and interference with their actions. If a man trips and falls on the way to the supermar-ket, we do not assume that he wanted to trip and fall, but if he succeeds in going to the market, we will not be easily persuaded that he did not want to do just that. Of course, our fellow may have gone to the market not because he enjoys shopping but rather be-cause he desired some sausage meat for lunch, which he very much wanted. Or he may have gone to the market to get food for the cat and to stop her meowing—which annoyed him enormously. But we can assume that when a person completes an action without interference, he or she has satisfied his or her own desire—whether that desire involves pleasure and pain, keeping a promise, or proving one's sainthood.

But if every action involves the satisfaction of one's own desire, then it is tempting to conclude that every act is at least self-interested, if not selfish. This gives us a more cynical explanation of saints and our own generous impulses: Whatever the motives of our actions, they (the saints) or we are satisfying desires, and so the actions are selfish. We might object here to the word "selfish" and insist on saving it for just those self-interested actions that also interfere with other people. Thus, buying a sausage and sharing it because one is both hungry and desirous of company is not selfish, but push-ing everyone else out of the way to eat the whole sausage oneself would be. Neverthe-less, in the sense that seems to count, all actions are selfish; it is just that some are obnoxiously so and others are quite acceptable to the rest of us (because they do not interfere with our own selfish desires). But if this is so, if there is a distinction to be made between those "selfish" actions that harm and those that help other people, we should suspect the true force of this "logical" argument. Perhaps the satisfaction of de-sire is irrelevant to the question of selfishness.

Against the view that all our actions are selfish, philosophers ever since Plato have vigorously argued that (a) at least some of our actions are not selfish but honestly based on generosity, charity, or moral principles; and (b) that we *ought* to act unselfishly. Even the ancient author Epicurus, whose name is almost synonymous with a life of self-indulgent pleasure, argued for moderation in the pursuit of pleasure and peace of mind. The English Bishop Joseph Butler presented several sermons in which he rejected the egoist claim and laid out the various reasons for accepting altruistic motives at face value. Most philosophers now reject the psychological and logical arguments that make all actions out to be selfish, and most also agree with the ethical thesis that we ought to act unselfishly, at least some of the time. But there is also a social dimension to the question of selfishness, and self-indulgence and exaggerated self-concern may be cultivated as part of some particular societies, for example, our own. This is a thesis recently and strikingly argued by Christopher Lasch, who argues that our selfishness is a cultural phenomenon. It consists not so obviously of straightforward self-interest but rather of the more subtle form of self-absorption: a constant concern with our private selves and a kind of oblivion to larger social concerns.

NTOZAKE SHANGE

get it & feel good

NTOZAKE SHANGE is a poet, novelist, playwright, and educator. Her most famous work is her play For Colored Girls Who Have Considered Suicide When the Rainbow Is Enuf. *Her plays have been produced both on Broadway and in regional theater across the world. She has received the Obie Award and the Outer Critics Circle Award.*

you cd just take what
he's got for you
i mean what's available
cd add up in the long run
if it's music/take it
say he's got good
dishwashing techniques
he cd be a marvelous
masseur/take it
whatever good there is to
get/get it & feel good

say there's an electrical
wiring fanatic/he cd
come in handy some day
suppose they know how to tend plants
if you want somebody
with guts/you cd go to a rodeo
a prize fight/or a gang war might be up your
    alley
there's somebody out there
with something you want/
not alla it/but a lil
bit from here & there can
add up in the long run

whatever good there is to get
get it & feel good
this one's got kisses
that one can lay
linoleum
this one likes wine
that one fries butter fish
real good
this one is a anarcho-musicologist
this one wants pushkin to rise again
& that one has had it with the past tense/

whatever good there is to get/
get it & feel good
this one cd make music
roll around the small of
yr back & that one jumps
up & down in the gardens
it cd be yrs
there really is enuf to get
by with in this world but
you have to know what yr looking
for/whatever good there is to get
get it & feel good
you have to know what
they will give up easily
what's available is not always
all that's possible
but there's so much fluctuation
in the market these days
you have to be
particular

whatever good there is to get
get it & feel good
whatever good there is to get
get it & feel good/get it & feel good
snatch it & feel good
grab it & feel good
steal it & feel good
borrow it & feel good
reach it & feel good
you cd
    oh yeah
        & feel good.

PLATO

The Ring of Gyges

PLATO's (427–347 B.C.) Republic is a blueprint for what would be, in Plato's opinion, the ideal society. Its central theme is justice, and the challenge with which Plato begins is the problem of the immoralist—the man who thinks that there is no reason not to be selfish and pursue one's own interests. Socrates' interlocutor Glaucon argues this thesis by using the myth of the "ring of Gyges," which makes its wearer invisible and allows him to get away with anything.

GLAUCON (TO SOCRATES):

I have never yet heard the superiority of justice to injustice
maintained by anyone in a satisfactory way. I want to hear
justice praised in respect of itself; then I shall be satisfied,
and you are the person from whom I think that I am most
likely to hear this; and therefore I will praise the unjust life
to the utmost of my power and my manner of speaking will
indicate the manner in which I desire to hear you too
praising justice and censuring injustice. Will you say
whether you approve of my proposal?

SOCRATES:

Indeed I do; nor can I imagine any theme about which a man of
sense would oftener wish to converse.

GLAUCON:

I am delighted to hear you say so, and shall begin by speaking, as
I proposed, of the nature and origin of justice.
They say that to do injustice is, by nature, good; to suffer
injustice, evil; but that there is more evil in the latter than
good in the former. And so when men have both done and
suffered injustice and have had experience of both, any
who are not able to avoid the one and obtain the other,
think that they had better agree among themselves to have
neither; hence they began to establish laws and mutual
covenants; and that which was ordained by law was termed
by them lawful and just. This, it is claimed, is the origin
and nature of justice;—it is a mean or compromise,
between the best of all, which is to do injustice and not be
punished, and the worst of all, which is to suffer injustice
without the power of retaliation; and justice, being at a

middle point between the two, is tolerated not as a good but
as the lesser evil, and honoured where men are too feeble to
do injustice. For no man who is worthy to be called a man
would ever submit to such an agreement with another if he
had the power to be unjust; he would be mad if he did.
Such is the received account Socrates, of the nature of
justice, and the circumstances which bring it into being.
Now that those who practise justice do so involuntarily and
because they have not the power to be unjust will best
appear if we imagine something of this kind: having given
to both the just and the unjust power to do what they will,
let us watch and see whither desire will lead them; then we
shall discover in the very act the just and unjust man to be
proceeding along the same road, following their interest,
which all creatures instinctively pursue as their good; the
force of law is required to compel them to pay respect to
equality. The liberty which we are supposing may be most
completely given to them in the form of such a power as is
said to have been possessed by Gyges, the ancestor of
Croesus the Lydian. According to the tradition, Gyges was
a shepherd in the service of the reigning king of Lydia;
there was a great storm, and an earthquake made an
opening in the earth at the place where he was feeding his
flock. Amazed at the sight, he descended into the opening,
where, among other marvels which form part of the story,
he beheld a hollow brazen horse, having doors, at which he
stooping and looking in saw a dead body of stature, as
appeared to him, more than human; he took from the corpse
a gold ring that was on the hand, but nothing else, and so
reascended. Now the shepherds met together, according to
custom, that they might send their monthly report about the
flocks to the king; into their assembly he came having the
ring on his finger, and as he was sitting among them he
chanced to turn the collet of the ring to the inside of his
hand, when instantly he became invisible to the rest of the
company and they began to speak of him as if he were no
longer present. He was astonished at this, and again
touching the ring he turned the collet outwards and
reappeared; when he perceived this, he made several trials
of the ring, and always with the same result—when he
turned the collet inwards he became invisible, when
outwards he was visible. Whereupon he contrived to be
chosen one of the messengers who were sent to the court;
where as soon as he arrived he seduced the queen, and with
her help conspired against the king and slew him, and took
the kingdom. Suppose now that there were two such magic

rings, and the just put on one of them and the unjust the
other; no man can be imagined to be of such an iron nature
that he would stand fast in justice. No man would keep his
hands off what was not his own when he could safely take
what he liked out of the market, or go into houses and lie
with any one at his pleasure, or kill or release from prison
whom he would, and in all respects be like a god among
men. Then the actions of the just would be as the actions of
the unjust; they would both tend to the same goal. And this
we may truly affirm to be a great proof that a man is just,
not willingly or because he thinks that justice is any good
to him individually, but of necessity; for wherever anyone
thinks that he can safely be unjust, there he is unjust. For all
men believe in their hearts that injustice is far more
profitable to the individual than justice and he who argues
as I have been supposing will say that they are right. If you
could imagine anyone obtaining this power of becoming
invisible, and never doing any wrong or touching what was
another's, he would be thought by the lookers-on to be an
unhappy man and a fool, although they would praise him to
one another's faces, and keep up appearances with one
another from a fear that they too might suffer injustice.
Enough of this.

Now, if we are to form a real judgement of the two lives in these
respects, we must set apart the extremes of justice and
injustice; there is no other way; and how is the contrast to
be effected? I answer: Let the unjust man be entirely unjust,
and the just man entirely just; nothing is to be taken away
from either of them, and both are to be perfectly furnished
for the work of their respective lives. First, let the unjust be
like other distinguished masters of craft; like the skillful
pilot or physician, who knows intuitively what is possible
or impossible in his art and keeps within those limits, and
who, if he fails at any point, is able to recover himself. So
let the unjust man attempt to do the right sort of wrongs,
and let him escape detection if he is to be pronounced a
master of injustice. To be found out is a sign of
incompetence; for the height of injustice is to be deemed
just when you are not. Therefore I say that in the perfectly
unjust man we must assume the most perfect injustice;
there is to be no deduction, but we must allow him, while
doing the most unjust acts, to have acquired the greatest
reputation for justice. If he has taken a false step he must be
able to recover himself; he must be one who can speak with
effect, if any of his deeds come to light, and who can force
his way where force is required, by his courage and

strength and command of wealth and friends. And at his side let us place the just man in his nobleness and simplicity, wishing, as Aeschylus says, to be and not to seem good. There must be no seeming, for if he seems to be just he will be honoured and rewarded, and then we shall not know whether he is just for the sake of justice or for the sake of honours and rewards; therefore, let him be clothed in justice only, and have no other covering; and he must be imagined in a state of life the opposite of the former. Let him be the best of men, and let him be reputed the worst; then he will have been put to the test and we shall see whether his justice is proof against evil reputation and its consequences. And let him continue thus to the hour of death; being just and seeming to be unjust. When both have reached the uttermost extreme, the one of justice and the other of injustice, let judgement be given which of them is the happier of the two.

SOCRATES:

Heavens! my dear Glaucon . . . how energetically you polish them up for the decision, first one and then the other, as if they were two statues.

EPICURUS

The Pursuit of Pleasure

EPICURUS *(c. 342–270 B.C.) was a Greek philosopher who argued that the good life consisted of pleasure. He is still regarded as one of the most articulate spokespersons for hedonism. His insistence on pleasure, however, is hardly of the "beer and pizza" variety, as the following selection from his* Menocceus *makes clear.*

LET no one when young delay to study philosophy, nor when he is old grow weary of his study. For no one can come too early or too late to secure the health of his soul. And the man who says that the age for philosophy has either not yet come or has gone by is like the man who says that the age for happiness is not yet come to him, or has passed away. Wherefore both when young and old a man must study philosophy, that as he grows old he may be young in blessings through the grateful recollection of what has been, and that in youth he may be old as well, since he will know no fear of what is to come. We must then meditate on the things that make our happiness, seeing that when that is with us we have all, but when it is absent we do all to win it.

The things which I used unceasingly to commend to you, these do and practise, considering them to be the first principles of the good life. First of all believe that god is a being immortal and blessed, even as the common idea of a god is engraved on men's minds, and do not assign to him anything alien to his immortality or ill-suited to his blessedness: but believe about him everything that can uphold his blessedness and immortality. . . .

Become accustomed to the belief that death is nothing to us. For all good and evil consists in sensation, but death is deprivation of sensation. And therefore a right understanding that death is nothing to us makes the mortality of life enjoyable, not because it adds to it an infinite span of time, but because it takes away the craving for immortality. For there is nothing terrible in life for the man who has truly comprehended that there is nothing terrible in not living. So that the man speaks but idly who says that he fears death not because it will be painful when it comes, but because it is painful in anticipation. For that which gives no trouble when it comes, is but an empty pain in anticipation. So death, the most terrifying of ills, is nothing to us, since so long as we exist death is not with us; but when death comes, then we do not exist. It does not then concern either the living or the dead, since for the former it is not, and the latter are no more.

But the many at one moment shun death as the greatest of evils, at another

yearn for it as a respite from the evils in life. But the wise man neither seeks to escape life nor fears the cessation of life, for neither does life offend him nor does the absence of life seem to be any evil. And just as with food he does not seek simply the larger share and nothing else, but rather the most pleasant, so he seeks to enjoy not the longest period of time, but the most pleasant.

And he who counsels the young man to live well, but the old man to make a good end, is foolish, not merely because of the desirability of life, but also because it is the same training which teaches to live well and to die well. Yet much worse still is the man who says it is good not to be born, but

> once born make haste to pass the gates of Death. (Theognis, 427)

For if he says this from conviction why does he not pass away out of life? For it is open to him to do so, if he had firmly made up his mind to this. But if he speaks in jest, his words are idle among men who cannot receive them.

We must then bear in mind that the future is neither ours, nor yet wholly not ours, so that we may not altogether expect it as sure to come, nor abandon hope of it, as if it will certainly not come.

We must consider that of desires some are natural, others vain, and of the natural some are necessary and others merely natural; and of the necessary some are necessary for happiness, others for the repose of the body, and others for very life. The right understanding of these facts enables us to refer all choice and avoidance to the health of the body and the soul's freedom from disturbance, since this is the aim of the life of blessedness. For it is to obtain this end that we always act, namely, to avoid pain and fear. And when this is once secured for us, all the tempest of the soul is dispersed, since the living creature has not to wander as though in search of something that is missing, and to look for some other thing by which he can fulfil the good of the soul and the good of the body. For it is then that we have need of pleasure, when we feel pain owing to the absence of pleasure; but when we do not feel pain, we no longer need pleasure. And for this cause we call pleasure the beginning and end of the blessed life. For we recognize pleasure as the first good innate in us, and from pleasure we begin every act of choice and avoidance, and to pleasure we return again, using the feeling as the standard by which we judge every good.

And since pleasure is the first good and natural to us, for this very reason we do not choose every pleasure, but sometimes we pass over many pleasures, when greater discomfort accrues to us as the result of them: and similarly we think many pains better than pleasures, since a greater pleasure comes to us when we have endured pains for a long time. Every pleasure then because of its natural kinship to us is good, yet not every pleasure is to be chosen: even as every pain also is an evil, yet not all are always of a nature to be avoided. Yet by a scale of comparison and by the consideration of advantages and disadvantages we must form our judgement on all these matters. For the good on certain occasions we treat as bad, and conversely the bad as good.

And again independence of desire we think a great good—not that we may at all times enjoy but a few things, but that, if we do not possess many, we may enjoy the few in the genuine persuasion that those have the sweetest pleasure in luxury who least need it, and that all that

is natural is easy to be obtained, but that which is superfluous is hard. And so plain savours bring us a pleasure equal to a luxurious diet, when all the pain due to want is removed; and bread and water produce the highest pleasure, when one who needs them puts them to his lips. To grow accustomed therefore to simple and not luxurious diet gives us health to the full, and makes a man alert for the needful employments of life, and when after long intervals we approach luxuries, disposes us better towards them, and fits us to be fearless of fortune.

When, therefore, we maintain that pleasure is the end, we do not mean the pleasures of profligates and those that consist in sensuality, as is supposed by some who are either ignorant or disagree with us or do not understand, but freedom from pain in the body and from trouble in the mind. For it is not continuous drinkings and revellings, nor the satisfaction of lusts, nor the enjoyment of fish and other luxuries of the wealthy table, which produce a pleasant life, but sober reasoning, searching out the motives for all choice and avoidance, and banishing mere opinions, to which are due the greatest disturbance of the spirit.

Of all this the beginning and the greatest good is prudence. Wherefore prudence is a more precious thing even than philosophy: for from prudence are sprung all the other virtues, and it teaches us that it is not possible to live pleasantly without living prudently and honourably and justly, nor, again, to live a life of prudence, honour, and justice without living pleasantly. For the virtues are by nature bound up with the pleasant life, and the pleasant life is inseparable from them. For indeed who, think you, is a better man then he who holds reverent opinions concerning the gods, and is at all times free from fear of death, and has reasoned out the end ordained by nature? He understands that the limit of good things is easy to fulfil and easy to attain, whereas the course of ills is either short in time or slight in pain: he laughs at destiny, whom some have introduced as the mistress of all things. He thinks that with us lies the chief power in determining events, some of which happen by necessity and some by chance, and some are within our control; for while necessity cannot be called to account, he sees that chance is inconstant, but that which is in our control is subject to no master, and to it are naturally attached praise and blame. For, indeed, it were better to follow the myths about the gods than to become a slave to the destiny of the natural philosophers: for the former suggests a hope of placating the gods by worship, whereas the latter involves a necessity which knows no placation. As to chance, he does not regard it as a god as most men do (for in god's acts there is no disorder), nor as an uncertain cause of all things: for he does not believe that good and evil are given by chance to man for the framing of a blessed life, but that opportunities for great good and great evil are afforded by it. He therefore thinks it better to be unfortunate in reasonable action than to prosper in unreason. For it is better in a man's actions that what is well chosen should fail, rather than that what is ill chosen should be successful owing to chance.

Meditate therefore on these things and things akin to them night and day by yourself, and with a companion like to yourself, and never shall you be disturbed waking or asleep, but you shall live like a god among men. For a man who lives among immortal blessings is not like to a mortal being.

THOMAS HOBBES

People Are Selfish

THOMAS HOBBES *(1588–1679) was an English philosopher famous for his work in political theory. He saw the fate of ancient Athens to be a warning against the excesses of democracy. His most famous work is* Leviathan *(1651), in which, among other things, he suggests, at least, that all people are selfish by nature.*

IT may seem strange to some man, that has not well weighed these things; that nature should thus dissociate, and render men apt to invade, and destroy one another: and he may therefore, not trusting to this inference, made from the passions, desire perhaps to have the same confirmed by experience. Let him therefore consider with himself, when taking a journey, he arms himself, and seeks to go well accompanied; when going to sleep, he locks his doors; when even in his house he locks his chests; and this when he knows there be laws, and public officers, armed, to revenge all injuries shall be done him; what opinion he has of his fellow subjects, when he rides armed; of his fellow citizens, when he locks his doors; and of his children, and servants, when he locks his chests. Does he not there as much accuse mankind by his actions, as I do by my words? But neither of us accuse man's nature in it. The desires, and other passions of man, are in themselves no sin. No more are the actions, that proceed from those passions, till they know a law that forbids them: which till laws be made they cannot know: nor can any law be made, till they have agreed upon the person that shall make it.

It may peradventure be thought, there was never such a time, nor condition of war as this; and I believe it was never generally so, over all the world: but there are many places, where they live so now. For the savage people in many places of America, except the government of small families, the concord whereof dependeth on natural lust, have no government at all; and live at this day in that brutish manner, as I said before. Howsoever, it may be perceived what manner of life there would be, where there were no common power to fear, by the manner of life, which men that have formerly lived under a peaceful government, use to degenerate into, in civil war.

But though there had never been any time, wherein particular men were in a condition of war one against another; yet in all times, kings, and persons of sovereign authority, because of their independency, are in continual jealousies, and in the state and posture of gladiators; having their weapons pointing, and their eyes fixed on one another; that is, their forts, garrisons, and guns upon the frontiers of their kingdoms; and continual spies upon their neighbours; which is a posture of war. But because they uphold thereby, the industry of their subjects; there does not follow from it, that misery, which accompanies the liberty of particular men.

To this war of every man, against every man, this also is consequent; that nothing can be unjust. The notions of right and wrong, justice and injustice have there no place. Where there is no common power, there is no law: where no law, no injustice. Force, and fraud, are in war the two cardinal virtues. Justice, and injustice are none of the faculties neither of the body, nor mind. If they were, they might be in a man that were alone in the world, as well as his senses, and passions. They are qualities, that relate to men in society, not in solitude. It is consequent also to the same condition, that there be no propriety, no dominion, no *mine* and *thine* distinct; but only that to be every man's, that he can get: and for so long, as he can keep it. And thus much for the ill condition, which man by mere nature is actually placed in; though with a possibility to come out of it, consisting partly in the passions, partly in his reason. . . .

JOSEPH BUTLER

Benevolence and Self-Interest

JOSEPH BUTLER *(1692–1752) was a bishop in England whose sermons were famous during his lifetime and have become philosophical classics since then. The following arguments against egoism (and in particular against Hobbes) are taken from his* Fifteen Sermons *(1726).*

SERMON I: UPON THE SOCIAL NATURE OF MAN

THE comparison will be between the nature of man as respecting self, and tending to private good, his own preservation and happiness; and the nature of man as having respect to society, and tending to promote public good, the happiness of that society. These ends do indeed perfectly coincide; and to aim at public and private good are so far from being inconsistent, that they mutually promote each other: yet in the following discourse they must be considered as entirely distinct; otherwise the nature of man as tending to one, or as tending to the other cannot be compared. There can no comparison be made, without considering the things compared as distinct and different.

From this review and comparison of the nature of man as respecting self, and as respecting society, it will plainly appear, that *there are as real and the same kind of indications in human nature, that we were made for society and to do good to our fellow-creatures, as that we were intended to take care of our own life and health and private good: and that the same objections lie against one of these assertions, as against the other.* For,

First, There is a natural principle of *benevolence* in man; which is in some degree to *society,* what *self-love* is to the *individual.* And if there be in mankind any disposition to friendship; if there be any such thing as compassion, for compassion is momentary love; if there be any such thing as the paternal or filial affections; if there be any affection in human nature, the object and end of which is the good of another, this is itself benevolence, or the love of another. Be it ever so short, be it in ever so low a degree, or ever so unhappily confined; it proves the assertion, and points out what we were designed for, as really as though it were in a higher degree and more extensive. I must, however, remind you that though benevolence and self-love are different; though the former tends most directly to public good, and the latter to private: yet they are so perfectly coincident that the greatest satisfactions to ourselves depend upon our having benevolence in a due degree, and that self-love is one chief security of our right behaviour towards society. It may be added, that their mutual coinciding, so that we can scarce promote one without the other, is equally proof that we were made for both.

Secondly, This will further appear, from observing that the *several passions* and *affections,* which are distinct, both from benevolence and self-love, do in general contribute and lead us to *public* good as really as to *private.* It might be thought too minute and particular, and would carry us too great a length, to distinguish between and compare together the several passions or appetites distinct from benevolence, whose primary use and intention is the security and good of society; and the passions distinct from self-love, whose primary intention and design is the security and good of the individual. It is enough to the present argument, that desire of esteem from others, contempt and esteem of them, love of society as distinct from affection to the good of it, indignation against successful vice, that these are public affections or passions; have an immediate respect to others, naturally lead us to regulate our behavior in such a manner as will be of service to our fellow-creatures. If any or all of these may be considered likewise as private affections, as tending to private good; this does not hinder them from being public affections too, or destroy the good influence of them upon society, and their tendency to public good. It may be added, that as persons without any conviction from reason of the desirableness of life, would yet of course preserve it merely from the appetite of hunger; so by acting merely from regard (suppose) to reputation, without any consideration of the good of others, men often contribute to public good. In both these instances they are plainly instruments in the hands of another, in the hands of Providence, to carry on ends, the preservation of the individual and good of society, which they themselves have not in their view or intention. The sum is, men have various appetites, passions, and particular affections, quite distinct both from self-love and from benevolence: all of these have a tendency to promote both public and private good, and may be considered as respecting others and ourselves equally and in common: but some of them seem most immediately to respect others, or

tend to public good; others of them most immediately to respect self, or tend to private good: as the former are not benevolence, so the latter are not self-love: neither sort are instances of our love either to ourselves or others; . . .

Thirdly, There is a principle of reflection in men, by which they distinguish between, approve, and disapprove their own actions. We are plainly constituted such sort of creatures as to reflect upon our own nature. The mind can take a view of what passes within itself, its propensions, aversions, passions, affections, as respecting such objects, and in such degrees; and of the several actions consequent thereupon. In this survey it approves of one, disapproves of another, and towards a third is affected in neither of these ways, but is quite indifferent. This principle in man, by which he approves or disapproves his heart, temper, and actions, is conscience; for this is the strict sense of the word, though sometimes it is used so as to take in more. And that this faculty tends to restrain men from doing mischief to each other, and leads them to do good, is too manifest to need being insisted upon. Thus a parent has the affection of love to his children: this leads him to take care of, to educate, to make due provision for them: the natural affection leads to this; but the reflection that it is his proper business, what belongs to him, that it is right and commendable so to do, this added to the affection becomes a much more settled principle, and carries him on through more labour and difficulties for the sake of his children, then he would undergo from that affection alone, if he thought it, and the course of action it led to, either indifferent or criminal. This indeed is impossible, to do that which is good and not to approve of it; for which reason they are frequently not considered as distinct, though they really are; for men often approve of the actions of others, which they will not imitate, and likewise do that which they approve not. It cannot possibly be denied that there is this principle of reflection or conscience in human nature. Suppose a man to relieve an innocent person in great distress; suppose the same man afterwards, in the fury of anger, to do the greatest mischief to a person who had given no just cause of offence; to aggravate the injury, add the circumstances of former friendship, and obligation from the injured person; let the man who is supposed to have done these two different actions, coolly reflect upon them afterwards, without regard to their consequences to himself: to assert that any common man would be affected in the same way towards these different actions, that he would make no distinction between them, but approve or disapprove them equally, is too glaring a falsity to need being confuted. There is therefore this principle of reflection or conscience in mankind. It is needless to compare the respect it has to private good, with the respect it has to public; since it plainly tends as much to the latter as to the former, and is commonly thought to tend chiefly to the latter. This faculty is now mentioned merely as another part of the inward frame of man, pointing out to us in some degree what we are intended for, and as what will naturally and of course have some influence. The particular place assigned to it by nature, what authority it has, and how great influence it ought to have, shall be hereafter considered.

From this comparison of benevolence and self-love, of our public and private affections, of the courses of life they lead to, and of the principle of reflection or conscience as respecting

each of them, it is as manifest, that *we were made for society, and to promote the happiness of it, as that we were intended to take care of our own life, and health, and private good.* . . .

The sum of the whole is plainly this. The nature of man considered in his single capacity, and with respect only to the present world, is adapted and leads him to attain the greatest happiness he can for himself in the present world. The nature of man considered in his public or social capacity leads him to a right behaviour in society, to that course of life which we call virtue. Men follow or obey their nature in both these capacities and respects to a certain degree but not entirely: their actions do not come up to the whole of what their nature leads them to in either of these capacities or respects: and they often violate their nature in both, *i.e.,* as they neglect the duties they owe to their fellow-creatures, to which their nature leads them; and are injurious, to which their nature is abhorrent; so there is a manifest negligence in men of their real happiness or interest in the present world, when that interest is inconsistent with a present gratification; for the sake of which they negligently, nay, even knowingly, are the authors and instruments of their own misery and ruin. Thus they are as often unjust to themselves as to others, and for the most part are equally so to both by the same actions. . . .

SERMON XI: UPON THE LOVE OF OUR NEIGHBOUR

Every man hath a general desire of his own happiness; and likewise a variety of particular affections, passions, and appetites, to particular external objects. The former proceeds from, or is, self-love, and seems inseparable from all sensible creatures, who can reflect upon themselves and their own interest or happiness, so as to have that interest an object to their minds: what is to be said of the latter is, that they proceed from, or together make up, that particular nature, according to which man is made. The object the former pursues is somewhat internal, our own happiness, enjoyment, satisfaction; whether we have or have not a distinct particular perception what it is, or wherein it consists: the objects of the latter are this or that particular external thing, which the affections tend towards, and of which it hath always a particular idea or perception. The principle we call self-love never seeks anything external for the sake of the thing, but only as a means of happiness or good: particular affections rest in the external things themselves. One belongs to man as a reasonable creature reflecting upon his own interest or happiness; the other, though quite distinct from reason, is as much a part of human nature.

That all particular appetites and passions are towards *external things themselves,* distinct from the *pleasure arising from them,* is manifested from hence, that there could not be this pleasure, were it not for that prior suitableness between the object and the passion: there could be no enjoyment or delight for one thing more than another, from eating food more than from swallowing a stone, if there were not an affection or appetite to one thing more than another.

Every particular affection, even the love of our neighbour, is as really our own affection, as self-love; and the pleasure arising from its gratification is as much my own pleasure, as the pleasure self-love would have from knowing I myself should be happy some time hence, would be my own pleasure. And

if, because every particular affection is a man's own, and the pleasure arising from its gratification his own pleasure, or pleasure to himself, such particular affection must be called self-love. According to this way of speaking, no creature whatever can possibly act merely from self-love; and every action and every affection whatever is to be resolved up into this one principle. But then this is not the language of mankind: or, if it were, we should want words to express the difference between the principle of an action, proceeding from cool consideration that it will be to my own advantage; and an action, suppose of revenge, or of friendship by which a man runs upon certain ruin, to do evil or good to another. It is manifest the principles of these actions are totally different, and so want different words to be distinguished by: all that they agree in is, that they both proceed from, and are done to gratify an inclination in a man's self. But the principle or inclination in one case is self-love; in the other, hatred, or love of another. There is then a distinction between the cool principle of self-love, or general desire of our own happiness, as one part of our nature, and one principle of action; and the particular affections towards particular external objects, as another principle of action. How much soever, therefore, is to be allowed to self-love, yet it cannot be allowed to be the whole of our inward constitution; because, you see, there are other parts or principles which come into it.

Further, private happiness or good is all which self-love can make us desire or be concerned about. In having this consists its gratification; it is an affection to ourselves—a regard to our own interest, happiness, and private good: and in the proportion a man hath this, he is interested, or a lover of himself. Let this be kept in mind, because there is commonly, as I shall presently have occasion to observe, another sense put upon these words. On the other hand, particular affections tend towards particular external things; these are their objects; having these is their end; in this consists their gratification: no matter whether it be, or be not, upon the whole, our interest or happiness. An action, done from the former of these principles, is called an interested action. An action, proceeding from any of the latter, has its denomination of passionate, ambitious, revengeful, or any other, from the particular appetite or affection from which it proceeds. Thus self-love, as one part of human nature, and the several particular principles as the other part, are themselves, their objects, and ends, stated and shown.

From hence it will be easy to see how far, and in what ways, each of these can contribute and be subservient to the private good of the individual. Happiness does not consist in self-love. The desire of happiness is no more the thing itself, than the desire of riches is the possession or enjoyment of them. People may love themselves with the most entire and unbounded affection, and yet be extremely miserable. Neither can self-love any way help them out, but by setting them on work to get rid of the causes of their misery, to gain or make use of those objects which are by nature adapted to afford satisfaction. Happiness or satisfaction consists only in the enjoyment of those objects which are by nature suited to our several particular appetites, passions, and affections. So that if self-love wholly engrosses us, and leaves no room for any other principle, there can be absolutely no such thing at all as happiness or en-

joyment of any kind whatever; since happiness consists in the gratification of particular passions, which supposes the having of them. Self-love then does not constitute *this* or *that* to be our interest or good; but our interest or good being constituted by nature and supposed self-love, only puts us upon obtaining and securing it. Therefore, if it be possible that self-love may prevail and exert itself in a degree or manner which is not subservient to this end, then it will not follow that our interest will be promoted in proportion to the degree in which that principle engrosses us, and prevails over others. Nay, further, the private and contracted affection, when it is not subservient to this end, private good, may, for anything that appears, have a direct contrary tendency and effect. And if we will consider the matter, we shall see that it often really has. Disengagement is absolutely necessary to enjoyment; and a person may have so steady and fixed an eye upon his own interest, whatever he places it in, as may hinder him from attending to many gratifications within his reach, which others have their minds free and open to. Overfondness for a child is not generally thought to be for its advantage; and, if there be any guess to be from appearances, surely that character we call *selfish* is not the most promising for happiness. Such a temper may plainly be, and exert itself in a degree and manner which may give unnecessary and useless solicitude and anxiety, in a degree and manner which may prevent obtaining the means and materials of enjoyment, as well as the making use of them. Immoderate self-love does very ill consult its own interest; and how much soever a paradox it may appear, it is certainly true, that, even from self-love, we should endeavour to get over all inordinate regard to, and consideration of, ourselves. Every one of our passions and affections hath its natural stint and bound, which may easily be exceeded; whereas our enjoyments can possibly be but in a determinate measure and degree. Therefore such excess of the affection, since it cannot procure any enjoyment, must in all cases be useless, but is generally attended with inconveniences, and often is down-right pain and misery. This holds as much with regard to self-love as to all other affections. The natural degree of it, so far as it sets us on work to gain and make use of the materials of satisfaction, may be to our real advantage; but beyond or beside this, it is in several respects an inconvenience and disadvantage. Thus it appears that private interest is so far from being likely to be promoted in proportion to the degree in which self-love engrosses us, and prevails over all other principles, that *the contracted affection may be so prevalent as to disappoint itself and even contradict its own end, private good. . . .*

RICHARD DAWKINS

The Selfish Gene

RICHARD DAWKINS *is a British biologist and the author of* The Selfish Gene, *an excerpt from which is reproduced here.*

THIS chapter is mostly about the much-misunderstood topic of aggression. We shall continue to treat the individual as a selfish machine, programmed to do whatever is best for his genes as a whole. This is the language of convenience. At the end of the chapter we return to the language of single genes.

To a survival machine, another survival machine (which is not its own child or another close relative) is a part of its environment, like a rock or a river or a lump of food. It is something that gets in the way, or something that can be exploited. It differs from a rock or a river in one important respect: it is inclined to hit back. This is because it too is a machine which holds its immortal genes in trust for the future, and it too will stop at nothing to preserve them. Natural selection favours genes which control their survival machines in such a way that they make the best use of their environment. This includes making the best use of other survival machines, both of the same and of different species.

In some cases survival machines seem to impinge rather little on each others' lives. For instance moles and blackbirds do not eat each other, mate with each other, or compete with each other for living space. Even so, we must not treat them as completely insulated. They may compete for something, perhaps earthworms. This does not mean you will ever see a mole and a blackbird engaged in a tug of war over a worm; indeed a blackbird may never set eyes on a mole in its life. But if you wiped out the population of moles, the effect on blackbirds might be dramatic, although I could not hazard a guess as to what the details might be, nor by what tortuously indirect routes the influence might travel.

Survival machines of different species influence each other in a variety of ways. They may be predators or prey, parasites or hosts, competitors for some scarce resource. They may be exploited in special ways, as for instance when bees are used as pollen carriers by flowers.

Survival machines of the same species tend to impinge on each others' lives more directly. This is for many reasons. One is that half the population of one's own species may be potential mates, and potentially hard-working and exploitable parents to one's children. Another reason is that members of the same species, being very similar to each other, being machines for preserving genes in the same kind of place, with the same kind of way of life, are particularly direct competitors for all the resources necessary for life. To a blackbird, a mole may be a competitor, but it is not nearly so important a competitor as another blackbird. Moles and blackbirds may compete for worms, but blackbirds and blackbirds compete with each other for worms *and* for everything else. If they are members of the same sex, they may also compete for mating partners. For reasons which we shall see, it is usually the males who compete with each other for females. This means that a male might benefit his own genes if he does something detrimental to another male with whom he is competing.

The logical policy for a survival machine might therefore seem to be to murder its rivals, and then, preferably, to eat them. Although murder and cannibalism do occur in nature, they are not as common as a naive interpretation of the selfish gene theory might predict. Indeed Konrad Lorenz, in *On Aggression,* stresses the restrained and gentlemanly nature of animal fighting. For him the notable thing about animal fights is that they are formal tournaments, played according to rules like those of boxing or fencing. Animals fight with gloved fists and blunted foils. Threat and bluff take the place of deadly earnest. Gestures of surrender are recognized by victors, who then refrain from dealing the killing blow or bite which our naive theory might predict.

This interpretation of animal aggression as being restrained and formal can be disputed. In particular, it is certainly wrong to condemn poor old *Homo sapiens* as the only species to kill his own kind, the only inheritor of the mark of Cain, and similar melodramatic charges. Whether a naturalist stresses the violence or the restraint of animal aggression depends partly on the kinds of animals he is used to watching, and partly on his evolutionary preconceptions—Lorenz is, after all, a 'good of the species' man. Even if it has been exaggerated, the gloved fist view of animal fights seems to have at least some truth. Superficially this looks like a form of altruism. The selfish gene theory must face up to the difficult task of explaining it. Why is it that animals do not go all out to kill rival members of their species at every possible opportunity?

The general answer to this is that there are costs as well as benefits resulting from outright pugnacity, and not only the obvious costs in time and energy. For instance, suppose that B and C

are both my rivals, and I happen to meet B. It might seem sensible for me as a selfish individual to try to kill him. But wait. C is also my rival, and C is also B's rival. By killing B, I am potentially doing a good turn to C by removing one of his rivals. I might have done better to let B live, because he might then have competed or fought with C, thereby benefiting me indirectly. The moral of this simple hypothetical example is that there is no obvious merit in indiscriminately trying to kill rivals. In a large and complex system of rivalries, removing one rival from the scene does not necessarily do any good: other rivals may be more likely to benefit from his death than oneself. This is the kind of hard lesson that has been learned by pest-control officers. You have a serious agricultural pest, you discover a good way to exterminate it and you gleefully do so, only to find that another pest benefits from the extermination even more than human agriculture does, and you end up worse off than you were before.

On the other hand, it might seem a good plan to kill, or at least fight with, certain particular rivals in a discriminating way. If B is an elephant seal in possession of a large harem full of females, and if I, another elephant seal, can acquire his harem by killing him, I might be well advised to attempt to do so. But there are costs and risks even in selective pugnacity. It is to B's advantage to fight back, to defend his valuable property. If I start a fight, I am just as likely to end up dead as he is. Perhaps even more so. He holds a valuable resource, that is why I want to fight him. But why does he hold it? Perhaps he won it in combat. He has probably beaten off other challengers before me. He is probably a good fighter. Even if I win the fight and gain the harem, I may be so badly mauled in the process that I cannot enjoy the benefits. Also, fighting uses up time and energy. These might be better conserved for the time being. If I concentrate on feeding and on keeping out of trouble for a time, I shall grow bigger and stronger. I'll fight him for the harem in the end, but I may have a better chance of winning eventually if I wait, rather than rush in now.

This subjective soliloquy is just a way of pointing out that the decision whether or not to fight should ideally be preceded by a complex, if unconscious, 'cost–benefit' calculation. The potential benefits are not all stacked up on the side of fighting, although undoubtedly some of them are. Similarly, during a fight, each tactical decision over whether to escalate the fight or cool it has costs and benefits which could, in principle, be analyzed. This has long been realized by ethologists in a vague sort of way, but it has taken J. Maynard Smith, not normally regarded as an ethologist, to express the idea forcefully and clearly. In collaboration with G. R. Price and G. A. Parker, he uses the branch of mathematics known as Game Theory. Their elegant ideas can be expressed in words without mathematical symbols, albeit at some cost in rigour.

The essential concept Maynard Smith introduces is that of the *evolutionarily stable strategy*, an idea which he traces back to W. D. Hamilton and R. H. MacArthur. A 'strategy' is a pre-programmed behavioural policy. An example of a strategy is: 'Attack opponent; if he flees pursue him; if he retaliates run away.' It is important to realize that we are not thinking of the strategy as being consciously worked out by the individual. Remember that we are picturing the animal as a robot survival machine with a pre-programmed computer controlling the muscles. To write the strategy out as a set of simple

instructions in English is just a convenient way for us to think about it. By
some unspecified mechanism, the animal behaves as if he were following
these instructions.

An evolutionarily stable strategy or
ESS is defined as a strategy which, if
most members of a population adopt it,
cannot be bettered by an alternative
strategy. It is a subtle and important
idea. Another way of putting it is to say
that the best strategy for an individual
depends on what the majority of the

population are doing. Since the rest of
the population consists of individuals,
each one trying to maximize his *own*
success, the only strategy that persists
will be one which, once evolved, cannot
be bettered by any deviant individual.
Following a major environmental
change there may be a brief period of
evolutionary instability, perhaps even
oscillation in the population. But once
an ESS is achieved it will stay: selection
will penalize deviation from it.

STEPHEN JAY GOULD

So Cleverly Kind an Animal

STEPHEN JAY GOULD *is a professor of paleontology at Harvard University and
the author of a great many scientific and popular articles and books on evolution,
including* The Panda's Thumb. *The following essay is taken from his monthly column
in* Natural History *magazine.*

IN *Civilization and Its Discontents,*
Sigmund Freud examined the agonizing dilemma of human social
life. We are by nature selfish and aggressive, yet any successful civilization
demands that we suppress our biological inclinations and act altruistically
for common good and harmony. Freud
argued further that as civilizations become increasingly complex and "modern," we must renounce more and more
of our innate selves. This we do imperfectly, with guilt, pain, and hardship;
the price of civilization is individual
suffering.

It is impossible to overlook the extent to
which civilization is built up upon a
renunciation of instinct, how much it
presupposes precisely the nonsatisfac-
tion . . . of powerful instincts. This "cultural frustration" dominates the large
field of social relationships between
human beings.

Freud's argument is a particularly
forceful variation on a ubiquitous theme
in speculations about "human nature."
What we criticize in ourselves, we attribute to our animal past. These are
the shackles of our apish ancestry—

brutality, aggression, selfishness; in short, general nastiness. What we prize and strive for (with pitifully limited success), we consider as a unique overlay, conceived by our rationality and imposed upon an unwilling body. Our hopes for a better future lie in reason and kindness—the mental transcendence of our biological limitations. "Build thee more stately mansions, O my soul."

Little more than ancient prejudice supports this common belief. It certainly gains no justification from science—so profound is our ignorance about the biology of human behavior. It arises from such sources as the theology of the human soul and the "dualism" of philosophers who sought separate realms for mind and body. It has roots in an attitude that I attack in several of these essays: our desire to view the history of life as progressive and to place ourselves on top of the heap (with all the prerogatives of domination). We seek a criterion for our uniqueness, settle (naturally) upon our minds, and define the noble results of human consciousness as something intrinsically apart from biology. But why? Why should our nastiness be the baggage of an apish past and our kindness uniquely human? Why should we not seek continuity with other animals for our "noble" traits as well?

One nagging scientific argument does seem to support this ancient prejudice. The essential ingredient of human kindness is altruism—sacrifice of our personal comfort, even our lives in extreme cases, for the benefit of others. Yet, if we accept the Darwinian mechanism of evolution, how can altruism be part of biology? Natural selection dictates that organisms act in their own self-interest. They know nothing of such abstract concepts as "the good of the species." They "struggle" continuously to increase the representation of their genes at the expense of their fellows. And that, for all its baldness, is all there is to it; we have discovered no higher principle in nature. Individual advantage, Darwin argues, is the only criterion of success in nature. The harmony of life goes no deeper. The balance of nature arises from interaction between competing teams, each trying to win the prize for itself alone, not from the cooperative sharing of limited resources.

How, then, could anything but selfishness ever evolve as a biological trait of behavior? If altruism is the cement of stable societies, then human society must be fundamentally outside nature. There is one way around this dilemma. Can an apparently altruistic act be "selfish" in this Darwinian sense? Can an individual's sacrifice ever lead to the perpetuation of his own genes? The answer to this seemingly contradictory proposition is "yes." We owe the resolution of this paradox to the theory of "kin selection" developed in the early 1960s by W. D. Hamilton, a British theoretical biologist. It has been stressed as the cornerstone for a biological theory of society in E. O. Wilson's *Sociobiology*. (I criticized the deterministic aspects of Wilson's speculations on human behavior in the last essay. I also praised his general theory of altruism, and continue this theme now.)

The legacy of brilliant men includes undeveloped foresight. English biologist J. B. S. Haldane probably anticipated every good idea that evolutionary theorists will invent during this century. Haldane, arguing about altruism one evening in a pub, reportedly made some quick calculations on the back of an envelope, and announced: "I will lay down my life for two brothers or eight cousins." What did Haldane mean by such a cryptic comment? Human chromosomes come in pairs: We receive one set from our mother's egg; the other from our father's sperm. Thus, we possess a paternal and a maternal copy of each gene (this is not true among males for genes located on sex chromosomes, since the maternal X chromosome is so much longer—i.e. has so many more genes—than the paternal Y chromosome; most genes on the X chromosome have no corresponding copy on the short Y.) Take any human gene. What is the probability that a brother will share the same gene? Suppose that it is on a maternal chromosome (the argument works the same way for paternal chromosomes). Each egg cell contains one chromosome of each pair—that is, one-half the mother's genes. The egg cell that made your brother either had the same chromosome you received or the other member of the pair. The chance that you share your brother's gene is an even fifty-fifty. Your brother shares half your genes and is, in the Darwinian calculus, the same as half of you.

Suppose, then, that you are walking down the road with three brothers. A monster approaches with clearly murderous intent. Your brothers do not see it. You have only two alternatives: Approach it and give a rousing Bronx cheer, thereby warning your brothers, who hide and escape, and insuring your own demise; or hide and watch the monster feast on your three brothers. What, as an accomplished player of the Darwinian game, should you do? The answer must be, step right up and cheer—for you have only yourself to lose, while your three brothers represent one and a half of you. Better that they should live to propagate 150 percent of

your genes. Your apparently altruistic act is genetically "selfish," for it maximizes the contribution of your genes to the next generation.

According to the theory of kin selection, animals evolve behaviors that endanger or sacrifice themselves only if such altruistic acts increase their own genetic potential by benefiting kin. Altruism and the society of kin must go hand in hand; the benefits of kin selection may even propel the evolution of social interaction. While my absurd example of four brothers and a monster is simplistic, the situation becomes much more complex with twelfth cousins, four times removed. Hamilton's theory does not only belabor the obvious.

Hamilton's theory has had stunning success in explaining some persistent biological puzzles in the evolution of social behavior in the Hymenoptera—ants, bees, and wasps. Why has true sociality evolved independently at least eleven times in the Hymenoptera and only once among other insects (the termites)? Why are sterile worker castes always female in the Hymenoptera, but both male and female in termites? The answers seem to lie in the workings of kin selection within the unusual genetic system of the Hymenoptera.

Most sexually reproducing animals are diploid; their cells contain two sets of chromosomes—one derived from their mother, the other from their father. Termites, like most insects, are diploid. The social Hymenoptera, on the other hand, are haplodiploid. Females develop from fertilized eggs as normal diploid individuals with maternal and paternal sets of chromosomes. But males develop from unfertilized eggs and possess only the maternal set of chromosomes; they are, in technical parlance, haploid (half the normal number of chromosomes).

In diploid organisms, genetic relationships of sibs and parents are symmetrical: parents share half their genes with their children, and each sib (on average) shares half its genes with any other sib, male or female. But in haplodiploid species, genetic relationships are asymmetrical, permitting kin selection to work in an unusual and potent way. Consider the relationship of a queen ant to her sons and daughters, and the relationship of these daughters to their sisters and brothers:

1. The queen is related by 1/2 to both her sons and daughters; each of her offspring carries 1/2 her chromosomes and, therefore, 1/2 her genes.

2. Sisters are related to their brothers, not by 1/2 as in diploid organisms, but only by 1/4. Take any of a sister's genes. Chances are 1/2 that it is a paternal gene. If so, she cannot share it with her brother (who has no paternal genes). If it is a maternal gene, then chances are 1/2 that her brother has it as well. Her total relationship with her brother is the average of zero (for paternal genes) and 1/2 (for maternal genes), or 1/4.

3. Sisters are related to their sisters by 3/4. Again, take any gene. If it is paternal, then her sister must share it (since fathers have only one set of chromosomes to pass to all daughters). If it is maternal, then her sister has a fifty-fifty chance of sharing it, as before. Sisters are related by the average of 1 (for paternal genes) and 1/2 (for maternal genes), or 3/4.

These asymmetries seem to provide a simple and elegant explanation for that most altruistic of animal behaviors—the "willingness" of sterile female workers to forego their own reproduction in order to help their mothers raise more sisters. As long as a worker can invest preferentially in her sisters, she will perpetuate more of her genes by helping her mother raise fertile sisters (3/4 relationship) than by raising fertile daughters herself (1/2 relationship). But a male has no inclination toward sterility and labor. He would much rather raise daughters, who share all his genes, than help sisters, who share only 1/2 of them. (I do not mean to attribute conscious will to creatures with such rudimentary brains. I use such phrases as "he would rather" only as a convenient shortcut for "in the course of evolution, males who did not behave this way have been placed at a selective disadvantage and gradually eliminated.")

My colleagues R. L. Trivers and H. Hare have recently reported the following important discovery in *Science* (January 23, 1976): they argue that queens and workers should prefer different sex ratios for fertile offspring. The queen favors a 1:1 ratio of males to females since she is equally related (by 1/2) to her sons and daughters. But the workers raise the offspring and can impose their preferences upon the queen by selective nurturing of her eggs. Workers would rather raise fertile sisters (relationship 3/4) than brothers (relationship 1/4). But they must raise some brothers, lest their sisters fail to find mates. So they compromise by favoring sisters to the extent of their stronger relationship to them. Since they are three times more related to sisters than brothers, they should invest three times more energy in raising sisters. Workers invest energy by feeding; the extent of feeding is reflected in the adult weight of fertile offspring. Trivers and Hare therefore measured the ratio of female/male weight for all fertile offspring taken together in nests of 21 different ant species. The average weight ratio—or investment ratio—is remarkably close to 3:1. This is impressive enough, but the clincher in the argument comes from studies of slave-making ants. Here, the workers are captured members of other species. They have no genetic relationship to the daughters of their imposed queen and should not favor them over the queen's sons. Sure enough, in these situations, the female/male weight ratio is 1:1—even though it is again 3:1 when workers of the enslaved species are not captured but work, instead, for their own queen.

Kin selection, operating on the peculiar genetics of haplodiploidy, seems to explain the key features of social behavior in ants, bees, and wasps. But what can it do for us? How can it help us understand the contradictory amalgam of impulses toward selfishness and altruism that form our own personalities. I am willing to admit—and this is only my intuition, since we have no facts to constrain us—that it probably resolves Freud's dilemma of the first paragraph. Our selfish and aggressive urges may have evolved by the Darwinian route of individual advantage, but our altruistic tendencies need not represent a unique overlay imposed by the demands of civilization. These tendencies may have arisen by the same Darwinian route via kin selection. Basic human kindness may be as "animal" as human nastiness.

But here I stop—short of any deterministic speculation that attributes *specific* behaviors to the possession of specific altruist or opportunist genes. Our genetic makeup permits a wide range of behaviors—from Ebenezer Scrooge before to Ebenezer Scrooge after. I do not believe that the miser hoards through opportunist genes or that the philanthropist gives because nature endowed him with more than the normal complement of altruist genes. Up-

bringing, culture, class, status, and all the intangibles that we call "free will," determine how we restrict our behaviors from the wide spectrum—extreme altruism to extreme selfishness—that our genes permit.

As an example of deterministic speculations based on altruism and kin selection, E. O. Wilson has proposed a genetic explanation of homosexuality (*New York Times Magazine,* October 12, 1975). Since exclusive homosexuals do not bear children, how could a homosexuality gene ever be selected in a Darwinian world? Suppose that our ancestors organized socially as small, competing groups of very close kin. Some groups contained only heterosexual members. Others included homosexuals who functioned as "helpers" in hunting or child rearing: they bore no children but they helped kin to raise their close genetic relatives. If groups with homosexual helpers prevailed in competition over exclusively heterosexual groups, then homosexuality genes would have been maintained by kin selection. There is nothing illogical in this proposal, but it has no facts going for it either. We have identified no homosexuality gene, and we know nothing relevant to this hypothesis about the social organization of our ancestors.

Wilson's intent is admirable; he attempts to affirm the intrinsic dignity of a common and much maligned sexual behavior by arguing that it is natural for some people—and adaptive to boot (at least under an ancestral form of social organization). But the strategy is a dangerous one, for it backfires if the genetic speculation is wrong. If you defend a behavior by arguing that people are programmed directly for it, then how do you continue to defend it if your speculation is wrong, for the behavior then becomes unnatural and worthy of condemnation. Better to stick resolutely to a philosophical position on human liberty; what free adults do with each other in their own private lives is their business alone. It need not be vindicated—and must not be condemned—by genetic speculation.

Although I worry long and hard about the deterministic uses of kin selection, I applaud the insight it offers for my favored theme of biological potentiality. For it extends the realm of genetic potential even further by including the capacity for kindness, once viewed as intrinsically unique to human culture.

Sigmund Freud argued that the history of our greatest scientific insights has reflected, ironically, a continuous retreat of our species from center stage in the cosmos. Before Copernicus and Newton, we thought we lived at the hub of the universe. Before Darwin, we thought that a benevolent God had created us. Before Freud, we imagined ourselves as rational creatures (surely one of the least modest statements in intellectual history). If kin selection marks another stage in this retreat, it will serve us well by nudging our thinking away from domination and toward a perception of respect and unity with other animals.

AYN RAND

The Virtue of Selfishness

AYN RAND *was immensely popular in the 1950s for her novels* The Fountainhead *and* Atlas Shrugged, *in which she argued for individualism and "the virtue of selfishness" against the reigning ethic of "altruism."*

IN popular usage, the word "selfishness" is a synonym of evil; the image it conjures is of a murderous brute who tramples over piles of corpses to achieve his own ends, who cares for no living being and pursues nothing but the gratification of the mindless whims of any immediate moment.

Yet the exact meaning and dictionary definition of the word "selfishness" is: *concern with one's own interests.*

This concept does *not* include a moral evaluation; it does not tell us whether concern with one's own interests is good or evil; nor does it tell us what constitutes man's actual interests. It is the task of ethics to answer such questions.

The ethics of altruism has created the image of the brute, as its answer, in order to make men accept two inhuman tenets: (a) that any concern with one's own interests is evil, regardless of what these interests might be, and (b) that the brute's activities are *in fact* to one's own interest (which altruism enjoins man to renounce for the sake of his neighbors).

For a view of the nature of altruism, its consequences and the enormity of the moral corruption it perpetrates, I shall refer you to *Atlas Shrugged*—or to any of today's newspaper headlines. What concerns us here is altruism's *default* in the field of ethical theory.

There are two moral questions which altruism lumps together into one "package-deal": (1) What are values? (2) Who should be the beneficiary of values? Altruism substitutes the second for the first; it evades the task of defining a code of moral values, thus leaving man, in fact, without moral guidance.

Altruism declares that any action taken for the benefit of others is good, and any action taken for one's own benefit is evil. Thus the *beneficiary* of an action is the only criterion of moral value—and so long as that beneficiary is anybody other than oneself, anything goes.

Hence the appalling immorality, the chronic injustice, the grotesque double standards, the insoluble conflicts and contradictions that have characterized human relationships and human societies throughout history, under all the variants of the altruist ethics.

Observe the indecency of what passes for moral judgments today. An industrialist who produces a fortune, and a gangster who robs a bank are regarded as equally immoral, since they both sought wealth for their own "selfish" benefit. A young man who gives up his career in order to support his parents and never rises beyond the rank of grocery clerk is regarded as morally superior to the young man who endures an excruciating struggle and achieves his personal ambition. A dictator is regarded as moral, since the unspeakable atrocities he committed were intended to benefit "the people," not himself.

Observe what this beneficiary-criterion of morality does to a man's

life. The first thing he learns is that morality is his enemy: he has nothing to gain from it, he can only lose; self-inflicted loss, self-inflicted pain and the gray, debilitating pall of an incomprehensible duty is all that he can expect. He may hope that others might occasionally sacrifice themselves for his benefit, as he grudgingly sacrifices himself for theirs, but he knows that the relationship will bring mutual resentment, not pleasure—and that, morally, their pursuit of values will be like an exchange of unwanted, unchosen Christmas presents, which neither is morally permitted to buy for himself. Apart from such times as he manages to perform some act of self-sacrifice, he possesses no moral significance: morality takes no cognizance of him and has nothing to say to him for guidance in the crucial issues of his life; it is only his own personal, private, "selfish" life and, as such, it is regarded either as evil or, at best, *amoral.*

Since nature does not provide man with an automatic form of survival, since he has to support his life by his own effort, the doctrine that concern with one's own interests is evil means that man's desire to live is evil—that man's life, as such, is evil. No doctrine could be more evil than that.

Yet that is the meaning of altruism, implicit in such examples as the equation of an industrialist with a robber. There is a fundamental moral difference between a man who sees his self-interest in production and a man who sees it in robbery. The evil of a robber does *not* lie in the fact that he pursues his own interests, but in *what* he regards as to his own interest; *not* in the fact that he pursues his values, but in *what* he chose to value; *not* in the fact that he wants to live, but in the fact that he wants to live on a subhuman level (see "The Objectivist Ethics").

If it is true that what I mean by "selfishness" is not what is meant conventionally, then *this* is one of the worst indictments of altruism: it means that altruism *permits no concept* of a self-respecting, self-supporting man—a man who supports his life by his own effort and neither sacrifices himself nor others. It means that altruism permits no view of men except as sacrificial animals and profiteers-on-sacrifice, as victims and parasites—that it permits no concept of a benevolent coexistence among men—that it permits no concept of *justice.*

If you wonder about the reasons behind the ugly mixture of cynicism and guilt in which most men spend their lives, these are the reasons: cynicism, because they neither practice nor accept the altruist morality—guilt, because they dare not reject it.

To rebel against so devastating an evil, one has to rebel against its basic premise. To redeem both man and morality, it is the concept of *"selfishness"* that one has to redeem.

The first step is to assert *man's right to a moral existence*—that is: to recognize his need of a moral code to guide the course and the fulfillment of his own life.

For a brief outline of the nature and the validation of a rational morality, see my lecture on "The Objectivist Ethics" which follows. The reasons why man needs a moral code will tell you that the purpose of morality is to define man's proper values and interests, that *concern with his own interests* is the essence of a moral existence, and that *man must be the beneficiary of his own moral actions.*

Since all values have to be gained and/or kept by men's actions, any breach between actor and beneficiary necessitates an injustice: the sacrifice of some men to others, of the actors to the nonactors, of the moral to the immoral. Nothing could ever justify such a breach, and no one ever has.

The choice of the beneficiary of moral values is merely a preliminary or introductory issue in the field of morality. It is not a substitute for morality nor a criterion of moral value, as altruism has made it. Neither is it a moral *primary;* it has to be derived from and validated by the fundamental premises of a moral system.

The Objectivist ethics holds that the actor must always be the beneficiary of his action and that man must act for his own *rational* self-interest. But his right to do so is derived from his nature as man and from the function of moral values in human life—and, therefore, is applicable *only* in the context of a rational, objectively demonstrated and validated code of moral principles which define and determine his actual self-interest. It is not a license "to do as he pleases" and it is not applicable to the altruists' image of a "selfish" brute nor to any man motivated by irrational emotions, feelings, urges, wishes or whims.

This is said as a warning against the kind of "Nietzschean egoists" who, in fact, are a product of the altruist morality and represent the other side of the altruist coin: the men who believe that any action, regardless of its nature, is good if it is intended for one's own benefit. Just as the satisfaction of the irrational desires of others is *not* a criterion of moral value, neither is the satisfaction of one's own irrational desires. Morality is not a contest of whims.

A similar type of error is committed by the man who declares that since man must be guided by his own independent judgment, any action he chooses to take is moral if *he* chooses it. One's own independent judgment is the *means* by which one must choose one's actions, but it is not a moral criterion nor a moral validation: only reference to a demonstrable principle can validate one's choices.

Just as man cannot survive by any random means, but must discover and practice the principles which his survival requires, so man's self-interest cannot be determined by blind desires or random whims, but must be discovered and achieved by the guidance of rational principles. This is why the Objectivist ethics is a morality of *rational self-interest*—or of *rational selfishness.*

Since selfishness is "concern with one's own interests," the Objectivist ethics uses that concept in its exact and purest sense. It is not a concept that one can surrender to man's enemies, nor to the unthinking misconceptions, distortions, prejudices and fears of the ignorant and the irrational. The attack on "selfishness" is an attack on man's self-esteem; to surrender one, is to surrender the other.

CHRISTOPHER LASCH

The Culture of Narcissism

CHRISTOPHER LASCH *was historian at the University of Rochester and a popular social critic. His book,* The Culture of Narcissism, *was a best-selling argument against our overly therapeutic and self-absorbed culture. An excerpt is included here.*

THE WANING OF THE SENSE OF HISTORICAL TIME

AS the twentieth century approaches its end, the conviction grows that many other things are ending too. Storm warnings, portents, hints of catastrophe haunt our times. The "sense of an ending," which has given shape to so much of twentieth-century literature, now pervades the popular imagination as well. The Nazi holocaust, the threat of nuclear annihilation, the depletion of natural resources, well-founded predictions of ecological disaster have fulfilled poetic prophecy, giving concrete historical substance to the nightmare, or death wish, that avant-garde artists were the first to express. The question of whether the world will end in fire or in ice, with a bang or a whimper, no longer interests artists alone. Impending disaster has become an everyday concern, so commonplace and familiar that nobody any longer gives much thought to how disaster might be averted. People busy themselves instead with survival strategies, measures designed to prolong their own lives, or programs guaranteed to ensure good health and peace of mind.

After the political turmoil of the sixties, Americans have retreated to purely personal preoccupations. Having no hope of improving their lives in any of the ways that matter, people have convinced themselves that what matters is psychic self-improvement: getting in touch with their feelings, eating health food, taking lessons in ballet or belly-dancing, immersing themselves in the wisdom of the East, jogging, learning how to "relate," overcoming the "fear of pleasure." Harmless in themselves, these pursuits, elevated to a program and wrapped in the rhetoric of authenticity and awareness, signify a retreat from politics and a repudiation of the recent past. Indeed Americans seem to wish to forget not only the sixties, the riots, the new left, the disruptions on college campuses, Vietnam, Watergate, and the Nixon presidency, but their entire collective past, even in the antiseptic form in which it was celebrated during the Bicentennial. Woody Allen's movie *Sleeper*, issued in 1973, accurately caught the mood of the seventies. Appropriately cast in the form of a parody of futuristic science fiction, the film finds a great many ways to convey the message that "political solutions don't work," as Allen flatly announces at one point. When asked what he believes in, Allen, having ruled out politics, religion, and science, declares: "I believe in sex and death—two experiences that come once in a lifetime."

To live for the moment is the prevailing passion—to live for yourself, not for your predecessors or posterity. We are fast losing the sense of historical continuity, the sense of belonging to a succession of generations originating in the past and stretching into the future. It is the waning of the sense of historical time—in particular, the erosion of any strong concern for posterity—that distinguishes the spiritual crisis of the seventies from earlier outbreaks of millenarian religion, to which it bears a superficial resemblance. Many commentators have seized on this resemblance as a means of understanding the contemporary "cultural revolution," ignoring the features that distinguish it from the religions of the past. A few years ago, Leslie Fiedler proclaimed a "New Age of Faith." More recently, Tom Wolfe has interpreted the new narcissism as a "third great awakening," an outbreak of orgiastic, ecstatic religiosity. Jim Hougan, in a book that seems to present itself simultaneously as a critique and a celebration of contemporary decadence, compares the current mood to the millennialism of the waning Middle Ages. "The anxieties of the Middle Ages are not much different from those of the present," he writes. Then as now, social upheaval gave rise to "millenarian sects."

Both Hougan and Wolfe inadvertently provide evidence, however, that undermines a religious interpretation of the "consciousness movement." Hougan notes that survival has become the "catchword of the seventies" and "collective narcissism" the dominant disposition. Since "the society" has no future, it makes sense to live only for the moment, to fix our eyes on our own "private performance," to become connoisseurs of our own decadence, to cultivate a "transcendental self-attention." These are not the attitudes historically associated with millenarian outbreaks. Sixteenth-century Anabaptists awaited the apocalypse not with transcendental self-attention but with ill-concealed impatience for the golden age it was expected to inaugurate. Nor were they indifferent to the past. Ancient popular traditions of the "sleeping king"—the leader who will return to his people and restore a lost golden age—informed the millenarian movements of this period. The Revolutionary of the Upper Rhine, anonymous author of the *Book of a Hundred Chapters,* declared, "The Germans once held the whole world in their hands and they will do so again, and with more power than ever." He predicted that the resurrected Frederick II, "Emperor of the Last Days," would reinstate the primitive German religion, move the capital of Christendom from Rome to Trier, abolish private property, and level distinctions between rich and poor.

Such traditions, often associated with national resistance to foreign conquest, have flourished at many times and in many forms, including the Christian vision of the Last Judgment. Their egalitarian and pseudohistorical content suggests that even the most radically otherworldly religions of the past expressed a hope of social justice and a sense of continuity with earlier generations. The absence of these values characterizes the survivalist mentality of the seventies. The "world view emerging among us," writes Peter Marin, centers "solely on the self" and has "individual survival as its sole good." In an attempt to identify the peculiar features of contemporary religiosity, Tom Wolfe himself notes that "most people, historically, have *not* lived their lives as if thinking, 'I have only one life to live.' Instead they have lived as if they are living their ancestors' lives and their offspring's lives. . . ." These observations go very close to the heart of the matter, but they call into question his characterization of the new narcissism as a third great awakening.

THE THERAPEUTIC SENSIBILITY

The contemporary climate is therapeutic, not religious. People today hunger not for personal salvation, let alone for the restoration of an earlier golden age, but for the feeling, the momentary illusion, of personal well-being, health, and psychic security. Even the radicalism of the sixties served, for many of those who embraced it for personal rather than political reasons, not as a substitute religion but as a form of therapy. Radical politics filled empty lives, provided a sense of meaning and purpose. In her memoir of the Weathermen, Susan Stern described their attraction in language that owes more to psychiatry and medicine than to religion. When she tried to evoke her state of mind during the 1968 demonstrations at the Democratic National Convention in Chicago, she wrote instead about the state of her health. "I felt good. I could feel my body supple and strong, and slim, and ready to run miles, and my legs moving sure and swift under me." A few pages later, she says: "I felt real." Repeatedly she explains that association with important people made her feel important. "I felt I was part of a vast network of intense, exciting and brilliant people." When the leaders she idealized disappointed her, as they always did, she looked for new heroes to take their place, hoping to warm herself in their "brilliance" and to overcome her feeling of insignificance. In their presence, she occasionally felt "strong and solid"— only to find herself repelled, when disenchantment set in again, by the "arrogance" of those whom she had previously admired, by "their contempt for everyone around them."

Many of the details in Stern's account of the Weathermen would be familiar to students of the revolutionary mentality in earlier epochs: the fervor of her revolutionary commitment, the group's endless disputes about fine points of political dogma, the relentless "self-criticism" to which members of the sect were constantly exhorted, the attempt to remodel every facet of one's life in conformity with the revolutionary faith. But every revolutionary movement partakes of the culture of its time, and this one contained elements that immediately identified it as a product of American society in an age of diminishing expectations. The atmosphere in which the Weathermen lived—an atmosphere of violence, danger, drugs, sexual promiscuity, moral and psychic chaos—derived not so much from an older revolutionary tradition as from the turmoil and narcissistic anguish of contemporary America. Her preoccupation with the state of her psychic health, together with her dependence on others for a sense of selfhood, distinguish Susan Stern from the kind of religious seeker who turns to politics to find a secularized salvation. She needed to establish an identity, not to submerge her identity in a larger cause. The narcissist differs also, in the tenuous quality of his selfhood, from an earlier type of American individualist, the "American Adam" analyzed by R. W. B. Lewis, Quentin Anderson, Michael Rogin, and by nineteenth-century observers like Tocqueville. The contemporary narcissist bears a superficial resemblance, in his self-absorption and delusions of grandeur, to the "imperial self" so often celebrated in nineteenth-century American literature. The American Adam, like his descendants today, sought to free himself from the past and to establish what Emerson called "an original relation to the universe." Nineteenth-century writers and orators restated again and again, in a great variety of forms, Jefferson's doctrine that the earth belongs to the living. The break with Europe, the abolition of primogeniture, and the looseness of family ties gave substance to their belief (even if it was finally an illusion) that Americans, alone among the people of the world, could escape the entangling influence of the past. They imagined, according to Tocqueville, that "their whole destiny is in their own hands." Social conditions in the United States, Tocqueville wrote, severed the tie that formerly united one generation to another. "The woof of time is every instant broken and the track of generations effaced. Those who went before are soon forgotten; of those who will come after, no one has any idea: the interest of man is confined to those in close propinquity to himself."

Some critics have described the narcissism of the 1970s in similar language. The new therapies spawned by the human potential movement, according to Peter Marin, teach that "the individual will is all powerful and totally determines one's fate"; thus they intensify the "isolation of the self." This line of argument belongs to a well established American tradition of social thought. Marin's plea for recognition of "the immense middle ground of human community" recalls Van Wyck Brooks, who criticized the New England transcendentalists for ignoring "the genial middle ground of human tradition." Brooks himself, when he formulated his own indictment of American culture, drew on such earlier critics as Santayana, Henry

James, Orestes Brownson, and Tocqueville. The critical tradition they established still has much to tell us about
the evils of untrammeled individualism,
but it needs to be restated to take
account of the differences between
nineteenth-century Adamism and the
narcissism of our own time. The critique
of "privatism," though it helps to keep
alive the need for community, has become more and more misleading as the
possibility of genuine privacy recedes.
The contemporary American may have
failed, like his predecessors, to establish
any sort of common life, but the integrating tendencies of modern industrial
society have at the same time undermined his "isolation." Having surrendered most of his technical skills to the
corporation, he can no longer provide
for his material needs. As the family
loses not only its productive functions
but many of its reproductive functions
as well, men and women no longer manage even to raise their children without
the help of certified experts. The atrophy
of older traditions of self-help has
eroded everyday competence, in one
area after another, and has made the individual dependent on the state, the corporation, and other bureaucracies.

Narcissism represents the psychological dimension of this dependence.
Notwithstanding his occasional illusions
of omnipotence, the narcissist depends
on others to validate his self-esteem. He
cannot live without an admiring audience. His apparent freedom from family
ties and institutional constraints does
not free him to stand alone or to glory in
his individuality. On the contrary, it
contributes to his insecurity, which he
can overcome only by seeing his
"grandiose self" reflected in the atten-
tions of others, or by attaching himself
to those who radiate celebrity, power,

and charisma. For the narcissist, the
world is a mirror, whereas the rugged
individualist saw it as an empty wilderness to be shaped to his own design. . . .

Today Americans are overcome not
by the sense of endless possibility but
by the banality of the social order they
have erected against it. Having internalized the social restraints by means of
which they formerly sought to keep
possibility within civilized limits, they
feel themselves overwhelmed by an annihilating boredom, like animals whose
instincts have withered in captivity. A
reversion to savagery threatens them so
little that they long precisely for a more
vigorous instinctual existence. People
nowadays complain of an inability to
feel. They cultivate more vivid experiences, seek to beat sluggish flesh to life,
attempt to revive jaded appetites. They
condemn the superego and exalt the lost
life of the senses. Twentieth-century
peoples have erected so many psychological barriers against strong emotion,
and have invested those defenses with
so much of the energy derived from forbidden impulse, that they can no longer
remember what it feels like to be inun-
dated by desire. They tend, rather, to be
consumed with rage, which derives
from defenses against desire and gives
rise in turn to new defenses against
rage itself. Outwardly bland, submissive, and sociable, they seethe with an
inner anger for which a dense, over-
populated, bureaucratic society can devise few legitimate outlets. . . .

Plagued by anxiety, depression,
vague discontents, sense of inner emptiness, the "psychological man" of the
twentieth century seeks neither individual self-aggrandizement nor spiritual
transcendence but peace of mind, under
conditions that increasingly militate
against it. Therapists, not priests or pop-

ular preachers of self-help or models of success like the captains of industry, become his principal allies in the struggle for composure; he turns to them in the hope of achieving the modern equivalent of salvation, "mental health." Therapy has established itself as the successor both to rugged individualism and to religion; but this does not mean that the "triumph of the therapeutic" has become a new religion in its own right. Therapy constitutes an antireligion, not always to be sure because it adheres to rational explanation or scientific methods of healing, as its practitioners would have us believe, but because modern society "has no future" and therefore gives no thought to anything beyond its immediate needs. Even when therapists speak of the need for "meaning" and "love," they define love and meaning simply as the fulfillment of the patient's emotional requirements. It hardly occurs to them—nor is there any reason why it should, given the nature of the therapeutic enterprise—to encourage the subject to subordinate his needs and interests to those of others, to someone or some cause or tradition outside himself. "Love" as self-sacrifice or self-abasement, "meaning" as submission to a higher loyalty—these sublimations strike the therapeutic sensibility as intolerably oppressive, offensive to common sense and injurious to personal health and well-being. To liberate humanity from such out-moded ideas of love and duty has become the mission of the post-Freudian therapies and particularly of their converts and popularizers, for whom mental health means the overthrow of inhibitions and the immediate gratification of every impulse.

Chapter 14

Can There Be Sexual Equality?

Story: *Driving the truck to work one day, Sandy noticed somebody by the side of the road with a flat tire. Sandy stopped and got out to help fix the flat. Because neither of them had a jack, Sandy had to hold up the rear end of the car while the owner replaced the tire. When they were done, Sandy reminded herself to buy a new jack on her way home.*

Story: *Sandy was putting the finishing touches on the pie when the kids rushed in the door. "What's for dinner? We're starved." "Wash your hands, kids, and set the table," Sandy replied. "We'll be eating as soon as Mom gets home from work."*

It is a rare person indeed who would read either of these stories without experiencing a "gender jolt" at the end of them. No matter what your views are about sexual equality, it is nevertheless true that we tend to make certain associations when it comes to gender. Even if your father does the cooking every night, you probably assumed that the person putting the finishing touches on the pie was a woman. Similarly, even if your mother is a body builder who drives a Harley, you probably assumed that the person holding up the rear of the car was a man.

One of questions of concern to philosophers is whether these characteristic associations are rooted in fundamental, irreversible differences between women and men, or whether they are a function of changeable social practices. Look around the world. How many women are truck drivers? Heads of large corporations? CIA agents? Roofing contractors? How many men are elementary school teachers? Are staying at home with their children? Are secretaries? Nurses? It is important to notice two things. First, men and women tend to occupy different roles in our culture. Second, the roles that women occupy tend to be subordinate to those of men. (This doesn't mean that women have no power, nor does it mean that all men have power. There are other factors, such as class and race, that affect the distribution of power.)

Some of the differences between men and women, their reproductive capacities, for example, are clearly not the result of social practices. Women have uteruses; for the time being, at least, men do not. To what extent do the physical differences between men and women *determine* their social roles (sometimes called "gender roles")? Should physical differences determine gender roles? You will see that Plato hedges on

591

an answer to this question. In the selection from *The Republic,* Socrates is discussing with Glaucon the education and training necessary for those who are going to rule Socrates' ideal city. Socrates makes it quite clear that education, more than any other single thing, determines what a person will be equipped to do. If men and women are educated in the same way, then they will be able to perform the same functions. The fact that women bear children, for example, does not entail that they should raise them. Rather, the raising of children should be done by those trained to do so, be they men or women. In principle, then, both men and women are capable of ruling the city as well. It is clear, however, that Socrates believes men to be naturally superior to women. Although there will be some men who are exceeded by women at performing a task, there will always be men who are better at it than any woman could be (except, he suggests, when making pancakes and jam). It is difficult to see how he can reconcile the view that men are naturally superior with the view that our capabilities are a result of education and training.

According to Mill, he can't. Confusions such as that of Socrates are the result of taking facts about the way things *are* as equivalent to facts about the way things *must be.* Suppose that you are in the hospital for a week and during that week you never encounter a male nurse. Are you entitled to conclude that men can't, by nature, be nurses? Or that women, by nature, are suited to nursing? Mill provides us with some reasons for questioning inferences like these. Was Socrates making such an inference when he claimed that men are naturally superior to women? If so, he finds himself in notable philosophical company. As you can see from the selections by Aristotle and Kant, philosophers' remarks about women tend to reinforce stereotypical associations. It is claimed that women are more emotional than men, are physically weaker than men, have a tendency to lie and to talk too much, and are lazier and more shameless than men.

Simone de Beauvoir, the foremother of contemporary feminism, sought to provide an account of the causes and effects of women's oppression. De Beauvoir argues that men have constructed women as what she calls "the Other" in order to establish the superiority of their own characteristics. The human tendency toward self-importance takes the form, in men, of casting feminine characteristics in a negative light. In fact, the feminine *is* the negative, the Other. By denying women's capacity to judge, man assures that whatever resistance women might show to this negative assessment of their abilities is itself dismissed as yet another error in judgment. Left with no other resources, women come to see themselves as men want them to be seen. They expect to be weak, silly, emotional, powerless, and dependent. They, too, see themselves as the Other.

De Beauvoir's rather gloomy picture may be an illuminating depiction of the origin and maintenance of woman's consciousness of herself as inferior to men. Marilyn Frye looks to those elements of our social relations that reinforce sexual inequality. According to Frye, sexism is the result of a particular social system of "sex-marking." She asks us to think about the variety of ways in which sex differences are reinforced by clothing and by manners of walking and speaking. In Frye's view, however, the reinforcement of sex differences is not life-enhancing. Rather it serves to maintain a system in which one group of people is subordinate to another. By continuing to emphasize the importance of sex differences, we further reinforce the relationship of domination and subordination whose purpose it serves.

The essay by bell hooks takes up further the joint issues of sexism and racism in her challenge to the American feminist movement. She argues that it has taken the experiences of white women as its focus and so has ignored the very different ways in which black women experience the oppressive forces in society. Indeed, she insists that white feminism, by casting all women equally as victims of male oppression, makes invisible the fact that white women have power over black women. She proposes that feminism attend to the "voices from the margin" in order to insure that it avoid perpetuating racism as it works to overcome sexism.

In thinking about the question of sexual equality, it is important to consider just what are the sources of inequality. In addition, it is important to reflect on how, ideally, you think things should be, and how you think we might best achieve those ends. You can begin by thinking about the ways in which you are affected by the importance that our society attaches to sex differences. If you think that you aren't, then remember the two stories with which we began.

PLATO

The Equality of Women

PLATO (427–347 B.C.) was born into a family of considerable wealth and power. In
Athens he came under the influence of Socrates and turned his attention to philosophy.
After Socrates was condemned to death for corrupting the minds of the youth of
Athens, Plato took it upon himself to continue Socrates' work. In this selection from
The Republic, Socrates, who serves as Plato's spokesman in the dialogue, discusses
his views about sexual equality with Glaucon.

W ELL, I replied, I suppose
that I must retrace my steps
and say what I perhaps
ought to have said before in the proper
place. The part of the men has been
played out, and now properly enough
comes the turn of the women. Of them I
will proceed to speak, and the more
readily since I am invited by you.

For men born and educated like our
citizens, the only way, in my opinion, of
arriving at a right conclusion about the
possession and use of women and children is to follow the path on which we
originally started, when we said that the
men were to be the guardians and
watchdogs of the herd.

True.

Let us further suppose the birth and
education of our women to be subject to
similar or nearly similar regulations;
then we shall see whether the result accords with our design.

What do you mean?

What I mean may be put into the
form of a question, I said: Are dogs divided into hes and shes, or do they both
share equally in hunting and in keeping
watch and in the other duties of dogs?
or do we entrust to the males the entire
and exclusive care of the flocks, while
we leave the females at home, under the
idea that the bearing and suckling their
puppies is labour enough for them?

No, he said, they share alike; the
only difference between them is that the
males are stronger and the females
weaker.

But can you use different animals for
the same purpose, unless they are bred
and fed in the same way?

You cannot.

Then, if women are to have the same
duties as men, they must have the same
nurture and education?

Yes.

The education which was assigned to
the men was music and gymnastic. Yes.

Then women must be taught music
and gymnastic and also the art of war,
which they must practise like the men?

That is the inference, I suppose.

I should rather expect, I said, that
several of our proposals, if they are carried out, being unusual, may appear
ridiculous.

No doubt of it.

Yes, and the most ridiculous thing of
all will be the sight of women naked in
the palaestra, exercising with the men,
especially when they are no longer
young; they certainly will not be a vision of beauty, any more than the enthusiastic old men who in spite of wrinkles

and ugliness continue to frequent the gymnasia.

Yes, indeed, he said: according to present notions the proposal would be thought ridiculous.

But then, I said, as we have determined to speak our minds, we must not fear the jests of the wits which will be directed against this sort of innovation; how they will talk of women's attainments both in music and gymnastic, and above all about their wearing armour and riding upon horseback!

Very true, he replied.

Yet having begun we must go forward to the rough places of the law; at the same time begging of these gentlemen for once in their life to be serious. Not long ago, as we shall remind them, the Hellenes were of the opinion, which is still generally received among the barbarians, that the sight of a naked man was ridiculous and improper; and when first the Cretans and then the Lacedaemonians introduced the custom, the wits of that day might equally have ridiculed the innovation.

No doubt.

But when experience showed that to let all things be uncovered was far better than to cover them up, and the ludicrous effect to the outward eye vanished before the better principle which reason asserted, then the man was perceived to be a fool who directs the shafts of his ridicule at any other sight but that of folly and vice, or seriously inclines to weigh the beautiful by any other standard but that of the good.

Very true, he replied.

First, then, whether the question is to be put in jest or in earnest, let us come to an understanding about the nature of woman: Is she capable of sharing either wholly or partially in the actions of men, or not at all? And is the art of war one of those arts in which she can or can not share? That will be the best way of commencing the enquiry, and will probably lead to the fairest conclusion.

That will be much the best way.

Shall we take the other side first and begin by arguing against ourselves; in this manner the adversary's position will not be undefended.

Why not? he said.

Then let us put a speech into the mouths of our opponents. They will say: 'Socrates and Glaucon, no adversary need convict you, for you yourselves, at the first foundation of the State, admitted the principle that everybody was to do the one work suited to his own nature.' And certainly, if I am not mistaken, such an admission was made by us. 'And do not the natures of men and women differ very much indeed?' And we shall reply: Of course they do. Then we shall be asked, 'Whether the tasks assigned to men and to women should not be different, and such as are agreeable to their different natures?' Certainly they should. 'But if so, have you not fallen into a serious inconsistency in saying that men and women, whose natures are so entirely different, ought to perform the same actions?'—What defence will you make for us, my good Sir, against any one who offers these objections?

That is not an easy question to answer when asked suddenly; and I shall and I do beg of you to draw out the case on our side.

These are the objections, Glaucon, and there are many others of a like kind, which I foresaw long ago; they made me afraid and reluctant to take in hand any law about the possession and nurture of women and children.

By Zeus, he said, the problem to be solved is anything but easy.

Why yes, I said, but the fact is that when a man is out of his depth, whether he has fallen into a little swimming bath or into mid-ocean, he has to swim all the same.

Very true.

And must not we swim and try to reach the shore: we will hope that Arion's dolphin or some other miraculous help may save us?

I suppose so, he said.

Well then, let us see if any way of escape can be found. We acknowledged—did we not? that different natures ought to have different pursuits, and that men's and women's natures are different. And now what are we saying?—that different natures ought to have the same pursuits,—this is the inconsistency which is charged upon us.

Precisely.

Verily, Glaucon, I said, glorious is the power of the art of contradiction!

Why do you say so?

Because I think that many a man falls into the practice against his will. When he thinks that he is reasoning he is really disputing, just because he cannot define and divide, and so know that of which he is speaking; and he will pursue a merely verbal opposition in the spirit of contention and not of fair discussion.

Yes, he replied, such is very often the case; but what has that to do with us and our argument?

A great deal; for there is certainly a danger of our getting unintentionally into a verbal opposition.

In what way?

Why, we valiantly and pugnaciously insist upon the verbal truth, that different natures ought to have different pursuits, but we never considered at all what was the meaning of sameness or difference of nature, or why we distinguished them when we assigned different pursuits to different natures and the same to the same natures.

Why, no, he said, that was never considered by us.

I said: Suppose that by way of illustration we were to ask the question whether there is not an opposition in nature between bald men and hairy men; and if this is admitted by us, then, if bald men are cobblers, we should forbid the hairy men to be cobblers, and conversely?

Yes, I said, a jest; and why? because we never meant when we constructed the State, that the opposition of natures should extend to every difference, but only to those differences which affected the pursuit in which the individual is engaged; we should have argued, for example, that a physician and one who is in mind a physician may be said to have the same nature.

True.

Whereas the physician and the carpenter have different natures?

Certainly.

And if, I said, the male and female sex appear to differ in their fitness for any art or pursuit, we should say that such pursuit or art ought to be assigned to one or the other of them; but if the difference consists only in women bearing and men begetting children, this does not amount to a proof that a woman differs from a man in respect to the sort of education she should receive; and we shall therefore continue to maintain that our guardians and their wives ought to have the same pursuits.

Very true, he said.

Next, we shall ask our opponent how, in reference to any of the pursuits or arts of civic life, the nature of a woman differs from that of a man?

That will be quite fair.

And perhaps he, like yourself, will reply that to give a sufficient answer on the instant is not easy; but after a little reflection there is no difficulty.

Yes, perhaps.

Suppose then that we invite him to accompany us in the argument, and then we may hope to show him that there is nothing peculiar in the constitution of women which would affect them in the administration of the State.

By all means.

Let us say to him: Come now, and we will ask you a question:—when you spoke of a nature gifted or not gifted in any respect, did you mean to say that one man will acquire a thing easily, another with difficulty; a little learning will lead the one to discover a great deal; whereas the other, after much study and application, no sooner learns than he forgets; or again, did you mean, that the one has a body which is a good servant to his mind, while the body of the other is a hindrance to him?—would not these be the sort of differences which distinguish the man gifted by nature from the one who is ungifted?

No one will deny that.

And can you mention any pursuit of mankind in which the male sex has not all these gifts and qualities in a higher degree than the female? Need I waste time in speaking of the art of weaving, and the management of pancakes and preserves, in which womankind does really appear to be great, and in which for her to be beaten by a man is of all things the most absurd?

You are quite right, he replied, in maintaining the general inferiority of the female sex: although many women are in many things superior to many men, yet on the whole what you say is true.

And if so, my friend, I said, there is no special faculty of administration in a state which a woman has because she is a woman, or which a man has by virtue of his sex, but the gifts of nature are alike diffused in both; all the pursuits of men are the pursuits of women also, but in all of them a woman is inferior to a man.

Very true.

Then are we to impose all our enactments on men and none of them on women?

That will never do.

One woman has a gift of healing, another not; one is a musician, and another has no music in her nature?

Very true.

And one woman has a turn for gymnastic and military exercises, and another is unwarlike and hates gymnastics?

Certainly.

And one woman is a philosopher, and another is an enemy of philosophy; one has spirit, and another is without spirit?

That is also true.

Then one woman will have the temper of a guardian, and another not. Was not the selection of the male guardians determined by differences of this sort?

Yes.

Men and women alike possess the qualities which make a guardian; they differ only in their comparative strength or weakness.

Obviously.

And those women who have such qualities are to be selected as the companions and colleagues of men who have similar qualities and whom they resemble in capacity and in character?

Very true.

And ought not the same natures to have the same pursuits?

They ought.

Then, as we were saying before, there is nothing unnatural in assigning music and gymnastic to the wives of the guardians—to that point we come round again.

Certainly not.

The law which we then enacted was agreeable to nature, and therefore not an impossibility or mere aspiration; and the contrary practice, which prevails at present, is in reality a violation of nature.

That appears to be true.

We had to consider, first, whether our proposals were possible, and secondly whether they were the most beneficial?

Yes.

And the possibility has been acknowledged?

Yes.

The very great benefit has next to be established?

Quite so.

You will admit that the same education which makes a man a good guardian will make a woman a good guardian; for their original nature is the same?

Yes.

I should like to ask you a question?

What is it?

Would you say that all men are equal in excellence, or is one man better than another?

The latter.

And in the commonwealth which we were founding do you conceive the guardians who have been brought up on our model system to be more perfect men, or the cobblers whose education has been cobbling?

What a ridiculous question!

You have answered me, I replied: Well, and may we not further say that our guardians are the best of our citizens?

By far the best.

And will not their wives be the best women?

Yes, by far the best.

And can there be anything better for the interests of the State than that the men and women of a State should be as good as possible?

There can be nothing better.

And this is what the arts of music and gymnastic, when present in such manner as we have described, will accomplish?

Certainly.

Then we have made an enactment not only possible but in the highest degree beneficial to the State?

True.

Then let the wives of our guardians strip, for their virtue will be their robe, and let them share in the toils of war and the defence of their country; only in the distribution of labours the lighter are assigned to the women, who are the weaker natures, but in other respects their duties are to be the same. And as for the man who laughs at naked women exercising their bodies from the best of motives, in his laughter he is plucking

A fruit of unripe wisdom,

and he himself is ignorant of what he is laughing at, or what he is about;—for that is, and ever will be, the best of sayings, *That the useful is the noble and the hurtful is the base.*

Very true.

ARISTOTLE

The Inequality of Women

ARISTOTLE (384–322 B.C.) was for eighteen years a student of Plato. After Plato's death, he turned to the study of biology. In addition to his biological studies, Aristotle virtually created the sciences of logic and linguistics. He developed extravagant theories in physics and made significant contributions to metaphysics, ethics, politics, and aesthetics.

WOMAN is more compassionate than man, more easily moved to tears. At the same time, she is more jealous, more querulous, more apt to scold and to strike. She is, furthermore, more prone to despondency and less hopeful than man, more devoid of shame or self-respect, more false of speech, more deceptive and of more retentive memory. She is also more wakeful, more shrinking, more difficult to rouse to action, and she requires a smaller amount of nutriment.

IMMANUEL KANT

The Inequality of Women

IMMANUEL KANT (1724–1804) was probably the greatest philosopher since Plato and Aristotle. He lived his entire life in East Prussia. He was a professor at the University in Konigsberg for over thirty years. He never married and his neighbors said that his habits were so regular that they could set their watches by him. His philosophical system was embodied in three volumes, The Critique of Pure Reason, The Critique of Practical Reason, *and* The Critique of Judgment.

THE person who is as silent as a mute goes to one extreme; the person who is loquacious goes to the opposite. Both tendencies are weaknesses. Men are liable to the first, women to the second. Someone has said that women are talkative because the training of infants is their special charge, and their talkativeness soon teaches a child to speak, because they can chatter to it all day long. If men had the care of the children they would take much longer to learn to talk. However that may be, we dislike anyone who will not speak: he annoys us; his silence betrays his pride. On the other hand, loquaciousness in men is contemptible and contrary to the strength of the male. All this by the way, we shall now pass to more weighty matters.

JOHN STUART MILL

The Subjection of Women

JOHN STUART MILL (1806–1873) was one of the documented geniuses of modern history. By the age of ten, he had accomplished more than most scholars do in a lifetime. He is best known for his moral and political writings, particularly On Liberty *and* Utilitarianism.

NEITHER does it avail anything to say that the *nature* of the two sexes adapts them to their present functions and position, and renders these appropriate to them. Standing on the ground of common sense and the constitution of the human mind, I deny that any one knows, or can know, the nature of the two sexes, as long as they have only been seen in their present relation to one another. If men had ever been found in society without women, or women without men, or if there had been a society of men and women in which the women were not under the control of the men, something might have been positively known about the mental and moral differences which may be inherent in the nature of each. What is now called the nature of women is an eminently artificial thing—the result of forced repression in some directions, unnatural stimulation in others. It may be asserted without scruple, that no other class of dependents have had their character so entirely distorted from its natural proportions by their relation with their masters; for, if conquered and slave races have been, in some respects, more forcibly repressed, whatever in them has not been crushed down by an iron heel has generally been let alone, and if left with any liberty of development, it has developed itself according to its own laws; but in the case of women, a hot-house and stove cultivation has always been carried on of some of the capabilities of their nature, for the benefit and pleasure of their masters. Then, because certain products of the general vital force sprout luxuriantly and reach a great development in this heated atmosphere and under this active nurture and watering, while other shoots from the same root, which are left outside in the wintry air, with ice purposely heaped all around them, have a stunted growth, and some are burnt off with fire and disappear; men, with that inability to recognize their own work which distinguishes the unanalytic mind, indolently believe that the tree grows of itself in the way they have made it grow, and that it would die if one half of it were not kept in a vapour bath and the other half in the snow.

Of all difficulties which impede the progress of thought, and the formation of well-grounded opinions on life and social arrangements, the greatest is now the unspeakable ignorance and inattention of mankind in respect to the influences which form human character. Whatever any portion of the human species now are, or seem to be, such, it is supposed, they have a natural tendency to be: even when the most elementary knowledge of the circumstances in which they have been placed, clearly points out the causes that made them what they are. . . . Because the Greeks cheated the Turks, and the Turks only plundered the Greeks, there are persons who think that the Turks are naturally more sincere: and because women, as is often said, care nothing about politics except their personalities, it is supposed that the general good is naturally less interesting to women than to men. History, which is now so much better understood than formerly, teaches another lesson: if only by showing the extraordinary susceptibility of human nature to external influences, and the extreme variableness of those of its manifestations which are supposed to be most universal and uniform. But in history, as in travelling, men usually see only what they already had in their own minds; and few learn much from history, who do not bring much with them to its study.

Hence, in regard to that most difficult question, what are the natural differences between the two sexes—a subject on which it is impossible in the present state of society to obtain complete and correct knowledge—while almost everybody dogmatizes upon it, almost all neglect and make light of the only means by which any partial insight can be obtained into it. This is, an analytic study of the most important department of psychology, the laws of the influence of circumstances on character. For, however great and apparently ineradicable the moral and intellectual differences between men and women might be, the evidence of their being natural differences could only be negative. Those only could be inferred to be natural which could not possibly be artificial—the residuum, after deducting every characteristic of either sex which can admit of being explained from education or external circumstances. The profoundest knowledge of the laws of the formation of character is indispensable to entitle any one to affirm even that there is any difference, much more what the difference is, between the two sexes considered as moral and rational beings; and since no one, as yet, has that knowledge (for there is hardly any subject which, in proportion to its importance, has been so little studied), no one is thus far entitled to any positive opinion on the subject. Conjectures are all that can at present be made; conjectures more or less probable, according as more or less authorized by such knowledge as we yet have of the laws of psychology, as applied to the formation of character.

Even the preliminary knowledge, what the differences between the sexes now are, apart from all question as to how they are made what they are, is still in the crudest and most incomplete state. Medical practitioners and physiologists have ascertained, to some extent, the differences in bodily constitution; and this is an important element to the psychologist: but hardly any medical practitioner is a psychologist. Respecting the mental characteristics of women; their observations are of no more worth than those of common men. It is a subject on which nothing final can be known, so long as those who alone can really know it, women themselves, have given but little testimony, and that little, mostly suborned. It is easy to know stupid women. Stupidity is much the same all the world over. A stupid person's notions and feelings may confidently be inferred from those which prevail in the circle by which the person is surrounded. Not so with those whose opinions and feelings are an emanation from their own nature and faculties. It is only a man here and there who has any tolerable knowledge of the character even of the women of his own family. I do not mean, of their capabilities; these nobody knows, not even themselves, because most of them have never been called out. I mean their actually existing thoughts and feelings. Many a man thinks he perfectly understands women, because he has had amatory relations with several, perhaps with many of them. If he is a good observer, and his experience extends to quality as well as quantity, he may have learnt something of one narrow department of their nature—an important department, no doubt. But of all the rest of it, few persons are generally more ignorant, because there are few from whom it is so carefully hidden. The most favorable case which a man can generally have for studying the character of a woman, is that of his own wife: for the opportunities are greater, and the cases of complete sympathy not so unspeakably rare. And in fact, this is the source from which any knowledge worth having on the subject has, I believe, generally come. But most men have not had the opportunity of studying in this way more than a single case: accordingly one can, to an almost laughable degree, infer what a man's wife is like, from his opinions about women in general. To make even this one case yield any results, the woman must be worth knowing, and the man not only a competent judge, but of a character so sympathetic in itself, and so well adapted to hers, that he can either read her mind by sympathetic intuition, or has nothing in himself which makes her shy of disclosing it. Hardly anything, I believe, can be more rare than this conjunction. It often happens that there is the most complete unity of feeling and community of interests as to all external things, yet the one

has as little admission into the internal life of the other as if they were common acquaintance. Even with true affection, authority on the one side and subordination on the other prevent perfect confidence. Though nothing may be intentionally withheld, much is not shown. In the analogous relation of parent and child, the corresponding phenomenon must have been in the observation of every one. As between father and son, how many are the cases in which the father, in spite of real affection on both sides, obviously to all the world does not know, nor suspect, parts of the son's character familiar to his companions and equals. The truth is, that the position of looking up to another is extremely unpropitious to complete sincerity and openness with him. The fear of losing ground in his opinion or in his feelings is so strong, that even in an upright character, there is an unconscious tendency to show only the best side, or the side which, though not the best, is that which he most likes to see: and it may be confidently said that thorough knowledge of one another hardly ever exists, but between persons who, besides being intimates, are equals. How much more true, then, must all this be, when the one is not only under the authority of the other, but has it inculcated on her as a duty to reckon everything else subordinate to his comfort and pleasure, and to let him neither see nor feel anything coming from her, except what is agreeable to him. All these difficulties stand in the way of a man's obtaining any thorough knowledge even of the one woman whom alone, in general, he has sufficient opportunity of studying. When we further consider that to understand one woman necessarily is not to understand any other woman; that even if he could study many women of one rank, or of one country, he would not thereby understand women of other ranks or countries; and even if he did, they are still only the women of a single period of history; we may safely assert that the knowledge which men can acquire of women, even as they have been and are, without reference to what they might be, is wretchedly imperfect and superficial, and always will be so, until women themselves have told all that they have to tell.

And this time has not come; nor will it come otherwise than gradually. It is but of yesterday that women have either been qualified by literary accomplishments, or permitted by society, to tell anything to the general public. As yet very few of them dare tell anything, which men, on whom their literary success depends, are unwilling to hear. Let us remember in which manner, up to a very recent time, the expression, even by a male author, of uncustomary opinions, or what are deemed eccentric feelings, usually was, and in some degree still is, received; and we may form some faint conception under what impediments a woman, who is brought up to think custom and opinion her sovereign rule, attempts to express in books anything drawn from the depths of her own nature. The greatest woman who has left writings behind her sufficient to give her an eminent rank in the literature of her country, thought it necessary to prefix as a motto to her boldest work, 'A man dares to have an opinion; a woman must submit to it.' The greater part of what women write about women is mere sycophancy to men. In the case of unmarried women, much of it seems only intended to increase their chance of a husband. Many, both married and unmarried, overstep the mark, and in-

culcate a servility beyond what is desired or relished by any man, except the very vulgarest. But this is not so often the case as, even at a quite late period, it still was. Literary women are becoming more freespoken, and more willing to express their real sentiments. Unfortunately, in this country especially, they are themselves such artificial products, that their sentiments are compounded of a small element of individual observation and consciousness, and a very large one of acquired associations. This will be less and less the case, but it will remain true to a great extent, as long as social institutions do not admit the same free development of originality in women which is possible to men. When that time comes, and not before, we shall see, and not merely hear, as much as it is necessary to know of the nature of women, and the adaptation of other things to it.

I have dwelt so much on the difficulties which at present obstruct any real knowledge by men of the true nature of women, because in this as in so many other things 'opinio copiae inter maximas causas inopiae est'; and there is little chance of reasonable thinking on the matter, while people flatter themselves that they perfectly understand a subject of which most men know absolutely nothing, and of which it is at present impossible that any man, or all men taken together, should have knowledge which can qualify them to lay down the law to women as to what is, or is not, their vocation. Happily, no such knowledge is necessary for any practical purpose connected with the position of women in relation to society and life. For, according to all the principles involved in modern society, the question rests with women themselves—to be decided by their own experience, and by the use of their own faculties. There are no means of finding what either one person or many can do, but by trying—and no means by which any one else can discover for them what it is for their happiness to do or leave undone.

One thing we may be certain of—that what is contrary to women's nature to do, they never will be made to do by simply giving their nature free play. The anxiety of mankind to interfere in behalf of nature, for fear lest nature should not succeed in effecting its purpose, is an altogether unnecessary solicitude. What women by nature cannot do, it is quite superfluous to forbid them from doing. What they can do, but not so well as the men who are their competitors, competition suffices to exclude them from; since nobody asks for protective duties and bounties in favour of women; it is only asked that the present bounties and protective duties in favour of men should be recalled. If women have a greater natural inclination for some things than for others, there is no need of laws or social inculcation to make the majority of them do the former in preference to the latter. Whatever women's services are most wanted for, the free play of competition will hold out the strongest inducements to them to undertake. And, as the words imply, they are most wanted for the things for which they are most fit; by the apportionment of which to them, the collective faculties of the two sexes can be applied on the whole with the greatest sum of valuable result.

The general opinion of men is supposed to be, that the natural vocation of a woman is that of a wife and mother. I say, is supposed to be, because, judging from acts—from the whole of the present constitution of society—one might infer that their opinion was the direct contrary. They might be supposed to think that the alleged natural vocation of women was of all things the most repugnant to their nature; insomuch that if they are free to do anything else—if any other means of living, or occupation of their time and faculties, is open, which has any chance of appearing desirable to them—there will not be enough of them who will be willing to accept the condition said to be natural to them. If this is the real opinion of men in general, it would be well that it should be spoken out. I should like to hear somebody openly enunciating the doctrine (it is already implied in much that is written on the subject)—'It is necessary to society that women should marry and produce children. They will not do so unless they are compelled. Therefore it is necessary to compel them.' The merits of the case would then be clearly defined. It would be exactly that of the slaveholders of South Carolina and Louisiana. 'It is necessary that cotton and sugar should be grown. White men cannot produce them. Negroes will not, for any wages which we choose to give. *Ergo* they must be compelled.' An illustration still closer to the point is that of impressment. Sailors must absolutely be had to defend the country. It often happens that they will not voluntarily enlist. Therefore there must be the power of forcing them. How often has this logic been used! and, but for one flaw in it, without doubt it would have been successful up to this day. But it is open to the retort—First pay the sailors the honest value of their labour. When you have made it as well worth their while to serve you, as to work for other employers, you will have no more difficulty than others have in obtaining their services. To this there is no logical answer except 'I will not': and as people are now not only ashamed, but are not desirous, to rob the labourer of his hire, impressment is no longer advocated. Those who attempt to force women into marriage by closing all other doors against them, lay themselves open to a similar retort. If they mean what they say, their opinion must evidently be, that men do not render the married condition so desirable to women, as to induce them to accept it for its own recommendations. It is not a sign of one's thinking the boon one offers very attractive, when one allows only Hobson's choice, 'that or none.' And here, I believe, is the clue to the feelings of those men, who have a real antipathy to the equal freedom of women. I believe they are afraid, not lest women should be unwilling to marry, for I do not think that any one in reality has that apprehension; but lest they should insist that marriage should be on equal conditions; lest all women of spirit and capacity should prefer doing almost anything else, not in their own eyes degrading, rather than marry, when marrying is giving themselves a master, and a master too of all their earthly possessions. And truly, if this consequence were necessarily incident to marriage, I think that the apprehension would be very well founded. I agree in thinking it probable that few women, capable of anything else, would, unless under an irresistible *entraînement,* rendering them for the time insensible to anything but itself, choose such a lot, when any other means were open to them of filling a conventionally honourable place in life: and if men are determined that the law of marriage shall be a law of despotism, they are quite right, in point of mere policy, in leaving to women only Hobson's choice. But, in that case, all that has been done in the modern world to relax the chain on the minds of women, has been a mistake. They never should have been allowed to receive a literary education. Women who read, much more women who write, are, in the existing constitution of things, a contradiction and a disturbing element: and it was wrong to bring women up with any acquirements but those of an odalisque, or of a domestic servant. . . .

When we consider how vast is the number of men, in any great country, who are little higher than brutes, and that this never prevents them from being able, through the law of marriage, to obtain a victim, the breadth and depth of human misery caused in this shape alone by the abuse of the institution swells to something appalling. Yet these are only the extreme cases. They are the lowest abysses, but there is a sad succession of depth after depth before reaching them. In domestic as in political tyranny, the case of absolute monsters chiefly illustrates the institution by showing that there is scarcely any horror which may not occur under it if the despot pleases, and thus setting in a strong light what must be the terrible frequency of things only a little less atrocious. Absolute fiends are as rare as angels, perhaps rarer: ferocious savages, with occasional touches of humanity, are, however, very frequent: and in the wide interval which separates these from any worthy representatives of the human species, how many are the forms and gradations of animalism and selfishness, often under an outward varnish of civilization and even cultivation, living at peace with the law, maintaining a creditable appearance to all who are not under their power, yet sufficient often to make the lives of all who are so, a torment and a burthen to them! It would be tiresome to repeat the commonplaces about the unfitness of men in general for power, which, after the political discussions of centuries, every one knows by heart, were it not that hardly any one thinks of applying these maxims to the case in which above all others they are applicable, that of power, not placed in the hands of a man here and there, but offered to every adult male, down to the basest and most ferocious. . . . I know that there is another side to the question. I grant that the wife, if she cannot effectually resist, can at least retaliate; she, too, can make the man's life extremely uncomfortable, and by that power is able to carry many points which she ought, and many which she ought not, to prevail in. But this instrument of self-protection—which may be called the power of the scold, or the shrewish sanction—has the fatal defect, that it avails most against the least tyrannical superiors, and in favor of the least deserving dependants. It is the weapon of irritable and self-willed women; of those who would make the worst use of power if they themselves had it, and who generally turn this power to a bad use. The amiable cannot use such an instrument, the high-minded disdain it. And on the other hand, the husbands against whom it is used most effectively are the gentler and more inoffensive; those who cannot be induced, even by provocation, to resort to any very harsh exercise of authority. The wife's power of being disagreeable generally only establishes a counter-tyranny, and makes victims in their turn chiefly of those husbands who are least inclined to be tyrants. . . .

With regard to the fitness of women, not only to participate in elections, but themselves to hold offices or practise professions involving important public responsibilities; I have already observed that this consideration is not essential to the practical question in dispute: since any woman, who succeeds in an open profession, proves by that very fact that she is qualified for it. And in the case of public offices, if the political system of the country is such as to exclude unfit men, it will equally exclude unfit women: while if it is not, there is no additional evil in the fact that the unfit persons whom it admits may be either women or men. As long therefore as it is acknowledged that even a few women may be fit for these duties, the laws which shut the door on those exceptions cannot be justified by any opinion which can be held respecting the capacities of women in general. But, though this last consideration is not essential, it is far from being irrelevant. An unprejudiced view of it gives additional strength to the arguments against the disabilities of women, and reinforces them by high consideration of practical utility.

Let us at first make entire abstraction of all psychological considerations tending to show, that any of the mental differences supposed to exist between women and men are but the natural effect of the differences in their education and circumstances, and indicate no radical difference, far less radical inferiority, of nature. Let us consider women only as they already are, or as they are known to have been; and the capacities which they have already practically shown. What they have done, that at least, if nothing else, it is proved that they can do. When we consider how sedulously they are all trained away from, instead of being trained towards, any of the occupations or objects reserved for men, it is evident that I am taking a very humble ground for them, when I rest their case on what they have actually achieved. For, in this case, negative evidence is worth little, while any positive evidence is conclusive. It cannot be inferred to be impossible that a woman should be a Homer, or an Aristotle, or a Michelangelo, or a Beethoven, because no woman has yet actually produced works comparable to theirs in any of those lines of excellence. This negative fact at most leaves the question uncertain, and open to psychological discussion. But it is quite certain that a woman can be a Queen Elizabeth, or a Deborah, or a Joan of Arc, since this is not inference, but fact. Now it is a curious consideration, that the only things which the existing law excludes women from doing, are the things which they have proved that they are able to do. There is no law to prevent a woman from having written all the plays of Shakespeare, or composed all the operas of Mozart. But Queen Elizabeth or Queen Victoria, had they not inherited the throne, could not have been entrusted with the smallest of the political duties, of which the former showed herself equal to the greatest.

If anything conclusive could be inferred from experience, without psychological analysis, it would be that the things which women are not allowed to do are the very ones for which they are peculiarly qualified; since their vocation for government has made its way, and become conspicuous, through the very few opportunities which have been given; while in the lines of distinction which apparently were freely open to them, they have by no means so eminently distinguished themselves. We know how small a number of reigning queens history presents, in comparison with that of kings. Of this smaller number a far larger proportion have shown talents for rule; though many of them have occupied the throne in difficult periods. It is remarkable, too, that they have, in a great number of instances, been distinguished by merits the most opposite to the imaginary and conventional character of women: they have been as much remarked for the firmness and vigour of their rule, as for its intelligence. When, to queens and empresses, we add regents, and viceroys of provinces, the list of women who have been eminent rulers of mankind swells to a great length. . . .

. . . Exactly where and in proportion as women's capacities for government have been tried, in that proportion have they been found adequate.

This fact is in accordance with the best general conclusions which the world's imperfect experience seems as yet to suggest, concerning the peculiar tendencies and aptitudes characteristic of women, as women have hitherto been. I do not say, as they will continue to be; for, as I have already said more than once, I consider it presumption in any one to pretend to decide what women are or are not, can or cannot be, by natural constitution. They have always hitherto been kept, as far as regards spontaneous development, in so unnatural a state, that their nature cannot but have been greatly distorted and disguised; and no one can safely pronounce that if women's nature were left to choose its direction as freely as men's, and if no artificial bent were attempted to be given to it except that required by the conditions of human society, and given to both sexes alike, there would be any material difference, or perhaps any difference at all, in the character and capacities which would unfold themselves. . . . even the least contestable of the differences which now exist, are such as may very well have been produced merely by circumstances, without any difference of natural capacity.

SIMONE DE BEAUVOIR

The Second Sex

SIMONE DE BEAUVOIR (1908–86) was a French philosopher best known for her extensive contributions to the development of feminist thought. A lifelong companion of Jean-Paul Sartre, her philosophical roots are in the existentialist tradition. Her book The Second Sex, *from which the following selection is taken, is a classic of feminist philosophy.*

FOR a long time I have hesitated to write a book on woman. The subject is irritating, especially to women; and it is not new. Enough ink has been spilled in the quarreling over feminism, now practically over, and perhaps we should say no more about it. It is still talked about, however, for the voluminous nonsense uttered during the last century seems to have done little to illuminate the problem. After all, is there a problem? And if so, what is it? Are there women, really? Most assuredly the theory of the eternal feminine still has its adherents who will whisper in your ear: "Even in Russia women still are *women*"; and other erudite persons—sometimes the very same—say with a sigh: "Woman is losing her way, woman is lost." One wonders if women still exist, if they will always exist, whether or not it is desirable that they should, what place they occupy in this world, what their place should be. "What has become of women?" was asked recently in an ephemeral magazine.

But first we must ask: what is a woman? *Tota mulier in utero,"* says one, "woman is a womb." But in speaking of certain women, connoisseurs declare that they are not women, although they are equipped with a uterus like the rest. All agree in recognizing the fact that fe-males exist in the human species; today as always they make up about one half of humanity. And yet we are told that femininity is in danger; we are exhorted to be women, remain women, become women. It would appear, then, that every female human being is not necessarily a woman; to be so considered she must share in that mysterious and threatened reality known as femininity. Is this attribute something secreted by the ovaries? Or is it a Platonic essence, a product of the philosophic imagination? Is a rustling petticoat enough to bring it down to earth? Although some women try zealously to incarnate this essence, it is hardly patentable. It is frequently described in vague and dazzling terms that seem to have been borrowed from the vocabulary of the seers, and indeed in the times of St. Thomas it was considered an essence as certainly defined as the somniferous virtue of the poppy.

But conceptualism has lost ground. The biological and social sciences no longer admit the existence of unchangeable fixed entities that determine given characteristics, such as those ascribed to woman, the Jew, or the Negro. Science regards any characteristic as a reaction dependent in part upon a *situation*. If today femininity no longer exists, then it never existed. But does the word *woman,* then, have no specific content? This is stoutly affirmed by those who hold to the philosophy of the enlightenment, of rationalism, of nominalism; women, to them, are merely the human beings arbitrarily designated by the word *woman.* Many American women particularly are prepared to think that there is no longer any place for woman as such; if a backward individual still takes herself for a woman, her friends advise her to be psychoanalyzed and thus get rid of this obsession. In regard to a work, *Modern Woman: The Lost Sex,* which in other respects has its irritating features, Dorothy Parker has written: "I cannot be just to books which treat of woman as woman. . . . My idea is that all of us, men as well as women, should be regarded as human beings." But nominalism is a rather inadequate doctrine, and the antifeminists have had no trouble in showing that women simply *are not* men. Surely woman is, like man, a human being; but such a declaration is abstract. The fact is that every concrete human being is always a singular, separate individual. To decline to accept such notions as the eternal feminine, the black soul, the Jewish character, is not to deny that Jews, Negroes, women exist today—this denial does not represent a liberation for those concerned, but rather a flight from reality. Some years ago a well-known woman writer refused to permit her portrait to appear in a series of photographs especially devoted to women writers; she wished to be counted among the men. But in order to gain this privilege she made use of her husband's influence! Women who assert that they are men lay claim none the less to masculine consideration and respect. I recall also a young Trotskyite standing on a platform at a boisterous meeting and

getting ready to use her fists, in spite of her evident fragility. She was denying her feminine weakness; but it was for love of a militant male whose equal she wished to be. The attitude of defiance of many American women proves that they are haunted by a sense of their femininity. In truth, to go for a walk with one's eyes open is enough to demonstrate that humanity is divided into two classes of individuals whose clothes, faces, bodies, smiles, gaits, interests, and occupations are manifestly different. Perhaps these differences are superficial, perhaps they are destined to disappear. What is certain is that right now they do most obviously exist.

If her functioning as a female is not enough to define woman, if we decline also to explain her through "the eternal feminine," and if nevertheless we admit, provisionally, that women do exist, then we must face the question: what is a woman?

To state the question is, to me, to suggest, at once, a preliminary answer. The fact that I ask it is in itself significant. A man would never get the notion of writing a book on the peculiar situation of the human male. But if I wish to define myself, I must first of all say: "I am a woman"; on this truth must be based all further discussion. A man never begins by presenting himself as an individual of a certain sex; it goes without saying that he is a man. The terms *masculine* and *feminine* are used symmetrically only as a matter of form, as on legal papers. In actuality the relation of the two sexes is not quite like that of two electrical poles, for man represents both the positive and the neutral, as is indicated by the common use of *man* to designate human beings in general; whereas woman represents only the negative, defined by limiting criteria, without reciprocity. In the midst of an abstract discussion it is vexing to hear a man say: "You think thus and so because you are a woman"; but I know that my only defense is to reply: "I think thus and so because it is true," thereby removing my subjective self from the argument. It would be out of the question to reply: "And you think the contrary because you are a man," for it is understood that the fact of being a man is no peculiarity. A man is in the right in being a man; it is the woman who is in the wrong. It amounts to this: just as for the ancients there was an absolute vertical with reference to which the oblique was defined, so there is an absolute human type, the masculine. Woman has ovaries, a uterus; these peculiarities imprison her in her subjectivity, circumscribe her within the limits of her own nature. It is often said that she thinks with her glands. Man superbly ignores the fact that his anatomy also includes glands, such as the testicles, and that they secrete hormones. He thinks of his body as a direct and normal connection with the world, which he believes he apprehends objectively, whereas he regards the body of woman as a hindrance, a prison, weighed down by everything peculiar to it. "The female is a female by virtue of a certain *lack* of qualities," said Aristotle; "we should regard the female nature as afflicted with a natural defectiveness." And St. Thomas for his part pronounced woman to be an "imperfect man," an "incidental" being. This is symbolized in Genesis where Eve is depicted as made from what Bossuet called "a supernumerary bone" of Adam.

Thus humanity is male and man defines woman not in herself but as relative to him; she is not regarded as an autonomous being. Michelet writes:

"Woman, the relative being. . . ." And Benda is most positive in his *Rapport d'Uriel:* "The body of man makes sense in itself quite apart from that of woman, whereas the latter seems wanting in significance by itself. . . . Man can think of himself without woman. She cannot think of herself without man." And she is simply what man decrees; thus she is called "the sex," by which is meant that she appears essentially to the male as a sexual being. For him she is sex—absolute sex, no less. She is defined and differentiated with reference to man and not he with reference to her; she is the incidental, the inessential as opposed to the essential. He is the Subject, he is the Absolute—she is the Other.

The category of the *Other* is as primordial as consciousness itself. In the most primitive societies, in the most ancient mythologies, one finds the expression of a duality—that of the Self and the Other. This duality was not originally attached to the division of the sexes; it was not dependent upon any empirical facts. It is revealed in such works as that of Granet on Chinese thought and those of Dumézil on the East Indies and Rome. The feminine element was at first no more involved in such pairs as Varuna-Mitra, Uranus-Zeus, Sun-Moon, and Day-Night than it was in the contrasts between Good and Evil, lucky and unlucky auspices, right and left, God and Lucifer. Otherness is a fundamental category of human thought.

Thus it is that no group ever sets itself up as the One without at once setting up the Other over against itself. If three travelers chance to occupy the same compartment, that is enough to make vaguely hostile "others" out of all the rest of the passengers on the train. In small-town eyes all persons not belonging to the village are "strangers" and suspect; to the native of a country all who inhabit other countries are "foreigners"; Jews are "different" for the anti-Semite, Negroes are "inferior" for American racists, aborigines are "natives" for colonists, proletarians are the "lower class" for the privileged. . . .

. . . The native traveling abroad is shocked to find himself in turn regarded as a "stranger" by the natives of neighboring countries. As a matter of fact, wars, festivals, trading, treaties, and contests among tribes, nations, and classes tend to deprive the concept *Other* of its absolute sense and to make manifest its relativity; willy-nilly, individuals and groups are forced to realize the reciprocity of their relations. How is it, then, that this reciprocity has not been recognized between the sexes, that one of the contrasting terms is set up as the sole essential, denying any relativity in regard to its correlative and defining the latter as pure otherness? Why is it that women do not dispute male sovereignty? No subject will readily volunteer to become the object, the inessential; it is not the Other who, in defining himself as the Other, establishes the One. The Other is posed as such by the One in defining himself as the One. But if the Other is not to regain the status of being the One, he must be submissive enough to accept this alien point of view. Whence comes this submission in the case of woman? . . .

History has shown us that men have always kept in their hands all concrete powers; since the earliest days of the patriarchate they have thought best to keep woman in a state of dependence; their codes of law have been set up against her; and thus she has been definitely established as the Other. This arrangement suited the economic interests of the males; but it conformed also to their ontological and moral pretensions. Once the subject seeks to assert himself, the Other, who limits and denies him, is none the less a necessity to him: he attains himself only through that reality which he is not, which is something other than himself. That is why man's life is never abundance and quietude; it is dearth and activity, it is struggle. Before him, man encounters Nature; he has some hold upon her, he endeavors to mold her to his desire. But she cannot fill his needs. Either she appears simply as a purely impersonal opposition, she is an obstacle and remains a stranger; or she submits passively to man's will and permits assimilation, so that he takes possession of her only through consuming her—that is, through destroying her. In both cases he remains alone; he is alone when he touches a stone, alone when he devours a fruit. There can be no presence of an other unless the other is also present in and for himself: which is to say that true alterity—otherness—is that of a consciousness separate from mine and substantially identical with mine.

It is the existence of other men that tears each man out of his immanence and enables him to fulfill the truth of his being, to complete himself through transcendence, through escape toward some objective, through enterprise. But this liberty not my own, while assuring mine, also conflicts with it: there is the tragedy of the unfortunate human consciousness; each separate conscious being aspires to set himself up alone as sovereign subject. Each tries to fulfill himself by reducing the other to slavery. But the slave, though he works and fears, senses himself somehow as the essential; and, by a dialectical inversion, it is the master who seems to be the inessential. It is possible to rise above this conflict if each individual freely recognizes the other, each regarding himself and the other simultaneously as object and as subject in a reciprocal manner. But friendship and generosity, which alone permit in actuality this recognition of free beings, are not facile virtues; they are assuredly man's highest achievement, and through that achievement he is to be found in his true nature. But this true nature is that of a struggle unceasingly begun, unceasingly abolished; it requires man to outdo himself at every moment. We might put it in other words and say that man attains an authentically moral attitude when he renounces *mere being* to assume his position as an existent; through this transformation also he renounces all possession, for possession is one way of seeking mere being; but the transformation through which he attains true wisdom is never done, it is necessary to make it without ceasing, it demands a constant tension. And so, quite unable to fulfill himself in solitude, man is incessantly in danger in his relations with his fellows: his life is a difficult enterprise with success never assured.

But he does not like difficulty; he is afraid of danger. He aspires in contradictory fashion both to life and to repose, to existence and to merely being; he knows full well that "trouble of spirit" is the price of development, that his distance from the object is the price of his nearness to himself; but he dreams of quiet in disquiet and of an opaque plenitude that nevertheless would be endowed with consciousness. This dream incarnated is precisely woman; she is the wished-for intermediary between nature, the stranger to man, and the fellow being who is too closely identical. She opposes him with neither the hostile silence of nature nor the hard

requirement of a reciprocal relation; through a unique privilege she is a conscious being and yet it seems possible to possess her in the flesh. Thanks to her, there is a means for escaping that implacable dialectic of master and slave which has its source in the reciprocity that exists between free beings.

We have seen that there were not at first free women whom the males had enslaved nor were there even castes based on sex. To regard woman simply as a slave is a mistake; there were women among the slaves, to be sure, but there have always been free women—that is, women of religious and social dignity. They accepted man's sovereignty and he did not feel menaced by a revolt that could make of him in turn the object. Woman thus seems to be the inessential who never goes back to being the essential, to be the absolute Other, without reciprocity. This conviction is dear to the male, and every creation myth has expressed it, among others the legend of Genesis, which, through Christianity, has been kept alive in Western civilization. Eve was not fashioned at the same time as the man; she was not fabricated from a different substance, nor of the same clay as was used to model Adam: she was taken from the flank of the first male. Not even her birth was independent; God did not spontaneously choose to create her as an end in herself and in order to be worshipped directly by her in return for it. She was destined by Him for man; it was to rescue Adam from loneliness that He gave her to him, in her mate was her origin and her purpose; she was his complement on the order of the inessential. Thus she appeared in the guise of privileged prey. She was nature elevated to transparency of consciousness; she was a conscious being, but naturally submissive. And therein lies the wondrous hope that man has often put in woman: he hopes to fulfill himself as a being by carnally possessing a being, but at the same time confirming his sense of freedom through the docility of a free person. No man would consent to be a woman, but every man wants women to exist. "Thank God for having created woman." "Nature is good since she has given women to men." In such expressions man once more asserts with naïve arrogance that his presence in this world is an ineluctable fact and a right, that of woman a mere accident—but a very happy accident. Appearing as the Other, woman appears at the same time as an abundance of being in contrast to that existence the nothingness of which man senses in himself; the Other, being regarded as the object in the eyes of the subject, is regarded as *en soi;* therefore as a being. In woman is incarnated in positive form the lack that the existent carries in his heart, and it is in seeking to be made whole through her that man hopes to attain self-realization. . . .

. . . Perhaps the myth of woman will some day be extinguished; the more women assert themselves as human beings, the more the marvelous quality of the Other will die out in them. But today it still exists in the heart of every man.

A myth always implies a subject who projects his hopes and his fears toward a sky of transcendence. Women do not set themselves up as Subject and hence have erected no virile myth in which their projects are reflected; they have no religion or poetry of their own: they still dream through the dreams of men. Gods made by males are the gods they worship. Men have shaped for their own exaltation great virile figures: Hercules, Prometheus, Parsifal; woman has only a

secondary part to play in the destiny of these heroes. No doubt there are conventional figures of man caught in his relations to woman: the father, the seducer, the husband, the jealous lover, the good son, the wayward son; but they have all been established by men, and they lack the dignity of myth, being hardly more than clichés. Whereas woman is defined exclusively in her relation to man. The asymmetry of the categories—male and female—is made manifest in the unilateral form of sexual myths. We sometimes say "the sex" to designate woman; she is the flesh, its delights and dangers. The truth that for woman man is sex and carnality has never been proclaimed because there is no one to proclaim it. Representation of the world, like the world itself, is the work of men; they describe it from their own point of view, which they confuse with absolute truth.

It is always difficult to describe a myth; it cannot be grasped or encompassed; it haunts the human consciousness without ever appearing before it in fixed form. The myth is so various, so contradictory, that at first its unity is not discerned: Delilah and Judith, Aspasia and Lucretia, Pandora and Athena—woman is at once Eve and the Virgin Mary. She is an idol, a servant, the source of life, a power of darkness; she is the elemental silence of truth, she is artifice, gossip, and falsehood; she is healing presence and sorceress; she is man's prey, his downfall, she is everything that he is not and that he longs for, his negation and his *raison d'être.* . . .

Man seeks in woman the Other as Nature and as his fellow being. But we know what ambivalent feelings Nature inspires in man. He exploits her, but she crushes him, he is born of her and dies in her; she is the source of his being and the realm that he subjugates to his will; Nature is a vein of gross material in which the soul is imprisoned, and she is the supreme reality; she is contingence and Idea, the finite and the whole; she is what opposes the Spirit, and the Spirit itself. Now ally, now enemy, she appears as the dark chaos from whence life wells up, as this life itself, and as the over-yonder toward which life tends. Woman sums up nature as Mother, Wife, and Idea; these forms now mingle and now conflict and each of them wears a double visage. . . .

This, then, is the reason why woman has a double and deceptive visage: she is all that man desires and all that he does not attain. She is the good mediatrix between propitious Nature and man; and she is the temptation of unconquered Nature, counter to all goodness. She incarnates all moral values, from good to evil, and their opposites; she is the substance of action and whatever is an obstacle to it, she is man's grasp on the world and his frustration; as such

she is the source and origin of all man's reflection on his existence and of whatever expression he is able to give to it; and yet she works to divert him from himself, to make him sink down in silence and in death. She is servant and companion, but he expects her also to be his audience and critic and to confirm him in his sense of being; but she opposes him with her indifference, even with her mockery and laughter. He projects upon her what he desires and what he fears, what he loves and what he hates. And if it is so difficult to say anything specific about her, that is because man seeks the whole of himself in her and because she is All. She is All, that is, on the plane of the inessential; she is all the Other. And, as the other, she is other than herself, other than what is expected of her. Being all, she is never quite *this* which she should be; she is everlasting deception, the very deception of that existence which is never successfully attained nor fully reconciled with the totality of existents.

MARILYN FRYE

Sexism

MARILYN FRYE *is a professor of philosophy at Michigan State University. Her extensive contributions to feminist thought are collected in* The Politics of Reality *(1983), from which the following selection is taken, and more recently in* Willful Virgin *(1994).*

THE first philosophical project I undertook as a feminist was that of trying to say carefully and persuasively what sexism is, and what

it is for someone, some institution or some act to be sexist. This project was pressed on me with considerable urgency because, like most women coming to a feminist perception of themselves and the world, I was seeing sexism everywhere and trying to make it perceptible to others. I would point out, complain and criticize, but most frequently my friends and colleagues would not see that what I declared to be sexist was sexist, or at all objectionable.

As the critic and as the initiator of the topic, I was the one on whom the burden of proof fell—it was I who had to explain and convince. Teaching philosophy had already taught me that people cannot be persuaded of things they are not ready to be persuaded of; there are certain complexes of will and prior experience which will inevitably block persuasion, no matter the merits of the case presented. I knew that even if I could explain fully and clearly what I was saying when I called something sexist, I would not necessarily be able to convince various others of the correctness of this claim. But what troubled me enormously was that I could not explain it in any way which satisfied *me*. It is this sort of moral and intellectual frustration which, in my case at least, always generates philosophy.

The following was the product of my first attempt to state clearly and explicitly what sexism is:

The term 'sexist' in its core and perhaps most fundamental meaning is a term which characterizes anything whatever which creates, constitutes, promotes or exploits any irrelevant or impertinent marking of the distinction between the sexes.

When I composed this statement, I was thinking of the myriads of instances in which persons of the two sexes are treated differently, or behave differently, but where nothing in the real differences between females and males justifies or explains the difference of treatment or behavior. I was thinking, for instance, of the tracking of boys into Shop and girls into Home Ec, where one can see nothing about boys or girls considered in themselves which seems to connect essentially with the distinction between wrenches and eggbeaters. I was thinking also of sex discrimination in employment—cases where someone otherwise apparently qualified for a job is not hired because she is a woman. But when I tried to put this definition of 'sexist' to use, it did not stand the test.

Consider this case: If a company is hiring a supervisor who will supervise a group of male workers who have always worked for male supervisors, it can scarcely be denied that the sex of a candidate for the job is relevant to the candidate's prospects of moving smoothly and successfully into an effective working relationship with the supervisees (though the point is usually exaggerated by those looking for excuses not to hire women). Relevance is an intrasystematic thing. The patterns of behavior, attitude and custom within which a process goes on determine what is relevant to what in matters of describing, predicting or evaluating. In the case at hand, the workers' attitudes and the surrounding customs of the culture make a difference to how they interact with their supervisor and, in particular, *make* the sex of the supervisor a relevant factor in predicting how things will work out. So then, if the company hires a man, in preference to a more experienced and knowledgeable woman, can we explain our objection to the decision by saying it involved distinguishing on the basis of sex when sex is irrelevant to the ability to do the job? No: sex is relevant here.

So, what did I mean to say about 'sexist'? I was thinking that in a case of a candidate for a supervisory job, the re-productive capacity of the candidate has nothing to do with that person's knowing what needs to be done and being able to give properly timed, clear and correct directions. What I was picturing was a situation purified of all sexist perception and reaction. But, of course, *if* the whole context were not sexist, sex would not be an issue in such a job situation; indeed, it might go entirely unnoticed. It is precisely the fact that the sex of the candidate *is* relevant that is the salient symptom of the sexism of the situation.

I had failed, in that first essay, fully to grasp or understand that the locus of sexism is primarily in the system or framework, not in the particular act. It is not accurate to say that what is going on in cases of sexism is that distinctions are made on the basis of sex when sex is ir-relevant; what is wrong in cases of sexism is, in the first place, that sex *is* relevant; and then that the making of distinctions on the basis of sex reinforces the patterns which make it relevant.

In sexist cultural/economic systems, sex is always relevant. To understand what sexism is, then, we have to step back and take a larger view.

Sex-identification intrudes into every moment of our lives and discourse, no matter what the supposedly primary focus or topic of the moment is. Elaborate, systematic, ubiquitous and redundant marking of a distinction between the two sexes of humans and most animals is customary and obligatory. One *never* can ignore it.

Examples of sex-marking behavior patterns abound. A couple enters a restaurant; the headwaiter or hostess addresses the man and does not address the woman. The physician addresses the man by surname and honorific (Mr. Baxter, Rev. Jones) and addresses the woman by given name (Nancy, Gloria). You congratulate your friend—a hug, a slap on the back, shaking hands, kissing; one of the things which determines which of these you do is your friend's sex. In everything one does one has two complete repertoires of behavior, one for interactions with women and one for interactions with men. Greeting, story-telling, order-giving and order-receiving, negotiating, gesturing deference or dominance, encouraging, challenging, asking for information: one does all of these things differently depending upon whether the relevant others are male or female.

That this is so has been confirmed in sociological and socio-linguistic research, but it is just as easily confirmed in one's own experience. To discover the differences in how you greet a woman and how you greet a man, for instance, just observe yourself, paying attention to the following sorts of things: frequency and duration of eye contact, frequency and type of touch, tone and pitch of voice, physical distance maintained between bodies, how and whether you smile, use of slang or swear words, whether your body dips into a shadow curtsy or bow. That I have two repertoires for handling introductions to people was vividly confirmed for me when a student introduced me to his friend, Pat, and I really could not tell what sex Pat was. For a moment I was stopped cold, completely incapable of action. I felt myself helplessly caught between two paths—the one I would take if Pat were female and the one I would take if Pat were male. Of course the paralysis does not last. One is rescued by one's ingenuity and good will; one can invent a way to behave as one says "How do you do?" to a human being. But the habitual ways are not for humans: they are one way for women and another for men. . . .

In order to behave "appropriately" toward women and men, we have to know which of the people we encounter are women and which are men. But if you strip humans of most of their cultural trappings, it is not always that easy to tell without close inspection which are female, which are male. The tangible and visible physical differences between the sexes are not particularly sharp or numerous and in the physical dimensions we associate with "sex differences," the range of individual variation is very great. The differences between the sexes could easily be, and sometimes are, obscured by bodily decoration, hair removal and the like. So the requirement of knowing everyone's sex in every situation and under almost all observational conditions generates a requirement that we all let others know our sex in every situation. And we do. We announce our sexes in a thousand ways. We deck ourselves from head to toe with garments and decorations which serve like badges and buttons to announce our sexes. For every type of occasion there are distinct clothes, gear and accessories, hairdos, cosmetics and scents, labeled as "ladies'" or "men's" and labeling us as females or males, and most of the time most of us choose, use, wear or bear the paraphernalia associated with our sex. It goes below the skin as well. There are different styles of gait, gesture, posture, speech, humor, taste and even of perception, interest and attention that we learn as we grow up to be women or to be men and that label and announce us as women or as men. It begins early in life: even infants in arms are color coded.

That we wear and bear signs of our sexes, and that this is absolutely compulsory, is made clearest in the relatively rare cases when we do not do so, or not enough. Responses ranging from critical to indignant to hostile meet mothers whose babies are not adequately coded; one of the most agitated criticisms of the sixties' hippies was that "you can't tell the boys from the girls." The requirement of sex-announcement is laden, indeed, with all the urgency of the taboo against homosexuality. One appears heterosexual by informing people of one's sex *very* emphatically and *very* unambiguously, and lesbians and homosexuals who wish *not* to pass as heterosexual generally can accomplish this just by cultivating ambiguous sex-indicators in clothes, behavior and style. The power of this ambiguity to generate unease and punitive responses in others mirrors and demonstrates the rigidity and urgency of this strange social rule that we all be and assertively act "feminine" or "masculine" (and not both) that we flap a full array of sex-signals at all times.

The intense demand for marking and for asserting what sex each person is adds up to a strenuous requirement that there *be* two distinct and sharply dimorphic sexes. But, in reality, there are not. There are people who fit on a biological spectrum between two not-so-sharply defined poles. In about 5 percent of live births, possibly more, the babies are in some degree and way not perfect exemplars of male and female. There are individuals with chromosome patterns other than XX or YY and individuals whose external genitalia at birth exhibit some degree of ambiguity. There are people who are chromosomally "normal" who are at the far ends of the normal spectra of secondary sex characteristics—height, musculature, hairiness, body density, distribution of fat, breast size, etc.—whose overall appearance fits the norm of people whose chromosomal sex is the opposite of theirs.

These variations notwithstanding, persons (mainly men, of course) with the power to do so actually *construct* a world in which men are men and women are women and there is nothing in between and nothing ambiguous; they do it by chemically and/or surgically altering people whose bodies are indeterminate or ambiguous with respect to sex. Newborns with "imperfectly formed" genitals are immediately "corrected" by chemical or surgical means, children and adolescents are given hormone "therapies" if their bodies seem not to be developing according to what physicians and others declare to be the norm for what has been declared to be that individual's sex. Persons with authority recommend and supply cosmetics and cosmetic regimens, diets, exercises and all manner of clothing to revise or disguise the too-hairy lip, the too-large breast, the too-slender shoulders, the too-large feet, the too-great or too-slight stature. Individuals whose bodies do not fit the picture of exactly two sharply dimorphic sexes are often enough quite willing to be altered or veiled for the obvious reason that the world punishes them severely for their failure to be the "facts" which would verify the doctrine of two sexes. The demand that the world be a world in which there are exactly two sexes is inexorable, and we are all compelled to answer to it emphatically, unconditionally, repetitiously and unambiguously.

Even being physically "normal" for one's assigned sex is not enough. One must *be* female or male, actively. Again,

the costumes and performances. Pressed to acting feminine or masculine, one colludes (co-lude: play along) with the doctors and counselors in the creation of a world in which the apparent dimorphism of the sexes is so extreme that one can only think there is a great gulf between female and male, that the two are, essentially and fundamentally and naturally, utterly different. One helps to create a world in which it seems to us that we *could* never mistake a woman for a man or a man for a woman. We never need worry.

Along with all the making, marking and announcing of sex-distinction goes a strong and visceral feeling or attitude to the effect that sex-distinction is the most important thing in the world: that it would be the end of the world if it were not maintained, clear and sharp and rigid; that a sex-dualism which is rooted in the nature of the beast is absolutely crucial and fundamental to all aspects of human life, human society and human economy. . . .

It is a general and obvious principle of information theory that when it is very, very important that certain information be conveyed, the suitable strategy is redundancy. If a message *must* get through, one sends it repeatedly and by as many means or media as one has at one's command. On the other end, as a receiver of information, if one receives the same information over and over, conveyed by every medium one knows, another message comes through as well, and implicitly: the message that this information is very, very important. The enormous frequency with which information about people's sexes is conveyed conveys implicitly the message that this topic is enormously important. I suspect that this is the single topic on which we most frequently receive information from others throughout our entire lives. If I am right, it would go part way to explaining why we end up with an almost irresistible impression, unarticulated, that the matter of people's sexes is the most important and most fundamental topic in the world.

We exchange sex-identification information, along with the implicit message that it is very important, in a variety of circumstances in which there really is no concrete or experientially obvious point in having the information. There are reasons, as this discussion has shown, why you should want to know whether the person filling your water glass or your tooth is male or female and why that person wants to know what you are, but those reasons are woven invisibly into the fabric of social structure and they do not have to do with the bare mechanics of things being filled. Furthermore, the same culture which drives us to this constant information exchange also simultaneously enforces a strong blanket rule requiring that the simplest and most nearly definitive physical manifestations of sex difference be hidden from view in all but the most private and intimate circumstances. The double message of sex-distinction and its pre-eminent importance is conveyed, in fact, in part *by* devices which systematically and deliberately cover up and hide from view the few physical things which do (to a fair extent) distinguish two sexes of humans. The messages are overwhelmingly dissociated from the concrete facts they supposedly pertain to, and from matrices of concrete and sensible reasons and consequences. . . .

If one is made to feel that a thing is of prime importance, but common sensory experience does not connect it with things of obvious concrete and practical importance, then there is mystery, and with that a strong tendency to the construction of mystical or metaphysical conceptions of its importance. If it is important, but not of mundane importance, it must be of transcendent importance. All the more so if it is *very* important.

This matter of our sexes must be very profound indeed if it must, on pain of shame and ostracism, be covered up and must, on pain of shame and ostracism, be boldly advertised by every means and medium one can devise.

There is one more point about redundancy that is worth making here. If there is one thing more effective in making one believe a thing than receiving the message repetitively, it is rehearsing it repetitively. Advertisers, preachers, teachers, all of us in the brainwashing professions, make use of this apparently physical fact of human psychology routinely. The redundancy of sex-marking and sex-announcing serves not only to make the topic seem transcendently important, but to make the sex-duality it advertises seem transcendently and unquestionably *true*. . . .

Sex-marking and sex-announcing are equally compulsory for males and females; but that is as far as equality goes in this matter. The meaning and import of this behavior is profoundly different for women and for men.

Imagine—

A colony of humans established a civilization hundreds of years ago on a distant planet. It has evolved, as civilizations will. Its language is a descendant of English.

The language has personal pronouns marking the child/adult distinction, and its adult personal pronouns mark the distinction between straight and curly pubic hair. At puberty each person assumes distinguishing clothing styles and manners so others can tell what type she or he is without the closer scrutiny which would generally be considered indecent. People with straight pubic hair adopt a style which is modest and self-effacing and clothes which are fragile and confining; people with curly pubic hair adopt a style which is expansive and prepossessing and clothes which are sturdy and comfortable. People whose pubic hair is neither clearly straight nor clearly curly alter their hair chemically in order to be clearly one or the other. Since those with curly pubic hair have higher status and economic advantages, those with ambiguous pubic hair are told to make it straight, for life will be easier for a low-status person whose category might be doubted than for a high-status person whose category might be doubted.

It is taboo to eat or drink in the same room with any person of the same pubic hair type as oneself. Compulsory hetero-gourmandism, it is called by social critics, though most people think it is just natural human desire to eat with one's pubic-hair opposite. A logical consequence of this habit, or taboo, is the limitation to dining only singly or in pairs—a taboo against banquetism, or, as the slang expression goes, against the group gulp.

Whatever features an individual male person has which tend to his social and economic disadvantage (his age, race, class, height, etc.), one feature which never tends to his disadvantage in the society at large is his maleness. The case for females is the mirror image of this. Whatever features an individual female person has which tend to her so-

cial and economic advantage (her age, race, etc.), one feature which always tends to her disadvantage is her femaleness. Therefore, when a male's sex-category is the thing about him that gets first and most repeated notice, the thing about him that is being framed and emphasized and given primacy is a feature which in general is an asset to him. When a female's sex-category is the thing about her that gets first and most repeated notice, the thing about her that is being framed and emphasized and given primacy is a feature which in general is a liability to her. Manifestations of this divergence in the meaning and consequences of sex-announcement can be very concrete.

Walking down the street in the evening in a town or city exposes one to some risk of assault. For males the risk is less; for females the risk is greater. If one announces oneself male, one is presumed by potential assailants to be more rather than less likely to defend oneself or be able to evade the assault and, if the male-announcement is strong and unambiguous, to be a noncandidate for sexual assault. If one announces oneself female, one is presumed by potential assailants to be less rather than more likely to defend oneself or to evade the assault and, if the female-announcement is strong and unambiguous, to be a prime candidate for sexual assault. Both the man and the woman "announce" their sex through style of gait, clothing, hair style, etc., but they are not equally or identically affected by announcing their sex. The male's announcement tends toward his protection or safety, and the female's announcement tends toward her victimization. It could not be more immediate or concrete; the meaning of the sex-identification could not be more different.

The sex-marking behavioral repertoires are such that in the behavior of almost all people of both sexes addressing or responding to males (especially within their own culture/race) generally is done in a manner which suggests basic respect, while addressing or responding to females is done in a manner that suggests the females' inferiority (condescending tones, presumptions of ignorance, overfamiliarity, sexual aggression, etc.). So, when one approaches an ordinary well-socialized person in such cultures, if one is male, one's own behavioral announcement of maleness tends to evoke supportive and beneficial response and if one is female, one's own behavioral announcement of femaleness tends to evoke degrading and detrimental response.

The details of the sex-announcing behaviors also contribute to the reduction of women and the elevation of men. The case is most obvious in the matter of clothing. As feminists have been saying for two hundred years or so, ladies' clothing is generally restrictive, binding, burdening and frail; it threatens to fall apart and/or to uncover something that is supposed to be covered if you bend, reach, kick, punch or run. It typically does not protect effectively against hazards in the environment, nor permit the wearer to protect herself against the hazards of the human environment. Men's clothing is generally the opposite of all this—sturdy, suitably protective, permitting movement and locomotion. The details of feminine manners and postures also serve to bind and restrict. To be feminine is to take up little space, to defer to others, to be silent or affirming of others, etc. It is not necessary here to survey all this, for it has been done many times and in illuminating detail in feminist writings. My point here is that though both men and women must behave in sex-announcing ways, the behavior which announces femaleness is in itself both physically and socially binding and limiting as the behavior which announces maleness is not.

The sex-correlated variations in our behavior tend systematically to the benefit of males and the detriment of females. The male, announcing his sex in sex-identifying behavior and dress, is both announcing and acting on his membership in a dominant caste—dominant within his subculture and to a fair extent across subcultures as well. The female, announcing her sex, is both announcing and acting on her membership in the subordinated caste. She is obliged to inform others constantly and in every sort of situation that she is to be treated as inferior, without authority, assaultable. She cannot move or speak within the usual cultural norms without engaging in self-deprecation. The male cannot move or speak without engaging in self-aggrandizement. Constant sex-identification both defines and maintains the caste boundary without which there could not be a dominance-subordination structure. . . .

The cultural and economic structures which create and enforce elaborate and rigid patterns of sex-marking and sex-announcing behavior, that is, create gender as we know it, mold us as dominators and subordinates (I do not say "mold our minds" or "mold our personalities"). They construct two classes of animals, the masculine and the feminine, where another constellation of forces might have constructed three or five categories, and not necessarily hierarchically related. Or such a spectrum of sorts that we would not experience them as "sorts" at all.

The term 'sexist' characterizes cultural and economic structures which create and enforce the elaborate and rigid patterns of sex-marking and sex-announcing which divide the species, along lines of sex, into dominators and subordinates. Individual acts and practices are sexist which reinforce and support those structures, either as culture or as shapes taken on by the enculturated animals. Resistance to sexism is that which undermines those structures by social and political action and by projects of reconstruction and revision of ourselves.

bell hooks

Black Women: Shaping Feminist Theory

bell hooks is the pen name of Gloria Watkins. She teaches English and African-American studies at Yale University. She has published numerous essays and books of cultural criticism. Her most recent book is Outlaw Culture: Resisting Representations *(1995).*

FEMINISM in the United States has never emerged from the women who are most victimized by sexist oppression; women who are daily beaten down, mentally, physically, and spiritually—women who are powerless to change their condition in life. They are a silent majority. A mark of their victimization is that they accept their lot in life without visible question, without organized protest, without collective anger or rage. Betty Friedan's *The Feminine Mystique* is still heralded as having paved the way for contemporary feminist movement—it was written as if these women did not exist. Friedan's famous phrase, "the problem that has no name," often quoted to describe the condition of women in this society, actually referred to the plight of a select group of college-educated, middle and upper class, married white women—housewives bored with leisure, with the home, with children, with buying products, who wanted more out of life. Friedan concludes her first chapter by stating: "We can no longer ignore that voice within women that says: 'I want something more than my husband and my children and my house.'" That "more" she defined as careers. She did not discuss who would be called in to take care of the children and maintain the home if more women like herself were freed from their house labor and given equal access with white men to the professions. She did not speak of the needs of women without men, without children, without homes. She ignored the existence of all non-white women and poor white women. She did not tell readers whether it was more fulfilling to be a maid, a babysitter, a factory worker, a clerk, or a prostitute, than to be a leisure class housewife.

She made her plight and the plight of white women like herself synonymous with a condition affecting all American women. In so doing, she deflected attention away from her classism, her racism, her sexist attitudes towards the masses of American women. In the context of her book, Friedan makes clear that the women she saw as victimized by sexism were college-educated, white women who were compelled by sexist conditioning to remain in the home. She contends:

> It is urgent to understand how the very condition of being a housewife can create a sense of emptiness, non-existence, nothingness in women. There are aspects of the housewife role that make it almost impossible for a woman of adult intelligence to retain a sense of human identity, the firm core of self or "I" without which a human being, man or woman, is not truly alive. For women of ability, in America today, I am convinced that there is something about the housewife state itself that is dangerous.

Specific problems and dilemmas of leisure class white housewives were real concerns that merited consideration and change but they were not pressing political concerns of masses of women. Masses of women were concerned about economic survival, ethnic and racial discrimination, etc. When Friedan wrote *The Feminine Mystique,* more than one third of all women were in the work force. Although many women longed to be housewives, only women with leisure time and money could actually shape their identities on the model

of the feminine mystique. They were women who, in Friedan's words, were "told by the most advanced thinkers of our time to go back and live their lives as if they were Noras, restricted to the doll's house by Victorian prejudices."

From her early writing, it appears that Friedan never wondered whether or not the plight of college-educated, white housewives was an adequate reference point by which to gauge the impact of sexism or sexist oppression on the lives of women in American society. Nor did she move beyond her own life experience to acquire an expanded perspective on the lives of women in the United States. I say this not to discredit her work. It remains a useful discussion of the impact of sexist discrimination on a select group of women. Examined from a different perspective, it can also be seen as a case study of narcissism, insensitivity, sentimentality, and self-indulgence which reaches its peak when Friedan, in a chapter titled "Progressive Dehumanization," makes a comparison between the psychological effects of isolation on white housewives and the impact of confinement on the self-concept of prisoners in Nazi concentration camps.

Friedan was a principal shaper of contemporary feminist thought. Significantly, the one-dimensional perspective on women's reality presented in her book became a marked feature of the contemporary feminist movement. Like Friedan before them, white women who dominate feminist discourse today rarely question whether or not their perspective on women's reality is true to the lived experiences of women as a collective group. Nor are they aware of the extent to which their perspectives reflect race and class biases, although there has been a greater awareness of biases in recent years. Racism abounds in the writings of white feminists, reinforcing white supremacy and negating the possibility that women will bond politically across ethnic and racial boundaries. Past feminist refusal to draw attention to and attack racial hierarchies suppressed the link between race and class. Yet class structure in American society has been shaped by the racial politic of white supremacy; it is only by analyzing racism and its function in capitalist society that a thorough understanding of class relationships can emerge. Class struggle is inextricably bound to the struggle to end racism. Urging women to explore the full implication of class in an early essay, "The Last Straw," Rita Mae Brown explained:

> Class is much more than Marx's definition of relationship to the means of production. Class involves your behavior, your basic assumptions about life. Your experience (determined by your class) validates those assumptions, how you are taught to behave, what you expect from yourself and from others, your concept of a future, how you understand problems and solve them, how you think, feel, act. It is these behavioral patterns that middle class women resist recognizing although they may be perfectly willing to accept class in Marxist terms, a neat trick that helps them avoid really dealing with class behavior and changing that behavior in themselves. It is these behavioral patterns which must be recognized, understood, and changed.

White women who dominate feminist discourse, who for the most part make and articulate feminist theory, have little or no understanding of white supremacy as a racial politic, of the psychological impact of class, of their political status within a racist, sexist, capitalist state.

• • •

A central tenet of modern feminist thought has been the assertion that "all women are oppressed." This assertion implies that women share a common lot, that factors like class, race, religion, sexual preference, etc. do not create a diversity of experience that determines the extent to which sexism will be an oppressive force in the lives of individual women. Sexism as a system of domination is institutionalized but it has never determined in an absolute way the fate of all women in this society. Being oppressed means the *absence of choices*. It is the primary point of contact between the oppressed and the oppressor. Many women in this society do have choices (as inadequate as they are), therefore exploitation and discrimination are words that more accurately describe the lot of women collectively in the United States. Many women do not join organized resistance against sexism precisely because sexism has not meant an absolute lack of choices. They may know they are discriminated against on the basis of sex, but they do not equate this with oppression. Under capitalism, patriarchy is structured so that sexism restricts women's behavior in some realms even as freedom from limitations is allowed in other spheres. The absence of extreme restrictions leads many women to ignore the areas in which they are exploited or discriminated against; it may even lead them to imagine that no women are oppressed.

There are oppressed women in the United States, and it is both appropriate and necessary that we speak against such oppression. French feminist Christine Delphy makes the point in her essay, "For a Materialist Feminism," that the use of the term oppression is important because it places feminist struggle in a radical political framework:

> The rebirth of feminism coincided with the use of the term "oppression." The ruling ideology, i.e. common sense, daily speech, does not speak about oppression but about a "feminine condition." It refers back to a naturalist explanation: to a constraint of nature, exterior reality out of reach and not modifiable by human action. The term "oppression," on the contrary, refers back to a choice, an explanation, a situation that is political. "Oppression" and "social oppression" are therefore synonyms or rather social oppression is a redundancy: the notion of a political origin, i.e. social, is an integral part of the concept of oppression.

However, feminist emphasis on "common oppression" in the United States was less a strategy for politicization than an appropriation by conservative and liberal women of a radical political vocabulary that masked the extent to which they shaped the movement so that it addressed and promoted their class interests.

Although the impulse towards unity and empathy that informed the notion of common oppression was directed at building solidarity, slogans like "organize around your own oppression" provided the excuse many privileged women needed to ignore the differences between their social status and the status of masses of women. It was a mark of race and class privilege, as well as the expression of freedom from the many constraints sexism places on working class women, that middle class white women were able to make their interests the primary focus of feminist movement and employ a rhetoric of commonality that made their condition synonymous with "oppression." Who was there to demand a change in vocabulary? What other group of women in the United States had the same access to universities, publishing houses, mass media, money? Had middle class black women begun a movement in which they had labeled themselves "oppressed," no one would have taken them seriously. Had they established public forums and given speeches about their "oppression," they would have been criticized and attacked from all sides. This was not the case with white bourgeois feminists for they could appeal to a large audience of women, like themselves, who were eager to change their lot in life. Their isolation from women of other class and race groups provided no immediate comparative base by which to test their assumptions of common oppression.

• • •

The ideology of "competitive, atomistic liberal individualism" has permeated feminist thought to such an extent that it undermines the potential radicalism of feminist struggle. The usurpation of feminism by bourgeois women to support their class interests has been to a very grave extent justified by feminist theory as it has so far been conceived. (For example, the ideology of "common oppression.") Any movement to resist the co-optation of feminist struggle must begin by introducing a different feminist perspective—a new theory—one that is not informed by the ideology of liberal individualism.

The exclusionary practices of women who dominate feminist discourse have made it practically impossible for new and varied theories to emerge. Feminism has its party line and women who feel a need for a different strategy, a different foundation, often find themselves ostracized and silenced. Criticisms of or alternatives to established feminist ideas are not encouraged, e.g., recent controversies about expanding feminist discussions of sexuality. Yet groups of women who feel excluded from feminist discourse and praxis can make a place for themselves only if they first create, via critiques, an awareness of the factors that alienate them. Many individual white women found in the women's movement a liberatory solution to personal dilemmas. Having directly benefited from the movement, they are less inclined to criticize it or to engage in rigorous examination of its structure than those who feel it has not had a revolutionary impact on their lives or the lives of masses of women in our society. Non-white women who feel affirmed within the current structure of feminist movement (even though they may form autonomous groups) seem to also feel that their definitions of the party line, whether on the issue of black feminism or on other issues, is the only legitimate discourse. . . .

•   •   •

We resist hegemonic dominance of feminist thought by insisting that it is a theory in the making, that we must necessarily criticize, question, re-examine, and explore new possibilities. My persistent critique has been informed by my status as a member of an oppressed group, experience of sexist exploitation and discrimination, and the sense that prevailing feminist analysis has not been the force shaping my feminist consciousness. This is true for many women. There are white women who had never considered resisting male dominance until the feminist movement created an awareness that they could and should. My awareness of feminist struggle was stimulated by social circumstance. Growing up in a Southern, black, father-dominated, working class household, I experienced (as did my mother, my sisters, and my brother) varying degrees of patriarchal tyranny and it made me angry—it made us all angry. Anger led me to question the politics of male dominance and enabled me to resist sexist socialization. Frequently, white feminists act as if black women did not know sexist oppression existed until they voiced feminist sentiment. They believe they are providing black women with "the" analysis and "the" program for liberation. They do not understand, cannot even imagine, that black women, as well as other groups of women who live daily in oppressive situations, often acquire an awareness of patriarchal politics from their lived experience, just as they develop strategies of resistance (even though they may not resist on a sustained or organized basis).

These black women observed white feminist focus on male tyranny and women's oppression as if it were a "new" revelation and felt such a focus had little impact on their lives. To them it was just another indication of the privileged living conditions of middle and upper class white women that they would need a theory to inform them that they were "oppressed." The implication being that people who are truly oppressed know it even though they may not be engaged in organized resistance or are unable to articulate in written form the nature of their oppression. These black women saw nothing liberatory in party line analyses of women's oppression. Neither the fact that black women have not organized collectively in huge numbers around the issues of "feminism" (many of us do not know or use the term) nor the fact that we have not had access to the machinery of power that would allow us to share our analyses or theories about gender with the American public negate its presence in our lives or place us in a position of dependency in relationship to those white and non-white feminists who address a larger audience.

The understanding I had by age thirteen of patriarchal politics created in me expectations of the feminist movement that were quite different from those of young, middle class, white women. When I entered my first women's studies class at Stanford University in the early 1970s, white women were revelling in the joy of being together—to them it was an important, momentous occasion. I had not known a life where women had not been together, where women had not helped, protected, and loved one another deeply. I had not known white women who were ignorant of the impact of race and class on their social status and consciousness (Southern white women often have a more realistic perspective on racism and classism than white women in other areas of the United States.) I did not feel sympathetic to white peers who maintained that I could not expect them to have knowledge of or understand the life experiences of black women. Despite my background (living in racially segregated communities) I knew about the lives of white women, and certainly no white women lived in our neighborhood, attended our schools, or worked in our homes.

When I participated in feminist groups, I found that white women adopted a condescending attitude towards me and other non-white participants. The condescension they directed at black women was one of the means they employed to remind us that the women's movement was "theirs"—that we were able to participate because they allowed it, even encouraged it; after all, we were needed to legitimate the process. They did not see us as equals. They did not treat us as equals. And though they expected us to provide first hand accounts of black experience, they felt it was their role to decide if these experiences were authentic. Frequently, college-educated black women (even those from poor and working class backgrounds) were dismissed as mere imitators. Our presence in movement activities did not count, as white women were convinced that "real" blackness meant speaking the patois of poor black people, being uneducated, streetwise, and a variety of other stereotypes. If we dared to criticize the movement or to assume responsibility for reshaping feminist ideas and introducing new ideas, our voices were tuned out, dismissed, silenced. We could be heard only if our statements echoed the sentiments of the dominant discourse.

Attempts by white feminists to silence black women are rarely written about. All too often they have taken place in conference rooms, classrooms, or the privacy of cozy living room settings, where one lone black woman faces the racist hostility of a group of white women. From the time the women's liberation movement began, individual black women went to groups.

Many never returned after a first meeting. Anita Cornwall is correct in "Three for the Price of One: Notes from a Gay Black Feminist," when she states, ". . . sadly enough, fear of encountering racism seems to be one of the main reasons that so many black women refuse to join the women's movement." Recent focus on the issue of racism has generated discourse but has had little impact on the behavior of white feminists towards black women. Often the white women who are busy publishing papers and books on "unlearning racism" remain patronizing and condescending when they relate to black women. This is not surprising given that frequently their discourse is aimed solely in the direction of a white audience and the focus solely on changing attitudes rather than addressing racism in a historical and political context. They make us the "objects" of their privileged discourse on race. As "objects," we remain unequals, inferiors. Even though they may be sincerely concerned about racism, their methodology suggests they are not yet free of the type of paternalism endemic to white supremacist ideology. Some of these women place themselves in the position of "authorities" who must mediate communication between racist white women (naturally they see themselves as having come to terms with their racism) and angry black women whom they believe are incapable of rational discourse. Of course, the systems of racism, classism, and educational elitism remain intact if they are to maintain their authoritative positions.

* * *

Racist stereotypes of the strong, superhuman black woman are operative myths in the minds of many white women, allowing them to ignore the extent to which black women are likely to be victimized in this society and the role white women may play in the maintenance and perpetuation of that victimization. In Lillian Hellman's autobiographical work *Pentimento,* she writes, "All my life, beginning at birth, I have taken orders from black women, wanting them and resenting them, being superstitious the few times I disobeyed." The black women Hellman describes worked in her household as family servants and their status was never that of an equal. Even as a child, she was always in the dominant position as they questioned, advised, or guided her; they were free to exercise these rights because she or another white authority figure allowed it. Hellman places power in the hands of these black women rather than acknowledge her own power over them; hence she mystifies the true nature of their relationship. By projecting onto black women a mythical power and strength, white women both promote a false image of themselves as powerless, passive victims and deflect attention away from their aggressiveness, their power, (however limited in a white supremacist, male-dominated state) their willingness to dominate and control others. These unacknowledged aspects of the social status of many white women prevent them from transcending racism and limit the scope of their understanding of women's overall social status in the United States.

Privileged feminists have largely been unable to speak to, with, and for diverse groups of women because they either do not understand fully the interrelatedness of sex, race, and class oppression or refuse to take this inter-relatedness seriously. Feminist analyses of woman's lot tend to focus exclusively on gender and do not provide a solid foundation on which to construct feminist theory. They reflect the dominant tendency in Western patriarchal minds to mystify woman's reality by insisting that gender is the sole determinant of woman's fate. Certainly it has been easier for women who do not experience race or class oppression to focus exclusively on gender. Although socialist feminists focus on class and gender, they tend to dismiss race or they make a point of acknowledging that race is important and then proceed to offer an analysis in which race is not considered.

As a group, black women are in an unusual position in this society, for not only are we collectively at the bottom of the occupational ladder, but our overall social status is lower than that of any other group. Occupying such a position, we bear the brunt of sexist, racist, and classist oppression. At the same time, we are the group that has not been so cialized to assume the role of exploiter/oppressor in that we are allowed no institutionalized "other" that we can exploit or oppress. (Children do not represent an institutionalized other even though they may be oppressed by parents.) White women and black men have it both ways. They can act as oppressor or be oppressed. Black men may be victimized by racism, but sexism allows them to act as exploiters and oppressors of women. White women may be victimized by sexism, but racism enables them to act as exploiters and oppressors of black people. Both groups have led liberation movements that favor their interests and support the continued oppression of other groups. Black male sexism has undermined struggles to eradicate racism just as white female racism undermines feminist struggle. As long as these two groups or any group defines liberation as gaining social equality with ruling class white men, they have a vested interest in the continued exploitation and oppression of others.

Black women with no institutionalized "other" that we may discriminate against, exploit, or oppress often have a lived experience that directly challenges the prevailing classist, sexist, racist social structures and its concomitant ideology. This lived experience may shape our consciousness in such a way that our world view differs from those who have a degree of privilege (however relative within the existing system). It is essential for continued feminist struggle that black women recognize the special vantage point our marginality gives us and make use of this perspective to criticize the dominant racist, classist, sexist hegemony as well as to envision and create a counter-hegemony. I am suggesting that we have a central role to play in the making of feminist theory and a contribution to offer that is unique and valuable. The formation of a liberatory feminist theory and praxis is a collective responsibility, one that must be shared. Though I criticize aspects of feminist movement as we have known it so far, a critique which is sometimes harsh and unrelenting, I do so not in an attempt to diminish a feminist struggle but to enrich, to share in the work of making a liberatory ideology and a liberatory movement.

Chapter 15
What Is the Right Thing for Me to Do?

Y̶ou once told your friend, "If you ever need me, I'll come right over," but now you've got to study for an exam you have in an hour and you promised you'd call your mother this morning and you're exhausted and now it's obvious that you aren't going to have time to do everything. What is the right thing for you to do? See your friend who seems to be in trouble? Study for your exam? Call your mom? Take a short nap? This happens to be an especially bad day for you, but you face similar decisions all the time and you know that, once in a while, it gets much worse. A friend of yours once had to decide whether to turn in his brother, who had committed a serious crime, to the police. Deciding whether to study, sleep, call your mother, or visit your friend is nothing by comparison. But the basic questions are the same: What is the right thing to do, and how do you decide what that is? This is the subject matter of **ethics.**

The field of ethics is concerned with the question, What should one do? but in a very special sense. There are a great many contexts in which we ask for guidance in getting what we want or achieving our goals, but these tend to be **prudential** concerns and not yet ethical. So, too, it is important in almost any public context to know what the law is—for example, whether in a certain country one drives on the right or left side of the road or whether in a particular park it is permissible to walk your dog without a leash. But such legal questions are not ethics either, although one would naturally expect some connection (sometimes troublesome) between the law and ethical concerns. One way of delineating ethics in particular is by reference to the questions, What *ought* I to do? What is the *right* thing to do? The right thing to do is usually in our own prudential interests, and it is usually within the law if not also specified by law. But what characterizes this special word "ought" is the existence of a set of rules or expectations that go beyond the interests of any individual and constitute a powerful force in our lives quite apart from the question of whether they are bound by law or not.

A familiar example is that one should not lie to one's friends. It may or may not be to your advantage to tell the truth, but in general (at least when you are not signing a contract or testifying in court) lying is not illegal. But lying to your friends is clearly unethical, or we might even say that it is **immoral.** The realm of ethics and morality includes a great many actions that deceive, hurt, or endanger the well-being of others or society as a whole, not only lying but cheating, stealing, killing, and a large number of related wrongdoings. Some of these are crimes, but not all are. "Honor thy father and mother" is considered by most people to be a central rule of morality, but (at least in our country) there is no law against dishonoring or embarrassing one's parents. What makes these the province of ethics and morality is that they are such basic concerns of all of us. The problem of ethical (or moral) philosophy is exactly what does define this set of basic concerns and, even more challenging, how these basic rules can be justified.

Imagine a person (you may not have to look far) who refused to do what she ought to do and demanded of you, "Why should I be moral?" What would you say? You might respond, "It is in your interests to be moral," but being moral is in fact not always in our interests and, even if it is, we would want to make some distinction between those who do the right thing because it is right and others who do it just because it happens to be to their advantage. (Knowing that a friend keeps his promises gives you a very different kind of confidence than knowing that he only keeps his promises when it is convenient.) One might insist that we should be moral because God wishes it (and will punish us if we aren't), but the temporal delay between moral transgression and divine punishment is such that many people either don't really believe it or they are willing to take the chance on a huge dose of confession and repentance later. Ethics and morality have also been justified on the basis that they serve the overall interests and well-being of society, but then the serious question arises of whether the most basic rules might in fact differ from society to society depending on their various needs and customs. In response to the possibility of such **relativism** (that is, the variance of the most basic rules of morality from one culture to another), some philosophers have defended universal principles of morality on the grounds that they satisfy the demands of human reason and thus apply everywhere regardless of the particular conditions or customs of a culture.

The following selections provide a spectrum of very different views of the nature and justification of morality. The foremost example of a moral code in our culture is the Ten Commandments in the Old Testament, coupled with the ethical precepts presented by Jesus, for instance, in the Sermon on the Mount. The basis and justification of that code, needless to say, is its divine origins. Selections from Confucius and the Koran follow. But there are other codes and other ways of justifying them. Aristotle, who wrote the most detailed manual of contemporary ethics in ancient Athens, justifies that code—whose ultimate goal is happiness—by appeal to a conception of human nature. Immanuel Kant, by way of contrast, justifies moral principles as the product of "pure practical reason" whose primary concern is **duty** and whose focus is not so much the consequences of our actions (including personal happiness) but rather the notion of a "good will," that is, good intentions based on the demands of the moral law. John Stuart Mill takes a very different approach to ethics; its primary concern is the happiness of all individuals—the common good, or what he calls "the greatest good of the greatest number."

Not every author takes the desirability of morality for granted, however. The German philosopher Friedrich Nietzsche believed that morality was basically a sham, a deceit that protected the weak and incompetent from the strong and creative. A. J. Ayer declares ethics to be nothing but an expression of emotion, and Simone de Beauvoir argues for the centrality of freedom in ethics. Mary Midgley attacks relativism with a particularly striking example of cross cultural moral judgment. Carol Gilligan has recently altered the face of ethical discussions by arguing that an ethics of care, typically associated with women, has been ignored in favor of a predominantly male ethic of rights. Novelist/journalist Joan Didion gives us her quite skeptical views on the very word "morality", and Cheshire Calhoun expands on Gilligan's theory to suggest a deep male bias in ethics.

THE BIBLE

The Ten Commandments and the Sermon on the Mount

The most influential source of Western morality has been THE BIBLE. *What follows from the King James version are the Ten Commandments and the Sermon on the Mount.*

A<small>ND</small> God spake all these words, saying,

2   I *am* the L<small>ORD</small> thy God, which have brought thee out of the land of Egypt, out of the house of bondage.

3   Thou shalt have no other gods before me.

4   Thou shalt not make unto thee any graven image, or any likeness *of any thing* that *is* in heaven above, or that *is* in the earth beneath, or that *is* in the water under the earth:

5   Thou shalt not bow down thyself to them, nor serve them: for I the L<small>ORD</small> thy God *am* a jealous God, visiting the iniquity of the fathers upon the children unto the third and fourth *generation* of them that hate me;

6   And shewing mercy unto thousands of them that love me, and keep my commandments.

7   Thou shalt not take the name of the L<small>ORD</small> thy God in vain; for the L<small>ORD</small> will not hold him guiltless that taketh his name in vain.

8   Remember the sabbath day, to keep it holy.

9   Six days shalt thou labour, and do all thy work:

10   But the seventh day *is* the sabbath of the L<small>ORD</small> thy God: *in it* thou shalt not do any work, thou, nor thy son,

nor thy daughter, they manservant, nor thy maidservant, nor thy cattle, nor thy stranger that is within thy gates:

11   For *in* six days the L<small>ORD</small> made heaven and earth, the sea, and all that in them *is,* and rested the seventh day: wherefore the L<small>ORD</small> blessed the sabbath day, and hallowed it.

12   Honour thy father and thy mother: that thy days may be long upon the land which the L<small>ORD</small> thy God giveth thee.

13   Thou shalt not kill.

14   Thou shalt not commit adultery.

15   Thou shalt not steal.

16   Thou shalt not bear false witness against thy neighbour.

17   Thou shalt not covet thy neighbour's house, thou shalt not covet thy neighbour's wife, nor his manservant, nor his maidservant, nor his ox, nor his ass, nor any thing that *is* thy neighbour's.

18   And all the people saw the thunderings, and the lightnings, and the noise of the trumpet, and the mountain smoking: and when the people saw *it,* they removed, and stood afar off. . . .

• • •

And seeing the multitudes, [Jesus] went up into a mountain: and when he was set, his disciples came unto him:

2   And he opened his mouth, and taught them, saying,

3   Blessed *are* the poor in spirit: for theirs is the kingdom of heaven.

4   Blessed *are* they that mourn: for they shall be comforted.

5   Blessed *are* the meek: for they shall inherit the earth.

6   Blessed *are* they which do hunger and thirst after righteousness: for they shall be filled.

7   Blessed *are* the merciful: for they shall obtain mercy.

8   Blessed *are* the pure in heart: for they shall see God.

9   Blessed *are* the peacemakers: for they shall be called the children of God.

10   Blessed *are* they which are persecuted for righteousness' sake: for theirs is the kingdom of heaven.

11   Blessed are ye, when *men* shall revile you, and persecute *you*, and shall say all manner of evil against you falsely, for my sake.

12   Rejoice, and be exceeding glad: for great *is* your reward in heaven: for so persecuted they the prophets which were before you.

13   ye are the salt of the earth: but if the salt have lost his savour, wherewith shall it be salted? it is thenceforth good for nothing, but to be cast out, and to be trodden under foot of men.

14   Ye are the light of the world. A city that is set on an hill cannot be hid.

15   Neither do men light a candle, and put it under a bushel, but on a candlestick; and it giveth light unto all that are in the house.

16   Let your light so shine before men, that they may see your good works, and glorify your Father which is in heaven.

17   Think not that I am come to destroy the law, or the prophets: I am not come to destroy, but to fulfil.

18   For verily I say unto you, Till heaven and earth pass, one jot or one tittle shall in no wise pass from the law, till all be fulfilled.

19   Whosoever therefore shall break one of these least commandments, and shall teach men so, he shall be called the least in the kingdom of heaven: but whosoever shall do and teach *them*, the same shall be called great in the kingdom of heaven.

20   For I say unto you, That except your righteousness shall exceed *the righteousness* of the scribes and Pharisees, ye shall in no case enter into the kingdom of heaven.

21   Ye have heard that it was said by them of old time, Thou shalt not kill; and whosoever shall kill shall be in danger of the judgment:

22   But I say unto you, That whosoever is angry with his brother without a cause shall be in danger of the judgment: and whosoever shall say to his brother, Raca, shall be in danger of the council: but whosoever shall say, Thou fool shall be in danger of hell fire.

23   Therefore if thou bring thy gift to the altar, and there rememberest that thy brother hath ought against thee;

24   Leave there thy gift before the altar, and go thy way; first be reconciled to thy brother, and then come and offer thy gift.

25   Agree with thine adversary quickly, whiles thou art in the way with him; lest at any time the adversary deliver thee to the judge, and the judge deliver thee to the officer, and thou be cast into prison.

26   Verily I say unto thee, Thou shalt by no means come out thence, till thou hast paid the uttermost farthing.

27   Ye have heard that it was said by them of old time, Thou shalt not commit adultery:

28   But I say unto you, That whosoever looketh on a woman to lust after her hath committed adultery with her already in his heart.

29   And if thy right eye offend thee, pluck it out, and cast *it* from thee: for it is profitable for thee that one of thy members should perish, and not *that* thy whole body should be cast into hell.

30   And if thy right hand offend thee, cut it off, and cast *it* from thee: for it is profitable for thee that one of thy members should perish, and not *that* thy whole body should be cast into hell.

31   It hath been said, Whosoever shall put away his wife, let him give her a writing of divorcement:

32   But I say unto you, That whosoever shall put away his wife, saving for the cause of fornication, causeth her to commit adultery: and whosoever shall marry her that is divorced committeth adultery.

33   Again, ye have heard that it hath been said by them of old time, Thou shalt not forswear thyself, but shalt perform unto the Lord thine oaths:

34   But I say unto you, Swear not at all; neither by heaven; for it is God's throne:

35   Nor by the earth; for it is his footstool: neither by Jerusalem; for it is the city of the great King.

36   Neither shalt thou swear by thy head, because thou canst not make one hair white or black.

37   But let your communication be, Yea, yea; Nay, nay: for whatsoever is more than these cometh of evil.

38   Ye have heard that it hath been said, An eye for an eye, and a tooth for a tooth:

39   But I say unto you, That ye resist not evil: but whosoever shall smite thee on thy right cheek, turn to him the other also.

40   And if any man will sue thee at the law, and take away thy coat, let him have *thy* cloak also.

41   And whosoever shall compel thee to go a mile, go with him twain.

42   Give to him that asketh thee, and from him that would borrow of thee turn not thou away.

43   Ye have heard that it hath been said, Thou shalt love thy neighbour, and hate thine enemy.

44   But I say unto you, Love your enemies, bless them that curse you, do good to them that hate you, and pray for them which despitefully use you, and persecute you;

45   That ye may be the children of your Father which is in heaven: for he maketh his sun to rise on the evil and on the good, and sendeth rain on the just and on the unjust.

46   For if ye love them which love you, what reward have ye? do not even the publicans the same?

47   And if ye salute your brethren only, what do ye more *than others*? do not even the publicans so?

48   Be ye therefore perfect, even as your Father which is in heaven is perfect.

•   •   •

Judge not, that ye be not judged.

2   For with what judgment ye judge, ye shall be judged: and with what measure ye mete, it shall be measured to you again.

3   And why beholdest thou the mote that is in thy brother's eye, but considerest not the beam that is in thine own eye?

4   Or how wilt thou say to thy brother, Let me pull out the mote out of thine eye; and, behold, a beam *is* in thine own eye?

5   Thou hypocrite, first cast out the beam out of thine own eye; and then shalt thou see clearly to cast out the mote out of thy brother's eye.

6   Give not that which is holy unto the dogs, neither cast ye your pearls before swine, lest they trample them under their feet, and turn again and rend you.

7   Ask, and it shall be given you; seek, and ye shall find; knock, and it shall be opened unto you:

8   For every one that asketh receiveth; and he that seeketh findeth; and to him that knocketh it shall be opened.

9   Or what man is there of you, whom if his son ask bread, will he give him a stone?

10   Or if he ask a fish, will he give him a serpent?

11   If ye then, being evil, know how to give good gifts unto your children, how much more shall your Father which is in heaven give good things to them that ask him?

12   Therefore all things whatsoever ye would that men should do to you, do ye even so to them: for this is the law and the prophets.

13   Enter ye in at the strait gate: for wide *is* the gate, and broad *is* the way, that leadeth to destruction, and many there be which go in thereat:

14   Because strait *is* the gate, and narrow *is* the way, which leadeth unto life, and few there be that find it.

15   Beware of false prophets, which come to you in sheep's clothing, but inwardly they are ravening wolves.

16   Ye shall know them by their fruits. Do men gather grapes of thorns, or figs of thistles?

17   Even so every good tree bringeth forth good fruit; but a corrupt tree bringeth forth evil fruit.

18   A good tree cannot bring forth evil fruit, neither *can* a corrupt tree bring forth good fruit.

19   Every tree that bringeth not forth good fruit is hewn down, and cast into the fire.

20   Wherefore by their fruits ye shall know them.

21   Not every one that saith unto me, Lord, Lord, shall enter into the kingdom of heaven; but he that doeth the will of my Father which is in heaven.

22   Many will say to me in that day, Lord, Lord, have we not prophesied in thy name? and in they name have cast out devils? and in thy name done many wonderful works?

23   And then will I profess unto them, I never knew you: depart from me, ye that work iniquity.

24   Therefore whosoever heareth these sayings of mine, and doeth them, I will liken him unto a wise man, which built his house upon a rock:

25   And the rain descended, and the floods came, and the winds blew, and beat upon that house; and it fell not: for it was founded upon a rock.

26   And every one that heareth these sayings of mine, and doeth them not, shall be likened unto a foolish man, which built his house upon the sand:

27   And the rain descended, and the floods came, and the winds blew, and beat upon that house; and it fell: and great was the fall of it.

28   And it came to pass, when Jesus had ended these sayings, the people were astonished at his doctrine:

29   For he taught them as *one* having authority, and not as the scribes.

CONFUCIUS

The Analects

CONFUCIUS (551–479 B.C.) was a famous Chinese poet and teacher. Self-educated, he sought to effect social change by holding a political office, but was unable to secure such a position. Instead, he acquired a small group of dedicated students, and spent his life teaching them his philosophical beliefs.

BOOK XVII

6. Tzu-chang asked Master K'ung about Goodness. Master K'ung said, He who could put the Five into practice everywhere under Heaven would be Good. Tzu-chang begged to hear what these were. The Master said, Courtesy, breadth, good faith, diligence and clemency. 'He who is courteous is not scorned, he who is broad wins the multitude, he who is of good faith is trusted by the people, he who is diligent succeeds in all he undertakes, he who is clement can get service from the people.'

8. The Master said, Yu, have you ever been told of the Six Sayings about the Six Degenerations? Tzu-lu replied, No, never. (The Master said) Come, then; I will tell you. Love of Goodness without love of learning degenerates into silliness. Love of wisdom without love of learning degenerates into utter lack of principle. Love of keeping promises without love of learning degenerates into villainy. Love of uprightness without love of learning degenerates into harshness.

BOOK IX

24. The Master said, First and foremost, be faithful to your superiors, keep all promises, refuse the friendship of all who are not like you; and if you have made a mistake, do not be afraid of admitting the fact and amending your ways.

BOOK I

8. The Master said, If a gentleman is frivolous, he will lose the respect of his inferiors and lack firm ground upon which to build up his education. First and foremost he must learn to be faithful to his superiors, to keep promises, to refuse the friendship of all who are not like him. And if he finds he has made a mistake, then he must not be afraid of admitting the fact and amending his ways.

BOOK II

6. Mêng Wu Po asked about the treatment of parents. The Master said, Behave in such a way that your father and mother have no anxiety about you, except concerning your health.

BOOK VI

25. Once when Yen Hui and Tzu-lu were waiting upon him the Master said, Suppose each of you were to tell his wish. Tzu-lu said, I should like to have carriages and horses, clothes and fur rugs, share them with my friends and feel no annoyance if they were returned

to me the worse for wear. Yen Hui said, I should like never to boast of my good qualities nor make a fuss about the trouble I take on behalf of others. Tzu-lu said, A thing I should like is to hear the Master's wish. The Master said, In dealing with the aged, to be of comfort to them; in dealing with friends, to be of good faith with them; in dealing with the young, to cherish them.

THE KORAN

The Unjust

THE KORAN, or Qur'an, is the sacred scripture of Islam. It chronicles the revelations of God to the prophet Mohammed. Originally the Koran was memorized by followers, and segments were used in prayer. It is hailed by Muslims to be the ultimate authority on all ethical and spiritual matters.

In the Name of Allah, the Compassionate, the Merciful

WOE to the unjust who, when others measure for them, exact in full, but when they measure or weigh for others, defraud them!

Do such men think that they will not be raised to life upon a fateful day, the day when all mankind will stand before the Lord of the Creation?

Truly, the record of the sinners is in Sidjeen. Would that you knew what Sidjeen is! It is a sealed book.

Woe on that day to the disbelievers who deny the Last Judgment! None denies it except the transgressors, the evil-doers who, when Our revelations are recited to them, cry: 'Fables of the ancients!'

No! Their own deeds have cast a veil over their hearts.

No! On that day a barrier shall be set between them and their Lord. They shall burn in Hell, and a voice will say to them: 'This is the scourge that you denied!'

But the record of the righteous shall be in Illiyun.

Would that you knew what Illiyun is! It is a sealed book, seen only by those who are closest to Allah.

The righteous shall surely dwell in bliss. Reclining upon soft couches they will gaze around them: and in their faces you shall mark the glow of joy. They shall drink of a pure wine, securely sealed, whose very dregs are musk (for this let all men emulously strive); a wine tempered with the waters of Tasnim, a spring at which the favoured will refresh themselves.

The evil-doers scoff at the faithful and wink at one another as they pass by them. When they meet their own folk they speak of them with jests and when they see them they say: 'These are erring men!' Yet they were not sent to be their guardians.

But on that day the faithful will mock the unbelievers as they recline upon their couches and gaze around them.

Shall not the unbelievers be rewarded according to their deeds?

ARISTOTLE

Happiness and the Good Life

ARISTOTLE's (384–322 B.C.) Nicomachean Ethics *was both a sociological summary of Athenian ethics in the fourth century B.C. and the classic philosophical theory of ethics. In the selection from Book I that follows, he argues his "teleological" view of ethics—that is, the idea that all human behavior is purposive and that the ultimate purpose of all our actions is happiness.*

1. Every art and every kind of inquiry, and likewise every act and purpose, seems to aim at some good; and so it has been well said that the good is that at which everything aims. But a difference is observable among these aims or ends. What is aimed at is sometimes the exercise of a faculty, sometimes a certain result beyond that exercise. And where there is an end beyond that act, there the result is better than the exercise of the faculty. Now since there are many kinds of actions and many arts and sciences, it follows that there are many ends also; *e.g.* health is the end of medicine, ships of shipbuilding, victory of the art of war, and wealth of economy. But when several of these are subordinated to some one art or science,—as the making of bridles and other trappings to the art of horsemanship, and this in turn, along with all else that the soldier does, to the art of war, and so on,—then the end of the master art is always more desired than the end of the subordinate arts, since these are pursued for its sake. And this is equally true whether the end in view be the mere exercise of a faculty or something beyond that, as in the above instances.

2. If then in what we do there be some end which we wish for on its own account, choosing all the others as means to this, but not every end without exception as a means to something else (for so we should go on *ad infinitum,* and desire would be left void and objectless),—this evidently will be the good or the best of all things. And surely from a practical point of view it much concerns us to know this good; for then, like archers shooting at a definite mark, we shall be more likely to attain what we want. . . . Though this good is the same for the individual and the state, yet the good of the state seems a grander and more perfect thing both to attain and to secure; and glad as one would be to do this service for a single

individual, to do it for a people and for a number of states is nobler and more divine.

This then is the aim of the present inquiry, which is a sort of political inquiry.

3.   We must be content if we can attain to so much precision in our statement as the subject before us admits of; for the same degree of accuracy is no more to be expected in all kinds of reasoning than in all kinds of handicraft. Now the things that are noble and just (with which Politics deals) are so various and so uncertain, that some think these are merely conventional and not natural distinctions. There is a similar uncertainty also about what is good, because good things often do people harm: men have before now been ruined by wealth, and have lost their lives through courage. Our subject, then, and our data being of this nature, we must be content if we can indicate the truth roughly and in outline, and if, in dealing with matters that are not amenable to immutable laws, and reasoning from premises that are but probable, we can arrive at probable conclusions. The reader, on his part, should take each of my statements in the same spirit; for it is the mark of an educated man to require, in each kind of inquiry, just so much exactness as the subject admits of: it is equally absurd to accept probable reasoning from a mathematician, and to demand scientific proof from an orator.

But each man can form a judgment about what he knows, and is called "a good judge" of that—of any special matter when he has received a special education therein, "a good judge" (without any qualifying epithet) when he has received a universal education. And hence a young man is not qualified to be a stu-

dent of Politics; for he lacks experience of the affairs of life, which form the data and the subject-matter of Politics. Further, since he is apt to be swayed by his feelings, he will derive no benefit from a study whose aim is not speculative but practical. But in this respect young in character counts the same as young in years; for the young man's disqualification is not a matter of time, but is due to the fact that feeling rules his life and directs all his desires. Men of this character turn the knowledge they get to no account in practice, as we see with those we call incontinent; but those who direct their desires and actions by reason will gain much profit from the knowledge of these matters. . . .

4.   Since . . . all knowledge and all purpose aims at some good, what is this which we say is the aim of Politics; or, in other words, what is the highest of all realizable goods? As to its name, I suppose nearly all men are agreed; for the masses and the men of culture alike declare that it is happiness, and hold that to "live well" or to "do well" is the same as to be "happy." But they differ as to what this happiness is, and the masses do not give the same account of it as the philosophers. The former take it to be something palpable and plain, as pleasure or wealth or fame; one man holds it to be this, and another that, and often the same man is of different minds at different times—after sickness it is health, and in poverty it is wealth; while when they are impressed with the consciousness of their ignorance, they admire most those who say grand things that are above their comprehension. Some philosophers, on the other hand, have thought that, beside these several good things, there is an "absolute" good which is the cause of their goodness. As it would hardly be worth while to

review all the opinions that have been held, we will confine ourselves to those which are most popular, or which seem to have some foundation in reason. . . .

5.   It seems that men not unreasonably take their notions of the good or happiness from the lives actually led, and that the masses who are the least refined suppose it to be pleasure, which is the reason why they aim at nothing higher than the life of enjoyment. For the most conspicuous kinds of life are three: this life of enjoyment, the life of the statesman, and, thirdly, the contemplative life. The mass of men show themselves utterly slavish in their preference for the life of brute beasts, but their views receive consideration because many of those in high places have the tastes of Sardanapalus. Men of refinement with a practical turn prefer honour; for I suppose we may say that honour is the aim of the statesman's life. But this seems too superficial to be the good we are seeking; for it appears to depend upon those who give rather than upon those who receive it; while we have a presentiment that the good is something that is peculiarly a man's own and can scarce be taken away from him. Moreover, these men seem to pursue honour in order that they may be assured of their own excellence,—at least, they wish to be honoured by men of sense, and by those who know them, and on the ground of their virtue or excellence. It is plain, then, that in their view, at any rate, virtue or excellence is better than honour; and perhaps we should take this to be the end of the statesman's life, rather than honour. But virtue or excellence also appears too incomplete to be what we want; for it seems that a man might have virtue and yet be asleep or be inactive all his life, and, moreover, might meet with the greatest disasters and misfortunes; and no one would maintain that such a man is happy, except for argument's sake. But we will not dwell on these matters now, for they are sufficiently discussed in the popular treatises. The third kind of life is the life of contemplation: we will treat of it further on. As for the money-making life, it is something quite contrary to nature; and wealth evidently is not the good of which we are in search, for it is merely useful as a means to something else. So we might rather take pleasure and virtue or excellence to be ends than wealth; for they are chosen on their own account. But it seems that not even they are the end, though much breath has been wasted in attempts to show that they are. . . .

7.   Leaving these matters, then, let us return once more to the question, what this good can be of which we are in search. It seems to be different in different kinds of action and in different arts,—one thing in medicine and another in war, and so on. What then is the good in each of these cases? Surely that for the sake of which all else is done. And that in medicine is health, in war is victory, in building is a house,—a different thing in each different case, but always, in whatever we do and in whatever we choose, the end. For it is always for the sake of the end that all else is done. If then there be one end of all that man does, this end will be the realizable good,—or these ends, if there be more than one.

By this generalization our argument is brought to the same point as before. This point we must try to explain more clearly. We see that there are many ends. But some of these are chosen only as means, as wealth, flutes, and the whole class of instruments. And so it is plain that not all ends are final. But the best of all things must, we conceive, be something final. If then there be only one final end, this will be what we are seeking,—or if there be more than one, then the most final of them. Now that which is pursued as an end in itself is more final than that which is pursued as means to something else, and that which is never chosen as means than that which is chosen both as an end in itself and as means, and that is strictly final which is always chosen as an end in itself and never as means.

Happiness seems more than anything else to answer to this description: for we always choose it for itself, and never for the sake of something else; while honour and pleasure and reason, and all virtue or excellence, we choose partly indeed for themselves (for, apart from any result, we should choose each of them), but partly also for the sake of happiness, supposing that they will help to make us happy. But no one chooses happiness for the sake of these things, or as a means to anything else at all. We seem to be led to the same conclusion when we start from the notion of self-sufficiency. The final good is thought to be self-sufficing [or all-sufficing]. In applying this term we do not regard a man as an individual leading a solitary life, but we also take account of parents, children, wife, and, in short, friends and fellow-citizens generally, since man is naturally a social being. Some limit must indeed be set to this; for if you go on to parents and descendants and friends of friends, you will never come to a stop. But this we will consider further on: for the present we will take self-suffing to mean what by itself makes life desirable and in want of nothing. And happiness is believed to answer to this description. And further, happiness is believed to be the most de-

sirable thing in the world, and that not merely as one among other good things: if it were merely one among other good things [so that other things could be added to it], it is plain that the addition of the least of other goods must make it more desirable; for the addition becomes a surplus of good, and of two goods the greater is always more desirable. Thus it seems that happiness is something final and self-sufficing, and is the end of all that man does.

But perhaps the reader thinks that though no one will dispute the statement that happiness is the best thing in the world, yet a still more precise definition of it is needed. This will best be gained, I think, by asking, What is the function of man? For as the goodness and the excellence of a piper or a sculptor, or the practiser of any art, and generally of those who have any function or business to do, lies in that function, so man's good would seem to lie in his function, if he has one. But can we suppose that, while a carpenter and a cobbler has a function and a business of his own, man has no business and no function assigned him by nature? Nay, surely as his several members, eye and hand and foot, plainly have each his own function, so we must suppose that man also has some function over and above all these.

What then is it? Life evidently he has in common even with the plants, but we want that which is peculiar to him. We must exclude, therefore, the life of mere nutrition and growth. Next to this comes the life of sense; but this too he plainly shares with horses and cattle and all kinds of animals. There remains then the life whereby he acts—the life of his rational nature, with its two sides or divisions, one rational as obeying reason, the other rational as having and exercising reason. But as this expression is ambiguous, we must be understood to mean thereby the life that consists in the exercise [not the mere possession] of the faculties; for this seems to be more properly entitled to the name.

The function of man, then, is exercise of his vital faculties [or soul] on one side in obedience to reason, and on the other side with reason. But what is called the function of a man of any profession and the function of a man who is good in that profession are, generically the same, *e.g.* of a harper and of a good harper; and this holds in all cases without exception, only that in the case of the latter his superior excellence at his work is added; for we say a harper's function is to harp, and a good harper's to harp well. Man's function then being, as we say, a kind of life—that is to say, exercise of his faculties and action of various kinds with reason—the good man's function is to do this well and beautifully [or nobly]. But the function of anything is done well when it is done in accordance with the proper excellence of that thing. If this be so the result is that the good of man is exercise of his faculties in accordance with excellence or virtue, or, if there be more than one, in accordance with the best and most complete virtue. But there must also be a full term of years for this exercise; for one swallow or one fine day does not make a spring, nor does one day or any small space of time make a blessed or happy man.

This, then, may be taken as a rough outline of the good; for this, I think, is the proper method,—first to sketch the outline, and then to fill in the details. But it would seem that, the outline once fairly drawn, any one can carry on the work and fit in the several items which time reveals to us or helps us to find. And this indeed is the way in which the arts and sciences have grown; for it requires no extraordinary genius to fill up the gaps. We must bear in mind, however, what was said above, and not demand the same degree of accuracy in all branches of study, but in each case so much as the subject-matter admits of and as is proper to that kind of inquiry. The carpenter and the geometer both look for the right angle, but in different ways: the former only wants such an approximation to it as his work requires, but the latter wants to know what constitutes a right angle, or what is its special quality; his aim is to find out the truth. And so in other cases we must follow the same course, lest we spend more time on what is immaterial then on the real business in hand. . . .

8.   . . . Now, good things have been divided into three classes, external goods on the one hand, and on the other goods of the soul and goods of the body; and the goods of the soul are commonly said to be goods in the fullest sense, and more good than any other. But "actions and exercises of the vital faculties may be said to be of the soul." So our account is confirmed by this opinion, which is both of long standing and approved by all who busy themselves with philosophy. But, indeed, we secure the support of this opinion by the mere statement that certain actions and exercises are the end; for this implies that it is to be ranked among the goods of the soul, and not among external goods. Our account, again, is in harmony with the common saying that the happy man lives well and does well; for we may say that happiness, according to us, is living well and doing well. And, indeed, all the characteristics that men expect to find

in happiness seem to belong to happiness as we define it. Some hold it to be virtue or excellence, some prudence, others a kind of wisdom; others, again, held it to be all or some of these, with the addition of pleasure, either as an ingredient or as a necessary accompaniment; and some even include external prosperity in their account of it. Now, some of these views have the support of many voices and of old authority; others have few voices, but those of weight; but it is probable that neither the one side nor the other is entirely wrong, but that in some one point at least, if not in most, they are both right.

First, then, the view that happiness is excellence or a kind of excellence harmonizes with our account; for "exercise of faculties in accordance with excellence" belongs to excellence. But I think we may say that it makes no small difference whether the good be conceived as the mere possession of something, or as its use—as a mere habit or trained faculty, or as the exercise of that faculty. For the habit or faculty may be present, and yet issue in no good result, as when a man is asleep, or in any other way hindered from his function; but with its exercise this is not possible for it must show itself in acts and in good acts. And as at the Olympic games it is not the fairest and strongest who receive the crown, but those who contend (for among these are the victors), so in life, too, the winners are those who not only have all the excellences, but manifest these in deed.

And, further, the life of these men is in itself pleasant. For pleasure is an affection of the soul, and each man takes pleasure in that which he is said to love,—he who loves horses in horses, he who loves sight-seeing in sight-seeing, and in the same way he who

loves justice in acts of justice, and generally the lover of excellence or virtue in virtuous acts or the manifestation of excellence. And while with most men there is a perpetual conflict between the several things in which they find pleasure, since these are not naturally pleasant, those who love what is noble take pleasure in that which is naturally pleasant. For the manifestations of excellence are naturally pleasant, so that they are both pleasant to them and pleasant in themselves. Their life, then, does not need pleasure to be added to it as an appendage, but contains pleasure in itself.

Indeed, in addition to what we have said, a man is not good at all unless he takes pleasure in noble deeds. No one would call a man just who did not take pleasure in doing justice, nor generous who took no pleasure in acts of generosity, and so on. If this be so, the manifestations of excellence will be pleasant in themselves. But they are also both good and noble, and that in the highest degree—at least, if the good man's judgment about them is right, for this is his judgment. Happiness, then, is at once the best and noblest and pleasantest thing in the world, and these are not separated.

For all these characteristics are united in the best exercises of our faculties; and these, or some one of them that is better than all the others, we identify with happiness.

But nevertheless happiness plainly requires external goods too, as we said; for it is impossible, or at least not easy, to act nobly without some furniture of fortune. There are many things that can only be done through instruments, so to speak, such as friends and wealth and political influence: and there are some things whose absence takes the bloom off our happiness, as good birth, the blessing of children, personal beauty; for a man is not very likely to be happy if he is very ugly in person, or of low birth, or alone in the world, or childless, and perhaps still less if he has worthless children or friends, or has lost good ones that he had. As we said, then, happiness seems to stand in need of this kind of prosperity; and so some identify it with good fortune, just as others identify it with excellence.

9. This has led people to ask whether happiness is attained by learning, or the formation of habits, or any other kind of training, or comes by some divine dispensation or even by chance. Well, if the Gods do give gifts to men, happiness is likely to be among the number, more likely, indeed, than anything else, in proportion as it is better than all other human things. This belongs more properly to another branch of inquiry; but we may say that even if it is not heaven-sent, but comes as a consequence of virtue or some kind of learning or training, still it seems to be one of the most divine things in the world; for the prize and aim of virtue would appear to be better than anything else and something divine and blessed. Again, if it is thus acquired it will be widely accessible; for it will then be in the power of all except those who have lost the capacity for excellence to acquire it by study and diligence. And if it be better that men should attain happiness in this way rather than by chance, it is reasonable to suppose that it is so, since in the sphere of nature all things are arranged in the best possible way,

and likewise in the sphere of art, and of each mode of causation, and most of all in the sphere of the noblest mode of causation. And indeed it would be too absurd to leave what is noblest and fairest to the dispensation of chance.

But our definition itself clears up the difficulty; for happiness was defined as a certain kind of exercise of the vital faculties in accordance with excellence or virtue. And of the remaining goods [other than happiness itself], some must be present as necessary conditions, while others are useful instruments to happiness. And this agrees with what we said at starting. We then laid down that the end of the art political is the best of all ends; but the chief business of that art is to make the citizens of a certain character—that is, good and apt to do what is noble. It is not without reason, then, that we do not call an ox, or a horse, or any brute happy; for none of them is able to share in this kind of activity. For the same reason also a child is not happy; he is as yet, because of his age, unable to do such things. If we ever call a child happy, it is because we hope he will do them. For, as we said, happiness requires not only perfect excellence or virtue, but also a full term of years for its exercise. For our circumstances are liable to many changes and to all sorts of chances, and it is possible that he who is now most prosperous will in his old age meet with great disasters, as is told of Priam in the tales of Troy; and a man who is thus used by fortune and comes to a miserable end cannot be called happy.

IMMANUEL KANT

Foundations of the Metaphysics of Morals

IMMANUEL KANT (1724–1804), the great German philosopher, wrote his short Foundations of the Metaphysics of Morals *as an anticipation of the more elaborate arguments in his* Critique of Practical Reason *(1788). In both books, he defends morality and moral principles as the product of practical reason, not feelings or "inclinations." Kant describes morality as concerning "a good will" rather than the consequences of an action or any other matters of good fortune which are not matters of intention. The principle of practical reason is called "the categorical imperative."*

NOTHING can possibly be conceived in the world, or even out of it, which can be called good without qualification, except a *good will*. Intelligence, wit, judgment, and other *talents* of the mind, however they may be named, or courage, resolution, perseverance, as qualities of tem perament, are undoubtedly good and desirable in many respects; but these gifts of nature may also become extremely bad and mischievous if the will which is to make use of them, and which, therefore, constitutes what is called *character,* is not good. It is the same with the *gifts of fortune*. Power, riches, honor, even health, and the general well-being and contentment with one's condition which is called *happiness,* inspire pride, and often presumption, if there is not a good will to correct the influence of these on the mind, and with this also to rectify the whole principle of acting, and adapt it to its end. The sight of a being who is not adorned with a single feature of a pure and good will, enjoying unbroken prosperity, can never give pleasure to an impartial rational spectator. Thus a good will

appears to constitute the indispensable condition even of being worthy of happiness.

There are even some qualities which are of service to this good will itself, and may facilitate its action, yet which have no intrinsic unconditional value, but always presuppose a good will, and this qualifies the esteem that we justly have for them, and does not permit us to regard them as absolutely good. Moderation in the affections and passions, self-control, and calm deliberation are not only good in many respects, but even seem to constitute part of the intrinsic worth of the person; but they are far from deserving to be called good without qualification, although they have been so unconditionally praised by the ancients. For without the principles of a good will, they may become extremely bad; and the coolness of a villain not only makes him far more dangerous, but also directly makes him more abominable in our eyes than he would have been without it.

A good will is good not because of what it performs or effects, not by its aptness for the attainment of some proposed end, but simply by virtue of the volition—that is, it is good in itself, and considered by itself is to be esteemed much higher than all that can be brought about by it in favor of any inclination, nay, even of the sum-total of all inclinations. Even if it should happen that, owing to special disfavor of fortune, or the niggardly provision of a stepmotherly nature, this will should wholly lack power to accomplish its purpose, if with its greatest efforts it should yet achieve nothing, and there should remain only the good will (not, to be sure, a mere wish, but the summoning of all means in our power), then, like a jewel, it would still shine by its own light, as a thing which has its whole value in itself. Its usefulness or fruitlessness can neither add to nor take away anything from this value. It would be, as it were, only the setting to enable us to handle it the more conveniently in common commerce, or to attract to it the attention of those who are not yet connoisseurs, but not to recommend it to true connoisseurs, or to determine its value. . . .

Everything in nature works according to laws. Rational beings alone have the faculty of acting according *to the conception* of laws, that is according to principles, *i.e.* have a *will.* Since the deduction of actions from principles requires *reason,* the will is nothing but practical reason. If reason infallibly determines the will, then the actions of such a being which are recognized as objectively necessary are subjectively necessary also, *i.e.* the will is a faculty to choose *that only* which reason independent of inclination recognizes as practically necessary, *i.e.* as good. But if reason of itself does not sufficiently determine the will, if the latter is subject also to subjective conditions (particular impulses) which do not always coincide

with the objective conditions; in a word, if the will does not *in itself* completely accord with reason (which is actually the case with men), then the actions which objectively are recognized as necessary are subjectively contingent, and the determination of such a will according to objective laws is *obligation,* that is to say, the relation of the objective laws to a will that is not thoroughly good is conceived as the determination of the will of a rational being by principles of reason, but which the will from its nature does not of necessity follow.

The conception of an objective principle, in so far as it is obligatory for a will, is called a command (of reason), and the formula of the command is called an Imperative. . . .

Now all *imperatives* command either *hypothetically* or *categorically.* The former represent the practical necessity of a possible action as means to something else that is willed (or at least which one might possibly will). The categorical imperative would be that which represented an action as necessary of itself without reference to another end, *i.e.* as objectively necessary.

Since every practical law represents a possible action as good, and on this account, for a subject who is practically determinable by reason, necessary, all imperatives are formulae determining an action which is necessary according to the principle of a will good in some respects. If now the action is good only as a means *to something else,* then the imperative is *hypothetical;* if it is conceived as good *in itself* and consequently as being necessarily the principle of a will which of itself conforms to reason, then it is *categorical.* . . .

When I conceive a hypothetical imperative, in general I do not know beforehand what it will contain until I am given the condition. But when I conceive a categorical imperative, I know at once what it contains. For as the imperative contains besides the law only the necessity that the maxims shall conform to this law, while the law contains no conditions restricting it, there remains nothing but the general statement that the maxim of the action should conform to a universal law, and it is this conformity alone that the imperative properly represents as necessary.

There is . . . but one categorical imperative, namely, this: *Act only on that maxim whereby thou canst at the same time will that it should become a universal law.*

Now if all imperatives of duty can be deduced from this one imperative as from their principle, then, although it should remain undecided whether what is called duty is not merely a vain notion, yet at least we shall be able to show what we understand by it and what this notion means.

Since the universality of the law according to which effects are produced constitutes what is properly called *nature* in the most general sense (as to form), that is the existence of things so far as it is determined by general laws, the imperative of duty may be expressed thus: *Act as if the maxim of thy action were to become by thy will a universal law of nature.*

We will now enumerate a few duties, adopting the usual division of them into duties to ourselves and to others, and into perfect and imperfect duties.

1. A man reduced to despair by a series of misfortunes feels wearied of life, but is still so far in possession of his reason that he can ask himself whether it would not be contrary to his duty to himself to take his own life. Now he inquires whether the maxim of his action could become a universal law of nature. His maxim is: From self-love I adopt it as a principle to shorten my life when its longer duration is likely to bring more evil than satisfaction. It is asked then simply whether this principle founded on self-love can become a universal law of nature. Now we see at once that a system of nature of which it should be a law to destroy life by means of the very feeling whose special nature it is to impel to the improvement of life would contradict itself, and therefore could not exist as a system of nature; hence that maxim cannot possibly exist as a universal law of nature, and consequently would be wholly inconsistent with the supreme principle of all duty.

2. Another finds himself forced by necessity to borrow money. He knows that he will not be able to repay it, but sees also that nothing will be lent to him, unless he promises stoutly to repay it in a definite time. He desires to make this promise, but he has still so much conscience as to ask himself: Is it not unlawful and inconsistent with duty to get out of a difficulty in this way? Suppose, however, that he resolves to do so, then the maxim of his action would be expressed thus: When I think myself in want of money, I will borrow money and promise to repay it, although I know that I never can do so. Now this principle of self-love or of one's own advantage may perhaps be consistent with my whole future welfare; but the question now is, Is it right? I change then the suggestion of self-love into a universal law, and state the question thus: How would it be if my maxim were a universal law? Then I see at once that it could never hold as a universal law of nature, but would necessarily contradict itself. For supposing it to be a universal law that everyone when he thinks himself in a difficulty should be able to promise whatever he pleases, with the purpose of not keeping his promise, the promise itself would become impossible, as

well as the end that one might have in view in it, since no one would consider that anything was promised to him, but would ridicule all such statements as vain pretences.

3. A third finds in himself a talent which with the help of some culture might make him a useful man in many respects. But he finds himself in comfortable circumstances, and prefers to indulge in pleasure rather than to take pains in enlarging and improving his happy natural capacities. He asks, however, whether his maxim of neglect of his natural gifts, besides agreeing with his inclination to indulgence, agrees also with what is called duty. He sees then that a system of nature could indeed subsist with such a universal law although men (like the South Sea islanders) should let their talents rest, and resolve to devote their lives merely to idleness, amusement, and propagation of their species—in a word, to enjoyment; but he cannot possibly *will* that this should be a universal law of nature, or be implanted in us as such by a natural instinct. For, as a rational being, he necessarily wills that his faculties be developed, since they serve him, and have been given him, for all sorts of possible purposes.

4. A fourth, who is in prosperity, while he sees that others have to contend with great wretchedness and that he could help them, thinks: What concern is it of mine? Let everyone be as happy as Heaven pleases, or as he can make himself; I will take nothing from him nor even envy him, only I do not wish to contribute anything to his welfare or to his assistance in distress! Now no doubt if such a mode of thinking were a universal law, the human race might very well subsist, and doubtless even better than in a state in which everyone talks of sympathy and good-will, or even takes care occasionally to put it into practice, but, on the other side, also cheats when he can, betrays the rights of men, or otherwise violates them. But

although it is possible that a universal law of nature might exist in accordance with that maxim, it is impossible to *will* that such a principle should have the universal validity of a law of nature. For a will which resolved this would contradict itself, inasmuch as many cases might occur in which one would have need of the love and sympathy of others, and in which, by such a law of nature, sprung from his own will, he would deprive himself of all hope of the aid he desires. . . .

We have thus established at least this much, that if duty is a conception which is to have any import and real legislative authority for our actions, it can only be expressed in categorical, and not at all in hypothetical imperatives. We have also, which is of great importance, exhibited clearly and definitely for every practical application the content of the categorical imperative, which must contain the principle of all duty if there is such a thing at all. We have not yet, however, advanced so far as to prove à *priori* that there actually is such an imperative, that there is a practical law which commands absolutely of itself, and without any other impulse, and that the following of this law is duty. . . .

Now I say: man and generally any rational being *exists* as an end in himself, *not merely as a means* to be arbitrarily used by this or that will, but in all his actions, whether they concern himself or other rational beings, must be always regarded at the same time as an end. All objects of the inclinations have only a conditional worth; for if the inclinations and the wants founded on them did not exist, then their object would be without value. But the inclinations themselves being sources of want are so far from having an absolute worth for which they should be desired, that, on the contrary, it must be the universal wish of every rational being to be wholly free from them. Thus the worth of any object which is *to be acquired* by our action is always conditional. Beings whose existence depends not on our will but on nature's, have nevertheless, if they are rational beings, only a relative value as means, and are therefore called *things;* rational beings, on the contrary, are called *persons,* because their very nature points them out as ends in themselves, that is as something which must not be used merely as means, and so far therefore restricts freedom of action (and is an object of respect). These, therefore, are not merely subjective ends whose existence has a worth *for us* as an effort of our action, but *objective ends,* that is things whose existence is an end in itself: an end moreover for which no other can be substituted, which they should subserve *merely* as means, for otherwise nothing whatever would possess *absolute worth;* but if all worth were conditioned and therefore contingent, then there would be no supreme practical principle of reason whatever.

If then there is a supreme practical principle or, in respect of the human will, a categorical imperative, it must be one which, being drawn from the conception of that which is necessarily an end for everyone because it is *an end in itself,* constitutes an *objective* principle of will, and can therefore serve as a universal practical law. The foundation of this principle is: *rational nature exists as an end in itself.* Man necessarily conceives his own existence as being so: so far then this is a *subjective* principle of human actions. But every other rational being regards its existence similarly, just on the same rational principle, that holds for me: so that it is at the same time an objective principle, from which as a supreme practical law all laws of the will must be capable of being deduced. Accordingly the practical imperative will be as follows: *So act as to treat humanity, whether in thine own person or in that of any other, in every case as an end withal, never as means only. . . .*

The conception of every rational being as one which must consider itself as giving all the maxims of its will universal laws, so as to judge itself and its actions from this point of view—this conception leads to another which depends on it and is very fruitful, namely, that of a *kingdom of ends.*

By a *kingdom* I understand the union of different rational beings in a system by common laws. Now since it is by laws that ends are determined as regards their universal validity, hence, if we abstract from the personal differences of rational beings, and likewise from all the content of their private ends, we shall be able to conceive all ends combined in a systematic whole (including both rational beings as ends in themselves, and also the special ends which each may propose to himself), that is to say, we can conceive a kingdom of ends, which on the preceding principles is possible.

JOHN STUART MILL

Utilitarianism

JOHN STUART MILL (1806–1873) was the most famous "utilitarian"—a movement started by Jeremy Bentham in the late eighteenth century. Here Mill defines utilitarianism as the ethics that prescribe doing "the greatest good for the greatest number," and he argues that all of our ethical thinking presupposes this principle.

THE creed which accepts [utility] as the foundation of morals, or the Greatest Happiness Principle, holds that actions are right in proportion as they tend to promote happiness, wrong as they tend to produce the reverse of happiness. By happiness is intended pleasure, and the absence of pain; by unhappiness, pain, and the privation of pleasure. To give a clear view of the moral standard set up by the theory, much more requires to be said; in particular, what things it includes in the ideas of pain and pleasure; and to what extent this is left an open question. But these supplementary explanations do not affect the theory of life on which this theory of morality is grounded—namely, that pleasure, and freedom from pain, are the only things desirable as ends; and that all desirable things (which are as numerous in the utilitarian as in any other scheme) are desirable either for the pleasure inherent in themselves, or as means to the promotion of pleasure and the prevention of pain.

Now, such a theory of life excites in many minds, and among them in some of the most estimable in feeling and purpose, inveterate dislike. To suppose that life has (as they express it) no higher end than pleasure—no better and nobler object of desire and pursuit—they designate as utterly mean and grovelling; as a doctrine worthy only of swine, to whom the followers of Epicurus were, at a very early period, contemptuously likened; and modern holders of the doctrine are occasionally made the subject of equally polite comparisons by its German, French, and English assailants.

When thus attacked, the Epicureans have always answered, that it is not they, but their accusers, who represent human nature in a degrading light; since the accusation supposes human beings to be capable of no pleasures except those of which swine are capable. If this supposition were true, the charge could not be gainsaid, but would then be no longer an imputation; for if the sources of pleasure were precisely the same to human beings and to swine, the rule of life which is good enough for the one would be good enough for the other. The comparison of the Epicurean life to that of beasts is felt as degrading, precisely because a beast's pleasures do not satisfy a human being's conceptions of happiness. Human beings have faculties more elevated than the animal appetites, and when once made conscious of them, do not regard anything as happiness which does not include their gratification. I do not, indeed, consider the Epicureans to have been by any means faultless in drawing out their scheme of consequences from the utilitarian principle. To do this in any sufficient manner, many Stoic, as well as Christian elements require to be included. But there is no known Epicurean theory of life which does not assign to the pleasures of the intellect, of the feelings and imagination, and of the moral sentiments, a much higher value as pleasures than to those of mere sensation. It must be admitted, however, that utilitarian writers in general have placed the superiority of mental over bodily pleasures chiefly in the greater permanency, safety, uncostliness, etc., of the former—that is, in their circumstantial advantages rather than in their intrinsic nature. And on all these points utilitarians have fully proved their case; but they might have taken the other, and, as it may be called, higher ground, with entire consistency. It is quite compatible with the principle of utility to recognize the fact, that some *kinds* of pleasure are more desirable and more valuable than others. It would be absurd that while, in estimating all other things, quality is considered as well as quantity, the estimation of pleasures should be supposed to depend on quantity alone.

If I am asked, what I mean by difference of quality in pleasures, or what makes one pleasure more valuable than another, merely as a pleasure, except its being greater in amount, there is but one possible answer. Of two pleasures, if there be one to which all or almost all who have experience of both give a decided preference, irrespective of any feeling of moral obligation to prefer it, that is the more desirable pleasure. If one of the two is, by those who are competently acquainted with both, placed so far above the other that they prefer it, even though knowing it to be attended with a greater amount of discontent, and would not resign it for any

quantity of the other pleasure which their nature is capable of, we are justified in ascribing to the preferred enjoyment a superiority in quality, so far outweighing quantity as to render it, in comparison, of small account.

Now it is an unquestionable fact that those who are equally acquainted with, and equally capable of appreciating and enjoying, both, do give a most marked preference to the manner of existence which employs their higher faculties. Few human creatures would consent to be changed into any of the lower animals, for a promise of the fullest allowance of a beast's pleasures; no intelligent human being would consent to be a fool, no instructed person would be an ignoramus, no person of feeling and conscience would be selfish and base, even though they should be persuaded that the fool, the dunce, or the rascal is better satisfied with his lot than they are with theirs. They would not resign what they possess more than he for the most complete satisfaction of all the desires which they have in common with him. If they ever fancy they would, it is only in cases of unhappiness so extreme, that to escape from it they would exchange their lot for almost any other, however undesirable in their own eyes. A being of higher faculties requires more to make him happy, is capable probably of more acute suffering, and certainly accessible to it at more points, than one of an inferior type; but in spite of these liabilities, he can never really wish to sink into what he feels to be a lower grade of existence. We may give what explanation we please of this unwillingness; we may attribute it to pride, a name which is given indiscriminately to some of the most and to some of the least estimable feelings of which mankind are capable: we may refer it to

the love of liberty and personal independence, an appeal to which was with
the Stoics one of the most effective
means for the inculcation of it; to the
love of power, or to the love of excitement, both of which do really enter into
and contribute to it: but its most appropriate appellation is a sense of dignity,
which all human beings possess in one
form or other, and in some, though by
no means in exact, proportion to their
higher faculties, and which is so essential a part of the happiness of those in
whom it is strong, that nothing which
conflicts with it could be, otherwise
than momentarily, an object of desire to
them. Whoever supposes that this preference takes place at a sacrifice of happiness—that the superior being, in
anything like equal circumstances, is
not happier than the inferior—confounds the two very different ideas, of
happiness, and content. It is indisputable that the being whose capacities
of enjoyment are low, has the greatest
chance of having them fully satisfied;
and a highly endowed being will always
feel that any happiness which he can
look for, as the world is constituted, is
imperfect. But he can learn to bear its
imperfections, if they are at all bearable;
and they will not make him envy the
being who is indeed unconscious of the
imperfections, but only because he feels
not at all the good which those imperfections qualify. It is better to be a
human being dissatisfied than a pig satisfied; better to be Socrates dissatisfied
than a fool satisfied. And if the fool, or
the pig, are of a different opinion, it is
because they only know their own side
of the question. The other party to the
comparison knows both sides.

It may be objected, that many who
are capable of the higher pleasures, occasionally, under the influence of temp-

tation, postpone them to the lower. But
this is quite compatible with a full appreciation of the intrinsic superiority of
the higher. Men often, from infirmity of
character, make their election for the
nearer good, though they know it to be
the less valuable; and this no less when
the choice is between two bodily pleasures, than when it is between bodily
and mental. They pursue sensual indul-
gences to the injury of health, though
perfectly aware that health is the greater
good. It may be further objected, that
many who begin with youthful enthusiasm for everything noble, as they advance in years sink into indolence and
selfishness. But I do not believe that
those who undergo this very common
change, voluntarily choose the lower
description of pleasures in preference to
the higher. I believe that before they devote themselves exclusively to the one,
they have already become incapable of
the other. Capacity for the nobler feelings is in most natures a very tender
plant, easily killed, not only by hostile
influences, but by mere want of substance; and in the majority of young
persons it speedily dies away if the occupations to which their position in life
has devoted them, and the society into
which it has thrown them, are not
favourable to keeping that higher capacity in exercise. Men lose their high aspirations as they lose their intellectual
tastes, because they have not time or
opportunity for indulging them; and
they addict themselves to inferior pleasures, not because they deliberately prefer them, but because they are either the
only ones to which they have access, or
the only ones which they are any longer
capable of enjoying. It may be questioned whether any one who has remained equally susceptible to both
classes of pleasures, ever knowingly

and calmly preferred the lower; though many, in all ages, have broken down in an ineffectual attempt to combine both.

From this verdict of the only competent judges, I apprehend there can be no appeal. On a question which is the best worth having of two pleasures, or which of two modes of existence is the most grateful to the feelings, apart from its moral attributes and from its consequences, the judgment of those who are qualified by knowledge of both, or, if they differ, that of the majority among them, must be admitted as final. And there needs be the less hesitation to accept this judgment respecting the quality of pleasures, since there is no other tribunal to be referred to even on the question of quantity. What means are there of determining which is the acutest of two pains, or the intensest of two pleasurable sensations, except the general suffrage of those who are familiar with both? Neither pains nor pleasures are homogeneous, and pain is always heterogeneous with pleasure. What is there to decide whether a particular pleasure is worth purchasing at the cost of a particular pain, except the feelings and judgment of the experienced? When, therefore, those feelings and judgment declare the pleasures derived from the higher faculties to be preferable *in kind,* apart from the question of intensity, to those of which the animal nature, disjoined from the higher faculties, is susceptible, they are entitled on this subject to the same regard.

I have dwelt on this point, as being a necessary part of a perfectly just conception of Utility or Happiness, considered as the directive rule of human conduct. But it is by no means an indispensable condition to the acceptance of the utilitarian standard; for that standard is not the agent's own greatest happi-ness, but the greatest amount of happiness altogether; and if it may possibly be doubted whether a noble character is always the happier for its nobleness, there can be no doubt that it makes other people happier, and that the world in general is immensely a gainer by it. Utilitarianism, therefore, could only attain its end by the general cultivation of nobleness of character, even if each individual were only benefited by the nobleness of others, and his own, so far as happiness is concerned, were a sheer deduction from the benefit. But the bare enunciation of such an absurdity as this last, renders refutation superfluous.

According to the Greatest Happiness Principle, as above explained, the ultimate end, with reference to and for the sake of which all other things are desirable (whether we are considering our own good or that of other people), is an existence exempt as far as possible from pain, and as rich as possible in enjoyments, both in point of quantity and quality; the test of quality, and the rule for measuring it against quantity, being the preference felt by those who in their opportunities of experience, to which must be added their habits of self-consciousness and self-observation, are best furnished with the means of comparison. This, being, according to the utilitarian opinion, the end of human action, is necessarily also the standard of morality; which may accordingly be defined, the rules and precepts for human conduct, by the observance of which an existence such as has been described might be, to the greatest extent possible, secured to all mankind; and not to them only, but, so far as the nature of things admits, to the whole sentient creation. . . .

. . . I must again repeat, what the assailants of utilitarianism seldom have the justice to acknowledge, that the happiness which forms the utilitarian standard of what is right in conduct, is not the agent's own happiness, but that of all concerned. As between his own happiness and that of others, utilitarianism requires him to be as strictly impartial as a disinterested and benevolent spectator. In the golden rule of Jesus of Nazareth, we read the complete spirit of the ethics of utility. To do as you would be done by, and to love your neighbour as yourself, constitute the ideal perfection of utilitarian morality.

FRIEDRICH NIETZSCHE

The Natural History of Morals

FRIEDRICH NIETZSCHE *(1844–1900) was a German philosopher who spent most of his life traveling in Northern Italy and Switzerland, toward the end of the nineteenth century. He was a harsh critic of Christianity and Judeo-Christian morality and argued that, contrary to their own protestations of piety, both religion and morality are in fact products of the resentment of the weak and a rejection of the ancient virtue of nobility. The following excerpt is from his book,* Beyond Good and Evil.

THE moral sentiment in Europe at present is perhaps as subtle, belated, diverse, sensitive, and refined, as the "Science of Morals" belonging thereto is recent, initial, awkward, and coarse-fingered:—an interesting contrast, which sometimes becomes incarnate and obvious in the very person of a moralist. . . . One ought to avow with the utmost fairness *what* is still necessary here . . . as preparation for a *theory of types* of morality. To be sure, people have not hitherto been so modest. All the philosophers, with a pedantic and ridiculous seriousness, demanded of themselves something very much higher, more pretentious, and ceremonious, when they concerned themselves with morality as a science: they wanted to *give a basis* to morality—and every philosopher hitherto has believed that he has given it a basis; morality itself, however, has been regarded as something "given." How far from their awkward pride was the seemingly insignificant problem—left in dust and decay—of a description of forms of morality. . . . They did not even come in sight of the real problems of morals— problems which only disclose themselves by a comparison of *many* kinds of morality. . . .

Apart from the value of such assertions as "there is a categorical imperative in us," one can always ask: What does such an assertion indicate about him who makes it? There are systems of morals which are meant to justify their author in the eyes of other people; other systems of morals are meant to tranquillise him, and make him self-satisfied; with other systems he wants to crucify and humble himself; with others he wishes to take revenge; with others to conceal himself; with others to glorify himself and gain superiority and distinction;—this system of morals helps its author to forget, that system makes him, or something of him, forgotten; many a moralist would like to exercise power and creative arbitrariness over mankind; many another, perhaps, Kant especially, gives us to understand by his morals that "what is estimable in me, is that I know how to obey—and with you it *shall* not be otherwise than with me!" In short, systems of morals are only a *sign-language of the emotions.*

. . . Every system of morals is a sort of tyranny against "nature" and also against "reason"; that is, however, no objection, unless one should again decree by some system of morals, that all kinds of tyranny and unreasonableness are unlawful. What is essential and invaluable in every system of morals, is that it is a long constraint. . . . The essential thing "in heaven and in earth" is that there should be long *obedience* in the same direction; there thereby results, and has always resulted in the long run, something which has made life worth living; for instance, virtue, art, music, dancing, reason, spirituality—anything whatever that is transfiguring, refined, foolish, or divine. The long bondage of the spirit, the distrustful constraint in the communicability of ideas, the discipline which the thinker imposed on himself to think in accordance with the rules of a church or a court, or conformable to Aristotelian premises, the persistent spiritual will to interpret everything that happened according to a Christian scheme, and in every occurrence to rediscover and justify the Christian God:—all this violence, arbitrariness, severity, dreadful-

ness, and unreasonableness, has proved itself the disciplinary means whereby the European spirit has attained its strength, its remorseless curiosity and subtle mobility; granted also that much irrecoverable strength and spirit had to be stifled, suffocated, and spoiled in the process (for here, as everywhere, "nature" shows herself as she is, in all her extravagant and *indifferent* magnificence, which is shocking, but nevertheless noble). . . . this tyranny, this arbitrariness, this severe and magnificent stupidity, has *educated* the spirit. . . .

In a tour through the many finer and coarser moralities which have hitherto prevailed or still prevail on the earth, I found certain traits recurring regularly together, and connected with one another, until finally two primary types revealed themselves to me, and a radical distinction was brought to light. There is *master-morality* and *slave-morality;*—I would at once add, however, that in all higher and mixed civilizations, there are also attempts at the reconciliation of the two moralities; but one finds still oftener the confusion and mutual misunderstanding of them, indeed, sometimes their close juxtaposition—even in the same man, within one soul. The distinctions of moral values have either originated in a ruling caste, pleasantly conscious of being different from the ruled—or among the ruled class, the slaves and dependents of all sorts. In the first case, when it is the rulers who determine the conception "good," it is the exalted, proud disposition which is regarded as the distinguishing feature, and that which determines the order of rank. The noble type of man separates from himself the beings in whom the opposite of this exalted, proud disposition displays itself: he despises them. Let it at once be noted that in this first kind of morality the antithesis "good" and "bad" means practically the same as "noble" and "despicable";—the antithesis "good" and "*evil*" is of a different origin. The cowardly, the timid, the insignificant, and those thinking merely of narrow utility are despised; moreover, also, the distrustful, with their constrained glances, the self-abasing, the dog-like kind of men who let themselves be abused, the mendicant flatterers, and above all the liars:—it is a fundamental belief of all aristocrats that the common people are untruthful. "We truthful ones"—the nobility in ancient Greece called themselves.

It is obvious that everywhere the designations of moral value were at first applied to *men,* and were only derivatively and at a later period applied to *actions;* it is a gross mistake, therefore, when historians of morals start questions like, "Why have sympathetic actions been praised?" The noble type of man regards *himself* as a determiner of values; he does not require to be approved of; he passes the judgment: "What is injurious to me is injurious in itself"; he knows that it is he himself only who confers honour on things; he is a *creator of values.* He honours whatever he recognizes in himself: such morality is self-glorification. In the foreground there is the feeling of plenitude, of power, which seeks to overflow, the happiness of high tension, the consciousness of a wealth which would fain give and bestow:—the noble man also helps the unfortunate, but not—or scarcely—out of pity, but rather from an impulse generated by the superabundance of power. The noble man honours in himself the powerful one, him also who has power over himself, who knows how to speak and how to keep silence, who takes pleasure in subjecting himself to severity and hardness, and has reverence for all that is severe and hard. "Wotan placed a hard heart in my breast," says an old Scandinavian Saga: it is thus rightly expressed from the soul of a proud Viking. Such a type of man is even proud of *not* being made for sympathy; the hero of the Saga therefore adds warningly: "He who has not a hard heart when young, will never have one."

The noble and brave who think thus are the furthest removed from the morality which sees precisely in sympathy, or in acting for the good of others, or in *désintéressement,* the characteristic of the moral; faith in oneself, pride in oneself, a radical enmity and irony towards "selflessness," belong as definitely to noble morality, as do a careless scorn and precaution in presence of sympathy and the "warm heart,"—It is the powerful who *know* how to honour, it is their art, their domain for invention. The profound reverence for age and for tradition—all law rests on this double reverence,—the belief and prejudice in favour of ancestors and unfavourable to newcomers, is typical in the morality of the powerful; and if, reversely, men of "modern ideas" believe almost instinctively in "progress" and the "future," and are more and more lacking in respect for old age, the ignoble origin of these "ideas" has complacently betrayed itself thereby.

A morality of the ruling class, however, is more especially foreign and irritating to present-day taste in the sternness of its principle that one has duties only to one's equals; that one may act towards beings of a lower rank, towards all that is foreign, just as seems good to one, or "as the heart desires," and in any case "beyond good and evil":

it is here that sympathy and similar sentiments can have a place. The ability and obligation to exercise prolonged gratitude and prolonged revenge—both only within the circle of equals,—artfulness in retaliation, *raffinement* of the idea in friendship, a certain necessity to have enemies (as outlets for the emotions of envy, quarrelsomeness, arrogance—in fact, in order to be a good *friend*): all these are typical characteristics of the noble morality, which, as has been pointed out, is not the morality of "modern ideas," and is therefore at present difficult to realise, and also to unearth and disclose.

It is otherwise with the second type of morality, *slave-morality.* Supposing that the abused, the oppressed, the suffering, the unemancipated, the weary, and those uncertain of themselves, should moralise, what will be the common element in their moral estimates? Probably a pessimistic suspicion with regard to the entire situation of man will find expression, perhaps a condemnation of man, together with his situation. The slave has an unfavourable eye for the virtues of the powerful; he has a scepticism and distrust, a *refinement* of distrust of everything "good" that is there honoured—he would fain persuade himself that the very happiness there is not genuine. On the other hand, *those* qualities which serve to alleviate the existence of sufferers are brought into prominence and flooded with light; it is here that sympathy, the kind, helping hand, the warm heart, patience, diligence, humility, and friendliness attain to honour; for here these are the most useful qualities, and almost the only means of supporting the burden of existence.

Slave-morality is essentially the morality of utility. Here is the seat of the origin of the famous antithesis "good" and "evil":—power and dangerousness are assumed to reside in the evil, a certain dreadfulness, subtlety, and strength, which do not admit of being despised. According to slave-morality, therefore, the "evil" man arouses fear; according to master-morality, it is precisely the "good" man who arouses fear and seeks to arouse it, while the bad man is regarded as the despicable being. The contrast attains its maximum when, in accordance with the logical consequences of slave-morality, a shade of depreciation—it may be slight and well-intentioned—at last attaches itself to the "good" man of this morality; because, according to the servile mode of thought, the good man must in any case be the *safe* man: he is good-natured, easily deceived, perhaps a little stupid, *un bonhomme.* Everywhere that slave-morality gains the ascendancy, language shows a tendency to approximate the significations of the words "good" and "stupid."

A. J. AYER

Emotivism

A. J. AYER is an English philosopher who was highly influential in the logical positivist movement, which tried to show that many of our ordinary ways of talking, including ethics, was nonsense. This excerpt is from his Language, Truth and Logic.

I T is our business to give an account of "judgements of value" which is both satisfactory in itself and consistent with our general empiricist principles. We shall set ourselves to show that in so far as statements of value are significant, they are ordinary "scientific" statements; and that in so far as they are not scientific, they are not in the literal sense significant, but are simply expressions of emotion which can be neither true nor false. . . .

The ordinary system of ethics, as elaborated in the works of ethical philosophers, is very far from being a homogeneous whole. Not only is it apt to contain pieces of metaphysics, and analyses of non-ethical concepts: its actual ethical contents are themselves of very different kinds. We may divide them, indeed, into four main classes. There are, first of all, propositions which express definitions of ethical terms, or judgements about the legitimacy or possibility of certain definitions. Secondly, there are propositions describing the phenomena of moral experience, and their causes. Thirdly, there are exhortations to moral virtue. And, lastly, there are actual ethical judgements. It is unfortunately the case that the distinction between these four classes, plain as it is, is commonly ignored by ethical philosophers; with the result that it is often very difficult to tell

from their works what it is that they are seeking to discover or prove.

In fact, it is easy to see that only the first of our four classes, namely that which comprises the propositions relating to the definitions of ethical terms, can be said to constitute ethical philosophy. The propositions which describe the phenomena of moral experience, and their causes, must be assigned to the science of psychology, or sociology. The exhortations to moral virtue are not propositions at all, but ejaculations or commands which are designed to provoke the reader to action of a certain sort. Accordingly, they do not belong to any branch of philosophy or science. As for the expressions of ethical judgements, we have not yet determined how they should be classified. But inasmuch as they are certainly neither definitions nor comments upon definitions, nor quotations, we may say decisively that they do not belong to ethical philosophy. A strictly philosophical treatise on ethics should therefore make no ethical pronouncements. But it should, by giving an analysis of ethical terms, show what is the category to which all such pronouncements belong. And this is what we are now about to do.

A question which is often discussed by ethical philosophers is whether it is possible to find definitions which would reduce all ethical terms to one or two fundamental terms. But this question, though it undeniably belongs to ethical philosophy, is not relevant to our present enquiry. We are not now concerned to discover which term, within the sphere of ethical terms, is to be taken as fundamental; whether, for example, "good" can be defined in terms of "right" or "right" in terms of "good," or both in terms of "value." What we are interested in is the possibility of reducing the whole sphere of ethical terms to nonethical terms. We are enquiring whether statements of ethical value can be translated into statements of empirical fact.

That they can be so translated is the contention of those ethical philosophers who are commonly called subjectivists, and of those who are known as utilitarians. For the utilitarian defines the rightness of actions, and the goodness of ends, in terms of the pleasure, or happiness, or satisfaction, to which they give rise; the subjectivist, in terms of the feelings of approval which a certain person, or group of people, has towards them. Each of these types of definition makes moral judgements into a subclass of psychological or sociological judgements; and for this reason they are very attractive to us. For, if either was correct, it would follow that ethical assertions were not generically different from the factual assertions which are ordinarily contrasted with them; and the account which we have already given of empirical hypotheses would apply to them also.

Nevertheless we shall not adopt either a subjectivist or a utilitarian analysis of ethical terms. We reject the subjectivist view that to call an action right, or a thing good, is to say that it is generally approved of, because it is not self-contradictory to assert that some actions which are generally approved of are not right, or that some things which are generally approved of are not good. And we reject the alternative subjectivist view that a man who asserts that a certain action is right, or that a certain thing is good, is saying that he himself approves of it, on the ground that a man who confessed that he sometimes approved of what was bad or wrong would not be contradicting himself. And a similar argument is fatal to utilitarianism. We cannot agree that to call an action right is to say that of all the actions possible in the circumstances it would cause, or be likely to cause, the greatest happiness, or the greatest balance of pleasure over pain, or the greatest balance of satisfied over unsatisfied desire, because we find that it is not self-contradictory to say that it is sometimes wrong to perform the action which would actually or probably cause the greatest happiness, or the greatest balance of pleasure over pain, or of satisfied over unsatisfied desire. And since it is not self-contradictory to say that some pleasant things are not good, or that some bad things are desired, it cannot be the case that the sentence "x is good" is equivalent to "x is pleasant," or "x is desired." And to every other variant of utilitarianism with which I am acquainted the same objection can be made. And therefore we should, I think, conclude that the validity of ethical judgements is not determined by the felicific tendencies of actions, any more than by the nature of people's feelings; but that it must be regarded as "absolute" or "intrinsic," and not empirically calculable. . . .

In admitting that normative ethical concepts are irreducible to empirical concepts, we seem to be leaving the way clear for the "absolutist" view of ethics—that is, the view that statements of value are not controlled by observation, ordinary empirical propositions are, but only by a mysterious "intellectual intuition." A feature of this theory, which is seldom recognized by its advocates, is that it makes statements of value unverifiable. For it is notorious that what seems intuitively certain to one person may seem doubtful, or even false, to another. So that unless it is possible to provide some criterion by which one may decide between conflicting intuitions, a mere appeal to intuition is worthless as a test of a proposition's validity. But in the case of moral judgements, no such criterion can be given. Some moralists claim to settle the matter by saying that they "know" that their own moral judgements are correct. But such an assertion is of purely psychological interest, and has not the slightest tendency to prove the validity of any moral judgement. For dissentient moralists may equally well "know" that their ethical views are correct. And, as far as subjective certainty goes, there will be nothing to choose between them. When such differences of opinion arise in connection with an ordinary empirical proposition, one may attempt to resolve them by referring to, or actually carrying out, some relevant empirical test. But with regard to ethical statements, there is, on the "absolutist" or "intuitionist" theory, no relevant empirical test. We are therefore justified in saying that on this theory ethical statements are held to be unverifiable. . . .

Considering the use which we have made of the principle that a synthetic proposition is significant only if it is empirically verifiable, it is clear that the acceptance of an "absolutist" theory of ethics would undermine the whole of our main argument. And as we have already rejected the "naturalistic" theories

which are commonly supposed to provide the only alternative to "absolutism" in ethics, we seem to have reached a difficult position. We shall meet the difficulty by showing that the correct treatment of ethical statements is afforded by a third theory, which is wholly compatible with our radical empiricism.

We begin by admitting that the fundamental ethical concepts are unanalysable, inasmuch as there is no criterion by which one can test the validity of the judgements in which they occur. So far we are in agreement with the absolutists. But, unlike the absolutists, we are able to give an explanation of this fact about ethical concepts. We say that the reason why they are unanalysable is that they are mere pseudo-concepts. The presence of an ethical symbol in a proposition adds nothing to its factual content. Thus if I say to someone, "You acted wrongly in stealing that money," I am not stating anything more than if I had simply said, "You stole that money." In adding that this action is wrong I am not making any further statement about it. I am simply evincing my moral disapproval of it. It is as if I had said, "You stole that money," in a peculiar tone of horror, or written it with the addition of some special exclamation marks. The tone, or the exclamation marks, adds nothing to the literal meaning of the sentence. It merely serves to show that the expression of it is attended by certain feelings in the speaker.

If now I generalise my previous statement and say, "Stealing money is wrong," I produce a sentence which has no factual meaning—that is, expresses no proposition which can be either true or false. It is as if I had written "Stealing money!!"—where the shape and thickness of the exclamation marks show, by a suitable convention, that a special sort of moral disapproval is the feeling which is being expressed. It is clear that there is nothing said here which can be true or false. Another man may disagree with me about the wrongness of stealing, in the sense that he may not have the same feelings about stealing as I have, and he may quarrel with me on account of my moral sentiments. But he cannot, strictly speaking, contradict me. For in saying that a certain type of action is right or wrong, I am not making any factual statement, not even a statement about my own state of mind. I am merely expressing certain moral sentiments. And the man who is ostensibly contradicting me is merely expressing his moral sentiments. So that there is plainly no sense in asking which of us is in the right. For neither of us is asserting a genuine proposition.

What we have just been saying about the symbol "wrong" applies to all normative ethical symbols. Sometimes they occur in sentences which record ordinary empirical facts besides expressing ethical feeling about those facts: sometimes they occur in sentences which simply express ethical feeling about a certain type of action, or situation, without making any statement of fact. But in every case in which one would commonly be said to be making an ethical judgement, the function of the relevant ethical word is purely "emotive." It is used to express feeling about certain objects, but not to make any assertion about them.

SIMONE DE BEAUVOIR

On Freedom and Morality

SIMONE DE BEAUVOIR *(1908–1986) was a French novelist and philosopher and a lifelong companion of Jean-Paul Sartre, with whom she shared a radical and profound view about the centrality of freedom in human life. In the following excerpt from her* Ethics of Ambiguity, *she contrasts the essential role of freedom to morality and its opposition to what she (and Sartre) calls mere "facticity" (thing-ness).*

THERE is no way for a man to escape from this world. It is in this world that—avoiding the pitfalls we have just pointed out—he must realize himself morally. Freedom must project itself toward its own reality through a content whose value it establishes. An end is valid only by a return to the freedom which established it and which willed itself through this end. But this will implies that freedom is not to be engulfed in any goal; neither is it to dissipate itself vainly without aiming at a goal. It is not necessary for the subject to seek to be, but it must desire that there *be* being. To will oneself free and to will that there be *being* are one and the same choice, the choice that man makes of himself as a presence in the world. We can neither say that the free man wants freedom in order to desire being, nor that he wants the disclosure of being by freedom. These are two aspects of a single reality. And whichever be the one under consideration, they both imply the bond of each man with all others.

This bond does not immediately reveal itself to everybody. A young man wills himself free. He wills that there be being. This spontaneous liberality which casts him ardently into the world can ally itself to what is commonly called egoism. Often the young man perceives only that aspect of his relationship to others whereby others appear as enemies. In the preface to *The Inner Experience* Georges Bataille emphasizes very forcefully that each individual wants to be All. He sees in every other man and particularly in those whose existence is asserted with most brilliance, a limit, a condemnation of himself. "Each consciousness," said Hegel, "seeks the death of the other." And indeed at every moment others are stealing the whole world away from me. The first movement is to hate them. But this hatred is naive, and the desire immediately struggles against itself. If I were really everything there would be nothing beside me; the world would be empty. There would be nothing to possess, and I myself would be nothing. If

he is reasonable, the young man immediately understands that by taking the world away from me, others also give it to me, since a thing is given to me only by the movement which snatches it from me. To will that there be being is also to will that there be men by and for whom the world is endowed with human significations. One can reveal the world only on a basis revealed by other men. No project can be defined except by its interference with other projects. To make being "be" is to communicate with others by means of being.

This truth is found in another form when we say that freedom cannot will itself without aiming at an open future. The ends which it gives itself must be unable to be transcended by any reflection, but only the freedom of other men can extend them beyond our life. I have tried to show in *Pyrrhus and Cineas* that every man needs the freedom of other men and, in a sense, always wants it, even though he may be a tyrant; the only thing he fails to do is to assume honestly the consequences of such a wish. Only the freedom of others keeps each one of us from hardening in the absurdity of facticity. And if we are to believe the Christian myth of creation, God himself was in agreement on this point with the existentialist doctrine since, in the words of an anti-fascist priest, "He had such respect for man that He created him free."

MARY MIDGLEY

Trying Out One's New Sword

MARY MIDGLEY *is a British philosopher who writes on a variety of topics in ethics, including a widely read book titled* Beast and Man.

ALL of us are, more or less, in trouble today about trying to understand cultures strange to us. We hear constantly of alien customs. We see changes in our lifetime which would have astonished our parents. I want to discuss here one very short way of dealing with this difficulty, a drastic way which many people now theoretically favour. It consists in simply denying that we can ever understand any culture except our own well enough to make judgments about it. Those who recommend this hold that the world is sharply divided into separate societies, sealed units, each with its own system of thought. They feel that the respect and tolerance due from one system to another forbids us ever to take up a critical position to any other culture. Moral judgment, they suggest, is a kind of coinage valid only in its country of origin.

I shall call this position 'moral isolationism'. I shall suggest that it is certainly not forced upon us, and indeed that it makes no sense at all. People usually take it up because they think it is a respectful attitude to other cultures. In fact, however, it is not respectful. Nobody can respect what is entirely unintelligible to them. To respect someone, we have to know enough about him to make a *favorable* judgment, however general and tentative. And we do understand people in other cultures to this extent. Otherwise a great mass of our most valuable thinking would be paralysed.

To show this, I shall take a remote example, because we shall probably find it easier to think calmly about it than we should with a contemporary one, such as female circumcision in Africa or the Chinese Cultural Revolution. The principles involved will still be the same. My example is this. There is, it seems, a verb in classical Japanese which means 'to try out one's new sword on a chance wayfarer'. (The word is *tsujigiri,* literally 'crossroads-cut'.) A samurai sword had to be tried out because, if it was to work properly, it had to slice through someone at a single blow, from the shoulder to the opposite flank. Otherwise, the warrior bungled his stroke. This could injure his honour, offend his ancestors, and even let down his emperor. So tests were needed, and wayfarers had to be expended. Any wayfarer would do—provided, of course, that he was not another Samurai. Scientists will recognize a familiar problem about the rights of experimental subjects.

Now when we hear of a custom like this, we may well reflect that we simply do not understand it; and therefore are not qualified to criticize it at all, because we are not members of that culture. But we are not members of any other culture either, except our own. So we extend the principle to cover all extraneous cultures, and we seem therefore to be moral isolationists. But this is, as we shall see, an impossible position. Let us ask what it would involve.

We must ask first: Does the isolating barrier work both ways? Are people in other cultures equally unable to criticize *us*? This question struck me sharply when I read a remark in *The Guardian* by an anthropologist about a South American Indian who had been taken into a Brazilian town for an operation, which saved his life. When he came back to his village, he made several highly critical remarks about the white Brazilians' way of life. They may very well have been justified. But the interesting point was that the anthropologist called these remarks 'a damning indictment of Western civilization'. Now the Indian had been in that town about two weeks. Was he in a position to deliver a damning indictment? Would we ourselves be qualified to deliver such an indictment on the Samurai, provided we could spend two weeks in ancient Japan? What do we really think about this?

My own impression is that we believe that outsiders can, in principle, deliver perfectly good indictments—only, it usually takes more than two weeks to make them damning. Understanding has degrees. It is not a slapdash yes-or-no matter. Intelligent outsiders can progress in it, and in some ways will be at an advantage over the locals. But if this is so, it must clearly apply to ourselves as much as anybody else.

Our next question is this: Does the isolating barrier between cultures block praise as well as blame? If I want to say that the Samurai culture has many virtues, or to praise the South American Indians, am I prevented from doing *that* by my outside status? Now, we certainly do need to praise other societies in this way. But it is hardly possible that we could praise them effectively if we could not, in principle, criticize them.

Our praise would be worthless if it rested on definite grounds, if it did not flow from some understanding. Certainly we may need to praise things which we do not *fully* understand. We say 'there's something very good here, but I can't quite make out what it is yet'. This happens when we want to learn from strangers. And we can learn from strangers. But to do this we have to distinguish between those strangers who are worth learning from and those who are not. Can we then judge which is which?

This brings us to our third question: What is involved in judging? Now plainly there is no question here of sitting on a bench in a red robe and sentencing people. Judging simply means forming an opinion, and expressing it if it is called for. Is there anything wrong about this? Naturally, we ought to avoid forming—and expressing—*crude* opinions, like that of a simple-minded missionary, who might dismiss the whole Samurai culture as entirely bad, because it is non-Christian. But this is a different objection. The trouble with crude opinions is that they are crude, whoever forms them, not that they are formed by the wrong people. Anthropologists, after all, are outsiders quite as much as missionaries. Moral isolationism forbids us to form *any* opinions on these matters. Its ground for doing so is that we don't understand them. But there is much that we don't understand in our own culture too. This brings us to our last question: If we can't judge other cultures, can we really judge our own? Our efforts to do so will be much damaged if we are really deprived of our opinions about other societies, because these provide the range of comparison, the spectrum of alternatives against which we set what we want to understand. We would have to stop using the mirror which an-thropology so helpfully holds up to us.

In short, moral isolationism would lay down a general ban on moral rea-soning. Essentially, this is the pro-gramme of immoralism, and it carries a distressing logical difficulty. Immoral-ists like Nietzsche are actually just a rather specialized sect of moralists. They can no more afford to put moraliz-ing out of business than smugglers can afford to abolish customs regulations. The power of moral judgment is, in fact, not a luxury, not a perverse indulgence of the self-righteous. It is a necessity. When we judge something to be bad or good, better or worse than something else, we are taking it as an example to aim at or avoid. Without opinions of this sort, we would have no framework of comparison for our own policy, no chance of profiting by other people's insights or mistakes. In this vacuum, we could form no judgments on our own actions.

Now it would be odd if Homo sapi-ens had really got himself into a posi-tion as bad as this—a position where his main evolutionary asset, his brain, was so little use to him. None of us is going to accept this sceptical diagnosis. We cannot do so, because our involvement in moral isolationism does not flow from apathy, but from a rather acute concern about human hypocrisy and other forms of wickedness. But we po-larize that concern around a few se-lected moral truths. We are rightly angry with those who despise, oppress or steamroll other cultures. We think that doing these things is actually *wrong*. But this is itself a moral judg-ment. We could not condemn oppres-sion and insolence if we thought that all our condemnations were just a trivial local quirk of our own culture. We

could still less do it if we tried to stop judging altogether.

Real moral scepticism, in fact, could lead only to inaction, to our losing all interest in moral questions, most of all in those which concern other societies. When we discuss these things, it be-comes instantly clear how far we are from doing this. Suppose, for instance, that I criticize the bisecting Samurai, that I say his behaviour is brutal. What will usually happen next is that some-one will protest, will say that I have no right to make criticisms like that of an-other culture. But it is most unlikely that he will use this move to end the dis-cussion of the subject. Instead, he will justify the Samurai. He will try to fill in the background, to make me understand the custom, by explaining the exalted ideals of discipline and devotion which produced it. He will probably talk of the lower value which the ancient Japanese placed on individual life generally. He may well suggest that this is a healthier attitude than our own obsession with se-curity. He may add, too, that the way-farers did not seriously mind being bisected, that in principle they accepted the whole arrangement.

Now an objector who talks like this is implying that it *is* possible to under-stand alien customs. That is just what he is trying to make me do. And he im-plies, too, that if I do succeed in under-standing them, I shall do something better than giving up judging them. He expects me to change my present judg-ment to a truer one—namely, one that is favourable. And the standards I must use to do this cannot just be Samurai standards. They have to be ones current in my own culture. Ideals like discipline and devotion will not move anybody unless he himself accepts them. As it happens, neither discipline nor devotion is very popular in the West at present. Anyone who appeals to them may well have to do some more arguing to make *them* acceptable, before he can use them to explain the Samurai. But if he does succeed here, he will have persuaded us, not just that there was something to be said for them in ancient Japan, but that there would be here as well.

Isolating barriers simply cannot arise here. If we accept something as a serious moral truth about one culture, we can't refuse to apply it—in however different an outward form—to other cultures as well, wherever circumstance admit it. If we refuse to do this, we just are not taking the other culture seriously. This becomes clear if we look at the last argument used by my objector—that of justification by consent of the victim. It is suggested that sudden bisection is quite in order, *provided* that it takes place between consenting adults. I cannot now discuss how conclusive this justification is. What I am pointing out is simply that it can only work if we believe that *consent* can make such a transaction respectable— and this is a thoroughly modern and Western idea. It would probably never occur to a Samurai; if it did, it would surprise him very much. It is *our* standard. In applying it, too, we are likely to make another typically Western demand. We shall ask for good factual evidence that the wayfarers actually do have this rather surprising taste—that they are really willing to be bisected. In applying Western standards in this way, we are not being confused or irrelevant. We are asking the questions which arise *from where we stand,* questions which we can see the sense of. We do this because asking questions which you can't see the sense of is humbug. Certainly we can extend our questioning by imag-

inative effort. We can come to understand other societies better. By doing so, we may make their questions our own, or we may see that they are really forms of the questions which we are asking already. This is not impossible. It is just very hard work. The obstacles which often prevent it are simply those of ordinary ignorance, laziness and prejudice.

If there were really an isolating barrier, of course, our own culture could never have been formed. It is no sealed box, but a fertile jungle of different influences—Greek, Jewish, Roman, Norse, Celtic and so forth, into which further influences are still pouring— American, Indian, Japanese, Jamaican, you name it. The moral isolationist's picture of separate, unmixable cultures is quite unreal. People who talk about British history usually stress the value of this fertilizing mix, no doubt rightly. But this is not just an odd fact about Britain. Except for the very smallest and most remote, all cultures are formed out of many streams. All have the problem of digesting and assimilating things which, at the start, they do not understand. All have the choice of learning something from this challenge, or alternatively, of refusing to learn, and fighting it mindlessly instead.

This universal predicament has been obscured by the fact that anthropologists used to concentrate largely on very small and remote cultures, which did not seem to have this problem. These tiny societies, which had often forgotten their own history, made neat, self-contained subjects for study. No doubt it was valuable to emphasize their remoteness, their extreme strangeness, their independence of our cultural tradition. This emphasis was, I think, the root of moral isolationism. But, as the tribal studies themselves showed, even there the anthropologists were able to interpret what they saw and make judgments—often favourable—about the tribesmen. And the tribesmen, too, were quite equal to making judgments about the anthropologists—and about the tourists and Coca-Cola salesmen who followed them. Both sets of judgments, no doubt, were somewhat hasty, both have been refined in the light of further experience. A similar transaction between us and the Samurai might take even longer. But that is no reason at all for deeming it impossible. Morally as well as physically, there is only one world, and we all have to live in it.

CAROL GILLIGAN

In a Different Voice

CAROL GILLIGAN *is a professor at Harvard University who has begun something of a revolution in ethical theory, pointing out that most of the history of ethics involves a strong male bias and that female ethics may in fact be very different.*

THE arc of developmental theory leads from infantile dependence to adult autonomy, tracing a path characterized by an increasing differentiation of self from other and a progressive freeing of thought from contextual constraints. The vision of Luther, journeying from the rejection of a self defined by others to the assertive boldness of "Here I stand" and the image of Plato's allegorical man in the cave, separating at last the shadows from the sun, have taken powerful hold on the psychological understanding of what constitutes development. Thus, the individual, meeting fully the developmental challenges of adolescence as set for him by Piaget, Erikson, and Kohlberg, thinks formally, proceeding from theory to fact, and defines both the self and the moral autonomously, that is, apart from the identification and conventions that had comprised the particulars of his childhood world. So equipped, he is presumed ready to live as an adult, to love and work in a way that is both intimate and generative, to develop an ethical sense of caring and a genital mode of relating in which giving and taking fuse in the ultimate reconciliation of the tension between self and other.

Yet the men whose theories have largely informed this understanding of development have all been plagued by the same problem, the problem of women, whose sexuality remains more diffuse, whose perception of self is so much more tenaciously embedded in relationships with others and whose moral dilemmas hold them in a mode of judgment that is insistently contextual. The solution has been to consider women as either deviant or deficient in their development.

That there is a discrepancy between concepts of womanhood and adulthood is nowhere more clearly evident than in the series of studies on sex-role stereotypes reported by Broverman, Vogel, Broverman, Clarkson, and Rosenkrantz. The repeated finding of these studies is that the qualities deemed necessary for adulthood—the capacity for autonomous thinking, clear decision making, and responsible action—are those associated with masculinity but considered undesirable as attributes of the feminine self. The stereotypes suggest a splitting of love and work that relegates the expressive capacities requisite for the former to women while the instrumental abilities necessary for the latter reside in the masculine domain. Yet, looked at from a different perspective, these stereotypes reflect a conception of adulthood that is itself out of balance, favoring the separateness of the individual self over its connection to others and leaning more toward an autonomous life of work than toward the interdependence of love and care. . . .

The revolutionary contribution of Piaget's work is the experimental confirmation and refinement of Kant's assertion that knowledge is actively constructed rather than passively received. Time, space, self, and other, as well as the categories of developmental theory, all arise out of the active interchange between the individual and the physical and social world in which he lives and of which he strives to make sense. The development of cognition is the process of reappropriating reality at progressively more complex levels of apprehension, as the structures of thinking expand to encompass the increasing richness and intricacy of experience.

Moral development, in the work of Piaget and Kohlberg, refers specifically to the expanding conception of the so-cial world as it is reflected in the understanding and resolution of the inevitable conflicts that arise in the relations between self and others. The moral judgment is a statement of priority, an attempt at rational resolution in a situation where, from a different point of view, the choice itself seems to do violence to justice.

Kohlberg, in his extension of the early work of Piaget, discovered six stages of moral judgment, which he claimed formed an invariant sequence, each successive stage representing a more adequate construction of the moral problem, which in turn provides the basis for its more just resolution. The stages divide into three levels, each of which denotes a significant expansion of the moral point of view from an egocentric through a societal to a universal ethical conception. With this expansion in perspective comes the capacity to free moral judgment from the individual needs and social conventions with which it had earlier been confused and anchor it instead in principles of justice that are universal in application. These principles provide criteria upon which both individual and societal claims can be impartially assessed. In Kohlberg's view, at the highest stages of development morality is freed from both psychological and historical constraints, and the individual can judge independently of his own particular needs and of the values of those around him.

That the moral sensibility of women differs from that of men was noted by Freud in the following by now well-quoted statement:

I cannot evade the notion (though I hesitate to give it expression) that for women the level of what is ethically normal is different from what it is in man. Their superego is never so inexorable, so impersonal, so independent of its emotional origins as we require it to be in men. Character-traits which critics of every epoch have brought up against women—that they show less sense of justice than men, that they are less ready to submit to the great exigencies of life, that they are more often influenced in their judgments by feelings of affection or hostility—all these would be amply accounted for by the modification in the formation of their superego which we have inferred above.

While Freud's explanation lies in the deviation of female from male development around the construction and resolution of the Oedipal problem, the same observations about the nature of morality in women emerge from the work of Piaget and Kohlberg. Piaget, in his study of the rules of children's games, observed that, in the games they played, girls were "less explicit about agreement [than boys] and less concerned with legal elaboration." In contrast to the boys' interest in the codification of rules, the girls adopted a more pragmatic attitude, regarding "a rule as good so long as the game repays it." As a result, in comparison to boys, girls were found to be "more tolerant and more easily reconciled to innovations."

Kohlberg also identifies a strong interpersonal bias in the moral judgments of women, which leads them to be considered as typically at the third of his six-stage developmental sequence. At that stage, the good is identified with "what pleases or helps others and is approved of by them." This mode of judgment is conventional in its conformity to generally held notions of the good but also psychological in its concern with intention and consequence as the basis for judging the morality of action.

That women fall largely into this level of moral judgment is hardly surprising when we read from the Broverman list that prominent among the twelve attributes considered to be desirable for women are tact, gentleness, awareness of the feelings of others, strong need for security, and easy expression of tender feelings. And yet, herein lies the paradox, for the very traits that have traditionally defined the "goodness" of women, their care for and sensitivity to the needs of others, are those that mark them as deficient in moral development. The infusion of feeling into their judgments keeps them from developing a more independent and abstract ethical conception in which concern for others derives from principles of justice rather than from compassion and care. Kohlberg, however, is less pessimistic than Freud in his assessment, for he sees the development of women as extending beyond the interpersonal level, following the same path toward independent, principled judgment that he discovered in the research on men from which his stages were derived. In Kohlberg's view, women's development will proceed beyond Stage Three when they are challenged to solve moral problems that require them to see beyond the relationships that have in the past generally bound their moral experience.

What then do women say when asked to construct the moral domain; how do we identify the characteristically "feminine" voice? A Radcliffe undergraduate, responding to the question, "If you had to say what morality meant to you, how would you sum it up?," replies:

> When I think of the word morality, I think of obligations. I usually think of it

as conflicts between personal desires and social things, social considerations, or personal desires of yourself versus personal desires of another person or people or whatever. Morality is that whole realm of how you decide these conflicts. A moral person is one who would decide, like by placing themselves more often than not as equals, a truly moral person would always consider another person as their equal . . . in a situation of social interaction, something is morally wrong where the individual ends up screwing a lot of people. And it is morally right when everyone comes out better off.

Yet when asked if she can think of someone whom she would consider a genuinely moral person, she replies, "Well, immediately I think of Albert Schweitzer because he has obviously given his life to help others." Obligation and sacrifice override the ideal of equality, setting up a basic contradiction in her thinking.

Another undergraduate responds to the question, "What does it mean to say something is morally right or wrong?," by also speaking first of responsibilities and obligations:

Just that it has to do with responsibilities and obligations and values, mainly values. . . . In my life situation I relate morality with interpersonal relationships that have to do with respect for the other person and myself. [Why respect other people?] Because they have a consciousness or feelings that can be hurt, an awareness that can be hurt.

The concern about hurting others persists as a major theme in the responses of two other Radcliffe students:

[Why be moral?] Millions of people have to live together peacefully. I personally

don't want to hurt other people. That's a real criterion, a main criterion for me. It underlies my sense of justice. It isn't nice to inflict pain. I empathize with anyone in pain. Not hurting others is important in my own private morals. Years ago, I would have jumped out of a window not to hurt my boyfriend. That was pathological. Even today though, I want approval and love and I don't want enemies. Maybe that's why there is morality— so people can win approval, love and friendship.

My main moral principle is not hurting other people as long as you aren't going against your own conscience and as long as you remain true to yourself. . . . There are many moral issues such as abortion, the draft, killing, stealing, monogamy, etc. If something is a controversial issue like these, then I always say it is up to the individual. The individual has to decide and then follow his own conscience. There are no moral absolutes. . . . Laws are pragmatic instruments, but they are not absolutes. A viable society can't make exceptions all the time, but I would personally. . . . I'm afraid I'm heading for some big crisis with my boyfriend someday, and someone will get hurt, and he'll get more hurt than I will. I feel an obligation to not hurt him, but also an obligation to not lie. I don't know if it is possible to not lie and not hurt.

The common thread that runs through these statements, the wish not to hurt others and the hope that in morality lies a way of solving conflicts so that no one will get hurt, is striking in that it is independently introduced by each of the four women as the most specific item in their response to a most general question. The moral person is one who helps others; goodness is service, meeting one's obligations and responsibilities to others, if possible, without sacrificing oneself. While the first of the four women ends by denying the conflict she initially introduced, the last woman anticipates a conflict between remaining true to herself and adhering to her principle of not hurting others. The dilemma that would test the limits of this judgment would be one where helping others is seen to be at the price of hurting the self.

The reticence about taking stands on "controversial issues," the willingness to "make exceptions all the time" expressed in the final example above, is echoed repeatedly by other Radcliffe students, as in the following two examples:

> I never feel that I can condemn anyone else. I have a very relativistic position. The basic idea that I cling to is the sanctity of human life. I am inhibited about impressing my beliefs on others.

> I could never argue that my belief on a moral question is anything that another person should accept. I don't believe in absolutes. . . . If there is an absolute for moral decisions, it is human life.

Or as a thirty-one-year-old Wellesley graduate says, in explaining why she would find it difficult to steal a drug to save her own life despite her belief that it would be right to steal for another: "It's just very hard to defend yourself against the rules. I mean, we live by consensus, and you take an action simply for yourself, by yourself, there's no consensus there, and that is relatively indefensible in this society now."

What begins to emerge is a sense of vulnerability that impedes these women from taking a stand, what George Eliot regards as the girl's "susceptibility" to adverse judgments of others, which

stems from her lack of power and consequent inability to do something in the world. While relativism in men, the unwillingness to make moral judgments that Kohlberg and Kramer and Kohlberg and Gilligan have associated with the adolescent crisis of identity and belief, takes the form of calling into question the concept of morality itself, the women's reluctance to judge stems rather from their uncertainty about their right to make moral statements or, perhaps, the price for them that such judgment seems to entail. This contrast echoes that made by Matina Horner, who differentiated the ideological fear of success expressed by men from the personal conflicts about succeeding that riddled the women's responses to stories of competitive achievement.

> Most of the men who responded with the expectation of negative consequences because of success were not concerned about their masculinity but were instead likely to have expressed existential concerns about finding a "non-materialistic happiness and satisfaction in life." These concerns, which reflect changing attitudes toward traditional kinds of success or achievement in our society, played little, if any, part in the female stories. Most of the women who were high in fear of success imagery continued to be concerned about the discrepancy between success in the situation described and feminine identity.

When women feel excluded from direct participation in society, they see themselves as subject to a consensus or judgment made and enforced by the men on whose protection and support they depend and by whose names they are known. A divorced middle-aged woman, mother of adolescent daughters, resident of a sophisticated university community, tells the story as follows:

As a woman, I feel I never understood that I was a person, that I can make decisions and I have a right to make decisions. I always felt that that belonged to my father or my husband in some way or church which was always represented by a male clergyman. They were the three men in my life: father, husband, and clergyman, and they had much more to say about what I should or shouldn't do. They were really authority figures which I accepted. I didn't rebel against that. It only has lately occurred to me that I never even rebelled against it, and my girls are much more conscious of this, not in the militant sense, but just in the recognizing sense. . . . I still let things happen to me rather than make them happen, than to make choices, although I know all about choices. I know the procedures and the steps and all. [Do you have any clues about why this might be true?] Well, I think in one sense, there is less responsibility involved. Because if you make a dumb decision, you have to take the rap. If it happens to you, well, you can complain about it. I think that if you don't grow up feeling that you ever had any choices, you don't either have the sense that you have emotional responsibility. With this sense of choice comes this sense of responsibility.

The essence of the moral decision is the exercise of choice and the willingness to accept responsibility for that choice. To the extent that women perceive themselves as having no choice, they correspondingly excuse themselves from the responsibility that decision entails. Childlike in the vulnerability of their dependence and consequent fear of abandonment, they claim to wish only to please but in return for their goodness they expect to be loved and cared for. This, then, is an "altruism" always at risk, for it presupposes an innocence constantly in danger of being compromised by an awareness of the trade-off that has been made. Asked to describe herself, a Radcliffe senior responds:

I have heard of the onion skin theory. I see myself as an onion, as a block of different layers, the external layers for people that I don't know that well, the agreeable, the social, and as you go inward there are more sides for people I know that I show. I am not sure about the innermost, whether there is a core, or whether I have just picked up everything as I was growing up, these different influences. I think I have a neutral attitude towards myself, but I do think in terms of good and bad. . . . Good—I try to be considerate and thoughtful of other people and I try to be fair in situations and be tolerant. I use the words but I try and work them out practically. . . . Bad things—I am not sure if they are bad, if they are altruistic or I am doing them basically for approval of other people. [Which things are these?] The values I have when I try to act them out. They deal mostly with interpersonal type relations. . . . If I were doing it for approval, it would be a very tenuous thing. If I didn't get the right feedback, there might go all my values.

Ibsen's play, *A Doll House,* depicts the explosion of just such a world through the eruption of a moral dilemma that calls into question the notion of goodness that lies at its center. Nora, the "squirrel wife," living with her husband as she had lived with her father, puts into action this conception of goodness as sacrifice and, with the best of intentions, takes the law into her own hands. The crisis that ensues, most painfully for her in the repudiation of that goodness by the very person who was its recipient and beneficiary, causes her to reject the suicide that she had initially seen as its ultimate expression and choose instead to seek new and firmer answers to the adolescent questions of identity and belief.

The availability of choice and with it the onus of responsibility has now invaded the most private sector of the woman's domain and threatens a similar explosion. For centuries, women's sexuality anchored them in passivity, in a receptive rather than active stance, where the events of conception and childbirth could be controlled only by a withholding in which their own sexual needs were either denied or sacrificed. That such a sacrifice entailed a cost to their intelligence as well was seen by Freud when he tied the "undoubted intellectual inferiority of so many women" to "the inhibition of thought necessitated by sexual suppression." The strategies of withholding and denial that women have employed in the politics of sexual relations appear similar to their evasion or withholding of judgment in the moral realm. The hesitance expressed in the previous examples to impose even a belief in the value of human life on others, like the reluctance to claim one's sexuality, bespeaks a self uncertain of its strength, unwilling to deal with consequence, and thus avoiding confrontation.

Thus women have traditionally deferred to the judgment of men, although often while intimating a sensibility of their own which is at variance with that judgment. Maggie Tulliver, in Eliot's *The Mill on the Floss,* responds to the accusations that ensue from the discovery of her secretly continued relationship with Phillip Wakeham by acceding to her brother's moral judgment while at the same time asserting a different set of standards by which she attests her own superiority:

> I don't want to defend myself. . . . I know I've been wrong—often continually. But yet, sometimes when I have done wrong, it has been because I have feelings that you would be the better for if you had them. If *you* were in fault ever, if you had done anything very wrong, I should be sorry for the pain it brought you; I should not want punishment to be heaped on you.

An eloquent defense, Kohlberg would argue, of a Stage Three moral position, an assertion of the age-old split between thinking and feeling, justice and mercy, that underlies many of the clichés and stereotypes concerning the difference between the sexes. But considered from another point of view, it is a moment of confrontation, replacing a former evasion, between two modes of judging, two differing constructions of the moral domain—one traditionally associated with masculinity and the public world of social power, the other with femininity and the privacy of domestic interchange. While the developmental ordering of these two points of view has been to consider the masculine as the more adequate and thus as replacing the feminine as the individual moves toward higher states, their reconciliation remains unclear.

JOAN DIDION

On Morality

JOAN DIDION *lives in Venice, California, and is the well-known author of* Slouching Toward Bethlehem *and* Play It As It Lays.

A S it happens I am in Death Valley, in a room at the Enterprise Motel and Trailer Park, and it is July, and it is hot. In fact it is 119°. I cannot seem to make the air conditioner work, but there is a small refrigerator, and I can wrap ice cubes in a towel and hold them against the small of my back. With the help of the ice cubes I have been trying to think, because *The American Scholar* asked me to, in some abstract way about "morality," a word I distrust more every day, but my mind veers inflexibly toward the particular.

Here are some particulars. At midnight last night, on the road in from Las Vegas to Death Valley Junction, a car hit a shoulder and turned over. The driver, very young and apparently drunk, was killed instantly. His girl was found alive but bleeding internally, deep in shock. I talked this afternoon to the nurse who had driven the girl to the nearest doctor, 185 miles across the floor of the Valley and three ranges of lethal mountain road. The nurse explained that her husband, a talc miner, had stayed on the highway with the boy's body until the coroner could get over the mountains from Bishop, at dawn today. "You can't just leave a body on the highway," she said. "It's immoral."

It was one instance in which I did not distrust the word, because she meant something quite specific. She meant that if a body is left alone for even a few minutes on the desert, the coyotes close in and eat the flesh. Whether or not a corpse is torn apart by coyotes may seem only a sentimental consideration, but of course it is more: one of the promises we make to one another is that we will try to retrieve our casualties, try not to abandon our dead to the coyotes. If we have been taught to keep our promises—if, in the simplest terms, our upbringing is good enough—we stay with the body, or have bad dreams.

I am talking, of course, about the kind of social code that is sometimes called, usually pejoratively, "wagon-train morality." In fact that is precisely what it is. For better or worse, we are what we learned as children: my own childhood was illuminated by graphic litanies of the grief awaiting those who failed in their loyalties to each other. The Donner–Reed Party, starving in the Sierra snows, all the ephemera of civilization gone save that one vestigial taboo, the provision that no one should eat his own blood kin. The Jayhawkers, who quarreled and separated not far from where I am tonight. Some of them died in the Funerals and some of them died down near Badwater and most of the rest of them died in the Panamints. A woman who got through gave the Valley its name. Some might say that the Jayhawkers were killed by the desert summer, and the Donner Party by the mountain winter, by circumstances beyond control; we were taught instead that they had somewhere abdicated their responsibilities, somehow breached their primary loyalties, or they would not have found themselves helpless in the mountain winter or the desert summer, would not have given way to acrimony, would not have deserted one another, would not have *failed.* In brief, we heard such stories as cautionary tales, and they still suggest the only kind of "morality" that seems to me to have any but the most potentially mendacious meaning.

You are quite possible impatient with me by now; I am talking, you want to say, about a "morality" so primitive that it scarcely deserves the name, a code that has as its point only survival, not the attainment of the ideal good. Exactly. Particularly out here tonight, in this country so ominous and terrible that to live in it is to live with antimatter, it is difficult to believe that "the good" is a knowable quantity. Let me tell you what it is like out here tonight. Stories travel at night on the desert. Someone gets in his pickup and drives a couple of hundred miles for a beer, and he carries news of what is happening, back wherever he came from. Then he drives another hundred miles for another beer, and passes along stories from the last place as well as from the one before; it is a network kept alive by people whose instincts tell them that if they do not keep moving at night on the desert they will lose all reason. Here is a story that is going around the desert tonight: over across the Nevada line, sheriff's deputies are diving in some underground pools, trying to retrieve a couple of bodies known to be in the hole. The widow of one of the drowned boys is over there; she is eighteen, and pregnant, and is said not to leave the hole. The divers

go down and come up, and she just stands there and stares into the water. They have been diving for ten days but have found no bottom to the caves, no bodies and no trace of them, only the black 90° water going down and down and down, and a single translucent fish, not classified. The story tonight is that one of the divers has been hauled up incoherent, out of his head, shouting— until they got him out of there so that the widow could not hear—about water that got hotter instead of cooler as he went down, about light flickering through the water, about magma, about underground nuclear testing.

That is the tone stories take out here, and there are quite a few of them tonight. And it is more than the stories alone. Across the road at the Faith Community Church a couple of dozen old people, come here to live in trailers and die in the sun, are holding a prayer sing. I cannot hear them and do not want to. What I can hear are occasional coyotes and a constant chorus of "Baby the Rain Must Fall" from the jukebox in the Snake Room next door, and if I were also to hear those dying voices, those Midwestern voices drawn to this lunar country for some unimaginable atavistic rites, *rock of ages cleft for me,* I think I would lose my own reason. Every now and then I imagine I hear a rattlesnake, but my husband says that it is a faucet, a paper rustling, the wind. Then he stands by a window, and plays a flashlight over the dry wash outside.

What does it mean? It means nothing manageable. There is some sinister hysteria in the air out here tonight, some hint of the monstrous perversion to which any human idea can come. "I followed my own conscience." "I did what I thought was right." How many madmen have said it and meant it? How many murderers? Klaus Fuchs said it, and the men who committed the Mountain Meadows Massacre said it, and Alfred Rosenberg said it. And, as we are rotely and rather presumptuously reminded by those who would say it now, Jesus said it. Maybe we have all said it, and maybe we have been wrong. Except on that most primitive level—our loyalties to those we love—what could be more arrogant than to claim the primacy of personal conscience? ("Tell me," a rabbi asked Daniel Bell when he said, as a child, that he did not believe in God. "Do you think God cares?") At least some of the time, the world appears to me as a painting by Hieronymous Bosch; were I to follow my conscience then, it would lead me out onto the desert with Marion Faye, out to where he stood in *The Deer Park* looking east to Los Alamos and praying, as if for rain, that it would happen: ". . . *let it come and clear the rot and the stench and the stink, let it come for all of everywhere, just so it comes and the world stands clear in the white dead dawn.*"

Of course you will say that I do not have the right, even if I had the power, to inflict that unreasonable conscience upon you; nor do I want you to inflict your conscience, however reasonable, however enlightened, upon me. ("We must be aware of the dangers which lie in our most generous wishes," Lionel Trilling once wrote. "Some paradox of our nature leads us, when once we have made our fellow men the objects of our enlightened interest, to go on to make them the objects of our pity, then of our wisdom, ultimately of our coercion.") That the ethic of conscience is intrinsically insidious seems scarcely a revelatory point, but it is one raised with increasing infrequency; even those who

do raise it tend to *segue* with troubling readiness into the quite contradictory position that the ethic of conscience is dangerous when it is "wrong," and admirable when it is "right."

You see I want to be quite obstinate about insisting that we have no way of knowing—beyond that fundamental loyalty to the social code—what is "right" and what is "wrong," what is "good" and what "evil." I dwell so upon this because the most disturbing aspect of "morality" seems to me to be the frequency with which the word now appears; in the press, on television, in the most perfunctory kinds of conversation. Questions of straightforward power (or survival) politics, questions of quite indifferent public policy, questions of almost anything: they are all assigned these factitious moral burdens. There is something facile going on, some self-indulgence at work. Of course we would all like to "believe" in something, like to assuage our private guilts in public causes, like to lose our tiresome selves; like, perhaps, to transform the white flag of defeat at home into the brave white banner of battle away from home. And of course it is all right to do that; that is how, immemorially, things have gotten done. But I think it is all right only so long as we do not delude ourselves about what we are doing, and why. It is all right only so long as we remember that all the *ad hoc* committees, all the picket lines, all the brave signatures in *The New York Times,* all the tools of agitprop straight across the spectrum, do not confer upon anyone any *ipso facto* virtue. It is all right only so long as we recognize that the end may or may not be expedient, may or may not be a good idea, but in any case has nothing to do with "morality." Because when we start deceiving ourselves into thinking not that we want something or need something, not that it is a pragmatic necessity for us to have it, but that it is a *moral imperative* that we have it, then is when we join the fashionable madmen, and then is when the thin whine of hysteria is heard in the land, and then is when we are in bad trouble. And I suspect we are already there.

CHESHIRE CALHOUN

Justice, Care, Gender Bias

CHESHIRE CALHOUN *teaches philosophy and is head of the women's studies program at Colby College in Maine.*

C AROL Gilligan poses two separable, though in her work not separate, challenges to moral theory. The first is a challenge to the adequacy of current moral theory that is dominated by the ethics of justice. The ethics of justice, on her view, excludes some dimensions of moral experience, such as contextual decision making, special obligations, the moral motives of compassion and sympathy, and the relevance of considering one's own integrity in making moral decisions. The second is a challenge to moral theory's presumed gender neutrality. The ethics of justice is not gender neutral, she argues, because it advocates ideals of agency, moral motivation, and correct moral reasoning which women are less likely than men to achieve; and because the moral dimensions excluded from the ethics of justice are just the ones figuring more prominently in women's than men's moral experience.

The adequacy and gender bias charges are, for Gilligan, linked. She claims that the ethics of justice and the ethics of care are two different moral orientations. Whereas individuals may use both orientations, the shift from one to the other requires a Gestalt shift, since "the terms of one perspective do not contain the terms of the other." The exclusion of the care perspective from the ethics of justice simultaneously undermines the adequacy of the ethics of justice (it cannot give a complete account of moral life) and renders it gender-biased.

Some critics have responded by arguing that there is no logical incompatibility between the two moral orientations. Because the ethics of justice does not in principle exclude the ethics of care (even if theorists within the justice tradition have had little to say about care issues), it is neither inadequate nor gender-biased. Correctly applying moral rules and principles, for instance, requires, rather than excludes, knowledge of contextual details. Both orientations are crucial to correct moral reasoning and an adequate understanding of moral life. Thus, the ethics of justice and the ethics of care are not in fact rivaling, alternative moral theories. The so-called ethics of care merely makes focal issues that are already implicitly contained in the ethics of justice.

Suppose the two are logically compatible. Would the charge of gender bias evaporate? Yes, so long as gender neutrality only requires that the ethics of justice could, consistently, make room for the central moral concerns of the ethics of care. But perhaps gender neutrality requires more than this. Since the spectre of gender bias in theoretical knowledge is itself a moral issue, we would be well advised to consider the question of gender bias more carefully before concluding that our moral theory speaks in an androgynous voice. Although we can and should test the ethics of justice by asking whether it could consistently include the central moral issues in the ethics of care, we might also ask what ideologies of the moral life are likely to result from the repeated inclusion or exclusion of particular topics in moral theorizing.

Theorizing that crystallizes into a tradition has nonlogical as well as logical implications. In order to explain why a tradition has the contours it does, one may need to suppose general acceptance of particular beliefs that are not logically entailed by any particular theory and might be denied by individual theorists were those beliefs articulated. When behavioral researchers, for example, focus almost exclusively on aggression and its role in human life, neglecting other behavioral motives, their doing so has the nonlogical implication that aggression is, indeed, the most important behavioral motive. This is because only a belief like this would explain the rationality of this pattern of research. Such nonlogical implications become ideolo-

gies when politically loaded (as the importance of aggression is when coupled with observations about women's lower level of aggression).

When understood as directed at moral theory's nonlogical implications, the gender-bias charge takes a different form. Even if the ethics of justice could consistently accommodate the ethics of care, the critical point is that theorists in the justice tradition have not said much, except in passing, about the ethics of care, and are unlikely to say much in the future without a radical shift in theoretical priorities; and concentrating almost exclusively on rights of noninterference, impartiality, rationality, autonomy, and principles creates an ideology of the moral domain which has undesirable political implications for women. This formulation shifts the justice-care debate from one about logical compatibility to a debate about which theoretical priorities would improve the lot of women.

I see no way around this politicization of philosophical critique. If we hope to shape culture, and not merely to add bricks to a philosophical tower, we will need to be mindful of the cultural/political use to which our thoughts may be put after leaving our word processors. This mindfulness should include asking whether our theoretical work enacts or discredits a moral commitment to improving the lot of women.

Providing us with some way of envisioning our shared humanity, and thus our equal membership in the moral community, is certainly an important thing for moral theory to do. But too much talk about our similarities as moral selves, and too little talk about our differences has its moral dangers. For one, unless we are also quite knowledgeable about the substantial differences between persons, particularly central differences due to gender, race, and class, we may be tempted to slide into supposing that our common humanity includes more substantive similarities than it does in fact. For instance, moral theorists have assumed that moral selves have a prominent interest in property and thus in property rights. But property rights may have loomed large on the moral horizons of past moral theorists partly, or largely, because they were themselves propertied and their activities took place primarily in the public, economic sphere. Historically, women could not share the same interest in property and concern about protecting it, since they were neither legally entitled to hold it nor primary participants in the public, economic world. And arguably, women do not now place the same priority. (I have in mind the fact that equal opportunity has had surprisingly little impact on either sex segregation in the workforce or on women's, but not men's, accommodating their work and work schedules to childrearing needs. One explanation is that income matters less to women than other sorts of considerations. The measure of a woman, unlike the measure of a man, is not the size of her paycheck.) Seyla Benhabib summarizes this point by suggesting that a singleminded emphasis on common humanity encourages a "substitutionalist universalism" where universal humanity "is defined surreptitiously by identifying the experiences of a specific group of subjects as the paradigmatic case of all humans."

In addition to encouraging us to overlook how our basic interests may differ depending on our social location, the emphasis on common humanity, because it is insensitive to connections between interests, social location, and power, deters questions about the possible malformation of our interests as a result of their development within an inegalitarian social structure. Both dangers plague the role-reversal test, some version of which has been a staple of moral theorizing. Although the point of that test is to eliminate egoistic bias in moral judgments, without a sensitivity to how our (uncommon) humanity is shaped by our social structure, role-reversal tests may simply preserve, rather than eliminate, inequities. This is because role-reversal tests either take individuals' desires as givens, thus ignoring the possibility that socially subordinate individuals have been socialized to want the very things that keep them socially subordinate (e.g., Susan Brownmiller argues that women have been socialized to want masochistic sexual relationships); or, if they take into account what individuals ought to want, role-reversal tests typically ignore the way that social power structures may have produced an alignment between the concept of a normal, reasonable desire and the desires of the dominant group (so, for example, much of the affirmative action literature takes it for granted that women ought to want traditionally defined male jobs with no consideration of the possibility that women might prefer retailoring those jobs so that they are less competitive, less hierarchical, and more compatible with family responsibilities).

In short, without adequate knowledge of how very different human interests, temperaments, lifestyles, and commitments may be, as well as a knowledge of how those interests may be malformed as a result of power inequities, the very egoism and group bias that the focus on common humanity was designed to eliminate may slip in as a result of that focus.

Chapter *16*

How Can We Get Along with One Another?

If you were asked to name the single thing that you spend the most time thinking about, the answer might very well be your relationships with other people. Throughout most of an ordinary day, we find ourselves wondering or worrying about our feelings about other people and their feelings about us. Did I really offend Bernie when I told him that his new haircut made him look like Pee Wee Herman? Does Delores really love me, or is she just using me to make José jealous? Should I go home to see my family during spring break instead of taking that trip to Florida? Will marriage destroy our love for each other? Will this one-night stand hurt my marriage? Should I tell my son that I dislike his fiance? Am I giving more to this relationship than I am getting out of it?

Although many philosophers have avoided reflecting on the nature of relationships (perhaps because they prefer to think that philosophy ought to concern itself with more enduring matters), others have viewed an understanding of human relationships as part of the central business of philosophy. Indeed, some philosophers believe that if philosophy is viewed as being somehow above matters of friendship, love, and fidelity, then the alleged wisdom of philosophers is not worth very much. For Socrates, who believed that the unexamined life is not worth living, the quality of a person's love and friendship was a measure of his or her goodness. As a result, he spent much time discussing exactly what he took real love to be. His immediate successors, Plato and Aristotle, treated friendship as a topic equal in importance to the nature of knowledge or the nature of goodness. With credentials such as these, it isn't surprising that serious consideration of relationships has seemed a worthy enterprise to a number of subsequent philosophers.

When you begin to reflect on the nature of relationships, one of the things that first becomes apparent is that they are both a source of pleasure and a source of pain. In a close relationship with another person, you sometimes feel that you are becoming nothing more than a fixture in his or her life. No matter how hard you try, you seem never to be able to satisfy your friend's desires. Experiencing yourself as chronically criticized, you begin to lose any sense of value. On the other hand, it is through relationships that you often experience your most intense feelings of self-affirmation, of connection, of worth. Under a lover's gaze, you can find yourself transformed: you are stunningly attractive, fiercely intelligent, astonishingly sensitive. It is interesting that self-affirmation is often accompanied by a sense that there are no boundaries between you and your friend or lover: Where before there were two, now there is one.

The quality of our relationships affects our perceptions of ourselves and our world. Indeed, some philosophers argue that, to understand what it is to be a person in the world, we must look to the particular ways in which it is possible to stand in relation to others. Martin Buber, for example, isolates two fundamental types of relationships. When we treat another person as an object (as we feel we have been treated in the first case described above), the type of relationship he or she stands in with respect to us is what Buber calls an "I–It" relationship. But, when we have a full, reciprocal relationship with another person (the kind described in the second case), our relationship is what Buber calls the "I–Thou" (or "I–You") variety. According to Buber, our very existence, the existence of the I, depends upon and grows out of these two types of relationships. Without them, there is no I at all. (You might want to compare Buber's concept of a person with that discussed in Chapter 8.) It is important to recognize that I–It relationships are not always entirely bad. Although our I–Thou relationships provide the most satisfaction, we gain much in the way of knowledge from our I–It relationships as well. Sometimes it may be that looking at things objectively ("objectification") is just what is needed in our attempt to understand a situation in which we have become excessively involved. At other times, of course, a tendency to objectify must be tempered by empathy or compassion, characteristics of an I–Thou relationship.

The concept of reciprocity is viewed by many as central to good relationships. According to Aristotle, reciprocity, while not always easy to measure "objectively," is nevertheless a definitive characteristic of what he calls "perfect" friendship. We have all had relationships in which the other person acts principally as a drain on our energy. One day, a crisis arises from a fight that he had with his father. The next day, he accuses his roommate of stealing his wallet. The next day, his boss warns him that he'll be fired if he's late to work one more time. Anything has the potential to become a crisis, and whenever there is one, you are expected to devote your full attention to it. When something else occupies your attention for a moment, you are accused of not really caring about his problems. Because his problems occupy so much of your time together, your own needs and desires are barely considered. A relationship such as this one can hardly be considered a real friendship, Aristotle would argue, because it fails to meet the condition of reciprocity. Instead, it is, at best, an "incidental" friendship, one whose principal aim is selfish benefit. For Aristotle, real friendship is a moral relationship; his understanding of it is closely allied to his views about the relationship between being good and having a virtuous character. (You may wish to refer to Chapter 15 for a discussion of Aristotle's ethical views.) Only good people can have real friendships, because only good people can wish well for another for his own sake. If he wishes the same for you in return, the condition of mutuality is satisfied and a real friendship is born. For Aristotle, real friendship is an exercise in rationality. Indeed, it is only in the context of real friendships that we are able to function rationally and effectively at all.

María Lugones provides an account of how those on the "outside" of white culture and those on the "inside" can have successful, nonexploitative relationships with one another. Her concern about such relationships stems from what has come to be called "the problem of difference" within feminism (see Chapter 14 for more on this), namely, that white middle-class women have tended to assume that their perspective on women's oppression is the only one. Hence, they have often marginalized the concerns and experiences of women of color and of working-class women. This arrogance of perception, argues Lugones, prevents the flourishing of real relationships between women from different economic, racial, and ethnic backgrounds. Lugones introduces the notion of "world"-traveling as a remedy for arrogant perception, one that establishes the possibility of multifaceted and respectful relationships.

While Buber and Aristotle assume that human relationships can be a source of satisfaction (and even, in the case of Buber, a source of identity), Jean-Paul Sartre has a more pessimistic, but some might say realistic, view. According to Sartre, human relationships are nothing more, or less, than a source of conflict. Fundamental to Sartre's existentialist perspective is his notion of freedom, which he calls "being-for-itself." A person is whatever she chooses to be. What she is, is always up to her. You are a student by choice, a baseball player by choice, a computer expert by choice. Even in prison, you are free to choose what sort of prisoner you want to be. We are in a continuous process of creating the world for ourselves according to our choices. (You might want to look at Chapter 18 for a more extensive look at Sartre's views about freedom.) Our experience of freedom is brought to an abrupt end when we instead experience ourselves as what Sartre calls "being-for-others." The experience of shame is one such case. Suppose that you go home for vacation and find yourself overwhelmed with curiosity about your younger sister's relationship with her boyfriend. One evening, he calls and you answer the phone. Instead of hanging up when your sister gets on the other phone, you listen in. The conversation gets rather hot and you find yourself incapable of putting down the phone. You look up after several minutes only to discover that your mother has been watching you. You are overcome with shame. Suddenly you see yourself not as you choose to be (a sophisticated college student, respectful of others' privacy), but rather as you are seen by someone else: as an eavesdropper. It is here that you experience yourself as "being-for" another. Others trap us in their gaze and so limit our freedom. This, according to Sartre, is the fundamental experience of human relationships. In his scheme, there is no room for Buber's I–Thou.

It is a commonplace in our culture to think that friendship and romantic love are profoundly different, and that what differentiates friendship and romantic love is that the latter, but not the former, involves a sexual relationship. In his essay, Laurence Thomas challenges this assumption by providing a careful analysis of the nature of what he calls "companion friendship". He points out the features that define companion friendship, such as self-disclosure, loyalty, and fidelity. He argues that the mere addition of sex to friendship cannot account for the significance of the apparent difference between it and romantic love.

Jane English claims that to view children as "owing" anything to their parents as a result of parental sacrifice is to undermine the possibility of love between parents and children. English asks that we see grown children's obligations as being like the obligations of friendship. Thus, if children do not feel that they are friends with their parents, they have no such obligations. You might want to consider English's argument in light of what you learned about the conditions of friendship and the nature of human relationships. In particular, you might compare her notion of reciprocity with that of Aristotle.

Finally, Nancy Aronie flips the coin of parent–child relationships considered by English. What exactly are the obligations of a mother trying earnestly to be sensitive to the needs of her young son? How do they compare to the obligations of friends, of lovers? Can a mother and a son stand in an I–Thou relationship? Are parents inevitably nothing more than impediments to freedom, doomed always to misunderstand their children? Once you start thinking about questions such as these, it becomes clear why some philosophers have taken the time to reflect carefully on the complex nature of human relationships.

MARTIN BUBER

I–Thou

MARTIN BUBER *(1878–1965), a religious existentialist, was born in Vienna but lived much of his life in Israel. His most famous book is* I–Thou, *though he also wrote extensively on religious issues.*

T HE world is twofold for man in accordance with his twofold attitude.

The attitude of man is twofold in accordance with the two basic words he can speak.

The basic words are not single words but word pairs.

One basic word is the word pair I–You.

The other basic word is the word pair I–It; but this basic word is not changed when He or She takes the place of it.

Thus the I of man is also twofold.

For the I of the basic word I–You is different from that in the basic word I–It.

Basic words do not state something that might exist outside them; by being spoken they establish a mode of existence.

Basic words are spoken with one's being.

When one says You, the I of the word pair I–You is said, too.

When one says It, the I of the word pair I–It is said, too.

The basic word I–You can only be spoken with one's whole being.

The basic word I–It can never be spoken with one's whole being. . . .

The life of a human being does not exist merely in the sphere of goal-directed verbs. It does not consist merely of activities that have something for their object.

I perceive something. I feel something. I imagine something. I want something. I sense something. The life of a human being does not consist merely of all this and its like.

All this and its like is the basis of the realm of It.

But the realm of You has another basis.

Whoever says You does not have something for his object. For wherever there is something there is also another something; every It borders on other Its; It is only by virtue of bordering on others. But where You is said there is no something. You has no borders.

Whoever says You does not have something; he has nothing. But he stands in relation.

The world as experience belongs to the basic word I–It. The basic word I–You establishes the world of relation. . . .

—What, then, does one experience of the You?

—Nothing at all. For one does not experience it.

—What, then, does one know of the You?

—Only everything. For one no longer knows particulars.

The You encounters me by grace—it cannot be found by seeking. But that I speak the basic word to it is a deed of my whole being, is my essential deed.

The You encounters me. But I enter into a direct relationship to it. Thus the relationship is election and electing, passive and active at once: An action of the whole being must approach passivity, for it does away with all partial actions and thus with any sense of action, which always depends on limited exertions.

The basic word I–You can be spoken only with one's whole being. The concentration and fusion into a whole being can never be accomplished by me, can never be accomplished without me. I require a You to become; becoming I, I say You.

All actual life is encounter.

ARISTOTLE

Friendship

ARISTOTLE (384–322 B.C.) was for eighteen years a student of Plato. After Plato's death, he turned to the study of biology. In addition to his biological studies, Aristotle virtually created the science of logic and linguistics. He developed extravagant theories in physics and made significant contributions to metaphysics, politics, and aesthetics.

IT will be natural to discuss friendship or love next, for friendship is a kind of virtue or implies virtue. It is also indispensable to life. For nobody would choose to live without friends, although he were in possession of every other good. Nay, it seems that if people are rich and hold official and authoritative positions, they have the greatest need of friends; for what is the good of having this sort of prosperity if one is denied the opportunity of beneficence, which is never so freely or so admirably exercised as towards friends? Or how can it be maintained in safety and security without friends? For the greater a person's importance, the more liable it is to disaster. In poverty and other misfortunes we regard our friends as our only refuge. Again, friends are helpful to us, when we are young, as guarding us from error, and when we are growing old, as taking care of us, and supplying such deficiencies of action as are the consequences of physical weakness, and when we are in the prime of life, as prompting us to noble actions, according to the adage, "Two come together"; for two people have a greater power both of intelligence and of action *than either of the two by himself.*

It would seem that friendship or love is the natural instinct of a parent towards a child, and of a child towards a parent, not only among men, but among birds and animals generally, and among creatures of the same race towards one another, especially among men. This is the reason why we praise men who are the friends of their fellow-men or philanthropists. We may observe too in travelling how near and dear every man is to his fellow-man.

Again, it seems that friendship or love is the bond which holds states together, and that legislators set more store by it than by justice; for concord is apparently akin to friendship, and it is concord that they especially seek to promote, and faction, as being hostility to the state, that they especially try to expel.

If people are friends, there is no need of justice between them; but people may be just, and yet need friendship. Indeed it seems that justice, in its supreme form, assumes the character of friendship.

Nor is friendship indispensable only; it is also noble. We praise people who are fond of their friends, and it is thought to be a noble thing to have many friends, and there are some people who hold that to be a friend is the same thing as to be a good man.

But the subject of friendship or love is one that affords scope for a good many differences of opinion. Some people define it as a sort of likeness, and define people who are like each other as friends. Hence the sayings "Like seeks like," "Birds of a feather," and so on. Others on the contrary say that "two of a trade never agree." Upon this subject *some philosophical thinkers* indulge in more profound physical speculations; Euripides asserting that

"the parched Earth loves the rain, And the great Heaven rain-laden loves to fall Earthwards";

Heraclitus that "the contending tends together," and that "harmony most beautiful is formed of discords," and that "all things are by strife engendered"; others, among whom is Empedocles, taking the opposite view and urging that "like desires like."

The physical questions we may leave aside as not being germane to the present enquiry. But let us investigate all such questions as are of human interest and relate to characters and emotions, e.g. whether friendship can be formed among all people, or it is impossible for people to be friends if they are vicious, and whether there is one kind of friendship or more than one. . . .

It is possible, I think, to elucidate the subject of friendship or love, by determining what it is that is lovable or an object of love. For it seems that it is not everything which is loved, but only that which is lovable, and that this is what is good or pleasant or useful. It would seem too that a thing is useful if it is a means of gaining something good or pleasant, and if so, it follows that what is good and what is pleasant will be lovable in the sense of being ends.

It may be asked then, Is it that which is good *in itself,* or that which is good relatively to us, that we love? For there is sometimes a difference between them; and the same question may be asked in regard to that which is pleasant. It seems then that everybody loves what is good relatively to himself, and that, while it is the good which is lovable in an absolute sense, it is that which is good relatively to each individual that is lovable in his eyes. It may be said that everybody loves not that which is good, but that which appears good relatively to himself. But this is not an objection that will make any difference;

for in that case that which is lovable will be that which appears to be lovable.

There being three motives of friendship or love, it must be observed that we do not apply the term "friendship" or "love" to the affection felt for inanimate things. The reason is (1) that they are incapable of reciprocating affection, and (2) that we do not wish their good; for it would, I think, be ridiculous to wish the good e.g. of wine; if we wish it at all, it is only in the sense of wishing the wine to keep well, in the hope of enjoying it ourselves. But it is admitted that we ought to wish our friend's good for his sake, and not for our own. If we wish people good in this sense, we are called well-wishers, unless our good wishes are returned; such reciprocal well-wishing is called friendship or love.

But it is necessary, I think, to add, that the well-wishing must not be unknown. A person often wishes well to people whom he has not seen, but whom he supposes to be virtuous or useful; and it is possible that one of these persons may entertain the same feeling towards him. Such people then, it is clear, wish well to one another; but they cannot be properly called friends, as their disposition is unknown to each other. It follows that, if they are to be friends, they must be well-disposed to each other, and must wish each other's good, from one of the motives which have been assigned, and that each of them must know the fact of the other wishing him well.

But as the motives of friendship are specifically different, there will be a corresponding difference in the affections and friendships.

The kinds of friendship therefore will be three, being equal in number to the things which are lovable, *or are objects of friendship or love,* as every such object admits of a reciprocal affection between two persons, each of whom is aware of the other's love.

People who love each other wish each other's good in the point characteristic of their love. Accordingly those whose mutual love is based upon utility do not love each other for their own sakes, but only in so far as they derive some benefit one from another. It is the same with those whose love is based upon pleasure. Thus we are fond of witty people, not as possessing a certain character, but as being pleasant to ourselves. People then, whose love is based upon utility, are moved to affection by a sense of their own good, and people whose love is based upon pleasure, by a sense of their own pleasure; and they love a person not for being what he is in himself, but for being useful or pleasant to them. These friendships then are only friendships in an accidental sense; for the person loved is not loved as being what he is, but as being a source either of good or of pleasure. Accordingly such friendships are easily dissolved, if the persons do not continue always the same; for they abandon their love if they cease to be pleasant or useful to each other. But utility is not a permanent quality; it varies at different times. Thus, when the motive of a friendship is done away, the friendship itself is dissolved, as it was dependent upon that motive. A friendship of this kind seems especially to occur among old people, as in old age we look to profit rather than pleasure, and among such people in the prime of life or in youth as have an eye to their own interest. Friends of this kind do not generally even live together; for sometimes they are not even pleasant to one another; nor do they need the intercourse of friendship, unless they bring some profit to one another, as the pleasure which they afford goes no further than they entertain hopes of deriving benefit from it. Among these friendships we reckon the friendship of hospitality, *i.e. the friendship which exists between a host and his guests.*

It would seem that the friendship of the young is based upon pleasure; for they live by emotion and are most inclined to pursue what is pleasant to them at the moment. But as their time of life changes, their pleasures are transformed. They are therefore quick at making friendships and quick at abandoning them; for the friendship changes with the object which pleases them, and friendship of this kind is liable to sudden change. Young men are amorous too, amorousness being generally a matter of emotion and pleasure; hence they fall in love and soon afterwards fall out of love, changing from one condition to another many times in the same day. But amorous people wish to spend their days and lives together, as it is thus that they attain the object of their friendship.

The perfect friendship or love is the friendship or love of people who are good and alike in virtue; for these people are alike in wishing each other's good, in so far as they are good, and they are good in themselves. But it is people who wish the good of their friends for their friends' sake that are in the truest sense friends, as their friendship is the consequence of their own character, and is not an accident. Their friendship therefore continues as long as their virtue, and virtue is a permanent quality.

Again, each of them is good in an absolute sense, and good in relation to his friend. For good men are not only good in an absolute sense, but serve each other's interest. They are pleasant too; for the good are pleasant in an ab-

solute sense, and pleasant in relation to one another, as everybody finds pleasure in such actions as are proper to him, and the like, and all good people act alike or nearly alike.

Such a friendship is naturally permanent, as it unites in itself all the proper conditions of friendship. For the motive of all friendship or affection is good or pleasure, whether it be absolute or relative to the person who feels the affection, and it depends upon a certain similarity. In the friendship of good men all these specified conditions belong to the friends in themselves; for other friendships *only* bear a resemblance to the perfect friendship. That which is good in an absolute sense is also in an absolute sense pleasant. These are the principal objects of affection, and it is upon these that affectionate feeling, and affection in the highest and best sense, depend.

Friendships of this kind are likely to be rare; for such people are few. They require time and familiarity too; for, as the adage puts it, it is impossible for people to know one another until they have consumed the proverbial salt together; nor can people admit one another to friendship, or be friends at all, until each has been proved lovable and trustworthy to the other.

People, who are quick to treat one another as friends, wish to be friends but are not so really, unless they are lovable and know each other to be lovable; for the wish to be friends may arise in a minute, but not friendship. . . .

It is the friendship of the good which is friendship in the truest sense, as has been said several times. For it seems that, while that which is good or pleasant in an absolute sense is an object of love and desire, that which is good or pleasant to each individual is an object of love or desire to him; but the love or desire of one good man for another depends upon such goodness and pleasantness as are at once absolute and relative to the good.

Affection resembles a feeling but friendship resembles a moral state. For while affection may be felt for inanimate as much as for animate things, the love of friends for one another implies moral purpose, and such purpose is the outcome of a moral state.

Again, we wish the good of those whom we love for their own sake, and the wish is governed not by feeling but by the moral state. In loving our friend too, we love what is good for ourselves; as when a good man becomes a friend, he becomes a blessing to his friend. Accordingly each of two friends loves what is good for himself, and returns as much as he receives in good wishes and in pleasure; for, as the proverb says, equality is friendship.

MARÍA LUGONES

Playfulness, "World"-Traveling, and Loving Perception

MARÍA C. LUGONES *teaches philosophy at Carleton College in Minnesota and radical grassroots politics at Escuela Popular Norteña. She is working on a book on pluralist feminism. She has written extensively on issues in feminist and cultural theory.*

"WORLDS" AND "WORLD" TRAVELING

SOME time ago I came to be in a state of profound confusion as I experienced myself as both having and not having a particular attribute. I was sure I had the attribute in question and, on the other hand, I was sure that I did not have it. I remain convinced that I both have and do not have this attribute. The attribute is playfulness. I am sure that I am a playful person. On the other hand, I can say, painfully, that I am not a playful person. I am not a

playful person in certain worlds. One of the things I did as I became confused was to call my friends, far away people who knew me well, to see whether or not I was playful. Maybe they could help me out of my confusion. They said to me, "Of course you are playful" and they said it with the same conviction that I had about it. Of course I am playful. Those people who were around me said to me, "No, you are not playful. You are a serious woman. You just take everything seriously." They were just as sure about what they said to me and could offer me every bit of evidence that one could need to conclude that they were right. So I said to myself: "Okay, maybe what's happening here is that there is an attribute that I do have but there are certain worlds in which I am not at ease and it is because I'm not at ease in those worlds that I don't have that attribute in those worlds. But what does that mean?" I was worried both about what I meant by "worlds" when I said "in some worlds I do not have the attribute" and what I meant by saying that lack of ease was what led me not to be playful in those worlds. Because you see, if it was just a matter of lack of ease, I could work on it.

I can explain some of what I mean by a "world." I do not want the fixity of a definition at this point, because I think the term is suggestive and I do not want to close the suggestiveness of it too soon. I can offer some characteristics that serve to distinguish between a "world," a utopia, a possible world in the philosophical sense, and a world view. By a "world" I do not mean a utopia at all. A utopia does not count as a world in my sense. The "worlds" that I am talking about are possible. But a possible world is not what I mean by a "world" and I do not mean a world-view, though something like a world-view is involved here.

For something to be a "world" in my sense it has to be inhabited at present by some flesh and blood people. That is why it cannot be a utopia. It may also be inhabited by some imaginary people. It may be inhabited by people who are dead or people that the inhabitants of this "world" met in some other "world" and now have in this "world" in imagination.

A "world" in my sense may be an actual society given its dominant culture's description and construction of life, in-cluding a construction of the relationships of production, of gender, race, etc. But a "world" can also be such a society given a non-dominant construction, or it can be such a society or *a* society given an idiosyncratic construction. As we will see it is problematic to say that these are all constructions of the same society. But they are different "worlds."

A "world" need not be a construction of a whole society. It may be a construction of a tiny portion of a particular society. It may be inhabited by just a few people. Some "worlds" are bigger than others.

A "world" may be incomplete in that things in it may not be altogether constructed or some things may be constructed negatively (they are not what 'they' are in some other "world.") Or the "world" may be incomplete because it may have references to things that do not quite exist in it, references to things like Brazil, where Brazil is not quite part of that "world". Given lesbian feminism, the construction of 'lesbian' is purposefully and healthily still up in the air, in the process of becoming. What it is to be a Hispanic in this country is, in a dominant Anglo construction purposefully incomplete. Thus one cannot really answer questions of the sort "What is a Hispanic?", "Who counts as a Hispanic?", "Are Latinos, Chicanos, Hispanos, black dominicans, white cubans, korean-colombians, italian-argentinians, hispanic?" What it is to be a 'hispanic' in the varied so-called hispanic communities in the U.S. is also yet up in the air. We have not yet decided whether there is something like a 'Hispanic' in our varied "worlds." So, a "world" may be an incomplete visionary non-utopian construction of life or it may be a traditional construction of life. A traditional Hispano construction of Northern New

Mexican life is a "world." Such a traditional construction, in the face of a racist, ethnocentrist, money-centered anglo construction of Northern New Mexican life is highly unstable because Anglos have the means for imperialist destruction of traditional Hispano "worlds."

In a "world" some of the inhabitants may not understand or hold the particular construction of them that constructs them in that "world." So, there may be "worlds" that construct me in ways that I do not even understand. Or it may be that I understand the construction, but do not hold it of myself. I may not accept it as an account of myself, a construction of myself. And yet, I may be *animating* such a construction.

One can "travel" between these "worlds" and one can inhabit more than one of these "worlds" at the very same time. I think that most of us who are outside the mainstream of, for example, the U.S. dominant construction or organization of life are "world travellers" as a matter of necessity and of survival. It seems to me that inhabiting more than one "world" at the same time and "travelling" between "worlds" is part and parcel of our experience and our situation. One can be at the same time in a "world" that constructs one as stereotypically latin, for example, and in a "world" that constructs one as latin. Being stereotypically latin and being simply latin are different simultaneous constructions of persons that are part of different "worlds." One animates one or the other or both at the same time without necessarily confusing them, though simultaneous enactment can be confusing if one is not on one's guard.

In describing my sense of a "world," I mean to be offering a description of experience, something that is true to experience even if it is ontologically problematic. Though I would think that any account of identity that could not be true to this experience of outsiders to the mainstream would be faulty even if ontologically unproblematic. Its ease would constrain, erase, or deem aberrant experience that has within it significant insights into non-imperialistic understanding between people.

Those of us who are "world"-travellers have the distinct experience of being different in different "worlds" and of having the capacity to remember other "worlds" and ourselves in them. We can say "That is me there, and I am happy in that 'world.'" So, the experience is of being a different person in different "worlds" and yet of having memory of oneself as different without quite having the sense of there being any underlying "I." So I can say "that is me there and I am so playful in that 'world.'" I say "That is *me* in that 'world'" not because I recognize myself in that person, rather the first person statement is non-inferential. I may well recognize that that person has abilities that I do not have and yet the having or not having of the abilities is always an "I have . . ." and "I do not have . . . ," i.e. it is always experienced in the first person.

The shift from being one person to being a different person is what I call "travel". This shift may not be willful or even conscious, and one may be completely unaware of being different than one is in a different "world," and may not recognize that one is in a different "world." Even though the shift can be done willfully, it is not a matter of acting. One does not pose as something else, one does not pretend to be, for example, someone of a different personality or character or someone who uses space or language differently than the other person. Rather one is someone who has that personality or character or uses space and language in that particular way. The "one" here does not refer to some underlying "I." One does not *experience* any underlying "I."

BEING AT EASE IN A "WORLD"

In investigating what I mean by "being at ease in a 'world'," I will describe different ways of being at ease. One may be at ease in one or in all of these ways. There is a maximal way of being at ease, viz. being at ease in all of these ways. I take this maximal way of being at ease to be somewhat dangerous because it tends to produce people who have no inclination to travel across "worlds" or have no experience of "world" travelling.

The first way of being at ease in a particular "world" is by being a fluent speaker in that "world." I know all the norms that there are to be followed, I know all the words that there are to be spoken. I know all the moves. I am confident.

Another way of being at ease is by being normatively happy. I agree with all the norms, I could not love any norms better. I am asked to do just what I want to do or what I think I should do. At ease.

Another way of being at ease in a "world" is by being humanly bonded. I am with those I love and they love me too. It should be noticed that I may be with those I love and be at ease because of them in a "world" that is otherwise as hostile to me as "worlds" get.

Finally one may be at ease because one has a history with others that is shared, especially daily history, the kind of shared history that one sees exemplified by the response to the "Do you remember poodle skirts?" question. There you are, with people you do not know at all. The question is posed and then they all begin talking about their poodle skirt stories. I have been in such situations without knowing what poodle skirts, for example, were and I felt so ill at ease because it was not *my* history. The other people did not particularly know each other. It is not that they were humanly bonded. Probably they did not have much politically in common either. But poodle skirts were in their shared history.

One may be at ease in one of these ways or in all of them. Notice that when one says meaningfully "This is *my* world," one may not be at ease in it. Or one may be at ease in it only in some of these respects and not in others. To say of some "world" that it is "*my* world" is to make an evaluation. One may privilege one or more "worlds" in this way for a variety of reasons: for example because one experiences oneself as an agent in a fuller sense than one experiences "oneself" in other "worlds." One may disown a "world" because one has first person memories of a person who is so thoroughly dominated that she has no sense of exercising her own will or has a sense of having serious difficulties in performing actions that are willed by herself and no difficulty in performing actions willed by others. One may say of a "world" that it is "my world" because one is at ease in it, i.e. being at ease in a "world" may be the basis for the evaluation.

Given the clarification of what I mean by a "world," "world"-travel, and being at ease in a "world," we are in a position to return to my problematic attribute, playfulness. It may be that in this "world" in which I am so unplayful, I am a different person than in the "world" in which I am playful. Or it may be that the "world" in which I am unplayful is constructed in such a way that I could be playful in it. I could practice, even though that "world" is constructed in such a way that my being playful in it is kind of hard. In describing what I take a "world" to be, I emphasized the first possibility as both the one that is truest to the experience of "outsiders" to the mainstream and as ontologically problematic because the "I" is identified in some sense as one and in some sense as a plurality. I identify myself as myself through memory and I retain myself as different in memory. When I travel from one "world" to another, I have this image, this memory of myself as playful in this other "world." I can then be in a particular "world" and have a double image of myself as, for example, playful and as not playful. But this is a very familiar and recognizable phenomenon to the outsider to the mainstream in some central cases: when in one "world" I animate, for example, that "world's" caricature of the person I am in the other "world." I can have both images of myself and to the extent that I can materialize or animate both images at the same time I become an ambiguous being. This is very much a part of trickery and foolery. It is worth remembering that the trickster and the fool are significant characters in many non-dominant or outsider cultures. One then sees any particular "world" with these double edges and sees absurdity in them and so inhabits oneself differently. Given that latins are constructed in Anglo "worlds" as stereotypically intense—intensity being a central characteristic of at least one of the anglo stereotypes of latins—and given that many latins, myself included, are genuinely intense, I can say

to myself, "I am intense" and take a hold of the double meaning. And furthermore, I can be stereotypically intense or be the real thing and, if you are Anglo, you do not know when I am which *because* I am Latin-American. As Latin-American I am an ambiguous being, a two-imaged self: I can see that gringos see me as stereotypically intense because I am, as a Latin-American, constructed that way but I may or may not *intentionally* animate the stereotype or the real thing knowing that you may not see it in anything other than in the stereotypical construction. This ambiguity is funny and is not just funny, it is survival-rich. We can also make the picture of those who dominate us funny precisely because we can see the double edge, we can see them doubly constructed, we can see the plurality in them. So we know truths that only the fool can speak and only the trickster can play out without harm. We inhabit "worlds" and travel across them and keep all the memories.

Sometimes the "world"-traveller has a double image of herself and each self includes as important ingredients of itself one or more attributes that are *incompatible* with one or more of the attributes of the other self: for example being playful and being unplayful. To the extent that the attribute is an important ingredient of the self she is in that "world," i.e., to the extent that there is a particularly good fit between that "world" and her having that attribute in it and to the extent that the attribute is personality or character central, that "world" would have to be changed if she is to be playful in it. It is not the case that if she could come to be at ease in it, she would be her own playful self. Because the attribute is personality or character central and there is such a good fit between that "world" and her being constructed with that attribute as central, *she* cannot become playful, she is unplayful. To become playful would be for her to become a contradictory being. So I am suggesting that the lack of ease solution cannot be a solution to my problematic case. My problem is not one of lack of ease. I am suggesting that I can understand my confusion about whether I am or am not playful by saying that I am both and that I am different persons in different "worlds" and can remember myself in both as I am in the other. I am a plurality of selves. This is to understand my confusion because *it is to come to see it as a piece* with much of the rest of my experience as an outsider in some of the "worlds" that I inhabit and of a piece with significant aspects of the experience of non-dominant people in the "worlds" of their dominators.

So, though I may not be at ease in the "worlds" in which I am not constructed playful, it is not that I am not playful *because* I am not at ease. The two are compatible. But lack of playfulness is not caused by lack of ease. Lack of playfulness is not symptomatic of lack of ease but of lack of health. I am not a healthy being in the "worlds" that construct me unplayful.

PLAYFULNESS

I had a very personal stake in investigating this topic. Playfulness is not only the attribute that was the source of my confusion and the attitude that I recommend as the loving attitude in travelling across "worlds," I am also scared of ending up a serious human being, someone with no multi-dimensionality, with no fun in life, someone who is just someone who has had the fun constructed out of her. I am seriously scared of getting stuck in a "world" that constructs me that way. A world that I have no escape from and in which I cannot be playful.

I thought about what it is to be playful and what it is to play and I did this thinking in a "world" in which I only remember myself as playful and in which all of those who know me as playful are imaginary beings. A "world" in which I am scared of losing my memories of myself as playful or have them erased from me. Because I live in such a "world," after I formulated my own sense of what it is to be playful and to play I decided that I needed to "go to the literature." I read two classics on the subject: Johan Huizinga's *Homo Ludens* and Hans-Georg Gadamer's chapter on the concept of play in his *Truth and Method*. I discovered, to my amazement, that what I thought about play and playfulness, if they were right, was absolutely wrong. Though I will not provide the arguments for this interpretation of Gadamer and Huizinga here, I understood that both of them have an agonistic sense of 'play.' Play and playfulness have, ultimately, to do with contest, with winning, losing, battling. The sense of playfulness that I have in mind has nothing to do with those things. So, I tried to elucidate both senses of play and playfulness by contrasting them to each other. The contrast helped me see the attitude that I have in mind as the loving attitude in travelling across "worlds" more clearly.

An agonistic sense of playfulness is one in which *competence* is supreme. You better know the rules of the game. In agonistic play there is risk, there is *uncertainty*, but the uncertainty is about who is going to win and who is going to lose. There are rules that inspire hostility. The attitude of *playfulness is conceived as secondary to or derivative from play.* Since play is agon, then the only conceivable playful attitude is an agonistic one (the attitude does not turn an activity into play, but rather presupposes an activity that is play). One of the paradigmatic ways of playing for both Gadamer and Huizinga is role-playing. In role-playing, the person who is a participant in the game has a *fixed conception of him or herself.* I also think that the players are imbued with *self-importance* in agonistic play since they are so keen on winning given their own merits, their very own competence.

When considering the value of "world"-travelling and whether playfulness is the loving attitude to have while travelling, I recognized the agonistic attitude as inimical to travelling across "worlds." The agonistic traveller is a conqueror, an imperialist. Huizinga, in his classic book on play, interprets Western civilization as play. That is an interesting thing for Third World people to think about. Western civilization has been interpreted by a white western man as play in the agonistic sense of play. Huizinga reviews western law, art, and many other aspects of western culture and sees agon in all of them. Agonistic playfulness leads those who attempt to travel to another "world" with this attitude to failure. Agonistic travellers fail consistently in their attempt to travel because what they do is to try to conquer the other "world." The attempt is not an attempt to try to erase the other "world." That is what assimilation is all about. Assimilation is the destruction of other people's "worlds." So, the agonistic attitude, the playful attitude given western man's construction of playfulness, is not a healthy, loving attitude to have in travelling across "worlds." Notice that given the agonistic attitude one *cannot* travel across

"worlds," though one can kill other "worlds" with it. So for people who are interested in crossing racial and ethnic boundaries, an arrogant western man's construction of playfulness is deadly. One cannot cross the boundaries with it. One needs to give up such an attitude if one wants to travel.

So then, what is the loving playfulness that I have in mind? Let me begin with one example: We are by the river bank. The river is very, very low. Almost dry. Bits of water here and there. Little pools with a few trout hiding under the rocks. But mostly is wet stones, grey on the outside. We walk on the stones for awhile. You pick up a stone and crash it onto the others. As it breaks, it is quite wet inside and it is very colorful, very pretty. I pick up a stone and break it and run toward the pieces to see the colors. They are beautiful. I laugh and bring the pieces back to you and you are doing the same with your pieces. We keep on crashing stones for hours, anxious to see the beautiful new colors. We are playing. The playfulness of our activity does not presuppose that there is something like "crashing stones" that is a particular form of play with its own rules. Rather *the attitude that carries us through the activity, a playful attitude, turns the activity into play.* Our activity has no rules, though it is certainly intentional activity and we both understand what we are doing. The playfulness that gives meaning to our activity includes uncertainty, but in this case the uncertainty is an *openness to surprise.* This is a particular metaphysical attitude that does not expect the world to be neatly packaged, ruly. Rules may fail to explain what we are doing. We are not self-important, we are not fixed in particular constructions of ourselves, which is part of saying that we are *open to self-construction.*

We may not have rules, and when we do have rules, *there are no rules that are to us sacred.* We are not worried about competence. We are not wedded to a particular way of doing things. While playful we have not abandoned ourselves to, nor are we stuck in, any particular "world." We *are there creatively.* We are not passive.

Playfulness is, in part, an openness to being a fool, which is a combination of not worrying about competence, not being self-important, not taking norms as sacred and finding ambiguity and double edges a source of wisdom and delight.

So, positively, the playful attitude involves openness to surprise, openness to being a fool, openness to self-construction or reconstruction and to construction or reconstruction of the "worlds" we inhabit playfully. Negatively, playfulness is characterized by uncertainty, lack of self-importance, absence of rules or a not taking rules as sacred, a not worrying about competence and a lack of abandonment to a particular construction of oneself, others and one's relation to them. In attempting to take a hold of oneself and of one's relation to others in a particular "world," one may study, examine and come to understand oneself. One may then see what the possibilities for play are for the being one is in that "world." One may even decide to inhabit that self fully in order to understand it better and find its creative possibilities. All of this is just self-reflection and it is quite different from resigning or abandoning oneself to the particular construction of oneself that one is attempting to take a hold of.

CONCLUSION

There are "worlds" we enter at our own risk, "worlds" that have agon, conquest, and arrogance as the main ingredients in their ethos. These are "worlds" that we enter out of necessity and which would be foolish to enter playfully in either the agonistic sense or in my sense. In such "worlds" *we* are not playful.

But there are "worlds" that we can travel to lovingly and travelling to them is part of loving at least some of their inhabitants. The reason why I think that travelling to someone's "world" is a way of identifying with them is because by travelling to their "world" we can understand *what is to be them and what it is to be ourselves in their eyes.* Only when we have travelled to each other's "worlds" are we fully subjects to each other (I agree with Hegel that self-recognition requires other subjects, but I disagree with his claim that it requires tension or hostility).

Knowing other women's "worlds" is part of knowing them and knowing them is part of loving them. Notice that the knowing can be done in greater or lesser depth, as can the loving. Also notice that travelling to another's "world" is not the same as becoming intimate with them. Intimacy is constituted in part by a very deep knowledge of the other self and "world" travelling is only part of having this knowledge. Also notice that some people, in particular those who are outsiders to the mainstream, can be known only to the extent that they are known in several "worlds" and as "world"-travellers.

Without knowing the other's "world," one does not know the other, and without knowing the other one is really alone in the other's presence because the other is only dimly present to one.

Through travelling to other people's "worlds" we discover that there are "worlds" in which those who are the victims of arrogant perception are really subjects, lively beings, resistors, constructors of visions even though in the mainstream construction they are animated only by the arrogant perceiver and are pliable, foldable, file-awayable, classifiable. I always imagine the Aristotelian slave as pliable and foldable at night or after he or she cannot work anymore (when he or she dies as a tool). Aristotle tells us nothing about the slave *apart from the master.* We know the slave only through the master. The slave is a tool of the master. After working hours he or she is folded and placed in a drawer till the next morning. . . .

So, in recommending "world"-travelling and identification through "world"-travelling as part of loving other women, I am suggesting disloyalty to arrogant perceivers, including the arrogant perceiver in ourselves, and to their constructions of women. In revealing agonistic playfulness as incompatible with "world"-travelling, I am revealing both its affinity with imperialism and arrogant perception and its incompatibility with loving and loving perception.

LAURENCE THOMAS

Friends and Lovers

LAURENCE THOMAS *teaches philosophy at Syracuse University and writes in the areas of social philosophy and moral psychology. His most recent book is* Vessels of Evil: American Slavery and the Holocaust *(1994).*

TIME was when it seemed rather easy to distinguish conceptually between romantic love and friendship. Supposedly, there were natural roles for women and natural roles for men; and it was natural for a person to fall in love with a person of the opposite gender: a woman with a man and a man with a woman. Sometimes members of the same gender fell in love with one another, but such romantic love, if it was called that, was considered perverted. In times past, romantic love was tied to the view that men and women complement one another in a deeper and more profound way than is possible for members of the same gender to comple-

ment one another, however close they might be as friends. The view has it that while ideally friends of the same gender flourish together, the extent to which persons of opposite genders flourish together far exceeds anything friendship might offer. A view of natural roles for women and men according to which women and men so complement one another yields a conceptual difference between friendship and romantic love. The former turns out to be an important but lesser form of interpersonal interaction. Let us refer to the conception of love suggested here as courtly romantic love.

Times are changing. Nowadays a great many liberals who align themselves with feminists subscribe to what I call an egalitarian conception of romantic love. This conception holds that whatever differences there are between women and men—it need not deny that there are any—the differences do not justify an assignment of social roles according to gender. It is not natural for women to care for the home and men to be the breadwinners; it is not natural for women to be subordinate to men; and so on. Indeed, the egalitarian conception rejects both the idea that the natural object of romantic love is a person of the opposite gender as well as the concomitant idea that romantic love between members of the same gender is perverted in some sense.

Given this conception of romantic love, a question that naturally arises is: What is the conceptual difference between it and friendship? The difference that most quickly comes to mind is sexual involvement: Romantic lovers are involved as sexual partners; friends are not. Indeed, it is not clear that one can point to anything else to distinguish these two interpersonal relationships. But can this difference bear the enormous weight that is put upon it? I do not believe so, as I try to show in this essay. That is, as a way of capturing what conceptually distinguishes friendship from egalitarian romantic love, sexual involvement with respect to the latter simply will not do. . . .

FRIENDSHIPS

Friends love one another, and for that very reason they take delight in one another's flourishing. There is an enormous bond of trust between them— a bond that is cemented by mutual self-disclosure. And they have a commanding perspective of one another's

lives—a perspective that comes in the wake of their mutual self-disclosure and their maximizing the amount of time that they spend together. Finally, friends are deeply loyal to one another. Obviously, not all who call themselves friends are friends in this way. There are, following Aristotle, lesser forms of friendship—friendships of convenience and utility. So let us refer to individuals who are friends in the way just delineated as companion friends.

As one might gather, what I take to be special about companion friends is that they share enormous amounts of private information about themselves with one another. I regard this as the predominant way in which such friends can and do contribute to one another's flourishing, where the emphasis here is upon the improvement of character and personality. Of course, I hardly mean to suggest that companion friends do not help one another in the usual sorts of ways. They speak to one another's needs, as their resources permit it. However, I assume that, by and large, companion friends are self-sufficient or, in any case, that the material help each provides the other is quite ancillary to the friendship. This assumption, far from revealing a Western bias, enables us to see more clearly how rich a friendship can be that does not turn upon material offerings.

There are a variety of ways in which the sharing of private and personal information enables friends to contribute to one another's flourishing. . . .

What we are entitled to discuss with others regarding their private lives is not so much a function of what we know about them as it is of the extent to which we have been invited by their self-disclosure to raise an issue with them. We may think of private information as information about a person that the members-at-large of any given community are not entitled to have at their disposal. One can be very public about things that are most private, as is the couple who openly talk about their sex life or the man who tells everyone what he earns. And that which is private can be known by several people: The five people who know that Jones was raped last year are those to whom Jones turned for comfort; those who have access to a faculty member's salary are the dean, the department head, and the appropriate members in the personnel department; the bank teller and the customer know that the customer just deposited a check for $25,000. Yet in each case the relevant information is private. Of course, whether a piece of information is private is not always obvious; indeed, whether it is may even be indeterminate. But this simply reveals what we already know, which is that life is full of different cases.

Now, it is because companion friends disclose considerable private information to one another that they can, without impropriety, raise issues and offer commentary concerning one another's behavior (words and deeds) that others cannot do without impropriety. Suppose, for instance, that contrary to what anyone would have thought, Murray uses formality to hide sexual attraction and has revealed this to Bower. Then Bower's querying Murray about her very formal behavior with so-and-so has a reasonableness to it that it could not otherwise have in the absence of this information about the way in which Murray uses formal behavior. What is more, Murray knows this.

Because companion friends invite one another, through reciprocal self-disclosure, to raise probing questions and press issues about one another's private lives, they can masterfully contribute to one another's moral flourishing in that through their interaction, self-examination and in turn self-understanding are facilitated. . . .

Mutual love, trust, and self-disclosure are among the factors that give rise to loyalty. Companion friends are quite loyal to one another. Now, loyalty is to be distinguished from altruism in the following way. Loyalty presupposes a pre-existing bond or tie; altruism does not. Perfect strangers can be quite altruistic toward one another, but they cannot be loyal to one another under such circumstances. Loyalty involves a commitment to the good of a specific individual, whereas altruism is simply a matter of bestowing benefits—benefits that can be distributed indiscriminately first to this one and then to that one, as the needs of individuals require. Altruistic people can move from one person to the next offering assistance. By contrast, loyal people stand by particular people (up to a point, at any rate) even when the evidence clearly suggests that the individuals will be defeated in their aims.

• • •

An important matter that I have not yet touched upon pertains to physical bonding between friends. In Western culture, at any rate, it would seem that there is far more physical bonding between women than men. It is not that men do not touch one another or show affection to one another; rather, it is that none of this has the spontaneity that is characteristic of female friendships. Male touching is very well defined: on the shoulder except when on the sports field, where the buttocks may be touched. A hug is appropriate given a crisis or as a greeting after an extremely long absence. In Europe there is the greeting that comes with a kiss, and men sometimes walk arm in arm in public. Still, none of this has the spontaneity of female affection. There is an expression of affection, which for lack of a better term I say comes under the rubric of mothering. In their comforting and encouraging of one another, women are much more physical and affectionate. As a token of encouragement a woman might give another close woman friend a kiss; or during trying times a woman might hold and rock a close woman friend. Male friendships do not exhibit this form of physical bonding. Since I believe that physical bonding is of the utmost importance in forming ties, what I infer from this is that female–female friendships have a depth to them that male–male friendships do not. The former reach the ideal of what I have called companion friendship to a much greater degree. I believe that these considerations give further support to the main claim of this paper.

More generally, I have said nothing about nonverbal behavior in friendships. That is not because I discount it; on the contrary, I take it to be of enormous importance. I have focused upon verbal behavior because of the absolutely indispensable role that conversation has in sharing information and establishing trust.

•   •   •

I believe that the sensual is a part of the richness of human life and that female–female friendships participate in that richness more fully than male–male friendships. And when I read a novel like Alice Walker's *The Color Purple* and appreciate the reality of sexism in general and, in particular, the reality that had not black women *physically* encouraged and comforted one another in both a racist and sexist world they most certainly would not have survived, I understand more fully that although the erotic is an important part of what the sensual is about, it is only a part.

ROMANTIC LOVE

Sexual passion is the fuel of romantic love—or so tradition has it. One is electrified by the features, style, and manners of one's would-be lover. The idea, presumably, is that when such electrification is reciprocated between two people, they are compatible enough to spend an eternity together; and the yearning that each has for the other is spoken to—not extinguished—through their sexual union. In the context of marriage, this union even has the blessings of Christianity, which (as traditionally interpreted) eschews sexual expression in all other respects.

For all the beauty that is now associated with the idea of romantic love, it may very well be that its origins are less than morally palpable. The Greeks thought that only men were capable of discerning and therefore experiencing true beauty. It was held natural for men to have greater affection for one another than for women because of the supposedly superior discerning and, more generally, intellectual powers of men; though since men want beautiful children, it was held natural for them to be attracted to beautiful women. The Judeo-Christian tradition, which does considerably better than the Greeks did in allowing women to appreciate beauty, still leaves much to be desired in terms of its attitude toward the intellectual powers of women. Women are still subordinate to men. Moreover, the woman is looking for a good provider for herself and her children; and the man is looking for a beautiful and faithful woman to provide for and to bear his children. Thus, on this view, women and men bring to their romantic relationship quite different gifts and natural talents, children aside. The woman is compassionate, caring, and understanding; the man is firm and decisive. He is the voice of reason and so the one who leads. Men and women find one another electrifying for rather different reasons quite apart from sexual attraction itself. This is romantic love traditionally construed—that is, what I call courtly romantic love.

As I have made clear, egalitarian romantic love does not have the asymmetry just sketched. What it does inherit from courtly romantic love, however, is the importance of sexual passion. . . . To sexual passion it would seem that this conception of romantic love adds only friendship, as there are no natural roles for women and men to play. Nor, in particular, is it held that sexual passion is more deeply kindled, or that romantic love is somehow more complete, when between women and men. Nor, again, does this conception of romantic love hold that fulfillment is tied to having offspring. It cannot, since it allows that equally fulfilling romantic love can occur between members of the same gender. Egalitarian romantic love, then, would seem to be reducible to sexual passion plus companion friendship.

Now, of course, there can be no ignoring the significance and power of sexual passion. One must allow, and not just for the sake of argument, that sexual intercourse between two individuals can make a qualitative difference in

their relationship. The issue, however, is whether the difference between friendship and romantic love can turn it on. I do not believe so.

FRIENDS AND LOVERS

The most pressing concern that arises when sexual intercourse is an expression of romantic love is that of fidelity—so much so that the two would seem to be conceptually linked. By contrast, the issue of fidelity or, rather, something that mirrors it does not seem to arise in the context of companion friendship; and this, too, seems be a conceptual truth. If so, then it would appear that the sexual component can, after all, bear the weight that the difference between romantic love and companion friendship puts upon it. Indeed, since fidelity is (or can be construed as) a moral issue, we have a moral difference between romantic love and companion friendship if, as a matter of conceptual truth, the issue of fidelity can arise in connection with the former only, and not the latter.

• • •

At this juncture let me pause just to record my awareness of the fact that the expressions "sexual intercourse" and "having sex" need not be strictly synonymous, with the latter having a wider range than the former; for the latter more clearly includes intimate physical activities that do not have coitus (vaginal penetration) as their final aim. Many individuals regard themselves as having (had) sex without having (had) sexual intercourse. The question of fidelity, of course, can be raised in either case, although it is clear that I am doing so primarily with sexual intercourse in mind. This is due to the historical fact that marriage has served as the paradigm context in which the issue of fidelity has been raised. In taking this route, I do not mean to disparage life styles or sexual orientations where coitus is not the final aim of intimate physical activity.

. . . The issue before us is whether the conceptual landscape of romantic love and companion friendship is as it is generally thought to be with respect to fidelity, and not what the practice is at present. It is indisputable that, currently, sexual involvement between romantic lovers is taken as the behavioral sign of union between them. A couple who have done everything else save have sex are thought to have yet a step to go. Indeed, it is regarded as necessary to consummate a marriage. Fidelity is important precisely because of the significance that the sex act has between romantic lovers. But the issue is not whether there is a widely held convention according to which the sex act between romantic lovers has the significance it has; for it is obvious that there is such a convention. Rather, the issue is whether it is a conceptual truth that this act must be taken to have this significance. And one does not show the latter simply by pointing to the universality of a convention.

Now, one extraordinarily compelling reason for maintaining that sexual intercourse need not have the significance that we now take it to have with regard to fidelity is that it has not always had that significance in Western culture. Fidelity as we now conceive of it is tied to monogamy, which was ushered in by Christianity. Monogamy just is the view that at any given time a person should be involved in a sexual relationship with only one other person. Thus it is not sexual intercourse as such that makes fidelity a pressing issue between romantic lovers; rather, a monogamous view of sexual intercourse does. A different issue altogether is whether a monogamous view of sexual intercourse is preferable to a nonmonogamous one. I have not dealt with this issue at all.

This is worth noting: A consideration that powerfully supports what has just been said is that even in the context of monogamous relationships, men have generally thought the requirement of fidelity did not hold as stringently for them as it did for their female lovers; and more than a few women have been understanding in this regard. It is no doubt true that sexism is operating rather explicitly here. But what follows from this? Not that the point made is mistaken, but that in a sexist world there has been a double standard with respect to fidelity.

Let us now look at companion friendships. Does it hold conceptually that nothing mirroring the issue of fidelity can arise in this context? I do not believe so. Fidelity has what we may call a possessive structure to it: There is something x which belongs to A and something y which belongs to B; and as a sign of unity between them A and B share x and y between them in that A allows B access to x and B allows A access to y; and none other has access to x and y. Indeed, x and y cannot be shared with any other without running the risk of rupturing the unity between A and B; and each believes this, as well as believing that the other believes this.

Well, suppose the widespread practice was that when two individuals took themselves to become companion friends, they purchased two very fine glasses of crystal. It is worth noting that the attitude of the friends toward the crystal would mirror the attitude of fidelity in romantic love. It would certainly be expected by both friends that neither would leave these crystal glasses out for anybody and everybody to use or give them over to day-to-day use. The expectation, surely, would be that they would use the crystal glasses on special occasions, and most preferably with one another.

Moreover, suppose that the companion friendship between, say, *A* and *B* dissolves and *A* goes on to form a new companion friendship with *C,* where *A* and *C* in turn purchase fine crystal. It is very unlikely that *A* will parade in front of *C* the crystal that belongs to *A* and *B*. And one reason for thinking this is that in general we are careful in how we exalt our past friendships in front of our present ones. In particular, we are careful not to speak so highly of past companion friendships as to suggest that the present ones are inferior to them. And this is rather like not making too much of a previous lover. It is one thing to have learned some invaluable lessons from previous lovers or companion friends and to have grown during the time spent with them; it is another thing entirely to suggest that a past relationship was superior to the present one. This is so, interestingly, even if it was the death of the previous friend or lover that ended the relationship. Of course, none of this is meant to deny that previous relationships can be better; the point, rather, is that normally we do not extol the virtues of previous ones to our present lover or companion friend—at least not to the point of making it clear that our present relationship is inferior to a previous one. These comparative

remarks are meant to show that the crystal example is not nearly as far-fetched as it might have first seemed. And this in turn supports the idea that something mirroring fidelity can hold among companion friendships.

A further consideration in support of this claim is that companion friends can be given to jealousy in precisely the same way that lovers are. Friends make time for one another; and if one fails to do so too often, this becomes a source of concern to the other—which holds, a fortiori, if it turns out too often that it is in order to do something with a third person that the other makes excuses. More to the point, a person who appears to be a potential threat to a friendship will be a cause of concern and will generally occasion feelings of jealousy. Furthermore, not only is it the case that sometimes a friend is jealous of the other's spouse-to-be, believing that the friendship will be qualitatively different on account of the marriage, but there are times when the spouse-to-be or the spouse-in-fact is jealous of the friend, believing that the friend is an obstacle to the marriage's flourishing in the desired way.

• • •

I have claimed that the crystal example can mirror sexual fidelity in important respects. I have not claimed that it is exactly the same as fidelity. There is clearly a difference in that revealing one's body before another is a form of self-disclosure. Obviously, the crystal scenario does not admit of this interpretation. And we might think that herein lies the difference, that revealing one's body before another is the ultimate form of self-disclosure. Perhaps. But this need not be so. For one thing, not all sexual intercourse admits of this sort of behavior. For another, revealing information about oneself really is the ultimate form of self-disclosure. To reveal to one's lover that one has been raped is a far deeper form of self-disclosure than is revealing one's body. This consideration is supported by the fact that in contexts where everyone is without clothing— nudist beaches and colonies, for instance—revealing one's body no longer has the air of self-disclosure, though the significance of sex itself hardly seems to be diminished on that account.

Two friends purchasing fine crystal is hardly the same as lovers engaging in sexual intercourse. There can be no doubt about that. But then, the issue was not that at all, but whether as a matter of conceptual truth nothing mirroring fidelity could obtain between friendships. And it is this that I have called into question, on the ground that fidelity has what I have called a possessive structure to it. I take my remarks about jealousy to underscore this point; for jealousy is a sign of possessiveness. Not for a moment do I suppose that possessiveness is out of place among either friends or romantic lovers. The point just is, however, that it is there in both relationships.

The argument has developed in two ways. First, I have argued that there is no conceptual reason why sexual intercourse must have the significance it has with regard to fidelity, since there is no logical reason to embrace the monogamous conception of sexual intercourse. Second, I have argued that there is no conceptual bar to friendship's having a component that mirrors fidelity.

My aim in this essay has been to show that if romantic love is understood as sex plus friendship, then we do not have much of a conceptual difference between romantic love and friendship. I have not denied that sex can make a qualitative difference in a relationship between two people. Quite the contrary, I have assumed that it does. Then I have argued that in the respect in which one might have thought it makes for a conceptual difference in the two forms of interpersonal relationships—merely, in connection with fidelity—sexual intercourse fails to do so.

I believe that upon reflection the conclusion I have reached should hardly come as a surprise. If companion friendship is as rich as I have claimed it to be, then one should not expect the act of sexual intercourse alone to yield a profoundly sharp difference between companion friendship and romantic love.

JEAN-PAUL SARTRE

Hell Is Other People

JEAN-PAUL SARTRE (1905–1980), a philosopher, novelist, playwright, and political activist, was one of the most controversial intellectual figures of the twentieth century. The founder and leading proponent of existentialism, Sartre took the principal task of philosophy to be the study of the essential structure of human consciousness. His greatest work is Being and Nothingness, *from which this selection is taken.*

WE have described human reality from the standpoint of negating conduct and from the standpoint of the *cogito.* Following this lead we have discovered that human reality is-for-itself. Is this *all* that it is? Without going outside our attitude of reflective description, we can encounter modes of consciousness which seem, even while themselves remaining strictly in for-itself, to point to a radically different type of ontological structure. This ontological structure is *mine;* it is in relation to myself as subject that I am concerned about myself, and yet this concern (for-myself) reveals to me a being which is *my* being without being-for-me.

Consider for example shame. Here we are dealing with a mode of consciousness which has a structure identical with all those which we have previously described. It is a nonpositional self-consciousness, conscious (of) itself as shame; as such, it is an example of what the Germans call *Erlebnis,* and it is accessible to reflection. In addition its structure is intentional; it is a shameful apprehension *of* something and this something is *me.* I am ashamed of what I *am.* Shame therefore realizes an intimate relation of myself to myself. Through shame I have discovered an aspect of *my* being. Yet although certain complex forms derived from shame can appear on the reflective plane, shame is not originally a phenomenon of reflection. In fact no matter what results one can obtain in solitude by the religious *practice* of shame, it is in its primary structure shame *before somebody.* I have just made an awkward or vulgar gesture. This gesture clings to me; I neither judge it nor blame it. I simply live it. I realize it in the mode of for-itself. But now suddenly I raise my head. Somebody was there and has seen me. Suddenly I realize the vulgarity of my gesture, and I am ashamed. It is certain that my shame is not reflective, for the presence of another in my consciousness, even as a catalyst, is incompatible with the reflective attitude; in the field of my reflection I can never meet with anything but the consciousness which is mine. But the Other is the indispensable mediator between myself and me. I am ashamed of myself *as I appear* to the Other.

By the mere appearance of the Other, I am put in the position of passing judgment on myself as on an object, for it is as an object that I appear to the Other. Yet this object which has appeared to the Other is not an empty image in the mind of another. Such an image, in fact, would be imputable wholly to the Other and so could not "touch" me. I could feel irritation, or anger before it as before a bad portrait of myself which gives to my expression an ugliness or baseness which I do not have, but I could not be touched to the quick. Shame is by nature *recognition.* I recognize that I *am* as the Other sees me. There is however no question of a comparison between what I am for myself and what I am for the Other as if I found in myself, in the mode of being of the For-itself, an equivalent of what I am for the Other. In the first place this comparison is not encountered in us as the result of a concrete psychic operation. Shame is an immediate shudder which runs through me from head to foot without any discursive preparation. In addition the comparison is impossible; I am unable to bring about any relation between what I am in the intimacy of the For-itself, without distance, without recoil, without perspective, and this unjustifiable being-in-itself which I am for the Other. There is no standard here, no table of correlation. Moreover the very notion of *vulgarity* implies an inter-monad relation. Nobody can be vulgar all alone!

Thus the Other has not only revealed to me what I was; he has established me in a new type of being which can support new qualifications. This being was not in me potentially before the appearance of the Other, for it could not have found any place in the For-itself. Even if some power had been pleased to endow me with a body wholly constituted before it should be for-others, still my vulgarity and my awkwardness could not lodge there potentially; for they are meanings and as such they surpass the body and at the same time refer to a witness capable of understanding them and to the totality of my human reality. But this new being which appears *for* the other does not reside in the

Other; I am responsible for it as is shown very well by the education system which consists in making children ashamed of what they are. . . .

. . . It is not true that I first am and then later "seek" to make an object of the Other or to assimilate him; but to the extent that the upsurge of my being is an upsurge in the presence of the Other, to the extent that I am a pursuing flight and a pursued-pursuing, I am—at the very root of my being—the project of assimilating and making an object of the Other. I am the proof of the Other. That is the original fact. But this proof of the Other is in itself an attitude toward the Other; that is, I can not *be in the presence of the Other* without being that "in-the-presence" in the form of having to be it. Thus again we are describing the for-itself's structures of being although the Other's presence in the world is an absolute and self-evident fact, but a contingent fact—that is, a fact impossible to deduce from the ontological structures of the for-itself.

These two attempts which I am are opposed to one another. Each attempt is the death of the other; that is, the failure of the one motivates the adoption of the other. Thus there is no dialectic for my relations toward the Other but rather a circle—although each attempt is enriched by the failure of the other. Thus we shall study each one in turn. But it should be noted that at the very core of the one the other remains always present, precisely because neither of the two can be held without contradiction. Better yet, each of them is in the other and endangers the death of the other. Thus we can never get outside the circle. . . .

Everything which may be said of me in my relations with the Other applies to him as well. While I attempt to free myself from the hold of the Other, the Other is trying to free himself from mine; while I seek to enslave the Other, the Other seeks to enslave me. We are by no means dealing with unilateral relations with an object-in-itself, but with reciprocal and moving relations. . . . Conflict is the original meaning of being-for-others.

JANE ENGLISH

What Do Grown Children Owe Their Parents?

JANE ENGLISH *(1947–1979) taught philosophy at the University of North Carolina at Chapel Hill until her untimely death in a climbing accident at the age of thirty-two.*

WHAT do grown children owe their parents? I will contend that the answer is "nothing." Although I agree that there are many things that children *ought* to do for their parents, I will argue that it is inappropriate and misleading to describe them as things "owed." I will maintain that parents' voluntary sacrifices, rather than creating "debts" to be "repaid," tend to create love or "friendship." The duties of grown children are those of friends and result from love between them and their parents, rather than being things owed in repayment for the parents' earlier sacrifices. Thus, I will oppose those philosophers who use the word "owe" whenever a duty or obligation exists. Although the "debt" metaphor is appropriate in some moral circumstances, my argument is that a love relationship is not such a case.

Misunderstandings about the proper relationship between parents and their grown children have resulted from reliance on the "owing" terminology. For instance, we hear parents complain "You owe it to us to write home (keep up your piano playing, not adopt a hippie lifestyle), because of all we sacrificed for you (paying for piano lessons, sending you to college)." The child is sometimes even heard to reply, "I didn't ask to be born (to be given piano lessons, to be sent to college)." This inappropriate idiom of ordinary language tends to obscure, or even to undermine, the love that is the correct ground of filial obligation.

FAVORS CREATE DEBTS

There are some cases, other than literal debts, in which talk of "owing," though metaphorical, is apt. New to the neighborhood, Max barely knows his neighbor, Nina, but he asks her if she will take in his mail while he is gone for a month's vacation. She agrees. If, subsequently, Nina asks Max to do the same for her, it seems that Max has a moral obligation to agree (greater than the one he would have had if Nina had not done the same for him), unless for some reason it would be a burden far out of proportion to the one Nina bore for him. I will call this a *favor:* when A, at B's request, bears some burden for B, then B incurs an obligation to reciprocate. Here the metaphor of Max's "owing" Nina is appropriate. It is not literally a debt, of course, nor can Nina pass this IOU on to heirs, demand payment in the form of Max's taking out her garbage, or sue Max. Nonetheless, since Max ought to perform one act of similar nature and amount of sacrifice in return, the term is suggestive. Once he reciprocates, the debt is "discharged"—that is, their obligations revert to the condition they were in before Max's initial request.

Contrast a situation in which Max simply goes on vacation and, to his surprise, finds upon his return that his neighbor has mowed his grass twice weekly in his absence. This is a voluntary sacrifice rather than a favor, and Max has no duty to reciprocate. It would be nice for him to volunteer to do so, but this would be supererogatory on his part. Rather than a favor, Nina's action is a friendly gesture. As a result, she might expect Max to chat over the back fence, help her catch her straying dog, or something similar—she might expect the development of a friendship. But Max would be chatting (or whatever) out of friendship, rather than in repayment for mown grass. If he did not return her gesture, she might feel rebuffed or miffed, but not unjustly treated or indignant, since Max has not failed to perform a duty. Talk of "owing" would be out of place in this case.

It is sometimes difficult to distinguish between favors and non-favors, because friends tend to do favors for each other, and those who exchange favors tend to become friends. But one test is to ask how Max is motivated. Is it "to be nice to Nina" or "because she did *x* for me"? Favors are frequently performed by total strangers without any friendship developing. Nevertheless, a temporary obligation is created, even if the chance for repayment never arises. For instance, suppose that Oscar and Matilda, total strangers, are waiting in a long checkout line at the supermarket. Oscar, having forgotten the oregano, asks Matilda to watch his cart for a second. She does. If Matilda now asks Oscar to return the favor while she picks up some tomato sauce, he is obliged to agree. Even if she had not watched his cart, it would be inconsiderate of him to refuse, claiming he was too busy reading the magazines. He may have a duty to help others, but he would not "owe" it to her. But if she has done the same for him, he incurs an additional obligation to help, and talk of "owing" is apt. It suggests an agreement to perform equal, reciprocal, canceling sacrifices.

THE DUTIES OF FRIENDSHIP

The terms "owe" and "repay" are helpful in the case of favors, because the sameness of the amount of sacrifice on the two sides is important; the monetary metaphor suggests equal quantities of sacrifice. But friendship ought to be characterized by *mutuality* rather than reciprocity: friends offer what they can give and accept what they need, without regard for the total amounts of benefits exchanged. And friends are motivated by love rather than by the prospect of repayment. Hence, talk of "owing" is singularly out of place in friendship.

For example, suppose Alfred takes Beatrice out for an expensive dinner and a movie. Beatrice incurs no obligation to "repay" him with a goodnight kiss or a return engagement. If Alfred complains that she "owes" him something, he is operating under the assumption that she should repay a favor, but on the contrary his was a generous gesture done in the hopes of developing a friendship. We hope that he would not want her repayment in the form of sex or attention if this was done to discharge a debt rather than from friendship. Since, if Alfred is prone to reasoning in this way, Beatrice may well decline the invitation or request to pay for her own dinner, his attitude of expecting a "return" on his "investment" could hinder the development of a friendship. Beatrice should return the gesture only if she is motivated by friendship.

Another common misuse of the "owing" idiom occurs when the Smiths have dined at the Joneses' four times, but the Joneses at the Smiths' only once. People often say, "We owe three dinners." This line of thinking may be appropriate between business acquaintances, but not between friends. After all, the Joneses invited the Smiths not in order to feed them or to be fed in turn, but because of the friendly contact presumably enjoyed by all on such occasions. If the Smiths do not feel friendship toward the Joneses, they can decline future invitations and not invite the Joneses; they owe them nothing. Of course, between friends of equal re-

sources and needs, roughly equal sacrifices (though not necessarily roughly equal dinners) will typically occur. If the sacrifices are highly out of proportion to the resources, the relationship is closer to servility than to friendship.

Another difference between favors and friendship is that after a friendship ends, the duties of friendship end. The party that has sacrificed less owes the other nothing. For instance, suppose Elmer donated a pint of blood that his wife Doris needed during an operation. Years after their divorce, Elmer is in an accident and needs one pint of blood. His new wife, Cora, is also of the same blood type. It seems that Doris not only does not "owe" Elmer blood, but that she should actually refrain from coming forward if Cora has volunteered to donate. To insist on donating not only interferes with the newlyweds' friendship, but it belittles Doris and Elmer's former relationship by suggesting that Elmer gave blood in hopes of favors returned instead of simply out of love for Doris. It is one of the heart-rending features of divorce that it attends to quantity in a relationship previously characterized by mutuality. If Cora could not donate, Doris's obligation is the same as that for any former spouse in need of blood; it is not increased by the fact that Elmer similarly aided her. It *is* affected by the degree to which they are still friends, which in turn may (or may not) have been influenced by Elmer's donation.

In short, unlike the debts created by favors, the duties of friendship do not require equal quantities of sacrifice. Performing equal sacrifices does not cancel the duties of friendship, as it does the debts of favors. Unrequested sacrifices do not themselves create debts, but friends have duties regardless of whether they requested or initiated the friendship. Those who perform favors may be motivated by mutual gain, whereas friends should be motivated by affection. These characteristics of the friendship relation are distorted by talk of "owing."

PARENTS AND CHILDREN

The relationship between children and their parents should be one of friendship characterized by mutuality rather than one of reciprocal favors. The quantity of parental sacrifice is not relevant in determining what duties the grown child has. The medical assistance grown children ought to offer their ill mothers in old age depends upon the mothers' need, not upon whether they endured a difficult pregnancy, for example. Nor do one's duties to one's parents cease once an equal quantity of sacrifice has been performed, as the phrase "discharging a debt" may lead us to think.

Rather, what children ought to do for their parents (and parents for children) depends upon (1) their respective needs, abilities, and resources and (2) the extent to which there is an ongoing friendship between them. Thus, regardless of the quantity of childhood sacrifices, an able, wealthy child has an obligation to help his needy parents more than does a needy child. To illustrate, suppose sisters Cecile and Dana are equally loved by their parents, even though Cecile was an easy child to care for, seldom ill, while Dana was often sick and caused some trouble as a juvenile delinquent. As adults, Dana is a struggling artist living far away, while Cecile is a wealthy lawyer living nearby. When the parents need visits and financial aid, Cecile has an obligation to bear a higher proportion of these burdens than her sister. This results from her abilities, rather

than from the quantities of sacrifice made by the parents earlier.

Sacrifices have an important causal role in creating an ongoing friendship, which may lead us to assume incorrectly that it is the sacrifices that are the source of the obligation. That the source is the friendship instead can be seen by examining cases in which the sacrifices occurred but the friendship, for some reason, did not develop or persist. For example, if a woman gives up her newborn child for adoption, and if no feelings of love ever develop on either side, it seems that the grown child does not have an obligation to "repay" her for her sacrifices in pregnancy. For that matter, if the adopted child has an unimpaired love relationship with the adoptive parents, he or she has the same obligations to help them as a natural child would have.

The filial obligations of grown children are a result of friendship, rather than owed for services rendered. Suppose that Vance married Lola despite his parents' strong wish that he marry within their religion, and that as a result, the parents refuse to speak to him again. As the years pass, the parents are unaware of Vance's problems, his accomplishments, the birth of his children. The love that once existed between them, let us suppose, has been completely destroyed by this event and thirty years of desuetude. At this point, it seems, Vance is under no obligation to pay his parents' medical bills in their old age, beyond his general duty to help those in need. An additional, filial obligation would only arise from whatever love he may still feel for them. It would be irrelevant for his parents to argue, "But look how much we sacrificed for you when you were young," for that sacrifice was not a favor but occurred as part of a friendship which existed at that time but is now, we have supposed, defunct. A more appropriate message would be, "We still love you, and we would like to renew our friendship."

I hope this helps to set the question of what children ought to do for their parents in a new light. The parental argument, "You ought to do x because we did y for you," should be replaced by, "We love you and you will be happier if you do x," or "We believe you love us, and anyone who loved us would do x." If the parents' sacrifice had been a favor, the child's reply, "I never asked you to do y for me," would have been relevant; to the revised parental remarks, this reply is clearly irrelevant. The child can either do x or dispute one of the parents' claims: by showing that a love relationship does not exist, or that love for someone does not motivate doing x, or that he or she will not be happier doing x.

Seen in this light, parental requests for children to write home, visit, and offer them a reasonable amount of emotional and financial support in life's crises are well founded, so long as a friendship still exists. Love for others does call for caring about and caring for them. Some other parental requests, such as for more sweeping changes in the child's lifestyle or life goals, can be seen to be insupportable, once we shift the justification from debts owed to love. The terminology of favors suggests the reasoning, "Since we paid for your college education, you owe it to us

to make a career of engineering, rather than becoming a rock musician." This tends to alienate affection even further, since the tuition payments are depicted as investments for a return rather than done from love, as though the child's life goals could be "bought." Basing the argument on love leads to different reasoning patterns. The suppressed premise, "If A loves B, then A follows B's wishes as to A's lifelong career" is simply false. Love does not even dictate that the child adopt the parents' values as to the desirability of alternative life goals. So the parents' strongest available argument here is, "We love you, we are deeply concerned about your happiness, and in the long run you will be happier as an engineer." This makes it clear that an empirical claim is really the subject of the debate.

The function of these examples is to draw out our considered judgments as to the proper relation between parents and their grown children, and to show how poorly they fit the model of favors. What is relevant is the ongoing friendship that exists between parents and children. Although that relationship developed partly as a result of parental sacrifices for the child, the duties that grown children have to their parents result from the friendship rather than from the sacrifices. The idiom of owing favors to one's parents can actually be destructive if it undermines the role of mutuality and leads us to think in terms of quantitative reciprocal favors.

NANCY SLONIM ARONIE

My Heartbreak Kid

NANCY SLONIM ARONIE *is a writer who lives in Connecticut. A former commentator on National Public Radio's "All Things Considered," she illuminates the dark side of life.*

I keep getting these lessons in detachment. One of the hardest ones was when I lost my brass heart necklace. I looked everywhere, and I missed it every time I saw teeny hearts on other necks. It wasn't a necklace I could easily replace and I know material things shouldn't be coveted, so I lived and presumably I grew. But detachment from people is still another lesson. Tougher to justify and impossible to replace.

These new lessons are manifest in creative, inventive, exciting young adult women. They come home with my creative, inventive, exciting young adult son. He says, "Mom, this is Bonnie," and I say, "Hi . . . Can you smush this garlic clove?" And we make wonderful Caesar salads together. Just when she learns just how much lemon juice we need, he arrives with Leah. "Mom, this is Leah. Can we have a ride to the mall?" Leah and I try on Norma Kamali markdowns together and just when we figure out how to remove the shoulder pads without ruining the look he brings home . . . Monica. Monica and I sit in the bleachers, cheering and praying that he'll make the foul shot and just when his game is college-scholarship-ready Monica is missing.

I thought I was the perfect new-age mother. I made sure he knew friendships with girls were available and valuable, that just because it was a girl didn't mean he had to get involved, that he could be supporting and silly and sharing with girlfriends, that that wouldn't preclude crushes and lovers, that both could co-exist.

So what happened to Bonnie and Leah and Monica? I miss them. After all, his wasn't the only relationship developing in the house. I don't have daughters. My close women friends live far away, my Mom has gone back to community college and I value these special friendships. They are fun and healthy.

"You can't keep doing this to me," I said.

"I'm not doing anything to anyone," he said.

When I asked him why he needed so many girlfriends he said he didn't need them; they were available and he thought valuable. The words had a new-age perfect mother ring to them.

Maybe they weren't friendships. Maybe they were crushes. Maybe it's his life. Maybe this is the ultimate lesson in detachment. Maybe I'll learn it.

All I know is last night he came home with another one and said, "Mom, this is Jennifer." I looked her straight in the eye, I looked at the unsmushed garlic clove and I said, "I don't want to get involved."

Chapter *17*

I Like It, but Is It Art?

No doubt you have some painting or poster on your wall that you look at apprecia-
tively from time to time. You probably also have a favorite record or cassette that you
play while you are relaxing. What is it that you like about them? Why do they give
you such special pleasure? Why not just hang an old newspaper on your wall and listen to the sound of two cats fighting while you relax? What is the special place in our
lives of those objects that we call "art"? What makes something, a piece of printed
paper or a piece of music, art? What makes something a piece of *good* art, as opposed
to bad art or not art at all?

The philosophy of art is as rich and varied as the arts themselves, ranging from questions of quality, such as, What is good art and what is bad art? and, What makes a
piece of music great? to questions of ontology, such as, What is an "original" work of
art? and, What makes an object a work of art in the first place? The subject of **aesthetics**—which originally meant the study of sensory experience but later came to mean
the study of beauty—is, like ethics, fundamentally a set of questions about values. The
ultimate question in the philosophy of art is not only what art is but also what its purpose, function, and importance are in our lives. Great literature, one might suggest, is
important because it provides information and carries down the essential stories of a
culture. But much of literature, especially poetry, and most of art and music do not
necessarily "tell a story" and may not actually convey any information (in the sense of
story). Sometimes, of course, the arts are decorative, a pleasant painting to cover an
otherwise bare wall, some soothing music to make a hectic day of running errands
more relaxing. But such daily uses of art seem to trivialize and demean it. Beethoven's
great symphonies, Rembrandt's striking self-portraits, the epics of Homer, Dante, and
Tolstoy—these works inspire an almost religious fervor, and we define an entire civilization in terms of them.

And yet, there is always that nagging question about the "subjectivity" of taste. "There
is no disputing over tastes," wrote David Hume, quoting some ancient writers. You
enjoy watching The Three Stooges re-runs on television; your friend prefers reading
Kafka. Is there a difference? You find yourself moved by a song that has been in the
Top 40 for five weeks, which you will tire of in another three weeks, and then never
hear again. Your friend prefers Bach's Brandenburg concertos, and although she admits
that they are hard to dance to, she nevertheless insists on her taste over yours. Is there
any ground for this claim, or is she just being a snob? Is there any arguing over tastes in
art? Is there, apart from established social conventions, any meaning to the term "good
taste"? Is it enough that we know what we like even if we don't know what's good?

717

Questions of taste sometimes extend, in a fascinating philosophical way, to the nature of the object itself. What justification could there be, for example, for celebrating the artistic merit of a seven-ton slab of concrete, carefully placed in the middle of an urban mall, at great expense to the taxpayers? What justification can there be to the introduction of a soup can label or, fifty years ago, a urinal into an art museum collection? What makes one piece a work of art and another just a photograph, or just a soup can label? And what distinguishes a copy—even a first rate copy—from the original? Why isn't the poster you buy in a museum shop for five dollars just as much a work of art as the original? In the case of music, this raises special problems: What counts as the original in any case? The first performance of a piece is often clumsy, badly done, perhaps confused, or even misinterpreted. Is this the original? Or is it the sheet music itself? The idea in the mind of the composer? Why is an original worth so much more, even more than a copy that may be superior to the original because of deterioration? Is this just a historical matter, a question of nostalgia and market value rather than aesthetics?

Until this century, there was more or less general agreement about what counted as art (or music or literature); the main source of disagreement involved questions of quality—Is this piece of art good art or bad art? The question is not just a matter of popular appeal. We all know that Rembrandt's paintings were often rejected by his clients and left to languish in Dutch attics, and that Beethoven and Stravinsky were sometimes booed on the first performances of their greatest works. We want to say that these works were great even when they were not appreciated and that we (in our superior wisdom and hindsight) recognize what their contemporaries did not. But today, matters have become even more complicated. We not only disagree on which contemporary pieces are good, great, or terrible, but we no longer even agree on what counts as art. A composer sits silently at a piano for ten minutes; a painting is a black canvas; a book of literature contains no punctuation and no recognizable grammar. And, as always, there is the question of "pop" culture; does it count as art or not?

Traditionally, there have been two answers to the question, What makes art good art? The first of these holds that a good or great work of art is so by virtue of inherent *objective* qualities—that is, in the object itself. In his classic *Poetics,* Aristotle defends this approach in his definition of tragedy. The second answer instead insists that what makes a work of art good or great is its effect on the observer or audience. The Russian novelist Leo Tolstoy, in particular, argued that the observer (in his case, the reader) should be "infected by the author's condition of soul." Unlike the first, objective answer, this *subjective* answer does not guarantee any agreement about taste because different audiences, different readers, or different observers may be affected very differently by the same piece. It might even suggest that anyone's reaction and judgment to a piece is as good as anyone else's reaction and judgment. Thus, it is still said today, "there is no disputing over tastes." In philosophy, however, there is still much disputing over the question of whether there is any disputing over tastes.

David Hume held that the maxim is true, that aesthetic judgment is subjective and a work of art is beautiful only if it evokes a certain kind of sentiment. Hume disagreed, however, with the conclusion that aesthetic judgments could not be agreed upon.

Beauty, he argued, appealed to the "common sentiments" of mankind, and although opinions might vary, the emotional response would be universal, or at least to every observer with sound judgment. The problem is that many people lack such judgment because they are uncultivated, uneducated, inexperienced, confused, or in poor health. Durable admiration—for example, the lasting admiration for the classics, for classical authors, for the great books and works of art—may be a reliable indicator of great art, but this may be of little help when we are trying to judge the value of works produced in our own time. Hume warns against the "caprices of mode and fashion" and "the mistakes of ignorance and envy."

What is the proper relation between art and society? How do the arts fit into the rest of our lives? In the particular case of music, Kathleen Higgins raises the question whether the pervasiveness and importance of music in our lives has been ignored in philosophy and aesthetics. She argues that music can give us special insight into ethics and the nature of social harmony. It is often said that art should stretch our experience and stimulate controversy, but the controversies thus stimulated can be ferocious indeed. For many years, the battle has raged in Hollywood between those who believe that adults should be allowed to choose to see (or not see) whatever movies they wish and those who believe that certain subjects and depictions are inappropriate or immoral and should be prohibited. Only recently, a similar battle emerged within the usually quiet confines of America's art museums, when a controversial photography exhibit over-stimulated critics and politicians who were usually rather indifferent to the art scene. We include several selections, from the infamous Hays Commission responsible for setting the standards for Hollywood movies until the sixties, and New York philosopher Paul Mattick discussing the ongoing debate over government sponsorship of the arts in regard to the recent debate over the function and responsibilities of the National Endowment for the Arts, which funded the controversial photography exhibit in question. Between these two very different views, German "Critical Theorist" Theodor Adorno discusses what he has called the "culture industry." Tom Wolfe then gives us a different picture of the function of art in America, and he compares our current attitudes toward art as fundamentally similar to a religion. He abandons aesthetic interpretation and instead emphasizes the social function of art, as a means of rejecting the world but at the same time legitimating wealth. Needless to say, his analysis has brought down the wrath of much of the art world. Finally, Lawrence Weschler describes one of the anomalies of contemporary art, the oddity of life not only imitating but in some cases getting confused with art.

ARISTOTLE

The Nature of Tragedy

ARISTOTLE's (384–322 B.C.) theory of tragedy remained the definitive work on the subject for over 2,000 years, and his view that tragedy depends on some fatal flaw in character is still the basis of many modern tragedies. In the following excerpt from the Poetics, *Aristotle describes the basic ingredients of this old and noble art form.*

L ET us proceed now to the discussion of Tragedy; before doing so, however, we must gather up the definition resulting from what has been said. A tragedy, then, is the imitation of an action that is serious and also, as having magnitude, complete in itself; in language with pleasurable accessories, each kind brought in separately in the parts of the work; in a dramatic, not in a narrative form; with incidents arousing pity and fear, wherewith to accomplish its catharsis of such emotions. Here by 'language with pleasurable accessories' I mean that with rhythm and harmony or song superadded; and by 'the kinds separately' I mean that some portions are worked out with verse only, and others in turn with song.

As they act the stories, it follows that in the first place the Spectacle (or stage-appearance of the actors) must be some part of the whole; and in the second Melody and Diction, these two being the means of their imitation. Here by 'Diction' I mean merely this, the composition of the verses; and by 'Melody', what is too completely understood to require explanation. But further: the subject represented also is an action; and the action involves agents, who must necessarily have their distinctive qualities both of character and thought, since it is from these that we ascribe certain qualities to their actions. There are in the natural order of things, therefore, two causes, Thought and Character, of their actions, and consequently of their success or failure in their lives. Now the action (that which was done) is represented in the play by the Fable or Plot. The Fable, in our present sense of the term, is simply this, the combination of the incidents, or things done in the story; whereas Character is what makes us ascribe certain moral qualities to the agents; and Thought is shown in all they say when proving a particular point or, it may be, enunciating a general truth. There are six parts consequently of every tragedy, as a whole (that is) of such or such quality, viz. a Fable or Plot, Characters, Diction, Thought, Spectacle, and Melody; two of them arising from the means, one from the manner, and three from the objects of the dramatic imitation; and there is nothing else besides these six. Of these, its formative elements, then, not a few of the dramatists have made due use, as every play, one may say, admits of Spectacle, Character, Fable, Diction, Melody, and Thought.

The most important of the six is the combination of the incidents of the story. Tragedy is essentially an imitation not of persons but of action and life, of happiness and misery. All human happiness or misery takes the form of action;

the end for which we live is a certain kind of activity, not a quality. Character given us qualities, but it is in our actions—what we do—that we are happy or the reverse. In a play accordingly they do not act in order to portray the Characters; they include the Characters for the sake of the action. So that it is the action in it, i.e., its Fable or Plot, that is the end and purpose of the tragedy; and the end is everywhere the chief thing. Besides this, a tragedy is impossible without action, but there may be one without Character. The tragedies of most of the moderns are characterless—a defect common among poets of all kinds, and with its counterpart in painting in Zeuxis as compared with Polygnotus; for whereas the latter is strong in character, the work of Zeuxis is devoid of it. And again: one may string together a series of characteristic speeches of the utmost finish as regards Diction and Thought, and yet fail to produce the true tragic effect; but one will have much better success with a tragedy which, however inferior in these respects, has a Plot, a combination of incidents, in it. And again: the most powerful elements of attraction in Tragedy, the Peripeties and Discoveries, are parts of the Plot. A further proof is in the fact that beginners succeed earlier with the Diction and Characters than with the construction of a story; and the same may be said of nearly all the early dramatists. We maintain, therefore, that the first essential, the life and soul, so to speak, of Tragedy is the Plot; and that the Characters come second—compare the parallel in painting, where the most beautiful colours laid on without order will not give one the same pleasure as a simple black-and-white sketch of a portrait. We maintain that Tragedy is primarily an imitation of action, and that it is mainly for the sake of action that it imitates the personal agents. Third comes the element of Thought, i.e., the power of saying whatever can be said, or what is appropriate to the occasion. This is what, in the speeches in Tragedy, falls under the arts of Politics and Rhetoric; for the older poets make their personages discourse like statesmen, and the modern like rhetoricians. One must not confuse it with Character. Character in a play is that which reveals the moral purpose of the agents, i.e., the sort of thing they seek or avoid, where that is not obvious—hence there is no room for Character in a speech on a purely indifferent subject. Thought, on the other hand, is shown in all they say when proving or disproving some particular point, or enunciating some universal proposition. Fourth among the literary elements is the Diction of the personages, i.e., as before explained, the expression of their thoughts in words, which is practically the same thing with verse as with prose. As for the two remaining parts, the Melody is the greatest of the pleasurable accessories of Tragedy. The Spectacle, though an attraction, is the least artistic of all the parts, and has least to do with the art of poetry. The tragic effect is quite possible without a public performance and actors; and besides, the getting-up of the Spectacle is more a matter for the costumier than the poet.

Having thus distinguished the parts, let us now consider the proper construction of the Fable or Plot, as that is at once the first and the most important thing in Tragedy. We have laid it down that a tragedy is an imitation of an action that is complete in itself, as a whole of some magnitude; for a whole may be of no magnitude to speak of. Now a whole is that which has beginning, middle, and end. A beginning is that which is not itself necessarily after anything else, and which has naturally something else after it; an end is that which is naturally after something itself, either as its necessary or usual consequent, and with nothing else after it; and a middle, that which is by nature after one thing and has also another after it. A well-constructed Plot, therefore, cannot either begin or end at any point one likes; beginning and end in it must be of the forms just described. Again: to be beautiful, a living creature, and every whole made up of parts, must not only present a certain order in its arrangement of parts, but also be of a certain definite magnitude. Beauty is a matter of size and order, and therefore impossible either (1) in a very minute creature, since our perception becomes indistinct as it approaches instantaneity; or (2) in a creature of vast size—one, say, 1,000 miles long—as in that case, instead of the object being seen all at once, the unity and wholeness of it is lost to the beholder. Just in the same way, then, as a beautiful whole made up of parts, or a beautiful living creature, must be of some size, but a size to be taken in by the eye, so a story or Plot must be of some length, but of a length to be taken in by the memory. As for the limit of its length, so far as that is relative to public performances and spectators, it does not fall within the theory of poetry. If they had to perform a hundred tragedies, they would be timed by water-clocks, as they are said to have been at one period. The limit, however, set by the actual nature of the thing is this: the longer the story, consistently with its being comprehensible as a whole, the finer it is by reason of its magnitude. As a rough general formula, 'a length which allows of the hero passing by a series of proba-

ble or necessary stages from misfortune to happiness, or from happiness to misfortune', may suffice as a limit for the magnitude of the story.

The Unity of a Plot does not consist, as some suppose, in its having one man as its subject. An infinity of things befall that one man, some of which it is impossible to reduce to unity; and in like manner there are many actions of one man which cannot be made to form one action. One sees, therefore, the mistake of all the poets who have written a *Heracleid,* a *Theseid,* or similar poems; they suppose that, because Heracles was one man, the story also of Heracles must be one story. Homer, however, evidently understood this point quite well, whether by art or instinct, just in the same way as he excels the rest in every other respect. In writing an *Odyssey,* he did not make the poem cover all that ever befell his hero—it befell him, for instance, to get wounded on Parnassus and also to feign madness at the time of the call to arms, but the two incidents had no necessary or probable connexion with one another—instead of doing that, he took as the subject of the *Odyssey,* as also of the *Iliad,* an action with a Unity of the kind we are describing. The truth is that, just as in the other imitative arts one imitation is always one thing, so in poetry the story, as an imitation of action, must represent one action, a complete whole, with its several incidents so closely connected that the transposal or withdrawal of any one of them will disjoin and dislocate the whole. For that which makes no perceptible difference by its presence or absence is no real part of the whole.

From what we have said it will be seen that the poet's function is to describe, not the thing that has happened, but a kind of thing that might happen, i.e., what is possible as being probable or necessary. The distinction between historian and poet is not in the one writing prose and the other writing verse—you might put the work of Herodotus into verse, and it would still be a species of history; it consists really in this, that the one describes the thing that has been, and the other a kind of thing that might be. Hence poetry is something more philosophic and of graver import than history, since its statements are of the nature rather of universals, whereas those of history are singulars. By a universal statement I mean one as to what such or such a kind of man will probably or necessarily say or do—which is the aim of poetry, though it affixes proper names to the characters; by a singular statement, one as to what, say, Alcibiades did or had done to him. In Comedy this has become clear by this time; it is only when their plot is already made up of probable incidents that they give it a basis of proper names, choosing for the purpose any names that may occur to them, instead of writing like the old iambic poets about particular persons. In Tragedy, however, they still adhere to the historic names; and for this reason: what convinces is the possible; now whereas we are not yet sure as to the possibility of that which has not happened, that which has happened is manifestly possible, else it would not have come to pass. Nevertheless even in Tragedy there are some plays with but one or two known names in them, the rest being inventions; and there are some without a single known name, e.g., Agathon's *Antheus,* in which both incidents and names are of the poet's invention; and it is not less delightful on that account. So that one must not aim at a rigid adherence to the traditional stories on which tragedies

are based. It would be absurd, in fact, to do so, as even the known stories are only known to a few, though they are a delight none the less to all.

It is evident from the above that the poet must be more the poet of his stories or Plots than of his verses, inasmuch as he is a poet by virtue of the imitative element in his work, and it is actions that he imitates. And if he should come to take a subject from actual history, he is none the less a poet for that; since some historic occurrences may very well be in the probable and possible order of things; and it is in that aspect of them that he is their poet.

Of simple Plots and actions the episodic are the worst. I call a Plot episodic when there is neither probability nor necessity in the sequence of its episodes. Actions of this sort bad poets construct through their own fault, and good ones on account of the players. His work being for public performance, a good poet often stretches out a Plot beyond its capabilities, and is thus obliged to twist the sequence of incident.

Tragedy, however, is an imitation not only of a complete action, but also of incidents arousing pity and fear. Such incidents have the very greatest effect on the mind when they occur unexpectedly and at the same time in consequence of one another; there is more of the marvellous in them then than if they happened of themselves or by mere chance. Even matters of chance seem most marvellous if there is an appearance of design as it were in them; as for instance the statue of Mitys at Argos killed the author of Mitys' death by falling down on him when a looker-on at a public spectacle; for incidents like that we think to be not without a meaning. A Plot, therefore, of this sort is necessarily finer than others.

Plots are either simple or complex, since the actions they represent are naturally of this twofold description. The action, proceeding in the way defined, as one continuous whole, I call simple, when the change in the hero's fortunes takes place without Peripety or Discovery; and complex, when it involves one or the other, or both. These should each of them arise out of the structure of the Plot itself, so as to be the consequence, necessary or probable, of the antecedents. There is a great difference between a thing happening *propter hoc* and *post hoc.*

A Peripety is the change of the kind described from one state of things within the play to its opposite, and that too in the way we are saying, in the probable or necessary sequence of events; as it is for instance in *Oedipus:* here the opposite state of things is produced by the Messenger, who, coming to gladden Oedipus and to remove his fears as to his mother, reveals the secret of his birth. And in *Lynceus:* just as he is being led off for execution, with Danaus at his side to put him to death, the incidents preceding this bring it about that he is saved and Danaus put to death. A Discovery is, as the very word implies, a change from ignorance to knowledge, and thus to either love or hate, in the personages marked for good or evil fortune. The finest form of Discovery is one attended by Peripeties, like that which goes with the Discovery of *Oedipus.* There are no doubt other forms of it; what we have said may happen in a way in reference to inanimate things, even things of a very casual kind; and it is also possible to discover whether some one has done or not done something. But the form most directly connected with the Plot and the action

of the piece is the first-mentioned. This, with a Peripety, will arouse either pity or fear—actions of that nature being what Tragedy is assumed to represent; and it will also serve to bring about the happy or unhappy ending. The Discovery, then, being of persons, it may be that of one party only to the other, the latter being already known; or both the parties may have to discover themselves. Iphigenia, for instance, was discovered to Orestes by sending the letter; and another Discovery was required to reveal him to Iphigenia.

Two parts of the Plot, then, Peripety and Discovery, are on matters of this sort. A third part is Suffering; which we may define as an action of a destructive or painful nature, such as murders on the stage, tortures, woundings, and the like. The other two have been already explained. . . .

The next points after what we have said above will be these: (1) What is the poet to aim at, and what is he to avoid, in constructing his Plots? and (2) What are the conditions on which the tragic effect depends?

We assume that, for the finest form of Tragedy, the Plot must be not simple but complex: and further, that it must imitate actions arousing fear and pity, since that is the distinctive function of this kind of imitation. It follows, therefore, that there are three forms of Plot to be avoided. (1) A good man must not be seen passing from happiness to misery, or (2) a bad man from misery to happiness. The first situation is not fear-inspiring or piteous, but simply odious to us. The second is the most untragic that can be; it has not one of the requisites of Tragedy; it does not appeal either to the human feeling in us, or to our pity, or to our fears. Nor, on the other hand, should (3) an extremely bad man be seen falling from happiness into misery. Such a story may arouse the human feeling in us, but it will not move us to either pity or fear; pity is occasioned by undeserved misfortune, and fear by that of one like ourselves; so that there will be nothing either piteous or fear-inspiring in the situation. There remains, then, the intermediate kind of personage, a man not preeminently virtuous and just, whose misfortune, however, is brought upon him not by vice and depravity but by some error of judgement, of the number of those in the enjoyment of great reputation and prosperity; e.g., Oedipus, Thyestes, and the men of note of similar families. The perfect Plot, accordingly, must have a single, and not (as some tell us) a double issue; the change in the hero's fortunes must be not from misery to happiness, but on the contrary from happiness to misery; and the cause of it must lie not in any depravity, but in some great error on his part; the man himself being either such as we have described, or better, not worse, than that. Fact also confirms our theory. . . .

The tragic fear and pity may be aroused by the Spectacle; but they may also be aroused by the very structure and incidents of the play—which is the better way and shows the better poet. The Plot in fact should be so framed that, even without seeing the things take place, he who simply hears the account of them shall be filled with horror and pity at the incidents; which is just the effect that the mere recital of the story in *Oedipus* would have on one. To produce this same effect by means of the Spectacle is less artistic, and requires extraneous aid. Those, however, who make use of the Spectacle to put before

us that which is merely monstrous and not productive of fear, are wholly out of touch with Tragedy; not every kind of pleasure should be required of a tragedy, but only its own proper pleasure. . . .

In the Characters there are four points to aim at. First and foremost, that they shall be good. There will be an element of character in the play, if (as has been observed) what a personage says or does reveals a certain moral purpose; and a good element of character, if the purpose so revealed is good. Such goodness is possible in every type of personage, even in a woman or a slave, though the one is perhaps an inferior, and the other a wholly worthless being. The second point is to make them appropriate. The Character before us may be, say, manly; but it is not appropriate in a female Character to be manly, or clever. The third is to make them like the reality, which is not the same as their being good and appropriate, in our sense of the term. The fourth is to make them consistent and the same throughout; even if inconsistency be part of the man before one for imitation as presenting that form of character, he should still be consistently inconsistent. . . .

As Tragedy is an imitation of personages better than the ordinary man, we in our way should follow the example of good portrait-painters, who reproduce the distinctive features of a man, and at the same time, without losing the likeness, make him handsomer than he is. The poet in like manner, in portraying men quick or slow to anger, or with similar infirmities of character, must know how to represent them as such, and at the same time as good men, as Agathon and Homer have represented Achilles.

DAVID HUME

Of the Standard of Taste

DAVID HUME *(1711–1776) wrote on art and manners in England as well as philosophy and history. It was Hume, more than anyone, who promoted the popular view that "there is no disputing of tastes."*

T HE great variety of Taste, as well as of opinion, which prevails in the world, is too obvious not to have fallen under every one's observation. Men of the most confined knowledge are able to remark a difference of taste in the narrow circle of their acquaintance, even where the persons have been educated under the same government, and have early imbibed the same prejudices. But those, who can enlarge their view to contemplate distant nations and remote ages, are still more surprised at the great inconsistence and contrariety. We are apt to call *barbarous* whatever departs widely from our own taste and apprehension: But soon find the epithet of reproach retorted on us. And the highest arrogance and self-conceit is at last startled, on observing an equal assurance on all sides, and scruples, amidst such a contest of sentiment, to pronounce positively in its own favour.

As this variety of taste is obvious to the most careless inquirer; so will it be found, on examination, to be still greater in reality than in appearance. The sentiments of men often differ with regard to beauty and deformity of all kinds, even while their general discourse is the same. There are certain terms in every language, which import blame, and others praise; and all men, who use the same tongue, must agree in their application of them. Every voice is united in applauding elegance, propriety, simplicity, spirit in writing; and in blaming fustian, affectation, coldness, and a false brilliancy: But when critics come to particulars, this seeming unanimity vanishes; and it is found, that they had affixed a very different meaning to their expressions. In all matters of opinion and science, the case is opposite: The difference among men is there oftener found to lie in generals than in particulars; and to be less in reality than in appearance. An explanation of the terms commonly ends the controversy; and the disputants are surprised to find, that they had been quarreling, while at bottom they agreed in their judgment. . . .

It is natural for us to seek a *Standard of Taste;* a rule, by which the various sentiments of men may be reconciled; at least, a decision, afforded, confirming one sentiment, and condemning another.

There is a species of philosophy, which cuts off all hopes of success in such an attempt, and represents the impossibility of ever attaining any standard of taste. The difference, it is said, is very wide between judgment and sentiment. All sentiment is right; because sentiment has a reference to nothing beyond itself, and is always real, wherever a man is conscious of it. But all determinations of the understanding are not right; because they have a reference to something beyond themselves, to wit, real matter of fact; and are not always comformable to that standard. Among a thousand different opinions which different men may entertain of the same subject, there is one, and but one, that is just and true; and the only difficulty is to fix and ascertain it. On the contrary, a thousand different sentiments, excited by the same object, are all right: Because no sentiment represents what is really in the object. It only marks a certain conformity or relation between the object and the organs or faculties of the mind; and if that conformity did not really exist, the sentiment could never possibly have being. Beauty is no quality in things themselves: It exists merely in the mind which contemplates them; and each mind perceives a different beauty. One person may even perceive deformity, where another is sensible of beauty; and every individual ought to acquiesce in his own sentiment, without pretending to regulate those of others. To seek the real beauty, or real deformity, is as fruitless an enquiry, as to pretend to ascertain the real sweet or real bitter. According to the disposition of the organs, the same object may be both sweet and bitter; and the proverb has justly determined it to be fruitless to dispute concerning tastes. It is very natural, and even quite necessary, to extend this axiom to mental, as well as bodily taste; and thus common sense, which is so often at variance with philosophy, especially with the skeptical kind, is found, in one instance at least, to agree in pronouncing the same decision.

But though this axiom, by passing into a proverb, seems to have attained the sanction of common sense; there is certainly a species of common sense which opposes it, at least serves to modify and restrain it. Whoever would assert an equality of genius and elegance between Ogilby and Milton, or Bunyan and Addison, would be thought to defend no less an extravagance, than if he had maintained a molehill to be as high as [a mountain], or a pond as extensive as the ocean. Though there may be found persons, who give the preference to the former authors; no one pays attention to such a taste; and we pronounce without scruple the sentiment of these pretended critics to be absurd and ridiculous. The principle of the natural equality of tastes is then totally forgot, and while we admit it on some occasions, where the objects seem near an equality, it appears an extravagant paradox, or rather a palpable absurdity, where objects so disproportioned are compared together.

It is evident that none of the rules of composition are fixed by reasonings *a priori,* or can be esteemed abstract conclusions of the understanding, from comparing those habitudes and relations of ideas, which are eternal and immutable. Their foundation is the same with that of all the practical sciences, experience; nor are they any thing but general observations, concerning what has been universally found to please in all countries and in all ages. Many of the beauties of poetry and even of eloquence are founded on falsehood and fiction, on hyperboles, metaphors, and an abuse or perversion of terms from their natural meaning. To check the sallies of the imagination, and to reduce every expression to geometrical truth and exactness, would be the most contrary to the laws of criticism; because it would produce a work, which, by universal experience, has been found the most insipid and disagreeable. But though poetry can never submit to exact truth, it must be confined by rules of art, discovered to the author either by genius or observation. If some negligent or irregular writers have pleased, they have not pleased by their transgressions of rule or order, but in spite of these transgressions: They have possessed other beauties, which were conformable to just criticism; and the force of these beauties has been able to overpower censure, and give the mind a satisfaction superior to the disgust arising from the blemishes. . . . If they are found to please, they cannot be faults; let the pleasure, which they produce, be ever so unexpected and unaccountable.

But though all the general rules of art are founded only on experience and on the observation of the common sentiments of human nature, we must not imagine, that, on every occasion, the feelings of men will be conformable to these rules. Those finer emotions of the mind are of a very tender and delicate nature, and require the concurrence of many favourable circumstances to make them play with facility and exactness, according to their general and established principles. The least exterior hindrance to such small springs, or the least internal disorder, disturbs their motion, and confounds the operation of the whole machine. When we would make an experiment of this nature, and would try the force of any beauty or deformity, we must choose with care a proper time and place, and bring the fancy to a suitable situation and disposition. A perfect serenity of mind, a recollection of thought, a due attention to the object; if any of these circumstances be wanting, our experiment will be fallacious, and we shall be unable to judge of the catholic and universal beauty. The relation, which nature has placed between the form and the sentiment will at least be more obscure; and it will require greater accuracy to trace and discern it. We shall be able to ascertain its

influence not so much from the operations of each particular beauty, as from the durable admiration, which attends those works, that have survived all the caprices of mode and fashion, all the mistakes of ignorance and envy. . . .

It appears then, that, amidst all the variety and caprice of taste, there are certain general principles of approbation or blame, whose influence a careful eye may trace in all operations of the mind. Some particular forms or qualities, from the original structure of the internal fabric, are calculated to please, and others to displease; and if they fail of their effect in any particular instance, it is from some apparent defect or imperfection in the organ. A man in a fever would not insist on his palate as able to decide concerning flavours; nor would one, affected with the jaundice, pretend to give a verdict with regard to colours. In each creature, there is a sound and a defective state; and the former alone can be supposed to afford us a true standard of taste and sentiment. If, in the sound state of the organ, there be an entire or a considerable uniformity of sentiment among men, we may thence derive an idea of the perfect beauty; in like manner as the appearance of objects in daylight, to the eye of a man in health, is denominated their true and real colour, even while colour is allowed to be merely a phantasm of the senses.

Many and frequent are the defects in the internal organs, which prevent or weaken the influence of those general principles, on which depends our sentiment of beauty or deformity. Though some objects, by the structure of the mind, be naturally calculated to give pleasure, it is not to be expected, that in every individual the pleasure will be equally felt. Particular incidents and situations occur, which either throw a false light on the objects, or hinder the true from conveying to the imagination the proper sentiment and perception.

One obvious cause, why many feel not the proper sentiment of beauty, is the want of that *delicacy* of imagination, which is requisite to convey a sensibility of those finer emotions. . . .

It is impossible to continue in the practice of contemplating any order of beauty, without being frequently obliged to form *comparisons* between the several species and degrees of excellence, and estimating their proportion to each other. A man, who had no opportunity of comparing the different kinds of beauty, is indeed totally unqualified to pronounce an opinion with regard to any object presented to him. By comparison alone we fix the epithets of praise or blame, and learn how to assign the due degree of each. . . .

But to enable a critic the more fully to execute this undertaking, he must preserve his mind free from all *prejudice,* and allow nothing to enter into his consideration, but the very object which is submitted to his examination. We may observe, that every work of art, in order to produce its due effect on the mind, must be surveyed in a certain point of view, and cannot be fully relished by persons, whose situation, real or imaginary, is not conformable to that which is required by the performance. . . .

It is well known, that in all questions, submitted to the understanding, prejudice is destructive of sound judgment, and perverts all operations of the intellectual faculties: It is no less contrary to good taste; nor has it less influence to corrupt our sentiment of beauty. It belongs to *good sense* to check its influence in both cases; and in this respect, as well as in many others, reason, if not an essential part of taste, is at

least requisite to the operations of this latter faculty. In all the nobler productions of genius, there is a mutual relation and correspondence of parts; nor can either the beauties or blemishes be perceived by him, whose thought is not capacious enough to comprehend all those parts, and compare them with each other, in order to perceive the consistence and uniformity of the whole. Every work of art has also a certain end or purpose, for which it is calculated; and is to be deemed more or less perfect, as it is more or less fitted to attain this end. The object of eloquence is to persuade, of history to instruct, of poetry to please by means of the passions and the imagination. These ends we must carry constantly in our view, when we peruse any performance; and we must be able to judge how far the means employed are adapted to their respective purposes. Besides, every kind of composition, even the most poetical is nothing but a chain of propositions and reasonings; not always, indeed, the justest and most exact, but still plausible and specious, however disguised by the coloring of the imagination. The persons introduced in tragedy and epic poetry, must be represented as reasoning, and thinking, and concluding, and acting, suitably to their character and circumstances; and without judgment, as well as taste and invention, a poet can never hope to succeed in so delicate an undertaking. Not to mention, that the same excellence of faculties which contributes to the improvement of reason, the same clearness of conception, the same exactness of distinction, the same vivacity of apprehension, are essential to the operations of true taste, and are its infallible concomitants. It seldom, or never happens, that a man of sense, who has experience in any art, cannot judge of its beauty; and it is no less rare to meet with a man who has a just taste without a sound understanding.

Thus, though the principles of taste be universal, and, nearly, if not entirely the same in all men; yet few are qualified to give judgment on any work of art, or establish their own sentiment as the standard of beauty. . . . Strong sense, united to delicate sentiment, improved by practice, perfected by comparison, and cleared of all prejudice, can alone entitle critics to his valuable character; and the joint verdict of such, wherever they are to be found, is the true standard of taste and beauty.

But where are such critics to be found? By what marks are they to be known? How distinguish them from pretenders? These questions are embarrassing; and seem to throw us back into the same uncertainty, from which, during the course of this essay, we have endeavoured to extricate ourselves.

But if we consider the matter aright, these are questions of fact, not of sentiment. Whether any particular person be endowed with good sense and a delicate imagination, free from prejudice, may often be the subject of dispute, and be liable to great discussion and enquiry: But that such a character is valuable and estimable will be agreed in by all mankind. Where these doubts occur, men can do no more than in other disputable questions, which are submitted to the understanding: They must produce the best arguments, that their invention suggests to them; they must acknowledge a true and decisive standard to exist somewhere, to wit, real existence and matter of fact; and they must have indulgence to such as differ from them in their appeals to this standard. It is sufficient for our present purpose, if we have proved, that the taste of all individuals is not upon an equal footing, and that some men in general, however difficult to be particularly pitched upon, will be acknowledged by universal sentiment to have a preference above others.

LEO TOLSTOY

What Is Art?

LEO TOLSTOY *(1828–1910), the author of such classics as* War and Peace *and* Anna Karenina, *also wrote extensively on art and religion. His theory of art as the sincere expression and communication of the artist's moral and religious feelings has been extremely influential and is still being vigorously argued by artists and writers today.*

EVERY work of art causes the receiver to enter into a certain kind of relationship both with him who produced, or is producing, the art, and with all those who, simultaneously, previously, or subsequently, receive the same artistic impression.

Speech, transmitting the thoughts and experiences of men, serves as a means of union among them, and art acts in similar manner. The peculiarity of this latter means of intercourse, distinguishing it from intercourse by means of words, consists in this, that whereas by words a man transmits his thoughts to another, by means of art he transmits his feelings.

The activity of art is based on the fact that a man, receiving through his sense of hearing or sight another man's expression of feeling, is capable of experiencing the emotion which moved the man who expressed it. To take the simplest example: one man laughs, and another who hears becomes merry; or a man weeps, and another who hears feels sorrow. A man is excited or irritated, and another man seeing him comes to a similar state of mind. By his movements or by the sounds of his voice, a man expresses courage and determination or sadness and calmness, and this state of mind passes on to others. A man suffers, expressing his sufferings by groans and spasms, and this suffering transmits itself to other people; a man expresses his feeling of admiration, devotion, fear, respect, or love to certain objects, persons, or phenomena, and others are infected by the same feelings of admiration, devotion, fear, respect, or love to the same objects, persons, and phenomena.

And it is upon this capacity of man to receive another man's expression of feeling and experience those feelings himself, that the activity of art is based.

If a man infects another or others directly, immediately, by his appearance or by the sounds he gives vent to at the very time he experiences the feeling; if he causes another man to yawn when he himself cannot help yawning, or to laugh or cry when he himself is obliged to laugh or cry, or to suffer when he himself is suffering—that does not amount to art.

Art begins when one person, with the object of joining another or others to himself in one and the same feeling, expresses that feeling by certain external indications. To take the simplest example: a boy, having experienced, let us say, fear on encountering a wolf, relates that encounter; and, in order to evoke in others the feeling he has experienced, describes himself, his condition before the encounter, the surroundings, the wood, his own lightheartedness, and then the wolf's appearance, its movements, the distance between himself and the wolf, etc. All this, if only the boy, when telling the story, again experiences the feelings he had lived through and infects the hearers and compels them to feel what the narrator had experienced, is art. If even the boy had not seen a wolf but had frequently been afraid of one, and if, wishing to evoke in others the fear he had felt, he invented an encounter with a wolf and recounted it so as to make his hearers share the feelings he experienced when he feared the wolf, that also would be art. And just in the same way it is art if a man, having experienced either the fear of suffering or the attraction of enjoyment (whether in reality or in imagination), expresses these feelings on canvas or in marble so that others are infected by them. And it is also art if a man feels or imagines to himself feelings of delight, gladness, sorrow, despair, courage, or despondency and the transition from one to another of these feelings, and expresses these feelings by sounds so that the hearers are infected by them and experience them as they were experienced by the composer.

The feelings with which the artist infects others may be most various—very strong or very weak, very important or very insignificant, very bad or very good: feelings of love for one's own country, self-devotion and submission to fate or to God expressed in a drama, raptures of lovers described in a novel, feelings of voluptuousness expressed in a picture, courage expressed in a triumphal march, merriment evoked by a dance, humor evoked by a funny story, the feeling of quietness transmitted by an evening landscape or by a lullaby, or the feeling of admiration evoked by a beautiful arabesque—it is all art.

If only the spectators or auditors are infected by the feelings which the author has felt, it is art.

To evoke in oneself a feeling one has once experienced, and having evoked it in oneself, then, by means of movements, lines, colors, sounds, or forms expressed in words, so to transmit that feeling that others may experience the same feeling—this is the activity of art.

Art is a human activity consisting in this, that one man consciously, by means of certain external signs, hands on to others feelings he has lived through, and that other people are infected by these feelings and also experience them. . . .

There is one indubitable indication distinguishing real art from its counterfeit, namely, the infectiousness of art. If a man, without exercising effort and without altering his standpoint on reading, hearing, or seeing another man's work, experiences a mental condition which unites him with that man and with other people who also partake of that work of art, then the object evoking that condition is a work of art. And however poetical, realistic, effectual, or interesting a work may be, it is not a work of art if it does not evoke that feeling (quite distinct from all other feelings) of joy and of spiritual union with

another (the author) and with others (those who are also infected by it).

It is true that his indication is an *internal* one, and that there are people who have forgotten what the action of real art is, who expect something else from art (in our society the great majority are in this state), and that therefore such people may mistake for this aesthetic feeling the feeling of diversion and a certain excitement which they receive from counterfeits of art. But though it is impossible to undeceive these people, just as it is impossible to convince a man suffering from color-blindness that green is not red, yet, for all that, this indication remains perfectly definite to those whose feeling for art is neither perverted nor atrophied, and it clearly distinguishes the feeling produced by art from all other feelings.

The chief peculiarity of this feeling is that the receiver of a true artistic impression is so united to the artist that he feels as if the work were his own and not someone else's—as if what it expresses were just what he had long been wishing to express. A real work of art destroys, in the consciousness of the receiver, the separation between himself and the artist—not that alone, but also between himself and all whose minds receive this work of art. In this freeing of our personality from its separation and isolation, in this uniting of it with others, lies the chief characteristic and the great attractive force of art.

If a man is infected by the author's condition of soul, if he feels this emotion and this union with others, then the object which has effected this is art; but if there be no such infection, if there be not this union with the author and with others who are moved by the same work—then it is not art. And not only is infection a sure sign of art, but the degree of infectiousness is also the sole measure of excellence in art.

The stronger the infection, the better is the art as art, speaking now apart from its subject matter, i.e., not considering the quality of the feelings it transmits.

And the degree of the infectiousness of art depends on three conditions:

1. On the greater or lesser individuality of the feeling transmitted:

2. on the greater or lesser clearness with which the feeling is transmitted:

3. on the sincerity of the artist, i.e., on the greater or lesser force with which the artist himself feels the emotion he transmits.

The more individual the feeling transmitted the more strongly does it act on the receiver; the more individual the state of soul into which he is transferred, the more pleasure does the receiver obtain, and therefore the more readily and strongly does he join it.

The clearness of expression assists infection because the receiver, who mingles in consciousness with the author, is the better satisfied the more clearly the feeling is transmitted, which, as it seems to him, he has long known and felt, and for which he has only now found expression.

But most of all is the degree of infectiousness of art increased by the degree of sincerity in the artist. As soon as the spectator, hearer, or reader feels that the artist is infected by his own production, and writes, sings, or plays for himself, and not merely to act on others, this mental condition of the artist infects the receiver; and contrariwise, as soon as the spectator, reader, or hearer feels that the author is not writing, singing or playing for his own satisfaction—does

not himself feel what he wishes to express—but is doing it for him, the receiver, a resistance immediately springs up, and the most individual and the newest feelings and the cleverest technique not only fail to produce any infection but actually repel.

I have mentioned three conditions of contagiousness in art, but they may be all summed into one, the last, sincerity, i.e., that the artist should be impelled by an inner need to express his feeling. That condition includes the first; for if the artist is sincere he will express the feeling as he experienced it. And as each man is different from everyone else, his feeling will be individual for everyone else; and the more individual it is—the more the artist has drawn it from the depths of his nature—the more sympathetic and sincere will it be. And this same sincerity will impel the artist to find a clear expression of the feeling which he wishes to transmit.

Therefore this third condition—sincerity—is the most important of the three. It is always complied with in peasant art, and this explains why such art always acts so powerfully; but it is a condition almost entirely absent from our upper-class art, which is continually produced by artists actuated by personal aims of covetousness or vanity.

Such are the three conditions which divide art from its counterfeits, and which also decide the quality of every work of art apart from its subject matter.

The absence of any one of these conditions excludes a work from the category of art and relegates it to that of art's counterfeits. If the work does not transmit the artist's peculiarity of feeling and is therefore not individual, if it is unintelligibly expressed, or if it has not proceeded from the author's inner need for expression—it is not a work of art. If all these conditions are present, even in the smallest degree, then the work, even if a weak one, is yet a work of art.

The presence in various degrees of these three conditions—individuality, clearness, and sincerity—decides the merit of a work of art as art, apart from subject matter. All works of art take rank of merit according to the degree in which they fulfil the first, the second, and the third of these conditions. In one the individuality of the feeling transmitted may predominate; in another, clearness of expression; in a third, sincerity; while a fourth may have sincerity and individuality but be deficient in clearness; a fifth, individuality and clearness but less sincerity; and so forth, in all possible degrees and combinations.

Thus is art divided from that which is not art, and thus is the quality of art as art decided, independently of its subject matter, i.e., apart from whether the feelings it transmits are good or bad.

KATHLEEN HIGGINS

The Music of Our Lives

KATHLEEN HIGGINS *teaches philosophy at the University of Texas at Austin. She has published several books, including* Nietzsche's Zarathustra *and* The Music of Our Lives *and numerous articles.*

"**B**ENEVOLENCE is akin to music," Confucius tells us; Plato claims that "musical training is a more potent instrument than any other, because rhythm and harmony find their way into the inward places of the soul, on which they mightily fasten, imparting grace, and making the soul to him who is rightly educated graceful, or of him who is ill-educated ungraceful." The pervasive influence of music, and its intimate connection with our ethical outlook, has been a matter of cross-cultural comment for millennia. The world's philosophical traditions have often treated music as a central tool for the promotion of harmonious living for both society and the individual.

But this idea seems foreign to most contemporary Americans. When I've mentioned my interest in . . . music and ethics, more than one acquaintance has asked, "Do you mean the controversy between Frank Zappa and Tipper Gore?" For most Americans, "rock lyrics gone wrong" is the paradigm case of music having an ethical impact. Only occasionally does one hear of the ethical impact of music apart from lyrics, and then usually as a complaint. Allan Bloom's controversial *Closing of the American Mind* devotes an entire chapter to lambasting the depravity of rock music, which in his view has "one appeal only, a barbaric appeal, to sexual desire." His vitriolic attack on a whole species of music lacks even the qualified tolerance that Nikita Khrushchev voiced when he conceded, "We are not against all jazz music. . . . But there is music which makes one feel like vomiting, and causes colic in one's stomach." Bloom at least "remembers" music serving a positive ethical function, although he despairs of its operation in a society that dances to rock 'n' roll.

Bloom is right in thinking that music can provide "cultivation of the soul" and express humanity's "noblest activities . . . while providing a pleasure extending from the lowest bodily to the highest spiritual" aspects of the human being. But he is wrong to withhold this praise from any but our tradition's classical repertoire. In this, he makes a common and pernicious rhetorical move. Bloom praises the glories of a fictitious past when everyday folks (at least the well-to-do) found spiritual sustenance in classical music (which in Bloom's usage comprises the output of a single continent over twice as many centuries). But this praise demeans our actual musical lives, in which most of us hear music almost continuously and have unprecedented resources for experiencing the wealth of music produced throughout the world and the course of our own history.

Bloom's move is pernicious because it reinforces the poverty that *does* characterize our everyday musical experience, while failing to acknowledge that it is a poverty of riches. Music is so pervasive in our environment that many of us are startled by silence; but we often feel its presence as an intrusion. For most of us, our everyday encounters with music are neither "encounters" nor "experience" in any meaningful sense. No wonder, then, that the thought of "spiritual experience" or "ethical edification" from music seems as foreign to us as Bloom's lament suggests.

The irony is that musical experience is more available than ever before. Developments in recording technology have done more than produce stars and millionaires. Recorded music can give us experiential access to an incredible range of music, a range spanning centuries and the world's cultures. While serious questions remain regarding the appropriate way to approach the music of other cultures, we have the unprecedented opportunity to *experience* it. But for the most part—with exciting exceptions like "Afro-Pop"—we take little advantage of this possibility, either as institutions or as individuals. We hear more music than our ancestors in any other era of history, and yet our sense of music's contribution to life is singularly impoverished. . . .

As a society we regard our everyday lives as virtually immune to transformative aesthetic experience, as John Dewey complained in *Art as Experience.* Dewey blamed this on Americans' tendency to put "art" on a distant pedestal. If what he says is true with respect to all art—and I think it is—his complaint is particularly apt with respect to music. Philosophy in America, moreover, has contributed to the problem by reinforcing the divorce between "objects worthy of its consideration" and the everyday world. To be sure, philosophical discussion may not have wide-ranging cultural impact on American musical habits, but that in itself is a manifestation of the dissociation between musical aesthetics and everyday life.

Contemporary American philosophy has little place for music, let alone for the music of everyday life. Musical aesthetics is a marginal phenomenon within aesthetics, and the whole field of aesthetics is treated as a "fringe" of philosophical concern. I suspect that, in response to this marginalization, aestheticians frequently adopt more "impressive" stylistic models from other, "technical" areas of philosophy, describing the arts in overly serious and somber dissections, with as many gestures toward precision as possible. Although most willingly admit that aesthetics cannot aspire to "more precision than it admits of," in Aristotle's phrase, recent writers have assumed that it admits of a remarkable degree of precision—distorting, I argue, both the arts and aesthetic sensibility.

In musical aesthetics, such endeavors have a built-in scaffold. Western musical notation is designed to provide precise indications of pitch and rhythm. Thus, musical aestheticians have frequently set to work on the musical score, ignoring or even denying the importance of the performer and, for that matter, the listener. Nelson Goodman, for instance, considers the score the sine qua non of the musical work, so much so that if one departs in the slightest detail from the written score, one has not, on his analysis, performed the work.

The problem with this is that the score just isn't the music. Not that most philosophers are likely to say that it is. Francis Sparshott calls it a "recipe" that provides an "opportunity" for the experiences of musical performance and listening. And few besides Goodman would consider it "the truth, the whole truth" about a musical work. But the score receives undue attention. And as a consequence, the sphere of discussion becomes quite narrow. Improvisation, for example, is treated as aberrant, even though this characterization describes most of the world's music. And nonnotated features of musical experience—the vital character of performance as well as the where, the when, and the circumstances of listening—are rarely discussed.

Conservatism, ethnocentrism, and divorce from experience characterize the now established philosophical approach to music. They result from what is seen as a requirement of philosophical procedure: restriction of one's topic to yield precise results. But such restrictive analysis involves deliberate disregard for the points of connection that one phenomenon may have with another. If the idea of discussing music's connection with ethics sounds bizarre to today's philosophical audience, this is partially due to a methodological obsession with keeping subject matters distinct and isolating music not only from morals and social philosophy but even from its performance and enjoyment. . . .

The thought that musical listening is a social phenomenon may seem out of date. In contemporary American society, it is only in the aberrant case that one experiences music in a live, group format. Our primary mode of musical production is recording technology (whether broadcast or personally employed). And through our use of such technology, our culture has become both predominantly passive and individualistic with respect to music. Passivity is encouraged by the fact that, although music is an accompaniment of the typical waking day, much of it is inflicted on us by someone else (a boss, a store manager, or a restaurant owner, for example). And while we choose our own radio stations when we drive, we still rely on stations and disc jockeys to tell us what is worth hearing.

Other features of our everyday experience encourage the impression that music is a matter of individual consumption. The availability of recorded music has made possible the development of a historically novel use of music: individual self-assertion, often in aggressive opposition to others. Such assertions are common in all walks of life. The person who accompanies his or her walking with a boom-box, the driver who blasts his radio station into the surrounding countryside, and the undergraduate who positions stereo speakers in a dormitory window are aggressively foisting their tastes on others. Each is using music for asocial, if not anti-social, ends. And most of us have been irritated at one time or another by the similarly asocial Walkman phenomenon, which enables people to appear in the midst of public bustle with their auditory capacities channeled into an entirely different world. Bloom casts the teenager with the Walkman as an icon of declining Western culture. I think he overstates the point; but the Walkman-wired cyclist I recently saw tying a shoe in front of oncoming traffic surely represents some kind of communicative breakdown.

With such conspicuous uses of music to tune out the immediate social environment, it is no wonder that many Americans besides philosophers do not consider music a particularly communal phenomenon. And yet it is not so many years since Woodstock, which reminded at least one generation that music can create a community, even if a short lived one. Events like Woodstock, even the well-attended local concert (of whatever musical discourse), make it obvious that a communal dimension of music is still evident to Americans who seek it out.

Furthermore, although our society's appropriation of music disguises its social dimension, this dimension remains inevitably a part of our awareness when we experience music. Music is, by its very nature, a social activity. Even the music heard through the earphones of a Walkman sounds like it comes from an external reality. In fact it does come from outside the individual listener. A social relationship between those who produce it and the listener still occurs, albeit a highly mediated one. But in addition, I believe that most listeners experience music, even that which comes to them through earphones, as a kind of communication between themselves and other human beings.

When one identifies with the gait and emotion suggested by music, one senses that one is joining an experience that others share. Even such intimate expressions of the longing individual soul as one hears in Bach's partitas for solo violin admit the listener into a communion of one soul with another. If only in a semiconscious way, one is aware of music as a shared experience—and of its potential to be shared by other listeners as well.

Usually it is not perversity or showing off when, in our society, the owner of records, tapes, or compact discs wants to play them for friends and acquaintances. The typical motivation is to share an experience. And when music is used to encourage a particular mood in guests, the host or hostess is also immersing him- or herself in musical experience with them. Again, when one hears music that inspires foot-tapping or the desire to dance, one is at least quasi-consciously motivated to put one's entire body into a context of social celebration.

Music is perhaps the most open medium of socially shared experience available in our culture. Contemporary American society has an impoverished range of social rituals, and most are linked to specific group memberships. Even worship services and baseball games typically involve reinforced awareness that one supports one doctrine or team as opposed to others. But although music can be employed to urge solidarity within a faction, it is almost uniquely suited to incite a sense of community among people who have little else in common besides appreciating it.

Merriam stresses the value of music for effecting a sense of communal solidarity:

> Music . . . provides a rallying point around which the members of society gather to engage in activities which require the cooperation and coordination of the group. Not all music is thus performed, of course, but every society has occasions signalled by music which draws its members together and reminds them of their unity. . . . Music is clearly indispensable to the proper promulgation of the activities that constitute a society; it is a universal human behavior—without it, it is questionable that man could truly be called man, with all that implies.

Even music's effectiveness in reinforcing the solidarity of a particular faction or social subgroup presupposes its more open-ended capacity to create a sense of community. Within such a subgroup of listeners, the shared experience of music is an effective means of minimizing the importance of personal differences. Music gives each listener a sense of full involvement as a self *and* a sense of other individuals sharing in this intense experience. A. R. Radcliffe-Brown describes this response to music in his description of the Andamanese dance:

> The pleasure that the dancer feels irradiates itself over everything around him and he is filled with geniality and good-will towards his companions. The sharing with others of an intense pleasure, or rather the sharing in a collective expression of pleasure, must ever include us to such expansive feelings.

Like any shared profound experience, listening to stirring music, which touches one's sense of what one is, has a socially binding effect on those who share the listening experience. The personal differences that divide the members of the audience seem less serious than this shared intense experience. And this is true whether the audience is construed as an open or closed group.

Music makes us feel ourselves to be connected with our larger social context. Because we respond to music physically, this connection is visceral as well as emotional. It is valuable to ethical living, for it extends one's sense of immediate concern beyond one's private person. It extends the range of one's identity by dissolving one's sense of a barrier between oneself and the rest of humanity.

THE HAYS COMMISSION

The Motion Picture Production Code

WILL H. HAYS *was known for his campaigns against "smut" before he became the first president of the Motion Picture Producers and Distributors in 1922. He inspired the Motion Picture Production Code, written in 1930, which censored the sexual and social content of films.*

Foreword

MOTION picture producers recognize the high trust and confidence that have been placed in them by the people of the world and that have made motion pictures a universal form of entertainment.

They recognize their responsibility to the public because of this trust and because entertainment and art are important influences in the life of a nation.

Hence, though regarding motion pictures primarily as entertainment without any explicit purposes of teaching or propaganda, they know that the motion picture within its own field of entertainment may be directly responsible for spiritual or moral progress, for higher types of social life, and for much correct thinking.

On their part, they ask from the public and from public leaders a sympathetic understanding of the problems inherent in motion picture production and a spirit of cooperation that will allow the opportunity necessary to bring the motion picture to a still higher level of wholesome entertainment for all concerned.

THE PRODUCTION CODE

General Principles

1. No picture shall be produced which will lower the moral standards of those who see it. Hence the sympathy of the audience shall never be thrown to the side of crime, wrongdoing, evil, or sin.

2. Correct standards of life, subject only to the requirements of drama and entertainment, shall be presented.

3. Law—divine, natural, or human—shall not be ridiculed, nor shall sympathy be created for its violation.

Particular Applications:

Crime

1. Crime shall never be presented in such a way as to throw sympathy with the crime as against law and justice, or to inspire others with a desire for imitation.

2. Methods of crime shall not be explicitly presented or detailed in a manner calculated to glamorize crime or inspire imitation.

3. Action showing the taking of human life is to be held to the minimum. Its frequent presentation tends to lessen regard for the sacredness of life.

4. Suicide, as a solution of problems occurring in the development of screen drama, is to be discouraged unless absolutely necessary for the development of the plot, and shall never be justified, or glorified, or used specifically to defeat the ends of justice.

5. Excessive flaunting of weapons by criminals shall not be permitted.

6. There shall be no scenes of law-enforcing officers dying at the hands of criminals, unless such scenes are absolutely necessary to the plot.

7. Pictures dealing with criminal activities in which minors participate, or to which minors are related, shall not be approved if they tend to incite demoralizing imitation on the part of youth.

8. Murder:

❦ The technique of murder must not be presented in a way that will inspire imitation.

❦ Brutal killings are not to be presented in detail.

❦ Revenge in modern times shall not be justified.

❦ Mercy killing shall never be made to seem right or permissible.

9. Drug addiction or the illicit traffic in addiction-producing drugs shall not be shown if the portrayal:

❦ Tends in any manner to encourage, stimulate, or justify the use of such drugs; or

❦ Stresses, visually or by dialog, their temporarily attractive effects; or

❦ Suggests that the drug habit may be quickly or easily broken; or

❦ Shows details of drug procurement or of the taking of drugs in any manner; or

❦ Emphasizes the profits of the drug traffic; or

❦ Involves children who are shown knowingly to use or traffic in drugs.

10. Stories on the kidnapping or illegal abduction of children are acceptable under the code only

❦ when the subject is handled with restraint and discretion and avoids details, gruesomeness and undue horror; and

❦ the child is returned unharmed.

Brutality

Excessive and inhuman acts of cruelty and brutality shall not be presented. This includes all detailed and protracted presentation of physical violence, torture, and abuse.

Sex

The sanctity of the institution of marriage and home shall be upheld. No film shall infer that casual or promiscuous sex relationships are the accepted or common thing.

1. Adultery and illicit sex, sometimes necessary plot material, shall not be explicitly treated, nor shall they be justified or made to seem right and permissible.

2. Scenes of passion:

❦ These should not be introduced except where they are definitely essential to the plot.

❦ Lustful and open-mouthed kissing, lustful embraces, suggestive posture and gestures are not to be shown.

❦ In general, passion should be treated in such manner as not to stimulate the baser emotions.

3. Seduction or rape:

❦ These should never be more than suggested, and then only when essential to the plot. They should never be shown explicitly.

❦ They are never acceptable subject matter for comedy.

❦ They should never be made to seem right and permissible.

4. The subject of abortion shall be discouraged, shall never be more than suggested, and when referred to shall be condemned. It must never be treated lightly

or made the subject of comedy. Abortion shall never be shown explicitly or by inference, and story must not indicate that an abortion has been performed. The word "abortion" shall not be used.

5. The methods and techniques of prostitution and white slavery shall never be presented in detail, nor shall the subjects be presented unless shown in contrast as such may not be shown.

6. Sex perversion or any inference of it is forbidden.

7. Sex hygiene and venereal diseases are not acceptable subject matter for theatrical motion pictures.

8. Children's sex organs are never to be exposed. This provision shall not apply to infants.

Vulgarity

Vulgar expressions and double meanings having the same effect are forbidden. This shall include, but not be limited to, such words and expressions as chippie, fairy, goose, nuts, pansy, S.O.B., son-of-a. The treatment of low, disgusting, unpleasant, though not necessarily evil, subjects should be guided always by the dictates of good taste and a proper regard for the sensibilities of the audience.

Obscenity

1. Dances suggesting or representing sexual actions or emphasizing indecent movements are to be regarded as obscene.

2. Obscenity in words, gesture, reference, song, joke, or by suggestion, even when likely to be understood by only part of the audience, is forbidden.

Blasphemy and Profanity

1. Blasphemy is forbidden. Reference to the Deity, God, Lord, Jesus, Christ shall not be irreverent.

2. Profanity is forbidden. The words "hell" and "damn," while sometimes dramatically

valid, will, if used without moderation, be considered offensive by many members of the audience. Their use shall be governed by the discretion and prudent advice of the Code Administration.

Costumes

1. Complete nudity, in fact or in silhouette, is never permitted, nor shall there be any licentious notice by characters in the film of suggested nudity.

2. Indecent or undue exposure is forbidden. The foregoing shall not be interpreted to exclude actual scenes photographed in a foreign land of the natives of that land, showing native life, provided:

❦ Such scenes are included in a documentary film or travelogue depicting exclusively such land, its customs, and civilization; and

❦ Such scenes are not in themselves intrinsically objectionable.

Religion

1. No film or episode shall throw ridicule on any religious faith.

2. Ministers of religion, or persons posing as such, shall not be portrayed as comic characters or as villains so as to cast disrespect on religion.

3. Ceremonies of any definite religion shall be carefully and respectfully handled.

Special Subjects

The following subjects must be treated with discretion and restraint within the careful limits of good tastes:

1. Bedroom scenes.

2. Hangings and electrocutions.

3. Liquor and drinking.

4. Surgical operations and childbirth.

5. Third-degree methods.

National Feelings

1. The use of the flag shall be consistently respectful.

2. The history, institutions, prominent people, and citizenry of all nations shall be represented fairly.

3. No picture shall be produced that tends to incite bigotry or hatred among peoples of differing races, religions, or national origins. The use of such offensive words as Chink, Dago, Frog, Greaser, Hunkie, Kike, Nigger, Spic, Wop, Yid should be avoided.

Titles

The following titles shall not be used:

1. Titles which are salacious, indecent, obscene, profane, or vulgar.

2. Titles which violate any other clause of this code.

Cruelty to Animals

In the production of motion pictures involving animals the producer shall consult with the authorized representative of the American Humane Association and invite him to be present during the staging of such animal action. There shall be no use of any contrivance or apparatus for tripping or otherwise treating animals in any unacceptably harsh manner.

THEODOR ADORNO AND MAX HORKHEIMER

The Culture Industry: Enlightenment as Mass Deception

THEODOR ADORNO *and* MAX HORKHEIMER *were two of the leading "Critical Theorists" who led the German philosophical revolt against National Socialism. This famous piece originated in their book,* The Dialectic of Enlightenment.

THE sociological theory that the loss of the support of objectively established religion, the dissolution of the last remnants of pre-capitalism, together with technological and social differentiation or specialization, have led to cultural chaos is disproved every day; for culture now impresses the same stamp on everything. Films, radio and magazines make up a system which is uniform as a whole and in every part. Even the aesthetic activities of political opposites are one in their enthusiastic obedience to the rhythm of the iron system. The decorative industrial management buildings and exhibition centers in authoritarian countries are much the same as anywhere else. The huge gleaming towers that shoot up everywhere are outward signs of the ingenious planning of international concerns, toward which the unleashed entrepreneurial system (whose monuments are a mass of gloomy houses and business premises in grimy, spiritless cities) was already hastening. Even now the older houses just outside the concrete city centers look like slums, and the new bungalows on the outskirts are at one with the flimsy structures of world fairs in their praise of technical progress and their built-in demand to be discarded after a short while like empty food cans. Yet the city housing projects designed to perpetuate the individual as a supposedly independent unit in a small hygienic dwelling make him all the more subservient to his adversary—the absolute power of capitalism. Because the inhabitants, as producers and as consumers, are drawn into the center in search of work and pleasure, all the living units crystallize into well-organized complexes. The striking unity of microcosm and macrocosm presents men with a model of their culture: the false identity of the general and the particular. Under monopoly all mass culture is identical, and the lines of its artificial framework begin to show through. The people at the top are no longer so interested in concealing monopoly: as its violence becomes more open, so its power grows. Movies and radio need no longer pretend to be art. The truth that they are just business is made into an ideology in order to justify the rubbish they deliberately produce. They call themselves industries; and when their directors' incomes are published, any doubt about the social utility of the finished products is removed.

Interested parties explain the culture industry in technological terms. It is alleged that because millions participate in it, certain reproduction processes are necessary that inevitably require identical needs in innumerable places to be satisfied with identical goods. The technical contrast between the few production centers and the large number of widely dispersed consumption points is said to demand organization and planning by management. Furthermore, it is claimed that standards were based in the first place on consumers' needs, and for that reason were accepted with so little resistance. The result is the circle of manipulation and retroactive need in which the unity of the system grows ever stronger. No mention is made of the fact that the basis on which technology acquires power over society is the power of those whose economic hold over society is greatest. A technological rationale is the rationale of domination itself. It is the coercive nature of society alienated from itself. Automobiles, bombs, and movies keep the whole thing together until their leveling element shows its strength in the very wrong which it furthered. It has made the technology of the culture industry no more than the achievement of standardization and mass production, sacrificing whatever involved a distinction between the logic of the work and that of the social system. This is the result not of a law of movement in technology as such but of its function in today's economy. The need which might resist central control has already been suppressed by the control of the individual consciousness. The step from the telephone to the radio has clearly distinguished the roles. The former still allowed the subscriber to play the role of subject, and was liberal. The latter is democratic: it turns all participants into listeners and authoritatively subjects them to broadcast programs which are all exactly the same. No machinery of rejoinder has been devised, and private broadcasters are denied any freedom. They are confined to the apocryphal field of the "amateur," and also have to accept organization from above. But any trace of spontaneity from the public in official broadcasting is controlled and absorbed by talent scouts, studio competitions and official programs of every kind selected by professionals. Talented performers belong to the industry long before it displays them; otherwise they would not be so eager to fit in. The attitude of the public, which ostensibly and actually favors the system of the culture industry, is a part of the system and not an excuse for it. If one branch of art follows the same formula as one with a very different medium and content; if the dramatic intrigue of broadcast soap operas becomes no more than useful material for showing how to master technical problems at both ends of the scale of musical experience—real jazz or a cheap imitation; or if a movement from a Beethoven symphony is crudely "adapted" for a film sound-track in the same way as a Tolstoy novel is garbled in a film script: then the claim that this is done to satisfy the spontaneous wishes of the public is no more than hot air. We are closer to the facts if we explain these phenomena as inherent in the technical and personnel apparatus which, down to its last cog, itself forms part of the economic mechanism of selection. In addition there is the agreement—or at least the determination—of all executive authorities not to produce or sanction anything that in any way differs from their own rules, their own ideas about consumers, or above all themselves.

In our age the objective social tendency is incarnate in the hidden subjective purposes of company directors, the foremost among whom are in the most powerful sectors of industry—steel, petroleum, electricity, and chemicals. Culture monopolies are weak and dependent in comparison. They cannot afford to neglect their appeasement of the real holders of power. . . . The dependence of the most powerful broadcasting company on the electrical industry, or of the motion picture industry on the banks, is characteristic of the whole sphere, whose individual branches are themselves economically interwoven. All are in such close contact that the extreme concentration of mental forces allows demarcation lines between different firms and technical branches to be ignored. The ruthless unity in the culture industry is evidence of what will happen in politics. Marked differentiations such as those of A and B films, or of stories in magazines in different price ranges, depend not so much on subject matter as on classifying, organizing, and labeling consumers. Something is provided for all so that none may escape; the distinctions are emphasized and extended. The public is catered for with a hierarchical range of mass-produced products of varying quality, thus advancing the rule of complete quantification. Everybody must behave (as if spontaneously) in accordance with his previously determined and indexed level, and choose the category of mass product turned out for his type. Consumers appear as statistics on research organization charts, and are divided by income groups into red, green, and blue areas; the technique is that used for any type of propaganda.

How formalized the procedure is can be seen when the mechanically differentiated products prove to be all alike in the end. That the difference between the Chrysler range and General Motors products is basically illusory strikes every child with a keen interest in varieties. What connoisseurs discuss as good or bad points serve only to perpetuate the semblance of competition and range of choice. The same applies to the Warner Brothers and Metro Goldwyn Mayer productions. But even the differences between the more expensive and cheaper models put out by the same firm steadily diminish: for automobiles, there are such differences as the number of cylinders, cubic capacity, details of patented gadgets; and for films there are the number of stars, the extravagant use of technology, labor, and equipment, and the introduction of the latest psychological formulas. The universal criterion of merit is the amount of "conspicuous production," of blatant cash investment. The varying budgets in the culture industry do not bear the slightest relation to factual values, to the meaning of the products themselves. Even the technical media are relentlessly forced into uniformity. Television aims at a synthesis of radio and film, and is held up only because the interested parties have not yet reached agreement, but its consequences will be quite enormous and promise to intensify the impoverishment of aesthetic matter so drastically, that by tomorrow the thinly veiled identity of all industrial culture products can come triumphantly out into the open, derisively fulfilling the Wagnerian dream of the *Gesamtkunstwerk* the fusion of all the arts in one work. The alliance of word, image, and music is all the more perfect than in *Tristan* because the sensuous elements which all approvingly reflect the surface of social reality are in principle embodied in the same technical process, the unity of which becomes its distinctive content. This process integrates all the elements of the production, from the novel (shaped with an eye to the film) to the last sound effect. It is the triumph of invested capital, whose title as absolute master is etched deep into the hearts of the dispossessed in the employment line; it is the meaningful content of every film, whatever plot the production team may have selected.

The man with leisure has to accept what the culture manufacturers offer him. Kant's formalism still expected a contribution from the individual, who was thought to relate the varied experiences of the senses to fundamental concepts; but industry robs the individual of his function. Its prime service to the customer is to do his schematizing for him. Kant said that there was a secret mechanism in the soul which prepared direct intuitions in such a way that they could be fitted into the system of pure reason. But today that secret has been deciphered. While the mechanism is to all appearances planned by those who serve up the data of experience, that is, by the culture industry, it is in fact forced upon the latter by the power of society, which remains irrational, however we may try to rationalize it; and this inescapable force is processed by commercial agencies so that they give an artificial impression of being in command. There is nothing left for the consumer to classify. Producers have done it for him. Art for the masses has destroyed the dream but still conforms to the tenets of that dreaming idealism which critical idealism balked at. Everything derives from consciousness: for Malebranche and Berkeley, from the consciousness of God; in mass art, from the consciousness of the production team. Not only are the hit songs, stars, and soap operas cyclically recurrent and rigidly invariable types, but the specific content of the entertainment itself is derived from them and only appears to change. The details are interchangeable. The short interval sequence which was effective in a hit song, the hero's momentary fall from grace (which he accepts as good sport), the rough treatment which the beloved gets from the male star, the latter's rugged defiance of the spoilt heiress, are, like all the other details, ready-made clichés to be slotted in anywhere; they never do anything more than fulfill the purpose allotted them in the overall plan. Their whole *raison d'être* is to confirm it by being its constituent parts. As soon as the film begins, it is quite clear how it will end, and who will be rewarded, punished, or forgotten. In light music, once the trained ear has heard the first notes of the hit song, it can guess what is coming and feel flattered when it does come. The average length of the short story has to be rigidly adhered to. Even gags, effects, and jokes are calculated like the setting in which they are placed. They are the responsibility of special experts and their narrow range makes it easy for them to be apportioned in the office. The development of the culture industry has led to the predominance of the effect, the obvious touch, and the technical detail over the work itself—which once expressed an idea, but was liquidated together with the idea. When the detail won its freedom, it became rebellious and, in the period from Romanticism to Expressionism, asserted itself as free expression, as a vehicle of protest against the organization. In music the single harmonic effect obliterated the awareness of form as a whole; in painting the individual color was stressed at the expense of pictorial composition; and in the novel psychology became more important than structure. The totality of the culture industry has put an end to this. Though concerned exclusively with effects, it crushes their insubordination and makes them subserve the formula, which replaces the work. The same fate is inflicted on whole and parts alike. The whole inevitably bears no relation to the details—just like the career of a successful man into which

everything is made to fit as an illustration or a proof, whereas it is nothing more than the sum of all those idiotic events. The so-called dominant idea is like a file which ensures order but not coherence. The whole and the parts are alike; there is no antithesis and no connection. Their prearranged harmony is a mockery of what had to be striven after in the great bourgeois works of art. In Germany the graveyard stillness of the dictatorship already hung over the gayest films of the democratic era.

The whole world is made to pass through the filter of the culture industry. The old experience of the movie-goer, who sees the world outside as an extension of the film he has just left (because the latter is intent upon reproducing the world of everyday perceptions), is now the producer's guideline. The more intensely and flawlessly his techniques duplicate empirical objects, the easier it is today for the illusion to prevail that the outside world is the straightforward continuation of that presented on the screen. This purpose has been furthered by mechanical reproduction since the lightning takeover by the sound film.

Real life is becoming indistinguishable from the movies. The sound film, far surpassing the theater of illusion, leaves no room for imagination or reflection on the part of the audience, who is unable to respond within the structure of the film, yet deviate from its precise detail without losing the thread of the story; hence the film forces its victims to equate it directly with reality. The stunting of the mass-media consumer's powers of imagination and spontaneity does not have to be traced back to any psychological mechanisms; he must ascribe the loss of those attributes to the objective nature of the products themselves, especially to the most characteristic of them, the sound film. They are so designed that quickness, powers of observation, and experience are undeniably needed to apprehend them at all; yet sustained thought is out of the question if the spectator is not to miss the relentless rush of facts. Even though the effort required for his response is semi-automatic, no scope is left for the imagination. Those who are so absorbed by the world of the movie—by its images, gestures, and words—that they are unable to supply what really makes it a world, do not have to dwell on particular points of its mechanics during a screening. All the other films and products of the entertainment industry which they have seen have taught them what to expect; they react automatically. The might of industrial society is lodged in men's minds. The entertainments manufacturers know that their products will be consumed with alertness even when the customer is distraught, for each of them is a model of the huge economic machinery which has always sustained the masses, whether at work or at leisure—which is akin to work. From every sound film and every broadcast program the social effect can be inferred which is exclusive to none but is shared by all alike. The culture industry as a whole has molded men as a type unfailingly reproduced in every product.

In the culture industry the notion of genuine style is seen to be the aesthetic equivalent of domination. Style considered as mere aesthetic regularity is a romantic dream of the past. The unity of style not only of the Christian Middle Ages but of the Renaissance expresses in each case the different structure of social power, and not the obscure experience of the oppressed in which the general was enclosed. The great artists were never those who embodied a wholly flawless and perfect style, but those who used style as a way of hardening themselves against the chaotic expression of suffering, as a negative truth. The style of their works gave what was expressed that force without which life flows away unheard. Those very art forms which are known as classical, such as Mozart's music, contain objective trends which represent something different to the style which they incarnate. As late as Schönberg and Picasso, the great artists have retained a mistrust of style, and at crucial points have subordinated it to the logic of the matter. What Dadaists and Expressionists called the untruth of style as such triumphs today in the sung jargon of a crooner, in the carefully contrived elegance of a film star, and even in the admirable expertise of a photograph of a peasant's squalid hut. [Style represents a promise in every work of art. That which is expressed is subsumed through style into the dominant forms of generality, into the language of music, painting, or words, in the hope that it will be reconciled thus with the idea of true generality. This promise held out by the work of art that it will create truth by lending new shape to the conventional social forms is as necessary as it is hypocritical. It unconditionally posits the real forms of life as it is by suggesting that fulfillment lies in their aesthetic derivatives. To this extent the claim of art is always ideology too.] However, only in this confrontation with tradition of which style is the record can art express suffering. That factor in a work of art which enables it to transcend reality certainly cannot be detached from style; but it does not consist of the harmony actually realized, of any doubtful unity of form and content, within and without, of individual and society; it is to be found in those features in which discrepancy appears: in the necessary failure of the passionate striving for identity. Instead of exposing itself to this failure in which the style of the great work of art has always achieved self-negation, the inferior work has always relied on its similarity with others—on a surrogate identity.

In the culture industry this imitation finally becomes absolute. Having ceased to be anything but style, it reveals the latter's secret: obedience to the social hierarchy. Today aesthetic barbarity completes what has threatened the creations of the spirit since they were gathered together as culture and neutralized. To speak of culture was always contrary to culture. Culture as a common denominator already contains in embryo that schematization and process of cataloging and classification which bring culture within the sphere of administration. And it is precisely the industrialized, the consequent, subsumption which entirely accords with this notion of culture. By subordinating in the same way and to the same end all areas of intellectual creation, by occupying men's senses from the time they leave the factory in the evening to the time they clock in again the next morning with matter that bears the impress of the labor process they themselves have to sustain throughout the day, this subsumption mockingly satisfies the concept of a unified culture which the philosophers of personality contrasted with mass culture.

TOM WOLFE

The Worship of Art: Notes on the New God

TOM WOLFE *is one of the founders of "the new journalism" and the author of such notorious works as* Electric Kool-Aid Acid Test *and the best-selling novel,* Bonfire of the Vanities. *He is also a rogue art critic, infuriating the art world and the architecture world, respectively, with his books* The Painted Word *and* From Bauhaus to Our House. *In the following essay, he suggests that art has become something of a new secular religion.*

LET me tell you about the night the Vatican art show opened at the Metropolitan Museum of Art in New York. The scene was the Temple of Dendur, an enormous architectural mummy, complete with a Lake of the Dead, underneath a glass bell at the rear of the museum. On the stone apron in front of the temple, by the lake, the museum put on a formal dinner for 360 souls, including the wife of the President of the United States, the usual philanthropic dowagers and corporate art patrons, a few catered names, such as Prince Albert of Monaco and Henry Kissinger, and many well-known members of the New York art world. But since this was, after all, an exhibition of the Vatican art collection, it was necessary to include some Roman Catholics. Cardinal Cooke, Vatican emissaries, prominent New York Catholic laymen, Knights of Malta—there they were, devout Christians at a New York art world event. The culturati and the Christians were arranged at the tables like Arapaho beads; one culturatus, one Christian, one culturatus, one Christian, one culturatus, one Christian, one culturatus, one Christian.

Gamely, the guests tried all the conventional New York conversation openers—real estate prices, friends who have been mugged recently, well-known people whose children have been arrested on drug charges, Brits, live-in help, the dishonesty of helipad contractors, everything short of the desperately trite subjects used in the rest of the country, namely the weather and front-wheel drive. Nothing worked. There were dreadful lulls during which there was no sound at all in that antique churchyard except for the ping of hotel silver on earthenware plates echoing off the tombstone facade of the temple.

Shortly before dessert, I happened to be out in the museum's main lobby when two Manhattan art dealers appeared in their tuxedos, shaking their heads.

One said to the other: "Who are these *unbelievable people?*"

But of course! It seemed not only *outré* to have these . . . these . . . these . . . these *religious types* at an art event, it seemed sacrilegious. The culturati were being forced to rub shoulders with heathens. That was the way it hit them. For today art—not religion—is the religion of the educated classes. Today educated people look upon traditional religious ties—Catholic, Episcopal, Presbyterian, Methodist, Baptist, Jewish—as matters of social pedigree. It is only art that they look upon religiously.

When I say that art is the religion of the educated classes, I am careful not to use the word in the merely metaphorical way people do when they say someone is religious about sticking to a diet or training for a sport. I am not using "religion" as a synonym for "enthusiasm." I am referring specifically to what Max Weber identified as the objective functions of a religion: the abnegation or rejection of the world and the legitimation of wealth. . . .

Today there are few new religions that appeal to educated people—Scientology, Arica, Synanon, and some neo-Hindu, neo-Buddhist, and neo-Christian groups—but their success has been limited. The far more common way to reject the world, in our time, is through art. I'm sure you're familiar with it. You're on the subway during the morning rush hour, in one of those cars that is nothing but a can of meat on wheels, jammed in shank to flank and haunch to paunch and elbow to rib with people who talk to themselves and shout obscenities into the void and click their teeth and roll back their upper lips to reveal their purple gums, and there is nothing you can do about it. You can't budge. Coffee, adrenaline, and rogue hate are squirting through your every duct and every vein, and just when you're beginning to wonder how any mortal can possibly stand it, you look around and you see a young woman seated serenely in what seems to be a perfect pink cocoon of peace, untouched, unthreatened, by the growling mob around her. Her eyes are lowered. In her lap, invariably, is a book. If you look closely, you will see that this book is by Rimbaud, or Rilke, or Baudelaire, or Kafka, or Gabriel García Marquez, author of *One Hundred Years of Solitude.* And as soon as you see this vision, you understand the conviction that creates the inviolable aura around her: "I may be forced into this rat race, this squalid human stew, but I do not have to be *of* it. I inhabit a universe that is finer. I can reject all this." You can envision her apartment immediately. There is a mattress on top of a flush door supported by bricks. There's a window curtained in monk's cloth. There's a hand-thrown pot with a few blue cornflowers in it. There are some Paul Klee and Modigliani prints on the wall and a poster from the Acquavella Galleries' Matisse show. "I don't need your Louis Bourbon bergères and your fabric-covered walls. I reject your whole Parish-Hadley world—through art."

And what about the legitimation of wealth? It wasn't so long ago that Americans of great wealth routinely gave 10 percent of their income to the church. The practice of tithing was a certification of worthiness on earth and an option on heaven. Today the custom is to give the money to the arts. When Mrs. E. Parmalee Prentice, daughter of John D. Rockefeller Sr. and owner of two adjoining mansions on East Fifty-third Street, just off Fifth Avenue, died in 1962, she did not leave these holdings, worth about $5 million, to her church. She left them to the Museum of Modern Art for the building of a new wing. Nobody's eyebrows arched. By 1962, it would have been more remarkable if a bequest of that size had gone to a religion of the old-fashioned sort. . . .

Today, what American corporation would support a religion? Most would look upon any such thing as sheer madness. So what does a corporation do when the time comes to pray in public? It supports the arts. I don't need to recite figures. Just think of the money raised since the 1950s for the gigantic cultural complexes—Lincoln Center, Kennedy Center, the Chandler Pavillion, the Woodruff Arts Center—that have become *de rigueur* for the modern American metropolis. What are they? Why, they are St. Patrick's, St. Mary's, Washington National, Holy Cross: the American cathedrals of the late twentieth century.

We are talking here about the legitimation of wealth. The worse odor a corporation is in, the more likely it is to support the arts, and the more likely it is to make sure everybody knows it. The energy crisis, to use an antique term from the 1970s, was the greatest bonanza in the Public Broadcasting Service's history. The more loudly they were assailed as exploiters and profiteers, the more earnestly the oil companies poured money into PBS's cultural programming. Every broadcast seemed to end with a discreet notice on the screen saying: "This program was made possible by a grant from Exxon," or perhaps Mobil, or ARCO. . . .

As you can imagine, this state of affairs has greatly magnified the influence of the art world. In size, that world has never been anything more than a village. In the United States, fashions in art are determined by no more than 3,000 people, at least 2,950 of whom live in Manhattan. I can't think of a single influential critic today. "The gallery-going public" has never had any influence at all—so we are left with certain dealers, curators, and artists. No longer do they have the servantlike role of catering to or glorifying the client. Their role today is to save him. They have become a form of clergy—or clerisy, to use an old word for secular souls who take on clerical duties.

• • •

It is in the area of public sculpture that the religion of art currently makes its richest contribution to the human comedy. . . .

. . . The Rockefellers' Number One Chase Manhattan Plaza was the first glass skyscraper on Wall Street. Out front, on a bare Bauhaus-style apron, the so-called plaza, was installed a sculpture by Jean Dubuffet. It is made of concrete and appears to be four toad stools fused into a gelatinous mass with black lines running up the sides. The title is *Group of Four Trees*. Not even *Group of Four Rockefellers*. After all, there *were* four at the time: David, John D. III, Nelson, and Laurance. But the piece has absolutely nothing to say about the glory or even the existence of the Rockefellers, Wall Street, Chase Manhattan Bank, American business, or the building it stands in front of. Instead, it proclaims the glory of contemporary art. It fulfills the new purpose of public sculpture, which is the legitimation of wealth through the new religion of the educated classes. . . .

If people want to place Turds in the Plazas as a form of religious offering of prayer, and they own the plazas, there isn't much anybody else can do about it. But what happens when they use public money, tax money, to do the same thing on plazas owned by the public? At that point you're in for a glorious farce. . . .

In 1976, the city of Hartford decided to reinforce its reputation as the Athens of lower central midwestern New England by having an important piece of sculpture installed downtown. It followed what is by now the usual procedure, which is to turn the choice over to a panel of "experts" in the field—i.e., the clerisy, in this case, six curators, critics, and academicians, three of them chosen by the National Endowment for the Arts, which put up half the money. So one day in 1978 a man named Carl Andre arrived in Hartford with thirty-six rocks. Not carved stones, not even polished boluses of the Henry Moore sort—rocks. He put them on the ground in a triangle, like bowling pins. Then he presented the city council with a bill for $87,000. Nonplussed and, soon enough, furious, the citizenry hooted and jeered and called the city council members imbeciles while the council members alternately hit the sides of their heads with their hands and made imaginary snowballs. Nevertheless, they approved payment, and the rocks—entitled *Stone Field*—are still there.

One day in 1981, the Civil Service workers in the new Javits Federal Building in Manhattan went outside to the little plaza in front of the building at lunchtime to do the usual, which was to have their tuna puffs and diet Shastas, and there, running through the middle of it, was a wall of black steel twelve feet high and half a city block long. Nonplussed and, soon enough, furious, 1,300 of them drew up a petition asking the GSA to remove it, only to be informed that this was, in fact, a major work of art, entitled *Tilted Arc*, by a famous American sculptor named Richard Serra. Serra did not help things measurably by explaining that he was "redefining the space" for the poor Civil Service lifers and helping to wean them away from the false values "created by advertising and corporations." Was it his fault if "it offends people to have their preconceptions of reality changed"? This seventy-three-ton gesture of homage to contemporary art remains in place.

The public sees nothing, absolutely nothing, in these stone fields, tilted arcs, and Instant Stonehenges, because it was never meant to. The public is looking at the arena of the new religion of the educated classes. At this point one might well ask what the clerisy itself sees in them, a question that would plunge us into doctrines as abstruse as any that engaged the medieval Scholastics. Andre's *Stone Field,* for example, was created to illustrate three devout theories concerning the nature of sculpture. One, a sculpture should not be placed upon that bourgeois device, the pedestal, which seeks to elevate it above the people. (Therefore, the rocks are on the ground.) Two, a sculpture should "express its gravity." (And what expresses gravity better than rocks lying on the ground?) Three, a sculpture should not be that piece of bourgeois pretentiousness, the "picture in the air" (such as the statues of Lee and Duke); it should force the viewer to confront its "object-ness." (You want object-ness? Take a look at a plain rock! Take a look at thirty-six rocks!). . . .

The public is nonplussed and, soon enough, becomes furious—and also uneasy. After all, if understanding such ar-

cana is the hallmark of the educated classes today, and you find yourself absolutely baffled, what does that say about your level of cultivation? Since 1975, attendance at museums of art in the United States has risen from 42 million to 60 million people per year. Why? In 1980 the Hirshhorn Museum did a survey of people who came to the museum over a seven-month period. I find the results fascinating. Thirty-six percent said they had come to learn about contemporary art. Thirty-two percent said they had come to learn about a particular contemporary artist. Thirteen percent came on tours. Only 15 percent said they were there for what was once the conventional goal of museumgoers: to enjoy the pictures and sculptures. The conventional goal of museumgoers today is something quite different. Today they are there to learn—and to see the light. At the Hirshhorn, the people who were interviewed in the survey said such things as: "I know this is great art, and now I feel so unintelligent." And: "After coming to this museum, I now feel so much better about art and so much worse about me."

In other words: "I believe, O Lord, but I am unworthy! Reveal to me Thy mysteries!"

PAUL MATTICK, JR.

Arts and the State

PAUL MATTICK, JR., *teaches philosophy at Adelphi University. He is the author of*
Social Knowledge: An Essay on the Nature and Limits of Social Science.

V ISITING the exhibition of
Robert Mapplethorpe's photographs at the Institute of
Contemporary Art in Boston a month
ago, it was hard at first to see what all
the fuss was about. The controversy that
has dogged the show since its organization by the Institute of Contemporary
Art in Philadelphia certainly made itself
felt in the huge numbers of visitors
(tickets sold out well in advance) and in
the aura of decorous excitement that en-
veloped those who managed to get in.
Most of the pictures, however, were un-
exciting. With the exception of a handful of striking images from the artist's
last years, we saw celebrity portraits
shot in 1940s fashion style, arty flowers, naked black men in a venerable
art-nude tradition. In a distinct area,
however, reached only by waiting in a
patient line of cultured scopophiles,
were the pictures which more than the
others had called down upon the National Endowment for the Arts, partial
funder of the Philadelphia I.C.A., the
wrath of America's self-appointed
guardians of morality.

There were more flowers, more
naked black men and a set of s&m pho-
tos that was undeniably gripping. Here
the subject matter overcame Mapplethorpe's tendency to artiness and
commercial finish in a set of documents
with the power of the once dark and
hidden brought to light. Here are some
things some people like to do, they say;
this is part of our world; you can look or

not, but now you know they exist, whatever you think of them. In an age saturated with sexual imagery of all kinds,
these pictures were perhaps not as disturbing as they might have been to more
innocent eyes. At any rate, the visiting
public was not so horrified as to fail to
crowd the museum store to purchase
bookfuls of Mapplethorpe's pictures
(along with black nude-emblazoned T-
shirts, floral porcelain plates and
bumper stickers proclaiming support for
freedom of the arts). Nonetheless, these
photographs, in the company of a few
other pictures and performances, have
evoked a storm of Congressional and
popular indignation that now threatens
to sweep away the N.E.A. itself. This, in
turn, has given rise to attempts to defend the current mode of state patronage
of the arts.

It is difficult to speak of real controversy in this area, as the two discourses
at work are to a great degree at cross-
purposes. That of the naysaying politicians tends toward expressions of
traditional American anti-intellectualism,
portraying state arts funding as the use,
basically for the gratification of a degenerate Eastern elite, of money better spent
on local pork barrels and military projects. Art, in this view, has a natural
affinity with sex, subversion and fraudu-
lence. On the other hand, the statements
of opposition to censorship and calls for
arts funding by artists, dealers, other art
professionals and liberal politicians take
as given the social value of the arts, their

consequent claim on the public purse and (with some disagreement) the current mode of distribution of the goodies. Without being in favor of either censorship or the diversion of yet more money to produce new bombers and missiles, one may step back and attempt to rethink the question.

Lacking a feudal heritage, a tradition of princely magnificence such as that which stands behind state cultural policy in European countries, the United States has no long history of governmental patronage of the arts. Under American law, corporations themselves were forbidden to engage in philanthropy, including support of the arts, until 1935. Washington was supposed, in this most purely capitalist of all nations, to spend only the minimum needed to control labor and defend business's national interests. Theater, including opera, functioned in the nineteenth century as a commercial enterprise across the country, and the visual arts were for the most part produced for private purchase. When growing economic power stimulated the mercantile and industrial upper classes of the later nineteenth century to call for the establishment of museums, symphony orchestras and other cultural institutions, they had to put up the money themselves. Thus, while the revolutionary regime in France, for example, took over the King's palace and its contents to create the Musée du Louvre for the nation, the United States did not have a National Gallery in Washington until Andrew Mellon gave his personal collection to the country and started building a structure to house it in 1938.

The arts began to attract more public attention with the start of the twentieth century, as can be seen in the national publicity gained by the Armory Show, which introduced European modernism to the United States in 1913. Whereas art and all those things called "culture" in general had earlier been largely identified with the European upper class, Regionalism, given national exposure by a *Time* cover story in 1934, claimed to be a uniquely American style. At the time of the New Deal, a few farsighted individuals conceived the idea of government aid to the arts as part of the general federal effort to combat the Depression. Two programs for the employment of artists, one run out of the Treasury Department and a much larger one as part of the Works Progress Administration, represented the national government's first entry into patronage (aside from the commissioning of official buildings, statuary and paintings). In the view of the organizers of these projects, their long-term rationale was support for the arts as a fundamental part of American life; but they could be realized, in the face of much opposition from Congress (and professional artists' associations, true to the principles of free enterprise), only as relief programs, employing otherwise starving (and potentially subversive) artists and preserving their productive skills during the emergency. Both programs died, after a period of reduction, with America's entry into the war.

Institutional concern with the arts developed markedly with the U.S. rise to world supremacy after the war. The war reversed the normal flow of American artists to Europe, bringing refugee artists to New York and California and thus stimulating artistic life, at least on the edges of North America. More important, its segue into the cold war joined to the growing desire of the American upper class to play social roles equal to its expanded global importance a new use for American modern art as a symbol of the advantages of a free society. New York abstraction, still unappreciated by any sizable public, was not only promoted by the mass media that had once publicized Regionalism but was shipped around the world, along with jazz music and industrial design, by government bodies like the United States Information Agency and by the Rockefeller-dominated Museum of Modern Art. In modern art, it seemed, America was now number one; while still incomprehensible (as critic Max Kozloff once observed), art that celebrated the autonomy of the creative individual no longer seemed so subversive. In the realm of classical music, Van Cliburn's victory in a piano competition in Moscow in 1958 was an event of political as well as cultural importance.

More fundamentally, beyond issues of international political prestige and the aristocratic pretensions of the very rich, the idea was gaining ground among America's elite—particularly in the Northeast but in a city like Chicago as well—that art is a Good Thing, a glamorous thing, even (more recently) a fun thing. This attitude rapidly trickled down to the middle class, whose self-assertion as leading citizens of an affluent and powerful nation was expressed in a new attachment to culture. As interest in art spread throughout the country, the 1950s saw galleries in department stores, rising museum and concert attendance and the commercial distribution of classical LPs and inexpensive reproductions of famous paintings. Studio training and art history departments proliferated in the universities. A handful of corporate executives, in alliance with cultural entrepreneurs like Mortimer Adler and R. M. Hutchins, discovered

that culture, whether classic or modern, could be both marketed and used as a marketing medium.

In part this reflected the changing nature of the business class; while fewer than 50 percent of top executives had some college education in 1900, 76 percent did by 1950. The postwar rise of the professional manager helped break down the traditional barrier between the worlds of business and culture, affecting the self-image of American society as a whole. To this was joined—with the growth of academia, research institutions and all levels of government—the emergence of the new professional-intellectual stratum, connected in spirit to the power elite in a way unknown to the alienated intelligentsia of yesteryear. In 1952 the editors of *Partisan Review* introduced a symposium on "Our Country and Our Culture" with the observation that just a decade earlier, "America was commonly thought to be hostile to art and culture. Since then, however, the tide has begun to turn. . . . Europe . . . no longer assures that rich experience of culture which inspired and justified a criticism of American life. . . . America has become the protector of Western civilization."

Thus politics, business and culture joined hands. Art's growing value as an area of investment and domestic public relations could only be reinforced by its emergence as a marker of international prestige. The Kennedys' Camelot was a watershed, with its transformation of the Europhilia typical of the American elite into the representation of the White House as a world cultural center. Kennedy counselor Arthur Schlesinger Jr. put it this way, in arguing for a government arts policy: "We will win world understanding of our policy and purposes not through the force of our arms or the array of our wealth but through the splendor of our ideals."

One must not exaggerate: The sums spent on its arts agency by the American government have always been derisorily small, both relative to other government programs and in comparison with the spending of other industrialized capitalist nations. West Germany, the world leader, spent about $73 per inhabitant on the arts last year; the Netherlands spent $33, and even Margaret Thatcher's Britain laid out $12; the United States indulged its culture-mongers with a measly 71 cents per capita. This amounted to less than 0.1 percent of the federal budget (the Smithsonian alone receives a larger appropriation than the N.E.A., as does the Pentagon's military band program, budgeted in 1989 at $193 million). Even this, however, has seemed too much to many conservative politicians, and the current effort to eliminate or restrict the N.E.A. must be seen as one more protest by conservative forces against a relatively novel effort with which they have never been happy.

• • •

Defenders of the N.E.A. and of freedom of state-funded expression tend, like their antagonists, to invoke "American values," celebrating the arts as a natural feature of a "free society."

The basic liberal argument was concisely stated by Richard Oldenburg, director of the Museum of Modern Art in New York, writing recently in MoMA's *Members Quarterly*. He identified the two fundamental issues at stake as the continuance of government arts funding and freedom of expression. The first is important because "support for the arts is support for creativity, a national resource essential to our future and a source of our pride and identity as a nation." And "creativity requires freedom of expression," including the liberty "to explore new paths which may occasionally test our tolerance." . . . As Anthony Lewis put it in a summertime column in *The New York Times,* "When politicians get into the business of deciding what is legitimate art, the game is up."

The other side has two basic responses to these claims. According to Congressman Philip Crane, "Funding art, whether that art is considered outstanding or obscene, is not a legitimate, nor is it a needed, function of the federal government." But in any case, he continues, if art is to receive state support, "Congress has a responsibility to its constituents to determine what type of art taxpayers' dollars will support." This does not constitute censorship, such arguments go: No one is preventing artists from doing whatever kind of work they wish; but the taxpayers are under no obligation to pay for work they find senseless or offensive.

LAWRENCE WESCHLER

Art and Money

LAWRENCE WESCHLER *(1952–) is a journalist and a writer. He has won several awards for his work, including a 1986 Guggenheim Fellowship for work on torture. He is currently a staff writer for* The New Yorker.

J. S. G. Boggs is a young artist who likes to invite you out to dinner at a restaurant, run up a tab of, say, eighty-seven dollars, and then, while sipping coffee, reach into his satchel and pull out a drawing he's been working on for several days. The drawing, on a small sheet of high-quality paper, might consist, in this instance, of a virtually exact rendition of the face side of a hundred-dollar bill. He next pulls out from his satchel a couple of precision pens—one green ink, the other black—and proceeds to apply the finishing touches to his drawing. This activity invariably causes a stir. Guests at neighboring tables crane their necks. Passing waiters stop to gawk. The maître d' eventually drifts over, stares for a while, and then remarks on the excellence of the young man's art. "Thank you," Boggs says. "I'm glad you like this drawing, because I intend to use it as payment for our meal."

At that moment, invariably, a chill descends upon the room. The maître d' blanches. You can just see his mind reeling ("Oh, no, not another nut case") as he begins to plot strategy: should he call the police? How is he going to avoid a scene? But Boggs almost immediately reestablishes a measure of equilibrium by reaching into his satchel and pulling out a real hundred-dollar bill—indeed, the very model for the drawing—and saying, "I mean, of course, if

you want, you can take this regular hundred-dollar bill here instead." Color is returning to the maître d's face. "But, as you can see," Boggs continues, "I'm an artist, and I drew this. It took me many hours to do it, and it's certainly worth something. I'm assigning it an arbitrary price, which just happens to coincide with its face value—one hundred dollars. That means that if you do decide to accept it as full payment for our meal, you're going to have to give me thirteen dollars in change. So you have to make up your mind whether you think this piece of art is worth more or less than this regular one-hundred-dollar bill. It's entirely up to you." Boggs smiles, and the maître d' blanches once again, because now he's into vertigo: the free-fall of worth and value.

Boggs has recently performed variations on this experiment at restaurants, hotels, airline-ticket counters, hot-dog stands, hardware stores, and the like, in the United States, England, Germany, France, Belgium, Ireland, Switzerland, and Italy. (Although he's American, he has been based in London for the past several years.) He has drawn large and small denominations of each of the local currencies, and he has evoked more and less hostile reactions from representatives of each of the local citizenries. Often, the maître d's and cab-drivers and shopkeepers have rejected his offer out of hand. But during the last two years Boggs has managed to gain acceptance of his proposal on more than seven hundred occasions, in transactions totalling well over thirty-five thousand dollars.

The entire game, of course, rests on the precision of Boggs' draftsmanship, which is remarkable, and yet Boggs always goes to great lengths to make sure that his patrons understand that he is not attempting to foist his drawings off as legal tender. For one thing, they're drawn on only one side of the paper; the other side is left blank except for Boggs' signature and documentation. And, in any case, as good as they are, one couldn't very well mistake them for the real thing.

Part 6

Justice and Responsibility

Chapter 18

Am I Free to Choose What I Do?

There is perhaps no topic in philosophy that inspires more public debate than the question of freedom and responsibility. Take the case of a criminal who was raised in a slum, surrounded by poverty, crime, and drugs. He went to a school in which the most academic activity was writing graffiti (most of it misspelled) on walls. He was abused as a child, beaten up as a teenager, and harassed as a young adult. His act of violence, his defense attorney argues, was nothing but the product of his environment and his upbringing. It is society's fault; he is not to blame. The prosecutor is incensed. Thousands of children grow up in similar circumstances, she argues, and they do not turn to crime. A person is free and responsible for what he or she does, she concludes, and crime must be paid for. In another case, a young would-be assassin is said to be "disturbed." He was taking drugs; he had delusions; he did not know right from wrong. His defense attorney also argues that he is not responsible. He had no choice in what he did. The public is enraged. How could a person not be responsible for an act that was planned in advance? And so the argument goes, on the front pages of our newspapers.

Freedom and responsibility go hand in hand. We hold people responsible because we believe that they are free to act or not act in certain ways. People have choices; they make decisions. They act on the basis of knowledge and in accordance with certain values. They are not robots. It is particularly disturbing, therefore, to realize that some of our basic beliefs about the universe contradict this treasured supposition. Once upon a time, people believed (much more than we do today) in **fate**—the idea that everything that happens is somehow ordained to happen beforehand. For example, the ancient Greeks accepted the idea that we are often caught in horrible conflicts from which there is no acceptable escape—which is what they called *tragedy*. Saint Augustine worried how it was possible for us to be free if God, in his omniscience, knew in advance everything that we would do. God may have given us "free will," but it doesn't seem to make much sense to speak of freedom of choice if what you were going to do is already known ahead of time (even if *you* didn't know it).

Modern science presents us with an even more formidable doubt about freedom. One of our basic beliefs about the world is that every event has a cause. Science may not yet have an explanation for a certain phenomenon because it may be very complicated. But we do not doubt that someday, with enough knowledge, we will explain it. And even if we cannot explain some strange event, we do not doubt that there is an explanation—even if we never find it out. This thesis is called **determinism,** which can be summarized as the principle that every event has a cause. But human actions and decisions are events, and if they too are caused or "determined" to be one way rather than another, then a very real question is whether or not it makes any sense to say that we are free to make our own decisions. We may only *seem* to be doing so, but this experience of making a decision, like our action itself, may be nothing but the result of a long sequence of causes and conditions that determine everything we do.

This is the "free will problem." It has tormented philosophers and juries for centuries, and it has practical implications that go far beyond criminal law. If we are in fact "pawns of the universe," then it not only makes no sense to hold us responsible for what we do, but what we do is just a matter of what or who controls the determining causes. It is with this in mind that Harvard psychologist and behaviorist B. F. Skinner attacks the idea of freedom and suggests that well-meaning behavioral psychologists could and should arrange a less chaotic and more civilized deterministic environment than the one we now live in. The result might be a more orderly world, but as author Anthony Burgess argues in his novel *A Clockwork Orange,* it would be a world in which something precious seems to be missing.

As science closes its explanatory grip on one realm of events after another, it would seem that determinism becomes less and less avoidable as a conclusion. But events in science itself sometimes undermine the determinist picture. In the heyday of **hard determinism** in about the eighteenth century (represented here by the French Baron d'Holbach), it made sense to think about the universe as composed of innumerable particles in causal relationship to one another, and this made the determinist thesis "hard" indeed. But twentieth-century physics has overthrown this picture of "matter in motion" and replaced it with a complicated model of subatomic "particles" that do not follow the classic laws of causality. Contemporary quantum theory, for instance, rejects the idea of predictable cause and effect relations at the fundamental level of reality, and without predictions and cause and effect, the determinist thesis does not have a foothold on our thinking. On the other hand, many scientists who accept the determinist picture insist that there is, nevertheless, room for freedom and responsibility. The great psychologist William James, for example, accepted the determinist premise but insisted that we still make decisions and can be held responsible for what we do—a position called **soft determinism.** Jean-Paul Sartre insists that, from one's own point of view, it makes no sense to believe that one's actions and decisions are determined.

In the following selections, we have included a discussion of the Greek tragedy of Agamemnon by Martha Nussbaum and Aristotle's classic definition of voluntary action as that which is done neither out of "compulsion" nor out of ignorance. Baron d'Holbach states the classic case for determinism. John Hospers uses the Freudian notion of the unconscious to throw into total confusion Aristotle's definition, since compelling forces are acting within us as well as on us from the outside. Jean-Paul Sartre offers an **existentialist** defense of freedom, which holds that even if determinism is true, there can be no escaping the freedom and responsibility that is always ours, in every action. B. F. Skinner presents his case for behaviorist control and novelist

Anthony Burgess replies. Bernard Williams discusses the controversial concept of "moral luck"—the extent to which our most deliberate decisions are nevertheless out of our control, and Jean Grimshaw discusses the problem of autonomy from the point of view of feminist ethics. Finally, Iris Young discusses the serious problem of **oppression,** the denial of freedom at the hands of others.

MARTHA NUSSBAUM

Agamemnon

MARTHA NUSSBAUM *is Professor of Classics and Philosophy at Brown University.*

AT the beginning of Aeschylus's *Agamemnon,* there is a strange and ominous portent. The king of birds appears to the king of the ships. Two eagles, one black, one white-tailed, in full view of the army, devour a pregnant hare with all her unborn young. It is difficult not to connect this omen with the coming slaughter, by this army, of innocent citizens at Troy. It is also difficult for an audience familiar with this story not to connect it with the imminent slaughter of the helpless girl Iphigenia, which will prove necessary for the departure of the expedition. But the omen receives from the prophet Calchas an oddly trivial interpretation. He 'knows the warlike devourers of the hare for the conducting chiefs'; and yet he predicts only that the army, in laying siege to Troy, will slaughter many herds of cattle before its walls. He finds the appropriate parallel to the eagles' cold-blooded and unreflective slaying of a hare to be human killing of animals, not human killing of other humans. In a sense he is correct. As an eagle kills a hare, so a human being might slaughter cattle: without compunction and to satisfy immediate needs. When the victims are human, we expect deliberations and feelings of greater complexity to be involved. The parallel does, then, have a point. And yet it is clear that this reading of the omen is not to be seen as sufficient. No significant omen merely predicts a beef dinner. Calchas is evasive. If, however, we connect his human/animal parallel with the omen's more sinister references, it does suggest further pertinent reflections. If we think of the omen as pointing towards the war crimes of the Greeks, we are reminded of the way in which circumstances of war can alter and erode the normal conventions of human behavior towards other humans, rendering them, in their indifference to the slain, either bestial or like killers of beasts. If we think of it as pointing to the murder of Iphigenia (for it is she who is 'stopped from her course' before the birth of children, she who is the particular victim of the 'king of ships'), we are introduced already to the central theme in the Chorus's blame of Agamemnon: he adopted an inappropriate attitude towards his conflict, killing a human child with no more agony, no more revulsion of feeling, than if she had indeed been an animal of a different species:

> Holding her in no special honor, as if it were the death of a beast where sheep abound in well-fleeced flocks, he sacrificed his own child.

The speaker is Clytemnestra; but she echoes here, as we shall see, the Chorus's own response to the tragic events.

The sacrifice of Iphigenia is regarded by the Chorus as necessary; but they also blame Agamemnon. Critics have usually explained away either the necessity or the blame, feeling that these must be incompatible. Some have introduced, instead, a hypothesis of 'overdetermined' or 'double' motivation that is explicitly said to exemplify Aeschylus's disregard for rational and logical thought. It is, however, possible to arrive at a coherent understanding of both aspects of the situation, if only we look more precisely at the nature and genesis of this necessity and also at what the Chorus finds blameworthy in the conduct of their chief. First of all, it is clear that the situation forcing the killing is the outcome of the contingent intersection of two divine demands and that no personal guilt of Agamemnon's own has led him into this tragic predicament. The expedition was commanded by Zeus to avenge the violation of a crime against hospitality. The Chorus asserts this with as much confidence as they assert anything about these events. In the first stasimon they say of the Trojans, 'They can speak of a stroke from Zeus: this, at least, one can make out.' Agamemnon is, then, fighting in a just cause, and a cause that he could not desert without the most serious impiety. The killing is forced by Artemis, who has in anger becalmed the expedition. Calchas divines that the only remedy for this situation is the sacrifice of Iphigenia. The anger of the goddess, said in other versions of the story to have been caused by a previous offense of Agamemnon's, is left, here, unexplained. Whether we are to infer that her anger is caused by her general pro-Trojan sympathies or by her horror, as protector of the young, at the impending slaughter of Trojan innocents, the force of Aeschylus's omission of a personal offense is to emphasize the contingent and external origin of Agamemnon's dreadful dilemma. It simply comes upon him as he is piously executing Zeus's command. (Later the men of the Chorus, singing of their vague foreboding of Agamemnon's death, invoke the image of a man who was sailing his ship on a straight course and came to grief on hidden rocks.) There is a background guilt at work in the situation: the guilt of Atreus, which is visited by Zeus upon his offspring. But this fact does not prevent us from asking precisely *how* the familiar guilt attaches itself to Agamemnon. And when we do so we must answer that Zeus has attached this guilt to him by placing him, a previously guiltless man, in a situation in which there is open to him no guilt-free course. Such situations may be repellent to practical logic; they are also familiar from the experience of life.

Agamemnon is told by the prophet that if he does not offer up his daughter as a sacrifice, the entire expedition will remain becalmed. Already men are starving, and winds blowing from the Strymon 'were wearing and wasting away the flower of the Argives'. If Agamemnon does not fulfill Artemis's condition, everyone, including Iphigenia, will die. He will also be abandoning the expedition and, therefore, violating the command of Zeus. He will be a *deserter.* It may, furthermore, depending upon our understanding of Artemis's requirements, be an act of disobedience against her. To perform the sacrifice will be, however, to perform a horrible and guilty act. We can see that one choice, the choice to sacrifice Iphigenia, seems clearly preferable, both because of consequences and because of the impiety involved in the other choice. Indeed, it is hard to imagine that Agamemnon could rationally have chosen any other way. But both courses involve him in guilt.

Agamemnon is allowed to choose: that is to say, he knows what he is doing; he is neither ignorant of the situation nor physically compelled; nothing forces him to choose one course rather than the other. But he is under necessity in that his alternatives include no very desirable options. There appears to be no incompatibility between choice and necessity here—unless one takes the ascription of choice to imply that the agent is free to do anything at all. On the contrary, the situation seems to describe quite precisely a kind of interaction between external constraint and personal choice that is found to one degree or another in any ordinary situation of choice. For a choice is always a choice among possible alternatives; and it is a rare agent for whom everything is possible. The special agony of this situation is that none of the possibilities is even harmless.

Agamemnon's first response is anger and grief: 'The Atreidae beat the ground with their staffs, and could not keep back their tears'. He then describes his predicament, apparently with full recognition of both competing claims. He acknowledges that there is wrong done whichever way he chooses:

A heavy doom is disobedience, but heavy, too, if I shall rend my own child, the adornment of my house, polluting a father's hands with streams of slaughtered maiden's blood close by the altar. Which of these is without evils? How should I become a deserter, failing in my duty to the alliance?

Agamemnon's statement of the alternatives shows us his sense that the *bet-ter* choice in the situation is the sacrifice: the future indicative in 'if I shall rend my own child' (*ei teknon daïxō*) is not parallel to the weak deliberative subjunctive of 'How should I become a deserter?' (pōs liponaus genōmai). But he indicates, too, that both choices involve evil.

So far, Agamemnon's situation seems to resemble the plight of Abraham on the mountain: a good and (so far) innocent man must either kill an innocent child out of obedience to a divine command, or incur the heavier guilt of disobedience and impiety. We might, then, expect to see next the delicate struggle between love and pious obligation that we sense in Abraham's equivocal words to Isaac, followed by a sacrifice executed with horror and reluctance. But something strange takes place. The Chorus had already prepared us for it in introducing their narrative: 'Blaming no prophet, he blew together with the winds of luck that struck against him'. The bold wind metaphor coined by the Chorus (the word *sumpneō* is used here, apparently, for the first time in Greek) expresses an unnatural cooperation of internal with external forces. Voicing no blame of the prophet or his terrible message, Agamemnon now begins to cooperate inwardly with necessity, arranging his feelings to accord with his fortune. From the moment he makes his decision, itself the best he could have made, he strangely turns himself into a collaborator, a willing victim.

ARISTOTLE

Voluntary and Involuntary Action

ARISTOTLE *(394–322 B.C.) uses Book III of his* Nicomachean Ethics *to understand the difference between voluntary and involuntary action. An excerpt follows.*

W E have found that moral excellence or virtue has to do with feelings and actions. These may be voluntary or involuntary. It is only to the former that we assign praise or blame, though when the involuntary are concerned we may find ourselves ready to condone and on occasion to pity. It is clearly, then, incumbent on the student of moral philosophy to determine the limits of the voluntary and involuntary. Legislators also find such a definition useful when they are seeking to prescribe appropriate rewards and punishments.

Actions are commonly regarded as involuntary when they are performed (*a*) under compulsion, (*b*) as the result of ignorance. An act, it is thought, is done under compulsion when it originates in some external cause of such a nature that the agent or person subject to the compulsion contributes nothing to it. Such a situation is created, for example, when a sea captain is carried out of his course by a contrary wind or by men who have got him in their power. But the case is not always so clear. One might have to consider an action performed for some fine end or through fear of something worse to follow. For example, a tyrant who had a man's parents or children in his power might order him to do something dishonourable on condition that, if the man did it, their lives would be spared; otherwise not. In such cases it might be hard to say whether the actions are voluntary or not. A similar difficulty is created by the jettison of cargo in a storm. When the situation has no complications you never get a man voluntarily throwing away his property. But if it is to save the life of himself and his mates, any sensible person will do it. Such actions partake of both qualities, though they look more like voluntary than involuntary acts. For at the time they are performed they are the result of a deliberate choice between alternatives, and when an action is performed the end or object of that action is held to be the end it had at the moment of its performance. It follows that the terms 'voluntary' and 'involuntary' should be used with reference to the time when the acts were being performed. Now in the imaginary cases we have stated the acts are voluntary. For the movement of the limbs instrumental to the action originates in the agent himself, and when this is so it is in a man's own power to act or not to act. Such actions therefore are voluntary. But they are so only in the special circumstances; otherwise of course they would be involuntary. For nobody would choose to do anything of the sort purely for its own sake. Occasionally indeed the performance of such actions is held to do a man credit. This happens when he submits to some disgrace or pain as the only way of achieving some great or splendid result. But if his case is just the opposite he is blamed, for it shows a degraded nature to submit to humiliations with only a paltry object in view, or at any rate not a high one. But there are also cases which are thought to merit, I will not say praise, but condonation. An example is provided when a man does something wrong because he is afraid of torture too severe for flesh and blood to endure. Though surely there are some things which a man cannot be compelled to do—which he will rather die than do, however painful the mode of death. Such a deed is matricide; the reasons which 'compelled' Alcmaeon in Euripides' play to kill his mother carry their absurdity on the face of them. Yet it is not always easy to make up our minds what is our best course in choosing one of two alternatives—such and such an action instead of such and such another—or in facing one penalty instead of another. Still harder is it to stick to our decision when made. For, generally speaking, the consequences we expect in such imbroglios are painful, and what we are forced to do far from honourable. Then we get praised or blamed according as we succumb to the compulsion or resist it.

What class of actions, then, ought we to distinguish as 'compulsory'? It is arguable that the bare description will apply to any case where the cause of the action is found in things external to the agent when he contributes nothing to the result. But it may happen that actions, though, abstractly considered, involuntary, are deliberately chosen at a given time and in given circumstances in preference to a given alternative. In that case, their origin being in the agent, these actions must be pronounced voluntary in the particular circumstances

and because they are preferred to their alternatives. In themselves they are involuntary, yet they have more of the voluntary about them, since conduct is a sequence of particular acts, and the particular things done in the circumstances we have supposed are voluntary. But when it comes to saying which of two alternative lines of action should be preferred—then difficulties arise. For the differences in particular cases are many.

If it should be argued that the pleasurable and honourable things exercise constraint upon us from without, and therefore actions performed under their influence are compulsory, it may be replied that this would make every action compulsory. For we all have some pleasurable or honourable motive in everything we do. Secondly, people acting under compulsion and against their will find it painful, whereas those whose actions are inspired by the pleasurable and the honourable find that these actions are accompanied by pleasure. In the third place it is absurd to accuse external influences instead of ourselves when we fall an easy prey to such inducements and to lay the blame for all dishonourable deeds on the seductions of pleasure, while claiming for ourselves credit for any fine thing we have done. It appears, then, that an action is compulsory only when it is caused by something external to itself which is not influenced by anything contributed by the person under compulsion.

Then there are acts done through ignorance. Any act of this nature is other than voluntary, but it is involuntary only when it causes the doer subsequent pain and regret. For a man who has been led into some action by ignorance and yet has no regrets, while he cannot be said to have been a voluntary agent—he

did not know what he was doing—
nevertheless cannot be said to have
acted involuntarily, since he feels no
compunction. We therefore draw a distinction. (*a*) When a man who has done
something as a result of ignorance is
sorry for it, we take it that he has acted
involuntarily. (*b*) When such a man is
not sorry, the case is different and we
shall have to call him a 'non-voluntary'
agent. For it is better that he should have
a distinctive name in order to mark the
distinction. Note, further, that there is
evidently a difference between acting *in
consequence* of ignorance and acting *in*
ignorance. When a man is drunk or in
passion his actions are not supposed to
be the result of ignorance but of one or
other of these conditions. But, as he
does not realize what he is doing, he is
acting *in* ignorance. To be sure every
bad man is ignorant of what he ought to
do and refrain from doing, and it is just
this ignorance that makes people unjust
and otherwise wicked. But when we use
the word 'involuntary' we do not apply
it in a case where the agent does not
know what is for his own good. For involuntary acts are not the consequence
of ignorance when the ignorance is
shown in our choice of ends; what does
result from such ignorance is a completely vicious condition. No, what I
mean is not general ignorance—which
is what gives ground for censure—but
particular ignorance, ignorance that is to
say of the particular circumstances or
the particular persons concerned. In
such cases there may be room for pity
and pardon, because a man who acts in
ignorance of such details is an involuntary agent. . . .

An involuntary act being one performed under compulsion or as the result of ignorance, a voluntary act would
seem to be one of which the origin or
efficient cause lies in the agent, he
knowing the particular circumstances in
which he is acting. I believe it to be an
error to say that acts occasioned by
anger or desire are involuntary. For in
the first place if we maintain this we
shall have to give up the view that any
of the lower animals, or even children,
are capable of voluntary action. In the
second place, when we act from desire
or anger are none of our actions voluntary? Or are our fine actions voluntary,
our ignoble actions, involuntary? It is an
absurd distinction, since the agent is one
and the same person. It is surely paradoxical to describe as 'involuntary' acts
inspired by sentiments which we quite
properly desire to have. There are some
things at which we *ought* to feel angry,
and others which we *ought* to desire—
health, for instance, and the acquisition
of knowledge. Thirdly, people assume
that what is involuntary must be painful
and what falls in with our own wishes
must be pleasant. Fourthly, what difference is there in point of voluntariness
between wrong actions which are calculated and wrong actions which are done
on impulse? Both are to be avoided; and
the further reflection suggests itself, that
the irrational emotions are no less typically human than our considered judgement. Whence it follows that actions
inspired by anger or desire are equally
typical of the human being who performs them. Therefore to classify these
actions as 'involuntary' is surely a very
strange proceeding. . . .

BARON D'HOLBACH

Are We Cogs in the Universe?

BARON D'HOLBACH (1723–1789) was a French aristocrat during the enlightenment who believed in a thoroughgoing materialism. He argued that the universe was nothing but "matter in motion" and human behavior nothing but the result of the deterministic behavior of this matter. He argues his version of "hard" determinism in the selection that follows.

IN whatever manner man is considered, he is connected to universal nature, and submitted to the necessary and immutable laws that she imposes on all beings she contains, according to their peculiar essences or to the respective properties with which, without consulting them, she endows each particular species. Man's life is a line that nature commands him to describe upon the surface of the earth, without his ever being able to swerve from it, even for an instant. He is born without his own consent; his organization does in nowise depend upon himself; his ideas come to him involuntarily; his habits are in the power of those who cause him to contract them; he is unceasingly modified by causes, whether visible or concealed, over which he has no control, which necessarily regulate his mode of existence, give the hue to his way of thinking, and determine his manner of acting. He is good or bad, happy or miserable, wise or foolish, reasonable or irrational, without his will being for anything in these various states. Nevertheless, in spite of the shackles by which he is bound, it is pretended he is a free agent, or that independent of the causes by which he is moved, he determines his own will, and regulates his own condition.

However slender the foundation of his opinion, of which everything ought to point out to him the error, it is current at this day and passes for an incontestable truth with a great number of people, otherwise extremely enlightened; it is the basis of religion, which supposing relations between man and the unknown being she has placed above nature, has been incapable of imagining how man could merit reward or deserve punishment from this being, if he was not a free agent. Society has been believed interested in his system; because an idea has gone abroad, that if all the actions of man were to be contemplated as necessary, the right of punishing those who injure their associates would no longer exist. At length human vanity accommodated itself to a hypothesis which, unquestionably, appears to distinguish man from all other physical beings, by assigning to him the special privilege of a total independence of all other causes, but of which a very little reflection would have shown him the impossibility.

The will, as we have elsewhere said, is a modification of the brain, by which it is disposed to action, or prepared to give play to the organs. This will is necessarily determined by the qualities, good or bad, agreeable or painful, of the object or the motive that acts upon his sense, or of which the idea remains with him, and is resuscitated by his memory. In consequence, he acts necessarily, his action is the result of the impulse he receives either from the motive, from the object, or from the idea which has modified his brain, or disposed his will. When he does not act according to this impulse, it is because there comes some new cause, some new motive, some new idea, which modified his brain in a different manner, gives him a new impulse, determines his will in another way, by which the action of the former impulse is suspended: thus, the sight of an agreeable object, or its idea, determines his will to set him in action to procure it; but if a new object or a new idea more powerfully attracts him, it gives a new direction to his will, annihilates the effect of the former, and prevents the action by which it was to be procured. This is the mode in which reflection, experience, reason, necessarily arrests or suspends the action of man's will: without this he would of necessity have followed the anterior impulse which carried him towards a then desirable object. In all this he always acts according to necessary laws from which he has no means of emancipating himself.

In short, the actions of man are never free; they are always the necessary consequence of his temperament, of the received ideas, and of the notions, either true or false, which he has formed to himself of happiness; of his opinions, strengthened by example, by education, and by daily experience. So many crimes are witnessed on the earth only because every thing conspires to render man vicious and criminal; the religion he has adopted, his government, his education, the examples set before him, irresistibly drive him on to evil: under these circumstances, morality preaches virtue to him in vain. In those societies where vice is esteemed, where crime is crowned, where venality is constantly recompensed, where the most dreadful disorders are punished only in those who are too weak to enjoy the privilege of committing them with impunity, the practice of virtue is considered nothing more than a painful sacrifice of happiness. Such societies chastise, in the lower orders, those excesses which they respect in the higher ranks; and frequently have the injustice to condemn those in the penalty of death, whom public prejudices, maintained by constant example, have rendered criminal.

Man, then, is not a free agent in any one instant of his life; he is necessarily guided in each step by those advantages, whether real or fictitious, that he attaches to the objects by which his passions are roused: these passions themselves are necessary in a being who unceasingly tends towards his own happiness; their energy is necessary, since that depends on his temperament; his temperament is necessary, because it depends on the physical elements which enter into his composition; the modification of this temperament is necessary, as it is the infallible and inevitable consequence of the impulse he receives from the incessant action of moral and physical beings.

JOHN HOSPERS

Meaning and Free Will

JOHN HOSPERS *was professor of philosophy at the University of Southern California and the author of a number of books on ethics. He ran several times for President of the United States on the Libertarian ticket. In the following he argues for a thoroughgoing determinism, not based on the model of physics but rather on psychoanalysis, which declares that all our behavior is based on unconscious motivation.*

PERHAPS the most obvious conception of freedom is this: an act is free if and only if it is a voluntary act. A response that occurs spontaneously, not as a result of your willing it, such as a reflex action, is not a free act. I do not know that this view is ever held in its pure form, but it is the basis for other ones. As it stands, of course, it is ambiguous: does "voluntary" entail "premeditated?" Are acts we perform semi-automatically through habit to be called free acts? To what extent is a conscious decision to act required for the act to be classified as voluntary? What of sudden outbursts of feeling? They are hardly premeditated or decided upon, yet they may have their origin in the presence or absence of habit-patterns due to self-discipline which may have been consciously decided upon. Clearly the view needs to be refined.

Now, however we may come to define "voluntary," it is perfectly possible to maintain that all voluntary acts are free acts and vice versa; after all, it is a matter of what meaning we are giving to the word "free" and we can give it this meaning if we choose. But it soon becomes apparent that this is not the meaning which most of us *want* to give it: for there *are* classes of actions which we want to refrain from calling "free" even though they are voluntary (not that we have this denial in mind when we use the word "free"—still, it is significant that we do not use the word in some situations in which the act in question is nevertheless voluntary).

When a man tells a state secret under torture, he does choose voluntarily between telling and enduring more torture; and when he submits to a bandit's command at the point of a gun, he voluntarily chooses to submit rather than to be shot. And still such actions would not generally be called free; it is clear that they are performed under compulsion. Voluntary acts performed under compulsion would not be called free; and the cruder view is to this extent amended.

For some persons, this is as far as we need to go. Schlick, for example, says that the free-will issue is the scandal of philosophy and nothing but so much wasted ink and paper, because the whole controversy is nothing but an inexcusable confusion between compulsion and universal causality. The free act is the uncompelled act, says Schlick, and controversies about causality and determinism have nothing to do with the case. When one asks whether an act done of necessity is free, the question is ambiguous: if "of necessity" means "by compulsion," then the answer is no; if, on the other hand, "of necessity" is a way of referring to "causal uniformity" in nature—the sense in which we may misleadingly speak of the laws of nature as "necessary" simply because there are no exceptions to them—then the answer is clearly yes; every act is an instance of some causal law (uniformity) or other, but this has nothing to do with its being free in the sense of uncompelled.

For Schlick, this is the end of the matter. Any attempt to discuss the matter further simply betrays a failure to perceive the clarifying distinctions that Schlick has made.

> Freedom means the opposite of compulsion; a man is *free* if he does not act under *compulsion,* and he is compelled or unfree when he is hindered from without in the realization of his natural desires. Hence he is unfree when he is locked up, or chained, or when someone forces him at the point of a gun to do what otherwise he would not do. This is quite clear, and everyone will admit that the everyday or legal notion of the lack of freedom is thus correctly interpreted, and that a man will be considered quite free . . . if no such external compulsion is exerted upon him.

This all seems clear enough. And yet if we ask whether it ends the matter, whether it states what we "really mean" by "free," many of us will feel qualms. We remember statements about human beings being pawns of their environment, victims of conditions beyond their control, the result of causal influences stemming from parents, etc., and we think, "Still, are we really free?" We do not want to say that the uniformity of nature itself binds us or renders us unfree; yet is there not something in what generations of wise men have said

about man being fettered? Is there not something too facile, too sleight-of-hand, in Schlick's cutting of the Gordian knot?

It will be noticed that we have slipped from talking about acts as being free into talking about human beings as free. Both locutions are employed, I would say about 50-50. Sometimes an attempt is made to legislate definitely between the two: Stebbing, for instance, says that one must never call acts free, but only the doers of the acts.

Let us pause over this for a moment. If it is we and not our acts that are to be called free, the most obvious reflection to make is that we are free to do some things and not free to do other things; we are free to lift our hands but not free to lift the moon. We cannot simply call ourselves free or unfree *in toto;* we must say at best that we are free in respect of certain actions only. G. E. Moore states the criterion as follows: we are free to do an act if we can do it *if we want to;* that which we can do if we want to is what we are free to do. Some things certain people are free to do while others are not: most of us are free to move our legs, but paralytics are not; some of us are free to concentrate on philosophical reading matter for three hours at a stretch while others are not. In general, we could relate the two approaches by saying that a *person* is free *in respect of* a given action if he can do it if he wants to, and in this case his *act* is free.

Moore himself, however, has reservations. . . . He adds that there *is* a sense of "free" which fulfills the criterion he has just set forth; but that there may be *another* sense in which man cannot be said to be free in all the situations in which he could rightly be said to be so in the first sense.

And surely it is not necessary for me to multiply examples of the sort of thing we mean. In practice most of us would not call free many persons who behave voluntarily and even with calculation aforethought, and under no compulsion either of any obvious sort. A metropolitan newspaper headlines an article with the words "Boy Killer Is Doomed Long before He Is Born," and then goes on to describe how a twelve-year-old boy has just been sentenced to thirty years in Sing Sing for the murder of a girl; his family background includes records of drunkenness, divorce, social maladjustment, epilepsy, and paresis. He early displays a tendency to sadistic activity to hide an underlying masochism and "prove that he's a man"; being coddled by his mother only worsens this tendency, until, spurned by a girl in his attempt on her, he kills her—not simply in a fit of anger, but calculatingly, deliberately. Is he free in respect of his criminal act, or for that matter in most of the acts of his life? Surely to ask this question is to answer it in the negative. Perhaps I have taken an extreme case; but it is only to show the superficiality of the Schlick analysis the more clearly. Though not everyone has criminotic tendencies, everyone has been moulded by influences which in large measure at least determine his present behavior; he is literally the product of these influences, stemming from periods prior to his "years of discretion," giving him a host of character traits that he cannot change now even if he would. So obviously does what a man is depend upon how a man comes to be, that it is small wonder that philosophers and sages have considered man far indeed from being the master of his fate. It is not as if man's will were standing high and serene above the flux of events that have

moulded him; it is itself caught up in this flux, itself carried along on the current. An act is free when it is determined by the man's character, say moralists; but when there was nothing the man could do to shape his character, and even the degree of will power available to him in shaping his habits and disciplining himself to overcome the influence of his early environment is a factor over which he has no control, what are we to say of this kind of "freedom?" Is it not rather like the freedom of the machine to stamp labels on cans when it has been devised for just that purpose? Some machines can do so more efficiently than others, but only because they have been better constructed.

It is not my purpose here to establish this thesis in general, but only in one specific respect which has received comparatively little attention, namely, the field referred to by psychiatrists as that of unconscious motivation. In what follows I shall restrict my attention to it because it illustrates as clearly as anything the points I wish to make.

Let me try to summarize very briefly the psychoanalytic doctrine on this point. The conscious life of the human being, including the conscious decisions and volitions, is merely a mouthpiece for the unconscious—not directly for the enactment of unconscious drives, but of the compromise between unconscious drives and unconscious reproaches. There is a Big Three behind the scenes which the automaton called the conscious personality carries out: the id, an "eternal gimme," presents its wish and demands its immediate satisfaction; the super-ego says no to the wish immediately upon presentation, and the unconscious ego, the mediator between the two, tries to keep peace by means of compromise.

To go into examples of the functioning of these three "bosses" would be endless; psychoanalytic case books supply hundreds of them. The important point for us to see in the present context is that it is the unconscious that determines what the conscious impulse and the conscious action shall be. Hamlet, for example, had a strong Oedipus wish, which was violently counteracted by super-ego reproaches; these early wishes were vividly revived in an unusual adult situation in which his uncle usurped the coveted position from Hamlet's father and won his mother besides. This situation evoked strong strictures on the part of Hamlet's super-ego, and it was this that was responsible for his notorious delay in killing his uncle. A dozen times Hamlet could have killed Claudius easily; but every time Hamlet "decided" not to: a free choice, moralists would say—but no, listen to the super-ego: "What you feel such hatred toward your uncle for, what you are plotting to kill him for, is precisely the crime which you yourself desire to commit: to kill your father and replace him in the affections of your mother. Your fate and your uncle's are bound up together." This paralyzes Hamlet into inaction. Consciously all he knows is that he is unable to act; this conscious inability he rationalizes, giving a different excuse each time.

We have always been conscious of the fact that we are not masters of our fate in every respect—that there are many things which we cannot do, that nature is more powerful than we are, that we cannot disobey laws without danger of reprisals, etc. Lately we have become more conscious, too, though novelists and dramatists have always been fairly conscious of it, that we are not free with respect to the emotions that we feel—whom we love or hate, what types we admire, and the like. More lately still we have been reminded that there are unconscious motivations for our basic attractions and repulsions, our compulsive actions or inabilities to act. But what is not welcome news is that our very acts of volition, and the entire train of deliberations leading up to them, are but facades for the expression of unconscious wishes, or rather, unconscious compromises and defenses.

A man is faced by a choice: shall he kill another person or not? Moralists would say, here is a free choice—the result of deliberation, an action consciously entered into. And yet, though the agent himself does not know it, and has no awareness of the forces that are at work within him, his choice is already determined for him: his conscious will is only an instrument, a slave, in the hands of a deep unconscious motivation which determines his action. If he has a great deal of what the analyst calls "free-floating guilt," he will not; but if the guilt is such as to demand immediate absorption in the form of self-damaging behavior, this accumulated guilt will have to be discharged in some criminal action. The man himself does not know what the inner clockwork is; he is like the hands on the clock, thinking they move freely over the face of the clock.

A woman has married and divorced several husbands. Now she is faced with a choice for the next marriage: shall she marry Mr. A, or Mr. B, or nobody at all? She may take considerable time to "decide" this question, and her decision may appear as a final triumph of her free will. Let us assume that A is a normal, well-adjusted, kind, and generous man, while B is a leech, an impostor, one who will become entangled constantly in quarrels with her. If she belongs to a certain classifiable psychological type, she will inevitably choose B, and she will do so even if her previous husbands have resembled B, so that one would think that she "had learned from experience." Consciously, she will of course "give the matter due consideration," etc., etc. To the psychoanalyst all this is irrelevant chaff in the wind—only a camouflage for the inner workings about which she knows nothing consciously. If she is of a certain kind of masochistic strain, as exhibited in her previous set of symptoms, she *must* choose B: her super-ego, always out to maximize the torment in the situation, seeing what dazzling possibilities for self-damaging behavior are promised by the choice of B, compels her to make the choice she does, and even to conceal the real basis of the choice behind an elaborate facade of rationalizations.

A man is addicted to gambling. In the service of his addiction he loses all his money, spends what belongs to his wife, even sells his property and neglects his children. For a time perhaps he stops; then, inevitably, he takes it up again, although he himself may think he chose to. The man does not know that he is a victim rather than an agent; or, if he sometimes senses that he is in the throes of something-he-knows-not-what, he will have no inkling of its character and will soon relapse into the illusion that he (his conscious self) is freely deciding the course of his own actions. What he does not know, of course, is that he is still taking out on his mother the original lesion to his infantile narcissism, getting back at her for her fancied refusal of his infantile wishes—and this by rejecting everything identified with her, namely education, discipline, logic, common sense,

training. At the roulette wheel, almost alone among adult activities, chance—the opposite of all these things—rules supreme; and his addiction represents his continued and emphatic reiteration of his rejection of Mother and all she represents to his unconscious.

This pseudo-aggression of his is of course masochistic in its effects. In the long run he always loses; he can never quit while he is winning. And far from playing in order to win, rather one can say that his losing is a *sine qua non* of his psychic equilibrium (as it was for example with Dostoyevsky): guilt demands punishment, and in the ego's "deal" with the super-ego the super-ego has granted satisfaction of infantile wishes in return for the self-damaging conditions obtaining. Winning would upset the neurotic equilibrium.

A man has wash-compulsion. He must be constantly washing his hands—he uses up perhaps 400 towels a day. Asked why he does this, he says, "I need to, my hands are dirty"; and if it is pointed out to him that they are not really dirty, he says "They feel dirty anyway, I feel better when I wash them." So once again he washes them. He "freely decides" every time; he feels that he must wash them, he deliberates for a moment perhaps, but always ends by washing them. What he does not see, of course, is the invisible wires inside him pulling him inevitably to do the thing he does: the infantile id-wish concerns preoccupation with dirt, the super-ego charges him with this, and the terrified ego must respond, "No, I don't like dirt, see how clean I like to be, look how I wash my hands!" . . .

Let us take, finally, a less colorful, more everyday example. A student at a university, possessing wealth, charm, and all that is usually considered essential to popularity, begins to develop the following personality-pattern: although well taught in the graces of social conversation, he always makes a *faux pas* somewhere, and always in the worst possible situation; to his friends he makes cutting remarks which hurt deeply—and always apparently aimed in such a way as to hurt the most: a remark that would not hurt A but would hurt B he invariably makes to B rather than to A, and so on. None of this is conscious. Ordinarily he is considerate of people, but he contrives always (unconsciously) to impose on just those friends who would resent it most, and at just the times when he should know that he should not impose: at 3 o'clock in the morning, without forewarning, he phones a friend in a near-by city demanding to stay at his apartment for the weekend; naturally the friend is offended, but the person himself is not aware that he has provoked the grievance ("common sense" suffers a temporary eclipse when the neurotic pattern sets in, and one's intelligence, far from being of help in such a situation, is used in the interest of the neurosis), and when the friend is cool to him the next time they meet, he wonders why and feels unjustly treated. Aggressive behavior on his part invites resentment and aggression in turn, but all that he consciously sees is other's behavior toward him— and he considers himself the innocent victim of an unjustified "persecution."

Each of these choices is, from the moralist's point of view, free: he chose to phone his friend at 3 a.m.; he chose to make the cutting remark that he did, etc. What he does not know is that an ineradicable masochistic pattern has set in. His unconscious is far more shrewd and clever than is his conscious intellect; it sees with uncanny accuracy just what

kind of behavior will damage him most, and unerringly forces him into that behavior. Consciously, the student "doesn't know why he did it"—he gives different "reasons" at different times, but they are all, once again, rationalizations cloaking the unconscious mechanism which propels him willy-nilly into actions that his "common sense" eschews.

The more of this sort of thing you see, the more you can see what the psychoanalyst means when he talks about "the illusion of free-will." And the more of a psychiatrist you become, the more you are overcome with a sense of what an illusion this precious free-will really is. In some kinds of cases most of us can see it already: it takes no psychiatrist to look at the epileptic and sigh with sadness at the thought that soon this person before you will be as one possessed, not the same thoughtful intelligent person you knew. But people are not aware of this in other contexts, for example when they express surprise at how a person whom they have been so good to could treat them so badly. Let us suppose that you help a person financially or morally or in some other way, so that he is in your debt; suppose further that he is one of the many neurotics who unconsciously identify kindness with weakness and aggression with strength, then he will unconsciously take your kindness to him as weakness and use it as the occasion for enacting some aggression against you. He can't help it, he may regret it himself later; still, he will be driven to do it. If we gain a little knowledge of psychiatry, we can look at him with pity, that a person otherwise so worthy should be so unreliable—but we will exercise realism too and be aware that there are some types of people that you cannot be good to: in "free" acts of their conscious volition, they will use your own goodness against you.

Sometimes the persons themselves will become dimly aware that "something behind the scenes" is determining their behavior. The divorcee will sometimes view herself with detachment, as if she were some machine (and indeed the psychoanalyst does call her a "repeating-machine"): "I know I'm caught in a net, that I'll fall in love with this guy and marry him and the whole ridiculous merry-go-round will start all over again."

We talk about free will, and we say, yes, the person is free to do so-and-so if he can do so *if* he wants to—and we forget that his wanting to is itself caught up in the stream of determinism, that unconscious forces drive him into the wanting or not wanting to do the thing in question. The idea of the puppet whose motions are manipulated from behind by invisible wires, or better still, by springs inside, is no mere figure of speech. The analogy is a telling one at almost every point. . . .

Now, what of the notion of responsibility? What happens to it on our analysis?

Let us begin with an example, not a fictitious one. A woman and her two-year-old baby are riding on a train to Montreal in mid-winter. The child is ill. The woman wants badly to get to her destination. She is, unknown to herself, the victim of a neurotic conflict whose nature is irrelevant here except for the fact that it forces her to behave aggressively toward the child, partly to spite her husband whom she despises and who loves the child, but chiefly to ward off super-ego charges of masochistic attachment. Consciously she loves the child, and when she says this she says it sincerely, but she must behave aggres-

sively toward it nevertheless, just as many children love their mothers but are nasty to them most of the time in neurotic pseudo-aggression. The child becomes more ill as the train approaches Montreal; the heating system of the train is not working, and the conductor advises the woman to get off the train at the next town and get the child to a hospital at once. The woman says no, she must get to Montreal. Shortly afterward, the child's condition worsens, and the mother does all she can do keep it alive, without, however, leaving the train, for she declares that it is absolutely necessary that she reach her destination. But before she gets there the child is dead. After that, of course, the mother grieves, blames herself, weeps hysterically, and joins the church to gain surcease from the guilt that constantly overwhelms her when she thinks of how her aggressive behavior has killed her child.

Was she responsible for her deed? In ordinary life, after making a mistake, we say, "Chalk it up to experience." Here we say, "Chalk it up to the neurosis." No, she is not responsible. She could not help it if her neurosis forced her to act this way—she didn't even know what was going on behind the scenes, she merely acted out the part assigned to her. This is far more true than is generally realized: criminal actions in general are not actions for which their agents are responsible; the agents are passive, not active—they are victims of a neurotic conflict. Their very hyperactivity is unconsciously determined.

To say this is, of course, not to say that we should not punish criminals. Clearly, for our own protection, we must remove them from our midst so that they can no longer molest and endanger organized society. And, of course, if we use the word "responsible" in such a way that justly to hold someone responsible for a deed is by definition identical with being justified in punishing him, then we can and do hold people responsible. But this is like the sense of "free" in which free acts are voluntary ones. It does not go deep enough. In a deeper sense we cannot hold the person responsible: we may hold his neurosis responsible, but he is not responsible for his neurosis, particularly since the age at which its onset was inevitable was an age before he could even speak.

The neurosis is responsible—but isn't the neurosis a part of *him*? We have been speaking all the time as if the person and his unconscious were two separate beings; but isn't he one personality, including conscious and unconscious departments together?

I do not wish to deny this. But it hardly helps us here; for what people want when they talk about freedom, and what they hold to when they champion it, is the idea that the *conscious* will is the master of their destiny. "I am the master of my fate, I am the captain of my soul"—and they surely mean their conscious selves, the self that they can recognize and search and introspect. Between an unconscious that willy-nilly determines your actions, and an external

force which pushes you, there is little if anything to choose. The unconscious is just *as if* it were an outside force; and indeed, psychiatrists will assert that the inner Hitler can torment you far more than any external Hitler can. Thus the kind of freedom that people want, the only kind they will settle for, is precisely the kind that psychiatry says that they cannot have. . . .

Let us . . . put the situation schematically in the form of a deductive argument.

1. An occurrence over which we had no control is something we cannot be held responsible for.

2. Events E, occurring during our babyhood, were events over which we had no control.

3. Therefore events E were events which we cannot be held responsible for.

4. But if there is something we cannot be held responsible for, neither can we be held responsible for something that inevitably results from it.

5. Events E have as inevitable consequence Neurosis N, which in turn has as inevitable consequence Behavior B.

6. Since N is the inevitable consequence of E and B is the inevitable consequence of N, B is the inevitable consequence of E.

7. Hence, not being responsible for E, we cannot be responsible for B.

JEAN-PAUL SARTRE

Freedom and Responsibility

JEAN-PAUL SARTRE'S (1905–1980) "existentialism" features a powerful emphasis on the freedom and responsibility of each individual. The following is taken from his Being and Nothingness.

ALTHOUGH the considerations which are about to follow are of interest primarily to the ethicist, it may nevertheless be worthwhile after these descriptions and arguments to return to the freedom of the for-itself and try to understand what the fact of this freedom represents for human destiny.

The essential consequence of our earlier remarks is that man being condemned to be free carries the weight of the whole world on his shoulders; he is responsible for the world and for himself as a way of being. We are taking the word "responsibility" in its ordinary sense as "consciousness (of) being the incontestable author of an event or of an object." In this sense the responsibility of the for-itself is overwhelming since he is the one by whom it happens that *there is* a world; since he is also the one who makes himself be, then whatever may be the situation in which he finds himself, the for-itself must wholly assume this situation with its peculiar coefficient of adversity, even though it be insupportable. He must assume the situation with the proud consciousness of being the author of it, for the very worst disadvantages or the worst threats which can endanger my person have meaning only in and through my project; and it is on the ground of the engagement which I am that they appear. It is therefore senseless to think of complaining since nothing foreign has decided what we feel, what we live, or what we are.

Furthermore this absolute responsibility is not resignation; it is simply the logical requirement of the consequences of our freedom. What happens to me happens through me, and I can neither affect myself with it nor revolt against it nor resign myself to it. Moreover everything which happens to me is *mine*. By this we must understand first of all that I am always equal to what happens to me *qua* man, for what happens to a man through other men and through himself can be only human. The most terrible situations of war, the worst tortures do not create a non-human state of things; there is no non-human situation. It is only through fear, flight, and recourse to magical types of conduct that I shall decide on the non-human, but this decision is human, and I shall carry the entire responsibility for it. But in addition the situation is *mine* because it is the image of my free choice of myself, and everything which it presents to me is *mine* in that this represents me and symbolizes me. Is it not I who decide the coefficient of adversity in things and even their unpredictability by deciding myself?

Thus there are no *accidents* in life; a community event which suddenly bursts forth and involves me in it does not come from the outside. If I am mobilized in a war, this war is *my* war; it is in my image and I deserve it. I deserve it first because I could always get out of it by suicide or by desertion; these ultimate possibles are those which must always be present for us when there is a question of envisaging a situation. For lack of getting out of it, I have *chosen* it. This can be due to inertia, to cowardice in the face of public opinion, or because I prefer certain other values to the value of the refusal to join in the war (the good opinion of my relatives, the honor of my family, *etc.*) Any way you look at it, it is a matter of a choice. This choice will be repeated later on again and again without a break until the end of the war. Therefore we must agree with the statement by J. Romains, "In war there are no innocent victims." If therefore I have preferred war to death or to dishonor, everything takes place as if I bore the entire responsibility for this war. Of course others have declared it, and one might be tempted perhaps to consider me as a simple accomplice. But this notion of complicity has only a juridical sense, and it does not hold there. For it depended on me that for me and by me this war should not exist, and I have decided that it does exist. There was no compulsion here, for the compulsion could have got no hold on a freedom. I did not have any excuse; . . . the peculiar character of human-reality is that it is without excuse. Therefore it remains for me only to lay claim to this war.

But in addition the war is *mine* because by the sole fact that arises in a situation which I cause to be and that I can discover it there only by engaging myself for or against it, I can no longer distinguish at present the choice which I make of myself from the choice which I make of the war. To live this war is to choose myself through it and to choose it through my choice of myself. There can be no question of considering it as "four years of vacation" or as a "reprieve," as a "recess," the essential part of my responsibilities being elsewhere in my married, family, or professional life. In this war which I have chosen I choose myself from day to day, and I make it mine by making myself. If it is going to be four empty years, then it is I who bear the responsibility for this.

Finally, . . . each person is an absolute choice of self from the standpoint of a world of knowledges and of techniques which this choice both assumes and illumines; each person is an absolute upsurge at an absolute date and is perfectly unthinkable at another date. It is therefore a waste of time to ask what I should have been if this war had not broken out, for I have chosen myself as one of the possible meanings of the epoch which imperceptibly led to war. I am not distinct from this same epoch; I could not be transported to another epoch without contradiction. Thus I *am* this war which restricts and limits and makes comprehensible the period which preceded it. In this sense we may define more precisely the responsibility of the for-itself if to the earlier quoted statement, "There are no innocent victims," we add the words, "We have the war we deserve." Thus, totally free, undistinguishable from the period for which I have chosen to be the meaning, as profoundly responsible for the war as if I had myself declared it, unable to live without integrating it in *my* situation, engaging myself in it wholly and stamping it with my seal, I must be without remorse or regrets as I am without excuse; for from the instant of my upsurge into being, I carry the weight of the world by myself alone without anything or any person being able to lighten it.

Yet this responsibility is of a very particular type. Someone will say, "I did not ask to be born." This is a naïve way of throwing greater emphasis on our facticity. I am responsible for everything, in fact, except for my very responsibility, for I am not the foundation of my being. Therefore everything takes place as if I were compelled to be responsible. I am *abandoned* in the world, not in the sense that I might remain abandoned and passive in a hostile universe like a board floating on the water, but rather in the sense that I find myself suddenly alone and without help, engaged in a world for which I bear the whole responsibility without being able, whatever I do, to tear myself away from this responsibility for an instant. For I am responsible for my very desire of fleeing responsibilities. To make myself passive in the world, to refuse to act upon things and upon Others is still to choose myself, and suicide is one mode among others of being-in-the-world. Yet I find an absolute responsibility for the fact that my facticity (here the fact of my birth) is directly inapprehensible and even inconceivable, for this fact of my birth never appears as a brute fact but always across a projective reconstruction of my for-itself. I am ashamed of being born or I am astonished at it or I rejoice over it, or in attempting to get rid of my life I affirm that I live and I assume this life as bad. Thus in a certain sense I *choose* being born. This choice itself is integrally affected with facticity since I am not able not to choose, but this facticity in turn will appear only in so far as I surpass it toward my ends. Thus facticity is everywhere but inapprehensible; I never encounter anything except my responsibility. That is why I cannot ask, "*Why* was I born?" or curse the day of my birth or declare that I did not ask to be born, for these various attitudes toward my birth—*i.e.,* toward the *fact* that I realize a presence in the world—are absolutely nothing else but ways of assuming this birth in full responsibility and making it *mine.* Here again I encounter only myself and my projects so that finally my abandonment—*i.e.,* my facticity—consists simply in the fact that I am condemned to be wholly responsible for myself. I am the being which *is* in such a way that in its being its being is in question. And this "is" of my being *is* as present and inapprehensible.

Under these conditions since every event in the world can be revealed to me only as an *opportunity* (an opportunity made use of, lacked, neglected, *etc.*), or better yet since everything which happens to us can be considered as a *chance (i.e.,* can appear to us only as a way of realizing this being which is in question in our being) and since other as transcendences-transcended are themselves only *opportunities* and *chances,* the responsibility of the for-itself extends to the entire world as a peopled-world. It is precisely thus that the for-itself apprehends itself in anguish; that is, as a being which is neither the foundation of its own being nor of the Other's being nor of the in-itselfs which form the world, but a being which is compelled to decide the meaning of being—within it and everywhere outside of it. The one who realizes in anguish his condition as *being* thrown into a responsibility which extends to his very abandonment has no longer either remorse or regret or excuse; he is no longer anything but a freedom which perfectly reveals itself and whose being resides in this very revelation. But as we pointed out . . . , most of the time we flee anguish in bad faith.

B. F. SKINNER

Freedom and the Control of Men

B. F. SKINNER was professor of psychology at Harvard and the best known American "behaviorist." In the following he argues his polemical thesis against the importance of what we call "freedom" and urges more scientific control over the conditions influencing people's behavior.

THE second half of the twentieth century may be remembered for its solution of a curious problem. Although Western democracy created the conditions responsible for the rise of modern science, it is now evident that it may never fully profit from that achievement. The so-called "democratic philosophy" of human behavior to which it also gave rise is increasingly in conflict with the application of the methods of science to human affairs. Unless this conflict is somehow resolved, the ultimate goals of democracy may be long deferred.

Just as biographers and critics look for external influences to account for the traits and achievements of the men they study, so science ultimately explains behavior in terms of "causes" or conditions which lie beyond the individual himself. As more and more causal relations are demonstrated, a practical corollary becomes difficult to resist: it should be possible to *produce* behavior according to plan simply by arranging the proper conditions. Now, among the specifications which might reasonably be submitted to a behavioral technology are these: Let men be happy, informed, skillful, well behaved, and productive.

This immediate practical implication of a science of behavior has a familiar ring, for it recalls the doctrine of human perfectibility of eighteenth- and nineteenth-century humanism. A science of man shares the optimism of that philosophy and supplies striking support for the working faith that men can build a better world and, through it, better men. The support comes just in time, for there has been little optimism of late among those who speak from the traditional point of view. Democracy has become "realistic," and it is only with some embarrassment that one admits today to perfectionistic or utopian thinking.

The earlier temper is worth considering, however. History records many foolish and unworkable schemes for human betterment, but almost all the great changes in our culture which we now regard as worthwhile can be traced to perfectionistic philosophies. Governmental, religious, educational, economic, and social reforms follow a common pattern. Someone believes that a change in a cultural practice—for example, in the rules of evidence in a court of law, in the characterization of man's relation to God, in the way children are taught to read and write, in permitted rates of interest, or in minimal housing standards—will improve the condition of men: by promoting justice, permitting men to seek salvation more effectively, increasing the literacy of a people, checking an inflationary trend, or improving public health and family relations, respectively. The underlying hypothesis is always the same: that a different physical or cultural environment will make a different and better man.

The scientific study of behavior not only justifies the general pattern of such proposals; it promises new and better hypotheses. The earliest cultural practices must have originated in sheer accidents. Those which strengthened the group survived with the group in a sort of natural selection. As soon as men began to propose and carry out changes in practice for the sake of possible consequences, the evolutionary process must have accelerated. The simple practice of making changes must have had survival value. A further acceleration is now to be expected. As laws of behavior are more precisely stated, the changes in the environment required to bring about a given effect may be more clearly specified. Conditions which have been neglected because their effects were slight or unlooked for may be shown to be relevant. New conditions may actually be created, as in the discovery and synthesis of drugs which affect behavior.

This is no time, then, to abandon notions of progress, improvement, or, indeed, human perfectibility. The simple fact is that man is able, and now as never before, to lift himself by his own bootstraps. In achieving control of the world of which he is a part, he may learn at last to control himself.

Timeworn objections to the planned improvement of cultural practices are already losing much of their force. Marcus Aurelius was probably right in advising his readers to be content with a haphazard amelioration of mankind. "Never hope to realize Plato's republic," he sighed, ". . . for who can change the opinions of men? And without a change of sentiments what can you make but reluctant slaves and hypocrites?" He was thinking, no doubt, of contemporary patterns of control based upon punishment or the threat of punishment which, as he correctly observed, breed only reluctant slaves of those who submit and hypocrites of those who discover modes of evasion. But we need not share his pessimism, for the opinions of men can be changed. The techniques of indoctrination which were being devised by the early Christian Church at the very time Marcus Aurelius was writing are relevant, as are some of the techniques of psychotherapy and of advertising and public relations. Other methods suggested by recent scientific analyses leave little doubt of the matter.

The study of human behavior also answers the cynical complaint that there is a plain "cussedness" in man which will always thwart efforts to improve him. We are often told that men do not want to be changed, even for the better. Try to help them, and they will outwit you and remain happily wretched. Dostoevsky claimed to see some plan in it. "Out of sheer ingratitude," he complained, or possibly boasted, "man will play you a dirty trick, just to prove that men are still men and not the keys of a piano. . . . And even if you could prove that a man is only a piano key, he would still do something out of sheer perversity—he would create destruction and chaos—just to gain his point. . . . And if all this could in turn be analyzed and prevented by predicting that it would occur, then man would deliberately go mad to prove his point." This is a conceivable neurotic reaction to inept control. A few men may have shown it, and many have enjoyed Dostoevsky's statement because they tend to show it. But that such perversity is a fundamental reaction of the human organism to controlling conditions is sheer nonsense.

So is the objection that we have no way of knowing what changes to make even though we have the necessary techniques. That is one of the great hoaxes of the century—a sort of booby trap left behind in the retreat before the advancing front of science. Scientists themselves have unsuspectingly agreed that there are two kinds of useful propositions about nature—facts and value judgments—and that science must confine itself to "what is," leaving "what ought to be" to others. But with what special sort of wisdom is the nonscientist endowed? Science is only effective knowing, no matter who engages in it. Verbal behavior proves upon analysis to be composed of many different types of utterances, from poetry and exhortation to logic and factual description, but these are not all equally useful in talking about cultural practices. We may classify useful propositions according to the degrees of confidence with which they may be asserted. Sentences about nature range from highly probable "facts" to sheer guesses. In general, future events are less likely to be correctly described than past. When a scientist talks about a projected experiment, for example, he must often resort to statements having only a moderate likelihood of being correct; he calls them hypotheses.

Designing a new cultural pattern is in many ways like designing an experiment. In drawing up a new constitution, outlining a new educational program, modifying a religious doctrine, or setting up a new fiscal policy, many statements must be quite tentative. We cannot be sure that the practices we

specify will have the consequences we predict, or that the consequences will reward our efforts. This is in the nature of such proposals. They are not value judgments—they are guesses. To confuse and delay the improvement of cultural practices by quibbling about the word *improve* is itself not a useful practice. Let us agree, to start with, that health is better than illness, wisdom better than ignorance, love better than hate, and productive energy better than neurotic sloth.

Perhaps the most crucial part of our democratic philosophy to be reconsidered is our attitude toward freedom—or its reciprocal, the control of human behavior. We do not oppose all forms of control because it is . . . "human nature" to do so. The reaction is not characteristic of all men under all conditions of life. It is an attitude which has been carefully engineered, in large part by what we call the "literature" of democracy. With respect to some methods of control (for example, the threat of force), very little engineering is needed, for the techniques or their immediate consequences are objectionable. Society has suppressed these methods by branding them "wrong," "illegal," or "sinful." But to encourage these attitudes toward objectionable forms of control, it has been necessary to disguise the real nature of certain indispensable techniques, the commonest examples of which are education, moral discourse, and persuasion. The actual procedures appear harmless enough. They consist of supplying information, presenting opportunities for action, pointing out logical relationships, appealing to reason or "enlightened understanding," and so on. Through a masterful piece of misrepresentation, the illusion is fostered that these procedures do not involve the control of behavior; at most, they are simply ways of "getting someone to change his mind." But analysis not only reveals the presence of well-defined behavioral processes, it demonstrates a kind of control no less inexorable, though in some ways more acceptable, than the bully's threat of force.

Let us suppose that someone in whom we are interested is acting unwisely—he is careless in the way he deals with his friends, he drives too fast, or he holds his golf club the wrong way. We could probably help him by issuing a series of commands: don't nag, don't drive over sixty, don't hold your club that way. Much less objectionable would be "an appeal to reason." We could show him how people are affected by his treatment of them, how accident rates rise sharply at higher speeds, how a particular grip on the club alters the way the ball is struck and corrects a slice. In doing so we resort to verbal mediating devices which emphasize and support certain "contingencies of reinforcement"—that is, certain relations between behavior and its consequences—which strengthen the behavior we wish to set up. The same consequences would possibly set up the behavior without our help, and they eventually take control no matter which form of help we give. The appeal to reason has certain advantages over the authoritative command. A threat of punishment, no matter how subtle, generates emotional reactions and tendencies to escape or revolt. Perhaps the controllee merely "feels resentment" at being made to act in a given way, but even that is to be avoided. When we "appeal to reason," he "feels freer to do as he pleases." The fact is that we have exerted *less* control than in using a

threat; since other conditions may contribute to the result, the effect may be delayed or, possibly in a given instance, lacking. But if we have worked a change in his behavior at all, it is because we have altered relevant environmental conditions, and the processes we have set in motion are just as real and just as inexorable, if not as comprehensive, as in the most authoritative coercion.

"Arranging an opportunity for action" is another example of disguised control. The power of the negative form has already been exposed in the analysis of censorship. Restriction of opportunity is recognized as far from harmless. As Ralph Barton Perry said in an article which appeared in the Spring, 1953, *Pacific Spectator,* "Whoever determines what alternatives shall be made known to man controls what that man shall choose *from.* He is deprived of freedom in proportion as he is denied access to *any* ideas, or is confined to any range of ideas short of the totality of relevant possibilities." But there is a positive side as well. When we present a relevant state of affairs, we increase the likelihood that a given form of behavior will be emitted. To the extent that the probability of action has changed, we have made a definite contribution. The teacher of history controls a student's behavior (or, if the reader prefers, "deprives him of freedom") just as much in *presenting* historical facts as in suppressing them. Other conditions will no doubt affect the student, but the contribution made to his behavior by the presentation of material is fixed and, within its range, irresistible.

The methods of education, moral discourse, and persuasion are acceptable not because they recognize the freedom of the individual or his right to dissent, but because they make only *partial*

contributions to the control of his behavior. The freedom they recognize is
freedom from a more coercive form of
control. The dissent which they tolerate
is the possible effect of other determin-
ers of action. Since these sanctioned
methods are frequently ineffective, we
have been able to convince ourselves
that they do not represent control at all.
When they show too much strength to
permit disguise, we give them other
names and suppress them as energetically as we suppress the use of force.
Education grown too powerful is rejected as propaganda or "brain-washing," while really effective persuasion is
described as "undue influence," "dema-
goguery," "seduction," and so on.

If we are not to rely solely upon accident for the innovations which give rise
to cultural evolution, we must accept
the fact that some kind of control of
human behavior is inevitable. We cannot use good sense in human affairs unless someone engages in the design and
construction of environmental conditions which affect the behavior of men.
Environmental changes have always
been the condition for the improvement
of cultural patterns, and we can hardly
use the more effective methods of science without making changes on a
grander scale. We are all controlled by
the world in which we live, and part of
that world has been and will be constructed by men. The question is this:
Are we to be controlled by accident, by
tyrants, or by ourselves in effective cultural design?

The danger of the misuse of power is
possibly greater than ever. It is not al-
layed by disguising the facts. We cannot

make wise decisions if we continue to
pretend that human behavior is not controlled, or if we refuse to engage in control when valuable results might be
forthcoming. Such measures weaken
only ourselves, leaving the strength of
science to others. The first step in a
defense against tyranny is the fullest
possible exposure of controlling techniques. A second step has already been
taken successfully in restricting the use
of physical force. Slowly, and as yet imperfectly, we have worked out an ethical
and governmental design in which the
strong man is not allowed to use the
power deriving from his strength to
control his fellow men. He is restrained
by a superior force created for that purpose—the ethical pressure of the group,
or more explicit religious and governmental measures. We tend to distrust superior forces, as we currently hesitate to
relinquish sovereignty in order to set up
an international police force. But it is
only through such counter-control that
we have achieved what we call peace—
a condition in which men are not permitted to control each other through
force. In other words, control itself must
be controlled.

Science has turned up dangerous
processes and materials before. To use
the facts and techniques of a science of
man to the fullest extent without making some monstrous mistake will be difficult and obviously perilous. It is no
time for self-deception, emotional indulgence, or the assumption of attitudes
which are no longer useful. Man is facing a difficult test. He must keep his
head now, or he must start again—a
long way back.

ANTHONY BURGESS

A Clockwork Orange

ANTHONY BURGESS *is the author of many novels, including* A Clockwork Orange.
In this excerpt from that book, a young hoodlum is reconditioned to be "good"
through experiments in which his viewing violent movies is accompanied by a drug
that makes him very ill. It works, but the prison chaplain points out the philosophical
problems it raises.

[T HE Prison Chaplain tells him:] 'Very hard ethical questions are involved,' he went on. 'You are to be made into a good boy, 6655321. Never again will you have the desire to commit acts of violence or to offend in any way whatsoever against the State's Peace. I hope you take all that in. I hope you are absolutely clear in your own mind about that.' I said:

'Oh, it will be nice to be good, sir.' But I had a real horrorshow smeck at that inside, brothers. He said:

'It may not be nice to be good, little 6655321. It may be horrible to be good. And when I say that to you I realize how self-contradictory that sounds. I know I shall have many sleepless nights about this. What does God want? Does God want goodness or the choice of goodness? Is a man who chooses the bad perhaps in some way better than a man who has the good imposed upon him? Deep and hard questions, little 6655321. But all I want to say to you now is this: if at any time in the future you look back to these times and remember me, the lowest and humblest of all God's servitors, do not, I pray, think evil of me in your heart, thinking me in any way involved in what is now about to happen to you. And now, talking of praying, I realize sadly that there will be little point in praying for you. You are passing now to a region where you will be beyond the reach of the power of prayer. A terrible terrible thing to consider. And yet, in a sense, in choosing to be deprived of the ability to make an ethical choice, you have in a sense really chosen the good. So I shall like to think. So, God help us all, 6655321, I shall like to think.' And he began to cry.

BERNARD WILLIAMS

Moral Luck

B. A. O. WILLIAMS *(1922–) is White Professor of Moral Philosophy at Oxford, and Monroe Deutsch Professor at Berkeley. In addition to his philosophical work, he was for many years a director of the English National Opera. His books include* Moral Luck *(1981), from which this selection is taken,* Utilitarianism and Beyond *(1982), and* Ethics and the Limits of Philosophy *(1985).*

LET us take first an outline example of the creative artist who turns away from definite and pressing human claims on him in order to live a life in which, as he supposes, he can pursue his art. Without feeling that we are limited by any historical facts, let us call him *Gauguin*. Gauguin might have been a man who was not at all interested in the claims on him, and simply preferred to live another life, and from that life, and perhaps from that preference, his best paintings came. That sort of case, in which the claims of others simply have no hold on the agent, is not what concerns me here, though it serves to remind us of something related to the present concerns, that while we are sometimes guided by the notion that it would be the best of worlds in which morality were universally respected and all men were of a disposition to affirm it, we have in fact deep and persistent reasons to be grateful that that is not the world we have.

Let us take, rather, a Gauguin who is concerned about these claims and what is involved in their being neglected (we may suppose this to be grim), and that he nevertheless, in the face of that, opts for the other life. This other life he might perhaps not see very determinately under the category of realising his gifts as a painter, but, to make things simpler, let us add that he does see it determinately in that light—it is as a life which will enable him really to be a painter that he opts for it. It will then be clearer what will count for him as eventual success in his project—at least, some possible outcomes will be clear examples of success (which does not have to be the same thing as recognition), however many others may be unclear.

Whether he will succeed cannot, in the nature of the case, be foreseen. We are not dealing here with the removal of an external obstacle to something which, once that is removed, will fairly predictably go through. Gauguin, in our story, is putting a great deal on a possibility which has not unequivocally declared itself. I want to explore and uphold the claim that in such a situation the only thing that will justify his choice will be success itself. If he fails—and we shall come shortly to what, more precisely, failure may be—then he did the wrong thing, not just in the sense in which that platitudinously follows, but in the sense that having done the wrong thing in those circumstances he has no basis for the thought that he was justified in acting as he did. If he succeeds, he does have a basis for that thought.

As I have already indicated, I will leave to the end the question of how such notions of justification fit in with distinctively moral ideas. One should be warned already, however, that, even if Gauguin can be ultimately justified, that need not provide him with any way of justifying himself to others, or at least to all others. Thus he may have no way of bringing it about that those who suffer from his decision will have no justified ground of reproach. Even if he succeeds, he will not acquire a right that they accept what he has to say; if he fails, he will not even have anything to say.

The justification, if there is to be one, will be essentially retrospective. Gauguin could not do something which is thought to be essential to rationality and to the notion of justification itself, which is that one should be in a position to apply the justifying considerations at the time of the choice and in advance of knowing whether one was right (in the sense of its coming out right). How this can be in general will form a major part of the discussion. I do not want, at this stage of the argument, to lay much weight on the notion of morality, but it may help to throw some light on the matter of prior justification if we bring in briefly the narrower question whether there could be a prior justification for Gauguin's choice in terms of moral rules.

A moral theorist, recognizing that some value attached to the success of Gauguin's project and hence possibly to his choice, might try to accommodate that choice within a framework of moral rules, by forming a subsidiary rule which could, before the outcome, justify that choice. What could that rule be? It could not be that one is morally justified in deciding to neglect other claims if one is a great creative artist: apart from doubts about its content, the saving clause begs the question which at the

relevant time one is in no position to answer. On the other hand, '. . . if one is convinced that one is a great creative artist' will serve to make obstinacy and fatuous self-delusion conditions of justification, while '. . . if one is reasonably convinced that one is a great creative artist' is, if anything, worse. What is reasonable conviction supposed to be in such a case? Should Gauguin consult professors of art? The absurdity of such riders surely expresses an absurdity in the whole enterprise of trying to find a place for such cases within the rules.

Utilitarian formulations are not going to contribute any more to understanding these situations than do formulations in terms of rules. They can offer the thought 'it is better (worse) that he did it', where the force of that is, approximately, 'it is better (worse) that it happened', but this in itself does not help towards a characterization of the agent's decision or its possible justification, and Utilitarianism has no special materials of its own to help in that. It has its own well-known problems, too, in spelling out the content of the 'better'—on standard doctrine, Gauguin's decision would seem to have been a better thing, the more popular a painter he eventually became. But there is something more interesting than that kind of difficulty. The Utilitarian perspective, not uniquely but clearly, will miss a very important dimension of such cases, the question of what 'failure' may relevantly be. From the perspective of consequences, the goods or benefits for the sake of which Gauguin's choice was made either materialise in some degree, or do not materialise. But it matters considerably to the thoughts we are considering, in what way the project fails to come off, if it fails. If Gauguin sustains some injury on the way to

Tahiti which prevents his ever painting again, that certainly means that his decision (supposing it now to be irreversible) was for nothing, and indeed there is nothing in the outcome to set against the other people's loss. But that train of events does not provoke the thought in question, that after all he was wrong and unjustified. He does not, and never will, know whether he was wrong. What would prove him wrong in his project would not just be that it failed, but that he failed.

This distinction shows that while Gauguin's justification is in some ways a matter of luck, it is not equally a matter of all kinds of luck. It matters how intrinsic the cause of failure is to the project itself. The occurrence of an injury is, relative to these undertakings at least, luck of the most external and incident kind. Irreducibly, luck of this kind affects whether he will be justified or not, since if it strikes, he will not be justified. But it is too external for it to unjustify him, something which only his failure as a painter can do; yet still that is, at another level, luck, the luck of being able to be as he hoped he might be. It might be wondered whether that is *luck* at all, or, if so, whether it may not be luck of that constitutive kind which affects everything and which we have already left on one side. But it is more than that. It is not merely luck that he is such a man, but luck relative to the deliberations that went into his decision, that he turns out to be such a man: he might (epistemically) not have been. That is what sets the problem.

In some cases, though perhaps not in Gauguin's, success in such decisions might be thought not to be a matter of epistemic luck relative to the decision. There might be grounds for saying that the person who is prepared to take the decision, and was in fact right, actually knew that he would succeed, however subjectively uncertain he may have been. But even if this is right for some cases, it does not help with the problems of retrospective justification. For the concept of knowledge here is itself applied retrospectively, and while there is nothing wrong with that, it does not enable the agent at the time of his decision to make any distinctions he could not already make. As one might say, even if it did turn out in such a case that the agent did know, it was still luck, relative to the considerations available to him at the time and at the level at which he made his decision, that he should turn out to have known.

Some luck, in a decision of Gauguin's kind, is extrinsic to his project, some intrinsic; both are necessary for success, and hence for actual justification, but only the latter relates to unjustification. If we now broaden the range of cases slightly, we shall be able to see more clearly the notion of intrinsic luck. In Gauguin's case the nature of the project is such that two distinctions do, roughly, coincide. One is a distinction between luck intrinsic to the project, and luck extrinsic to it; the other is a distinction between what is, and what is not, determined by him and by what he is. The intrinsic luck in Gauguin's case concentrates itself on virtually the one question of whether he is a genuinely gifted painter who can succeed in doing genuinely valuable work. Not all the conditions of the project's coming off lie in him, obviously, since others' actions and refrainings provide many necessary conditions of its coming off—and that is an important locus of extrinsic luck. But the conditions of its coming off which are relevant to unjustification, the locus of intrinsic luck, largely lie in him—which is not to say, of course, that they depend on his will, though some may. This rough coincidence of two distinctions is a feature of this case. But in others, the locus of intrinsic luck (intrinsic, that is to say, to the project) may lie partly outside the agent, and this is an important, and indeed the more typical, case.

JEAN GRIMSHAW

Autonomy and Identity in Feminist Thinking

JEAN GRIMSHAW *teaches Philosophy and Cultural Studies at Bristol Polytechnic in England. She has written extensively in feminist philosophy, and is the author of* Philosophy and Feminist Thinking *(1986).*

ISSUES about women's autonomy have been central to feminist thinking and action. Women have so often been in situations of powerlessness and dependence that any system of belief or programme of action that could count as 'fcminist' must in some way see this as a central concern. But what is meant by 'autonomy' and under what conditions is it possible? This has been an important and contentious question in philosophy. But questions about autonomy, and related questions about self and identity have also been important to feminism, and within feminist thinking it is possible to find radically different ways of thinking about these things. In this paper, I want to look at one kind of way in which some feminists have tried to conceptualise what it is for a woman to be 'autonomous', and at the implications this has for ways of thinking about the human self. I shall argue that this conception is not only philosophically problematic, but also has an implicit politics which is potentially damaging. And I shall try to suggest some ways of beginning to think about 'autonomy' which seem to me to be more fruitful and adequate, and to draw on different traditions of thinking about the self which have become influential in some recent feminist thinking.

Feminist thinking does not, of course, exist in a vacuum, and in thinking about women's autonomy, feminists have drawn on different (and conflicting) approaches to questions about the human self, some of which have a long history. I want to begin by going back to an argument that Aristotle put forward in the *Ethics,* since I think that the point at which his argument breaks down can illuminate the nature of the problem some feminist thinking has faced.

Aristotle's argument concerns the question of what it is that makes an action 'voluntary', done of a person's own free will, and in order to answer this question, he distinguished between actions whose origin was 'inside' a person, and those whose origin was 'outside', which resulted from external influences or pressure or compulsion. He discussed at some length the problems that arise over trying to define ideas such as 'compulsion', and in estimating the degree of severity of pressure that could make an action not voluntary. But in this sort of model of autonomy, what defines an action as autonomous is seen as its point of *origin;* it must have an 'immaculate conception', as it were, from *within* the self.

Now ultimately I think that it is this definition of 'autonomy' in terms of origin, and the associated distinction between an 'inner' self which can in some way spontaneously generate its 'own' actions, and 'external' influences which are not 'part' of the self, that will need challenging. But I think it is possible to defend the Aristotelian version of autonomy up to a point, provided notions of 'inside' and 'outside' the self are defined in a certain way. If a person is prevented from doing what they would otherwise intend or desire to do, or if they are coerced into doing what they would *not* otherwise want or desire to do, they are not acting autonomously. Under this interpretation, actions which originate from 'inside' the self are those which are seen as in accordance with conscious desires or intentions, and those which originate from 'outside' the self are those which one would not do if one were not coerced. The pressure here is to consider the sorts of circumstances which do, in fact, coerce people in these sorts of ways. And, of course, a central concern of feminism has been to identify and fight against the kinds of coercion to which women have been

subjected, including things like physical violence and economic dependence.

But it is at this point that an Aristotelian-type argument fails to be able to deal with the most difficult questions about autonomy. The Aristotelian view, as I have interpreted it, 'works' only to the extent that it is assumed that there is no problem about what I shall call 'the autonomy of desires'. Autonomy is defined as acting in accordance with desire (or intention). But what of the desires themselves? Are there *desires* (or intentions) which are not 'autonomous', which do not originate from 'within' the self, which are not authentic, not really 'one's own'?

Feminist writers have wanted, of course, to indict the various forms of brutality and coercion from which women have suffered. But this brutality and coercion has been seen not merely as a question of physical or 'external' coercion or constraint; the force of subjection has also been seen as a psychic one, invading women's very selves. The language of 'conditioning', 'brainwashing', 'indoctrination', and so forth, has been used to describe this force. The female self, under male domination, is riddled through and through with false or conditioned desires. But set against this conditioned, nonautonomous female self are various images of a female self that would be authentic, that would transcend or shatter this conditioning. I want now to look at some of these images of the female self in feminist discourse: my particular examples are from the work of Mary Daly, Marilyn Frye and Kate Millett.

Daly, Frye and Millett all stress the way in which women have been subject to the *power* of men. Much of Daly's book, *Gyn/Ecology* (1979), is an account of the barbarities inflicted on women such as suttee, clitorectomy, foot-binding and other forms of mutilation. Millett, in *Sexual Politics* (1977), sees patriarchal power as something so historically all-embracing that it has totally dominated women's lives. Frye, in *The Politics of Reality* (1983), uses the situation of a young girl sold into sexual slavery and then systematically brutalised and brainwashed into a life of service to her captors as an analogy for the situation of all women. And all three writers stress the way in which they see the female self as 'invaded' by patriarchal conditioning. Millet writes:

> When in any group of persons, the ego is subjected to such invidious versions of itself through social beliefs, ideology and tradition, the effect is bound to be pernicious. This should make it no very special cause for surprise that women develop group characteristics common to those who suffer minority status and a marginal existence.

Women, she argues, are deprived of all but the most trivial sources of dignity or self-respect. In her discussion of Lawrence's depiction of Connie in *Lady Chatterley's Lover*, what she sees Connie as relinquishing is 'self, ego, will, individuality' (243); all those things which, Millett argues, women had but recently achieved, (and for which Lawrence had a profound distaste).

Mary Daly's picture of the way in which women's selves are invaded by patriarchal conditioning is even more striking. She describes women, for example, as 'moronised', 'robotised', 'lobotomised', as 'the puppets of Papa'. At times she seems to see women as so 'brainwashed' that they are scarcely human; thus she describes them as 'fembots', even as 'mutants'. In Millett, Daly and Frye, women are seen primarily as *victims:* the monolithic brutality and psychological pressures of male power have reduced women almost to the state of being 'non-persons'. And indeed, as Daly sees women as having become 'mutants' or 'fembots', so Millett sees them as not having been allowed to participate in fully 'human' activities (which she characterises as those that are most remote from the biological contingencies of life), and Frye sees them as simply 'broken' and then 'remade' in the way that suits her masters.

But behind this victimised female self, whose actions and desires are assumed to be not truly 'her own', since they derive from processes of force, conditioning or psychological manipulation, there is seen to be an authentic female self, whose recovery or discovery it is one of the aims of feminism to achieve. The spatial metaphor implicit in the word 'behind' is not accidental, since this model of self is premised on the possibility of making a distinction between an 'inner' and an 'outer' self. Ibsen's Peer Gynt compared his quest for identity to the process of peeling layers off an onion; but after shedding all the 'false selves', he found that there was nothing inside, no 'core'. The sort of spatial metaphor implicit in Peer Gynt's account of himself is also apt in the accounts of self given by Daly, Millett and Frye, except that there *is* assumed to be a 'core'. This is clearest in the work of Daly. In *Gyn/Ecology*, discovering or recovering one's own self is seen as akin to a process of salvation or religious rebirth, and Daly writes of what she calls the unveiling or unwinding of the 'shrouds' of patriarchy to reveal the authentic female Spirit-Self underneath. And this Self is seen as a unitary and harmonious one. Splits and barriers within the psyche, she argues, as well as those between Selves, are the result of patriarchal conditioning. In the unitary and harmonious female Spirit-Self there will be no such splits.

Millett's picture of the authentic female self is rather different from that of Daly. It does not draw, as Daly's does, on religious metaphors of salvation and rebirth. It derives, rather, from a picture of the self as fundamentally a unitary, conscious and rational thing, a picture which, in Western philosophy, can be traced back to Descartes. It emerges most clearly in her discussion of Freud. She describes Freud's theory of the Unconscious as a major contribution to human understanding, but her account of the self owes, in fact, scarcely anything to Freud. She is scathingly critical of Freud's theory of penis envy: Freud, she argued, 'did not accept his patient's symptoms as evidence of a justified dissatisfaction with the limiting circumstances imposed on them by society, but as symptomatic of an independent and universal feminine tendency' (Millett, 1977, p. 179). He made a major (and foolish) confusion between biology and culture. Girls, Millett argues, are fully cognisant of male supremacy long before they see their brother's penis; and what they envy is not the penis, but the things to which having a penis gives the boy access—power, status and rewards. Freud ignored the more likely 'social' hypothesis for feminine dissatisfaction, preferring to ascribe it to a biologically based female nature. What we should be studying, Millett argues, are the effects of male-supremacist culture on the female ego. And what will undo these effects, she writes in the Postscript, is altered consciousness, and a process of 'human growth and true re-education'.

The 'social' factors of which Millett writes are here seen as pressures which are 'external' to the self, and which have the effect of thwarting the conscious and unitary rationality of female individuality, or the female ego. And the task is that of *removing* their influence. If, in *Lady Chatterley's Lover,* the scales were to fall from Connie's eyes and she were to see the worship of Mellor's phallus for what it is, a means of subordinating and oppressing women, she could free herself and develop her authentic will, ego and individuality.

The paradigm of coercion, writes Frye, is *not* the direct application of physical force. Rather, it is a situation in which choice and action *do* take place, and in which the victim acts under her own perception and judgment. Hence, what the exploiter needs is that

> the will and intelligence of the victim be disengaged from the projects of resistance and escape but that they not be simply broken or destroyed. Ideally, the disintegration and misintegration of the victim should accomplish the detachment of the victim's will and intelligence from the victim's own interests and their attachment to the interests of the exploiter. This will effect a displacement or dissolution of self-respect and will undermine the victim's intolerance of coercion. With that, the situation transcends the initial paradigmatic form or structure of coercion; for if people don't mind doing what you want them to do, you can't really be *making* them do it.

And, she writes:

> The health and integrity of an organism is a matter of its being organised largely towards its own interests and welfare. *She* is healthy and 'working right' when her substance is organised primarily on principles which align it to *her* interests and welfare. Co-operation is essential of

course, but it will not do that I arrange everything so that *you* get enough exercise: for me to be healthy, *I* must get enough exercise. My being adequately exercised is logically independent of your being so.

Frye is writing here as if it were possible to distinguish the interests of one self sharply from those of another, and as if, were the effects of male domination to be undone, it would not be too much of a problem for the self to know what its interests were.

In various ways then, underlying much of the work of these three writers is a set of assumptions about the self. First, that it is, at least potentially, a unitary, rational thing, aware of its interests. Second, that 'splits' within the psyche should be seen as resulting from the interference of patriarchal or male-dominated socialisation or conditioning. Third, that the task of undoing this conditioning is one that can be achieved solely by a rational process of learning to understand and fight against the social and institutional effects of male domination. And implicit in these assumptions about the self, I think, is a conception of autonomy. Frye writes that 'left to themselves' women would not want to serve men. Daly writes of unveiling or unwinding the 'shrouds' of patriarchy. Millett writes of the individuality and ego that women can discover in themselves once they recognise the effects of their patriarchal socialisation. And in all three, what is autonomous (or authentic) is what is seen as originating in some way from *within* the self; what is in some way *untainted* by the conditioning or manipulation to which a woman has previously been subjected.

IRIS YOUNG

Oppression

IRIS YOUNG *teaches feminism, philosophy, and politics at the University of Pittsburgh. She is author of* Justice and the Politics of Difference.

Someone who does not see a pane of glass does not know that he does not see it. Someone who, being placed differently, does see it, does not know the other does not see it.

When our will finds expression outside ourselves in actions performed by others, we do not waste our time and our power of attention in examining whether they have consented to this. This is true for all of us. Our attention, given entirely to the success of the undertaking, is not claimed by them as long as they are docile. . . .

*Rape is a terrible caricature of love from which consent is absent. After rape,
oppression is the second horror of human existence. It is a terrible caricature
of obedience.*

—Simone Weil

I have proposed an enabling conception of justice. Justice should refer not only to distribution, but also to the institutional conditions necessary for the development and exercise of individual capacities and collective communication and cooperation. Under this conception of justice, injustice refers primarily to two forms of disabling constraints, oppression and domination. While these constraints include distributive patterns, they also involve matters which cannot easily be assimilated to the logic of distribution: decision-making procedures, division of labor, and culture.

Many people in the United States would not choose the term "oppression" to name injustice in our society. For contemporary emancipatory social movements, on the other hand—socialists, radical feminists, American Indian activists, Black activists, gay and lesbian activists—oppression is a central category of political discourse. Entering the political discourse in which oppression is a central category involves adopting a general mode of analyzing and evaluating social structures and practices which is incommensurate with the language of liberal individualism that dominates political discourse in the United States.

A major political project for those of us who identify with at least one of these movements must thus be to persuade people that the discourse of oppression makes sense of much of our social experience. We are ill prepared for this task,

however, because we have no clear account of the meaning of oppression. While we find the term used often in the diverse philosophical and theoretical literature spawned by radical social movements in the United States, we find little direct discussion of the meaning of the concept as used by these movements.

I offer some explication of the concept of oppression as I understand its use by new social movements in the United States since the 1960s. My starting point is reflection on the conditions of the groups said by these movements to be oppressed: among others women, Blacks, Chicanos, Puerto Ricans and other Spanish-speaking Americans, American Indians, Jews, lesbians, gay men, Arabs, Asians, old people, working-class people, and the physically and mentally disabled. I aim to systematize the meaning of the concept of oppression as used by these diverse political movements, and to provide normative argument to clarify the wrongs the term names.

Obviously the above-named groups are not oppressed to the same extent or in the same ways. In the most general sense, all oppressed people suffer some inhibition of their ability to develop and exercise their capacities and express their needs, thoughts, and feelings. In that abstract sense all oppressed people face a common condition. Beyond that, in any more specific sense, it is not possible to define a single set of criteria that describe the condition of oppression of the above groups. Consequently, attempts by theorists and activists to discover a common description or the essential causes of the oppression of all these groups have frequently led to fruitless disputes about whose oppression is more fundamental or more grave. The contexts in which members of these groups use the term oppression to describe the injustices of their situation suggest that oppression names in fact a family of concepts and conditions, which I divide into five categories: exploitation, marginalization, powerlessness, cultural imperialism, and violence. . . .

One reason that many people would not use the term oppression to describe injustice in our society is that they do not understand the term in the same way as do new social movements. In its traditional usage, oppression means the exercise of tyranny by a ruling group. Thus many Americans would agree with radicals in applying the term oppression to the situation of Black South Africans under apartheid. Oppression also traditionally carries a strong connotation of conquest and colonial domination. The Hebrews were oppressed in Egypt, and many uses of the term oppression in the West invoke this paradigm.

Dominant political discourse may use the term oppression to describe societies other than our own, usually Communist or purportedly Communist societies. Within this anti-Communist rhetoric both tyrannical and colonialist implications of the term appear. For the anti-Communist, Communism denotes precisely the exercise of brutal tyranny over a whole people by a few rulers, and the will to conquer the world, bringing hitherto independent peoples under that tyranny. In dominant political discourse it is not legitimate to use the term oppression to describe our society, because oppression is the evil perpetrated by the Others.

New left social movements of the 1960s and 1970s, however, shifted the meaning of the concept of oppression. In its new usage, oppression designates the disadvantage and injustice some people suffer not because a tyrannical power coerces them, but because of the everyday practices of a well-intentioned liberal society. In this new left usage, the tyranny of a ruling group over another, as in South Africa, must certainly be called oppressive. But oppression also refers to systemic constraints on groups that are not necessarily the result of the intentions of a tyrant. Oppression in this sense is structural, rather than the result of a few people's choices or policies. Its causes are embedded in unquestioned norms, habits, and symbols, in the assumptions underlying institutional rules and the collective consequences of following those rules. It names, as Marilyn Frye puts it, "an enclosing structure of forces and barriers which tends to the immobilization and reduction of a group or category of people." In this extended structural sense oppression refers to the vast and deep injustices some groups suffer as a consequence of often unconscious assumptions and reactions of well-meaning people in ordinary interactions, media and cultural stereotypes, and structural features of bureaucratic hierarchies and market mechanisms—in short, the normal processes of everyday life. We cannot eliminate this structural oppression by getting rid of the rulers or making some new laws, because oppressions are systematically reproduced in major economic, political, and cultural institutions.

The systemic character of oppression implies that an oppressed group need not have a correlate oppressing group. While structural oppression involves relations among groups, these relations do not always fit the paradigm of conscious and intentional oppression of one group by another. Foucault suggests that to understand the meaning and operation of power in modern society we must look beyond the model of power as "sovereignty," a dyadic relation of ruler and subject, and instead analyze the exercise of power as the effect of often liberal and "humane" practices of education, bureaucratic administration, production and distribution of consumer goods, medicine, and so on. The conscious actions of many individuals daily contribute to maintaining and reproducing oppression, but those people are usually simply doing their jobs or living their lives, and do not understand themselves as agents of oppression.

I do not mean to suggest that within a system of oppression individual persons do not intentionally harm others in oppressed groups. The raped woman, the beaten Black youth, the locked-out worker, the gay man harrassed on the street, are victims of intentional actions by identifiable agents. I also do not mean to deny that specific groups are beneficiaries of the oppression of other groups, and thus have an interest in their continued oppression. Indeed, for every oppressed group there is a group that is *privileged* in relation to that group.

The concept of oppression has been current among radicals since the 1960s partly in reaction to Marxist attempts to reduce the injustices of racism and sexism, for example, to the effects of class domination or bourgeois ideology. Racism, sexism, ageism, homophobia, some social movements asserted, are distinct forms of oppression with their own dynamics apart from the dynamics of class, even though they may interact with class oppression. From often heated discussions among socialists, feminists, and antiracism activists in the last ten years a consensus is emerging that many different groups must be said to be oppressed in our society, and that no single form of oppression can be assigned causal or moral primacy. The same discussion has also led to the recognition that group differences cut across individual lives in a multiplicity of ways that can entail privilege and oppression for the same person in different respects. Only a plural explication of the concept of oppression can adequately capture these insights.

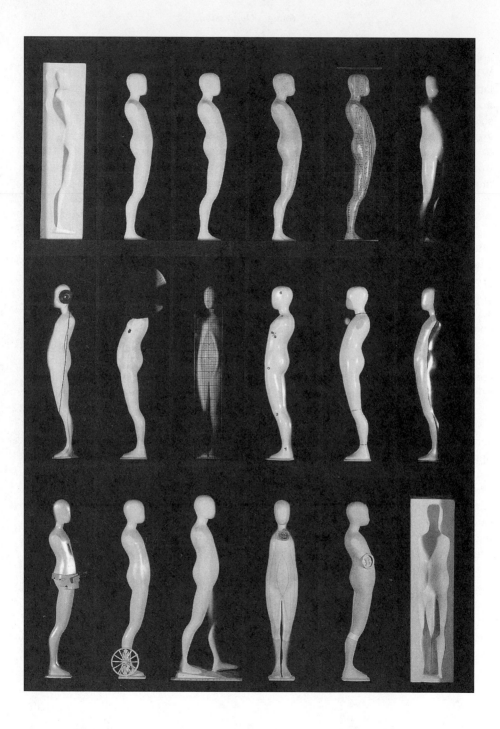

Chapter 19
What Do I Justly Deserve?

We demand and expect justice in society and we object when it is not in evidence. One person pays more in taxes than another person with the same income, and we want to know why. One child receives an excellent education, while another who is just as bright and talented does not, and we want to know why. One man is convicted of a criminal offense and is sentenced to lifetime imprisonment, while another is convicted of the same offense and is put on probation for two years, and we want to know why. One way to understand the theory of justice—admittedly a very modern way of doing so—is to think of a theory of justice as a general explanation about why people are treated differently. For example, some people *should* be taxed more because they have a different kind of income or fewer children to support. Some criminals should be punished more than others because they have committed prior offenses and are more likely to do so again. One person is called to serve in the army while another is allowed to pursue a career because his career is in "the national interest." A theory of justice is a kind of decision procedure through which legislators, judges, administrators, and, ultimately, all of us can figure out what is fair and what is not, who should get what and how much.

We often hear that "life isn't fair"—sometimes from someone who is trying to defend a recent injustice. This bit of cynicism isn't at all new; Plato considered it and rejected it more than twenty-five hundred years ago in *The Republic*. In the first of the following selections, Socrates considers the thesis that the only real justice is strength and that the strong can do whatever they can get away with. In other words, "might makes right." But Socrates shows that this cannot be what justice is. The strong can be wrong. A different way of understanding "life isn't fair" is the basis of Thomas Hobbes's famous account of justice in *The Leviathan*. In the state of nature, he argues, there is no such thing as justice, but in human society, justice comes about as a matter of **convention.** Thus, the question of whether life is fair or not is quite irrelevant, according to Hobbes; the important thing is that we are just and that we arrange our society so that justice is realized in it.

One of the presumptions of justice—although the word takes on many meanings and interpretations—is **equality.** Thus, John Stuart Mill defends his "utilitarian" theory of justice on the premise that everyone "counts for one and no more than one." John

Rawls presents a brief version of his influential recent theory of justice as fairness in which equality is also a central consideration, and Robert Nozick supplies a short rejoiner and a brief introduction to his own theory of "entitlements."

The final four selections are more practical in their focus—Joel Feinberg on economic income and distributive justice, Iris Young on "The Myth of Merit", Amartya Sen on world poverty in terms of basic human rights, and Malcolm X on the difference between human rights and civil rights.

PLATO

Does Might Make Right?

PLATO*'s (427–347 B.C.)* The Republic *takes justice as its central concern. In the following selection, Socrates holds that justice is a kind of harmony, in an individual as well as in the ideal state. He therefore argues against Thrasymachus, who insists that justice is whatever is in the interests of the stronger.*

LISTEN, then, [Thrasymachus] said; I proclaim that justice is nothing else than the interest of the stronger. And now why do you not praise me. But of course you won't.

Let me first understand you, [Socrates] replied. Justice, as you say, is the interest of the stronger. What, Thrasymachus, is the meaning of this? You cannot mean to say that because Polydamas is stronger than we are, and finds the eating of beef conductive to his bodily strength, that to eat beef is therefore equally for our good who are weaker than he is, and right and just for us?

That's abominable of you, Socrates; you take the words in the sense which is most damaging to the argument.

Not at all, my good sir, I said; I am trying to understand them; and I wish that you would be a little clearer.

Well, he said, have you never heard that forms of government differ; there are tyrannies and there are democracies, and there are aristocracies?

Yes, I know.

And the government is the ruling power in each state?

Certainly.

And the different forms of government make laws democratical, aristocratical, tyrannical, with a view to their several interests; and these laws, which are made by them for their own inter-ests, are the justice which they deliver to their subjects, and him who transgresses them they punish as a breaker of the law, and unjust. And that is what I mean when I say that in all states there is the same principle of justice, which is the interest of the government; and as the government must be supposed to have power, the only reasonable conclusion is, that everywhere there is one principle of justice, which is the interest of the stronger.

Now I understand you, I said; and whether you are right or not I will try to discover. But let me remark, that in defining justice you have yourself used the word 'interest' which you forbade me to use. It is true, however, that in your definition the words 'of the stronger' are added.

A small addition, you must allow, he said.

Great or small, never mind about that: we must first enquire whether what you are saying is the truth. Now we are both agreed that justice is inter-est of some sort, but you go on to say 'of the stronger'; about this addition I am not so sure, and must therefore con-sider further.

Proceed.

I will; and first tell me, Do you admit that it is just for subjects to obey their rulers?

I do.

But are the rulers of states absolutely infallible, or are they sometimes liable to err?

To be sure, he replied, they are liable to err.

Then in making their laws, they may sometimes make them rightly, and sometimes not?

True.

When they make them rightly, they make them agreeably to their interest; when they are mistaken, contrary to their interest; you admit that?

Yes.

And the laws which they make must be obeyed by their subjects,—and that is what you call justice?

Doubtless.

Then justice, according to your argument, is not only obedience to the interest of the stronger but the reverse?

What is that you are saying? he asked.

I am only repeating what you are saying, I believe. But let us consider: Have we not admitted that the rulers may be mistaken about their own interest in what they command, and also that to obey them is justice? Has not that been admitted?

Yes.

Then you must also have acknowledged justice not to be for the interest of the stronger, when the rulers unintentionally command things to be done which are to their own injury. For if, as you say, justice is the obedience which the subject renders to their commands, in that case, O wisest of men, is there any escape from the conclusion that the weaker are commanded to do, not what is for the interest, but what is for the injury of the stronger?

Nothing can be clearer, Socrates, said Polemarchus.

Yes, said Cleitophon, interposing, if you are allowed to be his witness.

But there is no need of any witness, said Polemarchus, for Thrasymachus himself acknowledges that rulers may sometimes command what is not for their own interest, and that for subjects to obey them is justice.

Yes, Polemarchus,—Thrasymachus said that for subjects to do what was commanded by their rulers is just.

Yes, Cleitophon, but he also said that justice is the interest of the stronger, and, while admitting both these propositions, he further acknowledged that the stronger may command the weaker who are his subjects to do what is not for his own interest; whence follows that justice is the injury quite as much as the interest of the stronger.

But, said Cleitophon, he meant by the interest of the stronger what the stronger thought to be his interest,—this was what the weaker had to do; and this was affirmed by him to be justice.

Those were not his words, rejoined Polemarchus.

Never mind, I replied, if he now says that they are, let us accept his statement. Tell me, Thrasymachus, I said, did you mean by justice what the stronger thought to be his interest, whether really so or not?

Certainly not, he said. Do you suppose that I call him who is mistaken the stronger at the time when he is mistaken?

Yes, I said, my impression was that you did so, when you admitted that the ruler was not infallible but might be sometimes mistaken.

You argue like an informer, Socrates. Do you mean, for example, that he who is mistaken about the sick is a physician in that he is mistaken? or that he who

errs in arithmetic or grammar is an arithmetician or grammarian at the time when
he is making the mistake, in respect of
the mistake? True, we say that the physician or arithmetician or grammarian has
made a mistake, but this is only a way of
speaking; for the fact is that neither the
grammarian nor any other person of skill
ever makes a mistake in so far as he is
what his name implies; they none of
them err unless their skill fails them, and
then they cease to be skilled artists. No
artist or sage or ruler errs at the time
when he is what his name implies;
though he is commonly said to err, and I
adopted the common mode of speaking.
But to be perfectly accurate, since you
are such a lover of accuracy, we should
say that the ruler, in so far as he is a
ruler, is unerring, and, being unerring,
always commands that which is for his
own interest; and the subject is required
to execute his commands; and therefore,
as I said at first and now repeat, justice
is the interest of the stronger.

Indeed, Thrasymachus, and do I
really appear to you to argue like an
informer?

Certainly, he replied.

And do you suppose that I ask these
questions with any design of injuring
you in the argument?

Nay, he replied, 'suppose' is not the
word—I know it; but you will be found
out, and by sheer force of argument you
will never prevail.

I shall not make the attempt, my dear
man; but to avoid any misunderstanding
occurring between us in future, let me
ask, in what sense do you speak of a
ruler or stronger whose interest, as you
were saying, he being the superior, it is
just that the inferior should execute—is
he a ruler in the popular or in the strict
sense of the term?

In the strictest of all senses, he said.
And now cheat and play the informer if
you can; I ask no quarter at your hands.
But you never will be able, never.

And do you imagine, I said, that I am
such a madman as to try and cheat
Thrasymachus? I might as well shave a
lion.

Why, he said, you made the attempt
a minute ago, and you failed.

Enough, I said, of these civilities. It
will be better that I should ask you a
question: Is the physician, taken in that
strict sense of which you are speaking, a
healer of the sick or a maker of money?
And remember that I am now speaking
of the true physician.

A healer of the sick, he replied.

And the pilot—that is to say, the true
pilot—is he a captain of sailors or a
mere sailor?

A captain of sailors.

The circumstance that he sails in the
ship is not to be taken into account; nei
ther is he to be called a sailor; the name
pilot by which he is distinguished has
nothing to do with sailing, but is significant of his skill and of his authority
over the sailors.

Very true, he said.

Now, I said, every art has an interest?

Certainly.

For which the art has to consider and
provide?

Yes, that is the aim of art.

And the interest of any art is the perfection of it—this and nothing else?

What do you mean?

I mean what I may illustrate negatively by the example of the body. Suppose you were to ask me whether the
body is self-sufficing or has wants, I
should reply: Certainly the body has
wants; for the body may be ill and
require to be cured, and has therefore

interests to which the art of medicine ministers; and this is the origin and intention of medicine, as you will acknowledge. Am I not right?

Quite right, he replied.

But is the art of medicine or any other art faulty or deficient in any quality in the same way that the eye may be deficient in sight or the ear fail of hearing, and therefore requires another art to provide for the interests of seeing and hearing—has art in itself, I say, any similar liability to fault or defect, and does every art require another supplementary art to provide for its interests, and that another and another end? Or have the arts to look only after their own interests? Or have they no need either of themselves or of another?—having no faults or defects, they have no need to correct them, either by the exercise of their own art or of any other; they have only to consider the interest of their subject-matter. For every art remains pure and faultless while remaining true—that is to say, while perfect and unimpaired. Take the words in your precise sense, and tell me whether I am not right.

Yes, clearly.

Then medicine does not consider the interest of medicine, but the interest of the body?

True, he said.

Nor does the art of horsemanship consider the interests of the art of horsemanship, but the interests of the horse; neither do any other arts care for themselves, for they have no needs; they care only for that which is the subject of their art?

True, he said.

But surely, Thrasymachus, the arts are the superiors and rulers of their own subjects?

To this he assented with a good deal of reluctance.

Then, I said, no science or art considers or enjoins the interests of the stronger or superior, but only the interest of the subject and weaker?

He made an attempt to contest this proposition also, but finally acquiesced.

Then, I continued, no physician, in so far as he is a physician, considers his own good in what he prescribes, but the good of his patient; for the true physician is also a ruler having the human body as a subject, and is not a mere money-maker; that has been admitted?

Yes.

And the pilot likewise, in the strict sense of the term, is a ruler of sailors and not a mere sailor?

That has been admitted.

And such a pilot and ruler will provide and prescribe for the interest of the sailor who is under him, and not for his own or the ruler's interest?

He gave a reluctant 'Yes.'

Then, I said, Thrasymachus, there is no one in any rule who, in so far as he is a ruler, considers or enjoins what is for his own interest, but always what is for the interest of his subject or suitable to his art; to that he looks, and that alone he considers in everything which he says and does.

When we had got to this point in the argument, every one saw that [Thrasymachus'] definition of justice had been completely upset.

THOMAS HOBBES

Justice and the Social Contract

THOMAS HOBBES *(1588–1679) was a political reformer and the author of a bold book,* The Leviathan, *in which, among other things, he argues against the divine right of kings. He begins the book by considering what life might be like in "the state of nature"—before the formation of societies (See pp. 570–571). In nature, he says, there is no such thing as justice. In nature, there is only a war,—"of all against all." Justice arises as part of the "social contract" which creates society. The following is from* The Leviathan.

T
O this war of every man, against every man, this also is consequent; that nothing can be unjust. The notions of right and wrong, justice and injustice have there no place. Where there is no common power, there is no law: where no law, no injustice. Force, and fraud, are in war the two cardinal virtues. Justice, and injustice are none of the faculties neither of the body, nor mind. If they were, they might be in a man that were alone in the world, as well as his senses, and passions. They are qualities, that relate to men in society, not in solitude. It is consequent also to the same condition, that there be no propriety, no dominion, no *mine* and *thine* distinct; but only that to be every man's, that he can get: and for so long, as he can keep it. And thus much for the ill condition, which man by mere nature is actually placed in; though with a possibility to come out of it, consisting partly in the passions, partly in his reason.

The passions that incline men to peace, and fear of death, desire of such things as are necessary to commodious living; and a hope by their industry to obtain them. And reason suggesteth convenient articles of peace, upon which men may be drawn to agreement. These articles, are they, which otherwise are called the Laws of Nature. . . .

The RIGHT OF NATURE, which writers commonly call *jus naturale,* is the liberty each man hath, to use his own power, as he will himself, for the preservation of his own nature; that is to say, of his own life; and consequently, of doing any thing, which in his own judgment, and reason, he shall conceive to be the aptest means thereunto.

By LIBERTY is understood, according to the proper signification of the word, the absence of external impediments: which impediments, may oft take away part of a man's power to do what he would; but cannot hinder him from using the power left him, according as his judgment, and reason shall dictate to him.

A LAW OF NATURE, *lex naturalis,* is a precept or general rule, found out by reason, by which a man is forbidden to do that, which is destructive of his life, or taketh away the means of preserving the same; and to omit that, by which he thinketh it may be best preserved. For though they that speak of this subject, use to confound *jus,* and *lex, right* and *law:* yet they ought to be distinguished; because RIGHT, consisteth in liberty to

do, or to forbear: whereas LAW, deter-
mineth, and bindeth, to one of them: so
that law, and right, differ as much, as
obligation, and liberty; which in one
and the same matter are inconsistent.

And because the condition of man, as
hath been declared in the precedent
chapter, is a condition of war of every
one against every one; in which case
every one is governed by his own reason; and there is nothing he can make
use of, that may not be a help unto him,
in preserving his life against his enemies; it followeth, that in such a condition, every man has a right to every
thing; even to one another's body. And
therefore, as long as this natural right of
every man to every thing endureth, there
can be no security to any man, how
strong or wise soever he be, of living
out the time, which nature ordinarily al-
loweth men to live. And consequently it
is a precept, or general rule of reason,
*that every man, ought to endeavour
peace, as far as he has hope of obtaining it; and when he cannot obtain it,
that he may seek, and use, all helps, and
advantages of war.* The first branch of
which rule, containeth the first, and fundamental law of nature; which is, *to seek
peace, and follow it.* The second, the
sum of the right of nature; which is, *by
all means we can, to defend ourselves.*

From this fundamental law of nature,
by which men are commanded to endeavour peace, is derived this second
law; that a man be willing, when others
are so too, as far-forth, as for peace, and
defense of himself he shall think it necessary, to lay down this right to all
things; and be contented with so much
liberty against other men, as he would
allow other men against himself. For as
long as every man holdeth this right, of
doing any thing he liketh; so long are all
men in the condition of war. But if other

men will not lay down their right, as
well as he; then there is no reason for
any one, to divest himself of his; for
that were to expose himself to prey,
which no man is bound to, rather than to
dispose himself to peace. This is that
law of the Gospel: *whatsoever you require that others should do to you, that
do ye to them.* And that law of all men,
*do not do to others what you do not
want them to do to you.*

Whensoever a man transferreth his
right, or renounceth it; it is either in
consideration of some right reciprocally
transferred to himself: or for some other
good he hopeth for thereby. For it is a
voluntary act: and of the voluntary acts
of every man, the object is some *good
to himself.* And therefore there be some
rights, which no man can be understood
by any words, or other signs, to have
abandoned, or transferred. As first a
man cannot lay down the right of resisting them, that assault him by force, to
take away his life; because he cannot be
understood to aim thereby, at any good
to himself. The same may be said of
wounds, and chains, and imprisonment;
both because there is no benefit consequent to such patience; as there is to the
patience of suffering another to be
wounded, or imprisoned: as also because a man cannot tell, when he seeth
men proceed against him by violence,
whether they intend his death or not.
And lastly the motive, and end for
which this renouncing, and transferring
of right is introduced, is nothing else
but the security of a man's person, in his
life, and in the means of so preserving
life, as not to be weary of it. And therefore if a man by words, or their signs,
seem to despoil himself on the end, for
which those signs were intended; he is
not to be understood as if he meant it, or

that it was his will; but that he was ignorant of how such words and actions were to be interpreted. . . .

A covenant not to defend myself from force, by force, is always void. For, as I have showed before, no man can transfer, or lay down his right to save himself from death, wounds, and imprisonment, the avoiding whereof is the only end of laying down any right; and therefore the promise of not resisting force, in no covenant transferreth any right; nor is obliging. For though a man may covenant thus, *unless I do so, or so, kill me;* he cannot covenant thus, *unless I do so, or so, I will not resist you, when you come to kill me.* For man by nature chooseth the lesser evil, which is danger of death in resisting; rather than the greater, which is certain and present death in not resisting. And this is granted to be true by all men, in that they lead criminals to execution, and prison, with armed men, notwithstanding that such criminals have consented to the law, by which they are condemned.

From that law of nature, by which we are obliged to transfer to another, such rights, as being retained, hinder the peace of mankind, there followeth a third; which is this, *that men perform their covenants made:* without which, covenants are in vain, and but empty words; and the right of all men to all things remaining, we are still in the condition of war.

And in this law of nature, consisteth the fountain and original of JUSTICE. For where no covenant hath preceded, there hath no right been transferred, and every man has right to every thing; and consequently, no action can be unjust. But when a covenant is made, then to break it is *unjust:* and the definition of INJUSTICE, is no other than *the not per-*

formance of covenant. And whatsoever is not unjust, is *just.*

But because covenants of mutual trust, where there is a fear of not performance on either part, as hath been said in the former chapter, are invalid; though the original of justice be the making of covenants; yet injustice actually there can be none, till the cause of such fear be taken away; which while men are in the natural condition of war, cannot be done. Therefore before the names of just, and unjust can have place, there must be some coercive power, to compel men equally to the performance of their covenants, by the terror of some punishment, greater than the benefit they expect by the breach of their covenant; and to make good that propriety, which by mutual contract men acquire, in recompense of the universal right they abandon: and such power there is none before the erection of a commonwealth. And this is also to be gathered out of the ordinary definition of justice in the Schools: for they say, that *justice is the constant will of giving to every man his own.* And therefore where there is no *own,* that is no propriety, there is no injustice; and where there is no coercive power erected, that is, where there is no commonwealth, there is no propriety; all men having right to all things: therefore where there is no commonwealth, there nothing is unjust. So that the nature of justice, consisteth in keeping of valid covenants: but the validity of covenants begins not but with the constitution of a civil power, sufficient to compel men to keep them: and then it is also that propriety begins.

A *commonwealth* is said to be *instituted,* when a *multitude* of men do agree, and *covenant, every one, with every one,* that to whatsoever *man,* or *assembly of men,* shall be given by the major part, the *right* to *present* the person of them all, that is to say, to be their *representative;* every one, as well he that *voted for it,* as he that *voted against it,* shall *authorize* all the actions and judgments, of that man, or assembly of men, in the same manner, as if they were his own, to the end, to live peaceably amongst themselves, and be protected against other men.

From this institution of a commonwealth are derived all the *rights,* and *faculties* of him, or them, on whom the sovereign power is conferred by the consent of the people assembled.

First, because they covenant, it is to be understood, they are not obliged by former covenant to any thing repugnant hereunto. And consequently they that have already instituted a commonwealth, being thereby bound by covenant, to own the actions, and judgments of one, cannot lawfully make a new covenant, amongst themselves, to be obedient to any other, in any thing whatsoever, without his permission. And therefore, they that are subjects to a monarch, cannot without his leave cast off monarchy, and return to the confusion of a disunited multitude; nor transfer their person from him that beareth it, to another man, or other assembly of men: for they are bound, every man to every man, to own, and be reputed author of all, that he that already is their sovereign, shall do, and judge fit to be done: so that any one man dissenting, all the rest should break their covenant made to that man, which is injustice: and they have also every man given the sovereignty to him that beareth their person; and therefore if they depose him, they take from him that which is his own, and so again it is injustice. Besides, if he that attempteth

to depose his sovereign, be killed, or punished by him for such attempt, he is author of his own punishment, as being by the institution, author of all his sovereign shall do: and because it is injustice for a man to do any thing, for which he may be punished by his own authority, he is also upon that title, unjust. And whereas some men have pretended for their disobedience to their sovereign, a new covenant, made, not with men, but with God; this also is unjust: for there is no covenant with God, but by mediation of somebody that representeth God's person; which none doth but God's lieutenant, who hath the sovereignty under God. But this pretence of covenant with God, is so evident a lie, even in the pretenders' own consciences, that it is not only an act of an unjust, but also of a vile, and unmanly disposition.

Secondly, because the right of bearing the person of them all, is given to him they make sovereign, by covenant only of one to another, and not of him to any of them; there can happen no breach of covenant on the part of the sovereign; and consequently none of his subjects, by any pretence of forfeiture, can be freed from his subjection. That he which is made sovereign maketh no covenant with his subjects beforehand, is manifest; because either he must make it with the whole multitude, as one party to the covenant; or he must make a several covenant with every man. With the whole, as one party, it is impossible; because as yet they are not one person: and if he make so many several covenants as there be men, those covenants after he hath the sovereignty are void; because what act soever can be pretended by any one of them for breach thereof, is the act both of himself, and of all the rest, because done in the person, and by the right of every one of them in particular. Besides, if any one, or more of them, pretend a breach of the covenant made by the sovereign at his institution; and others, or one other of his subjects, or himself alone, pretend there was no such breach, there is in this case, no judge to decide the controversy; it returns therefore to the sword again; and every man recovereth the right of protecting himself by his own strength, contrary to the design they had in the institution. It is therefore in vain to grant sovereignty by way of precedent covenant. The opinion that any monarch receiveth his power by covenant, this is to say, on condition, procedeth from want of understanding this easy truth, that covenants being but words and breath, have no force to oblige, contain, constrain or protect any man, but what it has from the public sword; that is, from the untied hands of that man, or assembly of men that hath the sovereignty, and whose actions are avouched by them all, and performed by the strength of them all, in him united. But when an assembly of men is made sovereign; then no man imagineth any such covenant to have passed in the institution; for no man is so dull as to say, for example, the people of Rome made a covenant with the Romans, to hold the sovereignty on such or such conditions; which not performed, the Romans might lawfully depose the Roman people. That men see not the reason to be alike in a monarchy, and in a popular government, proceedeth from the ambition of some, that are kinder to the government of an assembly, whereof they may hope to participate, than of monarchy, which they despair to enjoy.

Thirdly, because the major part hath by consenting voices declared a sovereign; he that dissented must now consent with the rest; that is, be contented to avow all the actions he shall do, or else justly be destroyed by the rest. For if he voluntarily entered into the congregation of them that were assembled, he sufficiently declared thereby his will, and therefore tacitly covenanted, to stand to what the major part should ordain: and therefore if he refuse to stand thereto, or make protestation against any of their decrees, he does contrary to his covenant, and therefore unjustly. And whether he be of the congregation, or not; and whether his consent be asked, or not, he must either submit to their decrees, or be left in the condition of war he was in before; wherein he might without injustice be destroyed by any man whatsoever.

Fourthly, because every subject is by this institution author of all the actions, and judgment of the sovereign instituted; it follows that whatsoever he doth, it can be no injury to any of his subjects; nor ought he to be by any of them accused of injustice. For he that doth anything by authority from another, doth therein no injury to him by whose authority he acteth: but by this institution of a commonwealth, every particular man is author of all the sovereign doth: and consequently he that complaineth of injury from his sovereign, complaineth of that whereof he himself is author; and therefore ought not to accuse any man but himself; no nor himself of injury; because to do injury to one's self, is impossible. It is true that they that have sovereign power may commit iniquity; but not injustice, or injury in the proper signification.

Fifthly, and consequently to that which was said last, no man that hath sovereign power can justly be put to death, or otherwise in any manner by his subjects punished. For seeing every subject is author of the actions of his sovereign; he punisheth another for the actions committed by himself.

JOHN STUART MILL

A Utilitarian Theory of Justice

JOHN STUART MILL (1806–1873) insists that justice is part and parcel of his ethical view, called "utilitarianism," which calls for "the greatest good for the greatest number." The problem for his view is that it is not clear how justice can be only a matter of utility rather than a question of rights and obligations. First, Mill analyzes the various ingredients in justice. Then he defends the idea that justice is indeed a function of utility. The following is from Mill's Utilitarianism.

IN the case of this, as of our other moral sentiments, there is no necessary connexion between the question of its origin and that of its binding force. That a feeling is bestowed on us by nature does not necessarily legitimate all its promptings. The feeling of justice might be a peculiar instinct, and might yet require, like our other instincts, to be controlled and enlightened by a higher reason. If we have intellectual instincts leading us to judge in a particular way, as well as animal instincts that prompt us to act in a particular way, there is no necessity that the former should be more infallible in their sphere than the latter in theirs; it may as well happen that wrong judgments are occasionally suggested by those, as wrong actions by these.

In the first place, it is mostly considered unjust to deprive anyone of his personal liberty, his property, or any other thing which belongs to him by law. Here, therefore, is one instance of the application of the terms "just" and "unjust" in a perfectly definite sense, namely, that it is just to respect, unjust to violate, the *legal rights* of anyone. But this judgment admits of several exceptions, arising from the other forms in which the notions of justice and injustice present themselves. For example, the person who suffers the deprivation may (as the phrase is) have forfeited the rights which he is so deprived of—a case to which we shall return presently. But also—

Secondly, the legal rights of which he is deprived may be rights which ought not to have belonged to him; in other words, the law which confers on him these rights may be a bad law. When it is so or when (which is the same thing for our purpose) it is supposed to be so, opinions will differ as to the justice of infringing it. Some maintain that no law, however bad, ought to be disobeyed by an individual citizen; that his opposition to it, if shown at all, should only be shown in endeavoring to get it altered by competent authority. This opinion (which condemns many of the most illustrious benefactors of mankind, and would often protect pernicious institutions against the only weapons which, in the state of things existing at the time, have any chance of succeeding against them) is defended by those who hold it on grounds of expediency, principally on that of the importance to the common interest of mankind, of maintaining inviolate the sentiment of submission to law. Other persons, again, hold the directly contrary opinion that any law, judged to be bad, may blamelessly be disobeyed, even though it be not judged to be unjust but only inexpedient, while others would confine the license of disobedience to the case of unjust laws; but, again, some say that all laws which are inexpedient are unjust, since every law imposes some restriction on the natural liberty of mankind, which restriction is an injustice unless legitimated by tending to their good. Among these diversities of opinion it seems to be universally admitted that there may be unjust laws, and that law, consequently, is not the ultimate criterion of justice, but may give to one person a benefit, or impose on another an evil, which justice condemns. When, however, a law is thought to be unjust, it seems always to be regarded as being so in the same way in which a breach of law is unjust, namely, by infringing somebody's right, which, as it cannot in this case be a legal right, receives a different appellation and is called a moral right. We may say, therefore, that a second case of injustice consists in taking or withholding from any person that to which he has a *moral right.*

Thirdly, it is universally considered just that each person should obtain that (whether good or evil) which he *deserves,* and unjust that he should obtain a good or be made to undergo an evil which he does not deserve. This is, perhaps, the clearest and most emphatic form in which the idea of justice is conceived by the general mind. As it involves the notion of desert, the question arises what constitutes desert? Speaking in a general way, a person is understood to deserve good if he does right, evil if he does wrong; and in a more particular sense, to deserve good from those to whom he does or has done good,

and evil from those to whom he does or has done evil. The precept of returning good for evil has never been regarded as a case of the fulfillment of justice, but as one in which the claims of justice are waived, in obedience to other considerations.

Fourthly, it is confessedly unjust to *break faith* with anyone: to violate an engagement, either express or implied, or disappoint expectations raised by our own conduct, at least if we have raised those expectations knowingly and voluntarily. Like the other obligations of justice already spoken of, this one is not regarded as absolute, but as capable of being overruled by a stronger obligation of justice on the other side, or by such conduct on the part of the person concerned as is deemed to absolve us from our obligation to him and to constitute a *forfeiture* of the benefit which he has been led to expect.

Fifthly, it is, by universal admission, inconsistent with justice to be *partial*— to show favor or preference to one person over another in matters to which favor and preference do not properly apply. Impartiality, however, does not seem to be regarded as a duty in itself, but rather as instrumental to some other duty; for it is admitted that favor and preference are not always censurable, and, indeed, the cases in which they are condemned are rather the exception than the rule. A person would be more likely to be blamed than applauded for giving his family or friends no superiority in good offices over strangers when he could do so without violating any other duty; and no one thinks it unjust to seek one person in preference to another as a friend, connection, or companion. Impartiality where rights are concerned is of course obligatory, but this is involved in the more general obligation of giving to everyone his right. A tribunal, for example, must be impartial because it is bound to award, without regard to any other consideration, a disputed object to the one of two parties who has the right to it. There are other cases in which impartiality means being solely influenced by desert, as with those who, in the capacity of judges, preceptors, or parents, administer reward and punishment as such. There are cases, again, in which it means being solely influenced by consideration for the public interest, as in making a selection among candidates for a government employment. Impartiality, in short, as an obligation of justice, may be said to mean being exclusively influenced by the considerations which it is supposed ought to influence the particular case in hand, and resisting solicitation of any motives which prompt to conduct different from what those considerations would dictate.

Nearly allied to the idea of impartiality is that of *equality,* which often enters as a component part both into the conception of justice and into the practice of it, and, in the eyes of many persons, constitutes its essence. But in this, still more than in any other case, the notion of justice varies in different persons, and always conforms in its variations to their notion of utility. Each person maintains that equality is the dictate of justice, except where he thinks that expediency requires inequality. The justice of giving equal protection to the rights of all is maintained by those who support the most outrageous inequality in the rights themselves. Even in slave countries it is theoretically admitted that the rights of the slave, such as they are, ought to be as sacred as those of the master, and that a tribunal which fails to enforce them with equal strictness is wanting in justice; while, at the same time, institutions which leave to the slave scarcely any rights to enforce are not deemed unjust because they are not deemed inexpedient. Those who think that utility requires distinctions of rank do not consider it unjust that riches and social privileges should be unequally dispensed; but those who think this inequality inexpedient think it unjust also. Whoever thinks that government is necessary sees no injustice in as much inequality as is constituted by giving to the magistrate powers not granted to other people. Even among those who hold leveling doctrines, there are differences of opinion about expediency. Some communists consider it unjust that the produce of the labor of the community should be shared on any other principle than that of exact equality; others think it just that those should receive most whose wants are greatest; while others hold the those who work harder, or who produce more, or whose services are more valuable to the community, may justly claim a larger quota in the division of the produce. And the sense of natural justice may be plausibly appealed to in behalf of every one of these opinions.

Justice implies something which it is not only right to do, and wrong not to do, but which some individual person can claim from us as his moral right. No one has a moral right to our generosity or beneficence because we are not morally bound to practice those virtues toward any given individual. And it will be found with respect to this as to every correct definition that the instances which seem to conflict with it are those which most confirm it. For if a moralist attempts, as some have done, to make out that mankind generally, though not any given individual, have a right to all the good we can do them, he at once, by that thesis, includes generosity and beneficence within the category of justice. He is obliged to say that our utmost exertions are *due* to our fellow creatures, thus assimilating them to a debt; or that nothing less can be a sufficient *return* for what society does for us, thus classing the case as one of gratitude; both of which are acknowledged cases of justice, and not of the virtue of beneficence; and whoever does not place the distinction between justice and morality in general, where we have now placed it, will be found to make no distinction between them at all, but to merge all morality in justice.

To recapitulate: the idea of justice supposes two things—a rule of conduct and a sentiment which sanctions the rule. The first must be supposed common to all mankind and intended for their good. The other (the sentiment) is a desire that punishment may be suffered by those who infringe the rule. There is involved, in addition, the conception of some definite person who suffers by the infringement, whose rights (to use the expression appropriated to the case) are violated by it. And the sentiment of justice appears to me to be the animal desire to repel or retaliate a hurt or damage to oneself or to those with whom one sympathizes, widened so as to include all persons, by the human capacity of enlarged sympathy and the human conception of intelligent self-interest. From the latter elements the feeling derives its morality; from the former, its peculiar impressiveness and energy of self-assertion. . . .

If the preceding analysis, or something resembling it, be not the correct account of the notion of justice—if justice be totally independent of utility, and be a standard *per se,* which the mind can recognize by simple introspection

of itself—it is hard to understand why that internal oracle is so ambiguous, and why so many things appear either just or unjust, according to the light in which they are regarded.

We are continually informed that utility is an uncertain standard, which every different person interprets differently, and that there is no safely but in the immutable, ineffaceable, and unmistakable dictates of justice, which carry their evidence in themselves and are independent of the fluctuations of opinion. One would suppose from this that on questions of justice there could be no controversy; that, if we take that for our rule, its application to any given case could leave us in as little doubt as a mathematical demonstration. So far is this from being the fact that there is as much difference of opinion, and as much discussion, about what is just as about what is useful to society. Not only have different nations and individuals different notions of justice, but in the mind of one and the same individual, justice is not some one rule, principle, or maxim, but many which do not always coincide in their dictates, and, in choosing between which, he is guided either by some extraneous standard or by his own personal predilections. . . .

. . . [for instance] in co-operative industrial association, is it just or not that talent or skill should give a title to superior remuneration? On the negative side of the question it is argued that whoever does the best he can deserves equally well, and ought not in justice to be put in a position of inferiority for no fault of his own; that superior abilities have already advantages more than enough, in the admiration they excite, the personal influence they command, and the internal sources of satisfaction attending them, without adding to these a superior share of the world's goods; and that society is bound in justice rather to make compensation to the less favored for this unmerited inequality of advantages than to aggravate it. On the contrary side it is contended that society receives more from the more efficient laborer; that, his services being more useful, society owes him a larger return for them; that a greater share of the joint result is actually his work, and not to allow his claim to it is a kind of robbery; that, if he is only to receive as much as others, he can only be justly required to produce as much, and to give a smaller amount of time and exertion, proportioned to his superior efficiency. Who shall decide between these appeals to conflicting principles of justice? Justice has in this case two sides to it, which it is impossible to bring into harmony, and the two disputants have chosen opposite sides; the one looks to what it is just that the individual should receive, the other to what it is just that the community should give. Each, from his own point of view, is unanswerable; and any choice between them, on grounds of justice, must be perfectly arbitrary. Social utility alone can decide the preference.

The considerations which have now been adduced resolve, I conceive, the only real difficulty in the utilitarian theory of morals. It has always been evident that all cases of justice are also cases of expediency; the difference is in the peculiar sentiment which attaches to the former, as contradistinguished from the latter. If this characteristic sentiment has been sufficiently accounted for; if there is no necessity to assume for it any peculiarity of origin; if it is simply the natural feeling of resentment, moralized by being made co-extensive with the demands of social good; and if this feeling not only does but ought to exist in all the classes of cases to which the idea of justice corresponds—that idea no longer presents itself as a stumbling block to the utilitarial ethics. Justice remains the appropriate name for certain social utilities which are vastly more important, and therefore more absolute and imperative, than any others are as a class (though not more so than others may be in particular cases); and which, therefore, ought to be, as well as naturally are, guarded by a sentiment, not only different in degree, but also in kind; distinguished from the milder feeling which attaches to the mere idea of promoting human pleasure or convenience at once by the more definite nature of its commands and by the sterner character of its sanctions.

JOHN RAWLS

Justice as Fairness

JOHN RAWLS *is a professor of philosophy at Harvard University and the author of*
A Theory of Justice. *In the following essay, he discusses some of the main ideas of his
theory "justice as fairness."*

1. It might seem at first sight that
the concepts of justice and fairness are the same, and that
there is no reason to distinguish them,
or to say that one is more fundamental
than the other. I think that this impression is mistaken. In this paper I wish to
show that the fundamental idea in the
concept of justice is fairness; and I wish
to offer an analysis of the concept of
justice from this point of view. To bring
out the force of this claim, and the
analysis based upon it, I shall then argue
that it is this aspect of justice for which
utilitarianism, in its classical form, is
unable to account, but which is ex
pressed, even if misleadingly, by the
idea of the social contract.

To start with I shall develop a particular conception of justice by stating and
commenting upon two principles which
specify it, and by considering the circumstances and conditions under which
they may be thought to arise. The principles defining this conception itself,
are, of course, familiar. It may be possible, however, by using the notion of
fairness as a framework, to assemble
and to look at them in a new way. Before stating this conception, however,
the following preliminary matters
should be kept in mind.

Throughout I consider justice only as
a virtue of social institutions, or what I
shall call practices. The principles of
justice are regarded as formulating restrictions as to how practices may define positions and offices, and assign
thereto powers and liabilities, rights and
duties. Justice as a virtue of particular
actions or of persons I do not take up at
all. It is important to distinguish these
various subjects of justice, since the
meaning of the concept varies according
to whether it is applied to practices, particular actions, or persons. These meanings are, indeed, connected, but they are
not identical. I shall confine my discussion to the sense of justice as applied to
practices, since this sense is the basic
one. Once it is understood, the other
senses should go quite easily.

Justice is to be understood in its customary sense as representing but *one* of
the many virtues of social institutions,
for these may be antiquated, inefficient,
degrading, or any number of other
things, without being unjust. Justice is
not to be confused with an all-inclusive
vision of a good society; it is only one
part of any such conception. It is important, for example, to distinguish that
sense of equality which is an aspect of
the concept of justice from that sense of
equality which belongs to a more comprehensive social ideal. There may well
be inequalities which one concedes are
just, or at least not unjust, but which,
nevertheless, one wishes on other
grounds, to do away with. I shall focus
attention, then, on the usual sense of
justice in which it is essentially the

elimination of arbitrary distinctions and the establishment, within the structure of a practice, of a proper balance between competing claims.

Finally, there is no need to consider the principles discussed below as *the* principles of justice. For the moment it is sufficient that they are typical of a family of principles normally associated with the concept of justice. The way in which the principles of this family resemble one another, as shown by the background against which they may be thought to arise, will be made clear by the whole of the subsequent argument.

2. The conception of justice which I want to develop may be stated in the form of two principles as follows: first, each person participating in a practice, or affected by it, has an equal right to the most extensive liberty compatible with a like liberty for all; and second, inequalities are arbitrary unless it is reasonable to expect that they will work out for everyone's advantage, and provided the positions and offices to which they attach, or from which they may be gained, are open to all. These principles express justice as a complex of three ideas: liberty, equality, and reward for services contributing to the common good.

•   •   •

The first principle holds, of course, only if other things are equal; that is, while there must always be a justification for departing from the initial position of equal liberty (which is defined by the pattern of rights and duties, powers and liabilities, established by a practice), and the burden of proof is placed on him who would depart from it, nevertheless, there can be, and often there

is, a justification for doing so. Now, that similar particular cases, as defined by a practice, should be treated similarly as they arise, is part of the very concept of a practice; it is involved in the notion of an activity in accordance with rules. The first principle expresses an analogous conception, but as applied to the structure of practices themselves. It holds, for example, that there is a presumption against the distinctions and classifications made by legal systems and other practices to the extent that they infringe on the original and equal liberty of the persons participating in them. The second principle defines how this presumption may be rebutted.

It might be argued at this point that justice requires only an equal liberty. If, however, a greater liberty were possible for all without loss or conflict, then it would be irrational to settle on a lesser liberty. There is no reason for circumscribing rights unless their exercise would be incompatible, or would render the practice defining them less effective. Therefore no serious distortion of the concept of justice is likely to follow from including within it the concept of the greatest equal liberty.

The second principle defines what sorts of inequalities are permissible; it specifies how the presumption laid down by the first principle may be put aside. Now by inequalities it is best to understand not *any* differences between offices and positions, but differences in the benefits and burdens attached to them either directly or indirectly, such as prestige and wealth, or liability to taxation and compulsory services. Players in a game do not protest against there being different positions, such as batter, pitcher, catcher, and the like, not to there being various privileges and powers as specified by the rules; nor do the citizens of a country object to there being the different offices of government such as president, senator, governor, judge, and so on, each with their special rights and duties. It is not differences of this kind that are normally thought of as inequalities, but differences in the resulting distribution established by a practice, or made possible by it, of the things men strive to attain or avoid. Thus they may complain about the pattern of honors and rewards set up by a practice (e.g., the privileges and salaries of government officials) or they may object to the distribution of power and wealth which results from the various ways in which men avail themselves of the opportunities allowed by it (e.g., the concentration of wealth which may develop in a free price system allowing large entrepreneurial or speculative gains).

It should be noted that the second principle holds that an inequality is allowed only if there is reason to believe that the practice with the inequality, or resulting in it, will work for the advantage of *every* party engaging in it. Here it is important to stress that *every* party must gain from the inequality. Since the principle applies to practices, it implies that the representative man in every office or position defined by a practice, when he views it as a going concern, must find it reasonable to prefer his condition and prospects with the inequality to what they would be under the practice without it. The principle excludes, therefore, the justification of inequalities on the grounds that the disadvantages of those in one position are outweighed by the greater advantages of those in another position. This rather simple restriction is the main modification I wish to make in the utilitarian principle as usually understood.

• • •

3. Given these principles one might try to derive them from a priori principles of reason, or claim that they were known by intuition. These are familiar enough steps and, at least in the case of the first principle, might be made with some success. Usually, however, such arguments, made at this point, are unconvincing. They are not likely to lead to an understanding of the basis of the principles of justice, not at least as principles of justice. I wish, therefore, to look at the principles in a different way.

Imagine a society of persons amongst whom a certain system of practices is *already* well established. Now suppose that by and large they are mutually self-interested; their allegiance to their established practices is normally founded on the prospect of self-advantage. One need not assume that, in all senses of the term "person," the persons in this society are mutually self-interested. If the characterization as mutually self-interested applies when the line of division is the family, it may still be true that members of families are bound by ties of sentiment and affection and willingly acknowledge duties in contradiction to self-interest. Mutual self-interestedness in the relations between families, nations, churches, and the like, is commonly associated with intense loyalty and devotion on the part of individual members. Therefore, one can form a more realistic conception of this society if one thinks of it as consisting of mutually self-interested families, or some other association. Further, it is not necessary to suppose that these persons are mutually self-interested under all circumstances, but only in the usual situations in which they participate in their common practice.

Now suppose also that these persons are rational: they know their own interests more or less accurately; they are capable of tracing out the likely consequences of adopting one practice rather than another; they are capable of adhering to a course of action once they have decided upon it; they can resist present temptations and the enticements of immediate gain; and the bare knowledge or perception of the difference between their condition and that of others is not, within certain limits and in itself, a source of great dissatisfaction. Only the last point adds anything to the usual definition of rationality. This definition should allow, I think for the idea that a rational man would not be greatly downcast from knowing, or seeing, that others are in a better position than himself, unless he thought their being so was the result of injustice, or the consequence of letting chance work itself out for no useful common purpose, and so on. So if these persons strike us as unpleasantly egoistic, they are at least free in some degree from the fault of envy.

Finally, assume that these persons have roughly similar needs and interests, or needs and interests in various ways complementary, so that fruitful cooperation amongst them is possible; and suppose that they are sufficiently equal in power and ability to guarantee that in normal circumstances none is able to dominate the others. This condition (as well as the others) may seem excessively vague; but in view of the conception of justice to which the argument leads, there seems no reason for making it more exact here.

Since these persons are conceived as engaging in their common practices, which are already established, there is no question of our supposing them to come together to deliberate as to how they will set these practices up for the first time. Yet we can imagine that from time to time they discuss with one another whether any of them has a legitimate complaint against their established institutions. Such discussions are perfectly natural in any normal society. Now suppose that they have settled on doing this in the following way. They first try to arrive at the principles by which complaints, and so practices themselves, are to be judged. Their procedure for this is to let each person propose the principles upon which he wishes his complaints to be tried with the understanding that, if acknowledged, the complaints of others will be similarly tried, and that no complaints will be heard at all until everyone is roughly of one mind as to how complaints are to be judged. They each understand further that the principles proposed and acknowledged on this occasion are binding on future occasions. Thus each will be wary of proposing a principle which would give him a peculiar advantage, in his present circumstances, supposing it to be accepted. Each person knows that he will be bound by it in future circumstances the peculiarities of which cannot be known, and which might well be such that the principle is then to his disadvantage. The idea is that everyone should be required to make *in advance* a firm commitment, which others also may reasonably be expected to make, and that no one be given the opportunity to tailor the canons of a legitimate complaint to fit his own special condition, and then to discard them when they no longer suit his purpose. Hence each person will propose principles of a general kind which will, to a large degree, gain their sense from the various applications to be made of them, the particular

circumstances of which being as yet unknown. These principles will express
the conditions in accordance with which
each is the least unwilling to have his
interests limited in the design of practices, given the competing interests of
the others, on the supposition that the
interests of others will be limited likewise. The restrictions which would so
arise might be thought of as those a person would keep in mind if he were de-
signing a practice in which his enemy
were to assign him his place.

The two main parts of this conjectural account have a definite significance. The character and respective
situations of the parties reflect the typical circumstances in which questions of
justice arise. The procedure whereby
principles are proposed and acknowledged represents constraints, analogous
to those of having a morality, whereby
rational and mutually self-interested persons are brought to act reasonably. Thus
the first part reflects the fact that questions of justice arise when conflicting
claims are made upon the design of a
practice and where it is taken for granted
that each person will insist, as far as possible, on what he considers his rights. It
is typical of cases of justice to involve
persons who are pressing on one another
their claims, between which a fair balance or equilibrium must be found. On
the other hand, as expressed by the second part, having a morality must at least
imply the acknowledgment of principles
as impartially applying to one's own
conduct as well as to another's, and
moreover principles which may constitute a constraint, or limitation, upon the
pursuit of one's own interests. There are,
of course, other aspects of having a
morality: the acknowledgment of moral
principles must show itself in accepting
a reference to them as reasons for limit-

ing one's claims, in acknowledging the
burden of providing a special explanation, or excuse, when one acts contrary
to them, or else in showing shame and
remorse and a desire to make amends,
and so on. It is sufficient to remark here
that having a morality is analogous to
having made a firm commitment in advance; for one must acknowledge the
principles of morality even when to
one's disadvantage. A man whose moral
judgments always coincided with his interests could be suspected of having no
morality at all.

Thus the two parts of the foregoing
account are intended to mirror the kinds
of circumstances in which questions of
justice arise and the constraints which
having a morality would impose upon
persons so situated. In this way one can
see how the acceptance of the principles
of justice might come about, for given
all these conditions as described, it
would be natural if the two principles of
justice were to be acknowledged. Since
there is no way for anyone to win special advantage for himself, each might
consider it reasonable to acknowledge
equality as an initial principle. There is,
however, no reason why they should regard this position as final; for if there
are inequalities which satisfy the second
principle, the immediate gain which
equality would allow can be considered
as intelligently invested in view of its
future return. If, as is quite likely, these
inequalities work as incentives to draw
out better efforts, the members of this
society may look upon them as concessions to human nature: they, like us,
may think that people ideally should
want to serve one another. But as they
are mutually self-interested, their acceptance of these inequalities is merely the
acceptance of the relations in which
they actually stand, and a recognition of

the motives which lead them to engage in their common practices. *They* have no title to complain of one another. And so provided that the conditions of the principle are met, there is no reason why they should not allow such inequalities. Indeed, it would be short-sighted of them to do so, and could result, in most cases, only from their being dejected by the bare knowledge, or perception, that others are better situated. Each person will, however, insist on an advantage to himself, and so on a common advantage, for none is willing to sacrifice anything for the others.

ROBERT NOZICK

Fairness versus Entitlement

ROBERT NOZICK *is a professor of philosophy at Harvard University, and in the following selection he expresses his reservations about the theory of justice formulated and made famous by his colleague, John Rawls.*

A principle suggested by Herbert Hart, which (following John Rawls) we shall call the *principle of fairness,* would be of service here if it were adequate. This principle holds that when a number of persons engage in a just, mutually advantageous, cooperative venture according to rules and thus restrain their liberty in ways necessary to yield advantages for all, those who have submitted to these restrictions have a right to similar acquiescence on the part of those who have benefited from their submission. Acceptance of benefits (even when this is not a giving of express or tacit undertaking to cooperate) is enough, according to this principle, to bind one. If one adds to the principle of fairness the claim that the others to whom the obligations are owed or their agents may *enforce* the obligations arising under this principle (including the obligation to

limit one's actions), then groups of people in a state of nature who agree to a procedure to pick those to engage in certain acts will have legitimate rights to prohibit "free riders." Such a right may be crucial to the viability of such agreements. We should scrutinize such a powerful right very carefully, especially as it seems to make *unanimous* consent to coercive government in a state of nature *unnecessary*! . . .

The principle of fairness, as we stated it following Hart and Rawls, is objectionable and unacceptable. Suppose some of the people in your neighborhood (there are 364 other adults) have found a public address system and decide to institute a system of public entertainment. They post a list of names, one for each day, yours among them. On his assigned day (one can easily switch days) a person is to run the public address system, play records over it, give news bulletins, tell amusing stories he has heard, and so on. After 138 days on which each person has done his part, your day arrives. Are you obligated to take your turn? You *have* benefited from it, occasionally opening your window to listen, enjoying some music or chuckling at someone's funny story. The other people *have* put themselves out. But must you answer the call when it is your turn to do so? As it stands, surely not. Though you benefit from the arrangement, you may know all along that 364 days of entertainment supplied by others will not be worth your giving up *one* day. You would rather not have any of it and not give up a day than have it all and spend one of your days at it. Given these preferences, how can it be that you are required to participate when your scheduled time comes? It would be nice to have philosophy readings on the radio to which one could tune in at any time, perhaps late at night when tired. But it may not be nice enough for you to want to give up one whole day of your own as a reader on the program. Whatever you want, can others create an obligation for you to do so by going ahead and starting the program themselves? In this case you can choose to forgo the benefit by not turning on the radio; in other cases the benefits may be unavoidable. If each day a different person on your street sweeps the entire street, must you do so when your time comes? Even if you don't care that much about a clean street? Must you imagine dirt as you traverse the street, so as not to benefit as a free rider? Must you refrain from turning on the radio to hear the philosophy readings? Must you mow your front lawn as often as your neighbors mow theirs?

At the very least one wants to build into the principle of fairness the condi-

tion that the benefits to a person from the actions of the others are greater than the costs to him of doing his share. How are we to imagine this? Is the condition satisfied if you do enjoy the daily broadcasts over the PA system in your neighborhood but would prefer a day off hiking, rather than hearing these broadcasts all year? For you to be obligated to give up your day to broadcast mustn't it be true, at least, that there is nothing you could do with a day (with that day, with the increment in any other day, by shifting some activities to that day) which you would prefer to hearing broadcasts for the year? If the only way to get the broadcasts was to spend the day participating in the arrangement, in order for the condition that the benefits outweigh the costs to be satisfied, you would have to be willing to spend it on the broadcasts rather than to gain *any* other available thing.

If the principle of fairness were modified so as to contain this very strong condition, it still would be objectionable. The benefits might only barely be worth the costs to you of doing your share, yet others might benefit from *this* institution much more than you do; they all treasure listening to the public broadcasts. As the person least benefited by the practice, are you obligated to do an equal amount for it? Or perhaps you would prefer that all cooperated in *another* venture, limiting their conduct and making sacrifices for *it*. It is true, *given* that they are not following your plan (and thus limiting what other options are available to you), that the benefits of their venture *are* worth to you the costs of your cooperation. However, you do not wish to cooperate, as part of your plan to focus their attention on your alternative proposal which they have ignored or not given, in your view at least, its proper due. (You want them, for example, to read the Talmud on the radio instead of the philosophy they are reading.) By lending the institution (their institution) the support of your cooperating in it, you will only make it harder to change or alter.

On the face of it, enforcing the principle of fairness is objectionable. You may not decide to give me something, for example a book, and then grab money from me to pay for it, even if I have nothing better to spend the money on. You have, if anything, even less reason to demand payment if your activity that gives me the book also benefits you; suppose that your best way of getting exercise is by throwing books into people's houses, or that some other activity of yours thrusts books into people's houses as an unavoidable side effect. Nor are things changed if your inability to collect money or payments for the books which unavoidably spill over into others' houses makes it inadvisable or too expensive for you to carry on the activity with this side effect. One cannot, whatever one's purposes, just act so as to give people benefits and then demand (or seize) payment. Nor can a group of persons do this. If you may not charge and collect for benefits you bestow without prior agreement, you certainly may not do so for benefits whose bestowal costs you nothing, and most certainly people need not repay you for costless-to-provide benefits which yet *others* provided them. So the fact that we partially are "social products" in that we benefit from current patterns and forms created by the multitudinous actions of a long string of long-forgotten people, forms which include institutions, ways of doing things, and language . . . does not create in us a general floating debt which the current society can collect and use as it will.

Perhaps a modified principle of fairness can be stated which would be free from these and similar difficulties. What seems certain is that any such principle, if possible, would be so complex and involved that one could not combine it with a special principle legitimating *enforcement* within a state of nature of the obligations that have arisen under it. Hence, even if the principle could be formulated so that it was no longer open to objection, it would not serve to obviate the need for other persons' *consenting* to cooperate and limit their own activities.

THE ENTITLEMENT THEORY

The subject of justice in holdings consists of three major topics. The first is the *original acquisition of holdings,* the appropriation of unheld things. This includes the issues of how unheld things may come to be held, the process, or processes, by which unheld things may come to be held, the things that may come to be held by these processes, the extent of what comes to be held by a particular process, and so on. We shall refer to the complicated truth about this topic, which we shall not formulate here, as the principle of justice in acquisition. The second topic concerns the *transfer of holdings* from one person to another. By what processes may a person transfer holdings to another? How may a person acquire a holding from another who holds it? Under this topic come general descriptions of voluntary exchange, and gift and (on the other hand) fraud, as well as reference to particular conventional details fixed upon in a given society. The complicated truth about this subject (with placeholders for conventional details) we shall call the principle of justice in transfer. (And we shall suppose it also includes principles governing how a person may divest himself of a holding, passing it into an unheld state.)

If the world were wholly just, the following inductive definition would exhaustively cover the subject of justice in holdings.

1. A person who acquires a holding in accordance with the principle of justice in acquisition is entitled to that holding.

2. A person who acquires a holding in accordance with the principle of justice in transfer, from someone else entitled to the holding, is entitled to the holding.

3. No one is entitled to a holding except by (repeated) application of 1 and 2.

The complete principle of distributive justice would say simply that a distribution is just if everyone is entitled to the holdings they possess under the distribution.

A distribution is just if it arises from another just distribution by legitimate means. The legitimate means of moving from one distribution to another are specified by the principle of justice in transfer. The legitimate first "moves" are specified by the principle of justice in acquisition. Whatever arises from a just situation by just steps is itself just. The means of change specified by the principle of justice in transfer preserve justice. As correct rules of inference are truth-preserving, and any conclusion deduced via repeated application of such rules from only true premises is itself true, so the means of transition from one situation to another specified by the principle of justice in transfer are justice-preserving, and any situation actually arising from repeated transitions in accordance with the principle from a just situation is itself just. The parallel between just-preserving transformations and truth-preserving transformations illuminates where it fails as well as where it holds. That a conclusion could have been deduced by truth-preserving means from premises that are true suffices to show its truth. That from a just situation a situation *could* have arisen via justice-preserving means does *not* suffice to show its justice. The fact that a thief's victims voluntarily *could* have presented him with gifts does not entitle the thief to his ill-gotten gains. Justice in holdings is historical; it depends upon what actually has happened. We shall return to this point later.

Not all actual situations are generated in accordance with the two principles of justice in holdings: the principle of justice in acquisition and the principle of justice in transfer. Some people steal from others, or defraud them, or enslave them, seizing their product and preventing them from living as they choose, or forcibly exclude others from competing in exchanges. None of these are permissible modes of transition from one situation to another. And some persons acquire holdings by means not sanctioned by the principle of justice in acquisition. The existence of past injustice (previous violations of the first two principles of justice in holdings) raises the third major topic under justice in holdings: the rectification of injustice in holdings. If past injustice has shaped present holdings in various ways, some identifiable and some not, what now, if anything, ought to be done to rectify these injustices? What obligations do the performers of injustice have toward those whose position is worse than it would have been had the injustice not been done? Or, than it would have been had compensation been paid promptly? How, if at all, do things change if the beneficiaries and those made worse off are not the direct parties in the act of injustice, but, for example their descendants? Is an injustice done to someone whose holding was itself based upon an unrectified injustice? How far back must one go in wiping clean the historical slate of injustices? What may victims of injustice permissibly do in order to rectify the injustices being done to them, including the many injustices done by persons acting through their government? I do not know of a thorough or theoretically sophisticated treatment of such issues. Idealizing greatly, let us suppose theoretical investigation will produce a principle of rectification. This principle uses historical information about previous situations and injustices done in them (as defined by the first two principles of justice and rights against interference), and information about the actual course of events that flowed from these injustices, until the present, and it yields a description (or descriptions) of holdings in the society. The principle of rectification presumably will make use of its best estimate of subjunctive information about what would have occurred (or a probability distribution over what might have occurred, using the expected value) if the injustice had not taken place. If the actual description of holdings turns out not to be one of the descriptions yielded by the principle, then one of the descriptions yielded must be realized.

The general outlines of the theory of justice in holdings are that the holdings of a person are just if he is entitled to them by the principles of justice in acquisition and transfer, or by the princi-

ple of rectification of injustice (as specified by the first two principles). If each person's holdings are just, then the total set (distribution) of holdings is just.

HISTORICAL PRINCIPLES AND END-RESULT PRINCIPLES

The general outlines of the entitlement theory illuminate the nature and defects of other conceptions of distributive justice. The entitlement theory of justice in distributions is *historical;* whether a distribution is just depends upon how it came about. In contrast, *current time-slice* principles of justice hold that the justice of a distribution is determined by how things are distributed (who has what) as judged by some *structural* principle(s) of just distribution. A utilitarian who judges between any two distributions by seeing which has the greater sum of utility and, if the sums tie, applies some fixed equality criterion to choose the more equal distribution, would hold a current time-slice principle of justice. As would someone who had a fixed schedule of trade-offs between the sum of happiness and equality. According to a current time-slice principle, all that needs to be looked at, in judging the justice of a distribution, is who ends up with what; in comparing any two distributions one need look only at the matrix presenting the distributions. No further information need be fed into a principle of justice. It is a consequence of such principles of justice that any two structurally identical distributions are equally just. (Two distributions are structurally identical if they present the same profile, but perhaps have different persons occupying the particular slots. My having ten and your having five, and my having five and your having ten are structurally identical distributions.) Welfare economics is the theory of current time-slice principles of justice. The subject is conceived as operating on matrices representing only current information about distribution. This, as well as some of the usual conditions (for example, the choice of distribution is in variant under relabeling of columns), guarantees that welfare economics will be a current time-slice theory, with all of its inadequacies.

Most persons do not accept current time-slice principles as constituting the whole story about distributive shares. They think it relevant in assessing the justice of a situation to consider not only the distribution it embodies, but also how that distribution came about. If some persons are in prison for murder or war crimes, we do not say that to assess the justice of the distribution in the society we must look only at what this person has, and that person has, and that person has, . . . at the current time. We think it relevant to ask whether someone did something so that he deserved to be punished, *deserved* to have a lower share. Most will agree to the relevance of further information with regard to punishments and penalties. Consider also desired things. One traditional socialist view is that workers are entitled to the product and full fruits of their labor; they have earned it; a distribution is unjust if it does not give the workers what they are entitled to. Such entitlements are based upon some past history. No socialist holding this view would find it comforting to be told that because the actual distribution A happens to coincide structurally with the one he desires D, A therefore is no less just than D, it differs only in that the "parasitic" owners of capital receive under A what the workers are entitled to under D, and the workers receive under A what the owners are entitled to under D, namely very little. This socialist rightly, in my view, holds onto the notions of earning, producing, entitlement, desert, and so forth, and he rejects current time-slice principles that look only to the structure of the resulting set of holdings. (The set of holdings resulting from what? Isn't it implausible that how holdings are produced and come to exist has no effect at all on who should hold what?) His mistake lies in his view of what entitlements arise out of what sorts of productive processes.

We construe the position we discuss too narrowly by speaking of *current* time slice principles. Nothing is changed if structural principles operate upon a time sequence of current time-slice profiles and, for example, give someone more now to counterbalance the less he has had earlier. A utilitarian or an egalitarian or any mixture of the two over time will inherit the difficulties of his more myopic comrades. He is not helped by the fact that *some* of the information others consider relevant in assessing a distribution is reflected, unrecoverably, in past matrices. Henceforth, we shall refer to such unhistorical principles of distributive justice, including the current time-slice principles, as *end-result principles* or *end-state principles*.

In contrast to end-result principles of justice, *historical principles* of justice hold that past circumstances or actions of people can create differential entitlements or differential deserts to things. An injustice can be worked by moving from one distribution to another structurally identical one, for the second, in profile the same, may violate people's entitlements or deserts; it may not fit the actual history.

JOEL FEINBERG

Economic Income and Social Justice

JOEL FEINBERG teaches philosophy at the University of Arizona. He has written extensively in ethics, in philosophy of law, and in social philosophy. This selection is from his 1973 book Social Philosophy.

T HE term "distributive justice" traditionally applied to burdens and benefits directly distributed by political authorities, such as appointed offices, welfare doles, taxes, and military conscription, but it has now come to apply also to goods and evils of a nonpolitical kind that can be distributed by private citizens to other private citizens. In fact, in most recent literature, the term is reserved for *economic* distributions, particularly the justice of differences in economic income between classes, and of various schemes of taxation which discriminate in different ways between classes. Further, the phrase can refer not only to acts of distributing but also to de facto states of affairs, such as the *fact that* at present "the five percent at the top get 20 percent [of our national wealth] while the 20 percent at the bottom get about five percent" There is, of course, an ambiguity in the meaning of "distribution." The word may refer to the *process* of distributing, or the *product* of some process of distributing, and either or both of these can be appraised as just or unjust. In addition, a "distribution" can be understood to be a "product" which is *not* the result of any deliberate distributing process, but simply a state of affairs whose production has been too compli-

cated to summarize or to ascribe to any definite group of persons as their deliberate doing. The present "distribution" of American wealth is just such a state of affairs.

Are the five percent of Americans "at the top" really different from the 20 percent "at the bottom" in any respect that would justicize the difference between their incomes? It is doubtful that there is any characteristic—relevant or irrelevant—common and peculiar to all members of either group. *Some* injustices, therefore, must surely exist. Perhaps there are some traits, however, that are more or less characteristic of the members of the privileged group, that make the current arrangements at least approximately just. What could (or should) those traits be? The answer will state a standard of relevance and a principle of material justice for questions of economic distributions, at least in relatively affluent societies like that of the United States.

At this point there appears to be no appeal possible except to *basic attitudes,* but even at this level we should avoid premature pessimism about the possibility of rational agreement. Some answers to our question have been generally discredited, and if we can see why those answers are inadequate, we might discover some important clues to the properties any adequate answer must possess. Even philosophical adversaries with strongly opposed initial attitudes may hope to come to eventual agreement if they share *some* relevant beliefs and standards and common commitment to consistency. Let us consider why we all agree (that is the author's assumption) in rejecting the view that differences in race, sex, IQ, or social "rank" are the grounds of just differences in wealth or income. Part of the answer seems obvious. People cannot by their own voluntary choices determine what skin color, sex, or IQ they shall have, or which hereditary caste they shall enter. To make such properties the basis of discrimination between individuals in the distribution of social benefits would be "to treat people differently in ways that profoundly affect their lives because of differences for which they have no responsibility." Differences in a given respect are *relevant* for the aims of distributive justice, then, only if they are differences for which their possessors can be held responsible; properties can be the grounds of just discrimination between persons only if those persons had a *fair opportunity* to acquire or avoid them. Having rejected a number of material principles that clearly fail to satisfy the "fair opportunity" requirement, we are still left with as many as five candidates for our acceptance. (It is in theory open to us to accept two or more of these five as valid principles, there being no a priori necessity that the list be reduced to one.) These are: (1) the principle of perfect equality; (2) the principle[s] of need; (3) the principles of merit and achievement; (4) the principle of contribution (or due return); (5) the principles of effort (or labor). I shall discuss each of these briefly.

EQUALITY

The principle of perfect equality obviously has a place in any adequate social ethic. Every human being is equally a human being, and . . . that minimal qualification entitles all human beings equally to certain absolute human rights: positive rights to noneconomic "goods" that by their very natures cannot be in short supply, negative rights not to be treated in cruel or inhuman ways, and negative rights not to be exploited or degraded even in "humane" ways. It is quite another thing, however, to make the minimal qualification of humanity the ground for an absolutely equal distribution of a country's *material wealth* among its citizens. A strict equalitarian could argue that he is merely applying Aristotle's formula of proportionate equality (presumably accepted by all parties to the dispute) with a criterion of relevance borrowed from the human rights theorists. Thus, distributive justice is accomplished between *A* and *B* when the following ration is satisfied:

$$\frac{A\text{'s share of } P}{B\text{'s share of } P} = \frac{A\text{'s possession of } Q}{B\text{'s possession of } Q}$$

Where *P* stands for economic goods, *Q* must stand simply for "humanity" or "a human nature," and since every human being possesses *that Q* equally, it follows that all should also share a society's economic wealth (the *P* in question) equally.

The trouble with this argument is that its major premise is no less disputable than its conclusion. The standard of relevance it borrows from other contexts where it seems very little short of self-evident, seems controversial at best, when applied to purely economic contexts. It seems evident to most of us that merely being human entitles *everyone*—bad men as well as good, lazy as well as industrious, inept as well as skilled—to a fair trial if charged with a crime, to equal protection of the law, to equal consideration of his interests by makers of national policy, to be spared torture or other cruel and inhuman treatment, and to be permanently ineligible for the status of chattel slave. Adding a right to an equal share of the economic pie, however, is to add a benefit of a wholly different order, one whose presence on the list of goods for which mere humanity is the sole qualifying condition is not likely to win wide assent without further argument

It is far more plausible to posit a human right to the satisfaction of (better: to an opportunity to satisfy) one's *basic* economic needs, that is, to enough food and medicine to remain healthy, to minimal clothing, housing, and so on. As Hume pointed out, even these rights cannot exist under conditions of extreme scarcity. Where there is not enough to go around, it cannot be true that everyone has a right to an equal share. But wherever there is moderate abundance or better—wherever a society produces more than enough to satisfy the *basic needs of everyone*—there it seems more plausible to say that mere possession of basic human needs qualifies a person for the opportunity to satisfy them. It would be a rare and callused sense of justice that would not be offended by an affluent society, with a large annual agricultural surplus and a great abundance of manufactured goods, which permitted some of its citizens to die of starvation, exposure, or easily curable disease. It would certainly be *unfair* for a nation to produce more than it needs and not permit some of its citizens enough to satisfy their

basic biological requirements. Strict equalitarianism, then, is a perfectly plausible material principle of distributive justice when confined to affluent societies and basic biological needs, but it loses plausibility when applied to division of the "surplus" left over after basic needs are met. . . .

Still, there is no way to *refute* the strict equalitarian who requires exactly equal shares for everyone whenever that can be arranged without discouraging total productivity to the point where everyone loses. No one would insist upon equal distributions that would diminish the size of the total pie and thus leave smaller slices for *everyone;* that would be opposed to reason. John Rawls makes this condition part of his "rational principle" of justice: "Inequalities are arbitrary unless it is reasonable to expect that they will work out to everyone's advantage. . . ." We are left then with a version of strict equalitarianism that is by no means evidently true and yet is impossible to refute. That is the theory that purports to apply not only to basic needs but to the total wealth of a society, and allows departures from strict equality when, *but only when,* they will work out to everyone's advantage. Although I am not persuaded by this theory, I think that any adequate material principle will have to attach great importance to keeping differences in wealth within reasonable limits, even after all basic needs have been met. One way of doing this would be to raise the standards for a "basic need" as total wealth goes up, so that differences between the richest and poorest citizens (even when there is no real "poverty") are kept within moderate limits.

NEED

The principle of need is subject to various interpretations, but in most of its forms it is not an independent principle at all, but only a way of mediating the application of the principle of equality. It can, therefore, be grouped with the principle of perfect equality as a member of the equalitarian family and contrasted with the principles of merit, achievement, contribution, and effort, which are all members of the nonequalitarian family. Consider some differences in "needs" as they bear on distributions. Doe is a bachelor with no dependents; Roe has a wife and six children. Roe must satisfy the needs of eight persons out of his paycheck, whereas Doe need satisfy the needs of only one. To give Roe and Doe equal pay would be to treat Doe's interests substantially *more* generously than those of anyone in the Roe family. Similarly, if a small private group is distributing food to its members (say a shipwrecked crew waiting rescue on a desert island), it would not be fair to give precisely the same quantity to a one hundred pounder as to a two hundred pounder, for that might be giving one person all he needs and the other only a fraction of what he needs— a difference in treatment not supported by any relevant difference between them. In short, to distribute goods in proportion to basic needs is not really to depart from a standard of equality, but rather to bring those with some greater initial burden or deficit up to the same level as their fellows.

The concept of a "need" is extremely elastic. In a general sense, to say that S needs X is to say simply that if he doesn't have X he will be harmed. A "basic need" would then be for an X in whose absence a person would be harmed in some crucial and fundamental way, such as suffering injury, malnutrition, illness, madness, or premature death. Thus we all have a basic need for foodstuffs of a certain quantity and variety, fuel to heat our dwellings, a roof over our heads, clothing to keep us warm, and so on. In a different but related sense of need, to say that S needs X is to say that without X he cannot achieve some specific purpose or perform some specific function. If they are to do their work, carpenters need tools, merchants need capital and customers, authors need paper and publishers. Some helpful goods are not strictly needed in this sense: an author with pencil and paper does not really need a typewriter to write a book, but he may need it to write a book speedily, efficiently, and conveniently. We sometimes come to rely upon "merely helpful but unneeded goods" to such a degree that we develop a strong habitual dependence on them, in which case (as it is often said) we have a "psychological" as opposed to a material need for them. If we don't possess that for which we have a strong psychological need, we may be unable to be happy, in which case a merely psychological need for a functional instrument may become a genuine need in the first sense distinguished above, namely, something whose absence is harmful to us. . . . The more abundant a society's material goods, the higher the level at which we are required (by the force of psychological needs) to fix the distinction between "necessities" and "luxuries"; what *everyone* in a given society regards as "necessary" tends to become an actual, basic need.

MERIT AND ACHIEVEMENT

The remaining three candidates for material principles of distributive justice belong to the nonequalitarian family. These three principles would each distribute goods in accordance, not with need, but with *desert;* since persons obviously differ in their deserts, economic goods would be distributed unequally. The three principles differ from one another in their conception of the relevant *bases of desert* for economic distributions. The first is the principle of *merit.* Unlike the other principles in the nonequalitarian family, this one focuses not on what a person has *done* to deserve his allotment, but rather on what kind of person he is—what characteristics he has.

Two different types of characteristic might be considered meritorious in the appropriate sense: skills and virtues. Native skills and inherited aptitudes will not be appropriate desert bases, since they are forms of merit ruled out by the fair opportunity requirement. No one deserves credit or blame for his genetic inheritance, since no one has the opportunity to select his own genes. Acquired skills may seem more plausible candidates at first, but upon scrutiny they are little better. First, all acquired skills depend to a large degree on native skills. Nobody is born knowing how to read, so reading is an acquired skill, but actual differences in reading skill are to a large degree accounted for by genetic differences that are beyond anyone's control. Some of the differences are no doubt caused by differences in motivation afforded different children, but again the early conditions contributing to a child's motivation are also largely beyond his control. We may still have some differences in acquired skills that are to be accounted for solely or primarily by differences in the degree of practice, drill, and perseverance expended by persons with roughly equal opportunities. In respect to these, we can propitiate the requirement of fair opportunity, but only by nullifying the significance of acquired skill as such, for now skill is a relevant basis of desert only to the ex-

tent that it is a product of one's own effort. Hence, *effort* becomes the true basis of desert (as claimed by our fifth principle, discussed below), and not simply skill as such. . . .

The most plausible nonequalitarian theories are those that locate relevance not in meritorious traits and excellences of any kind, but rather in prior doings: not in what one is, but in what one has done. Actions, too, are sometimes called "meritorious," so there is no impropriety in denominating the remaining families of principles in our survey as "meritarian." One type of action-oriented meritarian might cite *achievement* as a relevant desert basis for pecuniary rewards, so that departures from equality in income are to be justicized only by distinguished achievements in science, art, philosophy, music, athletics, and other basic areas of human activity. The attractions and disadvantages of this theory are similar to those of theories which I rejected above that base rewards on skills and virtues. Not all persons have a fair opportunity to achieve great things, and economic rewards seem inappropriate as vehicles for expressing recognition and admiration of noneconomic achievements.

CONTRIBUTION OR "DUE RETURN"

When the achievements under consideration are themselves contributions to our general economic well-being, the meritarian principle of distributive justice is much more plausible. Often it is conjoined with an economic theory that purports to determine exactly what percentage of our total economic product a given worker or class has produced. Justice, according to this principle, requires that each worker get back exactly that proportion of the national wealth he has himself created. This sounds very much like a principle of "commutative justice" directing us to *give back* to every worker what is really his own property, that is, the product of his own labor.

The French socialist writer and precursor of Karl Marx, Pierre Joseph Proudhon (1809–1865), is perhaps the classic example of this kind of theorist. In his book *What Is Property?* (1840), Proudhon rejects the standard socialist slogan, "From each according to his ability, to each according to his needs," in favor of a principle of distributive justice based on contribution, as interpreted by an economic theory that employed a pre-Marxist "theory of surplus value." The famous socialist slogan was not intended, in any case, to express a principle of distributive justice. It was understood to be a rejection of all consideration of "mere" justice for an ethic of human brotherhood. The early socialists thought it unfair, in a way, to give the great contributors to our wealth a disproportionately small share of the product. But in the new socialist society, love of neighbor, community spirit, and absence of avarice would overwhelm such bourgeois notions and put them in their proper (subordinate) place.

Proudhon, on the other hand, based his whole social philosophy not on brotherhood (an ideal he found suitable only for small groups such as families) but on the kind of distributive justice to which even some capitalists gave lip service:

The key concept was "mutuality" or "reciprocity." "Mutuality, reciprocity exists," he wrote, "when all the workers in an industry, instead of working for an entrepreneur who pays them and keeps their products, work for one another and thus collaborate in the making of a common product whose profits they share among themselves."

Proudhon's celebrated dictum that "property is theft" did not imply that all *possession* of goods is illicit, but rather that the system of rules that permitted the owner of a factory to hire workers and draw profits ("surplus value") from *their* labor robs the workers of what is rightly theirs. "This profit, consisting of a portion of the proceeds of labor that rightfully belonged to the laborer himself, was 'theft.'" The injustice of capitalism, according to Proudhon, consists in the fact that those who create the wealth (through their labor) get only a small part of what they create, whereas those who "exploit" their labor, like voracious parasites, gather in a greatly disproportionate share. The "return of contribution" principle of distributive justice, then, cannot work in a capitalist system, but requires a *fédération mutualiste* of autonomous producer-cooperatives in which those who create wealth by their work share it in proportion to their real contributions.

Other theorists, employing different notions of what produces or "creates" economic wealth, have used the "return of contribution" principle to support quite opposite conclusions. The contribution principle has even been used to justicize quite unequalitarian capitalistic status quos, for it is said that capital as well as labor creates wealth, as do ingenious ideas, inventions, and adventurous risk-taking. The capitalist who provided the money, the inventor who designed a product to be manufactured, the innovator who thought of a new mode of production and marketing, the advertiser who persuaded millions of customers to buy the finished product, the investor who risked his savings on the success of the enterprise—these are the ones, it is said, who did the most to produce the wealth created by a business, not the workers who contributed only their labor, and of course, these are the ones who tend, on the whole, to receive the largest personal incomes.

Without begging any narrow and technical questions of economics, I should express my general skepticism concerning such facile generalizations about the comparative degrees to which various individuals have contributed to our social wealth. Not only are there impossibly difficult problems of measurement involved, there are also conceptual problems that appear beyond all nonarbitrary solution. I refer to the elements of luck and chance, the social factors not attributable to any assignable individuals, and the contributions of population trends, uncreated natural resources, and the efforts of people now dead which are often central to the explanation of any given increment of social wealth. . . .

EFFORT

The principle of due return, as a material principle of distributive justice, does have some vulnerability to the fair opportunity requirement. Given unavoidable variations in genetic endowments and material circumstances, different persons cannot have precisely the same opportunities to make contributions to the public weal. Our final candidate for the status of a material principle of distributive justice, the *principle of effort,* does much better in this respect, for it would distribute economic products not in proportion to successful achievement but according to the degree of effort exerted. According to the principle of effort, justice decrees that hard-working executives and hard-working laborers receive precisely that same remuneration (although there may be reasons having nothing to do with justice for paying more to the executives), and that freeloaders be penalized by allotments of proportionately lesser shares of the joint products of everyone's labor. The most persuasive argument for this principle is that it is the closest approximation to the intuitively valid principle of due return that can pass the fair opportunity requirement. It is doubtful, however, that even the principle of effort fully satisfies the requirements of fair opportunity, since those who inherit or acquire certain kinds of handicap may have little opportunity to *acquire the motivation* even to do their best. In any event, the principle of effort does seem to have intuitive cogency giving it at least some weight as a factor determining the justice of distributions.

In very tentative conclusion, it seems that the principle of equality (in the version that rests on needs rather than that which requires "perfect equality") and the principles of contribution and effort (where nonarbitrarily applicable, and only *after* everyone's basic needs have been satisfied) have the most weight as determinants of economic justice, whereas all forms of the principle of merit are implausible in that role. The reason for the priority of basic needs is that, where there is economic abundance, the claim to life itself and to minimally decent conditions are, like other human rights, claims that all men make with perfect equality. As economic production increases, these claims are given ever greater consideration in the form of rising standards for distinguishing basic needs from other wanted goods. But no matter where that line is drawn, when we go beyond it into the realm of economic surplus or "luxuries," non egalitarian considerations (especially contribution and effort) come increasingly into play.

IRIS YOUNG

The Myth of Merit

IRIS YOUNG *teaches feminism, philosophy, and politics at the University of Pittsburgh. She is author of* Justice and the Politics of Difference.

A widely held principle of justice in our society is that positions and rewards should be distributed according to individual merit. The merit principle holds that positions should be awarded to the most qualified individuals, that is, to those who have the greatest aptitude and skill for performing the tasks those positions require. This principle is central to legitimating a hierarchical division of labor in a liberal democratic society which assumes the equal moral and political worth of all persons. Assuming as given a structural division between scarce highly rewarded positions and more plentiful less rewarded positions, the merit principle asserts that this division of labor is just when no group receives privileged positions by birth or right, or by virtue of arbitrary characteristics such as race, ethnicity, or sex. The unjust hierarchy of caste is to be replaced by a "natural" hierarchy of intellect and skill.

•   •   •

Use of a principle of merit to allocate scarce and desirable positions in a job hierarchy, and in the educational institutions that train people for those jobs, is just only if several conditions are met. First, qualifications must be defined in terms of technical skills and competence, independently of and neutral with respect to values and culture. By technical competence I mean competence at producing specified results. If merit criteria do not distinguish between technical skills and normative or cultural attributes, there is no way to separate being a "good" worker of a certain sort from being the sort kind of person— with the right background, way of life, and so on. Second, to justify differential job privilege the purely technical skills and competencies must be "job related," in that they operate as predictors for excellent performance in the position. Third, for merit criteria to be applied justly, performance and competence must be judged individually. In order to say that one individual is more qualified than another, finally, the performances and predicted performances of individuals must be compared and ranked according to measures which are independent of and neutral with respect to values and culture.

Proponents of a merit principle rarely doubt that these conditions can be met. Fishkin, for example, finds it obvious that the technical competence of individuals can be measured and predicted apart from values, purposes, and cultural norms. "It is hard to believe," he says, "in a modern industrial society, with a complex differentiation of tasks that qualifications that are performance related could not be defined so as to predict better performances." It may be hard to believe, but in fact such normatively and culturally neutral measures of individual performance do not exist for most jobs. The idea of merit criteria that are objective and unbiased with respect to personal attributes is a version of the ideal of impartiality, and is just as impossible.

First, most jobs are too complex and multifaceted to allow for a precise identification of their tasks and thus measurement of levels of performance of those tasks. Precise, value-neutral, task-specific measures of job performance are possible only for jobs with a limited number of definable functions, each of which is a fairly straightforward identifiable task, requiring little verbal skill, imagination, or judgment. Data entry work or quality control sorting may satisfy these requirements, but a great many jobs do not. A travel agent, for example, must keep records, communicate effectively on the telephone and through ever-changing computer networks of information, and study and keep at hand options in tour packages for many places. Service sector work, a vastly ex-

panding portion of jobs, in general can rarely be evaluated in terms of the criteria of productivity and efficiency applied to industrial production, because it makes much less sense to count services rendered than items that come off the assembly line.

Second, in complex industrial and office organizations, it is often not possible to identify the contribution that each individual makes, precisely because the workers cooperate in producing an outcome or product. The performance of a team, department, or firm may be measurable, but this is of little use in justifying the position or level of reward of any particular team members.

Third, a great many jobs require wide discretion in what the worker does and how best to do it. In many jobs the worker's role is more negative than positive; he or she oversees a process and intervenes to prevent something from going wrong. In automated processes, from individual machines to entire factories, for example, workers routinely contribute little to the actual making of things, but they must be vigilant in tending the machines to make sure the process goes as it should. The negative role increases worker discretion about whether, when and how often to intervene. Perhaps there is one easily identifiable and measurable way to perform many positive actions. But there are many ways of preventing a process from going wrong, and it is not usually possible to measure a worker's productivity level in terms of the costs that would have been incurred if she or he had not intervened, or the costs that would have been saved if she or he had intervened differently.

Finally, the division of labor in most large organizations means that those evaluating a worker's performance often are not familiar with the actual work process. Modern organizational hierarchies are what Claus Offe calls task discontinuous hierarchies. In a task continuous hierarchy, like that exemplified by medieval guild production, superiors do the same kind of work as their subordinates, but with a greater degree of skill and competence. In the task discountinuous hierarchies of contemporary organizations, job ladders are highly segregated. Superiors do not do the same kind of work as subordinates, and may never have done that sort of work. Thus the superior is often not competent to evaluate the technical work performance itself, and must rely on evaluating workers' attitudes, their compliance with the rules, their self-presentation, their cooperativeness— that is, their social comportment.

While these four impediments to a normatively and culturally neutral definition and assessment of job performance occur in many types of work, they are most apparent in professional and managerial work. These types of work usually involve a wide diversity of skills and tasks. Most or all of these tasks rely on the use of judgment, discretion, imagination, and verbal acuity, and none of these qualities is precisely measurable according to some objective, value-neutral scale. The achievement of professional and managerial objectives usually involves a complex series of social relationships and dependencies, to the extent that it is often unreasonable to hold professionals responsible for not meeting objectives. Professional and managerial jobs, finally, often are evaluated not only by superiors in a task discontinuous hierarchy, but by clients who are even less aware of the nature of the jobs and the skills required, and who are thus not in a position to apply criteria of technical performance that are normatively and culturally neutral.

* * *

AMARTYA SEN

Property and Hunger

AMARTYA SEN *is Professor of Economics at Harvard University and is author of many books, including* Ethics and Economics. *In this essay, he insists that questions of justice be appealed not just to abstract theory but to the concrete facts of human life— especially the facts revealed by economies and by pervasive human misery.*

I N an interesting letter to Anna George, the daughter of Henry George, Bernard Shaw wrote:

"Your father found me a literary dilettante and militant rationalist in religion, and a barren rascal at that. By turning my mind to economics he made a man of me." [I] am not able to determine what making a man of Bernard Shaw would exactly consist of, but it is clear that the kind of moral and social problems with which Shaw was deeply concerned could not be sensibly pursued without examining their economic aspects. For example, the claims of property rights, which some would defend and some (including Shaw) would dispute, are not just matters of basic moral belief that could not possibly be influenced one way or the other by any empirical arguments. They call for sensitive moral analysis responsive to empirical realities, including economic ones.

Moral claims based on intrinsically valuable rights are often used in political and social arguments. Rights related to ownership have been invoked for ages. But there are also other types of rights which have been seen as "inherent and inalienable," and the American Declaration of Independence refers to "certain unalienable rights," among which are "life, liberty and the pursuit of happiness." The Indian constitution talks even of "the right to an adequate means of livelihood." The "right not to be hungry" has often been invoked in recent discussions on the obligation to help the famished.

RIGHTS: INSTRUMENTS, CONSTRAINTS, OR GOALS?

Rights can be taken to be morally important in three different ways. First, they can be considered to be valuable *instruments* to achieve other goals. This is the "instrumental view," and is well illustrated by the utilitarian approach to rights. Rights are, in that view, of no intrinsic importance. Violation of rights is not in itself a bad thing, nor fulfillment intrinsically good. But the acceptance of rights promotes, in this view, things that are ultimately important, to wit, utility. Jeremy Bentham rejected "natural rights" as "simple nonsense," and "natural and imprescriptible rights" as "rhetorical nonsense, nonsense upon stilts." But he attached great importance to rights as instruments valuable to the promotion of a good society, and devoted much energy to the attempt to reform appropriately the actual system of rights.

The second view may be called the "constraint view," and it takes the form of seeing rights as *constraints* on what others can or cannot do. In this view rights *are* intrinsically important. However, they don't figure in moral accounting as goals to be generally promoted, but only as constraints that others must obey. As Robert Nozick has put it in a powerful exposition of this "constraint view": "Individuals have rights, and there are things no person or group may do to them (without violating their rights)." Rights "set the constraints within which a social choice is to be made, by excluding certain alternatives, fixing others, and so on."

The third approach is to see fulfillments or rights as goals to be pursued. This "goal view" differs from the instrumental view in regarding rights to be intrinsically important, and it differs from the constraint view in seeing the fulfillment of rights as goals to be generally promoted, rather than taking them as demanding only (and exactly) that we refrain from violating the rights of others. In the "constraint view" there is no duty to help anyone with his or her rights (merely not to hinder), and also in the "instrumental view" there is no duty, in fact, to help unless the right fulfillment will also promote some other goal such as utility. The "goal view" integrates the valuation of rights—their fulfillment and violation—in overall moral accounting, and yields a wider sphere of influence of rights in morality.

I have argued elsewhere that the goal view has advantages that the other two approaches do not share, in particular, the ability to accommodate integrated moral accounting including inter alia the intrinsic importance of a class of fundamental rights. I shall not repeat that argument here. But there is an interesting question of dual roles of rights in the sense that some rights may be *both* intrinsically important and instrumentally valuable. For example, the right to be free from hunger could—not implausibly—be regarded as being valuable in itself as well as serving as a good instrument to promote other goals such as security, longevity or utility. If so, both the goal view and the instrumental view would have to be simultaneously deployed to get a comprehensive assessment of such a right. This problem of comprehensiveness is a particularly important issue in the context of Henry George's discussion of rights, since he gave many rights significant dual roles.

The instrumental aspect is an inescapable feature of every right, since irrespective of whether a certain right is intrinsically valuable or not, its acceptance will certainly have other consequences as well, and these, too, have to be assessed along with the intrinsic value of rights (if any). A right that is regarded as quite valuable in itself may nevertheless be judged to be morally rejectable if it leads to disastrous consequences. This is a case of the rights playing a *negative* instrumental role. It is, of course, also possible that the instrumental argument will *bolster* the intrinsic claims of a right to be taken

seriously. I shall presently argue that such is the case in George's analysis with the right of labor to its produce.

There are two general conclusions to draw, at this stage, from this very preliminary discussion. First, we must distinguish between (1) the intrinsic value of a right, and (2) the overall value of a right taking note inter alia of its intrinsic importance (if any). The acceptance of the intrinsic importance of any right is no guarantee that its overall moral valuation must be favorable. Second, no moral assessment of a right can be independent of its likely consequences. The need for empirical assessment of the effects of accepting any right cannot be escaped. Empirical arguments are quite central to moral philosophy.

PROPERTY AND DEPRIVATION

The right to hold, use and bequeath property that one has legitimately acquired is often taken to be inherently valuable. In fact, however, many of its defenses seem to be actually of the instrumental type, e.g., arguing that property rights make people more free to choose one kind of a life rather than another. Even the traditional attempt at founding "natural property rights" on the principles of "natural liberty" (with or without John Locke's proviso) has some instrumental features. But even if we do accept that property rights may have some intrinsic value, this does not in any way amount to an overall justification of property rights, since property rights may have consequences which themselves will require assessment. Indeed, the causation of hunger as well as its prevention may materially depend on how property rights are structured. If a set of property rights leads, say, to starvation, as it well might, then the moral approval of these rights would certainly be compromised severely. In general, the need for consequential analysis of property rights is inescapable whether or not such rights are seen as having any intrinsic value.

Consider Henry George's formula of giving "the product to the producer." This is, of course, an ambiguous rule, since the division of the credits for production to different causal influences (e.g., according to "marginal productivities" in neoclassical theory, or according to human efforts in classical labor theory) is inevitably somewhat arbitrary, and full of problems involving internal tensions. But no matter how the ambiguities are resolved, it is clear that this rule would give no part of the socially produced output to one who is unemployed since he or she is producing nothing. Also, a person whose productive contribution happens to be tiny, according to *whichever* procedure of such accounting we use, can expect to get very little based on this so-called "natural law." Thus, hunger and starvation are compatible with this system of rights. George thought that this would not occur, since the economic reforms he proposed (including the abolition of land rights) would eliminate unemployment, and provision for the disabled would be made through the sympathetic support of others. These are empirical matters. If these empirical generalizations do not hold, then the outlined system of rights would yield a serious conflict. The property rights to one's product (however defined) might be of some intrinsic moral importance, but we clearly must also take note of the moral disvalue of human misery (such as suffering due to hunger and nutrition-related diseases). The latter could very

plausibly be seen as having more moral force than the former. A positive intrinsic value of the right to one's product can go with an overall negative value, taking everything into account.

This type of problem arises most powerfully in assessing the ethical force of some of the standard theories of rights. For example, neither a straightforward moral theory asserting inalienable property rights, nor an elaborate theory of an entitlement system of the kind outlined by Robert Nozick, can escape having to face the possibility that when applied to an actual society, the rights in question may yield hunger, starvation, and even large-scale famine. I have tried to argue elsewhere—not in the context of disputing these moral theories but in trying to understand the causation of famines in the modern world—that famines are, in fact, best explained in terms of failures of entitlement systems. The entitlements here refer, of course, to legal rights and to practical possibilities, rather than to moral status, but the laws and actual operation of private ownership economies have many features in common with the moral system of entitlements analyzed by Nozick and others.

The entitlement approach to famines need not, of course, be confined to private ownership economies, and entitlement failures of other systems can also be fruitfully studied to examine famines and hunger. In the specific context of private ownership economies, the entitlements are substantially analyzable in terms, respectively, of what may be called "endowments" and "exchange entitlements." A person's endowment refers to what he or she initially owns (including the person's own labor power), and the exchange entitlement mapping tells us what the person can obtain through exchanging what he or she owns, either by production (exchange with nature), or by trade (exchange with others), or a mixture of the two. A person has to starve if neither the endowments, nor what can be obtained through exchange, yields an adequate amount of food.

If starvation and hunger are seen in terms of failures of entitlements, then it becomes immediately clear that the total availability of food in a country is only one of several variables that are relevant. Many famines occur without any decline in the availability of food. For example, in the Great Bengal famine of 1943, the total food availability in Bengal was not particularly bad (considerably higher than two years earlier when there was no famine), and yet three million people died, in a famine mainly affecting the rural areas, through rather violent shifts in the relative purchasing powers of different groups, hitting the rural laborers the hardest. The Ethiopian famine of 1973 took place in a year of average per capita food availability, but the cultivators and other occupation groups in the province of Wollo had lost their means of subsistence (through loss of crops and a decline of economic activity, related to a local drought) and had no means of commanding food from elsewhere in the country. Indeed, some food moved *out* of Wollo to more prosperous people in other parts of Ethiopia, repeating a pattern of contrary movement of food that was widely observed during the Irish famine of the 1840s (with food moving out of famine-stricken Ireland to prosperous England which had greater power in the battle of entitlements). The Bangladesh famine of 1974 took place in a year of *peak* food availability, but several occupation groups had lost their entitlement to food

through loss of employment and other economic changes (including inflationary pressures causing prices to outrun wages). Other examples of famines without significant (or any) decline in food availability can be found, and there is nothing particularly surprising about this fact once it is recognized that the availability of food is only one influence among many on the entitlement of each occupation group. Even when a famine is associated with a decline of food availability, the entitlement changes have to be studied to understand the particular nature of the famine, e.g., why one occupation group is hit but not another. The causation of starvation can be sensibly sought in failures of entitlements of the respective groups.

The causal analysis of famines in terms of entitlements also points to possible public policies of prevention. The main economic strategy would have to take the form of increasing the entitlements of the deprived groups, and in general, of guaranteeing minimum entitlements for everyone, paying particular attention to the vulnerable groups. This can, in the long run, be done in many different ways, involving both economic growth (including growth of food output) and distributional adjustments. Some of these policies may, however, require that the property rights and the corresponding entitlements of the more prosperous groups be violated. The problem, in fact, is particularly acute in the short run, since it may not be possible to engineer rapid economic growth instantly. Then the burden of raising entitlements of the groups in distress would largely have to fall on reducing the entitlements of others more favorably placed. Transfers of income or commodities through various public policies may well be effective in quashing a famine (as the experience of famine relief in different countries has shown), but it may require substantial government intervention in the entitlements of the more prosperous groups.

There is, however, no great moral dilemma in this if property rights are treated as purely *instrumental*. If the goals of relief of hunger and poverty are sufficiently powerful, then it would be just right to violate whatever property rights come in the way, since—in this view—property rights have no intrinsic status. On the other hand, if property rights are taken to be morally inviolable irrespective of their consequences, then it will follow that these policies cannot be morally acceptable even though they might save thousands, or even millions, from dying. The inflexible moral "constraint" of respecting people's legitimately acquired entitlements would rule out such policies.

In fact this type of problem presents a reductio ad absurdum of the moral validity of constraint-based entitlement systems. However, while the conclusion to be derived from that approach might well be "absurd," the situation postulated is not an imaginary one at all. It is based on studies of actual famines and the role of entitlement failures in the causation of mass starvation. If there is an embarrassment here, it belongs solidly to the consequence-independent way to seeing rights.

I should add that this dilemma does not arise from regarding property rights to be of intrinsic value, which can be criticized on other grounds, but not this one. Even if property rights *are* of intrinsic value, their violation may be justified on grounds of the favorable consequences of that violation. A right, as was mentioned earlier, may be intrinsically valuable and still be justly violated taking everything into account.

The "absurdum" does not belong to attaching intrinsic value to property rights, but to regarding these rights as simply acceptable, regardless of their consequences. A moral system that values both property rights and other goals—such as avoiding famines and starvation, or fulfilling people's right not to be hungry—can, on the one hand, give property rights intrinsic importance, and on the other, recommend the violation of property rights when that leads to better overall consequences (*including* the disvalue of rights violation).

The issue here is not the valuing of property rights, but their alleged inviolability. There is no dilemma here either for the purely instrumental view of property rights or for treating the fulfillment of property rights as one goal among many, but specifically for consequence-independent assertions of property rights and for the corresponding constraint-based approaches to moral entitlement of ownership.

That property and hunger are closely related cannot possibly come as a great surprise. Hunger is primarily associated with not owning enough food and thus property rights over food are immediately and directly involved. Fights over that property right can be a major part of the reality of a poor country, and any system of moral assessment has to take note of that phenomenon. The tendency to see hunger in purely technocratic terms of food output and availability may help to hide the crucial role of entitlements in the genesis of hunger, but a fuller economic analysis cannot overlook that crucial role. Since property rights over food are derived from property rights over other goods and resources (through production and trade), the entire system of rights of acquisition and transfer is implicated in the emergence and survival of hunger and starvation.

THE RIGHT NOT
TO BE HUNGRY

Property rights have been championed for a long time. In contrast, the assertion of "the right not to be hungry" is a comparatively recent phenomenon. While this right is much invoked in political debates, there is a good deal of skepticism about treating this as truly a right in any substantial way. It is often asserted that this concept of "right not to be hungry" stands essentially for nothing at all ("simple nonsense," as Bentham called "natural rights" in general). That piece of sophisticated cynicism reveals not so much a penetrating insight into the practical affairs of the world, but a refusal to investigate what people mean when they assert the existence of rights that, for the bulk of humanity, are not in fact guaranteed by the existing institutional arrangements.

The right not to be hungry is not asserted as a recognition of an institutional right that already exists, as the right to property typically is. The assertion is primarily a moral claim as to what should be valued, and what institutional structure we should aim for, and try to guarantee if feasible. It can also be seen in terms of Ronald Dworkin's category of "background rights"—rights that provide a justification for political decisions by society in abstract. This interpretation serves as the basis for a reason to change the existing institutional structure and state policy.

It is broadly in this form that the right to "an adequate means of livelihood" is referred to in the Constitution of India: "The state shall, in particular, direct its policy towards securing . . . that the citizens, men and women equally, have the right to an adequate means of livelihood." This does not, of course, offer to each citizen a guaranteed right to an adequate livelihood, but the state is asked to take steps such that this right could become realizable for all.

In fact, this right has often been invoked in political debates in India. The electoral politics of India does indeed give particular scope for such use of what are seen as background rights. It is, of course, not altogether clear whether the reference to this right in the Indian constitution has in fact materially influenced the political debates. The constitutional statement is often cited, but very likely this issue would have figured in any case in these debates, given the nature of the moral and political concern. But whatever the constitutional contribution, it is interesting to ask whether the implicit acceptance of the value of the right to freedom from hunger makes any difference to actual policy.

It can be argued that the general acceptance of the right of freedom from acute hunger as a major goal has played quite a substantial role in preventing famines in India. The last real famine in India was in 1943, and while food availability per head in India has risen only rather slowly (even now the food availability per head is no higher than in many sub-Saharan countries stricken by recurrent famines), the country has not experienced any famine since independence in 1947. The main cause of that success is a policy of public intervention. Whenever a famine has threatened (e.g., in Bihar in 1967–68, in Maharashtra in 1971–73, in West Bengal in 1978–79), a public policy of intervention and relief has offered minimum entitlements to the potential famine victims, and thus have the threatening famines been averted. It can be argued that the quickness of the response of the respective governments (both state and central) reflects a political necessity, given the Indian electoral system and the importance attached by the public to the prevention of starvation. Political pressures from opposition groups and the news media have kept the respective governments on their toes, and the right to be free from acute hunger and starvation has been achieved largely because it has been seen as a valuable right. Thus the recognition of the intrinsic moral importance of this right, which has been widely invoked in public discussions, has served as a powerful political instrument as well.

On the other hand, this process has been far from effective in tackling pervasive and persistent undernourishment in India. There has been no famine in post-independence India, but perhaps a third of India's rural population is perennially undernourished. So long as hunger remains non-acute and starvation deaths are avoided (even though morbidity and mortality rates are enhanced by undernourishment), the need for a policy response is neither much discussed by the news media, nor forcefully demanded even by opposition parties. The elimination of famines coexists with the survival of widespread "regular hunger." The right to "adequate means" of *nourishment* does not at all seem to arouse political concern in a way that the right to "adequate means" to *avoid starvation* does.

The contrast can be due to one of several different reasons. It could, of course, simply be that the ability to avoid under-nourishment is not socially accepted as very important. This could be so, though what is socially accepted and what is not is also partly a matter of how clearly the questions are posed. It is, in fact, quite possible that the freedom in question would be regarded as a morally important right if the question were posed in a transparent way, but

this does not happen because of the nature of Indian electoral politics and that of news coverage. The issue is certainly not "dramatic" in the way in which starvation deaths and threatening famines are. Continued low-key misery may be too familiar a phenomenon to make it worthwhile for political leaders to get some mileage out of it in practical politics. The news media may also find little profit in emphasizing a non-spectacular phenomenon—the quiet survival of disciplined, non-acute hunger.

If this is indeed the case, then the implications for action of the goal of eliminating hunger, or guaranteeing to all the means for achieving this, may be quite complex. The political case for making the quiet hunger less quiet and more troublesome for governments in power in certainly relevant. Aggressive political journalism might prove to have an instrumental moral value if it were able to go beyond reporting the horrors of visible starvation and to portray the pervasive, non-acute hunger in a more dramatic and telling way. This is obviously not the place to discuss the instrumentalities of practical politics, but the endorsement of the moral right to be free from hunger—both acute and non-acute—would in fact raise pointed questions about the means which might be used to pursue such a goal.

MORAL ASSESSMENT AND SOCIAL RELATIONS

Henry George's advice to Bernard Shaw to study economics may well be supplemented by advising the economist to study politics and sociology, and the "moral scientist," to use an old-fashioned term, to study them all. When fulfillments of such rights as freedom from hunger are accepted as goals (among other possible goals), the moral assessment of actions and institutions will depend crucially on economic, social, and political analyses of how best to pursue these goals.

If there is one thing that emerges sharply from the discussion I have tried to present in this paper, it is the importance of factual analysis for moral assessment, including moral scrutiny of the acceptability and pursuit of specific rights. This is so even when the right in question is acknowledged to have intrinsic moral value, since valuing a right is not the same thing as accepting it. To affirm acceptability independently of consequences can be peculiarly untenable, as was discussed in analyzing entitlements and hunger. In assessing the claims of property rights, or the right not to be hungry, the examination cannot be confined to issues of basic valuation only, and much of the challenge of assessment lies in the empirical analysis of causes and effects. In the world in which we live—full of hunger as well as wealth—these empirical investigations can be both complex and quite extraordinarily important. The big moral questions are frequently also deeply economic, social, or political.

MALCOLM X

Human Rights, Civil Rights

MALCOLM X *(1925–1965), originally named Malcolm Little, was a controversial civil rights leader, a powerful organizer, and a spectacular spokesperson for human rights in America. Initially he advocated separatism and black nationalism, but as a result of his conversion to Islam and a pilgrimage he made to Mecca, he revised his political views. Shortly before he was assassinated he adopted a platform of brotherhood and equality. Here he distinguishes between human rights and civil rights.*

[INTERVIEWER]

One question that I've wondered about—in several of your lectures you've stressed the idea that the struggle of your people is for human rights rather than civil rights. Can you explain a bit what you mean by that?

MALCOLM X:

Civil rights actually keeps the struggle within the domestic confines of America. It keeps it under the jurisdiction of the American government, which means that as long as our struggle for what we're seeking is labeled civil rights, we

can only go to Washington, D.C., and then we rely upon
either the Supreme Court, the President or the Congress or
the senators. These senators—many of them are racists.
Many of the congressmen are racists. Many of the judges
are racists and oftentimes the president himself is a very
shrewdly camouflaged racist. And so we really can't get
meaningful redress for our grievances when we are
depending upon these grievances being redressed just
within the jurisdiction of the United States government.

On the other hand, human rights go beyond the jurisdiction of
this government. Human rights are international. Human
rights are something that a man has by dint of his having
been born. The labeling of our struggle in this country
under the title civil rights of the past 12 years has actually
made it impossible for us to get outside help. Many foreign
nations, many of our brothers and sisters on the African
continent who have gotten their independence, have
restrained themselves, have refrained from becoming
vocally or actively involved in our struggle for fear that
they would be violating U.S. protocol, that they would be
accused of getting involved in America's domestic affairs.

On the other hand, when we label it human rights, it
internationalizes the problem and puts it at a level that
makes it possible for any nation or any people anywhere on
this earth to speak out in behalf of our human rights
struggle.

So we feel that by calling it civil rights for the past 12 years,
we've actually been barking up the wrong tree, that ours is
a problem of *human* rights.

Plus, if we have our human rights, our civil rights are automatic.
If we're respected as a human being, we'll be respected as a
citizen; and in this country the black man not only is not
respected as a citizen, he is not even respected as a human
being.

And the proof is that you find in many instances people can come
to this country from other countries—they can come to this
country from behind the Iron Curtain—and despite the fact
that they come here from these other places, they don't
have to have civil-rights legislation passed in order for their
rights to be safeguarded.

No new legislation is necessary for foreigners who come here to
have their rights safeguarded. The Constitution is sufficient,
but when it comes to the black men who were born here—
whenever we are asking for our rights, they tell us that new
legislation is necessary.

Well, we don't believe that. The Organization of Afro-American
Unity feels that as long as our people in this country
confine their struggle within the limitations and under the
jurisdiction of the United States government, we remain
within the confines of the vicious system that has done
nothing but exploit and oppress us ever since we've been
here. So we feel that our only real hope is to make known
that our problem is not a Negro problem or an American
problem but rather, it has become a human problem, a
world problem, and it has to be attacked at the world level,
at a level at which all segments of humanity can intervene
in our behalf.

Chapter 20

How Should I Make a Living?

How do you intend to make a living? This might seem like a rather vulgar question for a philosophy course, but contrary to its reputation, philosophy is deeply involved in even the most practical aspects of our lives. In particular, the very question about "making a living"—as opposed to being granted the necessities of life by the government, for example—already points to an entire philosophy of life: the idea that you should *earn* your keep, that you have a *choice* in how you will do this, and that it is alright that you might or might not make more money and live more luxuriously than other people. The nineteenth-century name for the economic system that encourages this philosophical view of life and work is **capitalism,** and it is just as much a system of ethics as it is of economics. Although people all too often say that "business is unethical," the truth is that business is defined by its ethics. There are right and wrong ways for you to make money; it is not just a question of how much. **Business ethics** is the name of a new discipline (though it goes back to ancient times) that maps out the guidelines of ethics in business.

The broad principles of ethics—such as "treat people as ends and never merely as means" and "do not cause unnecessary harm"—apply in virtually every aspect of our lives, and perhaps too in every nation and culture. But most of ethics requires a more specific understanding of the particular practices in which human beings participate. The ethics of good sportsmanship will be very different (even when similar in vocabulary) from the ethics of war. Perhaps the most important single context for understanding ethics in contemporary American society is the world of business. It would not be an overstatement to say that a great many of our primary American values are either derived from or are part of business ethics. These include the traditional virtues of thrift, planning, and honoring one's contracts, as well as the skills of negotiation, trying to produce the highest quality product for the best price, and looking for the best bargain. Business—the production and sale of goods and services and the purchase of them—provides the context in which most of us live. Activities that once were the province of religion or the state (for example, the arts) are now very much part of the business world. And yet, it is often joked that "business ethics is a contradiction in terms" and that "there is no ethics in business." Such humor betrays an important problem in our thinking. On the one hand, business provides the value system upon which much of our society depends for its ethics and its understanding of what is right and wrong, fair and unfair. On the other hand, business itself is too often thought to be distinct from ethics, if not unethical, and value-free, except for the all-important "bottom line," the value of making a dollar (or a million of them).

Business ethics is a relatively new concern, in one sense. As a subject of serious concern, an attempt to understand how business actually works and what its implicit rules of fairness are, business ethics is only a few decades old. It is the product of both the power and success of American business and the increased awareness if not frequency of business scandals and abuses—automobiles that might have been fixed in the factory that explode upon collision, securities firms that fiddle with clients' funds or trade illegally on "insider" information, American companies abroad caught bribing foreign officials for contracts. But although the focus of business ethics is often upon such scandals and wrongdoing, the presumption is that most people and most companies in business are indeed ethical and conscientious. They really do try to serve not only their customers and stockholders but their employees and the surrounding community as well. So business ethics like ethics in general is the attempt to spell out the rules for proper conduct that are already followed by most of the businesspeople in America.

In another, less flattering sense, business ethics has been around since ancient times, but almost always in the form of an all-out attack on business and its values. The materialism on which a consumer society is based has often been thought to be unethical to the core. And the so-called profit motive, on which most of business is based, was condemned for centuries and even called a sin—"avarice." This entirely negative attitude toward business did not change in Europe until the seventeenth century, just about the time that America—the foremost business society—was being settled.

The philosophical problems of business fall roughly into two categories. First there are the very broad questions about business as such—what the nineteenth-century philosophers named capitalism. These include whether "free enterprise" is indeed the best way to make a society prosper and its citizens happy and whether it is a fair way to distribute the wealth, goods, and advantages of a society to all its citizens. The father of modern economics and most famous prophet of capitalism, Adam Smith, wrote in his *Wealth of Nations* that the free enterprise system was indeed the best way to make a society prosper and provide all its citizens with comforts and even luxuries unimaginable in any other society. (His book was published in England in 1776, the same year as the signing of the Declaration of Independence in America.)

But as capitalism (and the industrial revolution that provided its technology) developed in England and elsewhere, it became evident that not all people were prospering equally. Those who worked as much as 16 hours a day in the mines and factories—including many young children—remained desperately poor, while their bosses often became fabulously wealthy. The unfairness of this situation was particularly evident to a young German named Karl Marx, who had come to live in London in the mid-nineteenth century. He and his friend Friedrich Engels (who was himself a wealthy businessman) wrote what is still the most devastating attack on this new world. In fact, many of the reforms urged by Marx and Engels have been carried out in most businesses today. But the question remains to what extent business—the private production and sale of the material goods and services—is the best and fairest way of running the economy of a society. Many authors advocate more government control of who makes what and who gets what, or at least regulation of businesses so that certain minimal standards of quality, safety, and fairness are maintained. Many other authors and businesspeople insist that such control and regulation is best accomplished by businesses themselves and by the consumer, who in his or her freedom to buy or not buy a certain product in fact controls the business world more effectively than any government.

The second category of problems in business ethics is more particular and applies to the activities of particular businesses. The business world has changed a great deal since Adam Smith and Marx wrote their treatises on capitalism. They were looking at a world of small shopkeepers and (what we would consider) modest industries. The business world of today is dominated instead by enormous corporations, some of which have hundreds of thousands of employees and offices in almost every country in the world. Accordingly, many of the problems of business ethics today have to do with the size, the power, and consequently, the social responsibilities of corporations. It has been argued that corporations have only a single purpose—to make a profit, on the assumption that a corporation that is making a profit must also be providing quality goods and services to its consumers. It has also been argued that business is much more like a game of poker than it is a socially responsible institution, with the conclusion that businesspeople should not be expected to follow the same ethical principles as everyone else. On the other hand, it has been argued that businesses, like very powerful citizens, have special obligations which go beyond their responsibilities to their stockholders and customers. These arguments are kept in the public eye by such familiar headlines as "XYZ corporation indicted for taking kick-backs on defense contracts" or "Manufacturer knew that XXX causes cancer." One could even claim that a proper appreciation of business ethics is the condition for businesses' continued respect and success in the world.

The following selections include Adam Smith's classic statement about capitalism, an excerpt from Marx and Engels, and a recent sample of Marxist criticism by Paul Sweezy. Also included are Milton Friedman's controversial denial of the social responsibilities of business with Christopher Stone's rebuttal. As a bit of internal evidence in the conflict concerning the social responsibility of corporations, we include a memo from the Ford Motor Company concerning one of the more notorious cases of the past several decades. A study of over-the-border sweatshops raises questions about multicultural employment practices, and an essay by Joanne Ciulla raises deep questions concerning the meaning of work. Patricia H. Werhane enumerates the kinds of moral rights employees and employers must have to ensure justice in the workplace. Laurie Schrage and June O'Neill then present opposing views on the controversial problem of comparable worth, that is, whether legislation should enforce equality of pay between men and women for "comparable" jobs. Finally, we conclude the chapter with a few sage words on business by Confucius, writing some two millennia ago.

MICHAEL D'ANTONIO

On Ethics in Business

MICHAEL D'ANTONIO *writes for* Newsday.

I N the rough-and-tumble world of gold futures trading, Steve was known as a killer, a closer who could literally talk women with sick children out of their last dollars and into risky investments in gold and silver.

Technically, he was supposed to counsel potential buyers and advise them against investing if they didn't have the money or weren't in a position to take the risk. In practice, Steve (not his real name) used high-pressure techniques and glossed over the potential hazard in order to reel in profits. It pleased his bosses, who were concerned about the bottom line, but deep within his conscience it bothered Steve.

"If you didn't do it," he says, "it came out the next day at the morning meeting. You were a jerk, and schlemiel for letting them get away. It was clear that we were to lie, omit, or persuade, but we were to get the money.

"One case was this lady, maybe 57, worth about $350,000—not a lot these days. She had a kid who was in an accident. He was going to be in the hospital forever. Everything she had was accounted for except for about $5,000. I took it, knowing the market would go nowhere. She lost it. She sends me Christmas cards."

In the beginning, Steve says, he followed his conscience and advised some prospects against gold and silver investments, which "are as risky as betting football games." But as his pile of rejected leads grew, the morning sales meeting became unbearably humiliat-

ing. And despite nagging doubts about the morality of high-pressure tactics, he became what the bosses called "a closer, a killer." He buried his conscience and brought in the money.

Steve's, moral conflict—choosing between the demands of his job and the demand of conscience—posed the kind of ethical choice that adults confront in their public lives every day. Not life and death questions, these are seemingly simple matters of honesty. But increasingly, say some experts, Americans are setting aside traditional values of right and wrong and bypassing conscience.

It is apparently easy to cheat faceless victims—distant corporations, unknown stockholders, unseen employers. And today's technical, urban culture bombards inner morality with materialism. The researchers point to recent controversies in business and government, some involving hundreds of workers and executives, to support their claim of a widespread ethical breakdown.

- In May, E. F. Hutton, the investment firm, admitted to a long-running check-kiting scheme—systematic bank overdrafts—involving hundreds of employees and executives and billions of dollars.

- In April, government auditors charged that seven major defense contractors had submitted claims for expenses worth $109 million for clearly unauthorized items, including haircuts for executives.

❦ In March, six judges in Chicago were charged with taking bribes from lawyers and defendants.

❦ In 1984, National Semiconductor Corp. was convicted of deliberate fraud in its testing of computer chips used in high-tech armaments.

Although moral controversies are not unique to the 1980s, many ethicists, sociologists and psychologists say that today's moral lapses point to more widespread blurring of right and wrong.

The E. F. Hutton scandal was not the work of one or two "bad apples," but evidence of general moral decay, says psychologist Charles Ansell of Sherman Oaks, Calif. And researchers are beginning to explore the ways in which people bypass basic moral training in the competitive adult world.

"It's as simple as the Judeo-Christian maxim of doing unto others as you would have them do unto you," writes Ansell, who writes on behavior and morality. Moral judgment, ingrained in childhood, should become "an automatic sense that helps you make the right choice almost without thinking. Today, we are losing the sense of being inner-directed. Instead, we let the morals of the group, or organizations like our business, control us," he adds.

"The guy putting his hand into the cookie jar today is not thinking about what he is doing that is wrong. He is thinking about how he will look with more money in his hand."

On a personal level, the "loss of conscience," as Ansell calls it, opens a door to immoral behavior. He says it allows construction supervisors to engage in systematic payoffs to inspectors. It frees executives and employees of defense contractors to cooperate in fraud.

Ansell is convinced that 20th-century people suffer a kind of moral rootless-ness. "The 19th-century man was more inner-directed. He lived on his own, farming or in a small town, and he was forced to rely on an inner sense of what was right. And if he did something wrong, he saw his victim and had to deal with the consequences.

"Today's victim is faceless. If you rip off the telephone company, who is hurt? If you kite checks for your company, where is the victim? The person cheating the Pentagon doesn't see himself hurting anyone directly."

In general, Ansell lays blame on the pressures of modern life, including competition in business and the "facelessness" of a technological society, for individual immoral conduct. "We are so competitive, and part of competition is contempt for your opponent," he says. "The E. F. Hutton executive who finds himself involved in some scheme feels contempt for his victims." . . .

While the added pressures of modern life may erode morality, other analysts argue that institutions that used to be leading character-builders—family, religion and the schools—have declined to the point where they are becoming ineffective. And they say that too many people enter the adult world without a moral foundation.

"In past generations, ethical values were passed on by enduring institutions, especially the extended family," says philosopher Gary Edwards of the Ethics Resource Center in Washington. "There were grandparents, uncles and aunts to give you specific lessons, tell you stories with morals. And schools very self-consciously taught morals. They taught good citizenship."

Edwards says that popular educational movements in the 1950s and '60s and pressure from political groups forced moral lessons out of the public schools. Campaigns to drive prejudice out of public institutions also may have driven out baseline social values, he says. "We learned to be tolerant, and that's not a bad thing. But we came to be tolerant to a fault, and that meant people lost the courage of conviction."

Over a period of months, Steve tried to meet the standards set by his superiors. He talked people out of their money and committed what he calls "the sins of omission" as he described the risks of silver and gold futures. But the conflict bred what psychologist Ansell describes as immoral behavior sinking into self-contempt.

"I drank, skipped the morning meetings, played a lot of golf and left early. And the worst thing was looking my kids in the eye when I told them what was right and what was wrong," says Steve.

"Then one day they gobbled up my book [of clients] and were going to give all my leads to killers," he says. "When I told them they were wrong, they said I was a wimp, that I didn't understand the way the world works."

In the end, Steve quit. He went home and discussed his problem with his wife and two sons. "I told them I had cheated people, but I was stopping. I took a job running a restaurant, then driving a limo. I went from $1,500 a week to $450. At times I feel like I'm not such a macho guy because I didn't have what it takes for that life. I feel like a jerky idealist. But most of the time I feel good about myself. I never felt that way before."

ADAM SMITH

Benefits of the Profit Motive

ADAM SMITH's (1723–1790) Wealth of Nations *is often called the Bible of capitalism. It also marks the beginning of modern economic theory. The following selection from that work is a discussion of the value of the division of labor and the advantages of the capitalist system.*

THE greatest improvement in the productive power of labor, and the greater part of the skill, dexterity, and judgment with which it is anywhere directed, or applied, seem to have been the effects of the division of labor. . . .

To take an example, therefore, from a very trifling manufacture; but one in which the division of labor has been very often taken notice of, the trade of the pin-maker; a workman not educated to this business (which the division of labor has rendered a distinct trade), nor acquainted with the use of the machinery employed in it (to the invention of which the same division of labor has probably given occasion), could scarce, perhaps, with his utmost industry, make one pin a day, and certainly could not make twenty. But in the way in which this business is now carried on, not only the whole work is a peculiar trade, but it is divided into a number of branches, of which the greater part are likewise peculiar trades. One man draws out the wire, another straights it, a third cuts it, a fourth points it, a fifth grinds it at the top for receiving the head; to make the head requires two or three distinct operations; to put it on is a peculiar business, to whiten the pins is another; it is even a trade by itself to put them into the paper; and the important business of making a pin is, in this manner, divided into about eighteen distinct operations, which, in some manufactories, are all performed by distinct hands, though in others the same man will sometimes perform two or three of them. I have seen a small manufactory of this kind where ten men only were employed, and where some of them consequently performed two or three distinct operations. But though they were very poor, and therefore but indifferently accommodated with the necessary machinery, they could, when they exerted themselves, make among them about twelve pounds of pins in a day. There are in a pound upwards of four thousand pins of a middling size. Those ten persons, therefore, could make among them upwards of forty-eight thousand pins in a day. Each person, therefore, making a tenth part of forty-eight thousand pins, might be considered as making four thousand eight hundred pins in a day. But if they had all wrought separately and independently, and without any of them having been educated to this peculiar business, they certainly could not each of them have made twenty, perhaps not one pin in a day; that is, certainly, not the two hundred and fortieth, perhaps not the four thousand eight hun-

dredth part, of what they are at present capable of performing in consequence of a proper division and combination of their different operations.

In every other art and manufacture, the effects of the division of labor are similar to what they are in this very trifling one; though in many of them, the labor can neither be so much subdivided, nor reduced to so great a simplicity of operation. The division of labor, however, so far as it can be introduced, occasions, in every art, a proportionable increase of the productive powers of labor. . . .

This great increase of the quantity of work, which, in consequence of the division of labor, the same number of people are capable of performing, is owing to three different circumstances: first, to the increase of dexterity in every particular workman; secondly, to the saving of the time which is commonly lost in passing from one species of work to another; and lastly, to the invention of a great number of machines which facilitate and abridge labor, and enable one man to do the work of many.

First, the improvement of the dexterity of the workman necessarily increases the quantity of the work he can perform; and the division of labor, by reducing every man's business to some one simple operation and by making this operation the sole employment of his life, necessarily increases very much the dexterity of the workman. A common smith, who, though accustomed to handle the hammer, has never been used to make nails, if upon some particular occasion he is obliged to attempt it, will scarce, I am assured, be able to make about two or three hundred nails in a day, and those too very bad ones. A smith who has been accustomed to make nails, but whose sole or principal business has not been that of a nailer, can seldom with his utmost diligence make more than eight hundred or a thousand nails in a day. I have seen several boys under twenty years of age who had never exercised any other trade but that of making nails, and who, when they exerted themselves, could make, each of them, upwards of two thousand three hundred nails in a day. The making of a nail, however, is by no means one of the simplest operations. The same person blows the bellows, stirs or mends the fire as there is occasion, heats the iron, and forges every part of the nail: In forging the head too he is obliged to change his tools. The different operations into which the making of a pin or of a metal button is subdivided, are all of them much more simple; and the dexterity of the person, of whose life it has been the sole business to perform them, is usually much greater. The rapidity with which some of the operations of those manufactures are performed exceeds what the human hand could, by those who had never seen them, be supposed capable of acquiring.

Secondly, the advantage which is gained by saving the time commonly lost in passing from one sort of work to another is much greater than we should at first view be apt to imagine it. It is impossible to pass very quickly from one kind of work to another, that is carried on in a different place, and with quite different tools. A country weaver who cultivates a small farm must lose a good deal of time in passing from his loom to the field, and from the field to his loom. When the two trades can be carried on in the same workhouse, the loss of time is no doubt much less. It is even in this case, however, very considerable. . . .

Thirdly, and lastly, every body must be sensible how much labor is facili-

tated and abridged by the application of proper machinery. . . .

. . . A great part of the machines made use of in those manufactures in which labor is most subdivided were originally the inventions of common workmen, who, being each of them employed in some very simple operation, naturally turned their thoughts toward finding out easier and readier methods of performing it. Whoever has been much accustomed to visit such manufacturers must frequently have been shown very pretty machines which were the inventions of such workmen in order to facilitate and quicken their own particular part of the work. In the first fire-engines, a boy was constantly employed to open and shut alternately the communication between the boiler and the cylinder, according as the piston either ascended or descended. One of those boys, who loved to play with his companions, observed that, by tying a string from the handle of the valve which opened this communication to another part of the machine, the valve would open and shut without his assistance, and leave him at liberty to divert himself with his play-fellows. One of the greatest improvements that has been made upon this machine, since it was first invented, was in this manner the discovery of a boy who wanted to save his own labor. . . .

It is the great multiplication of the productions of all the different arts, in consequence of the division of labor, which occasions, in a well-governed society, that universal opulence which extends itself to the lowest ranks of people. Every workman has a great quantity of his own work to dispose of beyond what he himself has occasion for; and every other workman being exactly in the same situation, he is enabled to exchange a great quantity of his own goods for a great quantity, or, what comes to the same thing, for the price of a great quantity of theirs. He supplies them abundantly with what they have occasion for, and they accommodate him as amply with what he has occasion for, and a general plenty diffuses itself through all the different ranks of the society. . . .

This division of labor, from which so many advantages are derived, is not originally the effect of any human wisdom which foresees and intends that general opulence to which it gives occasion. It is the necessary, though very slow and gradual, consequence of a certain propensity in human nature which has in view no such extensive utility: the propensity to truck, barter, and exchange one thing for another.

. . . In almost every other race of animals each individual, when it is grown up to maturity, is entirely independent, and in its natural state has occasion for the assistance of no other living creature. But man has almost constant occasion for the help of his brethren, and it is in vain for him to expect it from their benevolence only. He will be more likely to prevail if he can interest their self-love in his favor, and show them that it is for their own advantage to do for him what he requires of them. Whoever offers to another a bargain of any kind, proposes to do this. Give me that which I want, and you shall have this which you want, is the meaning of every such offer; and it is in the manner that we obtain from one another the far greater part of those good offices which we stand in need of. It is not from the benevolence of the butcher, the brewer, or the baker, that we expect our dinner, but from their regard to their own inter-

est. We address ourselves, not to their humanity but to their self-love, and never talk to them of our own necessities but of their advantages. Nobody but a beggar chooses to depend chiefly upon the benevolence of his fellow-citizens. Even a beggar does not depend on it entirely. The charity of well-disposed people, indeed, supplies him with the whole fund of his subsistence. But though this principle ultimately provides him with all the necessaries of life which he has occasion for, it neither does nor can provide him with them as he has occasion for them. The greater part of his occasional wants are supplied in the same manner as those of other people, by treaty, by barter, and by purchase. With the money which one man gives him he purchases food. The old clothes which another bestows upon him he exchanges for other old clothes which suit him better, or for lodging, or for food, or for money, with which he can buy either food, clothes, or lodging, as he has occasion.

As it is by treaty, by barter, and by purchase that we obtain from one another the greater part of those mutual good offices which we stand in need of, so it is this same trucking disposition which originally gives occasion to the division of labor. In a tribe of hunters or shepherds a particular person makes bows and arrows, for example, with more readiness and dexterity than any other. He frequently exchanges them for cattle or for venison with his companions; and he finds at last that he can in this manner get more cattle and venison than if he himself went to the field to catch them. From a regard to his own interest, therefore, the making of bows and arrows grows to be his chief business, and he becomes a sort of armorer. Another excels in making the frames and covers of their little huts or movable houses. He is accustomed to be of use in this way to his neighbors, who reward him in the same manner with cattle and with venison till at last he finds it his interest to dedicate himself entirely to this employment, and to become a sort of house carpenter. In the same manner a third becomes a smith or a brazier; a fourth a tanner or dresser of hides or skins, the principal part of the clothing of savages. And thus the certainty of being able to exchange all that surplus part of the produce of his own labor, which is over and above his own consumption, for such parts of the produce of other men's labor as he may have occasion for, encourages every man to apply himself to a particular occupation, and to cultivate and bring to perfection whatever talent or genius he may possess for that particular species of business.

The difference of natural talents in different men is, in reality, much less than we are aware of; and the very different genius which appears to distinguish men of different professions, when grown up to maturity, is not upon many occasions so much the cause as the effect of the division of labor. The difference between the most dissimilar characters, between a philosopher and a common street porter, for example, seems to arise not so much from nature as from habit, custom, and education. When they came into the world, and for the first six or eight years of their existence, they were, perhaps, very much alike, and neither their parents nor playfellows could perceive any remarkable difference. About that age, or soon after, they come to be employed in very different occupations. The difference of talents comes then to be taken notice of, and widens by degrees, till at last the

vanity of the philosopher is willing to acknowledge scarce any resemblance. But without the disposition to truck, barter, and exchange, every man must have procured to himself every necessary and conveniency of life which he wanted. All must have had the same duties to perform, and the same work to do, and there could have been no such difference of employment as could alone give occasion to any great difference of talents. . . .

Every individual is continually exerting himself to find out the most advantageous employment for whatever capital he can command. It is his own advantage, indeed, and not that of the society, which he has in view. But the study of his own advantage, naturally, or rather necessarily, leads him to prefer that employment which is most advantageous to the society. . . .

As every individual, therefore, endeavors as much as he can both to employ his capital in the support of domestic industry, and so to direct that industry that its produce may be of the greatest value, every individual necessarily labors to render the annual revenue of the society as great as he can. He generally, indeed, neither intends to promote the public interest, nor knows how much he is promoting it. By preferring the support of domestic to that of foreign industry, he intends only his own security: and by directing that industry in such a manner as its produce may be of the greatest value, he intends only his own gain, and he is in this, as in many other cases, led by an invisible hand to promote an end which was no part of his intention. Nor is it always the worse for the society that it was no part of it. By pursuing his own interest he frequently promotes that of the society more effectually than when he really intends to promote it. I have never known much good done by those who affected to trade for the public good. It is an affectation, indeed, not very common among merchants, and very few words need be employed in dissuading them from it. . . .

If we examine, I say, all those things . . . we shall be sensible that without the assistance and cooperation of many thousands, the very meanest person in a civilized country could not be provided, even according to what we very falsely imagine, the easy and simple manner in which he is commonly accommodated. Compared indeed with the more extravagant luxury of the great, his accommodation must no doubt appear extremely simple and easy; and yet it may be true, perhaps, that the accommodation of a European prince does not always so much exceed that of an industrious and frugal peasant, as the accommodation of the latter exceeds that of many an African king, the absolute master of the lives and liberties of the thousand naked savages.

KARL MARX and FRIEDRICH ENGELS

The Immorality of Capitalism

KARL MARX *(1818–1883) and* FRIEDRICH ENGELS *(1820–1895) were the founders of modern communism. Their* Communist Manifesto, *reproduced in part here, was their 1848 battle cry, formulated in the name of the newly organized working class—the "proletariat."*

THE history of all hitherto existing society is the history of class struggles.

Freeman and slave, patrician and plebeian, lord and serf, guildmaster and journeyman, in a word, oppressor and oppressed, stood in constant opposition to one another, carried on an uninterrupted, now hidden, now open fight, a fight that each time ended, either in a revolutionary reconstitution of society at large, or in the common ruin of the struggling classes.

In the earlier epochs of history, we find almost everywhere a complicated arrangement of society into various orders, a manifold gradation of social rank. In ancient Rome we have patricians, knights, plebeians, slaves; in the Middle Ages, feudal lords, vassals, guildmasters, journeymen, apprentices, serfs; and in almost all of these particular classes, again, other subordinate gradations.

The modern bourgeois society that has sprouted from the ruins of feudal society has not done away with class antagonisms. It has only established new classes, new conditions of oppression, new forms of struggle in place of the old ones.

Our epoch, the epoch of the bourgeoisie, shows, however, this distinctive feature: it has simplified the class antagonisms. Society as a whole is more and more splitting up into two great hostile camps, into two great classes directly facing each other: *bourgeoisie* and *proletariat.*

From the serfs of the Middle Ages sprang the chartered burghers of the earliest towns. From these burghers the first elements of the bourgeoisie were developed.

The discovery of America, the rounding of the Cape, opened up fresh ground for the rising bourgeoisie. The East-Indian and Chinese markets, the colonization of America, trade with the colonies, the increase in the means of exchange and in commodities generally, gave to commerce, to navigation, to industry, an impulse never before known, and thereby, to the revolutionary element in the tottering feudal society, a rapid devilment.

The feudal system of industry, under which industrial production was monopolized by closed guilds, now no longer sufficed for the growing wants of the new markets. The guildmasters were pushed on one side by the manufacturing middle class; division of labor between the different corporate guilds vanished in the face of division of labor in each single workshop.

Meanwhile the markets kept on growing: demand went on rising. Manufacturing no longer was able to keep up with this growth. Then, steam and machinery revolutionized industrial production. The place of manufacture was taken by the giant, *modern industry;* the place of the industrial middle class, by industrial millionaires, the leaders of whole industrial armies, the modern bourgeois.

Modern industry has established the world market, for which the discovery of America paved the way. This market has given an immense development to commerce, to navigation, to communication by land. This development has, it its turn, reacted on the extension of industry; and in proportion as industry, commerce, navigation, railways extended, in the same proportion the bourgeoisie developed, increased its capital, and pushed into the background every class handed down from the Middle Ages.

We see, therefore, how the modern bourgeoisie is itself the product of a long course of development, of a series of revolutions in the modes of production and of exchange. . . .

The need of a constantly expanding market for its products chases the bourgeoisie over the whole surface of the globe. It must nestle everywhere, settle everywhere, establish connections everywhere.

The bourgeoisie has through its exploitation of the world market given a cosmopolitan character to production and consumption in every country. To the great chagrin of reactionaries, it has drawn from under the feet of industry the national ground on which it stood. All old-established national industries have been destroyed or are daily being destroyed. They are dislodged by new industries, whose introduction becomes a life and death question for all civilized nations, by industries that no longer work up indigenous raw material, but raw material drawn from the remotest zones; industries whose products are consumed, not only at home, but in every quarter of the globe. In place of the old wants, satisfied by the productions of the country, we find new wants requiring for their satisfaction the products of distant lands and climates. In place of the old local and national seclusion and self-sufficiency, we have intercourse in every direction, universal inter-dependence of nations. And as in material, so also in intellectual production. The intellectual creations of individual nations become common property. National one-sidedness and narrow-mindedness become more and more impossible, and from the numerous national and local literatures, there emerges a world literature.

The bourgeoisie, by the rapid improvement of all instruments of production, by the immensely facilitated means of communications, draws all, even the most backward, nations into civilization. The cheap prices of its commodities are the heavy artillery with which it batters down all Chinese walls, with which it forces the underdeveloped nations' intensely obstinate hatred of foreigners to capitulate. It compels all nations, on pain of extinction, to adopt the bourgeois mode of production; it compels them to introduce what it calls civilization into their midst, *i.e.,* to become bourgeois themselves. In one word, it creates a world in its own image.

The bourgeoisie has subjected rural areas to the rule of cities. It has created enormous cities, has greatly increased the urban population as compared with the rural, and has thus rescued a considerable part of the population from the idiocy of rural life. Just as it has made the country dependent on the cities, so has it made barbarian and semi-underdeveloped countries dependent on the civilized ones, nations of peasants on nations of bourgeois, the East on the West.

The bourgeoisie keeps more and more doing away with the scattered state of the population, of the means of production, and of property. It has agglomerated population, centralized means of production, and has concentrated property in a few hands. The necessary consequence of this was political centralization. Independent, or but loosely connected, provinces with separate interests, laws, governments, and systems of taxation became lumped together into one nation, with one government, one code of laws, one national class-interest, one frontier, and one customs-tariff.

The bourgeoisie, during its rule of scarcely one hundred years, has created more massive and more colossal productive forces than have all preceding generations together. Subjection of Nature's forces to man, machinery, application of chemistry to industry and agriculture, steam-navigation, railways, electric telegraphs, clearing of whole continents for cultivation, canalization of rivers, whole populations conjured out of the ground—what earlier century had even a presentiment that such productive forces slumbered in the lap of social labor?

We see then: the means of production and of exchange, on whose foundation the bourgeoisie built itself up, were generated in feudal society. At a certain stage in the development of these means of production and of exchange, the conditions under which feudal society produced and exchanged, the feudal organization of agriculture and manufacturing industry, in one word, the feudal relations of property became no longer compatible with the already developed productive forces; they became so many fetters. They had to be burst asunder; they were burst asunder.

Into their place stepped free competition, accompanied by a social and political constitution adapted to it, and by the economical and political sway of the bourgeois class.

A similar movement is going on before our own eyes. Modern bourgeois society with its relations of production, of exchange and of property, a society that has conjured up such gigantic means of production and of exchange, is like the sorcerer, who is no longer able to control the powers of the subterranean world which he has called up by his spells. For many decades now the history of industry and commerce has been but the history of the revolt of modern productive forces against modern conditions of production, against the property relations that are the conditions for the existence of the bourgeoisie and of its rule. It is enough to mention the commercial crises that by their periodical return put on trial, each time more threateningly, the existence of the entire bourgeois society. In these crises a great part not only of the existing products, but also of the previously created productive forces, are periodically destroyed. In these crises there breaks out an epidemic that, in all earlier epochs, would have seemed an absurdity—the epidemic of overproduction. Society suddenly finds itself put back into a state of momentary barbarism; it appears as if a famine, a universal war of devastation had cut off the supply of every means of subsistence; industry and commerce seem to be destroyed; and why? Because there is too much civilization, too much means of subsistence, too much industry, too much commerce. The productive forces at the disposal of society no longer tend to further the development of the conditions of bourgeois property; on the contrary, they have become too powerful for these conditions, by which they are fettered, and so soon as they overcome these fetters, they bring disorder into the whole of bourgeois society, endanger the existence of bourgeois property. The

conditions of bourgeois society are too narrow to comprise the wealth created by them. And how does the bourgeoisie get over these crises? On the one hand by enforced destruction of a mass of productive forces; on the other, by the conquest of new markets, and by the more thorough exploitation of the old ones. That is to say, by paving the way for more extensive and more destructive crises, and by diminishing the means whereby crises are prevented.

The weapons with which the bourgeoisie felled feudalism to the ground are now turned against the bourgeoisie itself.

But not only has the bourgeoisie forged the weapons that bring death to itself; it has also called into existence the men who are to wield those weapons—the modern working class— the proletarians.

In proportion as the bourgeoisie, *i.e.,* capital, is developed, in the same proportion is the proletariat, the modern working class, developed—a class of laborers, who live only so long as they find work, and who find work only so long as their labor increases capital. These laborers, who must sell themselves piecemeal, are a commodity, like every other article of commerce, and are consequently exposed to all the vicissitudes of competition, to all the fluctuations of the market.

Owing to the extensive use of machinery and division of labor, the work of the proletarians has lost all individual character, and, consequently, all charm for the workman. He becomes an appendage of the machine, and it is only the most simple, most monotonous, and most easily acquired knack that is required of him. Hence, the cost of production of a workman is restricted, almost entirely, to the means of subsistence that he requires for his maintenance, and for the propagation of his race. But the price of a commodity, and therefore also of labor, is equal to its cost of production. In proportion, therefore, as the repulsiveness of the work increases, the wage decreases. What is more, in proportion as the use of machinery and division of labor increases, in the same proportion the burden of toil also increases, whether by prolongation of the working hours, by increase of the work exacted in a given time or by increased speed of the machinery, etc.

Modern industry has converted the little workshop of the patriarchal master into the great factory of the industrial capitalist. Masses of laborers, crowded into the factory, are organized like soldiers. As privates of the industrial army they are placed under the command of a perfect hierarchy of officers and sergeants. Not only are they slaves of the bourgeois class, and of the bourgeois state; they are daily and hourly enslaved by the machine, by the foreman, and, above all, by the individual bourgeois manufacturer himself. The more openly this despotism proclaims gain to be its end and aim, the more petty, the more hateful, and the more embittering it is. . . .

But with the development of industry the proletariat not only increases in number; it becomes concentrated in greater masses, its strength grows, and it feels that strength more. The various interests and conditions of life within the ranks of the proletariat are more and more equalized, in proportion as machinery obliterates all distinctions of labor, and nearly everywhere reduces wages to the same low level. The growing competition among the bourgeoisie, and the resulting commercial crises, make the wages of the workers ever more fluctuating. The unceasing im-

provement of machinery, ever more rapidly developing, makes their livelihood more and more precarious; the collisions between individual workmen and individual bourgeoisie take more and more the character of collisions between two classes. Thereupon the workers begin to form combinations (trade unions) against the bourgeoisie; they club together in order to keep up the rate of wages; they found permanent associations in order to make provision beforehand for these occasional revolts. Here and there the contest breaks out into riots.

From time to time the workers are victorious, but only for a time. The real fruit of their battles lies not in the immediate result, but in the ever-expanding union of the workers. This union is helped by the improved means of communication that are created by modern industry and that place the workers of different localities in contact with one another. It was just this contact that was needed to centralize the numerous local struggles, all of the same character, into one national struggle between classes. But every class struggle is a political struggle. And that union, to attain which the burghers of the Middle Ages, with their miserable highways, required centuries, the modern proletarians, thanks to railways, achieve in a few years. . . .

Hitherto, every form of society has been based, as we have already seen, on the antagonism of oppressing and oppressed classes. But in order to oppress a class, certain conditions must be assured to it under which it can, at least, continue its slavish existence. The serf, in the period of serfdom, raised himself to membership in the commune, just as the petty bourgeois, under the yoke of feudal absolutism, managed to develop into a bourgeois. The modern laborer, on the contrary, instead of rising with the progress of industry, sinks deeper and deeper below the conditions of existence of his own class. He becomes a pauper, and pauperism develops more rapidly than population and wealth. And here it becomes evident that the bourgeoisie is unfit any longer to be the ruling class in society, and to impose its conditions of existence upon society as an overriding law. It is unfit to rule because it is incompetent to assure an existence to its slave within his slavery, because it cannot help letting him sink into such a state, that it has to feed him, instead of being fed by him. Society can no longer live under this bourgeoisie, in other words, its existence is no longer compatible with society.

The essential condition for the existence, and for the sway of the bourgeois class, is the formation and augmentation of capital; the condition for capital is wage labor. Wage labor rests exclusively on competition between laborers. The advance of industry, whose involuntary promoter is the bourgeoisie, replaces the isolation of the laborers, due to competition, by their revolutionary combination, due to association. The development of modern industry, therefore, cuts from under its feet the very foundation on which the bourgeoisie produces and appropriates products. What the bourgeoisie, therefore, produces, above all, is its own grave-diggers. Its fall and the victory of the proletariat are equally inevitable.

PAUL M. SWEEZY

A Primer on Marxian Economics

PAUL M. SWEEZY *is a well-known Marxist and social critic. The following essay is reprinted from* Business and Society Review.

I am a Marxist, and I am firmly convinced that only Marxism allows us to understand the functioning of capitalist societies. The essence of capitalism, as explained in the short second part of the first volume of Marx's *Capital,* is the accumulation of capital; which means continuous and perpetual expansion. To be healthy a capitalist enterprise must grow and grow and grow. The alternative is stagnation and eventual

death. And individual enterprises can grow only if the economy as a whole grows. This process has been going on in the United States ever since the first Europeans set foot on these shores.

The mechanism of growth is that society's surplus product—what is left over after a conventional and always relatively low level of subsistence is provided to the actual worker-producers—is appropriated and controlled by a small class of owners, in our day corporations and their stock- and bond-holders. Out of this surplus the owning class consumes enough to live well and in many cases in great luxury, but it cannot begin to consume the whole surplus, nor does it desire to do so. By far the larger part is accumulated, i.e., invested with a view to making profits and hence increasing the surplus still further in the future.

But this process can continue only so long as profitable markets grow in proportion to capital, and this is far from being guaranteed. If markets do not grow sufficiently, the result is an interruption of the process—crisis, depression, stagnation. It follows with iron logic that a high-priority pre-occupation of everyone in business and government is and must be the expansion of existing markets and the creation of new ones. And the means used, private and government alike, will be the most varied, the most ingenious, and, if need be, the most violent and ruthless imaginable. The list would be endless. I will mention only a few of the most important and commonly used: invention of new or seemingly new products, territorial expansion, penetration of rivals' markets, conquest of foreign peoples, credit creation and expansion, deficit financing, advertising, armaments, and wars. But despite all these methods to create and expand markets, periodic breakdowns of the accumulation process have occurred since the earliest days of capitalism and, as everyone now knows, continue to occur every few years. Right now we are in the worst period of stagnation since the Great Depression of the 1930s, with no signs of an early return to anything remotely approaching prosperity.

Let us now look at American capitalism against this background:

1. American capitalism in its roughly three centuries of existence has expanded enormously, has greatly increased the productivity of human labor, and has raised the per capita consumption of goods and services several-fold. The cost of these achievements, however, has been formidable. The system has exploited and often violently repressed not only its own work force (slave and free) but also vast numbers of people around the world whose economies and societies have been subordinated to the needs of American capitalism. The increased productivity of labor has been at the expense of dehumanizing the work process which absorbs the best part of the lives of most people. And in the long run perhaps the greatest, and ultimately fatal, flaw in capitalism is that an infinitely expanding system in a finite environment is a living contradiction, a time bomb bound sooner or later to explode with shattering and death-dealing ecological consequences. From the beginning, capitalism has always recklessly polluted and destroyed its environment, but until recently this did not seem to matter much. Now, however, the signs of overstrain are everywhere visible, and it is getting to be a commonplace that economic growth in the developed countries, and especially the United States, must be brought under control and decisively checked in the historically near future. What is unfortunately not so widely understood is that this implies the end of capitalism and its replacement by a planned system of production for use, rather than a market system of production for profit.

2. What about "equity" in American society? I suggest that there are two basic aspects to any meaningful concept of "equity." The first is that everyone without exception should have a sufficiency of the things needed to live a decent life: employment at useful work in humane

conditions, adequate housing, a healthy diet, good health care, security for the young, the old, and the infirm. The second is that inequalities in the provision of these necessities should be both small and declining over time. Judged by these criteria the American economy has obviously failed miserably in terms of equity.

3. The fact that income in the United States is distributed extremely unequally— that there is a small stratum of super-rich millionaires at the top and literally tens of millions of poverty-stricken at the bottom— is sufficient proof that some groups have profited inordinately while others have suffered because of the character and development of the American economic system. But it is necessary to add that in a society of exploiters and exploited, oppressors and oppressed, everyone, whether rich or poor, suffers from the alienation and dehumanization which are inherent in such a society.

MILTON FRIEDMAN

The Social Responsibility of Business Is to Increase Its Profits

MILTON FRIEDMAN *is a well-known economist, author, columnist, and defender of the free market system. The following is a notorious essay he wrote for the* New York Times *in 1970.*

WHEN I hear businessmen speak eloquently about the "social responsibilities of business in a free-enterprise system," I am reminded of the wonderful line about the Frenchman who discovered at the age of 70 that he had been speaking prose all his life. The businessmen believe that they are defending free enterprise when they declaim that business is not concerned "merely" with profit but also with promoting desirable "social" ends; that business has a "social conscience" and takes seriously its responsibilities for providing employment, eliminating discrimination, avoiding pollution and whatever else may be the catchwords of the contemporary crop of reformers. In fact they are—or would be if they or anyone else took them seriously—preaching pure and unadulterated socialism. Businessmen who talk this way are unwitting puppets of the intellectual forces that have been undermining the basis of a free society these past decades.

The discussions of the "social responsibilities of business" are notable for their analytical looseness and lack of rigor. What does it mean to say that "business" has responsibilities? Only people can have responsibilities. A corporation is an artificial person and in this sense may have artificial responsibilities, but "business" as a whole cannot be said to have responsibilities, even in this vague sense. The first step toward clarity to examining the doctrine of the social responsibility of business is to ask precisely what it implies for whom.

Presumably, the individuals who are to be responsible are businessmen, which means individual proprietors or corporate executives. Most of the discussing of social responsibility is directed at corporations, so in what follows I shall mostly neglect the individual proprietors and speak of corporate executives.

In a free-enterprise, private-property system, a corporate executive is an employee of the owners of the business. He has direct responsibility to his employers. That responsibility is to conduct the business in accordance with their desires, which generally will be to make as much money as possible while conforming to the basic rules of the society, both those embodied in law and those embodied in ethical custom. Of course, in some cases his employers may have a different objective. A group of persons might establish a corporation for an eleemosynary purpose   for example, a hospital or a school. The manager of such a corporation will not have money profit as his objectives but the rendering of certain services.

In either case, the key point is that, in his capacity as a corporate executive, the manager is the agent of the individuals who own the corporation or establish the eleemosynary institution, and his primary responsibility is to them.

Needless to say, this does not mean that it is easy to judge how well he is performing his task. But at least the criterion of performance is straightforward, and the persons among whom a voluntary contractual arrangement exists are clearly defined.

Of course, the corporate executive is also a person in his own right. As a person, he may have many other responsibilities that he recognizes or assumes voluntarily—to his family, his conscience, his feelings of charity, his church, his clubs, his city, his country. He may feel impelled by these responsibilities to devote part of his income to causes he regards as worthy, to refuse to work for particular corporations, even to leave his job, for example, to join his country's armed forces. If we wish, we may refer to some of these responsibilities as "social responsibilities." But in these respects he is acting as a principal, not an agent; he is spending his own money or time or energy, not the money of his employers or the time or energy he has contracted to devote to their purposes. If these are "social responsibilities," they are the social responsibilities of individuals, not of business.

What does it mean to say that the corporate executive has a "social responsibility" in his capacity as businessman? If this statement is not pure rhetoric, it must mean that he is to act in some way that is not in the interest of his employers. For example, that he is to refrain from increasing the price of the product in order to contribute to the social objective of preventing inflation, even though a price increase would be in the best interests of the corporation. Or that he is to make expenditures on reducing pollution beyond the amount that is in the best interests of the corporation or that is required by law in order to contribute to the social objective of improving the environment. Or that, at the expense of corporate profits, he is to hire "hard-core" unemployed instead of better qualified available workmen to contribute to the social objective of reducing poverty.

In each of these cases, the corporate executive would be spending someone else's money for a general social interest. Insofar as his actions in accord with his "social responsibility" reduce returns to stockholders, he is spending their money. Insofar as his actions raise the price to customers, he is spending the customers' money. Insofar as his actions lower the wages of some employees, he is spending their money.

The stockholders or the customers or the employees could separately spend their own money on the particular action if they wished to do so. The executive is exercising a distinct "social responsibility," rather than serving as an agent of the stockholders or the customers or the employees, only if he spends the money in a different way than they would have spent it.

But if he does this, he is in effect imposing taxes, on the one hand, and deciding how the tax proceeds shall be spent, on the other.

This process raises political questions on two levels: principle and consequences. On the level of political principle, the imposition of taxes and the expenditure of tax proceeds are governmental functions. We have established elaborate constitutional, parliamentary and judicial provisions to control these functions, to assure that taxes are imposed so far as possible in accordance with the preferences and desires of the public—after all, "taxation without representation" was one of the battle cries of the American Revolution. We have a system of checks and balances to separate the legislative function of imposing taxes and enacting expenditures from the executive function of collecting taxes and administering expenditure programs and from the judicial function of mediating disputes and interpreting the law.

Here the businessman—self-selected or appointed directly or indirectly by stockholders—is to be simultaneously legislator, executive and jurist. He is to decide whom to tax by how much and for what purpose, and he is to spend the proceeds—all this guided only by general exhortations from on high to restrain inflation, improve the environment, fight poverty and so on and on.

The whole justification for permitting the corporate executive to be selected by the stockholder is that the executive is an agent serving the interests of his principal. This justification disappears when the corporate executive imposes taxes and spends the proceeds for "social" purposes. He becomes in effect a public employee, a civil servant, even though he remains in name an employee of a private enterprise. On grounds of political principle, it is intolerable that such civil servants—insofar as their actions in the name of social responsibility are real and not just window-dressing—should be selected as they are now. If they are to be civil servants, then they must be elected through a political process. If they are to impose taxes and make expenditures to foster "social" objectives, then political machinery must be set up to make the assessment of taxes and to determine through a political process the objectives to be served.

This is the basic reason why the doctrine of "social responsibility" involves the acceptance of the socialist view that political mechanisms, not market mechanisms, are the appropriate way to determine the allocation of scarce resources to alternative uses.

On the grounds of consequences, can the corporate executive in fact discharge his alleged "social responsibilities"? On the one hand, suppose he could get away with spending the stockholders' or customers' or employees' money. How is he to know how to spend it? He is told that he must contribute to fighting inflation. How is he to know what action of his will contribute to that end? He is presumably an expert in running his company—in producing a product or selling it or financing it. But nothing about his selection makes him an expert on inflation. Will his holding down the price of his product reduce inflationary pressure? Or, by leaving more spending power in the hands of his customers, simply divert it elsewhere? Or, by forcing him to produce less because of the lower price, will it simply contribute to shortages? Even if he could answer these questions, how much cost is he justified in imposing on his stockholders, customers and employees for this social purpose? What is his appropriate share and what is the appropriate share of others? . . .

. . . the doctrine of "social responsibility" taken seriously would extend the scope of the political mechanism to every human activity. It does not differ in philosophy from the most explicitly collectivist doctrine. It differs only by professing to believe that collectivist ends can be attained without collectivist means. That is why, in my book "Capitalism and Freedom," I have called it a "fundamentally subversive doctrine" in a free society, and have said that in such a society, "there is one and only one social responsibility of business—to use its resources and engage in activities designed to increase its profits so long as it stays within the rules of the game, which is to say, engages in open and free competition without deception or fraud."

The Ford Pinto Memo

In the early 1970s, there were a number of fatal accidents involving Ford Pintos, in which the gas tank burst into flames following a relatively minor rear-end collision. Subsequent investigation established that the Ford Motor Company knew about the defect in advance and turned up a study that Ford had prepared for the federal government, breaking down "costs and benefits" of allowing the accidents to happen as opposed to fixing the defect. The summary of that study is reproduced here.

BENEFITS [of fixing the cars]

Savings : 180 burn deaths,
180 serious burn injuries,
2,100 burned vehicles

Unit Cost: $200,000 per death,
$67,000 per injury,
$700 per vehicle.

Total Benefit: $180 \times (200,000) + 180 \times (\$67,000) + 2,100 \times (\$700) = \$49.5$ million

COSTS

Sales : 11 million cars,
1.5 million light trucks

Unit Cost: $11 per car,
$11 per truck

Total Cost: $11,000,000 \times (\$11) + 1,500,000 \times (\$11) = \$137$ million

CALCULATION OF "COST OF DEATH" AT $200,000:		Property Damage	1,500
		Insurance Administration	4,700
		Legal and Court	3,000
		Employer Losses	1,000
Component	1971 Costs	Victim's Pain and Suffering	10,000
Future Productivity Losses		Funeral	900
Direct	$132,000	Asset (Lost Consumption)	5,000
Indirect	41,300	Miscellaneous	200
Medical Costs		Total per fatality	$200,725
Hospital	700		
Other	425		

CHRISTOPHER D. STONE

Why Shouldn't Corporations Be Socially Responsible?

CHRISTOPHER D. STONE *is a professor of law at the University of Southern California. The following is taken from his book,* Where the Law Ends.

THE opposition to corporate social responsibility comprises at least four related though separable positions. I would like to challenge the fundamental assumption that underlies all four of them. Each assumed in its own degree that the managers of the corporation are to be steered almost wholly by profit, rather than by what they think proper for society on the whole. Why should this be so? So far as ordinary morals are concerned, we often expect human beings to act in a fashion that is calculated to benefit others, rather than themselves, and commend them for it. Why should the matter be different with corporations?

THE PROMISSORY ARGUMENT

The most widespread but least persuasive arguments advanced by the "anti-responsibility" forces take the form of a moral claim based upon the corporation's supposed obligations to its shareholders. In its baldest and least tenable form, it is presented as though management's obligation rested upon the keeping of a promise—that the management of the corporation "promised" the shareholders that it would maximize the shareholders' profits. But this simply isn't so.

Consider for contrast the case where a widow left a large fortune goes to a broker, asking him to invest and manage her money so as to maximize her return. The broker, let us suppose, accepts the money and the conditions. In such a case, there would be no disagreement that the broker had made a promise to the widow, and if he invested her money in some venture that struck his fancy for any reason other than that it would increase her fortune, we would be inclined to advance a moral (as well, perhaps, as a legal) claim against him. Generally, at least, we believe in the keeping of promises; the broker, we should say, had violated a promissory obligation to the widow.

But that simple model is hardly the one that obtains between the management of major corporations and their shareholders. Few if any American shareholders ever put their money into a corporation upon the express promise of management that the company would be operated so as to maximize their returns. Indeed, few American shareholders ever put their money directly *into* a corporation at all. Most of the shares outstanding today were issued years ago and found their way to their current shareholders only circuitously. In almost all cases, the current shareholder gave his money to some prior shareholder, who, in turn, had gotten it from B, who, in turn, had gotten it from A, and so on back to the purchaser of the original issue, who, many years before, had bought the shares through an underwriting syndicate. In the course of these transactions, one of the basic elements that exists in the broker case is missing. The manager of the corporation, unlike the broker, was never even offered a chance to refuse the shareholder's "terms" (if they were that) to maximize the shareholder's profits.

There are two other observations to be made about the moral argument based on a supposed promise running from the management to the shareholders. First, even if we do infer from all the circumstances a "promise" running from the management to the shareholders, but not one, or not one of comparable weight running elsewhere (to the company's employees, customers, neighbors, etc.), we ought to keep in mind that as a moral matter (which is what we are discussing here) sometimes it is deemed morally justified to break promises (even to break the law) in the furtherance of other social interests of higher concern. Promises can advance moral arguments, by way of creating presumptions, but few of us believe that promises, per se, can end them. My promise to appear in class on time would not ordinarily justify me from refusing to give aid to a drowning man. In other words, even if management *had* made an express promise to its shareholders to "maximize your profits," (a) I am not persuaded that the ordinary person would interpret it to mean "maximize *in every way you can possibly get away with,* even if that means polluting the environment, ignoring or breaking the law"; and (b) I am not persuaded that, even if it were interpreted as so blanket a promise, most people would not suppose it ought—morally—to be broken in some cases.

Finally, even if, in the face of all these considerations, one still believes that there is an overriding, unbreakable, promise of some sort running from management to the shareholders, I do not think that it can be construed to be any stronger than one running to *existent* shareholders, arising from *their* expectations as measured by the price *they* paid. That is to say, there is nothing in the argument from promises that would wed us to a regime in which management was bound to maximize the income of shareholders. The argument might go so far as to support compensation for existent shareholders if the society chose to announce that henceforth management would have other specified obligations, thereby driving the price of shares to a lower adjustment level. All future shareholders would take with "warning" of, and a price that discounted for, the new "risks" of shareholding (i.e., the "risks" that management might put corporate resources to *pro bonum* ends).

JAMES W. RUSSELL

A Borderline Case: Sweatshops Cross the Rio Grande

JAMES W. RUSSELL *is a journalist who writes about political and economic issues.*

THE Third World and the First World meet in Juárez Avenue, a strip of bars, restaurants, and curio shops catering to tourists who spill over the border from El Paso. For Americans who went to photograph, purchase, or eat a bit of Mexicana, Ciudad Juárez is a convenient sally. They drive in, soak up the ambience around the "mariachi plaza," and go home.

But there is a permanent American presence in Ciudad Juárez, invisible to the sightseers though manifest to the city's inhabitants. To see it, one must take a frustrating drive through streets choked by traffic, bus fumes, and food vendors. On the outskirts of the city, in the barren Chihuahua desert, it rises like a gleaming mirage: row upon row of modern buildings and well-manicured lawns.

The buildings are *maquiladoras,* assembly plants run by foreign-based multinational corporations, most of which are headquartered in the United States. Juárez is home to about 125 foreign-owned factories that employ 45,000 people—a manufacturing nexus larger than Youngstown, Ohio, in its steel-producing heyday. Most of the *maquiladoras* operate within spanking new industrial parks, where security is tight and rent is cheap.

U.S. companies import American parts into Mexico, assemble the parts in *maquiladoras,* and export the products back to the United States. The finished goods are usually stamped, ASSEMBLED IN MEXICO OF U.S. MATERIALS. A host of U.S. corporate giants—including General Electric, Zenith, RCA, and General Motors—as well as many smaller subcontractors have set up shop along the 2,000-mile Mexican frontier, dominating the economies of such cities as Juárez, Tijuana, and Mexicali.

The companies have turned the border zone into a terminal on their global production line. More than 70 percent of *maquiladora* work involves electronics or apparel, both product lines that require intensive labor for final assembly. U.S. companies farm out, or "outsource," the fabrication work to Mexico to save on labor costs.

If the day trippers from the United States bring dollars and leave with knickknacks, the multinational employers bring capital and leave with ready profits—superprofits, in fact, derived from super-exploitation.

Maquiladora managers prefer to hire teen-aged women, believing them to be more dexterous and tractable than men. Since electronics assembly must be done in a clean, temperature-controlled environment, the new factories are air-conditioned, to protect the parts, not the workers, from sweltering desert heat that can send the mercury to 114 degrees. Garment manufacturers do not have that concern, so many of their factories are scattered about Juárez in old, uncooled buildings.

The *maquiladoras* are a tremendous boon to the corporations. Labor costs generally run 20 to 25 percent of what they would be in the United States; the work week is 25 percent longer; the pace of work is faster, and Mexico's high unemployment rate disciplines the labor force. Richard Michel, who manages General Electric's seven *maquiladoras* in Mexico, boasts of a 2 percent absentee rate in his factories, compared with 5 to 9 percent in the United States. Productivity, he adds, is 10 to 15 percent higher south of the Rio Grande.

Though *maquiladora* wages lag far behind those in the United States and represent a fraction of the workers' productive output, the pay is good by Mexican standards. However, border-zone wages are declining in real terms because of unfavorable exchange rates with the dollar. U.S. prices affect Mexican prices; moreover, the workers spend between a third and half of their earnings on the U.S. side.

Gustavo de la Rosa, a lawyer who specializes in *maquiladora* workers' cases, found that the government's peso devaluations have markedly reduced real pay in Juárez. In February 1981, 80 percent of the *maquiladora* employees were taking home the equivalent of $9.19 a day; one year later, take-home pay had slipped to $8.00; by late 1983, it had shrunk to $6.80.

Maria Munoz, who began sewing for Acapulco Fashions in Juárez at age sixteen, was earning $48 for a fifty-hour week in 1981—and she had accumulated eleven years of seniority. That year, she and her co-workers planned to strike for an 18 percent raise and a reduction in hours from fifty to forty-five. Preempting the strike, the company abruptly shut down operations. The managers of Acapulco Fashions returned to the United States carrying the workers' last paychecks and some $6,000 in credit union funds. The company never paid indemnities to the employees for closing down, as required by Mexican law.

In response, the workers seized the factory to prevent management from retrieving machinery and finished goods. Funds were raised from passing motorists and, after more than a year of occupying the plant, the workers sold the goods and machinery and divided the revenues. They recovered about half their losses. A small group continues to occupy the abandoned offices.

The story of Acapulco Fashions is unusual, not in its description of management but in its portrayal of border-zone labor relations. More revealing is the annual May Day in Juárez, when there are two parades—the government's and the Left's. Both take place on the city's main street, separated by ninety minutes.

In the first parade, most of the approximately 30,000 participants march behind banners of government-controlled unions. The signs proclaim loyalty to the ruling Partido Institucional Revolucionario (PRI). Other workers, including many from the *maquiladoras,* fall in behind company standards: Young women predominate the formations, which could be mistaken for girls' high school contingents. RCA goes so far as to dress up its workers in red-and-white cheerleader skirts, and male managers bark out marching orders through megaphones.

The second parade shatters the image of labor pliancy projected by the first. Dressed in red and black, members of the Comite de Defensa Popular (CDP) march behind portraits of Marx, Engels, Lenin, Pancho Villa, guerrilla leader Arturo Gamiz, the Haymarket martyrs, and effigies of Uncle Sam and a *charro syndicalista,* or sell-out labor leader.

Participation in the CDP-sponsored parade has steadily increased—from 2,000 three years ago to 15,000 last May—as the nation's economic crisis has intensified. The CDP, the largest left-wing organization in Juárez, is a leading political force in two dozen of the city's poor and squatter neighborhoods.

But the militance of the CDP has not moved *maquiladora* workers. A tenuous labor peace reigns within the assembly plants, though there have been isolated and sometimes violent confrontations.

The *maquiladoras* run smoothly, but not because the interests of the workers are protected. Between 1971 and 1978, the government's Board of Arbitration issued 482 judgments involving *maquiladora* employees. Only fourteen were favorable to the workers.

Mexican law requires that senior workers be assured job security, but there are many ways for multinational corporations to get around the requirement. Employers can slash hours or shut the plant down for a period, thereby forcing the employees to seek work elsewhere. Companies have also been known to swap workers, eliminating accrued seniority in the process. High turnover is seen as a key to high productivity, and workers are pressured to leave when they reach their late twenties.

The border cities were opened to *maquiladora* exploitation in 1965 with the inauguration of the Border Industrialization Program. A year earlier, the Bracero Program, which provided U.S. growers with seasonal armies of unorganized Mexicans, had been canceled. President Gustavo Diaz Ordaz was facing skyrocketing unemployment in the border region—and rising unrest.

In fact, guerrilla warfare had erupted in Chihuahua. Arturo Gamiz, a rural schoolteacher, had organized a base of guerrillas to combat fraudulent land reform, fight the sale of forest and mineral concessions to corporations, and defend the Tarahumara Indians. The Mexican Army engaged Gamiz and his followers in battle on September 23, 1965. Most of the guerrillas were killed, and their bodies were thrown into a common grave.

The Mexican government sensed that tensions in the border area would exacerbate as growing numbers of impoverished peasants left the land and filled the alrcady swollen ranks of the urban un-employed. So Diaz Ordaz designated the frontier region a free-trade zone, waived import duties, and granted tax breaks to the U.S.-based multinational companies.

This bonanza came at an opportune time for U.S. corporations. After a long period of unbridled expansion, they were facing heightened competition from Japan, West Germany, and other nations. As foreign garment and elec-tronics manufacturers began making in-roads into the U.S. market, labor costs became a vital factor in maintaining a competitive edge. U.S. multinational companies started shifting production to such cheap labor suppliers as South Korea, Taiwan, Singapore, and the Mexican border zone.

In choosing a Third World outpost, business executives consider three vari-ables: labor costs, freedom of opera-tions, and stability. Even before the Bracero Program ended, Mexico's bor-der cities suffered unemployment rates of 30 to 40 percent; wages, following the law of supply and demand, were ac-cordingly low. The unemployment rate in the region remains at least 40 percent [in 1984].

The Border Industrialization Pro-gram ensured multinational corpora-tions absolute freedom. The Mexican government absolved them of tax oblig-ations, and the U.S. government molded the U.S. tariff code to the companies' advantage. Two provisions pegged cus-toms duties of *maquiladora* products to the low wages paid in Mexico, not to the value added to the materials in the production process.

The PRI, which exercises firm con-trol over Mexican affairs, has coopted most of the popular movements, includ-ing the unions, and brutally suppressed the rest. It simply rigged the 1983 state elections: "Privately, PRI officials admit that votes were manipulated," *U.S. News & World Report* recently noted, "be-cause 'it was too dangerous to lose elec-tions during a major economic crisis.'"

Cheap labor, freedom from regula-tion, and political stability have con-spired to bring U.S. multinational corporations across the border. The total number of *maquiladoras* grew from twelve in 1965 to more than 600 by 1980.

The border zone is hardly unique: It competes with similar corporate havens in Asia and in other parts of Latin America. But the Mexican frontier has a special selling point—the "twin plant" concept. A firm can maintain its capital-intensive operations in the United States and meet its labor-intensive needs a short distance away. For example, U.S. workers can cut cloth—a task that is rel-atively skilled and requires major capi-tal investment—and *maquiladora* employees can then sew it.

Runaway plants deprive U.S. work-ers of jobs, and the *maquiladora* com-petition drives down wages in the United States, particularly along the border, where there is a palpable threat that more shops will flee to Mexico.

The damage north of the border has not been offset by benefits to the south. Unemployment in Mexico's frontier area has not been reduced, and living conditions have remained, at best, un-changed. The assembly plants have be-come magnets for displaced peasants; local newspapers warn that 100 families a day are moving into Juárez. A margin-alized, "surplus" population lives in cardboard shacks and feeds its young by begging or selling items scavenged from American parks, alleys, and dumps. Some of the poor become servants on the U.S. side; a full-time, resident maid in El Paso earns $30 to $40 a week.

The movement of women into the *maquiladoras* has strained traditional sex roles. Family strife has increased, and the idle men often turn to alcohol or crime. Many abandon their families to take jobs as undocumented workers in the United States. Spanish-language radio and television stations in El Paso and Juárez regularly broadcast appeals from wives searching for runaway husbands.

Desperation is what keeps the workers mute. Challenges to the system are few. The official unions enroll only a quarter of the work force, and seem to do little more than maintain discipline for the employers. The independent unions, which are more militant than the major labor groups, have yet to make significant inroads into the *maquiladoras.*

Opposition to the system is most visible among the squatter organizations, such as the CDP, and among the leftist electoral parties. A new and important component of the opposition is the Catholic lay communities.

As in the rest of Latin American, the currents of liberation theology flow through Juárez. When the 1979 Puebla Conference of the Latin American Church called for a Christian-based community movement to raise the social and political consciousness of the poor, a number of churches in Juárez responded.

One of them was Father Oscar Enriquez's parish in the working-class *colonia* of Alta Vista. From his church, Enriquez can see across the Rio Grande into the United States. He can also see the smoke of ASARCO's copper smelter as it poisons both sides of the border with lead and other toxic chemicals. Enriquez has become a leader of the Christian community movement, which now encompasses about seventy groups, with ten to fifteen members in each, that meet weekly to discuss social and political issues. The study groups have been growing, fostering a healthy skepticism toward capital among Juárez's citizens.

But even as the skepticism builds, new *maquiladoras* rise against the desert sky—concrete reminders that for the people of the Third World, growth is not necessarily development and industrialization is not necessarily salvation. If a tag could be placed on the profits of the corporate giants who have plants along the border strip, it might read, ASSEMBLED IN THE U.S. OF MEXICAN LABOR.

JOANNE CIULLA

Honest Work

JOANNE CIULLA *teaches business ethics and management at the Jepson School of Leadership at the University of Richmond. She has written numerous articles and reviews on the ethical environment of business.*

"Suppose that every tool we had could perform its function, either at our bidding, or itself perceiving the need," and "suppose that shuttles in a loom could fly to and fro and a plucker on a lyre all self-moved, then manufacturers would have no need of workers nor master of slaves."

—ARISTOTLE
Politics

I T'S been more than 2,300 years since Aristotle mused about a life without work. Today, the tools and machines that Aristotle dreamed of are becoming the furniture of everyday life in industrialized countries, as the demands of a competitive market catapult us toward a world in which machines replace or simplify most jobs. Aristotle might have rejoiced at this, but Americans don't. Instead of greeting this era with joy, we cling ever more tightly to our work.

Ours is a work-oriented society —one where "all play and no work makes Jack a big jerk." We live in a paradoxical culture that both celebrates work and continually strives to eliminate it. While we treasure economic efficiency, we seek interesting jobs that will offer fulfillment and meaning to our lives.

A SOURCE OF IDENTITY

Perhaps the demand for meaningful work grows because we see the supply shrinking.

For many people, work promises more than most jobs can deliver. The corporation is not capable of providing meaningful work for all of its employees.

As things now stand, we have gone beyond the work ethic, which endowed work with moral value, and expect our jobs to be the source of our identity, the basis of our individual worth and the mainspring of happiness. Furthermore, we want our work to substitute for the fulfillment that used to be derived from friends, family and community.

Over the past 60 years, management has capitalized on this "loaded" meaning of work. The social engineer has replaced the time-study man— corporations have become "cultures" that seek to transform employees into a happy family.

The problem of alienation has been licked by "entertaining" that encroaches on employees' leisure time in the guise of business dinners, corporate beer busts and networking parties. Managers, charged with the task of making work meaningful, create new ways of persuading employees to invest more of themselves in their work than their jobs may require. So, banal work is sometimes dressed up to look meaningful.

EMOTIONAL DEMANDS

Under the old school of scientific management, the alienated worker did what he or she was told, got paid and went home. The work might have been boring and the wages unfair, but at least everyone knew where they stood.

Today, the transaction is not as honest. While we still trade our labor, we are also required to give away a slice of our private lives.

Workers of the past were often overworked; today, many of us are overmanaged. The exhaustion that pains the faces of office workers at the end of the day may not be physical but emotional, because management may be demanding more of the self than the timely and efficient performance of the task at hand actually requires.

"WHAT DO YOU DO?"

Work determines our status and shapes our social interactions. One of the first things Americans ask when they met someone new is, "What do you do?" This used to be considered a rude question in Europe, but in recent years it's being asked more and more. To be retired or unemployed in a work-oriented society is to be relegated to the status of a nonentity.

Young people fanatically pursue careers as if a good job were the sole key to happiness—whether that happiness is derived from the status of the job itself or from the wages that they believe will eventually buy it. They are willing to take drug tests, wear the right clothes and belong to the right clubs, all in the name of obtaining a position that will eventually give them freedom to choose. Many argue that they'll work 70-hour weeks, make their fortunes and retire at 40—few ever do. This attitude

has taken a social toll in terms of loneliness, divorce, child abuse and sometimes even white-collar crime.

ONE-WAY COMMITMENTS

A consequence of this loaded meaning of work is that people willingly put their happiness in the hands of the market and their employers. Unlike social institutions such as church and community, corporations frequently do not possess a clear moral vision of what is good for people. It is ironic that in an era of hostile takeovers, corporations seem to offer less security but want more commitment and trust from their employees. Yet traits such as trust and loyalty are based on a reciprocal relationship.

In this environment, managers are challenged to find ways of motivating people who want jobs that satisfy a variety of abstract desires and needs, such as self-development and self-fulfillment.

While there doesn't seem to be much consensus on what "self-development" means or what people self-develop for, many feel that this is what they *should* want. So managers, consultants and psychologists guess at employees' needs and develop programs and policies that carry the implicit promise of fulfilling them. This results in a vicious circle—employees desire more, management promises more and the expectation of finding meaning in work rises. Both sides grope in the dark for ways to build a workplace "El Dorado."

The authenticity of a corporation's moral commitment is questionable if the drive for meaningful work is merely another motivating tool or a mask for authority. Young people who enter the work force are wise to attempts to manipulate them under the guise of caring and skeptical of programs prescribed by the latest management fad that are supposed to create excitement. Managers cannot continually jump-start employees into action. And unlike the organized workers of old, today's young worker doesn't rebel or exert power by picketing with his or her colleagues, but instead stages his or her own silent strike of passive resistance.

WORTHWHILE WORK

In Search of Excellence and the pop management books that followed it charged managers with the task of "making meaning." Peters and Waterman wrote, "We desperately need meaning in our lives and will sacrifice a great deal for it to the institution that provides it for us." We first have to ask: What is it that a corporation has a right to ask people to sacrifice? Their families? Their personal lives? Their leisure? Their beliefs?

Over the past 20 years, the workplace has become more appealing to people's tastes and lifestyles. But we're discovering that some of the values that have emerged from business life are not very attractive or satisfying. Corporate scandals and employee crimes have forced us to rethink the values that have been bred in the workplace and the marketplace. What we have seen in the 1980s is the moral crisis of work, which I would also characterize as a crisis of meaning.

What *is* meaningful work? Is it something that an institution can define or is it something that people discover? The British designer and social critic William Morris had some interesting insights into the nature of what he calls "worthwhile work."

Morris states that work can be either a "lightening to life" or "burden to life."

The difference lies in the fact that in the first type of work there is hope while in the second there is none. According to Morris, it is hope that makes work worth doing. He says, "Worthy work carries with it the hope of pleasure in rest, the hope of pleasure in our using what it makes, and the hope of pleasure in our daily creative skill."

MEANING IS INDIVIDUAL

The concept of hope is a useful one for understanding the nature of meaningful work.

Academics who write about work often make the mistake of assuming that everyone wants work like theirs. Interview a variety of workers, and you soon discover that this simply isn't true. There is a wide variance in the kinds of work that people like to do and the ways in which they find meaning.

Morris' characterization of worthy work has both a subjective and objective element to it. It is subjective in the sense that hope is a potential that the individual worker may or may not actualize. It is objective in the sense that leisure, usefulness and the exercise of skill require that these elements be present in the nature of the work itself. Morris further asserts, "If work cannot be made less repulsive by either shortening it, making it intermittent or having a special usefulness to the man who freely performs it, then the product of such work is not worth the price. "

And, while institutions can provide general frameworks for meaning, it is up to individuals to interpret these meanings for themselves. For example, our liberal society guarantees life and liberty, but it only offers us the *pursuit* of happiness. If a corporation defined and dictated "meaningful work," the freedom of employees to find it and shape it into the context of their lives would be diminished.

Employers do, however, have a moral responsibility to do all they can to redesign jobs and to carefully think through the impact of technology on employees.

Where jobs can't be made more interesting, companies need to think of ways to accommodate employees so that their jobs do not stand in the way of their leading satisfying lives outside of work.

TOWARD A MORE JUST WORKPLACE

Employers have an ethical obligation to recognize that employees have a right to meaningful lives. Businesses might begin by eliminating policies and practices that interfere with that right. Because not all jobs are exciting or en-

gaging, perhaps efforts should be made to make work fit better into people's lives instead of forcing people's lives to fit into work.

The main reasons people give for why they are unhappy at work are that they feel powerless, they do not trust the organization and they feel they are not being treated fairly.

Throughout history, work has involved a relationship of unequal power. Real innovation in management will come when issues like the balance of power are acknowledged and management seeks to create a more just workplace.

In the 8th century B.C., the Greek poet Hesiod pointed out that justice is what makes work worthwhile. He wrote, "Neither famine nor disaster ever haunt men who do true justice; but lightheartedly they tend the fields which are all their care."

PATRICIA H. WERHANE

A Bill of Rights for Employees and Employers

PATRICIA H. WERHANE *teaches business ethics at the University of Virginia. Much of her work focused on Wittgenstein, aesthetics, and professional ethics. Her books include:* Art and Nonart, Ethical Issues in Business, *and* Persons, Rights, and Corporations.

EMPLOYEE RIGHTS

1. Every person has an equal right to a job and a right to equal consideration at the job. Employees may not be discriminated against

on the basis of religion, sex, ethnic origin, race, color, or economic background.

2. Every person has the right to equal pay for work, where "equal work" is defined by the job description and title.

3. Every employee has rights to his or her job. After a probation period of three to ten years every employee has the right to his or her job. An employee can be dismissed only under the following conditions:

- ❦ He or she is not performing satisfactorily the job for which he or she was hired.

- ❦ He or she is involved in criminal activity either within or outside the corporation.

- ❦ He or she is drunk or takes drugs on the job.

- ❦ He or she actively disrupts corporate business activity without a valid reason.

- ❦ He or she becomes physical or mentally incapacitated or reaches mandatory retirement age.

- ❦ The employer has publicly verifiable economic reasons for dismissing the employee, e.g., transfer of the company, loss of sales, bankruptcy, etc.

- ❦ Under no circumstances can an employee be dismissed or laid off without the institution of fair due process procedure.

4. Every employee has the right to due process in the workplace. He or she has the right to a peer review, to a hearing, and if necessary, to outside arbitration before being demoted or fired.

5. Every employee has the right to free expression in the workplace. This includes the right to object to corporate acts that he or she finds illegal or immoral without retaliation or penalty. The objection may take the form of free speech, whistle-blowing, or conscientious objection. However, any criticism must be documented or proven.

6. The Privacy Act, which protects the privacy and confidentiality of public employees, should be extended to all employees.

7. The polygraph should be outlawed.

8. Employees have the right to engage in outside activities of their choice.

9. Every employee has the right to a safe workplace, including the right to safety information and participation in improving work hazards. Every employee has the right to legal protection that guards against preventable job risks.

10. Every employee has the right to as much information as possible about the corporation, about his or her job, work hazards, possibilities for future employment, and any other information necessary for job enrichment and development.

11. Every employee as the right to participate in the decision-making processes entailed in his or her job, department, or in the corporation as a whole, where appropriate.

12. Every public and private employee has the right to strike when the foregoing demands are not met in the workplace.

EMPLOYER RIGHTS

1A. Any employee found discriminating against another employee or operating in a discriminatory manner against her employer is subject to employer reprimand, demotion, or firing.

2A. Any employee not deserving equal pay because of inefficiency should be shifted to another job.

3A. No employee who functions inefficiently, who drinks or takes drugs on the job, commits felonies or acts in ways that prevent carrying out work duties has a right to a job.

4A. Any employee found guilty under a due process procedure should be reprimanded. (e.g., demoted or dismissed), and, if appropriate, brought before the law.

5A. No employer must retain employees who slander the corporation or other corporate constituents.

6A. The privacy of employers is as important as the privacy of employees. By written agreement employees may be required not to disclose confidential corporate information or trade secrets unless not doing so is clearly against the public interest.

7A. Employers may engage in surveillance of employees at work (but only at work) with their foreknowledge and consent.

8A. No employee may engage in activities that literally harm the employer, nor may an employee have a second job whose business competes with the business of the first employer.

9A. Employees shall be expected to carry out job assignments for which they are hired unless these conflict with common moral standards or unless the employee was not fully informed about these assignments or their dangers before accepting employment. Employees themselves should become fully informed about work dangers.

10A. Employers have rights to personal information about employees or prospective employees adequate to make sound hiring and promotion judgments so long as the employer preserves the confidentiality of such information.

11A. Employers as well as employees have rights. Therefore the right to participation is a correlative obligation on the part of both parties to respect mutual rights. Employers, then, have the right to demand efficiency and productivity from their employees in return for the employee right to participation in the workplace.

12A. Employees who strike for no reason are subject to dismissal.

Any employee or employer who feels he or she has been unduly penalized under a bill of rights may appeal to an outside arbitrator.

LAURIE SCHRAGE

Some Implications of "Comparable Worth"

LAURIE SCHRAGE *teaches philosophy at Pitzer College.*

THE passage of the Equal Pay Act in 1963 established the principle of "equal pay for equal work" in the American legal system. Workers who perform identical work must be paid equivalent wages, regardless of a worker's sex or race. However, due to historic occupational segregation, the vast majority of men and women do not perform work that is essentially similar in content. Moreover, occupational categories in which the incumbents are predominantly women (nurse, clerical worker, nursery school teacher, and the like) provide, on average lower wages than those awarded to jobs predominantly performed by men.

The persistent gap in wages between male and female dominated professions involving similar training, experience, and working conditions, indicates *prima facie* that wage differentials are affected by gender discrimination. For the past decade, feminist civil rights organizations have affirmed the existence of gender-based wage discrimination, and the need to compensate women more equitably for their work. The remedy they commonly advocate appeals to the principle of comparable worth: jobs which are dissimilar in content, but comparable in terms of their value to an employer, should be rewarded equally. While the idea of "equal pay for jobs of comparable worth" is widely accepted among feminists, it is established neither in the law nor in the academy.

Despite its narrow base of support, the comparable worth movement has made considerable progress. Several labor unions have successfully negotiated wage adjustments based on comparable worth studies, and many states have passed or rewritten legislation which will facilitate the litigation of comparable worth complaints. In response to these gains, conservative political economists have criticized the doctrine of comparable worth for promoting regulations that threaten to disrupt our free market economy. Business and management experts too have begun to question the validity of job evaluation techniques that have served management in the past, but which now form the basis of comparable worth demands.

Recently, comparable worth has attracted criticism not only from conservatives but from progressives as well. Critics on the left argue that comparable worth primarily serves the class interests of middle-class white women, and fails to address the needs of minorities, the poor, and working class people. Because the principle of comparable worth ties compensation to job merit—rather

than, for example, to employee need—its enforcement, these critics allege, will primarily benefit those in our society whose work carries high social status (in other words, white-collar, managerial and professional workers over blue-collar, skilled or unskilled manual laborers).

Although proponents of comparable worth have frequently addressed the concerns of conservative critics, they have not similarly confronted the issues raised by social progressives. Since comparable worth is motivated by a concern for equality, its proponents should be especially sensitive to the charge that their goals reflect some degree of middle-class elitism. This paper will examine the theoretical assumptions behind the demand for comparable worth, in order to see if it can be maintained in light of the criticisms raised by progressive theorists.

The demand for comparable worth contains five distinct components:

1) Work which is dissimilar in content, but which requires similar levels of training, experience, and responsibility, and is performed under similar conditions, is of comparable value to employers. Workers whose work is of comparable value should receive equal compensation from employers, regardless of race or sex.

2) The occurrence of systemic economic discrimination against women and minorities in our society can be inferred from a pervasive pattern of salary differentials—a pattern in which wages paid for work performed predominantly by women and minorities average approximately 60–75 percent of wages paid to white men for work of comparable value.

3) The job evaluation systems developed by business and management experts, and which have a long history of use by

employers, are helpful for comparing jobs in terms of their value to an employer.

4) However, job evaluation techniques that are currently in use must be reexamined to eliminate sex and ethnic bias both in their form (for example, how job factors are weighted, which factors are chosen, how jobs are described, and so forth) and in their application (for example, whether women and minorities participate in administering them).

5) Public and private employers must conduct their own bias-free job evaluation studies to determine the extent to which wage differentials in their institutions have been affected by race or gender, and must then make appropriate adjustments to their wage structure if inequalities are found to exist. If employers do not voluntarily undertake these actions, then such studies and adjustments should be brought about by union negotiations, or by state or federal law.

• • •

Economists report that "women who work full time all year earn about 60 percent of what full-time men earn." Despite the entrance of women in past years into jobs traditionally held by men, and despite a dramatic increase in the number of women in the work force, the gap in earnings between women and men has remained constant, or has even slightly increased, since 1955. Conversely, workers in male-dominated occupations earn 30–50 percent more than those in integrated or female-dominated occupations, and "the more an occupation is dominated by women, the less it pays."

Some of the differences in earnings between men and women can be explained by the amount of labor supplied, in other words, the number of hours worked. This is one example of a so-called "human capital" or "productivity-related job content" variable that economists and sociologists attempt to isolate and hold constant, in order to explain some portion of the wage gap. By identifying relevant variables, social scientists attempt to determine whether factors which are independent of employer bias (such as an employee's years of training, previous experience, or the level of responsibility a job demands) can account for salary differentials between male- and female-dominated occupations. While some portion of the earnings gap can be predicted by observing variation in "human capital" characteristics other than gender or race, even conservative critics find that these correlations leave a significant portion of the gap in wages (perhaps 60 percent) unexplained.

• • •

The theories of liberal economists generally make little use of the notion of discrimination because discrimination—as liberals conceive of it—is difficult to observe and measure. For them "discrimination in hiring and promotion" refers to the extent to which individual employers make decisions based upon their own biases or prejudices against particular segments of the population. To determine the extent of this phenomenon, one must measure the number of intentionally discriminatory acts of individuals. Thus, even where all Jills earn less than all Jacks, let alone in a single instance, commonsense will not dictate that discriminatory acts by employers have necessarily occurred. It is at least theoretically possible that all Jills have engaged in intentional action which is causally responsible for this state of affairs. Indeed, some would argue that given that all Jills have been socialized in a similar fashion, it is more plausible to assume that they have acted in a common fashion than to assume that their employers have. To assume common intentional action on the part of employers is to postulate a conspiracy, which is not only unlikely, but the product of paranoid thinking.

Some explanations of social phenomena employ a conception of discrimination that differs from the liberal model. By "discrimination in hiring and promotion," some theorists are referring to implicit principles of social organization which have adverse consequences for certain social groups, but which are generally not recognized by individuals because they are subsumed or entailed by the accepted, unquestioned values of their society. On this model sex discrimination is implicit in a society which is organized so that all Jills are paid less than all Jacks for comparable work. Employers may promote and perpetuate discrimination of this sort even if their

individual actions happen to be relatively free of personal bias or the intention to discriminate. Indeed, they perpetuate economic discrimination against women and minorities when their actions are merely consistent with dominant cultural beliefs and stereotypes. In short, one need not be aware of the principles which organize our social institutions in order to behave "normally," just as one need not be aware of the syntactical rules of one's native language in order to speak grammatically. Nevertheless, as social theorists, we can recognize the existence of rules which structure our social interaction, and which reproduce a social hierarchy that places women and minorities in the weakest economic positions. Because this type of discrimination focuses on structural features of cultural systems or institutions, it is variously referred to as "structural," "systematic" or "institutional discrimination."

JUNE O'NEILL

The Problem of "Comparable Worth"

JUNE O'NEILL *works at the Urban Institute in Washington, D.C.*

THE traditional goal of the feminist, at least as I understand it, has been equal opportunity for women, and that is the opportunity for women to gain access to schools, training, and jobs they choose to enter and on the same basis as men. This

goal, however, basically accepts the rules of the game as they operate in a market economy. In fact, the thrust has been to improve the way the market functions by removing discriminatory barriers that restrict the supply of workers to jobs.

By contrast, the recent policy of comparable worth would dispense with the rules of the game. In place of the goal of equality of opportunity, it would substitute a demand for equality of results, and it would do this essentially through regulation and legislation. In fact, after thinking about it, you wonder why one would bother to go through all these elaborate schemes and why not simply say all women should be paid the same as all men—and why even stop there? Because, in a sense, when you start thinking along these lines, you have to question why some women earn a great deal more than other women and why some men earn a great deal more than other men if they're each putting forth their maximum amount of effort in working according to their highest ability. I think therefore, comparable worth is a radical departure from the economic system we have and so should be scrutinized with great care.

The main points I will make are as follows: One, the concept of comparable worth rests on a misunderstanding of the role of wages and prices in our economy; two, the premises on which a comparable worth policy are based reflect confusion about the reasons why women and men are in different occupations and have different earnings. Both the occupational differences and the pay gap, to a large extent, are the result of differences in the roles of women and men in the family and the effect these role differences have on the accumulation of skills and other job choices that affect pay. Discrimination by employers may account for some of the occupational differences. But it does not, as comparable worth advocates claim, lower wages directly in women's occupations. Three, comparable worth, if implemented, would lead to capricious

wage differentials resulting in unintended shortages and surpluses of workers in different occupations with accompanying unemployment; moreover, it would encourage women to remain in traditional occupations. Four, policies are available that can be better targeted than comparable worth on any existing discriminatory or other barriers.

First, the concept of comparable worth. By comparable worth—the definition that I am working with is the view that employers should base compensation on the inherent value of the job rather than on strictly market considerations. In the free market, wages and prices are not taken as judgments of the inherent value of the work, of the worker, or of the goods, but reflect the balancing of what people are willing to pay for the services of these goods with how much it would cost to supply them. Market prices are the efficient signals that balance supply and demand. Thus, in product markets we do not require that nutrition dictate differences in price, for example, between soybeans and chocolates, or that the price of water be higher than the price of diamonds because it is so much more important to us. If I asked what the proper scale of prices should be for these products, I think most people would give a sensible answer, that there is no proper scale—it all depends. It depends on taste, the needs of millions of consumers, and various conditions that determine the cost of production and the price of these products.

What is true of the product market is also true of the labor market. There is simply no independent, scientific way to determine what pay should be in a particular occupation without recourse to the market. Job skills have costs of production, such as formal schooling and on-the-job training. Different jobs have different amenities that may be more or less costly for the employer to provide, such as part-time work, safe work, flexible hours, or a pleasant ambiance. And individuals vary in their talents and taste for acquiring skills and performing these different tasks. The skills required are constantly changing as the demand for products changes and as different techniques of production are introduced. Ten years ago, the demand for computer program operators was just not like it is today. The world is different. These changes can also vary by geographic region. In a market system, changing conditions are reflected in changing wage rates, which, in turn, provide workers with the incentive to acquire new skills or to migrate to different regions.

The wage pattern, that is, the net outcome of these forces, need not conform to anyone's independent judgment based on preconceived notions of comparability or of desirability. Some examples, I think, will help to indicate how really difficult it is to make those judgments.

Take college faculty that has a physics professor and an English professor. They both may have the same number of degrees; they both may have put in the same amount of work; they both may have the same publications—that is, the same number of publications and in the same quality journals. Should they be paid the same? Well, if they were paid the same, what would happen? The demand for physics teachers is different than that for English teachers. Presently, the pay for physics teachers is much higher than it is for English teachers, the reason being that physics teachers have demand in more parts of the economy than English teachers and physics also is an area that fewer people go into. It also so happens that physics is an area that has relatively more men than English. So, the question could be raised whether it is biases against women that result in pay differentials between the fields. It's very difficult to look at two occupations and decide what is comparable to what, what should be more highly rewarded than what.

CONFUCIUS

On Business

CONFUCIUS *(551–479 B.C.) was a famous Chinese sage and teacher. He sought to effect social change by holding a political office, but was unable to secure such a position. Instead, he acquired a small group of dedicated students, and his philosophy is now world-reknown. (China is one of the world's oldest business societies.)*

2. Tzu-chang asked Master K'ung, saying, What must a man do, that he may thereby be fitted to govern the land? The Master said, He must pay attention to the Five Lovely Things and put away from him

the Four Ugly Things. Tzu-chang said, What are they, that you call the Four Ugly Things? The Master said, Putting men to death, without having taught them (the Right); that is called savagery. Expecting the completion of tasks, without giving due warning; that is called oppression. To be dilatory about giving orders, but to expect absolute punctuality, that is called being a tormentor. And similarly, though meaning to let a man have something, to be grudging about bringing it out from within, that is called behaving like a petty functionary.

14. The Master said, He does not mind not being in office; all he minds about is whether he has qualities that entitle him to office. He does not mind failing to get recognition; he is too busy doing the things that entitle him to recognition.

7. The Master said, Gentlemen never compete. You will say that in archery they do so. But even then they bow and make way for one another when they are going up to the archery-ground, when they are coming down and at the subsequent drinking bout. Thus even when competing, they still remain gentlemen.

Tzu-chang said, What is meant by being bounteous without extravagance? The Master said, If he gives to the people only such advantages as are really advantageous to them, is he not being bounteous without extravagance? If he imposes upon them only such tasks as they are capable of performing, is he not getting work out of them without arousing resentment? If what he longs for and what he gets is Goodness, who can say that he is covetous? A gentleman, irrespective of whether he is dealing with many persons or with few, with the small or with the great, never presumes to slight them. Is not this indeed being 'proud without insolence'? A gentleman sees to it that his clothes and hat are put on straight, and imparts such dignity to his gaze that he imposes on others. No sooner do they see him from afar than they are in awe. Is not this indeed inspiring awe without ferocity?

the Four Ugly Things. Tzu-chang said, What are they that you call the Five Lovely Things? The Master said, A gentleman 'can be bounteous without extravagance, can get work out of people without arousing resentment, has longings but is never covetous, is proud but never insolent, inspires awe but is never ferocious.'

COPYRIGHTS AND ACKNOWLEDGMENTS

CHAPTER FOUR

CHAPTER FIVE

CHAPTER SIX

CHAPTER SEVEN

CARROLL, LEWIS "Humpty Dumpty" from *Through the Looking Glass,* New York: The Heritage Press, 1941.

NIETZCHE, FRIEDRICH "Communication and Consciousness" from *The Gay Science,* trans. Walter Kaufmann, New York: Random House, 1974.

ORWELL, GEORGE "Newspeak" excerpt from *1984,* Copyright © 1949 by Harcourt Brace Jovanovich, Inc., and renewed by Sonia Brownell Orwell, reprinted by permission of the publisher.

PINKER, STEVEN *The Language Instinct.* Copyright © 1994 by Steven Pinker. Reprinted by permission of William Morrow & Company, Inc.

ROSS, STEPHANIE "How Words Hurt" from *How Words Hurt: Attitudes, Metaphor and Oppression,* from Mary Vettering-Braggin, ed., *Sexist Language* (Totowa, NJ: Littlefield, Adams & Co., 1981), pp. 194–213.

SWIFT, JONATHAN "Getting Rid of Words" from *Gulliver's Travels,* London: John C. Nimms, 1886.

WHORF, BENJAMIN "Language, Thought, Reality" from *Language, Thought and Reality* by Benjamin Whorf. Copyright © by The MIT Press. Reprinted by permission of the publisher.

WITTGENSTEIN, LUDWIG "Meaning as Use" is reprinted with the permission of Macmillan Publishing Company for *Philosophical Investigations* by Ludwig Wittgenstein, translated from the German by G. E. M. Ascombe. Copyright © 1954 by Macmillan Publishing Company, copyright renewed 1981.

CHAPTER EIGHT

APPIAH, ANTHONY "But Would That Still Be Me?" from *The Journal of Philosophy LXXXVII,* 10 (October 1990). Reprinted by permission of The Journal of Philosophy, Inc.

HUME, DAVID "Of Personal Identity" from *A Treatise of Human Nature,* Book 1, Oxford: Clarendon Press, 1888.

LEIBER, JOHN "How to Build a Person" from *Beyond Rejection* by Justin Leiber, New York: Random House, 1980.

LOCKE, JOHN "Of Identity and Diversity" from *Essays Concerning Human Understanding,* Book 2, ed. Mary Whiton Calkins, The Open Court, 1905.

MACINTYRE, ALASDAIR "The Story-Telling Animal" from *After Virtue: A Study in Moral Theory* by Alasdair MacIntyre. Copyright © 1981 by Alasdair MacIntyre. Reprinted by permission of the University of Notre Dame Press.

MICHAELS, MEREDITH "Persons, Brains, and Bodies" from "Personal Identity" from *Introducing Philosophy,* Third Edition, by Robert Solomon, Copyright © 1985 by Harcourt Brace Jovanovich, Inc. Reprinted by permission of the publisher.

PERRY, JOHN "The First Night" reprinted from John Perry, *A Dialogue on Personal Identity and Immortality,* Hackett Publishing Co., Inc., 1978. With permission of the publisher.

CHAPTER NINE

ARISTOTLE "On Anger" trans. Jon Solomon, from *Rhetoric.* Reprinted by permission of Jon Solomon.

DESCARTES, RENE "The Passions of the Soul" from *The Philosophical Works of Descartes,* Volume 1, trans. Elizabeth S. Haldane and G. R. T. Ross (1967). Reprinted by permission of Cambridge University Press.

GRIFFITHS, MORWENNA "Feminism, Feelings, and Philosophy" from *Feminist Perspectives in Philosophy,* Morwenna Griffiths and Mary Whitford, eds., Indiana University Press, 1988, pp. 131–149. Reprinted by permission of Indiana University Press.

HUME, DAVID "On Pride" from *A Treatise of Human Nature,* Book 2, Oxford: Clarendon Press, 1888.

JAMES, WILLIAM "What Is an Emotion?" from *The Journal of Philosophy,* 1884.

PLATO "Aristophanes' Speech on Love" from *Symposium* by Plato. Translated by Alexander Nehamas and Paul Woodruff. Hackett Publishing Company, 1989, Indianapolis, IN and Cambridge, MA. With permission from the publisher.

SARTRE, JEAN-PAUL "Emotions as Transformations of the World" from *Sketch of a Phenomenological Theory* by Jean-Paul Sartre. Copyright © by Philosophical Library Publishers, a division of Allied Books. Reprinted by permission of Allied Books.

SOLOMON, ROBERT C. "What Love Is" from *Love: Emotion, Myth and Metaphors,* New York: Doubleday, 1981.

TAVRIS, CAROL "Uncivil Rites—The Cultural Rules of Anger" from *Anger: The Misunderstood Emotion* by Carol Tavris. Copyright © 1982 by Carol Tavris. Reprinted by permission of Simon & Schuster, Inc.

EPICURUS "The Pursuit of Pleasure" reprinted from *Epicurus: The Extant Remains,* translated by Cyril Bailey (1926) by permission of Oxford University Press.

GOULD, STEPHEN JAY "So Cleverly Kind an Animal" reprinted with permission of *Natural History,* November 1976. Copyright the American Museum of Natural History, 1976.

LASCH, CHRISTOPHER "The Culture of Narcissism" reprinted from "The Culture of Narcissism" by Christopher Lasch, by permission of W. W. Norton & Company, Inc. Copyright © 1979 by W. W. Norton & Company, Inc.

PLATO "The Ring of Gyges" from *Republic,* Book 2, trans. Benjamin Jowett, New York: Heritage Press, 1944.

RAND, AYN "The Virtue of Selfishness" from *The Virtue of Selfishness,* New York American Library, 1964.

SHANGE, NTOZAKE "get it and feel good" from *Nappy Edges* by Ntozake Shange. Copyright © 1972, 1974, 1975, 1976, 1977, 1978 by Ntozake Shange. Reprinted with permission from St. Martin's Press, Inc., New York, NY.

CHAPTER FOURTEEN

BEAUVOIR, SIMONE DE *The Ethics of Ambiguity,* translated by Bernard Frechtman. Copyright © 1948 by Philosophical Library. Published by arrangement with Carol Publishing Group.

FRYE, MARILYN "Sexism" from *Politics of Reality* by Marilyn Frye. Copyright © by The Crossing Press. Reprinted by permission of Marilyn Frye.

hooks, bell "Black Women: Shaping Feminist Theory" reprinted from *Yearning* by bell hooks with permission from the publisher, South End Press, 116 Saint Botolph St., Boston, MA 02115 U.S.A.

KANT, IMMANUEL "The Inequality of Women" from *Lectures on Ethics,* trans. Lois Infield, New York: Harper and Row, 1963.

MILL, JOHN STUART "The Subjugation of Women" from *The Subjugation of Women,* D. Appleton and Company, 1869.

PLATO "The Equality of Women" from *The Republic,* trans. Benjamin Jowett, New York: The Heritage Press, 1944.

CHAPTER FIFTEEN

ARISTOTLE "Happiness and the Good Life" from "The Goal of Human Activity" in *Nichomachean Ethics,* Book One, 1901.

AYER, A. J. "Emotivism" from *Language, Truth, and Logic* by A. J. Ayer. Copyright © Dover Publications. Reprinted by permission of the publisher.

BEAUVOIR, SIMONE DE "On Freedom and Morality" from *The Ethics of Ambiguity,* New Jersey: Citadel Press, 1948.

CALHOUN, CHESHIRE "Justice, Care and Gender Bias" from *The Journal of Philosophy LXXXV,* 9 (September 1988): pp. 451–455. Reprinted by permission.

CONFUCIUS "The Analects" reprinted with the permission of Macmillan Publishing Company from *The Analects of Confucius,* translated by Arthur Wiley. Copyright © 1938 by George Allen & Unwin, LTD.

DIDION, JOAN "On Morality" from *Slouching Towards Bethlehem* by Joan Didion. Copyright © 1965, 1968 by Joan Didion. Reprinted by permission of Farrar, Straus & Giroux, Inc.

GILLIGAN, CAROL "In a Different Voice," *Harvard Educational Review,* 47:4, pp. 481–517. Copyright © 1977 by the President and Fellows of Harvard College. All rights reserved.

MIDGLEY, MARY "Trying Out One's New Sword" from *Heart and Mind* by Mary Midgley. St. Martin's Press, 1981, pp. 69–75. Reprinted by permission of St. Martin's Press.

MILL, JOHN STUART "Utilitarianism" from *Utilitarianism* by John Stuart Mill, London: Longman, 1907.

NIETZSCHE, FRIEDRICH "The Natural History of Morals" from *Beyond Good and Evil* by Friedrich Nietzsche, translated by Helen Zimmern. Copyright © Allen & Unwin.

CHAPTER SIXTEEN

ARISTOTLE "Friendship" from *The Nichomachean Ethics,* Book 8, trans. J. E. C. Welldon, London Macmillan Publishing Company, 1912.

ARONIE, NANCY S. "My Heartbreak Kid" from *Northeast Magazine, Hartford Courant,* May 26, 1985. Copyright © by *Hartford Courant.* Used by permission of the author.

BUBER, MARTIN "I and Thou" from *I and Thou,* trans. Walter Kauffman, New York: Charles Scribner's Sons, 1970.

ENGLISH, JANE   "What Do Grown Children Owe Their Parents?" from *Having Children: Philosophical and Legal Reflections on Parenthood,* Onora O'Neill and William Ruddick, Editors. Copyright © by Oxford University Press. Reprinted by permission of Claire Miller and the Jane English Memorial Trust Fund.

LUGONES, MARIA   "Playfulness, World-Traveling, and Loving Perception" from *Hypatia,* vol. 2 (Summer 1987). Reprinted by permission of the author.

SARTRE, JEAN-PAUL   "Hell Is Other People" from *Being and Nothingness* by Jean-Paul Sartre. Copyright © by Philosophical Library Publishers, a division of Allied Books. Reprinted by permission of Allied Books.

THOMAS, LAURENCE   "Friends and Lovers" in *Person to Person,* edited by George Graham and Hugh LaFollette. Reprinted by permission of Temple University Press.

CHAPTER SEVENTEEN

ADORNO, THEODORE   *Dialectic of Enlightenment* from Horkheimer and Adorno, trans. John Cumming, Herder and Herder. Copyright © 1972. Reprinted by permission of The Continuum Publishing Company.

HAYS COMMISSION, THE   "The Motion Picture Production Code" reprinted by permission of The Motion Picture Association of America, Inc.

HIGGINS, KATHLEEN   "The Music of Our Lives" from *The Music of Our Lives* by Kathleen Higgins. Copyright © by Temple University Press, 1990, pp. 1–2, 150–154. Reprinted by permission of Temple University Press.

HUME, DAVID   "Of the Standard of Taste" from *Essays: Moral, Political, and Literary,* Volume 1, eds. T. H. Green and T. H. Grose, London: Logmans, Greem & Co. Ltd., 1882.

MATTICK, PAUL, JR.   "Who Should Support the Arts?" from the October, 1, 1990 issue of *The Nation.* Copyright © 1990 by The Nation Co., Inc. Reprinted by permission of the publisher.

TOLSTOY, LEO   "What Is Art?" Reprinted by permission of Macmillan Publishing Company from *What Is Art?* translated by Alymer Maude. Copyright © 1965, 1985 Macmillan Publishing Company.

WESCHLER, LAWRENCE   "Art and Money" from "Onward and Upward with the Arts" from *Shapinsky's Karma, Bogg's Bills, and Other True-Life Tales* by Lawrence Weschler. Reprinted by permission of Sterling Lord Literistic, Inc. Copyright © 1988 by Lawrence Weschler.

WOLFE, TOM   "The Worship of Art: Notes on the New God" copyright © 1984 by *Harper's Magazine.* All rights reserved. Reprinted from the October issue by special permission.

CHAPTER EIGHTEEN

ARISTOTLE   "Voluntary and Involuntary Action" from *The Nicomachean Ethics,* trans. J. E. C. Welldon, Book 3, London: Macmillan Publishing Company, 1912.

BURGESS, ANTHONY   "A Clockwork Orange" reprinted from *A Clockwork Orange* by Anthony Burgess, by permission of W. W. Norton & Company, Inc. Copyright © 1979 by W. W. Norton & Company, Inc.

GRIMSHAW, JEAN   "Autonomy and Identity in Feminist Thinking" from *Feminist Perspectives in Philosophy.* Morwenna Griffiths and Mary Whitford, eds. Indiana University Press, 1988, pp. 90–95. Reprinted by permission of Indiana University Press.

HOSPERS, JOHN   "Meaning and Free Will" from *Philosophy and Phenomenological Research,* vol. 10, no. 3 (March 1950). Copyright © by *Philosophy and Phenomenological Research.* Reprinted by permission of the publisher.

NUSSBAUM, MARTHA   "Agamemnon" from *The Fragility of Goodness* by Martha Nussbaum. Copyright © 1986 by The Cambridge University Press. Reprinted by permission of the publisher.

SARTRE, JEAN-PAUL   "Freedom and Responsibility" from *Being and Nothingness,* New York: Philosophical Library Publishers, 1943.

WILLIAMS, BERNARD   "Moral Luck" from *Moral Luck* by Bernard Williams. Copyright © by Cambridge University Press. Reprinted by permission of Cambridge University Press.

CHAPTER NINETEEN

FEINBERG, JOEL   "Economic Income and Social Justice" from *Social Philosophy* by Joel Feinberg. Copyright © 1973, pp. 107–117. Reprinted by permission of Prentice-Hall, Inc. Englewood Cliffs, NJ.

HOBBES, THOMAS   "Justice and the Social Contract" from *Leviathan,* Oxford: Oxford University Press, 1909.

MALCOLM X "Human Rights, Civil Rights" from his speech at Militant Labor Reform on "Prospects for Freedom in 1965." Reprinted by permission of Pathfinder Press. Copyright © 1965, 1990 by Pathfinder Press and Betty Shabazz.

MILL, JOHN STUART "A Utilitarian Theory of Justice" from *Utilitarianism,* 1907.

NOZICK, ROBERT "The Principle of Fairness" from *Anarchy, State, and Utopia* by Robert Nozick. Copyright © 1974 by Basic Books, Inc., a division of HarperCollins Publishers.

PLATO "Does Might Make Right?" from *Republic,* Book 1, trans. Benjamin Jowett, New York: Heritage Press, 1944.

RAWLS, JOHN "Justice as Fairness" reprinted by permission of the publishers from *A Theory of Justice* by John Rawls, Cambridge, MA: The Belnap Press of Harvard University Press, copyright © 1971 by President and Fellows of Harvard College.

SEN, AMARTYA "Property and Hunger" from *Economics and Philosophy,* vol. 4 (1988), pp. 57–68. Copyright © Cambridge University Press. Reprinted with the permission of Cambridge University Press.

YOUNG, IRIS *Justice and the Politics of Difference,* copyright © 1990 by Princeton University Press. Reprinted by permission of Princeton University Press.

CHAPTER TWENTY

CIULLA, JOANNE "Honest Work" from Joanne Ciulla, "Meaningful Work" *Benchmark Magazine* (Fall 1990), a publication of Xerox Corporation. Reprinted by permission.

CONFUCIUS "On Business" from *The Analects,* trans. A. Waley, New York: Random House, 1938. Reprinted by permission.

D'ANTONIO, MICHAEL "On Ethics in Business" Copyright © 1985 Newsday, Inc. Reprinted by permission of the publisher.

FRIEDMAN, MILTON "The Social Responsibility of Business Is to Increase Its Profits" from the *New York Times Magazine,* September 13, 1970. Copyright © 1970 by The New York Times Company. Reprinted by permission.

MARX, KARL and FRIEDRICH ENGELS "The Immorality of Capitalism" from "Bourgeois and Proletarians" from *The Communist Manifesto* by Karl Marx and Friedrich Engels. Copyright © 1934 by International Publishers Co., Inc., New York. Reprinted by permission of the publisher.

O'NEILL, JUNE from Comparable Worth, v. 1, US Commission on Civil Rights, 1984. Reprinted by permission of June O'Neill.

RUSSELL, JAMES W. "A Borderline Case" from "A Borderline Case: Sweatshops Cross the Rio Grande." New York: The Progressive, 1984.

SHRANGE, LAURIE "Some Implications of Comparable Worth" from *Social Theory and Practice.* Copyright © 1987 *Social Theory and Practice.*

SMITH, ADAM "Benefits of the Profit Motive" from *An Inquiry Into the Nature and Courses of the Wealth of Nations,* Book 1 and Book 4, ed. James Rogers, Oxford: Clarendon Press, 1880.

STONE, CHRISTOPHER D. "Why Shouldn't Corporations Be Socially Responsible?" from *Where the Law Ends* by Christopher D. Stone. Copyright © 1975 by Christopher D. Stone. Reprinted by permission of HarperCollins Publishers.

SWEEZY, PAUL M. "A Primer on Marxian Economics" copyright © by *Business & Society Review.* Reprinted by permission of the publisher.

WERHANE, PATRICIA H. "A Bill of Rights for Employees and Employers" from *Persons, Rights and Corporations.* Reprinted by permission of the author.

01 Shuku, *Pan Lang,* act. late fifteenth century–early sixteenth century, Japan, Muromachi period. Hanging scroll: ink on paper, 87.3 × 44.4 cm. William Sturgis Bigelow Collection. Courtesy of Museum of Fine Arts, Boston.   **02** Kandinsky, *Extended, 333,* 1926, oil on wood, 37½ × 17½; The Solomon R. Guggenheim Museum.   **03** Lucas Samaras, *Mirrored Room,* 1966. 8 × 8 × 10 ft. Albright-Knox Art Gallery, Buffalo, New York. Gift of Seymour H. Knox, 1966.   **04** Max Ernst, *Les Hommes n'en Sauront Rien.* Tate Gallery of London/Art Resource, NY.   **05** Ernst Barlach, *Hovering Angel.* Photo: Bildarchive, Rh: Museum, Koln Veroffentlichung nur mit Genehmigung des Archives.   **06** M. C. Escher, *Waterfall,* © 1961 M. C. Escher/Cordon Art-Baarn-Holland.   **07** Mary Cassat, *The Letter,* 1891; Color etching, 13⅝ × 9 in. (34.6 × 22.8 cm). Bibliotheque Nationale, Paris.   **08** George Grosz, *Republican Automatons* (1920), Watercolor, 23⅜ × 18⅜". Collection, The Museum of Modern Art, New York Advisory Committee Fund.   **09** Edvard Munch, *The Scream,* 1893, oil on canvas, 36 × 29 in. Kummune Kunstsamlingene, Munch-museet, Oslo.   **10** Alice Neel, *Nancy and the Rubber Plant,* 1975, oil on canvas 80 × 36 in. (203.2 × 91.4 cm). Courtesy Robert Miller Gallery, New York. **11** Jose Guadalupe Posada, Mexican, 1851–1913, *Calavera Don Quixote;* woodcut, modern restrike from relief zinc block, *c.* 1887, 35.7 × 19 cm. William McCallin McKee Fund, RO8286; photograph © 1994, The Art Institute of Chicago. All rights reserved.   **12** Pablo Picasso, *Les Demoiselles d'Avignon,* 1907. The Museum of Modern Art, New York; acquired through the Lillie P. Bliss Collection.   **13** August Macke, *Woman Looking in Shop Window,* 1912. Folkwang Museum, Essen. Liselotte Witzel, Essen.   **14** Miriam Schapiro, *Pas de Deux,* 1986, acrylic and fabric on canvas, 90 × 96 in. Collection: Dr. & Mrs. Acinapura. Courtesy Berneice Steinbaum Gallery, N.Y.C.   **15** Philip Evergood, *Through the Mill,* 1940, oil on canvas, 36 × 52 in. (91.4 × 132.1 cm). Collection of Whitney Museum of American Art, New York. Purchase 41.24. Copyright © 1995, Whitney Museum of American Art.   **16** Jessie Oonark, *Untitled,* 1972–75, stroud, felt and embroidery floss, 212 × 144 cm. Art Gallery of Ontario, Toronto.   **17** Andy Warhol, *Cambell's Soup,* 1965, oil on silkscreen on canvas, 36½ × 25 in. Collection, The Museum of Modern Art, New York; Philip Johnson Fund.   **18** Katsushika Hokusai, *Boat Being Carried by a Great Wave,* woodblock print. Courtesy Museum of Fine Arts, Boston. William S. and John T. Spaulding Collection.   **19** TROVA, Ernest (Ernest Tino Trova), study from *Falling Man Series.* Sixteen plaster figures, two plaster molds, with plastic devices, string, cloth, compass, etc., in a compartmented wood box, 48 × 323/4 × 63/4" (121.8 × 83.1 × 16.9 cm), each figure 12½" (31.8 cm) high. The Museum of Modern Art, New York.   **20** Florine Stettheimer, *The Cathedrals of Wall Street.* The Metropolitan Museum of Art, Gift of Ettie Stettheimer, 1953.